DICTIONARY OF AMERICAN HISTORY

DICTIONARY
OF
AMERICAN HISTORY

DICTIONARY OF AMERICAN HISTORY

REVISED EDITION

VOLUME V

National Urban League–Quasi-Judicial Agencies

Charles Scribner's Sons · New York

Printed in the United States of America
Library of Congress Catalog Card Number 76-6735
ISBN 0-684-13856-5

EDITORIAL STAFF

LOUISE BILEBOF KETZ, *Managing Editor*

JOSEPH G. E. HOPKINS, *Editorial Adviser*

COPY EDITORS

PATRICIA R. BOYD

NORMA FRANKEL

ROBERT HAYCRAFT

LELAND S. LOWTHER

PROOFREADERS

MARGARET DONOVAN

ROGER GREENE

PAULINE PIEKARZ

ANDREW J. SMITH

DORIS A. SULLIVAN

MARSHALL DE BRUHL, *Director, Reference Editorial*

DICTIONARY OF AMERICAN HISTORY

National Urban League–Quasi-Judicial Agencies

NATIONAL URBAN LEAGUE. Founded in New York in 1911 through the consolidation of the Committee for Improving the Industrial Condition of Negroes in New York (1906), the National League for the Protection of Colored Women (1906), and the Committee on Urban Conditions Among Negroes (1910), the National Urban League quickly established itself as the principal agency dealing with the problems of blacks in American cities. An interracial organization committed to integration, it relied on tools of negotiation, persuasion, education, and investigation to accomplish its economic and social goals. Concerned chiefly with gaining jobs for blacks, it has placed workers in the private sector, attacked the color line in organized labor, sponsored programs of vocational guidance and job training, and striven for the establishment of governmental policies of equal employment opportunity. During the Great Depression it lobbied for the inclusion of Afro-Americans in federal relief and recovery programs; in the 1940's it pressed for an end to discrimination in defense industries and for the desegregation of the armed forces.

As much concerned with social welfare as with employment, the Urban League has conducted scientific investigations of conditions among urban blacks as a basis for practical reform. It trained the first corps of professional black social workers and placed them in community service positions. It works for decent housing, recreational facilities, and health and welfare services, and it has counseled Afro-Americans new to the cities on behavior, dress, sanitation, health, and homemaking.

In the 1960's the Urban League supplemented its traditional social service approach with a more activist commitment to civil rights: it embraced direct action and community organization, sponsored leadership training and voter-education projects, helped organize massive popular demonstrations in support of the enforcement of civil rights and economic justice (the March on Washington of 1963 and the Poor People's Campaign of 1968), called for a domestic Marshall Plan, and began to concentrate on building ghetto power among Afro-Americans as a means to social change.

[Guichard Parris and Lester Brooks, *Blacks in the City: A History of the National Urban League;* Nancy J. Weiss, *The National Urban League, 1910–1940.*]

NANCY J. WEISS

NATIONAL WATERWAYS COMMISSION was established by Congress, Mar. 3, 1909, upon recommendation of the Inland Waterways Commission, to investigate water transportation and river improvement and report to Congress. The commission of twelve congressmen submitted a preliminary report in 1910 on Great Lakes and inland waterways commerce. It urged continuance of investigations by army engineers and completion of projects under way and opposed improvements not essential to navigation. A final report in 1912 favored the Lake Erie–Ohio River Canal, suggested further study on the Lake Erie–Lake

Michigan Canal, opposed the Anacostia-Chesapeake Canal, and urged regulation of all water carriers by the Interstate Commerce Commission.

[S. L. Miller, *Inland Transportation.*]

WILLIAM J. PETERSEN

NATIVE AMERICAN CHURCH. A development out of the Peyote Cult, the Native American Church is an amalgamation religion compounding some Christian elements with others of Indian derivation. It features as a sacrament the ingestion of the peyote cactus, which may induce multicolored hallucinations. Christian elements include the cross, the Trinity, and baptism. Christian ethics, theology, and eschatology have been incorporated, with modifications. The peyote rite is an all-night ceremonial, usually held in a Plains-type tipi. Singing, prayers, and testimonials are featured, in addition to the taking of peyote. First incorporated in Oklahoma in 1918, the Native American Church has become the principal religion of a majority of the Indians living between the Mississippi River and the Rocky Mountains, and it is also represented among the Navaho, in the Great Basin, in east-central California, and in southern Canada.

[Weston LaBarre, *The Peyote Cult;* James S. Slotkin, *The Peyote Religion.*]

KENNETH M. STEWART

NATIVISM, the policy of favoring native inhabitants of a country as against immigrants, has through the course of American history fostered antagonism toward the Roman Catholic church and its communicants rather than toward any particular alien group. Until well into the 20th century many Americans consistently held to the belief that this church endangered both the traditional Protestantism and the democratic institutions of the United States and viewed immigrants with alarm because many were Catholics rather than because of their alien birth.

This antipapal sentiment, brought to America by the first English colonists, was fostered in the new country by the 18th-century wars with Catholic France and Spain. Colonial laws and colonial writing both reflected this intolerance. The Revolution abruptly changed the American attitude toward Roman Catholicism, for the liberal spirit of the Declaration of Independence and the French alliance of 1778 both contributed toward a more tolerant spirit. It endured until the 1820's, despite the efforts of New England Federalists, who were largely responsible for the antialien sections of the Alien and Sedition Acts and the proposals of the Hartford Convention.

Anti-Catholic sentiment reappeared in the late 1820's, inspired by a mounting Catholic immigration and by the English propaganda that accompanied the passage of the Catholic Emancipation Act of 1829. Protestants, under the influence of the revivalism of Charles G. Finney, quickly rushed to the defense of their religion. *The Protestant* was founded in 1830, and a year later the New York Protestant Association began holding public discussions to "illustrate the history and character of Popery." By 1834 intolerance had grown to a point at which the mob destruction of an Ursuline convent at Charlestown, Mass., was condoned rather than condemned by the mass of the people. This sign of popular favor resulted in the launching of two new anti-Catholic papers, the *Downfall of Babylon* and the *American Protestant Vindicator;* the release of a flood of anti-Catholic books and pamphlets; and the formation of a national organization, the Protestant Reformation Society in 1836.

The sensational propaganda spread by the Protestant Reformation Society probably turned many Protestants against Catholicism, but it remained for the New York school controversy of the early 1840's to win over the churchgoing middle class. In this controversy Catholic protests against the reading of the King James version of the Scriptures in the public schools were immediately misrepresented by propagandists, who convinced Protestants that Catholics were opposed to all reading of the Bible. Alarmed, the churches took up the cry against Rome, giving nativists sufficient strength to organize the American Republican party with an anti-Catholic, antiforeign platform. Before more than local political success could be gained, a series of riots between natives and immigrants in Philadelphia in 1844 turned popular sentiment against the anti-Catholic crusade. For the remainder of the decade the Mexican War and the slavery controversy absorbed national attention.

Nativistic leaders, recognizing that the stigma of past sensationalism could be wiped out only by a new organization, formed the American Protestant Society in 1844 to take the place of the Protestant Reformation Society. This new body, by promising a labor of "light and love . . . for the salvation of Romanists," won the endorsement of nearly all Protestant sects and influenced hundreds of clergymen to deliver anti-Catholic sermons. Its methods proved so successful that in 1849 a merger was effected with two lesser anti-Catholic organizations, the Foreign Evangelical

Society and the Christian Alliance, to form the most important of the pre–Civil War societies, the American and Foreign Christian Union, pledged to win both the United States and Europe to Protestantism.

The propaganda machinery created by these organized efforts, combined with the heavy immigration from famine-stricken Ireland and Germany, so alarmed Americans that political nativism seemed again feasible. The Compromise of 1850, apparently settling the slavery question for all time, opened the way for the Know-Nothing, or American, party, which enjoyed remarkable success in 1854 and 1855, carrying a number of states and threatening to sweep the nation in the presidential election of 1856. Its brief career was abruptly halted by the passage of the Kansas-Nebraska Act, for as Americans became absorbed in the slavery conflict, they forgot their fears of Rome. The Civil War doomed both the Know-Nothing party and the American and Foreign Christian Union to speedy extinction.

After the war the nation's attention was so centered on the problems of reconstruction and economic rehabilitation that nativistic sentiments remained dormant until the 1880's. By that time mounting foreign immigration and unsettled industrial conditions had created a state of mind receptive to antialien propaganda, but instead of being directed against immigrants, this propaganda was again aimed almost exclusively at the Roman Catholic church. A "committee of one hundred" from Boston flooded the country with anti-Catholic documents; newspapers bent on exposing the "errors of Rome" were founded; and a fraudulent document alleged to be a papal bull calling for the massacre of all Protestants "on or about the feast of St. Ignatius in the Year of our Lord, 1893" was widely circulated and given credence. The American Protective Association, formed in 1887 to crystallize these prejudices, although pledging its members neither to vote for nor employ Catholics, scarcely mentioned Protestant aliens, indicating that religion and not birthplace was the point of objection.

The political failure of the American Protective Association combined with the interest aroused by the free silver campaign of 1896 to check nativistic agitation. In the years after 1898 there was another brief flurry occasioned by the continuing immigration and two events that centered attention on the Roman Catholic church: the celebration of the centenary of the erection of the diocese of Baltimore into a metropolitan see and the meeting in Chicago of the first American Catholic Missionary Conference. New

anti-Catholic organizations were formed, the most prominent being the Guardians of Liberty, the Knights of Luther, the Covenanters, and the American Pathfinders. Anti-Catholic newspapers, led by the *Menace,* began to appear, but before this phase of the movement could be translated into politics World War I intervened.

The next burst of nativistic excitement occurred during the 1920's. The United States, in the restless period that followed World War I, developed an intense nationalism that bred antagonism toward immigrants, Communists, and Catholics—toward all groups that were not conservative, Protestant Americans. During the early part of the decade the Ku Klux Klan shaped and fostered this prejudice. The Klan's excesses and political corruption brought about its decline, but intolerance did not abate—a fact clearly shown by the presidential campaign of 1928. The presence of Alfred E. Smith, a Catholic, as the Democratic candidate aroused a bitter nativistic propaganda that was important in causing his defeat.

The depression of the 1930's and World War II focused attention away from nativism, and the election of a Roman Catholic, John F. Kennedy, to the presidency in 1960 seemed to declare that it was substantially a dead issue.

[John Higham, *Strangers in the Land;* Ira M. Leonard and Robert Parmet, *American Nativism, 1830–1860;* Seymour Lipset and Earl Raab, *The Politics of Unreason.*]
RAY ALLEN BILLINGTON

NATIVISTIC MOVEMENTS, AMERICAN INDIAN. Nativistic movements, variously termed messianic cults, reversion or amalgamation religions, and revitalization movements, have arisen in many parts of the world, and they have been particularly common among North American Indians. Such movements typically arise among a people who face a crisis, whose survival is threatened, or whose way of life is in danger of destruction. The movements constitute attempts to revive or perpetuate parts of the native culture of the people.

After military defeats, and as the game animals were being killed off, American Indians became frustrated and disturbed, feeling that their backs were to the wall, so to speak; they longed for supernatural deliverance from their troubles. Prophets or messiahs to meet this need arose with promises of supernatural succor, withdrawal of intruders, and revival of the old ways. Typically, their messianic doctrines were messages of hope, coming from the Great Spirit or another high deity, promising that if the followers of the prophet conducted themselves properly, there would be a paradise on earth, enjoyed by the living and the resurrected dead. The conduct called for to bring about these anticipated conditions included return to aboriginal Indian ways of life and participation in prescribed ritual activities, which generally included singing and dancing.

The earliest nativistic movement on record among North American Indians started among the Tewa Indians of New Mexico in the late 17th century. The movement culminated in 1680 when the Pueblo Indians in Arizona and New Mexico, chafing under Spanish oppression, rebelled, under the leadership of Popé, a Tewa medicine man and prophet, and temporarily expelled the Spaniards from the Southwest.

Other nativistic movements arose among various Indian groups as the whites spread over the continent. In 1762 the Delaware Prophet appeared in the Lake Erie region, preaching a return to the old customs, and influenced Chief Pontiac to undertake his uprising the following year. The Shawnee Prophet, brother of Chief Tecumseh, in the early 19th century preached a doctrine similar to that of the Delaware Prophet. One of the followers of the Shawnee Prophet, named Kanakuk, himself became a prophet among the Kickapoo. There were also a Potawatomi prophet and a Winnebago prophet named Patheske. A Seneca prophet, Handsome Lake, calling for a reversion to the old Indian way of life, started a cult among the Iroquois in 1799 that has survived to the present. In southern California in 1801 a nativistic movement that began among the Chumash spread to the tribes of the interior and the Sierra Nevada. Later, in 1881, Nakaidoklini instigated a nativistic movement among the White Mountain Apache. In the Puget Sound area a Squaxin prophet named John Slocum founded the Indian Shaker religion in 1881, a cult that combines Christian elements with Indian-style visions. A number of nativistic movements began in the Columbia River area, including the Cult of the Dreamers, a revivalistic movement that had strong Roman Catholic overtones. The prophet was Smohalla, a Sahaptin who had frequented a Catholic mission in his youth and who, in 1884, started a nativistic religion that combined ancient Indian shamanistic elements with certain ceremonies of the Roman Catholic church.

The most famous of the messianic cults of the North American Indians was that of the Ghost Dance, which began in 1869 when a Paiute of Nevada named Wodziwob began to prophesy supernatural events allegedly revealed to him. A resurgence of the Ghost Dance in 1889, led by another Paiute messiah, named Wovoka, became a more militant movement when it spread into the Plains area, and it came to a climax in 1890 at the Battle of Wounded Knee in South Dakota.

[Ralph Linton, "Nativistic Movements," *American Anthropologist*, vol. 45; James Mooney, *The Ghost Dance Religion and the Sioux Outbreak of 1890.*]

KENNETH M. STEWART

NAT TURNER'S REBELLION (1831) was the most significant of a number of slave revolts that occurred in the United States. Under the leadership of Nat Turner, a group of Southampton County, Va., slaves conspired to revolt against the slave system.

Nat Turner was a thirty-one-year-old religious mystic who considered it God's work that he strike against slavery. He was literate and had, from time to time, served as a preacher. He had been owned by several different whites and on one occasion had run away from his owner after a change in overseers.

Southampton County, in which the uprising took place, is located in the tidewater section of Virginia near the North Carolina border. It was entirely agricultural and rural. In 1830 its population included 9,501 blacks and 6,574 whites.

On Aug. 21, 1831, Turner and six other slaves attacked and killed Turner's owner and the owner's family, gathered arms and ammunition as they could find it, and set out to gain support from other slaves. Turner's force grew to about seventy-five slaves, and they killed approximately sixty whites. On Aug. 23, while en route to the county seat at Jerusalem, the blacks encountered a large force of white volunteers and trained militia and were defeated. Turner escaped and attempted unsuccessfully to gather other supporters. He was captured on Oct. 30, sentenced to death by hanging on Nov. 5 after a brief trial, and executed on Nov. 11. Several of his followers had been hanged earlier.

The immediate effect of the rebellion on the actions of whites was the institution of a reign of terror resulting in the murder of a number of innocent blacks, the passage of more stringent slave laws, and the more vigorous enforcement of existing statutes. The immediate effect of the rebellion on the attitudes of blacks toward slavery and toward themselves is difficult if not impossible to document, but there is evidence that Turner was highly thought of. The long-range effect was to add to the conflict over slavery that led to the Civil War.

[Herbert Aptheker, *Nat Turner's Slave Rebellion;* Henry Irving Tragle, *The Southampton Slave Revolt of 1831.*]
HENRY N. DREWRY

NATURAL BRIDGE OF VIRGINIA, first mentioned by Frederick G. Burnaby, an English traveler, is a ninety-foot natural arch across Cedar Creek in Rockbridge County, Va. It was included in a grant of 157 acres made by King George III to Thomas Jefferson in 1774. Jefferson placed a log cabin there in 1802 to shelter visitors, and the first hotel was erected in 1815. The Jefferson estate sold the property in 1833, and a public highway now crosses the bridge.

[Chester Albert Reed, *The Natural Bridge of Virginia.*]
ALVIN F. HARLOW

NATURAL GAS INDUSTRY. Until the middle of the 19th century natural gas was primarily a curiosity, but thereafter its importance as an energy resource in the United States increased significantly. Gas springs had been found near Charleston, W. Va., as early as 1775. In 1796, M. Ambroise and Company, Italian fireworkers in Philadelphia, made the first recorded demonstration of burning natural gas in the United States. It aroused so much interest that in 1816 Rembrandt Peale put natural gas on display at his famous museum in Baltimore. But perhaps the best-known natural gas well during these years was in Fredonia, N.Y., discovered in 1824 by William A. Hart, a local gunsmith. This spring was used to fuel thirty streetlights in the village and led to the founding in 1858 of the Fredonia Gaslight and Waterworks Company, which undertook commercial exploitation of this new source of energy. During the next fifty years scores of promoters developed similar natural gas wells in Ohio and Indiana, supplying factories as well as homes. By 1900 the value of natural gas produced in the United States amounted to $24 million annually.

During the first four decades of the 20th century the natural gas industry grew, but its expansion was held up by a lack of suitable transportation. Increasing production of petroleum after 1900 boosted available natural gas enormously, since it appeared as a by-product. In 1920 the total annual value of natural gas produced had reached $196 million. Producers still faced serious problems in transporting the gas to the large urban centers that constituted their most lucrative markets. Ten years later engineers developed seamless electrically welded pipes that were capable of transmitting natural gas cheaply and efficiently over long distances, but in the midst of the Great Depression, investors were loath to develop such new pipelines to any appreciable extent.

World War II inaugurated a tremendous boom in natural gas consumption and production, as this energy resource became the foundation for a major new industry. In the ensuing thirty years prosperity and population growth stimulated investors to build thousands of miles of new pipelines from the vast natural gas fields in the Southwest to the great metropolitan areas of the East, the South, the Middle West, and the Far West. Natural gas quickly displaced coal and fuel oil in millions of homes and factories. It was far more versatile, and also cheaper, than its competitors. Gas could be used as readily for heating as for air conditioning and refrigeration. Moreover, it was cleaner and more convenient to use than coal or fuel oil and much easier to transport. Many industries came to utilize natural gas as a source of energy, including cement and synthetics manufacturers. In 1950 the natural gas industry served 8 million users with an income of about $1.5 billion; in 1960 it had 31 million customers and revenues totaling about $6 billion; and in 1970 natural gas producers supplied more than 42 million individuals and corporations, who paid $11 billion for the product. Between 1950 and 1970 the number of natural gas wells in the United States more than doubled, totaling about 120,000 in 1970. By then the natural gas industry had emerged as one of the ten most important in the nation.

This period of intensive growth was accompanied by increasing federal regulation of the industry. In the years between 1914 and 1938 state governments had been the prime regulators of gas production, seeking to reduce the excessive waste that was then so common. But their regulations varied greatly and frequently were not enforced. Thus, representatives of the industry as well as conservationists prevailed upon Congress in the New Deal era to extend federal control over the interstate transmission of natural gas. Their efforts resulted in the Natural Gas Act of 1938, which placed responsibility for national regulation in the hands of the Federal Power Commission. Since locally produced gas often mingled with gas crossing state boundaries, the commissioners found it difficult to determine clear boundaries of federal jurisdiction. Between 1942 and 1970 both the Federal Power Commission and the federal courts aggressively extended federal control over virtually all natural gas produced in the United States. In particular, the Supreme Court decision in *Phillips Petroleum Company* v. *Wisconsin*

(347 U.S. 672 [1954]) greatly expanded the Federal Power Commission's authority over the industry. Despite protests from natural gas producers that federal regulation was hampering their expansion, the natural gas industry became one of the most closely government-regulated industries in the nation.

[Paul McAvoy, *Price Formation in Natural Gas Fields;* Gerald D. Nash, *United States Oil Policy, 1890–1964;* Edward B. Swanson, *A Century of Oil and Gas in Books: A Descriptive Bibliography.*]

GERALD D. NASH

NATURALIZATION. Citizenship in the United States is acquired by birth—either in the United States or abroad to American citizen parents—or by naturalization. Naturalization is the formal and legal adoption of an alien into the membership of a political community. Under English practice, as late as the 19th century, naturalization was granted only through special acts of Parliament. But the American colonial assemblies, subject to frequent interference from Parliament, exercised a limited right to naturalize certain individuals and classes of persons. Upon achieving independence, the states were free to determine their own conditions for citizenship, but diversity in state legislation resulted. Therefore, the Constitution (Article I, Section 8, Clause 4) provided that Congress shall have power "to establish an uniform Rule of Naturalization." Since then it has been clear that the authority to grant naturalization rests exclusively with Congress.

Naturalization can occur in several ways. The principal methods of granting citizenship to aliens are through collective naturalization, judicial naturalization, and derivative naturalization. Collective naturalization entails the simultaneous grant of citizenship to groups of aliens, ordinarily following the acquisition of territory in which they reside, and it is usually accomplished by treaty or by statute. In the acquisition of several territories—for example, Louisiana, Florida, the Mexican cessions, and Alaska—such provisions were incorporated into the treaties of acquisition. The Texans received American citizenship through a joint resolution of Congress (1845). By statutes, citizenship was thereafter bestowed on the Hawaiians (1900), the Puerto Ricans (1917), the American Indians (1924), the U.S. Virgin Islanders (1927), and the Guamanians (1950).

Whereas these methods of collective naturalization do not necessarily require any individual applications or the issuance of formal citizenship papers, judicial naturalization, which is the most widely used and recognized form, is authorized by general legislation and entails an individual application by each alien seeking naturalization. Provisions for judicial naturalization have been on the statute books since the First Congress enacted a naturalization law in 1790. A major revision of the naturalization laws occurred in 1906 and instituted procedural reforms to eliminate widespread frauds in the naturalization process, particularly on the eve of elections. Other major revisions and recodifications of the naturalization laws occurred in 1940 and 1952.

Since the First Congress the process of individual naturalization has been entrusted to the courts. Brief deviations from this consistent practice occurred during World War I and during World War II, when administrative officers were authorized to grant naturalization to aliens serving overseas in the armed forces of the United States. The present statute authorizes the grant of naturalization by specified naturalization courts, which include all federal district courts and designated state courts. Since 1906 administrative officers, now in the Department of Justice, have been entrusted with important responsibilities in supervising the naturalization process and in assisting the courts.

In order to qualify for naturalization an alien must satisfy several preliminary requirements. First, he or she must have been lawfully admitted to the United States for permanent residence and have resided continuously thereafter in the country for five years. The requisite period of residence is reduced for certain special classes, including spouses of American citizens. In addition, the applicant for naturalization must establish that during the prescribed period of residence he has been of good moral character and attached to the principles of the Constitution of the United States. For many years the naturalization laws limited eligibility to "free white persons" and thus excluded blacks and Orientals. These racial disqualifications were gradually modified, and they were completely eliminated by the McCarran-Walter Act of 1952, which provides that the right to naturalization shall not be denied or abridged on the basis of race or sex.

The procedure is relatively simple. At one time a preliminary declaration of intention ("first papers") was required, but this requirement was eliminated in 1952. Now a person who believes himself or herself qualified for naturalization, after completing the requisite lawful residence, obtains a naturalization application from the Immigration and Naturalization Service and files it with that service, which processes the application and then notifies the applicant to appear in court with two witnesses in order to file a formal petition for naturalization. The applicant and the witnesses are questioned by a naturalization examiner, who conducts any necessary inquiries and investigations and makes a recommendation to the naturalization court. The next step is the final court hearing. In most instances this is a formality, since a favorable recommendation by the naturalization examiner is usually approved by the court without further inquiry. In exceptional cases the court conducts its own inquiry. The final step in the naturalization process is the court order, usually admitting the applicant to citizenship and directing that he or she take the oath of allegiance. Thereupon the applicant becomes a citizen of the United States, and the court issues a certificate of naturalization as evidence of his or her citizenship status.

Derivative naturalization is an automatic process and, like collective naturalization, does not depend upon the beneficiary's application. In appropriate cases, it results from the naturalization of another person, usually a spouse or parent.

Until 1922 an alien woman acquired derivative U.S. citizenship upon marriage to an American or upon the naturalization of her alien husband. As one aspect of the political emancipation of women the Cable Act of Sept. 22, 1922, provided that a married woman would thereafter retain and determine her own citizenship. Since then an alien woman who is married to a citizen of the United States does not automatically acquire U.S. citizenship. She may make her own application for naturalization, after her lawful admission for permanent residence, and her required period of residence is reduced to three years.

The naturalization laws have always provided for automatic acquisition of derivative citizenship by alien minor children upon the naturalization of their parents, although the conditions for such acquisition have varied. Under the present law, effective since 1952, an alien child generally acquires U.S. citizenship upon the naturalization of his parents if such naturalization and the child's acquisition of lawful permanent residence in the United States occur while the child is under the age of sixteen years.

[C. Gordon and B. Rosenfield, *Immigration Law and Procedure*.]

CHARLES GORDON

NATURAL RESOURCES, CONSERVATION OF. *See* **Conservation.**

NATURAL RIGHTS are commonly defined as rights that inhere in the individual anterior to the creation of government and are not relinquished upon entrance into civil society. The concept was brought to the American colonies through the writings of the English political philosopher John Locke and was stated in the New York assembly as early as 1714 by John Mulford. It was developed by the dissenting clergy in New England and became a part of the revolutionary philosophy. Samuel Adams conceived natural rights to be guaranteed by the British constitution, but the radical Thomas Paine thought they existed independent of charters and constitutions (*see* Rights of Man). His conception of popular sovereignty involved the basic notion that rights inhere in the individual, that governments exist only for the further protection of individual rights. This idea was in the mind of Thomas Jefferson when he wrote into the Declaration of Independence that all men "are endowed by their Creator with certain inalienable Rights," to secure which governments were instituted, and that among these rights are "Life, Liberty, and the pursuit of Happiness." From the revolutionary philosophy the idea was embodied in the state constitutions with some changes in phraseology (*see* Compact Theory).

Both Alexander Hamilton and Jefferson subscribed to the doctrine of natural rights, but neither permitted speculative theories to interfere with practical statesmanship. The first attack on natural rights came in the slavery controversy of the 1820's when Thomas Cooper of South Carolina, a prominent political agitator, repudiated the doctrine as a fabrication "by theoretical writers on a contemplation of what might usefully be acknowledged among men as binding on each other." There are no rights, he maintained, except those that society considers it expedient to grant. He was followed by John C. Calhoun, also from South Carolina, who rejected the individualistic political theory of the earlier centuries. In Calhoun's opinion, government was not a matter of choice but a fundamental necessity to the existence of man; it was therefore fallacious to assume a state of society anterior to the creation of government and from this to attempt to rationalize the formation of political institutions. Not all the defenders of slavery were willing to relinquish the doctrine of natural rights, but those who relied on the doctrine gave it an interpretation that obviated any objection to slaveholding.

Since the Civil War political theory in the United States, as elsewhere, has not adhered to the notion of individuality before organization. The dominant view is that natural rights have, at most, ethical significance and thus no place in political science. The doctrine is asserted occasionally in judicial decisions as a basis for the protection of the individual against arbitrary actions by government.

[Bernard Bailyn, *The Ideological Origins of the American Revolution;* Clinton Rossiter, *Seedtime of the Republic: The Origins of the American Tradition of Political Liberty.*]

WILLIAM S. CARPENTER

NAUTILUS, a "diving boat," armed with a torpedo, designed and built at Rouen, France, by Robert Fulton, was launched July 24, 1800. After several successful submersions of it, Fulton submitted his plans for submarine operations against England's navy to Napoleon Bonaparte, who advanced 10,000 francs for repairs and improvements to the *Nautilus*. Although Fulton blew up a French sloop with the *Nautilus,* at Brest, Aug. 11, 1801, he dismantled it when Napoleon offered no further encouragement.

[H. W. Dickinson, *Robert Fulton, Engineer and Artist;* W. B. Parsons, *Robert Fulton and the Submarine.*]

LOUIS H. BOLANDER

NAUVOO, MORMONS AT. In 1839, upon their expulsion from Missouri, the Mormons (Latter-Day Saints) purchased the embryonic town of Commerce in Hancock County, Ill., changed its name to Nauvoo, and prepared to make it the capital of their faith. The city grew rapidly, attracting Mormons from the East and converts from Europe, especially England. Figures are unreliable, but its population was probably 20,000 in 1845, which was larger than any other city in Illinois at the time.

Nauvoo seemed also to be prosperous. Evidences of wealth were the temple, begun in 1841 and completed five years later at a cost of $1 million, the Nauvoo House, and other pretentious structures. But the prosperity was hollow, being dependent principally upon the money brought to the community by the ever-growing stream of newcomers. By 1845 poverty was widespread, and if the exodus forced by the Mormon War had not taken place, economic collapse probably would have occurred.

[W. A. Linn, *The Story of the Mormons;* T. C. Pease, *The Frontier State, 1818–1848.*]

PAUL M. ANGLE

NAVAHO, or "Navajo" according to tribal preference, is a southwestern American Indian tribe paradoxical in several ways. Their culture, despite changes in their location and their subsistence patterns, remains remarkably intact. Further, even though they reside in the inhospitable San Juan plateau of northern Arizona and New Mexico, spilling over into the extreme south of Utah and Colorado, they constitute the largest contemporary American Indian tribe. In 1937 a report of the Bureau of Indian Affairs estimated the Navaho population at 45,000, and it had more than doubled by 1970.

The Athapascan language, spoken by the Navaho and Apache, is not indigenous to the area, and archaeologists continue to debate the question of precisely when the migration of these two tribes into the American Southwest occurred. It was probably late pre-Columbian times, about 1375–1475. The Athapascan incursions may have been a factor in the abandonment by the Pueblo of their great sites of Mesa Verde, Colo., and Chaco Canyon, N.Mex., and their general spread eastward, although the great drought of the end of the 13th century may also have played a role. Since the Athapascan languages are mainly focused in northwest Canada and central Alaska, it has been assumed that it is from this area that the Navaho and the Apache gradually made their way. An original hunting culture may be assumed, which changed as accommodation was made to desert conditions. Whereas the Apache retain some remnants of their northern origins, notably in their stress on the rituals surrounding girls' puberty, the Navaho were so heavily influenced by their Pueblo neighbors that much of their culture is clearly of Pueblo, and especially Hopi, origin. It must be stressed that the resemblance is superficial; to the extent that the Navaho adopted Pueblo culture, they so modified it that they created a mode of life distinctively their own.

The Navaho were drawn into the southwestern farming complex. But whereas the Pueblo chose to build permanent towns and to farm the lands adjacent, the Navaho spread out over a vast area, preferring to develop small, isolated family plots and moving to new fields as water and wood were available. From the Spanish the Navaho acquired domesticated sheep and, as a result, assumed a mixed farming-pastoral mode. The Navaho are the only American Indians who depend on livestock (exclusive of the horse), and they were successful in adapting their culture to this new economic base even though the problems associated with sheep raising, water supply, overgrazing, and soil conservation posed serious difficulties for so populous a group. Even in derivative cultural elements the stamp of the Navaho is distinctive. For weaving, they adopted a loom of European type, but the designs they employ are distinctive variations of basic southwestern artistic elements. Their clothing is Pueblo in origin, but again with a Navaho accent, at least for men; women's dress suggests 18th-century Mexico. A brush shelter, reminiscent of the Great Basin, was the rule among them but gave way to the hogan, a rounded, often octagonal dwelling, in the construction of which they relied on brush. Their corn cultivation is Pueblo; their sheep husbandry is Spanish; and their hunting and gathering techniques are suggestive of the Basin.

The names and structure of the matrilineal units on which Navaho social organization is based suggest the Hopi and Zuni. And the very existence of the Navaho as a tribe is based not on any political structure but rather on language and this network of maternal clans, some sixty in all, which are diffused through the group. Men live until marriage with the mother's clan. At marriage, men go to live in the grouping of the wife. Divorce is not unusual, the father leaving and the children remaining with the mother as members of her clan. Although a man may act as a leader of a local group, any authority he has is wholly informal. It was not until 1923 that the Navaho organized a tribal council.

It is in religion that the Navaho penchant for realigning borrowed cultural elements comes most to the fore. The paraphernalia of their religion is clearly Pueblo: corn pollen, rain symbolism, ritual curing, altars made of multicolored sands (the so-called "dry" paintings), masks, and so through a host of parallels. But while Pueblo religion aimed primarily at fertility and rain, Navaho ritual was directed toward curing. The Navaho developed a series of chants, rituals associated with the creation of a balance beween man and nature, and through these chants they sought the establishment of communal good through the restoration of the health of the ill. The various chants, or "ways," are extremely complex, highly ritualized, and reflective of a uniquely Navaho development.

Apart from the contacts that brought sheep into Navaho life, the group remained fairly aloof from Spanish contact. Always at war with their Pueblo neighbors, the Navaho extended their depredations to white settlers. Treaties of 1846 and 1849 failed to keep the Navaho at peace, and in 1863 Col. Christopher ("Kit") Carson led a punitive expedition against them, destroying their crops and rounding up their sheep; they were carried off into captivity at Bosque Redondo, N.Mex., on the Pecos River, supervised by a garrison at Fort Sumner. Continued resistance by the Navaho—and the great cost to the War Department of enforcing their confinement—led the federal government in 1868 to sign a treaty with the Navaho whereby a reservation of nearly 4 million acres was set aside for their use in New Mexico and Arizona. Since then they have increased remarkably in population but have generally maintained their composite yet vital culture.

Perhaps no other native American tribe has so influenced surrounding peoples as have the Navaho. They have created a special tone in developing their widely disseminated art forms. Their rugs, woven by women from wool and fibers, continue to be popular, although they do not reach the high standards of the beginning of the 20th century. Their silver necklaces, bracelets, rings, and other jewelry—made originally of Mexican coin silver by processes learned from Mexicans sometime in the 1850's—now incorporate locally mined turquoise, reaching the level of a fine art; it is now being copied by various of the Pueblo, notably the Zuni, as a source of cash.

[Clyde Kluckhohn, *The Navaho;* Dorothea Leighton and Clyde Kluckhohn, *The Children of the People;* E. Z. Vogt, *Peoples of Rimrock.*]

ROBERT F. SPENCER

NAVAL ACADEMY, UNITED STATES. Established by Secretary of the Navy George Bancroft in 1845 at Fort Severn in Annapolis, Md., the U.S. Naval Academy was first called the Naval School. At that time it offered a five-year course, of which three years were to be spent on board ship in actual service. The school was renamed the U.S. Naval Academy in 1851 and reorganized so as to offer a four-year course leading to a bachelor of science degree. The high standards of discipline and efficiency introduced in 1845 by the school's first superintendent, Cmdr. Franklin Buchanan, have been retained at the academy and have become a part of its tradition. Soon after the start of the Civil War, the Naval Academy moved to Newport, R.I., where it remained until the war's end. During this period the Annapolis buildings were used as an army hospital. After returning to Annapolis, the academy began adding new buildings, modernizing the curriculum, and giving more emphasis to athletics, all under the direction of Adm. David D. Porter, who became superintendent in 1865.

Throughout its history the Naval Academy has conservatively reflected the soundest trends in U.S. engineering institutions, while keeping uppermost the fundamental mission of educating professional officers rather than technicians. Bancroft Hall, named in honor of the school's founder, is by far the largest dormitory in the world, and is the heart of the program, providing the naval milieu and discipline twenty-four hours a day that infuses the midshipmen with a professional attitude. The curriculum offers twenty-six majors from English to aerospace engineering. The brigade of midshipmen is kept at a strength of approximately 4,500 by a dozen methods of entry, of which congressional appointment supplies the greatest number.

ROBERT W. DALY

NAVAL COMPETITION by the United States began when interference with its trade by both Germany and Great Britain caused the enactment of the so-called Plan of 1916. This called for the construction of 168 warships, including 10 battleships and 6 battle cruisers. By 1923 the United States would have a navy stronger than Great Britain. Japan's 1920 program surpassed even this.

By the Washington Conference of 1922 nine major powers abandoned their ambitious plans and proclaimed a naval holiday of ten years in building capital ships, except replacements. The United States accepted parity with Great Britain but because of its position on two oceans insisted on a 10-to-6 superiority over Japan. Competition thereupon broke out in other types of ships, especially cruisers. Between 1922 and 1928, Japan laid the keels of sixteen cruisers, Great Britain fifteen, France and the United States eight, and Italy six. France built forty-one destroyers, Japan thirty-nine, Italy twenty-nine, Great Britain eleven, and the United States none. France laid down forty-nine submarines, Japan thirty-one, Italy twenty-five, Great Britain nine, and the United States three. Great Britain wanted to increase the number of cruisers it had to seventy, which would have given it control of the wartime trade of belligerents and neutrals alike but was restrained by the treaties.

Upon the failure of the Geneva Three-Power Naval Conference of 1927, the Butler bill for seventy-one new ships was introduced in Congress, but although the construction of fifteen cruisers and one aircraft carrier was authorized in 1929, President Herbert Hoover delayed laying their keels. In the London Naval Treaty of 1930 the number of large cruisers was set at eighteen for the United States, fifteen for Great Britain, and twelve for Japan. Italy and France

refused to ratify the whole treaty and could thus build as many noncapital ships as they wished. As to replacements in capital ships, the five governments agreed to a naval holiday until 1936.

The United States did not exercise its right to a "treaty navy" between 1930 and 1934. As a result, in 1934, when Japan announced it would not renew the 1922 treaty or the London Treaty of 1930 when they both expired at the end of 1936, the United States found itself inferior to Japan in small cruisers, destroyers, and submarines and only slightly superior in large cruisers. It thereupon increased its building pace by authorizing increases to treaty strength. At the same time, at the London Naval Conference of 1935, the United States urged limitation and joined with France and Great Britain in qualitative restrictions on all classes of ships. Japan refused to participate further when its demand for full equality was denied. In 1938 it also refused to give assurance that it was not building larger battleships than the treaty allowed the signatories, whereupon they invoked the "escalator" clause but announced certain limits they would observe. In the United States, Congress authorized a 20 percent increase of the navy but made appropriations for only a part of this addition to U.S. naval power.

The haggling became pointless during World War II. The United States built only ten of the fifteen battleships allowed, because the Japanese by their attack on Pearl Harbor inadvertently vaulted the aircraft carrier to primacy. Between 1941 and 1945, the navy vastly augmented its fleet of 8 prewar carriers by an unmatchable 27 fleet carriers and 110 jeep carriers. Against that armada, the Japanese added an inadequate 17 to their 10 previous carriers, including hybrids created by removing the afterturrets from two battleships: a supreme irony was the complete conversion of the *Shinano,* sister to the *Yamato* and *Mushashi,* the largest battleships ever built.

Two world wars had exhausted the British economically, and they gracefully relinquished naval supremacy to the United States but maintained prestige through a small group of carriers of outstanding quality, many of whose innovations—such as the mirror-landing system and the angled flight deck—were adopted by the United States.

Russia, the emerging challenger, was a surprise. Its navy had been considered too trifling for consideration in the naval conferences before World War I. Indeed, in 1948 there was amusement among Western experts when Josef Stalin announced that the Soviet Union would build 1,000 submarines (*see* Arms Race

With the USSR). Western contempt stemmed from the total defeat inflicted by Adm. Heihachiro Togo upon Adm. Z. P. Rozhdestvenski at the 1905 Battle of Tsushima. The post-1917 Red Navy rarely had a unit on the open sea and then, more often than not, the vessel had been bought from French or Italian builders. Few doubted the valor of Soviet seamen, abundantly shown by the naval brigades that fought as infantry at Odessa, Leningrad, Moscow, and elsewhere during World War II. But not much seagoing war in the style of the great navies had been in evidence.

Actually, by the time of Pearl Harbor, Soviet submarine strength in the Pacific exceeded the combined strengths of Japan and the United States. In the 1950's the well-engineered Soviet ships in evidence led Westerners to assume the excellence of unseen Soviet submarines. In 1957, while the beeping of the first Sputnik astonished the world, the first ship-to-ship missiles appeared on Soviet warships, representing a quantum jump past conventional guns. At the time of the Cuban missile crisis there were too few such warships at Soviet Premier Nikita Khrushchev's command, but the Soviet navy and merchant marine continued unabated expansion into the 1970's.

The U.S. Navy had not developed a comparable missile. Its hierarchy considered aircraft carriers to be superior and to be a type of missile system—with a ship as the first stage, an airplane the second, and the plane's hardware the third. In any event, through the determination of Adm. Hyman Rickover, the U.S. Navy made its own quantum jump. After the 1955 success of the atomic-powered *Nautilus,* the first true submarine able to operate submerged as long as crew and provisions held out, the United States had an unprecedented naval capability. Largely because of W. F. Rayburn, the true submarine received an unprecedented punch with perfection of the Polaris ballistic missile, and in 1959 the nuclear-powered *George Washington,* the first of forty-one such submarines, cruised into the "opaque fortress of the sea" with a main battery of sixteen atomic-warheaded missiles with a range of over 1,000 miles.

Grim copying of Polaris submarines inevitably raised questions about the value of aircraft carriers. Congressmen were all too aware of the colossal costs, whose appreciation by the navy is seen in the winnowing of the 812 commissioned vessels of the 1960's to 502 in 1975. Costs had to be cut elsewhere in order to go forward with the nuclear carrier *Nimitz.* Its 1975 completion cost exceeded $1 billion and entailed $3 billion more for the antisubmarine and antimissile vessels with nuclear speeds to defend it in all kinds of weather. Although in wartime the ability of a *Nimitz* to operate a dozen years without refueling would be a strategic miracle, many critics think in terms of a half-hour's war, and some asked why, if the Russians were not building any carriers, the United States should. The fact was that the U.S. lead was so great that the Soviet navy could not realistically hope to catch up in the spectacular "hooklanding" system. They had to improvise a semblance of air power over the oceans by the aerial refueling of long-range landplanes. They waited for the perfection of safer aircraft types and between 1968 and 1973 sailed three helicopter carriers from the Black Sea.

The Strategic Arms Limitation Talks have frozen Polaris submarine numbers for the United States and the Soviet Union, but the U.S. Navy planned to have its first Trident submarine operational in 1978. It was to be nearly twice the size of the Polaris and to be armed with twenty-four missiles.

[Siegfried Breyer, *Guide to the Soviet Navy;* E. M. Eller, *The Soviet Naval Challenge;* U.S. Naval Institute, *Naval Review.*]

WALTER B. NORRIS
R. W. DALY

NAVAL HOME was opened in Philadelphia in 1826 as the Naval Asylum (the name being changed to Naval Home in 1889) to serve jointly as a general hospital and asylum for veteran naval seamen. Costs were defrayed from the pension fund contributed by naval personnel. The first superintendent was Lt. James B. Cooper, succeeded by Commodore James Biddle as governor in 1838. The Naval Asylum was also used as a school for midshipmen from 1839 to 1845. In 1842 Lt. Andrew H. Foote became governor for two years. That same year he induced most of the veterans to sign a temperance pledge, thus initiating a movement that resulted in the abolishment of grog in the navy in 1862. After the Civil War, hospitalization was restricted to veteran inmates of the asylum. In 1976 the Naval Home moved from Philadelphia to Gulfport, Miss., where new facilities accommodated 600 veterans, double the capacity of the former structure. The governor of the Naval Home during this move was Rear Adm. C. J. Van Arsdall, Jr. The former building in Philadelphia is maintained by the U.S. Park Service as a historical landmark.

[C. H. Stockton, *Origin, History, Laws and Regulations of the U.S. Naval Asylum.*]

DUDLEY W. KNOX

NAVAL LIMITATION CONFERENCES. *See* **Fourteen Points; Geneva Three-Power Naval Conference; Great Lakes Disarmament Agreement; Hague Peace Conferences; London Naval Treaty of 1930; London Naval Treaty of 1936; Washington, Naval Treaty of; Washington Conference on the Limitation of Armaments.**

NAVAL OBSERVATORY AND NAUTICAL ALMANAC OFFICE. The U.S. Naval Observatory was founded in 1842 as an outgrowth of the Depot of Charts and Instruments established by the secretary of the navy in 1830. The depot was an agency of the Bureau of Ordnance and Hydrography, whose function was to maintain navigational measuring instruments in good order. Before 1830 such equipment had been the responsibility of a ship's captain. The devices were not tested before purchase; and at the end of a voyage they were stored, after which most of the instruments and charts were unfit for use. To rectify these shortcomings, the depot was organized under the command of a naval officer who could make the necessary astronomical observations for their accurate calibration.

Lt. Louis M. Goldsborough, originator and first director of the depot, mounted a 30-inch transit instrument on rented grounds in Washington, D.C., to make star observations for rating chronometers. The depot's involvement in purely astronomical research began with its cooperation in the U.S. Exploring Expedition, under Charles Wilkes, in 1838–42. Moon culminations, occultations, and eclipses were measured by the expedition and at the depot to determine longitude differences. Several new instruments were purchased for this program, laying the foundation for a permanent observatory.

In 1842 Congress appropriated $25,000 for a permanent depot building on the bank of the Potomac River just north of Constitution Avenue. The new structure, planned by Lt. James M. Gilliss to be conducive to astronomical work, was occupied in late 1844, and regular observations began. During Commodore Matthew F. Maury's directorship (1844–61), observations were begun in preparation for a nautical almanac, wind and current charts for improved navigation were published, and the depot was officially recognized as the Naval Observatory. Astronomers were recruited in and out of the navy to provide a professional corps for the observatory's work.

Congress established the Nautical Almanac Office in 1849, under the superintendence of Capt. Charles H. Davis. The first volume of the *American Ephemeris and Nautical Almanac* appeared in 1855 and was divided into two sections containing tables of predicted positions of astronomical bodies, one section for navigators and the other for astronomers. Originally located in Cambridge, Mass., the office moved to Washington, D.C., in 1866 and became a department of the Naval Observatory in 1893, when the observatory was relocated at its present site. From its inception the Nautical Almanac Office conducted research on the theories of the motions of celestial objects and on the fundamental tables on which the *Almanac* is based. This research appears in a series of volumes entitled *The Astronomical Papers,* which were first published in 1882 and appear irregularly. The office pioneered in advocating cooperation among nations in the production of ephemerides.

The observatory's prime function, as it was in the past, is to provide accurate time and the astronomical data necessary for safe navigation at sea, in the air, and in space. It is the only such observatory in the United States. Time is determined from observations of the solar system and from the use of atomic clocks. In 1865, the observatory began transmitting time signals to fire and police stations in Washington, D.C., and to the Western Union Telegraph Company. The railroads began to use observatory time in 1883. With the development of longitude determination by radio signal in the 20th century, the observatory standardizes time signals and sends them out to ships at sea. A master clock that determines standard time for the United States is maintained at the observatory.

To provide accurate time of the earth's rotation on its axis (mean solar day) and of the earth's motion about the sun (ephemeris time), the observatory staff continues to make delicate measurements of the sun, moon, planets, and stars. This tradition dates from the early days of the depot, when Gilliss prepared the first American star catalog. Long series of observations were published over the years, and the data have been used both by the Nautical Almanac Office and by other astronomers. The observatory staff has also taken part in numerous expeditions to observe eclipses of the sun and transits of planets across the sun.

Observers were aided by occasional accessions of new equipment. By 1845, the observatory possessed a selection of meridian circles and transit instruments. A 9-inch equatorial telescope was obtained in 1844. In 1868 the superintendent proposed the construction of a new refractor because of the inadequacy of the earlier instruments. Congress appropriated $50,000 for the telescope and a contract was signed with Alvan Clark of Massachusetts for its construction. This 26-inch refractor, the largest of its kind at the time, was completed in 1872, and observations commenced in November 1873. It was used by Asaph Hall in the discovery of the two satellites of Mars in 1877. Modernized in 1960, the telescope is still used to photograph double stars.

For finer observations, prevented by the city lights of Washington, D.C., the observatory opened a facility at Flagstaff, Ariz., in 1955. A 40-inch reflector for observing comets and minor planets was transferred from Washington and a 61-inch astrometric reflector for measuring the distances of faint stars was installed in 1964.

[G. A. Weber, *The Naval Observatory*.]
ARTHUR L. NORBERG

NAVAL OIL RESERVES. In September 1909 Secretary of the Interior R. A. Ballinger suggested to President William Howard Taft that the United States should maintain naval oil reserves, and after the necessary legislation had been passed the president permanently withdrew from entry Naval Petroleum Reserve No. 1 (Elk Hills, Calif.) on Sept. 2, 1912; No. 2 (Buena Vista, Calif.) on Dec. 13, 1912; and No. 3 (Teapot Dome, Wyo.) on Apr. 30, 1915, altogether involving about 50,000 acres of public land. Less than 10 percent of the total area withdrawn from entry was free of pending prior claims. Although Secretary of the Navy Josephus Daniels, in his report to President Woodrow Wilson on Dec. 1, 1913, urged the passage of legislation permitting the Navy Department to take possession of the reserves, drill wells, erect refineries, and produce its own supply of fuel oil, such permission was not given. The reserves lay dormant until 1920, when an act of Congress authorized the Navy Department to take possession of that part of the reserves against which no claims were pending, to develop them, and to use, store, and exchange the products therefrom. It had become evident, meanwhile, that petroleum beneath the withdrawn area was probably being drained away through wells on adjoining land, and some leases for protective drilling were given during the few months Daniels remained in office. Edwin Denby, who became secretary of the navy under President Warren G. Harding, requested early in 1921 that the custody of the naval petroleum reserves be transferred to the Interior Department, which not only had been engaged in producing helium for the Navy Department but also

was the official agency for settling claims to public land. The power to determine general policy in regard to the reserves remained with the Navy Department, which proposed the lease of the Elk Hills and Teapot Dome reserves as a unit, exchanging the royalty oil not only for fuel oil but also for storage facilities at Pearl Harbor, Hawaii, and other strategic points. This was done in comparative secrecy, imposed by the Navy Department on the ground that the action taken was part of its war plans, but early in 1922 it came to the attention of the Senate, which began an investigation. This investigation, continuing with interruptions for several years, was, in part at least, an attempt to discredit the Republican administration. In this it was extremely successful; it was disclosed that Secretary of the Interior Albert B. Fall had received $100,000 from the president of the company that had leased Elk Hills and had engaged in involved financial dealings with the president of the company that leased Teapot Dome. Through the ensuing litigation the leases were cancelled and Fall was convicted on a charge of bribery, but the others were acquitted. (*See also* Elk Hills Oil Scandal.)

T. T. READ

NAVAL OPERATIONS, CHIEF OF. The post of CNO was established on Feb. 3, 1915, to give the navy a military chief "charged with the operations of the Fleet and with the preparations of plans for use in war" and was given the temporary rank of four-star admiral. The first CNO was William S. Benson. Legally, the CNO was only an adviser to the secretary of the navy, unable to issue orders except through the secretary's signature. Despite misgivings among senior naval officers, the structure adequately met the needs of World War I, when Secretary Josephus Daniels began, where he deemed appropriate, delegating some of his originating authority to the CNO. The real ambiguity stemmed from the four stars of the naval "commander in chief," presumably the military second-in-command but theoretically able to bypass the CNO to reach the secretary. Naval officers made a tradition of considering CNO senior, a tradition to which all successive commanders in chief subscribed. The CINCUS (an unhappy acronym for commander in chief, changed after Pearl Harbor to COMINCH) was, in practice, the commander of the Atlantic, the Pacific, or the Asiatic Fleet. In March 1942 the hazy relationship ended when the titles of CNO and COMINCH were merged in the person of Ernest J. King. His successful administration through

World War II resulted in the Jan. 12, 1946, general order abolishing COMINCH as such to vest CNO with clear authority and supremacy.

D. W. KNOX
R. W. DALY

NAVAL ORDNANCE. *See* **Ordnance, Naval.**

NAVAL RESEARCH LABORATORY (NRL). One of the signal features of World War I was the role played by science in stimulating military technology. On July 7, 1915, Secretary of the Navy Josephus Daniels wrote Thomas A. Edison, asking him to head a new Naval Consulting Board that would both initiate and evaluate new weapons for the fleet. At the board's first meeting, on Oct. 7, 1915, it was agreed that a naval laboratory should be constructed to provide facilities for research and development. Congress appropriated money for such a facility in 1916, but partly because of a disagreement over its location, ground was not broken until after the war—in December 1920, at a compromise site on the Potomac River in the southern corner of Washington, D.C. The laboratory was officially commissioned on July 1, 1923.

The naval service as a whole was not convinced of the utility of such a scientific establishment, and during the 1920's and 1930's the NRL was in constant danger of being closed. Although the facility compared well with similar laboratories in academic and industrial settings, it was administered in a way new to the navy, for while a naval officer served as director, civilian scientists were given a wide latitude in their work.

The earliest research concentrated successfully on two fields: sound and radio. Sonar (*sound navigation ranging*), in which inaudible high-frequency vibrations are bounced off submerged objects to locate them, was developed by 1935 and put into production by 1938. Radar (*radio detecting and ranging*) was proposed in the laboratory as early as 1922; and by 1932, airplanes fifty miles away could be detected by reflected radio waves.

Between 1935 and 1941 the laboratory's personnel grew from 91 to 396. With the coming of World War II the laboratory grew even faster; by 1945 the number of employees had risen to 1,069 and the budget had increased from $1.7 million to $13.7 million. Three important programs instituted after the war concerned upper-atmosphere research (using German V-2 rockets), guided missiles, and nuclear power. By 1971 NRL research was funded at $109 million and divided into four fields: space, oceanography, electronics, and materials. That same year the staff of 1,410 scientists and engineers published 520 papers and took out 76 patents.

[*NRL: 1971 Review;* R. M. Page, *The Origin of Radar;* A. Hoyt Taylor, *The First Twenty-Five Years of the Naval Research Laboratory.*]

CARROLL PURSELL

NAVAL RESERVE. *See* **Navy, United States.**

NAVAL STORES, a phrase applied to the resinous products of longleaf and other pines along the southeastern coast of America—tar, resin, pitch, and, to a lesser degree, turpentine—used aboard ships. Tar was used to preserve ropes from decay; pitch of resin was applied to seams in the planking to make them watertight; and turpentine was used in connection with paint. They were important in England's colonial commercial policy, for England had normally purchased these goods from Sweden, which meant an unfavorable balance of trade to the mercantilists and the strategic danger that an enemy might cut off the supply. Consequently, the British Board of Trade saw obtaining these stores from the colonies as an important move toward a self-sufficient empire and arranged for a bounty to be paid to colonial producers by the Royal Navy, which, however, objected to American tar as "of too hot a nature."

The Board of Trade tried without success to boost the manufacture of naval stores in New England, and a group of German Palatines operated for a while in upstate New York. The main source of supply was North Carolina, and the manufacture of naval stores was a major industry for "Tarheels." Later, the source of supply moved southward into Georgia and northern Florida. The tar and pitch were obtained by burning chunks of pinewood in kilns. Turpentine was procured by tapping the trees and distilling the sap.

The original naval aspect of these products ended with the coming of steam and of iron and steel hulls. Although one can still smell the tarred rope in shops serving yachtsmen, naval stores have otherwise lost their nautical aspect and have been absorbed among the numerous products of industrial chemistry. There is still a substantial trade based in Georgia, about half the product being exported.

[C. C. Crittenden, *The Commerce of North Carolina, 1763–1789;* T. W. Gamble, ed., *Naval Stores: History,*

Production, Distribution, and Consumption; J. J. Malone, Pine Trees and Politics: The Naval Stores and Forest Policy in Colonial New England.]

ROBERT G. ALBION

NAVAL WAR COLLEGE. *See* **Navy, United States.**

NAVAL WAR WITH FRANCE, also known as the **Quasi-War.** In consequence of the Franco-American misunderstanding of 1798–1800 the French, with no declaration of war, began to seize and plunder American merchant vessels. Despite U.S. attempts to settle the matter diplomatically, no solution could be reached. From March through July of 1798 Congress passed acts empowering the U.S. merchant marine to "repel by force any assault"; commissioning privateers; and ordering the navy to seize all armed French craft found along the U.S. coast or molesting trade. George Washington was recalled from retirement and appointed commander in chief of the army. The American navy of only three ships was rapidly enlarged by construction, purchase, and gifts to fifty-five vessels. The first went to sea on May 24, 1798. France, occupied with European wars and knowing the weakness of the untrained American navy, sent no heavy vessels to the western Atlantic, but placed its reliance on privateers supported by a few frigates and sloops of war.

As American vessels were commissioned, they were organized into small squadrons to guard the chief trade areas in the East and West Indies, and single vessels were detailed to convoy duty. Aside from numerous actions with privateers, the only engagements, each an American victory, were between the *Insurgente,* 40 guns, and the *Constellation,* 36; the *Vengeance,* 50, and the *Constellation,* 36; and the *Berceau,* 24, and the *Boston,* 32. Capt. Thomas Truxtun, commander of the *Constellation* in both engagements, was presented with two gold medals by Congress. Two vessels, the schooners *Enterprise* and *Experiment,* had especially notable careers, the former taking thirteen prizes on one cruise. No attempts to seize the French islands were made, but Capt. Henry Geddes with the ship *Patapsco* on Sept. 23, 1800, successfully dislodged the French forces that had taken possession of the Dutch island of Curaçao. About eighty-five French vessels were captured, not including recaptures of American craft and small boats. Although the French took only one American naval vessel, the schooner *Retaliation,* formerly the

Croyable, the first American capture in the war, several hundred American merchant vessels were seized by France both abroad and in home waters. These were condemned at farcical admiralty trials, and in most instances the crews were imprisoned and brutally treated.

On Sept. 30, 1800, a convention of peace, commerce, and navigation was concluded, and shortly thereafter hostilities ceased (*see* Convention of 1800). Claims arising from France's failure to meet its obligations under this treaty helped bring about the purchase of Louisiana. (*See also* French Spoliation Claims.)

[Alexander De Conde, *The Quasi War: The Politics and Diplomacy of the Undeclared War With France.*]

MARION V. BREWINGTON

NAVIGATION ACT OF 1817. The American movement toward national self-sufficiency that followed the War of 1812 was manifested in the tariff of 1816 and the Navigation Act of 1817. The latter was not different in spirit from earlier British and American commercial regulations (*see* Coasting Trade). It stated that all cargo between American ports must be carried in ships entirely owned by American citizens. Tonnage duties on vessels licensed for coastwise trade were set at six cents a ton on vessels manned by Americans and fifty cents for others.

[George Dangerfield, *The Awakening of American Nationalism, 1815–1828.*]

JOHN HASKELL KEMBLE

NAVIGATION ACTS had their origin in Britain's regulation of its coastwise trade, which was extended to the colonies as they developed. The first formal legislation affecting the colonies was enacted by Parliament in 1649 and in 1651. This legislation was modified, consolidated, and reenacted in 1660 and became the basic Navigation Act. This law and others were revised in the final act of 1696. The object was to protect British shipping against competition from Dutch and other foreign seamen. Under these acts no goods could be imported into or exported from any British colony in Asia, Africa, or America except in English vessels, English-owned, and manned by crews three-fourths English. Other clauses limited the importation of any products of Asia, Africa, or America into England to English vessels and provided that goods from foreign countries could be imported into England only in vessels of the exporting countries or in English ships.

Wherever the word "English" was used in these and subsequent acts it referred to the nationality of individuals and not to their place of residence. Thus American colonists were just as much English as their compatriots who resided in London. The net effect of these basic laws was to give Englishmen and English ships a legal monopoly of all trade between various colonial ports and between colonial ports and England. Even the trade between colonial ports and foreign countries was limited to English vessels. Thus foreign vessels were excluded entirely from colonial ports and could trade only at ports in the British Isles.

Another field of legislation related to commodities. Certain important colonial products were enumerated and could be exported from the place of production only to another British colony or to England. At first the list included tobacco, sugar, indigo, cotton wool, ginger, and fustic and other dyewoods. Later, the list was extended to include naval stores, hemp, rice, molasses, beaver skins, furs, copper ore, iron, and lumber.

Asian goods and European manufactures could be imported into the colonies only from England—though an exception was made in the case of salt or wine from the Azores or the Madeira Islands and food products from Ireland or Scotland.

The clauses of the Navigation Acts in which these commodities were enumerated were enforced by a system of bonds that required the master of the vessel to comply with the provisions of the acts. These operated in such a way as to give American shipowners a practical monopoly of the trade between the continental and West Indian colonies. Residents of Great Britain in turn had a general monopoly of the carrying of the heavy enumerated goods from the colonies to the British Isles.

Closely related to the Navigation Acts was another series of measures called Trade Acts, and usually confused with the Navigation Acts proper. Most of these were enacted after 1700, and they gradually developed into a complicated system of trade control and encouragement. The general plan was to make the entire British Empire prosperous and the trade of one section complementary to that of other sections.

Colonists were largely limited to buying British manufactures. This was not necessarily a disadvantage, because an elaborate system of export bounties was provided so that British goods were actually cheaper in the colonies than similar foreign goods. These bounties averaged more than £38,000 per year for the ten years preceding the Revolution. From 1757 to 1770 the bounties on British linens exported to the colonies totaled £346,232 according to British treasury reports. In addition to bounties there was a series of rebates, or drawbacks, of duties on European goods exported to the colonies. These, too, ran into formidable sums. Those to the West Indies alone amounted to £34,000 in 1774. The average payments from the British treasury in bounties and drawbacks on exports to the colonies in 1764 amounted to about £250,000 sterling per year.

Colonial production of articles desired in the British markets was encouraged by a variety of measures. Colonial tobacco was given a complete monopoly of the home market by the prohibition of its growth in England and the imposition of heavy import duties on the competing Spanish tobacco. Other colonial products were encouraged by tariff duties, so levied as to discriminate sharply in favor of the colonial product and against the competing foreign product. Some colonial commodities that were produced in greater volume than English demand called for were given rebates on reexportation so as to facilitate their flow through British markets to their foreign destinations. In other cases surplus colonial products, such as rice, were permitted to be exported directly to foreign colonies and to southern Europe without passing through England. In still other cases direct cash bounties were paid on such colonial products as hemp, indigo, lumber, and silk on their arrival in England. These alone totaled more than £82,000 from 1771 to 1775. Naval stores also received liberal bounties, totaling £1,438,762 from 1706 to 1774, and at the time of the Revolution were averaging £25,000 annually.

In the main the navigation system was mutually profitable to colonies and mother country. Occasionally colonial industry was discouraged by parliamentary prohibition if it threatened to develop into serious competition with an important home industry: notable are the laws forbidding the intercolonial export of hats made in the colonies and wool grown or manufactured in the colonies and the act forbidding the setting up of new mills for the production of wrought iron and steel. These laws produced some local complaint, although they evidently affected few people.

So long as the trade and navigation laws were limited to the regulation of trade and the promotion of the total commerce of the empire, they were generally popular in America; at least that was true after 1700. The attempt to use them as taxation measures was resisted. The enumerated products came largely from the colonies that remained loyal. The bounties went largely to the colonies that revolted. The New England shipping industry rested directly on the protection of the Navigation Acts. Consequently the First Continental Congress in its resolutions approved the navigation system, and Benjamin Franklin offered to have the acts reenacted by every colonial legislature in America and to guarantee them for a hundred years if taxation of America were abandoned.

[George E. Howard, *Preliminaries of the Revolution.*]
O. M. DICKERSON

NAVIGATOR, a handbook for western emigrants, with descriptions of river towns, was launched by Zadok Cramer of Pittsburgh about 1801 and went through twelve editions to 1824. The early editions contained directions for navigating the Ohio River (including the Allegheny and the Monongahela); later editions gave navigating directions for the Mississippi and descriptions of the Missouri and Columbia rivers. The publication was bought eagerly by emigrants going down the rivers in flatboats and was an effective aid to the western migration.

[C. W. Dahlinger, *Pittsburgh, A Sketch of Its Early Social Life.*]

SOLON J. BUCK

NAVY, CONFEDERATE, was established by act of the Confederate congress on Feb. 21, 1861. On the same day President Jefferson Davis appointed S. R. Mallory secretary of the Confederate navy; Mallory served for the duration of the war. By an act of Apr. 21, 1862, the navy was to consist of four admirals, ten captains, thirty-one commanders, and a specified number of subaltern officers. Some of these ranks were never filled because of the lack of ships.

As the states composing the Confederacy seceded, they had attempted to create state navies. A few revenue cutters and merchant steamers were seized and converted into men-of-war. These were turned over to the Confederate navy. Before the outbreak of hostilities Raphael Semmes was sent North to purchase ships and materials. No ships were secured but some materials were. Two U.S. shipyards fell to the Confederacy—one when the Gosport Navy Yard at Norfolk, Va., was abandoned and the other when the yard at Pensacola, Fla., was seized. All shipping in the Norfolk yard had been destroyed, but the Confederates raised the hull of the *Merrimack* and converted it into an ironclad ram. Much ordnance was secured from the Norfolk yard. The Pensacola yard was of little value. On May 9, 1861, Mallory commissioned James D. Bulloch to go to England to secure ships for

the Confederacy. Bulloch had some success, contriving to secure several ships that did much damage, as Confederate cruisers, to U.S. commerce.

The Confederacy had ample naval personnel, as 321 officers had resigned from the U.S. Navy by June 1, 1861, and tendered their services. Lack of all necessary facilities, however, and the increasing effectiveness of the Union blockade presented grave obstacles to the building of a Confederate navy. The Confederacy never possessed a mobile fleet. Its naval services may be roughly divided into three classes: (1) Ships serving in inland waters, both for offense and defense. Besides many miscellaneous craft, this group included twenty-one ironclads of varying armaments. (2) Commissioned cruisers, harrying the commerce of the Union abroad. This group numbered fifteen, including the *Alabama, Florida,* and *Shenandoah,* whose operations gave rise to the Alabama Claims against England. (3) Privateers.

The Confederacy is credited with introducing the ironclad vessel, which revolutionized naval warfare. Confederates also contributed to perfecting the torpedo.

[William M. Robinson, Jr., *The Confederate Privateers;* J. Thomas Scharf, *History of the Confederate States Navy.*]
HAYWOOD J. PEARCE, JR.

NAVY, DEPARTMENT OF THE. The unsatisfactory administration of naval affairs by the War Department led Congress to create the Department of the Navy in April 1798, following the recommendation of President John Adams. Benjamin Stoddert of Georgetown, in the District of Columbia, was appointed the first secretary and directed operations during the undeclared naval war with France (1798–1800). Experience during the War of 1812 demonstrated the need for adequate and responsible professional assistants for the secretary, and in 1815 the Board of Navy Commissioners, consisting of three senior officers, was created to meet that need. The first appointees were commodores John Rodgers, Isaac Hull, and David Porter—but by the rulings of the secretary the functions of the board were restricted to naval technology, naval operations being excluded from its purview. In 1842 an organization of technical bureaus was instituted, and it continued to be a main feature of the organization.

The first bureaus to be created were those of Navy Yards and Docks; Construction, Equipment, and Repairs; Provisions and Clothing; Ordnance and Hydrography; and Medicine and Surgery. The duties of the bureaus were performed under the authority of the secretary of the Department of the Navy, and their orders had full force and effect as emanating from him. In 1862 the five bureaus were supplanted by eight: two new bureaus were created, those of Navigation and of Steam Engineering, and the responsibilities of the Bureau of Construction, Equipment, and Repairs were divided between two bureaus, those of Construction and Repairs and of Equipment and Recruiting. The Bureau of Equipment was abolished in 1910, and in 1921 the Bureau of Aeronautics was established. The Office of the Judge Advocate General, independent of any bureau, was created in 1865.

The defect of inadequate professional direction of strategy and the general operations of the fleet was severely felt in all the nation's early wars. In the Civil War it was minimized by the advice of Gustavus V. Fox, a former naval officer who was appointed temporary assistant secretary. The office was created permanently in 1890 but is usually occupied by civilian appointees with jurisdiction over industrial functions. During the war with Spain in 1898 a temporary board of officers advised the secretary on strategy but had no responsibility or authority respecting fleet operations. In 1900 the secretary appointed a general board of high-ranking officers, which remained in existence as an advisory body without executive functions. But by 1909 the scope and extent of the Navy Department had grown too much to permit coordination of the bureaus by the office of the secretary, and in that year Secretary George von Lengerke Meyer appointed four naval officer–aides to assist him—one each for the functions of operations, personnel, matériel, and inspections. This functional organization seemed sound and worked well and was continued in principle. Secretary Josephus Daniels abolished the position of aide for personnel in 1913, but the duties were continued by the Bureau of Navigation. Similarly, the function of inspection was delegated to the Board of Inspection. Matters related to matériel passed largely to the jurisdiction of the assistant secretary. The creation by law in 1915 of a chief of naval operations served to rectify many previous administrative defects and to lead to further coordination within the department, the chief having authority commensurate with his great responsibilities as the principal adviser of the secretary and the person under the secretary having charge of the operations of the fleet. The Office of Operations absorbed many of the lesser boards and offices outside the normal province of the bureaus. During World War I the new organization worked extremely well.

World War II necessitated minor changes in organization that carried into 1947, when the National Security Act was passed. This act created the Department of Defense, within which the secretary of the navy lost cabinet status in 1949. By 1974 refinements in organization had resulted in a structure consisting of the secretary of the navy, an under-secretary, and four assistant secretaries for manpower and reserve affairs, installations and logistics, financial management, and research and development. The military arm has the chief of naval operations, a vice-chief, and six deputy chiefs for surface, submarine and air warfare, logistics, plans and policy, manpower, and reserve, supported by a complex system of bureaus and commands.

[A. W. Johnson, *Manuscript History of the Navy Department*.]

DUDLEY W. KNOX
R. W. DALY

NAVY, UNITED STATES. *This article discusses the U.S. Navy under the following headings:* The Revolution to the Mexican War; The Civil War to World War I; World War II to Vietnam; Peacetime Work; Training and Education; Fleets; Ships; Armament; Facilities; Naval Reserve.

The Revolution to the Mexican War. As colonials, Americans had served in the British navy and aboard merchantmen and had been expert privateers against Britain's foes. In seeking independence, it was natural for them to carry the struggle to sea. Such efforts were spontaneous and opportunistic, the most consequential resulting from the issuance of some 2,000 letters of marque.

The Continental navy was founded by the Continental Congress on Oct. 13, 1775, to perform duties that privateers shunned. Of twenty-seven small men-of-war at sea, only three survived hard fighting and cruising. Continental captains, including John Paul Jones, John Barry, Lambert Wickes, and Nicholas Biddle, were distinguished from privateers by eagerness to engage warships: Capt. Biddle blew up with the 32-gun frigate *Randolph* against the 64-gun ship-of-the-line *Yarmouth* on Mar. 7, 1778, while Jones gave the navy its battle cry of "I have not yet begun to fight!" in conquering the 44-gun frigate *Serapis* with the 42-gun merchantman *Bonhomme Richard* on Sept. 23, 1779. Eleven colonies also had navies that, when totaled, exceeded Continental numbers; Pennsylvania's was particularly aggressive under leaders like Capt. Joshua Barney.

During the Revolution, all maritime branches brought in about 800 prizes, whose cargoes were indispensable to the cause, especially before 1779 when the French alliance and sea power became effective. The British were further humiliated by the capture of 102 minor men-of-war mounting 2,322 guns, besides 16 privateers with 226 guns. It was the French navy that was decisive, by keeping the Royal Navy from relieving besieged Gen. Charles Cornwallis in the Yorktown campaign.

American navies vanished in peacetime. Nevertheless, independence brought problems. Barbary pirates and then warring British and French preyed on U.S. commerce. Consequently, the Navy Department was founded on Apr. 30, 1798. Benjamin Stoddert, as first secretary of the navy, directed twelve frigates and sloops commissioned to protect trade in the West Indies against French freebooters. Appropriately, the first man-of-war afloat was the 44-gun frigate *United States*.

In the Quasi-War with France (1798–1800), the U.S. Navy was expanded to forty-nine vessels through the conversion of merchantmen. Three French warships and eighty-one privateers were captured. Thomas Truxtun was the outstanding captain. In the 36-gun *Constellation,* he took the 40-gun *Insurgente* and shattered in night battle the 40-gun *Vengeance*. More enduringly, as a squadron commander Truxtun infused a professional order and attitude. Similarly, the Tripolitan War (1801–05) was most important for the example and training provided by Commodore Edward Preble.

By 1805, the officer cadre was firmly established. President Thomas Jefferson, alarmed by the implications of having fought offensively overseas, turned to gunboat construction to manifest intent to fight only defensively. Construction was halted on eight 74-gun ships that Stoddert had started. The 176 gunboats that were built proved useless in the War of 1812, while 22 seagoing vessels won glory. The *United States* and its sister *Constitution* under captains Stephen Decatur, Isaac Hull, and William Bainbridge won dazzling victories before preponderant British power closed American ports. Losing 12, the navy captured 15 minor warships and 165 merchantmen. The ubiquitous privateers took an additional 991 merchantmen and 5 small men-of-war. Significant as such successes were in hurting British trade and shortening the war, more significant were the victories of "pygmy fleets" on inland waters. Capt. Oliver Hazard Perry's victory on Lake Erie (Sept. 10, 1813), buttressed by Capt. Thomas Macdonough's on Lake Champlain (Sept.

11, 1814), settled much of the Canadian boundary. Daniel Todd Patterson's handful of ships was essential to the defense of New Orleans. The war stabilized the U.S. Navy, which was rewarded by a few 74-gun ships of the line. The *Independence,* commanded by William Crane and flying the commodore's pendant of William Bainbridge, was the first to go to sea, during the second war with Barbary pirates.

The Algerian War (1815), suppression of West Indian pirates (1816–29), and antislavery patrols (1820–50) provided training for the Mexican War. Then unchallenged, the navy of sixty-three vessels conducted blockade and amphibious operations, the latter destined to become a U.S. specialty. Captains John Sloat and Robert Stockton helped secure California. Captains David Conner and Matthew Perry had the bulk of the fleet in the Gulf of Mexico, making possible the transportation to, and landing at, Veracruz (Mar. 13, 1847) and maintenance of the lifeline for Gen. Winfield Scott's triumphal march to Mexico City.

The Civil War to World War I. When the Civil War began, Gideon Welles, the Union secretary of the navy, had only 8,800 personnel and forty-two of seventy-six vessels ready to close 185 registered harbors in 12,000 miles of indented coastline, exclusive of rivers. Stephen Russell Mallory, the Confederate secretary of the navy, began with 3,000 personnel and twelve sequestered vessels. By war's end, the Union navy had mushroomed to 58,000 sailors in 671 vessels. After Confederate confiscation of some federal ships, the Union lost 109 more. In action, thirty-four warships were sunk conventionally and fourteen by mines, while sixteen were captured. The rigors of blockade were witnessed by thirty-eight men-of-war lost to the sea, including the famous *Monitor*. Seven more burned accidentally. Confederate figures can only be approximated. Extant official records indicate that Mallory approximately doubled manpower and commissioned 209 vessels, always too little and too late.

The Union navy had three main missions: blockade, army cooperation, and commerce protection. Blockade was mounted through capturing a coaling base at Port Royal, S.C. (Nov. 7, 1861), between Charleston and Savannah, and was completed by the amphibious capture of the seaport of Wilmington, Del. (Jan. 15, 1865). Altogether, 1,504 blockade runners were captured or destroyed. Cooperating with the army, the navy helped take the Mississippi River, notably by seizing New Orleans (Apr. 25, 1862) and by providing assistance at Vicksburg (Mar. 13–July

4, 1863). Even more decisive was naval support along the rivers feeding into the Chesapeake Bay. Only on the high seas did the Confederate navy conspicuously succeed; the *Alabama* and 11 other ships took or sank 250 merchantmen. Prudently, one-third to one-half of northern shipowners sought foreign registry. Such shipping did not return to the flag. Since then, government subsidy of the merchant marine has been increasingly necessary.

The U.S. Navy withered in peace until given rationale by the historian Alfred Thayer Mahan, whose writings on sea power (1890–1914) became classics. A small "new navy" of only twenty-one modern warcraft was far readier than the Spaniards for the War of 1898, which was distinguished by the easy victories won by Commodore George Dewey at Manila (May 1) and by Commodore William Sampson at Santiago (July 3). The navy won national support and began its expansion to a position of supremacy. Unpleasant duty in helping to suppress insurrection in the newly acquired Philippines was followed by the world cruise of the "great white fleet" of sixteen new battleships (1907–09), which demonstrated the maturity of American engineering as well as the substance for the "big stick" policy then popular.

Through World War I, the navy had 497,030 personnel to man 37 battleships and 1,926 lesser vessels. Contracts for 949 others, including 32 battleships and battle cruisers, would have made the navy almost equal to all others combined, if completed. Operations were unglamorous. Since the British after the Battle of Jutland (1916) contained the German navy, the prime mission of the United States became the establishment of a bridge to France for 2,079,880 troops and their supplies. The submarine was the foe, combated defensively by convoy and escort and offensively by minefield and airplane. The U.S. Navy was brilliantly successful. Although primitive submarines sank nearly 13 million tons of shipping, including 124 American merchantmen, no American soldier was lost in a France-bound convoy. Only 1 of 178 submarines sunk fell to an American destroyer, but the stupendous North Sea mine barrage, 80 percent laid by the United States, sank or damaged about 17 more and reputedly broke the morale of German submariners. War losses were minimal for the navy, which lost 1,142 lives in forty-five miscellaneous men-of-war: thirteen were sunk by U-boats, three by mines, and twenty-nine by collision or mischance. The heaviest combat loss was the Coast Guard cutter *Tampa,* which went down with 111 men. (The Treasury Department's "navy" has been under naval control in all wars except those with Barbary pirates.)

Besides the portents of the submarine and airplane, the war had unveiled the amphibious potential that the navy had in the combat readiness and excellence of the marines. Quintupled from prewar strength to 67,000 men, the U.S. Marine Corps won immortality in France and a firm place in naval plans. In 1933 the Fleet Marine Force was created, a heavy-infantry organization dedicated to amphibious assault at a time when the perfecting of the aircraft carrier and naval gunfire promised to revolutionize war at sea.

World War II to Vietnam. When the storm of World War II broke, the U.S. Navy had the concepts, if not the numbers, for bold, flexible operations. Rebounding from the surprise attack on Pearl Harbor, the navy expanded to 3 million men and women serving on 8 battleships, 48 cruisers, 104 aircraft carriers, 349 destroyers, 203 submarines, 2,236 convoy-escort craft, 886 minesweepers, 4,149 large and 79,418 small amphibious craft, 1,531 auxiliaries, and 22,045 other types. American combat losses to Oct. 1, 1945, were 2 battleships, 5 heavy and 7 escort aircraft carriers, 10 cruisers, 79 destroyers, 52 submarines, 36 minesweepers, 69 PT boats, 172 large amphibious craft, and 254 other types. Casualties of the navy, marines, and Coast Guard totaled 56,206 dead, 8,967 missing, and 80,259 wounded. The U.S. Navy destroyed 132 German and 8 Italian submarines in supplementing air and British naval operations, but as the major combatant in the Pacific theater of war, the navy annihilated the initially triumphant Japanese, sinking 11 battleships, 15 fleet and 5 escort aircraft carriers, 33 cruisers, 119 destroyers, and countless lesser craft.

Fleet Adm. Ernest J. King, who commanded from 1941 to 1945, in his *U.S. Navy at War* divided the Pacific war into four stages. Phase one, from Dec. 7, 1941, to June 1942, was defensive. The period had ten naval engagements capped by the Battle of the Coral Sea (May 7–8, 1942), when Rear Adm. Frank J. Fletcher with the *Yorktown* and *Lexington* carrier task forces stopped a superior Japanese thrust at southeast New Guinea. Superb intelligence procedures detected Japanese intentions to take Midway Island. The ensuing battle (June 3–6, 1942) was the turning point of the war. Outnumbered American carriers decisively decimated their opposites in the first sea fight by fleets whose ships never sighted each other.

The defensive-offensive period of Midway was a brief phase two, merging with phase three, the offensive-defensive period that committed the marines to the long fight for Guadalcanal (Aug. 7, 1942–Feb. 9, 1943) and produced a dozen night battles amid shallows and islands, as well as supporting carrier engagements in the open sea. Together they exacted battle losses exceeding those at Jutland. The Japanese, rebuilding carrier strength after Midway, improvidently fed idle naval aviation into the fray, thus undermining their carrier potential in trying to stop the marine drive up the Solomons to join pressure with Gen. Douglas MacArthur's combined forces outflanking the Japanese naval and air bastion of Rabaul on New Britain. About this time, American submarines hit their stride with a deadliness that sank two-thirds of Japanese shipping, an attrition in itself sufficient to have produced eventual victory through the starvation of Japan.

The pure offensive, phase four, opened with the navy thrusting westward into the Marshall Islands. The Battle of the Philippine Sea, nicknamed the "Marianas Turkey Shoot" (June 19–20, 1944), disclosed the fatal deterioration of Japanese carrier aviation when 402 Japanese planes were downed with an American loss of only 17 planes. Saipan, Guam, Tinian, Peleliu, and Ulithi were milestones in the drive, forging a logistic line for naval juncture with the successful forces of MacArthur in a campaign for recapture of the Philippines. On Oct. 20, 1944, MacArthur landed at Leyte Island. The Japanese naval counterattack produced a complex of farflung actions (Oct. 23–26) that crushed Japan as a naval power and left the home islands completely vulnerable. Japan itself became the objective. To add fullest weight of air power to the assault on Japanese home industry and to supplement the mounting submarine blockade, marines took Iwo Jima at heavy cost (Feb. 19–Mar. 16, 1945), but the island thereafter provided essential fighter cover for long-range bombers. On Apr. 1, marines and army landed on Okinawa, within easy reach of southern Kyushu. Desperate kamikaze attacks failed to dislodge the supporting fleet, which sustained 5,000 fatalities, 368 damaged ships, and 36 minor vessels lost. When atomic attacks on Hiroshima and Nagasaki ended the war, the navy was preparing for the invasion of Kyushu and a drive on Tokyo itself. Strangulation by sea and air had produced the first unconditional surrender of a major nation without invasion.

In the war with Germany, the U.S. Navy was preoccupied anew with defense of sea communications and began as a junior partner to the British navy, which was mastering effective antisubmarine warfare in the period before U.S. belligerency. Concurrently, the Germans were perfecting submarine tactics, making the Battle of the Atlantic bitter and too often close. In the summer of 1943 the advent of American escort-carrier groups ("hunter-killers") gave defense the decisive edge. Allied forces destroyed 753 of a phenomenal 1,170 U-boats (the figures given by German Adm. Karl Doenitz), which sank 197 warships and 2,828 merchantmen totaling 14,687,231 tons (according to the historian Samuel Eliot Morison).

The liberation of Europe was predicated on reentry onto the Continent, which American amphibious techniques made possible. Beginning with a meager 102 vessels for landings in French Morocco (Nov. 8, 1942), the U.S. Navy multiplied amazingly to 2,489 amphibious craft for the Normandy invasion (June 6, 1944) and loaned an equal number to the British. The liberality of such lend-lease is the most convincing evidence that America had noncompetitively overtaken England in naval superiority. England was the recipient not only of amphibious craft but also of an impressive navy in the form of 38 escort-carriers, 189 blue-water convoy-escorts, 9 submarines, 187 minesweepers, and 415 specialized craft. The Soviet Union was second, receiving some 615 naval and military vessels and 90 merchantmen. France was third, with 145 minor men-of-war.

In the uncertainties of the nuclear age, the navy continued to perfect the potentials of carriers, submarines, and amphibians. Gradually budgeted down to 238 major combat craft, 393,893 personnel, and 74,396 marines, the navy was professionally keen in 1950 when the Korean War broke out. Besides vital close air support from carriers and amphibious outflanking as at the port of Inchon, naval gunfire proved invaluable in preventing free Communist use of the coasts. The 16-inch guns of the battleships were unexpectedly useful in firing across Communist territory from the seaward rear to knock out positions on reverse slopes of mountains, where Communist forces were otherwise safe from front-line fire. By the time of the armistice of July 27, 1953, the navy operated 408 major and 720 minor vessels, with reserves swelling manpower to 800,000 personnel and 248,612 marines. The navy lost 5 ships and had 87 damaged, while 564 downed aircraft added heavily to the 458 killed or missing and 1,576 wounded.

The U.S. Navy first became involved in Vietnam after the collapse of the French there in 1954. In August of that year the vanguard of an ultimate 100 amphibious and auxiliary vessels under Rear Adm. L. S. Sabin began evacuating more than 300,000 refugees from the new Communist government to the south from Haiphong. In 1955 a small group of advisers, rising to 60 by 1960 and to 742 by 1964, helped train South Vietnam's neophyte navy. The presence of American warships began in December 1961, with minesweepers assuming radar watch near the seventeenth parallel to assist Vietnamese patrols in finding possible infiltrators among the thousands of coastal fishing craft. A few months later, destroyer escorts briefly made the same surveillance in the Gulf of Thailand. By the end of 1964, when 23,000 U.S. troops were engaged in military operations in South Vietnam, naval commitment soon followed. In March 1965 the destroyers *Black* and *Higbee* started an anti-infiltration patrol-and-search operation code-named Market Time. This coast-surveillance force shortly became Task Force 115, using conventional warships to maintain radar coverage for directing scores of high-speed miniwarships appropriately named "Swift" boats and 26 U.S. Coast Guard small cutters, together with U.S. airplanes and the units of the Vietnamese navy. Broadened to include shore bombardment, this inshore blockade continued until the U.S. withdrawal in 1973.

In April 1966, another kind of naval operation began with Task Force 116, code-named Game Warden, which consisted of 120 boats designed to patrol within the numerous outlets of the Mekong River. Task Force 117, activated in June 1967, was the Riverine Assault Force, whose boats bore heavy weapons and were armored against small-arms fire. The pygmy capital-ship types with turrets were "monitors."

Training and expansion of the Vietnamese progressed so that the U.S. Navy could initiate transfer of its miniature men-of-war in February 1969, completed by 1971, releasing all but advisers, who left in 1972.

The major operation was inaugurated on Aug. 5, 1964, when airplanes from the *Constitution* and *Ticonderoga* of the Seventh Fleet struck targets in North Vietnam. Subsequently, the nuclear *Enterprise* and the fossil-fuel *America, Constitution, Coral Sea, Forrestal, Hancock, Kitty Hawk, Midway, Oriskany, Franklin D. Roosevelt,* and *Saratoga* rotated into duty. In May 1972, a concentration of six ships conducted the aerial mining of Haiphong and other North Vietnamese harbors in order to halt delivery by sea of munitions from Russia, China, and other Communist-bloc countries. Carrier operations caused the heaviest U.S. naval losses of personnel during the hostilities.

Peacetime Work. Although the U.S. Navy's primary occupation in peacetime is to prepare for hostilities, it has a rich history in diplomacy, humanitarianism, and exploration.

Throughout the 1900's, officers often acted on their own initiative to maintain or to advance U.S. foreign policy. Thus, in 1818, Capt. James Biddle and the *Ontario* began effective protection of Americans overseas by securing the freedom of some U.S. citizens imprisoned by the Spanish authorities in Valparaiso, Chile, during a revolution. In 1822, judicious conduct by Comdr. Robert Field Stockton of the *Alligator* helped to establish the country of Liberia. Lt. Charles Wilkes in 1842 negotiated a treaty with the Sultan of Sulu. The circumspect conduct of Capt. Lawrence Kearny and his squadron at Canton during Britain's first Opium War was crucial in bringing about the first U.S. treaty with China in 1844 on a "most-favored-nation" basis. Peacekeeping in the Caribbean dates from 1853 when Comdr. George N. Hollins and the *Cyane* brought disciplinary measures to Honduras, at a time when Comdr. Duncan Ingraham in the Mediterranean Sea at Izmir (Smyrna), Turkey, underscored the U.S. concept of *jus domus* by compelling an Austrian warship to release a naturalized American. Commodore Matthew Perry's spectacular "opening of Japan" in 1854 overshone the firm security simultaneously afforded by John Kelly and the *Plymouth* to Americans and foreigners beset by the Chinese in Shanghai. In 1859, a squadron under William B. Shubrick sailed down the Paraná River to quiet a bellicose Paraguay. Similarly, in 1873 a show of naval force off Cuba soothed the aftermath of the *Virginius* affair. In the same year in the Pacific, Capt. Richard Meade and the *Narragansett* laid effective claim to part of Samoa. The first treaty that Korea made with any Western power was negotiated in 1882 by Comdr. Robert W. Shufeldt on the *Swatara.*

The complete initiative of naval officers ended with the establishment of direct control from Washington, D.C., first made possible by underwater cable. By World War I, radio made such control almost instantaneous; this control was strikingly present in the 1962 Cuban missile crisis, when President John F. Kennedy personally gave orders over radiotelephone to the bridge of the commander whose destroyer was within hailing distance of the first Soviet merchantman sighted.

In foreign affairs, the post–World War II naval role was to show force in readiness to friends and possible foes. The permanent stationing of the Sixth Fleet helped avert Communist takeovers in Greece and Lebanon, dampened the Suez crisis, and limited the Six-Day War between Israel and the Arab states. The Seventh Fleet shielded Taiwan from Red China.

Apart from numerous rescues of persons innocently

trapped in shooting situations, the navy has often sped food, clothing, and medical aid to victims of major natural disasters, as the 1902 eruption of Mount Pelée that killed 40,000 on Martinique; the 1906 San Francisco earthquake; the 1908 earthquake in Sicily that killed 80,000; and the 1923 earthquake in Tokyo and Yokohama that killed 100,000. The development of long-range aviation made possible a swift response when earthquakes afflicted Ecuador in 1949, Chile in 1960, Yugoslavia in 1963, and Peru in 1970. Floods found navy and marine helicopter crews ready to sacrifice themselves to save others, as during the January 1969 rains on southern California. The outstanding example of aid to women and children victimized by war was by the cruiser-destroyer force of Rear Adm. Mark L. Bristol, which in 1919 entered the Black Sea to assist in the distribution of food and other supplies for relief. In 1920 the ships evacuated many persons fleeing the victorious Red Army in the Crimea. During the turbulence of 1920–22 in the Near East the navy covered the single-day embarkation of 30,000 Greeks from Izmir.

Navy hydrographers use ships' logs and observations for continual updating of charts and notices to mariners. The navy routinely charted U.S. shores until the formation of the Coast and Geodetic Survey. In the late 1830's, interest shifted to the exploration of foreign lands. Lt. Edwin J. De Haven with two vessels tried to find the British explorer Sir John Franklin and his companions, lost in the Arctic. Comdr. William Lynch charted the Jordan River and the Dead Sea in 1848 and the west coast of Africa in 1853. The Ringgold-Rodgers squadron in 1853–54 amplified the findings in the Pacific made by the earlier exploring expedition of Charles Wilkes (1838–42). Other officers surveyed the Isthmus of Panama for canal routes. Lt. Thomas Page charted southern South American rivers and thereby nearly caused a war with Paraguay. The possibilities of laying a transatlantic cable from Newfoundland to Ireland were inspired by the work of O. H. Berryman and given a sound basis by the work of Lt. Matthew Fontaine Maury.

Training and Education. In sailing ships, the ratings for noncommissioned officers or "mates" were the gunners, boatswains, quartermasters, carpenters, yeomen, storekeepers, and surgeon's mates. Ships powered by steam first needed the engineman, boilerman, and machinist and then the electrician, metalsmith, pipe fitter, molder, patternmaker, steelworker, and damage controlman. Aviation required its special varieties of ordnanceman. The development of radio

and electronics created the radioman, fire controlman, sonarman, radarman, and electronics technician. By 1973 there were twelve categories with sixty-nine ratings, including the ocean-systems technician, missile technician, and data-systems technician, required by modern naval technology.

Until the time of the Civil War, experienced seamen came directly into the navy from civilian vessels. The withering of the merchant marine largely brought about by the *Alabama* and other Confederate ships shrank the ready supply of seamen. In 1875, Capt. Stephen B. Luce hit upon the notion of recruiting boys and training them as naval apprentices, completely solving the problem.

By the mid-1970's there were hundreds of special schools for recruits. Entry to the first of the six grades of petty officer is usually accomplished by completing a basic school. After various periods of experience depending upon the rating and after passing examinations for promotion, a petty officer is able to advance higher by success at a second school and sometimes a third. The skills acquired in the rating, except for such outright military skills as that of gunner's mate, usually carry directly into a civilian counterpart.

Beyond training that is essentially military, the navy vigorously urges high school dropouts to volunteer for off-duty programs in order to win diplomas or certificates of equivalency. As for college-level opportunities conferring credit toward a degree, by the mid-1970's more than 6,000 correspondence courses, from language study to nuclear fission, were available. The special college-credit program begun aboard Polaris submarines to help ease the monotony of sixty-day submerged patrols has become available for all ships. Harvard University is one of the sponsoring institutions.

Stationed ashore and close to a college or university, navy personnel may have duties arranged to allow for part-time attendance at a school, a substantial part of the cost for the studies paid by the navy. A petty officer may attend a junior college full-time for an associate degree in arts, engineering, or science, and the whole cost is paid in exchange for a period of additional service. If a person has the requisite ability and volunteers for a scientific major desired by the navy, the navy pays for the whole four years and grants a commission. As of the 1970's every class entering the Naval Academy had eighty-five openings for young men from the fleet and another eighty-five for reservists.

By the mid-1970's young women had all the same opportunities as men plus the opportunities offered by the Bureau of Medicine for full-time attendance at a college studying for a degree in nursing or medical dietetics, with a commission upon graduation.

Also in the mid-1970's, members of minority groups were able to take advantage of Project BOOST (Broadened Opportunity for Officer Selection and Training), which provided them a maximum of two years in a preparatory school at San Diego, Calif., before competing in the examinations for entry to the Naval Academy or college with a Naval Reserve Officers' Training Corps (NROTC).

As for officers, by 1975 the greater number came from Officer Candidate School after having completed a bachelor's or higher degree in any accredited subject at a college or university (*see* Naval Reserve). After some years of duty, graduates from Officer Candidate School were able to qualify for regular commissions.

The traditional regular officer still comes from the Naval Academy, founded at Annapolis, Md., in 1845. The brigade of midshipmen at the academy is kept at a strength of approximately 4,200 by a dozen methods of entry, in which congressional appointment predominates.

Career officers gain professional depth at the Naval War College, conceived and established in 1884 at Newport, R.I., by Stephen B. Luce. The college had its purpose and value crystallized in the publications of its most illustrious faculty member, Alfred Thayer Mahan. By 1975 there were about 360 students, primarily from the navy but also including members of other services, government civilians, and foreign officers, enrolled at the college. On two-year assignment, officers explore and reflect upon strategy, tactics, logistics, and the philosophy of war, testing theories in war games, assisted by electronic displays and computers. The Naval War College has had a wide influence, notably in the adoption of all U.S. services of its "estimate of the situation" and "completed staff study" concepts.

Postgraduate education of officers in military "hardware" began modestly in 1904 with a handful of men taking courses in marine engineering given in the appropriate bureau. Success encouraged transfer to the Naval Academy, which in 1912 established a postgraduate department. Well received, the department flourished and was finally housed in the academy's erstwhile marine barracks. Capt. Ernest J. King was the first head of the newly named "PG School" after World War I. Congress in 1945 authorized the school to confer the master's degree and the

doctorate in technical fields, although by then a substantial number of students were primarily interested in refresher courses to enable them to enter civilian universities in pursuit of the same degrees. Relocated at Monterey, Calif., in 1954, the school was serving some 2,000 officers with an increasingly distinguished faculty by the mid-1970's.

The navy also strongly encouraged study at universities, not just in engineering but also in a considerable range of subjects from law to international relations. The latter subject, for instance, has about twelve officers a year entering the Fletcher School at Tufts University in Massachusetts. In exchange for full support, an officer must agree to an appropriately extended period of active service.

Many military installations have after-hours educational programs for which the navy pays part of the cost. An example is the master's in personnel administration conducted by George Washington University in Naval Academy classrooms for the officer-faculty.

Fleets. The squadron concept that began in the Quasi-War with France was the basic tactical organization until 1907, when the Atlantic, Pacific, and Asiatic fleets were formed. Within this structure the force concept grew into the now-familiar task force. In World War II there were eleven fleets with specific geographic areas of operations, except for the Tenth Fleet, which was charged with antisubmarine warfare. At that time, odd-numbered fleets were located in the Pacific, and even-numbered in the Atlantic. The most famous fleets in wartime were the Third, Fifth, and Seventh fleets, the latter with MacArthur. The Third and Fifth were in the Central Pacific and consisted largely of the same ships, designated Third when under Adm. William F. Halsey and Fifth when under Adm. Raymond A. Spruance.

Students reading World War II naval history may encounter numeral designations such as Task Element 38.4.6.2. In this designation, subdivision is indicated by italics:

3–.–.–.–. = *Third Fleet*
38.–.–.–. = *Task Force 8* of Third Fleet
38.4.–.–. = *Task Group 4* of Task Force 38
38.4.6.–. = *Task Unit 6* of Task Group 38.4
38.4.6.2. = *Task Element 2* of Task Unit 38.4.6

For purposes of administration, ships are also organized into type commands: for example, submarines, Atlantic (SUBLANT); submarines, Pacific (SUBPAC); and destroyers, Atlantic (DESLANT).

Basic tactical organizations are division (two or more vessels of the same type); squadron (generally two or more divisions); and flotilla (generally two or more similar squadrons).

By 1971 the Atlantic Fleet maintained the Second and Sixth fleets, the latter in the Mediterranean, while the Pacific Fleet had the First and Seventh fleets, the latter in Southeast Asian waters. Each great fleet has force subdivisions, such as amphibious, antisubmarine warfare, cruiser-destroyer, hunter-killer, mine, naval air, and submarine. There are five sea frontier commands for Alaska, Hawaii, the continental western and eastern coasts, and the Caribbean. Naval forces are assigned to Antarctica, the eastern Atlantic, Europe, Japan, Key West, Korea, the Middle East, the South Atlantic, and until 1973 to Vietnam. Such ships include the ships committed to the North Atlantic Treaty Organization (NATO). In 1973 some consolidation commenced, the First Fleet and the Pacific Antisubmarine Force merging into a new Second Fleet headquartered at Pearl Harbor.

Ships. The increasing power of cannon about the year 1700 required ships to have a defensive thickness of hull that gradually eliminated the adaptation of merchant vessels for war, except for their use as privateers. The principal types in the sail era were the ship of the line and the frigate. The Civil War witnessed the conversion of civilian vessels, even ferryboats, by the hundreds into gunboats and cruisers, a situation forced upon both the North and the South by the small prewar size of the U.S. Navy. Even so, the actual construction during the war was principally of ironclads. Later technology in steel brought into being the familiar battleships, aircraft carriers, cruisers, submarines, and destroyers, obviously built only for combat. Merchantmen continue to be valuable for wartime expansion of fleet auxiliaries, as for supply carriers and tankers.

Although the system of type designations of warships (such as CAG-2) reflects the considerable complexity of many specialized types of ships and may seem cryptic, this system is a form of shorthand describing a vessel's main mission and equipment.

The first letter in the designation identifies certain broad categories:

A = auxiliary vessel
B = capital gunship
C = cruiser or aircraft carrier
D = destroyer types
L = landing craft

M = mine warfare types
P = patrol types
S = submarines
Y = yard vessels

Some of the above letters may be doubled; they then mean:

BB = battleship
DD = destroyer
MM = fleet minelayer
SS = fleet submarine

The primary meaning does not necessarily carry over into a secondary position, as in

CA = heavy cruiser (8-inch guns)
CL = light cruiser (5-inch or 6-inch)
DL = frigate
MS = minesweeper

In the secondary position, most of the alphabet is used: for instance, AH for hospital auxiliary; AK for cargo ship; and AO for oiler auxiliary. The V in CV denotes an aircraft carrier.

Among letters used in the third and fourth positions, the most notable are B for ballistic missile; G for guided missile; H for helicopter; and N for nuclear-powered. Thus, SSBN is a nuclear-powered submarine armed with ballistic missiles, commonly called a Polaris sub; DDG is a destroyer with guided missiles; and CVH is a helicopter carrier.

A CAG-2 designation would thus signify: C (cruiser), A (heavy), G (guided missile). The number 2 indicates the place in the sequence in a type. The CAG-1 is the *Boston,* and the CAG-2, the *Canberra* (named for an Australian cruiser lost at the Battle of Savo Sound).

Traditionally battleships were named after states, carriers after battles or historic ships, cruisers after cities, submarines after sea creatures, and destroyers after naval heroes. There has been some modification of this practice. Names of fleet ballistic-missile submarines may honor outstanding Americans (*Patrick Henry,* SSBN-599), as have some carriers since 1955 (*James V. Forrestal,* CVA-59, A standing for "attack"). The torpedo-armed SSN's continue bearing the names of sea creatures, but the 688 begun in 1972 was named the *Los Angeles,* borrowing from the cruiser tradition. Increasingly, larger frigates that would once have been called destroyer flotilla leaders fittingly honor famous battle admirals (*George Dewey*, DLG-14), but the even larger DLGN-37 was laid down in 1972 as the *South Carolina*, hinting at the role of the future battleship.

From a 1969 peak of 932 commissioned vessels, of which 481 were combatants, the navy had been shrinking during the 1970's from the combined pressures of soaring costs and federal economizing. The 1974 plan was for 523 vessels in commission, of which 311 were combatants: 15 attack carriers, 7 cruisers, 29 frigates, 128 destroyer types, 12 diesel and 108 nuclear submarines, 15 amphibians, and 15 patrol types. Strength dropped to 502 in 1975. It is noteworthy that nuclear submarines constitute a substantial third, with the planned replacement of some of the 16-missile Polaris submarines with the colossal 24-missile Trident type.

Armament. For several centuries the main battery of line-of-battle warships was artillery, rivaled in World War II by aircraft and in the 1970's by rocketry.

The primary cannon of the Continental and U.S. navies were muzzle-loading smoothbore pieces known by weight of shot, from 24-pounders down through 18-, 12-, 9-, 6-, and 3-pounders. The largest could take up to three minutes to load, depending upon the efficiency of a crew. All were extremely inaccurate, with effective ranges of 1,200 yards at most, making for tactics of close combat, victory often gained by grappling and boarding. The main projectiles were solid spheres slightly less than the diameter of a bore and aimed to pierce a hull. Antipersonnel projectiles were grapeshot—small shot sewn into canvas—and canister, a can filled with musket balls, both kinds breaking open after firing to create giant shotgun effects. Antirigging langrage consisted of jagged-edged metal or even broken glass. Contrary to much fiction, very few exploding shells were fired from long guns until reliable, safe fuses appeared in the 1820's. Only privateers gambled with the early wooden fuses in long guns. The "bombs bursting in air" over Fort McHenry were fired from mortars. For incendiarism, a shot of lesser caliber could be heated white-hot and loaded against a green-wood core protecting the powder charge. The carcass was made by suspending a bag of gunpowder within a spherical framework of metal hoops, which was dipped into warmed tar to be shaped into rounded smoothness. Ignited by discharge, a carcass would burn until the gunpowder exploded to spew blazing tar.

As improving technology produced better tackle for handling weights, guns steadily grew in size. In the 1850's there was a whole new generation of cannon whose bores were measured in inches; these were scientifically perfected by John Dahlgren and others. The pair of XI-inch Dahlgrens of the *Monitor* fired 168-pound projectiles, the double-turreted *Miantonomoh* had XV-inch, but none was fitted with his monstrous XX-inch, if only because its projectiles weighed more than half a ton. These were the ultimate smoothbores, because technology concurrently mastered the rifling of iron and the ramming of a projectile to produce the muzzle-loading Parrott gun whose 30-pound shot flew more than two miles.

By the 1880's the revolution in steel made possible huge masses that could be easily machined; electric motors replaced muscles; and the modern, breech-loading rifle was born, doubling and redoubling in size until it reached the standard 16-inch gun of the battleships. The *New Jersey* hurled one-ton shells twenty miles onto coastal targets in Vietnam.

Cannon could be made even larger, as attested by the 18-inch guns of the Japanese *Yamato*, but the boundaries of prohibitive cost were well in view when airplanes came to offer a far cheaper means of accurately delivering ordance at comparatively vast ranges far beyond cannon possibilities. The challenge of the airplane arose during World War I, but the battleship was believed to have met the supposed deadliness of the torpedo plane, which had to attack on a straight course at suicidally slow speed to drop its delicate weapon. Level bombing had been inconclusive in the protracted tests by Gen. William ("Billy") Mitchell's airmen against the helplessly anchored *Ostfriedsland*, and although in 1936 during the Spanish Civil War the antiquated Republican battleship *Jaime I* was sunk by German level bombers, all major navies continued launching battleships. Late in the 1920's, accurate dive-bombing techniques were being pioneered by the U.S. Marines and U.S. Navy, techniques that would dominate during World War II in the Pacific. The new era dawned at the 1942 battles in the Coral Sea and at Midway, which were decided without any of the surface foes sighting each other.

In practical terms, the dive-bomber extended battle ranges to hundreds of miles. The 1944 advent of German rocketry simply spurred postwar development of airborne varieties into the 1972 "smart bombs" used against North Vietnam. Late in World War II, ground-scanning radar made high-level bombing somewhat more accurate, but carpet-bombing—a formation of airplanes salvoing together—remained the best means of hitting a desired target.

Those who expected gigantic missiles to supersede

the aircraft carrier, just as the carrier had superseded the battleship, were given pause by the 1945 atomic bombs. Total destruction is implicit both in the fitting of nuclear warheads in an aircraft's air-to-ground missiles for stand-off firing and in the placing of nuclear warheads on ballistic missiles. Indeed, there is a saying among Polaris submarine crews that "if we have to shoot, it means we've failed," pointing up the belief that the chief value of modern missiles is as a deterrent. As for critics of the aircraft carrier who claim it is fatally vulnerable to nonnuclear-warhead missiles, advocates point to the Japanese kamikazes as virtual missiles that were unable to drive the U.S. Navy away from the conquest of Okinawa.

Secondary batteries during the American Revolution were formed by cannon lighter than the main battery and generally mounted on fore and after castles. The Quasi-War with France found the new navy adopting the British carronade, which created an extremely unusual armament situation, insofar as this secondary weapon was usually more powerful than the main battery. Being about a third of the weight of its equivalent long gun and served by a fourth as many men, a stubby carronade within 300 yards intensified a broadside. Because of its lightness, it was ideal for mounting on the highest decking. A frigate such as the *Constitution* with a 24-pounder main battery could have 32-pounder or even 42-pounder carronades, sizes not in the U.S. Navy long-gun inventory until after the War of 1812. Carronades account for some discrepancies in accounts of sea battles; the *Constitution* might have had a dozen carronades to make a total of fifty-six muzzles, but it was still officially rated a forty-four, the number of its long guns.

The principle of using smaller guns to complement a main battery continued into the 20th century. The steel revolution and the development of breech-loading weapons vastly increased rates of fire, while improvements in mounting brought in the dual-purpose quick-firing gun that could be aimed at the horizon and upward to directly overhead. The 5-inch/38 was the most famous in World War II; it was a very effective antiaircraft weapon when fired with the VT, or proximity fuse. The common antiaircraft weapon in the 1970's was the radar-controlled 3-inch/70.

The machine guns introduced in the 1880's, such as the 1-pounder Hotchkiss, were comparatively heavy, being intended to sink torpedo boats. Antiaircraft was the primary mission of the .50 Browning, 20-mm Oerlikon, and 40-mm Bofors used in World War II.

The self-propelled torpedoes, first carried aboard tiny speedboats, never fulfilled their threat because they had to be launched at a few hundred yards, necessitating a run-in that afforded an alert man-of-war ample time. By 1900 the speedboat had been replaced by the larger vessel with greater speed originally known as the torpedo-boat destroyer, which carried the torpedoes in World War I and down to the mid-1970's. The ideal torpedo carrier turned out to be the submarine. As a result, one of a surface ship's best defenses is an antisubmarine torpedo.

Mines, known as "torpedoes" during the Civil War, made a deadly quantum jump from explosion by direct contact to explosion by detonator when the antenna mine was perfected by the Bureau of Ordnance during World War I. It made possible in World War I the laying of the stupendous North Sea mine barrage that diminished the zest of German submarine crews for trying to enter the North Atlantic. World War II brought the magnetic and acoustic types of mines, the sophisticated versions of which were air-dropped during 1972 in the approaches to Haiphong harbor in North Vietnam.

Facilities. The thirteen colonies had a very strong maritime tradition, and easily produced men-of-war for fighting in the Revolution. Construction of naval vessels by private companies has been done ever since. The naval base is centered on a navy yard, which is primarily devoted to the upkeep of ships and, in some cases, to the construction of ships as well. The first navy yard began operations in 1799 within the boundaries of the young nation's new capital, Washington, D.C. Initially engaged in the construction of small gunboats, the Washington Yard soon turned to the production of cannon to such an extent that it became known as the Naval Gun Factory. (It is now a naval museum.) In 1800, yards were established at Portsmouth, N.H., Boston, Mass., and Norfolk, Va.; in 1801 at Philadelphia, Pa., and Brooklyn, N.Y.; in 1825 at Pensacola, Fla.; in 1854 at Mare Island, Calif.; in 1901 at Charleston, S.C.; and in 1902 at Bremerton, Wash. A dozen more followed. Later some bases phased out shipbuilding. Pensacola, for example, concentrated on training naval aviators. By World War I, navy yards were generally kept free for the repairing of war-damaged units, letting private contractors build the new vessels needed, a procedure resumed during World War II. The Great Depression had shown the value of federal spending in priming the economy. After the peace of 1945, the government's desire to fend off a depression kept many private yards in business, enabling some, such as the Electric Boat Company of Groton,

Conn. (a submarine contractor), to become giants. Not one of the fifty-seven major units on the ways in 1973—including two aircraft carriers, nineteen submarines, and sixteen destroyers—was built in a navy dock.

During World War II, the navy had some 7,200 shore facilities, a figure that was cut back to 800 by 1949 and that has been dwindling ever since in recurrent budget squeezing by the government, compelling the navy to undergo sacrifices that would maximize forces at sea and underwrite research (*see* Naval Competition). The transfer of ownership of the tremendous Brooklyn Navy Yard to New York City in 1969 was a forecast of the wholesale shutdown in 1973 of 200 facilities. Ten shipyards, including historic Boston and San Francisco, were closed. Key West, the bulk of Newport, R.I., and Long Beach, Calif., closed down. Air bases were discontinued at famous Quonset Point, R.I.; Lakehurst, N.J.; Albany, Ga.; Imperial Beach, Calif.; and elsewhere. No less stunning were the closure of New York's Saint Alban's Naval Hospital and the decommissioning of the hospital ship *Repose*.

Since 1830 the navy has led in research and development with the opening in Washington, D.C., of the Naval Observatory and the Hydrographic Office, where Maury found world renown. The gun-testing station built in 1848 on the Potomac River moved its scientific personnel to the present Indian Head, Md., Naval Proving Ground in the 1890's. The Naval Torpedo Station (1869) at Newport developed the torpedo. The David Taylor Model Basin (1900) at Carderock, Md., is a leader in ship design. The naval aircraft factory begun at Philadelphia in 1917 completely relinquished production in the 1920's to civilian firms and went on in aerodynamic experimentation, notably in guided bombs before World War II. The Mine Laboratory (renamed the Naval Ordnance Laboratory), established in 1918 at White Oak, Md., developed the antenna mine. The Naval Research Laboratory (1923) at Anacostia in Washington, D.C., has evolved into one of the largest centers of applied and pure research, originally paying its way by the 1937 introduction of a practical, seagoing radar. In 1939 its scientists laid the foundation of what became the Manhattan Project for making the atomic bomb. By 1946 the complex of naval research centers required coordination, so the present Office of Naval Research began a systematic study of the basic sciences, including medicine. By the 1970's, there was little in science and technology that remained untouched by the navy.

Naval Reserve. During the years the American merchant marine was expanding, its seamen constituted a virtual reserve, epitomized by the volunteers who filled the ships during the Civil War. The ensuing decline of American shipping created a need for formal organization and recruiting. Massachusetts led the way on Mar. 18, 1890, by founding a naval militia, soon adopted by other seaboard states. Development paralleled the National Guard until militias were brought under federal control on Feb. 16, 1914. The National Naval Volunteers Act of Aug. 29, 1916, created the naval reserve as such, which absorbed the militias. Thereafter the naval reserve proliferated in conformance with technological advances to a complexity that in World War II provided about 90 percent of naval personnel.

The Act of July 9, 1952, created the present ready, standby, and retired categories, primarily differentiated by liability to recall to active duty. Normally, a reservist passes from the ready reserve through standby to retired status. Qualifications are maintained through drills in a broad program of some forty different types of pay and nonpay units, through two-week active-duty-for-training periods, officer schools, correspondence courses, and other ways approved by the chief of naval personnel. The success of the 1946 "weekend warrior" program for aviation units resulted in a selected reserve program for small ships, principally antisubmarine warfare types, which are kept ready by a small, permanent crew to be manned in a matter of hours by reserves who train afloat throughout the year, one weekend a month.

To supplement the traditional appointment of qualified officers from the merchant marine or from civilians with applicable specialties, the Student Navy Training Corps was established in 1917 at ninety colleges and universities. This became the basis for normal peacetime procurement and evolved into the present Naval Reserve Officers Training Corps (NROTC) at fifty colleges (1975 figure). Selected appointees receive pay throughout the four years of college work in fields of individual choice and concurrently take six hours a week of naval training plus appropriate summer cruises. After graduation and commissioning, they serve a stipulated time on active duty and then have the option, if recommended, of transferring into the regular navy for a career. The same NROTC units also have contract candidates who, after satisfactory grades and aptitude for the first two years, are paid during the last two. For non-NROTC collegiate institutions, there is the Reserve Officer Candidate (ROC) program, in which a college student may earn a commission by satisfactory completion of two six-week training courses during the summer. The Naval Aviation Cadet program is another means of entry. The major means for obtaining the number of junior officers needed annually is the Officer Candidate School at Newport, R.I. Every six weeks a class of college graduates starts the "ninety-day wonder" course. The navy and naval reserve have through such programs the largest percentage of college graduates in the armed services.

During the Vietnam War, service in the naval reserve was very popular, and every unit had long lists of waiting applicants. In the aftermath of the war, the navy commenced an augmentation policy demanding swifter readiness for call-up and more time on active duty, which, in the climate of the hoped for "zero draft," eroded the former popularity of the naval reserve.

[*American State Papers, Naval Affairs; Civil War Naval Chronology; Dictionary of American Naval Fighting Ships;* F. M. Bennett, *The Steam Navy of the United States;* W. R. Carter, *Beans, Bullets, and Black Oil;* F. E. Chadwick, *The Spanish-American War;* H. I. Chapelle, *History of the American Sailing Navy;* W. B. Clark, ed., *Naval Documents of the American Revolution;* E. J. King, *The U.S. Navy at War;* D. W. Knox, *The History of the U.S. Navy,* and *Barbary Wars;* D. W. Knox, ed., *Naval Documents of the Quasi-War With France;* A. T. Mahan, *The War of 1812;* S. E. Morison, *United States Naval Operations in World War II;* Secretary of the Navy, *Annual Reports* (since 1836); W. S. Sims, *Victory at Sea.*]

ROBERT W. DALY

NAVY YARDS. When piracy by the Barbary states of Morocco, Algiers, Tripoli, and Tunis led to the rebirth of the U.S. Navy, building yards were rented in Portsmouth, N.H.; Boston; New York; Philadelphia; Baltimore; and Norfolk, Va., to construct the six frigates authorized in 1794. During the growth of the fleet in the Quasi-War with France, Secretary of the Navy Benjamin Stoddert used some of the funds appropriated for the construction of 74-ton ships of the line and eighteen-gun sloops to purchase or construct six navy yards in 1800 and 1801—Portsmouth, N.H.; Boston (Charlestown); New York (Brooklyn); Philadelphia; Washington, D.C.; Norfolk (Gosport, now Portsmouth, Va.). The yards soon included manufacturing activities, repair shops, and storehouses, as well as shipbuilding. At the time of operations against pirates in the Gulf of Mexico and the Caribbean, a seventh navy yard was established at Pensacola, Fla., in 1825. The navy yard at Charleston, S.C., came into being in 1901.

On the West Coast, the navy yard at Mare Island, Vallejo, Calif., was established in 1854. Following the increased commitments in the Pacific, the Puget Sound Navy Yard, Bremerton, Wash., was activated in 1902, and another at Pearl Harbor, Hawaii, in 1908. Facilities at Hunter's Point, acquired in 1940 as an annex to Mare Island, became the San Francisco Navy Yard in 1945. Demands of the Korean War led to the Long Beach, Calif. (Terminal Island), yard in 1951.

Until the early 20th century, navy yards were used for a great variety of logistic-type activities of the Navy Department. Then on Sept. 14, 1945, multiple activities at the navy yards were split into separate commands. Since that date, the facilities for construction and repair have been designated naval shipyards.

Each of the navy yards (or shipyards) has had an eventful history—expanding rapidly in times of major shipbuilding programs, emergencies, and war and declining during periods of peacetime economy. The Norfolk site, for instance, had been used by the British before the Revolution and by the Virginia State Navy during that war. It was again in British hands for a time in 1779. Before acquisition by the U.S. Navy, it had been rented from the state of Virginia to construct the frigate *Chesapeake.* The Confederates occupied the navy yard in April 1861, capturing a valuable drydock, cannon, ordnance stores, and the U.S.S. *Merrimack,* which was converted to the iron-clad C.S.S. *Virginia.*

The Washington, D.C., yard and ships under construction were burned in 1814 to prevent capture and use by the British. In later years the increasing draft of ships and shallow approaches brought shipbuilding to a close there. Gradually this navy yard became the navy's principal ordnance manufacturing plant. Designated the U.S. Naval Gun Factory from 1945 to 1964, it was reassigned the historic name Washington Navy Yard in the latter year.

As of 1975 the active naval shipyards were at Portsmouth, N.H.; Philadelphia; Norfolk; Charleston; Puget Sound; Mare Island; Long Beach; and Pearl Harbor.

[Charles O. Paullin, *Paullin's History of Naval Administration 1775–1911;* U.S. Department of the Navy, *Annual Reports of the Secretary of the Navy.*]

EDWIN B. HOOPER

NAZARENE, CHURCH OF THE, was formed by the merger of three Pentecostal and Holiness churches in 1907–08: the Association of Pentecostal Churches in America, the Church of the Nazarene, and the Holiness Church of Christ. The church has dissociated itself from the more extreme Pentecostal groups and generally adheres to the teachings of late 19th-century Methodism. The Nazarenes believe that regeneration and sanctification are different experiences, and they practice faith healing and abstain from the use of tobacco and alcohol. The ecclesiastical structure of the church is similar to that of Methodism. The 1974 membership of the church was 417,200.

[John Leland Peters, *Christian Perfection and American Methodism;* Timothy Lawrence Smith, *Called Unto Holiness: The Story of the Nazarenes—The Formative Years.*]
GLENN T. MILLER

NC-4, FLIGHT OF. On May 8, 1919, three Curtis flying boats, with U.S. Navy crews aboard, took off from Rockaway, N.Y., for Plymouth, England, in an attempt to make the first west-to-east crossing of the Atlantic by plane. Stops were planned for Halifax, Nova Scotia; Trepassey, Newfoundland; the Azores; and Lisbon, Portugal. Sixty destroyers at intervals of seventy-five miles patrolled the course to give aid to the 400-horsepower seaplanes, if needed. All went well until the squadron approached the Azores, when two planes, lost in a fog, were forced down. The NC-1 sank, but its crew was rescued; the NC-3 "taxied" and drifted 209 miles to Ponta Delgada, Portugal. But the NC-4, commanded by Lt. Comdr. Albert C. Read, reached Horta, Portugal, safely on May 17 and two weeks later arrived at Plymouth, after touching at Lisbon and El Ferrol de Caudillo, Spain, with complete flying time of 53 hours and 58 minutes.

[Dudley W. Knox, *A History of the United States Navy.*]
CHARLES LEE LEWIS

NEAGLE, IN RE, 135 U.S. 1 (1890), a case in which the U.S. Supreme Court asserted the supremacy of federal law over state law. The case developed from the fact that, under presidential authority to see that the laws are faithfully executed, Benjamin Harrison, by executive order, directed David Neagle, a deputy U.S. marshal, to protect Justice Stephen J. Field of the Supreme Court against a threatened personal attack. At Stockton, Calif., as the justice was traveling in the performance of his official duties, Neagle shot and killed David S. Terry as Terry made a murderous assault on Field. Arrested by California state authorities and charged with murder, Neagle was brought before the federal circuit court on a writ of habeas corpus and released on the ground that he was being held in custody for "an act done in pursuance of a law

of the United States." His release was upheld by the Supreme Court.
P. ORMAN RAY

NEAR V. MINNESOTA, 283 U.S. 697 (1931), invalidated an act of the state of Minnesota that provided for the abatement as a public nuisance of a "malicious, scandalous, and defamatory newspaper, magazine, or other periodical." The *Saturday Press* of Minneapolis had been so abated, and the editor perpetually enjoined from further engaging in the business. The Supreme Court declared the statute unconstitutional on the ground that freedom of the press means freedom from previous restraint and that the right to criticize public officials is a fundamental principle of free democratic government.
HARVEY PINNEY

NEBBIA V. NEW YORK, 291 U.S. 502 (1934), a U.S. Supreme Court case that set forth a broad view of business "affected with a public interest." New York State in 1933 established a milk control board empowered to fix maximum and minimum retail prices. A dealer, convicted of underselling, claimed that price fixing violated the Fourteenth Amendment's due process clause, save as applied to businesses affected with a public interest, that is, to public utilities or monopolies. The Supreme Court, upholding the law five to four, declared "there is no closed class" of businesses "affected with a public interest"; such a class includes any industry that, "for adequate reason, is subject to control for the public good."

[W. Anderson, *American Government;* E. S. Bates, *The Story of the Supreme Court.*]
RANSOM E. NOBLE, JR.

NEBRASKA. The name "Nebraska" derives from the Oto word for the Platte River, used by the French explorer Étienne Veniard de Bourgmont in 1714. Although the region was visited occasionally by trappers and traders during the 18th century, significant interest in the area dates from the Louisiana Purchase (1803) and the explorations of Meriwether Lewis and William Clark in 1804–06. Manuel Lisa established Fort Lisa (1813–19) as a fur-trading post on a site that is now at the northern edge of the present city of Omaha. Fort Atkinson in the same area served as a military encampment (1818–27). Bellevue, at the southern edge of Omaha, became a permanent trading post in 1819 and remained the nucleus of white settlement.

The principal Indian tribes within Nebraska were the Omaha, Oto, Ponca, Missouri, Pawnee, Cheyenne, and Sioux. The Omaha, Oto, Ponca, and Missouri occupied land along the Missouri River; the Pawnee were in the central part of the state; the Sioux and Cheyenne roamed over the western section. The eastern tribes completed the cession of their lands in 1854; the Pawnee, in 1857; the Cheyenne, in 1861; and the Sioux, in 1876.

The early explorers were unfavorably impressed by the area between the Missouri River and the Rocky Mountains, and their reports—particularly those of Maj. Stephen H. Long (1819–24)—gave rise to the idea of the Great American Desert. During the 1840's the Overland Trail through the Platte Valley became a great continental highway. The reports of John C. Frémont popularized the route and also suggested ''Nebraska'' as an appropriate designation for the area of the Platte watershed.

Secretary of War William Wilkins proposed the organization of Nebraska Territory in 1844, and in the same year, Stephen H. Douglas introduced a Nebraska territorial bill in Congress. Northerners became interested in the organization of Nebraska Territory to compete with southern routes for the transcontinental railroad. The Nebraska question became embroiled in the controversy over the extension of slavery. Under the Missouri Compromise of 1820, slavery was excluded from the area; the Kansas-Nebraska Act of 1854, by which the territory was organized, provided for resolution of the question by the territorial governments. As originally proposed, Nebraska Territory included the area extending from the Missouri River on the east to the continental divide on the west; from the Niobrara River on the north to the Kansas and Arkansas rivers on the south. The Kansas-Nebraska Act changed the northern and southern boundaries to the Canadian border and forty degrees north latitude, respectively. Nebraska's area was reduced to approximately its present size by the creation of Colorado and Dakota territories in 1861. The northern boundary was changed from the Niobrara River to forty-three degrees north latitude between the Keya Paha and Missouri rivers in 1882.

Francis Burt of South Carolina became territorial governor on Oct. 16, 1854, at Bellevue. Two days later he died, and Secretary Thomas B. Cuming, originally from Michigan, became acting governor. The first territorial legislature convened at Omaha on Jan. 16, 1855. Territorial politics dealt chiefly with the location of the capital, slavery, the organization of legislative districts, the creation of counties, the disposal of public lands, and the problem of statehood. The territorial governors were Mark W. Izard of Arkansas, 1855–57; William A. Richardson of Illinois, 1857–58; Samuel W. Black of Pennsylvania, 1859–61; and Alvin Saunders of Iowa, 1861–67.

After Nebraska was admitted to the Union (Mar. 1, 1867), the first session of the state legislature established Lincoln as the capital. It also located the state university and the state penitentiary there. The state constitution, which had been hurriedly drawn, soon proved to be inadequate. A new constitution was rejected by the voters in 1871, but in 1875 another constitution was adopted. Although it has been amended many times, including forty-one amendments proposed by a convention in 1920, this constitution, with its stringent limitations on taxation and debt, remains in effect. A significant change occurred in 1934 when the voters approved an amendment providing for a unicameral legislature.

Nebraska's economy is based primarily on agriculture, and until the development of extensive irrigation, begun in the 1930's, was subject to frequent damage from drought. In 1970 it ranked third in the nation with respect to the raising of cattle on farms. The state's limited industry is principally in the processing of agricultural commodities.

Generally Nebraska has been a Republican state, although the voters have exhibited considerable independence and in times of economic stress have reacted vigorously against the Republican party, as they did in the 1890's and in the 1930's. The Populists gained a considerable following in the 1890's. The state's two leading political figures have been William Jennings Bryan, a Democrat who attracted strong Populist support, both as a member of the House of Representatives and as a presidential candidate, and Sen. George W. Norris, a Republican whose record exhibits a high degree of independence and who was reelected in 1936 as an Independent candidate.

[Everett Dick, *The Sod House Frontier;* James C. Olson, *History of Nebraska.*]

JAMES C. OLSON

NECESSITY, FORT. *See* **Great Meadows.**

NEEDHAM-ARTHUR EXPEDITIONS. With the completion in 1646 of Fort Henry (now Petersburg, Va.), commanded by the energetic and resourceful

Abraham Wood, there began a generation of exploration, impelled by hopes of revealing a passage to Asia, arable lands, minerals, gems, and peltries, culminating in the journeys of the English explorer James Needham and a youthful companion, Gabriel Arthur. Leaving the fort in May 1673, they traveled southwestwardly, arriving finally at a village, seemingly on or near the Little Tennessee River, thereby becoming the first Englishmen reported to have reached the Tennessee country. The Indians were reported by them to be called Tomahitans; whether they were Cherokee or pre-Cherokee, scholars disagree. Needham returned to Fort Henry, arriving Sept. 10, 1673. Within ten days he was on his way back to the Tomahita; en route he was treacherously slain by an Occaneechi companion. Meanwhile Arthur had joined Tomahita bands in journeys to Florida, South Carolina, the Ohio River vicinity, and apparently down the Tennessee River; he was probably the first white man to navigate that stream and to visit the Kentucky country. By June 1674 he was back at Fort Henry, where soon appeared a friendly Tomahita chieftain; he was so warmly welcomed by Wood and Arthur that he promised to return to the fort the ensuing autumn with many warriors and, presumably, with deerskins. Needham and Arthur had laid the foundations for English intercourse with the Indians of the southern Alleghenies.

[C. W. Alvord and L. Bidgood, *The First Explorations of the Trans-Allegheny Region by the Virginians, 1650–1674.*]

W. NEIL FRANKLIN

NEELY V. HENKEL, 180 U.S. 109 (1901), one of the cases arising from the Spanish-American War and concerning the status of former Spanish possessions. The Supreme Court held that Cuba, although temporarily under a military governor appointed by the American president, was foreign territory and not in any constitutional, legal, or international sense part of the United States.

[C. Warren, *The Supreme Court in United States History.*]

RANSOM E. NOBLE, JR.

NEGATIVE VOICE. After the admission in 1634 of deputies into the General Court of Massachusetts Bay, the assistants claimed a veto, or "negative voice," over their acts. This precipitated a major political and constitutional issue, resolved when, in 1644, the court constituted itself a bicameral body of assistants and deputies, each with veto on the other.

[C. M. Andrews, *The Colonial Period of American History,* vol. I.]

RAYMOND P. STEARNS

NEGRO. *See index listings under the headings* **Afro-American** *and* **Black.**

"NEGRO PLOT" OF 1741. Widespread fires broke out in New York City in the early part of 1741, starting at the fort at the lower end of Manhattan Island. A hysterical populace attributed these to a plot by blacks, actually believing that these supposed arsonists were being supported by Spaniards aiming to establish the Roman Catholic church in New York. Although no real foundation to support a conspiracy was ever established, thirty-one blacks and four whites were executed, and seventy transported.

[D. Horsmanden, *Journal of the Proceedings in the Detection of the Conspiracy.*]

RICHARD B. MORRIS

NELSON, FORT, at the Falls of the Ohio in present-day Kentucky, was named for Gov. Thomas Nelson of Virginia. Built in the summer of 1782, by Col. John Floyd, on orders from George Rogers Clark, Fort Nelson was erected to replace a small stockade fort built several years before. It served as Clark's headquarters until incorporated in the town of Louisville in 1785.

[L. Collins, *History of Kentucky.*]

THOMAS ROBSON HAY

NELSON-DAVIS QUARREL, in 1862, resulted from a severe rebuke received by Gen. Jefferson Columbus Davis from his commanding officer, Gen. William Nelson. On Sept. 29, 1862, Davis, in company with Gov. Oliver P. Morton of Indiana, sought out Nelson in the Galt Hotel in Louisville, Ky., presumably to start a quarrel. Having found Nelson, Davis demanded "satisfaction," but Nelson refused. Davis flipped a wadded card into Nelson's face; Nelson slapped Davis, who walked away. Davis borrowed a revolver, sought Nelson, and shot him. He died within an hour. Davis was indicted but, because of his political influence, was never tried.

[R. U. Johnson and C. C. Buel, eds., *Battles and Leaders of the Civil War,* vol. III.]

THOMAS ROBSON HAY

NESHAMINY, a creek that flows in a generally southerly direction into the Delaware River about three miles north of the Philadelphia city line. Near its banks was established in 1726 William Tennent's Log College for the training of Presbyterian ministers. Gen. George Washington encamped there, Aug. 10, 1777, while awaiting word of where the British army, then at sea, would land. He left Aug. 23 to meet the British force when it unexpectedly sailed up the Chesapeake. The Battle of Brandywine followed.

[William S. Baker, *Itinerary of General Washington.*]
HARRY EMERSON WILDES

NESTERS AND THE CATTLE INDUSTRY.

Beginning in the late 1860's cattle grazing on the open range of the western Plains from Texas to Montana became the major industry. The cattlemen divided the public domain into large grazing tracts, some of which they fenced. When farmers, contemptuously called nesters, attempted to settle on the range, the cattlemen kept them out by intimidation and in some rare instances by murder. The contest of the ranger and the granger continued from 1867 to 1886. Congress passed a law, Feb. 25, 1885, prohibiting interference with settlers, and President Grover Cleveland followed it with an enforcement proclamation, Aug. 7, 1885. Of greater potency was the great blizzard of January 1886. Freezing rain encased the buffalo grass, on which the cattle depended for winter feed, in a glare of ice. There followed driving snow and zero temperatures. Range cattle died of freezing and starvation, and most of the cattle barons were financially ruined. Commencing with the spring of 1886 homesteaders, streaming west in covered wagons on a 1,000-mile front, occupied the public domain on the Plains. In the mountain states the contest continued in isolated areas into the 20th century.

[Edward Everett Dale, *The Range Cattle Industry;* T. A. McNeal, *When Kansas Was Young.*]
BLISS ISELY

NETHERLANDS AWARD.

At the close of the War of 1812 the Treaty of Ghent established a mixed boundary commission to mark the northeastern boundary of the United States and Canada; it also provided that if the commission could not agree, the matter should be referred to the arbitration of some friendly sovereign or state. A special treaty of 1827 referred specific points of difference in the commission concerning that part of the line between the source of the Saint Croix and the "north west angle of Nova Scotia" to the arbitration of the king of the Netherlands, William I. Instead of deciding on the points in difference, as obliged by the treaty, the king, in 1831, laid down a compromise line that, roughly speaking, "split the difference." Great Britain did not object when the United States refused to accept the award on the valid ground that the king had exceeded his authority. After much further dispute the line was fixed by the Webster-Ashburton Treaty of 1842—which treaty line does not depart much from the compromise of the arbitrator in 1831.

[Samuel Flagg Bemis, *A Diplomatic History of the United States;* John Bassett Moore, *History and Digest of International Arbitrations to Which the United States Has Been a Party.*]
SAMUEL FLAGG BEMIS

NEUTRAL GROUND.

During the American Revolution, Westchester County, N.Y., especially the Bronx, then within that county, was known as neutral ground because it was not consistently occupied either by the British or by the Americans and the sympathies of its inhabitants were divided. In 1776 British Gen. William Howe began there his advance to White Plains.

After 1806 the region between the Arroyo Hondo, near Natchitoches, La., and the Sabine River, near Nacogdoches, Tex., was also called neutral ground as a result of the "neutral ground" agreement between Gen. James Wilkinson and Spanish Lt. Comdr. Simon de Herrera.

Another area received the designation "neutral ground" in 1830, when the Sioux on the north and the Sauk and Fox on the south each ceded twenty miles of land along a line from the Mississippi westward to the Des Moines River, leaving a neutral area forty miles wide, largely in present-day Iowa, in which they could hunt but must remain peaceful.

[Walter F. McCaleb, *The Aaron Burr Conspiracy;* Charles Pryer, *The Neutral Ground.*]
PHILIP COOLIDGE BROOKS

NEUTRALITY.

The concept of neutrality has two aspects: it is a legal status and a political policy. Both have figured prominently in American history from 1776 to 1941, but both have declined in importance since World War II.

The legal aspect of neutrality guided the relations between belligerents engaged in a recognized war and all other states not parties to the conflict. The purpose of neutrality was to reconcile the conflicting military necessities of belligerents that adversely affected neutrals with the neutrals' insistence that hostilities be limited to the territories, armies, navies, and civilian populations of the belligerent states.

Under traditional international law, a neutral state has the following duties toward belligerents: (1) impartiality; (2) abstention from assistance to belligerents; (3) prevention of the use of neutral territory as a base for belligerent operations; and (4) acquiescence in belligerent interference with neutral commerce to the extent permitted by international law. The belligerents had corresponding duties toward the neutral: (1) abstention from violations of neutral territory (including territorial waters and air space); (2) respect for the neutral's impartiality; and (3) abstention from interference with neutral commerce except under the guidelines of international law.

Historically, the principal area of application of neutral rights and duties was on the high seas. Neutrality was always a reflection of the legal status and material characteristics of war. The traditional law of neutrality developed in a period when recourse to war was a sovereign prerogative of all states. International law and diplomacy did not impose conditions on the decision of a state to go to war. The law was confined to the role of registering the fact of formal armed conflict and specifying the legal consequences of that fact.

This international law of neutrality developed in a period of limited wars, in the 17th and 18th centuries. The trend toward "total" wars, beginning as early as the Napoleonic Wars (1799–1815), was at odds with the traditional concept of neutrality. The intensity of the stakes, the technological changes in warfare, and the increased mobility of belligerents tended to make wars more bitter, destructive, and widespread in their effects. All of these factors mitigated against the traditional notion of neutrality as the international equivalent of forming a circle around two men engaged in a fist fight. By World War I the contradictions between the assumptions of traditional neutrality and the realities of modern total war were evident. They were not adequately recognized, however, until World War II.

The foregoing overview of the concept of neutrality as a legal status explains in part the troubled history of American neutrality. The United States came into existence just before such developments as the French Revolution and the Industrial Revolution unleashed the human and material forces that combined to make total war the central problem of the international community. Accordingly, the struggling American republic was obliged to seek neutral rights in an environment hostile to those rights.

For the United States, neutrality was a wise policy as well as a legal status. George Washington's administration rejected alliance with the new French republic and, indeed, with any foreign power. But the desire to avoid foreign entanglements did not preclude foreign trade. The United States wanted to avoid participation in foreign wars while profiting from them by trade with the belligerents. Under the circumstances, even the traditional 18th-century neutrality proved precarious. Violations of neutral rights, which had plagued European neutrals, were also inflicted on the United States. There were recurring threats of war with Great Britain and the undeclared war with France over neutral rights (1798–1800), all before the more comprehensive phase of European Napoleonic Wars.

Thomas Jefferson anticipated modern aspirations for alternatives to armed force in his attempts to protect American neutral rights through embargoes against belligerents who consistently violated those rights (1807–09). These embargoes apparently failed, although appraisal is difficult. It appears that the domestic American constituencies most adversely affected by British and French violations of their rights (mainly in the Northeast) preferred to take their chances with those belligerents rather than punish both the belligerents and themselves by embargoing trade. The Hawks of the period, not themselves the principal target of belligerent violations of U.S. neutral rights, wanted to fight for those rights, *inter alia,* because of their expansionist aspirations in the South and West.

Although the War of 1812 was supposedly fought with the protection of U.S. neutral rights as a major objective, the results were inconclusive. The end of the Napoleonic Wars in 1815 left a legacy of generally successful violation of neutral rights by the great maritime powers, Britain and France. The principal change in the law of neutrality of the 19th century came with the Declaration of Paris in 1856. This agreement abolished privateering—that is, commissioning of private ships so as to give them belligerent status to raid enemy shipping.

The United States did not adhere to the Declaration of Paris, because of the declaration's inadequate recognition of the rights of private neutral property on ships subject to search and seizure. However, the American posture as a leading proponent of neutral rights was altered considerably during the Civil War. Enforcement of the blockade of the Confederacy led to adoption of many of the same practices earlier objected to by the United States. As a belligerent rather than a neutral, the United States adopted the doctrine of continuous voyage, in order to deal with the problems of transshipment of supplies destined for the Confederacy through British and French possessions and Mexico. These departures from traditional neutral positions were later invoked against the United States when it was once again a neutral in the early years of World War I.

A major issue was raised in the wake of the Civil War in the Alabama Claims Arbitration (1871). The United States sought compensation from Great Britain for losses inflicted on U.S. shipping by Confederate raiders outfitted and based in British territory. The final settlement was more of a political compromise than a legal decision. In a precedent of continuing importance, Great Britain did agree that neutral territory henceforth should not be permitted to provide bases for belligerent operations. This precedent remains relevant even after the decline of the forms of maritime warfare that gave rise to it. Thus, connivance or acquiescence in the use of a state's territory as a base for civil war, terrorism, subversion, or other kinds of indirect aggression is contrary to contemporary international law.

The general U.S. policy of neutrality was potentially at variance with the Monroe Doctrine (1823), although the special interest claimed by the principle of European nonintervention in the Western Hemisphere was never brought to a major test. By the end of the 19th century the United States was adding a further special interest to its claims, this time in insistence on the Open Door policy for China. This policy, plus U.S. expansion in the Pacific, meant that the logic and integrity of a general posture of isolation and neutrality were questionable.

Efforts to codify the law of war and neutrality at sea at the Hague conferences of 1899 and 1907 were unsuccessful. A final attempt in the Declaration of London (1909) was never ratified. The greatest stumbling block was disagreement over the definition of "contraband of war," a term that came to include virtually all commerce with belligerents. World War I began with the law of neutrality in disarray. The United States attempted to maintain a policy of neutrality in this war and to protect its neutral rights. Both efforts were in vain.

World War I, the first modern total war, involved the continuous mobilization of the whole societies of the belligerents. Whatever distinctions had been previously possible between combatants and noncom-

batants, public and private property, free goods and contraband, were destroyed. The conduct of the war was incompatible with such distinctions and rights. Moreover, the heavy dependence of the Allies on U.S. trade and financial support made U.S. policies inherently unneutral and critically injurious from the German–Central Powers viewpoint.

Other factors affected the U.S. policy of neutrality and insistence on neutral rights: majority popular sentiment for the Allies over the Central Powers, effective Allied propaganda, heavy-handed Central Powers diplomacy, and attempts at subversion. But the essential element was Allied dependence on U.S. economic support—given at enormous profit—and the conviction of the Central Powers that this support must be interrupted. In a growing record of infringement of U.S. neutral rights the character of German violations arising out of submarine attacks overcame the substantial reaction against Allied practices. The United States went to war with neutral rights once again foremost among its war aims, although given the performance of the United States in the Civil War, it was not surprising that Allied total-war practices were immediately adopted and neutral rights virtually ceased.

American reaction against war, power politics, foreign entanglements, and allies who did not repay their war debts contributed to a return to an isolationist policy and to insistence on neutral rights in the interwar period. This trend was further encouraged by broad revulsion against the munitions industries, which, according to congressional investigations (1934–36), were greatly responsible for war and U.S. involvement therein. In the context of the failure of attempts at disarmament (for example, at the Geneva Conference, 1931–33), the failure of economic and other sanctions against Japan after its Manchurian takeover (1931–32) and Italy during its Ethiopian conquest (1935–37), and growing evidence of Nazi aggressive intentions, the United States continued to proclaim political and legal neutrality in preference to support for collective security.

The complicated development of U.S. neutrality laws in the late 1930's reflected the division between strong isolationist sentiment in Congress and increasing determination in the executive branch to resist aggression. Neutrality acts passed by Congress in 1935, 1936, 1937, and 1939 reflected these differences, as did the uneven record of their enforcement by the administration of Franklin D. Roosevelt.

These differences erupted in the debate over American neutrality from the outbreak of World War II

(September 1939) until the Pearl Harbor attack (Dec. 7, 1941). Roosevelt consistently sought liberalization of the U.S. neutrality laws, beginning with "cash-and-carry" armament sales by private concerns and proceeding to the "destroyer deal," whereby the U.S. government directly supplied navy vessels, field artillery, half a million rifles, and other arms and munitions to Britain in exchange for leases on Caribbean bases. Meanwhile, Roosevelt and Prime Minister Winston Churchill planned all manner of increased U.S. involvement, including participation in British convoys and consequent loss of U.S. naval vessels in combat. The concept of neutral impartiality was replaced with that of the arsenal of democracy.

U.S. interventions on behalf of Great Britain and its allies were clearly unneutral and would have justified a German declaration of war in defense of traditional neutral rights. Adolf Hitler's disinclination to take this course does not alter the lesson that the concept of neutrality cannot survive the conviction of a powerful neutral that one party to a conflict is an evil aggressor and the other a victim to be saved. This point is demonstrated in the case of the Declaration of Panama of October 1939, which sought to ban belligerent action within an enormous security zone enveloping the Western Hemisphere south of Canada. In addition to the practical impossibility of enforcing the declaration against German submarines, manifest nonapplication of the ban to Great Britain reflected U.S. unneutral policies.

Thus, technological advances in warfare, total-war attacks in an economically interdependent world, and aspirations for collective security against aggressors destroyed the foundations of neutrality as a policy and as a legal status. Since World War II these forces have continued to preclude a return to traditional neutrality. Although true collective security under the United Nations has not been feasible, nations such as the United States still distinguish illegal aggressors from their victims, as in the Korean conflict (1950–53). The duty to cooperate with collective security or collective defense measures—for example, under the North Atlantic Treaty Organization or the Organization of American States—generally overrides the presumption of neutral impartiality.

Ideological East-West rifts have produced a new concept of neutralism or nonalignment. Nations in the developing Third World have proclaimed their neutrality in the cold war's recurring conflicts and competitions. Additionally, some states such as Austria have become "neutralized," somewhat following the model of Switzerland. During the 1950's, Secretary of State John Foster Dulles and other U.S. statesmen denounced neutralism and sought unity in the non-Communist "Free World." By the 1970's the United States had become reconciled to neutralism and had moved cooperatively with the Soviet Union, the People's Republic of China, and other Communist states to soften the edges of ideological conflict. Nevertheless, a return to the international system in which neutrality developed appears remote.

[William W. Bishop, *International Law: Cases and Materials;* Edwin Borchard and William Potter Lage, *Neutrality for the United States;* Cecil V. Crabb, Jr., *The Elephants and the Grass: A Study in Nonalignment;* Charles G. Fenwick, *International Law;* Charles Cheney Hyde, *International Law;* Myres S. McDougal and Florentino P. Feliciano, *Law and Minimum World Public Order;* Roderick Ogley, *The Theory and Practice of Neutrality in the Twentieth Century;* Robert W. Tucker, *The Law of War and Neutrality at Sea;* Marjorie M. Whiteman, *Digest of International Law,* vols. 10 and 11.]

WILLIAM V. O'BRIEN

NEUTRALITY, PROCLAMATION OF. When news arrived in the United States in April 1793 of the declaration of war by France against Great Britain, and the extension of the wars of the French Revolution into a great maritime war, it was the general disposition of the U.S. government and the people, despite a strong predilection for the old ally France (*see* Franco-American Alliance), to remain neutral. In fact, France preferred its ally to be neutral, as a source of foodstuffs and naval stores to be moved in American neutral ships to France, despite the preponderant British navy, under the protection of the freedom of the seas if possible. President George Washington hurried from his home to Philadelphia, then the nation's capital, and after earnest discussion with his cabinet decided on a policy of strict neutrality. A proclamation to that effect was drawn up by Edmund Randolph, attorney general, and signed by the president and the secretary of state, Thomas Jefferson. At Jefferson's suggestion, the proclamation studiously avoided the word neutrality, hoping that the absence of this would be noted by Great Britain and persuade that power to make concessions of maritime practice to the United States in order to keep it neutral. The proclamation of Apr. 22, 1793—a landmark in the history of international law and neutral rights and obligations—enjoined upon citizens of the United States a friendly and impartial conduct and warned them against committing or abetting hostilities against any of the belligerent powers under penalty of "punishment or forfeiture under the law of nations," particularly if they should carry "articles which are deemed contraband by the modern usage of nations." Jefferson thought the use of the word "modern" very significant in that it might dispute the British traditional practice of including foodstuffs and naval stores in the category of contraband, which was contrary to American practice.

Despite the absence of the word "neutrality" in the proclamation, the belligerent powers, and the neutral world, regarded it as a genuine proclamation of neutrality—as indeed it was—and even the U.S. government soon lapsed into the habit of referring to the document as the proclamation of neutrality. The policy fixed by the proclamation was carefully carried out, in adherence to the strict letter of treaty obligations, and the executive rules proclaimed to enforce it were soon legislated into the Neutrality Act of June 5, 1794. It set American precedent and law for neutrality.

[Samuel Flagg Bemis, *Jay's Treaty, A Study in Commerce and Diplomacy,* and *A Diplomatic History of the United States;* Charles Marion Thomas, *American Neutrality in 1793.*]

SAMUEL FLAGG BEMIS

NEUTRALITY ACT OF 1939. In the spring and summer of 1938 impending war in Europe made the administration of Franklin D. Roosevelt and, in general, the public of the United States apprehensive lest the Neutrality Acts of 1935, 1936, and 1937 prevent Great Britain and France from purchasing arms, ammunition, and implements of warfare in the United States during the war. Under international law, as unamended by domestic legislation, belligerents had a right to purchase contraband of all kinds in a neutral state, and the power that controlled the seas would be able to secure their safe delivery. But the existing neutrality acts had superimposed restrictions and self-denials on American neutrality beyond what was called for by international law. These self-denials, particularly the embargo on the export of arms, ammunition, and implements of warfare to belligerents in time of war, had been accepted on the theory that they would serve to keep the United States out of the war.

The Neutrality Law of 1939 was approved on Nov. 4, after the war between Germany, on the one hand, and Poland, France, and the British Empire, on the other hand, had commenced in September. It was a relaxation of previously self-imposed obligations of neutrality and a deviation from strict juridical neutrality. It was in fact a diplomatic instrument, the purpose of which was to help the Allies win the war without American military involvement.

Briefly summarized, the act set forth the following: (1) "Whenever the President, or the Congress by concurrent resolution, shall find that there exists a state of war between two states, and that it is necessary to promote the security, preserve the peace of the United States or to protect the lives of citizens of the United States, the President shall issue a proclamation," putting into effect the statute. By the provisions of this section it is clear that the act did not apply to all wars: it did not apply to civil wars (as did the Neutrality Act of 1937), and it did not apply to those wars that both the president and Congress believed not to affect the peace or security of the United States or the lives of its citizens. For example, the law was immediately applied to the war between Germany and its enemies, but not to the subsequent war between Russia and Finland. (2) It omitted any embargo on arms, ammunition, or implements of war, or on anything else (in contrast to the neutrality legislation of 1935–37) but forbade American ships to carry arms, ammunition, or implements of war. (3) It forbade American ships to go to belligerent ports in Europe or North Africa, as far south as the Canary Islands. (4) It prohibited the arming of American merchant ships. (5) It gave discretionary power to the president to forbid American ships to enter such "combat zones" as he should proclaim. Roosevelt immediately proclaimed a zone that included the waters around the British Isles and European Atlantic waters, from the Spanish boundary to Bergen, Norway, including all the Baltic coasts. (6) It prohibited American citizens from traveling on belligerent vessels. (7) It allowed American ships to carry all goods except arms, ammunition, and implements of war—but did not exclude other contraband—to belligerent and neutral ports other than in Europe or North Africa or east of 66° west longitude and north of 35° north latitude. (These limits excluded them from the Saint Lawrence estuary and the port of Halifax, but allowed them to go to Saint John, in New Brunswick, Canada; Yarmouth, Nova Scotia; the Caribbean; Vancouver; and all belligerent ports in the Pacific and Indian oceans.) They could carry any goods—except arms, ammunition, and implements of war—to such ports without previous divesting of American title on leaving the United States. (8) All goods shipped to European belligerent ports on foreign ships must first have their title transferred from American ownership, so that they might never be the source of spoliation claims of any citizen of the United States. (This was in effect a pass-title-and-carry provision, not a cash-and-carry clause, as popularly called.) (9) Like the Neutrality Act of 1937, the act of 1939 forbade "any person within the United States to purchase, sell, or exchange bonds, securities, or other obligations" of a belligerent state, "or any person acting for or on behalf of any such state," but allowed dealing in securities issued previous to the act and did not prohibit "renewal or adjustment of existing indebtedness." (10) Like the previous neutrality legislation, the Neutrality Act of 1939 provided for the licensing of all munitions exports in time of peace or war.

[William L. Langer and S. Everett Gleason, *The Challenge to Isolation, 1937–1940.*]

SAMUEL FLAGG BEMIS

NEUTRALITY ACTS OF 1935, 1936, AND 1937 represented an effort to reorient American neutrality in anticipation of another conflict in Europe. The principal provisions of this legislation were (1) prohibition, in time of war between foreign states, or of foreign "civil strife," of the export from the United States of "arms, ammunition or implements of war," as the same shall be defined by presidential proclamation, "to any port of such belligerent state, or to any neutral port for transshipment to, or the use of, a belligerent country," with the exception of an American republic at war with a non-American state and not cooperating with a non-American state in such a war; (2) prohibition of loans or credits to a belligerent state (with the same exception) by an American national; (3) delegation of discretionary power to the president to forbid exportation on American ships to belligerent countries of articles or materials other than arms, ammunition, or implements of warfare, and to forbid the exportation of any American property in such articles or materials in foreign ships (the so-called "cash-and-carry" feature limited to two years, which expired May 1, 1939); (4) establishment of government licensing and control of the munitions industry in time of peace and war; (5) delegation of power to the president to forbid to belligerent submarines or armed merchant ships the use of American neutral ports; and (6) prohibition of the arming of American ships trading to belligerent countries.

Except for the first and second provisions, which were mandatory, the president retained a large measure of discretionary power in the execution of these acts, and even these provisions were brought measurably under his discretion (a) by the power he had to decide what was or was not a war (President Franklin D. Roosevelt did not recognize the second Sino-Japanese War as a war within the meaning of the act, although he did so judge the Italo-Ethiopian War) and (b) by phraseology that might exclude contiguous states—Mexico and Canada—from the operation of the cash-and-carry section.

After the outbreak of war in Europe in September 1939, this legislation was superseded by the Neutrality Act of that year.

[Samuel Flagg Bemis, *A Diplomatic History of the United States;* Edwin M. Borchard, "Neutrality," in Frank P. Davidson and George F. Viereck, Jr., eds., *Before America Decides.*]

SAMUEL FLAGG BEMIS

NEUTRAL RIGHTS. The United States entered an 18th-century international community in which there had developed some basic concepts of belligerent and neutral rights in time of war. War was a sovereign prerogative that engendered rights to prevent nonbelligerents from assisting the enemy. These rights primarily concerned maritime commerce. Direct assistance to belligerents through shipment of arms and other war materials—that is, contraband of war—could be prevented through blockades, interception, search and seizure, and conversion of unneutral ships and property to the use of the belligerent.

Neutral rights sought to limit belligerent interference with neutral impartiality, territory, commerce, and general international intercourse. Among the points most pressed by neutrals were the following: (1) blockades had to be real and effective, not "paper" proclamations; (2) "contraband" had to be limited to munitions and to material closely related to the conduct of war; (3) the right of neutrals to trade among themselves had to be respected, irrespective of the ultimate destination of commerce.

International law rights require a degree of general observance and/or enforcement. In retrospect, traditional neutral rights were defined by Great Britain and France. Despite the attempt by the United States to defend its neutral rights in the undeclared war with France (1798–1800), Thomas Jefferson's embargo of all belligerents (1807–09), and U.S. involvement in the War of 1812, the United States was never able to obtain satisfactory recognition of these rights. When the European nations ended privateering and sought to codify the maritime law of war in the Declaration of Paris in 1856, the United States refused to adhere because of inadequate protection for noncontraband neutral property. More unsuccessful codification attempts in the Hague conferences of 1899 and 1907 and in the London Declaration of 1909 meant that an authoritative definition of neutral rights was lacking as World War I began. Thus, neutral rights remained precarious and subject to the wills of great maritime powers even during the period when these rights were stoutly claimed by statesmen and legal publicists.

The virtual elimination of neutral rights was forecast by the trend toward "total war," discernible in the Napoleonic Wars (1799–1815) and in the American Civil War (1861–65). Ironically, the United States was obliged in the Civil War to adopt many of the policies against which it had protested as a neutral. For example, U.S. interpretations of continuous voyage and ultimate destination, justified as necessary to prevent shipment of contraband to the Confederacy from Europe via Caribbean ports and Mexico, contradicted U.S. objections to similar interpretations by European belligerents. Accordingly, U.S. defense of neutral rights in World War I was doubly difficult, because it ran counter to the necessities of modern total war, which greatly increased with the development of submarine warfare, and it sought legal rights that the United States itself had violated.

The importance of U.S. trade to the Allies, German submarine warfare, and Allied economic warfare against the Central Powers, all contributed to massive violations of neutral rights. Once German violations brought the United States into the war, the United States adopted Allied policies contrary to traditional neutral rights.

The interwar isolationist reaction in the United States prominently featured revived claims for neutral rights. After war broke out in 1939, President Franklin D. Roosevelt's interventionist policies overrode strong neutralist sentiments. By the time of the Japanese attack on Pearl Harbor, the United States had engaged in patently unneutral behavior toward Germany, as in the "destroyer deal" and U.S. participation in British convoys. The duty of a neutral to refrain from permitting its territory to serve as a base for belligerent operations—recognized by Britain in the Alabama Claims Arbitration (1871)—was manifestly violated by the United States.

Traditional neutral rights have been virtually eliminated by invocation of preferred status for belligerents engaged in collective security enforcement actions and in collective defense as provided in Article 51 of the UN Charter (for example, Korea and Vietnam); ideologically colored characterizations of belligerents as aggressors; and modern weaponry and communications that leave the neutral no place to hide and few rights to protect.

[Charles Cheney Hyde, *International Law;* Myres S. McDougal and Florentino P. Feliciano, *Law and Minimum World Public Order;* Robert W. Tucker, *The Law of War and Neutrality at Sea;* Marjorie M. Whiteman, *Digest of International Law,* vols. 10 and 11.]

WILLIAM V. O'BRIEN

NEVADA, meaning "snow covered," was the thirty-sixth state admitted to the Union. Prior to the 19th century the area's principal inhabitants were members of three Indian tribal groups—the Paiute, Shoshone, and Washo. Mexico laid claim to the territory after a successful revolt against Spain in 1821. From 1826 on, fur traders, emigrants, and explorers traversed the area, and in 1848 Mexico ceded the territory to the United States in the Treaty of Guadalupe Hidalgo. Two years later Congress established the territories of Utah and New Mexico as part of the Compromise of 1850, with most of what is now Nevada being a part of the Utah Territory.

The first permanent white settlement was a trading post set up by John Reese, a Mormon, in the Carson Valley in 1851. Following the recall of Mormons to the Salt Lake Valley by Brigham Young in 1857 and the large number of miners attracted to Virginia City in 1859 with the discovery of the Comstock Lode, Congress responded to the petitions of the people in the western part of the Utah Territory and created the separate Nevada Territory on Mar. 2, 1861.

President Abraham Lincoln strongly desired the admission of Nevada as a state, despite its small population, in order to secure three congressional votes for the Thirteenth Amendment. Congress passed the enabling act in March 1864, a constitution was approved by the people, and Lincoln proclaimed Nevada a state on Oct. 31, 1864.

Nevada prospered economically during the first fifteen years of statehood because of the gold and silver extracted from the Comstock Lode. The politics of the period were dominated by the mining interests and the Central Pacific Railroad. With the decline of the Comstock Lode in 1879, the economy became severely depressed, and many Nevadans turned to cattle and sheep raising. The Silver party was founded in 1892 and was an important force in Nevada politics until its fusion with the Democrats ten years later. The state gave its electoral votes to Gen. James B. Weaver, the Populist candidate for president, in 1892 because of his stand on free coinage of silver.

Mineral discoveries in the early years of the 20th century in Tonopah (silver), Goldfield (gold), and Ely (copper) set off a new mining boom. With the falloff of mineral production after World War I and the subsequent decline in the state's population, the legislature legalized gambling in 1931, an act that along with the construction of Hoover Dam in 1936 set the stage for a boom in tourism following World War II. The state's population tripled between 1950 and 1970 (from 160,083 to 488,738), with four-fifths of the people residing in the Las Vegas and Reno areas. State gambling and sales tax revenues continued to increase, even in the face of the national recession in the mid-1970's, and the state general fund showed healthy surpluses.

Nevada's electoral votes have gone to the winner in each presidential election from 1912 through 1972. Helped by the seniority rule, several U.S. senators from Nevada, including Key Pittman, Patrick A. McCarran, Alan Bible, and Howard Cannon, have been influential on the national scene.

[Eleanore Bushnell, *The Nevada Constitution;* Russell R. Elliott, *History of Nevada.*]

DON W. DRIGGS

NEW ALBION. *See* **Plowden's New Albion.**

NEW AMSTEL. *See* **New Castle.**

NEW AMSTERDAM was founded in July 1625, when the little settlement planted by the Dutch West India Company on Nut (now Governors) Island was transferred to the lower end of Manhattan Island. In accordance with the instructions of the company directors, a fort, pentagonal in shape, was built, and a street connecting the two gates was laid out, with a marketplace in the center; houses built around it were to be used as offices for the company and homes for the director and members of his council. In 1626, because of troubles with the Indians of the area, the families settled at Fort Orange, now Albany, were moved to New Amsterdam. Two roads (now Whitehall and Pearl streets) and two canals (now covered by the pavements of Broad and Beaver streets) formed the limits of the settlement. A wagon road led from the fort along present-day Broadway, Park Row, and Fourth Avenue up to about East 14th Street, east of which lay the five company farms and that of the director of the province.

The inhabitants of New Amsterdam had no voice in the government of the settlement, which was administered by the director of the province and his council,

appointed by the directors of the company. Obedience to the orders and laws of the company was expected. Life in New Amsterdam in the early years of the settlement was far from pleasant. The directors were autocratic, and members of the council quarreled with the director and with each other. Jonas Michaelius, the first ordained minister to New Netherland, who arrived in 1628, was sharply critical of conditions. He declared the people oppressed, the food supply scarce, and many of the inhabitants loafers who needed to be replaced by competent farmers and industrious laborers. Housing conditions were little better than at the beginning of the settlement. Although the population then numbered 270 men, women, and children, the majority of the people were still lodged in primitive huts of bark, huddled near the protecting ramparts of the fort. Religious services were held in the loft of the horse mill.

Despite difficulties the town grew and made progress. A new fort, girded with stone, was built. A barracks for the soldiers, a bakery, and more houses for company servants were constructed. A wooden church was begun, and shortly afterward a house for the minister was built.

In 1637 the brutal and unwise Indian policy of Director Willem Kieft resulted in a war that threatened to wipe out the settlement. Peace was made in 1645, but when Peter Stuyvesant arrived in 1647 to succeed Kieft, he found New Amsterdam in a state of complete demoralization. New ordinances were passed to curb drunkenness in the town, which boasted seventeen taphouses; three street surveyors were appointed to remedy the deplorable conditions of the houses, streets, and fences; and steps were taken to raise money to repair the fort, finish the church, and build a school.

In 1652, as a result of much popular agitation, Stuyvesant was instructed to give New Amsterdam a burgher government. Accordingly, in February of the following year, a schout, two burgomasters, and five schepens were appointed. These officials together constituted a court with both civil and criminal jurisdiction; it met once a week—and continued to function until merged in the supreme court of the state of New York in 1895. The magistrates met in the Stadt Huis, which had originally been built by Kieft as a tavern. In 1654 the magistrates received the power, if permitted by the council, to levy taxes and to convey lands. A painted coat of arms, a seal, and a silver signet were delivered to them with impressive ceremonies. In 1658 they were allowed to nominate their successors. Two years later the company granted additional prestige to the office of city schout, by removing from the schout his previous duties as sheriff, prosecutor, and president of the magistrates. In 1657 burgher rights were granted, and from that time on no merchant could do business, or craftsman ply his trade, without admission to the freedom of the city by the magistrates.

In 1655 a war with neighboring Indians was again threatened, but after some show of force a truce was patched up. A census taken in 1656 showed 120 houses and 1,000 inhabitants in the city. From the earliest days New Amsterdam had a cosmopolitan character: in 1644 the Jesuit missionary Isaac Joques reported that eighteen different languages were spoken in or about the town. New Amsterdam passed into the hands of the English, becoming New York City, with the fall of New Netherland in 1664. After the recapture of the colony by the Dutch in 1673, it was called New Orange, and then renamed New York after the restoration of the colony to England in 1674.

[Thomas J. Condon, *New York Beginnings: The Commercial Origins of New Netherland;* Allen W. Trelease, *Indian Affairs in Colonial New York, The Seventeenth Century.*]

A. C. FLICK

NEWARK, the largest city in New Jersey, with a population of 382,417 (1970), and the metropolitan center for nearly two million people. It is also the third oldest major city in the United States. Only Boston and New York were established earlier. Newark was founded by a group of Puritans who immigrated to the area from Connecticut in 1666 under the leadership of Robert Treat. The town, located on the Passaic River, was named Newark after the town in England from which Abraham Pierson, the spiritual leader of the settlers, emigrated. In 1713, Queen Anne granted it a township charter.

Rev. Aaron Burr, Sr., established the College of New Jersey in 1746, a college that later moved to Princeton and became Princeton University. In the colonial period, Newark remained a small town removed from the main transportation routes. During the American Revolution, the town was ravaged by the British and Hessian troops who followed George Washington's retreating army across New Jersey after its evacuation of Fort Lee in November 1776. The British subsequently raided the town several times during the war.

In the first half of the 19th century, Newark became a leading leather tanning center, developing a large trade with the South in such items as shoes, boots, carriages, and clothing. The growth of the city's economy resulted from the construction of the Morris Canal in 1832 and the New Jersey Railroad in 1835 and from a labor force swelled by the large influx of Irish and German immigrants. Newark was incorporated as a city in 1836. In the post–Civil War period, the city became a diversified industrial and manufacturing center, but leather remained its principal product.

With the construction of a rapid transit system to New York City in 1911, Port Newark in 1915, and Newark Airport in 1928, Newark became a major transportation and shipping center. It is also one of the leading insurance centers in the United States; both the Prudential and the Mutual Benefit Insurance companies were founded there.

The city contains the largest educational complex in the state, consisting of Essex County College, New Jersey Institute of Technology, New Jersey College of Medicine and Dentistry of Newark, and the Newark Campus of Rutgers University.

A major racial disturbance in 1967 resulted in the death of twenty-six people and the loss of more than $10 million in private property. In 1970, 54.2 percent of the city's population was black and 11.9 percent was Hispanic. In July 1970 Kenneth A. Gibson became the first black mayor of Newark.

Among the famous Newark residents were Seth Boyden, inventor of patent leather and malleable iron and a locomotive builder; Mary Mapes Dodge, author of *Hans Brinker, or the Silver Skates* (1865); Frederick T. Frelinghuysen, secretary of state in President Chester A. Arthur's cabinet; Rev. Hannibal W. Goodwin, inventor of flexible celluloid photographic film; William Pennington, governor of New Jersey and speaker of the U.S. House of Representatives in 1859; and Edward Weston, inventor of electrical machinery. Both Aaron Burr, vice-president of the United States in 1801–05, and Stephen Crane, author of the *Red Badge of Courage* (1895), were born in Newark.

[J. Atkinson, *The History of Newark, New Jersey;* J. T. Cunningham, *Newark.*]

WILLIAM C. WRIGHT

NEWBERRY V. UNITED STATES, 256 U.S. 232 (1921). Truman H. Newberry, in his Senate race against Henry Ford in the Michigan Republican primary of 1920, spent over $100,000, thereby violating a federal law of 1910, as amended in 1911. He claimed that he had not spent the money himself and had not known that it was being spent. In the following year the Supreme Court decided that a primary was not an essential part of an election, as that term was understood by the framers of the Constitution, whereupon the Senate voted that Newberry was entitled to his seat. These decisions proved so unpopular, and Newberry, because of them, such a liability to his party, that he was induced to resign his seat. This series of incidents resulted in the passage of the federal Corrupt Practices Act of 1925.

[Spencer Ervin, *Henry Ford vs. Truman H. Newberry: A Study in American Politics, Legislation and Justice;* Earl R. Sikes, *State and Federal Corrupt Practice Legislation.*]

W. BROOKE GRAVES

NEW BUDA. After the unsuccessful revolution in Hungary in 1848–49, many Hungarians fled to America. In 1850 a number of these exiles, under Count Ladislaus Ujházy, selected a tract of virgin prairie land in Decatur County, Iowa, near the Missouri border, which they named New Buda in honor of the Magyar capital of Hungary. Finding the Iowa climate unsuitable for raising grapes, Ujházy and some of the other settlers moved to Texas in 1853, but George Pomutz continued to promote settlement in New Buda, which he advertised as a "city," with parks, schools, and public buildings. In 1858 Congress, by special act, extended the right of preemption to the Hungarian exiles, but their culture and training did not fit them for pioneer life. Some of them later returned home. A few remained in Iowa, but New Buda soon disappeared.

[Lillian May Wilson, "Some Hungarian Patriots in Iowa," *The Iowa Journal of History and Politics,* vol. 11.]

RUTH A. GALLAHER

NEWBURGH ADDRESSES. The officers of the Continental Army, long unpaid, suspected, after Yorktown in 1781, that the Congress would be either unable or unwilling to settle their claims before demobilization. Respectful memorials begging relief availed nothing. At Newburgh, N.Y., winter quarters, exasperated officers were anonymously summoned to meet on Mar. 11, 1783, to consider measures redressing grievances. An eloquent, unsigned address was circulated, urging direct action—an appeal from "the justice to the fears of government." Coercion of Congress was pointedly suggested. Gen. George Washington, who was present in camp, with characteristic firmness intervened, denounced the "irregular invitation," and called a representative meeting for Mar. 15. A second anonymous address from the same pen then appeared, less vehement in tone. The commander in chief met a delegation and advised patience and confidence in the good faith of Congress. His enormous influence calmed the agitation; resolutions approving his counsel and reprobating the addresses were adopted. Maj. John Armstrong, Jr., a brilliant young soldier on Gen. Horatio Gates's staff, afterward general, minister to France, and secretary of war, was the writer of the two papers. Washington later expressed belief that his motives were patriotic, if misguided. Armstrong, writing in the *United States Magazine* in 1823, admitted his authorship.

[B. J. Lossing, *Pictorial Field-Book of the Revolution;* John Marshall, *Life of Washington.*]

CHARLES WINSLOW ELLIOTT

NEW CAESAREA, or New Jersey, were names given in the original deed of 1664 to territory leased to John Berkeley and Sir George Carteret. The word "Jersey" is a corruption of *Czar's-ey,* or *Caesar's-ey* (island of Caesar). The hybrid form, New Caesarea (or sometimes purified to the Latin *Nova Caesarea*), was rarely used. The name was chosen to honor Carteret's defense of the Channel Island of Jersey in 1649.

[F. B. Lee, *New Jersey as a Colony and as a State,* vol. I.]

C. A. TITUS

NEW CASTLE, a settlement in Delaware, was founded by the Dutch in 1651 as Fort Casimir, following the abandonment of Fort Nassau in Gloucester County, N.J. The Swedish Fort Christina (at present Wilmington) controlled the river trade with the Indians to the detriment of the Dutch at Fort Nassau. Fort Casimir was therefore established and became the key to the South, or Delaware, River. Differences between the Dutch and Swedes resulted in the surrender of Fort Casimir to the Swedish governor, Johan Rising, in May 1654. The fort, captured on Trinity Sunday, was renamed Fort Trefaldighet, or Fort Trinity. The following year a formidable force from New Amsterdam under Peter Stuyvesant recaptured it. This fort and all the other Swedish settlements in the Delaware River valley were under the jurisdiction of the Dutch West India Company until 1656. Fort Casimir was then transferred to the burgomasters of the city of Amsterdam and renamed New Amstel. With many difficulties the settlement continued under its new owners until 1664, when Sir Robert Carr, after aiding in the capture of New Amsterdam, arrived before New Amstel in September of the same year and demanded its surrender. The town was renamed New Castle by the representatives of the Duke of York, James Stuart (later James II), who continued to govern it (except for several months in 1673 when the Dutch regained control) until 1682. On Oct. 27, 1682, William Penn first landed on American soil at New Castle and received ownership of it and the surrounding territory from the Duke of York's agents. Under the Penn proprietorship New Castle was the seat of the assembly of the Lower Counties, as well as the seat of New Castle County. With the outbreak of the revolutionary war, New Castle remained the county seat, and it became the capital of Delaware. Because of British invasion in 1777, the capital was removed to Dover.

[Benjamin Ferris, *A History of the Original Settlements on the Delaware;* Amandus Johnson, *The Swedish Settlements on the Delaware.*]

LEON DEVALINGER, JR.

NEW DEAL is a term used to describe the various measures proposed or approved by President Franklin D. Roosevelt from his inauguration in 1933 to 1939 when, as he put it in 1943, "Dr. New Deal" had to make way for "Dr. Win-the-War." He first used the expression "New Deal" on July 2, 1932, when he addressed the Democratic convention in Chicago that had nominated him.

These measures fall into three general categories—relief, recovery, and reform—although there were some overlappings. Some of these measures were aimed at relieving the hardships caused by the economic depression that had started in October 1929. Others had as their chief purpose the recovery of the national economy. Still others were intended to reform certain practices that the president and his advisers regarded as harmful to the common good or were measures that they thought would further the general welfare. In many ways these laws curtailed traditional American individualism, and through them the government regulated aspects of its citizens' lives hitherto regarded as beyond its competence. The New Deal has been distinguished into two phases, the first New Deal, which lasted from 1933 to the beginning of 1935 and had recovery as its primary aim, and the second New Deal, running from 1935 to 1939, during which the chief objective was reform.

In implementing his program Roosevelt had the assistance of the members of his cabinet and numerous other advisers who were called the "New Dealers." Not all of those so termed agreed on principles or practices. There was much variety of opinion among them. As secretary of state, the president chose Cordell Hull of Tennessee, a Wilsonian Democrat with long congressional experience who was interested in free trade. William H. Woodin, a Pennsylvania industrialist, was made secretary of the Treasury but, due to ill health, was succeeded after a few months by Henry Morgenthau, Jr., of New York, a Dutchess County neighbor of the president. Henry A. Wallace, a progressive Republican from Iowa, an agricultural expert and the son of the secretary of agriculture under President Warren G. Harding, was named to the same post as his father. As secretary of the interior, Roosevelt appointed another progressive Republican, Harold L. Ickes of Illinois. Frances Perkins, a New York social worker, became secretary of labor and the first woman to hold a cabinet post. James A. Farley of New York, who had done so much as chairman of the Democratic National Committee to bring about Roosevelt's victory, became postmaster general. As secretary of commerce, the president chose Daniel C. Roper of South Carolina, a former commissioner of internal revenue who practiced law in Washington, D.C. Roosevelt appointed George H. Dern, a former governor of Utah, and Claude A. Swanson, a senator from Virginia, chiefs of the War and Navy departments, respectively. Homer S. Cummings of Connecticut was named attorney general. Those on whom Roosevelt leaned for advice who were not members of his official family became known as the "Brain Trust." Membership in this group shifted rather frequently. It included professors, social workers, lawyers, labor leaders, and financiers. Leading members of the group at one time or another were Raymond Moley, a Columbia professor who had worked under Roosevelt when he was governor of New York on ways to improve the administration of justice in the state; Rexford G. Tugwell—at one time a member of the faculties of the universities of Pennsylvania and Washington and Columbia University—who was concerned about the plight of the small farmers; and Adolph A. Berle, Jr., a lawyer and an authority on corporations who was also on the Columbia faculty. Iowa-born Harry L. Hopkins, a social worker who headed the New York State Temporary Relief Administration under Roosevelt, remained close to the president as director of relief agencies, secretary of commerce, and a roving diplomat.

On Mar. 6, 1933, in order to keep the banking system of the country from collapsing, Roosevelt availed himself of the powers given by the Trading With the

Enemy Act of 1917 and suspended all transactions in the Federal Reserve and other banks and financial associations. He also embargoed the export of gold, silver, and currency until Mar. 9 when Congress met in special session. On that day the Emergency Banking Relief Act was passed and signed. This gave the president the power to reorganize all insolvent banks and provided the means by which sound banks could reopen their doors without long delay. On Mar. 12 Roosevelt delivered the first of many ''fireside chats'' to reassure the country and win support for his policies. The Civilian Conservation Corps (CCC) was established on Mar. 31 to provide work for young men in reclamation projects and in the national parks and forests. About 250,000 youths were so employed at a wage of $30 a week, $25 of which was sent to their families. The Federal Emergency Relief Administration (FERA) was set up on May 12 and placed under the direction of Hopkins. This agency had an appropriation of $500 million, and it was authorized to match the sums allotted for the relief of the unemployed by state and local governments with federal funds. In 1933 there were nearly 13 million people out of work. By the Home Owners' Loan Act of June 13 the Home Owners' Loan Corporation (HOLC) was authorized to issue bonds to the amount of $3 billion to refinance the mortgages of owners who were about to lose their homes through foreclosure.

The first major recovery measure of the administration was the Agricultural Adjustment Act, which created the Agricultural Adjustment Administration (AAA). Passed on May 12, the act empowered the AAA to control the production of wheat, cotton, corn, rice, tobacco, hogs, and certain other commodities by paying cash subsidies to farmers who voluntarily restricted the acreage planted with such crops or who reduced the number of livestock. These cash subsidies were to be paid out of the proceeds of a tax levied on the processors of farm products. The act also authorized the federal government to make loans on crops to farmers so that they could hold them for better prices, and to buy surpluses outright. By these means it was hoped that demand would catch up with supply and that farm prices would rise. Those who favored inflation as the remedy for the country's ills succeeded in adding an omnibus amendment to the Agricultural Adjustment Act, proposed by Sen. Elmer Thomas of Oklahoma, which gave the president the power to inflate the currency by the coinage of silver at a ratio of his own choice, by printing paper money, or by devaluating the gold content of the dollar. Secretary Wallace and George N. Peek, a

former associate of Bernard Baruch on the War Industries Board during World War I and of Gen. Hugh S. Johnson in the Moline Plow Company and the first administrator of the AAA, undertook the job of persuading the farmers to curtail production.

Having tried to assist the farmer in recovery, the administration turned its attention to industry and labor. The National Industrial Recovery Act (NIRA), passed on June 16, set up the National Recovery Administration (NRA). Under governmental direction employers, employees, and consumers were to draft codes by which the various industries would be controlled. The employers were assured that these regulatory codes, which were similar to those drawn up by a number of trade associations in the 1920's, would be exempt from prosecution under the antitrust laws and that production would be limited to raise prices. Under section 7a the employee was promised collective bargaining and that minimum wages and maximum hours would be established. The NRA was placed under the direction of Gen. Hugh S. Johnson, a West Point graduate who had drafted and applied the Draft Act of 1917. Johnson threw himself into the work of codemaking with great energy and considerable showmanship. A great many codes were drawn up and the subscribing companies were allowed to stamp their product with the ''Blue Eagle,'' the symbol indicating that they had conformed to the code of their industry and were helping the country to recover. The second section of this act set up the Public Works Administration (PWA). Charge of this was given to Secretary Ickes, to the disappointment of Johnson, who did not think the NRA would be effective unless one office controlled both the regulation of industry and the disbursement of funds. The PWA was an extension of the policy of President Herbert Hoover to provide employment by the construction of public works. Under Ickes it was administered honestly but too slowly to be of assistance in recovery.

Three measures that were passed during the ''hundred days'' of this special session of the Seventy-third Congress belong more to the reform category than to relief or recovery. One was the Tennessee Valley Authority Act of May 18, which set up the Tennessee Valley Authority (TVA). This agency was to develop the economic and social well-being of an area that embraced parts of seven states. A corporation was organized and given the right of eminent domain in the valley. It was authorized, among other things, to erect dams and power plants, to improve navigation and methods of flood control, to undertake soil conservation and reforestation projects, and to sell electric power and fertilizers. Arthur E. Morgan, president of Antioch College, was named chairman of the TVA and David E. Lilienthal was made counsel. Lilienthal soon became the driving force in the authority.

Another reform was the Federal Securities Act of May 27. New issues of securities were to be registered with the Federal Trade Commission along with a statement of the financial condition of the company of issue. This statement was also to be made available to all prospective purchasers of the securities. The bill contained no provision for the regulation of stock exchanges. It was revised in 1934, and such regulatory power was entrusted to the Securities and Exchange Commission (SEC). The Glass-Steagall Banking Act, passed on June 16, separated investment from commercial banking so that there could no longer be speculation with the depositors' money. Another provision gave the Federal Reserve Board power over interest rates to prevent speculation with borrowed money. It also set up the Federal Deposit Insurance Corporation, by which the government guaranteed bank deposits below $5,000, later increased to $10,000 (by 1974, $40,000).

By Dec. 5, 1933, three-fourths of the state legislatures had ratified the Twenty-first Amendment to the Constitution, which repealed the Eighteenth Amendment. The states were henceforth to decide whether they would allow the sale of alcoholic beverages or not. As a national experiment, the "dry era" ended. Revenue from liquor taxes helped finance state and federal expenditures.

Despite all this legislation and activity, farm prices, industrial employment, and payrolls declined, and there was dissatisfaction with the recovery program. In an effort to raise prices the president experimented with an inflationary devaluation of the dollar by reducing its gold content, the third of the methods allowed him by the Thomas Amendment to the Agricultural Adjustment Act. This move in the direction of economic nationalism, based on the "commodity dollar" theory of George F. Warren of Cornell University, nullified the work of the International Monetary and Economic Conference then meeting in London. The resulting cheapening of American goods in foreign markets convinced European manufacturers that the United States was seeking an unfair advantage in world trade. It was also a blow to the more conservative advisers of the president, such as Lewis Douglas, the director of the budget, and the banker James Warburg, who wished to maintain the gold standard. The dollar was eventually stabilized by an

executive order of Jan. 31, 1934, which fixed the gold content of the dollar at 59.06 percent of its former value. Title to all gold in the Federal Reserve banks was transferred to the government, which was also buying gold in the world market above the current price. By the Gold Clause Act of 1935 no one has the right to sue the government because of gold-clause contracts or claims arising out of changes in the gold value of the dollar. The president also set up the Civil Works Administration (CWA) to "prime the pump" of recovery by increasing the purchasing power of the people at large. This was not intended to be a permanent solution to the problem of unemployment and was ended on Apr. 1, 1934.

While the president's policy of a managed currency was nationalistic in the sense that it was aimed at raising prices at home, it did not mean American isolation from world commerce. Partly to increase American foreign trade Roosevelt, after securing certain guarantees for American citizens from Maksim Litvinov, commissar for foreign affairs of the USSR, recognized the Soviet Union Nov. 16, 1933, and diplomatic representatives were exchanged. The Reciprocal Trade Agreement Act, which was passed on June 12, 1934, was also aimed at stimulating foreign commerce. After a long struggle between Hull and Peek, whom Roosevelt had made foreign trade adviser after he left the AAA, over the interpretation of the act, Hull's more international policy won out over Peek's idea that the act did not intend a general tariff reduction but merely provided a means for drawing up bilateral agreements with various countries. By the end of 1935 reciprocal trade agreements had been negotiated with fourteen countries and the process continued. Such treaties fitted in with the Good Neighbor policy of the administration, which brought an end to U.S. intervention in the internal affairs of Latin America and created a mutual security system for both continents.

During 1934 attempts were made to control the monopolistic tendencies of the larger companies under the NRA codes. During June the Railway Retirement Act was passed and the president appointed a committee to prepare plans for a general program of social security. In the same month the Frazier-Lemke Farm Bankruptcy Act became law. This made it possible for farmers to reacquire lost farms on reasonable terms and to stay bankruptcy proceedings for five years if creditors were unreasonable.

In his message to Congress of Jan. 4, 1935, Roosevelt emphasized the idea that reform was essential to recovery. He called for legislation that would provide assistance for the unemployed, the aged, destitute children, and the physically handicapped. He asked for laws concerning housing, strengthening the NRA, reforming public utilities holding companies, and improving the methods of taxation. Recovery was to be achieved by placing purchasing power in the hands of the many rather than by encouraging price rises in the hope that the benefits would seep down to the employees in the form of higher wages. This marks the opening of the second New Deal.

The Social Security Bill was introduced on Jan. 17, 1935. A federal tax on employers' payrolls was to be used to build up funds for unemployment insurance. A state that had approved insurance systems could administer up to 90 percent of the payments made within its borders. A tax of 1 percent, which would reach 3 percent by 1949, was levied on the wages of employees and the payrolls of employers to provide funds for old-age pension insurance. The bill was opposed by various groups. Among them were Dr. Francis E. Townsend's Old Age Revolving Pension movement, the American Federation of Labor (which was against the tax on wages), the National Association of Manufacturers, and the Communist party. It became law in August. On May 6, 1935, the Works Progress Administration (WPA) was established with Hopkins as director. Many projects were organized to spread employment and increase purchasing power. Critics of the administration considered many of them to be trivial and called them "boondoggling," as they had termed the jobs provided by the CWA. Among the agencies it established was the Resettlement Administration (RA), under Tugwell in the Department of Agriculture, the purpose of which was to remove farmers from submarginal to better land and to provide poorly paid workers with "Greenbelt towns" outside cities where they could supplement their salaries by part-time farming. An enthusiastic supporter of these ideas was Eleanor Roosevelt, the president's wife, whose political and social interests ranged widely. Another was the Rural Electrification Administration (REA), established May 11, which offered low interest loans to farmers' cooperatives to build power lines with WPA labor in localities where private companies thought investment unjustified. A third was the National Youth Administration (NYA), formed June 26, which aimed at keeping young people at school and out of the labor market. Money was turned over to school administrators who paid it out to students for various types of work about the school. The Federal Theatre Project provided work for many actors, directors, and stage crews; the Federal Writers' Project turned out a series of state guides; the

Historical Records Survey brought to light many documents in local archives. The wages paid WPA workers were higher than relief payments but lower than those paid by private enterprise. In 1936, after considerable pressure from the workers, the government raised wages on WPA projects to the prevailing level but reduced the number of hours worked a month so that wage totals remained at security level. The government wished the workers to return to private enterprise as soon as possible.

In June 1935 the president sent a special message to Congress on tax revision. Tax burdens, he said, should be redistributed according to ability to pay. Higher taxes on large individual incomes, inheritances, and gifts would lead to a wider distribution of wealth. The principle of ability to pay should also be extended to corporations. The Wealth Tax Act, which embodied these proposals, was opposed by Sen. Huey P. Long of Louisiana and his "Share Our Wealth" movement as too moderate, but it was passed on Aug. 30. Taxes on large individual incomes were steeply scaled to 75 percent on those over $5 million. Taxes on estates were increased. Excess profits taxes on corporations ranged from 6 percent on profits above 10 percent to 12 percent on profits above 15 percent. Income taxes on corporations were graduated from 12.5 percent to 15 percent. The act was regarded by many as a soak-the-rich scheme and as a punitive measure on the part of the administration, which had parted company with big business by this time.

The president submitted the Public Utility Holding Company Act to Congress, which was designed to prevent abuses in that field, especially those made possible by the pyramiding of such companies. The bill did not require the abolition of utility holding companies but imposed a "death sentence" on those that could not prove their usefulness in five years. The act as finally passed on Aug. 28, 1935, permitted two levels of holding companies but otherwise retained the "death sentence" clause.

Roosevelt requested the extension of the much criticized NRA for two more years. The Senate voted to extend it for ten months. At the same time it was considering the Wagner-Connery National Labor Relations Act, which was designed to strengthen section 7a of the NIRA. The bill proposed to outlaw employer-dominated unions and assure labor of its right to collective bargaining through representatives chosen by itself. While a number of the senators thought that this bill and section 7a overlapped, it passed on May 16. The bill, which did not become an administration measure until the NIRA was declared unconstitutional, became law on July 5, 1935. By it the National Labor Relations Board (NLRB) was set up to determine suitable units for collective bargaining, to conduct elections for the choice of labor's representatives, and to prevent interference with such elections.

The constitutionality of this controversial legislation became a central issue in 1935. Of the nine justices who then sat on the bench of the Supreme Court four were considered to be conservatives: Willis Van Devanter, George Sutherland, James Clark McReynolds, and Pierce Butler; three to be liberal: Louis Brandeis, Benjamin N. Cardozo, and Harlan F. Stone; while Chief Justice Charles Evans Hughes and Justice Owen J. Roberts were thought to occupy an intermediate position. On Jan. 7 the court decided that section 9c of the NIRA was an unconstitutional delegation of legislative authority by Congress to the executive. This led to doubts about the constitutionality of the whole act. On May 6 the court invalidated the Railroad Retirement Act, which raised the question of the constitutionality of the Social Security Act that was before Congress. On May 27 the Frazier-Lemke Farm Bankruptcy Act was declared unconstitutional because under it private property was taken without compensation. On the same day a unanimous court declared, in *Schechter Poultry Corporation* v. *United States,* that the legislature's delegation of the codemaking power to the president in the NIRA was an unconstitutional surrender of its own proper function. The court also found that the Schechter Corporation's activities, the sale of chickens in Brooklyn, N.Y., had only an indirect effect on interstate commerce. Roosevelt termed this a "horse-and-buggy" interpretation of the commerce clause.

A way out of this impasse was found in part by rewriting some of this legislation so as to meet the objections of the court. The Frazier-Lemke Farm Mortgage Moratorium Act of 1935 and the Wagner-Crosser Railroad Retirement Act replaced those found unconstitutional. The Guffey-Snyder Bituminous Coal Stabilization Act, passed on Aug. 30, practically reenacted the whole bituminous coal code of the NRA. The Wagner National Labor Relations Act replaced section 7a of the NIRA. When the court found the AAA unconstitutional in January 1936, because the tax on food processors was an unjust expropriation of money and because the powers of the states were invaded, it was replaced by the Soil Conservation and Domestic Allotment Act of Feb. 29, 1936, and later by the second Agricultural Adjustment Act of 1938. Rewriting did not save all this legislation. On May 18, 1936, the Guffey Snyder Act was invalidated. When, on June 1, a New York minimum wage law was declared unconstitutional because it violated freedom of contract, the president said that the court had created a "no man's land" where neither a state nor the federal government could act.

At the Democratic convention held in Philadelphia in June 1936, Roosevelt and Vice-President John Nance Garner were nominated practically without opposition. Alfred E. Smith and a number of conservative Democrats, who had joined with others to form the Liberty League, attempted to lead "Jeffersonian Democrats" out of the party but without much success. The convention also repealed the two-thirds rule with which Democratic conventions had been so long saddled. In his acceptance speech Roosevelt defended the measures of his administration and attacked his opponents, whom he termed "economic royalists." The Republicans nominated Gov. Alfred M. Landon of Kansas, who was strongly supported by publisher William R. Hearst, for president and Frank Knox of Illinois for vice-president. A third party was formed out of the followers of the Rev. Gerald L. K. Smith, who had taken over Long's "Share Our Wealth" movement after the senator was assassinated in 1935, of Dr. Francis Townsend, and of the Rev. Charles E. Coughlin of the Social Justice movement who had become strongly anti-Roosevelt. It was called the Union party and it nominated Rep. William F. Lemke of North Dakota for president. The Socialists nominated Norman Thomas and the Communists, Earl Browder. Labor took a very active part in the campaign and the new industrial labor organization, the Committee on Industrial Organization (CIO), under the leadership of John L. Lewis and Sidney Hillman, set up Labor's Nonpartisan League and raised a million dollars for the support of Roosevelt and other prolabor candidates of either party. After a stormy campaign the popular vote was 27,752,869 for Roosevelt and 16,674,665 for Landon. The electoral vote was 523 to 8. Only Maine and Vermont cast their votes for the Republican candidate.

After this resounding victory at the polls the president sent a proposal to Congress to reorganize the federal judiciary on Feb. 5, 1937. In his message he pointed out Congress' power over the federal judiciary and the difficulties arising from insufficient personnel, crowded dockets, and aged judges. He suggested that the number of federal judges be increased when the incumbent judges did not retire at seventy. He asked that cases involving the constitutionality of legislation be removed from the lowest court to the Supreme Court immediately and that such cases should have precedence there. This proposal shocked a great many people and Roosevelt was accused of trying to "pack" the court with judges who favored his legislation. During the debate over this bill the Democrats in Congress and throughout the country split. The situation was helped at this point by certain decisions of the Supreme Court. On Mar. 27 it upheld, by a vote of five to four, both the Washington State Minimum Wage Act, which was similar to the invalidated New York law, and the Frazier-Lemke Farm Mortgage Act. Justice Roberts joined Chief Justice Hughes and justices Brandeis, Cardozo, and Stone in these decisions. On Apr. 12 it found the Wagner Act, which had been declared unconstitutional by the circuit court of appeals in San Francisco, valid. On May 24 it declared the Social Security Act constitutional. Despite this change on the part of the Court and the fact that his party was divided on the matter, Roosevelt continued to press his judiciary reorganization bill. A substitute was proposed and the Judicial Procedure Reform Act was passed on Aug. 24. No mention of the appointment of new judges was made in the bill. This was the president's first important defeat at the hands of Congress.

During the summer of 1937 an economic recession started that lasted through 1938. Many attributed it to the administration's hostility to business and capital. High taxes, it was said, discouraged business expansion and personal initiative. Roosevelt again resorted to pump priming and expanded bank credits.

On Feb. 16, 1938, Congress passed a second Agricultural Adjustment Act. Like the first, it aimed at controlling surpluses but used different means. Whenever a surplus in an export crop that would cause a fall in prices appeared likely, the AAA would fix a marketable quota and the farmers who agreed not to market more than the product of the acreage allotted to them could store their surpluses under government seal until a shortage developed. In the interim they could receive loans on them. The AAA would also fix a parity price that represented the purchasing power of a unit of the crop concerned during the years 1909 to 1914. The farmer was to sell his surplus when the price was at parity or above. Thus, the "ever normal granary," a favorite project of Wallace, would be established. The act also had provisions taking care of the special problems raised by conditions in the Dust Bowl, the area of the semi-arid high Plains, and for soil conservation.

On June 25 the Fair Labor Standards Act was passed. The law sought an eventual minimum wage of 40 cents an hour and a maximum work week of 40 hours. Time-and-a-half was to be paid for overtime,

and labor by children under sixteen was forbidden. Exceptions were made for various localities. The National Housing Act of Sept. 1, 1937, made low-rent housing available in many cities. The second New Deal was written into law.

These measures had not gone unopposed. In addition an executive reorganization bill, which had been proposed by Roosevelt, like many of its predecessors was defeated largely because it was regarded as connected with his judiciary reorganization bill. The legislature also repealed the graduated tax on the undistributed profits of corporations of 1936. The president personally entered the congressional campaigns of 1938 and urged the voters not to reelect certain Democratic members of Congress who had not supported his program in recent sessions. Leading targets were Sen. Walter George of Georgia, Sen. Ellison DuRant ("Cotton Ed") Smith of South Carolina, Sen. Millard E. Tydings of Maryland, and Rep. John O'Connor of New York. Except for O'Connor the president was unsuccessful in his attempt to "purge" the party, and for the first time since 1928 the number of Republicans in Congress increased.

By 1938 the world situation had become very tense. Japan, Italy, and Germany were threatening international peace. The Democratic party was divided on foreign policy. The South, although not enthusiastic about all of Roosevelt's domestic policies, supported his program of resistance to aggression, while the Middle West and West were in favor of his domestic reforms but tended to isolationism. The Northeast alone supported him in both. In the face of world conditions, especially after the Munich crisis of September 1938, Roosevelt felt compelled to subordinate his domestic reforms to keep southern support for his foreign policy. His failure actively to support an antilynching bill indicated a new outlook. Henceforth, he would strive chiefly for party and domestic unity as the nations prepared for war.

[Irving Bernstein, *Turbulent Years: A History of the American Worker, 1933–1941;* James McGregor Burns, *Roosevelt: The Lion and the Fox;* William Leuchtenberg, *Franklin D. Roosevelt and the New Deal, 1932–1940;* Raymond Moley, *The First New Deal;* Dexter Perkins, *The New Age of Franklin D. Roosevelt;* Arthur M. Schlesinger, Jr., *The Age of Roosevelt: The Crisis of the Old Order, 1919–1933.*]

VINCENT C. HOPKINS

NEW DEAL INDIAN ADMINISTRATION. The Indian Reorganization Act of 1934, also known as the Wheeler-Howard Act, inaugurated a sweeping change in policy in American Indian affairs that has been called the Indian New Deal. It marked a change from the policy of enforced assimilation that had characterized Indian affairs for the preceding half century, and it still provides the legal basis for the federal administration of Indian affairs. John Collier, a social scientist who had done extensive research and fieldwork among Indians and who had served as executive secretary of the American Indian Defense Association, was appointed U.S. commissioner of Indian Affairs and served in that position until 1946.

The Indian Reorganization Act halted further allotment of Indian lands, and it authorized federal appropriations to buy back some lands that had been lost by the tribes. The tribes were granted increased self-determination, with the option to organize as corporate entities with elected tribal councils and chairmen and to borrow money from the federal government for business enterprises, such as cooperative cattle-raising. Special preference was to be given to Indians in hiring by the Bureau of Indian Affairs. The Indians were given back their constitutional right to religious freedom, which had been taken away during the first two decades of the 20th century by Indian Service officials who had been instructed to stop ceremonial rites that, in their opinion, violated Christian standards. Health and school services were approved. Each tribe was allowed to vote on acceptance or rejection of the provisions of the Indian Reorganization Act, and two-thirds of the eligible tribes approved it. Although much progress was made under the Indian Reorganization Act, it was never fully implemented, in part because of limitations on funds during the Great Depression and later because of the diversion of attention and funds with the outbreak of World War II. At the end of the war, pressures in Congress were strong for the termination of governmental services to American Indians, and it was near the end of the 1950's before there was a return to the principles embodied in the Indian Reorganization Act.

[William H. Kelly, *Indian Affairs and the Indian Reorganization Act: The Twenty Year Record;* Stephen J. Kunitz, "The Social Philosophy of John Collier," *Ethnohistory,* vol. 18.]

KENNETH M. STEWART

NEW DEPARTURE POLICY of the Democratic party in 1871 accepted the postwar constitutional amendments adopted after the Civil War as ending war issues and sought Liberal Republican cooperation in opposing the Radical Republicans. First proposed in formal resolution by Clement L. Vallandigham at Dayton, Ohio, on May 18, it resembled a suggestion by Horace Greeley in 1868. Eleven state Democratic conventions in the North and West endorsed the Dayton proposal. The New Departure policy paved the way for the Democratic–Liberal Republican alliance of the campaign of 1872 and Greeley's endorsement by both groups as candidate for president.

[J. L. Vallandigham, *Life of Clement L. Vallandigham.*]

CHARLES H. COLEMAN

NEW ECHOTA, TREATY OF, was signed Dec. 29, 1835, and proclaimed by President Andrew Jackson on May 23, 1836. For $5 million and 7 million acres of land the Cherokee agreed to give up all their territory east of the Mississippi and remove to the West within two years. The treaty was negotiated at New Echota, the Cherokee capital, in northern Georgia, between William Carroll and John F. Schermerhorn, the U.S. commissioners, and the faction of the Cherokee that favored a treaty, headed by Stand Watie and John Ridge. (*See also* Indian Removal.)

[J. P. Brown, *Old Frontiers, The Story of the Cherokee Indians From Earliest Times to the Date of Removal to the West, 1838.*]

E. MERTON COULTER

NEW ENGLAND, embracing the six states of Maine, New Hampshire, Vermont, Massachusetts, Rhode Island, and Connecticut, formed a distinct section with a character of its own from the beginning of European settlement in North America. It is significant that New England first developed the idea of a complete separation of the colonies from Great Britain, that it opposed westward expansion of the country, and that it was first to suggest secession from the Union (*see* Hartford Convention). Its sectionalism, separatism, and local character have many causes.

Geographically, the section is largely cut off from the rest of the continent by the northern spurs of the Appalachian mountain range, and it has no river system, such as the Mohawk-Hudson, giving it access to the hinterland. Although the Puritan outlook was widespread in the period of early English settlement in all the colonies, New England was settled by the strictest of the Puritans. In Massachusetts the government set up was a theocracy, which, owing to the transfer of the charter, was practically independent of England for a half-century. Connecticut and Rhode Island colonies never had royal governors. Owing to altered conditions in the home country, immigration almost ceased for two centuries after 1640. The early establishment of Harvard in 1636, though it was scarcely more than a grammar school, increased parochialism, for potential leaders who might have been broadened by going to Britain for their education remained in the narrow atmosphere of the colony. The poor soil and broken terrain prevented the development of large estates or staple crops, as well as of slavery. The section became a land of small farms and independent farmers as stubborn as their soil, of fishermen along the coast, and of traders overseas who, lacking furs and staple crops, had to be ingenious in finding ways of making money.

There were local differences, such as the religious intolerance of Massachusetts and the freedom of Rhode Island, but in the period from 1630 to 1830, roughly, the New England, or Yankee, character was becoming set in the section as a whole. The lack of immigrants and of outside contacts and control by the clerical oligarchy were factors of importance. Moreover, even when New Englanders migrated, they usually did so in groups of families or entire congregations; everywhere group solidarity helped to maintain customs and character.

The typical institutions of New England were thus developed almost in isolation—schools, the Congregational church, the town system of government, and the "New England conscience"—as was the New Englander's preoccupation with religious and spiritual matters. The opening of the Erie Canal in 1825, linking Lake Erie to New York City, isolated the section yet more, and for long, owing to characteristic insistence on short local lines, even its railroads did not link it to the nation. But training in mind, self-reliance, and ingenuity had developed the most skilled workmen in America, and New England developed manufactures, especially those calling for a high degree of individual skill, to an extent that no other section did. The growth of manufactures appeared to call for an increase in cheap labor, and after 1840 foreign immigration was so great as largely to change the population and character. For example, Puritan Massachusetts came to be an overwhelmingly Roman Catholic state.

The New England strain of character, set through its centuries of struggle and separatism, persisted, and contributed much to other sections by migration. Among the earliest movements were those to eastern Long Island and New Jersey—and even to South Carolina. Later there were settlements in Pennsylvania, the Mohawk Valley, Ohio, Illinois, Michigan, Wisconsin, and Oregon. There are towns and districts all across the northern United States that seem like transplanted bits of New England, and wherever groups of settlers went, they carried New England ideas of education, the Congregational church, the township and town meeting, and the peculiar flavor of the New England character and attitude. Sectional as it has been, the influence of New England on the rest of the United States has been out of all proportion to its size and population.

[J. T. Adams, *History of New England;* L. K. Mathews, *The Expansion of New England.*]

JAMES TRUSLOW ADAMS

NEW ENGLAND, DOMINION OF. By the 1680's the English government had for several decades had in mind the consolidation of the American colonies into a few large provinces for the sake of better administration of defense, commerce, and justice. The experiment in dominion government was first tried out in New England because of the necessity of replacing the old charter government of Massachusetts Bay Colony, after the annulment of the charter in 1684, with some form of royal control. The dominion was established in June 1686, in temporary form, under the presidency of a native New Englander, Joseph Dudley, but was formally inaugurated in December 1686 upon the arrival of Gov. Edmund Andros. Under his rule the former colonies or regions of Massachusetts, Plymouth, Rhode Island, Connecticut, New Hampshire, Maine, the county of Cornwall (northern Maine), and King's Province (a disputed region in southern New England) were consolidated into one province.

Governmental power was vested in the governor and a council, appointed by the king; there was no representative assembly. Andros' strict administration of the Navigation Acts, his attempts to establish English land law, and above all the menace of taxation without representation (though taxation under him was not excessive in amount) drew all groups into opposition. To strengthen the line of defense against the French, New York and New Jersey were added to the dominion in 1688, making a unit too large for one man to administer well. Upon arrival of news that James II had abdicated, the Puritan leaders rose in revolt against Andros and overthrew him in April 1689.

[V. F. Barnes, *The Dominion of New England.*]

VIOLA F. BARNES

NEW ENGLAND ANTISLAVERY SOCIETY, founded at Boston in 1832, later known as the Massachusetts Antislavery Society, was the first group in

America organized on the principle of the immediate abolition of slavery without compensation to slaveholders. Uncompromising in language, eschewing political action, hostile to the use of physical violence, and partial to many of the then considered un-American "isms" of the day, its members nevertheless revitalized the antislavery movement.

[A. B. Hart, ed., *Commonwealth History of Massachusetts,* vol. IV.]

LLOYD C. M. HARE

NEW ENGLAND COMPANY was the successor to the Dorchester Company, which began settlement of the Massachusetts Bay region, and precursor to the Massachusetts Bay Company. The New England Company came into existence as an attempt to revive the dying Dorchester plantation, which had originated chiefly as a fishing venture and had failed to establish a strong settlement. A new group of men interested primarily in making a plantation for religious purposes took over the Dorchester enterprise and then applied to the Council for New England for a patent, which they are reputed to have received under date of Mar. 19, 1628. The New England Company was an unincorporated, joint-stock venture, like so many that had attempted plantations under patents from trading companies but, under the leadership of John White, there was a strong Puritan influence in the enterprise. With funds subscribed the company dispatched a fleet with prospective settlers and supplies and appointed John Endecott governor of the tiny settlement already existing at Naumkeag (later Salem). Within the company doubts arose concerning the efficacy of the patent, which made the members decide to seek royal confirmation. Supported by important men at court, they succeeded in their endeavor and were able thenceforth to proceed in their project under the royal charter of Mar. 4, 1629, which released them from further dependence on the Council for New England.

[C. M. Andrews, *The Colonial Period in American History,* vol. I.]

VIOLA F. BARNES

NEW ENGLAND CONFEDERATION. *See* **United Colonies of New England.**

NEW ENGLAND COUNCIL. *See* **Council for New England.**

NEW ENGLAND EMIGRANT AID COMPANY, an important factor in the conflict in Kansas over the slavery issue and in the rise of the Republican party, was first incorporated by Eli Thayer, Apr. 26, 1854, as the Massachusetts Emigrant Aid Company, its name being changed the following year. Its plan of operations was to advertise Kansas, send emigrants in conducted parties at reduced transportation rates, and invest its capital in improvements in Kansas, from which it hoped to earn a profit. It sent about 2,000 settlers, who founded all the important free-state towns. It established ten mills and two hotels and assisted schools and churches. It aided the Free State party in various ways, and its officers sent the first Sharps rifles to the emigrants to defend themselves against raids by proslavery men. It raised and spent, including rents and sales, about $190,000. Its activities furnished the pretext for the fraudulent voting in Kansas by Missourians. It was blamed by President Franklin Pierce, Stephen A. Douglas, and the proslavery leaders for all the troubles in Kansas. Although the company failed financially, its friends believed it had saved Kansas from becoming a slave state. After the Civil War it undertook unsuccessful colonization projects in Oregon and Florida.

[L. W. Spring, *Kansas, The Prelude to the War for the Union;* Eli Thayer, *A History of the Kansas Crusade.*]

SAMUEL A. JOHNSON

NEW ENGLAND PRIMER, first published about 1690, combined lessons in spelling with a short catechism and with versified injunctions to piety and to faith in Calvinistic fundamentals. Crude couplets and woodcut pictures illustrated the alphabet. In it was first published the child's prayer that begins, "Now I lay me down to sleep." This eighty-page booklet, 4½ by 3 inches in size, was for a half century the only elementary textbook in America, and for a century more it held a central place in the education of children.

[P. L. Ford, *The New-England Primer;* C. F. Heartman, *The New England Primer.*]

HARRY R. WARFEL

"NEW ENGLAND WAY," a phrase used to refer to the ecclesiastical polity, its relation to the civil powers, and the practices of the Massachusetts Bay Colony churches, and sometimes, indiscriminately, to those of Connecticut or Rhode Island. Intended to prove that "Discipline out of the Word" enforced by godly magistrates was possible, Massachusetts considered its churches examples for Puritan reconstruction of the Church of England. English reformers inquired into the system (1637), and after the Long

Parliament began ecclesiastical "reform" (1641), interest in Massachusetts polity led John Cotton to expound its principles in *The Way of the Churches of Christ in New England . . .* (1645); the short title of his work, *The New England Way,* made permanent an expression already common.

Originally a platform of opposition to English prelacy, based upon teachings of Henry Jacob, William Ames, and others, the "New England Way," immature in the 1640's, developed into New England Congregationalism. The church, originating neither in princes nor parliaments but in God's Word, was a body of professed regenerates (the "elect") who subscribed to a "covenant" (or creed), selected officers, chose and ordained its minister, and was subject to no interchurch organizations save "consociations" for counsel and advice. Being "visible saints," they admitted only persons who approved the covenant and whose piety and deportment recommended them to the congregation. They denied separation from the Anglican church; they separated only from its "corruptions," considered themselves true "primitive churches of Christ," and were supremely intolerant of others. Magistrates, "nursing fathers of the churches," were limited in civil authority by the Word (in practice, as interpreted by ministers) and compelled both to conform and to purge churches and state of heterodoxy. Citizenship depended on church membership. Church and state were indissolubly united. The "New England Way" did not appeal to English Separatists, whose multiple sects required embracing toleration, or to Presbyterians, whose synods held great interchurch authority, or to parliamentarians, who required the church to be subject to parliamentary prerogative. Thus, in many particulars, the "New England Way" was impracticable as an English model, and New England Congregationalists parted company with their English brethren.

[Benjamin Hanbury, ed., *Historical Memorials Relating to the Independents and Congregationalists From Their Rise to the Restoration;* Perry Miller, *Orthodoxy in Massachusetts.*]

RAYMOND P. STEARNS

"NEW ERA," or **"New Economic Era,"** was a term used contemporaneously to describe the period just before the Great Depression began in 1929. Not only was it believed that the United States had entered an era of high wages and prices, "easy" credit, and satisfactory profits but also, apparently, it was the belief of those who used the expression that the conditions that they regarded as ideal would continue indefinitely. Those who spoke of the "New Era" failed to realize the dangers in the current stock market speculation, and they ignored unsatisfactory conditions in agriculture and certain other phases of economic activity.

[A. M. Schlesinger, *Political and Social Growth of the United States, 1852–1933.*]

ERIK McKINLEY ERIKSSON

NEW FRANCE. For a century after the discovery of America the kings of France, preoccupied with dynastic and civil wars, devoted little attention to New World enterprises. In 1524 Francis I sent out Giovanni da Verrazano, whose expedition provided a paper claim to much of North America, while the three expeditions of Jacques Cartier (1534–42) served to fix French attention on the region adjoining the Gulf of Saint Lawrence. The short peace with England between 1598 and 1610 made possible the first permanent French establishment in America, at Quebec in 1608. For over half a century the government followed the policy of making grants to various companies to exploit the colony, and despite the devotion of Samuel de Champlain, its growth was painfully slow.

In 1661 Louis XIV assumed direct control of the colony, and a notable renaissance ensued. Soldiers were sent out to defend it and families to establish homes. Numerous measures looking to its economic betterment were instituted, and the Iroquois, who had previously been dangerous enemies, were subdued. These things prepared the way for a remarkable geographical expansion, whereby the boundaries of New France were extended along the Great Lakes and the entire Mississippi Valley—notably by Simon François Daumont, Sieur de Saint Lusson; Louis Jolliet; Robert Cavelier, Sieur de La Salle; Louis Hennepin; and Daniel Greysolon, Sieur Duluth.

The revolution of 1688, which placed William III on the English throne, initiated the second Hundred Years' War between France and England. To Old World rivalries the colonies added their own, and the period 1689–1763 witnessed four international wars, in each of which the American colonies participated. The long conflict ended with the surrender of Canada to England (Sept. 8, 1760), while the remainder of New France was divided between England and Spain (*see* Fontainebleau, Treaty of; Paris, Treaty of). New France as a political entity thus ceased to exist, although the French people and culture remained permanently seated in the valley of the Saint Lawrence.

[Adam Shortt and Arthur G. Doughty, eds., *Canada and Its Provinces: A History of the Canadian People and Their Institutions by One Hundred Associates;* G. M. Wrong and H. H. Langton, eds., *Chronicles of Canada.*]

M. M. QUAIFE

NEW FREEDOM, a term generally accepted as descriptive of the political and economic philosophy underlying the domestic policies of President Woodrow Wilson at the opening of his first administration in 1913. Wilson's more significant utterances in the campaign of 1912 were published under the title *The New Freedom* early the following year. They constituted an earnest plea for a more humanitarian spirit in government and business and political reforms that would restore government to the people and break the power of selfish and privileged minorities. The growth of corporate power, he argued, had rendered obsolete many traditional concepts of American democracy. Wilson felt that government must have not a negative, but a positive, program in that regard and use its power "to cheer and inspirit our people with the sure prospects of social justice and due reward, with the vision of the open gates of opportunity for all."

[R. S. Baker, *Life and Letters of Woodrow Wilson.*]

W. A. ROBINSON

NEW FRONTIER, the term used to describe the economic and social programs of the presidency of John F. Kennedy (Jan. 20, 1961, to Nov. 22, 1963). The young, vigorous, articulate president inspired a new élan in the nation's political culture. His administration made innovations at home in economic and defense policies, a manned-flight moon program, and civil rights bills. Abroad, Kennedy supported the Bay of Pigs invasion of Cuba and the commitment of troops to Vietnam; he also formed the Peace Corps, favored reciprocal trade and the Alliance for Progress, protected Berlin, forced the Soviet Union to take its missiles out of Cuba, neutralized Laos, and signed the nuclear test ban treaty.

[Aida DiPace Donald, *John F. Kennedy and the New Frontier;* Arthur M. Schlesinger, Jr., *A Thousand Days;* Theodore C. Sorensen, *Kennedy.*]

AIDA DIPACE DONALD

NEW GRANADA TREATY. *See* **Bidlack Treaty.**

NEW HAMPSHIRE. The coast of New Hampshire and the Isles of Shoals were visited by many fisher-men in the 16th century. In 1603 Martin Pring sailed up the Piscataqua; it is believed that Samuel de Champlain landed at what is now Odiorne's Point in 1605, as did John Smith, whose *Description of New England* gave wide publicity to the region, in 1614. The Council for New England granted much of what is now Maine and New Hampshire in 1622 to Sir Ferdinando Gorges and Capt. John Mason and in 1629 regranted to Mason alone an area that he called New Hampshire. Later grants added to the Mason title. Under smaller grants from the council David Thomson settled at Odiorne's Point near Portsmouth in 1623, the first settlement in New Hampshire, and soon after Edward Hilton founded Dover. The Laconia Company settled Strawberry Bank as a trading post in 1630. Rev. John Wheelwright, with other religious dissenters from Massachusetts, founded Exeter in 1638, and Massachusetts encouraged the settlement of Hampton in 1639. These four towns were practically independent but weak. Massachusetts, disliking their Anglican or antinomian tendencies, laid claim to the region, holding "3 miles north of the Merrimac" to mean its source, and assumed control in 1641, making some religious concessions, especially in voting requirements. Although several Quakers were hanged in 1659–60, there was little other religious persecution in New Hampshire, and there were no trials for witchcraft. Farming, lumbering, shipbuilding, fishing, and the fur trade were the chief occupations. No Indian troubles developed until King Philip's War (1675–76), but only one more town was settled by 1675.

Mason's heirs succeeded in 1679 in having New Hampshire created a separate royal province, with a governor and a council chosen by the crown and an elected assembly. It was again ruled by Massachusetts for a time after the fall of Sir Edmund Andros and the Dominion of New England, becoming separate permanently in 1692, although it had the same governor as Massachusetts between 1699 and 1741. The boundary with Massachusetts was settled by the king in 1741. Soon afterward conflict developed with New York over the western line, and New Hampshire granted out 138 towns, the New Hampshire Grants, in what is now Vermont. The king settled this line in 1764.

Severe Indian attacks—as at Salmon Falls, Exeter, and Durham between 1689 and 1725—slowed up settlement. Immigration was chiefly from Massachusetts and Connecticut, the Scotch-Irish being an important group after 1719. After the Indian wars the province grew rapidly. By 1776 about 80,000 persons were liv-

53

ing along the coast, inland to the Merrimack and in the west along the Connecticut. The northern half of New Hampshire was still unsettled, and much of the rest so recently occupied as to be under frontier conditions. Portsmouth, the capital, was the only town of size and wealth. Economic differences were not great, and the colony was distinctly rural, provincial, and democratic. The first newspaper, the *New Hampshire Gazette,* was founded in 1756, and Dartmouth College in 1769.

As the Revolution approached, there were few Tories among the people of New Hampshire. The majority, after an attack on Fort William and Mary in 1774, drove out Gov. John Wentworth and created a new government in January 1776, the first of the colonies to do so. New Hampshire contributed significantly to the war: scores of privateers sailed from Portsmouth; three ships of the new navy were launched on the Piscataqua; Gen. John Stark won the Battle of Bennington (1777) with local troops; and the New Hampshire regiments did their full share. The economic distress after the war produced at Exeter a mild copy of Shays's Rebellion and a close contest in the ratification of the Constitution, which was finally secured June 21, 1788, as New Hampshire became the ninth and decisive state to ratify. For some time New Hampshire was Federalist, but a rising Jeffersonian Republican party under John Langdon won many state elections, prevented participation in the Hartford Convention of 1815, and passed the Toleration Act of 1819. Manhood suffrage had been secured by the constitution of 1784. A Democratic machine fashioned by Isaac Hill carried New Hampshire for Andrew Jackson and retained control until 1855, while the rest of New England was usually with the opposition; its peak occurred in the election of President Franklin Pierce in 1852. Since then the state has been generally Republican and for some decades after the Civil War was under the domination of the railroads.

The 19th century saw many economic changes in New Hampshire. Factories were built in many places, especially at Manchester, where the Amoskeag Company had the largest cotton mill in the world. After 1920 cotton manufacturing declined and was replaced by a more diversified industry. Agriculture suffered from western competition after 1825, knew a boom time with the introduction of merino sheep, and changed again toward the end of the century to dairying and truck farming. Lumbering—and the manufacture of paper and other wood products—was still important in the mid-1970's, although far less so than at

the beginning of the century. Beginning in the mid-1920's a resort and recreation business, especially in winter sports, began to be a major source of revenue. The state was hurt less than most by the depression of the 1930's, in part because of the large rural population and the diversification of its economic life. A significant shift occurred in New Hampshire's economy in the 1960's, as the traditional shoemaking, woodworking, and textile industries began to give way to the manufacture of electrical and electronic goods, to insurance and banking, and to other businesses and services.

The population of New Hampshire since the 1960's has experienced a more rapid growth rate than that of the rest of New England, and to the nearly pure Anglo-Saxon stock have been added many other national groups, the most numerous being the French Canadians. Even so, in 1970 New Hampshire ranked only forty-second among the states in population, with 737,681 residents.

[J. Belknap, *History of New Hampshire;* W. H. Fry, *New Hampshire as a Royal Province;* F. B. Sanborn, *New Hampshire;* E. S. Stackpole, *History of New Hampshire;* R. F. Upton, *Revolutionary New Hampshire.*]

EMIL W. ALLEN, JR.

NEW HAMPSHIRE GRANTS, a term applied in the early settlement to that section of territory now known as the state of Vermont. Benning Wentworth, first governor of New Hampshire, which colony claimed jurisdiction over the territory, began granting land to the settlers in 1749 in the name of the king of England. The first of the grants bore the name of Bennington. By 1761 the grants began to be issued rapidly, and a total of 138 townships had been chartered by 1764. At that point New York, which had set up counterclaims to the territory, with the attendant right to make grants, gained the support of the crown, and in 1765 began to charter townships within the grants, some of which conflicted with grants already made by New Hampshire. New York contended that the prior titles were invalidated, but the settlers, determined to keep their lands, formed a militia to protect them (*see* Green Mountain Boys) and declared themselves an independent republic. The controversy was ended only with the creation of the separate state of Vermont after the Revolution.

[W. H. Crockett, *History of Vermont.*]

LEON W. DEAN

NEW HARMONY SETTLEMENT, in Posey County, Ind., was founded in 1825 by Robert Owen, the English philanthropist and industrialist, on the site previously occupied by the Harmony Society of Pennsylvania. Owen attempted to put into practice the theories of socialism and human betterment that he had evolved. By December 1825 New Harmony had attracted a heterogeneous population of about 1,000 men, women, and children of all sorts and conditions. Following a preliminary organization the constitution of the New Harmony Community of Equality was adopted, Feb. 5, 1826. It provided for absolute equality of property, labor, and opportunity, together with freedom of speech and action. The absence of any real authority in the community government resulted in virtual anarchy, and after several abortive attempts to better conditions, Owen admitted the failure of the experiment on May 26, 1827. A number of communities modeled on New Harmony sprang up in other states at that time and were equally short-lived.

[G. B. Lockwood, *The New Harmony Communities,* and *The New Harmony Movement.*]

EDGAR B. NIXON

NEW HAVEN COLONY. Dissatisfied with government by king and council and with growing high-church Anglicanism in England, in the spring of 1637 John Davenport, Puritan divine, and Theophilus Eaton, merchant, led a group of Londoners to Massachusetts Bay. Both Davenport and Eaton were members of the Massachusetts Bay Company and probably intended to found a plantation within the limits of the Bay colony, where the group already had many friends. They were sympathetic to the principles of Congregationalism, to the attempt to limit political privileges to members of Congregational churches, and to Moses His Judicials, a code of laws recently prepared by the Puritan clergyman John Cotton for Massachusetts and at the time under consideration in that colony. They intended to found a commercial settlement, however, and by 1637 the best harbors of Massachusetts had been occupied. Moreover, at the time of their arrival the Antinomian controversy was at its height in Massachusetts and must have discouraged a group of Puritans seeking a new Jerusalem. Finally, the Pequot War had cleared the territory on the northern shore of Long Island Sound of Indians, and glowing reports of this region had reached Massachusetts. In the fall of 1637 Eaton and others set out to investigate this "promised land," and as a result of their explorations, the group decided to settle at Quinnipiac, later known as the town of New Haven.

With recruits gained in Massachusetts, the Davenport-Eaton company set out for Quinnipiac in the spring of 1638. They soon attracted kindred souls from Massachusetts, from Wethersfield on the Connecticut River, and from England. In addition to the town of New Haven, settlements appeared at Guilford, Milford, Stamford, Southold on Long Island, and, somewhat later, Branford. Without royal charter authorizing them to take possession of the soil and to organize a government, the settlers purchased land from the natives. In each town a church was gathered according to Congregational principles, and, following the gathering of a church, a plantation government was established based upon the Cotton code, adapted to meet the needs of a new and smaller community. At first Guilford and Milford were independent plantations, but Stamford, Southold, and Branford acquired their land from New Haven and always recognized the jurisdiction of the mother town. As a result of the formation of the United Colonies of New England in 1643, a colonial government, also based upon the Cotton code, was established, and the New Haven colony took its place as the smallest of the Puritan colonies of New England. Eaton was governor of this colony until his death in 1658. Throughout the existence of the colony, political privileges were restricted to members of Congregational churches. To train leaders for church and state, Davenport endeavored to found a colony grammar school and college at New Haven. A grammar school opened its doors in 1660 but closed two years later. The college of which Davenport dreamed did not materialize until long after his death (*see* Yale University).

During the early years of the colony the leaders had high hopes of establishing a commercial commonwealth that would extend from the western boundary of Saybrook on the Connecticut River to the Delaware River. As early as 1641 they acquired title to land on the Delaware from the Indians, but their plans brought the New Haven colony into conflict with New Sweden and New Netherland. Probably more than the other colonies of New England, the Puritans on Long Island Sound desired the English conquest of New Netherland. The first Anglo-Dutch war seemed to further their designs, but Massachusetts, not yet awakened to the possibility of extending its territory across the continent, blocked the plans of the merchants of the New Haven colony and Connecticut in 1653, and the end of the war in Europe halted an expedition that Oliver Cromwell had sent across the Atlantic to seize New Netherland in 1654. Hemmed in by Connecticut and the Dutch, the New Haven colony failed to develop into the great commercial commonwealth its founders had envisioned and turned to agriculture.

The Restoration in England found the New Haven colony without a leader capable of representing it at the court of Charles II. William Leete, governor, suggested that Connecticut's governor, John Winthrop the Younger, about to visit England to secure a royal charter for Connecticut, procure one charter under which two colonial governments might function. Winthrop succeeded in securing a charter that unquestionably included the New Haven colony, and, disregarding Leete's plan for two colonies, the magistrates of Connecticut hastened to extend their authority over their southern neighbor. The New Haven colony fought absorption, but a royal grant of the territory between the Connecticut and Delaware rivers to James, Duke of York, and the surrender of New Netherland to royal commissioners convinced the leaders that they would be better off under Connecticut than as part of the province of the Duke of York. In December 1664 the New Haven colony ceased to exist.

[I. M. Calder, *The New Haven Colony*.[

ISABEL M. CALDER

NEW HOPE CHURCH, BATTLES AT (May 24–28, 1864). While battling his way toward Atlanta, Union Gen. William Tecumseh Sherman attempted to pass to the right of the Confederate army, but Gen. J. E. Johnston, the opposing commander, detected the movement and blocked it in a series of sharp fights in the forests around New Hope Church, Ga. Losses on each side were about 3,000 men.

[R. U. Johnson and C. C. Buel, eds., *Battles and Leaders of the Civil War*.]

ALVIN F. HARLOW

NEW IRONSIDES, built in Philadelphia in 1861–62, was a screw sloop of the British *Warrior* type. It was 232 feet long, had a speed of 6 knots, and was protected by 4½ inches of rolled iron armor sloping at 17 degrees and extending 3 feet below the water line. Sixteen 11-inch Dahlgren smoothbores and two 8-inch Parrott rifles were its chief armament. It took part in all the Union attacks in Charleston harbor in 1863 and was hit many times, once even by a torpedo, without damage. After taking part in the attack on Fort Fisher, N.C., December-January 1864–65, it

was laid up at League Island in Philadelphia harbor, where it was destroyed by fire in 1866.

[F. M. Bennett, *Steam Navy of the United States.*]

WALTER B. NORRIS

NEW JERSEY became a historical entity when James, Duke of York, granted all his lands between the Hudson and Delaware rivers to John, Lord Berkeley, and Sir George Carteret. The two proprietors issued Concessions and Agreements on Feb. 10, 1665, setting forth their governmental and land policies. In March 1674, Berkeley sold his interest in New Jersey to a Quaker, John Fenwick, representing Edward Byllynge, for £1,000. Trustees for Byllynge, including William Penn, tried to establish a Quaker colony in West Jersey. Fenwick broke away from the Byllynge group and settled at Salem in November 1675, becoming lord proprietor of his "tenth" of the proprietary lands. The Quintpartite Deed of July 1676 separated the proprietary history of New Jersey into east and west, with Carteret as proprietor of East Jersey and Byllynge, William Penn, and two other Quakers as proprietors of West Jersey. A Council of Proprietors of West Jersey was formed with nine members in 1688.

Carteret's lands were sold upon his death to twelve men for £3,400 in February 1682. The Board of Proprietors of East Jersey was formed in 1684. Both East and West Jersey proprietors wished to end their political control of New Jersey, but the surrender of governmental authority was not accepted by the crown until 1702. Both groups retained the rights to the soil and to the collection of quitrents. The boards of proprietors are still in existence and hold meetings at Perth Amboy (for East Jersey) and Burlington (for West Jersey).

Riots over land titles in New Jersey occurred between the years 1745 and 1755. The first English settlers, who had come to East Jersey in the 1660's, felt they had no reason to pay proprietary quitrents since they had purchased the land from the Indians. James Alexander, an influential councillor of East Jersey, filed a bill in chancery court on Apr. 17, 1745, to settle the long-standing dispute. On Sept. 19, 1745, Samuel Baldwin, one of the claimants to land in East Jersey, was arrested on his land and taken to jail in Newark. He was set free by 150 men. Thus began sporadic rioting and the disruption of the courts and jails in most East Jersey counties. In 1752 the Elizabethtown people filed an answer to the Alexander bill.

By 1754, because they feared English retaliation, the coming of the French and Indian War, and unfavorable court decisions, the rioters ended their rebellion. The case was never legally resolved, since the bill in chancery was never heard.

Colonial New Jersey was characterized by ethnic and religious diversity. In East Jersey, Quakers, Baptists, and Congregationalists from New England and Scotch-Irish Presbyterians blended with Dutch settlers from New York. Most people lived in towns with individual landholdings of 100 acres, but the proprietors owned vast tracts of land. West Jersey was a sparsely settled area of large estates owned by English Quakers and Anglicans. Both sections remained agrarian and rural in the 18th century, but commercial farming did develop, and some towns, such as Burlington and Perth Amboy, became points of shipment to New York and Philadelphia. The attraction of fertile land and a tolerant religious policy saw the population of the colony expand to 120,000 by 1775.

From 1702, when East Jersey and West Jersey were reunited, to 1776, the province was ruled by a royal governor, an appointive council, and an assembly. Until 1738 the governor of New York was also governor of New Jersey. The governor's power was curtailed by the assembly's right to initiate money bills, which forced most governors to restrain their authority in order to receive their salaries. By 1763 the New Jersey assembly had gained the initiative in governmental affairs.

New Jersey played a small role in the imperial crisis after 1763, since it was divided by political factionalism and sectional conflict. The most important prerevolutionary incident was the robbery of the treasury of the East Jersey proprietors on July 21, 1768, which created tensions between the governor, William Franklin, and the assembly. By 1774, despite only tepid participation in boycotts and protests over the Stamp Act and Townshend duties, New Jersey was being pushed along toward revolt by the militancy of its larger and more powerful neighbors. With the closing of the port of Boston, the colony formed a provincial congress in May 1775 to assume all power. New Jersey participated in both sessions of the Continental Congress, which culminated in the Declaration of Independence, and established a state constitution on July 2, 1776.

Few states suffered as much or as long during the American Revolution. Both British and American armies swept across New Jersey, and Loyalists returned in armed forays and foraging expeditions. The battles of Trenton (Dec. 26, 1776), Monmouth (June 28, 1778), and Springfield (June 23, 1780) helped ensure American independence. Under the Articles of Confederation, New Jersey suffered from the aftershocks of war's devastation and a heavy state debt. At the Constitutional Convention of 1787, New Jersey's William Paterson assumed the role of advocate for the smaller states, presenting the New Jersey Plan.

In the Federalist era industry and transportation began to remold the state. In November 1791 Alexander Hamilton helped form the Society for the Establishment of Useful Manufactures, which began operating a cotton mill in the new city of Paterson. Hamilton was also involved in the organization of a similar industrial venture at Paulus Hook. He and other New York and New Jersey Federalists purchased land, and the group was incorporated as the Associates of New Jersey Company on Nov. 10, 1804. Both ventures only proved successful after 1820. A transportation revolution was stimulated by capital investment and new manufacturing opportunities. From 1800 to 1830 improved roads—notably the Morris Turnpike (1801)—invigorated the state's economy. Steamboats linked New Jersey to the ports of New York and Philadelphia. The construction of the Morris Canal (1824–38) and the Delaware and Raritan Canal (1826–38) brought coal and iron to eastern industry. John Stevens received a charter for the Camden and Amboy Railroad on Feb. 4, 1830, which was completed in 1834. All these transportation advances increased internal trade and stimulated manufacturing and urbanization.

By 1860 New Jersey had rapidly changed from a rural farming region into an urban, industrial state. Such cities as Camden and Hoboken were created by ship and rail facilities, while Newark and Jersey City prospered because of the concentration of industry there. The demand for labor created, in turn, a dramatic increase in the population of New Jersey cities. The need for unskilled workers in building and rail construction and in factories was met in part by new waves of immigrants. In the 1840's and thereafter, Germans, Irish, Poles, and other Europeans—Protestant, Jewish, and Roman Catholic—added to the ethnic and religious diversity of New Jersey. In the 20th century blacks from the South have swelled the urban population. With the invention of the automobile New Jersey's population decentralized into suburbs along the many major highways. The state has a varied contemporary economic landscape. Its principal industries include recreation facilities, particularly along the Jersey shore; scientific research; chemical and mineral refining; and insurance. In 1970, with a population of 7;168,164, New Jersey was the most urbanized state in the nation (88.9 percent).

The state's political development reflected the changing social and economic scene. The state constitution of 1776 provided for a weak executive with no veto powers, and until modern times the governor was less powerful than the state legislature and its party leaders. By 1800 both the Federalists and Democratic-Republicans had formed local organizations in New Jersey. The political competition of the Jacksonian era created the first ties between business and state government. With liberal incorporation laws and unremitting pressure upon legislators, industrial giants, such as Standard Oil and the Pennsylvania Railroad, controlled state politics. Toward the end of his 1911–13 governorship Woodrow Wilson attacked these corporations with his "Seven Sisters" monopoly legislation. After 1900 politics was increasingly dominated by the political parties that were controlled by urban bosses, such as Frank Hague of Jersey City. With the new state constitution of 1947 the governor became a more independent figure with wider powers. By the 1970's New Jersey had become an urbanized and industrialized state enjoying a high standard of living but also suffering the problems of environmental pollution, urban decay, racial tensions, and unemployment.

[John E. Bebout and Ronald J. Grele, *Where Cities Meet: The Urbanization of New Jersey;* Wheaton J. Lane, *From Indian Trail to Iron Horse;* Duane Lockard, *The New Jersey Governor: A Study in Political Power;* Richard P. McCormick, *New Jersey From Colony to State, 1609–1789;* John E. Pomfret, *The New Jersey Proprietors and Their Lands;* Rudolph J. Vecoli, *The People of New Jersey.*]

DENNIS PATRICK RYAN

NEW JERSEY PLAN. *See* **Constitution of the United States.**

NEW JERUSALEM, CHURCHES OF THE. The churches of the New Jerusalem follow the teachings of the 18th-century Swedish mystic Emanuel Swedenborg. Their members believe that all of reality is filled with the spirit and that, consequently, whenever scripture speaks of historical, natural, or scientific matters, it must be interpreted according to the "science of comprehension." The true nature of reality, they believe, will be revealed at the second ad-

vent when the "New Jerusalem" will be evident to all.

The Church of the New Jerusalem attracted its adherents through publications of Swedenborg's doctrines. The publications were particularly numerous in New England, where Swedenborg's writings influenced many American transcendentalists. The informal organization of the movement has meant that many of Swedenborg's followers did not join the churches but did study his works.

In 1974 the General Church of the New Jerusalem had more than 2,000 members, as did the General Convention, the Swedenborgian Church.

GLENN T. MILLER

NEWLANDS RECLAMATION ACT. *See* **Irrigation; Reclamation.**

NEW LIGHTS. George Whitefield, an English evangelist, appearing in New England in 1740, gave impetus to a religious movement led by Jonathan Edwards toward the old doctrine of sanctification by faith alone. This became a cult known as the New Lights, which split the Congregational establishment in New England and drew from other faiths also. It brought on a religious revival, known as the Great Awakening, which was characterized by extravagant demonstrations—the first of the sort in American history. Connecticut, where the controversy was violent, passed a law in 1742 to restrain the revivalists. Many New Lights leaders, including Edwards, eventually had to leave their parishes.

[G. P. Fisher, *History of Christian Doctrine;* F. H. Foster, *A Genetic History of the New England Theology.*]

ALVIN F. HARLOW

NEW LONDON, BURNING OF. On the morning of Sept. 6, 1781, a British fleet from New York landed Gen. Benedict Arnold and about 800 men near New London, Conn. Fort Trumbull was quickly taken and most of the warehouses and residences of the town were burned. The British withdrew the same evening. The attack on nearby Fort Griswold occurred simultaneously.

[F. M. Caulkins, *History of New London.*]

GEORGE MATTHEW DUTCHER

NEW MADRID, a small city in southeastern Missouri, was founded by a group of Americans under the leadership of George Morgan in 1789 in what was then Spanish Louisiana. Spain hoped to make Louisiana a buffer state between the United States and Mexico by settling it with discontented Americans (*see* Western Separatism). Morgan was representative of those discontented over the failure of the Confederation to bring order and prosperity. Many of the westerners who went with him did so because of the closure of the Mississippi by Spain, which made it difficult for residents of Kentucky and the upper Ohio to market their products (*see* Mississippi River, Free Navigation of). Morgan's grant, made to him by Don Diego de Gardoqui, Spanish minister to the United States, subject to the approval of the Spanish king, included the territory between Cape Cinque Hommes (Missouri) and the mouth of the Saint Francis River (Arkansas). Morgan himself led a party of seventy settlers and numerous Indians in four armed boats into Spanish territory early in 1789 and began to build the town on its present site. He took great pains to make his city beautiful and adopted a policy of advanced religious toleration, to the discomfort of the Spanish authorities. His Indian policy, also, was of a very liberal sort. Soon after getting his colony started he returned to the eastern seaboard, by way of New Orleans, where he had a discouraging interview with the Spanish governor, Esteban Miró. He never returned to New Madrid. Administration of the colony was taken over by the Spanish authorities, and a modification of Spanish policy with regard to the Mississippi, inspired by Gen. James Wilkinson, had the effect of discouraging American immigration until after the Louisiana Purchase.

[Louis Houck, ed., *The Spanish Régime in Missouri;* Max Savelle, *George Morgan, Colony Builder;* Arthur P. Whitaker, *The Spanish-American Frontier, 1783–1795.*]

MAX SAVELLE

NEW MARKET, BATTLE OF (May 15, 1864). Moving down the Shenandoah Valley from Winchester, Va., Union Gen. Franz Sigel engaged the combined Confederate forces of Gen. John D. Imboden and Gen. John C. Breckinridge at New Market, Va. The engagement, fought in a driving rain, resulted in a Confederate victory, important in that it afforded Gen. Robert E. Lee the opportunity of concentrating all his resources to the defense of Richmond.

[R. U. Johnson and C. C. Buel, eds., *Battles and Leaders of the Civil War.*]

ROBERT S. THOMAS

NEW MEXICO. The history of New Mexico is that of three peoples—the Indians, the Spanish, and the Anglo-Americans. Twentieth-century archaeological discoveries indicate the presence of Sandia and Folsom man in the state more than 10,000 years ago. When the Spanish first arrived in the 16th century, they found some twenty Indian pueblos, or towns, concentrated along the Rio Grande. Their inhabitants totaled approximately 20,000. The Pueblo civilization, built around the cultivation of corn, was one of the most highly developed of the cultures of native North American Indians.

The name New Mexico reflects Spanish hopes that the area would be as rich in minerals as Mexico, but the expedition in 1540 of Francisco Vásquez de Coronado dashed that dream. The conquest and settlement, led by Juan de Oñate in 1598, brought a few soldier-colonists, but Spanish occupation was, in the main, a missionary endeavor. Although Franciscan friars converted most of the Pueblo Indians to Christianity, many natives resented the intrusion of Hispanic civilization, and in 1680 they drove the white men out in a bloody uprising. The reconquest, led by Diego de Vargas, was accomplished by 1696, and the rest of the Spanish era saw the Pueblo living peacefully with their conquerors. Throughout the 18th century it was the nomadic tribes—Apache, Navaho, Ute, and Comanche—that threatened both the Spanish settlers and the Pueblo. This native harassment, along with the scarcity of water, led to the concentration of Spanish settlement in the north-central area of the state, along the upper Rio Grande and its tributaries.

Anglo-American intrusion into New Mexico began in the early 19th century with the quest for beaver by the mountain men; was continued with the opening of the Santa Fe trade in 1821; and was increased when the area became part of the United States as a result of the Mexican War. Territorial status was granted in 1850, but New Mexico waited until 1912 to become the forty-seventh state. The influx of Anglo-Americans increased rapidly after 1850. The Santa Fe Trail was utilized by many en route to California during the Gold Rush, but large numbers remained in New Mexico to seek a livelihood as traders and ranchers. There was usually harmony between the Hispanic majority and the recent arrivals, but friction did exist, primarily as a result of the manner in which Anglo-Americans obtained control of large areas of land. Again the nomadic Indians resisted this new invasion, which threatened their traditional mode of life. The Navaho were subdued in 1864, the Comanche in 1874, and the last of the Apache in 1886. During the Civil War a Confederate invasion force under Gen. Henry H. Sibley seized control of much of the state, but the invaders were driven out after a defeat at Glorieta Pass in 1862.

After the Civil War the Texas cattle frontier expanded into the state. The coming of the railroads in the 1880's fed an already existing mining boom and brought Anglo-American farmers in large numbers. The combination of agriculture and mining as the basis of the state's economy has continued: in the mid-1970's the state was a leading producer of petroleum, natural gas, and potash and had been the nation's principal producer of uranium since 1950. Cattle ranching continued to be important; and although there was considerable dry land farming, the most productive cultivated areas were irrigated. World War II and the cold war brought many military installations to New Mexico, notably the nuclear research center at Los Alamos and the White Sands Missile Range. These entailed large federal expenditures in the state and an expansion of manufacturing. Tourism was also a leading industry because of the state's natural beauty and the continuation of both Indian and Hispanic cultures in New Mexico.

Having been predominantly Republican as a territory, New Mexico voted more often than not for Democratic candidates in state elections in the period just after its admission to the Union. In 1950 it returned its allegiance to the Republican party, electing Republican Edwin L. Mechem to the governorship for four terms. Since then its Republican cast has wavered, owing partly to an influx of Texas Democrats. From its admission to the Union through 1972, New Mexico voted for the winning candidate in every presidential election. In population, New Mexico ranked thirty-seventh among the states in 1970, with 1,016,000 residents.

[Warren A. Beck, *New Mexico: A History of Four Centuries;* Warren A. Beck and Ynez Haase, *A Historical Atlas of New Mexico;* Richard Ellis, *New Mexico Past and Present: A Reader;* Frank Reeve, *History of New Mexico.*]

WARREN A. BECK

NEW NATIONALISM, the term used to describe the political philosophy of Theodore Roosevelt that the nation is the best instrument for advancing progressive democracy. In more detail, the phrase implied emphasis on the need for political, social, and industrial reforms, such as government regulation and control of corporations, better working conditions for labor, conservation of natural resources, and a con-

centration of more power directly in the people. Implied also were the ineffectiveness of the states in dealing with these problems and the consequent necessity of using the powers of the national government and of increasing those powers to the extent necessary. (*See also* New Freedom; New Deal.)

[Joseph Bucklin Bishop, *Theodore Roosevelt and His Time.*]

CLARENCE A. BERDAHL

NEW NETHERLAND. No serious attempt was made to plant a colony in New Netherland before the organization of the Dutch West India Company in 1621. In the spring of 1624 a group of thirty families, most of whom were Walloons, were sent in the ship *New Netherland.* A few of the emigrants remained at the mouth of the Hudson River but the greater part were settled up the river at Fort Orange, where the city of Albany now stands. A fort was also built on Nut (now Governors) Island. Shortly afterward Willem Verhulst was appointed *commies* and sailed for New Netherland. Three months after Verhulst's arrival in 1625 the thinly settled colony was reinforced by the coming of forty-two new emigrants. In addition one of the directors of the company sent 103 head of livestock, including horses, cows, hogs, and sheep. In July 1625 the settlement was moved from Nut Island to Manhattan Island and called New Amsterdam. A new fort was built.

Verhulst did not remain long in New Amsterdam. His own council found him guilty of mismanagement. He was dismissed, and Peter Minuit was appointed in his place as the first director general. Minuit negotiated the purchase of Manhattan from the Indians, paying the value of sixty guilders ($24) in trinkets, thus legalizing the occupation already in effect. In 1626, because of trouble with the Indians, Minuit moved the families at Fort Orange to Manhattan, leaving only a small garrison behind under Sebastian Crol.

Members of the settlement had no voice in its administration. Power was centered in the hands of the director and his council, who were appointed by and represented the company. The colonists for the most part were not free agents, but were bound by contracts to the company. Although farmers were allotted free land, they were obliged to stay in the colony for six years. The company had right of first purchase of the produce from their fields, and they could sell their farms only to one of the other colonists. Indentured husbandmen, under still more rigid restrictions, worked the company farms. Instructions in considerable detail were sent to the director by the company, and only in cases of urgent necessity was he allowed to modify his orders. New legislation was submitted to the executive committee of the company, as were appeals in judicial cases. The Reform Church was supported, though freedom of conscience was granted.

The first few years showed a moderate profit to the company from trade, but the efforts at colonization proved a loss. Among the directors of the company two parties appeared, one favoring active colonization of the province, the other desirous of restricting the company to its trading function. The former group was successful in 1629 in the passage of the Charter of Freedoms and Exemptions, which provided for the grant of great estates, called patroonships, to such members of the company as should found settlements of fifty persons within four years. The effect of patroonships under the charter has been overemphasized: with the single exception of Rensselaerswyck, they were unsuccessful. Another type of landholding provided for in the charter was destined to be of far greater importance: "private persons" were allowed to take possession of as much land as they could cultivate properly. In 1638, further to encourage colonization, trade restrictions in the colony were reduced, better provision was offered for transportation of settlers and their goods, and the fur-trade monopoly was discontinued. The revised charter of 1640 reduced the size of future patroonships and held out promises of local self-government.

In 1631 Minuit was recalled, and Wouter Van Twiller was named his successor. The administration of Van Twiller was marked by violent quarrels with his council and prominent colonists. In 1637 his failure to send reports to the company resulted in his recall and the appointment of Willem Kieft as director general. An adventurer with a bad record, Kieft did nothing to improve it during his administration. By the summer of 1641 his brutal and unwise Indian policy had created so dangerous a situation that he was constrained to ask the colonists to elect a board to advise with him, and the Twelve Men were chosen. Although they had been called only to give advice on Indian affairs, to Kieft's annoyance they drew up a petition asking for much-needed reforms. The Indian difficulties died down temporarily, but in September 1643 an unprovoked night attack on an Indian encampment, instigated by Kieft, caused the Indians to rise in fury. Safety was to be found only in the immediate vicinity of the fort. Distant Fort Orange alone was not molested. Kieft once more called for an election of representatives, and the Eight Men were chosen. In October 1643 and again in the following year they petitioned the company for aid, bitterly criticizing Kieft's management of Indian relations. Conditions in the province were desperate. The frightened settlers huddling in or near the fort faced starvation. Hostile bands of Indians, estimated as totaling 15,000, threatened attack, but they had no common and concerted plan. June brought reinforcements, but hostilities dragged on, and it was not until August 1645 that a general peace was signed. The Indian war had not extended to Fort Orange and the patroon's colony of Rensselaerswyck, although trade had suffered. Despite the restrictions imposed by the company this little settlement had grown by 1645 into a sizable colony.

The complaints of the Eight Men and similar protests from private persons resulted in the recall of Kieft, and on May 11, 1647, Peter Stuyvesant, his successor, arrived in New Amsterdam. The new director was honorable, active, and conscientious, but his autocratic disposition and his hostility to popular demands led to continual friction. Conditions in the province were bad; trade was in a state of confusion; morals were low; and money was urgently needed. In September 1647, as a means of raising revenue, Stuyvesant called for an election of representatives. The Nine Men were chosen. They met the requests of the director general fairly and expressed themselves as willing to tax themselves to help finish the church and reorganize the school. Then, despite protests from Stuyvesant, they drew up and sent to Holland two documents known as the Petition and the Remonstrance of New Netherland. The Petition was a concise statement of the unsatisfactory condition of the province with suggested remedies; the Remonstrance, a longer document, furnished in detail the facts on which the appeal was based. In April 1652 the company, inclined to grant some of the concessions asked, instructed Stuyvesant to give New Amsterdam a burgher government.

Although Stuyvesant made a sincere attempt to maintain friendly relations with the Indians, he had to fight three Indian wars. The first broke out in 1655 in New Amsterdam and extended to the Esopus settlement, near Kingston, and to Long Island. Five years later there was a serious outbreak at Esopus, which was aggravated when Stuyvesant sent some of the Indian captives to Curaçao as slaves. This incident rankled, and the Indians rose again; so it was not until May 1664 that a general peace was signed.

The gradual encroachment of settlers from New

England on territory claimed by the Dutch had been a source of trouble since the beginning of the colony. Rivalry over the fur trade and complaint from the English traders against the tariffs levied at New Amsterdam increased the ill feeling. Stuyvesant took up the quarrel vigorously. No decision was reached over the tariff and Indian trade disputes, but the question of boundaries was finally settled by the Treaty of Hartford in 1650. The last year of the Dutch regime in New Netherland was fraught with grave fear of Indian wars, rebellion, and British invasion. Stuyvesant tried vainly to put the province in a state of defense, but on Aug. 29, 1664, he was forced to surrender to an English fleet, which came to claim the province in the name of James, Duke of York.

[A. C. Flick, ed., *History of the State of New York,* vols. I, II.]

A. C. FLICK

NEW ORLEANS, located between Lake Pontchartrain and the Mississippi River about 100 miles from the Gulf of Mexico, was founded in 1718 by the French governor of Louisiana, Jean Baptiste Le Moyne, Sieur de Bienville, and named in honor of the regent of France, the Duc d'Orléans. An unprofitable port, it was transferred to Spain as part of Louisiana Territory west of the Mississippi by the Treaty of Paris of 1763 and then returned to France by the Treaty of San Ildefonso of 1800. In 1803 it was sold by Napoleon to the United States as part of the Louisiana Purchase.

New Orleans was at first a crude frontier town whose chief export was fur; it lacked the cultural polish of such older Atlantic ports as Charleston, S.C. In time, however, the descendants of the original French and Spanish settlers, known as Creoles, came to be large landowners noted for their stress on family tradition, social position, and hereditary wealth.

By 1800, as a result of the Treaty of Madrid of 1795, New Orleans had become a transshipment point to ocean vessels for flatboats and keelboats, and by 1812 steamboats were traveling the Mississippi. With the defeat of the British in the War of 1812, commerce burgeoned, and New Orleans became the Queen City of the South. By 1840 it led the nation in value of exports. It handled much more of exported western produce than all other ports together—and the shipping tonnage of its wharves was double that of New York. But the railroads, which its rivals from Mobile to New York began building at midcentury to tap the valley trade, proved its undoing. By 1860 its

receipt of western goods had declined to a mere 18 percent of the total volume handled, and its chief economic function became the marketing of cotton and sugar from its hinterland. With the destruction of the local slave economy as a result of the Civil War, the port's profit from that function declined, and it was not until World War I that it began to revive to its mid-19th-century level. The development of the petrochemical industry after World War II spurred an economic revival; by 1970 it had reached a position in exports second only to that of New York.

In the rank of urban population New Orleans had declined from third place in 1840 to nineteenth place in 1970, with a population of only 593,471. As Harold Sinclair observed, it became "a midget with a prodigious personality rather than one of the world's great ports."

New Orleans was built, said the *London Illustrated News* in 1853, "upon a site that only the madness of commercial lust could ever have attempted to occupy." It was frequently smitten by epidemics of yellow fever and cholera and menaced by hurricanes and floods (against which only frail levees protected it); it abounded with cockroaches and other vermin common to subtropical regions, as well as water moccasins and alligators on its outskirts. In many ways 19th-century New Orleans was more a Caribbean than a southern city. Yet its population was cosmopolitan, as a result of the heavy immigration of Irish and Germans, who in time outnumbered the native Creoles, and the migration of many easterners, who came there to make a quick fortune. It attracts hordes of tourists from all over the nation and the world with its annual Mardi Gras festival, the Sugar Bowl football game, and the French Quarter, or Vieux Carré, disparately unique in its Creole architecture and its continuing tradition of jazz, which was born there.

Because of extensive discoveries of oil and sulfur in Louisiana and in the Gulf of Mexico after World War II, the New Orleans area enjoyed a pronounced industrial boom, but the main economic function of the metropolis remained commercial—the export of most of the grain raised in the Mississippi Valley, for example. In population and economic importance, however, it was passed by other cities of the former slave states—Houston, Saint Louis, and Atlanta.

[Gerald M. Capers, *Occupied City: New Orleans Under the Federals, 1862–1865;* John G. Clark, *New Orleans 1715–1812: An Economic History;* Joy Jackson, *New Orleans in the Gilded Age;* Grace King, *New Orleans: The Place and the People;* Harold Sinclair, *Port of New Orleans.*]

GERALD M. CAPERS

NEW ORLEANS, the first steamboat on western waters, was built at Pittsburgh by Nicholas J. Roosevelt, under patents held by Robert Fulton and Robert R. Livingston, during 1810–11 (*see* Fulton's Folly). A sidewheeler of between 300 and 400 tons, the *New Orleans* left Pittsburgh on Oct. 20, 1811, braved the Falls of the Ohio and the New Madrid earthquake, and reached New Orleans, Jan. 10, 1812. It never returned to Pittsburgh, plying in the New Orleans–Natchez trade until snagged on July 14, 1814.

[W. J. Petersen, *Steamboating on the Upper Mississippi.*]

WILLIAM J. PETERSEN

NEW ORLEANS, BATTLE OF (Jan. 8, 1815). The United States declared war on Great Britain in June 1812 (*see* War of 1812), but the contest did not threaten Louisiana until near its close. After Napoleon Bonaparte's abdication early in 1814, England was free to concentrate its energies on the American war. A veteran army was dispatched to attack the South and West, the home of the "war hawks," leading proponents of the war. In the autumn of 1814 a British fleet of over fifty vessels, carrying 7,500 soldiers under Sir Edward Packenham, appeared in the Gulf of Mexico preparatory to attacking New Orleans, the key to the entire Mississippi Valley. The defenses of the city had been neglected, since the war up to that time had been waged mainly on the Canadian border. Under threat of British attack, Gov. William Claiborne undertook such defensive measures as he could with the limited means at his command. Gen. Andrew Jackson, who commanded the American army in the Southwest, reached New Orleans on Dec. 1, 1814, and immediately began preparations for defense.

Instead of coming up the Mississippi River as was expected, the superior British navy defeated the small American fleet on Lake Borgne, southwest of the river's mouth; landed troops on its border; and marched them across the swamps to the banks of the Mississippi, a few miles below New Orleans. Jackson had succeeded in assembling a force of between 6,000 and 7,000 troops, mainly Kentucky, Tennessee, and Louisiana militia, with a few regulars. After a few preliminary skirmishes late in December 1814 (*see* Villere's Plantation, Battle at), the British withheld their attack until their full strength could be brought to bear. In the decisive battle, on the morning of Jan. 8, 1815, the British undertook to carry the American position by storm (*see* Chalmette Plantation). So effective was the American defense that the

British were completely repulsed in less than a half-hour, losing over 2,000 men, of whom 289 were killed, including Packenham and most of the other higher officers. Because of the protection of their breastworks, the Americans lost only 71, of whom 13 were killed.

The British soon retired to their ships and departed. New Orleans and the Mississippi Valley were saved from invasion. Coming two weeks after the treaty of peace (*see* Ghent, Treaty of), the battle had no effect upon the peace terms; but it did have a tremendous effect upon the political fortunes of Andrew Jackson, the "hero of New Orleans."

[Alcée Fortier, *History of Louisiana;* Charles Gayarré, *History of Louisiana.*]

WALTER PRICHARD

NEW ORLEANS, CAPTURE OF (1862). At the outbreak of the Civil War the Union authorities recognized the strategic importance of seizing New Orleans, the commercial emporium of the entire Mississippi Valley and the second port of the United States. Because of pressing needs elsewhere and overestimation of the strength of their defenses, the Confederates had failed to render the approaches to New Orleans impregnable. In the spring of 1862 a naval squadron under Union Adm. David G. Farragut, carrying an army commanded by Gen. Benjamin F. Butler, entered the lower Mississippi. The chief defenses against approach by river to New Orleans were forts Jackson and Saint Philip, about sixty miles below the city, between which had been stretched a heavy chain cable, supported on rafts, with a secondary defense beyond it, consisting of a group of fire rafts loaded with pine knots and some armored rams. After firing upon the forts for some days, Farragut succeeded in cutting the chain and passing the forts in the night, without any very serious damage to his fleet, and shortly thereafter he appeared before New Orleans. Gen. Mansfield Lovell had only 3,000 Confederate troops to protect the city, and, realizing that resistance was useless, withdrew northward, leaving the city to fall into the hands of Union forces on May 1, 1862.

[Alcée Fortier, *History of Louisiana;* John Smith Kendall, *History of New Orleans.*]

WALTER PRICHARD

NEW ORLEANS, MARTIAL LAW IN. Reports of the mysterious advance of Aaron Burr and his men down the Mississippi during the fall of 1806 caused Gov. William Claiborne much anxiety at New Orleans. Uneasiness was increased by rumors that Gen. James Wilkinson and a detachment of troops were on the way to defend the city. Arriving in New Orleans late in November 1806, Wilkinson, with Claiborne's hesitant support, imposed martial law, forbade the movement of shipping, repaired fortifications, and arrested those suspected of being agents or friends of Burr. Those held appealed to local courts for release, but Wilkinson refused to yield to civil authority and even sent several east as military prisoners (*see* Bollman Case). The panic-stricken city began to throw off this virtual reign of terror as news of Burr's arrest arrived. It was not until Wilkinson left for Richmond in May 1807, to testify at the Burr trial, that calm returned to the city.

[W. F. McCaleb, *The Aaron Burr Conspiracy.*]
ELIZABETH WARREN

NEW ORLEANS RIOTS of 1873–74 resulted from the rivalries of two Reconstruction political factions, headed, respectively, by Republican W. P. Kellogg, the *de facto* governor, and Democrat John McEnery, who claimed the office as governor *de jure*. The disorders began Mar. 5, 1873, when some of McEnery's partisans attacked two police stations occupied by the metropolitan police. They were repulsed with a loss of two killed and several wounded. On Mar. 6 the members of McEnery's legislature were arrested, and they were not released until they had spent some hours in a local jail. Clashes between citizens and Republican officials also occurred elsewhere in Louisiana and were checked by the intervention of U.S. troops. Protests against such a use of the army, made by the McEneryites to President Ulysses S. Grant, were disregarded, whereupon the White League was organized, during the spring of 1874. It was responsible for the uprising against Kellogg in New Orleans on Sept. 14, 1874. In the fighting the metropolitan police were defeated with a loss of eleven killed and sixty wounded; the league suffered a loss of sixteen killed and forty-five wounded. McEnery took over the state government the following day, but U.S. troops were hurried into the city, and on Sept. 17 Kellogg was restored without opposition. The uprising was devoid of immediate results, but it is regarded as paving the way for the overthrow of the Republican regime in Louisiana three years later (*see* Home Rule in the South, Restoration of).

[Ella Lonn, *Reconstruction in Louisiana;* Albert Phelps, *Louisiana.*]

JOHN S. KENDALL

NEW PLYMOUTH COLONY was founded by a group of about a hundred English emigrants who came to New England in the *Mayflower* in 1620. The dominant element in this group consisted of religious dissenters who had separated from the Anglican church because of their dissatisfaction with its doctrines and practices. Some of these Separatists had come from Leiden in the Netherlands, where they had been living for more than a decade since leaving their original homes in northern England to escape persecution and association with their Anglican neighbors. After a brief sojourn in Amsterdam, they had settled in Leiden, where they had organized a flourishing church. Although they enjoyed religious freedom, they became dissatisfied in their new home. They were unwilling to give up the language and customs of England for those of Holland, had difficulty in making a comfortable living in a foreign land, and were disturbed about the enticements to worldliness and immorality to which their children were subjected. Accordingly, some of them (thirty-five in number) decided to join others of their religious persuasion in England and go to the New World. Both groups sailed on the *Mayflower* from Plymouth, England, Sept. 16, 1620. On Dec. 26, after five weeks spent in exploring Cape Cod, the *Mayflower* anchored in the harbor of what came to be Plymouth, Mass. The task of erecting suitable houses was rendered difficult by the lateness of the season, although the winter was a comparatively mild one. Nearly all the Indians in the vicinity had been destroyed by pestilence, and the few survivors gave no trouble. On the contrary, their deserted cornfields afforded the settlers quite an advantage. Partly because of poor housing, but more because of the run-down condition of the emigrants as a result of a lack of proper food on the voyage, there was great suffering the first winter and nearly half of them died. By spring there had come a turn for the better, and in a few years the menace of a food shortage was permanently removed.

The capital for the undertaking was furnished by a group of London merchants. An agreement was entered into between them and the settlers whereby a sort of joint-stock company was formed. The arrangement proved unsatisfactory to both the planters and their backers, and in 1627 the merchants sold their interests to the settlers and thus withdrew from the venture. From that time on the planters were the sole stockholders of the corporation, which had become a colony.

During the first decade of its existence Plymouth

was the only settlement in the area, but gradually other villages were established; so the town of Plymouth widened into the colony of New Plymouth.

Before embarking for America the Pilgrims had received assurances from James I that they would not be molested in the practice of their religion. A patent was also received from the Virginia Company authorizing them to settle on its grant and enjoy the right of self-government. But because they had landed outside the limits of the Virginia Company this patent was of no avail. The settlers, therefore, had no title to their lands and no legal authority to establish a government. It was not long, however, before a valid title to the land was obtained in the form of patents issued in 1621 and 1630 by the Council for New England—but the power to form a government was not conferred by these patents. Nevertheless a liberal government was founded for the colony, for the Pilgrims had, before landing, organized themselves into a body politic by entering into a solemn covenant that they would make just and equal laws and would yield obedience to the same. This agreement, known as the Mayflower Compact, had been signed by all the adult male settlers except eight, who were probably ill at the time. Laws were made by the General Court, at first a primary assembly and later a representative assembly of one house, the members of which were chosen annually by popular election. Administrative and certain important judicial functions were performed by the governor and the assistants, who were elected each year by the freemen, or qualified voters. On the death of the first governor, John Carver, in April 1621, William Bradford was chosen his successor. He was continued in office by reelection for more than thirty years.

New Plymouth was not well adapted to agriculture, since there was a scarcity of cultivable land in the colony. Nor was the location of the settlement so favorable for a profitable business in fishing and fur trading as were the locations of the other Puritan colonies. Consequently, the Pilgrims did not play a leading role in the history of colonial New England, although it was largely because of their initiative that the Congregational form of church government was adopted in that section. New Plymouth was quite overshadowed by its neighbors, Connecticut and Massachusetts Bay, and was absorbed by the latter in 1691.

[W. T. Davis, ed., *Bradford's History of Plymouth Plantation;* R. G. Usher, *The Pilgrims and Their History.*]

O. P. CHITWOOD

NEWPORT, a city in southeastern Rhode Island on Aquidneck Island, was founded in May 1639 by William Coddington, formerly an official in Massachusetts Bay, and John Clarke, a Baptist minister, who had previously been at Portsmouth, on the northern end of the island. In Newport was established the second Baptist church in America. From the beginning the city subscribed to the same principle of religious freedom that animated the Roger Williams settlement at Providence. Consequently it became a haven for the persecuted; the first Quakers arrived in 1657, and the first Jews in 1658, establishing there in 1763 Touro Synagogue, the oldest synagogue in the United States and now a national historic site.

Newport was an important colonial seaport: shipbuilding began about 1646; Long Wharf was a busy mart by 1685; and by the mid-18th century the city was at the height of its commercial glory. Rhode Island's first permanent newspaper, the *Newport Mercury,* was established in 1758 by James Franklin, Jr. During the Revolution the city was held by the British from 1776 to 1779, after which it became the headquarters for America's French allies under Jean Baptiste Donatien de Vimeur, Comte de Rochambeau (*see* Newport, French Army at). Newport lost many influential residents through the war, as rich Loyalists, notably the Wantons and the Brentons, fled the country, while many patriot families moved to the interior of the state.

The flight of the rich merchants led to Newport's economic decline after the Revolution, but about a century later it revived as a summer resort and social center. In 1885 the Naval War College was established at Coaster's Harbor Island near Newport, and it subsequently became an important naval base; the base was closed in 1974. During the 1950's and 1960's Newport was host to the annual Newport Jazz Festival and Newport Folk Festival. Yacht races, including the America's Cup Race, are held off Newport. Newport's population in 1970 was 34,562.

[R. M. Bayles, *History of Newport County, Rhode Island;* M. M. Shea, *The Story of Colonial Newport.*]

JARVIS M. MORSE

NEWPORT, FRENCH ARMY AT. The French fleet of forty-four vessels under Adm. Charles Louis d'Arsac, Chevalier de Ternay, bringing a force of 6,000 French soldiers under the command of Jean Baptiste Donatien de Vimeur, Comte de Rochambeau, arrived off Newport, R.I., on July 10, 1780, in support of the American Revolution. The landing of the troops began the next day, and Newport was illuminated in honor of the occasion. The presence of the French officers added to the gaiety of the social life. A printing press issued a newspaper in French. Some 600–800 cavalrymen were sent to Connecticut for the winter, and a part of the infantry was sent to Providence, R.I. On June 10, 1781, the French army left Newport by boat for Providence and thence marched to Yorktown, where it participated in the siege that resulted in the surrender of Gen. Charles Cornwallis and the end of the war.

[Edwin M. Stone, *Our French Allies.*]
HOWARD M. CHAPIN

NEWPORT BARRACKS, on the Kentucky side of the Licking River, opposite Cincinnati, was established about 1805 as an arsenal and was later used also as a recruit depot. Troops returned there at the end of the Mexican War; during the Civil War a small garrison was retained, after which Newport Barracks again became a recruit depot. It was menaced during the Civil War in the course of Confederate Gen. Braxton Bragg's invasion of Kentucky in 1862. Later the post was moved several miles inland and renamed Fort Thomas.

THOMAS ROBSON HAY

NEW SMYRNA COLONY. During 1767 and 1768 Andrew Turnbull, a Scottish physician who had traveled widely in the Mediterranean, brought some 1,400 persons from Greece, Italy, and Minorca to Florida, to cultivate sugarcane, rice, indigo, cotton, and other crops. The settlement was located within the grant of 60,000 acres of land adjacent to Mosquito Inlet that in 1767 had been made to Turnbull, Sir William Duncan, and Sir Richard Temple (the latter acting as trustee for Sir George Grenville). Colonists were to work for from seven to eight years and at the end of the period to receive tracts of fifty or more acres of land, according to the size of the family. The settlement, named New Smyrna, lasted until 1776, when the colonists marched in a body to Saint Augustine to ask for relief from their indentures, claiming cruel treatment. Only 600 by that time remained, and they settled in Saint Augustine after they had been released by the governor.

[Carita Doggett, *Dr. Andrew Turnbull and the New Smyrna Colony;* George R. Fairbanks, *Florida: Its History and Its Romance.*]
W. T. CASH

NEW SOUTH, a phrase originally used to designate the post-Reconstruction economic development of the South, particularly the expansion of industry, which has come to be applied to the post–Civil War South generally, with particular reference to the fundamental changes that have occurred. In the years immediately following Reconstruction, many southerners came to look upon the agrarian economy of the antebellum South as no longer viable and to believe that their region's future lay in the development of industry. F. W. Dawson, editor of the *Charleston* (S.C.) *News and Courier,* was an early prophet of this New South concept. He preached the South's need for more industry, arguing that the great significance of the Civil War was the white man's emancipation from slavery and cotton. Also influential and well known among those who advocated the growth of industry in the South was Henry W. Grady, longtime editor of the *Atlanta Constitution*. Grady orated to northern audiences as well as southern ones in his pursuit of an industrial economy for his native region, and his editorials in the late 19th century espoused this theme with vigor. Grady popularized the phrase "New South" in a famous address in New York in December 1886.

Southern politicians (*see* Bourbons) joined the South's opinion makers and economic leaders to turn the southern economy upside down; all these groups actively pursued the moneyed interests of the North and Europe. Northerners poured investments into the South at an amazing rate, especially after 1879, at the end of an economic depression, when both northern and foreign capital were seeking investment opportunities. Northern money meant northern control, and the South soon became an economic appendage of the North. This colonial status of the southern economy was well established in several industries before the end of the 19th century, and it continued to exist and to expand in the years following. Activities in regard to the public domain in the South illustrated the exploitative aspects of northern economic policy. Northern speculators acquired millions of acres of virgin timberlands from the national and southern state governments, making hundreds of millions of dollars as they denuded the land. Southern railroad development proved to be even more attractive to northern and foreign capital than southern real estate. Southern railroad mileage increased from 16,605 miles in 1880 to 39,108 in 1890, a 135.5 percent increase, in comparison with an 86.5 percent increase for the nation as a whole. In the 1880's more than 180 new railroad companies instituted activities in the region. Consolidations then took place, putting more economic power in the hands of northern bankers and financiers. The southern iron and steel industries followed the railroading pattern as the South felt the impact of great quantities of northern and English capital. Alabama's iron production in 1889 amounted to ten times the state's output a decade earlier. In the final quarter of the 19th century the South's pig iron production increased seventeenfold, more than twice the national rate. Great iron deposits, their proximity to coal and limestone, the rapidly developing transportation system, and northern investment capital all combined to increase the South's iron and steel output. Northern companies continued to control these industries in the 20th century.

The most important southern industry before the Civil War had been cotton textile manufacturing, and this industry expanded rapidly in the postwar years. Between 1860 and 1880 several southern states more than doubled their prewar production. In the following decades growth and production were so great that many people inaccurately assumed that 1880 marked the beginning of the industry in the South. In a dizzying period of expansion, the number of mills in the South rose from 161 in 1880 to 400 in 1900. The rate of growth in the 1890's was 67.4 percent, compared with the national increase of 7.5 percent. Capital investment in southern cotton mills increased by 131.4 percent between 1880 and 1900, while investments in New England mills increased by only 12.1 percent. World War I caused boom years for southern textile production and throughout the 1920's mill promoters continued their crusade for regional economic salvation through the textile industry. In the 20th century many New England mills with southern branches moved their major operations to the South, causing much social and economic distress for some areas of the Northeast.

The South led in tobacco manufacturing before the Civil War, and it resumed the lead early in the postwar period. The enlarged tobacco industry resulted mainly from mechanization and the increased demand for cigarettes. By the middle of the 20th century Americans were consuming more and more tobacco products per capita, despite cancer scares, and southern tobacco companies continued to expand and increase their output.

In addition to lumbering, railroading, and tobacco and textile manufacturing, the 20th-century South produced large quantities of furniture, paper, and aluminum. Also related to the South's natural resources, oil and its by-products, gas, and sulfur came to transform the western edge of the South. Petrochemicals became big business. World War II further stimulated southern industrial and economic development. Industries related to warfare, atomic energy, and the space age changed the southern landscape and gave southerners increased income and purchasing power. Billions of dollars worth of government contracts were awarded to companies in the southern states during the war years, and many army posts and camps were established or enlarged. Military research and the advent of space exploration altered Oak Ridge, Tenn.; Paducah, Ky.; Houston, Tex.; and Cape Canaveral, Fla. Thousands of related or lesser industries added to the South's drive toward industrialization.

Although the term "New South" was first used (and continues to be used) to describe the industrialized South, it is also commonly applied generally to the South since 1865, just as the term "Old South" describes the antebellum South. Used in this way, the phrase "New South" refers to a South that is changing not only economically but also politically, demographically, agriculturally, educationally, socially, racially, and intellectually. The so-called Solid South is disappearing slowly as the Republican party grows in the region. The face of the South is changing as rural dwellers move to the towns, as towns become cities, and as metropolitan sprawl characterizes such cities as Atlanta; Birmingham, Ala.; New Orleans; and Houston. Both blacks and whites have moved to the population centers seeking economic advancement and have added to urban problems. Even though the South remains an agricultural region, farming methods have changed; mechanization has taken the drudgery out of farm work; and hard-surfaced, farm-to-market roads have permitted farmers to live in towns and cities. The South's state educational systems have been upgraded as the states have increased expenditures for the education of their youth. As biracial school systems have declined, southern states have spent their money more wisely. The relationship of the races has been altered as blacks have pressed for and obtained better economic conditions, equal access to public accommodations, and more nearly equal education. While some white backlash has been apparent, white southerners on the whole have tolerated (if not entirely accepted) the new position of the Afro-American. In the 1970's the continued presence of the Ku Klux Klan, white citizens' councils, "segregation academies," and opposition to busing to achieve equal educational opportunities for all races were reminders that the New South was not yet all new, but the forces of change were overcoming these obstacles.

[Monroe Billington, *The American South: A Brief History;* Thomas D. Clark, *The Emerging South;* Paul Gaston, *The New South Creed: A Study in Southern Mythmaking;* George Brown Tindall, *The Emergence of the New South, 1913–1945;* C. Vann Woodward, *Origins of the New South, 1877–1913.*]

MONROE BILLINGTON

NEWSPAPERS. From the first New World printers with their toilsome, awkward handpresses to the specialized managers of the multifaceted journalistic enterprises nearly three centuries later; from the rabidly partisan sheets of the early 1800's by way of the literary grace of William Cullen Bryant's *New York Evening Post* (1829–78) and the Illinois martyrdom of Elijah Parish Lovejoy in defense of his weekly *Observer*'s right to speak out for abolition; from the robust paragraphs signed Mark Twain but contributed by a young newshawk named Samuel Langhorne Clemens in Virginia City, Nev., in 1862, to cartoonist Bill Mauldin's dog-tired foot soldiers, Willie and Joe, in the *Stars and Stripes* of World War II; from the small-town Main Street, shirt-sleeve reporting of William Allen White in his *Emporia* (Kans.) *Gazette,* beginning in 1895, to the sensation-filled mass-circulation tabloids of the big cities and the encyclopedic *New York Times,* the *Wall Street Journal,* and the *Christian Science Monitor* with their national distributions in the 1970's—the history of American newspapers has been a record of infinite variety in editorial leadership and outlook, in effort and application. It is a record of countless dissimilarities that are part and parcel of an individualized people's pattern of continuous innovation and change, in the press as everywhere else.

Publick Occurrences. The earliest colonial newspaper was *Publick Occurrences Both Forreign and Domestick,* which made its first and only appearance in Boston, Mass., on Sept. 25, 1690. It was immediately suppressed. Publisher Benjamin Harris, exiled London bookseller and printer of the *New England Primer,* and his printer, Richard Pierce, offended the colonial authorities by not obtaining official permission to publish. Moreover, portions of the contents were found objectionable, including "the passage referring to the French King and to the Maquas [Mohawk Indians]" that caused the governor and the council "much distaste." Arranged in double columns on three handbill-sized pages, it reported, in a news style anticipating those of modern newspapers, the Thanksgiving plans of "Plimouth" Indians, a suicide, the disappearance of two children, a decline in smallpox, a fire, and other events. Harris planned to issue it "once a month (or if any Glut of Occurrences happen, oftener). . . ." But after the authorities declared their "high resentment and Disallowance," there was no similar publication, so far as is known, for fourteen years. The only copy preserved was found in 1845 in the London Public Record Office.

Boston News-Letter. The next recorded attempt to establish a publication in the colonies was made by the *Boston News-Letter.* Successful in that it was not interrupted by the authorities, it or its successors continued to appear down to the Revolution. Issue No. 1 covered the week of Apr. 17, 1704. Boston Postmaster John Campbell was the original publisher and Bartholomew Green was the printer. They introduced their first illustration in the issue of Jan. 19, 1708. When Green became the owner and publisher in 1723, he renamed it the *Weekly News-Letter* and so it remained until 1763, when the name was changed to the *Boston Weekly News-Letter and New England Chronicle.* That was still the name when the British troops withdrew from Boston in 1776, whereupon publication ended. Campbell and those who followed him joined newspaper publication with job printing, the issuance of pamphlets and books, and the general retailing of printed matter and stationery.

Pennsylvania Gazette. The colonial *Pennsylvania Gazette,* made famous by Benjamin Franklin, was founded at Philadelphia on Dec. 24, 1728, by Samuel Keimer. Its original name was the *Universal Instructor in All Arts and Sciences: and Pennsylvania Gazette.* Although only the second newspaper in the Middle Colonies, it did not prosper, and on Oct. 2, 1729, it was purchased by Franklin, who had helped publish the *New England Courant* (1721) in Boston, and Hugh Meredith, who shortened the name to the *Pennsylvania Gazette.* After Meredith's retirement in 1732, Franklin used his ownership to turn it into the "most successful colonial newspaper." Franklin's innovations included the first weather report, an editorial column, the first cartoon, and humor. Essays and poetry had their place, but Franklin did not introduce them. David Hall joined in a partnership in 1748 that lasted until Franklin's retirement in 1766. The newspaper was published in York, Pa., for six months, beginning in December 1777, because of the British occupation of Philadelphia. The last issue was dated Oct. 11, 1815.

Zenger Case. The outstanding colonial case involving freedom of the press centered around John Peter Zenger and his *New-York Weekly Journal,* the first newspaper to be the organ of a political faction. In the early 1730's, New York became the focus of opposition to colonial policies on the part of merchants, lawyers, and other influential groups. Backed by this protest movement, Zenger, former printer for William Bradford's *New York Gazette,* first issued his paper on Nov. 5, 1733. Many articles were contributed, but Zenger, as publisher, was held responsible for them, and he produced his share of the criticism of colonial rule. Late in 1734 the Common Council ordered four numbers of the *Weekly Journal* to be burned. Zenger was arraigned and jailed for about ten months. In 1735 he was tried for seditious libel. Andrew Hamilton, who defended him, won acquittal with the plea that the jury had a right to inquire into the truth or falsity of the printed words. The paper, which appeared regularly because of the persistence of Zenger's wife, printed his report of the court proceedings and then issued separately in 1736 *A Brief Narrative of the Case and Tryal of John Peter Zenger*. The latter publication went through a series of printings and was widely circulated in the colonies and in England. Zenger was rewarded by being made New York public printer in 1737. The case set a precedent against judicial tyranny in libel suits.

Later Colonial Period. Following the success of the *Boston News-Letter,* by 1750 other colonial newspapers had been set up in Boston; New York; Philadelphia; Charleston, S.C.; Annapolis, Md.; Williamsburg, Va.; and Newport, R.I. By 1775, on the eve of the Revolution, there were thirty-seven papers in the seaboard colonies; the number would have increased rapidly but for the stringencies of the war for independence. The usual plan of the four-page weekly gazette was to devote the first page to foreign intelligence, the second page to domestic news, the third local matters, and the back page to advertisements. Since there was no other form of communication except by word of mouth, this was the means by which the colonists learned about deliberations in the councils, the actions of their governors, and other official matters. As a consequence the newssheets began to join the colonial peoples in common interests and eventual resistance to the crown. Other than the Bible and the almanac, the local gazette undoubtedly was the only printed material that entered most colonial homes.

Massachusetts Spy. Outstanding among patriotic gazettes in the years leading to the Revolution, the *Massachusetts Spy* won Isaiah Thomas a place of honor in preindependence journalism. Thomas, a Boston printer and publisher, became the partner of Zechariah Fowle in 1770 and in the same year founded the *Spy* in Boston to advance colonial interests. His devotion to the rank and file was widely known and appreciated, except by the royal governors. When the British troops took over Boston in 1773, Thomas moved his printing press to Worcester. En route he joined Paul Revere in the historic warning of Apr. 18, 1775, and he himself was a minuteman in the engagements at Lexington and Concord. The May 3, 1775, issue reported the news of those early clashes at arms. In Worcester he was also the official printer for the patriots. The *Spy* became the *Worcester Gazette* in 1781. Thomas' long association with the *Spy* and early journalism led him into such related fields as printing almanacs, music, and magazines; writing a history of printing; and, in 1812, founding the American Antiquarian Society, of which he was the first president.

Editors as Political Leaders. With the development of political factions, the early editors became in effect spokesmen for opposing groups. After the Revolution and in the first years of the new nation one journal after another enlisted in and led the public debate over political issues. Thus, the Federalist mouthpiece, the *Gazette of the United States,* later known (1804–18) as the *United States Gazette,* edited by John Fenno, espoused the principles of George Washington and John Adams so vigorously that Secretary of State Thomas Jefferson subsidized a competing *National Gazette,* begun Oct. 31, 1791, at Philadelphia, by appointing its editor, Philip Freneau, translator in the State Department. Freneau's criticisms of Alexander Hamilton brought on complaints from Washington, who held Jefferson responsible. The *National Gazette* ceased publication in 1793, soon after Jefferson's resignation from the secretaryship. In the meantime William Coleman and the *New York Evening Post* became linked to Hamilton, as Noah Webster and the *American Minerva* became associated with John Jay and Rufus King. Frequently political editors wrote so vitriolically and at such length that their articles were reprinted and circulated as partisan pamphlets.

Sedition Act Victims. Concern late in the 18th century over possible war with France brought on a suspicion of aliens, with the result that the Federalists put through Congress the Alien and Sedition Acts of 1798. Almost immediately the enforcement of these laws was directed against supporters of Jefferson, among them Democratic-Republican newspaper editors. Ten journalists were found guilty and fined and in several instances jailed for alleged seditious utterances. One of the first to feel the whip was William Duane, a New Yorker who, after serving as a printer in Ireland, Calcutta, and London, settled in Philadelphia, where he made the *Aurora* the foremost newspaper backing Jefferson. He opposed the restrictions of the Alien and Sedition Acts and in 1799 was arrested. Soon acquitted, he continued his criticism and again was arrested. Following Jefferson's election in 1800 the charges were dropped and Duane worked for repeal of the offensive statutes. Anthony Haswell, editor of the *Vermont Gazette or Freeman's Depository,* issued at Bennington, was among those jailed. Haswell, who was born in England, was both a soldier and editor during the Revolution, having edited the *Massachusetts Spy* in 1777. His Bennington gazette, the only publication in Vermont at the time, led to his indictment and trial for sedition in 1800. Haswell's imprisonment for two months amounted to political persecution. The $200 fine that he was required to pay was returned to his heir by act of Congress in 1844. There were to be other periods with civil liberties under restraint but no time when freedom of the press was so restricted.

Expansion Westward. Independence was followed by a veritable explosion of new journals. In the seven decades of colonial rule some 100 gazettes had been started, and during the conflict perhaps as many as 50 more were undertaken. Between the peace treaty in 1783 and the year 1800, at least 500 were begun in the original thirteen states. A careful historian of the early press, Douglas C. McMurtrie, concluded that inasmuch as about 200 more newspapers were launched in the new states from 1800 to 1820, some 1,200 newspapers were begun in less than forty years of independence as against about 150 in the eighty years prior to separation from the English crown. Venturesome printers soon moved west from the seaboard. The first newspaper beyond the Appalachians was the *Pittsburgh Gazette,* issued July 29, 1786, by Joseph Hall and John Scull. After seeing the promising site of Pittsburgh, Hugh Henry Brackenridge, a lawyer and veteran of the Revolution, urged the two young Philadelphia printers to move there and help develop the area. Even more daring was Kentuckian John Bradford, a surveyor, who transported a press through the wilderness and on Aug. 11, 1787, while the Constitutional Convention was deliberating in Philadelphia, founded the *Kentucke Gazette* in Lexington.

Along the Great Rivers. New territories meant new governments, with laws and proclamations, and for these as well as for frontier journals printing presses were a necessity. By Nov. 5, 1791, Robert Ferguson and George Roulstone had left North Carolina to begin publication of the *Knoxville Gazette* in Tennessee. William Maxwell set up the *Centinel of the North-Western Territory* in Cincinnati, Nov. 9, 1793; and Elihu Stout moved from Kentucky to Vincennes, where he was both public printer for Indiana Territory and publisher of the *Indiana Gazette,* beginning July 31, 1804. Meriwether Lewis and William Clark were hardly back from their expedition to the Pacific Northwest when Joseph Charless started the *Missouri Gazette,* July 12, 1808, in Saint Louis. Still another pioneer printer was Matthew Duncan, one-time Kentuckian who began the *Illinois Herald* in May 1814, at Kaskaskia, the first Illinois capital. Other newspapers in the new West included the *Mississippi Gazette* of Benjamin M. Stokes at Natchez, in 1799 or 1800; the *Mobile Centinel* of Samuel Miller and John B. Hood, May 23, 1811; and the *Detroit Gazette* of New Yorkers John P. Sheldon and Ebenezer Reed, July 25, 1817. By 1821 some 250 papers had come into being in the new West. Many were short-lived; most were struggles against odds, but as a whole they helped open up and tame the wilderness.

Assassination of Lovejoy. What doubtless was the most tragic occurrence in American journalism has been relatively little cited—the murder of Elijah Parish Lovejoy in Alton, Ill., in the struggle over slavery. Lovejoy, a native of Maine and a graduate of Waterville (now Colby) College, edited a Whig newspaper in Saint Louis in the late 1820's. After being licensed to preach, he published the Presbyterian weekly for the West, the *Saint Louis Observer.* Soon he was deep in the abolition movement, and rather than moderate his views to suit the Missouri critics, Lovejoy moved across and up the Mississippi River to Alton. There two of his presses were pushed into the river by his opponents. When he sought to protect a third press from attack by a mob, he was shot and killed on the night of Nov. 7, 1837. The fearless editor was not yet thirty-five years old. Lovejoy was the first editor to give his life in defense of freedom of the press in the United States, and his martyrdom fired the abolitionists all the way to New England. After blood had stained his press, there was no turning back in the antislavery crusade.

Coming of the Daily. The first gazettes did well to fare forth once a week, but in the larger communities semiweeklies and triweeklies made their appearance before independence was won. Philadelphia was the scene of Benjamin Towne's *Pennsylvania Evening Post and Daily Advertiser* in May 1783. The next year John Dunlap and David C. Claypoole brought out the *Pennsylvania Packet and Daily Advertiser,* while the *South-Carolina Gazette* was launched in Charleston. Then in 1785 two dailies were begun in New York City. Francis Childs' *New York Daily Advertiser* was the first daily that had not been published previously on a less frequent basis. By 1790 the total number of dailies had reached eight. The Sunday newspaper came slowly. The *Weekly Museum* with a Sunday date was started in Baltimore in 1797, but it lasted for only a few weeks. The Sunday *Observer* appeared in New York in 1809 and survived for some two years. The prevailing strictures against work on the Sabbath prevented early acceptance of newspapers for Sunday circulation and reading.

Penny Press. Newspapers left their gazette era behind with the coming of the "penny press." The first one-cent-a-copy venture to succeed was Benjamin H. Day's *New York Sun,* begun in 1833, and its success was immediate. Within two years it boasted the largest daily circulation in the world. At the time the older, well-established, generally dignified dailies sold for six cents, and they were quick to denounce the cut-price upstart as catering to the lower public tastes. Without question the penny press was directed at the common people, but also without question the interests of the common people had gone largely unrecognized in news reporting. Unfortunately, the *Sun* promoted sensationalism to the point of outright faking. James Gordon Bennett's *New York Morning Herald,* launched in 1835, began competing for news scoops and stressed writing that caught the reader's eye. Bennett also developed financial coverage and used steamships for transmitting foreign news on a regular basis. But Horace Greeley's *New York Weekly Tribune,* denouncing the "degrading police reports" of the penny papers, in 1841 undertook to raise standards by reporting new ideas by distinguished writers. The one-cent papers capitalized on street sales, giving rise to the newsboy who ran about the city with a bundle of newssheets, calling out the top headlines. The press was closer to ordinary people than ever before. And "yellow journalism" was on its way.

Civil War Coverage. By 1860 roving editors and correspondents had made Washington, D.C., a regular "beat," had written up the excitements of the West and the local color of the South, and had described European scenes and peoples in leisurely newsletters. Experimental war reporting, undertaken

in the Mexican War, became a major news activity in the Civil War. Sharing the soldiers' hardships and eluding censors, a network of news gatherers relayed eyewitness dispatches from the battlefronts. Outstanding among the war correspondents was Dublin-born Joseph B. McCullagh, who won a national reputation for his reports in the *Cincinnati Commercial* that stood the tests of reliability and fairness. When McCullagh's first Cincinnati newspaper, the *Gazette,* refused to print his account of the early fighting at Shiloh, which discredited the Union performance, "Little Mack" forthwith quit the *Gazette* and joined the *Commercial.* Meantime cameraman Mathew B. Brady compiled his monumental photographic record of the war and its participants. As interest in the conflict mounted, circulations rose rapidly and "extras" became commonplace. News columns held ascendancy over editorial commentary, with the readers seeking eagerly to learn the latest military developments and the conduct of the government in Washington, D.C. The southern press supported the Confederacy, and although northern editors generally upheld the Union cause, not a few were opposed to President Abraham Lincoln and some were openly Copperhead.

Yellow Journalism. After the Civil War the *New York Sun,* bought by Charles A. Dana in 1868, exalted artistic writing, while Henry Villard's *New York Evening Post* (1881), especially after Edwin L. Godkin became editor in chief in 1883, combined literary grace with Tammany exposures, and Joseph Pulitzer's *New York World* (1883) carried on its crusades for the working classes. But the sensationalism introduced to the press by Bennett's *Herald* in the 1830's was revived and extended by the new reliance on advertising. For by 1880 advertising met a major part of the costs of publishing a daily—and advertising rates were based on circulation. A consequence was hard-fought competition for both subscribers and street sales. To capture weekend readers, Pulitzer promoted the *New York Sunday World,* with special articles and features including a comic section, first produced in November 1894. Prominent among the comic strips was Richard F. Outcault's "Yellow Kid," a harum-scarum boy in long yellow garb. In less than a year, William Randolph Hearst, publisher of the *San Francisco Examiner,* entered the New York scene by purchasing the *Morning Journal* and going into headlong conflict with the *World* for circulation. The Cuban problem, the sinking of the *Maine,* and the Spanish-American War were exploited with banner headlines and irresponsible claims and charges. Coupled with detailed accounts of scandals and sob-sister stories, the total result became known as yellow journalism. Not all editors succumbed, but the malaise characterized an era.

Comic Strips and Funny Papers. A natural extension of the hearty humor of the 1870's and 1880's, the funny paper, as it was first called, abetted an expanding newspaperdom, bent on circulation and experimenting with color printing. James Swinnerton drew comic bear pictures for the *San Francisco Examiner* in 1892, and the *New York Daily News* printed an isolated comic strip as early as 1884. But the forerunner of the comic pages was Outcault's "Origin of a New Species," Sunday, Nov. 18, 1894, in the *New York World*. The bad-boy character featured in the comics, known as the Yellow Kid, proved exceedingly popular, and Hearst, then a newcomer to New York, bid him away from Pulitzer's *World* to the *New York Journal* in 1896. For a time both papers had Yellow Kids, and from the excessive competition with its shameless exploitations came the term "yellow journalism." Rudolph Dirks' Katzenjammer Kids, who first appeared in the *Journal* in 1897, set a pattern, also shaped by H. C. ("Bud") Fisher's six-days-a-week "A. Mutt," in the *San Francisco Chronicle* beginning in 1907.

Early comic characters such as Happy Hooligan, Buster Brown, Foxy Grandpa, Little Jimmy, Hans and Fritz, and Nemo, if not elevating, were relatively harmless. Yet critics denounced the funny paper's influence, and in 1937 the International Kindergarten Union asked parents to protect their children from it. The power of the comics over circulation was demonstrated when they set styles, gave turns to speech, and affected advertising. Arthur Brisbane rated the comics as second only to news in the newspapers, while surveys showed how attached readers were to their favorites. So important were the strips that two Washington, D.C., newspapers took to the Supreme Court their dispute over the right to print "Andy Gump." Syndicates grew up around the leading comics and bought them away from one another as fortune-making businesses developed from "Jiggs and Maggie," "Mutt and Jeff," "Toonerville Folks," and their contemporaries. As many as 2,500 newspapers used some 250 strips and single panels from some seventy-five agencies. At its peak *Hearst's Comic Weekly: Puck,* distributed by seventeen newspapers, with a total circulation of 5.5 million, ran fifty comics in its thirty-two pages. One syndicate claimed a circulation of more than 50 million. Comic section advertising skyrocketed from $360,000 in 1931 to more than $16.5 million in half a dozen years, cost per page reaching some $20,000.

After World War II the strips generally changed from comics to serial picture stories presenting everything from domestic affairs, ethnic life, military routine, the medical profession, and the conservation of natural resources to high adventure, international intrigue, crime and its detection, and the space age. A few educators found the new strips more degrading than ever, but experts in child care and development served as advisers for some, and the award-winning television program "Sesame Street" received high marks for beneficial influence. Syndicates employed translators to prepare the picture serials for demand all over the world. The leading characters became real in that they were a part of their readers' daily lives. When Orphan Annie's dog, Sandy, was lost, Henry Ford telegraphed her creator to do all he could to find it. Whether or not juveniles were harmfully affected by the worst of the strips, they continued to be popular, as Popeye supplanted Paul Bunyan, Clare Briggs' "Days of Real Sport" provided a genuine contribution to humor, and Gaar Williams recorded a nostalgic and precious past in "Among the Folks in History." By the mid-1970's some strips or panels were narrowly focused intellectual exercises, but Charles Schulz, with his "Peanuts" small-fry troupe (Charlie Brown, Linus, Lucy, Schroeder, Violet, Snoopy, Woodstock, and associates), produced a company so widely captivating that they turned up literally everywhere—on television, on the stage, in magazines, on stationery, on greeting cards, on clothing, and as art objects. These characters popularized the phrase "Happiness is . . . ," as their comic page neighbors helped shape the speech of the times. A "dagwood" was a tremendous, all-inclusive sandwich named after its creator, Dagwood Bumstead, the husband in "Blondie." "Grin and Bear It" often had the most incisive editorial comment of the day, much as Frank McKinney ("Kin") Hubbard's Hoosier philosopher, Abe Martin, had a generation earlier. Nor did the comic strips stop short of politics. Sen. Joseph R. McCarthy was readily recognizable in Walt Kelly's "Pogo," and "Doonesbury" used the White House as a backdrop and referred by name to the Watergate figures, including President Richard M. Nixon, and even went to Vietnam. Although appearing in comic strip format, Gary Trudeau's "Doonesbury" received a Pulitzer Prize for distinguished editorial cartooning in 1975.

Political Cartooning. The predecessor of 19th-century political cartoons appeared in early colonial times. Franklin's *Pennsylvania Gazette* in 1754 carried a drawing of a snake in eight disconnected pieces, each labeled for a colony. The caption, "Join, or Die," became a rallying cry for united action. Another influential colonial drawing was that of a snake warning the British, "Don't Tread on Me." The first cartoonist of national note, Thomas Nast, a native of Germany, devised the elephant and donkey symbols for the Republican and Democratic parties, respectively. After starting at fifteen as staff artist for *Frank Leslie's Illustrated Newspaper,* Nast became famous on *Harper's Weekly,* where he drew for a quarter century (1862–86). Lincoln called him the Union's "best recruiting sergeant." An uncompromising foe of the Tweed Ring, Nast portrayed Tammany as a predatory tiger. Walter H. McDougall appears to have been New York's first daily political cartoonist. The *New York World's* Rollin Kirby identified the Prohibition Amendment with a sour-visaged, long-nosed antisaloon character wearing a tall hat and carrying an umbrella. Oscar E. Cesare, born in Sweden, drew powerfully for peace in the *New York Evening Post* in the World War I period and then sketched world notables for the *New York Times.*

Chicago presented widely admired cartoonists in John T. McCutcheon and Carey Orr of the *Tribune,* Vaughan Shoemaker of the *Daily News,* and Jacob Burck of the *Sun-Times.* The national syndication of Jay N. Darling, known as Ding, a pioneer conservationist, embraced both world wars, while the wide distribution of William Henry (Bill) Mauldin followed his creation of Willie and Joe, battle-weary infantrymen, for the *Stars and Stripes* during World War II. The blunt, uninhibited conceptions of Daniel R. Fitzpatrick covered most of a half century, beginning in 1913, in the *Saint Louis Post-Dispatch.* The *Washington Post's* fearless Herbert L. Block—"Herblock"—hit so tellingly day after day that presidents Dwight D. Eisenhower and Richard M. Nixon would not look at his cartoons. Patrick B. Oliphant of the *Denver Post,* also syndicated, was merciless on the Watergate scandals. Don Hesse of the *Saint Louis Globe-Democrat* was representative of the syndicated conservative while Walt Partymiller of the *York* (Pa.) *Gazette and Daily* stood out among small-city cartoonists. Two of the most talented political cartoonists in the 20th century, Robert Minor and Arthur Henry (Art) Young, were highly esteemed, even though most of their work appeared in the radical press.

Era of Outstanding Editors. Beginning with William Cullen Bryant (*Evening Post*) and Benjamin H. Day (*Sun*), rivals in New York, the 19th century developed a galaxy of editor-publishers who not only became community and regional leaders but also in notable instances national figures. Among these,

James Gordon Bennett (*Morning Herald*), Horace Greeley (*Tribune*), Henry J. Raymond (*Daily Times*), Charles A. Dana (*Sun*), Edwin L. Godkin (*Evening Post*), Joseph Pulitzer (*World*), William Randolph Hearst (*Evening Journal*), and Adolph S. Ochs (*Times*) were situated in New York. Others of distinction issued newspapers over the country. They included Samuel Bowles (*Springfield* [Mass.] *Republican*), Joseph Medill (*Chicago Daily Tribune*), Henry Watterson (*Louisville Courier-Journal*), William B. McCullagh (*Saint Louis Globe-Democrat*), William Rockhill Nelson (*Kansas City Evening Star*), Clark Howell (*Atlanta Constitution*), James King (*San Francisco Bulletin*), and Harrison Gray Otis (*Los Angeles Times*). All these stamped journalism with their personalities, while such an extremist as Frederick G. Bonfils of the *Denver Post* became widely known for his gaudy excesses. King was so unrestrained in his attack on the corrupt elements in San Francisco's political and business life (1855–56) that he was shot and killed on May 14, 1856, by an enemy—a tragedy that led to the revival of the San Francisco Vigilance Committee.

In the 20th century editors of reputation included the McCormicks and the family of Marshall Field in Chicago and the Binghams in Louisville; Oswald Garrison Villard (*New York Evening Post*), Frank I. Cobb (*New York World*), Gardner Cowles (*Des Moines Register and Tribune*), Victor F. Lawson (*Chicago Daily News*), Lucius W. Nieman (*Milwaukee Journal*), Ernest Greuning (*Portland* [Maine] *Evening News*), Clark McAdams and Oliver K. Bovard (*Saint Louis Post-Dispatch*), John S. Knight (*Miami Herald*), Eugene C. Pulliam (*Arizona Republic*), William T. Evjue (*Madison* [Wis.] *Capital Times*), John N. Heiskell (*Arkansas Gazette*), Palmer Hoyt (*Portland Oregonian* and *Denver Post*), Douglas Southall Freeman (*Richmond News Leader*), Josephus and Jonathan Worth Daniels (*Raleigh News and Observer*), Thomas M. Storke (*Santa Barbara* [Calif.] *News-Press*), Ralph McGill (*Atlanta Constitution*), Virginius Dabney (*Richmond Times-Dispatch*), and George B. Dealey (*Dallas Morning News*). Kansas afforded the nation a remarkable pair of small-city editors with broad outlook in William Allen White of the *Emporia Gazette* and Edgar Watson Howe of the *Atchison Daily Globe.*

The World Wars and Indochina. Although the Hearst-Pulitzer rivalry helped bring on the Spanish-American War, the war itself was so short that the press could do little more than sensationalize developments. Reporter Richard Harding Davis and illustrator Frederic Remington were journalists who rose to national notice. World War I saw the press under heavy censorship on the one hand and acting largely as a propaganda machine on the other. George Creel's wartime Committee on Public Information produced more than 6,000 anti-German patriotic news releases, widely and dutifully printed in the press. Censorship at first was voluntary, but acts of Congress against espionage in 1917 and sedition in 1918 put newspapers under severe restraint. Editors and publishers generally fell in with the wishes of Washington, while the force of law bore against German-language and radical papers. Wartime controls barred two pacifistic Socialist dailies, the *New York Call* and the *Milwaukee Leader,* from the mails. Among the correspondents who made it the most closely covered war to that time were Floyd Gibbons, Irvin S. Cobb, William H. (Will) Irwin, Frank H. Simonds, Wythe Williams, Paul Scott Mowrer, Edgar Ansel, Raymond Gram Swing, Karl H. von Wiegand, Sigrid Schultz, Westbrook Pegler, Frazier Hunt, Edward Price Bell, and Walter Duranty.

World War II censorship began with the bombing at Pearl Harbor, and Congress quickly passed the first War Powers Act with the legislative basis for the Office of Censorship, of which Byron Price, executive news editor of the Associated Press, became director. Although war zone dispatches had to be cleared with military censors, most of the censorship was voluntary, self-applied as set out in a "Code of Wartime Practices for the American Press," issued Jan. 15, 1942. Several pro-Nazi and Fascist papers were ordered closed. A vast net of war correspondents spread around the globe. In a category by himself was Ernest T. (Ernie) Pyle, Hoosier reporter, who described in simple, homely, yet graphic, terms the battlefront existence of GI Joe in Africa, Europe, and the Pacific, where Pyle himself was killed. His colleagues included Herbert L. Matthews, Quentin Reynolds, George Fielding Eliot, Hal Boyle, Joseph Barnes, Richard L. Stokes, Raymond Clapper, Webb Miller, A. T. Steele, Joseph Driscoll, Drew Middleton, Edward W. Beattie, Wallace R. Deuel, and C. L. Sulzberger.

Censorship plus outright misstatement continued in the cold war years, as evidenced by the slow issuance of full facts from officialdom concerning the U-2 spy plane episode in 1960, the Bay of Pigs fiasco in 1961, and the Cuban missile crisis in 1962. In the Korean and Indochinese conflicts adverse news was not only frowned on officially but occasionally forbidden. Since the war in Indochina was never formally declared, actual censorship was difficult to apply. Manipulation took its place. Correspondents learned that too often the facts were not as presented in military briefings, as, for example, shortly before the Tet offensive. Thus, the newswriters began to dig for the truth for their publications. One was David Halberstam, whose *New York Times* reports led President John F. Kennedy to recommend his removal. The Associated Press's Malcolm Browne, United Press International's Neil Sheehan, and *Time*'s Charles Mohr joined in informing American readers that U.S. forces were indeed in combat when the official line was to the contrary.

The conclusion was inescapable that many of the untruths were deliberate, intended to deceive and, in so doing, to protect diplomatic and military mistakes. Inescapable too was the fact that the press played along far too frequently. When the My Lai massacre was brought to light, Seymour Hersch, then a freelance reporter, found it almost impossible to get newspapers to take his disclosures seriously. Hanoi's broad-scale operation, which finally brought Saigon's collapse and the end of the war, took the press, along with the military intelligence network, by surprise. The seizure of the cargo ship *Mayaguez* in 1975 by Cambodians retaught the press that the full information can be slow to emerge from the government in an embarrassing situation.

Tabloids. The post–World War I tabloid-sized newspaper had a forerunner in the diminutive *New York Daily Graphic,* 1873–89, which specialized in sensational pictures. Three decades passed before Joseph M. Patterson brought out his *New York Illustrated Daily News.* Launched on June 26, 1919, it was patterned on Alfred C. W. Harmsworth, Lord Northcliffe's successful London tabloid, the *Daily Mail,* half regular size for the convenience of riders of crowded subways. A largely uncultivated audience was quickly reached by the *News.* In two years "this unholy blot against the Fourth Estate," as one critic called it, had the largest circulation in New York, and twenty years later its distribution was nearly 2 million daily and more than 3 million on Sunday. Enticed by this mass welcome of the *Daily News,* Hearst produced the *New York Daily Mirror* in 1924 and Bernarr Macfadden attempted to build a daily circulation on cheap entertainment in the *Evening Graphic* (1924–32). Cornelius Vanderbilt, Jr., undertook a chain of "clean" tabloids, only to see it collapse in 1926–27. Crime, sex, sports, and comics were the main fare of tabloids; but some, including the *Chicago Sun-Times,* became popular pleaders for policies favorable to masses of city and suburban dwellers. In the 1950's and 1960's the tabloid-shaped *York* (Pa.) *Gazette and Daily,* published by Josiah W. Gitt, was as uninhibited a voice as the free press knew. In the 1970's the *New York Daily News* still enjoyed the nation's record circulation. Meanwhile it, like many other tabloids, had improved itself to serve its readers better.

Columnists. As the strong editors declined in number and the editorial pages tended toward a more common denominator, a new form of journalistic expression emerged—the signed column. Previously there had been well-heeded individual voices; before making up their own minds on the day's issues countless mid-19th-century citizens awaited the weekly *New York Tribune* to learn Greeley's views. The byline columnist, with regular offerings of opinion, came decades later with the syndication of Arthur Brisbane and Heywood Broun. Brisbane, who appeared on page 1 of the Hearst press, dealt briefly but positively with almost everything under the sun. Broun, whose far more literary essays decorated the *New York World*'s "opposite editorial page," discussed such heated problems as the Sacco-Vanzetti case, even to the point of being let go by his employers, the second generation of Pulitzers.

Although not the most widely read, former *World* editor Walter Lippmann was perhaps most highly esteemed for his thoughtful views, particularly on foreign affairs. Ranging from strongly liberal to equally strongly conservative were a spectrum of opinion shapers, among them Raymond Clapper, Dorothy Thompson, Arthur Krock, Thomas L. Stokes, Marquis W. Childs, Roscoe Drummond, George E. Sokolsky, James J. Kilpatrick, William S. White, Max Lerner, Mike Royko, William F. Buckley, and Carl T. Rowan. By the 1970's the *New York Times* shared its editorial columnists, via its wire service, to the extent that James Reston, Tom Wicker, William Safire, Anthony Lewis, C. L. Sulzberger, and William V. Shannon regularly spoke out far more vigorously than the local editors in whose pages they appeared. Some specialized. Drew Pearson, Robert S. Allen, and Jack Anderson engaged in disclosure reporting, often in the muckrakers' style. Even the humorists Franklin P. Adams, Don Marquis, O. O. McIntyre, Will Rogers, Kin Hubbard, Russell Baker, and Art Buchwald entered the public arena, the latter most irreverently. Sylvia Porter won an appreciative readership for her columns on business, economic, and consumer concerns. Other specialists centered on the military, the family, religion, movies, nature, gardening, sports, recreation, and a variety of other interests.

Ethnic Press. Newspapers in languages other than English and devoted to diverse social groups appeared in colonial times. Franklin's *Philadelphische Zeitung,* started in 1732 for German immigrants to Pennsylvania, was short-lived, but Christopher Sower's German-language paper, *Zeitung,* launched in 1739, caught on in Germantown, Pa. As Germans settled in Cincinnati, Saint Louis, Milwaukee, and other river and lake communities, a press in their language followed them. A Santo Domingoan, taking refuge in Louisiana, opened a French-language press as early as 1794. In Saint Louis the *Westliche Post* of Carl Schurz and Emil Preetorius provided immigrant Joseph Pulitzer with his first newspaper job in 1868. In the late 1800's papers in Italian, Polish, Spanish, Yiddish, and other tongues were published in the larger cities, where differing immigrant populations kept their customs and traditions alive in part through papers in their native languages. It was much the same for the agricultural Scandinavians who spread across the upper Mississippi Valley and onto the Plains.

The foreign-language press encouraged the characteristics of the ethnic groups being served. Differences to the point of antagonisms continued for decades; thus, papers in languages other than English tended to accent nationalistic concerns and religious rivalries. Refugees, many of whom reflected the revolutionary spirit of the 1840's, frequently brought radical ideas about government. A foremost outlet was the Jewish *Voice,* begun in New York in 1872 and emulated in Yiddish in other centers of Jewish population. The German-language press, which held to a generally high level, reached its peak in numbers in the mid-1890's. But as a whole the foreign-language press expanded until about 1914, when there were more than 1,300 such publications. World War I put the German press at a heavy disadvantage as only a few, led by the *New York Staats-Zeitung,* had sought to be "an American newspaper published in German." In World War II the Japanese-language press was looked upon by many as a disloyal force. Assimilation of later generations, along with wars and economic tribulations, undercut foreign-language newspapers until in 1970 only some 230 had survived. The largest circulation, about 76,000, was that of the New York daily *El Diario,* a tabloid in Spanish primarily for emigrants from Puerto Rico.

The story of the black press in the United States is an almost unknown chapter in American journalism. Rev. Samuel Cornish and John B. Russwurm brought out *Freedom's Journal* in 1827 in New York as the first paper written for black people. They began it, so they declared, because "too long others have spoken for us." Frederick Douglass, a former slave, issued the *North Star* in 1847 and sounded a continuing rallying cry for abolition in the years leading to the Civil War. W. E. B. Du Bois established *The Crisis* in 1910 as the voice of the National Association for the Advancement of Colored People, the crisis being, in his words, the idea that "mentally the Negro is inferior to the white."

By the mid-1970's, some 3,000 black-owned and black-conducted papers had been started, but the average life-span was only nine years. Thus, survivors in 1972 numbered fewer than 100. The largest black papers and their founding dates are the *New York Amsterdam News*, 1909; *Baltimore Afro-American*, 1892; *Chicago Defender*, 1905; *Pittsburgh Courier*, 1910; *Philadelphia Tribune*, 1884; and the Norfolk *Journal and Guide*, 1911. Once-high circulations fell after World War II; for example, the *Pittsburgh Courier*'s asserted 250,000 in 1945 dropped to 60,000. Others underwent similar losses.

In 1972 *Muhammad Speaks*, a leader in the black revolution, listed its circulation as 400,000. Unquestionably the new publications that espoused black power were outdistancing the older, essentially conservative black papers. Change also came in the field of integration. Robert S. Abbott of Chicago earned a national reputation as publisher of the oldest surviving black daily, and his nephew, John H. Sengstacke, in 1970 became the first black journalist elevated to the board of directors of the American Society of Newspaper Editors.

The American Indian press had to hoe a hard row. Efforts to produce a national paper met with language and distribution difficulties. In the mid-1970's *Wassaja*, with both news and comment, issued monthly from San Francisco's Indian Historical Press. Scattered sheets serving tribes and reservations, some begun in the early 1800's, survived for varying periods. New interest in the native Indian as a minority raised interest in Indian publications.

Ownerships, Chains, and Syndicates. The one-man editor-publisher practice of journalism, although persisting in rural areas, followed business trends into partnerships, companies, and corporations with many owners who held shares of stock. Chain ownership and management developed near the end of the 19th century. The Scripps brothers, Edward W., James E., and George H., with Milton A. McRae, began the first chain in the mid-1890's by establishing newspapers in medium-sized cities. By 1914 the Scripps-McRae League of Newspapers controlled some thirteen daily publications. In the 1920's the organization became the Scripps-Howard chain, after its new driving force, Roy W. Howard, who extended the enterprise from coast to coast and into New York City.

William Randolph Hearst was a close second in chain operation. After taking over the *San Francisco Examiner*, he bought the *New York Journal* in 1895 and soon moved into Chicago. By 1951 he owned seventeen dailies and two Sunday papers, to which he supplied national news, editorials, and features. Subsequently the Hearst organization retrenched, and its numbers declined while chain ownership generally expanded. In the mid-1970's the Gannett chain consisted of fifty-one newspapers, the largest number in one ownership. The Knight and Ridder chains merged in 1974 to form Knight-Ridder Newspapers with a national coverage of thirty-five newspapers in sixteen states and a combined circulation of 27 million. Important chains included Chicago Tribune, Cowles, Copley, Lee, Newhouse, and Thomson. Some of the newspapers with the largest circulations were chain owned, among them the *New York Daily News*, *Philadelphia Inquirer*, *Detroit Free Press*, *Chicago Tribune*, and *Los Angeles Times*. Approximately half the dailies were owned by companies or persons that owned other dailies. In nearly half the states more than 50 percent of the newspapers were chain owned and in Florida the total in chains was 83 percent. Chain newspapers accounted for nearly half of the total circulation in 1960, a proportion stepped up to about two-thirds in less than two decades. A continuation of these trends would place almost all dailies in chain ownership by 1990.

Another trend diversified even major newspaper companies. In 1975 the *New York Times*, the outstanding daily of record as well as the only standard-sized paper of general circulation in New York City, had many other business enterprises. These included daily and weekly newspapers in North Carolina and Florida; magazines for the family, golfers, tennis players, and medical circles; television and radio properties; book and music publishing; news and feature services; and teaching materials, filmstrips, a microfilm edition, a large-type weekly, an index service, and newsprint interests. Similarly the Dow Jones Company, publisher of the *Wall Street Journal*, owned and operated *Barron's*, the *National Observer*, the Ottway group of newspapers, a news service, a computerized news retrieval system, and ten daily printing plants nationwide.

Syndication began before the coming of chains, but the syndicate and chain operation went hand in hand. Hearst, for example, circulated feature material to syndicate subscribers who were not in his chain. The syndicate business grew to vast proportions, providing columnists and comics, religion and recipes, fashions and family counseling, and more in prepackaged daily installments.

Improvements in Production: Unions and Contracts. Newspaper production changed greatly as mechanical methods supplanted typesetting by hand and hand-fed presses. The steam-powered press was used in 1822, but a decade passed before it was common. The cylinder press, imported in 1824, took a larger sheet of paper. Although the stereotype was developed in the 1830's, its adoption awaited the coming in 1861 of the curve-shaped form that could be clamped on rotary-press cylinders. By 1863 newsprint was delivered in rolls instead of cut sheets; in another decade roll-fed presses were common. By 1876 these presses were equipped with folders so that a newspaper of several sections could be printed on as many presses, folded, and assembled for transportation and delivery. The outstanding contributors to printing-press development and manufacture in the 1800's were Robert Hoe, a native of England and founder of R. Hoe and Company, and his son Richard M. Hoe, holder of important patents for inventions and adaptations in press design.

Paper continued to be of the expensive rag manufacture until 1870, when wood-pulp paper began to take its place. From the mid-1840's the telegraph was employed in transmitting news, and it was a notable factor in reporting the Civil War. The *New York Daily Graphic* is credited with printing the first line engraving in March 1873, thus launching the photoengraving process. The *Daily Graphic* pioneered again in 1880 with the halftone reproduction from a photograph.

Although few occupations were as laborious as setting type by hand, the hand method was slow to yield to machine methods. James O. Clephane, a Washington stenographer, failed in his effort in 1876 to apply the typewriter principle, but his work inspired Ottmar Mergenthaler, a Baltimore machinist, who worked for a decade on a series of machines, each better than its predecessor. Finally Mergenthaler produced one that cast lines from molten metal, automatically spaced, by means of individual matrices assembled via a hand-operated keyboard and returned to a magazine after each use. Mergenthaler's first patent was issued in 1884, and on July 3, 1886, a "linotype" was successfully operated at the *New York Tribune*. Use of the machine spread quickly: 60 were in use in eighteen months, and by 1895 there were 3,100 speeding up typesetting across the country. The

speedup proved a boon to afternoon newspapers. The tramp printer's days were numbered, and a new era had come to printing.

The linotype fell prey to progress, and by the mid-1970's many newspaper composing rooms had removed their last "linos," as offset printing and other new techniques took over. Notable developments came, too, in color printing and rotogravure for feature sections, and some newspapers used color in their news and advertising columns. The wire services meantime developed the means by which a single impulse at the starting point caused a step in type production to be taken in the plants of many member newspapers.

As newspapers became mechanized, labor unions were formed to bargain collectively with employers. Although this movement began with typographers, pressmen, mailers, and related workers, unionization spread to reporters and other staff members with the formation of the American Newspaper Guild in the 1930's. Since about 1950, newspaper shutdowns occurred in many cities as contract disputes dragged on, sometimes for many weeks.

Elevation of Professional Standards. The press, which criticized the practices and morals of other social institutions, for decades ignored criticism raised by readers against its own performance. Protests grew until in 1922, under the impetus of Casper S. Yost, *Saint Louis Globe-Democrat* editorial page editor, a small group of journalists formed the American Society of Newspaper Editors. One of their early acts was to draw up a code of ethics with a strong emphasis on raising journalistic standards. Other organizations that sought to advance professional quality included the National Conference of Editorial Writers, the International Society of Weekly Newspaper Editors, and the Society of Professional Journalists: Sigma Delta Chi. The latter maintained a committee that called attention to infringements on freedom of the press and speech and issued annual reports on gains and losses.

Professional as well as public opinion continued to call for greater accountability, with the result that in 1972 a task force of the Twentieth Century Fund proposed the establishment of the National News Council to provide readers with a forum in which they might have their complaints heard on their merits. This council was incorporated on May 2, 1973, with nine professional and six public members and a professional staff in New York. It was charged with the investigation of complaints brought against national news associations or newspapers with national distribution—"the principal national suppliers of news." Many leading newspapers supported the idea, but others, including the *New York Times,* opposed it as a possible hindrance to press freedom. The council, with a grievance committee and one on freedom of the press, made a sustained but unsuccessful effort to obtain from President Nixon documentation for his charge that the reporting, after his dismissal of Special Watergate Prosecutor Archibald Cox and the resignation of Attorney General Elliott Richardson, was, in Nixon's words, the "most outrageous, vicious, and distorted" that he had ever seen. Council findings varied with the facts and the urgency of the case, and although many complaints were dropped after being reviewed, other protests were supported against print and electronic news handlers.

The Press and Watergate. The newspapers produced a mixed record with respect to the criminal acts and other scandals of the Nixon administration. A large number of news editors dismissed the Watergate break-in and burglary of the Democratic national headquarters in Washington, D.C., on June 17, 1972, as a "caper" worth little attention and so relegated it to a small, inconspicuous space. However, the *Washington Post* recognized that five men in business suits, wearing surgical gloves and equipped with a walkie-talkie, were not ordinary burglars. The *Post* not only placed the puzzling unlawful entry on page 1, but put a staff to work seeking the motive. Through one frustration after another, the *Post* editors, including Benjamin C. Bradlee and Barry Sussman, and two reporters, Bob Woodward and Carl Bernstein, dug for the facts. In the meantime the White House, as the public came to know later, engaged in a gigantic cover-up, led by Nixon himself. The presidential press secretary sought to mislead the news media by insisting that there was nothing to hide and by ridiculing the persistence of the *Post* staff.

As the screen of deception began to crack, other newspapers followed the *Post.* Early recruits to the investigative and reporting functions included the *New York Times, Los Angeles Times, Wall Street Journal,* and *Christian Science Monitor.* For example, disclosure that Spiro T. Agnew was under the federal inquiry that led to his no-contest plea and resignation from the vice-presidency first appeared in the *Wall Street Journal.* In time the press as a whole found it necessary to print Watergate and related news generously. When the electronic networks reported the shocking developments each day, newspapers had little choice but to do as much. Some of Nixon's defenders accused the media of seeking vindictively to destroy the president and his administration. That

thesis did not stand up in view of the fact that an overwhelming 94 percent of U.S. newspapers had supported Nixon in his bid for reelection in 1972. Over most of two years the *New York Times* devoted more space to the Senate hearings into Watergate scandals, Nixon's income taxes and associated matters, and the subsequent impeachment proceedings and pardon than to any other domestic concern. Eventually some of Nixon's strongest backers, such as the *Chicago Tribune* and the *Saint Louis Globe-Democrat,* altered their editorial position markedly and called him to strict account on his misconduct.

Newspapers and the Courts. The First Amendment to the Constitution prohibits Congress from passing any law "abridging the freedom of speech, or of the press," and the Supreme Court in *Gitlow* v. *New York* (1925) declared that "freedom of speech and of the press [are] protected by the due process clause of the Fourteenth Amendment from impairment by the states." Moreover, most states wrote strong free-press provisions into their constitutions. Even so, many issues arose, particularly in the half century after World War I, that brought press freedom into legal controversy.

Other than the cases related to World War I, the first important free-press test was decided by the Supreme Court in 1931 in *Near* v. *Minnesota.* At issue was a state law imposing prior censorship against comment on alleged wrongdoing by public officials. The law was voided unanimously. In 1937 the Supreme Court, in *Grosjean* v. *American Press Company,* invalidated Huey Long's newspaper gag act. In 1941, in *Times-Mirror Company* v. *Superior Court,* a five-to-four decision ruled in favor of wide latitude in critical comment on a pending case. The unanimous decision in *Craig* v. *Harney* in 1947 upheld the *Corpus Christi* (Tex.) *Call-Times'* defense against a contempt proceeding arising from comment on a trial involving private rather than public persons.

The 1960's and 1970's brought a series of major free-press cases. In *New York Times Company* v. *Sullivan,* involving the wording of a civil rights advertisement, the Supreme Court unanimously held in 1964 that a public official could not recover libel damages without proving malice. Also unanimously, the Supreme Court in *Brandenburg* v. *Ohio* voided a state criminal syndicalism law in 1969 as violating the rights of free speech and free press. The most important decision of the decade and one of the most important in American history came in the Pentagon Papers case in 1971. Involving the *New York Times* and the *Washington Post,* but also inferentially the press as a whole, the issue was whether the Nixon administration could enjoin publication of official papers relating to the Indochinese war. The holding of six justices was that the government did not meet its burden of showing justification for prior restraint. In a five-to-four decision in 1972 the Supreme Court ruled against Earl Caldwell of the *New York Times,* television newscaster Paul Pappas of New Bedford, Mass., and Paul Branzburg of the *Louisville Courier-Journal,* who argued against disclosing news sources before a grand jury. A crucial free-press victory came in 1974 in *Miami Herald Publishing Company* v. *Tornillo,* when the Supreme Court unanimously voided Florida's so-called right-of-reply statute requiring equal space in answering criticism.

Rather than disclose their news sources some reporters served contempt-of-court jail sentences. For example, William Farr of the *Los Angeles Times* served forty-six days in 1973 before being freed on appeal by Supreme Court Justice William O. Douglas. The press gained when Congress passed the 1975 Freedom of Information Act, which opened news sources in the federal government usually closed before.

The "New Journalism." In the late 1960's and into the 1970's unorthodox developments in the press came to be called the "new journalism." The term was used to embrace a wide range of writing—a partially imaginative "nonfiction" as news writing on current events as well as on the "pop culture"; school and campus and other so-called "underground" papers; the community-oriented journalism reviews, both professional and academic; the "alternative" weeklies that stressed local investigations and sharp commentaries; and publications that dealt with pointed problems, such as the environment, the feminist movement, and pressing social issues. The writers included Gay Talese, Tom Wolfe, Lillian Ross, Norman Mailer, Truman Capote, and Jimmy Breslin. Among the new-style papers were the *Maine Times,* Manhattan's *Village Voice,* the *Texas Observer, Cervi's Rocky Mountain Journal,* and the *San Francisco Bay Guardian.* A category of writers known as "advocates" included James F. Ridgeway, Nicholas von Hoffman, Gloria Steinem, Pete Hamill, and Jack Newfield. In the electronic media account was taken of "alternative broadcasting"—public access television and television sponsored by viewers. Although the field was subject to almost continuous change, the term "new journalism" persisted for want of a more exact description. Some of its critics held that it was neither new nor journalism.

Newspaper Rise and Decline. In the half century from 1800 to 1850, the number of dailies increased tenfold, from 24 to 254. Total daily circulation did not quite quadruple; it was 200,000 in 1800 and 758,000 in 1850. Through the 19th century each decade saw increases in the number of dailies, 387 in 1860 with a circulation of 1,478,000 to 574 in 1870 with a circulation of 2,601,000. Technological improvements made larger press runs possible, and as the number of dailies tripled—971 in 1880; 1,610 in 1889; 2,226 in 1899; and 2,600 in 1909—circulation rose at a faster rate. The circulation figures for those same years were 3,566,000; 8,387,000; 15,102,000; and 24,212,000. The 1909 total of 2,600 was essentially the high mark in the number of daily newspapers. By 1920 the total had declined to 2,324. Circulation continued to rise, reaching 31 million by 1920.

In the 1920–30 period the number of dailies decreased by about 100. In 1930 there were 2,219 dailies, but the total circulation reached 45,106,000. Under the pressure to combine, the number of dailies dropped in 1941 to 1,857, a decline that continued in the 1940's until the total fell to 1,744. After about 1945 there was a leveling off through the 1950's and 1960's. In the early 1970's the number of dailies held rather steady while the circulation total rose slightly. In 1970 there were 1,748 dailies, with a circulation of 62,107,000; by 1973 there were 1,774 dailies with a circulation of 63,147,000. A major influence was the rise of the electronic media as a means of communication. Where a century earlier, major cities might have had as many as 10 dailies, in 1974 only two cities—New York and Chicago—had 4 and only three—Philadelphia, Boston, and San Antonio—had 3 dailies.

News Wire Services. The major services for the transmission of news and pictures by wire or radio, the Associated Press and United Press International, were started in 1848 and 1907, respectively. The United Press Association merged with a Hearst wire service, the International News Service, in 1958 to form United Press International.

Education in Journalism. The American Press Institute at the Columbia University Graduate School of Journalism, the Nieman Foundation at Harvard, and other programs at academic institutions provided opportunities for practicing newspaper workers to improve their professional knowledge and abilities. The University of Missouri School of Journalism, dating back to 1908, maintained a national Freedom of Information Center. Programs of prizes and awards, such as those established by Joseph Pulitzer in 1917, emphasized meritorious service in reporting, correspondence, editorial writing, cartooning, criticism, and other areas. Many newspapers had overlooked their own shortcomings, and for years the press's own critics, Silas Bent, Will Irwin, A. J. Liebling, Oswald Garrison Villard, and George Seldes, wrote for a small but growing audience. By the mid-1970's the press was listening as never before and striving to work on a higher plane.

[W. K. Agee, ed., *The Press and the Public Interest;* James Aronson, *Deadline for the Media;* B. H. Bagdikian, *The Information Machines;* Alfred Balk, *A Free and Responsive Press;* J. A. Barron, *Freedom of the Press for Whom?;* Silas Bent, *Ballyhoo: The Voice of the Press;* S. M. Bessie, *Jazz Journalism;* W. G. Bleyer, *Main Currents in the History of American Journalism;* Herbert Brucker, *Communication Is Power;* F. L. Bullard, *Famous War Correspondents;* Robert Cirino, *Don't Blame the People;* H. M. Clor, ed., *The Mass Media and Modern Democracy;* E. E. Dennis and W. L. Rivers, *Other Voices: The New Journalism;* Edwin Emery and H. L. Smith, *The Press and America;* P. L. Fisher and R. L. Lowenstein, *Race and the News Media;* J. C. Goulden, *Truth Is the First Casualty;* Laurence Greene, *America Goes to Press;* Gerald Gross, ed., *The Responsibility of the Press;* W. A. Hachten, *The Supreme Court on Freedom of the Press;* Stephen Hess and Milton Kaplan, *The Ungentlemanly Art;* John Hohenberg, *Free Press, Free People;* R. M. Hutchins, *A Free and Responsible Press;* A. M. Lee, *The Daily Newspaper in America;* R. W. Lee, ed., *Politics and the Press;* A. J. Liebling, *The Wayward Pressman;* C. E. Lindstrom, *The Fading American Newspaper;* L. M. Lyons, ed., *Reporting the News;* R. E. McCoy, *Freedom of the Press;* A. K. MacDougall, ed., *The Press: A Critical Look From the Inside;* Lester Markel, *What You Don't Know Can Hurt You;* J. C. Merrill, *The Elite Press;* Dale Minor, *The Information War;* F. L. Mott, *American Journalism;* William Murrell, *A History of American Graphic Art;* R. E. Park, *The Immigrant Press and Its Control;* W. L. Rivers and M. J. Nyhan, *Aspen Notebook on Government and the Media;* Victor Rosewater, *History of Co-operative News-Gathering;* B. W. Rucker, *The First Freedom;* R. A. Rutland, *Newsmongers: Journalism in the Life of the Nation;* P. M. Sandman, D. M. Rubin, and D. B. Sachsman, *Media;* Martin Sheridan, *Comics and Their Creators;* Upton Sinclair, *The Brass Check;* I. F. Stone, *In a Time of Torment;* John Tebbell, *The Media in America;* O. G. Villard, *The Disappearing Daily;* E. S. Watson, *A History of Newspaper Syndicates in the United States.*]

IRVING DILLIARD

NEW SWEDEN COLONY. In March 1638 two ships, *Kalmar Nyckel* and *Fogel Grip,* brought to the Delaware River twenty-three Swedish soldiers and two officers to establish the first and only Swedish colony in the New World. They built a fort on the shore of a small river emptying into the Delaware, which stream they named Christina Kill (after the Swedish queen). The site of this first permanent settlement in the entire Delaware River valley, including Delaware, New Jersey, and Pennsylvania, is now within the boundaries of the city of Wilmington. Hav-

ing bought from the Indians a tract of land on the western side of the Delaware extending from Sankikan (now Trenton, N.J.) to Cape Henlopen at the mouth of Delaware Bay, they claimed this territory for their country, calling it New Sweden.

In 1640 a second expedition arrived with supplies and new colonists, the first governor, Peter Hollandaer, and the first clergyman, Reorus Torkillus. Another expedition arrived in 1641, and a fourth arrived in 1643, bringing a new governor, Johan Printz.

Printz started at once to extend his domain, building small forts on the eastern, or New Jersey, side of the Delaware, at Tinicum, near the present site of Philadelphia; at Upland (now Chester, Pa.); and at the mouth of the Schuylkill River. More ships came and more colonists; the forests were cleared and farms cultivated; and a village, Christinahamn, was laid out behind Fort Christina, their first establishment.

Printz ruled New Sweden with despotic power. Military leader, as well as civil governor, lawgiver, chief judge, and head of all the colony's activities, he was supreme over the whole Delaware Valley south of Sankikan. He was "a man of brave size, weighing over 400 pounds," headstrong, tyrannical, rough, violent, overbearing, arrogant, and arbitrary, but an intelligent man, a brave soldier, a strict disciplinarian, and an able administrator. In all, he was a colonial governor whose character and achievements have been unjustly slighted. He monopolized the fur trade, driving out the English who came from New Haven and the Dutch who came from New Amsterdam seeking to establish trading posts and settlements. By successive expeditions the colony increased to nearly 400 people.

Peter Stuyvesant, Dutch governor of New Amsterdam, built a fort at New Castle, Del., called Casimir. Printz's successor, Johan Rising, captured it in 1654 and again gave Sweden control of the whole valley. This so angered the Dutch in Holland that in 1655 they sent a warship to New Amsterdam, where it was joined by six others. With 300 fighting men Stuyvesant came down from Manhattan, recaptured Casimir, and, after a ten-day bloodless siege, also captured Fort Christina. Thus New Sweden disappeared from the map, and a Dutch province took its place.

[Christopher Ward, *The Dutch and Swedes on the Delaware.*]

CHRISTOPHER WARD

NEW SWEDEN COMPANY. Although several Swedish trading companies were formed during the second quarter of the 17th century, the organization that founded the first Swedish overseas colony was the New Sweden Company. Established in 1637 for the purpose of trading and planting colonies on the coast of North America from Newfoundland to Florida, this company secured its first foothold on American soil in the present state of Delaware in the year 1638 (see New Sweden Colony).

The principal promoters of the company were Axel Oxenstierna, regent and chancellor of Sweden; Samuel Blommaert of Holland, a director of the Dutch West India Company; Peter Minuit, formerly director of the colony of New Netherland at New Amsterdam; Adm. Klas Fleming of the Swedish navy; and Peter Spiring, diplomatic representative of Sweden in Holland. The cost of the first expedition, 36,000 florins, was subscribed to equally by Swedes and Hollanders; all the above-named persons, except Minuit, were among the subscribers. Minuit was chosen director of the expedition. In 1642 the company was reorganized and became entirely Swedish.

[Amandus Johnson, *The Swedish Settlements on the Delaware.*]

GEORGE H. RYDEN

NEW THOUGHT MOVEMENT, the name given to the liberal wing of the mind-healing movement in the United States. Members look upon Phineas P. Quimby as the pioneer whose ideas have been handed down to them through Julius and Horatio Dresser. The name was first used by the Church of the Higher Life, which was formed in Boston in 1894, having among its members some of Quimby's disciples. The first New Thought convention was held in San Francisco in the same year, and in successive years New Thought groups began to appear in various parts of the United States. In 1914 the International New Thought Alliance was formed, which adopted a constitution and set forth a series of affirmations, laying stress upon health, happiness, and success. New Thought groups do not profess to be churches; in fact, they ask no one to give up his church membership. Rather it is their design to make men and women efficient within their established patterns of life.

[Charles S. Braden, *Spirits in Rebellion: The Rise and Development of New Thought.*]

WILLIAM W. SWEET

NEWTON, BATTLE OF. *See* **Elmira, Battle of.**

NEW ULM, DEFENSE OF (1862). Citizens of New Ulm, Minn., a German town on the Minnesota River,

warned by refugees of a Sioux uprising, hastily barricaded the business section and repulsed a sharp Sioux raid on the afternoon of Aug. 19, 1862. Reinforced by volunteer companies led by Charles E. Flandrau, a jurist of nearby Saint Peter who took general command, some 250 guns faced the main attack on Aug. 23. In a desperate all-day battle against heavy odds, the defenders, after twenty-six had been killed, beat off the Sioux. Some minor skirmishing on Aug. 24 marked the final Sioux retreat.

[W. W. Folwell, *A History of Minnesota*, vol. II.]

WILLOUGHBY M. BABCOCK

"NEW WEST," a term used by American historian Frederick Jackson Turner—notably in his 1906 work *Rise of the New West*—and by the school of historians that adopted his view of the importance of the frontier in American history. The term was used specifically to refer to the states to the west of the Allegheny Mountains, including Ohio, Indiana, Illinois, Missouri, Kentucky, Tennessee, Alabama, Mississippi, and Louisiana, that were rapidly settled after 1815 and became "a dominant force in American life."

JOHN D. HICKS

NEW YORK, TREATY OF. *See* **McGillivray Incident.**

NEW YORK AND GENESEE COMPANY. Caleb Benton, Jared Coffin, John Livingston, and several wealthy residents of the Hudson River district formed a company in 1787 for the purpose of obtaining possession of the Indian country in New York State by leaseholding, ignoring the preemption rights of the state of Massachusetts. Livingston obtained the signatures of the Iroquois delegates on a 999-year lease for all the Iroquois lands in the state, at a rental fee of $2,000 per year plus a promised bonus of $20,000. The Indians denied the legality of the lease because it was not signed by the principal chiefs, and later legislative action nullified the agreement.

[Robert W. Bingham, *The Cradle of the Queen City.*]

ROBERT W. BINGHAM

NEW YORK CENTRAL RAILROAD. *See* **Railroads, Sketches.**

NEW YORK, CHICAGO AND SAINT LOUIS. *See* **Railroads, Sketches: Norfolk and Western.**

NEW YORK CITY, which covers 320.38 square miles, is divided into five boroughs: Manhattan (New York County), the Bronx (Bronx County), Queens (Queens County), Brooklyn (Kings County), and Staten Island (Richmond County). Its early importance and subsequent prominence were predicated upon the excellence of its ice-free, sheltered harbor and the attendant volume of its commerce. Possessing a shoreline of 578 miles, maintaining a considerable pier-modernization program, and served in 1975 by 180 steamship lines and 50 airlines, it is the premier port of the world in terms of the value of its sea and air commerce and the supportive facilities and services it provides.

On Sept. 8, 1664, during the first Anglo-Dutch War, Dutch Gov. Peter Stuyvesant reluctantly surrendered the city of New Amsterdam to a besieging English squadron commanded by Col. Richard Nicolls, who renamed it New York in honor of James, Duke of York, later James II. Nicolls became the first English governor. In August 1673, during the third Anglo-Dutch War, New York was reconquered by the Dutch under Capt. Anthony Colve, but it was returned to England in the concluding Treaty of Westminster in 1674. At first, the Duke of York, as the new proprietor, permitted a surprisingly liberal and tolerant administration, to insure the gratitude and loyalty of his Dutch and Walloon subjects and to promote commercial prosperity and thereby his revenues. On Apr. 27, 1686, Gov. Thomas Dongan granted the first English municipal charter to New York City, adding to earlier municipal prerogatives the right to eminent domain, the right to own and dispose of land, and the right to grant franchises.

In the century between English conquest and the termination of the French and Indian War in 1763, the city experienced constant growth in population. As the provincial capital, it was administered by governors who ran the gamut from excellent to deplorable, and there soon developed a remarkable political maturity, evidenced by the evolution of political parties with various ideological, religious, and economic bases: Whig versus Tory, Leislerian versus anti-Leislerian, assembly versus crown; Anglican versus Dissenter; and landowners, merchants, professionals, officeholders, and artisans in shifting and opposing alliances. This mounting awareness was responsible for a sophisticated and partisan cadre as issues sharpened.

The rebellion of 1689–91 led by Jacob Leisler helped to check the increasingly tyrannical policies of James II. Leisler was the *de facto* leader of the colony when Peter de Lanoy became the first popularly elected mayor of the city (Oct. 14, 1689, to Mar. 20, 1691)—and the last until 1834. It was the controversial Leisler's unjust execution for treason that divided the populace into Leislerians and anti-Leislerians.

Street lights and a night watch appeared in New York in 1697; a serious epidemic of yellow fever broke out in 1702; the public printer William Bradford published the first newspaper, the weekly *New York Gazette,* on Oct. 16, 1725; the first stage line ran to Philadelphia in 1730; a fire department was organized in 1731, the year Harlem at the northern end of Manhattan was annexed; and in April 1712 and February 1741 there occurred so-called black insurrections or conspiracies that resulted in harsh and tragic punishments. In 1735 John Peter Zenger, the courageous publisher of the Whiggish weekly *New York Journall,* was acquitted of seditious libel against royal Gov. William S. Cosby—a landmark victory for freedom of the press and for American legal interpretation over English common law. These years witnessed a steady growth of popular participation in government, of Whig partisan strength, and of the increasing power of the assembly in checking the governor's power.

The city played an important role in revolutionary activities. It was the site of the Stamp Act Congress in 1765, of anti-British violence, patriotic nonimportation agreements, and a lesser-known tea party on Apr. 22, 1774, in which eighteen cases of tea were dumped into the bay. The readily brawling Sons of Liberty and local committees of correspondence, aided by radical Whig leadership, drove the colony relentlessly toward revolution, even engaging in clashes with the British soldiery. From the New York Assembly came the suggestion that led to the First Continental Congress in 1774. With the outbreak of hostilities New York was vital to both British and American strategy. Although the province of New York remained in American hands, thus contiguously linking the northern and southern colonies, the city was not so fortunate. Gen. George Washington's army was defeated in the Battle of Long Island (Aug. 25–26, 1776) and on Manhattan Island in the weeks following and was compelled to withdraw northward to White Plains. The city suffered from the destructive and indifferent administration of the British military until war's end.

At the end of the struggle, and with independence, charters were reinstituted and municipal government restored; the Anglican church was disestablished; and the city began to recover economically. It grew both in population and commercial importance. In the first federal census (1790), New York's population was

33,131. By 1797, New York had moved ahead of Boston and Philadelphia in exports and imports. In population New York by 1830 had outstripped Philadelphia to become the nation's first city and the largest in the hemisphere. The population in that year was 202,589, having risen from 123,706 in 1820.

New York, between 1783 and 1861, faithfully mirrored the developments and issues of the intervening national historical eras. In 1784 the Bank of New York was founded. From 1785 until 1790 the city was the national capital and until 1797 the seat of the state government as well. In the early national period the elitist Federalist politics of Alexander Hamilton were dominant, but the Jeffersonian Republicans, led by Aaron Burr locally, gained control. After 1800 government in the city became more representative and democratic. The city suffered but little ill from the War of 1812 except a few years of decline in maritime activity, profits, and employment owing to Thomas Jefferson's embargo and a British naval blockade.

During the four decades preceding the Civil War the city gained from increasing immigration, banking, exchange and insurance activity, industry, and the growth of the railroads. By virtue of its harbor, the coming of the steamboat, the importance of the Hudson River and the Erie Canal, and a railroad trunk system that opened up the hinterland and the West along a low, water-level route, New York became a major market and entrepôt between Europe and the American continent.

Politically, in the struggle in this burgeoning urban milieu between the Jacksonian Democrats and nationalistic Whigs, the local Tammany Hall Democratic machine championed the president. Although it later divided into factions, New York remained a mainly Democratic bastion from that time. In 1834, Jacksonian Democrat Cornelius V. R. Lawrence became the first elected mayor since De Lanoy.

On the night of Dec. 16–17, 1835, occurred New York's Great Fire, in which nearly 700 buildings in the heart of the city were destroyed, including the Merchants Exchange and almost all of the remaining old Dutch structures. Another fire in 1845 ravaged the same area. The gloom of fires, epidemics, slums, and savage partisan politics was relieved by the construction of the Croton water system; the introduction of gas street lamps; the paving of streets; increased educational facilities at all levels; greater attention to charitable needs and social welfare; and increased ferry, rail, and streetcar transportation. In 1860 the population was 814,000.

As a banking and shipping center with numerous ties to southern planters and businessmen, New York was divided over the issues that led to the Civil War. Once hostilities commenced, however, the city supported the Union loyally and generously. Marring this commitment were the Draft Riots of July 1863, which caused extensive loss of life and property. The war was a watershed for the city: in the years following, New York became the unquestioned symbol of a booming, complex urban enclave and the marketplace of a maturing finance capitalism that had been stimulated by the needs of war. The city had a population of 942,292 in 1870. On Jan. 1, 1898, the present five boroughs were incorporated into the Greater City of New York after legislative action and plebiscites of approval.

After 1861 New York Democratic politics was dominated by Tammany Hall—under four so-called bosses, William M. Tweed, John Kelly, Richard Croker, and Charles F. Murphy. This machine survived in spite of occasional defeats, reform movements, legislative investigations, and public outcries. With Murphy's death in 1924, the Seabury investigations of 1930 and 1931, and the fusion mayoralty of Fiorello H. La Guardia, Tammany's decline became profound and irreversible. In the 20th century New York has been the focal point of progressivism, the muckraking movement, and reform. The city strongly supported the New Deal politics of President Franklin Delano Roosevelt, a former governor of New York.

New York has rightly been called the cultural capital of the United States. Its major opera and dance companies, world-famous symphony orchestra, libraries, museums, and theaters make it the center of the arts in the country. As the home of the two largest stock exchanges in the United States and the headquarters of hundreds of banks and corporations, New York is also the major financial center. In addition it is also the center of the publishing, broadcasting, and fashion industries in the United States.

New York runs one of the largest public education systems in the United States, which includes the multibranched City University of New York (CUNY). Private institutions of higher learning include Columbia, Fordham, Long Island, New York, Yeshiva, and St. John's universities and Manhattan College. In addition there are several medical schools and research institutions.

New York was faced in the 1970's with the enormous urban problems confronting the other cities in the nation. The city's size, however, not only magnified but intensified the problems. Its population in 1970 was 7,895,563, which included more than 1.5 million Afro-Americans and 1.2 million Hispanic-Americans. The shift toward an increased nonwhite population carried divisive overtones in housing, unemployment, welfare, education, and crime. A disastrous financial crisis in 1975 necessitated increased financial stringency that could only exacerbate the problems.

[William Thompson Bonner, *New York, The World's Metropolis;* I. N. Phelps Stokes, *Iconography of Manhattan Island.*]

MARK D. HIRSCH

NEW YORK CITY, CAPTURE OF (July 30, 1673). During the summer of 1673 rumors of the approach of a Dutch squadron with a design of recapturing the city reached New York. Gov. Francis Lovelace failed to take them seriously, and in July made a long-deferred visit to Gov. Fitz-John Winthrop of Connecticut, leaving Capt. John Manning in charge at Fort James. On July 28 a fleet of twenty-three ships, under the joint command of Cornelis Evertsen, Jr., and Jacob Binckes, appeared off Sandy Hook. Manning, putting up as brave a front as possible, demanded of the Dutch why they came ''in such a hostile manner,'' and hurriedly dispatched an express to Lovelace, in New Haven, begging him to return at once. The Dutch commanders replied they had come to take that which ''was theyr own.'' Manning tried frantically to raise volunteers. On July 30 the fleet came within musket shot of the fort, and Manning parleyed for delay until morning. He was given a respite of half an hour. When the time expired, the Dutch fleet opened fire. The fort held out for four hours and then surrendered.

[A. C. Flick, ed., *History of the State of New York,* vol. II.]

A. C. FLICK

NEW YORK CITY, PLOT TO BURN. As an aftermath of the Confederate raid on Saint Albans, Vt., in October 1864, an attempt was made to burn New York City. Originally planned for Nov. 8, the attempt was postponed to Nov. 25. Barnum's Museum, the Astor House, and a number of other hotels and theaters were fired with phosphorus and turpentine, but the damage was trifling.

[J. F. Rhodes, *History of the United States,* vol. V.]

THOMAS ROBSON HAY

NEW YORK CLEARINGHOUSE. *See* **Clearinghouse, New York.**

NEW YORK COLONY. The year after its addition to the Dominion of New England, 1689, was a time of anxiety, violence, and unrest in the colony of New York (*see* York's, Duke of, Proprietary). A declaration of war against France had followed the accession of William and Mary to the throne of England. A revolt in New England caused the arrest of Gov. Edmund Andros (*see* New England, Dominion of). His representative in New York, Capt. Francis Nicholson, fled, and Capt. Jacob Leisler seized control of the government. Albany attempted to resist Leisler's authority, but the burning of Schenectady by the French and Indians in 1690 forced the magistrates to yield. The government of William III, too weak to attempt anything in America, had left the colonies to their own resources. In the spring of 1690, with the cooperation of Massachusetts, Leisler called a meeting of the northern colonies in New York City. An attack on Montreal was planned. The expedition was a failure, and Leisler with a tactlessness that spoiled all of his efforts attempted to throw the blame on Fitz-John Winthrop of Connecticut, who had been in command. The following spring, on the arrival of Col. Henry Sloughter, who had been commissioned governor by William and Mary, Leisler and his chief associates were tried for treason and Leisler and Jacob Milbourne, his lieutenant, were executed. Leislerian and anti-Leislerian factions continued to disturb the colony for many years.

Gov. Benjamin Fletcher, who took office in 1692, interested himself energetically in the problems of defense and Indian relations. Acting on the advice of Peter Schuyler, mayor of Albany, he conciliated the Five Nations and bound them to a renewed alliance with England. This alliance, which had become a cardinal point of British policy in New York, was further strengthened in 1701, during the administration of Gov. Richard Coote, Earl of Bellomont, by the action of the Iroquois in conveying to the care of the king of England the western lands they claimed by conquest (*see* Iroquois Beaver Land Deed). Bellomont was shocked by his predecessor's generosity in granting enormous tracts of land to favored individuals and managed to have some of these grants set aside. An able man, and a friend of the small landowner, his administration was cut short by his death in 1701 (*see* New York State, Land Speculation in).

Edward Hyde, Viscount Cornbury, renewed the policy of making extravagant grants during his governorship, 1702–08. His arrogance and corruption greatly antagonized the assembly, which had been slowly growing in power and importance, and hastened the contest over the power of the purse, which was to agitate the province throughout the remainder of the colonial period. A short respite was granted the colony between the peace of Ryswick in 1697 and the beginning of Queen Anne's War in America in 1702. Although New York furnished its quota of men and money requested by the home government, the influence of the Albany traders tended to keep the colony neutral, when not specifically asked to take action. This tendency to neutrality and the trade between Albany and Montreal were the occasions of bitter complaint from the New England colonies.

Gov. Robert Hunter, whose administration between 1710 and 1719 witnessed the close of the war, was one of the ablest of the royal governors. By skillful management he compromised with the assembly and was able to bring a reasonable amount of stability and peace to the colony. One of the major problems of his administration was that of the Palatine refugees, who had been brought over to make naval stores. This unfortunate enterprise strained Hunter's personal credit in caring for the refugees—and Gov. William Burnet inherited the Palatine problem, which was finally solved by the settlement of most of the refugees on the Mohawk frontier to form a barrier against French attack.

The arrival of William Cosby as governor in 1732 witnessed the beginning of a period of violent popular agitation. Smarting under the accusations of maladministration printed in John Peter Zenger's small newspaper, the weekly *New York Journal,* Cosby ordered Zenger's arrest. In the trial that followed the principle that truth is the justification for making a public statement was established.

The French continued their encroachments on territory claimed by New York. In 1727 a fort was built by the British at Oswego to offset the rival French post at Niagara. In 1731 the French occupied Crown Point. Hostilities broke out again in 1744. George Clinton, then governor of New York, was a man of courage and ability, but he possessed little tact. His furious feud with James De Lancey, chief justice of the province, caused a bitter fight over the conduct of the war and the appropriation of funds by the assembly. As a result the only effective action taken by the colony was through the exertions on the western frontier of Sir William Johnson, who was able to exercise sufficient influence over the Six Nations to keep their friendship (*see* Indian Policy, Colonial).

In 1754 De Lancey was acting head of the provincial government. He presided over the famous Albany Congress, and in the fourth and final war with the French, which followed (*see* French and Indian War), he gave firm support to the king's commanders. In 1759 Jeffrey Amherst, British commander in chief in North America, compelled the French to abandon Ticonderoga and Crown Point, and Niagara was also captured. Throughout the war until the reduction of Montreal by Amherst in 1760 the western frontier of New York suffered cruelly.

The conviction had been growing in America that taxation should originate only in the colonial assemblies. The passage of the Stamp Act in 1765 aroused a storm of opposition. In October delegates from nine colonies met in New York to protest, and the following spring the act was repealed. In 1767, however, the Townshend Acts, putting a duty on glass, paint, paper, and tea, were passed. In protest the merchants of New York signed a nonimportation agreement, boycotting British goods. To add to the discontent in New York the currency bill of 1769 was disallowed (*see* Royal Disallowance). The Sons of Liberty again became active, and in 1770 the disturbances came to a climax in the Battle of Golden Hill. The duties on glass, paint, and paper were repealed and the agitation died down until the fall of 1773. In January 1774 a committee of correspondence was appointed to write to "sister colonies." In April of that year a group of New Yorkers disguised as Indians threw eighteen cases of tea into the harbor. Local and state revolutionary committees took over the government of the colony. On July 9, 1776, the fourth Provincial Congress of New York approved the Declaration of Independence, and on the following day declared that New York had begun its existence as a free state (*see* New York State).

[A. C. Flick, ed., *History of the State of New York,* vols. II, III.]

A. C. FLICK

"NEW YORK GETS THE NEWS," an expression pertaining to the reaction of patriots in New York City following the Battle of Lexington (Apr. 19, 1775). About noon on Sunday, Apr. 23, Israel Bissell, an express rider, arrived in New York City with the news of the battle in Massachusetts. The city was thrown into a state of great excitement. The arsenal was broken open, and about 600 muskets with ammunition were seized and distributed among citizens who formed a voluntary corps. They took possession of the customshouse and the public stores. They paraded in the streets. All business ceased. The posts were stopped and letters read. Acting Gov. Cadwallader Colden wrote that a "state of anarchy and confusion" prevailed. Summoning the council the following day, he was told that the militiamen were all Liberty Boys and would not aid the government. Assurance was given, however, that all was quiet in Dutchess and Queens counties. On May 1, 1775, a Committee of One Hundred was chosen and assumed control of the city. The militia was ordered to patrol the streets. It was forbidden to remove provisions from the city. Myles Cooper, president of King's College, and other pronounced Loyalists were forced to flee. The British troops stationed in the city were embarked on the warship *Asia* to prevent a clash with the excited populace.

[A. C. Flick, *The American Revolution in New York.*]

A. C. FLICK

NEW YORK, NEW HAVEN AND HARTFORD. *See* **Railroads, Sketches: Penn Central.**

NEW YORK STATE. In September 1609 Henry Hudson, in search of a northern passage to China, mistakenly brought his ship, the *Half Moon,* into New York harbor. He continued up the river named for him to the vicinity of Albany before deciding to return southward. By this trip up the river he discovered the fur-trading potentialities of the Hudson Valley and, as a result, extended the area of English claims and of conflict with the Dutch, who founded New Netherland colony in 1625. It was renamed New York after its conquest by the British in 1664.

Colonial New York was slow to develop in comparison to the other colonies because of French and Indian attacks on frontier settlements and also because of the adverse effects of a land system marked by speculation and large holdings. Calamitous fires in New York City in 1776 and 1778 caused half the city's population to move away, as that important center deteriorated under the British martial law that followed Gen. George Washington's defeat on Manhattan in 1776.

The Provincial Congress of New York on May 27, 1776, declared the right to self-government and on July 9 approved the Declaration of Independence. A convention framed a constitution that the legislature adopted on Apr. 20, 1777. Membership in the upper house (senate) and the governorship became elective, and eligibility to vote for members of the lower house (assembly) was extended to include most white adult males. To vote for governor and senators, one required a 100 freehold, five times greater than that needed to vote for assemblymen.

George Clinton defeated Philip Schuyler, the aristocracy's candidate for governor, and took office in July 1777. Serving six terms (1777–95), he directed the revolutionary militia and harassed the Tories. The flight of many aristocrats weakened the landed class, although patriot landlords—notably the Van Rensselaers and Livingstons—retained their lands until the 1840's, when rebellious tenants forced them to sell their interests.

Clinton championed state sovereignty but failed to prevent the Poughkeepsie Convention from ratifying the federal Constitution on July 26, 1788. Alexander Hamilton and John Jay led the Federalists, the latter serving two terms as governor (1795–1801). The Antifederalists became the Jeffersonian Republicans, later the Democratic party.

The Republican victory of 1800 returned Clinton to the governorship for his last term. Daniel D. Tompkins, another Republican governor, between 1807 and 1817, was in the forefront of the struggle against the British economic and military warfare that wreaked havoc on New York commerce. The followers of Tompkins and of Sen. Martin Van Buren captured control of the constitutional convention of 1821, which extended the suffrage to all white men twenty-one years or older who paid taxes, performed labor on the roads, or were enrolled in the militia. The foes of Tompkins and Van Buren rallied around De Witt Clinton who, as canal commissioner and as governor during 1817–22 and 1825–28, promoted the construction of the Erie Canal. The Democrats preached economy, although one branch favored state aid for an enlargement of the Erie Canal, which was authorized in 1835. The Whig party emerged in the 1830's, attracting anti-Masons and the enemies of Andrew Jackson. The party promoted internal improvements. Each party had a wing opposing the extension of slavery, although abolitionism enlisted only a handful. Antislavery feeling grew, and in 1848 some Democrats formed the Free Soil party, which threw the state and federal elections to the Whigs. The slavery issue also divided the Whigs, who collapsed after the passage of the Kansas-Nebraska Act. Thurlow Weed, Horace Greeley, and William Seward drifted into the newly formed Republican party, which also attracted some Free Soilers.

New York grew spectacularly, winning leadership in population and trade by 1820. Among the contributing factors were the opening up of central and western New York; the cession in 1786 by Massachusetts of sovereignty, but not the land, of the area west of Seneca Lake; turnpike and steamboat expansion; Manhattan's success in capturing the transatlantic, coastal, and interior trades; and an influx of New Englanders who dominated commercial, cultural, and political life. The completion of the Erie Canal (1825) made transportation cheaper, stimulated urban growth, and encouraged construction of branch canals. The Mohawk and Hudson Railroad in 1831 connected Albany with Schenectady. Scores of companies were formed, and by 1842 trains ran from Albany to Buffalo over short lines, incorporated in 1853 into the New York Central. After the construction of the cross-state lines—the Central and the Erie—promoters built a network of lines into every section of the state. Although most manufacturing took place in shops and homes in 1850, the factory system—and urbanization—took hold after Pennsylvania coal reached the cities. Wheat cultivation began to decline, but after 1850 dairying became the most important source of farm income.

New Yorkers were also founding churches, schools, and colleges; establishing newspapers; and promoting reform. Thousands joined churches. The Methodists and Baptists, hardly visible in 1776, made striking gains. The Presbyterians and Congregationalists, often allied, benefited from the Yankee invasion. Most fascinating was the emergence of new sects—Mormons, Adventists, and Spiritualists—and the establishment of the Oneida Community, a venture in communal living. The growth of the Roman Catholic church was outstanding. By 1855 it had outstripped any single Protestant denomination in membership.

Reform movements attracted support—temperance; women's rights; more humane treatment of criminals, the insane, and the blind; the curtailment of slavery; and free public education. Members of the feminist crusade, led by Elizabeth Cady Stanton, organized the famous Seneca Falls Convention in July 1848. Foes of slavery helped hundreds of runaway slaves and agitated against slavery. The district school law of 1812 granted state aid for local schools, which earned high praise by 1850.

In 1861 Gov. Edwin D. Morgan enthusiastically answered President Abraham Lincoln's call for men and supplies, but by July 1863 war weariness and an unfair draft had triggered riots, which Gov. Horatio Seymour, an antidraft Democrat, helped put down. The Civil War had a mixed effect on the economy, in general slowing the rate of growth.

Corruption—typified by Boss William Tweed, who dominated New York City politics in the 1860's and 1870's—inspired such reformers as governors Sam-

uel Tilden (1875–76) and Grover Cleveland (1883–85). Governors Theodore Roosevelt (1899–1900) and Charles Evans Hughes (1907–10) headed a distinguished list in the 20th century. Alfred E. Smith, a representative of the newer immigrant stock, reorganized state government during his four terms (1918–20, 1922–28). Gov. Franklin D. Roosevelt carried on Smith's progressivism, passing on the office to Herbert H. Lehman, who, during four terms between 1932 and 1942, regulated public utilities and aided labor. At the end of his twelve-year governorship (1942–54), Thomas E. Dewey left three legacies: the New York Thruway; the state university; and the Ives-Quinn Act, the first state law banning discrimination in hiring. Nelson A. Rockefeller in 1958 defeated W. Averell Harriman, a progressive Democratic governor. During his four terms Rockefeller expanded the state university, medical care, and conservation programs. These services and the construction of costly projects—for example, the Albany Mall—increased the debt and required increases in income, sales, and business taxes. Rockefeller resigned his office in 1973, and Lt. Gov. Malcolm Wilson became governor, only to lose to Rep. Hugh Carey in the next election. Carey faced several pressing problems: shrinking state revenues; rising demands by cities and citizens for more aid and services; and the imminent bankruptcy of New York City and the Urban Development Corporation. Carey and legislative leaders were able to patch together measures to rescue New York City, which had to agree to sharp cuts in its employees.

In 1970 New York State residents had a per capita income 22 percent above the national average. The state, however, ranked last in the nation in percentage of growth of total personal income from 1969 to 1973. Unlike the residents of other states, most New Yorkers are employed in clerical and sales work; nearly 70 percent of all personal income is derived from wages and salaries. New York's leading industries are printing and publishing, apparel, food, chemicals, and primary metals and fabricated metal products, including machinery and transportation equipment. New York State's mineral production is valued at nearly $300 million a year. In wholesale and retail trade New York leads the nation, and those industries employ more than 15 percent of the state's salary and wage earners. The port of New York handles about 35 percent of the nation's imports and 30 percent of the total value of exports. Because of its great financial institutions, stock exchanges, and banks, New York is the financial center of the world.

NEW YORK STATE, LAND SPECULATION IN

New York City banks handle about 30 percent of all U.S. commercial and business loans and about 75 percent of the financing of all U.S. foreign trade.

Having reinforced its early population growth by heavy influxes of European immigrants in the late 19th century, of southern blacks after World War I, and of Puerto Ricans after 1940, New York lost its population lead to California in 1963. In 1970 the state's population was 18,241,266.

[Robert A. Caro, *The Power Broker: Robert Moses and the Fall of New York;* David M. Ellis and others, *A History of New York State;* A. C. Flick, *History of the State of New York;* Michael Kammen, *Colonial New York;* Ronald A. Shaw, *Erie Water West: A History of the Erie Canal;* John H. Thompson, ed., *Geography of New York State.*]

DAVID M. ELLIS

NEW YORK STATE, LAND SPECULATION IN, was early encouraged by the Dutch practice of granting large tracts of land to individuals or associated groups for the promotion of settlement. This practice was continued and extended by the early English governors. Speculation became a fever, which did not abate until the outbreak of the Revolution. From 1690 to 1775 the majority of the prominent men of the colony were involved, either singly or in joint partnerships, in some sort of land speculation. Richard Coote, Earl of Bellomont, succeeded in having voided some of the extravagant grants made by Benjamin Fletcher, whom he followed as governor. But his activities were cut short by his death in 1701, and under Gov. Edward Hyde, Viscount Cornbury, the patenting of great tracts was resumed. The home government, awakened to some extent to the danger, attempted to set up safeguards. Starting with the brief administration of Gov. John Lovelace in 1709, the number of acres to be granted to a single individual was limited. Evasion, however, was common. The governors had come to regard the fees paid for granting patents as a part of their legitimate income. The practice grew up of granting land to a number of associates, often not the real owners. Careless surveys resulted in overlapping claims and litigation. Immigration and settlement were retarded, the settlers preferring the small freeholds offered by other colonies to the landlord-tenant relationship or higher prices in New York.

Although some of the estates and large holdings of Tory landowners were broken up, the newly created state government did little, at the conclusion of hostilities in the Revolution, to protect or encourage the small landowner. As new sections were opened to settlement by treaties with the Indians, or otherwise, speculators rushed in and bought up great tracts to sell to prospective settlers. Disputes over boundaries with neighboring states caused conflicting titles and claims to ownership of land. The royal governors of both New York and New Hampshire had issued grants in the present state of Vermont (*see* Green Mountain Boys), and the bitterness and confusion that resulted did not end until Vermont was admitted into the Union as an independent state in 1791. In 1786 the claim of Massachusetts to a vast tract east of the present western boundary of New York was settled by giving to Massachusetts the right of first purchase from the Indians and to New York the right of sovereignty to the disputed territory. In 1788 this vast tract was sold by Massachusetts to Oliver Phelps and Nathaniel Gorham, but one-third of the territory was all the Indians could be persuaded to part with at that time. The greater portion of the tract was sold to Robert Morris in 1790, and resold by him to Sir William Pulteney, John Hornby, and Patrick Colquhoun, who became known as the London Associates (*see* Pulteney Purchase). The remaining two-thirds, upon being relinquished by Phelps and Gorham because of financial difficulties, was also bought by Morris, who subsequently resold the greater part to a group of Dutch bankers, known as the Holland Land Company. The long-term contracts of sale, by which title did not pass until the final payment, were later to be the cause of considerable disturbance in the six western counties of New York (*see* Antirent War).

The difficulty of getting an immediate cash return from many of the settlers, and the competition of the hundreds of millions of acres available in New England, the Middle States, the South, and the West—much of it obtainable on the easiest terms and under the most favorable political conditions—caused the speculators in New York to turn their eyes abroad, where large cash sales could be made more easily. Tracts of land were hawked from one European capital to another. In 1786 with a desire to promote settlement on the unpatented land recently purchased from the Indians, the legislature of the state prepared to have the lands surveyed and offered for sale. Unfortunately, no effort was made to see that sales were made to actual settlers, and most of the territory fell into the hands of speculators, some of it eventually to reach the European market.

[Edith M. Fox, *Speculation in the Mohawk Valley;* R. L. Higgins, *Expansion in New York.*]

A. C. FLICK

NEW YORK UNDER THE DUKE OF YORK. *See* York's, Duke of, Proprietary.

NEW YORK WORLD'S FAIRS (1939–40, 1964–65). New York's first international exposition since 1853 was opened by President Franklin D. Roosevelt on Apr. 30, 1939, the 150th anniversary of the inauguration of George Washington as president. An optimistic expression of "things to come" dedicated to the "building of the world of tomorrow," the fair was constructed on 1,216.5 acres of a former dumping ground in Flushing Meadow and cost more than $155 million. Tree-lined avenues converged on the focal structures, the 728-foot triangular tapering shaft of the Trylon and the 180-foot-diameter Perisphere. Geographic zones divided the exhibits according to category: amusement, communication and business systems, community interests, food, government, production and distribution, and transportation. Prototype automobiles hinted at future technological achievements, and television was seen by many for the first time. Sixty-three nations and more than twenty states participated. The first season closed on Oct. 31. The outbreak of World War II precluded the participation of many nations in the fair's second season (May 11–Oct. 27, 1940). A financial failure, the fair attracted 44,932,978 visitors during its two-year run but returned only 40 cents on the dollar to bondholders.

The second fair followed four years of planning and construction under the direction of Robert Moses, who proposed to construct a permanent park on the site at the conclusion of the $500-million venture. Occupying the same site and designed to follow its layout, the fair was opened by President Lyndon B. Johnson, to the heckling of civil-rights demonstrators, on Apr. 22, 1964. Construction, hampered by union problems, rising costs, and a lack of technical specialists, was still in progress. The focal point and symbol, the Unisphere, was a stainless steel open model of the earth, the counterpart of the earlier Trylon and Perisphere. Although not sanctioned by the Bureau of International Expositions, the fair enjoyed the participation of private business concerns from sixty-two foreign nations, only nineteen of which were officially represented. There were nineteen federal and state pavilions. The fair's theme was "Man's Achievement in an Expanding Universe"; its avowed purpose, "Peace Through Understanding." The five areas—amusement, federal and state, industrial, international, and transportation—occupied 646

acres. A replica of a Belgian village, demonstrations of nuclear fusion, the exhibition of Michelangelo's *Pietà,* and a ride across the simulated surface of the moon were featured at the more popular exhibits. The first season closed on Oct. 18. An increase in the admission price from $2.00 to $2.50 and a decrease in attendance of 2.7 million marked the second season (Apr. 21–Oct. 17, 1965), which was highlighted by the visit of Pope Paul VI. The fair closed with a total attendance of 51,607,548—then the greatest on record—and $46 million in defaulted payments to the city of New York and holders of promissory notes. Bondholders received 19 cents on the dollar; plans for the projected park remained largely unrealized in 1975.

[Lucretia Lopez, *New York City and the Fair, 1964–1965;* Kathryn Maddrey, ed., *Official Guide: New York World's Fair 1964/1965;* Frank Monaghan, *Official Guide Book of the New York World's Fair* (1939).]

JOEL HONIG

NEZ PERCE WAR (1877). The various bands of the Nez Perce Indians, occupying a large area in the region where Washington, Oregon, and Idaho meet, had always been on friendly terms with the whites, and the Stevens Treaty of 1855 had guaranteed them a large reservation in their homeland. But when gold was discovered in 1860 swarms of miners and settlers intruded upon their lands. In 1863 some of the chiefs signed a new treaty, agreeing to move to the much smaller Lapwai Reservation in Idaho; but Chief Joseph and his southern Nez Perce refused to leave their Wallowa Valley home in northeastern Oregon, Joseph being under the influence of Smohalla, a nativistic prophet of a small Sahaptin tribe living along the Columbia River who preached that the Indians should reject the things of the white man and return to their native ways.

Joseph did not want war, and at the council held at Lapwai in May 1877 he agreed to move his people to the reservation. Hostilities were precipitated when a few young warriors killed some settlers in revenge for outrages. Troops under Gen. O. O. Howard moved against the Indians, who, fighting defensively, defeated the soldiers in several battles, notably at White Bird Canyon in Idaho on June 17. Joseph executed a skillful retreat across the Bitterroot Mountains in an attempt to reach Canadian territory, but on Oct. 15, 1877, within thirty miles of the border, he was surrounded by the troops of Gen. Nelson A. Miles and forced to surrender. With only 300 warriors, Joseph had opposed troops numbering 5,000, traveling more than 1,000 miles in four months with a band that included women and children.

[Merrill D. Beal, *"I Will Fight No More": Chief Joseph and the Nez Perce War;* Francis Haines, *The Nez Percés;* Alvin M. Josephy, *The Nez Percé Indians and the Opening of the Northwest.*]

KENNETH M. STEWART

NIAGARA, CARRYING PLACE OF. Passage by water between lakes Ontario and Erie being obstructed by Niagara Falls, a portage road fourteen miles in length on the east side of the Niagara River was maintained by the French in Canada. In 1720 Louis Thomas de Joncaire, who was appointed master of the portage, having obtained permission from the Seneca, constructed the Magazin Royal, a trading house of bark surrounded by a palisade, at the lower landing of the portage, now Lewiston, N.Y. This storehouse of the French trade was occupied by Joncaire until his death in 1739. Realizing the importance of the road, which was the means of communication between the posts below the falls and the upper lakes as well as the coveted Ohio region, Daniel de Joncaire, who had succeeded his father, erected Fort Little Niagara in 1751 at the upper landing. This was a palisaded post on the east shore of the river at the head of the portage road. The thoroughfare facilitated transportation of supplies destined for the new posts and those already established to the south and west. Although the English had established a post at Oswego, they were prevented from entering the upper lakes.

Fort Little Niagara was destroyed by its commandant on July 7, 1759, when the British attacked Fort Niagara. After becoming masters of the portage, the British fully realized its importance, and in 1764 they received from the Seneca by treaty the full right to its possession. Its importance was demonstrated in the relief of Detroit, during Pontiac's War, and in control of the upper lakes until relinquished, under the terms of Jay's Treaty, in 1796 (*see* Border Forts, Evacuation of).

[Frank H. Severance, *An Old Frontier of France.*]
ROBERT W. BINGHAM

NIAGARA, FORT. Having obtained permission from the Seneca, the French built a stone castle on the eastern shore of the Niagara River at Lake Ontario in 1726, six and one-half miles north of the Niagara Carrying Place. Palisades, ramparts, and other buildings soon followed, and the post became the principal guard of the coveted gateway to the rich fur lands in the West. During the French and Indian War a projected attack by the English under Gen. William Shirley in 1755 failed. Two years later a force of British and Indians under generals John Prideaux and William Johnson besieged the fortress. Prideaux was killed, and Johnson, succeeding to the command, captured the post on July 25. As a British fortress it was the scene of several Indian treaties, and during the Revolution the irregulars under John Butler and Guy Johnson issued from its gates bound on their devastating forays. After the war the surrounding territory was governed from Niagara until the fortress was relinquished to the American troops in August 1796 (*see* Border Forts, Evacuation of), in accordance with Jay's Treaty. Captured by the British on Dec. 19, 1813, it was returned to the United States under the Treaty of Ghent in 1814.

[Robert W. Bingham, *The Cradle of the Queen City;* Frank H. Severance, *An Old Frontier of France.*]
ROBERT W. BINGHAM

NIAGARA, GREAT INDIAN COUNCIL AT. Sir William Johnson, British superintendent of Indian affairs, in 1764 notified all the rebellious Indian nations of the intended expeditions of the English under Col. John Bradstreet and Col. Henry Bouquet, requesting those desirous of making peace to meet him at Niagara in July. In response, deputations including Ottawa, Huron, Menomini, Chippewa, Iroquois, and others began to arrive at Fort Niagara. By July 9, when the council convened, 2,060 Indians were assembled—the largest number ever gathered together for a peace conference. On July 18 a treaty was concluded with the Huron, by which they ceded lands in their country lying on both sides of the strait to Lake Saint Clair. The Seneca, who arrived later, signed a treaty on Aug. 6, which ceded to the crown the four-mile strip on each side of the Niagara River and gave the islands above the falls to Johnson. The other nations made no formal treaties, declaring they had come only to renew their friendship.

[A. C. Flick, ed., *The Sir William Johnson Papers,* vol. IV.]

ROBERT W. BINGHAM

NIAGARA CAMPAIGNS. On Oct. 13, 1812, Gen. Stephen Van Rensselaer crossed the Niagara River and attacked the British at Queenston, opposite Fort Niagara on the Niagara River, but lack of reinforcements finally caused the Americans to retire. On May

27, 1813, Col. Winfield Scott, assisted by Commodore Isaac Chauncey's fleet, captured Fort George, adjacent to Queenston, and the British abandoned the entire Niagara frontier to the American troops. Gen. George McClure, after destroying Fort George and burning the Canadian village of Newark on Dec. 10, retreated to Fort Niagara. The British captured Fort Niagara on Dec. 19 and burned the villages of Youngstown, Lewiston, and Manchester. Again crossing the river on Dec. 30, they defeated the Americans at Black Rock, burning that settlement and the village of Buffalo. The Americans, under Gen. Jacob Brown and Scott, captured Fort Erie, July 3, 1814, and marching north, defeated the enemy at Chippewa on July 5. After the Battle of Lundy's Lane on July 25, with both sides claiming victory, the Americans withdrew to Fort Erie. The British army under Gordon Drummond arrived before the fortress, Aug. 1, and began a siege that was raised, Sept. 17, by the sortie of Gen. Peter B. Porter's volunteers. This was the last important engagement in the campaigns on the Niagara.

[Louis L. Babcock, *The War of 1812 on the Niagara Frontier.*]

ROBERT W. BINGHAM

NIAGARA COMPANY. Various interests in the Indian lands in central New York, obtained through cooperation with the Phelps-Gorham Company, occasioned Col. John Butler, British commissioner of Indian affairs at Niagara, Canada, to form, with six associates, the Niagara Company in 1788. Each held fourteen shares consisting of 20,000 acres each in the Genesee lands. An investigation by the British authorities caused a relinquishment of the major part of the lands.

[Robert W. Bingham, *The Cradle of the Queen City.*]
ROBERT W. BINGHAM

NIAGARA FALLS. In the Niagara River between lakes Erie and Ontario is a great cataract on the boundary line between the United States and Canada, composed of the American Falls and the Canadian, or Horseshoe, Falls, separated by Goat Island. It rushes over the precipice to descend 167 feet to the lower river. From the head of the upper rapids, which extend one mile above the falls, to the end of the escarpment below, the river has a fall of 314 feet. Recognizing the falls to be a natural source of power, Augustus and Peter B. Porter in 1825 sought to interest eastern capitalists in their development. Their effort in 1847

to interest speculators in the construction of a canal was the beginning of the movement that culminated in 1886 with the formation of the Niagara Falls Power Company.

The first white man to view the cataract and describe it was the Recollect friar Louis Hennepin, who journeyed there in 1678. An obstacle to navigation, it occasioned the famous portage road that was so jealously guarded by both France and England (*see* Niagara, Carrying Place of). It made Fort Niagara the most coveted post in the New World and gave to the nation that held it absolute control of the upper lakes and the great natural resources that abounded in their valleys.

In 1950 the United States and Canada signed the Niagara Diversion Treaty, which provided for a minimum flow over the falls for scenic value and equal division of the rest of the flow between the two countries. The thirteen generators of the Robert Moses Power Plant (completed in 1961) at Lewiston, N.Y., have a capacity of 1.95 million kilowatts, which powers nearby industries and is transmitted to various cities. Power is produced on the Canadian side of the falls by the Sir Adam Beck Generating Stations at Queenston, Ontario. (*See also* Hydroelectric Power.)

[Edward D. Adams, *Niagara Power;* Lloyd Graham, *Niagara Country.*]
ROBERT W. BINGHAM

NIAGARA FALLS, PEACE CONFERENCE AT. *See* **Peace Movement in 1864.**

NIAGARA FALLS POWER. The hydroelectric power installation constructed at Niagara Falls during the 1890's was one of the most impressive and influential engineering achievements of the 19th century. This electrical "wonder of the world" established the superiority of polyphase alternating current to generate and distribute power for a large variety of applications over a sizable geographical area from a single central power station. The project enlisted the skills of many of the world's most eminent scientists and engineers and established the pattern followed in the "superpower" electrical distribution networks of the 20th century. The project stimulated an unanticipated growth in such energy-intensive electrochemical industries as the aluminum and carborundum industries, which soon located in the vicinity because of the availability of huge quantities of inexpensive power.

The installation also became one of the first big engineering projects to precipitate a confrontation between proponents of development and proponents of the preservation of natural beauty. A reflection of this confrontation was the creation of a reservation in the vicinity of the falls by the state of New York in 1885 and an explicit limitation on the amount of water that might be diverted for power generation to 200,000 horsepower by a legislative act in 1892. The federal government became involved through the Burton Act of 1906, which limited the quantity of power that might be brought in from the Canadian side. Similar concerns led the developers to retain a prominent architectural firm to design the powerhouses so that they would be in harmony with the environmental grandeur of the falls.

Niagara Falls was seen as an especially attractive source of power for a number of reasons. It was situated near the most highly populated and industrialized center of the country. The flowrate was very stable because the Great Lakes made an effective reservoir. The potential capacity was more than 6 million horsepower, which meant that if only 5 percent were actually utilized, it would still be an unprecedented supply from a single source.

The first serious proposal to harness the falls on a substantial scale was made by a civil engineer, Thomas Evershed, in 1885. Evershed, who had been employed to survey the newly created state reservation at the falls, proposed a design that would divert enough water through a tunnel to drive a number of mills located outside the reservation. His plan attracted the attention of a group of investment bankers, including J. P. Morgan and Edward D. Adams, who organized the Cataract Construction Company in 1890 to undertake the project. Adams, who was named president of the company, provided dynamic leadership and was perhaps more responsible for its ultimate success than any other individual. Construction of the tunnel began in 1890 and employed more than 1,000 men for about three years.

As part of his effort to obtain the best available technical advice, Adams appointed the five-man International Niagara Commission, headed by the distinguished British scientist-engineer William Thomson, Lord Kelvin. The commission in turn solicited design proposals from leading European and American manufacturing companies and independent consultant engineers. The design of the hydraulic turbines that they eventually accepted was submitted by Paul Piccard of a Swiss company. Because of tariff and transportation cost considerations the turbines were manufactured according to Piccard's design by the I. P. Morris Company of Philadelphia. The final

crucial decision was whether to use pneumatic or electrical means to transmit the power to remote locations, such as Buffalo, which was about twenty miles from the falls. Pneumatic transmission would have used compressed air to drive engines similar to existing steam engines. After an intensive and controversial debate over the merits and defects of pneumatic, direct-current, and alternating-current systems the final decision to adopt the still experimental polyphase system was made in May 1893. The dynamo designs proposed by the two major American firms, Westinghouse and General Electric, were rejected in favor of that of George Forbes, a British consultant hired by Adams. However, the Westinghouse Company was given the contract to manufacture the first three 5,000-horsepower units. These were completed in 1895, although several major changes had to be made in Forbes's original design.

Power was successfully transmitted to Buffalo in 1896, and the ten dynamos planned for use in the first powerhouse were in operation by 1899. The rapid growth in demand because of the electrochemical companies that located near the falls led to the construction of a second powerhouse, using General Electric machines, early in the 20th century. The Niagara Falls power stations were producing approximately one-fifth of the total electrical energy available in the United States in 1902. Additional development of the falls was authorized during World War I, and the total installed capacity of American and Canadian power plants at Niagara Falls reached almost 700,000 horsepower in 1926. Increased transmission voltages, which became standard during the 1920's, enabled Niagara Falls power to be transmitted economically to locations hundreds of miles from the falls and made feasible a superpower zone with interconnected systems throughout the region. A further increase in the quantity of water diverted for power generation was permitted by the Niagara Diversion Treaty between the United States and Canada in 1950. As a result a new plant, with a capacity of 1.95 million kilowatts, was completed in 1961. It was the largest single hydroelectric project in the Western Hemisphere up to that time.

[Edward Dean Adams, *Niagara Power: History of the Niagara Falls Power Company.*]

JAMES E. BRITTAIN

NIAGARA MOVEMENT, a black movement composed mainly of intellectuals and professionals, organized in 1905 under the leadership of W. E. B.

Du Bois and William Monroe Trotter for the purpose of initiating aggressive action to secure full citizens rights for black Americans. Its name came from the location of the organizational meeting in Niagara Falls, Ontario, Canada, to which Du Bois and his colleagues had gone after having been refused accommodations on the U.S. side of the border. The movement reflected the opposition among blacks both to the patterns of racial discrimination that had become standard practice in all parts of the country and to the accommodation and gradualism advocated by Booker T. Washington. It placed responsibility for the status of U.S. race relations on the attitudes and actions of whites and declared that blacks would be satisfied with nothing less than full civil rights. It called for the abolition of all legal distinctions based on race and color.

In 1906 the movement held its first national meeting at Harpers Ferry, W.Va., where it issued to the nation a strongly worded proclamation: "We claim for ourselves every right that belongs to freeborn Americans—political, civil and social. . . . We want full manhood suffrage, and we want it now, henceforth and forever." Among those attending the meeting were relatives of blacks who died in support of the abolitionist John Brown and a son of Frederick Douglass.

The selection of Harpers Ferry as the meeting place and the strength of its statements caused the Niagara movement to be viewed as radical and caused some black intellectuals and professionals to refuse to associate themselves with it. Strongly opposed to the movement was Booker T. Washington of Tuskegee Institute in Alabama, who because of his influence on the distribution of philanthropic gifts to education and on the appointment of blacks to government jobs was the strongest force in the black community of the nation. Washington's opposition, along with a split that developed between Du Bois and Trotter, weakened the movement to the point of ineffectiveness within a few years. In 1909, Du Bois and other blacks from the Niagara movement joined with a group of white liberals in the formation of the National Association for the Advancement of Colored People (NAACP).

The Niagara movement accomplished little during its brief history. Its importance lay in its outspoken opposition to Jim Crow laws, reflecting the dissatisfaction of Afro-Americans with their condition in the United States, and in its articulation of a position contrary to that of Washington. Coming as it did in the Progressive period, it revealed the lack of support for reform in race relations among white Progressive

leaders. It is important also as a forerunner of the NAACP.

[Francis L. Broderick, *W. E. B. Du Bois: Negro Leader in a Time of Crisis;* Stephen R. Fox, *The Guardian of Boston: William Monroe Trotter;* Elliott M. Rudwick, "The Niagara Movement," *Journal of Negro History,* vol. 42 (1957).]

HENRY N. DREWRY

NIAGARA SUSPENSION BRIDGES. Proposed 1844, chartered 1846, the first bridge over the Niagara Gorge was started by flying kites at the Whirlpool Rapids. A footbridge was completed in 1848, and the railroad bridge was finished by John A. Roebling in 1855. It was replaced in 1897 by a double-deck steel bridge, for railroad above and road below. The 10-foot-wide Upper Falls Bridge, or Falls View, begun during the winter 1867–68 by rope carried over the ice bridge, was opened in 1869. In 1887–88 wood was replaced by steel and the bridge widened, but it was blown down by a hurricane in 1889. The new steel bridge lasted from 1889 to 1897, when it was replaced by a steel arch bridge, crushed by ice in 1938. A new concrete bridge, the Rainbow Bridge, was authorized in 1939 and completed in 1941. The Lewiston suspension bridge, built 1850–51, lasted until 1861 and was replaced in 1899 by a suspension bridge.

AUGUSTUS H. SHEARER

NIBLO'S GARDEN, a famous 19th-century coffeehouse and theater on lower Broadway in New York City. Operas, concerts, and plays were presented there for several decades beginning in 1824. In 1866 Charles M. Barras' *The Black Crook* was first presented there—considered by some the first performance of the first American musical. Niblo's Garden was destroyed by fire in 1846, but it was rebuilt, and the new theater opened in 1849. It burned again in 1872, was rebuilt, and transformed into a concert hall. It was finally demolish in 1895.

[I. N. Phelps Stokes, *The Iconography of Manhattan Island.*]

ALVIN F. HARLOW

NICARAGUA, RELATIONS WITH, began officially eleven years after Nicaragua's separation from the Central American federation in 1838. Ephraim George Squier negotiated a first, unratified pact of friendship between Nicaragua and the United States in 1849. Attempts to ratify a pact in 1854, 1855, 1857, and 1859 also failed, but a successful treaty of amity, navigation, and commerce was signed in 1867. In the meantime, Nicaragua extended charters to the American Atlantic and Pacific Ship Canal Company in 1849, to the Accessory Transit Company in 1851, and to the Central American Transit Company in 1864, all three firms financed by U.S. money. The canal company failed, and the two transit companies were terminated in 1856 and 1868, respectively. Filibuster William Walker of Tennessee, who made himself president of Nicaragua in 1856–57, helped to bring an end to the enterprise of the Accessory Transit Company. The United States signed a treaty in 1884 promising an American-built canal in Nicaragua, but the U.S. Senate defeated its ratification by one vote. The Maritime Canal Company of Nicaragua, incorporated in 1889, labored unsuccessfully on the canal and had its concession canceled in 1898.

The 1903 decision to build the Panama Canal led the U.S. government to intervene in Central American affairs. The regime of José Santos Zelaya in Nicaragua (1893–1909) seemed a threat to Central American peace pacts drawn in Washington in 1907. The U.S. government showed sympathy for an anti-Zelaya rebellion that began in October 1909, and it refused to recognize Zelaya's successor, José Madriz (1909–10). The rebels quarreled among themselves after occupying Managua, the capital, in August 1910. The United States backed conservative Adolfo Díaz for the presidency (May 1911 to January 1917) and with him concluded arrangements for New York bankers to lend money to Nicaragua and to control Nicaragua's customs collections, national bank, and national railroad until the loans were repaid. When the position of Díaz was threatened, U.S. marines were deployed along the railroad in September 1912. The Bryan-Chamorro Treaty, establishing an intimate relationship between the two countries, was ratified in 1916. One hundred marines remained as a legation guard, while the U.S. government chose conservative successors to Díaz in 1917 and 1921. The loans were repaid in 1924, and the marines withdrew in August 1925.

A Nicaraguan civil war brought a second landing of U.S. marines, in greater numbers than before. They disembarked on Nicaragua's east coast in December 1926 and on its west coast in January 1927. Henry L. Stimson visited Nicaragua and secured agreement that Díaz would again serve as president until January 1929 but that his successor should be chosen in free elections supervised by the United States and that the marines would organize and train an efficient constabulary.

Under these terms, two liberal generals were elected to the presidency, José María Moncada (1929–33) and Juan Bautista Sacasa (1933–36). Nevertheless, another liberal general, Augusto César Sandino, fought against the marines and the new constabulary until the marines withdrew when Sacasa was inaugurated.

The head of the Nicaraguan constabulary, Anastasio Somoza García, arranged the murder of Sandino in February 1934, the resignation of Sacasa from the presidency in June 1936, and his own election to the presidency in December 1936. The Somoza family (father and two sons) continued to control Nicaragua into the 1970's, obtaining special favors from, and granting special favors to, the U.S. government. Notable examples of close cooperation between the two governments came at the time of the Guatemalan coup of 1954 and the Bay of Pigs invasion in Cuba in 1961.

[David I. Folkman, Jr., *The Nicaragua Route;* William Kamman, *A Search for Stability: United States Diplomacy Toward Nicaragua, 1925–1933;* Dana G. Munro, *Intervention and Dollar Diplomacy in the Caribbean, 1900–1921.*]

FRANKLIN D. PARKER

NICARAGUAN CANAL PROJECT. The idea of a waterway along the San Juan River and Lake Nicaragua to connect the Atlantic and Pacific oceans has long been considered. A Spanish engineer first surveyed the route in the 18th century. Independent Central America was interested, and Napoleon III considered the project. The route was the object of six treaties between the United States and Nicaragua during the 19th century, as well as of a treaty and an arbitration between Nicaragua and Costa Rica. England had claims that were considered in the negotiation of the Clayton-Bulwer (1850) and Hay-Pauncefote (1901) treaties. The Nicaraguan Canal Association, an American corporation, made a contract with Nicaragua in 1887 to build a canal, and the Maritime Canal Company was formed to carry it out. After a survey construction was undertaken, but it was suspended when funds could not be secured. The U.S. government in 1895 began investigations and received a favorable report on the project from the Ludlow Commission. In 1897–99 the Isthmian Canal Commission made a complete survey and report. By the Hay-Corea (1900) and the Sanchez-Merry (1901) protocols with Nicaragua and the Hay-Calvo protocol with Costa Rica (1900) steps were taken by the United States toward a Nicaraguan canal. Political considerations and other factors resulted in the adoption of the Panama route (*see* Panama Canal), and the Nicaraguan project was postponed. Nevertheless, it played an important part in the relations between the United States and Nicaragua after 1910. The Bryan-Chamorro Treaty, signed in 1914, gave the United States an option on the route. A new survey of the Nicaraguan route by army engineers was authorized by Congress on Mar. 2, 1929. The report, made in 1931, was favorable to a Nicaraguan canal whenever the Panama Canal should become inadequate.

[William Kamman, *A Search for Stability: United States Diplomacy Toward Nicaragua, 1925–1933.*]

ROSCOE R. HILL

NICKEL. *See* **Nonferrous Metals.**

NICOLET, EXPLORATIONS OF. The personal explorations of Samuel de Champlain terminated with his voyage to Georgian Bay and Huronia in 1615–16. Soon thereafter he adopted the policy of selecting promising youths to send among the Indians, to master, by such residence, the lore of the American wilderness.

Jean Nicolet, a native of Cherbourg, France, came to Canada in 1618 at about the age of twenty and was immediately sent by Champlain to Allumette Island in the Ottawa River, about seventy-five miles northwest of present-day Ottawa. After a two-year apprenticeship there he was assigned to the Nipissing living northward of the lake that bears their name. Here he remained several years, sharing the life of the Nipissing and keeping, for Champlain's benefit, a careful memoir of his observations. In 1633 he was called back and appointed interpreter at Three Rivers, about seventy-five miles northeast of present-day Montreal. From there, the following year, he was dispatched in search of the "People of the Sea," who were at war with the Huron, and who were surmised to have some connection with the realm of Tartary, which Marco Polo had described.

No direct record of Nicolet's voyage remains. Chiefly from contemporary Jesuit reports it is known that he journeyed by the Ottawa River north to Georgian Bay, passed through the Straits of Mackinac, and skirted the coast of Lake Michigan as far as Green Bay. Thereby he became the first known white visitor to Michigan and Wisconsin and the discoverer of Lake Michigan. On this achievement his fame chiefly rests. From the scanty contemporary sources, several modern historians have spun tales of the voyage that are largely fanciful.

[M. M. Quaife, *Wisconsin: Its History and Its People;* R. G. Thwaites, ed., *The Jesuit Relations,* vols. XVIII, XXIII.]

M. M. QUAIFE

NICOLLS' COMMISSION. In 1664 Charles II, determined to seize New Netherland, granted that site and adjacent lands to his brother James, Duke of York, who, in anticipation of the conquest, named Col. Richard Nicolls governor. The king provided a fleet and troops and named Nicolls head of a commission of four to visit New England and to investigate boundary disputes, state of defenses, laws passed during the Puritan revolution, attitude toward the new acts of trade, and in general the religious, economic, and political conditions. As they moved from place to place, the commissioners were to hear complaints and appeals and to make such decisions as to them seemed necessary. Their private instructions enlarged upon these powers and objectives and cautioned them to make it clear that the king had no intention of altering church government in the colonies in any way or of introducing any other form of worship there, but that he insisted on the freedom of conscience required by charter and denied to many people by the governments of the New England colonies. The king also enjoined the commissioners to endeavor to persuade those colonies to consent to the king's nominating or approving of their governors and appointing or recommending the chief officer of their militia. Although courteously received in southern New England, the commissioners met with difficulties in Massachusetts and opposition at every turn. In their final report they not only listed irregularities of all kinds as occurring in Massachusetts but also described an arrogant and defiant attitude that promised little hope of a friendly and peaceable settlement of the administration of a colonial policy in New England.

[J. R. Brodhead, *Documents Relative to the Colonial History of New York,* vol. III; H. L. Osgood, *The American Colonies in the Seventeenth Century,* vol. III.]

VIOLA F. BARNES

"NIGGER," a term of contempt used in reference to black Americans or to any dark-skinned peoples. During the late 1960's some militant Afro-American leaders of the civil rights movement either stressed the irrelevance of the word in the context of black pride or used its negative implications satirically.

In the Afro-American literature of that period, the word was used more openly by black characters in dialogue with other black characters than by white characters. Ed Bullins' play *The Electronic Nigger* attacked the pompous pseudointellectual in accord with the didactic purpose of black drama. Earlier use of the word by white authors occurred in Joseph Conrad's sea story *The Nigger of the "Narcissus"* (1897); Edward Sheldon's play *The Nigger* (1909), dealing with miscegenation; and Carl Van Vechten's novel *Nigger Heaven* (1926).

Many derivatives exist, such as niggertoe (Brazil nut) and niggerhead (a boulder with nodules). In some areas of the South the enunciation of "negro" is shortened to "nigra," creating a hybrid word with a blurred connotation. Ossie Davis, the black playwright and actor, writing in the *American Teacher* (April 1967), indicated that the English language was his enemy. He discussed the negative connotation of 60 of the 120 synonyms for the word "blackness" ("nigger" among them) in Roget's *International Thesaurus,* noting that not only black children but also white children received a skewed education in this "trap of racial prejudgment." He claimed that Roget lists 134 synonyms for whiteness, 44 of which are positive. His thesis is that words have power over attitudes and behavior, and he concludes that the weight of negative implication of words delineating blackness "teaches" denigration of blackness. Such continuing attention to the study of language and ethnicity and the reaction to political demands have served to decrease the public use of racial epithets and to increase attention to their psychological impact.

[Ossie Davis, *The Language Is My Enemy;* Arthur L. Smith, ed., *Language, Communication, and Rhetoric in Black America.*]

CECELIA HODGES DREWRY

NIGHT RIDERS, or the Silent Brigade, were armed bands who made war against monopolistic tobacco companies in Kentucky and Tennessee and attacked the tobacco farmers who refused to cooperate in the organized effort to break through the abusive control of the trust. They were publicly denounced, but perhaps secretly encouraged, by the leaders of the association—and hundreds of farmers who refused to join had their barns burned or crops destroyed.

After sporadic beginnings about 1903, their activities reached a peak during the Black Patch War of 1906–09, in southwest Kentucky and northern Tennessee. Large bands of armed, mounted men made successful raids on market towns, burning the warehouses of the tobacco trust at Russellville, Elkton,

Princeton, and Hopkinsville, Ky. Judges and juries were influenced or intimidated to prevent convictions.

After 1908, with the backing of Gov. Augustus E. Willson, several night riders were punished and others sued successfully in the federal courts. Although the tobacco cooperatives succeeded in raising prices, the criminal activities of some of their members caused the disbandment of the organizations between 1909 and 1921.

[J. O. Nall, *The Tobacco Night Riders.*]

W. C. MALLALIEU

NILES' WEEKLY REGISTER, a tabloid-size newspaper without pictures, founded in September 1811 at Baltimore by Hezekiah Niles. It was made up largely of extracts from other newspapers from all over the country. The aim was to provide an impartial chronicle of passing events, with a minimum of editorial opinion. It had a national circulation, was contemporarily respected and much quoted, and has since become popular with historians as source material. In 1837 its name was changed to *Niles' National Register,* which continued in publication until June 1849. The entire series has been reprinted in seventy-five volumes.

[James Melvin Lee, *History of American Journalism.*]

CULVER H. SMITH

NINE-POWER PACT, between the United States, Belgium, the British Empire, China, France, Italy, Japan, the Netherlands, and Portugal, was concluded at the Washington Naval Conference on Feb. 6, 1922. Japan's "Twenty-one Demands" on China in 1915 and the Japanese "Monroe Doctrine" had created a delicate international situation impairing the territorial integrity of China and endangering the Open Door principle.

In order to stabilize conditions in the Far East and to safeguard the rights and interests of China, the powers agreed to respect its sovereignty, independence, and territorial and administrative integrity; maintain the principle of the Open Door; and refrain from seeking special rights or privileges for their own citizens. The pact was an international guarantee of the Open Door and China's integrity and effected the cancellation of the Lansing-Ishii Agreement of 1917.

Completely disregarding the treaty, Japan, in 1931, seized Manchuria. Protesting, the United States proclaimed the Stimson nonrecognition doctrine in 1932. Following Japan's invasion of China in 1937, the

Brussels Conference (November 1937) censured Japan and reaffirmed the principles of the pact. Refusing to recognize Japan's "special position" in China, the United States in July 1939 notified Japan of its intention to terminate, at the end of six months, the Treaty of Commerce and Navigation of 1911.

[Norman D. Davis, *Europe and the East;* H. B. Morse and H. F. MacNair, *Far Eastern International Relations.*]
GLENN H. BENTON

NINETEENTH AMENDMENT. The movement for the enactment of the Nineteenth Amendment of the U.S. Constitution, which gave women the vote, began at the Seneca Falls Convention of 1848, when, on the insistence of Elizabeth Cady Stanton, a resolution was adopted declaring "that it is the duty of the women of this country to secure to themselves their sacred right to the elective franchise." Following the Civil War continuous work began for adoption of an amendment to the Constitution stating that "The right of citizens of the United States to vote shall not be denied or abridged by the United States or by any state on account of sex."

On Jan. 9, 1918, President Woodrow Wilson came out in favor of the amendment, and the next day the House of Representatives passed it; but the Senate failed to act before the congressional session ended. In May 1919, soon after the Sixty-sixth Congress met, the House again acted favorably, and in June 1919 the Senate gave approval. Wisconsin, the first state to ratify, acted June 10, 1919. On Aug. 26, 1920, Tennessee cast the decisive favorable vote, the thirty-sixth, making the measure part of the law of the land.

[E. C. Stanton, S. B. Anthony, M. J. Gage, I. H. Harper, eds., *The History of Woman Suffrage.*]
MARY WILHELMINE WILLIAMS

NINETY-SIX, a village in western South Carolina and a British fortified post during the revolutionary war, was besieged by the Americans under Gen. Nathanael Greene for twenty-eight days in May and June 1781. A desperate assault on June 17 failed, and the approach of Gen. Francis Rawdon-Hastings with 2,000 British soldiers forced Greene, who had only 1,000 men, to raise the siege on June 19. But the post was too far inland for Rawdon to hold, and he abandoned it June 29 and retired toward the coast.

[G. W. Greene, *Life of Major-General Nathanael Greene.*]
ALVIN F. HARLOW

"NINETY-TWO" AND "FORTY-FIVE" were political catchwords first used together in 1768. "Forty-five" referred to No. 45 of John Wilkes's newspaper *North Briton,* published in London, Apr. 23, 1763, which involved its publisher in a battle for the freedom of the press. "Ninety-two" was the number of the members of the Massachusetts Assembly who refused, June 30, 1768, to rescind the Massachusetts Circular Letter of Feb. 11, 1768, against the suppression of colonial liberties. A favorite toast became: "May the unrescinding ninety-two be forever united in idea with the glorious forty-five." These numbers were combined in great variety in the colonies before the Revolution.

[R. Frothingham, *The Rise of the Republic of the United States.*]
STANLEY R. PILLSBURY

NISQUALLY, FORT, ATTACK ON (May 1849). Established in 1833 on Puget Sound just north of Fort Vancouver, Fort Nisqually developed into an agricultural, commercial, and protective center. In May 1849, angered by the Oregon territorial government, the Snoquamish tried to capture it but failed. The defenders appealed to Gov. Joseph Lane, who sent the entire territorial army, consisting of a lieutenant and five men. The arrival from Honolulu of a steamer carrying two companies of artillery saved the day for the settlers in the area of Puget Sound.

[H. H. Bancroft, *History of Oregon;* Charles Wilkes, *Narrative of the United States Exploring Expedition.*]
ROBERT S. THOMAS

NITRATES. The element nitrogen, of which four-fifths of the atmosphere is composed, plays an important and complex role in nature. It is relatively inert in the atmosphere, but it is converted by lightning and radiation in the stratosphere, and above all by terrestrial microorganisms, into active compounds, the nitrates. Best known are potassium nitrate (saltpeter) and sodium nitrate. Potassium nitrate is associated with animal decay and was long obtained by sweeping up the earth around stables and human habitations. Sodium nitrate has occasionally been found, for reasons that are still mysterious, in a few mineral deposits, notably in Chile, whence its common name, Chile nitrate.

Man's interest in the nitrates stems from the invention of gunpowder, which is composed of about four-fifths saltpeter and one-fifth charcoal and sulfur. Possibly a Chinese or Indian invention, gunpowder became known in Europe about 1300, from which time the demand for it increased continually.

Saltpeter was already in short supply when North America was first settled, and in 1608 the settlers at Jamestown were enjoined to collect it. A succession of schemes failed to offset the fact that the climate of the British colonies, like that of Europe, was not conducive to the accumulation of saltpeter, and most of that which supplied the numerous European armies came from India. When the American Revolution cut off the colonies from this source, most of the colonial governments offered bounties for saltpeter, and some established "artificial nitrate works" where it was hoped (without much justification) to imitate nature in its production. The Continental army was saved from running out of gunpowder only by the French, who, faced with British control of Indian sources, had succeeded, by tremendous efforts, in developing a domestic supply.

In the first decade of the 19th century, saltpeter was found in large quantities in the caves of Kentucky and Tennessee—the Mammoth Cave in Kentucky, for one. Because of the animals that had lived there, the soil in these caves sometimes yielded 50 percent saltpeter. This supply was exploited throughout the American Civil War, when it was used by the Confederate armies—although 90 percent of their powder seems to have come through the blockade. Thereafter the United States obtained its nitrates from Chile—as did most of Europe—since a process had been developed in Europe for converting sodium nitrate into potassium nitrate.

The use of nitrates as fertilizers increased in importance in the 19th century, and an additional source was found in ammonia, a by-product of the coke oven. But this and other sources remained inadequate to meet an ever-increasing demand. By 1910 several processes had been developed in Europe to convert atmospheric nitrogen into the more active nitrate form. All were expensive and complex, and their development was restricted to countries without easy access to the Chile nitrate beds, notably Germany, which by 1900 was the world leader in chemical technology. At the outbreak of World War I it was not known which of several processes was most promising. The United States, although supplied by Chile, was concerned enough by 1917 to try several of the synthetic processes—notably the cyanamide process, in which atmospheric nitrogen is reacted with calcium carbide. As part of the effort to make nitrates synthetically, a dam was built at Muscle Shoals, Ala., on the Tennessee River, to produce the large quantities of hydroelectric power required. The American synthetic nitrate works were still only experimental when the war ended, and by then it had become clear that the most efficient method of nitrogen fixation (the conversion of atmospheric nitrogen to active nitrate) was the Haber process, introduced in Germany in 1912 by Fritz Haber. This process, in which nitrogen is reacted with hydrogen at high pressure, has since come to supply most of the world's nitrate requirements. It does not require large amounts of electric power, and the Muscle Shoals Dam became in the 1930's the basis of a regional electric-power system, the Tennessee Valley Authority.

Although nitrates have many uses, the predominating use by far continues to be in fertilizers.

[H. J. M. Creighton, "How the Nitrogen Problem Has Been Solved," *Journal of the Franklin Institute*, vol. 187 (1919); R. N. Maxon, "The Nitre Caves of Kentucky," *Journal of Chemical Education*, vol. 9 (1932); G. W. Rains, *History of the Confederate Powder Works*; O. W. Stephenson, "The Supply of Gunpowder in 1778," *American Historical Review*, vol. 30 (1925).]

ROBERT P. MULTHAUF

NIXON, RESIGNATION OF. On Aug. 9, 1974, in a letter delivered to Secretary of State Henry Kissinger at 11:35 A.M., President Richard M. Nixon wrote, "I hereby resign the office of President of the United States." He thus became the first president ever to do so. On the preceding evening, Nixon announced his decision in an address to the nation, and spoke regretfully of any "injuries" committed "in the course of events that led" to it. Nixon noted the painfulness of his decision: "I have never been a quitter. To leave office before my term is completed is opposed to every instinct in my body. But as president I must put the interests of America first."

On the morning of Aug. 9, Nixon bade an emotional, sometimes tearful, farewell to his cabinet and White House staff. He then flew home to California, where he had begun his political career. With Mrs. Nixon, their daughter Tricia, and her husband, Edward F. Cox, the outgoing president landed at El Toro Marine Base and was taken by helicopter to La Casa Pacifica, his seaside villa near San Clemente.

At the moment that Nixon's letter of resignation was handed to the secretary of state, Vice-President Gerald R. Ford assumed the powers of the president, and slightly more than half an hour later he took the oath of office. In his address, President Ford expressed prayerfully the hope, "May our former president, who brought peace to millions, find it for himself."

Nixon's resignation was rooted in the Watergate and other scandals that plagued his second term and eroded the political strength derived from his overwhelming reelection in 1972. Two late-hour events forced Nixon to resign. In late July 1974 the House Judiciary Committee adopted three articles of impeachment, delineating many specific charges against the president. Less than a week earlier, on July 24, the Supreme Court, in an 8–0 decision, had ruled, in *United States* v. *Nixon,* that he must provide quantities of tapes of White House conversations required in the criminal trials of his former subordinates. The tapes disclosed that Nixon had participated as early as June 23, 1972, in the cover-up of the Watergate burglary, thus contradicting his previous denials. His remaining congressional and public support swiftly collapsed and made his impeachment a certainty. Its course was halted by his resignation.

Nixon took the step after Republican Sen. Barry Goldwater of Arizona disclosed that no more than fifteen votes existed in the Senate against impeachment, far short of the thirty-four necessary if Nixon hoped to escape conviction. White House Chief of Staff Alexander M. Haig, Jr., and Kissinger urged Nixon to step down in the national interest.

By resigning, Nixon avoided the disgrace implicit in a successful impeachment, and he preserved the pension rights and other perquisites of a former president that would have been lost. In impeachment, the Senate would have rendered an authoritative judgment concerning Nixon's conduct. By resigning, he would be able to characterize his presidency himself in terms that were minimally culpable. He acknowledged only that "if some of my judgments were wrong—and some were wrong—they were made in what I believed at the time to be in the best interests of the nation."

On Sept. 8, 1974, President Ford pardoned Nixon for all federal crimes that he "committed or may have committed or taken part in" while in office. The pardoning of the former president prior to his possible indictment, trial, and conviction, although supported by a U.S. Supreme Court ruling in *Ex parte Garland,* 4 Wallace 333 (1867), provoked criticism that the pardon was a cover-up of Nixon's cover-up of Watergate.

LOUIS W. KOENIG

NOBEL PRIZES have stood as the cachet of international recognition and achievement in the areas of physics, chemistry, physiology or medicine, literature, and peace since their inception in 1901. (Awards in economics were established in 1969.) But Americans were slow to be recognized by the various Nobel Prize committees. During the first decade of the awards, only three prizes were awarded to Americans. The first was to Theodore Roosevelt, who received the Peace Prize in 1906. In the second decade, only four awards were given to Americans. But in later decades the number of prizes claimed by Americans (either born or naturalized citizens) grew remarkably. This increase was in part the result of the large number of scientists who fled from Europe to the United States during the rise of Nazi Germany.

In all, by 1974 thirty-two U.S. citizens had won (or shared) twenty-three awards in physics. Fifteen prizes had gone to twenty Americans in chemistry. The United States won its greatest number of prizes in the area of physiology or medicine, receiving twenty-five prizes among forty-three recipients. Only six writers had won the Nobel Prize in the field of literature, the most elusive prize category for Americans. The Peace Prize had been awarded to sixteen Americans, who received or shared fourteen prizes. The American Friends Service Committee shared this prize in 1947. The prize in economics, awarded by the Central Bank of Sweden, had been won four times by as many Americans.

In the area of economics, Americans won or shared 66.6 percent of all awards; in peace, 25.5 percent; in literature, 8.9 percent; in physiology or medicine, 38.5 percent; in chemistry, 22.7 percent; and in physics, 33.8 percent.

Unique among American prizewinners is Linus Carl Pauling, who won awards in two different fields, chemistry (1954) and peace (1962). Marie Curie is the only other prizewinner to have this distinction. The American physicist John Bardeen is the only American to have shared two prizes in the same field, physics (1956, 1972). Noteworthy is the fact that no American has ever declined an award. One hundred twenty-one Americans have won the Nobel Prize, 116 men and 5 women. U.S. citizens have won or shared 26.6 percent of all awards granted.

American winners of the Nobel Prize, which in 1974 amounted to $124,000, are listed below.

Economics: Paul A. Samuelson (1970); Simon S. Kuznets (1971); Kenneth J. Arrow (1972); Wassily Leontief (1973).

Literature: Sinclair Lewis (1930); Eugene O'Neill (1936); Pearl Buck (1938); William Faulkner (1949); Ernest Hemingway (1954); John Steinbeck (1962).

Chemistry: Theodore Richards (1914); Irving Langmuir (1932); Harold Urey (1934); James Sumner, John Northrop, Wendell Stanley (1946); William

Giauque (1949); Edwin McMillan, Glenn Seaborg (1951); Linus Carl Pauling (1954); Vincent Du Vigneaud (1955); Willard Libby (1960); Melvin Calvin (1961); Robert B. Woodward (1965); Robert S. Mulliken (1966); Lars Onsager (1968); Christian B. Anfinsen, Stanford Moore, William H. Stein (1972); Paul J. Flory (1974).

Peace: Theodore Roosevelt (1906); Elihu Root (1912); Woodrow Wilson (1919); Charles G. Dawes (1925); Frank B. Kellogg (1929); Jane Addams, Nicholas M. Butler (1931); Cordell Hull (1945); Emily G. Balch, John R. Mott (1946); American Friends Service Committee (1947); Ralph Bunche (1950); George C. Marshall (1953); Linus Carl Pauling (1962); Martin Luther King, Jr. (1964); Norman E. Borlaug (1970); Henry Kissinger (1973).

Physics: A. A. Michelson (1907); Robert A. Millikan (1923); Arthur Holly Compton (1927); Carl Anderson (1936); Clinton Davisson (1937); Ernest Lawrence (1939); Otto Stern (1943); Isidor Rabi (1944); Percy Bridgman (1946); Felix Bloch, Edward Purcell (1952); Willis Lamb, Jr., Polykarp Kusch (1955); William Shockley, John Bardeen, Walter Brattain (1956); Emilio Segrè, Owen Chamberlain (1959); Donald Glaser (1960); Robert Hofstadter (1961); Maria Goeppert-Mayer, Eugene P. Wigner (1963); Charles H. Townes (1964); Julian S. Schwinger, Richard P. Feynman (1965); Hans A. Bethe (1967); Luis W. Alvarez (1968); Murray Gell-Mann (1969); John Bardeen, Leon N. Cooper, John Schrieffer (1972); Ivar Giaever (1973).

Physiology or Medicine: Karl Landsteiner (1930); Thomas Hunt Morgan (1933); George R. Minot, William P. Murphy, George H. Whipple (1934); Edward Doisy (1943); Joseph Erlanger, Herbert S. Gasser (1944); Hermann J. Muller (1946); Carl and Gerty Cori (1947); Philip S. Hench, Edward C. Kendall (1950); Selman A. Waksman (1952); Fritz A. Lipmann (1953); John F. Enders, Thomas H. Weller, Frederick Robbins (1954); Dickinson W. Richards, André F. Cournand (1956); George W. Beadle, Edward L. Tatum, Joshua Lederberg (1958); Severo Ochoa, Arthur Kornberg (1959); Georg von Békésy (1961); James D. Watson (1962); Konrad Bloch (1964); Charles Huggins, Francis Peyton Rous (1966); Haldan K. Hartline, George Wald (1967); Robert W. Holley, H. Gobind Khorana, Marshall W. Nirenberg (1968); Max Delbruck, Alfred D. Hershey, Salvador E. Luria (1969); Julius Axelrod (1970); Earl W. Sutherland, Jr. (1971); Gerald M. Edelman (1972); Albert Claude, George E. Palade (1974).

LYLE CHURCHILL

NOBILITY, TITLES OF. Although sundry traces of feudalism appear in American colonial law and governmental practice and although British peerage and gentry played an important part in the founding and development of the thirteen colonies, conditions did not favor the establishment of a titled aristocracy. John Locke's fantastic scheme for granting titles of nobility in the Carolinas (1669) came to nothing (see Carolina, Fundamental Constitutions of). Few colonials were honored. William Phips, born in Maine, was knighted in 1687; William Pepperell, of the same region, was made a baronet in 1746; and William Johnson, of New York, received the same honor in 1755. The Revolution definitely committed the country to a republican system, and the Constitution, in Article I, Sections 9 and 10, prohibits the conferring of titles of nobility by either the United States or the states. Federal officials are likewise forbidden to accept titles from foreign states except with consent of the Congress. Federalist leaders were constantly charged with "aristocratic" leanings, but while frankly supporting the idea that the wise, the good, and the rich should dominate, they relied on restricted suffrage and natural influence to maintain their status.

[Broadus and Louise P. Mitchell, *A Biography of the Constitution of the United States: Its Origin, Formation, Adoption, Interpretation.*]

W. A. ROBINSON

NODDLES ISLAND SKIRMISH. On May 27, 1775, a band of colonials crossed to Noddles Island (now East Boston) to drive off livestock and secure fodder. There they battled a British marine guard, killing two and wounding two. After securing some of the livestock and firing several buildings and a quantity of hay, the colonials departed before British reinforcements from the fleet could land.

[Henry B. Dawson, *Battles of the United States by Sea and Land.*]

ROBERT S. THOMAS

NOGALES, TREATY OF. In the spring of 1792, complying with the Spanish plan of reorganizing and strengthening the defense of Louisiana, Manuel Gayoso de Lemos, commandant at Natchez, negotiated a treaty with the Choctaw and Chickasaw validating the Spanish seizure of Walnut Hills, the site of present-day Vicksburg, Miss., where Fort Nogales was erected. Thereafter Spanish officials began building a system of Indian alliances to support the military defense of the Mississippi. The capstone of this policy (see Chickasaw-Creek War) was the Treaty of Nogales, Oct. 28, 1793, negotiated with the Creek (who were induced to repudiate the Treaty of New York), Choctaw, Chickasaw, and Cherokee. This treaty reaffirmed the alliance and commerce treaties of 1784 and the reciprocal offensive-defensive alliance. The Indians agreed to defend Louisiana and Florida against attack and invoked Spanish assistance in securing boundary settlements with the United States. Annual supplies and presents were to be delivered to the Indians, and Spain guaranteed protection "in all cases in which they may need it." By inciting the Indians to burn and ravage the American settlements from Georgia to the Mississippi, the Spanish authorities hoped to compel the United States to respect Indian lands and thus create a barrier that would protect Louisiana. The United States protested this policy but received only evasive promises of correction. Meanwhile, Spanish authorities at New Orleans continued to stir the Indians to action and renewed separatist negotiations with the Kentuckians (see Spanish Conspiracy). Intrigue, uncertainty, and occasional Indian depredations continued until ended by Pinckney's Treaty of 1795, which provided for a new southern boundary and the Spanish evacuation of the posts on the Mississippi (see Guion's Expedition).

[S. F. Bemis, *Pinckney's Treaty*; Charles Gayarré, *History of Louisiana: Spanish Domination*.]

THOMAS ROBSON HAY

NOLAN, EXPEDITIONS OF. At least four expeditions into Texas were made by Philip Nolan, an American trader and filibuster from Kentucky. On the first expedition, 1792–94, he gathered and sold skins and drove a herd of horses to Louisiana. He made a second expedition to San Antonio, 1794–96. Through connivance with local Spanish officials he brought back 250 horses, which he sold in Natchez (then part of Louisiana) and in Kentucky.

Returning to Texas from Kentucky, Nolan met Andrew Ellicott going to Natchez to begin surveying the southern boundary. In 1797, protected by a Spanish passport, Nolan penetrated into Texas as far as the Rio Grande, returning with some 1,300 horses. When he proposed a fourth expedition, he was refused a passport and Spanish officials were warned to arrest him on sight, but he returned in 1798. In a skirmish near the present Waco, Tex., with a Spanish detachment sent from Nacogdoches, Nolan was killed, Mar. 21, 1801.

THOMAS ROBSON HAY

NO MAN'S LAND. *See* **Cimarron, Proposed Territory of.**

NOMINATING SYSTEM. In the operation of the American representative system of government some method of nominating candidates for the various offices is essential. To meet this need three chief methods have been devised: the caucus system, which prevailed prior to 1824; the convention system, which became the chief method about 1830; and the direct primary system, which was introduced in 1903.

Originated early in the 18th century, in connection with local elections, the caucus system was later adapted to the nomination of governors and other state officers. Members of the legislature belonging to the same party would meet to recommend candidates. The next development was the congressional caucus, wherein members of Congress having the same party affiliation would assemble for the purpose of recommending presidential and vice-presidential candidates. Used first in 1800, the congressional caucus functioned for the last time in the campaign of 1824. In a country that was becoming increasingly democratic, it was denounced as being out of tune with the times.

Meanwhile there was developing in the states the delegate convention system. Delaware took the lead in setting up a convention during the administration of President Thomas Jefferson. By 1830 state conventions prevailed everywhere except in the South.

Before the system was adapted to the national scene, there was a period of transition from the congressional caucus. In the campaign of 1824 William H. Crawford received the nomination of the Republican congressional caucus, but three of the presidential candidates, John Quincy Adams, Henry Clay, and Andrew Jackson, were nominated more informally by mass meetings, by newspapers, or by state legislative caucuses. In the next campaign, both Adams and Jackson were nominated by similar methods.

In 1831 the Anti-Masonic party, after a preliminary convention held in the previous year, inaugurated the national nominating convention. The National Republicans and the Democrats followed the example, with the result that the national nominating convention became the accepted method of nominating party candidates for the presidency and vice-presidency, while state conventions controlled the selection of candidates for state offices.

From the beginning the convention system was subjected to much severe criticism. As the years passed, the conviction grew that party conventions were so easily controlled by political bosses that their selections were not representative of the will of the party members. As an outgrowth of the dissatisfaction the direct primary system was developed. Originated in Wisconsin in 1903, the primary election system provides for the direct selection of party candidates by popular vote under state supervision. Generally, but not always, the primary election is closed to all but party members.

Advocated as a device to return government to the people, the primary system was adopted in some form in all but five states by 1915. By the next year, it had been adopted in twenty-two states for the selection of delegates to national nominating conventions. Although subjected to severe criticism, some of which has certainly been merited, the direct primary system has been firmly established as the most important nominating method in the 20th-century United States.

[Robert C. Brooks, *Political Parties and Electoral Problems*.]

ERIK MCKINLEY ERIKSSON

NONCONFORMISTS. *See* **Dissenters.**

NONFERROUS METALS. Of the major nonferrous metals—aluminum, copper, lead, zinc, nickel, and tin—all except tin are produced in commercial quantities in the United States. The small nickel industry has little or no impact on the world market, which has long been dominated by the International Nickel Company of Canada, Ltd. American production of copper, lead, zinc, and aluminum is influential in the world market and of great significance to the domestic economy. Moreover, the demand for metals with special qualities, such as light weight, high electrical conductivity, and noncorrosive finish, is increasing, and nonferrous metals represent the major source of supply to meet these demands.

During the latter part of the 19th century, following the already established pattern in other basic industries, the entire nonferrous metals industry underwent a period of rapid expansion and development, after which came concentration and consolidation. In the last decade of the century the Aluminum Company of America emerged to monopolize that industry, and the same period also witnessed the incorporation of Anaconda Copper Company, American Smelting and Refining, United States Mining Company, Phelps-Dodge Corporation, American Metals Company, and most of the other leading producers of zinc, lead, and copper. The large corporate units that characterize the

nonferrous metals industry resulted mostly from the advantages enjoyed by well-financed, large-scale operations in finding, extracting, processing, and marketing minerals.

The ''delivered price'' or ''basing point'' price system characteristic of the metals industries prevails throughout the nonferrous metals market. While in itself the system does not ensure price uniformity, in actual fact industries so in harmony on one aspect of pricing seldom have serious difficulty agreeing on others.

The first nonferrous metal to be mined and smelted in the United States was lead. English colonists exploited the small deposits along the eastern seaboard, and by 1720 the French had begun to work the Missouri lead mines. The Missouri mines have been in continuous production since the first underground mining began in 1798.

The opening of the Missouri lead region to American settlers and the discovery of lead in the Wisconsin-Illinois Fever River district occasioned one of the first mineral rushes into the American West by eager miners. The rapid influx of miners, coupled with strong pressure from aspiring entrepreneurs, prevented the federal government from enforcing its policy of retaining ownership of some mineral deposits and led it to grant leases to miners and smelters to exploit the deposits. Even in the Fever River district, where the federal leasing policy existed in some form until the 1840's, the government agents experienced chronic difficulty in collecting rents and regulating smelters. By the end of the 1840's the federal government had abandoned the leasing policy and opened mineral lands to unrestricted exploitation.

Development of the extensive western mines after the Civil War greatly augmented domestic lead production, and by 1881 the United States was the leading lead producer in the world. In the years immediately prior to World War I the United States annually accounted for more than one-third of the total output of lead. After World War II domestic production averaged slightly over 1 million tons annually, about 20 percent short of domestic consumption. Although traditional uses for lead in water pipes, paint, and pigments declined, the increased demand for automobile batteries, gasoline additives, and chemicals more than offset the loss of the former markets.

Unlike lead, zinc was not put into commercial production until toward the end of the 19th century. Only small quantities were smelted before the first commercially successful smelter in the United States began production in 1860. The then-known zinc deposits were not easily beneficiated, and the smelting process was difficult and expensive, rendering zinc metal too expensive for widespread use, and the only substantial demand for zinc was as a component in brass. The opening of the Joplin, Mo., zinc ore district in 1871–72 provided an easily mined, easily concentrated, and comparatively easily smelted ore. More important, the concurrent huge growth in the galvanizing and munitions industries created an effective demand for zinc metal. By 1907 the United States led the world in zinc production and ten years later annually supplied over 60 percent of the world output. Until World War II the United States continued to be a net exporter of zinc, and only since then has domestic production been insufficient to supply national demand. As long as the United States remained a net exporter, the domestic price, often protected by tariffs, operated without dependence on the world market.

Most zinc is now used for galvanizing and die-casting. The next most prevalent use has been in brass products and zinc pigments. The rapid growth of the zinc industry in the early 20th century is to be accounted for in part by the development of the froth flotation process for mineral concentration—a process that provided smelters with such additional ore supplies as practically to revolutionize the entire nonferrous metals industry prior to World War I. The later development of differential media separation, which provided an inexpensive means of separating different components of complex ores, allowed the economic exploitation of lower-grade and more complex ores than before and again greatly expanded domestic production.

Copper, perhaps the world's oldest metal, was being worked by American Indians for fishhooks and ornaments long before Europeans made contact with the Western Hemisphere, but the commercial copper industry in the United States started only in the 1840's with the discovery of old Indian mines in Michigan, and for the next forty years the Lake Superior region produced most of the copper in the United States. With the discovery of the great western mines, especially at Butte, Mont., in the 1880's the United States became the principal producer of copper in the world—a position it has retained. Whereas the Lake Superior copper occurs as native metal and requires no complicated metallurgical process, some of the more complex western ores require leaching with an acidified solution and the separation of the copper from the resulting copper sulfate solution by an electrolytic process.

The most dramatic development in copper mining and manufacturing occurred at the beginning of the 20th century when massive deposits of porphyry ores, often containing no more than 1 percent of copper, were first successfully exploited. D. C. Jackling, a prominent American mining engineer, demonstrated that the huge porphyry deposits at Bingham, Utah, could be profitably developed by utilizing open-pit mining and large-scale operations that permit significant economies of scale. A large portion of the world copper supply subsequently came to be produced from porphyry ore bodies.

The rapid growth of the copper industry paralleled the expansion of the major copper-consuming industries—the electrical, automobile, construction, and mechanical refrigeration industries. In addition, large quantities of copper are used as alloys, especially by the American brass industry. Aluminum and magnesium under favorable price ratios are close substitutes for copper in transmission lines and in certain die castings, but for the most part the demand for copper has been increasing within normal price ranges.

Although aluminum is the most abundant of all metallic elements found in the earth's crust, it was the last of the common nonferrous metals to be commercially exploited. Until the introduction of the electrolytic process in 1886, developed simultaneously but independently by Charles Martin Hall and Paul Louis Toussaint Héroult, the price of aluminum had been much too high for industrial uses. Within five years after its development the Hall-Héroult process reduced the price from more than $8 to less than $1 a pound. In 1888 Hall convinced a group of Pittsburgh entrepreneurs to form the Pittsburgh Reduction Company, later the Aluminum Company of America (Alcoa), to exploit his process, and until 1941 Alcoa was the sole producer of primary aluminum in the United States. In 1937 the Justice Department filed an antitrust suit against Alcoa but lost the appeal in 1945 when Judge Learned Hand ruled that whereas Alcoa had had a monopoly earlier, the existence and pending disposal of government-built wartime facilities threatened that monopoly. Judge Hand ruled that pending "judicious" disposal of the government facilities, remedial action should be held in abeyance. The lease and ultimate sale of these facilities to the Reynolds Metals Company and Kaiser Aluminum and Chemical Company ended the Alcoa monopoly, and since 1946 a number of metal firms have entered the aluminum reduction industry. However, Alcoa still exerts strong leadership in the industry.

The demand for aluminum accelerated rapidly after

World War II as both domestic and world production increased and the price of aluminum dropped, making it competitive with other nonferrous metals for a great variety of uses. In the 1970's the United States accounted for nearly 40 percent of the world output and consumed approximately the same proportion. Leading domestic consumers included the building and construction, transportation, electrical, and containers and packaging industries.

[Charles C. Carr, *Alcoa: An American Enterprise;* W. Y. Elliott, ed., *International Control of Non-Ferrous Metals;* William B. Gates, Jr., *Michigan Copper and Boston Dollars;* Isaac F. Marcosson, *Metal Magic: The Story of the American Smelting and Refining Company;* James D. Norris, *AZn: A History of the American Zinc Company;* Edward H. Robie, ed., *Economies of the Metals Industry;* U.S. Bureau of Mines, *Minerals Yearbook* (published annually).]
                                                    JAMES D. NORRIS

NONIMPORTATION AGREEMENTS were the American colonies' chief weapon against Great Britain in the struggle for American liberty from 1765 to 1775. For a decade before the outbreak of the revolutionary war, Americans attempted to force the mother country to recognize their political rights by means of economic coercion—and it was the failure to achieve their purpose by this means that led many colonial Whigs reluctantly to regard war as the only safeguard of their liberties.

Nonimportation was first used against Great Britain by the New York merchants when, in 1765, they countermanded their orders for British merchandise and declared that they would order no more goods until the Stamp Act was repealed—an example that was quickly followed by the Boston and Philadelphia merchants. Thoroughly alarmed at the prospect of losing their lucrative colonial trade, the British merchants and manufacturers lobbied so vigorously in Parliament that the Stamp Act was repealed, largely through their efforts.

Many colonial Whigs concluded from this victory that they had found a certain defense against the centralizing schemes of British imperialists. Although Englishmen might be deaf to appeals to natural law and charter rights, they seemed to lose no time in coming to terms with the colonies when pinched in their pocketbooks. When the Townshend duties threatened colonial liberty, Americans again resorted to a boycott of British goods. Beginning in Boston in 1768, the nonimportation agreement was rapidly extended over the colonies with varying degrees of thoroughness and effectiveness. Tory merchants who refused to join the agreement were terrorized by mobs and compelled to cease importing British goods.

Leadership of the movement soon passed from the Whig merchants to the radical Sons of Liberty, who insisted that it be protracted until all colonial grievances—not merely the Townshend duties—had been redressed.

In 1770 the British government repealed all the Townshend duties except the tax on tea. This concession proved fatal to the nonimportation agreement. The New York merchants, outraged by Newport's open flouting of the agreement and suspicious of Boston's good faith, determined in 1770 to open their port to all British merchandise except tea. Although Boston and Philadelphia attempted to continue the struggle, New York's defection soon brought about the collapse of the boycott.

Economic coercion of the mother country was again attempted by the formation of the Continental Association in 1774. This differed from previous colonial boycotts in that it was imposed by the Continental Congress; contained provisions for nonexportation as well as nonimportation; and was controlled by the people, working through committees, rather than by the merchants. Nevertheless, the Continental Association failed to fulfill the hopes of conservative patriots who regarded it as a certain means of averting war. The British merchants and manufacturers, upon whom Americans relied to exert pressure upon the British government for a redress of colonial grievances, discovered new sources of trade to replace the lost American market; instead of rallying to the defense of the colonies, they permitted the ministry a free hand in dealing with the American controversy. The supineness of the British merchants and manufacturers destroyed the plans of conservative American Whigs for a peaceful settlement, and the Continental Association had not been in effect six months before it was clear that the dispute between mother country and colonies was not to be decided by a bloodless economic war.

[Lawrence Gipson, *The Coming of the Revolution;* A. M. Schlesinger, *The Colonial Merchants and the American Revolution, 1763–1776.*]
                                                    JOHN C. MILLER

NONINTERCOURSE ACT. Commercial restrictions were an early and prominent ingredient in American foreign policy. President George Washington and the Federalists experimented with them, but it remained for President Thomas Jefferson and his Republicans to realize their fullest possibilities. In the first decade of the 19th century there were four major acts restricting commerce, the partial Nonintercourse Act of Apr. 18, 1806, suspended on Dec. 19 of that year; the Embargo Act of Dec. 22, 1807, which expired in March 1809; the total Nonintercourse Act of Mar. 1, 1809; and the so-called Macon's Bill Number Two of May 1, 1810. Of these four acts, the Embargo Act was the most significant, its two successors marking a progressive weakening of confidence in the efficacy of commerce as a coercive instrument.

The act of Mar. 1, 1809, was a somewhat impotent successor to Jefferson's pet measure, the Embargo Act. A face-saving device, it was far from comforting to the retiring president; at the same time it testified to American commercial desperation. Designating Great Britain and France as countries with which the United States would hold no commercial relations, it offered to restore relations with whichever of those nations first withdrew the obnoxious orders and decrees (see Napoleon's Decrees; Orders in Council). It was a marked recession from the late embargo, which retained American shipping in home ports, for there was nothing in the Nonintercourse Act of 1809 to prevent a general European trade in which the offender nations might indirectly benefit.

The attempt to pit the French and English against one another in a rivalry for America's commercial favors was rather an entreaty than a threat. And even this was weakened by a time limit on the act, limiting enforcement at the outset to the close of the next session of the Congress.

Although the Nonintercourse Act prohibited direct commerce, it permitted indirect commerce. Its successor, Macon's Bill Number Two, was even milder. Direct commerce with Great Britain and France was reopened, saving only that restrictions should be renewed against one nation in the event that the other repealed its offending legislation. The restrictive system had been tried and found wanting, the embargo alone being a true pathmarker on the road to peace.

How the European powers responded to these successive acts is another story. In the diplomatic duel of which they were a part, Napoleon Bonaparte probably played the shrewder role; when war supplanted these commercial gestures, the United States was at his side.

[Henry Adams, *History of the United States*, vol. V; H. S. Commager, ed., *Documents of American History*.]
LOUIS MARTIN SEARS

NONINTERVENTION POLICY. In 1936 the United States for the first time bound itself to a policy of nonintervention in the affairs of other states. At Buenos Aires, on the occasion of the Special Inter-American Conference for the Maintenance of Peace, the United States joined the other American republics in signing, without reservation, a protocol that declared "inadmissible the intervention of any of them [the high contracting parties], directly or indirectly, and for whatever reason, in the internal or external affairs of any other of the parties." The moment was auspicious in the history of the relations between the United States and Latin America and the achievement considerable in view of the fact that the United States had, up to that time, consistently refused to renounce the right of categorical intervention.

From the earliest years of the 20th century, American intervention in the affairs of the nations of the Caribbean and of Central America had been a common practice. The purpose was to eliminate European influence in the area and to establish American hegemony, to make the approaches to the Panama Canal more secure. European nations had been in the habit of sending naval vessels, bombing port facilities, and landing troops both to protect the lives and property of their nationals during the frequent revolutions and to collect the debts owed their citizens —which Latin-American leaders repeatedly refused to honor. So they tended to establish footholds in the territory of the republics and gain influence.

In 1904, President Theodore Roosevelt hit upon the idea of the United States creating such conditions in the neighboring republics as would make European intervention unnecessary. America itself would intervene to bring about political and financial stability. In December 1904, in a message to Congress, he presented the administration's position, which came to be known as the Roosevelt Corollary to the Monroe Doctrine. "Chronic wrongdoing," he said, "may in America, as elsewhere, ultimately require intervention by some civilized nation, and in the Western Hemisphere the adherence of the United States to the Monroe Doctrine may force the United States, however reluctantly, in flagrant cases of such wrongdoing or impotence, to the exercise of an international police power." Pursuant to that policy, the United States in the next decade and a half interfered in the affairs of Cuba, Nicaragua, the Dominican Republic, Haiti, and other countries by landing troops, taking over customshouses, supervising elections, and forcing treaties on them that made them virtual protectorates of the United States. Such action aroused great hostility in Latin America and earned for the powerful northern republic the designation "Colossus of the North."

Frequent efforts were made to bind the United States to a policy of nonintervention. The doctrines proposed by the Argentine statesmen Carlos Calvo and Luis M. Drago that "the public debt cannot occasion armed intervention'' and that ''sovereignty is inviolable'' were two such attempts. Others took place at the several conferences of American states, most notably the sixth conference, held at Havana in 1928, when a draft resolution containing the clause ''No state may intervene in the internal affairs of another'' was offered. That resolution and other tries were rejected by the United States. At Havana, Charles Evans Hughes, chief of the American delegation, went so far as to defend the right of ''interposition of a temporary character'' when ''government breaks down and American citizens are in danger of their lives.''

Still, in the 1920's and 1930's the United States did begin to retreat from an interventionist policy. Troops were withdrawn from the Dominican Republic (1924), Nicaragua (1933), and Haiti (1934); treaties with several republics that gave the United States the legal right to intervene were terminated; and the Roosevelt Corollary was exorcised from the Monroe Doctrine in a memorandum prepared by Undersecretary of State J. Reuben Clark in 1928 and published two years later. While the Republican administrations of the 1920's took significant steps in the direction of ending interventionism, not one of the presidents was willing to renounce the right to intervene. That was left for Franklin D. Roosevelt to do. Roosevelt had on numerous occasions before reaching the White House expressed his opposition to ''arbitrary intervention in the domestic affairs of our neighbors,'' and the Democratic party platform in 1932 pledged ''no interference in the internal affairs of other nations.'' At the seventh International Conference of American States, held in December 1933 at Montevideo, Secretary of State Cordell Hull signed the Convention on the Rights and Duties of States, which contained, in Article VIII, the words ''No state has the right to intervene in the internal or external affairs of another.'' The Latin-American victory was not complete: Hull reserved the right to intervene ''by the law of nations as generally recognized.'' Three years later, at Buenos Aires, that reservation was abandoned.

[D. A. Graber, *Crisis Diplomacy: A History of U.S. Intervention Policies and Practices;* Ann Van Wynen and A. J. Thomas, Jr., *Non-Intervention: The Law and Its Import in the Americas.*]

ARMIN RAPPAPORT

NONPARTISAN LEAGUE, NATIONAL,

an agrarian uprising in the Northwest, formed in 1915, aroused one of the most bitter political controversies in American history. In immediate origin it was a revolt of the spring wheat farmers against the evils of the grain trade, but in part it was a culmination of the Progressive movement in the Northwest. Marketing unrest, centering in North Dakota, was directed chiefly against the Minneapolis Chamber of Commerce, which, it was charged, exercised a monopolistic control over the wheat trade. Led by the Equity Cooperative Exchange after 1908, the farmers of North Dakota attempted to break the hold of the combine by establishing their own terminal facilities. When in 1915 the conservative administration of Gov. Louis B. Hanna refused to carry out plans—twice approved by the voters—for a state-owned terminal elevator, the state was ready for revolt.

The man of the hour was Arthur Charles Townley, a bankrupt flax farmer of western North Dakota and Socialist party organizer. In the spring of 1915 Townley, with the assistance of Equity and Socialist party leaders, launched the Nonpartisan League, demanding, particularly, state-owned elevators, mills, and packing plants; state hail insurance; state rural credits; and taxation reform. Capitalizing on bitterness and directed by men skilled in the art of organizing farmers, the league won a sweeping victory in the 1916 election: a ticket headed by a dirt farmer, Lynn J. Frazier, captured the primaries of the Republican party and was easily elected. In 1918 and 1920 the league was again successful. In 1919 the entire league program was enacted into law.

After 1916 the league spread into neighboring states, its growth facilitated by a series of poor crops in the spring wheat region. Many Progressive leaders, including Charles A. Lindbergh, league candidate in Minnesota for the Republican gubernatorial nomination in 1918, joined the movement, and the organizing genius of Townley, coupled with an effective publicity service, built up a formidable organization. Strong financial resources, which came from high membership fees, enabled the league to carry the fight to its enemies. North Dakota, Minnesota, South Dakota, and Montana were most strongly organized, but many members were reported in Wisconsin, Iowa, Nebraska, Kansas, Colorado, Oklahoma, Idaho, Washington, and Oregon. In each state the program of the league was modified to take advantage of local conditions, but state ownership of marketing facilities was the principal point in each platform. In states having large industrial populations, league leaders broadened their program to include the demands of the workingman and were generally able to effect a coalition of farmer-labor forces. In no state was the league so successful as in North Dakota. The strategy of the league was to capture the primaries of the dominant party; this was accomplished in several states, but outside North Dakota conservative elements were powerful enough to prevent victory at the general elections. No attempt was made by the league to influence the presidential election of 1920.

The strength of the league began to wane after 1920. The depression following World War I, severe in the agricultural states by 1921, made difficult the payment of dues, and without money the organization weakened. The nationalistic reaction that followed the war also weakened the movement. During the war the league's advocacy of conscription of wealth had resulted in accusations of disloyalty, and these, combined with the cry of socialism, brought the league into disrepute in many quarters. In North Dakota, influenced by charges of mismanagement of the industrial program and by several banking scandals involving league leaders, the voters recalled Frazier in 1921. By 1924 the organization had almost disappeared; but the left-wing political revolt that it had created lived on—in Minnesota as the Farmer-Labor party, in North Dakota and other states as a faction within existing parties.

[Paul R. Fossum, *The Agrarian Movement in North Dakota;* Herbert E. Gaston, *The Nonpartisan League.*]

ROBERT H. BAHMER

NONRECOGNITION POLICY. Nonrecognition is not simply the absence of recognition; it is a positive policy taken deliberately in response to a specific act and in a particular situation. Whereas recognition implies neither approval nor disapproval and involves no moral judgment, nonrecognition registers disapproval and is meant to be punitive. The most prominent example of nonrecognition is to be found in the Stimson (or Hoover-Stimson) Doctrine. On Jan. 7, 1932, Secretary of State Henry L. Stimson announced the U.S. government's decision not to recognize the new state of Manchukuo carved out of the territory of the Republic of China by force by the Japanese army. The basis for the policy, said the secretary, was that the situation was brought about in violation of a treaty, the Pact of Paris of 1928, which both Japan and the United States had signed. The pact had outlawed war as an instrument of national policy. Some two months later, on Mar. 11, 1932, the American position was multilateralized when fifty-four nations, members of the League of Nations, approved a resolution of the assembly of the league paralleling the Stimson Doctrine.

While the nonrecognition policy was first fully and specifically used in 1932, it was not without precedent. In 1915, when Japan presented China with the Twenty-one Demands—which, if accepted by China, would have made that country virtually a protectorate of Japan—Secretary of State William Jennings Bryan warned the Japanese that the United States would not recognize any agreement forced on China that impaired the treaty rights of American citizens. Six years later, Secretary of State Charles Evans Hughes directed a similar warning to Japan when that country seemed on the verge of wresting a portion of Russian territory in Siberia by force. The Stimson Doctrine was also applied in the Western Hemisphere. In 1933, at the seventh international Conference of American States held at Montevideo, the American republics acknowledged "an obligation not to recognize territorial acquisition and special advantages which may have been obtained by force." In subsequent conferences in 1936, 1938, and 1945, the principle was reiterated and accepted as the public law of the Americas.

There was another face to the nonrecognition policy that related to governments coming to power by force and violence and in disregard of constitutional methods. President Woodrow Wilson initiated the practice of refusing to recognize such new governments and applied it first to the regime of Victoriano Huerta in Mexico in 1913 and later to the Federico Tinoco government in Costa Rica in 1917 and to that of Álvaro Obregón in 1920 in Mexico. Wilson was not acting without precedent. In 1907 the five Central American republics agreed among themselves not to recognize new governments sprung from revolutions until they had received the sanction of free elections. In 1933, as part of a network of treaties adopted at a conference in Washington, D.C., the five republics renewed the agreement. Meanwhile, Wilson's two successors in the White House, Warren G. Harding and Calvin Coolidge, continued Wilson's policy of nonrecognition. The third Republican president in the decade, Herbert Hoover, changed the policy. In 1932, Stimson announced that a revolutionary government in Chile would be recognized if it passed the three traditional criteria: control of the country, support of the majority of the people, and ability to discharge its international obligations. At the same time, Stimson declared his government's intention to abide by the treaty of 1923 and not recognize revolutionary governments in Central America. Two years later, when the five Central American nations repudiated the principle of nonrecognition of revolutionary governments, the United States followed suit. The application of the nonrecognition policy to mainland China after 1949 may be said to be a return to the Wilsonian position. The Communists came to power in China by force and by nonconstitutional means, having deposed the Nationalist regime by revolution and without benefit of the ballot.

[Robert Langer, *The Seizure of Territory: The Stimson Doctrine and Related Principles in Legal Theory and Diplomatic Practice.*]

ARMIN RAPPAPORT

NONSENSE, FORT. At the terminal point of a high ridge extending into Morristown, N.J., from the southwest, and overlooking the town, are the remains of a redoubt known as Fort Nonsense. Popular belief has long connected these earthworks with the second encampment of the American army at Morristown (1779–80) when Gen. George Washington, merely to save his men from the demoralizing effects of an inactive camp life, put them to work building a fort never intended for use.

[A. M. Sherman, *Historic Morristown.*]

C. A. TITUS

NONSLAVEHOLDERS IN THE SOUTH. According to the census of 1860 there were 383,637 slaveholders in the fifteen slaveholding states. The white population of those states numbered 8,039,000. Assuming that slaveholders were heads of families, and assuming five persons to the family, it is seen that only about 2 million persons were included in the slaveholding class.

The nonslaveholders fall into two classes. One, far the more numerous, included small farmers, artisans, and tradesmen. Members of this class might be industrious and intelligent, and were usually expected to rise into the ranks of the slaveholders. Many, born into this class, reached high position in the antebellum South, including Gov. Joseph E. Brown of Georgia; Gov. John Letcher of Virginia; Christopher G. Memminger, Confederate secretary of the treasury; and Andrew Johnson, later president of the United States.

Another class of southern nonslaveholding whites, whose number it is impossible to estimate, but which was relatively small, has been conventionally designated as "poor whites." Such persons were squatters or tenants, in wilderness or piney-wood clearings, or

might form squalid communities of their own in barren lands, avoided by whites and blacks alike.

[U. B. Phillips, *Life and Labor in the Old South.*]

HAYWOOD J. PEARCE, JR.

NONVOTING. The extent of nonvoting is the proportion of the franchised electorate that does not turn out to vote. A description of the historical pattern of nonvoting must account for the extent of the franchise as well as the nature of electoral contests.

Only a small proportion of the U.S. population voted in the early 19th century, but the removal of the last property qualifications for voting for white males and the enfranchisement of blacks was marked by an increase in the numbers voting from the end of the Civil War until the close of the century. No increase in turnout was evident in the elections immediately following the enfranchisement of women (1920) or of eighteen- to twenty-one year olds (1972).

At the turn of the century nonvoting increased, because many blacks were denied access to the polls in the South and perhaps because party competition declined as the Democratic party became dominant in the South and the Republican party dominated the politics of many northern states. Nonvoting decreased in the 1930's, 1950's, and 1960's, probably because of the interest aroused by the issues and candidates associated with national elections in those decades.

The nonvoting population is made up of habitual nonvoters and intermittent nonvoters. From the end of World War II habitual nonvoters constituted about 15 percent of the national electorate. They overrepresented these population groupings: southerners, females, blacks, residents of central cities and of rural areas, and people with only a grade-school education or less. In the 1960's and 1970's the proportion of habitual nonvoters living in the South declined markedly, and the decline was greatest among blacks.

In most American elections the proportion of qualified voters failing to turn out is greater than that of the habitual nonvoters, so that the numbers of intermittent nonvoters swell the ranks of nonvoters. Intermittent nonvoting is associated with the social and political attributes of the voters as well as with electoral procedures and the characteristics of electoral contests. The number of intermittent nonvoters is disproportionately high among females, nonwhites, adults under thirty, the lower economic classes, the less well educated, and people who have not identified with a political party or shown a sustained interest in politics. State and local registration requirements and procedures demand added time and awareness on the part of the electorate and contribute to nonvoting, as do electoral contests in which the issues and candidates have little salience or popular appeal.

Nonvoting is used as an indicator of popular interest in public affairs and popular satisfaction with public policies and government officials. But whether nonvoting is a direct indication of lack of interest or satisfaction in politics has not been established. While some studies of voting behavior contend that a high turnout indicates interest and involvement on the part of the electorate, data suggest that in high-turnout elections uninterested voters are mobilized and many voters are expressing dissatisfaction with the government.

[William H. Flanigan, *Political Behavior of the American Electorate.*]

SHEILAH R. KOEPPEN

NOOTKA SOUND CONTROVERSY arose from conflicting British and Spanish claims to the northwest coast of North America. In 1789 expeditions from both countries arrived to occupy Nootka Sound, on the west coast of Vancouver Island. The Spaniards seized the Englishmen and their vessels and sent them to Mexico. The Spanish court demanded that the British court disavow the acts of its commander, but the British refused, making counterdemands. Each prepared for war and applied to its allies for assurances of support. Britain's responded affirmatively. Spain sought support under the Family Compact. Being in the throes of revolution, France responded tardily and unsatisfactorily; and revolutionary contagion was feared by Spain. By a convention signed Oct. 28, 1790, Spain conceded most British demands. In the Oregon controversy with the United States Britain claimed its gains under the 1790 convention, and the United States claimed what Spain retained, having acquired Spain's claims in the Adams-Onís Treaty of 1819.

WILLIAM R. MANNING

"NO PEACE BEYOND THE LINE," a phrase that colorfully reflects the international rivalry for the New World, had its origins in the refusal of Spain and Portugal to concede rights to others within the monopolies fixed by the line of demarcation. Diplomats, unable to agree on this question, elected, as in the Franco-Spanish peace of 1559 and the Anglo-Spanish

Treaty of 1604, to omit all reference to it, rather than to sacrifice the benefits of a European peace. Thus, it was understood (in 1559 by oral agreement) that European treaties lost their force west of the prime meridian (sometimes identified as passing through the Azores and sometimes as being identical with the demarcation line) and south of the Tropic of Cancer. Beyond these indefinite "lines of amity" hostile acts did not technically break the peace in Europe, though they might well strain it to a breaking point. The Treaty of Madrid in 1670, and subsequent agreements among the maritime powers reached through the years prior to 1685, mark the most significant steps in the gradual abandonment of this rule for one holding that the peace of Europe governed as well "beyond the line."

[F. G. Davenport, *European Treaties Bearing on the History of the United States and Its Dependencies;* A. P. Newton, *The European Nations in the West Indies, 1493–1688.*]

WESLEY FRANK CRAVEN

NORFOLK, a city in southeastern Virginia, was founded in 1682 and first became a port for the planters of northeastern North Carolina, who were unable to use the shallow and treacherous waters of the Albemarle and Pamlico sounds. During the first half of the 18th century, when the increasing size of the English tobacco ships made it difficult for them to take on goods directly at the plantation wharves, Norfolk also became the chief port for the Chesapeake region. Tobacco, wheat, corn, naval stores, and provisions were the chief products of the backcountry shipped from Norfolk. Tobacco and wheat were sent to England in exchange for manufactured goods, and the naval stores and provisions went to the West Indies to be exchanged for sugar, molasses, and rum.

During the American Revolution, Norfolk was occupied by John Murray, Lord Dunmore, with a mixed force of British, Tories, and blacks. The patriots drove him out, but realizing that the place could not be defended against the British navy, they burned the town. After the Revolution, Norfolk was rebuilt. During the French Revolution and Napoleonic Wars, it enjoyed great prosperity through its trade with the British and French West Indies. But it declined as a commercial port after the Treaty of Ghent in 1815 because of restrictions on trade with the British West Indies and the imposition of protective tariffs. Competition from Baltimore and New York, failure to secure railroad connections with the interior of

Virginia, and destruction of the navy yard during the Civil War also retarded growth.

After the Civil War Norfolk became the terminus of several important railway systems, making its port one of the nation's chief points of export for coal, tobacco, and cotton. Both World War I and World War II caused rapid expansion of the naval yard and other military facilities at Norfolk and made the city's continued prosperity heavily dependent on them. After World War II Norfolk made a strenuous effort to broaden its economic base to provide greater stability. The port expanded its general cargo facilities, and a 468-acre industrial park attracted new industries. Improved highway and tunnel connections speeded travel between Norfolk and adjoining communities. During the 1950's and 1960's, Norfolk also undertook extensive urban redevelopment and housing projects. The city had a population of 307,951 in 1970.

[T. J. Wertenbaker, *Norfolk: Historic Southern Port.*]
WILLIAM WILLINGHAM

NORFOLK AND WESTERN. *See* **Railroads, Sketches.**

"NORMALCY." In an address before the Home Market Club at Boston, May 14, 1920, Sen. Warren G. Harding said, in part, "America's present need is not heroics but healing, not nostrums but normalcy. . . ." The word "normalcy" came quickly to symbolize to many powerful American economic interests the immediate abandonment of the chief foreign and domestic policies of the administrations of President Woodrow Wilson. Specifically, it signified a return to a high protective tariff, a drastic reduction in income and inheritance taxes, "putting labor in its place," a restoration of subsidies and bounties to favored corporate groups, an absence of government interference in private enterprise, and a vigorous nationalistic foreign policy. The "back to normal" slogan was used with great effectiveness by Harding in his successful campaign for the presidency later in the year.

[C. A. and M. R. Beard, *The Rise of American Civilization.*]

THOMAS S. BARCLAY

NORMANDY INVASION, Allied landings in France on June 6, 1944 (D Day), the prelude to the defeat of Nazi Germany in World War II. Known as Operation Overlord, the invasion was scheduled for June 5 but was postponed because of stormy weather. It involved 5,000 ships, the largest armada ever assembled, and was overall the greatest amphibious operation in history, although more men went ashore on the first day in the earlier Allied invasion of Sicily.

Under command of Gen. Dwight D. Eisenhower, with Gen. Bernard L. Montgomery as ground commander, approximately 130,000 American, British, and Canadian troops landed on beaches extending from the mouth of the Orne River near Caen to the base of the Cotentin Peninsula, a distance of some fifty-five miles. Another 23,000 landed by parachute and glider. Allied aircraft during the day flew 11,000 sorties. Airborne troops began landing soon after midnight; American seaborne troops at 6:30 A.M.; and, because of local tidal conditions, British and Canadian troops at intervals over the next hour. The Allies chose Normandy because of its relatively short distance from British ports and airfields, the existence of particularly strong German defenses of the Atlantic Wall at the closest point to Britain in the Pas de Calais, and the need for early access to a major port (Cherbourg).

On beaches near Caen christened Gold, Juno, and Sword, one Canadian and two British divisions under the British Second Army made it ashore with relative ease, quickly establishing contact with a British airborne division that had captured bridges over the Orne and knocked out a coastal battery that might have enfiladed the beaches. By nightfall the troops were short of the assigned objectives of Bayeux and Caen but held beachheads from two to four miles deep.

The U.S. First Army under Lt. Gen. Omar N. Bradley sent the Fourth Infantry Division of the VII Corps ashore farthest west on Utah Beach, north of Carentan, at one of the weakest points of the Atlantic Wall. The 82nd and 101st Airborne divisions landing behind the beach helped insure success. Although the air drops were badly scattered and one division landed amidst a reserve German division, most essential objectives were in hand by the end of the day.

Under the V Corps, two regiments of the First Infantry Division and one of the Twenty-ninth landed on Omaha Beach, between Bayeux and Carentan. Sharp bluffs, strong defenses, lack of airborne assistance, and the presence of a powerful German division produced near-catastrophic difficulties. Throughout much of the day the fate of this part of the invasion hung in the balance, but inch by inch American troops forced their way inland, so that when night came the beachhead was approximately a mile deep.

At a nearby cliff called Pointe du Hoe, the First Ranger Battalion eliminated a German artillery battery.

The invasion sector was defended by the German Seventh Army, a contingent of Army Group B, under overall command of Field Marshal Gerd von Rundstedt. Deluded by Allied deception measures, based in large part on intelligence known as ULTRA, obtained as a result of the British having broken the German wireless enciphering code, the Germans believed, even after the landings had begun, that a second and larger invasion would hit the Pas de Calais and for several weeks held strong forces there that might have been decisive in Normandy. German defense was further deterred by difficulty in shifting reserves, because of preinvasion bombing of French railroads, disruption of traffic by Allied fighter bombers that earlier had driven German planes from the skies, and French partisans. The bad weather of June 5 and continuing heavy seas on June 6 lulled German troops into a false sense of security. Reluctance of staff officers back in Germany to awaken the German dictator, Adolf Hitler, for approval to commit reserves delayed a major counterattack against the invasion. The only counterattack on the first day, by a panzer division against the British, was defeated by fire from naval guns.

At the end of D Day only the Canadians on Juno and the British on Gold had linked their beachheads. More than five miles separated the two American beachheads; the Rangers at Pointe du Hoe were isolated and under siege; and the Fourth Division at Utah Beach had yet to contact the American airborne divisions. Nevertheless, reinforcements and supplies were streaming ashore, even at embattled Omaha Beach, and unjustified concern about landings elsewhere was to continue to hamper German countermeasures. By the end of the first week, all Allied beachheads were linked and sixteen divisions had landed; only thirteen German divisions opposed them. By the end of June a million Allied troops were ashore.

Several innovations aided the invasion and subsequent buildup. Amphibious tanks equipped with canvas skirts that enabled them to float provided early fire support on the beaches. Lengths of big rubber hose (called PLUTO, for Pipe Line Under the Ocean) were laid on the floor of the English Channel for transporting fuel. Given the code name Mulberry, two artificial prefabricated harbors were towed into position at Omaha Beach and Arromanches. These consisted of an inner breakwater constructed of hollow concrete caissons six stories high, which were sunk and anchored in position, and a floating pier that rose and fell with the tide while fixed on concrete posts resting on the sea bottom. Old cargo ships sunk offshore formed an outer breakwater. Although a severe storm on June 19 wrecked the American Mulberry, the British port at Arromanches survived. A sophisticated family of landing craft delivered other supplies directly over the beaches.

Allied casualties on D Day were heaviest at Omaha Beach (2,500) and lightest at Utah (200). American airborne divisions incurred 2,499 casualties. Canadian losses were 1,074; British, 3,000. Of a total of more than 9,000 casualties, approximately one-third were killed.

[Anthony Cave Brown, *Bodyguard of Lies;* Gordon A. Harrison, *Cross-Channel Attack;* Cornelius Ryan, *The Longest Day.*]

CHARLES B. MacDONALD

NORRIDGEWOCK FIGHT (Aug. 23, 1724), at the site of Madison, Maine, was the crucial point of Dummer's War. Capt. Jeremiah Moulton, with about eighty men, attacked the stockaded Abnaki town. The Indians rallied, fired two ineffective volleys, and then ran to the Kennebec River, where they were slaughtered in crossing. Between 80 and 100 Indians, including 7 noted chiefs and the Jesuit missionary Sebastian Rasles, were killed. English losses were two soldiers wounded and a Mohawk ally killed.

[F. H. Eckstorm, "The Fight at Norridgewock," *New England Quarterly,* vol. 7.]

FANNIE HARDY ECKSTORM

NORRIS DAM. *See* **Hydroelectric Power.**

NORRIS FARM EXPORT ACT, often called the McNary Act, was introduced in Congress, May 31, 1921, by Sen. George W. Norris. After a stormy legislative history it was approved Aug. 24, 1921. In form, it was an amendment to the War Finance Corporation Act. The corporation was authorized to make advances up to $1 billion to finance agricultural exports.

JAMES D. MAGEE

NORRIS–LA GUARDIA ANTI-INJUNCTION LAW, passed by Congress in 1932, was a legislative attempt to circumvent Supreme Court limitations on the activities of organized labor groups, especially as those limitations were imposed between the enactment of the Clayton Antitrust Act in 1914 and the end of the 1920's. Based on the theory that the lower courts are creations not of the Constitution but of Congress, and that Congress therefore has wide power in defining and restricting their jurisdiction, the act forbids issuance of injunctions to sustain antiunion contracts of employment, to prevent ceasing or refusing to perform any work or remain in any relation of employment, or to restrain acts generally constituting component parts of strikes, boycotts, and picketing.

ROYAL E. MONTGOMERY

NORSEMEN IN AMERICA. The Norse discovery and attempted colonization of part of the eastern coast of North America during the late 10th and early 11th centuries A.D. was the logical end of a sequence of Norse voyages across the North Atlantic Ocean: the voyages to the British Isles in the 790's, to the Faeroe Islands by 820, to Iceland about 870, to Greenland in the 980's; the sighting of America in 985–86; and the first landing there about 1000. The causes of this westward progress lay in Scandinavian history, geography, and economics, and specifically in a search for habitable land and for the benefits of trade. The evolution of the seagoing ship of all work—whose best exemplar is the Gokstad ship now preserved in Oslo—capable of transporting men, animals, and goods over considerable distances, provided the means.

The first voyages, dated about 986–1020, reached large and inexactly defined areas called Helluland, Markland, and Vinland by the sagas. It is likely that they took place in favorable climatic conditions. All planned and recorded voyages during this period were mounted by the Norse colonies in Greenland, and gaps in information, together with hard times in the colonies after 1300, make it difficult to trace a consistent American connection. There is, even so, an Icelandic annal for 1121, "Eirik the Greenlanders' Bishop Went to Look for Vinland," somewhat expanded in a legend of the Vinland Map. And an annal for 1347 tells of a small Greenland ship being driven by a storm to Iceland after a voyage to Markland-Labrador.

The voyages of about 986–1020, as recorded at least 200 years later in *The Greenlanders' Saga* and *Eirik the Red's Saga,* with early documentary support and the promise of archaeological confirmation from Helge Ingstad's excavations at L'Anse aux Meadows

in northern Newfoundland, are the basis of the best-known claim for a Norse arrival in North America. The details are not to be relied on, but the claim appears irrefutable. A further claim inviting favorable consideration is that once the Norsemen were settled in Greenland they set about exploiting not only their own northern hunting grounds but also parts of the Canadian littoral as well; whether this led to a racial blending with the Eskimo awaits proof. Third and more speculative is the theory of a late immigration, perhaps Norse or Norse-Eskimo, from Greenland into Arctic Canada after the unexplained but disastrous end of the western settlement (Vestribygð, near modern Godthaab) about 1340. But the documentary evidence lends itself to likelier explanations, and the archaeological evidence relating to such phenomena as bear traps; eider-duck shelters; rectangular houses; iron nails and knives; and tall, blond, or bearded Eskimos, is variously interpreted.

Thus, while a Norse acquaintance with some eastern coastal regions of North America, and in particular of modern Canada, is acknowledged by modern scholarship, its extent is debatable and its duration uncertain. A fixed point is that there were Norsemen at L'Anse aux Meadows about 1000. As hunters, fishers, and garnerers of natural resources, the Norsemen made many unrecorded but vaguely traceable voyages for at least 350 years thereafter, not only to regions in the general latitude of the two Greenland colonies (58° and 64° north latitude), but well south and north of these. They must at times have wintered away from home, doubtless at regularly frequented bases, but that they established a single long-lasting colony anywhere in America is not proven. The number of Norsemen engaged in such enterprises was always small; and at an unknown time, in worsened circumstances, suddenly or desultorily, they left off trafficking. Most probably they withdrew to Greenland or were absorbed by the local populations, but here, too, nothing is proven. (*See also* Vinland.)

[Helge Ingstad, *Land Under the Pole Star;* R. A. Skelton et al., *The Vinland Map and the Tartar Relation.*]

GWYN JONES

NORTH AFRICAN CAMPAIGN. Although the British and the Italians, later augmented by the Germans, engaged in combat in Libya and Egypt between 1940 and 1942, the North African campaign opened on Nov. 8, 1942, when Anglo-American ground, sea, and air forces under U.S. Gen. Dwight D. Eisenhower landed in French Morocco and Algeria near

Casablanca, Algiers, and Oran and met bitter French resistance. An armistice brought the fighting to an end on Nov. 11, and the French forces soon joined the Allies.

Allied units under British Gen. Kenneth Anderson tried to take Bizerte and Tunis quickly, but Italian and German troops dispatched from Italy under the command of Gen. Jürgen von Arnim took a firm hold over northern Tunisia and stopped them. Field Marshal Erwin Rommel's Italo-German army, defeated at El Alamein, Egypt, in October, was retreating across Libya and at the end of the year would take defensive positions in the old French fortifications around Mareth, Tunisia, to halt the pursuing British under Gen. Bernard L. Montgomery.

Bad weather brought large-scale operations to a close. The Axis forces built up strength, but the Allies suffered from a supply line too small to support the units required, thinly dispersed troops over a large area, unsatisfactory command arrangements, American battle inexperience and overconfidence, and obsolete weapons and equipment in French hands.

In February 1943 the Axis forces, in a series of engagements called the Battle of Kasserine Pass, drove the Americans and French back about fifty miles in southern Tunisia, inflicting severe damage and panic. In accordance with agreements at the Casablanca Conference, British Gen. Harold Alexander took command of Anderson's and Montgomery's ground troops. Together with Gen. George S. Patton, Jr., who was put at the head of the American units, he restored confidence.

In March, the Allies attacked and pushed Rommel's army into the northern corner of Tunisia. The final offensive started on Apr. 22, and Bizerte and Tunis fell on May 7. Arnim surrendered, and the last organized Axis resistance in North Africa ended on May 13, with more than 250,000 prisoners taken. With all of North Africa in Allied hands, the stage was set for operations directed on Europe.

[George F. Howe, *Northwest Africa: Seizing the Initiative in the West.*]

MARTIN BLUMENSON

NORTH AMERICAN LAND COMPANY was
organized in Philadelphia in 1795 by Sen. Robert Morris, John Nicholson, and James Greenleaf to develop and sell 4 million acres in Pennsylvania, Virginia, North Carolina, South Carolina, Georgia, and Kentucky. Capital stock was $3 million, divided into 30,000 shares at $100 each. Repeated attempts to

sell stock failed because of financial stress in the United States and abroad, unsettled European conditions, and the unpopularity of stock companies. Greenleaf's nefarious land operations cost Morris £30,000; the Bank of England suspended specie payments; Morris' notes were foreclosed—and all contributed to the company's decline. In April 1797 Morris threw the remaining lands into the Pennsylvania Property Company in a last futile attempt to recoup a fortune.

[E. P. Oberholtzer, *Robert Morris.*]

JULIAN P. BOYD

NORTH ANNA, BATTLE OF (May 23–25, 1864).
Failing to break Gen. Robert E. Lee's lines at Spotsylvania, Va., Gen. Ulysses S. Grant moved toward Hanover Courthouse, May 20, 1864. Lee, outmarching him, fortified behind the North Anna River at Hanover Junction, covering Richmond. Arriving there May 23, Grant's army in sharp fighting forced the river crossings and entrenched. But finding Lee's position too strong to warrant a general assault, Grant on May 26 moved by his left toward the Pamunkey at Hanovertown.

[O. L. Spaulding, *The United States Army.*]

JOSEPH MILLS HANSON

NORTH ATLANTIC TREATY ORGANIZATION
(NATO) came into existence through a treaty negotiated by twelve nations (Belgium, Canada, Denmark, France, Iceland, Italy, Luxembourg, Netherlands, Norway, Portugal, the United Kingdom, and the United States). The treaty was signed in Washington, D.C., on Apr. 4, 1949. Greece and Turkey acceded to the treaty on Feb. 15, 1952, and the Federal Republic of Germany on May 6, 1955, bringing the total membership to fifteen. Headquarters were established in Brussels, Belgium.

At the close of World War II the United States, the United Kingdom, and France retained military forces in Berlin. The Soviet Union and its Communist satellite allies assumed a belligerent attitude toward Western Europe. This was met by the Truman Doctrine, Mar. 12, 1947, which stated that it was "the policy of the United States to support free peoples who are resisting attempted subjugation by armed minorities or by outside pressure," and by the Marshall Plan of economic assistance announced June 5, 1947, which together were resisted by the Soviet Union "as an instrument of American imperialism." In the face of

Soviet belligerence, these two programs of military and economic assistance emphasized the need on the part of the United States to join in the promotion and support of a defensive alliance. The Truman Doctrine and the Marshall Plan only caused the Soviet Union to be more threatening and induced the signing of a treaty of mutual assistance in Brussels on Mar. 17, 1948, by Belgium, France, Luxembourg, the Netherlands, and the United Kingdom. In September 1948, a military body called the Western Union Defense Organization was created within the provisions of the Brussels treaty. It was soon realized that such mutual-defense agreements for those countries within the United Nations could give no immediate protection unless backed by more powerful military strength. Hence, a greater single defense system, including and superseding the Brussels treaty provisions, was necessary. To this action by Western European powers the Soviet Union countered with the Berlin blockade (June 1948 to May 1949), which was answered by an airlift initiated by the United States, the United Kingdom, and France.

The time had come to do something positive and effective. A plan was put forward and promptly adopted under the name of the North Atlantic Treaty Organization, which initially was set up in Western Europe as a defense mechanism against Soviet-led communism. This constituted a first phase of NATO responsibility that extended from 1949 to 1955 and was marked by the death of Joseph Stalin, the beginning of the end of the cold war, and the creation of the Soviet-led Warsaw Pact of 1955. The second phase, 1955 to 1964, was marked by more varied Soviet Communist activities in every quarter of the globe, including Soviet attempts to renew diplomatic activities practically suspended since 1949. This expansion of diplomacy required NATO, while maintaining and perfecting its defense arrangements, to exercise an increasing degree of consultation and cooperation among its members over an ever-widening political front.

The third phase, beginning in 1965, was marked by a growing feeling of East-West détente, notably on the bilateral level between individual NATO members and satellite members as well as with the Soviet Union itself, largely in the form of cultural and scientific agreements and exchanges. In spite of temporary setbacks, such as the Soviet invasion of Czechoslovakia (1968), NATO continued the process of adapting its defense machinery, notably in the fields of nuclear planning and policymaking and crisis management. The decision of the French government to

withdraw its forces from the integrated NATO commands (1967) necessitated the adaptation of existing structures and their relocation.

Since the formation of NATO there have been many administrative and organizational changes, but always the primary objective has been defense against aggression. Many problems have been met and dealt with, such as the Korean War, brought about in 1950 by a Communist attack; the invasion of Czechoslovakia; and problems of control of atomic power and nuclear weapons.

NATO has played a decisive role in the maintenance of world peace. While the military role of NATO has been of prime importance, the regular and continued consultation between the fifteen member nations has been no less important. The developing work of NATO over the years and its continuous adaptation to ever-changing circumstances have demonstrated its flexibility and ability to meet these changes.

Beginning in the late 1960's some people felt that the organization was no longer as necessary as it had been at its inception, because of the apparent decline in the Soviet Union's aggressive and belligerent attitude, the Chinese-Soviet impasse, and the rising cost of weaponry and occupying forces.

In accordance with provisions of the peace settlement ending World War II and of later agreements, NATO military forces from the United States, the United Kingdom, and France have occupied Berlin, although France has withdrawn its military support but not its membership in NATO. SACLANT (Supreme Allied Command Atlantic), a naval arm of NATO, has been constantly on the alert to insure the freedom and integrity of the North Atlantic Ocean and to deny use of the North Atlantic to any enemy submarines able to interrupt and destroy convoys and to shell coastal city fortifications.

The apparent reduction in Soviet Communist belligerency during the late 1960's and early 1970's tended to soften the ties to NATO of some of its members. Furthermore, money and trade differences between NATO members presented problems that caused a reluctance on the part of some members to incur the increasing expense of NATO membership. This attitude was strengthened by a continued discussion and hope of effective arms control. Likewise, there were calls in 1970 for a reduction of U.S. commitments to NATO, particularly a reduction of occupying ground forces. These proposals were strongly opposed by member nations and by President Richard M. Nixon. It was argued that a reduction of this nature would weaken NATO's defenses; weaken the bargaining power of the United States in its efforts to improve East-West relations; undermine the credibility of the United States regarding the defense of Western Europe; and increase European fear that the United States might disregard allied interests to reach agreement with the Soviet Union.

In this connection it should be noted that the primary reason for U.S. membership in NATO was to prevent the Soviet Union and its satellites from using force as an instrument of national policy.

[Richard J. Barnet and Marcus G. Raskin, *After Ten Years;* John J. McCloy, *Atlantic Alliance: Origin and Future;* Robert E. Osgood, *NATO.*]

THOMAS ROBSON HAY

NORTH CAROLINA. Under authority of Queen Elizabeth I the first English colony in America was planted on Roanoke Island in 1585, with Ralph Lane as governor. Sir Walter Raleigh was promoter. The settlers soon returned to England and the second attempt at settlement, in 1587 with John White as governor, became known as the Lost Colony. In 1629 Charles I granted Carolana, as it was first called, to Sir Robert Heath, who failed to plant a colony. About the middle of the 17th century, settlers from Virginia began to locate along the Albemarle Sound, and in 1663 Charles II granted Carolina to eight lords proprietors. In 1665 a second charter fixed the boundaries of Carolina at 39°30′ on the north, 29° on the south, and westward to the Pacific Ocean. In 1664 the proprietors created two counties—Albemarle and Clarendon (Cape Fear region)—in what is now North Carolina and offered land grants, tax exemption, and other inducements to settlers. Clarendon was soon abandoned, and it was half a century before the Cape Fear country was settled. Until 1689, Albemarle had a proprietary governor and an elective legislature. From that date until 1711, North Carolina, as the northern portion of Carolina came to be called, was ruled by a deputy governor from Charles Town, although it had its own legislature. In 1712 an independent governor was appointed for North Carolina, and in 1729 it became a royal colony.

North Carolina grew slowly during the proprietary period because of its dangerous coast and other geographical handicaps; the neglect of the proprietors; the weakness and inefficiency of its governors; Indian wars; piracy; friction over the established church, particularly with the Quakers and Baptists; and the uncertainty of land titles and unpopularity of quitrents. Only five towns were founded during this period:

Bath (1706), New Bern (1710), Edenton (1712), Beaufort (1715), and Brunswick (1725).

From 1729 to 1775 government improved, population increased and spread, agriculture and industry developed, many churches and a few schools were established, a new and more permanent capital (Edenton) was designated, and three newspapers began publication. The lower Cape Fear was settled soon after 1713, and the upper Cape Fear after 1740, largely by Scottish Highlanders. During the next thirty years thousands of Scotch-Irish and Germans moved from Pennsylvania into the Piedmont, and by 1775, settlers had reached the mountains.

North Carolina patriots openly resisted the Stamp Act; organized nonimportation associations to boycott British goods; called a meeting in defiance of the governor and chose delegates to the Continental Congress; set up a temporary government in 1775; crushed the Tories at Moores Creek Bridge, Feb. 27, 1776, ending British plans to occupy the South early in the war; and, at Halifax, Apr. 12, 1776, authorized their delegates in the Continental Congress to vote for independence—the first state to take such action. The Battle at Guilford Courthouse was the most important revolutionary battle in the state, but North Carolina troops fought valiantly elsewhere and also conquered the Cherokee in the West. The University of North Carolina, the first state university in the Union, was chartered in 1789 and opened its doors in 1795. The state's first constitution, drafted in 1776, set up a government characterized by a weak executive, property and religious tests for voting and officeholding, and a bicameral legislature elected annually.

The chief problems confronting the new state were lack of specie and depreciation of paper currency; backwardness of agriculture, industry, commerce, and education; Tories and their property; tramontane lands; and relations with the central government. The state ceded its western lands in 1789, and Tennessee was created therefrom. North Carolina rejected the federal Constitution in 1788 but ratified it in 1789, thus being the penultimate state to accept that document. The state was Federalist for less than a decade and then was Democratic from 1800 to the 1970's with the exception of the years of Whig supremacy (1840–52); the Reconstruction era; the "fusion" period (1896–1900); and in 1972, when a Republican was elected governor.

Prior to 1840, North Carolina was one of the most backward states in the Union. Unscientific farming and soil exhaustion, lack of manufactures and adequate transportation facilities, commercial dependence on Virginia and South Carolina, emigration, and a planter-controlled government that was unwilling to spend money for internal improvements and education were all contributing factors. The state constitution was revised in 1835, and a more democratic government was created, with the western part of the state predominant in influence. The Whigs, championing internal improvements, rose to power, and the state enjoyed two decades of progress—under Whig rule in the 1840's and under the Democrats in the 1850's. Railroads and plank roads were constructed; cotton mills and other industries were established; a public school system was begun; and many other progressive measures were adopted.

Although North Carolinians held over 300,000 slaves in 1860, Union sentiment was strong, and it was not until May 20, 1861, that the state seceded, after President Abraham Lincoln had called on it for troops for the federal army. It contributed about 125,000 men to the southern cause; sustained about one-fourth of the Confederate losses; fed and clothed its own soldiers; led all the states in blockade-running; and probably received less Confederate patronage than any southern state. Battles were fought at Plymouth, New Bern, Fort Fisher, Bentonville, and elsewhere; and "the last surrender of the Civil War," that of Joseph E. Johnston to William T. Sherman, occurred at the Bennett House near Durham.

North Carolina was almost prostrate at the close of the war, although it did not suffer as much as some of the southern states did under Reconstruction. It was readmitted to the Union in 1868, after it had ratified the Fourteenth Amendment and had drafted a new state constitution. Some of the most significant innovations made by this document were the popular election of all state and county officials; the adoption of the township-county commission form of government; and provision for a "general and uniform system of public schools." After Reconstruction, thirty amendments were added to the constitution (1875–76). Secret political societies were made illegal; white and black schools were to be kept separate; marriages between whites and blacks were forbidden; residence requirements for voting were raised to circumvent the Fifteenth Amendment; and the legislature was given virtual control over county government.

After the Civil War, farm tenancy replaced the old plantation economy and tended to increase to such an extent that by the 1930's it became one of the state's greatest social and economic problems. Tobacco and furniture manufacturing became major industries; the textile industry expanded; and railroad construction was revived. As late as 1900, however, North Carolina was still one of the most backward states. Transportation facilities were inadequate; the state ranked near the bottom in education; and farmers were poverty-stricken as a result of low prices for their crops, high prices for what they purchased, and excessive interest and freight rates.

Since 1900, when North Carolina's population was 1,893,810, the state has made phenomenal progress. It has become one of the leading agricultural states of the nation, ranking first in tobacco production and having high rank in many other crops as well as in per acre yields. By the mid-1970's it led all the states in tobacco and cotton-textile manufacturing and ranked first in the South in furniture production. It was the pioneer state of the South in good road construction. By 1970 the state's population had increased to 5,082,000.

The passage of several bond issues in the 1960's and 1970's, as well as generous legislative support, enabled the public school system to expand and to attain high standards of excellence. School desegregation was accomplished with a minimum of difficulty. Increased urbanization; improved means of communication, particularly a network of interstate highways; a number of large trucking firms; the development of deep-water ports at Wilmington and Morehead City; and the growth of industry have altered the rural outlook of the state. An outstanding state museum of art, a state symphony orchestra, a state zoo, an opera company, a ballet troupe, state support for several outdoor dramas, the opening of a large number of state historic sites and recreational parks, attention to the improvement of air and water resources, the development of an extensive system of community colleges and technical institutes, and the reorganization of state-supported institutions of higher education, including the School of the Arts, have had the support of North Carolinians since World War II. The development of Research Triangle Park as a center of industrial and scientific research since 1955 has been phenomenal. Located on a 5,000-acre tract in the triangle formed by Duke University at Durham, North Carolina State University at Raleigh, and the University of North Carolina at Chapel Hill, the facilities in the region have attracted thousands of highly skilled specialists. The development of beach resorts along the coast, both summer and winter resorts in the mountains and in the

Piedmont, and the growth of retirement and second-home communities have greatly altered the face of North Carolina.

[Hugh T. Lefler, *North Carolina: The History of a Southern State;* Hugh T. Lefler and William S. Powell, *Colonial North Carolina: A History.*]

WILLIAM S. POWELL

NORTH CAROLINA RAILROAD was built, 1848–56, by the state of North Carolina from Goldsboro to Charlotte, by way of Greensboro, Salisbury, and Concord, a distance of 232 miles. It was considered ''the greatest internal improvement ever undertaken by the state.'' It connected with several roads already constructed in eastern North Carolina and gave the state its first east-west rail connection. Three-fourths of the stock, originally valued at $3 million, is owned by the state. In 1871 the road was leased to the Richmond and Danville Company, and in 1895 to the Southern Railway Company for a term of ninety-nine years.

[C. K. Brown, *A State Movement in Railroad Development.*]

HUGH T. LEFLER

NORTH CHURCH. *See* **Old North Church.**

NORTH DAKOTA was formed by a division of Dakota Territory in 1889. The state, 70,665 square miles, is largely a cool, semiarid grassland. The Dakota Territory, organized in 1861, had come into being soon after a trickle of land speculators had founded the towns of Sioux Falls and Yankton. Although traders interested in the commerce of the Selkirk settlement had put a steamboat on the Red River of the North in 1859, settlement in northern Dakota did not really get under way until railroads reached that river in 1871. Throughout the territorial period southern Dakota, settled earlier and with a larger population, dominated the territory, even though a tricky maneuver had moved the capital from Yankton to Bismarck in 1883. The region was settled in two booms, the first in 1878–86 and the second in 1898–1915. Four developments were responsible for settlement: a surge of immigration, the development of a gradual-roller milling process for hard spring wheat, the growth of flour milling in Minneapolis, and the building of railroads that tied North Dakota to the Minneapolis market. By the 1890 census, at the

end of the first surge of settlement, the state's population was 190,983. By 1900 North Dakota had a population of 319,146 and ranked with Minnesota and Kansas as a leading wheat state. The peak of homesteading came in 1906 when original entries were filed on 2,736,460 acres. In 1910, with settlement nearing completion, 71 percent of the population of 577,056 was of foreign stock. Of this, 29 percent was Scandinavian, 20 percent German, and 9 percent Canadian.

For years North Dakota was a colonial hinterland for the Twin Cities—Minneapolis and Saint Paul—which were not only the market for its wheat but also the headquarters for its railroads, its country and terminal grain elevators, and its bankers. Revolting against the exploitation inherent in colonial status, angry farmers joined the Populists in the 1890's, elected Eli C. D. Shortridge governor in 1892, overthrew the political machine of Alexander McKenzie, and made the socialistic Nonpartisan League the dominant power in state government from 1917 to 1921. In 1919 the legislature established a state-owned bank and a state-owned terminal elevator and flour mill.

In the 1920's there were many bank failures and farm bankruptcies in North Dakota, and in the 1930's there was a disastrous drought that further depressed farm income. The agrarian revolt continued with a wheat pool from 1922 to 1930; the North Dakota Farmers' Union, organized in 1927; and the governorship of William Langer, 1933–34 and 1937–39. The Farmers' Union secured the passage of an anticorporation farming law in 1932 and stimulated the growth of cooperative grain elevators and oil companies. Langer raised wheat prices by an embargo on shipments and stopped farm mortgage foreclosures by a moratorium. The 1940's brought good rains and farm prosperity. Although the population had begun to decline after reaching a peak in 1930, emigration reduced it to 617,761 by 1970. Drillers discovered oil at Tioga in 1951, the U.S. Corps of Engineers completed Garrison Dam in 1953, and the U.S. Air Force built bases at Grand Forks and Minot in 1956.

The anticapitalist ideology of the agrarian revolt tended to make North Dakotans noninterventionists. Probably a majority opposed entry into both World War I and World War II. In the 1930's North Dakota's Sen. Gerald P. Nye conducted the investigation of the munitions industry that led to the neutrality laws of 1935–37.

A majority of North Dakotans have been Republicans, although party loyalty is tempered by country-bred independence. Energetic and ambitious, North Dakotans have had a strong faith in education. In 1970 the state had 431 full-time college students for each 10,000 of population, compared with 287 for the United States. Although the growing size of farms (average 993 acres in 1973) reduced the rural population, North Dakota remained essentially rural and farm production remained the backbone of its economy. In 1970, the population density was only nine persons per square mile and the largest city, Fargo, had a population of only 53,365; Bismarck, the capital, had a population of 34,703. Fifty-six percent of the people lived in small towns or the countryside. The state thus maintained its rural characteristics—relatively low crime and divorce rates, frequent church attendance, and a neighborly friendliness.

[Elwyn B. Robinson, *History of North Dakota*.]

ELWYN B. ROBINSON

NORTHEAST BOUNDARY. The Definitive Treaty of Peace of 1783 designated the northeastern boundary of the United States as the Saint Croix River to its source, thence a line due north to the highlands dividing the rivers tributary to the Saint Lawrence River from those tributaries to the Atlantic, thence along the highlands to the most northwestern head of the Connecticut, down the latter to the forty-fifth parallel and along the parallel to the St. Lawrence (*see* Red Line Map). The controversy concerning the identity of the true Saint Croix was settled in 1798 by a mixed commission selected under a provision of Jay's Treaty. Unsuccessful attempts to decide on the line of the highlands were made in 1803 and 1807 by the negotiation of draft treaties that were never ratified. Another attempt was made in 1814 by a provision of the Treaty of Ghent, resulting in the appointment of a joint mixed commission, which, after working on the problem for six years, 1816–22, by examination of costly joint frontier surveys and acrimonious arguments, reached no agreement except an agreement to disagree and adjourned without resorting to the provision for selection of a friendly umpire.

Under a treaty of 1827 the question of the location of highlands and the ratification of the old survey of 1774 west of the Connecticut River was submitted for arbitration by the king of the Netherlands, William I, who, in 1831, proposed a compromise line along the upper Saint John and the Saint Francis tributary and westward to the line claimed by the United States (*see*

Netherlands Award). This proposal, not contemplated in the terms of the arbitration, the American government after some delay declined to accept.

Confronted by new border controversies and irritations resulting from the advance of settlements in part of the disputed territory, President Andrew Jackson suggested a renewal of diplomatic efforts, which were delayed for various reasons. The negotiations were continued in a tone that became more and more acrid until it impressed upon both contesting parties the necessity of a peaceful compromise to prevent border conflict in territory where each party had agreed to refrain from any extension of jurisdiction during the period of the negotiations for peaceful adjustment. From the devious negotiations and increasing danger finally emerged a friendlier attitude, and in 1842 it found practical expression in the Webster-Ashburton Treaty.

Early in 1838 Secretary of State John Forsyth contemplated the expediency of an attempt at direct negotiations for the establishment of a conventional line, but he obtained no encouragement from Massachusetts, while Maine, early in 1839, precipitated the border clash known as the Aroostook War. Meanwhile the situation had been complicated by unsettled questions concerning the British destruction of the *Caroline* on the Niagara River in 1837. (*See also* McLeod Case.)

In 1841 Secretary of State Daniel Webster, who succeeded Forsyth, determined to end the long dispute by conciliatory compromise. After declining the British proposal for arbitration by a commission of three European kings, he stated his decision to attempt a settlement on the basis of a conventional line, resulting in the British decision to appoint Alexander Baring, Lord Ashburton, as a special minister to conduct the negotiations at Washington. Webster tactfully prepared the way for the cooperation of Maine and Massachusetts.

The negotiators were at last successful in reaching an agreement to accept as the boundary the upper Saint John to the Saint Francis, thence a direct southwest line to a point near the southwest branch of the Saint John, thence a line via the crest of the hills to the northwest branch (Hall Stream) of the Connecticut River, and west of the Connecticut on the old survey line of the forty-fifth parallel to the Saint Lawrence. These agreements, and provisions for certain equivalents for loss of American territory in Maine, and other coincidental agreements were included in the Webster-Ashburton Treaty, which was signed at Washington, D.C., on Aug. 9, 1842.

[J. M. Callahan, *American Foreign Policy in Canadian Relations;* Albert B. Corey, *The Crisis of 1830–1842 in Canadian-American Relations.*]

J. M. CALLAHAN

NORTHERN PACIFIC RAILROAD. See Railroads, Sketches: Burlington Northern.

NORTHERN SECURITIES COMPANY V. UNITED STATES, 193 U.S. 197 (1904), started out as a rather ordinary contest between competitive railroad trunk lines over control of an intermediate feeder line and ended up as a struggle for supremacy between John Pierpont Morgan, James J. Hill, and their associates on one side and Edward H. Harriman and affiliated financial interests on the other. The former controlled the Northern Pacific and Great Northern railways. The latter controlled the Union Pacific system. The immediate occasion of the rivalry was an effort by Harriman to wrest from Morgan and Hill a special interest in the Chicago, Burlington and Quincy, thereby effecting an entrance into Chicago.

At first by stealthy moves and then by frenzied bidding culminating in the "Northern Pacific panic" of 1901, Harriman contrived to acquire a sufficient interest to give him a majority of the voting rights outstanding in Northern Pacific stock. He was checkmated by Morgan's threat to call for redemption the preferred stock, which represented a large part of Harriman's holdings. Negotiations ensued for a friendly settlement, and out of them emerged the Northern Securities Company. It was a holding company that took over all the contestants' stock interests in the Great Northern, Northern Pacific, and Burlington lines—and in this company the Morgan and Hill group held a controlling interest.

Challenged for violation of the Sherman Antitrust Act, the defendants contended that that act did not embrace the mere transfer of proprietary interests in any enterprise from one person to another and that if it was held to embrace such transfer, it was beyond the constitutional power of Congress to regulate, *a fortiori* to prohibit it. It was especially urged that if, as in this case, the purchasing party was a corporation duly organized by a sovereign state and expressly authorized to make the acquisitions attacked, the application of the Sherman Act's prohibitions would invade powers constitutionally reserved to the states.

The decision of the Supreme Court upheld the government's contention that the holding company had been used as an illegal device for restraining interstate trade, since its necessary effect was to eliminate competition in transportation service over a large section of the country.

[J. C. Gray, "The Merger Case," *Harvard Law Review,* vol. 17 (1904); H. R. Seager and C. Gulick, *Trust and Corporation Problems.*]

MYRON W. WATKINS

NORTHFIELD BANK ROBBERY. After some days of preliminary scouting, eight men, probably including Frank and Jesse James, and headed by Thomas ("Cole") Younger, a former Confederate guerrilla, rode into Northfield, Minn., about noon on Sept. 7, 1876. While three men attempted to hold up the First National Bank and killed teller Joseph Heywood, the remainder engaged in a wild gun battle with citizens, during which two bandits were killed and a bystander mortally wounded. On Sept. 21 posses surrounded four of the gang near Madelia—two having escaped—and after sharp firing in which one bandit was killed, the three Younger brothers, badly wounded, surrendered.

[John J. Lemon, *The Northfield Tragedy;* Thomas C. Younger, *The Story of Cole Younger.*]

WILLOUGHBY M. BABCOCK

NORTH SEA MINE BARRAGE, a World War I minefield 230 miles long and from fifteen to thirty-five miles wide, laid in 1918 between the Orkney Islands off northern Scotland and Norway to blockade German submarines. The mine, invented by Ralph C. Browne, of Salem, Mass., and perfected by S. P. Fullinwider and T. S. Wilkinson, Jr., of the U.S. Navy, could be placed as deep as 240 feet below the surface. It also had a long wire antenna that would explode the contents, 300 pounds of TNT, on contact with any metallic object.

The various parts were manufactured in different American factories, shipped to the west coast of Scotland, transported to Inverness on the east coast, and there assembled. From there minelayers, protected by screens of destroyers, cruisers, and battleships, planted the mines. Altogether 70,263 were laid, 56,571 by the United States and the rest by Britain. On one occasion more than 5,000 were dropped within four hours. After a few disastrous attempts on Mar. 3, 1918, in which 43 percent of the mines planted were lost in the operation, the real work began on June 7 and continued until Oct. 24. The cost of the mine barrage was $80 million.

From the day the work began, German U-boats

were damaged or destroyed. The exact number is unknown but is estimated at seventeen. The moral effect was perhaps greater in shattering the morale of German submarine crews and thus helping to produce the revolt of German seamen that marked the beginning of the defeat of Germany.

[Allan Westcott, ed., *American Sea Power Since 1775.*]

WALTER B. NORRIS

NORTHWEST ANGLE, a projection of land extending north of the forty-ninth parallel at the Lake of the Woods on the northern boundary of Minnesota. This area of about 130 square miles, separated from the rest of Minnesota by the southwest bay of the Lake of the Woods, is the northernmost territory in the United States proper. Ignorance of the geography of the region in 1783, when the Definitive Treaty of Peace was negotiated, resulted in this curious projection of the international boundary. The treaty provided that the northern boundary of the United States should extend due west from the northwest point of the Lake of the Woods to the Mississippi River. After explorers proved that the source of the Mississippi was not due west of the lake but considerably south, a proposal that the boundary should be drawn from the northwest point of the lake south to the forty-ninth parallel was adopted in the Convention of 1818. The Northwest Angle Inlet was designated as the northwest point of the lake in negotiations conducted in 1824, 1825, and 1842. Surveys of the boundary in this vicinity and decisions relating to it continued, however, and a treaty defining the boundary was made in 1925.

[John E. Parsons, *West on the 49th Parallel: Red River to the Rockies, 1872–1876.*]

T. C. BLEGEN

NORTHWEST BOUNDARY CONTROVERSY. The Definitive Treaty of Peace of 1783 between the United States and Great Britain provided that the boundary between the United States and British North America should proceed by various streams from the western head of Lake Superior to "the most Northwestern point" of the Lake of the Woods in Minnesota, "and from thence on a due west course to the Mississippi River." The negotiators had before them John Mitchell's Map of North America of 1755, which shows the Mississippi flowing out from under an insert map of Hudson Bay, which had been set into the upper left corner of the map. They assumed that the river rose north of a line due west from the north-

westernmost point of the Lake of the Woods. Actually, the source of the river is 152 miles south of that latitude. Thus a serious boundary gap was left by the peace settlement. It first became a matter of dispute in 1792, when Great Britain unsuccessfully proposed to close it by a boundary rectification that would have extended British territory south to the navigable waters of the Mississippi, thus giving Canada an access to that river, the free navigation of which had been guaranteed by the treaty of peace to the citizens and subjects of both parties. Jay's Treaty of 1794 established a mixed commission to determine the northwestern boundary, but it never met. In 1803 Rufus King signed a convention to close the gap by drawing a line from the Lake of the Woods to the source of the Mississippi River, but the Senate did not ratify it for fear of prejudicing the northern boundary of Louisiana, just acquired from France. In 1807 the United States proposed drawing a line north or south from the northwestern corner of the Lake of the Woods to the forty-ninth parallel and thence west along that parallel. The British negotiators accepted the proposal with the proviso that the words were added, "as far [along the forty-ninth parallel] as the territories of the United States extend in that quarter." James Monroe and William Pinkney, the American negotiators, rejected this phraseology because it implied a limitation of American territory anywhere along that line. During the negotiations for peace at Ghent in 1814 the British negotiators reverted to the project of setting up between the Ohio and Mississippi and the Great Lakes a "neutral Indian barrier state"—a proposal first introduced in 1792—and when this fell to the ground, they eluded discussion of the boundary west of the Lake of the Woods lest they recognize the American title to Louisiana, which they desired to annul. The peace treaty provided for mutual restoration of occupied territory without stipulating boundaries.

After the Napoleonic Wars Great Britain's need for repose caused it to cease contesting the American title to Louisiana, and the northwestern boundary gap disappeared in the Convention of 1818, which provided that the boundary should proceed from the northwesternmost corner of the Lake of the Woods to the forty-ninth parallel and along that parallel to the Rocky Mountains. Beyond the mountains the western territory and rivers claimed by either party were to be free and open for a term of ten years (extended indefinitely in 1826) to the vessels, citizens, and subjects of both parties to the treaty without prejudice to the claims of either. The northwest boundary controversy thus graduated from the closed northwest boundary gap to the Oregon issue, terminated in the Oregon Treaty of 1846 by extending the line of the forty-ninth parallel through to the Pacific Ocean.

[Samuel Flagg Bemis, "Jay's Treaty and the Northwest Boundary Gap," *American Historical Review,* vol. 27, and *A Diplomatic History of the United States.*]

SAMUEL FLAGG BEMIS

NORTH WEST COMPANY, a major fur trading firm organized in the winter of 1783–84, was never an incorporated company as were its chief rivals, the Hudson's Bay Company and the American Fur Company. It resembled a modern holding company, the constituent parts of which were chiefly Montreal firms and partnerships engaged in the fur trade. It came into existence during the period of the American Revolution and ended by coalescing with the Hudson's Bay Company in 1821. In the interim it had reorganized in 1783; added the firm of Gregory, McLeod and Company, its chief rival, in 1787; split into two factions in the later 1790's; reunited in 1804; joined forces with the American Fur Company temporarily in 1811; been ejected from effective work on the soil of the United States in 1816; and established its posts over much of Canada and the northern United States. Its main line of communication was the difficult canoe route from Montreal, up the Ottawa River, and through lakes Huron and Superior to its chief inland depot—Grand Portage before 1804 and Fort William thereafter. Beyond Lake Superior the route to the Pacific was the international boundary waters to Lake of the Woods (Minnesota), the Winnipeg River, Lake Winnipeg, the Saskatchewan River, the Peace River, and the Fraser River. Many lines branched from this main one, south into the Wisconsin, Dakota, Minnesota, and Oregon countries, north to Lake Athabasca and the Mackenzie River area. Attempts were made by the company, but unavailingly, to gain access to the interior through Hudson Bay, whose basin was the exclusive trading area of the Hudson's Bay Company. Excessive competition between the two companies was raised to fever pitch after Thomas Douglas, Earl of Selkirk, established his colony in the Red River valley in 1811, and it led to actual warfare. Thereafter, but only at the cost of sinking its individuality under the charter rights and acquiring the name of the Hudson's Bay Company, the North West Company got its cheaper transportation route. When this union occurred in 1821 the Scottish, Yankee, English, and French-Canadian employees of the North West Company had behind them nearly fifty years of valorous exploration and trailblazing; they had forced the Hudson's Bay Company to build forts in the interior, and they had developed the voyageur to the acme of his unique serviceability.

[Gordon C. Davidson, *The North West Company;* Douglas MacKay, *The Honourable Company;* W. Stewart Wallace, ed., *Documents Relating to the North West Company.*]

GRACE LEE NUTE

NORTHWEST CONSPIRACY. Military reverses in 1863–64 led to a Confederate effort to promote insurrection in the Northwest. Using the Sons of Liberty and other disaffected elements, it was planned to liberate Confederate prisoners at camps Douglas and Chase, in Chicago, Ill., and Columbus, Ohio, and at other prison camps; arm them from seized federal arsenals; and with the aid of the Sons of Liberty overthrow the governments of Ohio, Indiana, Illinois, and Missouri. It was further planned that a Northwestern confederacy, allied with the Confederate states, would be formed; peace terms would be dictated to a dismembered North.

Clement L. Vallandigham, supreme commander of the Sons of Liberty, then in Canada, refused to cooperate with Jacob Thompson, Confederate commissioner in Canada. Other less scrupulous Copperhead leaders accepted funds and promised cooperation. An uprising planned for July 20 was postponed to Aug. 16, and again to Aug. 29, the date of the Democratic National Convention at Chicago. The federal government learned of the plan and reinforced the guard at Camp Douglas, where the first blow was to be struck; the uprising did not take place, although sixty Confederates under Capt. T. H. Hines were present in Chicago.

Abandoning hope of Copperhead assistance, the Confederates proceeded in September and October to create diversions on the Canadian border, most important of which were John Yates Beall's raid to liberate prisoners on Johnson Island in Lake Erie and the raid on Saint Albans, Vt.

The Northwest conspiracy failed because Copperheads (or Peace Democrats) refused to take arms against the federal government and because Copperhead violence would endanger Democratic prospects in the campaign of 1864.

[E. J. Benton, *The Movement for Peace Without a Victory During the Civil War.*]

CHARLES H. COLEMAN

NORTHWEST ORDINANCES. *See* **Northwest Territory; Ordinances of 1784, 1785, and 1787.**

NORTHWEST PASSAGE. From 1497 to 1800, when it was believed that the riches of the Orient could be reached via a ship route around the northern extremities of North America, a northwest passage was the goal of many explorers. Further stimulus was provided by the papal bull of 1493 that barred all southern trade routes to countries other than Spain and Portugal. The most important explorers of this period were John Cabot (1497–98), Jacques Cartier (1534–35), Martin Frobisher (1576), John Davys (1585–87), and Henry Hudson (1610–11). They covered most of the shoreline and inlets of the northeastern section of the North American continent. By directing attention to certain areas for further search while negating others, they contributed to future exploration for a passage. William Baffin (1610), however, gave the quest a decided setback when, as a result of his one voyage to the Arctic, he declared that Baffin Bay was entirely landlocked.

Later the search for a water route took a more practical bent, a filling-in of geographical and scientific data. After the Napoleonic Wars, British naval officers under the supervision of John Barrow, second secretary of the admiralty, renewed exploration of the North American Arctic. The combined exploits of expeditions led by W. E. Parry (1819–20, 1821–23), John Franklin and John Richardson (1819–22, 1825–27), John Ross (1829–33), and R. J. L. M. McClure (1850–54) resulted in eventual success. Roald Amundsen (1903–06), a Norwegian, was the first to sail all the way from the Atlantic to the Pacific. Henry A. Larsen (1940–42), a sergeant in the Royal Canadian police, crossed eastward in the schooner *Saint Roch* along the same shallow route. In 1944, Larsen made the return journey in the same ship, following a deep-water route this time. In 1954 Capt. O. C. S. Robertson of the Royal Canadian Navy traversed the deep-water route westward with the icebreaker *Labrador*. In 1956 three U.S. Coast Guard vessels—*Storis, Spar,* and *Bramble*—led by the Canadian icebreaker *Labrador,* made the passage westward through the treacherous Bellot Strait, between Boothia Peninsula and Somerset Island.

The Northwest Passage consists of five possible routes through the Canadian Arctic archipelago, but only two are practical and only one is deep enough for large ships. The deep-water route extends westward from Baffin Bay through Lancaster Sound, Barrow Strait, Viscount Melville Sound, Prince of Wales Strait, and Amundsen Gulf to emerge into the Beaufort Sea. In an attempt to determine the type of tanker needed to reach Alaska's oil-rich north shore by a northern route, a $50 million project was begun in 1969 by three major oil companies. The *Manhattan*, the largest and most powerful ship built in the United States, was converted to a research vessel and the world's largest icebreaker. Accompanied by other icebreakers, the *Manhattan* sailed on Aug. 24, 1969, entering the Northwest Passage on Sept. 5. On Sept. 14 it reached Point Barrow, after breaking through 650 miles of ice. Although the voyage was made during the most favorable season for ice navigation, hull damage was sustained. Atomic submarines also have navigated an under-the-ice route across the North Pole via the Bering Strait to the Atlantic Ocean east of Greenland. Continued advances in technology may well render surface ship transport through the Northwest Passage economically feasible in the future.

[Ernest S. Dodge, *Northwest by Sea;* Bern Keating, *The Northwest Passage;* L. P. Kirwan, *A History of Polar Exploration;* Jeannette Mirsky, *To the North;* U.S. Department of the Navy, *Toward the Poles.*]

EDWIN A. MACDONALD

NORTHWEST TERRITORY, officially the "Territory Northwest of the River Ohio," included the Old Northwest when it was established by Congress July 13, 1787. The Ordinance of 1785 had already provided for the survey of the public land in townships, each six miles square and divided into thirty-six sections of 640 acres. Payment for the land was permitted in specie, or in Continental certificates, and, for one-seventh, the land warrants issued to revolutionary soldiers were accepted. The ordinance set aside section sixteen in each township for the support of education.

The Ordinance of 1787 outlined the governmental framework. At first there would be an arbitrary administration, with a governor, three judges, and a secretary elected by and responsible to Congress. When the population included 5,000 free white males of voting age, the territory would have local autonomy, with a legislative assembly, although Congress would still choose the governor. Finally, when any one of the stipulated divisions contained 60,000 free inhabitants, it would be admitted into the Union as a state. An important clause in the ordinance forbade slavery in the Old Northwest. The two ordinances, modified to meet changing conditions, remained the basic principles for the organization of the Old Northwest and set precedents for later territorial development.

In 1787 the Northwest Territory had a widely scattered population of some 45,000 Indians and 2,000

French. The first legal American settlement was made at Marietta (present-day Ohio), Apr. 7, 1788. Gov. Arthur Saint Clair inaugurated the territorial government, July 15, 1788, forming Washington County between the eastern boundary and the Scioto. In January 1790 he established Hamilton County between the Scioto and Miami rivers and in March he set up Saint Clair County along the Mississippi north of the Ohio. Winthrop Sargent, secretary of the territory, then organized Knox County between the Miami and Saint Clair County, and in 1796 he formed Wayne County with Detroit as the county seat. From these basic counties others were set off as population increased.

Because of a fear of attacks by Indians the earliest settlements were confined to the Ohio Valley, but after Gen. Anthony Wayne's decisive victory at Fallen Timbers, Aug. 20, 1794, and the subsequent Treaty of Greenville the greater part of Ohio was opened up. Population increased so rapidly that the autonomous stage of government was inaugurated Sept. 4, 1799, with the first meeting of the territorial assembly. Owing to the distance between many of the settlements a division of the territory became necessary, and in 1800 the area west of a line north from the mouth of the Kentucky River was set off as Indiana Territory. The diminished Northwest Territory was further decreased in 1803, when Michigan was annexed to Indiana.

A movement for statehood began, which was aided by the Jeffersonian Republican national victory in 1800. Although the territory had approximately only 42,000 inhabitants on Apr. 30, 1802, Jefferson approved the necessary enabling act. With the first meeting of the state legislature, Mar. 1, 1803, the Northwest Territory gave place to the state of Ohio.

[B. W. Bond, Jr., *Civilization of the Old Northwest;* R. C. Downes, *Frontier Ohio, 1788–1803.*]

BEVERLEY W. BOND, JR.

NORUMBEGA, a name of Indian origin applied vaguely to the New World north of Florida by 16th- and 17th-century cartographers. Samuel de Champlain in 1604 used the name to designate the Penobscot River, but no place by that name, as described by early explorers, ever existed.

[B. F. De Costa, "Norumbega and Its English Explorers," in Justin Winsor, *Narrative and Critical History,* vol. III.]

ELIZABETH RING

NORWEGIAN CHURCHES. Norwegian-American churches established in the 19th century reflected the Lutheran religious emphases in the homeland. Low-church revivalism, led by Elling Eielsen, a self-taught layman, formed the basis for the Eielsen Synod (1846). This body splintered when the majority organized Hauge's Synod (1876), named in memory of the Norwegian revivalist Hans Nielsen Hauge. Representatives of a more traditional Lutheranism, led by university-trained immigrant clergymen, organized (1853) the Norwegian Synod (popular name), which soon formed ties with the German Missouri Synod (popular name). By 1870 individuals who found the atmosphere in both of these groups uncongenial formed two new bodies, the Norwegian Augustana Synod and the Norwegian-Danish Conference. The predestination controversy within the Missouri-influenced Norwegian Synod led to the formation in the 1880's of the Anti-Missourian Brotherhood, which assumed leadership in a union movement that created the United Church (1890), consisting of the Anti-Missourians, the Augustanans, and the Conference. Polity and property disputes in the new body produced the Lutheran Free Church (1897). A second offshoot, the Lutheran Brethren, formed in 1900. Negotiations, begun in 1905, brought 98 percent of the Norwegian Lutherans into the Norwegian Lutheran Church of America (1917). An ultraconservative minority, the Norwegian Synod of the American Lutheran Church, was formed in 1918. The Norwegian Lutheran Church of America, known as the Evangelical Lutheran Church between 1946 and 1960, was united with the American Lutheran (German background) and the United Evangelical Lutheran (Danish background) churches to form The American Lutheran Church (1960). The Lutheran Free Church joined The American Lutheran Church in 1963. Membership in this church in the mid-1970's was about 2.5 million.

[E. Clifford Nelson, *The Lutheran Church Among Norwegian-Americans,* vol. II; E. Clifford Nelson and Eugene L. Fevold, *The Lutheran Church Among Norwegian-Americans,* vol. I.]

E. CLIFFORD NELSON

NORWEGIAN IMMIGRATION. *See* **Immigration.**

"NOT WORTH A CONTINENTAL." Five days after the Battle of Bunker Hill (June 17, 1775) the Continental Congress authorized the issuance of bills of credit to the amount of $2 million. During the remainder of the revolutionary war forty emissions were made in a total amount of $241,552,780. Depreciation eventually became marked. With an exchange value in the closing year of the war as low as 1,000 to 1, these bills of credit became a symbol of absolute worthlessness, whence the expression "not worth a continental."

[D. R. Dewey, *Financial History of the United States.*]
J. HARLEY NICHOLS

NOVA CAESAREA. *See* **New Caesarea.**

"NO-WIN POLICY," a derogatory term first used in 1950–51 by militant groups in America who opposed President Harry S. Truman's strategy of limited war in Korea and argued for an "all-out" effort to achieve "total victory." The Truman administration held fast to a posture of both limited objectives (avoiding general war with China or Russia) and limited means (no use of nuclear weapons) in Korea. After repelling the initial North Korean aggression and restoring the division of Korea at the thirty-eighth parallel, the administration was prepared, on behalf of both the United States and the United Nations, to negotiate a truce.

The concept of limited military objectives at that time ran hard against the grain of both the American experience and the American temperament in war: in World War I, Americans had fought "to make the world safe for democracy"; in World War II, their national leaders had demanded "unconditional surrender" of Adolf Hitler, Benito Mussolini, and the Japanese warlords. Traditionalists, including advocates of "preventive war" and other political hawks, thus objected to the Truman strategy of restraint as a "no-win policy"; they failed to grasp, or refused to accept, that his posture was dictated by a concern to save the world from a nuclear holocaust. In April 1951, Gen. Douglas MacArthur epitomized the traditional view in his pronouncement (set forth in a letter to Rep. Joseph W. Martin) that "there is no substitute for victory." Five days later, Truman removed MacArthur from command of all U.S. and UN forces in Korea and Japan.

The term "no-win policy" was later used by right-wingers to express opposition to the whole broad strategy of coexistence with the Soviet Union and Communist China pursued by presidents Dwight D. Eisenhower, John F. Kennedy, and Lyndon B. Johnson.

TOWNSEND HOOPES

NUCLEAR PHYSICS. *See* **Physics, Nuclear.**

NUCLEAR TEST BAN TREATY was largely a result of worldwide public pressure to eliminate the health hazard of radioactive fallout from exploding atom bombs. By 1954 governments felt that pressure to be sufficiently strong to deal with the problem seriously. Previously, banning nuclear tests had been a minor aspect of general and futile disarmament talks. On May 10, 1955, the Soviet Union seized the initiative by making the test ban a major point in its general disarmament proposal. Although in the course of time it changed the details of the proposal, it consistently favored a simple prohibition of testing nuclear devices. The American government rejected this idea for several years, arguing that without an international inspection system a test ban or disarmament in general would be dangerous to national security and that, besides, a "clean" bomb would soon be developed, making a test ban superfluous. The resulting debate between the Soviet Union, the United States, and Great Britain merely served to arouse public opinion further. The controversial issue figured prominently in the American presidential elections of 1956 and 1960. On Jan. 12, 1957, the American government felt obliged to announce the conditions under which it would consider a test ban and thereby allowed the problem to be dealt with separately from general disarmament negotiations. But it took another six and a half years before an independent agreement could be reached, and, ironically, by that time the motivation for conciliatory attitudes had changed in the United States and the Soviet Union, although not in Britain.

The negotiations during this period paralleled the vicissitudes of the cold war. For instance, in 1958 the three governments each renounced independently any further tests but soon after resumed them, mainly for political reasons. After the U-2 spy plane incident and the cancellation of the Paris summit conference in 1960, negotiations slowed down considerably and at times were even integrated again with the hopeless general disarmament talks. In spite of public demands in many countries for a test ban, it was clear that the negotiations were decisively affected by considerations of foreign policy, national security, and cold war propaganda. A gradual rapprochement between the United States and the Soviet Union on the test ban question was caused by changing incentives on both sides to reach agreement. In the United States, preoccupation with a nuclear balance of power and a general inspection system for disarmament was partly replaced by a desire to prevent the enlargement of the "nuclear club." In the Soviet Union the growing split with China made a test ban agreement desirable. Very likely also, the development of reconnaissance satellites made on-site inspection increasingly unimportant to the United States and the Soviet Union.

On Aug. 27, 1962, the United States, in a major concession, and the United Kingdom presented a draft treaty resembling a Soviet proposal of Nov. 28, 1961, both calling for the end of tests in the atmosphere, in space, and under water. The problem of underground tests was left unmentioned because the parties were too far apart in their views. The Cuban missile crisis and its settlement provided the final impetus to conclusive action. On Aug. 5, 1963, the United States, Great Britain, and the Soviet Union signed an agreement in Moscow, open for signature to all other nations. All test explosions of nuclear weapons or other devices in the atmosphere, in space, and under water were prohibited. The signatories also promised not to participate in any way in such tests by others. More than 100 acceded to the treaty. Among them was India but not France and China. The treaty was hailed as a precedent for other disarmament measures, as a means for stopping the spread of nuclear weapons to other nations, and as a major contribution to the reduction of international tensions. Subsequent events showed that these hopes were not fully realized.

[Arthur H. Dean, *Test Ban and Disarmament: The Path of Negotiation;* Harold K. Jacobson and Eric Stein, *Diplomats, Scientists, and Politicians: The United States and the Nuclear Test Ban Negotiations;* Mary Milling Lepper, *Foreign Policy Formulation: A Case Study of the Nuclear Test Ban Treaty of 1963;* David E. Mark, *Die Einstellung der Kernwaffenversuche.*]

WERNER LEVI

NUECES RIVER, which empties into Corpus Christi Bay, was the subject of two boundary disputes, first between the Texas Republic and Mexico (1836–46) and next between the United States and Mexico (1846–48). Although Texas had never extended west of the Nueces as a Spanish or a Mexican province, the Texas Republic claimed the Rio Grande as its boundary. After annexation to the United States, the claims of Texas were supported when President James K. Polk sent troops beyond the Nueces, and then asked Congress to declare war against Mexico for attacking them because they were on American soil. Mexico claimed the Americans were invaders. The Rio Grande became the boundary of Texas by the Treaty of Guadalupe Hidalgo in 1848.

L. W. NEWTON

NULLIFICATION, the act by which a state suspends, within its territorial jurisdiction, a federal law. The doctrine of nullification evolved from the theory that the Union was the result of a compact between sovereign states, that the Constitution was a body of instructions drawn up by the states for the guidance of the general government, that the states were the rightful judges of infractions of the Constitution, and that the states were not bound by the acts of their agent when it exceeded its delegated powers. The right of nullification was first asserted by Virginia and Kentucky in their resolutions of 1798. The Kentucky resolutions of 1799 boldly asserted that nullification was the "rightful remedy" for infractions of the Constitution. Only fifteen years later the fundamental principles of nullification were again invoked by the action of the Hartford Convention of 1814. Georgia not only nullified the decisions of the Supreme Court in its controversy with the Cherokee in the early 1830's but also prevented their enforcement (*see Cherokee Nation* v. *Georgia*). Several northern states nullified the Fugitive Slave Law of 1850 by the passage of personal liberty laws.

The most notable example of nullification occurred in South Carolina after opposition to the protective tariff began to develop in the South in the 1820's. This hostility mounted to such proportions that the legislature of South Carolina in 1828 printed and circulated Sen. John C. Calhoun's *Exposition,* which reaffirmed the doctrines of 1798 and formulated a program of action—the interposition of the state's veto through the people in sovereign convention assembled. The South Carolinians then waited, expecting the administration of President Andrew Jackson to reduce the tariff. When Congress enacted a tariff act in 1832 that proclaimed protection a permanent policy, the nullifiers carried the issue to the people. They won control of the legislature and called a state convention (Nov. 19, 1832). This body adopted the Ordinance of Nullification declaring the tariff acts of 1828 and 1832 oppressive, unconstitutional, null and void, and not binding on the people of South Carolina. Appeals to the federal courts were forbidden, and state officials were required to take an oath to support the ordinance. The legislature later passed acts necessary to put the ordinance into effect. South Carolina expected other southern states to follow its lead, but none supported nullification, although several protested against protective tariffs.

Jackson issued a proclamation on Dec. 10, 1832, in which he denounced nullification as rebellion and treason and warned the people of South Carolina that he would use every power at his command to enforce the laws. In a message to Congress he urged modification of the tariff and, later, asked the passage of a "force act" to enable him to use the army and navy in enforcing the law. Before the date set for the ordinance to take effect, Feb. 1, 1833, measures for reducing the tariff were introduced in Congress. Consequently, a South Carolina committee, empowered by the convention to act, suspended the ordinance until Congress should take final action. Both the Force Act and the Compromise Tariff were passed by Congress, and both were approved by the president early in March. The convention reassembled on Mar. 11, 1833, and rescinded the Ordinance of Nullification, but nullified the Force Act. The nullifiers, who had claimed their action peaceable, argued that the reduction of the tariff duties amply justified their position and action.

The doctrine of nullification was again raised in 1954, when the Supreme Court declared racial segregation unconstitutional in *Brown* v. *Board of Education of Topeka*. No state, however, chose to call a special state convention to nullify the decision, but chose instead to evade compliance, especially through state legislation and litigation.

[H. V. Ames, *State Documents on Federal Relations;* Frederic Bancroft, *Calhoun and the South Carolina Nullification Movement;* C. S. Boucher, *The Nullification Controversy in South Carolina;* John R. Schmidhauser, *The Supreme Court as Final Arbiter in Federal-State Relations, 1789–1957.*]

FLETCHER M. GREEN

NUMBER 4, now Charlestown, N.H., settled in 1740, was then the most northerly English post in the Connecticut Valley, many miles off in the wilderness. Its chief building was a strong fort built in 1744. Attacked frequently by the French and Indians, it was of great military importance in blocking this line of approach to Massachusetts, which had claimed title also since 1736 and maintained a garrison there. It was a base for several advances on Canada, and during the Revolution for Gen. John Stark's troops before the Battle of Bennington.

[Jeremy Belknap, *History of New Hampshire;* H. H. Saunderson, *History of Charlestown.*]

HERBERT W. HILL

NURSING. The origins of American nursing can be traced, in part, to the humanitarian ideals, sanitary reforms, and scientific progress characteristic of medicine in the late 19th century. Although no longer monopolized by the moralism of the religious orders, nursing attracted many women because of its ideals of service. The hygienic values of the sanitary reformers were incorporated into the designs of hospitals, by then viewed as institutions exclusively devoted to the care of the sick. In these hospitals, physicians could attend to a larger number of patients and they could offer an ever-increasing array of technically effective services. With the advent of new diagnostic and therapeutic instruments (for example, thermometers, sphygmomanometers, hypodermic needles) and the rise of the new surgery made possible by anesthetics and antiseptic techniques, patients needed responsible attendants, and physicians needed knowledgeable assistants. By 1873 four hospitals were operating schools of nursing: the New England Hospital for Women and Children in Boston; Massachusetts General Hospital in Boston; New Haven Hospital in New Haven, Conn.; and Bellevue Hospital in New York City. These early schools, though, provided mostly apprenticeship training, at best.

Hospital administrators soon realized that improved nursing care diminished mortality and morbidity on the wards and that young, idealistic women could be encouraged to care for the sick in return for training and "board and keep." In 1873 there were 178 hospitals in the United States; by 1909 the number had increased to more than 4,000. By 1893 there were 225 hospital nursing schools, and by 1900, at least 432. The students learned from older nurses, matrons, or superintendents, and physicians who volunteered to give lectures or demonstrations. In 1907 Columbia University appointed Mary Adelaide Nutting as the first full-time American professor of nursing.

Nutting had been one of the first graduate nurses to urge the establishment of a professional journal for nursing. After several years of struggle, the *American Journal of Nursing* appeared in 1900. Prior to that, Nutting's predecessors at the Johns Hopkins Hospital School of Nursing, Isabel Hampton and Lavinia Dock, had been instrumental in the establishment of two professional nurse associations: the American Society of Superintendents of Training Schools for Nurses of the United States and Canada (1894) and the Nurses Associated Alumnae of the United States and Canada (1896). By 1912 the former group, now known as the National League of Nursing Education, and the latter group, now known as the American Nurses' Association, adopted the *American Journal of Nursing* as their official publication. In recognition of the growing number of public health nurses who worked in homes, clinics, schools, and industries, the National Organization for Public Health Nursing was organized in 1912.

By 1914 forty-one states had adopted nurse practice acts, thereby establishing state boards of nurse examiners. The graduates of schools approved by these boards were authorized to use the title "Registered Nurse" (RN). Many of these state boards established criteria for evaluating schools, but standards were not very high.

With cues from the successful reforms in medical education, nurse educators undertook a thorough evaluation of nursing schools between 1913 and 1937. The National League of Nursing Education prepared a standardized curriculum that was gradually adopted. Between 1929 and 1937, nursing schools reduced their enrollment, made admission qualifications more rigid, eliminated monthly stipends for hospital services, and discharged students with poor grades. A truly national program of accreditation became effective with the formation of the National Nursing Accrediting Service in January 1949.

As the demand for nurses became particularly acute during and after World War II, the problems of balancing quality and quantity loomed large. Fraught with considerable intramural squabbling, several kinds of educational programs evolved. The majority remained in hospitals; they included short-term training programs for practical or vocational nurses and diploma programs that afforded eligibility for licensure after two or three years of study. In 1957, 81.9 percent of American nursing schools were under hospital or noncollegiate control. Of nurses graduating in 1963, 82.5 percent received diplomas from 874 hospital schools. Some nurse educators believed that nursing education must be interdigitated with baccalaureate education. The University of Minnesota offered the first baccalaureate degree program in 1909. By 1929 there were 32 such programs; by 1962, 174. In that year, 13.8 percent of 31,000 nurse graduates had received baccalaureate degrees. The third major approach involved numerous junior colleges that appeared after World War II. In 1962, 3.7 percent of nursing graduates were trained in 69 associate degree programs mostly affiliated with these junior colleges. By 1973 there were 574 such programs, along with 305 baccalaureate degree programs and 494 diploma programs. The trend has been toward an increase in baccalaureate and associate degree programs and a decrease in diploma programs.

After 1925 nurses experienced severe social and scientific stresses in their quest for professional status. Primarily women until the 1960's, nurses have participated in the many vicissitudes of the woman's rights movement. The demands of marriage and family together with the competitive attractions of other occupations and professions have influenced the evolution of nursing in a profound way. Professionally, nurses have acquired an extraordinary new array of scientific and technical responsibilities. Rapidly accepting many new tasks in operating rooms, on the wards, and in outpatient clinics, nurses have even begun to specialize in the same fashion as physicians. Furthermore, the advent of the pediatric nurse practitioner program in the 1960's has given rise to a new group of nurse professionals whose functions are very similar to those of some orthodox medical practitioners.

[Richard A. Shryock, *The History of Nursing.*]
CHESTER R. BURNS

NUTRITION AND VITAMINS. Although some interest in nutrition had been evinced earlier, especially with regard to the diet of workingmen, and although agricultural experiment stations had been dealing with nutrition as a function of animal husbandry, American scientific interest in the field began late in the 19th century.

The original thrust of American interest is to be found in W. O. Atwater's compilation of food-composition tables based on chemical analysis that was published by the Department of Agriculture in 1896. Breaking foods down primarily into percentages of protein, carbohydrates, and fats and indicating caloric values for each food, these tables became basic to the scientific and economic dietetics of the period. Biochemistry and the study of metabolism turned the study of nutrition in new directions. The investigation of the role of proteins by T. B. Osborne and R. H. Chittenden, starting in 1890, led to the study of amino acids; the existence of one or more "essential" amino acids was recognized by 1914 (L. B. Mendel and Osborne).

Other researchers (A. Harden, W. J. Young, C. F. Cori, G. T. Cori) elucidated the biochemistry of carbohydrate utilization by the body. Still others dispelled the notion that fats were not essential in the diet, their work culminating, in 1929–30, in the recognition of indispensability of unsaturated fatty acids in human diet (G. O. Burr and M. M. Burr). Americans also played a part in the understanding of the nutritive role of inorganic and trace elements.

It was becoming evident by 1913 that sound nutrition and the metabolic processes also depended on what European researchers were calling "vitamines." In the era of vitamin research that followed, American scientists played a prominent role, although hardly independent from the work of scientists in other countries. Outstanding among the many great contributors to the field were Elmer V. McCollum, who, with his associates, recognized the existence of fat-soluble A (later called vitamin A) and water-soluble B (later shown to be a complex of vitamins) in 1914–15 and distinguished vitamin D from vitamin A in 1922; Osborne and Mendel, who recognized vitamin A almost simultaneously with McCollum; J. Goldberger, who, from 1915 on, established pellagra as a deficiency disease; H. M. Evans and K. S. Bishop, who discovered vitamin E in 1922; C. A. Elvehjem and associates, whose accomplishments included the identification, in 1937, of nicotinic acid (niacin) as a factor whose absence caused pellagra; and Karl A. Folkers, who played a leading role in the synthesis of vitamin B_6 (1939), pantothenic acid (1940), biotin (1943), and vitamin B_{12} (1948).

The ability of the pharmaceutical and chemical industries to crystallize and synthesize vitamins and to produce them on a large scale had a twofold consequence. First was the availability to the public of enormous quantities of vitamins, puffed to the medical profession and to the public by persistent and persuasive advertising. At times the taking of multivitamins or of particular vitamins has reached fad proportions. A U.S. Census estimate placed the value, on the manufacturers' level, of the domestic sale of vitamins, nutrients, and hematinics at almost $500 million in 1970. This suggests an overuse of vitamins, both in terms of questionable use and effectiveness for well-nourished people and in terms of possible dangers from excessive intake. In 1972 the Food and Drug Administration took steps, on these grounds, to limit the amounts of vitamins A and D compounded into vitamin pills.

The second consequence of the technological potential in the production of vitamins is the restoration, enrichment, fortification, or supplementation of foods by the addition of vitamins and other dietary essentials. In the United States, such procedures are not required by federal law, but when voluntarily undertaken they must conform with standards set by law. The process began with the addition of skim-milk solids to bread mix after a suggestion made to the National Bakers Association by McCollum in 1923. In 1924 potassium iodide was added to salt. In 1936 evaporated and whole milk were fortified with vitamin D. Since then nonfat dried milk, corn products, rice, pastas, and cereal breakfast foods have all been enriched or fortified. The enrichment of certain breads and flour became compulsory during World War II, and after the war approximately thirty states adopted laws requiring such enrichment. Nonetheless, in 1974 the National Research Council's Food and Nutrition Board found that significant numbers of Americans suffered from a variety of vitamin and mineral deficiencies and recommended that all foods made of wheat, corn, or rice be enriched with ten named essential nutrients. (The board, whose existence reflected the disclosure of widespread nutritional problems by Selective Service medical examinations during World War II, has established standards known as recommended dietary allowances. First issued in 1943, the allowances have been revised and updated at intervals since then.)

The persistence of undernutrition and malnutrition in American life was generally recognized. Statistics indicated that deaths from avitaminosis and other vitamin deficiencies still totaled 2,543 in 1968, although this was a low 1.3 per 100,000 population. Presidents from Franklin D. Roosevelt to Richard M. Nixon called the matter to public attention, and a National Nutrition Conference for Defense (1941) and a White House Conference on Food, Nutrition and Health (1969) dealt with the problem, the latter labeling hunger and malnutrition "a national emergency." In 1968 the Senate established the Select Committee on Nutrition and Human Needs, which has been carrying on an almost continuous series of hearings, conferences, and publications. Twelve million Americans, the select committee noted in 1973, were still undernourished and although some progress had been made, the next year it was reported that the needy in the United States were hungrier than four years earlier. (In 1974 National Nutrition Policy Study hearings held by the select committee produced recommendations for the "institutionalization" of governmental nutritional responsibilities and efforts. A panel of experts recommended a unified National Nutrition Plan; a Federal Food and Nutrition Office with responsibility for implementing the plan; a National Nutrition Center in the Department of Health, Education, and Welfare to administer nutrition programs; and more. Some of these had already been recommended at the White House Conference five years earlier.)

The response to the apparent need, although undernutrition rather than malnutrition was often the primary consideration, began much earlier than these activities. A school lunch program, begun originally under the Works Progress Administration (WPA) auspices, came into its own under the National School Lunch Act of 1946. A milk program (1954), a school breakfast program (1966), and assistance to day-care centers and the like (1968) were added, and in 1975 it was estimated that 9 million children were involved in the program.

A second program, begun in the 1930's, was a federal program of donating commodities to low-income families through state and local governments. Originally the Commodity Distribution Program gave little consideration to questions of nutrition. In 1961 and 1968 steps were taken to insure variety as well as quantity of the food offered, with special emphasis on proteins and vitamin-fortified foods. Department of Agriculture figures showed that 3,205,013 individuals were participating in the commodity distribution programs in April 1969.

The third program, inaugurated in 1939, was the food-stamp program. It did not become available to every county and city that wanted it until 1964 but developed into a primary weapon for combating undernutrition and malnutrition and by 1975 the select committee declared it to be "no longer an experiment. . . . It works." In 1975 the select committee estimated that 18 million people were reached by the program and an unfriendly observer estimated that the program would cost $6.6 billion per year by 1976. (Various programs for nutrition of the elderly sought to tie them into the food-stamp program in 1970 and to provide them with the equivalent of the school lunch program in 1972.)

The success of these programs in terms of providing nutrition for all Americans has been hampered by many problems other than those peculiar to the scientific and administrative aspects of the problem. Financing was always a problem, aggravated by the government's tendency to deal with hunger rather than with nutrition. The nutrition programs also had to contend with rivalries between the administration and Congress, with problems of federal-state relationships, with problems of welfare reform in general, and with problems of racial discrimination. Basic, too, was the problem of serving two masters: the agricultural community interested in price maintenance and marketing of surplus crops on the one side and the nutritionists concerned with undernutrition and malnutrition on the other. Finally, the world's population explosion and the concomitant pressure on the food supply, coupled with rising food costs and a

general inflation at home, made it increasingly difficult to realize a domestic program that would banish hunger and provide proper nutrition.

Proper nutrition was not solely a problem of the poor in the United States. Malnutrition was to be found in all strata of society, reflecting ignorance of sound nutrition practices and the inertia of traditional food habits; the impact of processing, preserving, and freezing food; the decreasing consumption, perhaps as a concomitant of the last, of fresh vegetables and fruits. Overnutrition—a consequence of excessive ingestion of fat, sugar, and alcohol and of a sedentary life—and the atherosclerosis and heart disease that come out of it, have turned the attention of nutritionists in a new direction. (In 1968 over 1 million Americans died from heart disease—three times as many as from malignant neoplasms—a rate of 512.1 per 100,000 population. In 1973 the Select Committee noted that 30 percent of Americans were overweight.) Twentieth-century technology and life-style thus have had an impact on nutrition that has extended beyond the perimeters of economic disadvantage.

[A. M. Beeuwkes et al., *Essays on History of Nutrition and Dietetics;* E. V. McCollum, *A History of Nutrition;* J. R. K. Robson et al., *Malnutrition: Its Causes and Controls.*]

DAVID L. COWEN

OATHS. *See* **Test Laws.**

OATMAN GIRLS. The Oatman family of overland emigrants to California was attacked in 1851 by western Yavapai—mistakenly identified as Apache—in southwestern Arizona about eighty miles from Fort Yuma. Six of the nine members of the party were slain. A son, Lorenzo, was left for dead by the Indians but managed to make his way back to the Pima villages. The two surviving girls, Olive, aged fifteen, and Mary Ann, aged seven, were taken as captives to the Yavapai camp. In 1852 the Yavapai traded the girls to the Mohave for horses and food. Mary Ann died during a famine, but Olive lived with the Mohave for four years. In 1856 the Mohave released Olive and allowed her to be escorted to Fort Yuma.

[Kenneth M. Stewart, "A Brief History of the Mohave Indians Since 1850," *Kiva,* vol. 34; E. B. Stratton, *The Captivity of the Oatman Girls.*]

KENNETH M. STEWART

OATS, like most cultivated plants, were domesticated from wild varieties at an unknown time and place.

They spread from western Europe to other parts of the world and were brought to North America by New World explorers. Bartholomew Gosnold planted oats on the Elizabeth Islands in Buzzards Bay about 1600, and the Jamestown colonists planted them in 1611. They were grown early in Newfoundland and New Netherland and spread throughout the English colonies. George Washington had several hundred acres in oats at his Mount Vernon farm.

Oats thrive in a cool climate with abundant rainfall but can be grown from Alaska to Texas. Oat breeders have been concerned with developing more productive varieties but even more with varieties resistant to rust, smut, and other diseases to which oats are particularly susceptible. During the 1960's, efforts were made to breed oats with a higher protein content. Oats are particularly suitable for rotation crops and for farm use as livestock feed. Long the outstanding feed for horses, oat production has declined sharply in the United States with the comparative disappearance of horses from American streets and farms.

In 1839, when the United States produced 123 million bushels, New York and Pennsylvania were the leading producers. In 1909, when production exceeded 1 billion bushels, Illinois and Iowa were the leading states. Peak production occurred in 1917 with over 1.5 billion bushels. Production in 1974 was 621 million bushels, with Minnesota and Iowa the leading producers.

[U.S. Department of Agriculture, *Yearbooks* (1922, 1936).]

WAYNE D. RASMUSSEN

OBERLIN MOVEMENT, in its antislavery aspect was an evangelical agitation throughout the West against slavery. In essence the movement began in 1834 at Lane Theological Seminary in Cincinnati, with an eighteen-day "debate" among the students on slavery. Conducted by a quondam revivalist, Theodore D. Weld, the discussion converted the whole student body, northerners and southerners alike, to the duty of antislavery agitation. When the trustees of the seminary attempted by repressive regulations to end the agitation, most of the students promptly withdrew, and enrolled next year at Oberlin College in Ohio. These antislavery evangelists proceeded to convert the community, the Western Reserve, and much of Ohio and the West to the abolition cause.

[G. H. Barnes, *The Antislavery Impulse, 1830–1844.*]

GILBERT HOBBS BARNES

OBERLIN-WELLINGTON RESCUE CASE grew out of the release in 1858 by a rescue party from Oberlin, Ohio, of a fugitive slave in the custody of a federal officer, at the village of Wellington, nine miles south of Oberlin. The rescuers, mostly citizens of Oberlin and students of the college, were indicted under the Fugitive Slave Act of 1850. From their jail in Cleveland they published a newspaper, *The Rescuer;* through the barred windows they addressed mass meetings of sympathizers; and in their cells they entertained correspondents of eastern newspapers and deputations from churches and philanthropic societies. The indictments were shortly dismissed and the rescuers freed.

[H. H. Catterall, *Judicial Cases Concerning American Slavery and the Negro;* J. H. Shipherd, *History of the Oberlin-Wellington Rescue.*]

GILBERT HOBBS BARNES

OBLONG, a narrow strip of land, 61,440 acres, along the eastern borders of Dutchess, Putnam, and Westchester counties, which was ceded to New York by Connecticut in 1731, in return for a rectangular strip along Long Island Sound and west of the boundary line that had been confirmed by the crown in 1700. The survey of the boundary line made at this time was satisfactory to neither New York nor Connecticut, and bickering continued until 1860, when a survey was made that satisfied both states.

In 1731 the oblong was patented in London to Sir Joseph Eyles and Company. The colonial government of New York patented the same tract to Thomas Hawley and associates. The consequent litigation was terminated by the Revolution, the American patentees remaining in possession.

[Frank Hasbrouck, *History of Dutchess County.*]

A. C. FLICK

OBSERVATORIES, ASTRONOMICAL. The first astronomical observations in the New World were made by the early European navigators and explorers. Amerigo Vespucci cataloged the southern stars as seen from the coast of South America in 1499 and 1501. The scientifically inclined residents of colonial America, like their counterparts in England, used both the telescope and the unaided eye to determine latitude and longitude and to view the sun, moon, stars, planets, comets, and solar and lunar eclipses. Although numerous observations were made, only temporary viewing platforms—like that established by David Rittenhouse for the 1769 transit of Venus—were used.

During the first fifty years of the new republic serious agitation for the establishment of permanent astronomical observatories was mounted by Ferdinand R. Hassler, the first director of the U.S. Coast Survey, and by President John Quincy Adams, who urged the erection of what he called "lighthouses of the skies." The first fruits of their urgings were soon forthcoming.

As astronomical apparatus became increasingly available between 1830 and the Civil War, private individuals such as William Mitchell on Nantucket, Mass., routinely observed the heavens. Lewis M. Rutherfurd in New York City experimented with celestial photography and spectroscopy. Small schools, such as Transylvania College (now a university) at Lexington, Ky., taught practical, as well as theoretical, astronomy. In addition about twenty-five notable observatories were built and equipped with equatorial refracting telescopes for viewing celestial bodies and with meridian instruments for measuring their positions. Support for these new observatories and their functions varied greatly. The U.S. Naval Observatory, Washington, D.C., established by Congress in 1842, served as the national observatory. Private colleges, often with the assistance of wealthy alumni, built observatories on their campuses. And in many communities local citizens pooled their resources to finance observatories. Some observatories served commercial interests by supplying standard time for ships and railroads and served as bases from which terrestrial distances could be measured. Most college observatories were used for teaching, but some discouraged students in favor of scientific research. In some instances, as in the case of Harvard (1839), the community paid for a research observatory; in others, such as Cincinnati Astronomical Society (1843), hundreds of citizens contributed to the observatory fund so that they might all share in the enjoyment of a first-class telescope. In still other instances, notably Dudley Observatory set up in Albany, N.Y., in 1853, differences between the democratic motivations of the sponsors and the professional aspirations of the astronomers led to open conflict.

Between the Civil War and World War II astronomical observatories proliferated across the United States. They were built on almost every college campus and in the backyards of countless amateur astronomers. Telescopes became a popular outlet for philanthropy; indeed, they were often seen as avenues to immortality—San Francisco philanthropist James Lick's ashes repose in the great telescope that bears his name. As the 19th century progressed, air pollution and the proliferation of electric lights impeded observations in urban areas. New observatories and branches of old ones were built in the countryside and on high mountains, in the western states, in South America, and in Africa.

The American mania for getting there first was reflected in the telescope race run in the second half of the 19th century. Five times Alvan Clark and Sons of Cambridgeport, Mass., produced refractors larger than any previous ones: 18.5 inches (1863), Dearborn Observatory in Chicago, later relocated to Evanston, Ill., at Northwestern University; 26 inches (1872), U.S. Naval Observatory; 30 inches (1883), Pulkovo Observatory, near Leningrad, Russia; 36 inches (1887), Lick Observatory, near San Jose, Calif.; and 40 inches (1897), Yerkes Observatory, at Williams Bay, Wis. (still the largest refractor in use in the mid-1970's). A similar series of improvements occurred in the early 20th century, this time with reflectors: 60 inches (1908), Mount Wilson, Calif.; 100 inches (1918), Mount Wilson; and 200 inches (1948), Palomar Mountain, Calif.

In a well-equipped observatory of the late 19th century it was usual to find apparatus for celestial photography, spectroscopy, and photometry, in addition to the more traditional astronomical apparatus. Long-exposure photographs revealed otherwise invisible celestial objects and produced pictures from which celestial distances and magnitudes could be more precisely measured. Analyses of the position and intensity of the spectral lines provided, for the first time, information about the temperature, density, chemical composition, and evolution of celestial bodies. Photometry, the precise measurement of celestial brightnesses, led to an improved understanding of stellar structure.

Because refracting telescopes—those with a large lens—do not focus light of all colors at the same place, a refractor designed for visual observations cannot produce first-rate photographs. In the second half of the 19th century many visual refractors were adapted for photography either by the addition of a photographic correcting lens or by the substitution of a photographic lens for the regular visual one. Increasingly, astronomers recognized the advantages of reflecting telescopes for celestial photography, and instrumentmakers learned to satisfy their demands. They also learned to make the spectroscopes and photometers needed for astrophysical researches.

In the years after World War II, primarily because of federal largesse, the number of working astronomers vastly increased, and their instruments developed dramatically. The range of radiation that astronomers were able to study increased severalfold: radio telescopes ''see'' the radio waves that reach the earth; rockets carry infrared and ultraviolet detectors above the obscuring atmosphere. Apollo missions into outer space permitted an intimate examination of the moon, while unmanned missions led to a better understanding of other planets. Contributions were also made by orbiting solar observatories and Skylab. The application of electronics to conventional earth-based instruments greatly increased their range and precision, and electronic computers quickly solved countless problems that could take months if done by hand. In the period 1968–72 a general disillusionment with science coincided with a reduction in financial support for astronomy.

[*Bulletin of the American Astronomical Society,* vol. 1 (1969); Elias Loomis, *The Recent Progress of Astronomy;* David Musto, ''A Survey of the American Observatory Movement, 1800–1850,'' *Vistas in Astronomy,* vol. 9 (1967).]

DEBORAH JEAN WARNER

OCALA PLATFORM was adopted at a meeting of a number of farmers' organizations, including the Southern Alliance and the National Farmers Alliance, held at Ocala, Fla., December 1890. It demanded, among other things, the abolition of national banks, a graduated income tax, free and unlimited coinage of silver, the establishment of subtreasuries where farmers could obtain money at less than 2 percent on nonperishable products, and the election of U.S. senators by a direct vote of the people.

[John D. Hicks, *The Populist Revolt.*]

W. T. CASH

OCCUPATIONS, CHANGES IN. In the early days of settlement and continuing through the first decades of the 19th century, agriculture was the dominant activity of almost all American workers. The first reliable estimates of occupation for the work force of the United States—based on the 1820 census of population—show farm workers constituting over 70 percent of the economically active population. Since then each succeeding census has shown a smaller proportion, and the decline has been at an accelerating pace over virtually all of the census intervals. By 1970, only a little over 3 percent of all employed persons were engaged in farm work and no state in the Union had as much as 25 percent of its workers in agricul-

ture. The rapid expansion of population during the 19th century resulted in growing numbers of workers in agriculture, despite their decline in relative importance. But since 1910, when there were over 11 million farm workers, even the absolute numbers have declined. In 1970, fewer than 3 million Americans were reported as working on farms. Concomitant with the decline in the number of farm workers were the very rapid increases in nonfarm activities. The nature of these activities has also changed sharply, particularly in the course of the 20th century.

Throughout the 19th century, declines in the proportion of workers in farm occupations were offset primarily by increases in the proportion of manual workers, as the developing industrial sector steadily replaced the farm as the work site. Factories, mines, railroads, and construction absorbed many immigrant workers and provided manual jobs for increasing numbers of natives, particularly in the northeastern section of the country. A lesser, but still increasing, proportion of workers was engaged in the distribution of goods, as proprietors and sales workers in retail establishments; they constituted the majority of what are now called white-collar workers. As late as 1900, only about 4 percent of American workers were in professional occupations and about 3 percent were in clerical pursuits. Over the succeeding seventy years, the increase in these two groups of occupations far outpaced that of any other, and by 1970 one out of every three employed persons was either a professional or clerical worker. The other white-collar occupations—that is, sales workers and proprietors and managers in nonfarm enterprises—increased at a much more moderate rate; although they included the majority of white-collar jobs before World War I, they accounted for only a third by the mid-1970's.

As a result of the spectacular growth in professional and clerical occupations, most of the decline in the proportions of farm workers in the 20th century, from 38 percent in 1900 to less than 4 percent in 1970, has been offset by increases in the proportion of white-collar workers, in contrast to the situation in the 19th century. These shifts in workers' occupations reflect the changes in the structure of the U.S. economy from one in which the production of goods was paramount toward one in which the production of services assumed increasing importance.

The alterations in the types of work performed by the country's labor force have been accompanied by major changes in other characteristics of workers. First, although data to measure the change are unfortunately not available for earlier decades, there can be little doubt that the majority of workers were self-employed through most of the pre–Civil War period; that is, they were independent farmers or artisans or shopkeepers, relying for their incomes on the profits of their own enterprises. By the mid-1970's the vast majority of the labor force worked for wages or salaries: in 1975, nine out of ten workers were employees. The second notable change was the substantial increase in employment of women during the course of the 20th century, particularly since World War II. At the close of the Civil War about 15 percent of all workers were women. This proportion increased slowly to 20 percent after World War I. Since then, the rate has accelerated, and by 1970, 38 percent of all American workers were women. Over half of these women were in professional or clerical occupations, leading many people to believe that the increase in opportunities in these fields may be an underlying cause of the growth in the employment of women.

[U.S. Bureau of the Census, *Comparative Occupation Statistics in the United States: 1870–1940,* and *Occupational Trends in the United States, 1900–1950.*]

ANN R. MILLER

OCEANOGRAPHIC SURVEY. The U.S. Naval Oceanographic Office and the National Ocean Survey conduct oceanographic surveys on the high seas and in foreign and U.S. coastal waters. Other organizations undertake surveys for specific purposes, but these are the federal organizations charged with the responsibility of conducting oceanographic surveys to meet national requirements. The participation of the United States in the field of worldwide oceanographic surveys is characterized in the history of the U.S. Naval Oceanographic Office.

The U.S. Coast Survey was founded in 1807 to conduct surveys of coastal waters, but in the two decades after 1844 it also conducted extensive explorations of ocean tides, currents, and bottom deposits. Subsequently, it participated in research in deep-sea biology and other aspects of ocean science. River and harbor, as well as coastal, surveys were taken over by the navy in 1818 and returned to the Coast Survey in 1832. The navy established the Depot of Charts and Instruments in 1830 to supply accurate nautical charts, books, and navigational instruments to the navy and American shipping interests, which had formerly been compelled to rely on foreign charts and various commercial sources. The depot, in 1854, was separated into the Hydrographic Office and the Naval Observatory, which were given individual status in 1866 by an act of Congress.

The first survey made by the U.S. Navy was of fishing banks off the coast of Massachusetts and resulted, in 1837, in the publication of four engraved charts. The exploring expedition of Charles Wilkes (1838–42), which ranged from the eastern Atlantic to the coasts of both the Americas and thence deep into the western and southwestern reaches of the Pacific, made surveys that formed the basis for charts issued prior to the Civil War. Extensive supplementary surveys were also conducted in 1848, 1850, and 1853. Matthew C. Perry's expedition to Japan in 1852 provided a wealth of data supplementing the earlier works of Wilkes.

In 1842 Matthew Fontaine Maury, in command of the depot between 1842 and 1861, laid the foundation for systematic ocean surveying by initiating an extensive uniform system for collecting oceanographic, meteorological, and navigational data. The data, obtained from the logbooks of naval and merchant vessels, contributed to the issue in 1847 of a "track chart," the prototype of the modern pilot chart. The production of trade-wind charts, thermal charts, whale charts, and storm and rain charts was commenced shortly afterward. Maury himself wrote the first authoritative sailing directions and, in 1855, published *The Physical Geography of the Sea,* a work that is the basis of modern oceanography.

The expeditions of 1874–84 succeeded by use of the telegraph in accurately establishing the longitude of thirty positions girdling the globe, and established a level of accuracy in the survey that was not improved until the advent of the radio time signal in 1911. In 1921 the United States became a member of the International Hydrographic Bureau established in Monaco for the exchange of information on an international basis.

In 1922 the introduction of a practical sonic depth-finder and the application of photogrammetry to aerial photography, both initiated by the U.S. Navy, marked the beginning of a new era in ocean surveying. The sonic depthfinder allowed more accurate charts of the ocean depths to be constructed; aerial photography allowed a true relationship of land and water areas to be shown quickly.

After World War II, the U.S.S. *San Pablo* and the U.S.S. *Rehoboth* (two converted seaplane tenders) were employed on oceanographic/acoustic surveying. The National Oceanographic Data Center was established within the Hydrographic Office in 1960 as a repository of collected data to serve both federal agencies and private organizations. The center was transferred to the National Oceanic and Atmospheric Administration when the latter was established in 1970, as was the National Oceanographic Instrumentation Center, previously a component of the U.S. Naval Oceanographic Office.

In recognition of its broader responsibilities in oceanography, the Hydrographic Office was officially redesignated the U.S. Naval Oceanographic Office in July 1962 by act of Congress. In the mid-1970's the Naval Oceanographic Office maintained a fleet of eleven ships and three aircraft. All ships are equipped with the latest in electronic surveying equipment, including modern electronic devices for making measurements of temperature, chemical constituents, precise depth, and geomagnetic and gravity determinations. In addition, more extensive use is made of underwater acoustics in probing the oceans and their bottom structures. Aircraft and satellites using remote sensing devices are now being employed to survey rapidly oceanic variables such as the radiated temperature of the sea and the physical shape and slope of the sea surface.

[National Academy of Sciences–National Research Council, "A History of Oceanography: A Brief Account of the Development of Oceanography in the United States," in *Oceanography, 1960 to 1970;* U.S. Navy Hydrographic Office, *American Practical Navigator—An Epitome of Navigation.*]

U.S. NAVAL OCEANOGRAPHIC OFFICE

OCEANOGRAPHY. Serious scientific study of the sea began in the United States in the 1840's. Before that time efforts to understand the marine environment had been sporadic. Benjamin Franklin, the outstanding American scientist in the 18th century, had studied the surface currents and temperatures of the North Atlantic. President Thomas Jefferson founded the U.S. Coast Survey in 1807, but it did little offshore until Alexander Dallas Bache, Franklin's great-grandson, became superintendent (1843–67). Under Bache's leadership, the Coast Survey was in the forefront of the exploration of the ocean—its tides, currents, bottom deposits, and chemical composition. Rivaling the survey's efforts, which were carried out at sea by naval officers serving temporarily, were the navy's own efforts under Lt. Matthew Fontaine Maury, head of the Depot of Charts and Instruments from 1842 to 1861. He, too, devoted his attention and that of his staff to the ocean as physical environment, especially after Congress expressly authorized ships for his use in the 1850's. The depot's investigations

reached farther out into the Atlantic because the survey was limited by law until 1959 to the coastal waters of the United States. Another major effort before the Civil War was the U.S. Exploring Expedition (1839–42) under Lt. Charles Wilkes, Maury's predecessor at the depot, but the expedition contributed little to oceanography. Techniques for obtaining marine organisms had not yet been developed, and Wilkes's efforts in physical oceanography were perfunctory.

Both Maury and Bache sent the specimens of the sea bottom brought back by their ships to Jacob W. Bailey of the U.S. Military Academy, who became, with C. G. Ehrenberg of Berlin, one of the two leading students of marine sediments in the world. Progress in marine science depends heavily on new techniques; for example, the exploration of the sea bottom benefited greatly from the invention by Maury's assistant, John M. Brooke, of a sounder that brought substantial samples back to the surface. Exploring the life in the sea began when Bache offered a survey steamer to Louis Agassiz, an immigrant from Switzerland, in 1847. Foremost student of fish in his day, Agassiz made several cruises along the American coast. By the late 1860's his assistant, Count L. F. de Pourtalès, had developed a technique of deep-sea dredging for animals and had mapped the sediments of the East Coast. Agassiz's attempt to extend these techniques on the cruise of the Coast Survey ship *Hassler* from New York to California in 1871–72 failed because of faulty equipment.

Also in 1871 Agassiz's student Spencer F. Baird founded the U.S. Fish Commission, which established seaside laboratories at Woods Hole, Mass., in 1885. In a series of cruises, financed largely by himself, Agassiz's son, Alexander, explored widely in Atlantic and Pacific waters aboard Fish Commission and Coast Survey vessels. With the shift from coastal to inland exploration that followed the Civil War, the Coast Survey ceased to dominate the American scientific scene, but excellent work on tides and currents continued to be done, especially by the civilian William Ferrel and the naval officer John E. Pillsbury. Yet by 1913, when the International Ice Patrol was founded in response to the *Titanic* disaster of 1912, American oceanography—the world's leader until the 1870's—was practically moribund. Leadership in marine science had passed first to the British with the Challenger Expedition of 1872–76 and then to the Scandinavians, becoming consolidated in Europe with the founding of the International Council for the Exploration of the Sea in 1901.

The *Titanic* sinking and the development of submarines during World War I jointly stimulated research into underwater sound. The result was the greatest American technical advance since Brooke's sediment-retrieving sounder: the sonic depthfinder, perfected in the early 1920's. The rebuilding of American marine research began at the same time, led by Alexander Agassiz's students, W. S. Ritter and Charles A. Kofoid, who developed the Scripps Institution in San Diego, and Henry B. Bigelow, who led a long series of cruises to the Gulf of Maine. In connection with the International Ice Patrol, the U.S. Coast Guard began research in northern waters that complemented Bigelow's. When about 1927 Frank R. Lillie of the University of Chicago became president of the U.S. National Academy of Sciences following his term as director of the Marine Biological Laboratory at Woods Hole, he persuaded the Rockefeller Foundation to make a major effort in oceanography. The result was the founding of the Woods Hole Oceanographic Institution in 1930 and the strengthening of ongoing programs, principally at the University of Washington and the Scripps Institution of Oceanography of the University of California.

The coming of World War II brought a considerable expansion of oceanography to meet the demands of submarine and antisubmarine warfare. After 1945 Texas A. & M., Miami, Rhode Island, Columbia, New York, Oregon State, and Johns Hopkins universities began substantial programs of teaching and research. A federal sea grant program, established in 1966 in imitation of the land grant college program that followed the Morrill Act of 1862, expanded oceanography still further, and this emphasis on education led the Woods Hole Oceanographic Institution to grant degrees.

Before the Civil War, problems of physical oceanography were dominant in American marine science as it attempted to aid ship navigation. From about 1870 to about 1940, biological concerns dominated, in part because of interest in the problems of fisheries. Beginning in 1940, physical problems again came to the fore, at that time because of submarine warfare. With the growth of funds for science, the adaptation of geophysical exploration and deep drilling techniques from the oil industry shifted interest to the ocean basins as the most accessible repository of information about the earth's structure and history.

By 1870 the currents and winds of the ocean had been mapped and their dynamics were on the threshold of being understood in a general way. By 1940 the major sedimentary provinces of the ocean floor had been delineated; the organisms that live in the ocean had been classified and their life cycles investigated; and the use of marine organisms had vastly increased knowledge in experimental embryology and physiology. The physical oceanography of the 1940's had two major outcomes. First, there was substantial progress in making physical oceanography a fully mathematical science, leading to a detailed, quantitative understanding of tides and currents, productive of new observations as well as of new theories. Second, sonic, seismic, gravity, and magnetic observations at sea led to a new picture of the earth's history, according to which continents split apart, the sea floor between them spread, and the ocean floor bent down to form deep trenches. This startling view is being confirmed by the study of the sediments retrieved from deep-sea drilling.

[Margaret Deacon, *Scientists and the Sea, 1650–1900;* Susan Schlee, *The Edge of an Unfamiliar World: A History of Oceanography.*]

HAROLD L. BURSTYN

OFFICE OF ECONOMIC OPPORTUNITY (OEO), created by the Economic Opportunity Act of 1964, was the coordinating agency for the War on Poverty begun by President Lyndon B. Johnson. As originally passed, the Economic Opportunity Act called for a Job Corps; Neighborhood Youth Corps; work training and work study programs; community action programs (dubbed CAP), including Head Start; adult education; loans for the rural poor and small business; work experience programs; and Volunteers in Service to America (VISTA). Although the OEO was located in the Executive Office of the President to provide strong presidential coordination of its components, the War on Poverty was in fact a loosely structured and shifting collection of semiautonomous programs involving little direct presidential control.

During OEO's initial years of operation two programs came under major congressional attack: the Job Corps and CAP. In the case of Job Corps, Congress reacted in 1966 and 1967 to reports of high costs and disorders at Job Corps camps by setting cost and enrollment limits and by imposing strict behavior standards on the camps. In addition, many of the original OEO programs were transferred from OEO to other agencies and departments (particularly Health, Education, and Welfare; and Labor) because of congressional criticism.

Objections to CAP stemmed from a provision of the 1964 law requiring "maximum feasible participation'' of residents of the areas served by each local program. Most local CAP agencies were private organizations, and in many cases enlisted militant poor residents with whom city officials clashed. In 1966, Congress amended the law to require greater representation of the poor on local community action agencies and to limit salaries of local CAP employees; in 1967 the so-called Green amendment required that all local CAP agencies be under the aegis of state or local governments rather than private bodies.

Another recurring controversy in OEO revolved around provisions for a governor's veto over certain OEO programs. In the original act of 1964, governors were given a veto over proposed work training programs in their states, and then in 1965 this provision was modified to allow the OEO director to override a governor's veto. The issue arose again in 1967 and 1969, when Sen. George Murphy of California proposed legislation to provide a governor's veto on legal aid programs. California's Gov. Ronald Reagan did veto continuation of the California Rural Legal Assistance Program in 1971, but a three-judge commission ruled in favor of the continuance of the program.

After his inauguration in 1969, President Richard M. Nixon announced his intention to transfer successful OEO programs to operating departments, retaining OEO only as a laboratory and research agency. As congressional conservatives attempted to turn all OEO activities over to the states, Nixon signed bills extending OEO in 1969 and 1972. The administration's fiscal 1974 budget contained no funds for OEO, however, effectively terminating the agency on June 30, 1973, despite a previously approved extension through fiscal 1974. While Congress was working on the fiscal 1974 budget, two separate court decisions first ordered an end to the dismantling of OEO and then removed the acting OEO director because his nomination had not been submitted for Senate approval.

After surviving an additional year on a continuing appropriation, OEO was finally terminated on Jan. 4, 1975. Extensive lobbying in 1974 by governors, mayors, and antipoverty workers had rescued OEO's programs, however. In the compromise bill signed by President Gerald Ford, community action, economic development, community food and nutrition, comprehensive health services, Head Start, and a number of minor programs were continued through fiscal 1977. Most of these programs were transferred to the independent Community Services Administration; a few were transferred to the Department of Health, Education, and Welfare.

[Joseph A. Kershaw, *Government Against Poverty;* Sar A. Levitan, *The Great Society's Poor Law;* Daniel P. Moynihan, *Maximum Feasible Misunderstanding.*]

ROBERT EYESTONE

OFFICE OF EMERGENCY PREPAREDNESS.
See **Federal Agencies.**

OFFICE OF MANAGEMENT AND BUDGET (OMB) was established by President Richard M. Nixon's Reorganization Plan 2 in 1971. By executive order, OMB was created from the reorganization of the Bureau of the Budget, the agency within the Executive Office of the President responsible for the formulation of the national budget since 1939. (Prior to 1939 the Budget and Accounting Act of 1921 had placed the Bureau of the Budget in the Treasury Department.) The director of OMB is selected by the president and has cabinet-level status within the federal bureaucracy.

The primary function of OMB is to assist the president in preparing the national budget and to ''supervise and control the administration of the budget.'' In addition, it has a number of other functions of considerable significance and influence. It is charged with aiding the president in achieving governmental efficiency; advising him about the administration's legislative program and coordinating the legislative requests of agencies; developing information systems and assembling statistical data; monitoring the performance and efficiency of federal programs; developing programs for recruiting, training, and evaluating career personnel; and coordinating all programs of the executive branch in order to achieve maximum efficiency and efficacy. In short, the reorganization and change in agency title from Bureau of the Budget to Office of Management and Budget reflect an expansion of the managerial responsibilities and influence of the agency.

In fulfilling its primary responsibility, the preparation of the national budget, OMB addresses itself not only to fiscal policy but also to the administration's policy goals for the fiscal year in terms of substantive aims. In the budgetary process agencies present program plans and appropriation requests to OMB, where they are examined in detail. Beginning in the mid-1960's the Bureau of the Budget instituted an evaluation process known as ''Planning, Programming, Budgeting'' (PPB) for assessing agency programs and appropriation requests in terms of the efficiency with which stated program goals are met by the available alternative means, or cost effectiveness. The objective of PPB is the achievement of program objectives by choosing the alternative having the optimal cost-benefit ratio.

The Office of Management and Budget, the Department of the Treasury, and the Council of Economic Advisors work together in formulating government fiscal policy and in coordinating the relationships of government programs and spending with the economy in general. Once the programs and appropriations of all agencies within the eleven cabinet departments are evaluated, OMB prepares the annual budget that the president submits to Congress each January.

[Aaron Wildavsky, *The Politics of the Budgetary Process.*]

STEFAN J. KAPSCH

OFFICE OF SCIENTIFIC RESEARCH AND DEVELOPMENT. Drawing on his emergency powers, President Franklin D. Roosevelt created the Office of Scientific Research and Development (OSRD) by executive order in 1941. A civilian agency, its mission was to coordinate and facilitate weapons research and medical research as part of the national mobilization during World War II. Vannevar Bush, the president of the Carnegie Institution of Washington, D.C., became the director of the new agency. The National Defense Research Committee (NDRC), which Roosevelt had established in 1940 to coordinate weapons research, and the Committee on Medical Research (CMR), which was to oversee wartime research in medicine, became the two main operational units of OSRD. Hundreds of research scientists participated in the various committees and specialized sections of OSRD, including many of the leading university scientists and industrial researchers in the United States. In addition to Bush, the most influential men in OSRD were James B. Conant, chemist and president of Harvard University; Karl T. Compton, physicist and president of Massachusetts Institute of Technology; A. Newton Richards, physiological chemist and vice-president for medical affairs at the University of Pennsylvania; and Frank B. Jewett, president of the National Academy of Sciences and president of Bell Telephone Laboratories, the leading industrial laboratory in the United States at the time. Weapons experts from the army and navy worked with OSRD but were not dominant.

Bush enjoyed close working relations with Roosevelt and Harry L. Hopkins, one of Roosevelt's closest advisers. He also developed strong political support

in Congress. The result was that throughout the war OSRD received handsome budgetary support and maintained a stout independence, remaining largely free of military interference. OSRD relied heavily on decentralization to carry out its functions. Instead of developing research laboratories of its own, it initiated a system of contract research, in which university and industrial scientists could be utilized without being brought directly into the military services.

OSRD performed its wartime mission with great success. It was responsible, for instance, for the advanced development of radar and the introduction of proximity fuses—each of which made a major impact on the conduct of the war. It coordinated the development of mass-production methods for penicillin and hastened the development of DDT. It designed the DUKW, an amphibious vehicle used extensively in the Pacific campaign. Work on the atomic bomb was initiated by OSRD and later transferred to the Manhattan District of the Army Corps of Engineers. Its achievements in the application of science and technology to modern warfare were unparalleled.

Remarkably effective during the war, OSRD also had long-range historical significance. It pioneered the contract system of research, which revolutionized the pursuit of science in the United States after the war. It demonstrated the central importance of science and technology to national defense and propelled science into a permanent alliance with the federal government. It also provided scientists with a taste of federal financial support for scientific research, support that increased after Sputnik. In short, OSRD established the pattern of national science policy in the United States for a generation after World War II.

OSRD went out of existence in 1947. The task of coordinating and supporting scientific research was taken over by such emerging federal agencies as the Atomic Energy Commission, the National Institutes of Health, the Office of Naval Research, and later the National Science Foundation. Its history spanned scarcely more than five years, but it left an important legacy in the history of science and technology in the United States.

[James Phinney Baxter, *Scientists Against Time;* Vannevar Bush, *Pieces of the Action;* National Academy of Sciences, *Federal Support of Basic Research in Institutions of Higher Learning.*]

DONALD C. SWAIN

OFFICE OF STRATEGIC SERVICES. On June 13, 1942, President Franklin D. Roosevelt created the Office of Strategic Services (OSS) as a means of centralizing the fragmented and uncoordinated intelligence activities of the nation. An earlier attempt to do so, through the Office of the Coordinator of Information (COI), formed July 11, 1941, had failed to achieve any real success because of unclear lines of authority and bureaucratic jealousies among the various government agencies concerned. As a part of the plan for establishing OSS, some of the COI functions, such as domestic information activities, were transferred to the newly formed Office of War Information. OSS was charged with others: the collection and analysis of strategic information and the planning and performance of special operations, particularly in the realms of espionage and sabotage. The Joint Chiefs of Staff were to supervise and direct OSS activities; Col. William J. ("Wild Bill") Donovan was named director. Donovan, a lawyer, World War I hero, and confidant of the president, had been in contact with the British Special Operations Executive (SOE) since 1941, and to a large extent OSS was modeled after that group.

Throughout its existence the organization of OSS constantly changed as it grew to an eventual strength of 12,000 personnel drawn from all walks of life, including the military. Basically, OSS consisted of a headquarters and various subordinate offices in and near Washington, D.C., and a series of field units, both in the United States and in overseas areas generally associated with a theater of operations. Two exceptions were Latin America, where the Federal Bureau of Investigation was charged with intelligence activities, and the South West Pacific theater. (Gen. Douglas MacArthur's refusal to accept OSS there may have been a manifestation of the skepticism many of the nation's leaders felt toward such an unorthodox, irregular, and clandestine organization.)

There were three branches of OSS that exemplify the breadth and scope of its operations. The secret intelligence branch dealt with sabotage, spying, demolitions, secret radio communications, and paramilitary functions. The morale operations branch handled the propaganda functions vested in OSS. The research and analysis office gathered extensive information on all aspects of the areas in which U.S. forces operated. Even the most trivial data were collected and used to further the war effort. All three of these branches and others as well had agents in both enemy and neutral areas.

It is with the secret intelligence area that much of the glamour of OSS is associated. Many of its operations were in fact more dramatic than the fictionalized accounts found in books and films. In Burma, for example, a small OSS unit of twenty men (Detachment 101) operated behind Japanese lines with such success that it—along with an allied Kachin guerrilla band—is credited with killing or wounding more than 15,000 of the enemy. Beginning in 1943, OSS personnel, along with British and other Allied teams, took part in the Jedburgh operation, which sent hundreds of three-man teams into France and the Lowlands to organize and aid underground forces in advance of the invasion of Europe. In 1944 another group smuggled an Italian inventor out of his German-occupied homeland to the United States, where he was able to produce an effective countermeasure to the torpedo he had designed for the Germans.

The end of World War II brought the demise of OSS, by an executive order effective Oct. 1, 1945. The functions, personnel, and records of the office were divided between the departments of state and war. It was the experience gained by the OSS that laid the foundation for the Central Intelligence Agency, established in 1947.

[Corey Ford, *Cloak and Dagger: The Secret Story of OSS;* Richard W. Rowan, *Secret Service: Thirty-Three Centuries of Espionage.*]

JOHN E. JESSUP, JR.

OFFICERS' RESERVE CORPS of the U.S. Army and Air Force was established by the National Defense Act of June 1916 as part of the Organized Reserve Corps and reorganized by amendments to the act in 1920. Its primary function has been to provide school-trained personnel, educated in leadership and military tactics. The members are assigned to units of the Organized Reserve Corps and to inactive regiments of the regular army.

During the early years of the corps, active duty training was limited to fourteen days out of every five years and offered full officer's pay with allowance in grade. Later, the minimum requirement was increased to one weekend a month, but some areas require fewer days of active duty. Inactive training has also been available without monetary compensation, in evening and correspondence classes. Between 1933 and 1939 the corps assisted with the administration of the Civilian Conservation Corps.

By 1919 the corps consisted of 45,573 officers; this number rose to 133,485 by 1933, and declined to 111,169 in 1936. The number has continued to fluctuate, but there has been a steady decline since the beginning of the Vietnam War. In 1960 there were

50,000 army and 22,000 air force reserve officers; by 1970 these figures had dropped to 30,432 and 12,333, respectively.

The Reserve Officers' Training Corps (ROTC) had been the major means of filling the corps. Established at colleges throughout the country, it provided the opportunity for young men subject to the draft to enter the army or air force as officers. The major purpose of the ROTC is the development of a strong and well-trained officer. Before the establishment of an all-volunteer army in the 1970's, it was felt that better training could be provided during the time served in the ROTC than during the regular service period under the selective service program. In the 1960's and 1970's student opposition to war caused a drop in ROTC enrollment and even the removal of corps units from several schools. This fact, coupled with the general dissension in the United States over the military establishment, brought about a reduction in the number of officer trainees enrolled in the corps.

[Maurice Matloff, ed., *American Military History;* Walter Mills, *American Military Thought;* O. L. Spaulding, *The United States Army in War and Peace.*]

LORING D. WILSON

OFFICIAL RECORDS. *See* **Archives.**

OGALLALA, a city in western Nebraska on the South Platte River, named for one of the most powerful bands of Teton Sioux, was established by two brothers, Philip J. and Thomas Lonergan, in 1869, when they brought a herd of cattle from Frio County, Texas (*see* Cattle Drives), and wintered them at Ogallala, then only a water-tank station on the new Union Pacific Railroad.

Shipping facilities for cattle were established by the railroad at Ogallala in 1874, and the town became the terminus for one of the important Texas cattle trails. This cattle-drive business was in part diverted to Cheyenne, Wyo., in 1876, when the latter became a shipping point, but for many years Ogallala continued as a cow town with a lively reputation. In its early days it was a rendezvous for many desperate western characters, including "Doc" Middleton, Nebraska outlaw leader; Luke Short, noted quick-shot gunman; and the Joel Collins gang of train robbers. Ogallala became a city of diversified agriculture in the 20th century; the population in 1970 was 4,976.

[A. T. Andreas, *History of Nebraska; Nebraska History Magazine* (1933).]

PAUL I. WELLMAN

OGDEN PURCHASE. In 1826 the Ogden Company purchased from the Iroquois, mainly Seneca, the lands in New York State comprising the reservations of Caneadea, Caughnawaga, Big Tree, Squawkie Hill, Gardeau, and portions of Buffalo Creek, Tonawanda, and Cattaraugus, for the sum of $48,260. With the understanding that the Indians were to be moved to lands in the West, in 1838 a majority of the chiefs were prevailed upon to sell the remainder of their reservations in New York State to the company for $202,000. As there was strong opposition to the sale by many of the Indians and their white friends, concessions were made whereby the Indians were allowed to retain their lands on the Cattaraugus and Allegheny reserves.

ROBERT W. BINGHAM

OGDENSBURG, an industrial city and port in northern New York on the Saint Lawrence River. In 1749 Father François Picquet founded the Indian mission of La Présentation on the site of the present city and erected a small fort that was soon partially destroyed by the Mohawk. The post was repaired, but fearing future attacks, Picquet persuaded the French governor to erect a stronger fortification. The purpose of the post was to shelter those Indians of the Five Nations, principally the Onondaga, who desired to settle under French protection.

After the abandonment of Fort Frontenac in 1758, the sustenance of Fort Niagara and the posts to the south and west depended on La Présentation, and the British garrisoned the post in 1760, renaming it Fort William Augustus as a protection for their fur trade. In 1776 the fort was repaired and remained under British control as Fort Oswegatchie until relinquished to the Americans by the terms of Jay's Treaty in 1796, and permanent settlement was begun under the proprietorship of Col. Samuel Ogden in 1792.

In 1812 an attack by a British flotilla was repulsed by Gen. Jacob Jennings Brown's troops who had been sent to reinforce the garrison, and in 1813 the British captured and destroyed part of the town. Ogdensburg was incorporated as a town in 1818 and chartered as a city in 1868.

The city developed into an important port of entry and railroad center with extensive trade in lumber and grains. On Aug. 17–18, 1940, near the city, President Franklin D. Roosevelt and Canadian Prime Minister William L. Mackenzie King signed the Ogdensburg Agreement to defend North America from Nazi aggression. The city's population in 1970 was 14,554.

[P. S. Garand, *The History of the City of Ogdensburg.*]

ROBERT W. BINGHAM

OGDEN'S HOLE, a rendezvous for trading in the early days of the fur trappers (*see* Trappers' Rendezvous), occupied a sheltered cove in the Rocky Mountains near the northeast shore of the Great Salt Lake in Utah. It was named after Peter Skene Ogden, a Hudson's Bay Company trapper, as was the present city of Ogden, which stands on the same site.

[H. M. Chittenden, *History of the Fur Trade of the Far West*.]

CARL L. CANNON

OGDEN **V.** *SAUNDERS,* 12 Wheaton 213 (1827), a suit involving the constitutionality of many state bankruptcy laws, was brought before the U.S. Supreme Court by David Bayard Ogden, who sought a discharge in bankruptcy under New York legislation enacted in 1801. In March 1827 the Court by a close division (four to three) upheld the validity of the legislation in dispute but restricted its application to the state in which it was enacted. Chief Justice John Marshall gave his only dissenting opinion upon a constitutional question in this important, although not altogether popular, decision.

[J. P. Hall, *Cases on Constitutional Law;* Charles Warren, *The Supreme Court in U.S. History*.]

RAY W. IRWIN

OHIO. The earliest known inhabitants of Ohio were the prehistoric peoples lumped together by modern archaeologists as the Mound Builders. They lived chiefly in the Ohio, Miami, Muskingum, and Scioto valleys. They were sedentary farmers and the impressive mounds that they built were chiefly burial tombs, although some were built as temples and fortresses. Some extant examples include Hopewell, Fort Ancient, and Great Serpent Mound. The Indians inhabiting Ohio in the historic era were descendants of the Mound Builders; important tribes were the Iroquois, Erie, Ottawa, Shawnee, and Miami. In 1655 the Erie were virtually destroyed in a bloody war with the Iroquois.

Although there is some question, Robert Cavelier, Sieur de La Salle, is believed to have been the first white explorer of Ohio (1669). He claimed the whole region for France. By the beginning of the 18th century, a rich fur trade had been established, with both French and British fur traders moving in and out of the area. The British contested the French claims and established (1747) the Ohio Company to extend Virginia's dominion into Ohio. They built a fort and trading post in 1748 at Pickawillany in the heart of the French trading area on the Miami River. The French

sent an expedition to destroy it and other British outposts. The expedition met with some success, but at the end of the French and Indian War in 1763 the British triumphed. The French gave up all claim to what later became known as the Old Northwest. New disputes broke out almost immediately. British treaties with the various Indian tribes were aimed at limiting and containing white settlement (and therefore protecting their lucrative fur trade). The land-hungry colonies to the east (Virginia, Massachusetts, New York, and Connecticut) objected to the treaties and, for the most part, ignored them. They began laying claim to land west of the Alleghenies, including land guaranteed by the British to the Indians. In 1774, by the Quebec Act, Britain made all of the Ohio country a part of Canada, an act that enraged the colonies. It quickly became one of the grievances that led to the American Revolution.

The Ohio Indians were allied with the British during the Revolution. American troops under George Rogers Clark attacked British forts in the Old Northwest and succeeded in neutralizing the area. Indian forces under British command in turn attacked American settlements across the Ohio River in Kentucky. The Treaty of Paris (1783), which ended the war, ceded the Old Northwest, including Ohio, to the United States, and Virginia, Massachusetts, and Connecticut quickly pressed claims to various parts of the territory. The claims were ceded to the national government by the Ordinance of 1787, except for a strip in northern Ohio, the Western Reserve, which was retained by Connecticut, and the Virginia Military District in southern Ohio, which Virginia had reserved for land for revolutionary war veterans. The ordinance cleared the way for settlement; it created the Northwest Territory, gave full citizenship rights to settlers there, and guaranteed them eventual self-government. Land companies were formed and settlement began. The first permanent white settlement was established at Marietta in 1788. Losantiville (Cincinnati) was founded later the same year. The Ohio Company of Associates, formed in 1786, was the most important of the land companies. The Connecticut Land Company was formed to settle the Western Reserve, purchasing the Ohio tract from Connecticut in 1795 for $1.2 million. In 1796 Moses Cleaveland, one of its directors, established the first settlement (Cleveland) in the reserve.

The sudden influx of settlers was opposed by the Indians, who saw their best hunting lands being systematically deforested and turned into farm country. With the support of the British, who still entertained designs on the area, the Indians kept up a relentless guerrilla war against the white encroachers. In 1794 a decisive battle was won by the American troops under Gen. Anthony Wayne at Fallen Timbers. Ohio was more or less pacified, and the British withdrew their support of the Indians under the terms of Jay's Treaty (1794).

In 1800 Congress divided the Northwest Territory. The western part became the Indiana Territory; present-day Ohio retained the name Northwest Territory. Two years later legislation was passed clearing the way for statehood, and in 1803 Ohio was admitted as the seventeenth state. Chillicothe was made the first state capital (the capital was moved permanently to Columbus in 1816), and Edward Tiffin was selected the first governor.

New Indian troubles soon arose. The Shawnee leader Tecumseh, with the aid of his brother Tenskwata, known as the Shawnee Prophet, had considerable success in uniting the Indians of the Old Northwest. Tecumseh argued that Indian lands were held in common by all Indians and could not be bargained away by individual tribes or chiefs. He called upon all Indians to renounce their treaties with the whites and to take up arms and drive the whites from the Indians' ancestral hunting grounds. His ambitions were dashed at the Battle of Tippecanoe in Indiana Territory in November 1811; the Indian defeat there marked the end of their organized military effort. Tecumseh himself retreated to Canada, where he joined the British.

Ohioans, like most westerners, were in favor of the War of 1812, chiefly because they looked on the British as the instigators and allies of the Indians. Great numbers of Ohio volunteers served in all theaters of the war. The British invaded northern Ohio but were repulsed, particularly at Fort Meigs (near Toledo). British ambitions in Ohio ceased after the American navy established control over Lake Erie. Tecumseh was killed in the Battle of the Thames (1813). His death marked the end of Indian threats in Ohio. The Treaty of Ghent (1814) ended once and for all British hopes in the Ohio country.

With both British and Indian threats forever ended, Ohio entered into its greatest period of growth. Settlements were established in all parts of the state, and they all prospered from the rich farmlands. Settlers came from every part of the nation, particularly the South, the Middle States, and New England. And for the first time immigrants began arriving in Ohio directly from Europe. Transportation from the East was greatly improved by the completion of the Erie Canal in 1825 and the opening of the National Road in

1833. The population of the state, which had reached 581,434 by 1820, almost doubled by 1830.

In the 1830's a territorial dispute erupted between Ohio and the Michigan Territory over a portion of northwestern Ohio. It was known as the Toledo War, and fighting broke out and continued sporadically until Congress, in 1836, resolved the dispute in favor of Ohio.

Ohio was an overwhelmingly agricultural state in the early 19th century, and its farmers were producing surpluses that had to reach their markets, mostly in the East. During the 1830's a great transportation building program began. The Ohio and Erie Canal connected the Ohio River with Lake Erie; the Miami and Erie Canal connected Cincinnati and Dayton in 1830 and was extended to Toledo in 1845. Numerous smaller feeder canals were built, and a statewide road system was developed. By the middle of the 19th century, Ohio led the country in the production of horses, sheep, wool, and corn. It was one of the leading U.S. producers of cattle, wheat, hogs, and oats.

The first railroads were built in Ohio in the 1830's, and by midcentury most major cities were connected by rail. Late in the decade rail links to the eastern seaboard were established in all parts of the state. That tie with the East was to have great influence on the future commercial and industrial life of the state. The first half of the century had seen Ohio take its place as a major agricultural producer; the second half saw its rise as a commercial and manufacturing center.

Despite a large southern population, Ohio remained firmly within the Union during the Civil War. The state had long been a center of abolitionist sentiment and had supported a network of Underground Railroad stations. Except for minor border skirmishes, Ohio was out of the main war theater and suffered little damage, although nearly 25,000 of its men were killed in the war. Prominent Ohioans who served in the Union cause in the Civil War were Salmon P. Chase, secretary of the Treasury; Edwin M. Stanton, secretary of war; and generals Ulysses S. Grant and William Tecumseh Sherman.

Ohio's industrialization came into full flower after the war. Northern Ohio—Cleveland, Youngstown, and Canton in particular—became the center of the iron and steel and heavy machinery industries. John D. Rockefeller started the Standard Oil Company at Cleveland. By 1870 Akron was the national center for the rubber industry. Toledo was a glassmaking center and Cincinnati was one of the great meat-packing centers in the nation.

Ohio's industrial and commercial importance was reflected in its role in national politics. Just as Virginia was dominant in the early years of the republic, Ohio now supplied many of the national leaders. Between 1869 and 1923 seven native sons of Ohio served as president: Ulysses S. Grant, Rutherford B. Hayes, James A. Garfield, Benjamin Harrison, William McKinley, William Howard Taft, and Warren G. Harding. All were conservative Republicans.

A wave of reform hit Ohio in the early years of the 20th century, particularly in local government. Samuel M. ("Golden Rule") Jones, who served as mayor of Toledo for most of the years between 1897 and 1903, won national attention for his municipal reforms. He instituted a civil service, inaugurated an eight-hour day for city workers, and advocated public ownership of utilities. Organized labor became politically powerful in the state during the same period, offsetting somewhat the almost total control that big business had previously exercised.

Ohio prospered during the 1920's but suffered greatly during the Great Depression. There was also much labor strife during that period: the Akron sitdown strikes (1935–37) and the Little Steel Strike (1937) are prominent examples. Ohio labor and industry quickly converted to war production in World War II, and the state prospered as a major producer of war material. This prosperity continued after the war. The opening of the Saint Lawrence Seaway in 1959 made ocean ports of Cleveland and Toledo.

Although Ohio was always considered a Republican state, the Democratic party showed increasing strength during the second half of the 20th century. The support of organized labor was a strong factor in this. Evidence of a strong two-party system in Ohio may be shown by the fact that in 1970 the state sent to the U.S. Senate Robert A. Taft, Jr., the Republican grandson of William Howard Taft; four years later, the state elected as its second senator the Democrat John H. Glenn, Jr.

[D. W. Bowman, *Pathway to Progress, A Short History of Ohio;* Federal Writers' Project, *Ohio Guide;* Grace Gouldy, *This Is Ohio;* Walter Havighurst, *The Heartland: Ohio, Indiana, Illinois;* F. A. Ogg, *The Old Northwest;* E. H. Roseboom and F. P. Weisenburger, *A History of Ohio.*]

DONALD W. HUNT

OHIO, ARMY OF THE. On Nov. 9, 1861, the Union troops operating in Kentucky were organized as the Army of the Ohio, under the command of Gen. Don Carlos Buell. During the year 1862 they fought at Shiloh, Tenn. (April), repelled Confederate Gen.

Braxton Bragg's invasion of Kentucky (July), and fought at the siege of Corinth, Miss. (October). On Oct. 30, 1862, Gen. William S. Rosecrans relieved Buell, and the Army of the Ohio became the Army of the Cumberland.

A new Army of the Ohio was later formed and Gen. Horatio G. Wright placed in command. He was succeeded by Gen. Ambrose E. Burnside in March 1863. In the fall of 1863 the army was ordered to the defense of Knoxville. Burnside was replaced in December by Gen. John G. Foster, who, on Jan. 28, 1864, gave way to Gen. John M. Schofield, who commanded the Army of the Ohio until Jan. 17, 1865, when it was merged into the Department of the Cumberland. In this interval the army participated in the Atlanta campaign and was then detached to aid Union Gen. George H. Thomas in repelling Confederate Gen. John Bell Hood's invasion of Tennessee.

[F. Phisterer, *Statistical Record.*]
THOMAS ROBSON HAY

OHIO, FALLS OF THE, opposite Louisville, Ky., are really rapids caused by ledges covering the riverbed for half a mile. Flatboats often went down the falls in high water, but steamboat freight and passengers were usually transported overland from the harbor just above the falls. The alleged discovery of the falls in 1669 by Robert Cavelier, Sieur de La Salle, has been questioned, but Pierre Joseph de Céloron (1739) preceded all known British explorers. In December 1773 John Murray, Earl of Dunmore, then governor of Virginia, granted land at the falls to John Connolly, who, with John Campbell, sent a few temporary settlers (1775). On May 27, 1778, about twenty families accompanying Lt. Col. George Rogers Clark's band of soldiers (*see* Clark's Northwest Campaign) settled on Corn Island at the falls, moving to the mainland at Christmas. The name Louisville was adopted presumably because of the Franco-American alliance of the same year. Connolly's claim was escheated because of his Tory activities, and town trustees were authorized to sell lots to settlers (1780). Most of the money went to pay Campbell's claims against Connolly. In 1795 elected trustees were authorized to levy taxes and supervise town affairs. The westward movement and the introduction of the steamboat in 1811 stimulated trade. Population growth finally brought about incorporation as the city of Louisville in 1828. (*See also* Louisville and Portland Canal.)

[J. S. Johnston, ed., *Memorial History of Louisville.*]
W. C. MALLALIEU

OHIO, FORKS OF THE, was the name given to the junction of the Allegheny and Monongahela rivers, where they form the Ohio River. Historically, the name is often applied to the surrounding country or is used as the equivalent of such names as Fort Duquesne, Fort Pitt, or Pittsburgh.

As many floods have amply demonstrated, the Allegheny, the Monongahela, and the Ohio rivers are topographically great gorges through which the western drainage of the Appalachian system of the north flows off to the Mississippi River. These gorges were the natural approach to the Middle West from the Middle Atlantic seaboard. The Forks of the Ohio thus became a natural gateway to the West in American westward migration.

Strangely enough, the Ohio Company of Virginia, organized in 1747, failed to grasp at once the significance of the Forks and the point of land lying between the Allegheny and the Monongahela, but planned to establish a post down the Ohio at a point now known as McKees Rocks, named after Alexander McKee, noted Tory, who was one of the early residents of the area. Neither such famous fur traders as Aernout Viele and George Croghan nor explorers as Pierre Joseph de Céloron and Christopher Gist seem to have appreciated the importance of the Forks of the Ohio. It remained for George Washington, on his journey to Fort LeBoeuf in December 1753, to note its significance and through his widely published diary to give it, after 1754, enduring fame. In Washington's words, "I spent some time in reviewing the Rivers and the Land in the Fork; which I think extremely well situated for a Fort, as it has the absolute Command of both Rivers."

The Ohio Company in February 1754 began construction of a rude fort on the point. Before its completion, the French captured it. From April 1754 to late 1758, Fort Duquesne, under French control, dominated not only the Forks of the Ohio but also the entire country eastward to the Alleghenies and westward to the Mississippi River. Captured and renamed Pittsburgh by Gen. John Forbes, and protected by Fort Pitt, the region remained under British supervision for more than a decade, mainly as a garrison and trading post. Slowly, with settlement of the region, the trading post became a commercial village. It was chartered as a borough in 1794.

[S. J. Buck and E. H. Buck, *The Planting of Civilization in Western Pennsylvania.*]

ALFRED P. JAMES

OHIO AND ERIE CANAL. *See* **Ohio State Canals.**

OHIO COMPANY OF ASSOCIATES developed as a result of the interest in western settlement shown by a group of revolutionary war officers. Two New Englanders, generals Rufus Putnam and Benjamin Tupper, were its leading spirits. Because of their activity, "A Piece Called Information" appeared in several Massachusetts newspapers in January 1786, inviting officers and soldiers to form "an association by the name of the Ohio Company." All persons interested were to elect delegates to meet at the Bunch of Grapes Tavern in Boston on Mar. 1. Eleven men met on that date and organized the company. They planned to raise $1 million, to be subscribed in shares of $1,000 each, payable in Continental certificates, plus $10 in gold or silver, the fund to be used to purchase land "north westerly of the River Ohio."

A year elapsed before 250 shares had been subscribed and the company was ready to ask Congress for land. Gen. Samuel Parsons proving unsatisfactory as an agent, Rev. Manasseh Cutler was selected to represent the company before Congress. By skillful lobbying and by effecting an alliance with a group of New York speculators headed by William Duer, Cutler arranged a joint purchase: nearly 5 million acres for the Scioto Company and 1.5 million acres for the Ohio Company. Reservations of one section in each township for schools, another for religion, three for later disposal by Congress, and two whole townships for a university increased the Ohio Company's total to 1,781,760 acres. The company was to pay $500,000 down and the same amount when the survey was completed, but payment could be made in government securities, worth perhaps twelve cents on the dollar. The tract lay north of the Ohio River between the seventh range and the western limit of the seventeenth of the Seven Ranges. Cutler also helped in the formation and adoption of the Ordinance of 1787.

The Ohio Company later encountered financial difficulties and could not complete its payments. Nevertheless, Congress granted title to 750,000 acres and added 214,285 acres to be paid for with army warrants (*see* Land Bounties) and 100,000 acres to be granted free to actual settlers. More than two-thirds of the shareholders remained in the East, thus adding absentee ownership to the complications of inaugurating settlement on the exposed frontier. It required many years to arrange for the division of the lands and other assets among the 817 shareholders. Meetings were still being held as late as 1831, although nearly all the assets had long since been allocated. The great achievement of the company was the successful beginning of organized settlement north of the Ohio River at Marietta, Ohio, in 1788.

[A. B. Hulbert, ed., *The Records of the Ohio Company,* Marietta College Historical Collections, vols. I, II; E. O. Randall and D. J. Ryan, *History of Ohio,* vol. II.]

EUGENE H. ROSEBOOM

OHIO COMPANY OF VIRGINIA, a partnership of Virginia gentlemen, a Maryland frontiersman, and a London merchant organized in 1747 to engage in land speculation and trade with the Indians in the territory claimed by Virginia west of the Appalachian Mountains. The company petitioned the crown for a grant of 500,000 acres of land in the upper Ohio Valley or elsewhere in the West, 200,000 acres to be granted at once on condition that 200 families be settled on the land within seven years. Early in 1749 the governor of Virginia was directed to make the grant. The company built a storehouse for trade goods on the Potomac River opposite the mouth of Wills Creek within the present limits of Cumberland, Md., and sent Christopher Gist on exploring expeditions in 1750 and 1751. The Indians having been induced at the Treaty of Logstown (1752) to permit settlement south of the Ohio River, a road was opened across the mountains, probably in 1752, and in 1753 Gist and a number of others sent out by the company settled in what is now Fayette County, Pa. In the same year the company built another storehouse on the Monongahela River at the site of Brownsville, Pa. (*see* Redstone Old Fort), and early in 1754 it began, with the cooperation of the governor of Virginia, the erection of Fort Prince George at the Forks of the Ohio. The capture of this uncompleted fort by the French in 1754, and the war that ensued (*see* French and Indian War), resulted in the withdrawal of the settlers, and plans of the company to renew its activities in the region after the fall of Fort Duquesne were frustrated by the prohibition of settlement west of the mountains to conciliate the Indians (*see* Proclamation of 1763). An agent dispatched by the company to England to seek a renewal of its grant was unsuccessful in his quest, and in 1770 he exchanged its claims for two shares in the Vandalia Company. The Ohio Company was significant as a manifestation of the intention of England, and also of Virginia, to expand across the mountains into the Ohio Valley; and its activities played a part in bringing on the final contest between the French and the English for control of the interior.

[C. W. Alvord, *Mississippi Valley in British Politics;* K. P. Bailey, *The Ohio Company of Virginia.*]

SOLON J. BUCK

OHIO IDEA refers to the proposal to redeem the Civil War five-twenty bonds in greenbacks instead of coin (1867–68). Put forth as an inflationary measure by the *Cincinnati Enquirer,* the proposal was so popular that both political parties in the Middle West were forced to endorse it, although neither committed itself outright to inflation.

[C. M. Destler, "Origin and Character of the Pendleton Plan," *Mississippi Valley Historical Review,* vol. 24; D. R. Dewey, *Financial History of the United States.*]

CHESTER MCA. DESTLER

OHIO-MICHIGAN BOUNDARY DISPUTE. The Ordinance of 1787 and the Ohio Enabling Act of 1802 defined the northern boundary of the proposed state of Ohio as an east-and-west line drawn through "the southerly bend or extreme of Lake Michigan." Ohio was supposed to include Maumee Bay on Lake Erie, since 18th-century maps generally placed the southern end of Lake Michigan north of its true location. Advised by an old trapper that such a line would intersect Lake Erie south of Maumee Bay, the Ohio constitutional convention (1802) changed the boundary to make it reach that lake at the northernmost cape of Maumee Bay. Congress never formally assented to the change, and Michigan Territory later claimed the boundary as stated in the ordinance. A long controversy ensued, reaching a climax in the bloodless Toledo War of 1835–36. Congress, after much difficulty, compromised matters by giving the disputed strip to Ohio (some 400 square miles) but compensated Michigan with statehood and a tract of 9,000 square miles on the Upper Peninsula.

[E. O. Randall and D. J. Ryan, *History of Ohio,* vol. III.]

EUGENE H. ROSEBOOM

OHIO NATIONAL STAGE COMPANY, with its headquarters at Columbus, Ohio, operated stagecoaches on the western division of the National Road after its completion to that city in 1833. The company established branch lines to all parts of Ohio and western Pennsylvania, and by 1844 had become a near monopoly, having absorbed all its rivals but one. Railroad competition ended its importance in the 1850's.

[A. B. Hulbert, *The Cumberland Road, Historic Highways of America,* vol. X.]

EUGENE H. ROSEBOOM

OHIO RIVER, EARLY DISCOVERY OF, cannot be fixed with certainty. In the first half of the 17th century rumors came to the French in Canada and the English in Virginia of a great river beyond the mountains, and occasional explorers may even have reached the Ohio Valley.

From the Indians Robert Cavelier, Sieur de La Salle, had heard of the "great river" (in the Iroquois tongue, "Ohio") that, flowing westward, plunged over a waterfall. He became convinced he could descend it to the Gulf of California and perhaps even to China. Leaving Montreal July 6, 1669, La Salle with twenty men went up the Saint Lawrence, along the southern shore of Lake Ontario, and across country to the Grand River valley in northeastern Ohio. From there they pushed on to the Allegheny and down the Ohio to the marshy country below the falls opposite present-day Louisville, Ky. Whether La Salle accompanied his men to the Ohio or to the falls, as he claimed, or abandoned the expedition before it reached the river, is a question still raised by historians.

News of La Salle's voyage quickly spread. Louis Jolliet's map in 1674 gave the general course of the Ohio as far as the falls, and Jean Baptiste Louis Franquelin's map in 1682 showed that it flowed into the Mississippi River. Later French explorers located the chief tributaries from the north, notably the Wabash. Frequently these early maps showed the Wabash as the main river into which the Ohio flowed, and to the latter many of them gave the alternative name La Belle Rivière.

The Virginians, too, sought the great river west of the Appalachian Mountains that reputedly flowed into the South Sea. About 1648 Virginia Gov. William Berkeley proposed an expedition across the mountains, and other adventurous souls followed his example, although none of these plans materialized. It was left to Abraham Wood, a fur trader at Fort Henry (now Petersburg) on the Appomattox River, actually to mark the path from Virginia across the mountains. According to unverified reports, Wood himself, between 1654 and 1664, discovered several branches of the Ohio and the Mississippi. If so, he even preceded La Salle in the Ohio Valley. Certainly in 1671 he dispatched a trading party that crossed to the New River on the western slope of the Appalachians. In the 18th century Gov. Alexander Spotswood urged an English advance from Virginia, and in 1716 at the head of the romantic Knights of the Golden Horseshoe he reached the south branch of the Shenandoah River.

Gradually the Virginia explorers, now joined by the fur traders from Pennsylvania, opened up the

chief passes across the Appalachians, marking out the courses of the rivers that flowed from the summit of the mountains to the Ohio, and thus coming into the chief theater of French enterprise. By the middle of the 18th century these English explorations, together with those of the French fur traders, had made it possible to draw up a fairly accurate map of the entire Ohio Valley.

[Francis Parkman, *Discovery of the Great West;* Justin Winsor, *Narrative and Critical History of America,* vol. IV.]

BEVERLEY W. BOND, JR.

OHIO STATE ANTISLAVERY SOCIETY. Organized in 1835 by abolitionist converts of Theodore D. Weld and his helpers (*see* Oberlin Movement), the Ohio Society shortly became second only to the New York Society among the state auxiliaries of the American Antislavery Society. During the decade after 1840 its leaders, Salmon P. Chase, Gamaliel Bailey, Leicester King, and Joshua R. Giddings, converted the society to political action. By 1848 it had practically merged with the Free Soil party.

[G. H. Barnes, *The Antislavery Impulse, 1830–1844;* T. C. Smith, *The Liberty and Free Soil Parties in the Northwest.*]

GILBERT HOBBS BARNES

OHIO STATE CANALS. Surveys for canals were authorized by the Ohio legislature in 1822, and in 1825 the building of two major canals was authorized. One, the Ohio and Erie, was to leave Lake Erie at the village of Cleveland, follow the Cuyahoga Valley for several miles, then continue via Akron, Massillon, Coshocton, Newark, in Licking County, and the Scioto Valley to the Ohio River at Portsmouth. The other, the Miami and Erie, was to run at first only from the Ohio at Cincinnati up to Dayton, with a later extension to Lake Erie. Work began at once, and by 1832 the whole 308-mile course of the Ohio and Erie Canal was open. The extension of the Miami and Erie Canal to the Maumee River at Defiance and via that stream to Toledo and Lake Erie was begun in 1833 and was theoretically open to the Maumee by 1836, but boats did not get through to Toledo until 1843. Ohio was blessed with wise and honest management in the building of its canals, and for several years they contributed enormously to the state's growth and prosperity. Beginning in 1835–36 the legislature authorized the building of several branch canals that were of little value and that only laid serious financial burdens upon the state. The halcyon days of the Ohio canals were from 1845 to 1857. Then railroad competition began slowly throttling them. After 1863 bits of the two main canals began to be obliterated, although the last of them did not vanish until around 1910.

[Alvin F. Harlow, *Old Towpaths*.]

ALVIN F. HARLOW

OHIO VALLEY forms a natural link between the Appalachians and the Mississippi Valley. Also, it binds together the Gulf coast and the Great Lakes region. Its strategic location, its numerous navigable streams, its fertile soil, and its natural resources mark a region admirably adapted to early settlement. At first Robert Cavelier, Sieur de La Salle, was enthusiastic over its possibilities, but the Iroquois controlled the upper Ohio Valley, and instead, the French turned to the Maumee-Wabash region.

Gradually, traders came to the Ohio Valley from Virginia and Pennsylvania, and occasionally from South Carolina. Logstown, eighteen miles below the Forks of the Ohio, developed a flourishing trade with the Indians. This English advance soon provoked a struggle with the French. In 1749 Pierre Joseph de Céloron made his famous voyage down the Allegheny and the Ohio rivers to the Miami, planting a lead plate at each important tributary to assert French claims. The English lost the opportunity to found an adequate stronghold, and the French established a series of forts in the upper Ohio Valley, even though Virginia Gov. Robert Dinwiddie sent George Washington to warn them from land the English claimed. In 1758 the English captured Fort Duquesne at the Forks of the Ohio, rechristening it Fort Pitt, and during the Revolution it became the strategic center from which the Americans controlled the Ohio Valley. Settlers now flocked in. The Ohio became the dividing line between free and slave territory. Nevertheless, a community of interests developed among the populations of both banks of the river. Virginians, Kentuckians, and Ohioans united in the War of 1812 to fight the British and the Indians. Since the end of the Civil War this community of interests has grown even stronger. Problems of transportation, of flood control, and of water pollution have come into the foreground, and, in place of consideration by individual states, have demanded action by the entire Ohio Valley as a distinct sectional division of the United States.

[D. B. Crouse, *The Ohio Gateway;* A. B. Hulbert, *The Ohio River, A Course of Empire;* F. J. Turner, "The Ohio Valley in American History," *The Frontier in American History*.]

BEVERLEY W. BOND, JR.

"OH! SUSANNA," a song of the old black minstrel or nonsense type, was written and composed by Stephen Collins Foster and published in the spring of 1848. It was one of Foster's earliest successful songs, although he is said to have received only $100 for it. It became very popular that summer, when there was much immigration to Oregon. Parodies began to be written in which "Oregon" was substituted for "Alabama" in the original version. In the spring of 1849, when the gold rush started, "California" was the next substitution, and the whimsical ballad became in effect the theme song of America's most remarkable mass movement. It was sung on vessels rounding Cape Horn and by the campfires of the overland voyagers. In the East, it was played at balls as a polka or quadrille and by military bands as a quickstep and was arranged with variations for band and solo piano. "Oh! Susanna" has remained an American favorite and has gained popularity even in foreign countries.

[John Tasker Howard, *Stephen Foster, America's Troubadour*.]

ALVIN F. HARLOW

OIL EXCHANGES, EARLY. After the completion of the Drake oil well in 1859 in Titusville, Pa., and the drilling of others, buyers and sellers of petroleum gathered on the streets, in hotels, and in telegraph offices especially at Titusville or Oil City, Pa., in order to buy and sell oil. The organization of the Titusville Board of Trade in 1865, the assignment of a special railway passenger car to oilmen traveling between Oil City and Titusville after 1866, and the establishment of the Oil Dealers' Exchange at Petroleum Centre in 1867 represented steps in the development of regular oil exchanges. The first permanently organized oil exchange was established at Titusville in January 1871, a second at Franklin, and a third at Oil City in April and May respectively.

[Paul H. Giddens; *The Birth of the Oil Industry*.]

PAUL H. GIDDENS

OIL INDUSTRY. *See* **Petroleum Prospecting and Technology.**

OIL SCANDALS. *See* **Elk Hills Oil Scandal; Naval Oil Reserves; Teapot Dome Oil Scandal.**

OISE-AISNE OPERATION (Aug. 18–Nov. 11, 1918). Exploiting the success of the Franco-American Aisne-Marne operation in reducing the Marne salient,

French Gen. Henri Pétain ordered Gen. Jean Marie Degoutte's Sixth Army and Gen. Charles Mangin's Tenth Army to continue their offensive between the Aisne and the Oise. The American Third Corps, commanded by Maj. Gen. Robert Lee Bullard, was in Degoutte's army east of Soissons when the attack was resumed. The American Seventy-seventh Division, under generals George B. Duncan, Evan M. Johnson, and Robert Alexander, and the Twenty-eighth Division, under Maj. Gen. Charles H. Muir, were in line, left to right, behind the Vesle River. After indecisive fighting along this stream the two divisions crossed, Sept. 4, with the general French advance, and against strong opposition by German Gen. Von Boehn's Seventh Army, pushed across the watershed toward the Aisne. The Twenty-eighth Division was relieved on Sept. 8; the Seventy-seventh on Sept. 16, after progressing ten kilometers and crossing the Aisne Canal.

Placed in line in Mangin's army north of Soissons, the Thirty-second Division attacked toward Juvigny on Aug. 28, which was taken on Aug. 30. On Sept. 2, after repeated attacks, the division reached the National Road at Terny.

[Joseph M. Hanson, "History of the American Combat Divisions," *The Stars and Stripes;* J. J. Pershing, *My Experiences in the World War.*]

JOSEPH MILLS HANSON

OJIBWA. *See* **Chippewa.**

OKANOGAN, FORT, located on the juncture of the Columbia River and the mouth of the Okanogan River, was built by the Pacific Fur Company in 1811 as an Indian trading post. In 1813 it passed to the North West Fur Company, and in 1821 to the Hudson's Bay Company, which claimed indemnity for it when the territory under dispute passed from Britain to the United States (*see* Oregon Question). Formerly of great importance as a trade-route center, by 1860 Fort Okanogan had almost disappeared.

[E. Voorhis, *Historic Forts and Trading Posts.*]

CARL L. CANNON

OKEECHOBEE, BATTLE OF (Dec. 25, 1837), the bloodiest engagement of the second Seminole War. Regular and volunteer troops under Col. Zachary Taylor met Seminole warriors in a swamp on the north shore of Lake Okeechobee, Fla. Taylor had the advantage of numbers, the Indians the advantage of position. Taylor attacked, sending Missouri volunteers across the swamp toward a hummock where the enemy

waited. Exposed to a galling fire, many Missourians fell, regulars taking their places. After three hours Taylor, by a flank movement, drove the Indians before him. Twenty-six whites were killed; 112 were wounded. Indian losses were not determined accurately, but at least fourteen perished. Without great immediate consequence, this conflict ultimately proved an important factor in effecting the removal of the Indians from Florida. It also brought Taylor to the fore as a determined and courageous, if not brilliant, commander.

[John T. Sprague, *Origin, Progress, and Conclusion of the Florida War.*]

HOLMAN HAMILTON

OKINAWA lies at the midpoint of the Ryukyu Island chain, which forms a 750-mile arc between Japan and Taiwan. A minor Japanese base during most of World War II, Okinawa became important when U.S. planners decided to seize it as a staging point for their projected invasion of Japan. On Apr. 1, 1945, American forces began a struggle that ended on June 21 with more than 115,000 Japanese defenders vanquished.

Gen. Mitsuru Ushijima, commanding Japan's Thirty-second Army, allowed Gen. Simon Bolivar Buckner's four assault divisions of the U.S. Tenth Army to storm ashore virtually unopposed. Instead of trying to defend the beaches, Ushijima's troops burrowed into caves and tunnels in a succession of low ridges lying between the beaches and Shuri, the capital. Invading U.S. Army and U.S. Marine Corps attackers eliminated them with "blowtorch" (flamethrower) and "corkscrew" (demolition charge) tactics at heavy cost to themselves.

Driven late in May from their Shuri line, the Japanese retreated to Okinawa's southern tip, where both commanders perished at the battle's end. Ushijima died by ritual suicide (hara-kiri), and Buckner was killed by the explosion of one of the last artillery shells fired by the Japanese. Earlier, on the adjacent islet of Ie Shima, the famous war correspondent Ernie Pyle had been killed by a burst fired from a by-passed Japanese machine gun.

Equally bitter was the fighting at sea. Japan's air forces hurled more than 4,000 sorties, many by kamikaze suicide planes, at U.S. and British naval forces. The bulk of the kamikaze attacks was absorbed by radar picket destroyers stationed north of Okinawa. U.S. losses totaled thirty-eight ships of all types sunk and 368 damaged; 4,900 U.S. Navy men died; and U.S. Army and U.S. Marine fatalities numbered 7,900 men. Japan's naval losses included the super battleship *Yamato,* torpedoed by U.S. carrier aircraft while trying to raid the beachhead.

[J. H. Belote and W. M. Belote, *Typhoon of Steel: The Battle for Okinawa.*]

JAMES H. BELOTE
WILLIAM M. BELOTE

OKLAHOMA. Before the arrival of Europeans in what is now the state of Oklahoma, various Indian groups lived there, conventionally identified as the Fourche Mailine people, the Grove focus, the Gibson focus, and the Fulton focus. In the northeast as early as A.D. 500, a village-dwelling people who built the Spiro Mound, lived and flourished. Later, in the better-watered eastern prairies, the Caddoan, a semi-cultural people known as Wichita, Taovaya, and Tawakoni, occupied village sites after A.D. 1000 and raised various crops, including corn. In the postcontact period, aside from the Caddoan in the east, bands of nomadic Osage, Kiowa Apache, and Comanche wandered the western plains.

Oklahoma, included in the vast Louisiana Territory, was part of the spoils over which Spain and France struggled for two centuries. First claimed by Spain through the explorations of Francisco Vásquez de Coronado in 1541 and of Hernando de Soto in the same year, Oklahoma was later claimed by France because of activity of Robert Cavelier, Sieur de La Salle, along the Mississippi River in 1682. At the conclusion of the Seven Years War in 1763, France ceded the territory to Spain, only to regain it in 1800 by the Treaty of San Ildefonso. In 1803 the United States purchased from France the Louisiana Territory, including all of Oklahoma except the panhandle. American exploration was conducted by James Wilkinson in 1805–06, Richard Sparks in 1806, Zebulon M. Pike in 1806–07, and George Sibley in 1811.

Except for the panhandle and a small area in the northeast, Oklahoma became the home of the Five Civilized Tribes. Forced from their homes in the southeast between 1817 and 1842, the Cherokee, Chickasaw, Choctaw, Creek, and Seminole settled in assigned tracts and, by 1856, had established their own autonomous national governments patterned after that of the United States. The hardships endured by the Indians during removal were exemplified by the experiences of the Cherokee in 1838 on their "Trail of Tears." Like their former southern neighbors, these five tribes adopted the institution of slavery and, although lacking unanimity, joined the Confederacy during the Civil War. Ravaged by war, the tribes, considered vanquished nations by the federal govern-

ment, relinquished their slaves and annuities and lost half their lands. The federal government, through treaties, relocated Plains Indians, including the Comanche, Cheyenne, Arapaho, Osage, and Pawnee, and eastern tribes, such as the Seneca, Shawnee, and Wyandot, in reservations on these lands in western Oklahoma.

Following the Civil War, white interests in the Indian Territory increased. The movement of vast cattle herds from Texas over the Shawnee Trail, Chisholm Trail, and Great Western Trail through Oklahoma encouraged organized use of the rich western grazing lands between 1866 and 1890. Coal discovered in the Choctaw region by C. C. McAlester in 1870 encouraged whites to exploit the territory's mineral wealth, while the construction of some fifteen railroads through Indian lands by 1907 had introduced thousands of whites to the economic potential of these lands.

With increased economic activity, pressure grew for the opening of Indian lands to white settlement—specifically the opening of the unassigned lands, the Cherokee Outlet, Greer County, and No Man's Land. Between 1879 and 1884 numerous attempts were made by organized immigrant groups called boomers, led by such people as C. C. Carpenter, David L. Payne, and William L. Couch, to settle clandestinely on the unassigned lands. Their efforts were deterred by federal authorities. Meanwhile the United States acquired the unassigned lands on Mar. 2, 1889, and on Apr. 22 some 50,000 persons participated in the first run on government land to claim their quarter sections.

Implementation of the Dawes General Allotment Act of 1887 and the Springer Amendment to the Indian Appropriation Act of 1889 (by which the president was authorized to negotiate for surplus Indian lands after allotment) opened more Indian territory to white settlement. Between 1891 and 1895 four runs were made upon lands acquired from various tribes. The first was in September 1891, when 20,000 persons scrambled to make claims on former Iowa, Sauk, Fox, and Shawnee-Potawatomi lands; the second, in April 1892, on Cheyenne and Arapaho lands; the third and most famous, in September 1893, when the Cherokee Strip and Tonkawa and Pawnee lands were opened to 100,000 individuals; and the fourth, in May 1895, on the Kickapoo lands. In July 1901, Kiowa-Comanche lands were opened, but to avoid incidents, land was distributed by lottery. Greer County, in the southwest, was added to Oklahoma by a U.S. Supreme Court decision in 1896. The last opening occurred in 1906 when former Kiowa, Comanche, Apache, Wichita, and Caddoan lands, or the "Big Pasture Lands," were auctioned in 160-acre tracts to the highest bidder. Each opening, however, had its "Sooners," or squatters, who had settled on lands illegally and resisted removal.

The western half of Indian Territory was made Oklahoma Territory on May 2, 1890, and for seventeen years it was under a territorial government while Indian territory was governed by the five separate Indian nations. As the twin territories developed economically, the population grew. Although whites settled in Indian Territory, they were, in most instances, squatters. Pressure developed from the whites within the twin territories for statehood, and between 1889 and 1906 thirty-one bills were introduced in Congress for either separate or joint statehood. Generally, for both economic and political reasons, whites wanted joint statehood while the Indian nations favored separate states. The Eufaula Convention in 1902 and 1903 favored statehood, and in Muskogee in August 1905, representatives from the Indian nations drafted a constitution for the proposed Indian state of Sequoyah. Congress rejected separate statehood, and on Nov. 16, 1907, the twin territories entered the Union as Oklahoma.

Between 1904 and 1907 Oklahoma experienced a prosperous period in oil production. Wild boomtowns, such as Burbank, sprang into existence and flourished, although many had become ghost towns by 1930. Indians became both rich and impoverished because of the boom.

Following the prosperous years of World War I, Oklahoman business and farming faced critical readjustments. Politics were also hectic during the 1920's: two governors, one in 1924 amidst visible Ku Klux Klan activity and another in 1929, were impeached. The economic depression of the 1930's was extremely serious in the rural areas, and by 1935, 61 percent of the farms in Oklahoma were operated by tenant farmers. Conditions were worsened by the drought of 1934–36; western Oklahoma was part of the Dust Bowl. Many Oklahomans went to Texas or California to become migrant farm laborers, referred to as Okies. Oklahoma experienced prosperity during World War II: petroleum, coal, lead, zinc, food, and cotton production increased. Forty-one military installations, including Fort Sill, an artillery base, and two major airfields—Tinker Air Field and Will Rogers Field—were located in the state. In the postwar period, Oklahoma ranked fourth nationally in the production of petroleum, natural gas, and stone. The manufacturing of transportation and farm equipment and clay and glass items, as well as a large cattle industry, gives the state a diversified economy. A turning point occurred in Oklahoma in 1951, when for the first time more of its population was urban than rural; of the state's 1970 population of 2,559,259, 68 percent was urban.

Oklahoma is basically a Democratic state: through the 1972 election it had supported ten Democratic presidential candidates in seventeen national elections; it elected its first Republican governor, Henry Bellman, in 1962.

[Edwin C. McReynolds, *Oklahoma: A History of the Sooner State;* Muriel H. Wright, *A Guide to the Indian Tribes of Oklahoma.*]

THOMAS H. SMITH

OKLAHOMA OPENINGS, the opening of former Indian lands in western Oklahoma to white settlement. The first was that of the Unassigned Lands, which, under the authority of an act of Congress, President Benjamin Harrison proclaimed would be open to settlement under the homestead laws at high noon, Apr. 22, 1889. This resulted in a "run" in which some 50,000 people took part, each seeking to be the first to settle on one of the 160-acre homestead tracts. Other former Indian lands opened by "runs" were those of the Iowa, Sauk and Fox, and Shawnee-Potawatomi in 1891, the Cheyenne-Arapaho lands in 1892, the Cherokee Strip and Pawnee and Tonkawa lands in 1893, and the Kickapoo lands in 1895. In an effort to avoid the disorder incident to the runs the Kiowa-Comanche and Wichita lands were opened in 1901 by a lottery in which qualified homesteaders wanting lands registered and were allowed to choose homesteads in the order in which their names were drawn. In 1906 the so-called Big Pasture Lands were opened by an auction sale in which tracts of 160 acres were sold to the highest bidder, only qualified homesteaders being allowed to bid.

[J. S. Buchanan and E. E. Dale, *A History of Oklahoma;* E. E. Dale and J. L. Rader, *Readings in Oklahoma History.*]

EDWARD EVERETT DALE

OKLAHOMA SQUATTERS were settlers upon lands not yet opened to white settlement or to which the title was in dispute. As early as 1819 white settlers attempted to occupy lands in the southeastern part of Oklahoma that were claimed by the Osage, but they were removed by the military. The region between the two branches of Red River, known as Greer County, was claimed by both Texas and the United States; it was also entered by settlers soon after 1880, although a presidential proclamation warned them not to occupy it until the question of title had been settled.

During the period from 1879 to 1885 a large number of so-called boomers, under the leadership of C. C. Carpenter, David L. Payne, and W. L. Couch, sought to settle as squatters upon the unassigned lands of central Oklahoma, but were removed by U.S. soldiers. Just prior to each of the various openings of lands to settlement a number of people entered upon the land before the date set for the opening. These were known as Sooners. Many other white persons entered the Indian Territory without the permission of the governments of the Five Civilized Tribes and stubbornly resisted removal. These were in reality squatters, although they were commonly called intruders.

[J. S. Buchanan and E. E. Dale, *A History of Oklahoma;* E. E. Dale and J. L. Rader, *Readings in Oklahoma History.*]

EDWARD EVERETT DALE

OLD AGE. The number of persons over sixty-five years of age in the United States increased both absolutely and as a proportion of total population during the first three-quarters of the 20th century. In 1900, 3.1 million (about 4 percent of the population) were in this age category; by 1974, the number was estimated at 21.8 million (10.3 percent of the total). The growth in absolute numbers came partly from increased longevity (average life expectancy increased from 47.3 to 71.3 years during the period), partly from high immigration in the early 1900's (15 percent of those over sixty-five in 1970 were foreign born, a substantially higher percentage than for any younger age group), and partly from the high birth rates prevailing when the native population in that age group was born. Increased longevity and immigration are not expected to play an important part in future growth, and the rate of increase of those over sixty-five, although their numbers will continue to rise through the remainder of the 20th century, is expected to fall, reaching a minimum in the decade 1990–2000, when the low birth cohorts of the depression decade 1930–40 enter that age group.

The increase in numbers has been accompanied by a decline in the proportions working. In 1900 about 70 percent of men over sixty-five were employed; by 1970 the figure was 25 percent. Concern for the economic welfare of the aged brought enactment of the first Social Security Act in 1935, under which both employer and employee are taxed, and the employee becomes eligible for a lifetime monthly benefit at the age of sixty-five, or at the age of sixty-two with reduced lifetime benefits. About 90 percent of workers are now covered, and a substantial proportion of the remaining 10 percent is insured under the federal retirement system. Since 1966 certain persons over seventy-two not covered by the act during their working lives have also become eligible for benefits. At the end of 1974, 26.9 million persons were receiving monthly benefits under the retirement provisions, 16 million as retired workers and the remainder as dependents or survivors of such workers. Additionally, 2.3 million disabled workers under the age of sixty-five (of whom about 60 percent were aged 55–64), and 1.7 million of their dependents, received benefits under disability provisions enacted in 1957. In 1965 hospital insurance (Medicare) for those over sixty-five was added to the basic benefits, and a program of voluntary low-cost medical insurance was instituted.

Of those over sixty-five in 1974, 88 percent received some cash benefit under the act. Benefits are generally determined by previous earnings. At the end of 1973 the average retired-worker family received $184.40 per month, an amount just above the poverty ("low-income") level for single individuals over sixty-five and considerably below that for two-person families with heads over sixty-five at that date. Most persons receiving benefits have additional income from other sources (including public assistance). Nevertheless, about 16 percent of the population over sixty-five was living in poverty status in 1973.

[Social Security Administration, *Social Security Bulletin,* various issues; U.S. Bureau of the Census, *Some Demographic Aspects of Aging in the United States.*]

ANN R. MILLER

OLD CHILLICOTHE INDIAN TOWN. See **Chillicothe.**

OLD COURT–NEW COURT STRUGGLE, a political contest in Kentucky that reached its climax during the years 1824 to 1826, and that involved the immunity of the state supreme court (called court of appeals) from legislative control and the finality of its decisions on constitutional questions. The controversy was engendered by the financial and business disturbances that eventuated in the panic of 1819 and that lingered on for nearly a decade, and by the efforts of the legislature to mitigate distress by passing measures of doubtful validity. The immediate cause of the clash was the action of the appellate court, October 1823, in affirming, in the cases of *Blair* v. *Williams* and *Lapsley* v. *Brashears,* the principle that stay laws unduly restricting the time for issuing executions on judgments and laws granting excessive indulgence to debtors upon replevin bonds were violations of both state and federal constitutions in that such hindrances and burdens upon the rights and remedies of creditors impaired the obligation of contracts. In retaliation, the advocates of relief for the large debtor class, who controlled the legislature, undertook in December 1824 to abolish the court of appeals by passing a reorganizing act, repealing the law under which that court had been organized and setting up an entirely new court in its place. This act was promptly declared unconstitutional by the "old court," but in defiance of the adjudication the new appointees proceeded to organize a "new court." The bench and bar of the state were divided in allegiance between the rival courts, which functioned simultaneously during the ensuing two years, but a majority of both judges and lawyers adhered to the "old court." An acrimonious contest between the two court parties engaged the attention of the people of the state preceding the elections of 1825 and 1826. The "old court" finally triumphed, and in December 1826 an act was passed repealing the reorganizing act of two years before. The objectives of the "new court" party were not unlike those of many countries that, during and after World War I and in the years of depression following the economic crash of 1929, sought by moratoriums and other devices to ease the hardships of debtors.

[Robert M. Ireland, *The County Courts in Antebellum Kentucky;* Niels H. Sonne, *Liberal Kentucky, 1780–1828.*]
SAMUEL M. WILSON

OLD DOMINION. When Charles II was restored to the throne in 1660, his authority was promptly and enthusiastically recognized by the Virginia burgesses. Thereupon Charles elevated Virginia to the position of a "dominion" by quartering the arms of the old seal of the London Company on his royal shield along with the arms of England, Scotland, and Ireland. The burgesses, recalling that they were the oldest as well as the most loyal of the Stuart settlements in the New World, adopted the name, the Old Dominion.

[John Fiske, *Old Virginia and Her Neighbors.*]
JAMES E. WINSTON

OLD FIELD SCHOOLS were quite common in parts of the southern states before the Civil War. They acquired the name from the practice of establishing schools at convenient places in the neighborhood, generally on a neglected or abandoned field not suitable for farming. Most of them had only one teacher, generally a man, who was often indifferently trained. The curriculum usually consisted of the merest rudiments of learning. The schoolhouses and equipment were generally crude, and discipline was often quite rigid. Some of these schools grew into rather pretentious institutions and went under the name of academies.

[Edgar W. Knight, *Public Education in the South.*]
EDGAR W. KNIGHT

"OLD FUSS AND FEATHERS," a nickname applied to Gen. Winfield Scott. The connotation was affectionate or derisive, depending on the user's opinion of Scott. The sobriquet referred to the general's love of military pageantry, show uniforms, and meticulousness in military procedure and etiquette. Soldiers, who appreciated his talents, seldom used it maliciously.

CHARLES WINSLOW ELLIOTT

"OLD HICKORY." Because of his endurance and strength, Andrew Jackson was given this nickname in 1813 by his soldiers during a 500-mile march home from Natchez, Miss., to Nashville, Tenn. He was affectionately known by this name among his friends and followers for the rest of his life.

[J. Parton, *Life of Andrew Jackson,* vol. I.]
P. ORMAN RAY

OLD IRONSIDES. See Constitution.

OLD NORTH CHURCH, the name more commonly used for Christ Church in Boston. Erected in 1723, it was the second Episcopal church to be established in Boston and is the oldest church edifice in the city. The bells in its tower, cast in England in 1744, were probably the first to peal in North America. It was in the steeple of the Old North Church that two signal lights were hung to indicate to Paul Revere that the British were approaching Lexington on the night of Apr. 18, 1775 (*see* Revere's Ride).

[Justin Winsor, *Memorial History of Boston.*]
ALVIN F. HARLOW

OLD NORTHWEST included some 248,000 square miles, approximately between the Ohio and Mississippi rivers and the Great Lakes. The Definitive Treaty of Peace of 1783 awarded this territory to the United States and, after the different states had ceded their claims (*see* Western Lands), it became a public domain organized as the Northwest Territory.

[F. A. Ogg, *The Old Northwest.*]
BEVERLEY W. BOND, JR.

"OLD OAKEN BUCKET," a poem written by Samuel Woodworth, journalist, playwright, and poet, about 1817, and originally entitled "The Bucket." One version as to the inception of this poem has it that Woodworth remarked after drinking a glass of water at home one day, "How much more refreshing it would be to drink from the old oaken bucket hanging in my father's well"; upon which his wife remarked, "That's a splendid idea for a poem." The other version is that when Woodworth once praised some brandy at a bar, the saloonkeeper, an old friend, reminded him how much better the water once tasted from the old well bucket they knew in childhood; whereupon Woodworth immediately wrote the poem. It was included in the McGuffey readers and was set to music by Frederick Smith, who merely adapted a tune composed by the English composer George Kiallmark for Thomas Moore's "Araby's Daughter." Sung to this air, the "Old Oaken Bucket" became one of the most popular of the nostalgic songs of home during the 19th century.

[Louis R. Dressler, *Favorite Masterpieces;* F. A. Woodworth, ed., *Poetical Works of Samuel Woodworth.*]
ALVIN F. HARLOW

"OLD ROUGH AND READY." His physical prowess and zeal and the informality of his military attire earned this sobriquet for Gen. Zachary Taylor during the Seminole War in 1841. The nickname was of great service to him in winning votes during his successful bid for the presidency in 1848.

[Joseph Reese, *Life of General Zachary Taylor.*]
ALVIN F. HARLOW

OLD SOUTH CHURCH, Boston, was built in 1729 to replace the original structure of 1670. Here was held the Boston Massacre town meeting that forced the royal governor to withdraw the British troops from Boston in 1770; here were delivered massacre anniversary orations by Joseph Warren, John Hancock,

and others; and here also was held the Tea Party meeting from which the "Indians" went to dump the hated tea into Boston Harbor.

[H. A. Hall, *History of the Old South Church.*]
R. W. G. VAIL

OLEANA, an immigrant colony in northern Pennsylvania, was established in 1852 by the Norwegian violinist Ole Bull, who bought 120,000 acres of land in Potter County and planned a "New Norway." Immigrants began to arrive in September and the village of Oleana was founded. Poor management and unfavorable land and market conditions, coupled with brazen frauds practiced upon the founder by land sharpers, brought about the quick collapse of the colony. An ironic Norwegian ballad (1853) described Oleana as a land where "cakes rain down from out the skies," Münchener beer runs in the creeks, everybody plays the fiddle, and "little roasted piggies, with manners quite demure, Sir,/They ask you, 'Will you have some ham?'—and then you say, 'Why sure, Sir.'/Ole-Ole-Ole, oh, Oleana!'"

[T. C. Blegen, *Norwegian Migration to America, 1825–1860.*]
T. C. BLEGEN

OLENTANGY, BATTLE OF (June 6, 1782). Near a fork of the Olentangy River, a few miles from present-day Bucyrus, Ohio, the retreating frontier militia of Col. William Crawford's expedition fought off the pursuing Indians (Shawnee, Delaware, and Wyandot) and British Rangers. Three Americans were killed and eight wounded. This success saved the little army, then commanded by Col. David Williamson in place of Crawford, who had been captured by the Indians.

[E. O. Randall and D. J. Ryan, *History of Ohio,* vol. II.]
EUGENE H. ROSEBOOM

OLIVE BRANCH PETITION. After the first armed clashes at Lexington and Bunker Hill in Massachusetts in 1775, the newly organized Continental Congress decided to send a petition to George III, setting forth the grievances of the colonies. Knowing the king's violent opposition to the idea of dealing with the colonies as a united group, each of the congressional delegates signed the paper as an individual. Further, to show their amicable intent, they made Richard Penn, descendant of William Penn and a staunch Loyalist, their messenger. When Penn reached London on Aug. 14, 1775, the king refused to see him or to receive his petition through any channel.

[Edmund C. Burnett, *The Continental Congress;* Merrill Jensen, *The Founding of a Nation.*]

ALVIN F. HARLOW

OLNEY COROLLARY. In his dispatch of July 20, 1895, to Thomas F. Bayard, ambassador to Great Britain, Secretary of State Richard Olney applied the Monroe Doctrine to the Venezuela–British Guiana boundary dispute by a much broader interpretation than that previously current. He declared that the doctrine as a part of "public law" had made it the traditional policy of the United States to oppose a forcible increase by any European power of its territorial possessions in the Americas; that by withholding from arbitration part of the territory in dispute with Venezuela, Great Britain was constructively extending its colonization; and that since the United States was "entitled to resent and resist any sequestration of Venezuelan soil by Great Britain, it is necessarily entitled to know whether such sequestration has occurred or is now going on." The British were asked to reply before December, when Congress would convene. Miscalculating the date when Congress would open its session, the British reply, which made no concessions, arrived on Dec. 7, Congress having convened on Dec. 2. On Dec. 17 President Grover Cleveland asked Congress to appoint a commission to fix the true boundary, beyond which Britain should not be allowed to push. Great Britain backed down, and the subject of arbitration was reopened. Olney's loose construction of the doctrine went much beyond the language used by James Monroe and John Quincy Adams and was at once challenged by various American authorities on the subject.

[Paul R. Fossum, "The Anglo-Venezuelan Boundary Controversy," *Hispanic American Historical Review,* vol. 8 (1928); Walter La Feber, "The Background of Cleveland's Venezuelan Policy," *American Historical Review,* vol. 56 (1961).]

ALLAN NEVINS

OLNEY-PAUNCEFOTE TREATY was a general treaty of Anglo-American arbitration drafted primarily by Secretary of State Richard Olney and Sir Julian Pauncefote, British ambassador to the United States. Such a treaty had been considered for some years and was suggested anew by British Prime Minister Robert Gascoyne-Cecil, Lord Salisbury, in January 1896. Salisbury proposed one of limited terms;

Olney believed in giving arbitration the greatest possible scope and in making the awards securely binding. The treaty he and Pauncefote drew up during 1896 made pecuniary and most other nonterritorial disputes completely arbitrable; territorial disputes, and any "disputed questions of principle of grave importance," were arbitrable subject to an appeal to a court of six, and if more than one of the six dissented, the award was not to be binding. Parliament promptly ratified the treaty. President Grover Cleveland sent it to the Senate on Jan. 11, 1897, with his strong approval, but it lay over until the Republican administration came into office. Then, although President William McKinley and Secretary of State John Hay earnestly supported it, ratification failed.

[Nelson M. Blake, "The Olney-Pauncefote Treaty of 1897," *American Historical Review,* vol. 50 (1945); Henry James, *Richard Olney and His Public Services.*]

ALLAN NEVINS

OLUSTEE, BATTLE OF (Feb. 20, 1864), between 5,500 Union troops, under Gen. Truman Seymour, and 5,200 Confederates, under Gen. Joseph Finnegan, resulted in a Confederate victory and thwarted the Union purpose of gaining possession of the interior of Florida. Losses in killed, wounded, and missing were: Union, 1,861; Confederate, 946.

[William Watson Davis, *Civil War and Reconstruction in Florida.*]

W. T. CASH

OLYMPIC GAMES. The participation of the United States in the Olympic Games is the sole responsibility of the U.S. Olympic Committee (USOC), recognized by the International Olympic Committee as the official agency to select, train, transport, clothe, house, and feed 450 American amateur athletes for the Olympic Summer Games and about 130 for the Olympic Winter Games, conducted quadrennially. The budget for the Olympic movement in the United States has grown to about $10.8 million for the four-year period (1970's). It has been the policy of the USOC to enter a full complement of athletes in competition in the sixteen individual sports and in all the five team sports for which the United States qualifies to participate in the Olympic Summer Games and in the six individual sports and ice hockey on the Olympic Winter Games program.

From the inauguration of the Olympic Games at Athens, Greece, in 1896 to the 1972 games the United States has won 583 gold medals, 412 silver medals, and 373 bronze medals, a total of 1,368 medals out of the 6,658 presented. No other nation even approached the U.S. total in number of medals won—although the Olympic Games must be recognized strictly as competition among athletes and not as a display of a nation's strength. For the Olympic Winter Games the United States trailed Norway and the Soviet Union, having won 27 gold medals, 37 silver medals, and 23 bronze medals, a total of 87 out of the 777 medals presented since the inaugural Olympic Games in Chamonix, France, in 1924.

The United States has the distinction of winning the first gold medals awarded at both Athens and Chamonix. James B. Connolly withdrew from Harvard College to compete in 1896 and was victor in the triple jump in track and field. In the Olympic Winter Games the first champion crowned was Charles Jewtraw in the 500-meter speed skating event.

Although the United States has been represented in all sports on the Olympic Games programs, it usually excels in men's track and field, men's and women's swimming and diving, basketball, and rowing. Over the years the United States has enjoyed modest success in boxing, shooting, wrestling, yachting, speed skating, and figure skating. The United States cannot be considered competitive in cycling, fencing, men's gymnastics, judo, luge (tobogganing), cross-country skiing, and ski jumping or in the team sports of field hockey, team handball (a popular Central European sport), volleyball, and, until 1972, soccer.

It is estimated that at the beginning of a four-year period of preparation for the Olympic Games more than 5 million athletes consider themselves candidates for the fewer than 600 places on the teams for the Olympic Summer and Winter Games. Selection trials are held to select the team members, and invitations, in general, are extended to those athletes who have proved themselves in national and international competitions. There are no upper or lower age limits for Olympic athletes. The youngest gold medalist from the United States was Marjorie Gestring, thirteen, when she competed at Berlin in 1936.

Outstanding U.S. athletes include the following:

Track and Field, Men's: James B. Connolly (1896); Lee Q. Calhoun (1956, 1960); Harrison Dillard (1948, 1952); Robert Mathias (1948, 1952); Jesse Owens (1936); Al Oerter (1956, 1960, 1964, 1968); Alvin Kraenzlein, winner of four gold medals (1900); and Ray Ewry, winner of eight gold medals in the standing jumps (1900, 1904, 1908).

Track and Field, Women's: Mildred ("Babe") Didrikson (1932); Wilma Rudolph (1960).

Basketball: Bob Kurland (1948, 1952); Bill Russell (1956); Oscar Robertson (1960); Jerry West (1960); Bill Bradley (1964); Jerry Shipp (1964); Spencer Haywood (1968).

Swimming, Men's: Duke P. Kahanamoku (1912, 1920); John Weissmuller (1924, 1928); Mike Burton (1968, 1972); Mark Spitz, winner of two gold medals in 1968 and seven in 1972.

Swimming, Women's: Gertrude Ederle, the first woman to swim the English Channel (1924); Chris von Saltza (1960); Sharon Stouder (1964); Deborah Meyer (1968); Melissa Belote and Sandra Neilson (1972).

Diving, Men's and Women's: Patricia Keller McCormick, the only person to win the springboard and platform diving events twice (1952, 1956); Sammy Lee (1948, 1952); Victoria M. Draves (1948); Robert Webster (1960, 1964).

Boxing: Floyd Patterson (1952); Cassius Clay, later known as Muhammad Ali (1960); Joe Frazier (1964); George Foreman (1968). Each became the world's professional heavyweight champion.

Wrestling: Jack van Bebber (1932); Henry Wittenberg (1948); Douglas Blubaugh (1960); Dan Gable and Wayne Wells (1972).

Rowing: John B. Kelly, Sr. (1920).

Equestrian: William Steinkraus (1968).

Shooting: William McMillan (1960); Lones Wigger (1964, 1972).

Weightlifting: John Davis (1948, 1952); Tommy Kono (1952, 1956).

Figure Skating: Dick Button (1948, 1952); Tenley Albright (1956); Peggy Fleming (1968).

Skiing: Andrea Lawrence-Mead (1952); Barbara Ann Cochran (1972).

Speed Skating: Irving Jaffee (1928, 1932); Anne Henning and Dianne Holum (1972).

Among the 879 gold medalists from the Olympic Summer Games and the 50 from the Winter Games, by 1972 only one person had won a gold medal in each set of games—Edward Eagan of the United States was 1924 light heavyweight boxing champion and eight years later was a member of the winning U.S. team in the four-man bobsledding competition.

[Arthur Daley and John Kieran, *The Olympic Games;* Dick Schaap, *An Illustrated History of the Olympic Games;* U.S. Olympic Committee, *The Olympic Games.*]

PHILIP O. KRUMM

OMAHA. Inhabitants of northeastern Nebraska on the Missouri River, the Omaha tribe represented that segment of Plains culture defined as sedentary and agricultural. Like other such riverine Plains groups, the Omaha tended toward permanent villages and seasonal bison hunts. Material culture, including such elements as the tipi, was more elaborate than among the nomadic Plains tribes. The Omaha are noted for the complexity of their patrilineal organization. The tribe spoke Siouan and was most closely related to the Ponca, Kansa, and Osage. The Omaha had an estimated population of 2,800 in 1780.

[Alice C. Fletcher and Francis LaFlesche, "The Omaha Tribe," Bureau of American Ethnology, *Annual Report* (1906).]

ROBERT F. SPENCER

OMNIBUS BILL, reported on May 8, 1850, by the special Senate Committee of Thirteen, was an attempt at a comprehensive adjustment of the territorial question. On June 17 the popular sovereignty feature was applied to the provisions concerning Utah. The opposition of President Zachary Taylor and of the northern and southern opponents of compromise prevented the adoption of the bill even by the Senate. In the contemporary figure of speech, the "omnibus" experienced such rough going that it jolted out all of its occupants but one. On July 31 the sections relating to California, New Mexico, and Texas were stricken, and on the following day the Senate adopted the Utah bill. Later legislation (*see* Compromise of 1850) included substantially the ground of the originally proposed compromise.

ARTHUR C. COLE

OÑATE'S EXPLORATIONS. The explorations of the Spanish explorer Juan de Oñate, 1598–1608, were in reality rediscoveries of regions previously seen by Juan Vásquez de Coronado and Antonio de Espejo, but they brought to light better trails and established Spain on the Rio Grande. Oñate, who previously had colonized San Luis Potosi, was appointed in 1595 to colonize and govern a new Mexico to be founded on the Rio Grande. He advanced from the Mexican frontier with 400 men, of whom 130 had families, and took formal possession near El Paso on Apr. 30, 1598. Later in the summer he founded San Juan, north of present-day Santa Fe. In the next three years he and his subordinates explored and subjugated what are now New Mexico and northeastern Arizona. Oñate's first extensive journey from the Rio Grande was eastward in 1601, down the Canadian River and northeastward to the grasshouse Indian village of Quivira, which the historian Herbert E. Bolton locates on the Arkansas in the present state of Kansas.

Returning to New Mexico, Oñate suppressed a brewing revolt. Late in 1604 he marched westward across the present northern part of Arizona to Bill Williams River, followed it to the Colorado, and marched down that river to the Gulf of California, returning in 1605. He was recalled from the governorship in 1608.

[Herbert E. Bolton, *Spanish Exploration in the Southwest.*]

BLISS ISELY

ONEIDA COLONY, established in 1848 between Syracuse and Utica, in New York State, was America's most radical experiment in social and religious thinking. From literal concepts of perfectionism and Bible communism the colony advanced into new forms of social relationships: economic communism, the rejection of monogamy for complex marriage, the practice of an elementary form of birth control (*coitus reservatus*), and the eugenic breeding of stirpicultural children. John Humphrey Noyes, leader of the group, was a capable and shrewd Yankee whose sincere primitive Christianity expressed itself in radically modern terms. His fellow workers had experienced complete religious conversion and boldly followed him into a communal life that rejected the evils of competitive economics while it kept realistically to the methods of modern industry, believing that socialism is ahead of and not behind society.

From the inception of the colony the property grew to about 600 acres of well-cultivated land, with shoe, tailoring, and machine shops, the latter producing commercially successful traps and flatware among other items; canning and silk factories; and great central buildings and houses for employees. The group also formed a branch colony in Wallingford, Conn. Assets had reached more than $550,000 when communism was dropped. Health was above the average, women held a high place, children were excellently trained, work was fair and changeable, and entertainment was constant.

In 1879, forced by social pressure from without and the dissatisfaction of the young within, monogamy was adopted, and within a year communism was replaced by joint-stock ownership. In its new form, Oneida continued its commercial success, but as a conventional company. During the 20th century, the Oneida Company was noted for its production of fine silver and stainless steel flatware.

[W. A. Hinds, *American Communities;* J. H. Noyes, *History of American Socialism;* R. A. Parker, *A Yankee Saint.*]

ALLAN MACDONALD

ONION RIVER LAND COMPANY. A survey by Ira Allen in 1772 of the land in the New Hampshire grants of 1749–64 (now in the state of Vermont) convinced him of the value of the region around the Onion River (now the Winooski) and the shores of Lake Champlain. In 1773 four Allen brothers, with a cousin, formed the Onion River Land Company and bought land from claimants under New Hampshire titles, securing at least 77,000 acres and possibly much more. The venture was a pure land speculation, since they had full knowledge of the disputed title. Ethan Allen managed the sales and political affairs, while Ira laid out a road and selected the site of Burlington. Settlement began at once, but financial success depended on destroying the claims of New York State, and to do this the Allens resorted to mob violence and the destruction of property, the building of forts, and the use of the Green Mountain Boys, of whom Ethan Allen was colonel. New York outlawed them, but ceased to claim jurisdiction of the disputed area when the Revolution broke out. About 16,000 acres were sold by 1775. After Ethan's death the affairs of the company became confused, and the only survivor, Ira, after having his property seized and after being thrown briefly into prison, was reduced to poverty. The partners benefited little financially, but their interest in making good their titles was important for the early history and independence of Vermont.

[John Pell, *Ethan Allen;* J. B. Wilbur, *Ira Allen, Founder of Vermont.*]

HERBERT W. HILL

ONIONS, apparently native to Asia, were unknown to the American Indians and were first brought to America from Europe by the early colonists. Wethersfield, Conn., soon became a noted onion-growing center. Barnstable, Mass., was a slightly less important onion producer. Records show that Wethersfield was shipping onions as early as 1710; and a century later it was sending out a million bunches annually, most going to the West Indies. It supplied quantities of onions to the army and navy during the revolutionary war. But as onion culture spread to all parts of the country, Wethersfield lost its preeminence. Extensive production of Bermuda onions began soon after 1900 in Texas, California, and Louisiana, and by the early 1970's Texas and California were leading all other states in onion production. In 1972 the United States produced 1.39 million short tons of onions, valued at nearly $140 million.

[Percy Wells Bidwell, "Rural Economy in New England," *Transactions of Connecticut Academy of Arts and Sciences,* vol. XX; Norris Galpin Osborn, *History of Connecticut.*]

ALVIN F. HARLOW

ONONDAGA, GREAT COUNCIL HOUSE AT. *See* **Iroquois.**

"ONONTIO," meaning "great mountain," was the Iroquois name for the French governors of Canada. It was a translation of the surname of Charles Huault de Montmagny, who succeeded Samuel de Champlain as governor of New France in 1636. In 1645 Montmagny called a grand council at the mission settlement of Sillery to consider the fate of two Iroquois prisoners. As a matter of policy their lives were spared, and one of the prisoners in a speech expressing his gratitude addressed Montmagny as "Onontio," thus it is said using this term for the first time.

[F. Parkman, *The Jesuits in North America.*]

A. C. FLICK

ONTARIO, LAKE, the smallest of the five Great Lakes, was discovered by Samuel de Champlain and Étienne Brulé in 1615. Champlain with a party of Huron Indians had traveled diagonally across Ontario from Lake Simcoe to the eastern end of the lake, somewhere in the neighborhood of Kingston, on his way to attack the Iroquois in what is now northern New York. Brulé's course is more problematical, but he seems to have gone south from Lake Simcoe and to have reached Lake Ontario at Toronto. The lake appears as "Lac St Louis" on Champlain's map of 1632; as "Ontario ou Lac St Louis" on Nicolas Sanson's map of 1656; and as "Ontario" on Guillaume Delisle's map of 1700. Popple has "Lake Ontario or Frontenac" on his 1733 map, but thereafter the name Ontario appears alone. Ontario means "high rocks near the water."

The lake was the scene of naval or military engagements between 1756 and 1759 and again in 1813; and for many generations it formed part of one of the principal water thoroughfares of the fur trade. Fort Frontenac was built in 1673, by Hugues Randin, where the city of Kingston now stands. It was destroyed by Jacques René Brisay, Marquis de Denonville, in 1689, rebuilt by Louis de Buade, Comte de Frontenac, in 1695, and captured and destroyed by the English in 1758. Kingston was founded in 1783 by United Empire Loyalists. Fort Toronto was built in 1750, where the city of the same name stands today, but there was a trading post here before 1730. Fort Oswego, built by Gov. William Burnet of New York in 1727, was destroyed by Louis Joseph de Montcalm in 1756, rebuilt by British Lt. Gen. Frederick Haldimand in 1759 and renamed Fort Ontario. In 1678 Robert Cavelier, Sieur de La Salle, built a small post at the mouth of the Niagara River that was burned in 1680 and rebuilt in stone by Gaspard-Joseph Chaussegros de Léry in 1726. Fort Niagara went through many vicissitudes, and finally was surrendered by the English to the United States in 1796 (see Border Forts, Evacuation of). The first sailing ships on Lake Ontario, or on any of the Great Lakes, were four built by La Salle at Fort Frontenac in 1678 or earlier to provide transportation between the fort and his post at the mouth of the Niagara.

Lake Ontario and Oswego, the main U.S. port on the lake, became important during the 19th century for the shipping of grain and lumber from the Middle West and Canada, and of coal from Pennsylvania by way of the Welland Canal (first opened in 1829), connecting lakes Erie and Ontario. With the opening of the Saint Lawrence Seaway in 1959, shipping through Lake Ontario increased greatly. A combined traffic amounting to more than 65 million tons of freight was passing through the seaway and the Welland Canal by the early 1970's.

[George A. Cuthbertson, *Freshwater;* Arthur Pound, *Lake Ontario.*]

LAWRENCE J. BURPEE

"ON TO RICHMOND." On June 28, 1861, an editorial advocating an aggressive military policy—reputedly written by Charles A. Dana, but really by another staff writer—entitled "Forward to Richmond," appeared in the *New York Tribune.* Other newspapers took up the phrase, shortening it to "On to Richmond," and it actually influenced federal military policy.

[James Harrison Wilson, *Life of Charles A. Dana.*]
ALVIN F. HARLOW

"ON TO WASHINGTON." When the Union army was fleeing from the field after the Battle of Bull Run, July 21, 1861, the cry "On to Washington" was raised among the pursuing Confederate troops, but they themselves became too disorganized to achieve the objective. Newspapers throughout the South then took up the phrase and urged it repeatedly.

[Jefferson Davis, *Rise and Fall of the Confederate Government.*]
ALVIN F. HARLOW

OPEN COVENANTS, OPENLY ARRIVED AT. The first of President Woodrow Wilson's famous Fourteen Points included in his address to Congress of Jan. 8, 1918, read: "Open covenants of peace, openly arrived at, after which there shall be no private international understandings of any kind but diplomacy shall proceed always frankly and in the public view."

This proposal was concordant with the then popular slogan, "no secret treaties," although more far-reaching. In a letter to Secretary of State Robert Lansing (Mar. 12, 1918) Wilson wrote: ". . . certainly when I pronounced for open diplomacy, I meant not that there should be no private discussion of delicate matters, but that no secret agreements of any sort should be entered into and that all international relations, when fixed, should be open, above-board, and explicit."

The point for open diplomacy was a basis for Article XVIII of the Covenant of the League of Nations, which provided for the registration and publication of treaties and which stated that no treaty or international engagement shall be binding until registered.

[Thomas A. Bailey, *Woodrow Wilson and the Lost Peace;* N. Gordon Levin, Jr., *Woodrow Wilson and World Politics: America's Response to War and Revolution.*]
HUNTER MILLER

OPEN DOOR POLICY. Three interrelated doctrines—equality of commercial opportunity, territorial integrity, and administrative integrity—constituted the American idea of the Open Door in China. Formally enunciated by Secretary of State John Hay in 1899 and 1900, the Open Door policy emerged from two major cycles of American expansionist history; the first, a maritime cycle, gained impetus from the new commerial thrust of the mid-19th century and blended into the new cycle of industrial and financial capitalism that emerged toward the end of the century and continued into the 1930's. Thereafter, its vitality ebbed away as political and economic forces posed a new power structure and national reorganization in the Far East.

The first cycle of Open Door activity developed through the mid-19th-century interaction of the expansion of American continental and maritime frontiers. The construction of the transcontinental railroads gave rise to the idea of an American transportation bridge to China. The powers behind the lush China trade, headquartered in the mid-Atlantic and New England coastal cities, established commercial positions on the north Pacific coast and in Hawaii in order to transfer furs and sandalwood as items in the trade with the Chinese. The resulting expansion of maritime commerce was coordinated with the American investment in whaling; the great interest in the exploration of the Pacific Ocean and the historic concern for the development of a short route from the Atlantic to the Pacific across Central America; a growing American diplomatic, naval, and missionary interest in eastern Asia; the opening of China to American trade on the heels of the British victory in the Anglo-Chinese War of 1839–42 via the Cushing Treaty of 1844; and the push into the Pacific led by Secretary of State William H. Seward that culminated in the purchase of Alaska in 1867 and the Burlingame Treaty of 1868.

Throughout this period the United States adapted British commercial policy to its own ends by supporting the notion of free and open competition for trade in international markets, while denouncing British colonial acquisitions and preferential trade positions. The European subjection of China by force and the imposition of the resulting treaty system gave American maritime interests an opportunity to flourish without a parallel colonial responsibility or imperial illusion. The expansionist thrust of this cycle of mercantile exchange and trade reached its peak with the onset of the Spanish-American War in 1898 and the great debate over the annexation of Hawaii and the Philippines during President William McKinley's administration.

The second cycle of expansionist development sprang from the advent of industrial capitalism and the requirements of commercial American agriculture for export markets, bringing together a peculiarly complex mixture of farm and factory interests that had traditionally clashed over domestic economic policy and legislation. A mutually advantageous world view of political economy was welded as both interests prepared to move into and expand the China market. As the increasing commercialization of American agriculture led to a need for greater outlets for American grain and cotton manufactured goods, China was becoming also a potential consumer of the products of American heavy industry, including railroad equipment, and of oil products. At the same time, outlets were needed for the investment of growing American fortunes, and it was speculated that the modernization of China through the expansion of communication and transportation would, in turn, increase the demand for the products of American economic growth.

Critics of Secretary of State John Hay's policy assert that the Open Door formula "was already an old and hackneyed one at the turn of the century," that its "principles were not clear and precise," and that it could not "usefully be made the basis of a foreign policy." It may well be that American announcements on behalf of China's territorial integrity did create an erroneous "impression of a community of outlook among nations which did not really exist." But it was a foreign policy expressive of national ambition and protective of American interests, actual and potential. It was stimulated by international rivalry at the end of the 19th century for control of ports, territories, spheres of influence, and economic advantage at the expense of a weak China. It was manipulated through the influence of British nationals in the Imperial Maritime Customs Service (established by the foreign treaty system) who were intent on protecting their vested administrative interests even at the expense of their own country's position in China. And it was a time-honored administrative tactic that attempted to strengthen the American position in China by cloaking its claims in the dress of international morality on behalf of China's territorial and political independence while simultaneously protecting the interests of the powers in maintaining the trade and political positions already acquired there. Dealing as Hay did from an American bias in developing a position of power without admitting the power of an already existing ambition in China, the tactic of the Open Door served full well to initiate a chain of Open Door claims that steadily expanded up to World War I and beyond.

Hay's Open Door notes to Germany, Russia, and England in 1899, and later to the other powers, are conventionally interpreted as an attempt to bluff them into accepting the American position in China, whereas actually they announced the decision of the United States to press its interests on its own behalf.

From that time forward the United States mingled in the international rivalries in Manchuria as well as in China proper. At first anti-Russian in Manchuria and intent on extending American railroad, mining, and commercial privileges there, the United States then became anti-Japanese after the Russo-Japanese War of 1905, although it was not able to make a definitive commitment of national resources and energy. Influenced by the caution of President Theodore Roosevelt, in the Taft-Katsura Agreement of 1905 and the Root-Takahira Agreement of 1908, the United States recognized Japan's growing power in eastern Asia in return for stated Open Door principles and respect for American territorial legitimacy in the Far East. Later, during the administration of President William Howard Taft, the United States attempted to move into Manchuria and China proper via Open Door proposals on behalf of American railroad and banking investment interests in 1909 and 1913, and in so doing made overtures of cooperation with the European powers as well as with Russia and Japan. During President Woodrow Wilson's administrations the United States veered from side to side: it attempted to protect its stake in China by opposing Japan's 21 Demands on China in 1915, and then it attempted to appease Japan's ambitions in Manchuria by recognizing the Japanese stake there in the Lansing-Ishii Agreement of 1917.

Five years later, at the Washington Armament Conference negotiations, the Open Door outlook was embedded in the details of the Nine-Power Treaty, which called for the territorial and administrative integrity of China and equality of trade opportunity without special privileges for any nation; there also began plans for the abolition of extrality, the system of legal rights and privileges that foreigners enjoyed in China, which placed them beyond the reach of the government.

During the period 1929–33, Manchuria came to the forefront of American Open Door concerns, with the invocation of the Kellogg-Briand Pact of 1927 against Japan's use of force in Manchuria. By 1931, Secretary of State Henry L. Stimson had established the continuity of American policy by linking the principles of the Kellogg-Briand Pact with those expressed in the Nine-Power Treaty of 1922. A year later, in 1932, Stimson made history by articulating his non-recognition doctrine, regarding Japan's conquest of Manchuria and the establishment of the puppet state of Manchukuo.

From that point onward, throughout the 1930's and on to World War II, the United States, led by Secretary of State Cordell Hull, maintained growing opposition to Japan's aggrandizement in the sphere of China and the enlargement of Japan's ambitions throughout Southeast Asia.

[John K. Fairbank, *The United States and China;* George Kennan, *American Diplomacy 1900–1950;* William A. Williams, *The Shaping of American Diplomacy.*]

CHARLES VEVIER

OPEN-MARKET OPERATIONS is a term used to describe the purchase and sale of government securities and other assets held by a central bank. In open-market operations the initiative is taken by a central bank, whereas in discount operations the initiative is taken by the borrowing bank. At times it is difficult to affix initiative. The sale of securities by a central bank may force a commercial bank to borrow from a central bank in order to replenish reserves depleted by open-market operations.

In the United States open-market operations are under the complete control of the Federal Open Market Committee, consisting of the seven members of the board of governors of the Federal Reserve System and five representatives of the twelve Federal Reserve banks. The assets that may be bought and sold include gold coin and bullion; bills of exchange; cable transfers and bankers acceptances; U.S. securities, both direct and guaranteed; and municipal warrants. In practice, purchases and sales are usually limited to U.S. direct obligations, principally short-term.

The purpose of open-market operations is to raise or lower money-market rates of interest, thereby exerting control over credit conditions; to facilitate U.S. Treasury financing; and to affect the foreign-exchange value of the dollar.

Open-market operations, for the purposes employed in the United States, are to be found generally in developed nations that have active capital markets. In developing nations, open-market operations may be used to finance particular industries and sectors of the economy.

A record of the reasons for undertaking specific operations in the United States is released approximately ninety days following the decision taken and published in monthly issues of the *Federal Reserve Bulletin.*

[B. H. Beckhart, *The Federal Reserve System.*]

BENJAMIN HAGGOTT BECKHART

OPEN-RANGE CATTLE PERIOD. While cattle were pastured on unoccupied public lands quite early, and especially in Texas in the years before the Civil War, the period of open-range grazing, in a larger sense, began about 1866 and closed early in the last decade of the 19th century. During the years following the close of the Civil War a vast stream of cattle poured north out of Texas to cow towns in Kansas and Nebraska. From these towns the fat, mature animals were shipped to market while young steers and breeding animals were driven farther north or west to stock new ranges. It has been estimated that nearly 5.5

million cattle were driven north from Texas in the period from 1866 to 1885, and this does not include large numbers driven west or northwest into New Mexico and Colorado (*see* Cattle Drives).

Most of the cattle driven north each year were spread out over ranges in the public domain throughout western Kansas, Nebraska, Dakota, Montana, Wyoming, and other western states and territories. They were held there for growth and fattening, the boundaries of each ranchman's pasturelands being determined by that unwritten law of the range known as "cow custom." A ranch headquarters was usually established near the center of the range and along its borders were placed cow camps at which riders were stationed to look after the cattle and to keep them within the limits of their own range. Despite their efforts, some would stray across the line onto the pasturelands of neighboring ranchmen, which made it necessary to hold roundups each spring and autumn. At the spring roundup calves were branded and at the fall roundup the fat, mature animals of each ranchman were separated from the remainder and placed in the "beef herd" to be shipped to market for slaughter.

All the ranchmen of a large area designated as the roundup district participated in the roundups. Each ranchman usually sent a wagon and several cowboys to share in the work. In some states or territories, notably Wyoming, the districts and the dates and manner of conducting roundups were designated by law. A roundup foreman was chosen to have charge of the work and the method of disposing of mavericks, or unbranded animals, was often fixed by statute.

Cattle were driven over the state lands of western Texas and northward from Texas over the great Indian reservations of Indian Territory as well as those farther north, and over the public domain of the central and northern Plains. All of this great region constituted the so-called cow country. Settlers steadily advanced westward along its eastern border, taking up homesteads, but the area lost to grazing was for a time replaced by the opening up of large tracts of hitherto unwatered lands for use as pasturage with the construction of dams across ravines, and the drilling of deep wells from which water was pumped by windmills.

The first shipments of dressed beef to Europe began in 1875. Shipments steadily increased until more than 50 million pounds were exported in 1878 and more than 100 million pounds in 1881. Most of this was sent to Great Britain, where the enormous influx of American beef so alarmed the cattle growers of north Britain that a parliamentary commission was sent to the United States to visit the range area and report on conditions. Its report, made in 1884, told of such great profits made in ranching as to cause much excitement among the English and Scottish investors, and huge sums of British capital were sent to America for investment in ranching enterprises. Many individual Scots or English came to the cow country to give their personal attention to ranching. By 1884 it was estimated that more than $30 million of British capital had been invested in ranching on the Great Plains. (*See also* Foreign Investments in the United States.)

Among the large Scottish or English enterprises were the Prairie Land and Cattle Company, the Matador, and the Espuela Land and Cattle Company. An enthusiasm for grazing cattle on the open range amounting almost to a craze had also swept over the United States before 1885. Prominent lawyers, U.S. senators, bankers, and other businessmen throughout the East formed cattle companies to take advantage of the opportunities offered for ranching on the great open ranges of the West. The destruction of the buffalo herds made it necessary to feed the many large tribes of western Indians, and this resulted in the awarding of valuable beef contracts for that purpose with the privilege of pasturing herds upon the various reservations.

The invention of barbed wire and the rapid extension of its use after 1875 brought about the enclosure of considerable tracts of pastureland. Laws were enacted by Congress forbidding the fencing of lands of the public domain, and orders of the Indian Bureau prohibited the enclosure of lands on Indian reservations. While such laws and orders were not strictly enforced, they were not without effect.

Perhaps the year 1885 marks the peak of the open-range cattle industry. By that time most of the range was fully stocked and much of it overstocked. During the summer of 1886 large herds were driven north from Texas and spread over the ranges in the most reckless fashion possible. Then came the terrible winter of 1886–87 in which hundreds of thousands of cattle died of cold and starvation. Spring came to find nearly every ranchman on the central and northern Plains facing ruin. The open-range cattle industry never recovered from the results of that tragic winter. The range area was being rapidly settled by homesteaders. Large Indian reservations were thrown open to settlement. The use of barbed wire was becoming universal, and the public domain was passing into the hands of private owners who enclosed their lands with wire fences. In many regions cattle were being replaced by sheep. No date can be given for the end of the open-range cattle period, but by 1890 it was close at hand, and by the end of the century it virtually belonged to the past.

[Lewis Atherton, *The Cattle Kings;* Edward E. Dale, *Cow Country;* Henry D. McCallum and Frances T. McCallum, *The Wire That Fenced the West;* Orin J. Oliphant, *On the Cattle Ranges of the Oregon Country.*]

EDWARD EVERETT DALE

OPEN SHOP. *See* **Closed Shop.**

ORANGE, FORT. *See* **Albany.**

ORATORY. Although such Indian orators as Pontiac and Red Jacket had stirred their people to defend their hunting grounds, the eloquence of the colonists was dormant until the Revolution aroused the talents of Samuel Adams, James Otis, and the burning enthusiasm of Patrick Henry. In three great speeches: on the "Parson's Cause" (1763), on the Stamp Act (1765), and in the "Liberty or Death" speech (1775), Henry left his mark upon U.S. history; even though he lost his three-week fight against ratifying the Constitution (1788), he triumphed by aiding the adoption of the first ten amendments (*see* Bill of Rights). John Randolph's perennial invective held sway in Congress until the period of controversy and compromise over the nature of the Union brought forth Henry Clay, John Calhoun, and Daniel Webster. Clay was remarkable for the frequency and fluency of his persuasive utterance; Calhoun for subject mastery and logical presentation; Webster for his magnificent voice, memory, and presence. In his plea for Dartmouth College (1818), his commemorative address at Bunker Hill (1825), and his deliberative oration in "Reply to Sen. Robert Y. Hayne of South Carolina" (1830), Webster attained the summit of eloquence in three distinct types of speech. The roll of eminent speakers of the middle period would include John Quincy Adams, Thomas Hart Benton, Thomas Corwin, Seargent Smith Prentiss, Robert Toombs, and William Yancey. The sonorous voice and superb confidence of Stephen A. Douglas were matched by the admirable directness of Abraham Lincoln in their debates (1858), which marked the apogee of this style of political campaigning. Lincoln's inaugural addresses have been the best of their kind.

Except for Charles Sumner, Albert J. Beveridge, and the elder Robert La Follette, the greatest orators since the Civil War have not been in Congress. A consummate speaker who achieved popular success in unpopular causes was Wendell Phillips. His Phi Beta Kappa oration at Harvard (1881) equaled those of Edward Everett (1824) and Ralph Waldo Emerson (1837). Civic reform enlisted the abilities of George W. Curtis; agnosticism those of Robert G. Ingersoll; and the "New South" (1886) those of Henry W. Grady. The greatest pulpit orators have been Henry Ward Beecher, Phillips Brooks, and Harry Emerson Fosdick. Foremost among legal advocates have been William Pinkney, Rufus Choate, and Clarence Darrow; Choate was especially noted for adaptability to any mood or subject. The Populist orators were the precursors of William Jennings Bryan, Theodore Roosevelt, and Woodrow Wilson as molders of public opinion. Bryan was supreme in voice, Roosevelt in vigor, and Wilson in earnest sincerity. All were effective phrasemakers and had great skill in moral suasion. Franklin D. Roosevelt, whose clarity of expression was evident in his first inaugural address (1933) and in his "fireside chats," remained unrivaled as an orator among important U.S. public figures during his lifetime. Since World War II the emphasis on oratory has declined, and few notable orators have appeared. The civil-rights leader Martin Luther King, Jr., was one of these few. King's memorable, eloquent speech "I Have a Dream" (1963) caused many Americans to give their support to him and to his movement. Coretta King, his widow, possessed similar qualities of eloquence and persuasion, as revealed in a series of addresses and sermons delivered after 1968.

[Henry Hardwicke, *History of Oratory and Orators;* Edgar D. Jones, *Lords of Speech;* James A. Woodburn and Alexander Johnston, eds., *Representative American Orations.*]

HARVEY L. CARTER

ORDER OF AMERICAN KNIGHTS, a Civil War secret order of northern Peace Democrats or Copperheads that was particularly strong in the Northwest. It was formed through the reorganization of the Knights of the Golden Circle in 1863. Again reorganized in 1864, when C. L. Vallandigham became supreme commander, the order took the name of Sons of Liberty.

[E. C. Kirkland, *The Peacemakers of 1864.*]

CHARLES H. COLEMAN

ORDER OF THE STAR-SPANGLED BANNER. *See* **American Party.**

161

ORDERS IN COUNCIL are executive edicts in Great Britain issued in the name of the king, "by and with the advice of his privy council." They have the force of law until superseded by acts of Parliament. Among the many orders in council promulgated in British history, two are of primary interest for their influence upon the United States. They are the orders in council of Jan. 7 and Nov. 11, 1807, which were Britain's reply to Napoleon's Berlin Decree, Nov. 21, 1806, imposing a blockade of the British Isles.

Aimed at neutral commerce in general, in an endeavor to overthrow the economic foundations of Napoleon's power, these orders in council affected principally the United States as the chief of neutral carriers. The orders of Jan. 7 placed French commerce under a blockade and forbade neutrals to trade from one port to another under Napoleon's jurisdiction. Commercial strangulation of Europe under French control advanced a further step when, by the orders of Nov. 11, it was stipulated that neutral ships, meaning American, might not enter any ports "from which . . . the British flag is excluded, and all ports or places in the colonies belonging to his majesty's enemies, shall, from henceforth, be subject to the same restrictions . . . as if the same were actually blockaded by his majesty's naval forces, in the most strict and rigorous manner."

These orders were superseded on Apr. 26, 1809, by a blockade of the Netherlands, France, and Italy; and in June 1812, too late to avert the War of 1812, the orders were actually repealed, subject to certain modifications, in what constituted a major victory for American diplomacy.

[H. S. Commager, ed., *Documents of American History; L. M. Sears, A History of American Foreign Relations*.]
LOUIS MARTIN SEARS

ORDINANCES OF 1784, 1785, AND 1787 were enacted in connection with the development of a policy for the settlement of the country northwest of the Ohio River (*see* Northwest Territory). The establishment of the government of the Confederation was delayed several years over the issue of the disposition of the western lands. Seven states had western land claims, six had none; and the latter refused to join the Confederation until the former should cede their lands to the new government, to be utilized for the common benefit of all the states.

In 1780 New York led the way by giving up all claim to the western lands, whereupon Congress passed a resolution pledging that the lands the states might cede to the general government would be erected into new states that should be admitted to the Union on a basis of equality with the existing states. This vital decision made possible the future extension of the nation across the continent, for it is unthinkable that without it the people west of the Alleghenies would ever have submitted to a state of permanent dependence upon the original states.

Connecticut and Virginia followed New York, and the Confederation was established, Mar. 1, 1781. With the close of the Revolution the problems of reorganization became more insistent, and among them the disposition of the western country loomed foremost. Among various projects propounded, one by Thomas Jefferson, which Congress enacted (Apr. 23), became known as the Ordinance of 1784. It provided for an artificial division of the entire West into sixteen districts, each district eligible for statehood upon attaining a population of 20,000. Although subsequently repealed, the Ordinance of 1784 contributed to America's developing colonial policy its second basic idea: the establishment of temporary governments, under the fostering oversight of Congress, until a population sufficient for statehood should be attained (*see* Territorial Governments).

Next year (May 20, 1785) the ordinance "for ascertaining the mode of disposing of lands in the Western territory" was enacted. Since the dawn of civilization individual landholdings had been bounded and identified by such marks as trees, stakes, and stones, and in the absence of any scientific system of surveying and recording titles of ownership to them, confusion, with resultant disputes and individual hardships, existed. In its stead, the Ordinance of 1785 provided a scientific system of surveying and subdividing land with clear-cut establishment of both boundaries and titles. The unit of survey is the township, six miles square, with boundaries based on meridians of longitude and parallels of latitude. The townships are laid out both east and west and north and south of base lines crossing at right angles; within, the township is subdivided into thirty-six square-mile sections, and these, in turn, into minor rectangles of any desired size.

In March 1786 a group of New Englanders organized at Boston the Ohio Company of Associates. The leaders were able men of affairs who had very definite ideas concerning the colony they proposed to found. They opened negotiations with Congress, which made the desired grant of land, and on July 13, 1787, enacted the notable ordinance (which the petitioners had drafted) for the government of the territory northwest of the Ohio. It provided for a temporary government by agents appointed by Congress; but when the colony numbered 5,000 adult free males, a representative legislature was to be established, and upon the attainment of 60,000 population the territory would be admitted to statehood.

The ordinance also provided for the future division of the territory into not less than three nor more than five states; and it contained a series of compacts, forever unalterable save by common consent, safeguarding the rights of the future inhabitants of the territory. These established religious freedom, prohibited slavery, and guaranteed the fundamental rights of English liberty and just treatment of the Indians; a notable summary of the fundamental spirit of New England was supplied in the declaration that "Religion, morality, and knowledge being necessary to good government and the happiness of mankind, schools and the means of education shall forever be encouraged."

The Ordinance of 1784 contributed a fundamental idea to America's colonial system. Those of 1785 and 1787 still remain as landmarks in the orderly development of the American scheme of life.

[B. A. Hinsdale, *The Old Northwest;* W. E. Peters, *Ohio Lands and Their Subdivisions;* M. M. Quaife, *Wisconsin, Its History and Its People.*]

M. M. QUAIFE

ORDNANCE originally referred to military firearms: gun tubes, ammunition, and auxiliary equipment supporting the immediate firing process. Since about 1890, however, technical revolutions in weaponry have continually broadened the meaning of the term, and in America it now stands for all types of weapons and weapons systems.

Army Ordnance. In the United States the manufacture of ordnance has been traditionally a federal concern. In 1794, Congress authorized the establishment of arsenals for the development and manufacture of ordnance at Springfield, Mass., and at Harpers Ferry, Va., and in 1812 created a U.S. Army Ordnance Department to operate them. A major achievement during this early period was the introduction of interchangeable parts for mass-produced firearms by Eli Whitney.

In the 19th century five more arsenals were added to satisfy the army's demand for small arms, powder, shot, and cannon. Although Civil War needs sent arsenal and private ordnance production soaring, this hyperactivity ended abruptly in 1865. The navy had been given an Ordnance Bureau in 1842 but continued to rely heavily on army and civilian producers.

During the early 20th century the pace of ordnance development accelerated rapidly and was accompanied by a growing gap between the designer-manufacturer and the user. Until 1917, the Ordnance Department, under Maj. Gen. William B. Crozier, dominated the army's weapons acquisition process; after 1917 and between the two world wars the combat arms determined their own needs, and the department devoted itself to planning industrial mobilization. But the growing cost and sophistication of ordnance were making the centralization of procurement a necessity.

Another new factor was the increasing importance of private industry. World War I had shown the importance of private ordnance-producing resources, or at least the need to be able to mobilize those resources quickly, but the United States abandoned its policy of restricting peacetime ordnance production to federal arsenals with great reluctance. On June 16, 1938, the Educational Orders Act authorized the immediate placement of ordnance contracts with civilian firms in order to strengthen outside procurement procedures and ease a future transition to a wartime economy. In World War II, private arms production dwarfed governmental efforts, especially in weapons carriers and auxiliary equipment; at the same time, as ordnance continued to grow more complex, public and private defense production became more integrated.

From 1945 to 1973 worldwide commitments forced the United States to remain in a state of semimobilization and made dependence on arsenal production alone impractical. Ordnance was increasingly discussed in terms of weapons systems, which bore little resemblance to the firearms of 1860 or even 1917, and the army soon joined the naval and air arms in their dependence on private industry for a great proportion of their ordnance and ordnance-supporting equipment. In recognition of these trends President John F. Kennedy's defense reorganizations of 1961–63 placed the three service staffs on a functional basis, established three large matériel commands, and continued the centralization of the ordnance selection process. The manufacture of ordnance had become one of America's largest enterprises and demanded constant executive attention.

JEFFREY J. CLARKE

Naval Ordnance. Naval ordnance includes all the weapons and their control systems used by naval forces. These can be classed by type (guns, mines, torpedoes, depth charges, bombs, rockets, missiles); by warheads (conventional or nuclear); by launching platform (surface, airborne, underwater); or by targets (submarine, air, surface).

Until the mid-19th century, U.S. Navy ships were armed with carriage-mounted, muzzle-loading, smooth-bore cannons, principally of iron, firing solid shot at point-blank range. At the time of the Civil War, pivot mounts, turrets, rifled guns, and explosive projectiles were beginning to be used. By World War I, directors, rangekeepers (computers), and breech-loading steel guns were in use. By World War II, radar and automatic controls had been added. Battleship 16-inch guns were capable of firing 2,700-pound armor-piercing projectiles at ranges up to twenty miles; proximity fuses for use against aircraft were developed; and bombardment rockets were also added.

Moored mines, contact-activated or controlled from the shore, were used in the Civil War. Starting in World War II, additional sensors were developed (magnetic, pressure, and acoustic). Preceded by spar-mounted "torpedoes" of the Civil War, self-propelled torpedoes were introduced into the U.S. Navy in the latter part of the 19th century. Homing torpedoes first appeared in World War II. World War I aircraft were armed with machine guns and crude bombs. Gyroscopic bombsights and aircraft rockets were in use in World War II.

Introduced in combat against Japanese ships in 1945, the first homing missile was the Bat, an air-launched, antiship, radar-homing, glider bomb. Since then a variety of ship, air, and submarine guided missiles have been developed. The first of the navy's long-range ballistic missiles, introduced in 1960, was the submerged-launched, 1,200-mile Polaris, made possible by solid propellants, inertial guidance, small thermonuclear warheads, and sophisticated fire control and navigational systems. Its successor, Poseidon, has a 2,500-nautical-mile range and was later equipped with multiple warheads. A Trident missile system, with greater range and improved capabilities, was being developed in the mid-1970's.

EDWIN B. HOOPER

[C. M. Green, H. C. Thomson, and P. C. Roots, *The Ordnance Department: Planning Munitions for War;* Ordnance School, *ST 9-173: History of the Ordnance Corps;* Taylor Peck, *Round-Shot to Rockets;* Breford Roland and William Boyd, *U.S. Navy Bureau of Ordnance in World War II.*]

OREGON, an Indian name, possibly of Algonkin origin, was originally applied to the legendary great "River of the West" and then to the land drained by that river, the Columbia. It appears in print in Jonathan Carver's semifictional *Travels Through the Interior Parts of North America* (1788). The region to which "Oregon" referred, on the Northwest Coast, may have been reached by sea by the Spanish Bartolomé Ferrelo in 1543, by the English Sir Francis Drake in 1578, and by the Spanish Martin d'Aguilar in 1603, who reported the existence of a great river. Almost two centuries later, Russian expansion into Alaska inspired further Spanish exploration around Vancouver Island, beginning with Juan Pérez in 1774. On Mar. 7, 1778, Capt. James Cook, on his third expedition to the Pacific, sighted the Oregon coast off Yaquina Bay as he sailed north to Nootka Sound. His tremendous profits from sea-otter furs sold in Canton led many British and American traders to the coast. On May 11, 1792, Capt. Robert Gray of Boston discovered and entered the "River of the West," which he named the Columbia for his ship. On learning of the river, Capt. George Vancouver of the British navy, then on the coast, sent a party under Lt. William Broughton, who surveyed the stream for approximately 120 miles.

Overland exploration to the Northwest Coast was initiated by the Canadians; Alexander Mackenzie was first to reach the Pacific at the mouth of the Bella Coola in northern British Columbia in 1793. Inspired by his example, President Thomas Jefferson sent the first U.S. expedition (1804–06), led by Meriwether Lewis and William Clark, with instructions to find the "River Oregon," which they identified as the Columbia. It was to the Columbia that John Jacob Astor's partners went in 1811 to found Astoria, the first settlement in Oregon, and to develop the fur trade, the major economic activity of the next thirty years.

Astor and the men of his Pacific Fur Company, of the North West Company (which bought them out in 1813), and of the Hudson's Bay Company (which took over in 1821) referred to the new country as the Columbia, or the Columbia District. It was first referred to officially as Oregon when in 1822 John Floyd of Virginia introduced in Congress a bill to provide "that all that portion of the territory of the United States north of the forty-second degree of latitude, and west of the Rocky Mountains, shall constitute the Territory of Oregon."

Under a treaty of 1818 between Great Britain and the United States the Northwest was jointly occupied without formation of a government. In 1819 a treaty with Spain set the boundary at 42° north latitude, and

OREGON

in 1824 and 1825 the Russians relinquished their claims south of 54°40′. Thus, the maximum boundaries of Oregon were defined, including British Columbia, Washington, Oregon, Idaho, and parts of Montana and Wyoming. Over the years the joint occupation became a political and diplomatic issue in both Great Britain and the United States. Great Britain claimed all land north of the Columbia River, including what is now Washington, and American politicians felt that the United States should have all the coast. The militant slogan "Fifty-four Forty or Fight" was used by those advocating the ouster of Great Britain. The decline of furs to the south led the Hudson's Bay Company to move its headquarters to Vancouver Island, and President James K. Polk was able to negotiate the treaty of 1846, which established the continental boundary as the forty-ninth parallel from the Rockies to Puget Sound, and left Vancouver Island to the British. This cut off New Caledonia (British Columbia) from Oregon.

Man has lived in the Oregon region for about 10,000 years, and settlement must have come in waves from Asia. On the coast, from the Columbia north, the dominant tribe met by the whites were the Chinook, related to the more sophisticated native Americans of Puget Sound and Alaska. In the Willamette and other valleys linguistic groups west of the Cascades were isolated by mountains or headlands. With the coming of the fur traders the Chinook jargon was developed—incorporating elements of Chinook, Nootka, English, Spanish, and French—and used by the various tribes and the white men with whom they traded. According to the jargon, Oregon was the Indians' "Siwash Illahie."

About 1830 the first employees of the old Pacific Fur Company, or freemen, who had not contracted for service with the Hudson's Bay Company, settled as farmers in the Willamette Valley with their Indian families. They were soon joined by other Americans. In 1834 members of the Oregon Methodist Mission under Jason Lee settled in the region, followed in 1838 by the Roman Catholic mission under Father François Norbert Blanchet. The missions of Marcus Whitman and Henry Spaulding were located east of the mountains. These missions aroused American interest in the Oregon Country and resulted in the migration of independent settlers beginning in 1839. Each year saw larger numbers of Americans coming over the Oregon Trail to obtain donation land claims, primarily in the fertile Willamette Valley. It was these Americans who guaranteed their squatters rights

to their land by organizing a provisional territorial government at Champoeg with the adoption of the Organic Act on July 5, 1843, to meet civil and military needs until the U.S. territorial government in Oregon was established by Gov. Joseph Lane on Mar. 3, 1849. In 1853 Washington Territory was separated from Oregon; and when Oregon was granted statehood on Feb. 14, 1859, on the eve of the Civil War, its present eastern boundary was delineated.

Indians in northwestern Oregon were decimated by the white man's diseases, and the remnants were placed on reservations under a treaty of 1855. Gold rushes of the early 1850's produced the Rogue River War (1855–56), and similar rushes in eastern Oregon during the Civil War and afterward produced wars that resulted in the confinement of the rest of the Indians to reservations. By 1860 there were 54,465 settlers in Oregon, many of whom had come over the Oregon Trail; at least two-thirds were southern in origin. Agriculture, which they established, has changed but is still of major importance, including wheat, food-processing crops, and seeds as well as stock raising. In 1967 the 2 million mark in population was passed. Lumbering from the start was important. Tourism, metals fabrication, and wood products are Oregon's other major industries. In government, Oregon has contributed innovations, such as the Oregon System, establishing the initiative and referendum in 1902, the gas tax in 1919, and the bottle bill in 1973. Perhaps the nation knows the state best for its independent political thinkers and the beauty of its land—the coast, Mount Hood, Crater Lake, and the Wallowa Mountains.

[Dorothy O. Johansen and Charles M. Gates, *Empire of the Columbia: A History of the Pacific Northwest.*]

DAVID DUNIWAY

OREGON, a U.S. battleship, was built in San Francisco, 1891–96. At the outbreak of the Spanish-American War, the *Oregon*, under Capt. Charles E. Clark, made a famous, 14,700-mile run, Mar. 19 to May 26, 1898, from the Golden Gate through the Strait of Magellan to Key West, Fla. Joining Adm. William T. Sampson's blockading squadron off Santiago de Cuba, the *Oregon*, because it was almost opposite the harbor entrance, was able to engage effectively all the Spanish cruisers on July 3. The *Oregon*'s trip gave dramatic evidence of the need for quicker communication by water between the Pacific and Atlantic coasts, and it was thus an important factor leading to the construction of the Panama Canal.

165

Later attempts at preserving the *Oregon* as a historic ship failed, and it was used as a barge in World War II.

[F. S. Hill, *Twenty-Six Historic Ships.*]
WALTER B. NORRIS

OREGON CARAVANS. From 1842 until the era of transcontinental railways, beginning in 1869 with the completion of the Union Pacific, each year saw emigrants following the Oregon Trail to the Pacific coast. Travel was by covered wagons, usually drawn by oxen, although mules and horses were also widely used. Because of the danger from Indian attack and the keenly felt need of mutual assistance, caravans were commonly organized at the Missouri frontier. Often notices that indicated a time and place of assembly were sent out by men interested in securing the protection of a group. Officers were elected, rules of conduct adopted, and a guide agreed upon. If forceful leaders were found a considerable degree of discipline and effective order was maintained. The parties that made the toilsome and dangerous trek with greatest safety were those who created and maintained the most effective organization.

[Charles H. Carey, *A General History of Oregon Prior to 1861.*]
ROBERT MOULTON GATKE

OREGON LAND FRAUDS were brought to light during the administration of President Theodore Roosevelt. They were effected under the Homestead Act (1862), under the Timber and Stone Act (1878), and under exchange of state school lands for government timberlands. The device of securing state school lands of little or no value at a cost of $1.25 an acre and exchanging them for valuable timberlands was in operation as early as 1890. The system of dummy entries on homestead and timberlands under which large lumber companies, often controlled by capitalists from Wisconsin, Michigan, or Minnesota, acquired immense tracts of valuable timberland was extensively used in the period from 1890 to 1904. The great increase in entries in Oregon under the Timber and Stone Act (from 646 in 1901 to 4,209 in 1903, and 3,260 in 1904) seems to indicate the height of the period of fraud.

These frauds were made possible by the connivance and assistance of state and federal government officials. They were exposed through the investigations of Francis J. Heney and William J. Burns. Heney secured thirty-three convictions out of thirty-four prosecutions. One of those convicted was John M. Mitchell of Oregon.

[Stephen Arnold Douglas Puter, *Looters of the Public Domain.*]
R. C. CLARK

OREGON MEMORIAL OF 1838. During the period of joint occupation of Oregon by both the United States and Great Britain, there was great uncertainty among the settlers concerning land titles. When Jason Lee, the head of the Methodist mission established in Oregon in 1834 went East in 1838 he carried a petition addressed to Congress. It was dated Mar. 16, 1838, and signed by thirty-six residents of Oregon, including a few French Canadian settlers. This number included a large percentage of all the settlers in the Willamette Valley. The petition asked that the United States take possession of Oregon, which they believed to be "the germ of a great state." The memorial was presented to the Senate by Sen. Lewis F. Linn of Missouri, chairman of the committee on territories, on Jan. 28, 1839. Lee also had correspondence with Rep. Caleb Cushing of Massachusetts, and both Linn and Cushing were stimulated by the memorial and by Lee's correspondence to interest Congress in extending control over Oregon. This congressional agitation over Oregon in turn greatly stimulated the popular interest in and ultimate settling of Oregon. In connection with the memorial, Lee urged that protection be extended to the infant colony and that the pioneers be given security in the title to their lands (*see* Oregon Treaty of 1846).

[Charles H. Carey, *A General History of Oregon Prior to 1861.*]
ROBERT MOULTON GATKE

OREGON MISSIONS. Attention was called to the need for Christian work among the Indians of the Pacific Northwest by an appeal made to Gen. William Clark of Saint Louis in 1831 by four Flathead Indians, who had journeyed from the Oregon Country asking that they be given religious instructors. A description of this visit was first published in the *Christian Advocate and Journal* of New York in 1833 and was widely copied in other religious journals. The Methodists immediately recommended the establishment of an Oregon mission, and Jason Lee, a young New Englander, was appointed to head it. By September 1834, he and his party had reached Fort Vancouver, on the Columbia River. A mission among the Flathead being found to be impracticable, Lee established a mission in the Willamette Valley. A year later the American Board of Commissioners for Foreign Missions resolved to found a mission in the Pacific Northwest and commissioned Marcus Whitman and Henry H. Spalding to carry out the enterprise. Work was begun near what is now Walla Walla, Wash., and soon a prosperous mission was in operation. Both Lee and Whitman became interested in bringing colonists to Oregon, a policy that their mission boards did not approve. Largely because of this fact Lee was removed. Whitman and his wife with twelve other persons were murdered by the Indians in 1847.

Roman Catholic missionaries were also active in the same region, where their work was favored by the Hudson's Bay Company as being less likely to interfere with the fur trade. Under the intrepid Jesuit, Father Pierre Jean De Smet (1840–46), Catholic missions were established in the region and within a few years 6,000 converts were claimed.

[C. J. Brosnan, *Jason Lee, Prophet of the New Oregon;* Clifford M. Drury, *Marcus Whitman, Pioneer and Martyr;* E. Lavelle, *The Life of Father DeSmet, S.J., 1801–1873.*]

WILLIAM W. SWEET

OREGON PAROCHIAL SCHOOL CASE, *Pierce* v. *Society of the Sisters of the Holy Names of Jesus and Mary,* 268 U.S. 510 (1925), a case in which the Supreme Court by unanimous opinion invalidated an Oregon statute adopted in 1922 by initiative and referendum (*see* Oregon System), under which all children would have been required to attend the public schools. Ostensibly an education law and as such within the reserved powers of the state, it was well known from discussion in the course of the referendum that it was aimed at the parochial schools. It was not a compulsory education law or a reasonable regulation of school standards. The Supreme Court ruled, in effect, that children are not public wards, that parents have a right to control the selection of schools for their children, and that the owners and teachers of those private schools have a right to conduct their activities. The statute was an obvious abridgment of liberty under the due process clause of the Fourteenth Amendment. This decision, generally regarded as a wise and wholesome exposition of American ideals, is frequently cited in refutation of the common misconception that the Fourteenth Amendment is useful only as a protection of "property rights."

W. A. ROBINSON

OREGON QUESTION was the question of national ownership of the Pacific Northwest. By successive treaties the territory was defined until it meant the territory west of the Rocky Mountains, north of 42° and south of 54°40'. All or major portions of this vast territory were the subject of the conflicting claims of ownership of Spain, Great Britain, the United States, and Russia.

Spain's exclusive claims, based on the discoveries of Spanish explorers along the coast of the Pacific Northwest, and on special claims of dominance in the Pacific Ocean, were successfully challenged by Great Britain in the Nootka Convention (1790); and in the Adams-Onís Treaty (1819) Spain surrendered to the United States all claims north of the forty-second parallel. Russia, whose claims were the weakest of any of the four powers, withdrew all claims south of 54°40' by separate treaties with the United States (1824) and Great Britain (1825). With the boundary between the United States and British America having been drawn as far west as the Rockies by the Convention of 1818, the boundaries of Oregon were determined, and the territory was left by the same treaty in joint occupation of the two claimants, the United States and Great Britain.

Until the final division of the territory between the two powers in June 1846 by the extension of the forty-ninth parallel to the sea, deflecting southward to leave Vancouver Island (*see* Haro Channel Dispute) to the British, the Oregon question was the subject of intermittent correspondence between the two governments. British claims were repeatedly summarized as depending on the discoveries of Sir Francis Drake, Capt. James Cook, and Capt. George Vancouver; the Nootka Convention with Spain; and the exploration and occupation of the British fur companies. The American claims were based on the discovery of the Columbia River by Capt. Robert Gray (1792); explorations by Meriwether Lewis and William Clark (1804–06); the establishment of the Astoria fur-trading post (1811) by the Pacific Fur Company, and its restoration under the Convention of 1818; the Spanish claims; and American settlements that started with the Oregon missions (1834) and had constantly increased after 1842.

American public interest became centered on Oregon by successive unsuccessful efforts to make land claims available for American settlers. Under the leadership of Rep. John Floyd of Virginia such an effort was first made in 1821. Later congressional leadership concerning Oregon passed to Sen. Lewis F. Linn of Missouri. The first missionary settlements aroused widespread interest, and each successive group of settlers that poured into Oregon after 1842 built up the interest. By 1844 the popular feeling over Oregon found expression in the political slogan "Fifty-four Forty or Fight," widely used in the campaign in which James K. Polk was elected president. Action followed quickly upon Polk's taking office. On Apr. 27, 1846, Congress authorized the president to give Great Britain notice of the termination of the joint occupation treaty. The British government was distinctly a peace government, and the American government clearly overstated its claims, so by June 15, 1846, a compromise treaty settled the Oregon question by continuing the boundary east of the Rockies (forty-ninth parallel) to the sea (see Oregon Treaty).

[Charles H. Carey, *A General History of Oregon Prior to 1861.*]

ROBERT MOULTON GATKE

OREGON SHORT LINE RAILWAY, a subsidiary corporation of the Union Pacific Railway incorporated by Congress in 1881 and completed early in 1882 to run 550 miles from Granger, Wyo., on the main line of the Union Pacific to Huntington, Oreg., where it connected with the line of the Oregon Railroad and Navigation Company built to Portland, Oreg., in 1884. It was built to develop the Pacific Northwest and to secure its traffic for the Union Pacific. In 1897 this road was sold under foreclosure and organized independently, but was reacquired by the Union Pacific in 1899, with which it was completely merged.

[Robert G. Athearn, *Union Pacific Country.*]

R. C. CLARK

OREGON SYSTEM. In 1902 Oregon adopted a constitutional amendment establishing a system of direct voter participation in lawmaking. The initiative permits a specified percentage of voters to place a law or constitutional amendment before the voters for their final action without reference to the legislature. By the referendum a law passed by the legislature can be referred to the people for final acceptance or rejection. Closely associated with these two features were other features commonly known as parts of the Oregon system, including the recall, direct primary, presidential preference primary, and state printed campaign textbooks.

[James D. Barnett, *The Operation of the Initiative, Referendum, and Recall in Oregon.*]

ROBERT MOULTON GATKE

OREGON TRAIL was first dimly traced across the country from the Missouri River to the Columbia River by explorers and fur traders. After 1842 it was worn into a deeply rutted highway by the pioneers in their covered wagons. In 1805 the course of Meriwether Lewis and William Clark in the region of the Snake and Columbia rivers covered a portion of what was later to be the famous pioneer highway. A few years later (1808) a party of the Missouri Fur Company traveled through the South Pass in Wyoming, and thus discovered an important part of the trail. A party of fur traders from Astoria, under Robert Stuart, returned to the East in 1812 largely following the route that later became the Oregon Trail. Two independent American fur traders, Capt. Benjamin L. E. de Bonneville and Capt. Nathaniel J. Wyeth, between the years 1832 and 1836, led their companies over this route. Knowledge of the trail as a passable route was current among the traders on the frontier and became common property. For the companies of settlers this knowledge was available in two forms: traders who had been over the route and were willing to hire out as guides; and printed guidebooks compiled by enterprising travelers. These guidebooks appeared surprisingly early and the copies that reached the end of the trail were thumbed and worn.

The distances on the trail were calculated with a high degree of accuracy. One of the old guidebooks (J. M. Shively, *Route and Distances to Oregon and California* [1846]) gives a tabulation of the distances of the established trail. The points used to mark the way were selected for a variety of reasons—conspicuous landmarks, difficult streams to ford, and infrequent posts at which a few supplies might be obtained. This guidebook marks the way from the Missouri River to the mouth of the Columbia River as follows:

	Miles
From Independence to the Crossings of Kansas	102
Crossings of Blue	83
Platte River	119
Crossings of South Platte	163
To North Fork	20
To Fort Larima [Laramie]	153
From Larima to Crossing of North Fork of the Platte	140
To Independence Rock on Sweet Water	50
Fort Bridger	229
Bear River	68
Soda Springs	94
To Fort Hall	57
Salmon Falls	160
Crossings of Snake River	22

	Miles
To Crossings of Boise River	69
Fort Boise	45
Dr. Whitman's Mission	190
Fort Walawala [Walla Walla]	25
Dallis Mission [The Dalles]	120
Cascade Falls, on the Columbia	50
Fort Vancouver	41
Astoria	90

The author could well have left off the last ninety miles and given the distance into the Willamette Valley, which was the destination of most of the travelers.

The interest in Oregon became so widespread along the frontier about 1842 that emigrating societies were formed to encourage people to move to Oregon. By lectures, letters, and personal visits, members of these societies secured recruits for the long journey. Independence, Mo., was the most frequent place of departure, and shortly after leaving there the companies commonly organized a government by electing officers and adopting rules of conduct (see Oregon Caravans). The emigrants gathered in time to leave in the early spring, so as to take advantage of the fresh pasturage for their animals and to allow all possible time for the long journey.

From Independence the companies followed the old Santa Fe Trail, a two days' journey of some forty miles to where a crude signpost pointed to the "Road to Oregon." At Fort Laramie, where the trail left the rolling plains for the mountainous country, there was an opportunity to overhaul and repair wagons. The next point where repairs could be made with outside help was Fort Bridger, some 394 miles beyond Laramie and about 1,070 miles from Independence. The trail used South Pass through the Rockies. It is a low pass less than 7,500 feet above sea level and was easily passable for the heavy covered wagons. The difficulties of travel greatly increased on the Pacific side. Much barren country had to be crossed under conditions that wore out and killed the already exhausted horses and oxen. At Fort Hall, in the Snake River country, the first emigrants gave up their wagons and repacked on horses; but after a short while determined individuals refused to do this and worked a way through for their wagons. The Grande Ronde Valley, in northeast Oregon, offered grass to recruit the worn beasts of burden before the travelers attempted the almost impassable way through the Blue Mountains. Emerging from these mountains the emigrants followed the Umatilla River to the Columbia River, which they followed to Fort Vancouver, the

last portion often being made on rafts. The journey of some 2,000 miles over the Oregon Trail was the greatest trek of recorded history.

The wagon traffic on the Oregon Trail during the 1840's and 1850's became so heavy that the road was a clearly defined and deeply rutted way across the country. When the ruts became too deep for travel, parallel roads were broken. So deeply worn was the Oregon Trail that generations after the last covered wagon had passed over it hundreds of miles of the trail could still be traced. To the awed Indians it seemed the symbol of a nation of countless numbers.

The 2,000 miles of the Oregon Trail tested human strength and endurance as it has rarely been tested. The trail was littered with castoff possessions, often of considerable monetary as well as great sentimental value. Worn draft animals that could no longer drag the heavy wagons and even the most prized possessions had to be left standing beside the trail. Carcasses of the innumerable dead cattle and horses were left along the trail while the bodies of the human dead were buried in shallow graves. The diaries of the overland journey note with fearful monotony the number of new graves passed each day. Cholera was then the terrible scourge of these pioneers.

From 1842 through the 1850's the companies came over the trail in large numbers, to dwindle away in the 1860's. The bitter experiences of the first companies, who knew so little about equipment, were passed on to the later companies, and as the years went by the travelers were able to use better-adapted equipment. Specially constructed wagons became available; oxen largely replaced horses; and supplies were selected more wisely. The route became easier to follow and even included crude ferries at some of the most difficult river crossings. Nevertheless, up to the day that the last covered wagon was dragged over the rutted highway, the Oregon Trail was the way of hardship and danger that tested the pioneer stock of the West.

[David Lavendar, *Westward Vision: The Story of the Oregon Trail*.]

ROBERT MOULTON GATKE

OREGON TREATY OF 1846 fixed the boundary between the United States and British America at the forty-ninth parallel west of the Rocky Mountains except at the western terminus of that line, where it was to swerve southward around Vancouver Island and out through Juan de Fuca Strait, north of what is today Clallam County, Wash. By the Convention of 1818, renewed in 1827, the United States and Great Britain had agreed that the country claimed by either west of the Rockies be free and open to the citizens of the two powers (*see* Joint Occupation). Acting under a joint resolution of Congress (Apr. 27, 1846), President James K. Polk transmitted the year's notice for the termination of that treaty, expressing the hope that this would hasten a friendly settlement (*see* Oregon Question). George Hamilton Gordon, Lord Aberdeen, the British foreign minister, then drafted a treaty (May 18, 1846), which was accepted by President Polk and the Senate (June 15, 1846). The election of Polk as president in 1844 on a platform that demanded the whole Oregon Country, its rapid settlement by Americans, the purpose of the Hudson's Bay Company to move its main establishment from Fort Vancouver on the Columbia River to Victoria on Vancouver Island, and the adoption by Great Britain and the United States of mutual beneficial tariff policies in 1846—repeal of the British Corn Laws (June 26) and passing of the Walker tariff (July 30)—were factors in influencing a settlement of this boundary dispute at this time.

[S. F. Bemis, *A Diplomatic History of the United States;* R. C. Clark, *A History of the Willamette Valley, Oregon.*]

R. C. CLARK

ORGANIC LAW, as used in the United States, has two meanings. In one sense, it refers to any fundamental set of rules and principles establishing the organs of government, distributing the powers of government among them, and defining the reciprocal rights and duties of the government and the people. In other words, it is synonymous with the term "constitution" in its broadest significance. A second and more restricted use of the term is in its application to the acts of Congress providing a form of government for the territories. These organic acts serve as a fundamental law for a territory until its government as a state is provided for in a constitution framed for that purpose and adopted by the people of the territory, pursuant to an enabling act passed by Congress.

[C. Kettleborough, ed., *The State Constitutions.*]

HARVEY WALKER

ORGANIZATION FOR ECONOMIC COOPERATION AND DEVELOPMENT (OECD), headquartered in Paris, is an organization in which membership was ratified by the United States on Mar. 16, 1961. It began its existence on Sept. 30, 1961, when it replaced the Organization for European Economic Cooperation (OEEC), originally organized in 1948 to administer the Marshall Plan and the cooperative ef-

forts for European recovery from the economic disaster of World War II. The United States was not a member of OEEC. Its membership in OECD constitutes the first step taken by the United States in economic internationalism.

Originally a twenty-nation association (Austria, Belgium, Denmark, France, the Federal Republic of Germany, Greece, Iceland, Ireland, Italy, Luxembourg, the Netherlands, Norway, Portugal, Spain, Sweden, Switzerland, Turkey, the United Kingdom, the United States, and Canada), OECD had been expanded by the addition of three new members by 1971 (Japan, in 1964; Finland, 1968; and Australia, 1971). New Zealand and Yugoslavia have special status, not full membership, in OECD.

The purpose of OECD is to achieve economic growth in member countries, to contribute to sound economic expansion, and to increase the expansion of world trade. Broadly speaking, the objective is to foster the free international flow of payments, services, and capital globally, combined with the utilization of human resources and scientific developments, on international levels. Likewise, OECD is concerned with developments in the fields of industry and agriculture, the use of nuclear energy for peaceful purposes, and environmental problems. In pursuance of these objectives OECD serves as a clearinghouse of information.

[Organization for Economic Cooperation and Development, *History, Aims, Structure.*]

THOMAS ROBSON HAY

ORGANIZATION OF AFRO-AMERICAN UNITY was founded by Malcolm X on Mar. 8, 1964, following his break with the Black Muslims, and was dominated by him until his assassination on Feb. 21, 1965. He and his organization rejected the racist teachings of the Black Muslims but remained devoted to the cause of black liberation. During the final year of his life, the creative marriage of black nationalism and Marxism by Malcolm X laid the ideological foundation for the black revolutionary movement of the late 1960's.

Malcolm X was born Malcolm Little on May 19, 1925, in Omaha, Nebr., the son of a West Indian mother and a black nationalist preacher. After his father's death Malcolm was forced to live in state institutions until, as a young man, he went to live with his sister in Boston. There and in New York, Malcolm worked at the unskilled jobs available to poor blacks and eventually gained the underworld skills of a hustler. In 1946 he was arrested in Boston for burglary;

while in prison he became converted to the Black Muslim religion. Shortly after his release in 1952, he was accepted into the movement and rose rapidly to a position of leadership. His background, intelligence, and oratory aided him in building the Black Muslims into a national movement. He dominated the Black Muslims from 1954, when he became head of the Black Muslims in Harlem, until his break with Elijah Muhammad in December 1963.

[*The Autobiography of Malcolm X;* John Henrik Clarke, ed., *Malcolm X: The Man and His Times;* Peter Goldman, *The Death and Life of Malcolm X.*]

RICHARD P. YOUNG

ORGANIZATION OF AMERICAN STATES

(OAS) had its genesis in the Ninth International Conference of American States, assembled in Bogotá, Colombia, in March 1948. At that meeting a charter was adopted formalizing the inter-American system, its key structural features being (1) a council of the OAS to manage the organization's business, (2) subsidiary councils (cultural, economic and social, and juridical), and (3) the Pan-American Union, to function as the general secretariat. General inter-American conferences were to be held every five years, and provision was made for the convocation of consultative meetings of foreign ministers to deal with threats to the Western Hemisphere.

Regular inter-American conferences under the OAS aegis began in 1954 in Caracas, Venezuela, and special conferences have been held at Punta del Este, Uruguay (1961); Washington, D.C. (1964); Rio de Janeiro (1965); and Buenos Aires (1967). Matters dealt with have included internal organizational rearrangements, hemispheric security, and the formation of the Alliance for Progress. Consultative meetings occurred in Washington (1951, 1964, 1965, 1967), Santiago, Chile (1959), San José, Costa Rica (1960), Punta del Este (1962), and Buenos Aires (1967). The principal issues were the stance of the Americas in the Korean conflict, the aggression of the Dominican Republic against Venezuela, the threat of communism and the Cuban revolution, and U.S. intervention in the Dominican Republic.

Given the distribution of economic and military power in the Western Hemisphere, U.S. participation in the OAS has been crucial in most respects. It was on U.S. initiative that the organization came into being, and its operational costs are defrayed mostly by the United States. Thus, it is not surprising that the choice of issues considered and the nature of the resolutions passed by that body have tended to reflect U.S. interests and positions, although not as categorically as political realities might lead one to expect.

[Mary Margaret Ball, *The OAS in Transition.*]

FRANCISCO S. PÉREZ-ABREU

ORGANIZED LABOR. *See* **Labor.**

ORIENTAL RELIGIONS AND SECTS have come to the United States from a variety of sources. Buddhism, the most prominent non-Western faith, is practiced by about 10 percent of Japanese-Americans. The primary form of Buddhism in the United States is the Jōdo-Shinshu sect, the most popular in Japan, which was introduced by two priests in San Francisco in 1898. It has a U.S. membership of approximately 100,000, served by eighty religious leaders, and is centered on the West Coast. Since World War II, Zen Buddhism has grown in popularity among non-Asian Americans. Traced back to the teachings of Bodhidharma in the first quarter of the 6th century, Zen has tended to become secularized in the 20th century. Its emphasis is on the inner discipline of the soul: the teacher poses a seemingly cryptic saying, or *kōan*, which the initiate must understand in order to move toward enlightenment, or *satori*. Such enlightenment produces a new way of viewing the reality of the world. While the growth of the counterculture contributed to the popularity of Zen in the United States in the mid-20th century, its basic appeal to Americans lies in its undogmatic and nonmetaphysical character.

Hinduism was introduced into the United States by the Swami Vivekananda, who appeared at the World's Parliament of Religions in Chicago in 1893. He founded the Vedanta Society in 1897, dedicated to the idea of a world religion rooted in Indian concepts. The Self-Realization Fellowship, founded by Paramhansa Yogananda in 1920, has tended to teach a practical form of Hinduism that stresses peace, health, and greater personal powers. It claims to have 200,000 members. In the late 1960's, interest in Hinduism was revived through the teachings of Maharishi Mahesh Yogi, a member of the order of Shankara and the leader of the International Meditation Society. Touring the United States and establishing meditation centers, he has influenced many, especially in the youth culture.

Baha'i, or Bahaism, arose in the 19th century from the teachings of 'Ali Muhammad, a member of the Shi'ite sect of Islam, who claimed to be a messenger from God, or B'ab. He declared that the laws of

Mohammed were abrogated and envisioned a world-wide religion. He was succeeded by Mirza Husayn 'Ali, who was succeeded by 'Abdu'l-Baha, the world-wide popularizer of the movement in the 1890's. He introduced the new faith at the World's Parliament of Religions in 1893 and broke ground for a temple in Wilmette, Ill., in 1912. Bahaism is a syncretistic faith that stresses the inspiration of the founders of all religions and looks toward a worldwide reign of peace, love, and holiness. Doctrinally, its teachings are a philosophical version of the major themes of Judaism, Christianity, and Islam.

American theosophical sects often draw their inspiration from the traditional Eastern religions. Helena Petrovna Blavatski has been one of the leading spokesmen for the movement through her writings, for example, *Isis Unveiled* (1877), *The Secret Doctrine* (1888), and *The Key to Theosophy* (1889). Although theosophy is more a stream of thought, there are some organized theosophical groups, among them the Theosophical Society, the Liberal Catholic Church, the I Am movement, and Rosicrucian societies. All stress the possibility of mystical experience.

[Charles Braden, *These Also Believe: A Study of Modern American Cults and Minority Religious Movements;* John Ferraby, *All Things Made New: A Comprehensive Outline of the Baha'i Faith;* Thomas Merton, *Mystics and Zen Masters;* Bishop Kenyru T. Tsuji, *The Buddhist Churches of America.*]

GLENN T. MILLER

ORIGINAL PACKAGE DOCTRINE for determining the point at which goods pass from federal control over interstate commerce to state control over local or intrastate commerce was first enunciated by the Supreme Court in *Brown* v. *Maryland* (1827). It was a tax case under a Maryland act of 1821 requiring importers and dealers in foreign goods within the state to take out a $50 license. The state's power to impose such a fee was questioned, and the Court held, in respect to such goods, that "while remaining the property of the importer, in his warehouse, in the original form or package in which it was imported, a tax upon it is too plainly a duty on imports to escape the prohibition of the Constitution."

The later and better-known case of *Leisy* v. *Hardin* (135 U.S. 100 [1890]), in which the Supreme Court ruled that Iowa state laws could not be applied to interstate freight shipments as long as they remained in the original package, unsold, resulted in the immediate passage by Congress of the Wilson Original Package Act to protect the internal police powers of the

states. Such shipments were still in interstate commerce and were, therefore, under federal—not state—jurisdiction. Thus goods in interstate shipment have not "arrived" for purposes of regulation by the state until they have been delivered into the hands of the consignee, and the original package has been broken. Goods have not arrived for purposes of taxation by the state until they have come permanently at rest within the borders of the state, and until they have become mingled with the wealth of the state, whether or not the original package has been broken. In most cases, the change for both purposes occurs simultaneously.

[Charles K. Burdick, *The Law of the American Constitution;* W. W. Willoughby, *Constitutional Law of the United States;* James T. Young, *The New American Government and Its Work.*]

W. BROOKE GRAVES

ORISKANY, BATTLE OF (Aug. 6, 1777). The British threefold plan of campaign for 1777 included in its strategy the advance of Lt. Col. Barry St. Leger across New York from Fort Oswego on the west bank of the Oswego River, to meet generals John Burgoyne and William Howe in Albany. On Aug. 3, St. Leger with an army of approximately 1,200, mostly Tories under Col. John Butler and Sir John Johnson and Indians led by Joseph Brant, a Mohawk chief, appeared before Fort Stanwix on the Mohawk River, east of Oneida Lake, and demanded its surrender. In the meantime Gen. Nicholas Herkimer had called out the Tryon County militia. On Aug. 4, with an army of about 800 men, he left Fort Dayton. The following evening he sent three messengers to advise Col. Peter Gansevoort, the commanding officer at Fort Stanwix, that he planned to fall upon St. Leger's rear when Gansevoort attacked in front. Three guns were to be fired as a signal. The next morning the Americans advanced to a point about eight miles from the fort. There, Herkimer wished to stop until he received the signal. His caution seemed excessive to his officers. A violent quarrel followed, and against his better judgment Herkimer gave the order to advance.

Brant's Indians had reported Herkimer's approach to St. Leger and a detachment of Tories and Indians under Sir John Johnson had been sent to ambush the advancing Americans. About two miles west of Oriskany Creek the main body of the Americans entered a ravine, followed by the heavy baggage wagons. A deadly volley from both sides met them. The rearguard, still on the hill above, retreated. The main body was thrown into confusion but rallied, and one of the bloodiest battles of the Revolution took place. A sudden thundershower added to the tumult. Early in the conflict a ball killed Herkimer's horse and shattered his own leg. He had his saddle placed at the foot of a beech tree and lighting his pipe calmly continued to give orders. Suddenly the signal guns were heard. The expected sortie was taking place. The Indians fled and the Tories retreated from the Oriskany battlefield, but the weakened American forces were unable to proceed to the relief of the fort. Gansevoort and his men captured much-needed supplies and ammunition during the sortie, and St. Leger, unable to force the surrender of the fort, on Aug. 22 retreated to Oswego (*see* British Campaign of 1777).

[J. A. Scott, *Fort Stanwix and Oriskany.*]
A. C. FLICK

ORLEANS, FORT, was built in 1723 on an island in the Missouri River, at the mouth of Grand River, by Étienne Venyard, Sieur de Bourgmont, under instructions from the Company of the Indies to hold the line of the river against Spanish incursions from the southwest. It was also the French intention, by constructing another fort on the Kansas River and placating the Indians, to open a trade route to Sante Fe. Orleans was the first fort built on the Missouri.

[J. Winsor, *The Mississippi Basin.*]
CARL L. CANNON

ORLEANS, TERRITORY OF, now the state of Louisiana, was so called only during the period of American territorial government. The region it included was probably first visited by the survivors of Hernando de Soto's expedition in 1543, and as part of Louisiana was claimed by Robert Cavelier, Sieur de La Salle, for France in 1682. Under the French the province was successively governed under charter to Antoine Crozat (1712–17), by the Scottish financier John Law's Western Company and the India Company (1717–31), and finally as a crown colony. Jean Baptiste Le Moyne, Sieur de Bienville, governor of Louisiana, founded New Orleans in 1718 and made it the capital in 1722. Louisiana was ceded to Spain in 1762 (*see* Fontainebleau, Treaty of), returned to France in 1800 (*see* San Ildefonso, Treaty of), and sold to the United States in 1803 (*see* Louisiana Purchase). The actual transfer occurred Dec. 20, 1803. The Territory of Orleans, as organized by the act approved Mar. 26, 1804, included the present state of Louisiana except for the part east of the Mississippi River and north of Lake Pontchartrain. A

governor, secretary, three judges, and a council of thirteen members, all appointed by President Thomas Jefferson, constituted the government as first organized, but a popularly elected legislature was provided by the act approved Mar. 2, 1805. William C. C. Claiborne was governor throughout the territorial period. Orleans, under the present name of Louisiana, was admitted as a state Apr. 30, 1812.

[Charles Gayarré, *History of Louisiana;* Dunbar Rowland, ed., *Claiborne Letter Books.*]
EDGAR B. NIXON

ORTHODOX CHURCHES. *See* **Eastern Orthodoxy.**

OSAGE, one of the southern Siouan tribes of the western division, were found in historical times in Missouri in two principal bands, the Great Osage and the Little Osage. In 1802 nearly half of the Great Osage under a chief named Big Track migrated to the Arkansas River, leaving the remainder of the tribe on the Osage River in Missouri.

By a treaty negotiated in 1808 at Fort Clark the Osage ceded to the United States all their lands in Missouri and Arkansas, and subsequently they were found in the present Oklahoma. Entering into later treaties, they gave up more land and agreed to remove to what is now Kansas. By an act of Congress in 1870 their reservation was established comprising the present Osage County, Okla. Their population was estimated at more than 5,000 in 1845; but by 1855, after hundreds died from smallpox, they were reduced to 3,500. The Osage are among those tribes that have enjoyed large incomes from the production of oil from their tribal holdings (*see* Indian Oil Lands).

[John Joseph Mathews, *The Osages, Children of the Middle Waters.*]
GRANT FOREMAN

OSAGE, FORT, was established under direction of Gen. William Clark in September 1808 on the south bank of the Missouri River, nineteen miles east of present-day Kansas City, Kans., and manned by a company of infantry for protection of a government post for trade with the Osage tribes. To shorten lines of the Missouri defense in the War of 1812, it was evacuated in June 1813 but reoccupied in 1816. It maintained its importance as the most western outpost of the U.S. government until the abandonment of government trade with the Indians in 1822 and the establishment of Fort Leavenworth in 1827.

[Kate L. Gregg, *Westward With Dragoons*.]

KATE L. GREGG

OSAGE HEDGE, or *Maclura*, universally used on the prairies for fences, is a thorn-bearing tree that grows up to forty feet in height and that produces a pale-green fruit larger than an orange, from which the tree gets its name—Osage orange. The French observed the Osage Indians using the tough, springy yellow wood for bows and named the tree *bois d'arc* or bow wood. The first nurseries on the treeless prairies raised millions of these Osage orange, or, as they were commonly called, "hedge" plants, and sold them to the settlers for fences. The wood, although knotty and crooked, was used for tool handles, tongues for implements, and fence posts that lasted for years. Hedge also furnished excellent wood for fuel. The thorn on the Osage orange gave an inventor the idea for perfecting barbed wire, which largely replaced hedge as a fencing agent. In the 20th century hedge has fallen into disfavor because it saps crops and obscures the roadway. Miles of this once-prized fence have been grubbed out at great expense.

[Everett Dick, *The Sod House Frontier;* Walter P. Webb, *The Great Plains*.]

EVERETT DICK

OSAWATOMIE, BATTLE OF (Aug. 30, 1856). The town of Osawatomie was attacked by about 250 proslavery men (supposedly Missourians) and was defended by John Brown with 40 men. The Free State men were soon dislodged from their position along the creek bank and fled, after which the town was sacked. Each side lost about six killed and several wounded.

[L. W. Spring, *Kansas, The Prelude to the War for the Union*.]

SAMUEL A. JOHNSON

OSBORN V. BANK OF THE UNITED STATES, 9 Wheaton 738 (1824), a Supreme Court decision upholding a circuit court ruling against the taxing by a state of branches of the second Bank of the United States. The jealousies of local banks and the restrictions on credits by the second bank in the crisis of 1818 led to the enactment by the Ohio legislature, February 1819, of a tax of $50,000 on each branch of the second bank in the state. The auditor was given unlimited right of search, even to entering the vaults

of the bank to collect the tax. Ralph Osborn, state auditor, sent an agent, John L. Harper, to the Chillicothe branch, and on Sept. 17, 1819, he took $100,000 from its vaults, the taxes due from the two branches. After considerable delay the U.S. circuit court ruled against Osborn, who appealed to the Supreme Court. Chief Justice John Marshall's opinion, following the precedent of *McCulloch* v. *Maryland* (1819), sustained the circuit court and held the Ohio law taxing the branches of the Bank of the United States unconstitutional. Even though the Ohio legislature had in 1820 passed a set of pronounced states' rights resolutions and had followed them with a law withdrawing the protection of state laws from the Bank of the United States, no attempt was made to nullify the Supreme Court decision.

[E. H. Roseboom and F. P. Weisenburger, *A History of Ohio*.]

EUGENE H. ROSEBOOM

OSGOODITES, a New Hampshire religious sect, followers of Jacob Osgood (1777–1844), who left the Freewill Baptists to form a new church in 1812, claiming special powers of prophecy and healing from God. The sect's religious services were noted for singing, exhortations, and very frank comments on whatever or whomever displeased them. They were otherwise good neighbors, honest, abstemious, and law-abiding, although they would not vote, hold office, or serve in the militia, then compulsory. After Osgood's death their number declined, and all were gone by 1890.

[J. O. Lyford, *History of the Town of Canterbury*.]

HERBERT W. HILL

OSTEND MANIFESTO. Expansionist ardor, unsatisfied even by the Mexican cession of 1848, was largely responsible for this blunder in U.S. Cuban policy. American slaveholders had dreaded the possibility of emancipation or revolution and the creation of a new Santo Domingo almost within sight of U.S. shores. Cuba, furthermore, offered tempting possibilities for annexation and the establishment of another slave state. On Apr. 7, 1853, President Franklin Pierce appointed Pierre Soulé minister to Spain with instructions to negotiate for the purchase of Cuba. Soulé failed completely; but in 1854 Spain was embarrassed by revolutionary outbreaks, and it was hoped that holders of Spanish bonds, tempted by the prospect of American cash reinforcing a dubious security, might exert pressure on the Madrid government. Soulé, James Buchanan, minister to Great Britain, and John

Y. Mason, minister to France, were instructed by Secretary of State William L. Marcy to confer on the Cuban situation. They met at Ostend (Oostende), Belgium, in October 1854, signing the notorious manifesto on Oct. 15. In effect, the conferees declared that should Spain refuse to sell, and should the United States consider Spain's further possession of Cuba inimical to U.S. domestic interests, forcible seizure would be fully justified. The document caused a profound sensation, and amid a storm of foreign and domestic denunciation, Secretary Marcy disavowed the declaration.

[F. E. Chadwick, *The Relations of the United States and Spain;* A. A. Ettinger, *The Mission of Pierre Soulé, 1853–1855.*]

W. A. ROBINSON

OSTEOPATHY, the general application of manipulative methods based upon recognition of the importance of structural integrity of the body, and linked with general application of the science of natural immunity, was developed by Andrew T. Still (1828–1917). It was a revolt against the use of drugs and primitive surgical treatment. Although emphasizing manipulative methods, osteopathy is a complete therapeutic system, including surgery, obstetrics, and other specialities. Still promulgated osteopathy at Baldwin, Kans., in 1874, then moved to Kirksville, Mo., in 1875, where he practiced osteopathy with the help of his sons, whom he had trained, and established the American School of Osteopathy in 1892 with seventeen students. By 1916 a full four-year course had been established and by 1974 there were nine colleges in the United States offering the course. At least three years of study at an accredited college or university is required for admission to an osteopathic school. A degree of doctor of osteopathy (D.O.) is awarded upon completion of the course, after which a one-year internship is required in many states. The number of doctors practicing osteopathy grew to 3,000 in 1904, 9,969 in 1939, and more than 12,000 by 1975. Vermont, the first state to legalize the practice (1896), has been followed by all the other states and the District of Columbia. The American Osteopathic Association was organized in 1897, followed by component societies in practically every state, as well as affiliated societies of specialists and educators.

[E. R. Booth, *Booth's History of Osteopathy;* Ray G. Hulburt, "A. T. Still, Founder of Osteopathy," *Missouri Historical Review* (1924); A. T. Still, *Autobiography.*]

RAY G. HULBURT

OSWEGATCHIE, FORT. *See* **Ogdensburg.**

OSWEGO, a city on Lake Ontario in New York State, began as an Indian trading post in 1722, where, despite French claims to the region, English and Dutch traders began to assemble and to carry on a thriving trade. In 1726–27 Gov. William Burnet dispatched a number of soldiers and workmen to construct a fort on the west bank of the Oswego River near its mouth. Intruding into the line of French fortifications that controlled the Great Lakes and the waterways to the south, this post was the most important English fortification west of the Hudson, for it created a barrier to further French encroachments into northern New York.

From this point, on June 28, 1755, was launched the first English vessel to sail on the Great Lakes, and on Aug. 18 Gen. William Shirley arrived with an expedition destined for an attack on Fort Niagara. This move was deferred, but on the east side of the Oswego River, a quarter of a mile from Fort Oswego, the British erected a post that they named Fort Ontario. In 1756 these establishments came under attack by the French, and on Aug. 13–14 they were captured and destroyed by Louis Joseph de Montcalm. Abandoned by the French, the ruins were later converted into a fortified camp for the British troops under Col. John Prideaux.

In 1759–60 the British rebuilt Fort Ontario, and it again became a base for military operations. In July and August 1760 it was the rendezvous of Gen. Jeffery Amherst's army, augmented by 1,300 French Iroquois who came to make peace with the British (*see* French and Indian War). It was there on July 24, 1766, that Sir William Johnson met in council the great Ottawa chieftain, Pontiac, who signed a peace treaty with Great Britain. Fort Ontario continued as a peaceful trading post until 1774, when it was dismantled, with only a few men left to keep it from falling into decay. In 1777 Oswego served as Lt. Col. Barry St. Leger's base in his operations in the Mohawk Valley in connection with Gen. John Burgoyne's invasion.

In the War of 1812, Oswego was a naval base and the headquarters of Commodore Isaac Chauncey (*see* Montreal, Wilkinson Expedition Against). On May 6, 1814, it was attacked and captured by the British. The settlement was incorporated as a village in 1828 and chartered as a city in 1848.

The completion of the New York State barge system in 1917 brought new prosperity to Oswego's port, which handled shipments from Canada, Pennsylvania, and the Middle West. In 1959, with the opening of the Saint Lawrence Seaway, Oswego became a major Great Lakes port. The construction of the Nine Mile Point Nuclear Station along with other power installations has given the city further importance as a center of hydronuclear electric power for New York State. The population in 1970 was 23,844.

[Frank H. Severance, *An Old Frontier of France*.]
ROBERT W. BINGHAM

OTSEGO LANDS consisted of a tract of 100,000 acres on the west side of the Susquehanna River and Otsego Lake, embracing the present town of Cooperstown, N.Y., and extending north and south of it. The Otsego tract was purchased from the Indians by George Croghan and patented to him and his associates in 1769. With future financial profits in mind, Croghan began a series of improvements including the clearing of land and the construction of two houses and a bridge near Oak Creek. But he became involved in financial difficulties and mortgaged his holdings (*see* Burlington Company). Because he was unable to sell land to actual settlers, the greater part of the tract passed to William Cooper and Andrew Craig of Burlington, N.J. Both Cooper and Craig at once began developing the land for sale. Cooper laid out Cooperstown (1789), built Otsego Hall, and made a fortune from the sale of his land to settlers from New England. His posthumous publication *Guide in the Wilderness* (1810), intended to be a treatise on the most-approved methods of settling virgin country, is a record of his successful methods. In 1790 Cooper moved his family from Burlington and made his permanent home at Cooperstown. Many years later his son, James Fenimore Cooper, was to romanticize the region in novels and tales of frontier life.

[A. T. Volwiler, "George Croghan and the Development of Central New York, 1763–1800," *Quarterly Journal of the New York State Historical Association*, vol. 4.]
A. C. FLICK

OTTAWA. *See* **Algonquin.**

OUIATENON, FORT, was first established by the French in 1720 on the north bank of the Wabash River near present-day Lafayette, Ind. It was a transfer point on the fur-trading route from Fort Miami (Fort Wayne) to Vincennes and Kaskaskia (in southern Illinois). It lost its significance as a transfer point and fur-trading center after the revolutionary war and in 1791 was abandoned.

[L. Esarey, *History of Indiana*.]
THEODORE G. GRONERT

"OUR COUNTRY, RIGHT OR WRONG." At a dinner in his honor at Norfolk, Va., Apr. 4, 1816, Capt. Stephen Decatur offered the following toast: "Our country! In her intercourse with foreign nations may she always be in the right and always successful, right or wrong." This toast, popularly quoted incorrectly, was a reflection of the development of U.S. nationalism incident to the War of 1812.

[Charles Lee Lewis, *The Romantic Decatur*.]
CHARLES LEE LEWIS

"OUR FEDERAL UNION! IT MUST BE PRESERVED!" President Andrew Jackson's volunteer toast at the Thomas Jefferson anniversary dinner, Apr. 13, 1830, was a rejoinder to previous speakers who had eulogized states' rights and had hinted at disunion. Delivered in a most dramatic setting, with John C. Calhoun, the exponent of nullification, at the table, and described by onlookers as ringing through the banquet hall like one of the old warrior's strident commands on the field of battle, these words not only clarified the position of the chief executive on the nullification question but served to strengthen the hearts of Unionists throughout the nation. It unquestionably contributed to the successful meeting of the ominous crisis of 1833 (*see* Force Acts).

[J. S. Bassett, *Life of Andrew Jackson*.]
W. A. ROBINSON

OVERLAND COMPANIES, or overland emigrant companies, were composed of groups of families who traveled from points east of the Mississippi River to the Pacific coast, usually Oregon or California, by wagon train, as opposed to those who went by ship around Cape Horn or by the Isthmus of Darien (present-day Isthmus of Panama).

The first of the large overland movements was the "great migration" of 1843 to Oregon, which established the Oregon Trail. The second large movement was the California gold rush of 1849. A company was usually organized by a group of friendly families, although sometimes other unattached persons were accepted into membership. Rules to regulate the movement of the train and the action of individuals were drawn up and accepted before the start of the trek. One of the members, usually the most influential man, was elected captain; he had as much authority as a sea or army captain in making and enforcing the orders of the day. A council of ten or twelve older men was sometimes chosen to make policy. Other active younger men were appointed hunters to supply the party with meat. All able-bodied men were regarded as a standing army if defense against an Indian attack was necessary.

[S. Dunbar, *History of Travel in America*.]
CARL L. CANNON

OVERLAND EXPRESS. *See* **Pony Express.**

OVERLAND FREIGHTING. Before the completion of the Union Pacific, the first transcontinental railway, in 1869, most freight was carried by wagons. More specifically, the term "overland freighting" has been applied to the carrying industry on the Overland Trail from points on the Missouri River to the Rocky Mountains or California.

As soon as Salt Lake City was founded (1847) and gold discovered in California (1849), a certain amount of hauling began. This was greatly increased during the campaign of Col. Albert S. Johnston against the Mormons (1857) and by the discovery of gold in Colorado in the late 1850's (*see* Pikes Peak Gold Rush). The outfitting towns along the Missouri River (*see* Independence) were the eastern termini of the freighting routes that, for the most part, crossed the Platte Valley or the Kansas Valley to the Rocky Mountains.

Large freighting companies were established to take care of this business. The best known of these was the firm of Russell, Majors and Waddell, which used the towns of Atchison and Leavenworth, Kans., Saint Joseph, Mo., and Nebraska City, Nebr., as shipping points. At the outfitting towns there were acres of wagons, huge herds of oxen, great pyramids of extra axletrees, and battalions of drivers and other employees. In 1859 this firm alone used 45,000 oxen, and from Apr. 25 to Oct. 13, 1860, shipped from Nebraska City 2,782,258 pounds of freight. There were many other, both large and small, concerns in the business of hauling freight. Even pioneer farmers with one or two wagons sought a share of the lucrative business. In 1864 an army officer estimated that for several months during the summer no less than 1,000 tons of merchandise a day poured into Denver, Colo.

Russell, Majors and Waddell ran twenty-six wagons in a train with an average load of 6,000 pounds each. Each wagon was drawn by six yoke of oxen. The train was presided over by the wagon boss. An assistant boss, a night herder, a man to drive the extra animals, and a spare driver or two brought the number of men in a train up to at least thirty-one. Their covered wagons strung out in line of travel like a fleet of ships with their white sails unfurled. The wagon master was admiral of this little fleet, and his word was law. He rode ahead, directed the course, selected a campsite, and started and stopped the train. He and his assistant were on hand at once when one of the wagons had trouble.

It was customary to rise at three in the morning, get onto the road early, and drive until ten, when breakfast was eaten. The oxen were then allowed to rest until the afternoon, when a second drive was made. The train averaged from twelve to fifteen miles a day. When it reached the bedground, the boss directed the bullwhackers, as the drivers were called, in forming an elliptical corral with their wagons.

The time required for a trip from Kansas City to Salt Lake City was about fifty days; the return trip was made in about forty. The freight rate differed with the season and the danger from Indians.

Some freighting concerns used mule teams. In 1860 a steam wagon, made on the order of a modern steam tractor, was tried out at Nebraska City, with the idea of hauling freight overland, but its great weight, its imperfect mechanism, and the difficulty with which fuel could be secured for it caused its promoters to abandon the plan. As the railroads were built across the Plains the freighting outfits continued to operate over the gradually narrowing gap until finally the railroad usurped the freighting of goods overland.

[Henry Inman, *The Great Salt Lake Trail;* Alexander Majors, *Seventy Years on the Frontier*.]
EVERETT DICK

OVERLAND MAIL AND STAGECOACHES followed the covered wagon into the trans-Missouri West. Monthly government mail services were established from Independence, Mo., to Santa Fe and to Salt Lake City in 1850. Thirty days were allowed for the one-way trip on each line. A similar service was begun between Salt Lake City and Sacramento, Calif., in 1851. As a result of the small remuneration for the service, only one team was usually employed for the trip, and no way stations were maintained.

Because of these limited facilities, practically all mail for California went by steamer, via Panama, with a thirty-day schedule from New York to San Francisco.

Proponents of overland mail service advocated an adequate subsidy for the maintenance of stations and changes of teams. They finally pushed their bill through Congress. Under it, the semiweekly Southern, or Butterfield, Overland Mail Company on a twenty-five-day schedule was inaugurated in 1858. The choice of a southern route, via El Paso and Tucson, angered proponents of the central route (via Salt Lake City). The postmaster general defended the southern route as the only one feasible for year-round travel. To disprove this, the Pony Express was established on the central route (1860) by William H. Russell, together with Alexander Majors—two members of the firm of Russell, Majors and Waddell, which carried the semimonthly stagecoach mail on this road.

With the outbreak of the Civil War the Southern Overland Mail was moved to the central route in Union-controlled territory and was made a daily service (*see* Central Overland California and Pikes Peak Express). Coaches were scheduled to carry letter mail from the Missouri River to California in twenty days, other mail in thirty-five days. The contract provided annual compensation of more than $1 million. Ben Holladay purchased the line and contract in 1862. A vigorous organizer, he quickly improved the line and extended branches to Oregon and Montana. Indians interrupted the coaches and destroyed many stations in 1864, but the distribution of additional soldiers cleared the road. Wells Fargo purchased Holladay's lines in 1866 and continued operations until the completion of the first transcontinental railroad in 1869 (*see* Union Pacific Railroad). Coaches continued for many years to serve localities not reached by rail.

The Concord stagecoach, manufactured by Abbot, Downing and Company of Concord, N.H., was the great overland carrier of passengers, mail, and express before 1869. It was swung on leather thoroughbraces in lieu of springs and accommodated nine inside passengers and others on the top. Leather boots at front and rear carried the mail and express. The coach was drawn by four or six horses or mules and usually made 100 miles in twenty-four hours. The driver was the lion of the road, the only one, as Mark Twain on his stage trips says, "they bowed down to and worshipped." The stagecoach was a symbol and an institution of the prerailroad West.

[L. R. Hafen, *The Overland Mail, 1849–1869.*]
LeRoy R. Hafen

OVERLAND TRAIL, or Overland Route, was a variation of the Oregon Trail, being a short route from the northeastern part of present-day Colorado, near the forks of the Platte River, to Fort Bridger (Wyoming). It was popularized and named in 1862 when Ben Holladay's Overland Stage Line was moved to it from the old emigrant road along the North Platte River. Shorter distance and less Indian danger induced the change of stage route. The Overland Trail followed the south bank of the South Platte to Latham, near present-day Greeley, Colo., up the Cache la Poudre River, across the Laramie Plains, over Bridger's Pass (in central Wyoming), and thence west to Fort Bridger. Its route west of Latham was previously called the Cherokee Trail, having been crossed by Cherokee goldseekers in 1849. The Lincoln Highway and the Union Pacific Railroad follow approximately the Overland Trail through western Wyoming. Some emigrants used this trail in the middle 1860's, but it was never as popular as the older route, the Oregon Trail.

[L. R. Hafen, *The Overland Mail, 1849–1869.*]
LeRoy R. Hafen

OVERSEER, the title given the general manager of a large agricultural unit in the antebellum South. The smooth and efficient operation of the plantation depended on him. It was his duty to maintain discipline, divide the labor, issue all supplies, care for the livestock, keep all tools and buildings in repair, and harvest the crops. His annual salary ranged from $120 or less to $1,500, depending on the locality and the overseer's individual ability and integrity. The typical overseer was a native southerner, half literate, crude, and mediocre in ability, and often scorned by his employer and by the slaves subject to his control.

[U. B. Phillips, *Life and Labor in the Old South.*]
Ralph B. Flanders

OWEN, FORT. Maj. John Owen built his trading post and stockade on the Bitterroot River, Mont., in 1851, adjacent to the site of Saint Mary's Jesuit Mission to the Flathead Indians. In 1874 Owen was taken to an insane asylum. His post was closed and became dilapidated. It was repaired in 1876 to serve as a refuge for settlers during an Indian outbreak, then abandoned again and allowed to fall into ruin.

[Seymour Dunbar and Paul C. Phillips, eds., *The Journals and Letters of Major John Owen;* Gilbert J. Garraghan, S.J., *The Jesuits of the Middle United States.*]
Alvin F. Harlow

OWENITES. *See* **New Harmony Settlement.**

OXEN were used from the time of the early settlements in America as draft animals and for plowing. Their slowness of pace was counterbalanced on rough, muddy pioneer roads by their great superiority to the horse in strength and endurance. They were used in logging and in early canal and railroad building. On the Middlesex Canal in Massachusetts, about 1805, one yoke of oxen, in a test, drew a raft containing 800 tons of timber, but at the rate of only one mile per hour, which was considered too slow to be permitted on the towpath. During the 19th century small farmers in the South were happy to have a yoke of "steers," or even one "steer" for general use. Oxen were still used, although rarely, as late as the 1920's.

Oxen drew many of the household wagons of the pioneers in all the great westward migrations—to the Ohio country, to Tennessee, Kentucky, the prairie states, and finally in 1848–49 on the long treks over plains and mountains to Oregon and California. Next they were employed in enormous numbers for freighting in the West. Two large loaded wagons were often hooked together and drawn over rough trails by six, eight, or ten yoke of oxen. Several rigs of this sort, traveling together for safety, were called, in western parlance, a "bull train." The freighting firm of Russell, Majors and Waddell, while they were hauling supplies for the army from the Missouri River to Utah in 1857–58 (*see* Mormon War), are said to have worked 40,000 oxen and only 1,000 mules. When the gold rush to the Black Hills (South Dakota) began in 1875, one company, freighting from Sioux City, Iowa, to Deadwood, S.Dak., used from 2,000 to 3,000 oxen and 1,000 to 1,500 mules. Another concern, operating between Yankton and Deadwood, made use of 4,000 oxen at the height of the rush.

[Alvin F. Harlow, *Old Waybills;* Ezra Meeker, *The Ox Team, or The Old Oregon Trail.*]

ALVIN F. HARLOW

OXFORD MOVEMENT, also called the Tractarian movement, was a religious revival that began in 1833 in the Church of England and that emphasized the Catholic heritage of the Anglican communion in its doctrine, polity, and worship. In America, where it was commonly called Puseyism, after Edward B. Pusey, canon of Christ Church at Oxford, the movement found congenial soil in circles of the Episcopal church already influenced by the high churchmanship of Bishop John H. Hobart of New York (1811–30),

particularly in the General Seminary in New York City. Opposition by those who believed the movement endangered the protestantism of the church reached considerable proportions during the 1840's, but efforts to obtain a condemnation of Tractarianism by the General Convention of 1844 were unsuccessful. Several conversions to Roman Catholicism, notably that of Bishop Levi S. Ives of North Carolina in 1852, increased party tension. In the decade following the Civil War controversy centered about ceremonial innovations by the Anglo-Catholics; and the General Convention of 1874 passed a canon designed to prevent liturgical practices inconsistent with the church's doctrines. Nonetheless, the movement exercised a permanent influence throughout the Episcopal church, and even in other denominations, both as to the external ceremonial of the liturgy and in a larger emphasis upon the sacramental forms of religious devotion.

[W. W. Manross, *A History of the American Episcopal Church.*]

MASSEY H. SHEPHERD, JR.

OYSTER RIVER RAID (July 18, 1694). An Indian war party, recruited in Maine and accompanied by several Frenchmen, surprised the settlement on Oyster River in the town of Dover (New Hampshire). A few garrison houses were successfully defended, but ninety-four persons were killed or captured.

[J. Scales, "The Oyster River Massacre," *Proceedings of the New Hampshire Historical Society,* vol. V.]

W. A. ROBINSON

PACIFIC CABLE. *See* **Cables.**

PACIFIC COAST, FAKE EXPLORATION OF. The first individuals to attain fame in connection with the Pacific coast of the United States were the fakers: authentic persons (with one exception) who professed to have made miraculous discoveries; that is, men who found inlets and passages where none existed or located real ones, without actually going to those places, by means of their dynamic imaginations. The earliest of these men was Capt. Lorenzo Ferrer Maldonado, who declared that in 1588 he had voyaged in high latitudes from the Atlantic Ocean through a strait into a large sea and then through another strait that debouched on the western coast of the North American continent.

In Venice in April 1596, Michael Lok, an English

merchant, encountered Juan de Fuca, a Greek whose real name was Apostolos Valerianos, who claimed to be a mariner and pilot in the service of Spain. He stated that in 1592 he had made a voyage along the Pacific coast, during which he had discovered the strait that now bears his name. Since the strait really exists many persons have claimed that de Fuca really made the voyage.

The most colorful of the pretenders was Adm. Bartholomew de Fonte, whose person and deeds seem to have been created by James Petiver, a London author. In the April and June 1708 issues of the *Monthly Miscellany, or Memoirs for the Curious,* published in London, appeared a letter purportedly written many decades earlier by de Fonte. De Fonte claimed that he had sailed north from Callao, Peru, on Apr. 3, 1640, and at fifty-three degrees north latitude, discovered a great river. He ascended the river to a lake, where he left his ships and by boat descended a river flowing eastward until he came to the Atlantic Ocean, where he supposedly found a Boston vessel at anchor. Publication of the letter created a heated controversy that lasted for several decades.

[James Burney, *A Chronological History of the Voyages and Discoveries in the South Sea or Pacific Ocean,* vol. III; H. R. Wagner, ''Apocryphal Voyages to the Northwest Coast of America,'' *Proceedings of the American Antiquarian Society* (1931).]

FRANK EDWARD ROSS

PACIFIC FUR COMPANY, organized by John Jacob Astor in 1810, was the western subsidiary of his American Fur Company. By the combined work of these two companies he hoped to control the American fur market. Astor supplied capital up to $400,000 and was to bear any losses for the first five years. He retained 50 percent of the stock and prorated the remainder among his field partners. Alexander Mackay, Duncan McDougal, Donald MacKenzie, David Stuart, and Wilson Price Hunt, all former employees of Astor's Canadian rival, the North West Fur Company, except Hunt, were the chief partners. The plan of operations centered on the chief depot, Astoria, at the mouth of the Columbia River in Oregon, at which point the sea otter pelts gathered in coasting trade and beaver pelts from the interior would be made ready for shipment. Vessels from the East Coast would bring supplies to Astoria and then carry the pelts to Canton, China, and return to the United States with a cargo of Chinese goods. There was also to be a chain of posts along the Columbia and Missouri river routes. The wreck of

two of the ships, unfortunate management in the field, and the War of 1812 resulted in the failure of the Pacific Fur Company, and Astoria and its equipment were sold by the field partners, at a great sacrifice, to the North West Company.

[George W. Fuller, *A History of the Pacific Northwest.*]
ROBERT MOULTON GATKE

PACIFIC ISLANDS. *See* **Trust Territory of the Pacific.**

PACIFIC NORTHWEST, a region of the United States comprising the states of Oregon, Washington, and Idaho. The close economic ties and the common historical heritage of the states—all part of Old Oregon—underscore the unity of the region. The section is best referred to as the Pacific Northwest to avoid confusion with the Old Northwest, the country of the Ohio River and Great Lakes region.

[Dan Elbert Clark, *The West in American History.*]
ROBERT MOULTON GATKE

PACIFIC RAILROAD. *See* **Railroads, Sketches: Union Pacific.**

PACIFIC REPUBLIC MOVEMENT, advocating the separation of the region west of the Rockies into one or more independent states, was especially active on the eve of secession and during the first year of the Civil War. The first push to create a Pacific coast republic was begun by Oregon Democrats when obliged to submit to the rule of Whig party officials (1849–53) and by the people of California when Congress delayed admission of their state to the Union (1848–50). Congressmen from Oregon and California, among them senators Joseph H. Lane, William Gwin, and Multon S. Latham, were charged with a plot to establish a Pacific republic, which was advocated by prosouthern newspapers in these states, such as the *Portland Standard,* the *San Francisco Chronicle,* the *Sonora Democrat,* and the *Los Angeles Star.* The Knights of the Golden Circle, a secret organization of southern sympathizers, took an oath to support a Pacific coast republic and were said to have plotted to seize customhouses and arsenals. It was argued that by the establishment of an independent republic, participation in the fratricidal strife between North and South could be avoided.

[Joseph Ellison, "The Sentiment for a Pacific Republic," *Proceedings of the Pacific Coast Branch of the American Historical Association* (1929); Dorothy Hull, "The Movement in Oregon for the Establishment of a Pacific Coast Republic," *Oregon History Quarterly,* vol. 17.]

R. C. CLARK

"PACIFICUS" AND "HELVIDIUS."

On Apr. 22, 1793, President George Washington issued the proclamation of neutrality designed to keep the United States out of the war between Great Britain and France. The proclamation was defended by Secretary of the Treasury Alexander Hamilton in a series of articles written under the pseudonym of "Pacificus" in the *Gazette of the United States* (June 29–July 27, 1793). James Madison, then a member of the House of Representatives, replied to these in a series of letters in the same paper as "Helvidius" (Aug. 24–Sept. 18, 1793).

[L. M. Sears, *A History of American Foreign Relations.*]

STANLEY R. PILLSBURY

PACIFISM.

Four unique types of pacifism have entered American life and politics: (1) conscientious objection to war, resulting in personal refusal to participate in war or military service; (2) opposition to, and renunciation of, all forms of violence; (3) a strategy of nonviolent action to overcome specific injustices or to bring about radical change in the social order; and (4) a "positive testimony" to a way of life based on conviction of the power of love to govern human relationships.

Conscientious objection to war was a central doctrine of the "historic peace churches" (Brethren, Mennonites, and Quakers), which held war to be in fundamental contradiction to their religious faiths. In prerevolutionary Pennsylvania, Quakers tried with some success to apply their pacifist convictions in the colony that William Penn had established as a "holy experiment," a colony where they could live at peace with each other and with all persons, including their Indian neighbors. The Revolution, however, split the Quakers on the issue of political pacifism and led to their permanent withdrawal as an organized religious body from political responsibility. This returned pacifism to the individual for decision—on refusing to fight, pay taxes for military purposes, or in other ways support the war "system."

The number of objectors and the form of their objection varied with the moral appeal of each war, reaching a climax of opposition to U.S. military action in Vietnam and Cambodia in the late 1960's. Probably one out of five of those of draft age during this period were exempted from military service because of conscientious objection (although many of these were ostensibly deferred for other reasons, because local draft boards did not wish to acknowledge such claims formally). An unprecedented, though unspecified, number of draftees were discharged from military service or were absent without leave (AWOL) because of objections after induction. In addition, a substantial number were imprisoned because they refused to fight or to be inducted.

During this time, pacifist ranks reached out to most denominations, and many of the country's religious leaders were included. Also, persons whose objection to war stemmed from humanitarian or philosophical convictions, rather than religious training and belief—the criterion for conscientious objection specified in the Selective Training and Service Act of 1940—were legitimized by a succession of Supreme Court decisions.

Meanwhile, pacifists in the 20th century had again gone political in attempts to prevent war and keep the United States out of war. They were a principal force in the American peace movement and were often at odds with those who urged a collective-security system with international military sanctions as the most effective approach to maintaining peace.

The second form of pacifism abjures violence in any form and sees violence operating not only in outright war but also through social institutions that permit human exploitation and discrimination and that rely on repression and force to maintain "law and order." Consequently, the major goal of such pacifists has been social reform. The core of the American antislavery movement was largely pacifist. For example, in the 1750's John Woolman preached to his fellow Quakers that slavery was incompatible with their professed respect for "that of God in every man." Social pacifism also infused the struggle for prison reform, the fight against capital punishment, the championing of women's rights, efforts to improve care of the mentally ill and retarded, and the securing of civil rights for all minorities.

Social-reform pacifists were in direct conflict with those who insisted that effective action demanded violence. They found themselves denounced as softheaded dupes, if not outright lackeys, of the entrenched oppressors. To this, pacifism responded with its third pattern—a strategy of nonviolent direct action. Modeled on Mahatma Gandhi's philosophy of civil disobedience (*satyagraha*), sit-ins (put to an early test by some unions in the industrial conflicts of the 1930's), marches (which achieved dramatic impact with the "stride toward freedom" from Selma to Montgomery, Ala., of Martin Luther King, Jr., who called for an end to racial discrimination), vigils (usually conducted by smaller groups with a strong religious motif), and boycotts (as notably organized by César E. Chavez, 1965–70, on behalf of grape pickers striking against California growers) became expressions of nonviolent protest. These actions were characterized by extraordinary self-discipline, even when met by violent counteraction.

Pacifist influence was fractured by a succession of violent events. The assassination of King silenced the most effective spokesman for nonviolence at a time when militants among blacks and others in the civil rights movement were clamoring for confrontation by force. Later, a sense of helplessness swept over the peace movement when President Richard M. Nixon moved to extend the war into Cambodia and substituted massive, electronically controlled bombing and mining for the presence of most American draftees in Vietnam. But backlash against the civil rights and peace movements demonstrated that a wide base of nonpacifist values existed throughout America, especially in middle-income ethnic groups. The collapse of the George S. McGovern campaign for the presidency in 1972 seemed to bury the hopes for effective political expression of pacifist concerns, leaving a vacuum of disillusionment that militants eagerly sought to fill.

Two influences combined to generate a fourth type of pacifism. Many conscientious objectors became increasingly troubled by the essentially negative posture of their position. Mere objection, whether to war or to injustice generally, failed to satisfy their concern with creating the conditions for a human community. Second, there was a growing feeling that societies, and American society in particular, were past reforming and that peace would have to be sought within a small group of kindred souls. Both influences moved toward a definition of pacifism as a total philosophy of life and toward experimentation with human relationships in which love would replace violence. These two expressions of pacifism, however, differed in focus. The first emphasized an outward "testimony" by which the principles of cooperative community could be demonstrated to others as a viable way of life. This was the original intent of the Civilian Public Service program, which had been organized voluntarily by the historic peace churches to offer an alternative to military service during World

War II. Conscientious objector units worked, with commendable accomplishments, on conservation and park projects, in fire fighting and disaster relief, in mental health hospitals and schools for retarded children, and as "guinea pigs" for medical research. The effectiveness of the testimony-by-work approach was seriously undermined, however, by Selective Service control and the inescapable consciousness that the testifiers were in fact conscripts, not volunteers.

The second approach rejected society in favor of a commune of persons willing to live simply on a share-alike basis and as independently as possible from the requirements of the so-called system (including fixed employment). The new communes followed the long tradition in America of experimental communities devoted to the ideal of self-sufficient and harmonious living.

In the mid-1970's pacifism in America seemed to have returned to its pristine base of individual conviction. But the activism of the 1960's had left both a commitment to conscientious objection to war and a sensitivity to social injustice that encompassed a much broader reach of American life than ever before.

[American Friends Service Committee, *Speak Truth to Power;* Peter Brock, *Pacifism in the United States: From the Colonial Era to the First World War;* Charles Chatfield, *For Peace and Justice: Pacifism in America, 1914–1941;* Merle E. Curti, *Peace or War: The American Struggle, 1636–1936;* Martin Luther King, Jr., *The Trumpet of Conscience;* Peter Matthiessen, *Sal si puedes: César Chavez and the New American Revolution;* Mulford Q. Sibley, *The Quiet Battle;* Mulford Q. Sibley and Philip E. Jacob, *Conscription of Conscience: The American State and the Conscientious Objector, 1940–1947.*]

PHILIP E. JACOB

PACKAGING. The United States in the early 1800's was a predominantly rural society. Little merchandise was packaged; barrels, wooden boxes, and burlap sacks lined the walls of each general store. Syrup, cider, and vinegar were decanted from barrels and carboys into the consumers' bottles or jars; beer was obtained from the corner saloon in a pail.

Modern packaging began in the late 1890's. Gradually, more and more consumer goods were packed in suitable containers rather than being sent to the retail store in bulk. From 1920 on, packaging of industrial goods increased in importance. By the mid-1970's, more than 8,000 packages containing different consumer commodities competed for the consumer's dollar in an average supermarket.

The definition of packaging has been broadened by

many authorities to include "containerization"—the use of bulk containers in which small packaged commodities are loaded for shipment between countries or between points in the United States. Containerization provides greater efficiency of storage and transfer of commodities, while also encouraging improvements in the design and operation of warehouses and transport vehicles.

Traditionally packaging has been designed to provide protection against waste and loss, identification, attractiveness and salability, light weight, economy of space, saving, low cost, and convenience. Important developments since 1950 include the development of composite film structures, shrink packaging, and thermoformed containers, as well as improvements in metal cans, glass and plastic bottles, aerosols, and point-of-sale packages. Trends noted in consumerism, especially since 1960, are encouraging the development of packages that are designed for the convenience of the consumer, use recycled materials or are recyclable, use child-protective closures, and give consumers better information on which to base buying decisions.

[Lawrence J. Rinaldi, *Containerization;* William C. Simms, ed., *Modern Packaging Encyclopedia and Planning Guide, 1974–75.*]

CLARENCE J. MILLER

PACKERS' AGREEMENT. The investigation of the meatpacking industry begun in 1917 by the federal government resulted in the exposure of monopoly and unfair practices. Public opinion forced the larger packers in 1920 to agree voluntarily with the government to sell all holdings in public stockyards, stockyard railroads, cold storage warehouses, and terminals; dispose of their interests in all market newspapers; give up the selling of all products unrelated to the meat industry; abandon the use of all transportation facilities for the carrying of any but their own products; and submit to federal injunction forbidding monopoly.

[William B. Colver, "Federal Trade Commission and the Meat Packing Industry," *Annals of the American Academy of Political and Social Science* (1919); Lewis H. Haney, *The Case Against the Meat Packers.*]

ERNEST S. OSGOOD

PACKERS AND STOCKYARDS ACT, passed in August 1921 after several years of controversy, made it unlawful for packers to manipulate prices, to create monopoly, and to award favors to any person or local-

ity. The regulation of stockyards provided for non-discriminatory services, reasonable rates, open schedules, and fair charges. The administration of the law was under the direction of the secretary of agriculture, who entertained complaints, held hearings, and issued "cease and desist" orders. The bill was a significant part of the agrarian legislation of the early 1920's.

[A. Capper, *The Agricultural Bloc.*]

THOMAS S. BARCLAY

PACKETS, SAILING. The packet, or sailing liner, as distinguished from the "regular trader" and the transient, or tramp, was one of a line of privately owned vessels sailing in regular succession on fixed dates between specified ports; it rendered a service later continued by the steamship lines. The New York packets served as the chief link between the Old World and the New World, played an essential part in attracting the movements of commerce toward New York, demonstrated the value of shipping-line arrangements, and incidentally made more money than most clippers or whalers. Driven to the limit through ocean gales in all seasons, the packets never lacked for adventure.

The British government mail brigs, which carried no freight, and local New York steamers were partial precedents for the first transatlantic packet, the Black Ball Line, which began monthly service between New York and Liverpool in 1818. By 1822 the Red Star Line, the Blue Swallowtail Line, and doubled Black Ball service made weekly sailings between the two ports, augmented later by the Dramatic Line and "New Line." Meanwhile New York inaugurated similar service with London and Le Havre between 1822 and 1824. Rival efforts of Philadelphia, Boston, and Baltimore met with slight success.

The history of these New York ocean packets falls into three periods of some twenty years each. Until 1838 their functional importance was at its height, for they conveyed most of the news, cabin passengers, and fine freight between Europe and America. During the next twenty years, with steamships cutting into those lucrative fields, sailing packets carried immigrants. During this period the ships increased in size and speed. After the 1850's, losing even the steerage trade, they become mere freighters on schedule. The last ocean packet sailing was made in 1881.

The packet principle was successfully extended to coastal runs. By 1826 lines of full-rigged ships were connecting New York with the cotton ports (such as New Orleans and Baltimore), while lesser lines of brigs or schooners plied other coastal runs. The former group brought cotton to New York for shipment to Europe and helped to distribute New York's imports.

[R. G. Albion, *Square-Riggers on Schedule: The New York Sailing Packets to England, France, and the Cotton Ports.*]

ROBERT G. ALBION

PACK TRAINS, organized by trans-Allegheny pioneers, were a means of transport for western products that were traded for indispensable goods from the East. After crops were harvested in autumn, the neighbors of a frontier community organized a caravan of packhorses, each horse girthed with a wooden packsaddle and laden with goods for barter—mainly peltry and some ginseng, potash, flax, and whiskey. Feed was also carried, part to be cached in the mountains for the return journey. The string of customarily ten to twenty horses, under command of a master driver and two or three "understrappers," usually followed an old Indian trail; the belled horses plodded in single file some fifteen to twenty-five miles before they were hobbled for the night's bivouac. The main Pennsylvania trails were the Kittanning from the Allegheny River down the Juniata Valley, and the Raystown Path from the Ohio to the eastern cities; on the main southerly route Baltimore, the earliest depot, was replaced as trading spread farther west by other Maryland cities—Frederick, Hagerstown, and Cumberland. The pack trains returned with salt, iron, sugar, lead, and perhaps some urban "luxuries," such as crockery.

From its communal beginnings, packing became a professional vocation. The widening of the trails to permit wagon passage, James O'Hara's enterprise in bringing salt down the Allegheny River to Pittsburgh, and the safety of keelboat transportation on the Ohio after 1795 pushed the primitive pack trains into farther frontiers. Pack trains shared the Santa Fe Trail with freighters' wagons, served remote fur-trading and mining posts, and were much used by troops operating against hostile Indians.

[W. C. Langdon, *Everyday Things in American Life.*]

E. DOUGLAS BRANCH

PADLOCK INJUNCTION. In such cases when the use of the usual processes of the criminal law were insufficient to abate a public nuisance, such as a gambling operation or a house of prostitution, the courts could issue an order to the police to padlock the premises, protecting the lock against molestation by an injunction. Thus, anyone who tampered with the lock was held in contempt of court and punished accordingly. The padlock injunction was used extensively during Prohibition (1919–33) to permanently close premises used for bootlegging. Interpretation of the due process clause of the U.S. Constitution since Prohibition, particularly under Chief Justice Earl Warren, has eliminated the actual padlocking of premises.

HARVEY WALKER

PAINTING. 17th Century. American painting in the 17th century followed no coherent pattern of development. American works of this period are basically transplants from the artistic traditions of European mother countries. Some of the paintings were done by Europeans working in America. Other paintings were imported by settlers from Europe or are portraits painted when the American patron revisited the mother country. Few pictures survive that were painted in the colonies.

The 17th century was an age of exploration; the earliest pictures done in America were watercolors and drawings by explorers. The artists recorded the flora and fauna of the New World or made topographical views of a given region. French, Spanish, Dutch, and English explorers painted in America. Spanish works date to the early 16th century. Two of the most notable artist-explorers were a Frenchman, Jacques Le Moyne, and an Englishman, John White. They drew pictures of the Indians, especially their costumes and activities. Le Moyne painted in a mannerist style with strong emphasis on the customs of the native Americans, which he considered curious. White used a style more analogous to late Gothic views in conceptual perspective. Le Moyne worked in Florida about 1564; White painted in Virginia in 1590. No pictures produced in the South during the 17th century have come to light. Portraits of southern colonists are known but appear to have been painted in England.

New England was more productive. Some portraits were imported. Sir Richard Saltonstall and John Winthrop, first governor of Massachusetts Bay Colony, both brought portraits from England; Edward Winslow had his portrait painted in London when he returned there in 1646. A few painters settled and worked in New England. Probably the first artist by trade to arrive was Augustine Clemens, who emigrated to Boston in 1635. He was trained as a painter in provincial Reading, northwest of London, where a style based on a mixture of traditional late Gothic linear motifs and Dutch baroque realism flourished. Clemens is listed as a glazier in the ship's manifests, but by 1652 he was described as a painter. One of his works was probably the portrait of Dr. John Clarke, Clemens' next-door neighbor, dated 1664. The style of the portrait is close to works done in Reading.

Other pictures of Boston sitters exist. They reveal a wide range of styles and ability. The widely known portraits of John Freake and of Elizabeth Freake with baby Mary may have been done by Samuel Clemens, Augustine's son. Painted in 1674, they boast an inventive combination of naive solutions in drawing and sophisticated composition and design. The painter (or painters) of the portraits of John Wheelwright, John Davenport, and Richard Mather was probably completely untrained. The last-mentioned may be by the Harvard graduate and printer John Foster, whose woodcut of Mather is related to the portrait. Several anonymous limners painted the portraits of Abigail Adams; the Gibbs children, Robert, Margaret, and Henry; and other colonial sitters in Massachusetts.

Toward the end of the century the baroque style emerged more strongly. Thomas Smith, who painted a portrait of President William Ames of Harvard as early as 1680, is the earliest identified painter to use the baroque style. Smith's self-portrait is the best known of his work. Three other pictures are attributed to Smith—two of military leaders, George Curwin and Thomas Savage, and one of his daughter, Maria Catherine Smith. They are similar in style but have certain notable differences in execution. Except for the picture of Maria Smith, each composition contains scenes of battle and personal items. While these elements are seen in European works of the period, Smith's own portraits eschew the symbolic poses indicating one's status that are used in European portraiture; Smith relies instead on the character of the face and various autobiographical objects to convey the personality of the sitter.

The baroque style emerged earlier in New York, then called New Amsterdam. The colonists in New Amsterdam came from Holland, where Rembrandt (van Rijn) and Frans Hals were at the height of their careers. The baroque style was not filtered through an intermediate source. As in Boston, many pictures were imported. Peter Stuyvesant brought several paintings from Holland, one of which was attributed to an important Dutch painter, Geerard Donck.

Henri Couturier, a Huguenot, recorded in the Leiden guild of painters, was probably in New Amsterdam by 1663. There is written evidence that he painted pictures of Stuyvesant and his sons, although the extant pictures of these subjects cannot be positively identified as being from the hand of Couturier. The first painter to land in New Amsterdam was Evert Duyckinck. Like Clemens in Boston, he was listed as a glazier when he arrived in 1638. In 1693 Duyckinck was recorded as a painter, but no pictures by him have been discovered. However, he founded a dynasty of painters in New York that lasted for three generations. Portraits by his son Gerret are known, but they belong to the 18th century.

By 1700, no real traditions had emerged. A school of painters in New York was developing, but it remained for an influx of English and continental painters who settled permanently in America to establish painting in the colonies.

18th Century. American painting in the 18th century closely followed English and continental styles, which were adapted to reflect the new culture and tastes of America. But patronage was very different in America. It was not royal or papal, but middle-class and mercantile. Americans were among the earliest to explore neoclassicism and may have been the first to develop romantic painting—both developments strongly rooted in bourgeois aesthetics. Thus, American painting was colonial rather than provincial. Even though it imitated European painting, it was imbued with an interest in line, geometry, and direct observation, unlike European work.

Four phases of development occurred in American painting during the 18th century. In the first phase, a period from 1700 to 1727, artistic activity was halting, and no major artists predominate. The period 1727–51 was characterized by an influx of various English artists, especially John Smibert, and the establishment of the American school by Robert Feke. The third phase, 1751–74, witnessed the emergence of talented colonial painters, such as Benjamin West and John Singleton Copley, alongside a continuing stream of foreign émigrés. The final phase reflected the influence of West, who trained nearly all the major artists during the period 1775–1800. In the first three phases, portraiture dominated; in the last phase, genre, still life, and, most important, landscape began to be produced.

Before 1727 the names of few painters were known. Pastelist Henrietta Johnson worked in South Carolina, and Christopher Witt painted in Philadelphia. Various artists worked in New England, but they are identified only by the names of the people

PAINTING

they painted, such as the Pierpont limner and the Pollard limner. The most important group of painters of the period was concentrated in New York City and the Hudson River valley, sometimes known as patroon painters. Their pictures were generally painted with broken brush strokes, strong colors, and stylized modeling; the compositions often followed English mezzotint prints imported to America. Several distinctly related subgroups of pictures can be distinguished. One of the principal subgroups is composed of pictures that all bear the Latin inscription *Aetatis Suiae* on them; examples are found in the vicinity of Albany, N.Y. Another subgroup, which has strongly rounded brush strokes, comes from Westchester County and may be by Gerret Duyckinck. Finally, some rather sophisticated pictures from New York City form a subgroup. The only patroon artist known is Pieter Vanderlyn of Kingston, N.Y., who painted the portrait of Mrs. Petrus Vas.

The best paintings of the period in America were from the brush of Justus Englehardt Kühn and Gustavus Hesselius, who emigrated to the Chesapeake area from Germany and Sweden, respectively. They were trained in the late baroque tradition and brought the elaborate trappings of court painting. Kühn's American subjects were painted in grand gardens and formal settings. Hesselius painted allegorical subjects, but his finest pictures were of four Delaware Indian chiefs. For a time Hesselius was occupied with music and built organs. His later painting (1752–55) was much like Feke's. With the arrival of Peter Pelham in 1727 American painting changed. Although trained as an engraver in London, Pelham also brought the latest painting techniques to Boston. About that same time Charles Bridges appeared in Virginia, John Watson in New Jersey, and Smibert in Boston. Of these, Smibert was by far the most significant. He set out in 1728 with Rev. George Berkeley and others to found a college in Bermuda. They landed in Newport, R.I., to await funds for the college. When the money was not forthcoming, the group disbanded and Smibert went to Boston to set up a studio. He remained there for some twenty years. In 1724 George Vertue, an English critic, rated Smibert a better artist than William Hogarth, but few would agree that Hogarth did not surpass him; still, Smibert's paintings were the best in America to that time. He was called in 1740 to both New York and Philadelphia to paint. The first art exhibition in America was held in his studio in 1730, and after Smibert's death in 1751 the studio became a museum and was

visited by most of the major American artists of the 18th century.

Although Smibert did much to establish painting in America, the first important native American painter was Feke. Born about 1707 on Long Island, Feke may have learned his trade in New York City (reports of some European training cannot be substantiated). Feke probably painted as early as 1735, but his first major work was the portrait of Isaac Royall and his family done in 1741, a landmark of 18th-century painting. In 1742 Feke married, settled in Newport, and began painting portraits of the ministers of that area. In 1746 he went to Philadelphia, where his career enlarged, and he painted many socially prominent Philadelphians, including Benjamin Franklin. In 1748 he went to Boston, where he produced more than twenty portraits, considered his best work. Among them are the Bowdoin family portraits. In 1749 he returned to Philadelphia. Feke disappeared from history in 1751, after a short but important career in which he produced some of the most beautiful pictures of the 18th century.

After Smibert's death and the disappearance of Feke in 1751, a new period of American painting began. At first, American artists followed the style of Feke. Both John Greenwood and Joseph Badger of Boston, who painted as early as the mid-1740's, imitated Feke in their works after 1749. John Hesselius, the son of Gustavus Hesselius, copied many of Feke's works and may have been his student. In time these artists influenced Copley and Charles Willson Peale, who were the most important artists in America in the second half of the century. For this reason Feke may be considered the founder of the American school. At the same time a number of English artists came to America, and colonial patrons even appear to have preferred them for a period of time. The most prominent were John Wollaston and Joseph Blackburn. Wollaston came from London in 1749 to New York City. He painted in Pennsylvania, Maryland, Virginia, and South Carolina. Blackburn arrived in 1754 and painted in Rhode Island, Massachusetts, and New Hampshire. Other European painters who painted in the colonies were Lorenz Kilburn in New York; Jeremiah Theüs in Charleston, S.C.; William Williams in Philadelphia; and Cosmo Alexander in Newport.

West and Copley, the two most famous American painters of the 18th century, began painting in this period. West was born in Swarthmore, Pa., in 1738, and painted as early as 1747. His first work was a

186

landscape on a wood panel for the Pennsylvania Hospital. He progressed under the sponsorship of William Henry of Lancaster, Pa., and his style showed the influence of Feke and John Hesselius. By 1759 he could paint well, and such portraits as that of Thomas Mifflin reveal the influence of Wollaston, who worked in Philadelphia in 1758. The next year a group of Philadelphians, recognizing West's talents, pooled some resources to send him to England. They hoped he would return to practice and improve art in the colonies. Although he did not intend it, he remained in England for the rest of his life. In London he became a leading painter and the second president of the Royal Academy of Art. West was a pioneer of all the newest European styles—neoclassicism, history painting, and romanticism. His *Death on the Pale Horse* (1817) anticipated by many years the work of the French romantic painters Jean Géricault and Ferdinand Delacroix.

Although Copley also eventually went to England, enjoyed fame there, and became West's chief rival for the presidency of the Royal Academy, he had stayed in America longer and developed colonial art to its zenith. Copley was born on July 3, 1738, probably in Boston. His father died shortly thereafter, and his mother struggled for a living selling tobacco on Boston's Long Wharf. In 1748 she married Pelham. This was a fortunate circumstance for American art, since the young Copley was introduced to printmaking and met such painters as Greenwood through his stepfather. He augmented his early training by copying European prints and studying the work of Blackburn, who came to Boston in 1754. Copley's work until 1765 followed the society portrait format of Feke and Blackburn, but Copley's ability to render objects with intense verisimilitude slowly emerged, culminating in the famous *Boy With a Squirrel,* which Copley sent to the 1766 Royal Academy show in London. Sir Joshua Reynolds, the leading British painter of the time and president of the Royal Academy, and West both praised it with some minor reservations. During the next ten years Copley incorporated the realism of this work into his society commissions and became increasingly successful, but an ambition to go to England, sparked by the success of the *Boy With a Squirrel,* grew. By 1774 the gathering clouds of the American Revolution cut into his portrait business, and he decided to travel to Europe. Copley apparently intended to stay only long enough to improve his painting, but, like West, he never returned.

After Copley's departure the most important painter in the colonies was Peale, one of West's first pupils. Peale, who had briefly studied with John Hesselius in Annapolis, Md., and visited Copley in Boston, was sent to England in 1765 by a group of Philadelphians, as West had been earlier, to learn painting. In London he studied with West while the latter was pursuing his neoclassical style. Peale's first works, portraits of William Pitt and John Beale Boardly, were influenced by the neoclassical style, but he soon formulated his own style based on aspects of Hogarth and Reynolds. Peale's work often revealed a great interest in nature, and actual landscapes appear in the background of his portraits. Later in his career, in 1802, he founded a museum that encompassed both painting and natural history; he specialized in painting portraits of historical figures and habitat groups for his museum. Some of his best pictures were autobiographical scenes of his museum and his scientific expeditions, painted toward the end of his life.

Peale was one in a long line of artists who started painting in America as amateurs, traveled to London to study with West, and returned to paint in America. Two, John Trumbull and Ralph Earl, were from Connecticut. Trumbull, the son of the governor of Connecticut and aide-de-camp to George Washington, first studied painting at Harvard by copying Copley portraits there. He always had a more intellectual approach to art and became interested in history painting at the suggestion of Thomas Jefferson. Earl was more common; in fact, after learning high-style English portrait techniques under West, he returned to Connecticut and deliberately changed to a style akin to folk painting, which emphasized pattern and stylized line. Curiously, both Earl and Trumbull acquired a great interest in landscape and went beyond the academic tradition, which used idealized formulas based on the work of Claude Lorrain, to paint actual places.

Gilbert Stuart was the best and most influential pupil of West. He began painting in Newport about 1770. After an abortive apprenticeship with Alexander, he went to London in 1775. He returned in 1793 and painted great numbers of new federal leaders, the most famous of his portraits being those of Washington. During his career he worked in New York, Philadelphia, Washington, D.C., and Boston, and his style influenced nearly all portrait painters in America for many years.

These products of West's school still competed with continental and English artists painting in America—Pierre Charles L'Enfant and Charles

PAINTING

Fevret de Saint-Mémin came from France, Christian Gullagher came from Denmark, and Robert Edge Pine and Edward Savage from England. The latter Englishmen specialized in pictures of Washington and the events of the Revolution. Francis Guy, John Shaw, and William R. Birch settled in Philadelphia in the 1790's. These painters brought new interests in genre, landscape, and marine painting, reflecting the interests of Trumbull, Earl, and Peale, who were also exploring these subjects. This laid the foundation for painting in the 19th century, which developed the genre, landscape, and marine themes.

R. PETER MOOZ

Romantic Painting. Although the 19th century saw the fullest expression of romanticism, the origins of that movement lie in the 18th century. For all its preoccupation with classicism, the 18th century provided the foundation for attitudes in art that would eventually turn from formalist concepts of rational order to expressions of intuitive impulse. In literature George Gordon, Lord Byron, defined the new order as the "expression of excited passion." And in art, even as Greek and Roman antiquities were being held up as models of excellence by the European academies, Edmund Burke was promulgating his *Philosophical Enquiry Into the Origin of Our Ideas of the Sublime and the Beautiful* (1756), a theory of aesthetics that is at the center of the romantic tradition. Burke argued that the true expression of art is to be found in the pleasurable or terrifying emotions that certain objects evoke and rejected the classical notion that beauty resided in the object itself. Artists began turning away from the works of man; nature, especially in its wilder aspects, allowed painters to explore the emotions, using landscape painting as a vehicle for expression. Narrative painting also assumed a romantic character as painters of historical, religious, and genre subjects gave greater emphasis to the drama of the setting.

One of the earliest precursors of the romantic style in America was William Williams, an English adventurer-artist who worked in Philadelphia from 1747 until the outbreak of the Revolution. Many of his conversation-piece portraits, such as *Gentleman and Wife* (1775), contain moody, theatrical backgrounds suggesting dramatic action. Williams' only recognized pupil, West, who became the foremost painter in Britain, was a continuing influence on many young Americans who came to him for instruction. West at first joined the neoclassicists at the Royal Academy and then gradually turned to romantic concepts, as in his *Saul and the Witch of Endor* (1777). His career culminated in *Death on the Pale Horse,* a work of gigantic size and programmatic scope. West's fully developed study for this painting, completed in 1802, was the sensation of the Paris Salon of that year, and its impact on French art may be conjectured in the emergence of romantic painting in France under Delacroix and Géricault.

West's principal American disciples, Copley, Trumbull, and Washington Allston, each turned to historical narrative painting in the romantic mode. Copley's *Watson and the Shark* (1778), painted in London, reveals West's influence in the direction of forceful romantic realism. Trumbull's most successful efforts were achieved in history painting, principally a series of four subjects commemorating pivotal events in the Revolution. Of particular interest is the preparatory study for *Battle of Bunker's Hill* (1786) with its turbulent action. Of the three, Allston was most thoroughly influenced by literary values. His career culminated unsuccessfully in the monumental, never-completed *Belshazzar's Feast,* begun in 1817, which may be considered the terminal effort of the school of West. Only sporadically thereafter did any American artist attempt to achieve a canvas of similar size and programmatic scope. Rembrandt Peale was momentarily swept up in the fervor of romantic literature; his immense and lugubrious *The Court of Death* (1820) stands as an isolated effort in a career otherwise given over entirely to portraiture. At midcentury the influence of the Düsseldorf Academy briefly returned American art to projects equally ambitious. The central work of this school and period was created by Emanuel Leutze, whose *Washington Crossing the Delaware* (1851) marks the turning point from romanticism to sentimentality in the idiom of history painting.

Portraiture, long the staple product of the American artist, also turned from the neoclassical mode of the federal period to romanticism. Allston's principal pupil, Samuel F. B. Morse, a founder of the National Academy of Design before turning to scientific pursuits, was a prime mover in the establishment of the romantic poetry of mood in American painting. The portrait of his daughter, *The Muse: Susan Walker Morse* (ca. 1835–37), forcefully conveys the emotionalism of the romantic point of view within the context of a portrait. The most prolific portrait painter of the period was Thomas Sully, a Philadelphia artist who had studied in London under the celebrated English romanticist Sir Thomas Lawrence. His large works, charged with dramatic chiaroscuro, such as

188

the portrait of Thomas Handasyd Perkins (1832), earned him preeminence in the field.

Landscape painting came into prominence in America during the second quarter of the 19th century with a group of New York artists who formed what is loosely known as the Hudson River school, although there was never any formal association as such. Two of its senior members, Thomas Doughty and Asher B. Durand, came to painting after following careers in other fields and were largely self-taught. Doughty's intensely somber and frequently imaginary landscapes, such as In Nature's Wonderland (1835), epitomize a kind of rustic romanticism. Durand's work, although much more sophisticated, offers further example of the school's gentle lyricism and instantiates the bond that existed between artists and writers of the period. His Kindred Spirits (1849), for example, celebrates the close bond of friendship between the painter Thomas Cole and the poet William Cullen Bryant, whose figures are central to the composition of this Catskill Mountain landscape painting. The acknowledged leader of the school, Cole, idealized the Hudson River valley landscape and offered interpretations of nature in his paintings that transcend mere description of visual phenomena. While The Pic-Nic (1846) offers a glowing, autumnal scene in the Catskill Mountains, the picture is covertly a digression on the romantic notion of the harmony of man and nature. Similarly, his ambitious allegorical fantasies, such as the four-part serial composition The Voyage of Life (1842) and the five-part work The Course of Empire (1836), reflect romanticism's preoccupation with the transitoriness of life. Cole's only student, Frederick E. Church, carried landscape painting into a new realm of romantic interpretation of nature, in vast panoramic views of often exotic content, as in Rainy Season in the Tropics (1866). Church was part of a second generation of painters after Cole who developed a new style of painting called luminism. This approach combined a meticulous study of nature with an extremely delicate treatment of atmospheric color; it affected to minimize as much as possible the presence of the artist in the creation of the work of art. Along with Church, the notable practitioners of luminism were Fitz Hugh Lane, who was a marine painter, and Martin J. Heade, John F. Kensett, and Sanford R. Gifford, who were landscape painters.

The romantic tradition was strong also in the work of American genre painters, coming to its fullest expression in the mid-19th century. The intuitive aspects of romanticism permitted a full range of talents to flourish. Romantic literature of the period

often furnished the artist with subject matter. The writings of Washington Irving and James Fenimore Cooper gave impetus to the wild visions of John Quidor and Charles Deas. Quidor, although working in a quasi-primitive style, created an authentic mood of Gothic horror in The Money Diggers (1832). Scenes of everyday life, properly in the genre idiom, were usually portrayed with benign humor. William Sidney Mount devoted his entire career to depicting life in rural Long Island. His paintings—for example, Eel Spearing at Setauket (1845)—are rendered with extreme purity of color and drawing, imbuing his countryfolk with a kind of gentle nobility. The western frontier had its own exponent of romantic realism, George C. Bingham. Bingham's frontiersmen—trappers, river men, politicians—are portrayed with evident good humor, as in The County Election (1851–52), and he frequently turned to history for thematic material. His grandly theatrical Daniel Boone Escorting a Band of Pioneers (ca. 1851) offers a highly romanticized version of the crossing at the Cumberland Gap. Genre and history were also mingled in the work of David G. Blythe, whose slightly primitive style often aimed at political satire, as in The Lawyer's Dream (ca. 1858–60). Explorer-artists working in the western Plains added to the store of romantic myth surrounding the American Indian. George Catlin and Alfred Jacob Miller created an extremely large body of work concerning the life of the Plains Indians, whom they idealized in styles ranging from romantic realism to fantasy. Seth Eastman was one of the few explorer-artists who remained consistently objective in his paintings; yet, even with Eastman, the Rousseauean notion of the "noble savage" lingers on, as in Lacrosse Playing Among the Sioux Indians (1857).

By the third quarter of the 19th century enough Americans had emerged as painters of fantasy to indicate that this was an important aspect of American romantic tradition. More often than not, these artists were personally detached from the mainstream of society and lived lives of dreamers and recluses. The enigmatic William Rimmer, a Boston painter, was beset by strange inner fears that he externalized in pictures of dreamlike images, on the order of Flight and Pursuit (1872). The heavily worked paintings of Albert P. Ryder are intensely subjective images taken from literature, as in The Flying Dutchman (before 1890), and deeply personal rumination; yet they possess an enamellike beauty of unusual order. Ralph A. Blakelock concentrated almost exclusively on landscape subjects of a darkly brooding intensity; his

Vision of Life (ca. 1895) is a summation of the romantic impulse to celebrate mood over explicit content. One of the few painters of fantasy who can be credited with having an academic orientation was Elihu Vedder. While his deliberate choice of this field over landscape painting, for which he was also highly qualified, led to a certain stiffness and artificiality, Vedder created many pictures of genuine fantasy. His *Questioner and the Sphinx* (1863) possesses an authentic dreamlike ambiguity.

Inevitably, the realist painters of the late 19th century, such as Winslow Homer and Thomas Eakins, can be credited with having created certain paintings that partake of the romantic impulse. Homer's *The Gulf Stream* (1899) and Eakins' *The Pathetic Song* (1881) are singular examples of the lingering effect of romanticism. In such pictures the poetry of mood is present in large measure; yet the works of the realists and the later impressionists do not aim at generating emotional response from the viewer, and without that necessary ingredient, true romantic painting ceased to occupy a central place in American art.

DONELSON F. HOOPES

Early Naturalism. The concept of naturalism in American painting of the 19th century is not so easy to isolate as the neoclassicism and overt romanticism that preceded it, nor is there an absolute continuity from one period to the next. As early as the second decade of the century both Charles Willson Peale and his younger brother James were painting landscapes, portraits, and still lifes that were remarkably free of both sentiment and allegory. The elder Peale's views of his farm, Belfield, and his portraits of Andrew Jackson, his brother, and his third wife, and the younger Peale's still-life paintings were the first endeavors in realistic, yet unidealized, painting and the beginning of a tradition that was to last for half a century.

The portraits of Chester Harding, with their careful and unpretentious craftsmanship, and many of those by Morse provided uncompromising likenesses without the brilliant surfaces and colorism of the Stuart-Sully tradition and often without their charm. Morse's *Old House of Representatives* (1821–22) and his *View From Apple Hill* (1828–29), despite the idealization of the figures in the latter, are convincing representations of forms in space, and these less pretentious works place him among the pioneers of naturalism. In many of his later landscapes and portraits, he must be identified with romanticism.

Both Doughty and Durand were trained as engravers, and their technical background and interest in drawing from nature kept them closer to naturalism than such romantic landscapists as Cole. Doughty's later work was influenced by Dutch 17th-century landscape painting and became more specific in locale and confined to a narrower color range. Durand, even when presenting allegory, as in the famous *Kindred Spirits,* gives the feeling of specific observation, believable space, and sensitivity to the qualities of light. The last of these characteristics is also to be found in the work of such members of the next generation of landscapists as Jasper F. Cropsey and the pre–Civil War work of George Inness. Both Cropsey and Inness were somewhat freer and had a greater feeling for color than their predecessors, but they shared a dedication to direct observation and realism.

Another category of naturalist endeavor was the painting of the flora and fauna of the United States as practiced first by Alexander Wilson and later by the better-known John James Audubon. While the artists may have been motivated by impulses similar to those of the painters of the Indian and the western frontier, the need for careful delineation of form and accuracy of color, combined with Audubon's lively line, produced watercolors of unprecedented vitality and fidelity to nature. His hundreds of bird paintings and the animal works done with the help of his sons clearly defined both the method and the style for the several naturalist painters who succeeded Audubon.

Genre painting had existed in the United States since the early 1820's, but it was usually derived from European models and included foreign subjects. From the 1830's through the 1850's American subjects made their appearance, and the direct observation of nature was integrated with the subjects. Such a point of view was first manifest in the paintings of rural Long Island in the 1830's by Mount. Mount expressed his desire to study the natural object and to portray it without reference to allegory, sentiment, or moral commentary. His *Bargaining for a Horse* (1835), *Eel Spearing at Setauket* (1845), and *The Power of Music* (1847) are examples of his well-conceived figures in a natural atmosphere. He produced his simple, yet original, compositions for thirty years and influenced numerous other painters to follow his lead, although the majority of them were too easily led into sentimentality and rhetorical exaggeration.

The genre paintings of Bingham are much more anecdotal than the majority of Mount's, and many of his larger canvases—*The Verdict of the People* (1854–55) and others—are crowded and contrived in comparison to those of his slightly older contemporary. Nevertheless, Bingham's handling of his picturesque subjects and the treatment of both form and light place him squarely in the naturalist tradition. In *Fur Traders Descending the Missouri* (ca. 1845), for example, the precise observation of the texture of garments, water, foliage, and other objects is blended with a presentation of atmospheric effects that are matched only by the best work of Mount. The works of these genre painters are definitely part of the mainstream of naturalism and set the stage for the next generation of American realists, including Eakins and Homer.

DAVID M. SOKOL

American Renaissance. The decades from 1880 to 1930 are generally called the American Renaissance because all the arts flourished as never before or since in America. One of these arts was mural decoration. The first great example of mural decoration in America is that of Constantino Brumidi in the national Capitol. He worked at about the time of the Civil War but had no followers. The next, executed in the late 1870's, were William Morris Hunt's two murals done for the New York State capitol in Albany, neither of which survives, and John La Farge's decoration of the interior of Boston's Trinity Church. Shortly afterward several Vanderbilt mansions in New York City boasted the work of Pierre Victor Galland and Paul J. A. Baudry.

Nothing occurred on a grand scale until 1893, with the opening of the World's Columbian Exposition in Chicago. Francis D. Millet, an artist who was to spend much of his working life in England, was put in charge of the mural work at the fair, and he invited Charles Yardley Turner, Kenyon Cox, Edward Emerson Simmons, William de Leftwich Dodge, Edwin Howland Blashfield, and others to Chicago. What was extraordinary was that these men, nearly all of them trained as easel painters in Paris, were launched on careers of mural painting. One of the first big commissions that followed was for inside the Library of Congress, where Blashfield, Cox, Elihu Vedder, John W. Alexander, and many others did murals. Mural decoration found its way into hotels, theaters, courthouses, schools, private houses, churches, libraries, and state capitols. It is impossible not to be struck by the quantity of the work and the enthusiasm of the artists. These men felt that they were fulfilling the noblest aim of their art, the decoration of interiors, especially the interiors of public buildings. Although much has gone, some of it has survived, notably in state capitols.

After 1920 a later generation of mural decorators faced a shrinking market. Still, there were enough commissions to keep the industry alive. Allyn Cox, Kenyon Cox's son, painted the murals in the William A. Clark Library in Los Angeles. One of the more ambitious schemes was that of Ezra Winter for the Great Hall of the Cunard Building in New York City. Then mural decoration in the traditional sense vanished with the panic of 1929 and the triumph of modern art.

While mural painting flourished for the first time in America, American easel painting became caught up in current European fashion. In the latter half of the 19th century painting in the Western world turned to a preoccupation with nature in the form of realism and the replacement of the ancient technique of transparent glazes with the use of opaque pigment, called direct painting. The artist painted for himself, not on commission, except for portraits. What had been essentially an art of decoration, creating beauty to embellish a room, became a form of self-expression. The center of the change was Paris.

Although a few American painters went to Antwerp, Belgium, and Düsseldorf and Munich in Germany, most found their way to Paris. Toward the end of the 1870's the first flood of French-trained men returned. They announced their presence in 1877 by founding the Society of American Artists in New York City to promote naturalism and direct painting. Not long afterward, they won over the National Academy of Design, the nation's chief artistic organization at the time. Eakins, somewhat older than most of the dominant group of the 1870's, is the outstanding example of the artist interpreting nature realistically on the French model.

So much were Americans part of the Paris scene at the time that a good number of them remained abroad, finding it just as easy to find a market for their work in the French capital as in New York or Boston, if not easier. The most successful of them was John Singer Sargent, who after an initial success in Paris made London his headquarters, achieving international prominence. Another was James McNeil Whistler.

The tragedy of the American easel painters—after 1880 the number of them increased at a staggering rate—was that in accepting the new interpretation of nature and the use of opaque paint they led the American collector to French artists who were more skilled than they. Well-to-do Americans bought the work of the 19th-century Frenchmen and then, after 1900, the work of the old masters. American easel painters were left behind as fortunes were spent on the work of 16th-century Italians, 17th-century Dutchmen, and 18th-century Frenchmen and Englishmen.

America succumbed to every artistic fashion coming from Europe. After 1890, influenced by Mary Cassatt, an American impressionist living in France, Americans bought French impressionists—that is, artists who painted impressions of nature rather than doing realistic studies. An American impressionist school developed and counted, besides Cassatt, Childe Hassam, J. Alden Weir, and John H. Twachtman.

A few painters, old and young, worked independently of European fashion and along traditional lines. Among the older artists were the landscapists Homer, William Trost Richards, and Thomas Moran. Vedder looked to the Italian Renaissance, as did the younger George de Forest Brush. Also, the market for illustration expanded in the 1890's. Frederic Remington, Howard Pyle, and Maxfield Parrish were among the better known who profited by the coming of the glossy magazine.

About 1910 yet another artistic fashion came out of Europe—modern art, reflecting the total rejection of the traditional outlook. Once again foreign artists, rather than Americans, were the chief beneficiaries of American patronage. The 1920's saw the world of easel painting moving slowly into chaos, with the art museum taking over from such artists' organizations as the National Academy of Design and the Pennsylvania Academy of Art. In the next decade even impressionism bowed out before modern art.

HENRY HOPE REED

20th Century. The course of 20th-century American painting can be seen as a series of revolutions against previous styles and approaches. Opposing themselves to the prevailing esotericisms of the late 19th century—the strange visions of Ryder, the near abstractions of Whistler, the remote, moody late landscapes of George Inness—a group of artists concentrated on the everyday activities of ordinary lower- and middle-class New Yorkers. This so-called Ash Can school—which included John Sloan, Maurice B. Prendergast, and their spokesman, Robert Henri—brought forth a revolution in subject rather than in style during the first two decades of the century. During the second and third decades other painters were following the leads of European avant-gardists. From 1910 until about 1915 Stanton Macdonald-Wright and Morgan Russell, dubbing themselves synchromists, produced nonobjective and nearly nonobjective paint-

ings based on the emotive effects of colors. From about 1915 to 1930 Max Weber; John Marin; Joseph Stella; Stuart Davis, who favored bright metallic color and such modern-day motifs as gas pumps and telephone poles; and others fragmented and recombined parts of city scenes after the manner of European cubists. During the 1920's Charles Sheeler, Georgia O'Keeffe, and Charles Demuth simplified sometimes to a geometrical core objects pushed starkly up to the frontal plane—a style called precisionism from the dry, linear handling.

The late 1920's and 1930's brought a reaction against the European-based modernism of the 1920's as a concurrent spirit of isolationism took hold. The regionalists Grant Wood, Thomas Hart Benton, and James Steuart Curry focused on what they saw as authentically American types—the rural people of the southern, western, and midwestern parts of the country. The theme of the city continued with Edward Hopper, who visualized the city not as a place of frequent companionship, as had the Ash Can school, but as one of brooding loneliness; and Charles Burchfield maintained the visionary approach of Ryder in his pictures of decaying Victorian houses. Moved in part by the economic hardships brought on by the Great Depression, Ben Shahn, William Gropper, and the German immigrant George Grosz used their posterlike art as a means of social protest condemning legislative favoritism, judicial injustice, and the greed of the rich. Affected by neither modernism nor social protest was the school of illustrators centered at Chadds Ford, Pa., from the early part of the century, which included N. C. Wycth, father of the more famous Andrew Wyeth, and Maxfield Parrish.

By the mid-1940's a new wave of modernism, abstract expressionism, had asserted itself in opposition to the naturalism of the 1930's. The great size and forceful impact of the canvases reflected America's preeminence politically and economically at the end of World War II. The painters came from far and wide—Arshile Gorky from Armenia, Willem de Kooning from Holland, Mark Rothko from Russia, Jackson Pollock from Wyoming—to congregate in New York, whose vastness and dynamism contributed to the violence and boldness that permeated the paintings. Then, too, the presence in New York of such major modernist European émigrés as Piet Mondrian and Salvador Dali encouraged these painters. The painter Hans Hofmann, born in Germany in 1880, was an inspiration for the group in the 1940's, as well as a major theoretician of nonobjective painting. The abstract expressionists worked their way through the cubism of Pablo Picasso and the surrealism of Joan Miró to arrive at a variety of nonobjective approaches, which seemed underived and placed a premium value on spontaneity of execution. They insisted that their work transcended decoration and, as equivalents of the inner state of consciousness, would suggest to the observer coded expressions of his own experience. With abstract expressionism New York surpassed the European capitals as the international center of avant-garde art.

Unassociated with abstract expressionism during the 1940's and 1950's were the West Coast painter Mark Tobey, whose gossamer-thin, seemingly endless webs of lines were related to the unity preached by his Baha'i faith, and Milton C. Avery, whose flattened landscapes and figures were presented with a childlike directness.

By 1960 abstract expressionism had run its course as a vital avant-garde direction. By the mid-1950's Jasper Johns was painting a series of American flags and other recognizable objects, and Robert Rauschenberg was combining silk-screened images with splatters of paint, after the manner of the abstract expressionists. The pop artists of the early and mid-1960's—Andy Warhol, Roy Lichtenstein, and James Rosenquist—did away completely with the gestural, improvisational approach of the abstract expressionists. They worked in the glossy, impersonal format of the subjects to which they turned—items and images commonly seen in supermarkets and on billboards. Some of Lichtenstein's and Warhol's large paintings were nearly duplications of comic-strip frames and labels on soup cans, respectively. In keeping with the anonymity prescribed by the pop artists, Philip Pearlstein presented his figures matter-of-factly and blocklike, frequently cut by the frame with the dry unconcern often accorded still-life objects. In the late 1960's photorealism was in vogue among such painters as Richard Estes, who sought to simulate in his oils the high finish of photographs turned out more or less mechanically through chemical processes.

The nonobjective painters of the 1960's, the post painterly abstractionists, in contrast to the abstract expressionists before them, avoided all marks of the manipulation of the paint, as well as the notion of forms existing in some sort of spatial receptacle. Canvases were often left unprimed so that the acrylic paint could seep into the fabric and the sensation of depth thus be avoided. Jules Olitski sprayed his paint onto the canvas in tiny droplets to produce something of the look of the atmosphere, and Morris Louis inclined his canvas to let his thinned-out paint flow into the vague shapes of veils and other configurations. In their paintings the color sensation itself matters; the sorts of psychic innuendoes in which abstract expressionism abounded are absent. In the paintings of the hard-edge post painterly abstractionists, the surfaces are smooth and enamellike, and the color areas are precisely demarcated. Ellsworth Kelly showed a preference for flaring curves; there is the suggestion of the extension of his painted shapes beyond the painted surface. Frank Stella introduced the nonrectilinear canvas, whose shape determined the configurations of the painted surface. A branch of the hard-edge painters, the op (optical) artists, including Richard Anuskiewicz and Victor Vasarely, schooling themselves in color theory and perception, played with a variety of optical illusions to induce such aftereffects in the observer as the perception of negative colors and of movement.

ABRAHAM A. DAVIDSON

[Virgil Barker, *American Painting;* John I. H. Baur, *Revolution and Tradition in Modern American Art;* Waldron P. Belknap, Jr., *American Colonial Painting: Materials for a History;* Mary Black and Jean Lipman, *American Folk Painting;* Wolfgang Born, *American Landscape Painting;* Alan Burroughs, *Limners and Likenesses;* Wayne Craven, Wendy Shadwell, and Robert Strunsky, *Catalogue of American Portraits in the New-York Historical Society;* Louisa Dresser and Alan Burroughs, *XVIIth Century Painting in New England;* James Thomas Flexner, *American Painting: First Flowers of Our Wilderness, American Painting: The Light of Distant Skies, Nineteenth Century American Painting,* and *That Wilder Image: The Native School From Thomas Cole to Winslow Homer;* Alfred V. Frankenstein, *After the Hunt: William Harnett and Other Still Life Painters, 1879–1900;* Wendell D. Garrett and others, *Arts in America: The Nineteenth Century;* Henry Geldzahler, *American Painting in the Twentieth Century;* William H. Gerdts and Russell Burke, *American Still-Life Painting;* Lloyd Goodrich and John I. H. Baur, *American Art in Our Century;* George C. Groce and David H. Wallace, eds., *Dictionary of Artists in America, 1564–1860;* Neil Harris, *The Artist in American Society: The Formative Years, 1790–1860;* John K. Howat, *The Hudson River and Its Painters;* Oliver W. Larkin, *Art and Life in America;* Jean Lipman and Alice Winchester, *The Flowering of American Folk Art, 1776–1876;* Nina F. Little, *American Decorative Wall Paintings, 1700–1850;* Russell Lynes, *The Art-Makers of Nineteenth Century America;* John W. McCoubrey, *American Tradition in Painting;* Barbara Novak, *American Painting of the Nineteenth Century: Realism, Idealism, and the American Experience;* Jules D. Prown, *American Painting: From Its Beginnings to the Armory Show;* Edgar P. Richardson, *Painting in America: From 1502 to the Present;* Barbara Rose, *American Painting: The 20th Century;* Hermann Warner Williams, Jr., *Mirror to the American Past, A Survey of American Genre Painting:*

1750–1900; John Wilmerding, *History of American Marine Painting;* Louis B. Wright and others, *Arts in America: Colonial Period.*]

PAIRING, a practice whereby two members of Congress of opposing parties who plan to be absent agree that, during a specified period, they will refrain from voting in person, but will permit their names to be recorded on opposite sides of each question, thereby not affecting the vote. It was first used in the House of Representatives as early as 1824 and was first openly avowed in 1840, but pairing was not officially recognized in the House rules until 1880. Pairing is also permitted in the Senate, and is customary, though not universal, in state legislatures.

[R. Luce, *Legislative Procedure;* D. Tacheron and M. Udall, *The Job of the Congressman.*]

P. ORMAN RAY

PAIUTE. The western Great Basin of the United States, an arid desert with basin-range topography, spreads east of the Sierra Nevada from southeastern Oregon through southern California, across Nevada and northern Arizona, and well into Utah. This topographically defined area was the aboriginal homeland of the many localized bands of Paiute, of whom there were an estimated 7,500 in 1845. The environment and the mode of subsistence of these peoples precluded any extensive tribal development. Dependent on the gathering of wild seeds and fruits, such as pine nuts and juniper berries, and, indeed, on all wild foods that the area offered, the local groupings were small; they wandered in areas familiar to them and met at times with neighboring groups for social activities and marriage arrangements. Theirs were the essentially impoverished cultures of the West, and they were contemptuously dismissed by the first settlers and travelers as "Diggers." Although it is true that the cultural inventory of these peoples was not large, it is worth noting that they achieved a wholly adequate mode of life in the face of highly adverse conditions of territory and climate.

Lacking tribes as such, the Paiute are generally classified on the basis of language. Two main languages appear in the area, both branches of Shoshonean, a subdivision of the major Uto-Aztecan phylum. A typical Basin adaptation was achieved especially by the southern Paiute. The northern Paiute were less well defined and spread as a linguistic unit from southeastern Oregon to southeastern California. They were variously identified as Paiute, Mono-Paviotso, and Paviotso and show a gradual fading into the Californian focus. The northern Paiute were contacted late by Europeans, being first encountered in 1825 by the trader and explorer Jedediah Smith. The southern Paiute, on the other hand, were described by the Spanish priest Silvestre Vélez de Escalante in 1776. The advent of miners and prospectors and the introduction of livestock and the horse combined to break down the native culture patterns. It was a northern Paiute, Wovoka, who in 1889 originated the second Ghost Dance movement, an anguished attempt at revival of a dying cultural system.

[Robert H. Lowie, *Notes on Shoshonean Ethnography;* Julian H. Steward, *Basin-Plateau Aboriginal Socio-political Groups.*]

ROBERT F. SPENCER

PALATINE JURISDICTIONS. The palatine lords of the medieval period of European history enjoyed within their domains virtually regal authority and unusual immunities from royal interference. Of diverse origins, these palatine jurisdictions represented, among other things, a feudal solution for the problem of governing remote areas, as is suggested by the northern and western locations of the three English palatinates of Durham, Cheshire, and Lancashire.

In America the bishopric of Durham is of greatest importance. Although, in substance, little of the independence of palatine jurisdictions remained by the 17th century, English colonizers undertook to transplant in America the system it represented. The obvious risks assumed by promoters of colonization led to a demand for exceptional rights and powers in controlling their settlements. Where the grant was to a member of the landed classes there was a disposition to follow customary forms and define these powers in terms of feudal prerogatives. Thus, proprietary projects frequently looked to the enjoyed jurisdictional rights similar to those of palatine lords. Several grants (notably Maryland in 1632 and Carolina in 1663) even stipulated that the grantees should enjoy an authority equal to that of the bishop of Durham "at any time" theretofore. Such efforts, largely abortive but extending well into the 18th century, to transfer to America outworn feudal usages, provide a key to many troublesome chapters of colonial history.

[G. G. Lapsley, *The County Palatine of Durham;* C. M. Andrews, *The Colonial Period of American History,* vols. II, III.]

WESLEY FRANK CRAVEN

PALATINES were German Protestants from the Rhenish or Lower Palatinate, who in 1708–09, because of devastation by war, religious persecution, famine, or the enticing advertisements circulated by William Penn and other colonial proprietors, made their way to England to petition for assistance from Queen Anne to settle in America. Completely dependent on the English government for subsistence, they soon became a pressing problem. In July 1709 an abortive attempt was made to settle 794 families in Ireland, and in August of that same year a group of 600 were sent to North Carolina. By far the greater part of the refugees, however, were settled in the Hudson Valley, in New York, with the expectation that they would manufacture naval stores, an occupation in which they were totally inexperienced. With the failure of this project many left for Pennsylvania or New Jersey; and 150 families, led by Conrad Weiser, went to Schoharie, N.Y. On his arrival in 1720, Gov. William Burnet of New York was ordered to move the Palatines to the frontier, and a number of families were settled on the Mohawk near Ilion, in Herkimer County, formerly known as German Flats.

[Walter Knittle, *Early 18th Century Palatine Emigration.*]

A. C. FLICK

PALEONTOLOGY, the study of fossil remains, may have begun in the New World with the discovery of elongate shells of an extinct squid that had a special significance for some medicine men of High Plains Indian tribes. In the 1700's giant fossil teeth led the European settlers to speculate on the former presence in America of monstrous beasts. Because of Thomas Jefferson's paleontological interests, the White House was the scene of one of the first scientific exhibitions of fossils. Jefferson believed no animal to be extinct and thought that the large claws, for example, that he himself had found in Virginia caves indicated the presence of lions in the interior of America. (The claws are now associated with the extinct giant ground sloth.)

During the first quarter of the 19th century, the scientific study of fossils was placed on a firm geologic base by the concepts of stratigraphic succession and correlation. It was realized that different rocks are of different relative ages because they are deposited in successive layers. Each layer contains different kinds of fossils; and by studying the fossils from rocks in one area, it is possible to compare them to fossils of another area and thereby to determine their geologic history. This approach, which originated in Europe, has obvious applicability in such practical fields as mining. Some of the state geological surveys that were established during the period 1820–50 included

paleontology among their published results, although many state legislators did not share the paleontologists' interest in fossil plants and animals and a number of scientific administrators were dismissed for spending appropriated money to support this supposedly esoteric science.

The plan for a geological survey of New York State included the study of fossils as an integral part. Timothy Conrad was appointed paleontologist of the survey in 1837 and did pioneer work in establishing that the rocks within the state are from the Silurian and Devonian ages; he worked out their general sequence and correlated them with rocks and fossils that had recently been described in England. He later did equally fundamental studies on the younger invertebrates in the coastal plain of the eastern and southern states and was among the first to describe fossils from the Pacific northwest.

Conrad was succeeded as state paleontologist in 1843 by James Hall. Hall described the fossils of New York, and his volumes on paleontology have become classics. He was the second most prolific producer of fossil descriptions, after his Bohemian contemporary Joachim Barrande. At one stage of his career, Hall was involved simultaneously with the geological surveys of three states. At another time he sold his own collection while pleading with the New York State legislature to buy other fossil collections for him to study. He made the fossils of New York among the best known in the world, and in 1878 he was elected president of the First International Geological Congress.

After the Civil War, paleontology became a central part of the state surveys. Generally scientists were contracted to describe the fossils of a state but were sometimes paid on a piecework basis. By the turn of the 20th century, the fossils and rock strata of a number of the older states were reasonably well known.

With the Charles Wilkes exploring expedition (1838–42), which employed James Dwight Dana as geologist-paleontologist, the federal government began to assume a role in investigations of natural history and natural resources. During the period 1840–60, a series of expeditions, mainly led by the U.S. Army, explored the western territories in order to determine the route for a western railroad. But these expeditions also added to the knowledge of fossils and provided support for struggling paleontologists.

As in many other fields, all study of fossils by federal institutions was virtually halted by the Civil War. After the war, four separate territorial surveys collected and described fossils. In 1879 these groups were combined in the U.S. Geological Survey. Although a few fossils had been described earlier in government documents, F. B. Meek deserves to be called the first federal (albeit nonsalaried) paleontologist. He began as Hall's assistant (1852), but after leaving Albany in 1858, he went to the Smithsonian Institution and made his living as a self-employed paleontologist. During his career, Meek worked on invertebrates of every major group from the Cambrian to the present. He was the first to work extensively on rocks of nonmarine origin and the first to assign a geologic age to many of the rock units in the western United States.

Meek was succeeded by C. A. White, who published in state and territorial surveys and later in the publications of the U.S. Geological Survey. By 1900 the number of federal paleontologists had increased to about 10, the most prominent of whom was C. D. Walcott. With scant formal training, Walcott made major contributions to the study of the Cambrian system and of trilobites (extinct crablike arthropods). He also did important work in Precambrian paleontology and studied some of the algae, among the most ancient of large marine plants. Walcott became the third director of the Geological Survey and subsequently fifth secretary of the Smithsonian Institution.

Because the field was so small, a single person produced much of the literature on a large group of fossils. E. O. Ulrich and George H. Girty, both strong-willed and prolific writers, dominated the study of Lower Paleozoic and Upper Paleozoic rocks, respectively, during the first three decades of the 20th century; T. W. Stanton studied fossils from somewhat younger rocks, and W. H. Dall worked on recent mollusks and allied, relatively young fossils. These federal invertebrate paleontologists largely shaped the science.

Although invertebrate paleontology has been emphasized here, there is a threefold split that characterizes the study of fossils. Vertebrate fossils have aroused the most public interest but have attracted relatively few workers. Invertebrate fossils have received more scientific investigation but less public attention; and fossil plants have attracted neither until recently, notwithstanding their clear importance. Plant studies may be divided into two arbitrary groups. The coal-bearing deposits of eastern North America incorporate impressive fossil floras. J. S. Newberry, trained as a physician, worked on the plants of Ohio (1869–74); but it is representative of the breadth of research of early paleontologists that he

is as well known for his work on Paleozoic invertebrates of the West and was also among the first in the United States to describe fossil fish. The leading paleobotanical specialist was Leo Lesquereux, a political refugee who had been active in Europe as a botanist. He described the fossil plants of Illinois, but the culmination of his efforts was the three-volume *Coal Flora of Pennsylvania* (1879–84). His paleobotanical work was refined and extended by David White of the U.S. Geological Survey. Emphasis in this field has shifted to the study of "coal balls," in which plant fragments are preserved without being compressed.

The younger, nonmarine beds of the western part of the United States also yielded a large number of plants, which again were first described by Lesquereux. Lester Ward and Frank Knowlton, both with the Geological Survey, later described these plants and found apparent differences in the age of the beds. Knowlton studied the plants, and Stanton the shells, from similar beds in Montana.

Bones are the fossils best known to the average person; and if there is one fossil particularly associated with North America, it is the large vertebrate. Just prior to the Civil War vast deposits of extinct mammal remains were found in the Badlands of South Dakota. These remains were described over a period of years by Joseph Leidy, a distinguished anatomist from Philadelphia. This work, completed in 1869, attracted the attention of O. C. Marsh and Edward D. Cope, whose rivalry in pursuit of the big bones soon made bitter enemies of these former friends. Leidy left paleontology because of their excesses. Both Marsh and Cope were wealthy, and each spent great sums collecting fossils in the West. With the construction of the transcontinental railway there was a scramble for bones of the large early mammals and the still older and larger dinosaurs. Marsh and Cope telegraphed descriptions from the field in order to obtain scientific priority and even posted armed guards to protect collecting localities. Their feuding, particularly virulent during the 1870's, eventually affected the Geological Survey and was a factor in forcing the resignation of J. W. Powell as the second director. Vertebrate paleontology has subsequently produced much excellent work and a number of outstanding scientists, but no more banner headlines.

The concept of evolution had essentially no impact on the field of paleontology in America. Louis Agassiz was a leading opponent of Charles Darwin, but after his initial opposition he tacitly accepted Darwinian evolution. A few invertebrate paleontologists attempted to find evolutionary principles in the history of certain fossil groups, especially cephalopods, gastropods, and trilobites; and Cope is remembered by the evolutionists for Cope's law—increase in size of animals through geologic time—but generally evolution was ignored. The pursuit of stratigraphic paleontology did not depend on a belief in organic evolution. The work of the 19th- and early 20th-century paleontologists was to date the sedimentary rocks of North America, and this they achieved. A handful of people wrote a staggering number of descriptions and developed to a fine art relative age dating by fossils.

For the most part, paleontologists were self-taught. Some learned by working under Hall at Albany and eventually escaped from his tyranny to do their own work. After the Civil War, a number of home-trained paleontologists came from the Cincinnati area, where fossils were so prolific that they were washed into the streets after every rain. Marsh was the first professor of paleontology in the United States, having been appointed in the 1870's to a chair at Yale, where he ran a "school"—a very hard school—for his preparators. But it was not until the 20th century that a few professors gave formal training in paleontology to a few graduate students.

Traditionally, paleobotanists have come from botany departments, and today a few such departments include a full-time paleobotanist. Vertebrate paleontologists studied in zoology departments, but the first formal training in the field came in the early 1900's, with teachers such as S. W. Williston at Kansas and Chicago and E. C. Case at Michigan. Training in invertebrate paleontology began earlier and was linked to the rise of geology departments. Several professors, S. Weller at Chicago, and especially C. Schuchert at Yale, trained an inordinate proportion of the next generation of paleontologists, before and after World War I.

After World War I a new field opened for paleontology—namely, the study of microfossils, which can be seen only with the aid of a hand lens. One-celled organisms that secrete a calcareous shell were known for many years and had been described as fossils. J. A. Cushman demonstrated that these forms change rapidly through time and can be used to date rocks. Because these small fossils could be recovered from the drill cuttings of oil wells, they found an obvious economic applicability. The years 1920–40 were the era of "the bug picker," and the efflorescence of oil discovery during that time was a direct result of this work.

The principles of subsurface paleontology developed by the micropaleontologists have been trans-ferred to other groups of still smaller organisms. During the period 1940–60, palynology, the study of spores and pollen, was recognized as a separate subdiscipline. With the development of more sophisticated optical techniques, remains of fossils may be found in the future in virtually every sedimentary rock. The new techniques have been used to push the record of life on earth back through time, and simple organisms that are more than 3 billion years old are now known.

Since World War II, there has been an explosive expansion of the field of paleontology, comparable to that in other fields of science. It is estimated that the number of paleontologists in the United States in the mid-1970's was about 2,000, probably a tenfold increase over the total number for the first 150 years. Although a slow growth in government employment of paleontologists has been compensated for by the continuing interest of oil companies, the 1970's could be characterized as the era of academic paleontology, for the majority of the profession were on college campuses.

Three separate trends characterize this phase of paleontology. First, there has been a major effort to systematize knowledge. The *Treatise on Invertebrate Paleontology,* edited by R. C. Moore, which was begun in 1953, is a multivolume work that draws upon international collaborators and has, through investigations undertaken for this study, revitalized all of systematics. Second, interest in former environments has risen steadily, so that one can be a paleoecologist, interested in a community of fossils rather than a systematist interested in a particular group. The foundation for this work was established by the massive *Treatise on Ecology and Paleoecology* (1957), edited by H. S. Ladd. Lastly, many paleontologists have become interested in evolution, and there is a continual exchange between them and biologists on the subject; no single unifying book or series exists, but hundreds of papers document this new outlook.

[C. L. Fenton and M. Fenton, *The Fossil Book;* G. P. Merrill, *The First One Hundred Years of American Geology.*]

ELLIS L. YOCHELSON

PALMER'S DISCOVERY OF ANTARCTICA. According to the logbook of the sloop *Hero,* a vessel of only 40 tons burden, Capt. Nathaniel Brown Palmer, a twenty-one-year-old American, discovered the mainland of Antarctica on Nov. 18, 1820, about eighty days before the reputed date of discovery by Capt. John Davis. Three important things are proved by the logbook and contemporary documents. First, the motive for the voyage was the gathering and sale of fur-seal skins and seal oil. Secondly, Palmer discovered Port Williams (Port Foster), the breached volcanic crater in Deception Island; he explored many parts of the South Shetland Islands, including Yankee Sound (McFarlane Strait) and Yankee Harbor (Hospital Cove), making creditable maps. Most important of all, the log demonstrates that Palmer was the first person to see and to visit any part of the Antarctic mainland.

Palmer made his initial landfall at 63°45′ south latitude and 60°10′ west longitude on that part of the mainland now known as Palmer Peninsula. It had been improperly called Graham Land, which, since Lincoln Ellsworth's air voyage in 1935, is known to be continental and not insular. R. T. Gould's theory that the English explorer Edward Bransfield may have anticipated Palmer in seeing Antarctica is not based upon any existing logbook. Bransfield discovered Trinity Island, but the third-hand record of his supposed momentary glimpse of a peak through fog, on Jan. 30, 1820, was not necessarily one on the Antarctic mainland but was perhaps an iceberg or one of the islands northeast of Palmer Peninsula. Jule Dumont d'Urville in 1842 and Otto Nordenskjöld in 1911 both concluded that Bransfield never saw Antarctica. Palmer's landfall, on the other hand, is not nebulous, but based upon specific records. He subsequently explored other parts of the Antarctic coast going as far as Marguerite Bay, and, jointly with George Powell, discovered the South Orkney Islands in December 1821.

[Edmund Fanning, *Voyages Round the World;* A. W. Greely, "American Discoverers of the Antarctic Continent," *National Geographic Magazine,* vol. 23; W. H. Hobbs, "The Discoveries of Antarctica Within the American Sector," *Transactions of the American Philosophical Society,* new series, vol. 31.]

LAWRENCE MARTIN

PALMETTO COCKADES, emblems adopted by the States' Rights party in South Carolina during the nullification controversy—a dispute in 1832 in which supporters of states' rights tried unsuccessfully to declare the national protective tariff acts of 1828 and 1832 null and void. The cockade was in the form of a small rosette of blue ribbon on the center of which was fastened a gilt palmetto button, and when displayed on a nullifier's hat was not infrequently regarded by members of the opposing Union party as an invitation to a fight.

[Chauncey S. Boucher, *The Nullification Controversy in South Carolina.*]

JAMES W. PATTON

PALMITO RANCH, BATTLE OF (May 13, 1865), the last land battle of the Civil War. On May 12, Union Col. Theodore H. Barrett, stationed near the mouth of the Rio Grande in Texas, drove out a small group of Confederates at Palmito Ranch, twelve miles below Brownsville. The following day the southern troops moved back into their former position with reinforcements, including six 12-pounders. Barrett, unable to dislodge them, began a retreat. A three-hour running fight began in which Barrett reported a loss in killed and missing of 111 men.

[Dudley G. Wooten, *History of Texas,* vol. II; H. H. Bancroft, *History of North Mexican States and Texas.*]

J. G. SMITH

PALO ALTO, BATTLE OF (May 8, 1846), the first battle of the Mexican War. Gen. Zachary Taylor's army of about 2,200 men met a Mexican force of nearly three times its number under Gen. Mariano Arista twelve miles northeast of the modern city of Brownsville, Tex. Almost entirely an artillery duel, it demonstrated the superiority of Taylor's cannon, strengthened American morale, and resulted in an American victory, the full effect of which was not felt until the following day at Resaca de la Palma.

[J. H. Smith, *The War With Mexico.*]

HOLMAN HAMILTON

PAMPHLETEERING is the carrying on of controversy by means of separately issued tracts, or pamphlets, which, because they are inexpensive to produce, provide a means of propagating new or unpopular ideas. English practice had established the method as effective in religious controversy and in political contests of the commonwealth period. Sermons, often with a political tinge, were effective as pamphlets in colonial America; and the writings of James Otis, Stephen Hopkins, John Dickinson, and others debated the issue of taxation by Parliament. Leaders of the Revolution wrote many pamphlets to justify their course, and some tracts were issued by the Loyalists. The ablest pamphleteer of the Revolution was Thomas Paine. His *Common Sense* was one of the strongest and most effective arguments for independence, and *The Crisis* papers were a powerful buttress to the morale of the patriot cause.

Issues confronting the new government, and especially the question of adopting the federal Constitution, were freely aired in pamphlets. While the newspapers carried some of the debate, such as *The Federalist* papers, John Jay, Noah Webster, Pelatiah Webster, Tench Coxe, and David Ramsay wrote pamphlets in favor of adoption, and Elbridge Gerry, George Mason, Melancthon Smith, Richard Henry Lee, Luther Martin, and James Iredell produced pamphlets in opposition.

Multiplication of newspapers in the early national period made pamphlet warfare less common, but the pamphlet was still the recourse for the impecunious or irresponsible agitator. Religious enthusiasts, reform groups, and propagators of Utopian societies or economic panaceas still found the pamphlet an effective agent. Political campaigns flooded the country with pamphlets to augment the circulation of newspapers or to make irresponsible attacks. Toward the end of the 19th century Socialists and Populists used pamphlets to gain converts, and a Free Silverite produced the notorious *Coin's Financial School*. Government propagandists during World War I utilized the pamphlet to sustain morale or refute criticism, and pacifists found it most useful. After World War I the use of the pamphlet declined. Throughout the rest of the century the pamphlet was used for information purposes, by government organizations, religious organizations, and learned societies, rather than in support of controversial issues.

[Bernard Bailyn and J. N. Garrett, eds., *Pamphlets of the American Revolution;* Frank Freidel, ed., *Union Pamphlets of the Civil War, 1861–1865;* Paul Smith, compiler, *English Defenders of American Freedom, 1774–1778.*]

MILTON W. HAMILTON

PAN-AFRICANISM began at the end of the 19th century under the leadership of American and West Indian blacks. It is the belief that, despite linguistic, tribal, or religious differences, Africans are one people whose goal is African unity. Whether this meant political unity under one government or a voluntary association of independent nations has been a matter of opinion. Until the end of World War II, the movement was directed mainly against the evils of colonialism; and at four conferences between 1900 and 1927 attention was focused on political restrictions and racial indignities suffered by Africans at the hands of Europeans.

The first Pan-African Congress was organized by Henry Sylvester-William, a West Indian lawyer. The thirty delegates who met in London were from England, the United States, and the West Indies. The American W. E. B. Du Bois, the leading figure in this early phase of the movement, articulated the feelings of this group of intellectuals with these prophetic words: "The problem of the twentieth century is the problem of the color line—the relation of the darker to the lighter races of men in Asia and Africa, in America and the islands of the sea." As its aim the conference sought to bring to the attention of the world the fate of African blacks under colonial control, who had no voice in deciding their destiny. It had limited success, if any at all. The British government promised to consider the interest of Africans in its policies, but in practice neither Britain nor any other European nation took positive action.

At the end of World War I, despite opposition by the U.S. government, Du Bois was able to gather fifty-seven blacks in Paris, including a number of Africans, to appeal to the Peace Conference of Versailles for a code of laws to protect Africans. But statesmen from America and Europe were unwilling to extend to Africans the principle of self-determination that the conference adopted for Europeans. The chief value of the Paris meeting was the opportunity it provided for African and American blacks to meet.

Du Bois was still the leading spokesman at the Second Pan-African Congress in 1921, but by that time the majority of those attending were from Africa. The third congress, in 1923, and the fourth, in 1927, were even less influential than the earlier two and served to do little more than keep Pan-Africanism alive.

The Fifth Pan-African Congress, which met in Manchester, England, in 1945, reflected a major change in aim. Two hundred black delegates from all parts of the English-speaking world participated. Africans dominated the group, which included labor leaders and politicians as well as intellectuals. At the age of seventy-three Du Bois was still the symbolic leader, but active leadership was provided by a group of young energetic Africans. Included in this group were Jomo Kenyatta of Kenya, Peter Abrahams of South Africa, Nnamdi Azikiwe of Nigeria, and Kwame Nkrumah of the Gold Coast (later Ghana). The main theme was national independence and the strategies for attaining it.

The national movements among various groups of Africans and the successful move to independence, beginning with that of Ghana in 1957, created problems for Pan-Africanism and somewhat altered its direction. Nkrumah, as prime minister of Ghana, defined it as an effort to create a third force in the world to which the industrialized nations would be compelled to give attention and provide assistance. The Organization of African Unity (OAU) was created in 1963 as the instrument for maintaining solidarity and accomplishing this end. But the subsequent inability of the OAU to deal satisfactorily with crisis within Africa limited the effectiveness of this aspect of Pan-Africanism. Furthermore, nationalism within the various black African countries appeared to be a stronger force than Pan-Africanism. After 1968, with the creation of a number of regional economic organizations, the major efforts at international cooperation in Africa began to focus on the economic sphere.

In the 1920's Marcus Garvey created the first mass movement of American blacks. His idea of "Africa for the Africans" called for the return of U.S. blacks to a "redeemed" Africa as a solution to the problems of segregation and discrimination. His Back-to-Africa movement transported few Americans or West Indians to that continent, but it did expand the concept of black unity beyond the circle of intellectuals to which Du Bois appealed. Although Du Bois and Garvey agreed on the general concept of African unity, they disagreed about methods and were hostile toward each other throughout most of Garvey's career.

[Adekunle Ajala, *Pan-Africanism Evolution, Progress and Prospect;* J. Ayadele Langley, *Pan-Africanism and Nationalism in West Africa;* George Padmore, ed., *History of the Pan-African Congress.*]

HENRY N. DREWRY

PANAMA, DECLARATION OF, was adopted at Panama City on Oct. 3, 1939, by the Consultative Meeting of Foreign Ministers of the American Republics. To deal with conditions created by the outbreak of war in Europe in early September 1939, sixteen resolutions or sets of resolutions and declarations were adopted. These dealt with such matters as economic cooperation, continental solidarity, neutrality, humanization of war, and contraband of war. But the most widely publicized was No. XIV, entitled "Declaration of Panama," which consisted of a preamble and four declarations. The first declaration stated that American waters should be "free from the commission of any hostile act by any non-American belligerent nation, whether such hostile act be attempted or made from land, sea or air." These waters were defined to include a strip averaging about 300 miles in width extending southward from the eastern end of the United States–Canada boundary, around South America, and northward to the western end of the boundary between the United States and Canada.

In the second declaration it was stated that the republics would attempt, "through joint representations," to secure compliance with the declaration by the belligerents. Provision was made in the third declaration for further consultation, if necessary, to "determine upon the measures" to be undertaken "to secure the observance" of the declaration. The fourth declaration provided for individual or collective patrols by the republics of "the waters adjacent to their coasts . . . whenever they may determine that the need therefor exists."

ERIK MCKINLEY ERIKSSON

PANAMA CANAL, a fifty-one-mile waterway through the Isthmus of Panama, connecting the Atlantic and Pacific oceans. During the 15th and 16th centuries, explorers sought a passage through the American continental barrier that would permit navigation between Europe and China. These early efforts resulted in extensive colonization by Spain, which had developed preliminary plans for a canal by the end of the 18th century. But Spain abandoned these plans when its colonies revolted early in the 19th century, the occasion for President James Monroe's announcement of the Monroe Doctrine, which eventually came to stand for the proposition that any canal across the American isthmus should be controlled by the United States. This policy was explicitly stated by President Rutherford B. Hayes in 1880 and thereafter on numerous occasions by the president and the Congress.

During the last half of the 19th century, U.S. interest in a canal was limited almost exclusively to the Nicaraguan route, although in 1846 the United States had concluded a commercial treaty with the Republic of New Granada (now Colombia), under which that country agreed that transportation across the Isthmus of Panama, then a part of New Granada, should be open and free to the United States, which in turn guaranteed the neutrality of the isthmus. In 1849 U.S. private interests obtained an exclusive concession from Nicaragua for construction of a canal there, but the Clayton-Bulwer Treaty of 1850 with Great Britain precluded exclusive construction or control of a canal by either country.

Also in 1850, a New York corporation was granted an exclusive concession by New Granada to construct a railroad across the Isthmus of Panama. The railroad, completed in 1855, was an immediate financial success, largely because of traffic generated by the gold rush, and served as an important factor in subsequent developments on the isthmus.

In 1881, under a concession granted by Colombia

in 1878, the French engineer Ferdinand de Lesseps commenced construction of a canal on the Panama route. This attempt failed because of a combination of fiscal problems and unspeakable health conditions on the isthmus, but the engineering plans were sound and a substantial amount of excavation had been completed before work was abandoned in 1889, when the French Canal Company went into bankruptcy.

In 1898 the voyage of the U.S.S. *Oregon* around Cape Horn at the outbreak of the Spanish-American War added military necessity to the arguments for construction of a canal. (Earlier arguments were based on commercial advantage.) The first Isthmian Canal Commission, appointed in the United States in 1899, submitted a report in 1901 recommending the Nicaraguan route; and in 1901 the United States negotiated the Hay-Pauncefote Treaty with Great Britain permitting U.S. control, operation, and protection of a canal. The treaty provided for the canal's neutrality by adopting rules from the 1888 Convention of Constantinople, which dealt with the Suez Canal.

After the 1901 report of the Isthmian Canal Commission, the French New Panama Canal Company (the name given to the bankrupt French Canal Company after reorganization in 1894) offered to sell its assets to the United States for $40 million; and Philippe Bunau-Varilla, a brilliant engineer who had been associated with the French project, came to the United States to extend his considerable persuasive influence for construction of the canal in Panama.

In January 1902 the Isthmian Canal Commission filed a supplementary report recommending construction of a canal on the Panama route if the United States could obtain the assets of the New Panama Canal Company for $40 million and if Colombia would grant the United States perpetual control over the territory required for the canal. The Spooner Act of June 28, 1902, authorized construction of the canal on the conditions laid down by the commission and directed that if those conditions were not met within a reasonable time, the canal should be built in Nicaragua. On Jan. 22, 1903, the United States and Colombia signed the Hay-Herrán Treaty meeting the requirements of the Spooner Act, but Colombia refused to ratify the treaty in spite of vigorous efforts by representatives of Panama, who advocated construction of the canal there.

After the rejection of the treaty by Colombia, Panama revolted and declared its independence on Nov. 3, 1903. The United States recognized the new government of Panama on Nov. 6; and on Nov. 13, Bunau-Varilla, who had been appointed as Panama's minister to the United States, signed a treaty with the United States providing for the construction and operation of the canal in Panama. The treaty was ratified by Panama on Dec. 2, 1903, approved by the U.S. Senate on Feb. 23, 1904, and proclaimed on Feb. 26, 1904.

In the 1903 treaty, Panama granted to the United States in perpetuity the use, occupation, and control of a zone of land for the construction, operation, maintenance, sanitation, and protection of a transisthmian canal. Within that zone, Panama granted to the United States all the rights, power, and authority "which the United States would possess and exercise if it were the sovereign of the territory . . . to the total exclusion of the exercise by the Republic of Panama of any such rights, power or authority." The United States guaranteed the independence of the Republic of Panama and agreed to pay Panama $10 million in cash and an annuity of $250,000.

After the promulgation of the treaty, the United States moved immediately to begin construction. The threat to the project posed by yellow fever, malaria, and other tropical diseases was eliminated by the construction of a modern water and sewer system for the Canal Zone and the cities of Panama and Colón and by the brilliant and energetic program of the health authorities under the direction of Col. William C. Gorgas. The Isthmian Canal Commission was designated by the Spooner Act to construct the canal, but the exigencies of the work soon required a consolidation of responsibility and authority. As chief engineer (1905–07) and chairman, John F. Stevens is principally credited with the successful organization, planning, and implementation of the first phases of actual construction. After Stevens resigned in 1907, the canal was completed under the leadership of Lt. Col. G. W. Goethals (1907–14). By an act signed into law by President Theodore Roosevelt on June 29, 1906, Congress resolved a bitter controversy by directing the construction of a lock canal rather than a sea-level canal. Thereafter, the work proceeded with increasing momentum to conclusion. The canal was opened to commerce on Aug. 15, 1914.

Once completed, the canal was operated under the terms of the Panama Canal Act of Aug. 24, 1912, and under executive orders issued by the president pursuant to that act. In 1928, Congress authorized the codification of all laws applicable in the Canal Zone and in 1934 enacted the Canal Zone Code.

By an act of Congress (Thompson Act) approved in 1950, the operation of the canal was transferred to the Panama Railroad Company, which was renamed the

Panama Canal Company and put under the management of a board of directors. The agency previously responsible for the operation of the canal was renamed the Canal Zone government and was made responsible for the various duties connected with the civil government of the Canal Zone. The governor of the Canal Zone is appointed by the president of the United States and is ex officio a member of the board of directors and president of the Panama Canal Company. Since 1951, all expenses for operating the canal, including interest, depreciation, and the net cost of the Canal Zone government, as well as the cost of capital improvements, have been met from revenues.

After the independence of Panama and the location of the canal there were assured, Panama became dissatisfied with the terms of the 1903 treaty, largely because of the sweeping rights of sovereignty granted to the United States and the restraints against Panamanian exploitation of the commercial opportunities created by the canal. These problems began to develop even before construction was completed, and the subsequent history of relations between the two countries reflects almost continuous effort to reach accommodation on the disputed points.

After Panama refused to ratify a treaty signed in 1926 dealing with only a few of the economic issues, a treaty signed on Mar. 2, 1936, was ratified in 1939. That treaty abrogated provisions of the 1903 treaty guaranteeing the independence of Panama by the United States and requiring Panamanian compliance with sanitary ordinances prescribed by the United States. The 1936 treaty also increased Panama's annuity to $430,000 and placed certain restrictions on residence, importations, and commercial activities in the Canal Zone. Moreover, the United States relinquished the right to take land for canal use in addition to that previously acquired under the 1903 treaty.

An executive agreement signed on May 18, 1942, included provisions for transfer to Panama of the water and sewer systems built by the United States in the cities of Panama and Colón, along with certain real estate in Panama. The agreement also covered the highway construction by the United States in Panama and put further restrictions on employment in the Canal Zone.

Another agreement, also signed on May 18, 1942, provided for the lease to the United States of a number of defense sites in Panama. This agreement was to terminate one year after the date of the definitive peace treaty ending World War II and was renewable by mutual consent. After the surrender of Japan,

however, Panama stated that the agreement had expired; and the Panama National Assembly, intimidated by a mob of 10,000 nationalists opposing the U.S. military bases, refused to extend the agreement, resulting in the abandonment of the defense sites by the United States.

The 1955 Eisenhower-Remón Treaty further increased Panama's annuity to $1,930,000, provided for the return to Panama of real estate owned by the United States in Panama, withdrew from Panamanian employees living in Panama the privilege of making purchases in Canal Zone stores, granted to Panama the right to tax Panamanians employed in the Canal Zone, provided for equality of opportunity and treatment for Panamanians in Canal Zone employment, and provided for construction of a bridge over the canal at the Pacific entrance.

After the 1955 treaty, the issues in dispute focused increasingly on demands for recognition of Panama's sovereignty in the Canal Zone, particularly after Egypt's nationalization of the Suez Canal in 1956. Serious riots along the border occurred in 1959 and again in 1964, requiring the use of U.S. military forces to protect the Canal Zone.

At the time of the 1964 riots, which resulted in numerous casualties and extensive property damage, Panama broke off diplomatic relations with the United States and accused it of aggression in the United Nations and the Organization of American States (OAS). Panama also appealed to the International Commission of Jurists, which exonerated the United States of the charges made by Panama. Through the efforts of the OAS, diplomatic relations were resumed in April 1964, when negotiations for a new treaty were begun. Concurrently, the United States established the Atlantic-Pacific Interoceanic Canal Study to examine the feasibility of constructing a new sea-level canal. The commission submitted its report in December 1970, recommending the construction of a sea-level canal in Panama at a cost of $2.88 billion, subject to negotiation of a suitable treaty with Panama and availability of funds.

On July 3, 1967, the treaty negotiators announced that they had reached agreement on three related treaties: (1) a treaty abrogating the 1903 treaty, recognizing Panamanian sovereignty, and providing for the operation of the existing canal until the end of the century by a joint authority composed of U.S. and Panamanian members, with royalty payments (about $20 million a year) to Panama based on the tonnage of cargo moving through the canal; (2) a treaty granting the United States an option to build a sea-level canal and providing for operation of such a canal by a joint authority for sixty years after its opening or until 2067, whichever is first; and (3) a treaty providing for U.S. military bases in Panama for a period generally coterminous with the periods of operation of any canal by the proposed joint authority.

The 1967 drafts had not been signed when Arnulfo Arias was elected president of Panama. He took office on Oct. 1, 1968. Ten days later Panama's National Guard, the only military force in the country, staged a coup; a military junta took over the government, with ultimate authority consolidated in Brig. Gen. Omar Torrijos, the commandant of the guard. The new government was recognized by the United States on Nov. 13, 1968. On Aug. 5, 1970, Panama formally rejected the 1967 draft treaties because it was dissatisfied with the length of time that would elapse before sole possession and control of the canal would be vested in Panama, with continued limitations on Panama's political jurisdiction and administrative control in the Canal Zone, with the scope of action allowed the United States under the defense treaty, and with the amount of financial benefits that would accrue to Panama.

When the 1967 drafts were rejected, Panama expressed a willingness to reopen negotiations for a new treaty. The United States agreed and negotiations were resumed in 1970.

[Miles P. Du Val, *Cadiz to Cathay: The Story of the Long Diplomatic Struggle for the Panama Canal*]

W. M. WHITMAN

PANAMA CITY, the capital city of Panama, from the time of its foundation in 1519 has been important as the western terminus of the transit route across the Isthmus of Panama. It was the center from which the exploration and conquest of the Pacific coast of Central and South America were carried on, and a point of transshipment throughout the colonial period for goods going to Peru. The city was moved to its present location in 1674 after the English buccaneer Henry Morgan sacked and destroyed it three years earlier. It became the capital of the Republic of Panama in 1903. Although not a part of the Canal Zone, it is almost completely surrounded by zone territory, and is the Pacific terminus of the Panama Railroad.

[C. L. G. Anderson, *Old Panama and Castilla del Oro.*]

DANA G. MUNRO

PANAMA CONGRESS. On Sept. 6, 1815, while in exile, Simón Bolívar wrote his so-called prophetic *Letter From Jamaica,* expressing a wish that someday a "congress of representatives of the republics, kingdoms, and empires of America" might meet on the Isthmus of Panama "to deal with the high interests of peace and war." On Dec. 7, 1824, Bolívar sent invitations for such a congress to Colombia, Mexico, Central America, Brazil, the United Provinces of Buenos Aires, and Peru. The United States was eventually invited at the insistence of Colombia and Mexico. The congress finally met at Panama City from June 22 to July 15, 1826. Ten meetings were held, but only Colombia, Peru, Mexico, and Central America were represented. One United States delegate died before reaching the meeting and the other, learning the congress had adjourned, never departed. The delegates signed a treaty of perpetual union and confederation and a convention providing for a common army and navy to defend the interests of the union. Other matters were discussed, but none of the acts was ratified by all of the governments. The congress adjourned to meet in Mexico, but never reconvened.

[J. B. Lockey, *Pan-Americanism, Its Beginnings.*]

A. CURTIS WILGUS

PANAMA-PACIFIC INTERNATIONAL EXPOSITION, held in San Francisco from Feb. 4 to Dec. 4, 1915, celebrated the opening of the Panama Canal and the discovery of the Pacific Ocean by Vasco Núñez de Balboa, who crossed the Isthmus of Panama in 1513. Approximately 13 million visitors thronged the exposition's 635 acres, and the official balance sheet showed an ultimate profit of more than $2 million. Despite the fact that World War I was in progress during the exposition, thirty-one foreign nations participated—twenty-five officially and six unofficially. Twenty-five American states, Hawaii, the Philippines, and New York City erected their own exhibit buildings. Notable were the landscaping, lighting effects, and the architectural unity achieved through the use of Spanish and Italian Renaissance and Spanish Baroque styles. This exposition was the first held in America that did not stress the industrial or scientific phases of modern life. Its greatest accomplishments were cultural and artistic.

FRANK MONAGHAN

PANAMA RAILROAD was built by an American company (1849–55) at a cost of about $8 million. Until the building of transcontinental railways in the

United States, the Panama Railroad carried many thousands of passengers on their way from New York to California, and its operation was exceedingly profitable. Later, the French Panama Canal Company purchased nearly all of the capital stock. These French shares were subsequently transferred to the U.S. government in 1902 with other assets of the French company, and the remainder of the stock was also acquired. Since 1951 the line has been operated by the Panama Canal Company, the U.S. government corporation that also operates the Panama Canal.

[Ian Cameron, *The Impossible Dream: The Building of the Panama Canal;* Sheldon B. Liss, *The Canal: Aspects of United States Panamanian Relations.*]

DANA G. MUNRO

PANAMA REVOLUTION. On Aug. 12, 1903, the Colombian senate refused to ratify the Hay-Herrán Treaty authorizing the construction of an interoceanic canal at Panama by the United States. The evident purpose was to obtain greater financial benefits, either from the United States or from the French New Panama Canal Company, which had already agreed to sell its interests to the United States. This caused much discontent in Panama, then under Colombian rule, and on Nov. 3 a group of revolutionists, aided by the commander of the local garrison, seized control of the city and proclaimed the Republic of Panama. The movement was financed by the French engineer Philippe Bunau-Varilla, working in the interests of the French canal company.

Colombian forces had been sent to Colón, on the opposite side of the isthmus, just before the outbreak, but they were prevented from crossing to Panama by the commander of the U.S.S. *Nashville,* which had likewise just arrived. This action was based on the Bidlack Treaty of 1846 under which the United States considered itself authorized to intervene to maintain freedom of transit across the isthmus. Its effect was to prevent the suppression of the revolt. On Nov. 6, furthermore, the United States recognized the independence of Panama. The revolutionists appointed Bunau-Varilla Panamanian minister at Washington, and on Nov. 18 he signed a treaty with Secretary of State John Hay by which the United States was given the exclusive right to build and control a canal and in return guaranteed Panama's independence (*see* Hay–Bunau-Varilla Treaty). Thereafter the United States refused to permit Colombia to make any attempt to restore its authority on the isthmus.

The Colombian government asserted that the revolt had been instigated and aided by the United States,

and that the action of the American forces in preventing Colombian troops from crossing the isthmus was improper. President Theodore Roosevelt and Secretary Hay denied that any responsible American official had been in communication with the revolutionists before the revolt. They defended the action of the American forces as justifiable under the Bidlack Treaty. With regard to the unusually prompt recognition of Panama's independence, they argued that the building of the canal was necessary to the United States and the world, that Colombia's refusal of permission had been unreasonable, and that the people of Panama had been justified in revolting against an action that had threatened to injure their vital interests. Nevertheless, the U.S. government made reparation to Colombia in April 1921 in the amount of $25 million.

[Alexander DeConde, *A History of American Foreign Policy;* G. H. Stuart, *Latin America and the United States.*]

DANA G. MUNRO

PANAMA TOLLS QUESTION. A bill enacted late in 1912 to regulate the Panama Canal once it was completed exempted coastwise vessels of the United States from payment of tolls. In its original form it had exempted all American vessels, but under British protest it had been modified. The British government repeated its protest, pointing out that the exemption violated the Hay-Pauncefote Treaty of 1901, which said that the canal was "to be open to British and American vessels on equal terms." It asked for repeal of the exemption clause or arbitration of the dispute. The American government, in reply, defended exemption but expressed willingness to arbitrate. Many Americans opposed exemption as a violation of the treaty. President Woodrow Wilson, on Mar. 5, 1914, asked Congress to repeal the exemption clause, which was done; on June 15, 1914, the president signed the repeal bill. Since the canal was not then completed, no tolls had yet been charged.

[M. W. Williams, *Anglo-American Isthmian Diplomacy, 1815–1915.*]

MARY WILHELMINE WILLIAMS

PAN-AMERICAN CONFERENCES. *See* **Latin America, Relations With.**

PAN-AMERICAN EXPOSITION, held at Buffalo, N.Y., witnessed the assassination of President William McKinley after the delivery of his Pan-American speech in the fair's Temple of Music on Sept. 6, 1901. The fair was originally scheduled to open on May 1, but the opening of the exposition was again delayed, until after the president's funeral. The exposition reopened in November. It was designed to show the progress of a century in the New World and to promote commercial and social interests; its cost was almost $2.5 million. The New York State Building, an imitation of the Parthenon in Greece, now houses the Buffalo Historical Society. The exposition presented a comprehensive picture of the beauties and possibilities of modern electricity.

FRANK MONAGHAN

PAN-AMERICAN UNION, an international agency of Western Hemisphere nations with headquarters in Washington, D.C. It was founded on Apr. 14, 1890, as the International Bureau of the American Republics at the First International Conference of American States (the modern inter-American conferences) and in 1910 was renamed the Pan-American Union. Created originally to collect and distribute commercial information, by 1975 it had also organized seven inter-American conferences (Mexico City, 1901; Rio de Janeiro, 1906; Buenos Aires, 1910; Santiago, 1923; Havana, 1928; Montevideo, 1933; and Lima, 1938) and sought to promote inter-American cooperation. But its limited diplomatic machinery served few multilateral functions; and it was powerless to stop several intraregional conflicts between the two world wars, most notably the bloody Chaco War (1932–35) between Bolivia and Paraguay.

The union became the permanent secretariat of the Organization of American States (OAS) when it was created by twenty-one American republics at Bogotá on Apr. 30, 1948. The secretary-general of the union is elected by the OAS Council for a ten-year term and is the highest international administrative officer of the OAS. After a reorganization in 1958, the union was composed of the departments of economic and social affairs, legal affairs, cultural affairs, technical cooperation, and statistics and public information, and the offices of secretariat services, financial services, and publication services. Under the direction of the OAS Council and through its technical and information offices, the Union promotes economic, social, juridical, and cultural relations among OAS members. In addition, it prepares the programs and regulations of OAS conferences, serves as the distributor of documents and the custodian of archives of conferences and instruments of ratification of inter-

American agreements, and submits annual reports to each inter-American conference on the work accomplished by the various OAS organs. Since the creation of the OAS in 1948, the volume of work of the union has continued to grow, especially after the expansion of economic and social programs in the Western Hemisphere under the Charter of Punta del Este (August 1961), which created the Alliance for Progress.

[Gordon Connell-Smith, *The Inter-American System;* Ann Van Wynen Thomas and A. J. Thomas, Jr., *The Organization of American States.*]

GARY W. WYNIA

PANAY **INCIDENT.** On Dec. 12, 1937, Japanese bombers, engaged in war with China, bombed and sank the clearly marked U.S. gunboat *Panay* and three Standard Oil supply ships twenty-seven miles above Nanking on the Yangtze River. The ships were engaged in evacuating American officials from China. Several crew members were killed and a number of other Americans wounded. Secretary of State Cordell Hull demanded full redress. Japan accepted responsibility, made formal apologies, promised indemnities and appropriate punishment, and gave future assurances. Hull accepted these assurances and the incident was closed. Indemnities were later set at more than $2 million.

[Alexander DeConde, *A History of American Foreign Policy.*]

OSCAR OSBURN WINTHER

PANHANDLE, a long, usually narrow, tract of land appended to the main area of a state. There are several such areas in the United States. The panhandle of West Virginia extends northward between Pennsylvania and Ohio. This is the rather accidental result of the definition of Pennsylvania's western boundary and the grant by Virginia of its western lands. The panhandle of Oklahoma is a long strip about twenty-five miles wide, lying between Texas on the south and Colorado and Kansas on the north. The panhandle of Texas is a large, nearly square area, including the northern portion of the state.

The term "panhandle" is also applied to the northern portion of Idaho where it projects between Washington and Montana, and also occasionally to the projection at the southeast corner of Missouri; the western portion of Nebraska where it extends north of Colorado; the addition to Pennsylvania at its northwestern corner along the shore of Lake Erie; and the long western extension of Florida.

ERWIN N. GRISWOLD

PANIC OF 1785 put an end to the business boom following the American Revolution and ushered in a period of hard times, which, severest in 1785–86, lasted until 1788. Its causes lay in the overexpansion, extravagance, and debts incurred following the victory at Yorktown; the deflation that accompanied the end of army contracts and privateering; the blow to American manufactures from large imports of British goods; and the lack of adequate credit facilities and a sound circulating medium. The depression was accentuated by the absence of any central mechanism for promoting interstate trade and by state laws interfering with it; by the British refusal to conclude a commercial treaty; and by disorders among debtor groups (*see* Shays's Rebellion). The deep alarm of business and propertied groups gave strength to the demand for a stronger federal government (*see* Convention of 1787).

[Bray Hammond, *Banks and Politics in America From the Revolution to the Civil War;* Curtis Nettels, *The Emergence of a National Economy, 1775–1815.*]

ALLAN NEVINS

PANIC OF 1792. The economic prosperity that accompanied the launching of the federal government developed into a speculative boom by late 1791. Schemes for internal improvements; the chartering by state legislatures of inadequately financed banks; and speculation in bank scrip, government securities, and western lands brought a collapse in 1792. Much of the bank scrip proved to be of no value, and there were many bank failures with huge losses.

[W. B. Smith and A. H. Cole, *Fluctuations in American Business, 1790–1860.*]

CHARLES MARION THOMAS

PANIC OF 1819 resulted from a sharp contraction of credit initiated by the second Bank of the United States. The bank was seeking to curb speculation in commodities and in western lands encouraged by many state banks and some of the branches of the Bank of the United States, following the War of 1812. A period of severe depression, especially in the southern and western states, followed the contraction. Many banks suspended specie payments and many failed, and the Bank of the United States went

through a trying period of recrimination, congressional investigation for alleged mismanagement, and financial rehabilitation. Prices declined; cotton, for example, fell 50 percent within a year. Hezekiah Niles, a contemporary editor, was "sickened to the heart" at the large numbers of sheriff's sales and imprisonments for debt. Although the situation alarmed the administration, John Quincy Adams, then secretary of state, believed that the government could do nothing "but transfer discontents, and propitiate one class . . . by disgusting another." Nevertheless, manufacturers clamored for more protection, and debtors demanded relief legislation, which was enacted in several western states. By 1823 the economic picture improved.

[S. Rezneck, "The Depression of 1819–1822," *American Historical Review* (1933); Murray Rothbard, *The Panic of 1819.*]

SAMUEL REZNECK

PANIC OF 1837. During the period 1830–36 enormous state debts had piled up from the construction of canals and railroads and in the chartering of new banks among the settled states. At the same time many state banks, which after 1833 held deposits of government funds, expanded their credit; land speculation was common in all sections of the country; and imports exceeded exports. In 1836 three events occurred that precipitated a crisis. To check the land speculation President Andrew Jackson, on July 11, 1836, issued a specie circular, which required all payments for public lands to be made in specie, thus cramping the operations of the banks financing the western land speculation. On June 23, 1836, Congress passed an act to distribute the surplus revenue in the U.S. Treasury among the states, thereby causing the depository banks to contract their credit. To make matters worse, a financial crisis in England caused many British creditors to call in their loans, while the failure of American crops lessened the purchasing power of farmers. On May 10, 1837, the New York banks suspended specie payment, a move followed by most of the banks in the country. After resumption in 1838, Philadelphia banks suspended specie payments, Oct. 9, 1839, and there were additional widespread suspensions in 1842. The depression lasted until 1843 and was most severely felt in the West and the South. There was a general suspension of public works, a demand for more stringent banking laws, widespread unemployment, and state defalcations and repudiations. The Independent Treasury System was established in 1840 partly as a result of the panic, and the universal distress contributed to the defeat of Martin Van Buren for president and the return of the Whigs to power in that same year.

[R. C. McGrane, *The Panic of 1837;* W. B. Smith, *Economic Aspects of the Second Bank of the United States.*]
REGINALD C. MCGRANE

PANIC OF 1857 followed the boom decade after the Mexican War (1846–48). This period saw speculation and expansion run riot in railroad construction, manufacturing, the wheat belt, and land; state banking was poorly regulated. The opening of the California gold fields also contributed to the general spirit of speculation.

The failure of the Ohio Life Insurance Company of Cincinnati in August 1857 pricked the bubble. The panic spread from the Ohio Valley into the urban centers of the East, and, with the approach of winter, unemployment grew, breadlines formed, and ominous signs of social unrest appeared.

The depression was most serious in the rising industrial areas of the East and wheat belt of the West. Faced by British competition and balked by southern low tariff policies, the industrial East turned to the new Republican party. The Middle West, hit by bank failures and faced with southern hostility to free land, likewise turned to the new party. The cotton belt was less affected by the panic—cotton crops were good, prices were high, and banks were sound. These factors brought overconfidence in the South, an impulse to protection in the East, and a drive for free land in the West. In the election of 1860, therefore, economic conditions were no less potent an issue than the moral issue of slavery.

[L. C. Helderman, *National and State Banks—A Study of Their Origins;* G. W. Von Vleck, *The Panic of 1857.*]
L. C. HELDERMAN

PANIC OF 1873 was precipitated by the failure of a number of important eastern firms, including the New York Warehouse and Securities Company on Sept. 8; Kenyon, Cox and Company on Sept. 13; and the most famous banking house, Jay Cooke and Company, on Sept. 18. Days of pandemonium followed. President Ulysses S. Grant hurried to New York, the stock exchange closed for ten days, and bankruptcy overtook a host of companies and individuals. Some of the causes of the panic and ensuing depression were worldwide: a series of wars, including the Austro-Prussian, Franco-Prussian, and American civil conflicts; excessive railroad construction in middle

Europe, Russia, South America, and the United States; commercial dislocations caused by the opening of the Suez Canal; and worldwide speculation, overexpansion, and extravagance. Other causes were more peculiar to the United States: currency inflation and credit inflation; governmental waste; the losses from the Boston and Chicago fires; overinvestment in railroads, factories, and buildings; and an adverse trade balance. Even in 1872 the United States had suffered more than 4,000 business failures for a total of some $121 million.

The depression following the panic proved one of the worst in American history. During 1876–77 business failures numbered more than 18,000, a majority of American railroads went into bankruptcy, and more than two-thirds of the iron mills and furnaces lay idle. By the beginning of 1875 fully 500,000 men were out of work, and in the absence of organized public relief, destitution and hunger far outstripped the efforts of charity to keep up. Wage reductions caused strikes among the coal miners of Pennsylvania and textile operatives of New England and a railroad walkout in 1877 (*see* Railroad Strikes of 1877). The latter was accompanied by appalling violence. Beggary, prostitution, and crime increased, while political and economic radicalism gained ground. In 1878 the depression began to lift, and in the following year economic conditions greatly improved.

[Eric Goldman, *Rendezvous With Destiny;* A. D. Noyes, *Forty Years of American Finance;* Walter T. K. Nugent, *Money and American Society, 1865–1880.*]
ALLAN NEVINS

PANIC OF 1893, a spectacular financial crisis the background of which is found in the usual factors of the business cycle, together with an inflexible banking system. Capital investments in the 1880's had exceeded the possibilities of immediately profitable use, and the trend of prices continued generally downward.

The uneasy state of British security markets in 1890, culminating in the liquidation of the British banking house of Baring Brothers and Company, stopped the flow of foreign capital into American enterprise, and the resale of European-held securities caused a stock market collapse in New York and substantial exports of gold. The panic that seemed inevitable that autumn turned instead to uneasy stagnation as the huge exports of agricultural staples the next two years reestablished gold imports and postponed the crisis. A high degree of uncertainty returned in the winter of 1892–93, aided by the well-publicized danger that the country would be forced off the gold standard by the decline in the U.S. Treasury's gold reserve, which bore the brunt of the renewed exports of gold and also suffered from decreased federal revenues and heavy expenditures, including the purchases of silver under the Sherman Silver Purchase Act of 1890.

The Philadelphia and Reading Railroad failed in February, and the gold reserve fell below the accepted minimum of $100 million in April 1893. The National Cordage Company failed in May and touched off a stock market panic. Banks in the South and West were especially hard pressed, and nearly 600 in the entire country suspended, at least temporarily. By the end of 1893 about 4,000 banks had collapsed, and there were more than 14,000 commercial failures. This condition continued throughout the summer, and all currency was at a premium in New York in August.

Many of President Grover Cleveland's advisers had been urging him to force repeal of the Silver Purchase Act, since his election the previous November. The panic atmosphere furnished the opportunity, and repeal was advanced as the one absolute cure for the depression. By Oct. 30 it had passed both houses of Congress. In the meantime, imports of gold had stabilized the monetary situation in New York somewhat, but the depression continued. The winter of 1893–94 and the summer following witnessed widespread unemployment, strikes met by violence, and a march on Washington, D.C., by a group of jobless men seeking relief, known as "Coxey's Army"—all part of the human reaction to the tragedy. The depression did not lift substantially until the poor European crops of 1897 stimulated American exports and the importation of gold. The rising prices that followed helped to restore prosperous conditions.

[J. A. Barnes, *John G. Carlisle: Financial Statesman;* O. M. W. Sprague, *History of Crises Under the National Banking System;* Otto C. Lightner, *History of Business Depressions.*]

ELMER ELLIS

PANIC OF 1907, which broke in October of that year, is sometimes called the "rich man's panic." It came as a surprise, although a succession of speculative excesses had preceded it: in life insurance (witness the Charles Evans Hughes investigations in New York in 1905); in railroad combinations; in western mining stocks, especially copper, during 1906; in inadequately regulated trust companies that competed with banks; and in coastal shipping combines. Bank credit expanded rapidly between 1897 and 1906—the

amount in checking accounts grew by 161 percent and bank clearings tripled. The year 1906 also witnessed several profit dampening reforms, such as the Hepburn Act, which gave the Interstate Commerce Commission power to set maximum railroad rates; the Pure Food and Drug Act; and the New York State insurance reform law. And on Aug. 3, 1907, Judge Kenesaw Mountain Landis imposed a shocking $29.24 million fine (reversed on appeal) on Standard Oil of Indiana for granting illegal rebates. Yet the economy seemed to be healthy in January 1907, and most financiers believed that improved banking controls made it impossible for panics like those of 1873 and 1893 to happen again.

When Henry H. Rogers of Standard Oil had to pay 8 percent interest to float a $20 million bond issue in February 1907, a sharp drop in the stock market took place, the so-called silent panic. The economy seemed to recover, but the Charles Morse shipping combination collapsed that summer. The failure in October of F. Augustus Heinze's United Copper Company was followed by runs on the Heinze-Morse chain of banks. The Knickerbocker Trust Company closed on Oct. 22 and its president committed suicide. Runs on the Trust Company of America and several others followed, and there was panic on the stock markets.

To halt the panic, Secretary of the Treasury George B. Cortelyou authorized large deposits in several banks. Investment banker J. P. Morgan headed a banking group that used a borrowed emergency fund of nearly $40 million to rescue banks and firms they deemed savable and whose survival was crucial. In order to rescue the brokerage house of Moore and Schley, Morgan arranged, after gaining President Theodore Roosevelt's approval, to have the United States Steel Corporation buy the brokers' holdings of the stock of a major rival, the Tennessee Coal, Iron and Railroad Company. This arrangement also strengthened the steel trust. By the end of the year things were normal again.

Although the panic did not lead to heavy unemployment or to a wave of bankruptcies, or affect agriculture, it seriously damaged the image of the big financiers. Many Americans questioned the desirability of letting one private citizen, Morgan, wield such enormous power in a crisis. The panic also had repercussions overseas. The United States temporarily imported a large amount of gold, and interest rates abroad rose, which led to grumblings that the United States, lacking a central bank to soften a crisis, was "an international financial nuisance."

On Mar. 30, 1908, Congress passed the Aldrich-Vreeland Currency Act, one part of which provided for the issuance of emergency bank currency in the event of another currency stringency. A second part of the act created the National Monetary Commission—headed by Sen. Nelson Aldrich of Rhode Island—to propose needed bank reforms. It produced the Aldrich Report of 1911, which was in turn a major step in setting up the Federal Reserve System in 1913-14.

The bank failures of the panic of 1907 also contributed to the establishment in 1910 of the Postal Savings System, the purpose of which was to protect the savings of the poor, especially the immigrant poor.

[F. L. Allen, *The Great Pierpont Morgan;* O. C. Lightner, *The History of Business Depressions;* John Moody, *Masters of Capital;* A. D. Noyes, *Forty Years of American Finance;* U.S. Department of Commerce, *Historical Statistics of the United States: Colonial Times to 1957.*]

DONALD L. KEMMERER

PANIC OF 1920. *See* **Depression of 1920.**

PANIC OF 1929 had so many causes that, historically, the remarkable fact is that its magnitude surprised many economists who were keeping a close watch on the situation. Wesley C. Mitchell, however, one of the greatest American economists, was never carried away by the climate of speculative prosperity. Writing in the spring of 1929 he said that "recent developments may appear less satisfactory in retrospect than they appear in prospect. . . . Past experience . . . suggests that the pace will slacken presently, and that years may pass before we see such another well-maintained advance." Basic among the factors leading to the instability feared by Mitchell were a volume of annual private and corporate savings in excess of the demand for real capital formation, a large export trade in manufactured goods supported by foreign lending, a low-discount Federal Reserve policy designed to support the British pound, an increasing use of stock-exchange securities rather than commercial paper for bank loans, the failure of wages or mass consumption to continue to rise much after 1926, a rapid increase in urban and suburban mortgage debt on speculative properties, sharply rising local government indebtedness, and increasing depression in a large part of the agricultural sector.

Some of these factors have been common to all American boom periods. The three that particularly characterized and ultimately undermined the pre-1929 boom were an insufficient increase in consumer demand to encourage the use of savings in productive domestic investment, the financial relations with foreign nations, and the change in the character of bank assets.

The period of prosperity from 1924 to late 1926 had been largely aided by installment buying of consumer durable goods, particularly automobiles; real estate investment; and construction. When this boom ended with a temporarily saturated automobile market in 1927, a depression of some duration was to be expected, but the speculative construction boom, supported greatly by state and local expenditures, showed surprising vitality until mid-1929; the Federal Reserve Board pursued a relatively easy money policy; and exports continued to be buoyed up by large foreign lending. To this extent the boom of 1927-29 may be regarded as partly dependent on government policies ranging all the way from borrowing too freely for street paving in new developments to failure to aid declining agriculture. But to put the blame on government at all levels would be to neglect the optimism of American big businessmen and financiers and their failure to face the long-run instabilities in the situation until a runaway stock-market boom had made orderly retreat impossible.

It is estimated—reliable data are still restricted by government regulations—that the income of the top 10 percent of receivers, who in those days did nearly all the net saving, was advancing rapidly. When the opportunities for real, labor-employing investment sagged after 1926, the money of the top-income group went into luxury purchases and the stock, bond, or mortgage markets. This development in turn gave the incentive of "easy money" to all kinds of speculative operators. In utilities and railroads, particularly, the pyramided, or many-staged, holding company structure was used by such insiders as Samuel Insull, Sidney Z. Mitchell, and Mantis J. and Oris P. Van Sweringen to put together and control vast business empires in which the costs of management and the burden of indebtedness rose rapidly. Investment trust companies, formed to give small investors the security of diversification, also became agencies for gaining control of companies—in other words, power structures for the insiders. Banks, in order to keep their depositors' money employed, often made large loans on the security of huge blocks of the common stock of a single company.

In June of 1929, sensitive economic indices began turning downward and some bankers were becoming alarmed by the continued rise of the stock market; in

August the Federal Reserve Board tightened credit by raising the discount rate. The immediate effect of this action was adverse, as some of the Federal Reserve Bank officers had feared. Higher interest rates attracted not only more domestic capital into call loans on the stock market but also much foreign capital as well, applying a final lash of the whip to the runaway boom in security prices.

The stock market reached its peak right after Labor Day, 1929. It declined only slightly during September and early October, but on Friday, Oct. 18, it began to decline rapidly; from then until mid-November there was a series of panic days, the first of which was Oct. 24 and the worst, Oct. 29, the most devastating day in the history of the stock exchange. Yet during the whole month-long decline, the Standard and Poor stock-market index fell less than 40 percent and public statements held that no harm had been done to normal business.

Some of the unseen factors that were to turn the stock-market decline into an unforeseen and unprecedented depression were big bank loans that could not be liquidated, forcing the banks, by law, to post capital sufficient to cover the deficiency between a loan and the market value of its collateral; the pressure of the failure of weak banks on stronger ones; the collapse of Central European finance in 1931; the decline in the total of all forms of government spending for public works from 1930 to 1936; a monetary policy by the Federal Reserve banks that vacillated between meeting domestic needs and meeting foreign needs; and the failure of any large capital-consuming technological development to restimulate private investment. One might also add the general failure of economists, politicians, and businessmen to understand the relations of income distribution, demand, and investment, which were to be clarified in the mid-1930's by John Maynard Keynes.

[John Kenneth Galbraith, *The Great Crash, 1929;* Wesley C. Mitchell, *Recent Economic Changes,* vol. II.]

THOMAS C. COCHRAN

PANIC OF 1937. *See* **Business Cycles.**

PANICS AND DEPRESSIONS. *See articles on Panics and* **Business Cycles; Depression of 1920.**

PAN-INDIANISM. The Pan-Indian movement represents a growing nationalism among American Indians of different tribes, who are increasingly able to overlook their deep-rooted tribal differences in recognition of their common Indianness. Recognizing that they have interests and problems in common, since World War II Indians have been coming together in a number of intertribal organizations, to affirm and intensify their Indian identity vis-à-vis all non-Indians.

The Pan-Indian movement incorporates elements from a variety of Indian cultures, but the influence of the Plains culture predominates. Pan-Indian gatherings often feature the Plains style of war bonnet and Plains styles of dancing, which have become symbols of Indianness to Indians of a variety of tribes in cultural areas outside of the Plains. There are intertribal federations, powwows at which Indians of many tribes get together for dancing and celebration, fraternal Pan-Indian groups, and intertribal groups devoted to Indian history or art. Intertribal visiting and intertribal marriages are on the increase.

A number of relatively new Pan-Indian organizations have developed in recognition of the need for unity among Indian Americans. The oldest of the major intertribal organizations created by and for the Indian people is the National Congress of American Indians, founded in 1944, which uses the political technique of lobbying to advance Indian interests. More militant organizations, the National Indian Youth Council and the American Indian Movement (AIM), were founded in 1961 and 1968. AIM made headlines with its occupation of the Washington, D.C., offices of the Bureau of Indian Affairs in 1972 and with its seizure of the village of Wounded Knee, S.Dak., in 1973. Other current Pan-Indian organizations include American Indians United, the United Native Americans, and the League of Nations, Pan-Am Indians.

[Hazel W. Hertzberg, *The Search for an American Indian Identity.*]

KENNETH M. STEWART

PANMURE, FORT, was the former French settlement Fort Rosalie at Natchez, Miss., as renamed after British occupancy in 1764. Bernardo Galvez captured it for Spain in 1779, and the Spanish retained it until 1798, when it was surrendered to the United States in accordance with Pinckney's Treaty in 1795. The fort was demolished in 1805.

[Dunbar Rowland, ed., *Mississippi,* vol. I; Joseph Dunbar Shields, *Natchez: Its Early History.*]

WALTER PRICHARD

PANOCHE GRANDE CLAIM of William McGarrahan was a celebrated land fraud comparable in its notoriety to the Crédit Mobilier scandal. The land claimed by McGarrahan, known as the Panoche Grande Rancho, was located in San Benito County, Calif., and included the New Idria Quicksilver Mine, already established by 1854. (New Idria Mine continued to be an important source of mercury well into the second half of the 20th century, having the largest mercury ore deposits in the United States.) Based on a pretended land grant that was supposed to have been made to Vicente P. Gomez by the governor of Mexico in 1844, the claim was purchased Dec. 22, 1857, by McGarrahan after squatters had discovered mercury in the area. Since Pacificus Ord had already purchased half the alleged claim, he and McGarrahan owned it jointly, until Ord gave the latter full power of attorney and the right to sell one-third of the alleged Gomez grant. In 1862 McGarrahan sold this interest to the Panoche Grande Quicksilver Company for $1, and he subsequently received from the company full paid stock for the entire claim. Because the original Gomez claim was not confirmed after the American conquest of California, and because it was denied by the U.S. Supreme Court a number of times, McGarrahan took his case to nearly every Congress during the 1860's, but to no avail. In the struggle for control of the New Idria Mine, McGarrahan was charged with constant lobbying and malpractice.

[R. J. Parker, "William McGarrahan's Panoche Grande Claim," *Pacific Historical Review*, vol. 5.]

ROBERT J. PARKER

PANTON, LESLIE AND COMPANY, originally set up as Panton, Forbes and Company, was organized in East Florida during the American Revolution by William Panton, Thomas Forbes, and other Loyalists to build up trade and influence with the Creek Indians. Spain permitted the company to remain in operation after the war but realized, with the departure of the British in 1784, that it needed the good will of the Indians as protection against the Anglo-American frontiersmen. Thus, in 1785 Spain gave the firm the entire Creek trade, adding that of the Choctaw and Chickasaw in 1788. Well organized both in England and America and exempted from duties, the company drove most competitors from the Creek, Choctaw, Cherokee, and Chickasaw nations and was the principal instrument with which Spain won and held the friendship of the Indians. The Indians bought supplies from the company and munitions furnished to the company by Spain. These were the Indians' principal resources in their struggles with the Americans.

Before Pinckney's Treaty of 1795, in which Spain accepted American boundary claims in East Florida and West Florida, the company helped promote trouble between the Indians and Americans to keep out rivals. After 1795, when Spain withdrew to the thirty-first parallel, the company confined itself to business and was able to keep most of the trade, although the U.S. government tried to compete with it. The firm and its successor, Forbes and Company (Panton died in 1801), continued to handle most of the Indian trade until about 1817.

[A. P. Whitaker, *The Spanish-American Frontier, 1783–1795,* and *The Mississippi Question, 1795–1803.*]

DUVON CLOUGH CORBITT

PAOLI, BATTLE OF (Sept. 21, 1777), was fought when the British, under Gen. Charles Grey, in an early morning attack, surprised Gen. Anthony Wayne's division of 1,500 men encamped near Paoli Inn, Pa. Under orders from Gen. George Washington to harass the British in order to delay Gen. William Howe's advance on Philadelphia, Wayne maneuvered to join Gen. William Smallwood for a concerted attack. Tory spies had revealed Wayne's position to Grey and, advancing in overwhelming numbers under cover of darkness, the British killed 300 and wounded 70.

[Gilbert Cope and J. Smith Futhey, *History of Chester County.*]

JULIAN P. BOYD

PAPAL STATES, DIPLOMATIC SERVICE TO. During the period 1797–1867 eleven American consuls resident in Rome were accredited to the papal government. There were also consulates in Civita Vecchia and Ancona. Formal diplomatic relations were inaugurated in 1848 with the appointment of Jacob L. Martin as chargé d'affaires for the United States, a post that later carried with it the title of minister. The last American minister to the papal states was Rufus King, as the legation was suppressed in 1867 through failure of Congress to continue the appropriation for its support. This action was protested by King as based on misunderstanding of a papal regulation regarding Protestant services in Rome. While the legation lasted, relations between the two governments were friendly. During the Civil War the papal authorities withheld recognition from the Confederacy on the ground that the North represented legitimate government in the United States and, after the conflict, delivered over to Washington John H. Surratt, who had enlisted in the papal army while under indictment for complicity in President Abraham Lincoln's assassination.

[L. F. Stock, *United States Ministers to the Papal States: Instructions and Despatches, 1848–1868.*]

GILBERT J. GARRAGHAN

PAPER AND PULP INDUSTRY. The first paper mill in the American colonies was established in 1690 at Germantown, near Philadelphia, Pa., by William Rittenhouse. Among his three partners was William Bradford, first printer in Pennsylvania and New York. Paper was made by hand, a single sheet at a time, from macerated rags, called pulp. Rags were the sole raw material. A hand mold, a sievelike device, was dipped into a vat of rag fibers in water and then raised. By a "shake," an even layer of wet fibers was achieved on the mold's surface. Removal of the wet mat from the mold and subsequent pressing and drying required two additional men. The three-man team produced about five reams of paper per day.

The establishment of new mills depended on population density both for markets and for adequate rag supplies. Practices and problems remained the same into the 19th century. According to census figures, by 1810 there were 202 mills in sixteen states. Employment numbered over 2,500, including ragpickers. The 19th century brought great change. The first paper machine in the colonies for making a continuous sheet was installed by Thomas Gilpin in Wilmington, Del., in 1817, greatly increasing production. Scientific and technical developments between 1828 and 1909 made straw and then wood usable as raw materials, making possible even greater production. Between 1865 and 1885 a larger number of patents related to papermaking were issued by the U.S. Patent Office than had been known in the history of any country.

The 20th century brought continuous scientific and technical improvement of 19th-century inventiveness, creating a forest-based, capital-intensive industry. In markets after World War II, American paper met challenges from plastics and, through "disposables," challenged textiles. Machine speeds of paper production rose from 1,000 feet per minute in 1920 to 5,000 for some types of paper by 1973; widths reached 390 inches. Leading the world, 1973 U.S. paper production was over 60 million tons, more than 90 percent of which was domestically consumed; per capita consumption was over 625 pounds per year.

The shores of the Fox River from Neenah and Menasha, Wis., to its outlet in Green Bay are said to be the most concentrated papermaking area in the world. Georgia leads all states in total tonnage of paper produced according to 1973 figures. Recycling fiber has received increased attention in the 1970's as a method of conserving fiber resources. Approximately 21 percent of all fiber used for papermaking in 1973 was reclaimed fiber.

U.S. newsprint consumption in 1973 approached 10.75 million tons, of which 32 percent was produced domestically and 64 percent was imported from Canada. Besides printing, principal uses of paper include facial tissues and other hygienic products, packaging, and functional and decorative building and construction products.

[Dard Hunter, *Papermaking: The History and Technique of an Ancient Craft;* David C. Smith, *History of Papermaking in the United States (1691–1969).*]

ARNOLD E. GRUMMER

PAPER MONEY. *See* **Money.**

PARAGUAY EXPEDITION. On Feb. 1, 1855, the U.S.S. *Water Witch,* temporarily commanded by W. N. Jeffers, was fired on and the helmsman killed while surveying a channel of the Paraná River, which was claimed to be Paraguayan territory. Unable to secure redress, the United States, in December 1858, assembled a squadron of nineteen ships and 1,708 men in the Río de la Plata under W. B. Shubrick. Two ships, the *Fulton* and the *Water Witch,* proceeded to Asunción, supported by the remainder lower down the river. Shubrick and the American commissioner, James B. Bowlin, easily secured an apology and $10,000 for the family of the helmsman and concluded a treaty that granted free navigation.

[T. J. Page, *The LaPlata, The Argentine Confederation, and Paraguay.*]

WALTER B. NORRIS

PARAPSYCHOLOGY, a term denoting the organized experimental study of purported "psychic" abilities, such as telepathy (the knowledge of human thoughts without sensory communication), clairvoyance (the knowledge of physical objects without sensory aid), psychokinesis (the ability to influence an object physically without contact with it), and precognition (the knowledge of future events). The term, originally German, found its way into English in the 1930's and has supplanted the older term "psychical research'' in America and to a degree in Great Britain.

Organized psychical research came into being in the United States in 1885 with the founding of the American Society for Psychical Research. The Society for Psychical Research, with which the American society maintained close connections, had been formed in England in 1882. With popular interest in spiritualism then at its height, there was concern on the part of some intellectuals in both countries that spiritualist or psychic phenomena be investigated scientifically; this was certainly a motive behind the formation and continuation of these societies. The most prominent American supporter of psychical research at this time was William James, although most American psychologists were, and are, hostile to the subject. Many famous mediums were studied, the most noteworthy being Leonora E. Piper, extensively investigated by James himself. The three principal leaders of American psychical research in its early years were Richard Hodgson, John Hervey Hyslop, and Walter Franklin Prince.

Funds and fellowships for the conduct of psychical research were established in three American universities—Harvard, Stanford, and Clark—in the first two decades of the 20th century, but the work done there was greatly overshadowed by the work done in the early 1930's by Joseph Banks Rhine with associates in the Psychology Department of Duke University. Asking subjects to guess cards from a deck of twenty-five containing five different symbols (star, square, circle, cross, and wavy lines) and employing statistical techniques to evaluate the results, Rhine ran thousands of tests with Duke students, some of whom achieved striking extra-chance results in card guessing either telepathically or clairvoyantly. The results were published in 1934 in *Extra-Sensory Perception;* the methods described there soon became standard experimental procedure, and Rhine's term ESP (extrasensory perception) has become a common label for psychic abilities. A parapsychology laboratory was subsequently set up at Duke and was for a long time the focus of American parapsychology. Rhine established the *Journal of Parapsychology* in 1937, and in the 1940's he carried his investigations on into psychokinesis and precognition.

Parapsychology aroused controversy and hostility in scientific and academic quarters; objections were made both to its experimental and statistical methods and to its philosophical implications. Fifty years after university studies began, the subject was still not yet well established academically and had not yet devel-

oped a clear professional structure and status. In the popular mind, and to some degree in the field, the connections with spiritualism and the occult remained close. But by the 1970's research in parapsychology was being pursued at various academic centers, including the University of Virginia, the City University of New York, and Maimonides Hospital in New York City, as well as at the American Society for Psychical Research and at private foundations in Durham, N.C., and elsewhere. This later experimental work was broadly diversified, with researchers attempting to bring physiology, psychiatry, and studies of animal behavior to bear on parapsychology.

[Rhea A. White and Laura A. Dale, *Parapsychology: Sources of Information.*]

SEYMOUR H. MAUSKOPF
MICHAEL R. MCVAUGH

PARATROOPS, light infantry, trained and equipped with parachutes, who jump behind enemy lines from aircraft. When used as shock troops, they are dropped within supporting distance of friendly lines to disrupt the enemy's rear area and seize such key points as bridges, road junctions, and communications centers. They are usually employed in conjunction with an amphibious landing, as at Normandy, or a large-scale ground offensive, as at Arnhem in the Netherlands; they are also used as highly mobile reinforcements. As light infantry these troops lack heavy weapons, although they carry such substitutes as recoilless artillery; they cannot remain in the field long without heavy aerial resupply or contact with ground forces.

Paratroops were first used by the French on a small scale during World War I. An American, Col. William C. (''Billy'') Mitchell, planned a parachute assault on the city of Metz, France, but the armistice occurred before the attack was mounted. Between the wars the United States did little to develop an airborne arm, but German success with paratroops early in World War II spurred the formation of five airborne divisions, the 11th, 13th, 17th, 82nd, and 101st. American paratroops participated in combat on all fronts. The first jump supported Allied amphibious landings in North Africa; others followed in Sicily, Normandy, southern France, the Netherlands, and Germany. Except in North Africa all these operations involved at least a division-size unit. Although airborne operations were staged in the Pacific in New Guinea and the Philippines, none involved units larger than a regiment. There were two airborne operations by U.S. troops during the Korean War, and there was one during the Vietnam War. As of

1975 the army had only one airborne unit, the 82nd Airborne Division; the 101st Airborne is an airmobile unit.

[John R. Galvin, *Air Assault: The Development of Air Mobility;* Charles B. MacDonald, *Airborne.*]

WARNER STARK

PARDON. *See* **Amnesty.**

PARIS, DECLARATION OF (1856). At the end of the Crimean War (1854–56), the representatives of Austria, France, Great Britain, Prussia, Russia, Sardinia, and Turkey adopted a declaration concerning maritime law that stated (1) privateering is and remains abolished; (2) the neutral flag covers enemy goods, with the exception of contraband of war; (3) neutral goods, with the exception of contraband of war, are not liable to capture under the enemy's flag; and (4) blockades, in order to be binding, must be effective, that is to say, maintained by a force sufficient to prevent access to the coast of the enemy.

Other powers were invited to adhere to the declaration in its entirety. Secretary of State William H. Marcy declined to accede because the United States was still a small naval power and unwilling to abandon privateering unless the large naval powers would deny the right of belligerent public warships to capture private property, contraband excepted. Later, during the Civil War, the United States endeavored to accede, in order to outlaw Confederate privateering, but the powers declined. The United States never pursued privateering after the War of 1812.

[Carlton Savage, *Policy of the United States Toward Maritime Commerce in War,* vol. I.]

SAMUEL FLAGG BEMIS

PARIS, PACT OF. *See* **Kellogg-Briand Pact.**

PARIS, PEACE OF (1783). During the American Revolution, Great Britain became successively engaged in war with the American colonies, France, Spain, and the Netherlands. When the conflict came to an end treaties of peace between those four powers respectively and Great Britain were made. Preliminary articles were signed at Paris between the United States and Great Britain on Nov. 30, 1782, and between the Netherlands and Great Britain on Sept. 2, 1783. On Sept. 3, 1783, three definitive treaties of peace between Great Britain and the United States, France, and Spain were signed.

The Definitive Treaty of Peace, between the United States and Great Britain, was signed at Paris because the British plenipotentiary, David Hartley, declined to go to Versailles for that purpose, although that course was desired by the American commissioners—John Adams, Benjamin Franklin, and John Jay. The signing of the treaty with the United States took place in the morning, and after word thereof was received at Versailles the treaties with France and Spain were there signed between noon and one o'clock. Thus, it is erroneous to speak of the Definitive Treaty of Peace between the United States and Great Britain as the Treaty of Versailles.

[Richard B. Morris, *The Peacemakers: Great Powers and American Independence;* Richard W. Van Alstyne, *Empire and Independence: The International History of the American Revolution.*]

HUNTER MILLER

PARIS, TREATY OF (1763), between Great Britain, France, and Spain, brought to an end the French and Indian War. In 1755 Great Britain had been willing to limit its jurisdiction in the interior of North America by a line running due south from Cuyahoga Bay on Lake Erie to the fortieth parallel and southwest to the thirty-seventh parallel, with the proviso that the territory beyond that line to the Maumee and Wabash rivers be a neutral zone. The British claimed, however, an area that would have included all the land between the Penobscot and Saint Lawrence rivers and the Gulf of Saint Lawrence and the Bay of Fundy, as well as the peninsula of Nova Scotia. The result of the British victory was an extension of British demands on France to include the cession of all of Canada to Great Britain and the advancement of the boundary of the continental colonies westward to the Mississippi River. Both these demands, together with the right to navigate the Mississippi, were granted to Great Britain in the treaty. Cuba, conquered by the British, was returned to Spain, which to offset this gain ceded East Florida and West Florida to Britain. As compensation for its losses, Spain received from France by the Treaty of Fontainebleau (1762) all the territory west of the Mississippi River and the island and city of New Orleans. France retained only the islands of Saint Pierre and Miquelon off the south coast of Newfoundland, together with the privilege of fishing and drying fish along the northern and western coasts of Newfoundland as provided in the Treaty of Utrecht (1713). In the West Indies, Great Britain retained the islands of Saint Vincent, Tobago, and Dominica; Saint Lucia, Martinique, and Guadeloupe were returned to France. The Treaty of Paris left only two great colonial empires in the Western Hemisphere, the British and the Spanish.

[Kate Hotblack, "The Peace of Paris, 1763," *Transactions of the Royal Historical Society*, vol. 2, 3rd series; Theodore C. Pease, *Anglo-French Boundary Disputes in the West, 1749–1763*; Max Savelle, *The Diplomatic History of the Canadian Boundary, 1749–1763*.]

MAX SAVELLE

PARIS, TREATY OF (1898), terminated the Spanish-American War. Under its terms Spain relinquished all authority over Cuba and ceded to the United States Puerto Rico, the Philippine Islands, and Guam, in exchange for $20 million as the estimated value of public works and nonmilitary improvements in the Philippines. Hostilities had been suspended Aug. 12, and on Oct. 1 the five U.S. commissioners, headed by former Secretary of State William R. Day, opened negotiations with the Spanish commissioners in Paris. The most difficult questions encountered were the disposition of the Philippines, which Spain was reluctant to relinquish, and of the $400 million Spanish debt charged against Cuba, which the Spanish wished assumed by either Cuba or the United States. Eventually Spain yielded on both points. An attempt by the U.S. commissioners to secure the island of Kusaie in the Carolines was blocked by Germany, which had opened negotiations for the purchase of these islands. The treaty was signed Dec. 10. The Senate, after bitter debate over the adoption of an imperialistic policy, exemplified in the annexation of the Philippines, consented to ratification by a close vote on Feb. 6, 1899. The treaty was proclaimed Apr. 11, 1899.

[E. J. Benton, *International Law and Diplomacy of the Spanish-American War*; Julius W. Pratt, *Expansionists of 1898*.]

JULIUS W. PRATT

PARIS AGREEMENT (1925) was an arrangement among Germany's reparations creditors (except the United States) to distribute the annuities paid to them after World War I. The payments had been scaled down from the original reparations bill by the Dawes Plan (1924), after Germany had defaulted in early 1923. The share of the United States in this distribution was confirmed by the American-German debt agreement of June 23, 1930.

[Harold G. Moulton and Leo Pasvolsky, *War Debts and World Prosperity*.]

SAMUEL FLAGG BEMIS

PARIS CONFERENCES (after World War II). During 1946 the United States participated in two lengthy international conferences at Paris called for the purpose of drafting a postwar European settlement. The Council of Foreign Ministers, made up of representatives from the United States, the Soviet Union, Great Britain, and France, met from Apr. 25 to May 16 and from June 15 to July 12 in an effort to agree on peace treaties for the former Axis satellites, Finland, Bulgaria, Romania, Hungary, and Italy. After extended argument, compromise agreements were reached that allowed the convening of the Paris Peace Conference on July 29, 1946, composed of the twenty-one nations that had been at war with Germany. Concluding on Oct. 15, this conference could, and did, recommend modifications in the draft peace treaties to the Big Four, but the essential elements of the treaties had been hammered out in the preliminary foreign ministers meetings.

The Paris conferences of 1946 were important as a step in the growing tension between the United States and the Soviet Union. The bitterness and acrimony that marked the foreign ministers' efforts to agree on relatively minor matters—such as the Italian-Yugoslav boundary, Italian reparations, disposition of the Italian colonies, and rules for the international navigation of the Danube—indicated that agreement on the far more complex German peace treaty was some distance away. Furthermore, each nation used these public forums for propaganda attacks on the other, thus intensifying tensions. Final provisions of the satellite peace treaties were agreed to at the New York foreign ministers meeting on Nov. 4–Dec. 12, 1946, and the treaties were signed by the United States in Washington, D.C., on Jan. 20, 1947, and by the other powers at Paris on Feb. 10.

Another Big Four foreign ministers conference was held at Paris from May 23 to June 20, 1949. This conference dealt mainly with the German problem, which revolved largely around the Big Four's inability to agree on terms for a peace treaty for that country. The meeting at Paris had been agreed to by the United States, Great Britain, and France in return for Soviet agreement to drop the blockade of Berlin, which had been begun in 1948 in protest against the Western powers' decision to create an independent West Germany. At the conference the West rejected a Soviet plan for German reunification, and the Soviets turned down a Western proposal for extension of the new West German constitution to East Germany.

In 1959 the heads of state of the United States, Great Britain, France, and the Soviet Union agreed to hold a summit conference in Paris in May 1960 for the purpose of discussing the mutual reduction of tensions. This conference had been agreed to as an outcome of Premier Nikita S. Khrushchev's determination to sign a peace treaty with the East Germans that would have impaired Western access rights to Berlin. Plans for the conference went awry two weeks before its opening when an American reconnaissance aircraft (the U-2) was shot down over the Soviet Union. When President Dwight D. Eisenhower refused to disavow responsibility or apologize for the flight, Khrushchev dramatically refused to participate in the summit conference and canceled an invitation for Eisenhower to visit the Soviet Union.

The longest series of negotiations at Paris in which the United States participated was the talks regarding the settlement of the Vietnam War, which began in 1968 and did not end until 1973. Following President Lyndon B. Johnson's agreement to restrict the bombing of North Vietnam and his withdrawal from the presidential campaign in March 1968, the North Vietnamese agreed to meet with the Americans at Paris to discuss a settlement of the war. The talks were later broadened to include the South Vietnamese and the Viet Cong. Negotiations were held on a weekly basis for the next four years, resulting in a gradual narrowing of differences. In 1969, Henry Kissinger, then special adviser for national security affairs to President Richard M. Nixon, began secret meetings at Paris with North Vietnamese politburo member Le Duc Tho. These meetings were made public early in 1972 and by the fall of that year had brought the two sides close to agreement. Differences of interpretation arose that led to a temporary suspension of the talks in December 1972, before the peace settlement of 1973.

[Council on Foreign Relations, *The United States in World Affairs, 1945–47, 1949, 1960;* U.S. Department of State, *Foreign Relations of the United States, 1946,* vols. III and IV, and *Paris Peace Conference, 1946: Selected Documents.*]

JOHN LEWIS GADDIS

PARISH, the unit for ecclesiastical administration, particularly of the Roman Catholic church, throughout the United States. In it is also the civil or political unit for local administrative purposes, corresponding to the county in other states. The French and Spanish population of Louisiana disliked the county system established after the Louisiana Purchase (1803), and the parish soon replaced the county as the local civil or political unit in the state.

[Alcée Fortier, ed., *Louisiana,* vol. II.]

WALTER PRICHARD

PARITY in naval defense was a principle used as a basis for the limitation of naval armaments adopted at the Washington Conference of 1921–22. As proposed by the American delegation, U.S. superiority in capital-ship tonnage was reduced to equality with the British and to five-thirds of Japan's tonnage. Aircraft carrier allowances in the same proportion were agreed upon, but the total tonnage of other types of ships remained unlimited until the London Treaty of 1930 with America's corresponding ratio somewhat reduced. Restrictions on naval base facilities in the Orient resulted in Japan having virtual parity with Britain or America for operations in those waters. With the notable naval concessions made by other powers in 1922, Japan consented to withdraw from current military occupation of northern China and to sign the Nine-Power Treaty guaranteeing future political and territorial integrity of China. Japan refused to renew the naval limitation treaties on their expiration in 1936, except on a basis of parity in ships, which Britain and America declined since this would give Japan great superiority in Far East operations. Meantime, by failure to build to its treaty allowances, the United States had dropped well below its parity ratio.

[Dudley W. Knox, *A History of the U.S. Navy.*]

DUDLEY W. KNOX

PARKER'S FORT was established at the headwaters of the Navasota River in Limestone County, Tex., in 1835. Around it grew up the first settlement in that region. In May 1836 the settlement was attacked by 300 Comanche and Caddo. All the Texans were killed except Cynthia Ann Parker, a child, who was carried into captivity, grew up with the Indians, married Peta Nocone, a chief of the Kwahadi, and had a son, Quanah Parker, who became chief of his tribe and a pacific influence in mediating between Indians and whites.

[F. W. Johnson and E. C. Barker, *History of Texas.*]

CARL L. CANNON

PARKS, NATIONAL, AND NATIONAL MONUMENTS. Of the 31 million acres in the National Park System in 1975, 15.6 million were in the thirty-eight national parks and 9.8 million in the eighty-one national monuments. Often called the crown jewels of the park system, national parks can be established only by act of Congress. Congress may also authorize national monuments, but most of them have been established by presidential proclamation under the Antiquities Act of 1906, which was passed to protect endangered archaeological and scientific sites on federal lands. Whereas the term "monument" is used in Europe principally to describe works of nature and in America most commonly to refer to statues or stone shafts, both meanings are included in the National Park System's usage—which comprehends, for example, both Death Valley and the Statue of Liberty.

Every president from Theodore Roosevelt to Lyndon B. Johnson proclaimed at least one national monument to protect scientific or historical sites, placing them under the supervision of the Department of the Interior, Department of Agriculture, or War Department, and in a number of instances the designation served to protect significant areas until park status could be conferred on them. National parks that were formerly national monuments are Lassen Volcanic, Grand Canyon, Acadia, Zion, Carlsbad Caverns, Bryce Canyon, Grand Teton, Olympic, Petrified Forest, Arches, and Capitol Reef.

The sixty-two areas transferred to the National Park Service by executive order in 1933 included the Statue of Liberty, nine other national monuments of the War Department, and Fort McHenry National Park, which was redesignated a national monument in 1939. The order also transferred fourteen national monuments from the Department of Agriculture's Forest Service to the Park Service, including Mount Olympus, Wash., most of which became Olympic National Park in 1938. Bandelier National Monument in New Mexico, containing ruins of cliff dwellings, was transferred from the Department of Agriculture to the National Park Service in 1932; Custer Battlefield, Mont., from the War Department in 1940; and Fort Sumter, S.C., from the Department of the Army in 1948.

A national park must possess nationally significant lands or waters of such superior quality, beauty, or scientific importance that it is imperative to protect them. While both national parks and national monuments must possess features that merit commitment to national care, a national park should contain two or more such features whereas a national monument need not. National parks are relatively spacious; national monuments may be any size. The two largest National Park Service areas in 1975 were national monuments in Alaska, Glacier Bay and Katmai, both of which may become national parks. All national parks are categorized as natural, rather than historical, areas except Mesa Verde, Colo.

The thirty-five national monuments categorized as natural areas are Glacier Bay and Katmai, Alaska; Chiricahua, Organ Pipe Cactus, Saguaro, and Sunset Crater, Ariz.; Channel Islands, Devils Postpile, Joshua Tree, Lava Beds, Muir Woods, and Pinnacles, Calif.; Death Valley, Calif.-Nev.; Black Canyon of the Gunnison, Colorado, Florissant Fossil Beds, and Great Sand Dunes, Colo.; Dinosaur, Colo.-Utah; Biscayne, Fla.; Craters of the Moon, Idaho; Agate Fossil Beds, Nebr.; Lehman Caves, Nev.; Capulin Mountain, Fossil Butte, and White Sands, N.Mex.; John Day Fossil Beds and Oregon Caves, Oreg.; Badlands and Jewel Cave, S.Dak.; Cedar Breaks, Natural Bridges, Rainbow Bridge, and Timpanogos Cave, Utah; Devils Tower, Wyo.; and Buck Island Reef, V.I.

The forty-six national monuments categorized as historical areas are Russell Cave, Ala.; Canyon de Chelly, Casa Grande Ruins, Hohokam-Pima, Montezuma Castle, Navajo, Pipe Spring, Tonto, Tumacacori, Tuzigoot, Walnut Canyon, and Wupatki, Ariz.; Cabrillo, Calif.; Yucca House, Colo.; Hovenweep, Colo.-Utah; Castillo de San Marcos, Fort Jefferson, and Fort Matanzas, Fla.; Fort Frederica, Fort Pulaski, and Ocmulgee, Ga.; Effigy Mounds, Iowa; Saint Croix Island, Maine; Fort McHenry, Md.; Grand Portage and Pipestone, Minn.; George Washington Carver, Mo.; Custer Battlefield, Mont.; Homestead and Scotts Bluff, Nebr.; Aztec Ruins, Bandelier, Chaco Canyon, El Morro, Fort Union, Gila Cliff Dwellings, Gran Quivira, and Pecos, N.Mex.; Castle Clinton and Fort Stanwix, N.Y.; Statue of Liberty, N.Y.-N.J.; Mound City Group, Ohio; Fort Sumter, S.C.; Alibates Flint Quarries and Texas Panhandle Pueblo Culture, Tex.; Booker T. Washington and George Washington Birthplace, Va.

Legislation presented in Congress on Dec. 17, 1973, would preserve for all present and future generations scenic, wildlife, and archaeological wonders of Alaska. The polar bear would come under National Park Service protection for the first time. Wolf packs, mountain goats, brown grizzly bears, caribou, Dall sheep, endangered species of whale, rare birds, and birds migrating to six continents would be protected, as would Eskimo and Indian cultures, archaeological sites, mountain ranges, unspoiled river valleys, glaciers larger than Rhode Island, and tundra and mountain wilderness. Four new national parks, four new national monuments, and two other parklands would achieve this purpose. The proposed national parks would take in 21.48 million acres, added to which would be a 3.18-million-acre expansion of Mount McKinley National Park, to include the south half of North America's highest peak.

[John Ise, *Our National Park Policy;* National Park Service, *Index of the National Park System,* and *Public Use of the National Parks;* Thomas A. Sullivan, *Proclamations*

PARKS, NATIONAL, AND NATIONAL MONUMENTS

NATIONAL PARKS

NAME	LOCATION	ORIGIN	ACREAGE	1974 VISITORS
Yellowstone	Wyo.-Idaho-Mont.	1872	2,219,823	1,937,800
Sequoia	Calif.	1890	386,823	686,900
Yosemite	Calif.	1890	760,917	2,343,100
Mount Rainier	Wash.	1899	235,404	1,495,500
Crater Lake	Oreg.	1902	160,290	525,000
Wind Cave	S.Dak.	1903	28,060	855,700
Platt	Okla.	1906	912	3,903,500
Mesa Verde	Colo.	1906	52,036	446,700
Glacier	Mont.	1910	1,013,598	1,406,600
Rocky Mountain	Colo.	1915	263,793	2,501,100
Hawaii Volcanoes	Hawaii	1916	229,177	1,613,100
Lassen Volcanic	Calif.	1916	106,372	408,700
Mount McKinley	Alaska	1917	1,939,492	425,500
Grand Canyon	Ariz.	1919	1,218,375	2,028,200
Acadia	Maine	1919	37,601	2,734,900
Zion	Utah	1919	146,571	941,300
Hot Springs	Ark.	1921	5,801	2,314,500
Carlsbad Caverns	N.Mex.	1923	46,755	672,400
Bryce Canyon	Utah	1924	37,277	410,300
Great Smoky Mountains	N.C.-Tenn.	1926	517,014	10,447,200
Shenandoah	Va.	1926	190,445	2,215,300
Mammoth Cave	Ky.	1926	52,129	1,740,000
Grand Teton	Wyo.	1929	310,418	2,936,800
Isle Royale	Mich.	1931	539,280	13,900
Everglades	Fla.	1934	1,400,533	1,000,000

PARK SERVICE, NATIONAL, AND NATIONAL PARK SYSTEM

NATIONAL PARKS

NAME	LOCATION	ORIGIN	ACREAGE	1974 VISITORS
Big Bend	Tex.	1935	708,118	191,300
Olympic	Wash.	1938	897,886	2,479,300
Kings Canyon	Calif.	1940	460,136	1,224,400
Virgin Islands	V.I.	1956	14,470	298,200
Haleakala	Hawaii	1960	27,824	441,300
Petrified Forest	Ariz.	1962	94,189	789,200
Canyonlands	Utah	1964	337,570	59,000
Guadalupe Mountains	Tex.	1966	79,972	39,400
Redwood	Calif.	1968	62,286	328,300
North Cascades	Wash.	1968	504,785	885,300 *
Voyageurs	Minn.	1971	219,128	no count
Arches	Utah	1971	73,398	171,300
Capitol Reef	Utah	1971	241,865	234,000

* Includes visits to two adjacent national recreation areas.

and Orders Relating to the National Park Service up to Jan. 1, 1945; Hillary A. Tolson, *Laws Relating to the National Park Service,* supp. II.]

JOHN VOSBURGH

PARK SERVICE, NATIONAL, AND NATIONAL PARK SYSTEM. The U.S. Congress established the National Park Service, within the Department of the Interior, in an act signed by President Woodrow Wilson on Aug. 25, 1916. The new agency was to provide strong central administration of the loosely managed national parks and monuments. The heart of the act, written by landscape architect Frederick Law Olmsted, Jr., declared that the "fundamental purpose of the parks [was] . . . to conserve the scenery and the natural and historic objects and the wildlife therein and to provide for the enjoyment of the same in such manner and by such means as will leave them unimpaired for the enjoyment of future generations."

Over the years the areas under the management of the National Park Service came to include recreational and cultural areas as well as natural wonders and historic monuments and became known informally as the national park system, a name recognized officially by Congress in 1953. Since many of the areas administered by the National Park Service had been set aside as federal preserves before the establishment of the service—the first being Yellowstone National Park in 1872—Congress in 1970 designated 1872 as the date of origin of the National Park System. Recognizing the expanded purpose of the National Park System, it declared that the areas were "preserved and managed for the benefit and inspiration of all the people."

The first director of the National Park Service, from 1917 until 1929, was a Chicago manufacturer, Stephen T. Mather, who had complained to the secretary of the interior in 1914 about conditions in the parks. The secretary, Franklin K. Lane, a fellow Californian and college friend of Mather, had replied: "If you don't like the way the national parks are being run, come down and run them yourself." As Lane's assistant between 1915 and 1917, and subsequently as director of the National Park Service, Mather acquainted the American public with the parks and fought off efforts of livestock, power, irrigation, mining, lumber, and hunting interests to use parklands and waters. He won the support of John D. Rockefeller, Jr., who provided financial aid vital to the acquisition of Acadia, Grand Teton, and Great Smoky Mountains national parks; and gave additional funds for many other national parks. His son, Laurance S. Rockefeller, contributed the first 5,000 acres of Virgin Islands National Park and additions to Haleakala National Park, Hawaii.

Between 1929 and 1940 the National Park Service was directed by two former assistants of Mather, each of whom made his own special contribution. Horace M. Albright, director from 1929 to 1933, expanded the role of the Park Service in the preservation of historic sites. Under Albright's aegis a plan long favored by Mather, Albright, and President Herbert Hoover was consummated when President Franklin D. Roosevelt transferred forty-eight War Department areas and fourteen Department of Agriculture areas to the National Park Service in 1933. Albright's administrative initiative is also reflected in the fact that he brought the Civilian Conservation Corps into the parks. Following Albright, Arno B. Cammerer, director between 1933 and 1940, added to the National Park System the first rural roadway park, Blue Ridge Parkway, and the first national seashore, Cape Hatteras, N.C. He set up four regional offices and assured massive park improvements. He developed his predecessor's focus on the Park Service's historical functions, under the Historic Sites Act of 1935.

During World War II the National Park System was not only weakened by a curtailment of funds but also threatened by wartime demands to use the parks for lumbering, mining, grazing, and farming; to whittle down Olympic National Park; and to flood parklands with federal dam waters. When the Department of the Interior approved the construction of dams at Dinosaur National Monument, the director, Newton B. Drury, resigned, and the dams were never built. The effects of wartime budgetary neglect had become serious for the nation's parks when Conrad L. Wirth became director of the Park Service in 1951. With the support of President Dwight D. Eisenhower, he launched a $750-million, ten-year improvement plan. Called Mission 66, for its 1966 proposed completion date, it produced 100 visitor centers, 575 camp-

grounds, 12,393 picnic grounds, thousands of miles of roads and trails, and hundreds of other benefits, including 459 historic buildings.

After Wirth, George B. Hartzog, Jr., administered the parks during a record expansion period, from 1964 to 1973, and introduced a series of innovative programs. With strong support from presidents Lyndon B. Johnson and Richard M. Nixon, he developed new urban parks and projects. The National Park Service also responded to the urban dweller's needs by creating seven new national parks during Hartzog's directorship; public use increased from 133 million visits in 1963 to 213 million in 1972. The greatly increased use of the parks called for a new focus of concern by Hartzog's successor, Ronald H. Walker, who became director in 1973. While limiting visits to overused areas and fostering safety precautions, he stressed the expansion of interpretive services to inform the public about the diversity of the park system and urged public use of lesser-known areas and of parklands within a day's drive of urban centers.

In 1975 the National Park System included 286 areas, in every state of the Union except Delaware: 74 natural areas, encompassing 25,826,745 acres; 167 historical areas, 501,375 acres; and 45 recreational areas, 4,698,955 acres. Under the 1971 Alaska Native Claims Settlement Act about 32.26 million acres were placed under protection until Dec. 18, 1978, for possible addition to the National Park System.

[William C. Everhart, *The National Park Service;* John Ise, *Our National Park Policy;* Robert Shankland, *Steve Mather of the National Parks;* Donald C. Swain, *Wilderness Defender.*]

JOHN VOSBURGH

PARLIAMENT, BRITISH, is significant in American history mainly as the embodiment of those rights and liberties possessed under the British constitution by all Englishmen. To the American colonist, who regarded these privileges as belonging to himself as well as to the Briton in Europe, it was a cherished ideal, and all the provincial assemblies save that of Pennsylvania accepted its bicameral principle. In fact, the chief object of every colonial assembly was to run a course similar to that of Parliament and secure the right to participate in the benefits that Parliament had wrested from the crown.

The part played by Parliament in the administration of the colonies before 1763 was very small, for North America was regarded as an appurtenance of the crown and governed by ordinances of the Privy Council. Only in matters of combined domestic and colonial interest, or involving the welfare of the empire as a whole, did Parliament legislate for the colonies, as in the Molasses Act of 1733, designed to promote trade between New England and the British West Indies and to benefit West Indian planters.

Not until the firm establishment of the principle of parliamentary supremacy in England, concurrent with the close of the French and Indian War, did Parliament seriously set itself to the direction of colonial affairs (see Colonial Policy, British). It quickly made itself odious to Americans by asserting its authority in regard to colonial taxation and appropriation, which the assemblies had long looked upon as their exclusive domain. Americans felt that Parliament had no right to assume powers that the crown had formerly been unable to make good, and the uncompromising attitude of the ministry of George Grenville concerning the Stamp Act (1765) precipitated a crisis in which colonial opinion everywhere stiffened against Parliament. Two years later, the passage of the Townshend Acts widened the breach, and in 1773 the resolution of the British prime minister, Frederick, Lord North, to "try the issue [of taxation] in America" led directly to the Revolution.

[Louis B. Namier and John Brooke, *The History of Parliament, The House of Commons, 1754–1790.*]

FRANK J. KLINGBERG

PAROLE SYSTEM is a phase of penology usually associated with the indeterminate sentence (in which the exact duration of the sentence is determined by the administrative authorities, within the limits of a maximum or minimum sentence already set), based upon the idea of making prisoners useful members of society. An offender is released (paroled) from prison upon certain conditions, but remains under supervision of state authorities during the balance of his term. If the conditions are violated, he may be returned to prison. First used in New York State in 1876, parole has been adopted by most of the states and by the federal government.

[J. P. Bramer, *A Treatise Giving the History, Organization, and Administration of Parole.*]

P. ORMAN RAY

PARSON BROWNLOW'S BOOK was the popular short title of a powerful propaganda book written in 1862 by William G. Brownlow, a fearless and militant Unionist of Tennessee during the Civil War. Under the title *Sketches of the Rise, Progress, and Decline of Secession; With a Narrative of Personal Adventures Among the Rebels,* it was written and pub-

lished while Parson Brownlow was an exile in the North. He studded its 458 pages with "rebel atrocities" and scathing denunciations of the Confederates; and a New York artist reinforced the effect with a dozen illustrations.

[E. M. Coulter, *William G. Brownlow, Fighting Parson of the Southern Highlands.*]

E. MERTON COULTER

PARSON'S CAUSE. During the colonial period tobacco was a medium of exchange, and ministers' salaries had been fixed (1748) at 17,200 pounds of tobacco a year. To remedy the distress from fluctuating crops and prices, laws were passed in 1755 and again in 1758 permitting tobacco payments to be commuted in paper money at twopence per pound. As tobacco sold for sixpence a pound the ministers considered themselves losers, assailed the law both in Virginia and England, and obtained a royal veto in 1759 (see Royal Disallowance), which was not published in Virginia until 1760. In the meantime, ministers' salaries for 1758 had been settled in paper money at the prescribed rate. With the announcement of the veto, ministers started suits for the difference between what they were paid and the value of their tobacco quota at current prices. In Hanover County the court ruled the act of 1758 was invalid from its passage, and the Rev. James Maury, rector of a parish in Louisa County, brought suit to recover on his salary (1762). Patrick Henry defended the parish, presenting no witnesses but assailing the ministers and the practice of vetoing laws necessary for the public good. The jury awarded Maury one penny damages. In 1764 the general court of the province held the law good until it was vetoed and left the ministers without any remedy. This was appealed to the Privy Council where the appeal was dismissed (1767). A general two-penny act was passed in 1769, and the ministers gave up the agitation. Henry's speech was publicized about fifty years later when he had become a national hero, and the reference in the Declaration of Independence to vetoing "Laws, the most wholesome and necessary for the public good" probably refers to this issue.

[George E. Howard, *Preliminaries of the Revolution.*]

O. M. DICKERSON

PARTIES, POLITICAL. *See* **Political Parties.**

PARTISAN BANDS constitute a type of irregular soldiery found mainly in civil war and warfare in defense

PARTY EMBLEMS

of invaded territory. In many ways partisan bands resemble guerrillas and are commonly accused by the enemy of carrying on guerrilla warfare, but a slight distinction exists. Guerrillas are sometimes unorganized or, if organized at all, somewhat independent of any regular army and thereby almost without any constituted authority, while partisan bands are loosely organized and nominally under some constituted government.

In American history partisan bands have played a romantic if somewhat indecisive role. They first appeared in the series of wars between the British and French that went on at intervals from 1689 to 1763. In these wars groups of frontiersmen, in defense of their homesteads, formed irregular military bands. They called themselves and were by others called "rangers." Sometimes they made expeditions into the enemy's strongholds, as in Col. John Armstrong's raid on Kittanning, on the Allegheny River in western Pennsylvania, in 1756. On the opening of hostilities in the American Revolution partisan bands appeared, among them the Green Mountain Boys in the North and the followers of Col. Andrew Pickens, Lt. Col. Francis Marion, and Col. Thomas Sumter in the South. In the Civil War partisan bands or corps came into existence, of which Mosby's Rangers, led by Maj. John S. Mosby, were merely the most famous. Smaller bands existed in Kentucky, Kansas, Missouri, Arkansas, and Indian Territory. Of these Gen. Albert Pike's partisan band of Confederates, composed largely of Indians, was possibly the most significant.

At the Hague Conferences of 1899 and 1907 efforts were unsuccessfully made to bring partisan bands or guerrillas under regular military rules and control.

ALFRED P. JAMES

PARTY EMBLEMS. *See* **Emblems, Party.**

PARTY GOVERNMENT, defined as the existence of cohesive political coalitions, programmatic in appeal, and democratically responsive to their electors, has never existed in the United States. The problems of judging the realities of American politics in relation to some standard of responsible party government have intrigued commentators from the days of James Bryce, Woodrow Wilson, A. Lawrence Lowell, and Moisei Yakovlevich Ostrogorski in the late 19th century down to and including more recent students of party behavior, such as Elmer E. Schattschneider,

James MacGregor Burns, and Austin Ranney, who made their mark principally in the third quarter of the 20th century.

The difficulties that arise in assessing the American experience with political parties derive from a variety of sources: the competing, and intrinsically more rational, model of party behavior that evolved in Great Britain; the continuing attempt to place party appeals and voter support within an intelligible framework; and the frustration implicit in attempting to master the diversity and inconsistency in performance and organization that has characterized American party operations from the community, county, state, and national operations to the independent candidate groupings and the insularity of many legislative party concerns—a network of relationships that defies systematic description.

The British experiment with political parties resulted in policy-oriented and comparatively cohesive groups, characterized by centralized decision making, clear lines of authority, and even sanctions applicable by a dissatisfied leadership to recalcitrant elected party members. For many the British party system epitomizes a responsibility obviously lacking in its American counterpart. In large part the parliamentary system of government permits the kind of order and appeal to clear issues that a national-level separation of powers superimposed on a federal arrangement of governing units does not. Whether such institutional factors alone explain the continuing excessive decentralization and fragmentation of parties in the United States remains a moot point. Many critics have come to believe that American parties could, while not necessarily aping the British model, improve considerably in organizational coherence, responsibility for the enactment of avowed policies, and cooperativeness both between differing levels of party agencies and between the presidential and congressional wings of the two major political coalitions.

Equally discontented have been those who have attempted to identify the basis for cleavage between the two principal parties. The 18th-century conservative British statesman Edmund Burke once wrote that a "party is a body of men recruited, for promoting by their joint endeavors the national interest, upon some particular principle in which they are all agreed." The perspective has an intuitive appeal. Yet although scholarship has shown that there is, in the United States, a greater consensus on issues on the basis of party allegiance than had been realized—especially on social and economic issues—anyone who seeks to assess American parties in relation to such criteria

222

courts disappointment. The major American parties, the Democrats and the Republicans, cast a wide net, including in their membership approximately 75 percent of the adult population. These parties arc best understood as loose coalitions of groups that represent an impressively wide variety of interests. Their *raison d'être* is to win elective office. To the extent that the Democratic and Republican parties can be distinguished, they divide in relation to their group support in the electorate. One legacy of the Great Depression was the realignment of party appeals along self-consciously economic lines: broadly speaking, those who are better off economically tend to support the Republican party and the less well-to-do are disproportionately Democratic in their sympathies. The lines between the two parties are not always clear-cut, an understandable condition given the multiplicity of forces that influence party support and the numbers and diversity of the people involved.

While there are identifiable social and economic cleavages between the two parties, organizationally the parties are seldom more than ad hoc groups, suitable for little more than intermittent attempts to secure public office. The necessity to win at least some votes from those identified with the opposition party or not identified with either party (an especially critical factor for the minority party) further mutes the independence of their policy appeals. The major parties cluster toward the center of the ideological spectrum, and the result is often a confusion of party stands and dissatisfaction with party performance, a condition that has plagued both parties.

Political parties were not anticipated by the founding fathers of the United States and are not provided for in the body of the American Constitution. They arose from need, from an attempt to provide voters with some organized policy alternatives and to make the government and its leaders directly responsive to the electors. Their conception during the 1790's was mainly the work of Thomas Jefferson, James Madison, and the New York political leader Martin Van Buren, who carried the effort to a second generation of leaders. In an attempt to counter what Jefferson considered the dangerous tendencies of Hamiltonian policies, adopted by the dominant Federalists, and to ensure the election of Jeffersonian Republicans (the forerunners of 20th-century Democrats), he began to organize those sympathetic to his views to do battle in the election of 1800.

Jefferson succeeded only too well. The period 1800–28 was an era of one-party dominance. With no competitors to contend with, the majority party split into warring factions, and the split culminated in the bitter election of 1824. Four years later Andrew Jackson won the presidency and a new period of party vitality began. The years 1828–40 were remarkable ones for party growth, marked by the emergence of a second competitive major party, the Whigs; the creation of the national convention for presidential nominations; the establishment of the nucleus for the national committees and the national party structure; the introduction of the personalized national campaign; the enfranchisement of a mass electorate; the democratization of the presidency; and, at the same time, a widening of the split between the presidential and congressional factions of the respective parties. Notable changes in party procedures after that period have been few; the most innovative was the presidential primary, which found increasing favor after the election of 1912.

The slavery issue and its resultant regional and constitutional stresses tore the Democratic coalition apart. The Republican party supplanted the Whigs as the major opposition, and in 1860, only four short years after its founding, claimed the presidency. While the Republicans generally managed to control both the presidency and the Congress, a competitive party system functioned during the forty years following the Civil War. The election of 1896, in which the Democratic party adopted the agrarian populism of its candidate, William Jennings Bryan, clarified the distinctions between the two parties, to the detriment of the Democrats. The election foreshadowed a Republican dominance that lasted until the economic realignment of the years 1928–36. With the election of Franklin D. Roosevelt in 1932 the Democratic party came to represent the views of the majority of party identifiers in the United States, a condition that has continued (and even accelerated) despite the election of a Republican president in 1952, 1956, 1968, and 1972. The basic division of electoral groups between the parties dates from the same period. The 1970's seemed to be experiencing another era of party change, at least in the structure and operations of the major parties, the strength of group attachments both to the parties and individually, and, more significantly, to the party system overall. Perhaps the most noteworthy development of the 1960's and 1970's has been the marked increase in the proportion of independents, those not affiliated with either of the two major parties.

Party government has never been a part of the American experience. On the contrary, throughout their long history parties have had to fight, with varying degrees of success, periodic reform movements, intended in actuality to destroy the party system, and to introduce an idyllic, but unworkable, nonpartisanship. Political parties in the United States have much to be proud of: they have consistently taken the lead in extending the franchise and in democratizing an increasingly impersonal government; they constitute the principal means of organizing the electorate; they are the principal vehicle for recruiting people to seek office; they hold those in power at least partly accountable for their actions; and they provide the cohesion and unity that does exist in the fragmented American system of government.

[American Political Science Association, *Toward a More Responsible Two-Party System*; J. M. Burns, *The Deadlock of Democracy*; R. Hofstadter, *The Idea of a Party System*; V. O. Key, Jr., *Politics, Parties and Pressure Groups*; A. Ranney, *The Doctrine of Responsible Party Government*; E. E. Schattschneider, *Party Government*.]

WILLIAM CROTTY

PASS CHRISTIAN, in southeastern Mississippi, about sixty miles east of New Orleans, was an early French settlement on the Gulf coast. The U.S. flag was hoisted here on Jan. 9, 1811, after the annexation of West Florida, and British and American fleets fought a battle here on Dec. 14, 1814 (*see* Borgne, Battle at Lake), just prior to the British attack on New Orleans. In 1970 the population of the town was 2,979.

[Dunbar Rowland, ed., *Mississippi*, vol. II, and *History of Mississippi, The Heart of the South*.]

WALTER PRICHARD

PASSES, MOUNTAIN. America is traversed from north to south by two mountain chains, the Appalachians and Rockies, which formed barriers to the westward movement. Early hunters in search of pelts and pioneers who coveted western lands met the difficulty by finding natural outlets through the mountains. In the Appalachians these were generally called "gaps" and in the Rockies "passes." Early trails were, when possible, water trails so that the Mohawk and the Ohio rivers were the key routes to the Great Lakes and the Mississippi Valley. The Iroquois and French barred the Mohawk route on the north, and the Cherokee and other confederate tribes barred routes through the lowlands south of the Appalachians. Accordingly, the confluence of the Allegheny and Monongahela rivers to form the Ohio at Pittsburgh (*see* Ohio, Forks of the), and the breaks in the mountain ridges in the corner between Virginia and North

Carolina leading into Kentucky, were the points of easiest passage. Such gaps in the Appalachians were frequently the result of troughs cut through the mountain slopes by rivers seeking an outlet to the Ohio or the Atlantic Ocean. The Virginia coast range is low, but early maps show only three passes into the Shenandoah Valley—Williams, Ashby, and Vestal gaps, all in Fairfax County.

The most important pass in the Kentucky approach was the Cumberland Gap, which led by way of the Holston and Clinch rivers in eastern Tennessee over and through the mountains and thence along the Kentucky River and its tributaries to the Falls of the Ohio. This was known as Boone's Wilderness Road, and gaps noted by early travelers include Flower Gap, from tidewater to the sources of Little River; Blue Ridge Gap, another passage from tidewater to the Shenandoah Valley; and Moccasin Gap, between the north fork of the Holston and Clinch rivers.

On the Virginia road by Braddock's Road to Pittsburgh was encountered Chester's Gap in the Blue Ridge Mountains. On the Forbes Road, running west from Philadelphia to Pittsburgh, Miller's Run Gap was crossed northwest of the present site of Ligonier, in Westmoreland County, Pa.

The Rockies, because of their uninterrupted length and great height, offered a more serious problem. Their secrets were unlocked for the most part by early Spanish missionaries at the south; and fur traders, emigrants, and army explorers at the north and center. The earliest approaches were made in the south by the Spaniards pushing into California from New Mexico. After Mexico revolted and American trade with Santa Fe began, fur trappers thrust westward from Taos and Santa Fe to San Diego and Los Angeles. The river valleys unlocking the southern route to the West were the Gila and the Colorado. The Colorado trail, known as the Spanish Trail, went north from Taos, crossed the Wasatch Mountains and Mojave Desert, and entered California by the Cajon Pass. The Gila route was the shorter trail from Santa Fe, going west across the mountains and, by way of Warner's pass, eventually reaching San Diego.

By following the Arkansas River west to Pueblo, Colo., and crossing the mountains by a choice of three or four different passes—the Williams or Sandy Hill, the Roubideau or Mosca, and the Sangre de Cristo or Music passes—Taos could be reached by turning south, or California by turning northwest on a route traced by John C. Frémont. This route crossed the Great Basin of Utah and Nevada and surmounted the Sierra Nevada passes in California. The most important of these passes were the Walker, the Carson, the Virginia, the Frémont, the Sonora, the Donner, and the Truckee. After the eastern escarpment had been scaled, there still remained mountain folds in the Sierra Nevada that impeded progress to the coast. The Tehachapi Pass into San Joaquin Valley crossed one such fold.

The central approach to the Rockies was by way of the Platte River, which sends fingers high up into the mountains. The most important pass in the entire Rocky Mountain chain, South Pass, was on this route. It has easy grades and was used by many travelers bound for California who turned south at Fort Hall, Idaho (*see* Oregon Trail).

Of all river approaches the Missouri was the most effective and was the route used by Meriwether Lewis and William Clark, who crossed the Rockies by Lemhi, Clark, and Gibbon passes. Other useful passes of the Northwest were the Nez Perce and Lo Lo through the Bitterroot Mountains on the Montana and Idaho border. The Bozeman Pass offered access from the valley of the Gallatin River to that of the Yellowstone River. For traveling south from Oregon to California the Siskiyou Pass proved useful.

Important passes in the midcontinental region were the Union, crossing the Wind River Mountains in southwestern Wyoming; Cochetope Pass over the San Juan Mountains in southwestern Colorado, used by Frémont and others in passing from Colorado to Utah; and Muddy Pass, two degrees south of South Pass, useful in crossing the Atlantic and Pacific divides from Platte headwaters. Bridger's Pass, discovered in the early days of the fur trade, crossed the divide south of South Pass and saved distance on the California route; for this reason, it was used by the Pony Express.

[F. S. Dellenbaugh, *Frémont and '49;* E. W. Gilbert, *Exploration of Western America;* A. B. Hulburt, *Historic Highways of America.*]

CARL L. CANNON

PASSPORTS were issued by local authorities and notaries as well as the secretary of state until 1856 when, because of the refusal of foreign governments to recognize those issued by local authorities, issuance was confined to the U.S. Department of State. Except for the Civil War period, passports were not required of foreign travelers in the United States until 1918. The requirement was made permanent in 1921.

[E. M. Borchard, *The Diplomatic Protection of Citizens Abroad.*]

L. J. MEYER

PATENTS AND U.S. PATENT OFFICE. The American legal and administrative system for issuing letters patent to inventors has attempted since the colonial period to encourage invention and the growth of industry by granting monopolies. Detailed requirements for this valuable privilege have been imposed to prevent the continuance of the monopoly beyond a limited period. The rare colonial approval of monopolies for the purchase, production, and sale of commodities derived from the British crown's authority to grant such monopolies in the national interest. This authority was restricted in scope by *Darcy* v. *Allien* (1602), which invalidated the patent of Queen Elizabeth I for the manufacture of playing cards because she failed to show that the process was an invention; the monopoly was therefore not considered to be in the national interest. Monopolistic practices, such as engrossing, regrating, and forestalling, had already been declared illegal under the common law. These decisions served as the basis for the 1623 Statute of Monopolies, which authorized monopolies only to "the true and first inventor" of a new manufacturing process. The monopolies were limited to fourteen years, presumably an adequate period to train apprentices in the new technology and to receive the deserved monetary benefits. Continuation of the monopoly was to be prevented when the apprentices became independent.

With this background the general court of Massachusetts Bay Colony granted monopolies for stated periods, with the objective of encouraging domestic industry. Benefits to inventors or innovators were either in the form of monopolies or monetary grants by the colony for each sale of the patented item. Since the Articles of Confederation made no mention of patents, individual states continued the precedent established in colonial Massachusetts. Maryland, for example, granted patents to James Rumsey for his steamboat and to Oliver Evans for his milling machinery. Evans' invention was also patented in most other states.

In 1790 Congress passed the first patent law under the constitutional power, provided in Article I, Section 8, "to promote the Progress of Science and useful Arts, by securing for limited Times" exclusive rights of inventors to their discoveries. The act provided that petitions for patents would be forwarded to the secretaries of state and war and to the attorney general, that any two members of this patent board could approve a fourteen-year patent, and that the attorney general was to submit the approved patent for the president's signature. When Thomas Jefferson was secretary of state, he played the leading role in this procedure, and his department was the registry for the system. Jefferson, a notable inventor, had a deep interest in science and technology. Because of his abhorrence of monopoly, he applied strictly the rule of novelty and usefulness to each application. Only three patents were approved in 1790.

Objections to delays in processing petitions and the narrow interpretation of the 1790 act resulted in passage in 1793 of a new law, providing for termination of the board and an administrative structure for examining the merits of the petitions. The secretary of state was to register the patents and appoint a board of arbiters when two or more petitioners claimed the same invention (known as an interference proceeding). The law left to the courts any disputes about the validity of the petitioners' claims. But it seemed to many that the courts were excessively concerned with patent litigation and that the judges were in general unqualified to adjudicate disputes about claims of priority and technical questions. The volume of petitions under the 1793 act caused Secretary of State James Madison to establish in 1802 the Patent Office, under Commissioner William Thornton, to administer the department's responsibilities for the patent system. It was Thornton who, in September 1814, saved the patent files from destruction by British troops.

Chiefly through the efforts of Sen. John Ruggles, a persistent critic, the patent law was again completely rewritten on July 4, 1836. The new law gave the Patent Office responsibility for examining petitions and for ruling on the validity of the claims for an invention, its usefulness, and its workability. The law provided that the fourteen-year monopoly could be extended for an additional seven years if a special board (later, the commissioner of patents) found that the patentee encountered unusual problems in producing and marketing his device. In 1861 Congress withdrew this authority to extend patents and reserved such grants to itself; to give the patentee additional time for producing and marketing new products, Congress increased the monopoly period to seventeen years.

In 1839, Congress initiated a historically important program for the Patent Office by authorizing it to disseminate seeds and to collect and publish data of interest to farmers. The agricultural division of the office was thus the predecessor of the Department of Agriculture, established in 1862. Since 1930 the Patent Office has issued patents for a "distinct and new variety" of asexually produced plants, thus renewing an early interest in promoting agriculture.

Congress codified and modified the various patent laws in 1870. It added the power to issue trademark patents to the authority under an 1842 act for granting design patents. The 1870 act delegated copyright responsibilities, some of which had been in the Patent Office, to the Library of Congress. It also sanctioned the procedures for adjudicating interferences by establishing the Office of the Examiner of Interferences. During the next decades the Patent Office, which had been transferred to the Department of the Interior when that was created in 1849 and to the Department of Commerce in 1925, developed its basic organization and essential procedures. Executive and managerial authority were vested in the commissioner of patents, one or more assistant commissioners, and the Office of Administration. The solicitor assumed jurisdiction over all legal matters and, particularly, the extensive litigation to which the commissioner was a party. A registry office, under several name changes, registered patent applications and assignments of approved patents, published and distributed patent specifications, and organized a scientific and technical library. The chief operating function of examining the claims assigned by the registry unit was delegated to several patent examining divisions. Separate units processed trademark applications. Boards with important staff functions—such as the Trademark Trial and Appeal Board, the Board of Patent Interferences, and the Board of Appeals—began adjudicating appeals to reverse examiners' findings with regard to invention and design patents, trademark disputes, and interferences. An office was also established to study and advise the commission on policies and actions under international patent and trademark agreements. Beginning in the 1960's the Patent Office included advisers on the use of automatic data-processing systems for recording, classifying, and examining patents.

Although the patent system has long played a significant role in the history of American science and technology, it has had considerable adverse criticism. Critics—for example, in the 1938 hearings of the Temporary National Economic Committee—have claimed that the system has fostered monopoly by creating producers who, by superior technology protected by a series of patents and delays in patent proceedings, corner a large part of the market. Critics have also accused the system of suppressing inventions to delay change. Advocates, probably a large majority, have called attention to the incentive of reward, to antitrust proceedings when companies become too dominant in an industry, to the right of a patentee not to sell his product, and to the importance of Patent Office publications in disseminating specifications and drawings of inventions. Since the founding of Thomas Edison's laboratory in 1876, most of the significant inventions have been developed by institutional research sponsored by the federal government, universities, and private companies.

[Levine H. Campbell, *The Patent System of the United States, so far as It Relates to the Granting of Patents: A History;* Harry Kursh, *Inside the U.S. Patent Office;* U.S. Patent Office, *Rules of Practice in Patent Cases.*]

MEYER H. FISHBEIN

PATERSON PLAN. *See* Constitution of the United States.

"PATHFINDER," a sobriquet given to John Charles Frémont following the publication in 1845 by the U.S. government of his *Report of the Exploring Expedition to the Rocky Mountains in the Year 1842, and to Oregon and North California in the Years 1843–44,* which met with instant popularity and quickly ran through four editions.

[Allan Nevins, *John Charles Frémont.*]

OSGOOD HARDY

PATHFINDER OF THE SEAS. *See* Maury's Charts.

PATRIOT WAR (1837–38), between Canadian rebels and their American supporters and the British in Canada, was the result of a desire to free Canada from British control. It was spurred on by the promise of bounties in money and land and by Canadian refugees who joined in the fray. The "Patriots" were mostly American farmers and unemployed artisans, recruited by William Lyon Mackenzie, a defeated leader of one of the Canadian rebellions, in the border counties from Vermont to Michigan. Without the benefit of united and effective leadership and with inadequate and undisciplined ranks, they made three different extensive plans in 1838 for widespread contemporaneous attacks along the Canadian border, with a view to the eventual joining of forces and the establishment of a republic in Canada. With the failure of these plans, the movement came completely under the domination of a secret society, the Hunters and Chasers of the Eastern Frontier. International complications were averted as a consequence of the coopera-

tion and vigorous action of the British and American authorities. Congress passed a stronger neutrality act in March 1838, and federal troops were sent to the frontier. In the border states the militia was called out, and civil and criminal suits were instituted. On their side, the Canadian and British authorities used military and civil measures to prevent retaliatory attacks (*see* Canadian-American Relations). A serious repercussion of the Patriot War was the arrest of the Canadian Alexander McLeod on Nov. 12, 1840, in New York City and the subsequent controversy (*see* Caroline Affair).

[Albert B. Corey, *The Crisis of 1830–1842 in Canadian-American Relations;* Orrin E. Tiffany, "The Relations of the United States to the Canadian Rebellion of 1837–38," *Buffalo Historical Society Publications,* vol. 8.]

ALBERT B. COREY

PATRONAGE, POLITICAL, in the United States, includes all the forms of largesse at the disposal of successful candidates for public office. In the absence of limitations on the officeholder, all public jobs and all public contracts are subject to dispensation at the discretion of the principal officer of the governmental unit involved. The privilege of that dispensation is usually employed to further the personal interests of the officeholder or the interests of the party he represents. In its most extreme form such political patronage is known as the spoils system, after a remark made in 1832 by Sen. William Marcy of New York, "To the victor belong the spoils." Originally involving only the awarding of jobs, political patronage has come to include the vast range of favors distributed by expanding governmental bureaucracies, whose increased spending, much of it discretionary, has brought greater opportunities to political supporters. These favors may vary in scope from mundane ones, such as state legislators securing vanity license plates for constituents, to more tangible ones, such as the granting of franchises or judgeships. On a larger scale, political patronage may involve construction and defense contracts, or at least favored treatment in efforts to secure such contracts. Senators and representatives have considerable ability to influence the location of dams, post offices, military installations, and university facilities in their home states and districts and to control federal committee assignments and judicial appointments in a way that will benefit their constituents and strengthen their political bases.

Political patronage was first implemented on a national scale in the United States during the administration of President Andrew Jackson (1828–36), and state and local government officeholders were not slow in adopting the system. By 1880, governments were in many cases mere appendages of political machines that grew out of the excesses of the spoils system. The taxpayer's dollar was directed more to supporting the officeholder's party than to supplying public services.

The assassination of President James A. Garfield in 1881 by a disappointed officeseeker awoke the American public and Congress to the harmful effects of an unrestrained spoils system. The National Civil Service League, founded in 1881, led a reform movement that succeeded in gaining congressional passage of the Pendleton Act in 1883. It provided for the creation of a civil service commission, for the establishment of the principle of open competitive examinations for admission to public employment, and for the protection of classified civil servants from discrimination or removal on account of political or religious beliefs. The employees of Congress and of the federal courts are not included in the classified civil service, and there is a distinct tendency toward nepotism and political patronage in filling such positions.

By and large, state governments still use the patronage system. According to the National Civil Service League, virtually all of the fifty states had some sort of merit system by 1975, although the number of employees actually hired under merit principles was unknown. Statutory merit systems are not consistently enforced. City governments have been subjected to tremendous public pressure to remove public employment from political patronage. Despite the efforts of reformers, only 75 percent of all American cities had any kind of formal merit system by 1950, and only 25 percent had one covering all employees. Traditionally, counties have been the strongholds of political parties and, as such, are slow to adopt a civil service system. On the local level, however, such as the rural town and the school district, there is either a tradition to maintain or a standard to meet. Patronage exists in the schools, but certain minimum standards must be enforced in order to secure state subsidies. Generally, rural communities are too small and too poor to support an effective personnel program based on merit, and the few positions that are available are considered patronage for the mayor.

It should not be assumed that everyone appointed to public office for political reasons is incompetent. Many of the most conscientious and capable officeholders have secured their appointments through political patronage. The recruitment of new and energetic talent into government is often accomplished through patronage, and it helps to assure the continuation of a competitive two-party system.

Political patronage is used for many purposes. The political parties use it to reward and maintain the loyalty of party workers. Officeholders use it to build political machines that can assure their continuation in office. Constituents are befriended with small favors that reinforce their belief that their representatives are concerned about them. Even the most respected American presidents have not hesitated to use their patronage power to obtain congressional support for their policies.

Patronage is also used to obtain financial support for political campaigns. Those who have received or who expect to receive some financial benefit from the operation of the government, such as the awarding of contracts or orders for the supplies, material, and equipment needed for government use, usually respond with rebates or contributions to campaign funds. The limitation of official discretion in such matters usually takes the form of a law requiring the acceptance of competitive bids and the awarding of the contract to the lowest bidder. Such laws are in effect for large purchases by the federal government and for most state and local governments, but they can be and are evaded.

With the Watergate revelations acting as an impetus, many states and the national government have enacted more stringent campaign expenditure and disclosure laws. These laws in general tend to limit the amounts that can be spent in a given campaign and in some cases, particularly at the federal level, the amount any one individual may contribute to a campaign.

[Theodore Lowi, *At the Pleasure of the Mayor—Patronage and Power in New York City, 1898–1958;* Wallace S. Sayre, ed., *The Federal Government Service;* Frank J. Sorauf, "The Silent Revolution in Patronage," in Edward Banfield, ed., *Urban Government—A Reader in Administration and Politics;* Martin Tolchin and Susan Tolchin, *To the Victor . . . Political Patronage From the Clubhouse to the White House.*]

DONALD HERZBERG

PATRONS OF HUSBANDRY was founded as a farmers' lodge on Dec. 4, 1867, in Washington, D.C., and served as the vehicle through which the Granger movement operated. It had a secret ritual like the Masons and admitted both men and women to membership. Each local unit was known as a "Grange." In 1876 the order reached its peak membership of 858,050, but by 1880 the collapse of the Granger movement had reduced this figure to

124,420. Thereafter, by abandoning business and politics for its original program of social and educational reforms, the order began a slow and steady growth that, by 1934, enabled it to claim again over 800,000 members, mainly in New England, the North Central states, and the Pacific Northwest, although by 1974 membership had declined to about 600,000. Of late years it has not hesitated to support legislation, both state and national, deemed of benefit to farmers.

[Edward Wiest, *Agricultural Organization in the United States.*]

JOHN D. HICKS

PATROONS. On June 7, 1629, the directorate of the West India Company granted, and the States General of the Netherlands approved, a charter of freedoms and exemptions, which provided for the grant of great estates, called patroonships, to those members of the company who were able to found settlements of fifty persons within four years after giving notice of their intentions. The patroon, after extinguishing the Indian title by purchase, was to hold the land as a "perpetual fief of inheritance" with the fruits, plants, minerals, rivers, and springs thereof. He was to swear fealty to the company and have the right of the high, middle, and low jurisdiction. Before the end of January 1630, patroonships had been registered by Michiel Pauw, for Pavonia, on the west side of the Hudson River, across from Manhattan Island; by Samuel Godyn, for the west side of the Delaware River; by Albert Coenraets Burgh, on the east side of the Delaware River; by Samuel Blommaert, for the Connecticut River; and by Kiliaen van Rensselaer, for Rensselaerswyck, around Fort Orange on the Hudson. With the single exception of Rensselaerswyck, these grants were unsuccessful. The difficulties of transportation across the Atlantic Ocean, lack of cooperation from the company, quarrels with the authorities at New Amsterdam, Indian troubles, and the difficulties of management from 3,000 miles away were all factors in their failure. In 1640 the revised charter reduced the size of future patroonships, but the same factors contributed to prevent the success of these smaller grants. At the close of Dutch rule all but two of the patroonships had been repurchased by the company.

[A. C. Flick, ed., *History of the State of New York,* vol. I.]

A. C. FLICK

PAULISTS. The Society of Missionary Priests of Saint Paul the Apostle, popularly known as the Paulist Fathers, was founded in New York City in 1858 by Father Isaac Thomas Hecker. Associated with him were Fathers Augustine Hewit, George Deshon, Francis Baker, and Clarence Walworth. The first religious society of men in the Roman Catholic church established in the United States, its mission is to help men to discover Jesus Christ, with a special concern for the peoples of North America.

Paulist missions to Catholics and lectures for non-Catholics, the special apostolate of the Paulists, began with the inception of the society in 1858. Utilizing the written as well as the spoken word, Father Hecker established *The Catholic World* in 1865. The following year he founded the Catholic Publication Society, which is now known as the Paulist Press.

The Paulist mission to those not of the Catholic faith has taken form in information centers, trailer missions, radio and television, and the university apostolate.

In 1975 there were 232 priests in the society, staffing forty-two foundations—thirty-nine in the United States, two in Canada, and one in Rome.

[James M. Gillis, C.S.P., *The Paulists;* Vincent F. Holden, *Yankee Paul.*]

LAWRENCE V. McDONNELL, C.S.P.

PAULUS HOOK, SURPRISE OF (Aug. 19, 1779). The British forts on lower Manhattan and at Paulus Hook, N.J., directly opposite, commanded the entrance to the Hudson River. In a bayonet attack at dawn, Maj. Henry Lee, with 200 men, surprised the garrison at Paulus Hook, captured 159 prisoners and regained New Bridge (Hackensack) with the loss of two men. Congress rewarded Lee with a gold medal and distributed $15,000 among his men. The capture of Stony Point, further up the Hudson, in July and the capture of Paulus Hook made the British cautious and limited the field of their activities.

[F. B. Lee, *New Jersey as a Colony and as a State,* vol. II.]

C. A. TITUS

PAUPERISM. *See* Poverty and Pauperism.

PAVING. All the earliest paving in America seems to have been done with cobblestones. The first mention of paving is found in a court record in New Amsterdam in 1655, a reference to repairs of the paving in Pearl Street. Brouwer Street was paved with cobbles in 1658 and thereafter called Stone Street, even to the present time. Several other short New York streets were paved before 1700. In Boston, State and Washington streets were undoubtedly cobble paved in the 17th century. In 1719 it was said that some citizens of Philadelphia had laid stone to the middle of the street in front of their own property, but the city was notorious for muddy thoroughfares for many decades thereafter. Alongside some city streets very narrow brick or slab stone sidewalks were laid as early as 1700—often long before the vehicular way was even macadamized. Some macadamizing with broken stone or gravel and some cobble paving were done in the 18th century, but even in 1800 most city streets were still given over to dust or mud. In fact, some downtown business streets in New York were quagmires as late as 1850, and in Chicago for long after that. In 1832 what is said to have been the first granite or Belgian block pavement in America was laid in New York. That city also introduced wood paving in 1835, laid in hexagonal blocks—said to be a "Russian idea." Later, square blocks were used. Wooden paving was easy on horses, and the clumping of their hoofs was muffled by it, but in wet weather it was apt to swell and rise in hillocks. With the coming of the automobile and the disappearance of the horse, the arguments for it lost force. When Chicago burned in 1871, the weather had been so dry that even the wooden paving burned. In New Orleans, built on soft alluvial soil, many streets were surfaced with thick wooden planks laid crosswise—some streets until well into the 20th century. The first brick street paving was laid in Charleston, W.Va., in 1870. When asphalt was first tried in New York in 1877, it was pronounced a failure; but it shortly afterward became popular, although its habit of softening and consequent roughening in hot weather was a defect. After 1900 it began slowly to be replaced by concrete, which for some years had been vying with sawed Bedford stone in popularity for sidewalks. Various mixtures of crushed stone with tar, bitumen, asphalt, and cement were developed for streets and roads as the automobile era dawned, but for the main highways, concrete came to be the only material considered. Glass paving bricks were announced in 1905 but never came into use, and rubber paving was tried in 1923. By 1970 the surface paving of streets in most major cities was a bituminous mixture from either asphalts (petroleum products) or tars (coal products).

ALVIN F. HARLOW

PAWNEE. When first contacted by Europeans, perhaps as early as 1541 by the expedition of Francisco Vásquez de Coronado, the Pawnee, an American Indian tribe in the Great Plains, lived in the present state of Nebraska on the middle course of the Platte River and the Republican fork of the Kansas River. Three main branches or bands of the Pawnee spoke a single Caddoan language, while a fourth group, virtually a separate tribe, the Skidi, spoke a variant dialect. The Caddoan languages were spoken in the regions to the south, by the Caddo and Wichita, for example. If Caddoan, as some suggest, relates to a broader Hokan, sometimes designated as a Hokan-Siouan phylum, the origins of the Pawnee as well as those of the Arikara, a prominent related offshoot, may be traced to the southeast. Such a notion is borne out by the retention by the Pawnee of river-bottom agriculture, a trait carried by the Arikara from the Pawnee to the Siouan Mandan and Hidatsa. A large Plains tribe, with perhaps 10,000 members in 1780, the Pawnee stressed both the permanent farming village and forays far afield for horses and military honors. Although the Pawnee shared basic elements of Plains Indian culture with neighboring tribes, they were known for the ceremony of the morning star, a ritual involving human sacrifice for communal good. Somewhat off the paths of east-west settlement, the Pawnee enjoyed fairly benign relations with Europeans and were often employed as U.S. Army scouts.

[George E. Hyde, *Pawnee Indians.*]

ROBERT F. SPENCER

PAWNEE ROCK, a pioneer landmark of uplifted sandstone, which has since been largely quarried away, on the old Santa Fe Trail near what is now Pawnee Rock, Kans. It was the scene of tribal warfare between the Pawnee and Cheyenne and furnished cover from which marauding bands of Plains Indians frequently launched attacks on passing wagon trains.

[Henry Inman, *The Old Santa Fé Trail.*]

JOHN FRANCIS, JR.

PAWTUCKET, a city in northeastern Rhode Island, located at Pawtucket Falls, the head of navigation on the Blackstone River, four miles north of Providence. The area was deeded to Roger Williams in 1638, but the first permanent settlement did not begin until 1671, when Joseph Jenckes established an iron forge. Ironmaking was the only important industry until 1793, the year Samuel Slater installed the first Arkwright machinery for spinning cotton in America at Pawtucket Falls. From then until World War II, Pawtucket was one of the nation's leading textile manufacturing centers. Pawtucket was chartered as a city in 1885.

In addition to textiles and iron manufacture, the city developed into a manufacturing center for wire and cables and electronic equipment. After World War II, when most of the textile industry moved its factories to the South, Pawtucket's share of this industry lessened, but state aid has revived it somewhat. The population of the city in 1970 was 76,984.

[Robert Grieve, *Illustrated History of Pawtucket.*]

PAXTON BOYS. During Pontiac's War (1763) some fifty-seven rangers from Paxton, Pa., killed twenty defenseless and peaceable Conestoga Indians near Lancaster in December 1763. Gov. John Penn issued two proclamations commanding magistrates to bring the culprits to trial, but the juries and justices of the frontier towns were sympathetic, and nothing was done. Aside from the brutality of this event, it is important as evidence of the hatred of the frontiersmen for the eastern domination of the province, a hatred that grew out of unequal representation in the assembly and the assembly's failure to provide defense for the frontiers. The Conestoga massacre projected the Paxton Boys into one of the bitterest political campaigns in the history of Pennsylvania. Numerous pamphlets were written (one by Benjamin Franklin), and in January 1764, 600 armed "back inhabitants" marched on Philadelphia, intent on destroying their political opponents. Franklin was chiefly responsible for quelling this rebellion.

Lazarus Stewart, as head of the Paxton Boys, disgusted with the proprietary government and with writs hanging over him, moved with his followers to the Wyoming Valley, an area near present-day Wilkes-Barre, Pa., in 1769. There he was granted a township by the Susquehanna Company of Connecticut, engaged in the Pennamite Wars that followed, and was killed in the Wyoming massacre of 1778.

[Francis Parkman, *Conspiracy of Pontiac;* B. J. Wallace, *Insurrection of the Paxton Boys.*]

JULIAN P. BOYD

PAYNE-ALDRICH TARIFF. *See* **Tariff.**

PAYNE'S LANDING, TREATY OF, was made on the Oklawaha River in north central Florida, May 9, 1832, by James Gadsden for the United States, with fifteen Seminole chiefs, providing for a delegation of Indians to proceed to the West and decide whether

land set apart for them there was acceptable. If so, the Seminole were to remove within the next three years, giving up all their Florida lands and receiving an equal amount in the West in addition to certain money compensations. Disputes over this treaty and other problems led to the second Seminole War.

[Grant Foreman, *Indian Removal;* C. J. Kappler, ed., *Indian Affairs, Laws and Treaties,* vol. II.]

E. MERTON COULTER

PEABODY FUND, the pioneer educational foundation in the United States, was established in 1867 by George Peabody, a native of Massachusetts who subsequently became a banker in London. His first gift was $1 million, to which two years later he added a like sum to encourage and assist educational effort in "those portions of our beloved and common country which have suffered from the destructive ravages, and not less disastrous consequences, of civil war." When he made his second gift Peabody said to the trustees of the fund: "This I give to the suffering South for the good of the whole country." To administer the fund he named sixteen northern and southern men of prominence and distinction, who selected Barnas Sears, president of Brown University, as the first general agent of the fund. Upon his death in 1880 Sears was succeeded by Jabez L. M. Curry, former president of Howard College in Alabama and later U.S. ambassador to Spain, who was succeeded in 1907 by Wickliffe Rose, dean of the George Peabody College for Teachers in Nashville. Through the tactful and energetic work of these agents the fund greatly assisted general education and teacher training for both whites and blacks in the states that had formed the Confederacy and in West Virginia, and proved to be a most wholesome influence during the dark days that followed the war. When the fund was dissolved in 1914 the bulk of the capital went to the endowment of Peabody College; some went to southern universities for schools of education; and some to the John F. Slater Fund. During its life the Peabody Fund distributed from income about $3.65 million.

[Edgar W. Knight, *Public School Education in North Carolina.*]

EDGAR W. KNIGHT

PEACE COMMISSION OF 1778. The surrender of Gen. John Burgoyne's army at Saratoga on Oct. 17, 1777, inspired the British government to propose peace to the colonies, an offer based on repeal of the obnoxious parliamentary legislation since 1763 and a constitutional arrangement of home rule within the empire. Following the necessary authorization from Parliament, the government sent to Philadelphia in 1778 a commission headed by Frederick Howard, Earl of Carlisle, and including William Eden and George Johnstone. It was really an effort to secure a reconciliation with the colonies before France should make an alliance with them. But the Continental Congress refused to hold parley with the commission, although the terms that it was ready to offer would have been satisfactory before the signing of the Declaration of Independence. Furthermore, the arrival of the French treaties of Feb. 6, 1778, extinguished all hope of negotiation. The Carlisle peace mission seems to have been the first concrete suggestion by the British government of the idea of dominion self-government.

[Sir George O. Trevelyan, *American Revolution.*]
SAMUEL FLAGG BEMIS

PEACE CONFERENCE AT BUENOS AIRES. On Jan. 30, 1936, President Franklin D. Roosevelt wrote directly to the presidents of the Latin-American republics suggesting that a conference be convened at Buenos Aires to discuss the maintenance of peace in the Western Hemisphere by ratifying pending inter-American peace instruments, by amending existing peace treaties, or by creating new peace agreements. The invitations were enthusiastically received and many program topics were suggested. These were finally formulated by the governing board of the Pan-American Union into a program consisting of the following general headings: (1) organization of peace; (2) neutrality; (3) limitation of armaments; (4) juridical problems; (5) economic problems; and (6) intellectual cooperation, or "moral disarmament."

The conference met at Buenos Aires Dec. 1–23, 1936, with Secretary of State Cordell Hull leading the U.S. delegation and with Roosevelt delivering the opening address in person. The conference was presided over by Carlos Saavedra Lamas, the Argentine minister of foreign affairs. The delegates voted in favor of consulting together and cooperating to settle all threats to American peace from within and without through the use of conciliation and arbitration. The questions of organizing an American league of nations and the establishment of an inter-American court of justice were postponed for consideration at the eighth International American Conference at Lima, Peru, in December 1938. In all, seventy acts were approved, including the exchange of students and teachers as a means of promoting moral disarmament.

[Pan-American Union, *Report on the Proceedings of the Conference Submitted to the Governing Board of the Pan-American Union by the Director General* (1937).]
A. CURTIS WILGUS

PEACE CONFERENCES, as here defined for the United States, are those international conferences in which the nation has participated in an effort to establish procedures for settling international disputes without resort to the use of force. These efforts can be divided into four categories: (1) arbitration, the voluntary submission of a dispute to an impartial body for a decision that the disputants agree in advance to accept; (2) efforts to facilitate negotiations between disputants, either through the extension of good offices or through mediation; (3) the establishment of permanent international structures to preserve peace; and (4) direct negotiations with other countries to settle disputes.

Arbitration has the longest history of the four. The first arbitration agreement in which the United States participated was written into Jay's Treaty of 1794 with Great Britain. The Treaty of Ghent of 1814, also with Great Britain, established arbitration boards to handle conflicts over boundaries arising out of the settlement. The most notable 19th-century example of arbitration in which the United States was involved was the Treaty of Washington of 1871, in which Great Britain and the United States agreed to submit to an arbitration commission claims arising out of the depredations of the *Alabama* and other British-built Confederate warships. By the turn of the century considerable sentiment had built up in favor of having the United States sign with other nations bilateral treaties providing for the automatic submission of certain classes of disputes to arbitration. Secretary of State Elihu Root negotiated a series of twenty-four such agreements in 1908 and 1909, of which all but three were ratified. Secretary of State William Jennings Bryan renewed some of the Root treaties in 1913 and 1914 and negotiated others. A third group of arbitration treaties was signed between 1928 and 1931.

These agreements had little practical effect. The tendency of arbitration boards to resolve conflicts by splitting the difference between disputants made American diplomats reluctant to employ the procedure for the settlement of significant territorial or financial issues. Disputes involving vital interests were excluded from the arbitration treaties negotiated between 1908 and 1931, and the Senate insisted on the right to reject the use of arbitration in each case. As a result arbitration was employed only rarely as a means of settling international disputes, and then only in situations of minor significance.

The use of mediation in the resolution of international conflicts has not been frequent, but the results obtained have been more significant than those derived from arbitration. The United States accepted Russian mediation in setting up negotiations with Great Britain leading to a settlement of the War of 1812 but rejected British mediation in two other important 19th-century conflicts, the Mexican War and the Civil War. Mediation has been employed by the United States, with varying degrees of success, in its relations with Latin America. The United States successfully mediated an end to the struggle between Spain and the Latin-American countries of Chile, Peru, Ecuador, and Bolivia in 1869 but failed in several efforts between 1879 and 1884 to mediate the War of the Pacific. President Theodore Roosevelt employed mediation successfully in two important situations: settlement of the Russo-Japanese War in 1905 and resolution of the first Morocco crisis at the Algeciras Conference in 1906. President Woodrow Wilson made several efforts to mediate World War I before the United States entered that struggle, none of them successful. Since World War I most efforts at mediation have been carried out through international organizations rather than through individual countries, although Secretary of State Henry Kissinger had some success in mediating differences between Egypt and Israel following the 1973 Yom Kippur War.

Participation in international organizations has become the principal way in which the United States has sought to establish procedures for maintaining peace, but Americans for many years avoided such participation as inconsistent with their traditions of isolationism and neutrality. The United States took part in no international conferences at all until 1861 and for the rest of the 19th century associated itself only with noncontroversial international projects, such as the Universal Postal Union and the Geneva convention on the treatment of the wounded in warfare. One important exception was the Commercial Union of the American Republics (later the Pan-American Union), which evolved out of the first general meeting of Western Hemisphere nations at Washington, D.C., in 1889, but its primary function was the facilitation of trade, not the peaceful resolution of disputes.

The first significant participation by the United States in an international conference to establish peacekeeping mechanisms came at the first Hague Conference, in 1899. The meeting of twenty-six nations had been called by Czar Nicholas II of Russia in hopes of reaching agreements that would prevent war, but its main energies were devoted instead toward humanizing the rules of warfare. The United States confined its participation in the conference to urging the use of arbitration and mediation. The second Hague Conference, in 1907, produced further refinements in the rules of warfare but resulted in no significant action to prevent war. The United States also participated in a conference of leading maritime powers at London in 1908–09. The resulting Declaration of London, establishing rules for blockades and contraband, was approved by the Senate in 1912 but failed to go into effect because of British opposition.

The outbreak of World War I greatly increased American interest in the possibility of creating an international organization to prevent war. Wilson endorsed this concept in 1916, and following the Allied victory in 1918, he devoted great effort toward the establishment of such an organization as part of the peace settlement. The result was the League of Nations, an international organization of nations whose members were obliged, in the words of Article X of the covenant, "to respect and preserve as against external aggression the territorial integrity and existing political independence of all Members of the League." Article XVI required members to apply economic and, if necessary, military sanctions against aggressors. Wilson himself did not regard these as ironclad commitments requiring the United States to resist aggression anywhere at any time, but many Americans, including a substantial portion of the Senate, did. Because of this, and because Wilson refused to accept reservations making clear the nonbinding nature of the commitment, the Senate refused to approve U.S. membership in the League of Nations.

Nonetheless, the United States did not, between World War I and World War II, exclude itself from other international peacekeeping efforts. The United States called the Washington Naval Conference of 1921–22, which imposed limitations on the construction of certain classes of warships, and participated in conferences at Geneva in 1927 and between 1932 and 1934 and at London in 1930, which attempted, generally without success, to extend the disarmament agreements reached at Washington, D.C. Secretary of State Frank B. Kellogg was a prime mover behind the multilateral Kellogg-Briand Pact of 1928, the signatories of which renounced the use of war as an instrument of national policy except in cases of self-defense. The question of U.S. membership in the Permanent Court of International Justice, established by the League of Nations in 1920, was also widely debated during the period, although because of the Senate's refusal to accept membership without reservations, the United States never joined.

World War II revived interest in the possibility of creating an international structure to maintain peace. Convinced that the United States had made a great mistake by repudiating Wilson's advocacy of the League of Nations, State Department planners began working, even before the United States entered the war, to create a new international organization to safeguard peace in the postwar period. President Franklin D. Roosevelt and Secretary of State Cordell Hull carefully sought to avoid Wilson's mistakes by consulting Congress at every step of this process. Their efforts paid off when the Senate endorsed U.S. membership in the United Nations in July 1945, by a vote of eighty-nine to two.

The United Nations resembled the League of Nations in its structure, but unlike the league, it did not require member nations automatically to apply sanctions against aggressors. The General Assembly, in which all members had one vote, could only recommend action. The Security Council could take action but only with the approval of its five permanent members, the United States, Great Britain, the Soviet Union, France, and China, each of which had the right of veto. In the end, the United Nations could be effective only if the great powers were in agreement; in disputes between the great powers themselves the world organization could do little.

At the insistence of the United States a provision was inserted into the UN charter allowing members to create regional security organizations outside the framework of the world organization. As tensions between the United States and the Soviet Union intensified, revealing the limitations of the United Nations as a peacekeeping agency, the U.S. government began looking toward the formation of such organizations as a means of promoting security; it was a prime mover in the establishment of the Organization of American States in 1948, the North Atlantic Treaty Organization in 1949, the Southeast Asia Treaty Organization in 1954, and the Central Treaty Organization in 1959. The relative ineffectiveness of the latter two organizations, together with a general feeling that the United States had become overcommitted, caused the U.S. government to deemphasize the role of regional security organizations by the mid-1960's.

American interest in the United Nations remained low, partly because of the continuing inability of that organization to deal effectively with conflicts involving the great powers and partly because of the decreasing influence of the United States in the world body as a result of the proliferation of new member-states in Asia and Africa.

After the Cuban missile crisis of 1962 the United States relied with increasing frequency on direct negotiations with its principal adversary, the Soviet Union, as a means of relaxing international tensions. A similar tendency appeared to be evolving in relations with the People's Republic of China following President Richard M. Nixon's visit to that country in 1972. During the 1970's American diplomats showed less interest in arbitration, mediation, and international organization as mechanisms for the peaceful resolution of disputes between nations than at any other time in the 20th century.

[Richard W. Leopold, *The Growth of American Foreign Policy;* Roland N. Stromberg, *Collective Security and American Foreign Policy: From the League of Nations to NATO.*]

JOHN LEWIS GADDIS

PEACE CORPS. *See* **ACTION.**

PEACE DEMOCRATS. *See* **Copperheads.**

PEACE MOVEMENT OF 1864. Efforts to end the Civil War in 1864 began in July with negotiations between Horace Greeley of the *New York Tribune* and Confederate commissioners James P. Holcombe, Clement C. Clay, and Jacob Thompson at Niagara Falls, Canada. President Abraham Lincoln's terms, presented by Greeley, were reunion and emancipation. A meeting with the commissioners by Greeley and John Hay, Lincoln's private secretary, showed the impossibility of an agreement. In August an equally futile visit was made by Jeremiah Black, friend of Thompson and Secretary of War Edwin Stanton, whom he claimed to represent. In Richmond, James F. Jaquess and James R. Gilmore, with Lincoln's permission, interviewed President Jefferson Davis in July, without result.

Lincoln's message to Congress in December stipulated a cessation of resistance to the Union as the only basis for peace. Visits to Davis by Francis P. Blair, Sr., in January 1865, led to the abortive Hampton

Roads Conference on Feb. 3. Thus ended hope for a negotiated peace.

[E. C. Kirkland, *The Peacemakers of 1864*.]
CHARLES H. COLEMAN

PEACE MOVEMENTS. Two kinds of peace movement have been prevalent in America. One kind has opposed particular wars in which the United States has been involved; the other, most active in peacetime, has concentrated on advocating long-term mechanisms for the peaceful settlement of international disputes. Pacifists have taken part in both kinds of peace movement, but they have rarely constituted the most important segment.

Between the American Revolution and World War I, the major American wars were opposed by disparate groups that were unsympathetic to the purposes of a specific war. Opposition to the War of 1812 was centered among conservative Federalists in New England, who flirted with the idea of seceding from the Union in the Hartford Convention of 1814. They opposed the disruption of trade with Britain that the war entailed, and they feared that the territorial expansion desired by the promoters of the war would diminish the power of the eastern states in national politics. The Mexican War (1846–48), on the other hand, was opposed most strongly by northern critics of slavery, who attacked the war as a slaveholders' plot to add new land for the expansion of slavery. These same people, except for a small group of pacifists, strongly supported the northern cause in the Civil War. Opposition to the Civil War was generally of a conservative, often racist, nature, based on opposition to the use of the federal government's power to take action against slavery. The Spanish-American War of 1898 was almost universally popular in the United States at first; the opposition that emerged was directed at the decision of President William McKinley's administration to keep the Philippines and suppress the Filipinos by force, an opposition centered among reformers who saw imperialism as contrary to American ideals.

During the long intervals between these wars, the second type of peace movement grew at a more or less steady pace. The first local peace society was formed by David Low Dodge in New York in 1815, and the nationwide American Peace Society followed in 1828. Led chiefly by William Ladd, this group flourished during the social reform agitation of the 1830's, distributing tracts attacking the folly of war and advocating proposals such as a congress of na-

tions and arbitration treaties. In 1846 Elihu Burritt and others who objected to the moderate policies of Ladd's successors formed the League of Universal Brotherhood, which within a few years claimed 20,000 American and 20,000 British members. Its members took an oath never to support any war for any purpose. It undertook peace propaganda and was in large measure responsible for a series of "universal peace congresses" held in various European cities between 1848 and 1853.

Except for a small number of people who clung to an absolute pacifism—notably Burritt and William Lloyd Garrison—the great majority of those active in the peace groups supported the Civil War. The American Peace Society spoke for them when it claimed that the war was an unlawful rebellion against authority, not a genuine war, and George Beckwith, the society's leader, repeatedly spoke against any concessions to the Confederacy. The society continued in existence during the war, however, and resumed its propaganda activities after the armistice. It was joined by the Universal Peace Union, founded by pacifists in 1866 and headed by Alfred Love, a Philadelphia merchant. Both organizations placed considerable stress on arbitration of disputes between nations, and their pressure helped encourage a growing willingness on the government's part to negotiate treaties promising to submit future disputes to arbitration. The Universal Peace Union, unlike most peace groups before or since, also concerned itself with labor disputes in the United States; it took a middle-ground position favoring arbitration as an alternative to strikes and lockouts. As before the Civil War the peace movement consisted mainly of upper-middle-class people, such as lawyers, preachers, and merchants, although there were few wealthy businessmen in its ranks.

The Spanish-American War and, more important, the American conquest of the Philippine Islands that followed Spain's surrender marked the first large-scale use of American troops outside the North American continent. The American Anti-Imperialist League, formed in 1899 and centered in Boston, organized a persistent opposition to the American invasion. The Democratic party's 1900 presidential candidate, William Jennings Bryan, made opposition to the Philippine annexation his main campaign issue and received much support for it even though he lost the election. Bryan's defeat, together with the waning of Filipino military resistance, did much to deflate the antiimperialist movement. During its heyday it had managed to offer principled opposition to an American war and also to point out (as the traditional peace movement had not done) the connection between economic expansionism and war.

During the next decade and a half, before the outbreak of World War I in 1914, the traditional peace movement flourished as never before. It acquired some wealthy backers, such as Andrew Carnegie, who sponsored the Carnegie Endowment for World Peace. Most of the new converts to the peace movement were far from being pacifists; their primary concern was with the fashioning of mechanisms to ensure international order without war. Their growth reflected the new status of the United States as the world's leading manufacturing power with a strong stake in international diplomacy. At the same time, there was increasing concern within churches, especially of the Protestant denominations, about peace: for example, it has been estimated that more than 50,000 sermons were preached in behalf of peace on the Sunday before Christmas in 1909.

After the outbreak of war in Europe in 1914, most of the peace movement came to reconcile itself to the idea of American intervention, which came in April 1917. New organizations, such as the American Union Against Militarism, the Emergency Peace Federation, and the Women's Peace Party, took on the burden of trying to stave off American entry into the war. The main left-wing groups of that period, the Socialist party and the Industrial Workers of the World, also vigorously denounced the war as a dispute between rival imperialists. Once war was declared, the nominal peace groups generally gave full support, as when the American Peace Society newspaper seriously declared, "We must aid in the starving and emaciation of a German baby in order that he, or at least his more sturdy little playmate, may grow up to inherit a different sort of government from that for which his father died."

Some opposition groups did remain active during the war. The American Union Against Militarism spawned a civil liberties bureau, later to become the American Civil Liberties Union, which worked on behalf of conscientious objectors to conscription during the war. Liberal and Socialist critics of the war formed the People's Council of America for Democracy and Terms of Peace to advocate an early peace. But governmental repression on all levels was fierce. The People's Council searched in vain for a city to meet in; dozens of Socialist publications were denied access to the mails; hundreds of national and local leaders of the Industrial Workers of the World were

jailed; and 2,000 people were arrested altogether on charges of disloyal speech. The fact that considerable grass-roots opposition to the war still existed was shown by the increased vote given to Socialist party candidates in many local elections; but the opposition was given no room to mobilize on a national level.

In the two decades after the 1918 armistice a strong disenchantment with the aims and results of World War I spread among the American public. It was reflected not only in revisionist writings about the war but also in the renewed growth of peace organizations. Both the more conservative groups aligned with the Carnegie Endowment and such pacifist groups as the Fellowship of Reconciliation flourished during that period. Peace activity was especially marked on college campuses, as an estimated half million students took part in rallies against war at the peak of the student activity in 1936. Disillusionment with war was so widespread that Congress passed a series of neutrality acts in the 1930's aimed at preventing the United States from being drawn into a future war. As war drew nearer in Europe and Asia at the end of the decade, the antiwar consensus eroded and the neutrality legislation was circumvented or repealed. German attacks against France and Britain in 1940 and Russia in 1941 reconciled most people, including a great majority of liberals and radicals, to American support for the Allies. Once the United States entered the war officially in December 1941, American participation received a more nearly unanimous domestic support than in any previous war in the nation's history. Public opposition to the war was almost nonexistent. Of the prewar peace groups, the most active during the war were those that worked to influence the government in the direction of creating a permanent world organization on the basis of the wartime alliance. Pacifists still refused to accept the war—while preferring the Allied cause to that of Germany and Japan—but a great many of those who had espoused an absolute pacifism in the 1930's abandoned their previous position.

With the breakup of the wartime alliance and the beginning of the cold war against the Soviet Union in the late 1940's, the wartime consensus on foreign policy at first fell apart and was then reimposed by repression. In the immediate aftermath of World War II, war weariness and demonstrations by soldiers who wanted to come home forced a much more rapid demobilization of the armed forces than had been planned. But cold war tensions soon made possible a peacetime draft and increasingly tight alliances with conservative regimes around the world. Critics of the government's stance came to be branded either as subversives or as dupes of world communism. The outbreak of war in Korea (1950) exacerbated this tendency, and pacifist, as well as radical, groups were reduced to the lowest point of their peacetime influence in at least half a century. The Korean War was by no means popular in the United States, but this fact sprang simply from war weariness, and there was no peace movement of any size that could claim credit for the war's unpopularity.

The Korean armistice in 1953 and a general relaxation of cold war tensions in the mid-1950's, together with a decline in the worst aspects of repression, enabled a peace movement to emerge again in 1957. The issue of nuclear testing was seized upon, both as a symbol of the menace of nuclear war and as an immediate hazard. Thousands of scientists signed a petition against atmospheric nuclear testing, and the National Committee for a Sane Nuclear Policy (SANE) was formed in 1958 by liberals and pacifists. Women Strike for Peace, the Student Peace Union, and the Committee for Nonviolent Action were formed within the space of a few years. Agitation by this new peace movement contributed to the defeat of the proposals under President John F. Kennedy's administration for a far-reaching civil defense program (which the peace groups argued would make war seem more acceptable) and, on the other hand, helped lead to the negotiation of a limited ban on nuclear testing by the United States and the Soviet Union in 1963. The peace movement was not able to slow the steady increase in military appropriations, which accelerated under Kennedy.

The American intervention in Vietnam, which reached major proportions in 1965, elicited a strong and ultimately effective peace movement. The first national demonstrations against the war, called by the Students for a Democratic Society, drew upward of 20,000 young people to Washington, D.C., in April 1965. Within two years, perhaps as many as half a million persons took part in the spring 1967 antiwar marches in New York City and San Francisco. On college campuses a draft-resistance movement gained momentum, and on scores of campuses there were obstructive sit-ins against recruiters for the armed forces and for the Dow Chemical Company, which manufactured napalm used in Vietnam. As more and more liberals joined radicals in turning against the war, President Lyndon B. Johnson's popularity within his own Democratic party began to suffer

badly. Amid poll reports that showed him a certain loser to antiwar Sen. Eugene McCarthy in the Wisconsin presidential primary, Johnson withdrew as a presidential candidate in March 1968.

During the administration of President Richard M. Nixon the ranks of protesters swelled. Probably several million persons took part in activities during the antiwar moratorium in October 1969, and on Nov. 15 the largest antiwar demonstration in the nation's history took place in Washington, D.C. In May 1970 hundreds of college campuses were shut down during a nationwide student strike to protest an American invasion of Cambodia. Because of general disillusionment and the growing protest movement, the Democratic majority in Congress began to pressure the Nixon administration for an end to the war. The administration signed a peace treaty on Vietnam in January 1973 and in the summer of that year was forced by Congress to end American bombing of Cambodia, the last element of direct participation by American forces in the Indochina war.

[Charles Chatfield, *For Peace and Justice;* Merle Curti, *The American Peace Crusade;* H. C. Peterson and Gilbert Fite, *Opponents of War, 1917–1918;* Thomas Powers, *The War at Home;* Daniel B. Schirmer, *Republic or Empire;* Lawrence S. Wittner, *Rebels Against War.*]

JAMES P. O'BRIEN

PEACE RESOLUTIONS OF BRITISH PARLIAMENT. Although Great Britain had suffered some disastrous defeats during the American Revolution, culminating in Gen. Charles Cornwallis' surrender at Yorktown in 1781, it was by no means crushed; the triumph of the liberal parliamentary opposition in 1782 made possible negotiations for peace. The historic resolution, introduced on Feb. 22 by Gen. Henry Seymour Conway, finally passed the House of Commons by a majority of nineteen votes on Feb. 28, 1782. The resolution prayed that the war in America might no longer be pursued for the impracticable purpose of reducing the inhabitants of that country to obedience by force. On Mar. 4 Conway carried unanimously another motion "that the house will consider as enemies of the King and country all who shall advise, or by any means attempt, the further prosecution of offensive war for the purpose of reducing the revolted colonies to obedience by force."

[George Otto Trevelyan, *George the Third and Charles Fox.*]

SAMUEL FLAGG BEMIS

"PEACE WITHOUT VICTORY." In his address to the Senate on Jan. 22, 1917, President Woodrow Wilson attempted to state the terms of peace that in his opinion would create "a stable Europe." The peace, he said,

> must be a peace without victory. . . . Victory would mean peace forced upon the loser, a victor's terms imposed on the vanquished. It would be accepted in humiliation, under duress. . . . Only a peace between equals can last. . . . The right state of mind, the right feeling between nations, is as necessary for a lasting peace as is the just settlement of vexed questions of territory or racial and national allegiance.

At that time Wilson was still hoping to mediate between the European powers at war and was not expecting the rupture with Germany that came in less than two weeks.

[R. S. Baker and W. E. Dodd, eds., *The Public Papers of Woodrow Wilson.*]

BERNADOTTE E. SCHMITT

PEACHTREE CREEK, BATTLES ON (July 1864). As the Confederate army fell back on Atlanta, the Confederate government became impatient and alarmed. Confederate Gen. J. E. Johnston was replaced by Gen. John Bell Hood because he had failed to arrest Union Gen. William Tecumseh Sherman's advance (*see* Davis-Johnston Controversy).

On the night of July 19, 1864, the Union army began crossing Peachtree Creek to start a vigorous movement against the Atlanta defenses. Hood adopted Johnston's plan, already formulated, to attack the Union army as it crossed. The Confederate movement was delayed until the late afternoon of July 20 and then was only partially successful. Poor staff work and confusion in orders and judgment resulted in uncoordinated attacks. Sherman's center, already across Peachtree Creek, could not be dislodged. Darkness ended the fighting. July 21 was passed in artillery bombardments, isolated actions, and maneuvering for position.

During the night Hood learned that Sherman's left under Union Gen. James B. McPherson, moving to cut the Confederate communications into Atlanta, was exposed and vulnerable. Late at night Confederate Gen. William J. Hardee was ordered to withdraw his command and march to attack McPherson. As soon as McPherson could be forced back the remainder of the Confederate army would move forward. Because of the distances involved, Hardee could not attack until about noon. McPherson was taken by surprise and only saved from defeat by the fortuitous arrival of the Seventeenth Corps, led by Union Gen. Francis P. Blair, Jr. The remainder of Hood's army did not attack until nearly four hours after Hardee had moved forward. Sherman was able to reinforce McPherson and halt Hardee. McPherson was killed in the battle, and night closed with Hardee in possession of the field. The losses on both sides were heavy in this the bloodiest fight of the Atlanta campaign. Union casualties numbered about 1,600 killed, wounded, and missing; Confederate casualties, about 2,500.

[R. U. Johnson and C. C. Buel, eds., *Battles and Leaders of the Civil War*, vol. IV.]

THOMAS ROBSON HAY

PEACOCK-EPERVIER ENGAGEMENT (Apr. 29, 1814). The new American sloop *Peacock* (twenty-two guns), commanded by Capt. Lewis Warrington, captured the British brig *Epervier* (eighteen guns), commanded by Capt. R. W. Wales, off Cape Canaveral, Fla. The *Peacock*, slightly superior in all respects, lost the use of its foresails at the outset, but drove forty-five shots into its opponent's hull and killed nine and wounded fourteen of the crew. The American losses were two wounded. The prize was brought safely into Savannah on May 1.

[A. T. Mahan, *Sea Power in Its Relation to the War of 1812.*]

WALTER B. NORRIS

PEA RIDGE, BATTLE OF (Mar. 7-8, 1862), also known as the Battle of Elkhorn Tavern, an engagement in northwestern Arkansas near the Missouri state line. In the struggle for control of the trans-Mississippi, a Confederate army under Maj. Gen. Earl Van Dorn maneuvered against a Union army of about equal strength under Brig. Gen. Samuel R. Curtis. They met in northwestern Arkansas in the vicinity of Sugar Creek and Elkhorn Tavern, at the crest of Pea Ridge. A fierce two-day fight ensued with alternating success for each side. In the first day's fighting, at a critical moment, two of the Confederate leaders, Ben McCulloch and James M. McIntosh, were killed. Superior leadership and equipment finally brought victory to the Union army. This battle ended organized fighting in the trans-Mississippi. All troops were soon transferred to the line of the Mississippi River.

[R. U. Johnson and C. C. Buel, eds., *Battles and Leaders of the Civil War*, vol. I.]

THOMAS ROBSON HAY

PEARL HARBOR

PEARL CASE. Shortly after the suppression in 1848 of the underground railroad for fugitive slaves going north from Washington, D.C., the "underground station" in Washington, probably embarrassed by the accumulation of fugitives, sent seventy-seven of them down the Potomac River on the schooner *Pearl*. They were apprehended and brought back to Washington. The trial of the fugitives' white "conductors," Daniel Drayton and Edward Sayres, was published throughout the North, abolitionists making the case a national issue; and in Congress, antislavery members led by Joshua R. Giddings provoked a three-day debate "worth thousands to the cause."

[H. H. Caterall, *Judicial Cases Concerning American Slavery and the Negro;* M. C. McDougall, *Fugitive Slaves.*]
GILBERT HOBBS BARNES

PEARL HARBOR. Pearl Harbor naval base on the south coast of Oahu, Hawaiian Islands, six miles west of Honolulu, is large enough to accommodate the entire U.S. fleet. First in 1845 and again in 1875 attention was called to Pearl Harbor as a defense post for Hawaii and for the west coast of the United States. In 1887 the Hawaiian government granted the United States exclusive use of Pearl Harbor as a fueling and naval repair station. In 1908 the Navy Department dredged and widened the entrance channel. In 1919 a huge drydock was completed, and in 1926 the channel was again deepened and widened. It was designated as a naval, military, and airplane base, and all needed facilities were established, including ammunition dumps, machine shops, radio towers, a hospital, an airplane base on Ford Island in the harbor, barracks for military and naval personnel, and extensive fuel oil storage facilities. Pearl Harbor served as a port of observation in the mid-Pacific, as a defense lookout for the west coast of the United States and Alaska, and as a base for the Pacific fleet.

On July 16, 1940, a militant government came into power in Japan, favoring Germany in its war against the Soviet Union and Western Europe. Relations with the United States became strained. President Franklin D. Roosevelt proposed a meeting with the Japanese prime minister, Prince Fumimaro Konoye, to adjust differences between the two countries, but the offer only strengthened the hands of the Japanese militarists. Further negotiations between the two governments followed, but to no avail. The war in Europe seemed to be favoring Germany, with which the Japanese wanted to form an alliance, as the United States government was trying to halt Japanese aggression in

Manchuria and to prevent the making of an alliance with Germany.

On Oct. 18, 1941, a new Japanese government, more militant than its predecessor, came into power, headed by Hideki Tojo, and all efforts at conciliation failed. On Nov. 14, 1941, U.S. army and navy commanders in the Pacific area, including Pearl Harbor, were warned to be on the alert for a surprise Japanese attack; on Nov. 27 a dispatch declaring itself to be a "war warning" was sent to Pearl Harbor—but American authorities thought that the Philippines or Malaysia would be the target.

In the meantime a Japanese carrier task force had left the Kurile Islands in northern Japanese waters on Nov. 25, moving eastward for a surprise attack on the American naval base at Pearl Harbor, despite the opposition of the Japanese Emperor Hirohito and his supporters. Despite the several warnings—all of them vague and uncertain, however, about the objective of the rumored Japanese attack—the commanders at Pearl Harbor, both naval and military, were unimpressed and continued to concentrate on their training programs rather than on making preparations for any sort of a surprise naval attack. No effective security patrol had been established.

On Saturday, Dec. 6, 1941, many army and navy personnel were on the usual weekend shore leave, some to return to their posts late that night and some early the next day. At about 3:30 A.M., local mean time, on Dec. 7, a patrolling minesweeper reported the presence of an unidentified midget submarine outside the harbor to the destroyer *Ward,* also on night patrol. No report was made to the commandant until the *Ward* radioed at 6:54 A.M. that it had sunk a submarine, but the information was delayed in reaching the high command; also the harbor gate had not been closed. Virtually the entire U.S. fleet of ninety-four vessels, including eight battleships, was concentrated at Pearl Harbor; the disposition of troops, airplanes, and antiaircraft guns made effective defense nearly impossible.

At 7:55 A.M. on Dec. 7, 1941—a "day that will live in infamy"—the first waves of Japanese bombers attacked airfields and the fleet, particularly the battleships, anchored in the harbor. A second wave came over at 8:50 A.M. Not a single American plane in the area could be got into the air except a fighter squadron at Haleiwa, some miles away, which the Japanese had overlooked. Several of the smaller vessels were able to get into action briefly against Japanese submarines. When the last attacking Japanese planes returned to their carriers at about 9:45 A.M. Pearl Harbor was a smoking shambles. The attackers were unopposed. Every American airplane was either destroyed or disabled; the battleships were sunk or disabled; and other naval craft in the harbor had suffered a like fate. Of the personnel in the area, 2,403 were lost; the wounded totaled 1,176. Fortunately, the three carriers of the Pacific fleet were not in the harbor.

Word of the disaster reached Washington, D.C., at about 2:00 P.M., eastern standard time. The next day, Dec. 8, Roosevelt appeared before Congress and asked for recognition of a state of war. It was granted promptly, with one dissenting vote.

When news of the attack on Pearl Harbor reached the people of the United States, the nation was shocked that such a thing could happen at a time when it was generally known that relations with a boasting, belligerent Japan were strained almost to the breaking point. It was necessary for the president to do something without delay to satisfy public clamor, and so, on Dec. 18, 1941, he appointed a commission under the chairmanship of Owen J. Roberts of the U.S. Supreme Court to inquire into the matter and make an immediate report fixing the responsibility. The report, rendered in January 1942, placed the responsibility and the blame squarely on Rear Adm. H. E. Kimmel and Gen. Walter C. Short, the navy and army commanders at Pearl Harbor. There were many responsible people in and out of Washington who felt that the commission had not reached the heart of the matter, but merely produced scapegoats to satisfy the public—that Kimmel and Short had been sacrificed to political expediency. Both of them were relieved of their commands and retired. Adm. Harold R. Stark, chief of naval operations, was reduced in authority and transferred to an innocuous assignment in Great Britain; Gen. George C. Marshall, army chief of staff, went unscathed. It was generally considered that while none could be accused of culpable negligence, a lamentable lack of judgment could be charged to Kimmel, Short, and Stark.

As time passed, however, it came to be generally agreed that responsibility for their faulty evaluation must be shared by those in Washington who had been slow in relaying information about the fast-moving developments to the commanders in Hawaii. Moreover, everyone concerned had underestimated Japanese capabilities.

[E. J. King and W. M. Whitehill, *Fleet Admiral King: A Naval Record;* Samuel Eliot Morison, *The Rising Sun in the Pacific, 1931–1942.*]

THOMAS ROBSON HAY

PEARL RIVER, in the central part of the present state of Mississippi, was involved in the maneuvers by which Americans seized West Florida from Spain. After the West Florida rebellion (1810) Spain unsuccessfully attempted to make Pearl River the eastern limit of American territorial expansion. Congress in 1812 attached West Florida, from the Mississippi to the Pearl, to Louisiana, the area east of the Pearl to Mobile being attached to Mississippi Territory.

[Peter J. Hamilton, *Colonial Mobile.*]

MACK SWEARINGEN

PEARY'S POLAR EXPEDITIONS (1891–1909). Robert Edwin Peary was sent in 1891 by the Philadelphia Academy of Natural Sciences to explore northern Greenland. Wintering at McCormick Bay near the seventy-eighth parallel, he started on Apr. 30, 1892, with Eivind Astrup, and crossed the ice cap to Independence Bay on the northeastern coast of the island. The following year he returned to Greenland in the *Falcon,* and after spending two winters at Bowdoin Bay repeated the feat in 1895, with H. J. Lee and Matthew Henson.

In 1898 the Peary Arctic Club was organized in New York to finance an expedition under Peary to discover the North Pole. He sailed that year in the *Windward,* given him by Alfred Charles Harmsworth (later Lord Northcliffe), British newspaper publisher; wintered at Cape d'Urville; and spent the following year exploring Ellesmere Island, west of northern Greenland, and Grinnell Land in the central part of Ellesmere Island. Proceeding along the Greenland coast in 1900 he reached Cape Morris K. Jesup in Hazen Land, now Peary Land, where he struck northward over the ice to latitude 83°52′. Here he was forced back, but continued eastward along the coast to Wyckoff Island. Two years later he made another attempt, starting this time from Cape Hecla in Grant Land, the northernmost part of Ellesmere Island, only to be stopped by snow at latitude 84°17′.

The Peary Arctic Club was still willing to back Peary and in 1905 sent him out in the specially constructed *Roosevelt* to make another attempt. He wintered at Cape Sheridan, on the northern part of Ellesmere Island, near Robeson Channel, and the following year started northward from Point Moss with Capt. Robert A. Bartlett, equipped with dogs and sledges. In six weeks he reached latitude 87°6′ when open water forced him to turn back. Later in the season he led an expedition westward along the coast to Cape Thomas Hubbard, the northern extremity of Axel Heiberg Island, west of Ellesmere Island.

Elated at his success the club again sent Peary out in the *Roosevelt* in 1908. Wintering once more at Cape Sheridan he gathered a large party the following February at Cape Columbia, along the northern coast of Ellesmere Island, which he divided into detachments that were to precede him, establish caches, and return. At latitude 87°47′ he parted from Bartlett and proceeded with only Matthew Henson and four Eskimos. On Apr. 6, 1909, he reached the North Pole. Widely acclaimed as the discoverer of the North Pole, Peary in 1911 was given the rank of rear admiral by Congress.

[Eivind Astrup, *With Peary Near the Pole;* Fitzhugh Green, *Peary, The Man Who Refused to Fail;* Josephine Diebitsch Peary, *My Arctic Journal;* Robert E. Peary, *Northward Over the Great Ice,* and *The North Pole.*]

N. M. CROUSE

PECK, FORT, was built in 1867 for the trading firm of Durfee and Peck about two and a half miles above the Big Dry on the north side of the Missouri River, in what is now Valley County, Mont. The firm owned a number of steamboats and carried goods and equipment to soldiers and Indians. The fort had a stockade of logs and a staff of fifteen to twenty men. In 1874 the owners sold the post to the federal government, which maintained it as an Indian agency until 1879, when it was abandoned.

CARL L. CANNON

PECOS, a town in New Mexico, about thirty miles southeast of Santa Fe, was known as Cicuye to the first Spaniards who, under Francisco Vásquez de Coronado, reached the place in 1540. Pecos was then, and long after, the largest and most populous settlement of the Pueblo in New Mexico. After the conversion of the Indians to Christianity, especially as a result of the work of Luis Descalona, a Franciscan priest who accompanied Coronado to Cicuye and who remained behind when Coronado returned to Mexico in 1542, their town was a flourishing mission with church, school, and friary, especially during the 18th century, though it suffered repeatedly from epidemics and Comanche raids. The town was abandoned in 1838. The ruins of the massive church and ancient pueblo remains are part of the Pecos National Monument, authorized June 1965.

[A. F. Bandelier, *Report on the Ruins of the Pueblo of Pecos;* F. W. Hodge, *Handbook of American Indians.*]

FRANCIS BORGIA STECK

PECOS TRAIL. *See* **Goodnight-Loving Trail.**

PECULIAR INSTITUTION, a euphemistic term that southerners used as a pseudonym for slavery. John C. Calhoun defended the "peculiar labor" of the South in 1828 and the "peculiar domestick institution" in 1830. The term came into general use in the 1830's when the abolitionist followers of William Lloyd Garrison began to attack slavery.

[Augustin Cochin, *The Results of Slavery;* A. B. Hart, *Slavery and Abolition.*]

FLETCHER M. GREEN

PEDDLERS. As soon as the settlements in America were sufficiently advanced to produce surpluses and to demand the surplus commodities of each other, these commodities were transported by pack on back, by horse, by boat, or by carriage. Clocks and tinware are outstanding examples of commodities distributed by the colonial peddler (*see* Yankee Notions). At times the peddler provided the back settlements with their only contacts with the rest of the world, and at times he was guilty of gross deception in selling his wares. With improvements in transportation and communication, peddling as formerly understood declined in importance, although there were 16,594 people in the United States who followed the occupation in 1860. In the 20th century the peddler has been referred to as a door-to-door salesman.

[Richardson Wright, *Hawkers and Walkers in Early America.*]

FRED M. JONES

PEGGY STEWART, BURNING OF. "I would not be surprised to hear that you made a Bon Fire of the Peggy Stewart as I have a hint that a certain T[homas] W[illiams] has ship'd Tea on Board of her." So wrote J. J. Johnson, London representative of the Annapolis firm of Wallace, Davidson, and Johnson on Aug. 4, 1774. The *Peggy Stewart* had reached Annapolis by Oct. 14, 1774, with about a ton of tea consigned to Williams and Company. Williams paid the duty on the tea, but permission was not given to land it, even when Anthony Stewart, owner of the *Peggy Stewart*, and Williams offered to land it and destroy it. The threatening mob finally allowed Stewart to run the vessel aground on Windmill Point and burn it to the water's edge on Oct. 19 (now celebrated in Maryland as "Peggy Stewart Day").

["Account of the Destruction of the Brig 'Peggy Stewart,' " *Pennsylvania Magazine of History and Biography,* vol. 25 (1901); W. B. Norris, *Annapolis: Its Colonial and Naval History.*]

JAMES A. ROBERTSON

PEJEPSCOT PURCHASE, a tract of land, indefinite in extent, on the Androscoggin River (Maine), purchased Nov. 5, 1714, from the estate of Richard Wharton, by a group of eight proprietors—Thomas Hutchinson, John Wentworth, Adam Winthrop, John Watts, David Jeffries, Stephen Minot, Oliver Noyes, and John Ruck—most of them of Boston. The title rested on the Council for New England grant of June 16, 1632, to Thomas Purchase and George Way, supplemented by Indian deeds. The proprietors, the first of their kind active in Maine, may be credited with the early settlement of Brunswick (incorporated 1717) and Topsham, protected by Fort George, built in 1715 partly at the proprietors' charge. The threat of Indian wars lessened interest in the area from 1720 to 1737, after which the settlements grew rapidly. A dispute with the Kennebec proprietors, who claimed the same land, was settled by compromise in 1766. Other land disputes were settled by legislative action in 1814. With the final distribution of their lands soon after, the proprietors disbanded.

[G. A. and H. W. Wheeler, *History of Brunswick, Topsham and Harpswell, Including the Ancient Territory Known as Pejepscot.*]

ROBERT E. MOODY

PEKING CONGRESS met from October 1900 until the following September to adjust and settle the political, social, economic, and religious questions arising from the Boxer Rebellion. William W. Rockhill, who had suggested the wording of the Open Door memorandum to Secretary of State John Hay, headed the American delegation. By the provisions of the protocol, adopted Sept. 7, 1901, China agreed to punish the officials responsible for the murder of foreigners, allowed the diplomatic corps the right to a fortified legation quarter in Peking, and agreed that alien troops might be maintained in China to protect the communication lines running from Peking to the sea. Against the desire of the Americans, China agreed,

also, to pay an inflated indemnity of $333 million, of which 7.3 percent, or $24.5 million, was to be paid to the United States. In 1908 the U.S. government returned nearly $11 million of the American share to China. The sum thus remitted was devoted by the Chinese to an education fund, mainly to enable Chinese students to study in the United States. In 1924 the U.S. government canceled the unpaid balance ($6.1 million) of the indemnity owed the United States.

[Sir Edward Hertslet, *China Treaties;* John V. A. MacMurray, *Treaties and Agreements With or Concerning China.*]

HARRY EMERSON WILDES

PEKING TARIFF CONFERENCE was opened in October 1925 as a result of China's appeal for restoration of its customs autonomy. The U.S. delegation, led by Silas Hardy Strawn, urged tariff autonomy provided that Chinese *likin* (provincial taxes on goods in transit) were also abolished. Great Britain supported the proposal, but Japan opposed the plan. China asked also for abolition of extraterritoriality and for the removal of foreign control over both the customs service and the salt-tax administration. Civil wars in China, together with antiforeign agitation, forced a two months' recess of the conference, but in March 1926 the American proposals alone were accepted, effective January 1929. The extraterritoriality problem was referred to a special conference for solution.

HARRY EMERSON WILDES

PELELIU, one of the southernmost of the Palau Islands, a part of Micronesia that came under Japanese control after World War I. During World War II the islands were an important Japanese defense position; the main air base was located on Peleliu. Most American planners viewed the Palaus as a stepping-stone on the way back to the Philippines, although some thought they might be bypassed; the islands were strongly defended by more than 40,000 Japanese, and Allied victories elsewhere made their occupation seem less important. The decision was made in mid-1944 to seize three of the southern Palaus.

First to be invaded was Peleliu, defended by about 10,000 Japanese under Col. Kunio Nakagawa. After a three-day pre-assault bombardment the U.S. First Marine Division, under Gen. William H. Rupertus, landed early on Sept. 15, 1944. The Japanese, strongly entrenched in the island's central ridge system, fought back stubbornly, killing more than 200 and wounding more than 900 marines during the first day. By the end of the second day, despite continued heavy casualties, the First Division had secured Peleliu airfield and pushed Nakagawa's men back into higher ground. Fighting in temperatures as high as 115°F and short on water, the invaders attacked a series of interlocking Japanese cave positions. Most of these were occupied by the end of the month, but the Americans had to commit additional troops, a regiment of the army's Eighty-first Division, in order to do the job.

Resistance on Peleliu did not cease until the end of November, with the death of the last Japanese defenders. The island cost the Americans nearly 2,000 lives, but its value seems doubtful. Airfields on Peleliu and elsewhere in the Palaus could not support the Philippine invasion in the manner expected, and it is questionable whether Japanese forces in the Palaus could have interfered with subsequent American operations.

[Robert Ross Smith, *The Approach to the Philippines*, United States Army in World War II.]

STANLEY L. FALK

PEMAQUID PAVEMENTS were the unusually extensive stone remains of former constructions seen at Pemaquid Point in Maine until the mid-19th century, when most of them were taken up and used for local buildings. It was conjectured that these were remains of early fortifications, roadways, drying floors for fish, tannery pits, cellars, or drainage systems. The discovery of a reddish stone native to Florida, called coquina, and coins and weapons of Spanish make, in excavations among these ruins, lent color to the theory that Pemaquid Point might have been occupied as a fishing base by the Spanish from Saint Augustine early in the 16th century.

[Henry Cartland, *Twenty Years at Pemaquid;* Arlita D. Parker, *A History of Pemaquid.*]

ROBERT P. TRISTRAM COFFIN

PEMAQUID POINT, the peninsula on the Maine coast between the Kennebec River region and Penobscot Bay in present-day Lincoln County, plays an important, if shadowy, role in the early history of American colonization. Pavements found there, never satisfactorily explained, give weight to legends of very early occupation by Europeans (*see* Pemaquid Pavements). Mystery shrouds its beginnings, but it, with nearby Monhegan Island, was a center of European fisheries probably from the late 16th century on.

There was an Abnaki settlement on Pemaquid Point when George Weymouth landed, June 3, 1605, at New Harbor. James Rosier, who accompanied Weymouth, described the peninsula. The English seized five Indians and took them home for exhibit. Men of the Popham plantation visited the place in 1607. In 1616 Capt. John Smith found a dozen European fishing vessels there. Pemaquid was linked for many years with the colonial interests of Bristol, England; Robert Aldworth and Giles Elbridge, Bristol merchants, farmed its fisheries and furs. John Witheridge, a Devonian, was trading with the natives there in 1624. Englishmen were settled permanently at Pemaquid by 1625; and that year John Brown bought land from the great chief Samoset. Abraham Shurt obtained a grant at Pemaquid in 1631 and built a palisaded post. The ship *Angel Gabriel* was wrecked at Pemaquid in 1631. Dixie Bull, the pirate, captured the place and obtained £500 worth of furs. It was the most vital eastern outpost against the French colonization of Maine. Together with New York, New Jersey, and Delaware, it was granted to the Duke of York in 1664, and was administered as a part of the "County of Cornwall" and the colony of New York under Sir Edmund Andros. It was reclaimed by Massachusetts after the Duke of York became James II.

Pemaquid was a key position, heavily fortified, in the Indian wars. The early fort was taken by the Indians in 1676; the second, Fort Charles, in 1689; and Fort William Henry, built by Sir William Phips in 1692 at a cost of £20,000, with walls 6 feet thick and 22 high, was captured by the French and Indians in 1696.

[H. O. Thayer, "Beginnings at Pemaquid," *Maine Historical Society Collections,* 2nd series, vol. 2; Henry S. Burrage, *The Beginnings of Colonial Maine.*]

ROBERT P. TRISTRAM COFFIN

PEMAQUID PROPRIETORS, claimants to lands at Pemaquid Point on the Maine coast as heirs of Nicholas Davison, who succeeded to the title held under the grant of Feb. 29, 1631, issued by the Council for New England to Robert Aldworth and Giles Elbridge, of 12,000 acres of land plus 100 acres for each colonist. Shem Drowne of Boston, whose wife was one of the Davison heirs, organized the group in 1735, took possession in 1737, had a map made before 1741, and arranged three divisions of the lands in 1743 and 1744. The claim included all of the town of Bristol and parts of Newcastle and Nobleborough (Maine). Other claims, based on Indian deeds, covered much of the same ground, and the land titles of the settlers were in such confusion that the Massachusetts legislature in 1811 appointed a commission to recommend a solution. In 1813 the claims under Indian deeds were disallowed, but by agreement the Pemaquid proprietors did not dispossess any settlers, accepting equivalents in unsettled lands elsewhere.

[John Johnston, *A History of the Towns of Bristol and Bremen in the State of Maine, Including the Pemaquid Settlement.*]

ROBERT E. MOODY

PEMBINA, in northeastern North Dakota at the junction of the Red and Pembina rivers, was a strategic fur trade point for the North West Company in its war with the Hudson's Bay Company. The Red River valley to the south of this point belonged by charter to the Hudson's Bay Company, but its rival early took possession of it, and its fur resources were exploited by the traders of the North West Company. Charles Chaboillez, who established the first trading post in North Dakota in 1797, and Alexander Henry, Jr., who occupied the post in 1801, were both with the North West Company. Pembina was also one of the best-known outfitting points for the buffalo hunters of the prairies to the west and south. Their Red River carts and ponies returned with loads of pemmican, buffalo robes and skins, and dried meat. The pemmican was usually sold in Fort Garry (present-day Winnipeg), where it was in great demand as a winter food. In 1812 the first permanent settlement in North Dakota was made at Pembina by a group of pioneers from Scotland led by Thomas Douglas, Lord Selkirk. There Rev. George A. Belcourt built the first church in North Dakota. The federal government sent two expeditions from Fort Snelling, south of Minneapolis, to Pembina, in 1823 (*see* Long's Explorations) and 1849, for the purpose of locating the international boundary line of 1818.

O. G. LIBBY

PEMBROKE RESOLVES were drawn up by the citizens of Pembroke, Mass., in 1772 in response to the plea of the Boston committee of correspondence that the New England towns protest against the British ministry's plan of having the Massachusetts judges' salaries paid by the crown—a step that colonial patriots believed certain to create an arbitrary judiciary. The Pembroke men declared that British oppression called for the use of "every rightful art and energy of Policy, Stratagem, and Force." The Pembroke Resolves were given wide publicity in England by Solic-

itor General Alexander Wedderburn, who regarded them as proof of the alarming growth of American republicanism and sedition.

[J. C. Miller, *Sam Adams, Pioneer in Propaganda.*]

JOHN C. MILLER

PEMMICAN. *See* **Agriculture, American Indian.**

PEMMICAN WAR. In August 1812 the Hudson's Bay Company established an agricultural colony near Winnipeg, Canada, in the Red River valley, the center of the pemmican-producing area. Pemmican was vital to the rival North West Company since it was the principal diet of the voyageurs. From Pembina, N.Dak., Miles McDonnell, governor of the Red River settlement, issued a proclamation, Jan. 8, 1814, forbidding the exportation from the colony of pemmican and other supplies. This brought on the Pemmican War between the two companies. Many acts of violence occurred on what is now U.S. soil. The British government finally intervened, and the two firms were merged in 1821.

[R. E. Pinkerton, *Hudson's Bay Company.*]

FRANK EDWARD ROSS

PENDERGAST MACHINE. From 1890 to 1939 a Democratic political organization called the Pendergast machine dominated politics in Kansas City, Mo. The first permanent political club in the city, it was founded in 1890 by James Pendergast, and as a councilman, he used the patronage and power at his disposal to aid the working class. When he died in 1911, his younger brother Thomas took charge. Thomas Pendergast continued to provide services for the poor, and he built a large following among the middle class and among businessmen by providing both legal and illegal favors. From the time of his appointment to a county judgeship in 1922 until his election to the U.S. Senate in 1934, Harry S. Truman, a Missouri Democrat, was a beneficiary of the vote-getting ability of the machine, but it is generally agreed that he avoided involvement in the machine's corruption. Throughout the 1930's Pendergast continued to control enough votes to direct state politics, but the machine came to an end when he went to prison for tax fraud in 1939.

[L. W. Dorsett, *The Pendergast Machine.*]

LYLE W. DORSETT

PENDLETON ACT (Jan. 16, 1883), the federal government's central civil service law, was written by Dorman B. Eaton, sponsored by Sen. George H. Pendleton of Ohio, and forced through Congress by public opinion. It exempted public officials from political assessments. The Civil Service Commission was reestablished to prepare rules for a limited classified civil service, which the president could expand at discretion. Competitive examinations were to determine the qualifications of applicants, while appointments were to be apportioned among the states according to population.

[C. R. Fish, *The Civil Service and the Patronage.*]
CHESTER MCA. DESTLER

PENINSULAR CAMPAIGN (1862), an advance against Richmond, began on Apr. 4, 1862, when Maj. Gen. George B. McClellan got his Union army of approximately 100,000 under way from Fortress Monroe, its base, to attack the Confederate capital by way of the peninsula formed by the York and James rivers. McClellan had counted on a larger force and on aid from the navy on the James River. Because his arrangements for the defense of Washington, D.C., were unsatisfactory to the administration, 45,000 troops were withheld from his command. The navy was unable to help because of the menace of the *Merrimack* and Confederate shore batteries.

The campaign had three phases. The early Union advance was marked by Confederate resistance behind entrenchments across the peninsula from Yorktown. On Apr. 5 McClellan besieged Yorktown, which was evacuated on May 3. He then pushed slowly forward, fighting at Williamsburg on May 5, reaching and straddling the Chickahominy River on May 20 and facing a strengthened Confederate force under Gen. Joseph E. Johnston.

Help expected from Union Gen. Irvin McDowell's 40,000 men was lost to McClellan in May when Confederate Gen. T. J. ("Stonewall") Jackson's Shenandoah Valley campaign scattered or immobilized the Union armies before Washington. The first phase of the campaign ended with the indecisive two-day Battle of Fair Oaks (or Battle of Seven Pines), May 31 and June 1. Johnston was wounded on June 1 and Robert E. Lee succeeded to his command.

After Fair Oaks came the second phase, three weeks without fighting, marked by Confederate Gen. J. E. B. Stuart's spectacular cavalry raid around the Union army, June 11–13.

McClellan, reinforced, intended to take the offensive again, but Lee forestalled him and opened the third phase of the campaign by attacking the Union right at Mechanicsville on June 26. This began the Seven Days' Battles, during which McClellan changed his base to the James River and retreated, fighting at Gaines' Mill on the 27th, at Allen's Farm and Savage's Station on the 29th, at Glendale on the 30th, and at Malvern Hill on July 1. On the night of July 1 the Union Army withdrew to its base at Harrison's Landing and the unsuccessful Union campaign ended. With the appointment on July 11 of Gen. Henry W. Halleck to command all land forces of the United States, withdrawal of the Army of the Potomac from the peninsula began.

Union casualties in the campaign were approximately 15,000, with 1,700 killed; Confederate losses were about 20,000, with 3,400 killed. The Union forces greatly outnumbered the Confederate at the start of the campaign; toward its close the opposing forces were nearly equal.

[Bruce Catton, *The Army of the Potomac,* vol. I; R. U. Johnson and C. C. Buel, eds., *Battles and Leaders of the Civil War,* vol. II; Alexander S. Webb, *The Peninsula: McClellan's Campaign of 1862.*]
EDWIN H. BLANCHARD

PENITENT BROTHERS, or *Los Hermanos Penitentes,* is a religious organization in New Mexico that traces its origin to the 16th-century *conquistadores* and through them to medieval Europe. The local organizations are frequently incorporated as *cofradias* and are protected by law. The avowed purpose of the Penitent Brothers is the celebration in actual dramatization of the Passion of Jesus Christ as observed by medieval Spanish Christians, thus preserving the concept of the expiation of sins through physical suffering. They have been driven to secrecy by the unpleasant notoriety given the flagellant exercises of their Lenten ceremonies.

[Alexander M. Darley, *The Passionists of the Southwest;* Alice Corbin Henderson, *Brothers of Light.*]
DOROTHY WOODWARD

PENNAMITE AND YANKEE WARS. *See* **Yankee-Pennamite Wars.**

PENN CENTRAL. *See* **Railroads, Sketches.**

PENN'S DELAWARE TERRITORIES. *See* **Delaware Counties Act of Union; Lower Counties-on-Delaware.**

PENN'S FRAME OF GOVERNMENT, approved and signed in England by the first Pennsylvania colonists and published by William Penn, Apr. 25, 1682, consisted of twenty-four articles, to which was appended (May 5) the Laws Agreed Upon in England—a bill of rights emphasizing religious liberty. Defining free government as one "where the laws rule and the people are a party to those laws," Penn proceeded to establish a governor and council with large governing powers, including the sole power of originating laws, and an assembly with power limited to approval of laws promulgated by the council. Both bodies were to be elected by the freemen, one third of the council and the entire assembly to be chosen annually. The Charter of 1701, the joint work of Penn and the assembly, eliminated the council and gave the assembly complete control over legislation and taxation. Another provision of this charter, by which the province was governed until 1776, led to the separation of Delaware from Pennsylvania.

[C. M. Andrews, *The Colonial Period of American History,* vol. III.]

C. A. TITUS

PENN'S HOLY EXPERIMENT. *See* **Holy Experiment.**

PENNSYLVANIA. At the time of settlement by Europeans in the early 17th century Pennsylvania was inhabited by some 15,000 Indians divided into three main tribal groups, the Delaware, Susquehanna, and Shawnee. Possession of the territory was disputed by the English, Dutch, and Swedes. English claims rested principally on the voyage of John Cabot in 1498, whereas Henry Hudson sailing under the Dutch flag had entered the Delaware River on the *Half Moon* in 1609 and Dutch trading posts were subsequently established. In 1637 the Swedes started trade; in 1638 they built Fort Christina, and in 1643, the first permanent settlement and capital within Pennsylvania on Tinicum Island, at the mouth of the Schuylkill River. The Dutch seized New Sweden in 1655, only to lose it to the English in 1664. The territory then was governed under James, Duke of York. Charles II in 1681 made Quaker leader William Penn the governor and proprietor, partly to clear a debt of £16,000 owed Penn's father, Adm. William Penn, and to establish a firmer English control over this key area. Penn made his colony a haven for persecuted Quakers and others under the liberal Frame of Government of 1682 and the Charter of Privileges of 1701, which he consid-

ered the basis for a "holy experiment." After his death in 1718 the colony was governed briefly by his wife, Hannah Penn; thereafter the proprietorship fell to his sons, John, Richard, and Thomas, and finally to his grandson, John Penn. The Revolution ended the proprietorship in 1776, but political battles had led in the intervening years to a strong colonial assembly.

The liberal government, abundant land, and economic opportunity combined to attract to the new colony thousands of immigrants from Europe who sought greater religious and political freedom as well as a chance for a more prosperous life. The English Quakers of southeastern Pennsylvania were joined in increasing numbers by Germans after 1700, mainly from the Palatinate, who moved into central Pennsylvania, and by 1728 by Scotch-Irish from northern Ireland, who moved farther west. Philadelphia grew quickly into the largest city in colonial America and by 1776 was the second largest in the British Empire. Its economy was enriched by growing agricultural wealth from prosperous inland farms providing surpluses for export, shipbuilding on the Delaware, the charcoal iron industry, an interior fur trade, and a developed commercial leadership. A rich cultural and intellectual life evolved, which led Philadelphia to be called the Athens of America.

The Penns fell heir to major boundary disputes with Maryland, Virginia, and Connecticut because of vague "sea-to-sea" charters. The Maryland dispute was settled by the Mason-Dixon line survey in 1769; the Connecticut claim was not adjusted until after some bloodshed in 1782; the Virginia altercation was settled in 1779 in the courts. The colonial era also saw Pennsylvania drawn into the final stages of the war for empire between France and England, as the French sought to occupy the upper Ohio Valley, to control the fur trade and a link between Canada and the lower Mississippi. Forts were built by the French at the present sites of Erie, Waterford, Franklin, and Pittsburgh; the most famous key outpost was Fort Duquesne, built on the site of present-day Pittsburgh in 1754. English efforts to dislodge the French led to Gen. Edward Braddock's defeat in 1755 but were followed in 1758 by the capture of Fort Duquesne by Gen. John Forbes, who then built Fort Pitt. The conquest of Canada in 1760 ended the French threat, but Pontiac's War threatened western Pennsylvania, which was saved only by Col. Henry Bouquet's relief of beleaguered Fort Pitt in 1763.

By 1776 Pennsylvania had grown to be the third largest colony in population, although next to the last to be founded. The three original counties had grown to eleven, reaching west of the Alleghenies. The population was estimated at 275,000.

Pennsylvania was bound to have an important role in the Revolution despite the pacifism of a majority of Quakers and many German settlers. John Dickinson and Benjamin Franklin were leaders in developing early resistance to English tax measures. The first Continental Congress met in Carpenters' Hall in Philadelphia in 1774, and the second in the Pennsylvania State House (Independence Hall) in 1776; continuing to meet there, the Continental Congress made the city the nation's capital except when Adm. Richard Howe's occupation of 1777–78 forced a withdrawal to Lancaster and York. At the Pennsylvania State House both the Pennsylvania constitution of 1776 and the Declaration of Independence were drawn up. After the war Independence Hall, Philadelphia, was the seat of the Constitutional Convention (May–September 1787), and Pennsylvania was the second state to ratify the new federal Constitution, on Dec. 12, 1787. Philadelphia was the national capital from 1790 to 1800, when the capital was relocated in Washington, D.C. The state capital was also relocated in the same year, in Lancaster, and thence to Harrisburg in 1812. A new state constitution was adopted in 1790.

After the Revolution there came several decades of major developments for Pennsylvania. The population grew and soon filled out the frontier. A rising tide of democracy made Pennsylvania a stronghold of the Jeffersonian and Jacksonian democracy, of which the Whiskey Rebellion against federal excise taxation in western Pennsylvania in 1794 was a manifestation. A new and more democratic state constitution was adopted in 1838. The antislavery movement flourished after early Quaker opposition to slavery, and Pennsylvania Rep. David Wilmot spearheaded the drive against the extension of slavery into territory gained by the United States through the Mexican War. The need for Philadelphia to maintain access to the expanding interior and the West, both as markets and as sources of materials, such as coal and iron, to be sold and manufactured, led to early improvements in transportation. The Philadelphia-Lancaster Turnpike, first in the nation, was completed in 1794; many miles of state canals were constructed and linked by the Allegheny Portage Railroad over the Alleghenies in 1835; pioneer railroads were built in the mining regions; and a great growth of commerce and shipbuilding took place. The revolution in industry made Philadelphia a textile center, and the use of anthracite as a fuel in furnaces expanded the iron industry. Oil was discovered near Titusville in 1859.

Just before the Civil War, Pennsylvania provided its only president, James Buchanan (1857–61). During the war Gettysburg was the scene of the war's most decisive battle, July 1–3, 1863—and Pennsylvania furnished men and leaders, including generals George B. McClellan, Winfield S. Hancock, and George Meade and Adm. David D. Porter, for the Union army and navy. A Philadelphia banker, Jay Cooke, became the leading financier of the Civil War, and Philadelphia continued as a financial leader in the nation until after 1870.

The cultural and intellectual growth of the state continued, with special emphasis on science and invention, and the later years of the 19th century saw a continued growth of industry, with steel replacing iron, notably under the leadership of Andrew Carnegie. The state led in oil production and refining before 1900, as well as in the lumber and leather industries. It was first in anthracite and bituminous coal mining. Pennsylvanian Thomas A. Scott contributed importantly to national railroad development, and John A. Roebling applied his genius to bridge building. George Westinghouse invented the air brake, revolutionizing railroading, and practical use of alternate-current electricity. William Kelly of Pittsburgh pioneered in blast furnaces in the making of steel. The development of large-scale industry induced the organization of labor, which had started in Philadelphia much earlier. Labor disorders took place in the 1870's; the famous strike against the Carnegie steel mills at Homestead occurred in 1892 and the great anthracite strike in 1902. Notable labor leaders included Terence Powderly, John Mitchell, and William Wilson.

The 20th century saw Pennsylvania upholding the nation's war efforts with its men and leadership and its mills and mines. World War I leaders included generals Tasker H. Bliss and Peyton C. March and Adm. William S. Sims. The most notable Pennsylvanian of World War II was Gen. George C. Marshall. Predominantly Republican in politics after 1870, the state developed an effective two-party system after the 1930's and elected three Democratic governors between 1954 and 1970. The Great Depression and a sharp decline in the coal-mining industry, especially anthracite, to which was added a less dominant role in the nation's steel production, created serious economic problems for Pennsylvania. To the decline in anthracite and steel production could be added the increase in population, so that by 1970, a number of Pennsylvania's 11,793,909 inhabitants were on welfare or relief. Although beset with problems, Pennsylvania continued to hold a high place in the nation's cultural and intellectual affairs, and any listing of prominent persons in these areas of national life reveals a large number of actors, writers, musicians, scientists, humanitarians, and educators with Pennsylvania roots.

[P. S. Klein and A. Hoogenboom, *A History of Pennsylvania;* S. K. Stevens, *Pennsylvania, Birthplace of a Nation.*]

S. K. STEVENS

PENNSYLVANIA, INVASION OF (1863). The Confederate victory at Chancellorsville, Va., early in May 1863 presented Gen. Robert E. Lee with two problems: the reorganization of the army and the determination of what to do next. As to the first, Lee decided to divide his army into three corps—Gen. James Longstreet remained in command of the first; generals Richard S. Ewell and A. P. Hill commanded the other two. The cavalry was increased and the artillery reorganized. All this involved the mixing of old and new units, the breaking up of associations of long standing, and the introduction of many new leaders. While these changes were being made, Lee was developing a plan for future operations. He thought a victory on northern soil essential to Confederate success. He would free Virginia from the danger of invasion and meet and destroy his opponent. Confederate President Jefferson Davis, not appreciating the tremendous moral effect of the Emancipation Proclamation, still looked to foreign recognition as a means of saving the Confederacy, meantime adhering to his original military policy of holding territory regardless of its importance or strategic value. Others urged troop transfers on interior lines within the Confederacy. Key areas were menaced—Union Gen. Ulysses S. Grant was threatening Vicksburg, and Confederate Gen. Braxton Bragg in Tennessee felt too weak to take the offensive (*see* Tullahoma Campaign). Lee's plan of invading the North was adopted. He believed that success would relieve pressure on other areas and that northern public opinion would force a peaceable settlement.

The delicate operation of maneuvering Union Gen. Joseph Hooker out of his positions behind the Rappahannock River was begun on June 3, 1863. Lee planned to use the Shenandoah and Cumberland valleys as covered avenues of approach into Pennsylvania. By June 12 Hooker had begun to move northward so as to keep between Lee and the capital at Washington, D.C. On June 23, while the Confederate army was crossing the Potomac River, Confederate

Gen. J. E. B. Stuart and his cavalry rode off to harass Hooker's army. Stuart then passed between it and Washington, crossed into Maryland, and rejoined Lee in Pennsylvania on July 2. In retrospect it was a fatal detachment. On June 27 Hooker, feeling he had lost the support of his government, resigned, and Gen. George G. Meade succeeded him. The Confederate army, living off the country, was moving into Pennsylvania when Lee learned that Meade was in pursuit; on June 29 he ordered a concentration of his scattered army. Stuart's unfortunate absence deprived Lee of exact knowledge of enemy movements and position. As a result, Hill's troops, investigating the character and strength of a Union cavalry force in Gettysburg, inadvertently and accidentally brought on the three-day battle that ended in Confederate defeat.

All during July 4 Lee waited in position for Meade's counterattack, but none was made. After dark the Confederate army began to withdraw. The retreat, skillfully conducted, was made in driving rain that turned the roads into quagmires. By July 6 the army was at Hagerstown, in northern Maryland, drawn up to repel Meade's expected attack. But Meade did not begin pursuit until July 5, moving cautiously as he went. Lee moved back slowly to the Potomac at Williamsport, about seven miles southwest of Hagerstown, where flood waters compelled another halt. Meade, following, hesitated to attack, and by the time he reached a decision the river had fallen sufficiently to permit Lee's army to cross over into Virginia during July 13 and 14. Early in August the Confederate army had taken position south of the Rapidan River to protect Richmond from any move by Meade's army. On Aug. 8 Lee, assuming complete responsibility for the failure of the campaign, asked President Davis to select someone else to command the army. Davis refused, asking, "Where am I to find the new commander?" In disaster Lee blamed no one but himself and in disaster his faith was unshaken.

[D. S. Freeman, *R. E. Lee.*]

THOMAS ROBSON HAY

PENNSYLVANIA, UNIVERSITY OF, in Philadelphia, emerged from a sequence of experimental trusts. Starting from a 1740 plan for a charity school, a subsequent plan for a public academy was implemented in 1749, through Benjamin Franklin's *Proposals* and the *Constitutions,* which he wrote with the attorney general of the province. The resulting institution was historic because never before in the history of higher education had an educational institution been founded on purely secular and civil objectives, without patronage from a religious group, a private sponsor, or a government. Instruction began at the academy in 1751 and included some classes for poor children. In 1755 Franklin's commitment to higher education was epitomized in a rechartering that denominated the school a "College and Academy."

During the eight years (1749–57) that Franklin shepherded the infant institution, he exemplified the spirit of compromise needed to moderate the conflict and bitterness that can strangle academic progress. Instead of insisting on the primarily utilitarian curriculum he preferred, he agreed to a major classical emphasis in order to attract important trustees, and thus, there emerged a balance between classical and scientific education unique in the colonies. Through the succeeding two centuries the example of resilience set by Franklin more than once moderated academic fright over prospective change and permitted some venturesome innovations—for example, the first medical school in the colonies (1765) and the first department of botany (1768).

The self-perpetuating board of trustees, established in 1749 and continuing from then on, began a close connection between the school and the old aristocracy of Philadelphia and environs that lasted through most of two centuries. Perhaps it accounted in part for an action by the Pennsylvania legislature in 1779 by which the rights and property of the trustees were confiscated and the corporate title was changed to "Trustees of the University of the State of Pennsylvania," the first designation of any institution as a university in the emerging nation. The rights and property were restored to the "college" in 1789, apparently with the idea that the "university" would function somewhat separately. This anomaly ended in 1791 when the college and university were amalgamated as the University of Pennsylvania, privately controlled and funded, except for some state aid—an independent status that has been retained.

Little momentum was achieved between 1790 and 1850; the medical school was faltering, and the pioneer law professorship of 1790–91 (the first in the United States) failed (until 1850) to inspire the establishment of a law school. Fortunately, vigor was on the point of resuming, as proved by the addition of the Towne Scientific School (1875), the School of Dentistry (1878), the Wharton School of Business (1881), the Graduate School of Arts and Sciences (1882), and the Veterinary School (1884). Affiliation with the Free Museum of Science and Arts (since 1938, the University Museum) was established in 1887.

The 20th century brought medicine forward at the university: the Graduate School of Medicine was founded in 1919; the School of Nursing in 1935; and the School of Allied Medical Professions in 1950. The university became affiliated with several hospitals and divers medical facilities. The spectrum of academic inquiry was broadened further with the founding of the Moore School of Electrical Engineering in 1923, the College of Liberal Arts for Women in 1933, the Fels Institute of State and Local Government in 1937, and the Annenberg School of Communications in 1959.

Such rapid and varied growth called for taking stock, and in 1954 the university commissioned a critical five-year survey by outside specialists. Adoption of many of the suggested alterations resulted in the expenditure of $100 million for new buildings and a proliferation of experiments in curricula, student lifestyles, and community relations. The total yearly operating expenditures of the university were well over $280 million in 1975. Franklin's little Academy, which opened its doors in 1751 to 145 pupils, had become a multiform university of approximately 20,500 students in 1975.

[E. P. Cheyney, *History of the University of Pennsylvania, 1740–1940*.]

JEANNETTE P. NICHOLS

PENNSYLVANIA AND OHIO CANAL, planned as a shortcut from Pennsylvania to Lake Erie, ran from the Ohio River near Pittsburgh to Akron, where it connected with the Ohio and Erie Canal. The Ohio legislature in 1836 subscribed to one-third of its entire stock issue, and the canal was opened in 1840. In 1854 the Cleveland and Mahoning Railroad obtained a controlling interest in it, and it soon fell into disuse. By 1874 the canal was permanently closed.

[Alvin F. Harlow, *Old Towpaths*.]
ALVIN F. HARLOW

PENNSYLVANIA CANAL SYSTEM. Not only was Pennsylvania jealous of New York's fame through the building of the Erie Canal, but Philadelphia's western trade was menaced by it. In 1826 the Pennsylvania legislature passed an act for state construction of a waterway from Philadelphia to Pittsburgh (known as the Main Line), and ground was broken at once. From Philadelphia to Columbia along the Susquehanna River, a distance of 81.6 miles, a railroad instead of a

249

canal was built and opened in 1834. The canal began at Columbia and followed the Susquehanna and Juniata rivers to Hollidaysburg, from which the Portage Railroad carried the line over the mountains to Johnstown; from there the canal continued to Pittsburgh. Several auxiliary canals were authorized, and work on them began in 1828. Leaving the Main Line at the mouth of the Juniata, one of the canals ran up the Susquehanna to Northumberland where the river forked; one line followed the west branch of the Susquehanna past Lewisburg and Williamsport, and the other followed the north branch past Wilkes-Barre toward the New York state line. The Delaware Division, following the Delaware River from the mouth of the Lehigh River down to tidewater at Bristol (in southeast Pennsylvania), was in effect a continuation of the Lehigh Canal, privately built from mines at Mauch Chunk (now Jim Thorpe, Pa.) and above, down to the Delaware. Some short branch canals were built; the Monongahela River was improved with locks and dams; and a canal was projected from the Ohio River near Pittsburgh to Lake Erie, of which only thirty-one miles were ever built. By 1840 there were 606 miles of canal and 118 miles of railroad in the system, and the expense incurred and authorized then stood at $32 million, although the original estimate had been $5 million. On Feb. 1, 1840, for the first time in its history, Pennsylvania defaulted in the payment of interest on its bonds. Thoroughly alarmed, the legislature halted construction throughout the whole system, and in some places it was never resumed. Although the tolls could not pay expenses and interest, the system was enormously useful in getting the state's coal and other products to market, in capturing a considerable portion of the trade of the Ohio and Mississippi valleys, and, in general, in developing Pennsylvania into one of the nation's greatest commercial and industrial states.

On Apr. 13, 1846, the Pennsylvania Railroad was chartered by the state legislature to build a line paralleling the main canal from Philadelphia to Pittsburgh; but prosperity was returning, and although the canal debt had by 1848 risen to $40 million, the state was still hopeful. But the yearly balance sheets proved that these internal improvements were being operated at a loss. The governor was authorized to offer the Main Line for sale. In 1857 the Pennsylvania Railroad bought it for $7.5 million and promptly shut down the Portage Railroad. In 1863–64 it abandoned the west end of the canal, from Johnstown to Pittsburgh. The eastern section was turned over to a subsidiary corporation, the Pennsylvania Canal Company, in 1866. In 1858 the state sold the Delaware, Susquehanna, north branch and west branch divisions to the Sunbury and Erie Railroad for $3.5 million. The railroad resold all these to companies organized to operate them. The North Branch canal was extended to Athens, Pa., three miles south of the New York state line, where it connected with the New York State canal system, but the portion of it above Wilkes-Barre was wrecked by a flood in 1865, and the Lehigh Valley Railroad was built on its right of way. In 1871 the Pennsylvania Canal Company operated 358 miles of the old system—the east end of the Main Line and portions of the Susquehanna, north and west branch divisions—and carried more than one million tons of freight, but thereafter its business declined. In 1889 the eastern fragment of the Main Line was wrecked by a flood and never fully rebuilt. In 1904 the last mile of canal along the Susquehanna was abandoned. The Delaware Division, leased in 1866 by the Lehigh Coal and Navigation Company, continued to operate as long as its sister canal, the Lehigh, functioned. Both ceased operation in 1931.

[Alvin F. Harlow, *Old Towpaths*.]

ALVIN F. HARLOW

PENNSYLVANIA-CONNECTICUT BOUNDARY DISPUTE had its origin in the overlapping territorial jurisdictions of the charters granted by Charles II to Connecticut "from sea to sea" (1662) and to William Penn (1681). The crown attorney general, Sir William Jones, admitted when Penn's charter was before him in 1681 that Connecticut had a real but impracticable claim to the lands within the whole breadth of the forty-first degree of latitude. Connecticut made no effort to give force to that right until 1774, when it gave official support to the demands of the Susquehanna Company (formed 1753) to the Wyoming Valley in what is now the northeastern portion of Pennsylvania. A year later this territory was made a county under Connecticut jurisdiction, and its inhabitants maintained possession by force of arms in the Pennamite Wars. County officials were appointed by Connecticut authority, its representatives sat in the Connecticut legislature, and its companies of militia were organized under the Connecticut line from 1775 to 1782. In the latter year, by reason of a petition from Pennsylvania to the Continental Congress, an interstate commission was organized under the terms set forth in Article IX of the Articles of Confederation, and on Dec. 30, 1782, this commission unanimously awarded jurisdiction of the territory in dispute to Pennsylvania. This was the only interstate trial held under the Articles of Confederation, and while the official dispute between Connecticut and Pennsylvania lasted only from 1775 to 1782, the actual conflict of private titles under the two charters originated about 1750 and was not finally settled until the first quarter of the 19th century.

[J. P. Boyd, ed., *The Susquehannah Company Papers.*]

JULIAN P. BOYD

PENNSYLVANIA DUTCH. *See* **Pennsylvania Germans.**

PENNSYLVANIA GAZETTE was established by Samuel Keimer at Philadelphia, Dec. 24, 1728, under the title the *Universal Instructor in All Arts and Sciences: and Pennsylvania Gazette,* as the second newspaper in the Middle Colonies. It was not successful, and on Oct. 2, 1729, Keimer sold it to Benjamin Franklin and Hugh Meredith, who continued it as the *Pennsylvania Gazette*. Meredith retired in 1732 and Franklin became sole owner, competing with Andrew Bradford's *American Weekly Mercury*. Franklin's ingenuity soon made the *Gazette* the most successful colonial newspaper. He introduced the editorial column, humor, the first weather report, and the first cartoon, exerting tremendous influence on journalism. On Jan. 12, 1748, he admitted his foreman David Hall to a partnership that continued until 1766 when Franklin retired. That year Hall formed a partnership with William Sellers, his journeyman, that lasted until Hall's death in 1772, when his son, William Hall, succeeded him. Occupation of Philadelphia by the British necessitated issuing the paper at York, Pa., from December 1777 to June 1778. Sellers died in 1804, and four years later William Hall, Jr., took George W. Pierie into partnership. Hall died in 1813 and Pierie in 1814. Although stating that the newspaper would probably be resumed in May 1816, the issue of Oct. 11, 1815, proved to be the last one of the *Pennsylvania Gazette*.

[Clarence S. Brigham, "Bibliography of American Newspapers, 1690–1820," *Proceedings of the American Antiquarian Society,* vol. 32.]

JULIAN P. BOYD

PENNSYLVANIA GERMANS, commonly but erroneously called "Pennsylvania Dutch," are a distinctive people with a history all their own and should not be confused with the general mass of German-Americans. Among the first settlers entering Pennsyl-

vania under Penn's charter, they increased somewhat slowly at first, but after 1727, when the heavy Palatine immigration set in, their increase was rapid. At the time of the Revolution the Pennsylvania Germans composed about a third of the population of the province.

Settling in the southeastern part of the colony, between the English on the east and the Scotch-Irish on the west, they occupied a well-defined geographic area, frequently referred to as Pennsylvania-German Land, where they still predominate overwhelmingly. This region embraces the counties of Northampton, Lehigh, Berks, Lancaster, Lebanon, and York, and adjacent districts, although many Pennsylvania Germans are found elsewhere in the state. In the area occupied by them in predominant numbers they developed a distinctive civilization that, by reason of the Pennsylvania-Dutch dialect and a strong ethnic consciousness, together with a certain conservatism, tends to perpetuate itself. Although considerably modified by the assimilating influences about them, the distinctive characteristics of the Pennsylvania Germans have persisted to a remarkable degree, especially in the rural districts.

[Richard O'Connor, *The German-Americans;* Ralph Wood, ed., *The Pennsylvania Germans.*]

WAYLAND F. DUNAWAY

PENNSYLVANIA HOSPITAL in Philadelphia is the oldest hospital in the United States. Chartered in 1751, it was founded by Benjamin Franklin and Thomas Bond. The buildings originally erected for it (1755–94), at Eighth and Spruce streets, are still in use. John Morgan, William Shippen, Jr., Benjamin Rush, and Philip Syng Physick were early members of its staff, and the board of managers has always consisted of representative citizens of Philadelphia. Its records show the admission of many victims of the French and Indian wars, including soldiers from Gen. Edward Braddock's army in 1755. During the Revolution its facilities were used by both the British and Continental armies during their occupation of Philadelphia. The earliest clinical lectures in America were given in its wards by Thomas Bond, and the oldest clinical amphitheater (1804) is still shown.

[T. G. Morton, *History of the Pennsylvania Hospital.*]

FRANCIS R. PACKARD

PENNSYLVANIA-MARYLAND BOUNDARY DISPUTE grew out of the ambiguous terms of territorial grants made by the crown to William Penn (1681) and to George Calvert, First Lord Baltimore (1632). Shortly after his arrival in America, Penn held a conference with Charles Calvert, Third Lord Baltimore, and presented a letter from Charles II ordering both parties to determine the boundaries and Baltimore to take two degrees northward, sixty miles to a degree. Baltimore objected to the two degrees and Penn then urged him to take two and a half, measuring northward from Watkins Point on Chesapeake Bay. Fortunately for Penn, Baltimore declined this proposition, which would have put his northern line twenty miles above Philadelphia. Baltimore then issued a proclamation offering lands in the disputed area in larger quantities and at cheaper prices than Penn was willing to grant. Thereupon Penn appealed to the Privy Council. In 1685 an order in council was issued that the region bounded on the east by the Atlantic Ocean and the river and bay of Delaware, and on the west by Chesapeake Bay, should be divided into equal parts by a line drawn from the latitude of Cape Henlopen, on the western side of Delaware Bay, northward to forty degrees north latitude, the eastern half of which should belong to the king and the western half to Baltimore. From this time on invasions from Maryland into the Delaware counties were made; Pennsylvania settlers were brought before Maryland courts, their houses burned, and their crops and cattle destroyed or stolen. In 1708 Baltimore petitioned the crown to set aside the order of 1685 on the ground that it had been surreptitiously obtained and was false in its statements. Penn countered with another petition and was sustained. Baltimore again petitioned in 1709 but was dismissed, and the order of 1685 was commanded to be put in execution. Actual jurisdiction over the lower counties had been exercised by Pennsylvania since 1693, and on four occasions between 1704 and 1724 the Maryland assembly admitted they were annexed to Pennsylvania. Charles Calvert, Fourth Lord Baltimore, effected an agreement with Penn's widow in 1724, but her death and the infancy of the Pennsylvania proprietors delayed its execution. In 1731 Baltimore petitioned the crown to order the Penns to join with him in settling the boundaries, and in 1732 an agreement with the Penn family was drawn up. Commissioners were appointed to run the line but could not agree. In 1735 the Penns presented in chancery a bill that gave an exhaustive statement of all of the points at issue. This case was dragged on at enormous expense. Eminent crown lawyers were employed on both sides, and ancient documents were examined in England and America. Finally in 1750 Lord Chancellor Philip Yorke, First Earl of Hardwicke, pro-

nounced his decree: that the agreement of 1732 should be enforced, and that commissioners to ascertain the boundaries should be appointed within three months. But again a deadlock ensued, when the Penns received in chancery an order to reopen the proceedings. In 1760 Baltimore entered into a final agreement with the Penns and in 1762 the chancellor ordered it to be executed. Commissioners were again appointed, but the actual running of the lines was entrusted to two expert surveyors from England, Charles Mason and Jeremiah Dixon. In 1767 Mason and Dixon finally located at 39°44′ the northern line of Maryland, which has since borne their names, and thus brought to an end a tedious and costly dispute that had lasted through most of a century. This boundary was ratified by an order in council, Jan. 11, 1769.

[W. R. Shepherd, *History of Proprietary Government in Pennsylvania.*]

JULIAN P. BOYD

PENNSYLVANIA PRISON SYSTEM was first developed in Cherry Hill Penitentiary, erected at Philadelphia, 1829–35. Prisoners were confined in large, solitary cells, which flanked corridors that branched out from a central control room like the spokes of a great stone wheel. Separate walled exercise yards adjoined the backs of most of the cells. The inmates spent their years of confinement in solitude, laboring at various handicrafts, and saw no one except prison officers or the chaplain. The system required a minimum of discipline and was widely copied in Europe; but its great expense prevented its spread in the United States, and the practice of solitary confinement was abandoned even at Cherry Hill in the 1880's.

[Harry E. Barnes, *The Evolution of Penology in Pennsylvania;* Blake McKelvey, *American Prisons.*]

BLAKE MCKELVEY

PENNSYLVANIA RAILROAD. *See* **Railroads, Sketches: Penn Central.**

PENNSYLVANIA TROOPS, MUTINIES OF. On Jan. 1, 1781, Pennsylvania troops stationed at Morristown, in northern New Jersey, mutinied. They killed or wounded several officers, and on Jan. 3 started for Philadelphia to place before the Continental Congress demands for back pay, food, clothing, and adjustment of enlistment terms. At Trenton the troops were met by Joseph Reed, president of the

Supreme Executive Council of Pennsylvania, who on Jan. 11 secured acceptance by the mutineers of an agreement adjusting their demands. They then returned to Morristown.

On June 13, 1783, some Pennsylvania troops, in Philadelphia for discharge, presented a memorial demanding pay due them. Lancaster detachments soon joined the malcontents. Irresolution characterized the reply by Congress, then sitting in Philadelphia. The mutineers became insolent in their demands and conduct, and on June 21 they made a public demonstration. Congress, still temporizing, adjourned to Princeton, N.J. The mutineers, hearing of the approach of troops from Gen. George Washington's army under Gen. Robert Howe, dispersed or surrendered. Congress did not sit again in Philadelphia until 1790.

[L. C. Hatch, *The Administration of the American Revolutionary Army.*]

THOMAS ROBSON HAY

PENNSYLVANIA-VIRGINIA BOUNDARY DISPUTE had its origin in the ambiguous terms of the grant of 1681 to William Penn and the claim of Virginia to extend "from sea to sea, west and northwest" over any territory not covered by royal grants. The questions at issue were whether the thirty-ninth or the fortieth parallel was the southern boundary of Pennsylvania and how the western boundary, which was to be five degrees west of the Delaware River, should be drawn. Prior to the French and Indian War Virginia claimed most of what is now southwestern Pennsylvania, including the district around the Forks of the Ohio, and attempted to settle it by means of the Ohio Company. The survey of Charles Mason and Jeremiah Dixon, 1763–67, made it clear that Pennsylvania extended some distance west of the mountains, and in 1773 Pennsylvania established Westmoreland County in the disputed territory. Early in 1774 John Connolly, acting on instructions from the governor of Virginia, took possession of Fort Pitt and organized a company of Virginia militia in the region; and in 1775 Virginia included the disputed territory in the District of West Augusta and set up a court at Pittsburgh.

The efforts of rival magistrates to exercise jurisdiction over each other resulted in disorders in 1774 and 1775, but the advent of the Revolution and the consequent necessity of cooperation against Tories and Indians put a stop to them. Thereafter the authority of Pennsylvania was generally recognized in what is now Westmoreland County and that of Virginia in the Monongahela Valley. In 1779 joint commissioners of the two states agreed to settle the dispute by extending the Mason-Dixon line, which is about a quarter of a degree south of the fortieth parallel, to a point five degrees west of the Delaware River and by running the western boundary of Pennsylvania due north from that point. The Pennsylvania assembly promptly ratified the commissioners' decision, but the Virginia assembly waited until commissioners had confirmed the land claims of Virginians in the region and then ratified with the proviso that such claims should be valid.

[S. J. Buck and E. H. Buck, *The Planting of Civilization in Western Pennsylvania;* Boyd Crumrine, "The Boundary Controversy Between Pennsylvania and Virginia, 1748–1785," *Annals of Carnegie Museum,* vol. 1.]

SOLON J. BUCK

PENOBSCOT, the peninsula at the mouth of Maine's largest river of the same name, held by five different nations in turn, was the strategic center of the battleground of the French and the English for the possession of Maine. Explored by both, it was the site of Fort Pentegoet, founded by the French fur trader Claude de Saint-Étienne de la Tour about 1625. It was also the site of a trading post established by the Plymouth Plantation about 1626. Sacked by the French in 1631 and captured by them in 1633, it was held, in spite of Myles Standish's attack in 1635, by Charles de Menou d'Aulnay (later governor of Acadia), until its recapture by the Puritans in 1654. Returned to the French by the Treaty of Breda (1667), in 1670 it became the seat of the picturesque Baron Vincent de Castine, who left the French army to become an Indian nabob and philosopher, husband of a Penobscot princess, and founder of a trading post at Penobscot. Castine and his half-breed son became the leaders of the Indians in King Philip's War (1675–76) against the British. Castine's stronghold at Penobscot did not become completely English until Quebec fell in 1759.

[Henry S. Burrage, *The Beginnings of Colonial Maine;* Robert P. Tristram Coffin, *Kennebec.*]

ROBERT P. TRISTRAM COFFIN

PENOBSCOT EXPEDITION (1779), an attempt by Massachusetts to dislodge the British from Bagaduce (now Castine), on the Penobscot peninsula of Maine, which they had occupied in June 1779. Nineteen armed vessels with more than 2,000 men, commanded by Capt. Dudley Saltonstall, together with twenty-four transports carrying about 900 militia under Gen. Solomon Lovell, with Paul Revere as chief of artillery, arrived at Penobscot Bay on July 25, 1779. Lovell's forces made a courageous landing, but Saltonstall failed to cooperate. When British naval reinforcements arrived on Aug. 13, Saltonstall hardly attempted a defense and lost nearly all his vessels, most of them being fired by their crews to prevent capture. Ill-conceived, ill-planned, and worse executed, the expedition cost Massachusetts £1,739,000 in inflated currency and nearly its whole trading fleet.

[G. W. Allen, *A Naval History of the American Revolution*.]

ROBERT E. MOODY

PENOLE, a compound of crushed parched corn, sugar or molasses, and cinnamon, the last optional. Originating in the Spanish Southwest, penole was of great value to early travelers whose rations were reduced to essentials, particularly travelers to the Far West. The traveler, without necessarily cooking it, mixed penole with water and found it nutritious if not delicious. A man could live for a month on half a bushel.

[W. J. Ghent, *Road to Oregon*.]

CARL L. CANNON

PENSACOLA, a city in northwestern Florida on the Gulf of Mexico. The first settlement at Pensacola, soon abandoned, was that of Tristán de Luna y Arellano and a party of 2,000 settlers in 1559. Almost 150 years later, in November 1698, Andrés de Arriola reached Pensacola Bay and established Fort San Carlos de Austria near the present site of Fort Barrancas as a protection against French encroachments. Within a few months the French settled the lower Mississippi region. In 1719, when war was declared, Jean Baptiste Le Moyne, Sieur de Bienville, seized the town, only to have his prize at once recaptured. The French attacked a second time and burned the settlement; but after peace was made Pensacola was restored to Spain (1723). The Spaniards now made their settlement on Santa Rosa Island, near the entrance to Pensacola Bay, from which a hurricane in 1754 drove them back to the mainland.

In 1763 the British obtained Florida and divided it at the Apalachicola River into two provinces, Pensacola becoming the government seat of West Florida. The trading house of Panton, Leslie and Company was organized with headquarters at Pensacola, and the town, until then a wretched place of "forty huts and a barracks," rose to its most prosperous period before the Civil War. During the American Revolution, Pensacola was involved in intrigues and, after Spain entered the war against England, was captured by Bernardo de Gálvez in May 1781.

Florida was restored to Spain in 1783 by the Definitive Treaty of Peace, and Pensacola lost its importance, although it remained the headquarters of Panton, Leslie and Company. During the War of 1812 the British attempted to use the town as a base of operations, whereupon it was seized by Gen. Andrew Jackson (1814), and the British were expelled. Jackson again occupied Pensacola in 1818 on the grounds that Spain was harboring hostile Seminole. After fourteen months it was restored to the Spanish authorities.

When the United States obtained Florida, the formal cession took place in Pensacola on July 17, 1821 (*see* Adams-Onís Treaty; Florida, Purchase of). In 1822 the first Florida territorial legislative council met there, and the town was soon full of land speculators attracted by the road then being started from Pensacola to Saint Augustine on the Atlantic coast. A second real estate boom took place because of a projected railroad, but the scheme collapsed, and by 1839 Pensacola's population was less than 2,000.

On Jan. 12, 1861, Fort Barrancas and the navy yard were surrendered to the Confederates, but Fort Pickens on Santa Rosa Island remained in Union hands. From this base Union troops retook the city in 1862.

After the Civil War Pensacola grew in importance as a port, especially for the commercial fishing industry. In 1914 the navy yard was reopened as the U.S. Naval Air Station, with a large aviation school. By 1900 the city's population had risen to 17,747. In 1970 it was 59,507.

[Richard C. Campbell, *Colonial Florida;* Dorothy Dodd, "The New City of Pensacola," *Florida Historical Quarterly* (1931); John Lee Williams, *Territory of Florida*.]

KATHRYN T. ABBEY

PENSACOLA, CONGRESS OF, was held in 1765 to define boundaries and ensure peace between the Indians and the British, who had acquired the Floridas two years earlier. It was attended by chiefs and warriors of the upper and lower divisions of the Creek nation, private traders, the British governor and council of West Florida, and Indian Superintendent John Stuart. The resultant treaty laid down a definite boundary—a line running along the coast and about fifteen miles inland—between Indian and British territories and provided for the elimination of certain irregularities in the fur trade, notably by annexing to the treaty a tariff of rates at which traders must dispose of their goods. Although it had soon to be revised, the treaty served to allay Anglo-Creek friction at a time when English relations with Indian nations along the entire frontier were highly unsettled.

[C. E. Carter, "British Policy Towards the American Indians in the South, 1763–8," *English Historical Review,* vol. 33; D. Rowland, ed., *Mississippi Provincial Archives, 1763–1766: English Dominion,* vol. I.]

W. NEIL FRANKLIN

PENSION ACT, ARREARS OF, passed Jan. 25, 1879, was the most significant and costly piece of pension legislation of the post–Civil War period. It was passed in response to a definite, well-organized, skillful lobby, led by the *National Tribune,* the "soldier sheet" of that day. Briefly stated, the act provided that all pensions that had been granted under previous laws, and all that were to be granted in the future, were to commence from the date of discharge. The rates for the period during which arrears of pensions were to be granted were to be the same as those for which the pension was originally allowed. The bill was admittedly a bid for the soldier vote. It received only four negative votes in the House of Representatives and only four negative votes in the Senate, excluding the southern congressmen and senators, most of whom refrained from voting. While under discussion the estimated cost of the bill was placed at $35 million. But within two years President Chester A. Arthur had placed the cost at $250 million. For years this act continued to prove the most burdensome piece of pension legislation in U.S. history.

[John W. Oliver, *History of the Civil War Military Pensions;* U.S. Commissioner of Pensions, *Annual Reports* (1880 and following).]

JOHN W. OLIVER

PENSION PLANS. In the mid-1970's more than 48 million active and retired American workers participated in the major private and government retirement programs in the United States, exclusive of the federal retirement program, Old-Age, Survivors, Disability, and Health Insurance (OASDHI). These included private pension and deferred profit-sharing plans, retirement programs for federal civilian employees, the federally administered railroad retirement system, and state and local government employee retirement systems. In terms of coverage, the federal OASDHI retirement program is the most comprehensive, since 90 percent of all persons earning wages or salaries or who are self-employed in the United States are covered under its provisions.

Private pension plans constitute the largest of the major retirement programs (other than OASDHI), having more than 35 million persons on their rolls in 1970 and assets and reserves well in excess of $137 billion. They fall into two major groups, those administered by life insurance companies and noninsured plans. Some pension arrangements combine both insured and noninsured features.

Noninsured plans include pension plans administered by trustees, pay-as-you-go plans, and deferred profit-sharing plans. In trustee plans contributions are paid into a trust, usually held by a bank that invests the contributions and pays benefits in accordance with the term of the trust and plan provisions. Pay-as-you-go plans meet benefit payments out of current revenue. Deferred profit-sharing plans are financed completely or partially from the employer's profits, with shares apportioned to the participants in some manner that takes into account either or both compensation and length of service.

Pension plans insured with life insurance companies in 1970 covered 11 million persons and had reserves of $41 billion. Group annuities, of which there are several types, have always been the most important kind of contractual arrangement devised by life insurance companies to underwrite pension plans. Group annuity contracts are used to provide regular income to each individual in a group (usually employees) payable upon the retirement of the individual. There are other kinds of contracts designed for smaller groups, or designed to provide benefits in addition to retirement benefits or for self-employed individuals.

Formal retirement plans for private industry were introduced by the American Express Company in 1875 and were soon widely adopted by railroads. By the late 1920's, about 80 percent of all railroad employees had coverage, but only about 10 percent of all American workers in private industry enjoyed this benefit. The private pension plans in existence at that time were chiefly in large-scale enterprises in basic industry and were established on the initiative of employers. Several developments during the 1930's and 1940's led to a marked expansion of the private pension rolls. First, the establishment of the federal Social Security program in 1935, by creating a floor of income protection, made the idea of pension planning much more widely applicable. Second, although wage controls were imposed as a World War II economic stabilization measure, contributions to pension plans that conformed to standards prescribed by the Treasury Department were permitted because they were not considered wage or salary increases. Pension plans were also aided by high wartime tax rates, since employers' contributions were deductible from taxable income, making it possible to retain valued employees by indirectly increasing their compensation.

A powerful impetus to the growth of private pension plans came from the trade union drive in the postwar years for the inclusion of pensions and other supplementary benefits in collective bargaining contracts. Up to that time, provisions for pensions were not common in collective bargaining contracts, and, in fact, trade unions had earlier viewed pensions as a device to hinder labor organization. Labor's drive for negotiated pension plans was strengthened in 1949 both by the Supreme Court decision in the Inland Steel Case to the effect that employers were required to bargain on pensions and by findings of the steel industry fact-finding board that held that the industry had an obligation to provide its workers with pensions and welfare benefits. The establishment of pension plans in the basic mass-production industries had brought more than 5 million workers within the scope of collectively bargained plans by 1950.

In terms of worker coverage the 1950's witnessed the most rapid expansion of the private pension movement. In each year, on the average, more than 1 million workers were added to private pension rolls. The rate of expansion slackened during the 1960's, but the total number of active workers covered reached 30 million in 1970, or about 50 percent of all private wage-earning and salaried workers. While the addition of active workers declined somewhat there was a marked increase in the number of retired annuitants; almost 3 million were added during the 1960's. During the same period private pension reserves and assets grew at an annual average of $7 billion.

The ability of private pension plans to provide the promised retirement benefits to participating employees has been questioned in legislative and other studies. The issues raised include (1) adequacy of retirement and survivor benefits, (2) termination of employment prior to normal retirement without forfeiture of accrued pensions, (3) provision of information to employees about provisions of pension plans, (4) adequacy of retirement funds to pay accrued benefits, (5) provision of means to enable workers to transfer pension credits from employer to employer, (6) protection for employees when a plan is terminated, and (7) safeguards against mismanagement of

pension funds. In order to increase the protection of private pension plan participants, the Employee Retirement Income Act was enacted by Congress in 1974. Among its major provisions are the establishment of minimum participation standards in regard to age and length of service, the accelerated vesting of benefits for participants after ten to fifteen years of service, and the current funding of normal (annual) costs of pension plans together with the systematic amortization of accumulated unfunded pension liabilities. The act also provides for pension plan termination insurance.

[Merton C. Bernstein, *The Future of Private Pensions;* Dan M. McGill, *Fundamentals of Private Pensions;* Roger F. Murray, *Economic Aspects of Pensions: A Summary Report;* U.S. Senate Committee on Labor and Public Welfare, Subcommittee on Labor, *Interim Report of Activities of the Private Welfare and Pension Plan Study* (1971).]

IRVING STONE

PENSIONS, MILITARY AND NAVAL. The United States has granted pensions to participants in all its wars, including Indian wars, and to members of the regular army and navy in peacetime. They may be classified as (1) pensions for injuries incurred in the service or to dependents of those whose death was caused by the service; (2) qualified service pensions for service of specified length combined with some other qualification, such as age, disability, or indigence; and (3) pensions for service alone, usually granted to aged survivors long after the war. These pensions developed independently of the retirement system for regular and lengthy service, which was generally accorded half-pay after a stipulated minimum service. Since World War II even the reserve components of the services have a retirement schedule. It is based on 2.5 percent of highest base pay per full year of active duty or cumulative years of training through a minimum of twenty years of satisfactory federal service, such a year being one in which a reservist earns the equivalent of at least fifty days' duty. Payment for the regular commences on retirement; for the reservist, it is deferred to age sixty-two. Even retirements for physical disability are not true pensions, since all recipients are liable to recall to active duty in wartime or national emergency.

The systems grew haphazardly. Before 1817 American wars were fought mainly by volunteer armies. Pensions were offered as inducements to enlistment in colonial wars and in the Revolution. Early federal enactments granting pensions to persons who had served in the Revolution provided only for disabilities incurred in the service. The first service pension law was enacted in 1818, and the first pensions for widows of soldiers of the Revolution were granted in 1836.

A separate system for the regular army and navy was established in 1790. The acts raising troops for the War of 1812 and the Mexican War promised the volunteers the same pensions as the regulars, and acts increasing these pensions before 1862 applied alike to the army and navy, the War of 1812, and the Mexican War. The first service pension was granted for the War of 1812 in 1871, and for the Mexican War in 1887.

Two innovations appeared during the Civil War. First, the "general laws" of 1862, providing uniform pensions on account of death or disability of service origin for both regulars and volunteers of the armed forces, applied to future wars. Second, certain specific disabilities were pensioned in 1864 at higher rates than under the general laws. Thereafter both the number of these disabilities and the rates rose rapidly.

A combination of political factors, including patriotism, the soldier vote, veterans lobbies, and pension attorneys, led to the establishment in the United States of the most generous pension system in the world. President Grover Cleveland's vetoes of private pension bills and of the Dependent Pension Bill of 1887 made the subject an issue in the election of 1888. The act of 1890 gave a qualified service pension to Civil War veterans who, from any cause, were incapacitated for performing manual labor. In 1904 an administrative order made age above sixty-two years a pensionable disability under this act. Congress recognized this principle in acts of 1907 and 1912, which graduated payment according to age and length of service. The first Civil War pension for service alone was enacted in 1920. At the beginning of the Spanish-American War, volunteers and state militia were specifically granted the same pensions as regulars. In 1920 a qualified service pension was given to all above sixty-two years of age.

The philosophy of veteran treatment was transformed by World War I and its aftermath. Subsequently the able-bodied veteran shared immediate and substantial benefits with his less fortunate comrades-in-arms. The new policy began during the war with enactments of a liberal life insurance program and a $60 discharge allowance. Thereafter, benefits progressively grew, largely through the persistent, indefatigable efforts of the American Legion, organized in 1919, almost simultaneously with the federal Veterans Bureau, created to oversee the traditional caretaking of casualties. Able-bodied veterans were soon lobbying for what was called the Bonus Bill, predicated on $1 per day for domestic service and $1.25 per day for overseas service. In 1924 Congress passed the bill over President Calvin Coolidge's veto. Sums exceeding claims of $50 were paid in life insurance certificates maturing in 1945, when the principal was to be paid. Compound interest and an adjustment scale made an average claim of $400 worth $1,000 at maturity. The depression came, and veterans organizations militated for preferential treatment. In 1931 Congress overrode President Herbert Hoover's veto to authorize veteran borrowing from the Treasury of amounts up to 50 percent of their certificates. The next year the Bonus Expeditionary Force marched on Washington, D.C., in a futile effort to force premature, lump-sum payment. In 1935 President Franklin D. Roosevelt's veto of a bill for such payment was sustained. In 1936 his veto was overridden and the then enormous sum of $2.491 billion was disbursed. It was an omen. From the Revolution to 1930 all federal disbursements to veterans totaled about $15 billion, a sum that by 1973 would cover only a year and a half of Veterans Administration (VA) commitments.

Established in 1930, the VA expanded rapidly in scope and complexity, originally befriending 4.6 million veterans, 3.7 percent of the U.S. population. By 1971 veterans numbered 28.3 million, a sizable 13.7 percent of the citizenry, counting 4,000 from the Spanish-American War, 1,408,000 from World War I, 14,294,000 from World War II, 4,626,000 from the Korean War, 4,837,000 from the Vietnam War, and 3,119,000 from peacetime service. It was estimated that they had about 97.6 million relatives, making 47 percent of the U.S. population actual or potential beneficiaries of the VA.

The major benefits provided by the VA are medical care, insurance, education and training, loans, and guardianship of minors and incompetents. Some 60 percent of the budget goes to compensation and pensions, the former to recompense veterans for the loss of earning power because of injury or disease arising from military service. Pensions recognize an obligation to give aid when necessary for non-service-connected disease or death. Disability pensions by no means underwrite lives of affluence. The monthly averages of 1971 were Vietnam, $128; Korea, $119; World War II, $114; World War I, $103; and the Spanish-American War, $140. In 1972 Frederick Fraske, the last surviving veteran of the Indian wars, received $135 per month, or $1,620 for the year, tax free but still far below the designated poverty level. (Fraske died in 1973.) Some 20 percent of the VA budget goes for medical programs. In 1972 the VA maintained 166 hospitals and 298 other facilities, such as nursing homes and clinics, serving 912,342 inpatients. Hospitalization increases with the aging of veterans. The VA is the fourth largest ordinary life insurer in the United States.

After World War II, GI bills of rights gave education or training to nearly 16 million veterans, besides their dependents. For World War II service, such benefits expired on July 25, 1956; for service in Korea, on Jan. 31, 1965; and service after the Korean War generally provided an eligibility of eight years from the day of release from active duty. The first GI bill was generous, covering up to forty-eight school months all the costs of tuition, fees, and study materials and providing living allowances of a monthly $65–160, scaled to the number of a veteran's dependents. Considering inflation in general and rising tuitions in particular, the 1972 Vietnam veteran was a poor relation, limited to thirty-six school months and provided with only $220 per month if single (up to $298 for a man with two dependents plus $18 for each additional dependent). Since 1944 the VA has guaranteed or insured loans for homes, farms, or businesses. In mid-1971 there were 7,782,000 loans on the books, nearly 99 percent for homes. At the same time the guardianship program took care of 648,000 minors and incompetent adults.

It should be noted that as World War I poison gas fatally eroded the vitality of thousands of veterans in postwar years, the barbarism of Viet Cong and North Vietnamese booby traps produced unusual wounds of body and mind in servicemen who participated in the Vietnam War. The fighting created a high rate of total impairment, about 9 percent of the compensated wounded—about 22,000 men. The number that became addicted to "hard" drugs in the course of service is unknown but estimated to be unprecedented, and the VA in 1972 was greatly expanding drug dependence treatment centers, opening the thirty-second and planning more.

By 1972 the VA had a staff of 182,546 people, almost exactly ten times the size of the regular army at the outbreak of the Civil War, underscoring the great expansion in veteran benefits since then. In an effort to reduce federal spending, the administration, in February 1973, proposed to save $100 million by nearly halving the benefits of some 200,000 veterans who had become physically handicapped from fighting in the Vietnam War. The 90 percent rating for a

veteran with a leg amputated at the hip, a monthly $275, would have been reduced to 40 percent, or $106. The reaction of the public defeated the proposal. The fiscal 1974 VA budget was $11.7 billion.

[Administrator of Veterans Affairs, *Annual Reports.*]

DONALD L. McMURRY
R. W. DALY

PENSIONS, OLD AGE. *See* **Old Age; Pension Plans; Social Security; Townsend Plan.**

PENTAGON PAPERS. The so-called Pentagon Papers comprise a forty-seven-volume study of the American involvement in the Vietnam War. Commissioned by Secretary of Defense Robert S. McNamara under the administration of President Lyndon B. Johnson, during an interval of impasse and frustration in the war, the study includes internal working papers from the four presidential administrations of the years 1945–68, with analytical commentary, or about 4,000 pages of documents and 3,000 pages of analysis, prepared by thirty-six military and civilian analysts. Initially, twenty sets of the papers were printed early in President Richard M. Nixon's administration, which largely ignored them until they were published in the *New York Times.*

While working for the Rand Corporation in 1969 in Santa Monica, Calif., which contributed to the Pentagon Papers study, Daniel Ellsberg decided that the American people should know about the actions of their government as depicted in the papers; aided by Anthony J. Russo, he copied the study and released it to newspapers. In 1971 the *New York Times* and other newspapers published the papers. After several installments appeared, the Justice Department obtained an injunction barring further publication. However, in *The New York Times* v. *United States* (1971), the Supreme Court ruled that the government failed to satisfy the exacting burden of proof necessary to justify prior restraint and had therefore infringed on the First Amendment's guarantees of freedom of the press.

Subsequently, Ellsberg and Russo were indicted for espionage, theft, and conspiracy; but in 1973, U.S. District Judge William M. Byrne, Jr., terminated the case on grounds of gross government misconduct. Byrne cited many violations of procedure and an alleged break-in by government officials at the office of Ellsberg's psychiatrist in a quest for evidence to discredit the defendant. During the case White House officials improperly approached Byrne concerning his possible appointment to the vacant Federal Bureau of Investigation directorship, which raised questions of propriety.

The Pentagon Papers are a mine of historical raw material, an inside view of government decisionmaking, available for scholarly scrutiny extraordinarily soon after the events they generated. The papers drew upon sealed files of the Defense Department, important presidential orders, and diplomatic papers. But the papers are also incomplete, for they do not include secret and important White House documents revelatory of presidential attitudes and purposes; nor do the papers include important and voluminous documents concerning the war's diplomacy.

The papers can be interpreted in conflicting ways, largely depending on the evaluator's own assessment of U.S. involvement in the Vietnam War: If it is deemed a horrendous mistake, the papers are a chronicle of failure, instigated by outmoded cold war doctrines and President John F. Kennedy's 1960 inaugural commitment to pay any price and bear any burden to bar the loss of further territory to Communist control. But the Pentagon Papers can also be interpreted as proving the viability of such concepts and as detailing the remarkable collaboration of four administrations, of both major parties, in perpetuating a commitment to an ally and in long pursuing a costly, eventually unattainable, goal—the prevention of victory in Vietnam to Communist forces.

The papers support several particular findings. For example, the war was closely controlled by civilian leaders; military leaders, reluctant to undertake the venture and doubting its strategic significance, were constantly concerned that they would not be allowed to enlarge the war sufficiently to establish a clear advantage over Communist forces. And the papers reveal that the United States entered the war and increased its commitment always by thoroughly deliberated steps, not by casual decision or through faulty intelligence.

Although civilian leaders controlled the war, military considerations surpassed political factors at most stages. Each presidential administration was captive to a resolve not to abandon the war—not to repeat the 1938 appeasement of Munich (which American leaders well remembered), not to sacrifice Vietnam as Czechoslovakia had been sacrificed before World War II. The Pentagon Papers reflect a belief in the domino theory, the supposition that the fall of one Asian nation into Communist hands would lead progressively to the fall of others. Even the Soviet–Communist China split did not raise doubts among American decisionmakers about the necessity of continuing the war. Each president, caught in a dilemma caused by anxiety to avoid defeat by a minor enemy and by fear of bringing Communist China or the Soviet Union into the war, was reluctant to escalate the war, a mood that was camouflaged by expansive public rhetoric urging the nation to "stay the course" and "pay the price."

The Pentagon Papers are replete with the cold, assured prose of efficiency experts, social-science gamesmanship, and probability theory: The war's choices are "options," countries and peoples are "audiences," and threats and escalations become "scenarios." They show that, generally, the executive decisionmakers constituted a tightly knit inner government that easily perpetuated itself from one presidency to the next.

[Mike Gravel, ed., *The Pentagon Papers;* Lyndon Baines Johnson, *The Vantage Point.*]

LOUIS W. KOENIG

PENTECOSTAL CHURCHES. The Pentecostal movement is a relatively late arrival on the American religious scene. Generally the Pentecostalists tend to be conservative on the question of the inspiration of the Bible, to stress the necessity of an emotional conversion, to practice the ministry of healing, and to believe in the experience of the Spirit. The presence of the Spirit may manifest itself in "speaking in tongues" (hence, their name), movements of the body, or a deep inner joy. Some Pentecostalists view the experience of receiving the Spirit as "the second blessing" and identify this experience with entire sanctification or holiness. In addition to the Pentecostal churches themselves, there is a widespread movement in the principal Protestant denominations that stresses many of the same experiences and beliefs.

Pentecostalism appears to have begun in the disputes over the place of "entire sanctification" in 19th-century Methodism. Although John Wesley's doctrine stressed the gradual growth of the Christian toward perfection, many revivalists were teaching the doctrine as if it called for a second experience of the Spirit, following conversion. In 1900, Bethel College, a Bible school, was founded by Charles F. Parham to train men in the doctrine of "Spirit baptism." Although the school closed, its students spread throughout the South and the West. W. J. Seymour, a convert, carried the faith to Los Angeles, where he founded the Azusa Street Mission in 1906. The strength of the revival there enabled the movement to grow rapidly.

While Pentecostalism has spread rapidly and widely in the United States, it has become fragmented into many competing denominations. The Assemblies of God, a denomination founded in 1904, is closest in organization to the principal Protestant denominations, for unlike earlier Pentecostalists, members of this group have a trained ministry and a church structure that combines Congregational and Presbyterian elements. The International Church of the Foursquare Gospel represents another style of the Pentecostal church; founded by evangelist Aimee Semple Mc-Pherson in the early 1920's, the church was entirely dominated by her during her lifetime, and after 1944 largely controlled by her son.

In 1974 the membership of the Pentecostal churches was as follows: Apostolic Faith, 4,800 members; Apostolic Overcoming Holy Church of God, 75,000; Church of God, Cleveland, Tenn., 258,000; Church of God in Christ, 425,000; Church of God of Prophecy, 48,700; Congregational Holiness Church, 3,000; Elim Missionary Assemblies, 3,500; International Church of the Foursquare Gospel, 40,000; International Pentecostal Assemblies, 6,500; Open Bible Standard Churches, 30,000; (Original) Church of God, 18,000; Pentecostal Assemblies of the World, 45,000; Pentecostal Church of America, 115,000; Pentecostal Holiness Church, 67,000; United Holy Church of America, 13,500; and United Pentecostal Church, 200,000.

[Charles W. Conn, *Like A Mighty Army Moves the Church of God;* Robert Glenn Gromacki, *The Modern Tongues Movement;* Walter J. Hollenweger, *The Pentecostals: The Charismatic Movement in the Churches;* William Wood, *Culture and Personality Aspects of the Pentecostal Holiness Religion.*]

GLENN T. MILLER

PENTEGOET, FORT, located in what is now Castine, Maine, was the advanced eastern post of the French in New England. Erected about 1625 by Claude de Saint-Étienne de la Tour, a French fur trader, it was seized by a group of Englishmen from the Plymouth Plantation a year later. After the English trading post established by the New Englanders was sacked in 1631 and then captured in 1633 by the French, Fort Pentegoet remained one of the French strongholds during the French and Indian War.

[G. A. Wheeler, "Fort Pentegoet and the French Occupation of Castine," *Maine Historical Society Collections,* 2nd series, vol. IV.]

ELIZABETH RING

PEONAGE, involuntary servitude under which a debtor is forced to make payment to a master by his labor. It differs from slavery, serfdom, and contract labor by both the necessary element of indebtedness and the indefinite term of service. While not wholly confined to blacks in the United States, peonage developed in the South after the abolition of slavery. Fines imposed for petty crime were paid by an employer who then exacted work from the sentenced person. Where agricultural laborers or tenants were advanced cash or supplies, any attempt to leave was interpreted under state statutes as obtaining credit under false pretenses, a criminal offense. Peonage did not lose its legal sanction until 1910, when the U.S. Supreme Court declared such state laws to be in violation of the Thirteenth and Fourteenth amendments (*Bailey* v. *Alabama,* 219 U.S. 219).

[Pete Daniel, *The Shadow of Slavery: Peonage in the South, 1901–1969;* Robert J. Harris, *The Quest for Equality: The Constitution, Congress & the Supreme Court.*]

RUPERT B. VANCE

PEOPLE'S PARTY. *See* **Populist Party.**

PEORIA, a city in central Illinois on Peoria Lake (part of the Illinois River), was the site of the first permanent French settlement in Illinois Country. Robert Cavelier, Sieur de La Salle, built Fort Crèvecoeur in 1680 near the lower outlet of Peoria Lake. In 1691–92 Henry de Tonti and François de la Forest erected Fort Saint Louis, later named Fort Pimitoui, which probably survived until the transfer of the Illinois Country to Great Britain in 1763. In 1778 a new village was founded on a nearby site, also within the limits of the present city. At the outbreak of the War of 1812 the village was believed to be an outpost for Indian raids. The first of two militia expeditions in 1812 destroyed an Indian village at the head of the lake, while the second, led by Capt. Thomas E. Craig, plundered and partly burned the French settlement. Fort Clark was built the following year.

American settlement began in the area of Fort Clark in 1819. The name of the community was changed to Peoria in 1825 when Peoria County was founded. Incorporated as a town in 1835 and chartered as a city in 1845, Peoria's growth was slow until the late 19th century. Because of its location in a rich agricultural region, the city became an important corn trading center and manufacturer of agricultural and earthmoving equipment. A port of entry on the Illinois River and a railroad center, Peoria was Illinois's second largest city from 1880 until the 1950's, when its population declined by 7.7 percent, the first such decline in its history. Peoria's population in 1970 was 126,963.

[Daniel J. Elazar, *Cities of the Prairie: The Metropolitan Frontier and American Politics.*]

PAUL M. ANGLE

PEQUOT TRAIL. The Pequot prior to 1637 occupied the region from the Niantic River in Connecticut eastward some distance into Rhode Island. The name Pequot Trail has been attached to a much-used Indian route through this region from New London, across the Pawcatuck River, to Westerly, East Greenwich, and Providence, all in Rhode Island. White settlers early laid out a road along or near the route, which by 1691 was a part of the post road between New York and Boston. In the 19th century the trail was paralleled successively by a turnpike and by the Shore Line of the New Haven Railroad and in the 20th century by a highway.

[F. S. M. Crofut, *Guide to the History and Historic Sites of Connecticut.*]

GEORGE MATTHEW DUTCHER

PEQUOT WAR (1636–37). Prior to any white settlement in Connecticut trouble had developed between Dutch traders and the Pequot, who were located in the southeastern part of the region and who claimed control over the tribes farther west. Capt. John Stone, an English trader, and several companions were killed by the Pequot on board their ship in the Connecticut River in 1633, as was Capt. John Oldham in 1636 at Block Island, at the entrance to Long Island Sound, which led to a fruitless attack by a Massachusetts Bay expedition.

Both sides began preparations for further hostilities. Capt. John Underhill with a score of men arrived early in 1637 to strengthen Saybrook Fort, located at the mouth of the Connecticut River, while in April some Pequot made an attack on Wethersfield further north, near Hartford, killing nine persons. It was this latter event that led the general court of the recently settled river towns—Windsor, Hartford, and Wethersfield—on May 1, 1637, to declare war on the Pequot. Ninety men were levied, supplied, and placed under command of Capt. John Mason. Accompanied by eighty Mohegan under Uncas, they soon made their way down the river to Saybrook. Joined by

Capt. Underhill and twenty Massachusetts men, Mason took his party in boats to the country of the Narraganset, where he conferred with their chief, Miantonomo, and received further aid. A two-day march overland brought the party to the Pequot fort near present-day Mystic. The fort was surprised and burned (May 26). Only seven Indians escaped the slaughter. Mason and his men attacked a second Pequot stronghold two miles away the same night. About 300 braves from other Pequot towns decided that their only safety was in flight and started with their women and children for the Hudson River. Meanwhile, the Mason party, reinforced by forty Massachusetts men, returned to Saybrook, while Capt. Israel Stoughton and 120 additional Massachusetts men arrived at New London harbor. After a conference, it was decided to pursue the fleeing Pequot, who were soon caught in Sasqua swamp, near present-day Southport, Conn. Through the intervention of Thomas Stanton the women and children were led out of the swamp before the attack was made. The fight on July 13 resulted in the escape of about 60 Pequot and the capture of 180, who were allotted to the Mohegan, Narraganset, and Niantic and absorbed into their tribes. Many of those who escaped were hunted down, while chief Sassacus was slain by the Mohawk and his scalp sent to Hartford. The Pequot, as a separate tribe, ceased to exist.

[Alden T. Vaughan, *New England Frontier: Puritans and Indians, 1620–1675.*]

GEORGE MATTHEW DUTCHER

PERDICARIS AFFAIR of 1904 was a spectacular prelude to U.S. secret participation in the Algeciras Conference. On May 18, 1904, Ion Perdicaris, an American citizen, and his stepson, Cromwell Varley, a British subject, were abducted from their villa near Tangier by the Riffian bandit Ahmed ibn-Muhammed Raisuli. The United States, with British support and the use of French good offices, demanded that the Moroccan sultan secure Perdicaris' release and dispatched the warship *Brooklyn* to Tangier. Meanwhile, the U.S. State Department came to suspect that Perdicaris had divested himself of American citizenship but ultimately determined the question in his favor. On June 22 Secretary of State John Hay sent the famous dispatch demanding "Perdicaris alive or Raisuli dead," just as Perdicaris was in fact being released. Hay's dispatch, hailed as robust-Rooseveltian, took the country by storm, but the dubious character of Perdicaris' citizenship was concealed until after President Theodore Roosevelt's election on Nov. 8.

[E. N. Anderson, *The First Moroccan Crisis, 1904–1906;* S. F. Bemis, *Diplomatic History of the United States;* A. L. P. Dennis, *Adventures in American Diplomacy, 1896–1906.*]

HAROLD E. DAVIS

PERDIDO, a river flowing through southwest Alabama to the Gulf of Mexico. As a result of frontier conflict between French and Spanish colonists in 1719, the Perdido became the boundary between French Louisiana and Spanish Florida. British East Florida and West Florida were divided at the Apalachicola River in 1763, but since 1783 the Perdido has been the limit of East Florida, now the state of Florida.

[Caroline M. Brevard, *History of Florida From the Treaty of 1763 to Our Own Times.*]

PHILIP COOLIDGE BROOKS

PERMANENT COURT OF ARBITRATION, commonly known as the Hague Court of Arbitration, operates under the Convention for the Pacific Settlement of International Disputes, which dates from the First Hague Peace Conference (1899). The United States led in drafting this treaty, which provided for resolving differences through good offices, mediation, and arbitration. The court established was to be "competent for all arbitration cases, unless the parties agree to institute a special Tribunal." Twenty-six signatory states ratified this convention, but it contained no provision for later members, a shortcoming remedied at the Second Hague Conference (1907) when the text was expanded from sixty-one to ninety-seven articles. Over forty nations subsequently signed, accepting the principle of arbitration as a means of resolving disputes.

The establishment of the court reflected a belief, which gained widespread acceptance in the 19th century, that nations would resort to such machinery to avert conflicts, but this dream did not materialize. Between 1899 and 1932, only twenty-one minor matters were referred to arbitration under the court, and it has not been used since 1932. The United States sought to make it an effective agency by submitting the Pious Fund case to it in 1902, and subsequently the United States agreed to hearings on five more issues.

The reluctance of nations to utilize the court stems from its lack of any compulsory feature requiring states to submit their differences to it and from confusion over its structure and use. It was actually neither permanent nor a court, but was a facilitating agency in the form of a panel of names from which a tribunal could be created according to need. Furthermore, the Permanent Court of International Justice, organized in 1921, deprived the earlier tribunal of considerable influence as governments utilized the newer body. The arbitration court heard only four cases after the new agency appeared.

Yet the Permanent Court of Arbitration has survived as a functional, if not functioning, agency. In addition to a panel of judges, it comprises an international bureau at The Hague, with a secretary and staff to handle operational details, and an administrative council to approve budgets and prepare reports. The United States has always named its four judges to the panel because these men nominate members to the International Court of Justice subject to election by the United Nations.

[Calvin D. Davis, *The United States and the First Hague Peace Conference;* Manley O. Hudson, *International Tribunals, Past and Future;* James Brown Scott, *The Hague Conferences of 1899 and 1907.*]

WARREN F. KUEHL

PERRY-ELLIOTT CONTROVERSY. At the Battle of Lake Erie (Sept. 10, 1813), a major engagement of the War of 1812, Jesse D. Elliott, commander of the *Niagara,* did not move his ship up to support the *Lawrence,* commanded by Oliver Hazard Perry, until the *Lawrence* was practically destroyed. This action led to much private recrimination, until in 1818, Elliott challenged Perry to a duel, and Perry preferred charges against Elliott for his conduct during the engagement. The charges were pigeonholed by the administration of President James Monroe, but in 1821, after Perry's death, the controversy was revived. In 1839, when James Fenimore Cooper, in his *History of the Navy of the United States of America,* failed to criticize Elliott, he was violently attacked by friends of Perry, mostly Whigs. Cooper thereupon successfully sued for libel. His restatement of the 1818 incident at the trial constituted the core of his *Battle of Lake Erie,* published in 1843. Although another libel suit was also won by Cooper, his 1839 history was excluded for a time from the school libraries of New York State. Later naval historians, Alfred T. Mahan, for example, tended to criticize Elliott for inaction.

[T. R. Loundbury, *James Fenimore Cooper;* A. T. Mahan, *Sea Power in Its Relations to the War of 1812.*]

WALTER B. NORRIS

PERRY'S EXPEDITION TO JAPAN. In response to a growing desire in the United States for commercial relations with Japan, closed to foreigners for almost two and a half centuries except for a carefully restricted trade with the Dutch, President Millard Fillmore dispatched an expedition to Japan in 1852 under the command of Commodore Matthew Calbraith Perry. Its objectives were to arrange for the protection of American seamen and property involved in shipwrecks off the Japanese coast; to obtain permission for American vessels in the Asiatic trade to secure provisions, water, and fuel; and to induce the Japanese government to open up one or more of its ports for trade. A further goal suggested by Perry was the acquisition of one of the outlying Japanese islands for use as an American naval base or coaling station, but this proposed move was rejected by the president.

Perry's mission, although pacific in character, was intended to impress upon the Japanese, through a show of force, the determination of the United States to enter into treaty relations. Thus, a considerable squadron, first of four war vessels and later of seven, was provided Perry. A first visit was made to the Bay of Yedo (Tokyo) in July 1853, and Perry formally delivered a letter from President Fillmore to the emperor of Japan. Perry informed the Japanese authorities that he would return early the next year for a definite answer to the proposals embodied in the letter, and he then withdrew his ships to the China coast.

A second visit took place in February 1854, and conversations were commenced, near the site of present-day Yokohama, looking toward conclusion of a treaty of peace and amity. Perry's firm insistence on American rights, backed up by the strength of his naval force, and conditions within the empire combined to convince the Japanese authorities to abandon their traditional policy of seclusion. On Mar. 31, 1854, the Treaty of Kanagawa, opening Japan to trade and also providing for the care of shipwrecked Americans and for facilities to supply American ships, was duly signed.

[Foster Rhea Dulles, *Yankees and Samurai;* Samuel Eliot Morison, *Old Bruin: Commodore Matthew C. Perry, 1794–1858;* Matthew C. Perry, *The Japan Expedition, 1852–1854: The Personal Journal of Commodore Matthew C. Perry.*]

FOSTER RHEA DULLES

PERRYVILLE, BATTLE OF (Oct. 8, 1862). After Confederate Gen. Braxton Bragg had attended the inauguration of the secessionist governor of Kentucky (*see* Kentucky, Invasion of), he set about gathering his scattered army to form a junction with reinforcements, commanded by Gen. Edmund Kirby-Smith, coming from Cumberland Gap. On Oct. 8, 1862, Bragg's army was drawn up in battle array near Perryville. Union troops under Gen. Don Carlos Buell, marching from Louisville, unexpectedly encountered the Confederate force. A bloody battle followed. The Confederates achieved a tactical success and remained in possession of the battlefield. During the night Bragg withdrew eastward to join Kirby-Smith. The following day a retirement southward toward Knoxville, Tenn., was begun.

[R. U. Johnson and C. C. Buel, eds., *Battles and Leaders of the Civil War,* vol. III.]

THOMAS ROBSON HAY

PERSONAL LIBERTY. *See* Liberty, Concept of.

PERSONAL LIBERTY LAWS, state enactments intended to impede the return of fugitive slaves. They were considered by slaveowners as a gross infringement of rights guaranteed them by the U.S. Constitution, and they were enumerated among the grievances justifying secession in 1861. The Constitution required that fugitive slaves be delivered to the person having legal claim to them (Article IV, Section II). These general provisions required implementation, and Congress provided it in the first Fugitive Slave Act, Feb. 12, 1793. Procedures for recovery were prescribed, and, admittedly, safeguards against abuses, such as the seizure of free blacks under perjured testimony or affidavits, were entirely inadequate. With the rise of sectional antagonism and the tendency to treat slavery as a moral question, the recovery of fugitives became increasingly difficult. Indiana (1824) and Connecticut (1838) had provided for jury trials for fugitives, but the bulk of personal liberty laws were adopted after 1842 when the U.S. Supreme Court, in *Prigg* v. *Pennsylvania* (16 Peters 539), declared that state officials could not be required to enforce the Fugitive Slave Act. Several states responded by forbidding their officers to perform any duties under the 1793 act or to use state jails or prisons for holding fugitive slaves.

After 1850, when the second Fugitive Slave Act, adopted at the end of a decade of growing tension, strengthened federal enforcement of Article IV, Section II, the scope of personal liberty laws was greatly enlarged, ostensibly to establish and safeguard traditional individual rights. Rigorous requirements for identification and proof of ownership had to be met, perjury and illegal seizures were heavily penalized, and the use of the jury was in effect a promise that the runaway and those who assisted him would have full measure of "liberty" while the pursuer would encounter equal measure of obstruction. South Carolina in 1860 named thirteen states in which laws "nullify or render useless" any attempt to carry out the guarantees under which the slaveholding states had accepted the Constitution.

[F. E. Chadwick, *Causes of the Civil War;* A. B. Hart, *Slavery and Abolition;* M. G. MacDougall, *Fugitive Slaves;* W. H. Siebert, *Underground Railroad.*]

W. A. ROBINSON

PERTH AMBOY, a city in New Jersey, settled in 1683–86. It became the capital (1686) and port of entry of East Jersey. Winning, through the *Hester* case (1700), its contest for commercial independence, Perth Amboy was important during the 18th century as a slave port and transfer point to the overland stage. It was a favorite residence of the colonial governors. During the Revolution, the city was occupied by the British in 1776–77. It was one of the twin capitals of New Jersey until 1790.

In the first half of the 19th century, Perth Amboy was known primarily as a summer resort. It began to attract heavy industry in the late 1800's and has become an important shipbuilding and oil-refining center, as well as a major East Coast port. The city's population in 1970 was 38,798.

[W. A. Whitehead, *Contributions to the Early History of Perth Amboy.*]

C. A. TITUS

PET BANKS. When in 1833 the administration of President Andrew Jackson determined to remove the governmental deposits from the Bank of the United States, certain state banks, popularly called "pet banks," were selected to receive future deposits. By Nov. 1, 1836, eighty-nine such banks in various states were acting as depositories of the federal government.

[D. R. Dewey, *Financial History of the United States.*]

ERIK MCKINLEY ERIKSSON

PETERHOFF **ADMIRALTY CASE** elaborated the status of a blockaded river serving both a neutral and a belligerent, and applied the ultimate destination rule to conditional and absolute contraband. The English-owned *Peterhoff* was captured Feb. 25, 1863, near

Saint Thomas, Danish West Indies, en route to Matamoras, Mexico. The Rio Grande offered port facilities to both Matamoros and Brownsville, Tex., then part of the Confederacy. The river mouth was considered within the federal blockade. The *Peterhoff* was laden with all three classes of goods—noncontraband, conditional contraband, and absolute contraband. The U.S. Supreme Court freed the ship and its noncontraband cargo, as the blockade, though it included the Rio Grande, could not preclude free use of the port for goods legally consigned to the neutral city. The seizure of the remainder of the cargo was sustained.

[John Bassett Moore, *International Law Digest.*]

JIM DAN HILL

PETER PARLEY, the pen name of Samuel G. Goodrich (1793–1860), poet, miscellaneous writer, and publisher. Impressed with the "monstrous, false and pestilent" nature of such nursery tales as "Little Red Riding Hood," "Puss in Boots," "Blue Beard," and "Jack the Giant-Killer," Goodrich set out with didactic fervor to create books consisting of "beauty instead of deformity, goodness instead of wickedness, decency instead of vulgarity." Goodrich's first attempt was *The Tales of Peter Parley About America* (1827). Its popularity led him, with the occasional assistance of fellow New Englanders, including Nathaniel Hawthorne, William Andrus Alcott, and James Russell Lowell, to compile during the next thirty years a total of 116 Peter Parley books and 54 others. As many as 10 million copies of Goodrich's books were in circulation. They ranged from toy books for nurseries to books for amusing and instructing youths—tales of travel, history, nature, and art and works designed to cultivate a love of truth, charity, piety, virtue, and patriotism. Widely used as textbooks, Goodrich's works gave impetus to the movement to make schoolbooks attractive and entertaining.

[S. G. Goodrich, *Recollections of a Lifetime.*]

HARRY R. WARFEL

PETERSBURG, SIEGE OF (1864–65). Severely repulsed by the Confederate forces of Gen. Robert E. Lee at Cold Harbor (June 3, 1864), Gen. Ulysses S. Grant decided to approach Richmond, Va., from the south, through Petersburg. On June 12, Grant started moving his army south toward the James River, which it crossed by ferry and pontoons at Wyanoke Neck, June 14–16. His leading corps attacked Petersburg on June 15. After three days of fighting, the federal troops captured the eastern defenses. Lee's army then arrived, occupied a shorter line nearer the city, and repulsed the last assaults.

Grant then began siege operations on the eastern front. At the same time, he persistently pushed his left flank southwestward to envelop Petersburg and cut the railways leading south. His first advance, June 21–22, was driven back. The Battle of the Crater, July 30, resulted in another defeat for Grant's troops. Again striking westward, the Union forces, after severe fighting Aug. 18–21 around Globe Tavern, succeeded in cutting the Weldon Railroad. In September, Grant extended his right flank across the James. Grant's capture, Sept. 29, of Fort Harrison, eight miles south of Richmond, compelled Lee, also, to move much of his army north of the James and to keep it there. Thus weakened southwest of Petersburg, the Confederates lost further territory on Sept. 30 when Grant's left pushed forward to Peebles Farm, within two miles of the Boydton Plank Road. But an attempt to cut this highway by advancing across Hatcher's Run was decisively repulsed by Lee on Oct. 27, and field operations virtually ceased during the winter.

Foreseeing that when spring came his attenuated line, now thirty-five miles long, would be broken by superior numbers, Lee, on Mar. 25, 1865, assaulted Fort Stedman, desperately attempting to penetrate Grant's right and cut his supply railroad to City Point. The attack failed and Grant countered on Mar. 29 by sending Gen. Philip Sheridan, with heavy cavalry and infantry forces, to Dinwiddie Courthouse to destroy the Southside Railroad. Sheridan was defeated on Mar. 31 by Gen. George Edward Pickett's and other divisions. He received reinforcements and on Apr. 1 routed Pickett at Five Forks, rendering the railroad indefensible. Lee evacuated Petersburg and Richmond on Apr. 2 and retreated westward.

[Douglas S. Freeman, *R. E. Lee*, vol. IV; R. U. Johnson and C. C. Buel, eds., *Battles and Leaders of the Civil War*, vol. IV.]

JOSEPH MILLS HANSON

PETITION, RIGHT OF, guarantees a citizen the opportunity to communicate with his government. In the United States it arises from the First Amendment to the Constitution, which provides that "Congress shall make no law respecting . . . the right of the people peaceably to assemble, and to petition the Government for a redress of grievances." Most state constitutions make a similar provision, and the Supreme Court extended the First Amendment right of petition, through the Fourteenth Amendment, to prohibit infringement by a state, in *De Jonge* v. *Oregon,* 299 U.S. 353 (1937). Originally, peaceful assembly was part of the right to petition. Its independent standing shows both the early importance of petition and the growth of protected expression. Lobbying and bills for private relief are covered. The right has been extended beyond grievances to encompass anything within the jurisdiction of government, including issues of highest national policy. There is no right to action on a petition, only to consideration.

In 1215, Articles 40 and 61 of the Magna Charta established a limited right of petition to four of twenty-five English barons acting as guardians of the charter. Until 1414, when it declared itself "as well assenters as petitioners," even Parliament stood only as a petitioner. The Declaration of Right of 1689 protected the British subject from government retaliation for exercising the right of petition by providing that "Prosecutions for such Petitioning are Illegall." The use of petitions increased greatly in the 18th and 19th centuries but is now of little significance in Parliament and is limited by technical requirements.

Although the American Declaration of Independence proclaimed, "We have Petitioned for Redress in the most humble terms: Our repeated Petitions have been answered only by repeated injury," American history is marked by government opposition to the right of petition. Following passage of the gag resolutions of May 1836, which tabled petitions to abolish slavery, former president John Quincy Adams, then a representative from Massachusetts, said, "I hold this . . . to be a direct violation of the Constitution." But in January 1840 the House of Representatives enacted a standing rule providing "no petition . . . praying the abolition of slavery . . . shall be received by this House, or entertained in any way whatever." The rule was repealed in December 1844. Jacob Coxey's army of the unemployed invoked the right of petition in 1894, only to be arrested for walking on the grass of the Capitol. In 1918 petitioners seeking repeal of espionage, sedition, and military recruitment laws were jailed. Veterans petitioning Congress for bonuses were routed by soldiers and their camps burned in 1932.

The 1960's and 1970's witnessed a great increase in mass petitioning. In 1965, Martin Luther King, Jr., led petitioners from Selma to the state capitol in Montgomery, Ala., seeking the right of blacks to vote, but the governor failed to appear to receive their petition. The Poor People's Campaign in 1968 presented to all three branches of the federal government the most comprehensive petitions in American history, with the warning "Heed the poor, America." The Vietnam Veterans Against the War petitioned the Congress to end the war in Indochina, by activity ranging from formal testimony to hurling their medals for service, heroism, and combat wounds on the Capitol steps in 1971.

What has become the American right of petition was slowly wrested from a monarch who originally did not have to hear any grievance and could do no wrong for which redress could be obtained in law. The U.S. Supreme Court, in its first test of the right, said, "The very idea of a government, republican in form, implies a right on the part of its citizens . . . to petition for a redress of grievances" (*United States* v. *Cruikshank,* 92 U.S. 542 [1876]). No right more sensitively measures the vitality of a republic and its responsiveness to the people.

RAMSEY CLARK

PETITION AND REMONSTRANCE OF NEW NETHERLAND, documents drawn up by a group of Dutch colonists protesting the government of New Netherland. In order that the colonists might be induced to contribute to the expenses of the government, Peter Stuyvesant in 1647 permitted the election of a board known as the Nine Men. In spite of Stuyvesant's objections, this board drew up and, on July 26 and 28, 1649, signed two documents of protest to the home government. Adriaen van der Donck, Jacob van Couwenhoven, and Jan Evertsen Bout were chosen to present the appeals to the States General. The petition was a short, concise statement of the condition of the province, with suggested remedies. The remonstrance was a long essay that gave in more detail and in historic perspective the facts and grievances upon which the petitioners based their appeal for changes. The autocratic proceedings and personal characters of governors William Kieft and Stuyvesant and their councillors were set forth in forcible terms, questions were raised about the expenditures of public funds, and the administration of justice was severely criticized. "A suitable municipal government . . . adapted to this province, and somewhat resembling the laudable government of our fatherland," was requested. The need for more farmers as colonists was stated and concessions in trading rights asked. Although a new charter with enlarged trading rights was granted by the Amsterdam Chamber of the Dutch West India Company, the arbitrary powers of the governor were confirmed, and Stuyvesant continued his autocratic course until

April 1652, when he was instructed by the Amsterdam Chamber to give New Amsterdam a "burgher government."

[A. C. Flick, ed., *History of the State of New York,* vol. I.]
A. C. FLICK

PETITIONS, ANTISLAVERY, to Congress, first became a major weapon of abolition agitation in 1836. In that year petitions for legislation against slavery so clogged the congressional schedule that the Democratic majority in the House of Representatives resolved thereafter to table antislavery petitions without a hearing or any other action. This, the first gag rule, was continued in varying forms until 1844. Abolitionists argued that the rule, by preventing as it did the reading of antislavery petitions in the House, denied them their constitutional right of petition. Although the right of petition was not actually involved in the gag rule, the abolitionists' contention was accepted in the North and was propounded on the floor of Congress by John Quincy Adams.

In order to exploit the issue of the right of petition, the American Anti-Slavery Society initiated a nationwide organization for sending petitions to Congress. During the ensuing years this organization deluged Congress with petitions and diffused antislavery doctrine throughout the North. Its effect on the state and national antislavery societies was disastrous; for the petitioning organization, once it was in operation, neither needed nor desired centralized direction. The success of the petition campaign thus led directly to the collapse of the antislavery societies.

[G. H. Barnes, *The Antislavery Impulse, 1830–1844.*]
GILBERT HOBBS BARNES

PETROCHEMICAL INDUSTRY. Although petroleum has been known since remote antiquity as a more or less flammable "rock-oil" oozing from the earth in various places, it was long considered a nuisance. In the early 19th century the Kanawha River in West Virginia was called "Old Greasy" because of the unwanted petroleum dumped into it from the wells of local saltmakers. But by the 1850's it was recognized that distillation could separate the oil into fractions having various useful properties, notably kerosine, useful as a source of both heat and light. After 1859, when Edwin L. Drake drilled the first commercial well on Oil Creek, at Titusville, Pa., petroleum was no longer a neglected material.

The following half-century saw the rise of the petroleum industry, owing largely to the perfection of the internal-combustion engine and the automobile and the resultant wide demand for gasoline, a more volatile fraction than kerosine. But aside from the adjustment of the distilling process to favor the production of this fraction, and its treatment with sulfuric acid to remove impurities, little attention was given to its chemical character. Although coal had been subjected to extensive chemical study after it was realized in the 1860's that some of its ingredients could be profitably converted into dyestuffs, the study of petroleum had been relatively neglected—both because the United States, the principal center of the petroleum industry, was far behind Europe in chemical research and because the demand for gasoline expanded at a rate that made other possible products seem relatively inconsequential. The most volatile fractions (containing from one to four carbon atoms) were allowed to escape into the atmosphere; the gasoline (primarily the eight-carbon hydrocarbon, octane) and kerosine fractions were collected; and the heavier residue was extracted for greases or tar or discarded.

The chemical consideration of petroleum began in an effort to maximize gasoline production by cracking the heavier, or less volatile, fractions, that is, breaking their molecules, usually by heating them to high temperatures, into smaller fragments—ideally into the compound octane. The first commercially successful process was developed by William M. Burton at the Standard Oil Company of Indiana in 1913. By 1936 more than half of the gasoline sold was the product of cracking.

Studies of the ingredients of petroleum in order to improve the cracking process gave the industry a better conception of the chemical variety of its raw material, a variety that was further increased by compounds created in the cracking process. An elaborate program to ameliorate the undesirable engine characteristic known as knocking, which was accomplished by the addition of a mixture of lead and bromine compounds (ethyl), cast further light on petroleum chemistry. In 1926 the industry established a research fund, and some companies established research laboratories, notably the Universal Oil Products Company of Chicago, which in 1931 secured the services of Vladimir N. Ipatiev, an eminent organic chemist from Russia, the only other country in which significant petroleum resources were then exploited.

As the meat-packing industry had earlier begun to utilize its wasted by-products, until "only the squeal of the hog" remained, so the petroleum industry began in 1928 to collect and bottle for sale the for-

merly wasted gases propane and butane and to sort out and seek uses for its greases and tars. But not until the 1940's did the industry adopt the practice that had characterized the German coal industry more than a half-century earlier, the production of pure chemical compounds and their conversion into a wide range of commercial products. The close relationship between petroleum and coal could hardly have been overlooked after the Germans had made artificial gasoline from coal in the 1920's; in the 1940's they made artificial rubber from coal, while Americans were making rubber of petroleum. After World War II the chemical potentialities of petroleum came to be fully exploited, and because of its convenience it replaced other natural raw materials, animal, vegetable, and —to the extent it has replaced coal—mineral. Rubber, refrigerants, plastics, paints, fibers, detergents, and many other commonplace products came to be derived from petroleum.

The term "petrochemical industry" has no official status; it merely represents an awareness that the petroleum industry is no longer merely a producer of fuels. It reflects former corresponding developments in the coal industry, especially in Germany, which gave rise to the "coal tar dye industry." In the early 1970's some 65 percent of the total U.S. production of chemicals was derived from petroleum and natural gas.

ROBERT P. MULTHAUF

PETROGRAPHY deals with the systematic description of rocks. The term is sometimes loosely used as synonymous with "petrology," which, being the broad science of rocks, is concerned not only with precise description but also with understanding the origin (petrogenesis), modification (metamorphism), and ultimate decay of rocks. Petrography as a science began with a technique invented by the Scottish physicist William Nicol, about 1825, for producing polarized light by cutting a crystal of iceland spar (calcite) into a special prism, which is still known as the Nicol prism. Addition of two such prisms to the ordinary microscope, which until then had been used only for magnification, converted the instrument into a polarizing, or petrographic, microscope. By means of transmitted light and Nicol prisms, it became possible to deduce the internal crystallographic character of even very tiny mineral grains, thereby greatly advancing the specific knowledge of a rock's constituents.

But it was a later development that truly laid the foundations of petrography. This was a technique, perfected by Henry C. Sorby in England, and others, about 1840, whereby a slice of rock was affixed to a microscope slide and then ground so thin that light could be transmitted through mineral grains that otherwise appeared opaque. Moreover, the position of adjoining grains was not disturbed, thus permitting analysis of rock texture. In 1975 thin-section petrography remained the standard method of rock study—and since textural details contribute greatly to a knowledge of the sequence of crystallization of the various mineral constituents in a rock, petrography ranges into petrogenesis and thus into petrology.

One notable American contribution to petrographic instrumentation was the development of the polarizing plate by Edwin H. Land in the 1930's; by 1947 this synthetic material had largely superseded Nicol prisms in petrographic microscopes. Developments in the making of optical glass for lenses to very specific and advantageous formulations resulted in some measure from research at the Geophysical Laboratory of the Carnegie Institution of Washington, D.C. Perfection of reflection microscopes and of polished sections extended petrographic investigations to include opaque ores.

It was in Europe, principally in Germany, that petrography burgeoned in the last half of the 19th century, and American geologists went to Germany for their introduction to this new science. This period coincided with the exploration of the western United States. Notable among the early surveys was the U.S. Geological Exploration of the Fortieth Parallel under the direction of Clarence King, who became the first director of the U.S. Geological Survey in 1878. The sixth volume of the report of the exploration, *Microscopical Petrography* (1876), was at King's invitation prepared by Ferdinand Zirkel of Leipzig, at the time acknowledged as one of the two leading petrographers in the world. This publication, in a sense, introduced petrography to the United States. Subsequent monographs and other publications of the U.S. Geological Survey, as well as some of the state surveys, were replete with beautifully lithographed plates of distinctive rock types as seen in thin sections. Many of these became collectors' items, for they are models of scientific accuracy and artistic merit. Based on petrographic methods many new and interesting rock types were discovered, and because names of rocks commonly reflect the geography of a type locality, some exotic names have resulted: for example, shonkinite, from the Shonkin Sag, Mont.; ouachitite, from the Ouachita Mountains, Ark.; and uncompahgrite, from Uncompahgre Peak, Colo.

Descriptions of rocks are not confined to thin-section studies. One of the earliest members of the U.S. Geological Survey, George F. Becker, recognized that in order to understand rock minerals properly, it would be necessary to synthesize them from chemically pure components. This awareness led to the establishment of the Geophysical Laboratory of the Carnegie Institution in 1905, of which Arthur L. Day was first director. From the foundation of the laboratory chemical principles were applied in investigating sequences and stability ranges of rock minerals, and in parallel studies improved methods of accurate chemical analyses of rocks were developed. Working with colleagues at the Geological Survey, Henry S. Washington, a chemist at the Geophysical Laboratory, brought out *The Quantitative Classification of Igneous Rocks* in 1903, a work that had enormous impact, worldwide, on petrography and petrology. This was followed in 1917 by *Chemical Analyses of Igneous Rocks,* U.S. Geological Survey Professional Paper 99, perhaps still the largest compendium of chemical analyses of rocks ever brought together. Each analysis, of which there are several thousand, was converted to the author's special classification—a classification still in use, along with the more conventional mineralogical and textural classifications.

Meantime, the physicochemical studies of rock-forming minerals at the laboratory were leading to new principles and new interpretations of the origin of rocks, culminating with *The Evolution of the Igneous Rocks* in 1928 by Norman L. Bowen—a publication that has perhaps had wider influence in petrology than any other emanating from America.

Until the 1920's, when the National Research Council first established a committee on sedimentation, petrographers were concerned chiefly with igneous rocks, although to some extent also with metamorphic rocks, for it was these two categories (sometimes grouped as the crystalline rocks) that contained the widest variety of minerals, presented the best-formed crystals, and occurred in the most interesting combinations. Sedimentary rocks, by contrast, appeared relatively uniform and monotonous. Recognition of the economic importance of sediments (especially for their hydrocarbon content) led to an upsurge in sedimentary petrography. Many new authoritative works were published, dealing with the special types of petrographic investigations that are appropriate for sediments.

Some of the most exciting developments in petrography involve the moon rocks that first became available for study in 1969. Never before had so many and such highly sophisticated methods of petrographic study been so thoroughly applied: X-ray studies of many kinds, electron microprobes, spectrographic and isotopic analyses, and a host of other advanced techniques, together with the classic petrographic studies. The studies are aided by the fact that since the moon is without atmosphere and apparently without water, moon rocks are not subject to the types of decay that affect most rocks on the earth's surface and tend to obscure thin-section observations and to contaminate (or at least render difficult) chemical studies. Petrographers may well look to the moon for their best illustrations in microscopic petrography.

[A. Holmes, *Petrographic Methods and Calculations;* A. Johannsen, *A Descriptive Petrography of the Igneous Rocks;* H. B. Milner, *Sedimentary Petrography;* F. J. Pettijohn, *Sedimentary Rocks;* R. L. Stanton, *Ore Petrology;* F. J. Turner, *Metamorphic Petrology.*]

IAN CAMPBELL

PETROLEUM INDUSTRY. References to petroleum have appeared in accounts of the New World ever since Gonzalo Fernández de Oviedo y Valdés, Spanish governor of Cartagena, Colombia, first mentioned an asphalt deposit in Cuba in 1526. Oil was found floating on streams in New York (where the first occurrence in North America was reported in 1627), Pennsylvania, Kentucky, and western Virginia. After techniques for drilling salt wells were introduced in 1806, oil also appeared, unsought and unwanted, in wells in these areas. Early colonists used petroleum to caulk ships, and Indians used it as medicine, a use that was quickly adopted by the colonists. By the 1830's druggists in the East sold petroleum as a liniment, and in the 1840's several companies sold bottled and branded petroleum as a patent medicine.

One of these companies was the Pennsylvania Rock Oil Company, formed in 1854 by G. A. Bissell, a New York lawyer, and J. G. Eveleth, to exploit an oil spring near Titusville, Pa. To analyze the oil from the spring, they engaged Benjamin Silliman, professor of chemistry at Yale, who in an epochal report of 1855 indicated that petroleum, properly refined, would make a profitable illuminant. The partners hired Edwin L. Drake, an unemployed railroad conductor, to develop their property. In April 1859, Drake employed a salt-well driller, "Uncle Billy" Smith, to drill for oil; on Aug. 27, 1859, at a depth of 69.5 feet, oil appeared in the drill-hole. The new well probably produced from eight to ten barrels a day when pumped. Prospectors rushed to the area as the

news spread, and by 1861 they were producing more than 2 million barrels annually.

Techniques for distilling and refining paraffin-type oils from cannel coals and oil shales, developed during the 1850's, were transferred to petroleum refining. The basic processes had been patented by James Young, a Scottish chemist, in 1850. Abraham Gesner, a Canadian surgeon working independently in New York, patented another process in 1854. The first to market a coal-oil illuminant (in 1856), Gesner called his product "kerosine," from the Greek *keros* ("wax" = "paraffin") and *elaion* ("oil"). Coal oil proved highly popular, being cheaper than lard and sperm oils and safer than camphene, the most widely used illuminant. But with the increasing supply of petroleum, coal-oil refiners began using that for raw material, and such processing was well developed by 1862.

Crude oil was originally teamed in barrels to barges along the Allegheny River or to railroads, but Samuel Van Syckle broke the pattern in 1865 by successfully pumping crude oil through five miles of 2-inch pipe from the Pithole field in western Pennsylvania to a railroad terminal. Van Syckle's success marked the demise of the teamster, who had charged three times more than he, and invited many competitors. In 1865, too, railroad tank cars appeared. The first were simply two wooden tubs mounted on a flatcar, but the horizontal metal type with an expansion dome, introduced in 1868, greatly increased stability and safety in transit.

The petroleum industry early exhibited wide fluctuations in price and output, which persisted until the 1930's. New discoveries would attract producers and refiners and output would burgeon and then decline, leaving excess refining capacity and eager producers waiting for the next cycle. This erratic exploitation was unwittingly encouraged by the courts, which permitted a surface owner to take all the oil he could from his wells, even though he diminished the flow from neighboring wells. This "rule of capture," developed from precedents involving water rights, was first applied in Pennsylvania, in the case of *Brown* v. *Vandergrift* (1875); it became the law in almost all oil-producing states.

After various voluntary attempts to stabilize production failed, the Standard Oil Company sought to accomplish the same end by monopolizing the industry. Incorporated in 1870 by John D. Rockefeller and his brother William, the company combined superior efficiency, offers of monopoly profits to competitors who merged with it, and outright threats to increase its market share from 10 percent in 1872 to almost 90 percent by 1880. It could not, however, control entry as new fields opened in Indiana and Ohio in 1882, California in 1893–94, Kansas and Oklahoma in 1906, and along the Texas Gulf in 1901. By 1911, when the U.S. Supreme Court dissolved the combine into thirty-four separate companies for violating the Sherman Antitrust Act, the company's market share had fallen to 65 percent. Nonetheless, the industry, except for the sector producing crude oil, has traditionally been characterized by large firms: in 1967 the twenty largest oil companies controlled 83 percent of refining capacity in the United States, and all of them were among the 200 largest industrial corporations in the country.

Around the turn of the century the industry began to change from producing primarily illuminants to supplying increasing proportions of fuel and motive-energy products. Improvements in the production and distribution of gas and electricity made them increasingly cheap and popular substitutes for kerosine. The crude oils of California and the Gulf Coast yielded comparatively lower proportions of kerosine and high fractions of fuel oil, depressing the latter's price and making it competitive with coal. Gasoline grew to become the industry's leading seller, first as an industrial solvent and then as an automotive fuel. From 1919 to 1975 between 40 percent and 45 percent of the industry's output consisted of automotive gasoline.

The most significant innovations in 20th-century refining techniques involved efforts to increase gasoline yields by cracking—breaking down long hydrocarbon molecules under heat and pressure. Standard Oil Company (Indiana) produced the first commercially cracked gasoline in 1914, following five years of experimentation directed by William M. Burton, vice-president for refining. Within ten years four other major processes were successfully competing with Burton's. Because the patents on all methods were widely licensed, cracking spread swiftly: about one-third of all gasoline was cracked by 1929 and one-half by 1939; the figure had increased to about 65 percent or 70 percent by 1975. In 1936–37 higher octane ratings at lower cost became available when Eugene J. Houdry, a French engineer, perfected a commercial method of using chemical catalysts in the cracking process.

The twin pressures of a severely depressed demand (the result of the Great Depression) and unprecedented flush production in Oklahoma and eastern Texas between 1929 and 1932 induced federal and state governments to enact measures, which continued in effect into the 1970's, to conserve crude-oil production. In 1930 the Federal Oil Conservation Board, consisting of the secretaries of war, navy, commerce, and the interior, published the federal government's first forecast of demand. Under the short-lived National Recovery Administration's petroleum code of 1933 the Bureau of Mines inaugurated regular monthly forecasts of demand, used by state regulatory commissions to establish production quotas among producers in their states. The major oil-producing states agreed, with the blessing of Congress, to coordinate conservation legislation in the Interstate Oil Compact of 1935. The Connally "Hot Oil" Act of 1935 prohibited interstate shipment of oil produced in violation of state conservation laws.

World War I had placed little strain on the industry until 1917, and even at their peak military requirements probably did not exceed 15 percent of U.S. crude-oil output. World War II, however, created extraordinary demands that required the rationing of civilian supplies after 1942; in 1945 military procurement equaled one-third of the 1.7 billion barrels of crude oil produced, and this rate of crude production itself threatened to reduce the amount of oil ultimately recoverable from the then-existing fields.

From 1945 to 1970 domestic demand nearly tripled, while domestic crude-oil production only doubled. American firms, investing in foreign production properties, caused the United States to reverse its historic position in world petroleum markets and become a net importer of oil after 1948. In 1959 the federal government inaugurated a program of oil-import quotas, ostensibly to protect domestic supplies for defense. These quotas were removed in 1973 as the prospects dimmed for obtaining sufficient low-cost foreign oil to supplement costly American crude. In 1970–72 the Organization of Petroleum Exporting Countries, a consortium of Persian Gulf states that produced 35 percent of the world's oil supply, imposed higher taxes on foreign concessions. Simultaneously the growth in demand was accelerated by rising income, heavier and more complicated automobiles, and newly imposed environmental standards. Automobile emission devices, for example, reduced mileage per gallon of gasoline, as did the increased use of auxiliary equipment on cars. Clean-air ordinances hastened industry's shift from sulfur-laden coal to fuel oil. The consequent fear of shortage increased pressure on the federal government to grant approval, formerly delayed because of ecological considerations, for the development of an estimated

40-billion-barrel untapped reserve in Alaska. It remained to be seen whether, in the face of these conflicting pressures, petroleum would continue in its role as one of the cheapest energy sources in the United States.

[Melvin G. de Chazeau and Alfred E. Kahn, *Integration and Competition in the Petroleum Industry;* Thomas G. Moore, "The Petroleum Industry," in Walter Adams, ed., *The Structure of American Industry;* Harold F. Williamson and Arnold R. Daum, *The American Petroleum Industry: The Age of Illumination, 1859–1899;* Harold F. Williamson and others, *The American Petroleum Industry: The Age of Energy, 1899–1959.*]

GILBERT KLOSE

PETROLEUM PROSPECTING AND TECHNOLOGY. The American petroleum industry was born on the banks of Oil Creek near Titusville, Pa., in 1859. The presence of oil in the area had long been known from oil seeps on the surface. Petroleum obtained as a by-product of drilling salt wells had been marketed as a medicine, but the well drilled by Edwin L. Drake in 1859 was the result of a belief that petroleum could be used successfully as an illuminant and that salt-drilling techniques could be applied directly to oil. The success of these efforts set off an oil prospecting boom that was characterized by an ever-widening search for the mineral.

As the demand for petroleum increased while obvious locations to drill for it did not, many theories about finding oil appeared. One of the most popular early ones involved use of the divining rod, which had been employed since the 16th century in the search for minerals and water. Initially there was no understanding of the geology of petroleum deposits, and spiritualists and "oil smellers" were sometimes employed in the search for them.

Within a decade of the drilling of Drake's well, more sophisticated theories about finding oil were developed. It was recognized by some that petroleum was trapped in sand rocks at different subterranean levels. Three such strata were soon discovered and classified along Oil Creek. In 1867 C. D. Angell hypothesized that petroleum was to be found in narrow belts several miles long and that its presence was not necessarily revealed by surface manifestations. This hypothesis eventually led to prospecting by creekology-trendology, which involved the determination of the direction of rock layers and of whether or not they slanted to form oil traps. Nevertheless, until well past the turn of the 20th century the most popular prospecting approach was to search for surface evidence of the presence of petroleum.

A typical oil strike led quickly to a flurry of drilling that often drained a newly discovered pool. Since subterranean chambers of oil flowed to the point at which a well was drilled, petroleum could be drained from adjacent lands whose mineral rights belonged to persons other than the driller—and under the "rule of capture" the petroleum belonged to the person who brought it to the surface. As a result the drilling of a successful well was quickly followed by the drilling of others, closely spaced. This procedure produced gluts of oil followed by a famine, thus giving continuing impetus to petroleum prospecting.

Pennsylvania remained the center of petroleum production until the 1880's, and many of the most famous American petroleum prospectors, called "wildcatters," acquired skills and techniques there that they later applied in other parts of the country. Two of the most famous wildcatters were John H. Galey and James M. Guffey. After opening the famous McDonald field in western Pennsylvania in 1891, they moved on to Neodesha, Kans., in 1893, to Corsicana, Tex., in 1894, and to the Gulf coast at the turn of the century. In their expanding search for oil they helped to open a new era for the American petroleum industry, which was being threatened by the decline of Appalachian production.

Geology remained of little help in finding oil. In Texas a state-appointed committee had reported that there were no prospects for petroleum in that state, and the state geologist was equally skeptical. At Beaumont, Tex., however, Patillo Higgins was convinced that a sulfurous gas seeping from a big salt mound indicated the presence of petroleum. The heavy tools that had been used in Pennsylvania to pound a hole in the ground did not work well in the salt mound, and Higgins exhausted his resources with no success. When oil was discovered at Corsicana, through the use of a new rotary drilling technique, interest in using this method on the Beaumont salt mound was kindled.

Anthony F. Lucas was convinced that sulfur, oil, and salt were somehow related; and he took over from Higgins. Discouraged by his slow progress, Lucas eventually turned to Guffey and Galey, who agreed to continue drilling with Lucas as a minor partner. Galey, literally relying on his ability to smell oil, picked the spot to drill, and on Jan. 10, 1901, the fabulous Spindletop well came in, flowing up to 100,000 barrels a day. There was no longer any question about the presence of petroleum in Texas, which became a major petroleum-producing state. Unfortunately for Galey, a restless wildcatter, the lure of prospecting led him to sell his Spindletop interest to Guffey. For the remainder of his career Galey never made another major oil strike.

Location of petroleum deposits by surface oil seepage led to discoveries in Louisiana, California, and Mexico, but the systematic application of geology played a minor role. Benjamin Silliman, a geologist and chemist at Yale University, had predicted the commercial value of Drake's well, and he had prospected for oil in Pennsylvania and California, with mixed results. The assistant state geologist of California had carefully reported every known oil seep in the state, but years passed before any oil prospector used that information to advantage. In 1913, Charles N. Gould of the Oklahoma Geological Survey gave a paper in which he suggested a significant relationship between the structure of rocks and the occurrence of oil and gas. This suggestion led to the search for anticlines, or arching rock structures, which dominated oil prospecting methods for the next fifteen years.

The Gulf Oil Company hired the first company geologist in 1911. By 1915 oil companies were hiring most of the graduates in geology at the University of Oklahoma. Thereafter courses in petroleum geology expanded in popularity and availability, and their graduates found places in both large and small oil companies.

Meanwhile new geophysical techniques were being developed, most notably by Everette L. DeGolyer, whose brilliant concepts further revolutionized oil finding. He saw the possibilities of using a torsion balance to detect differences in the gravitational attraction of the earth caused by the presence of rocks of different specific gravities, and he hypothesized the presence of petroleum traps under such circumstances. His technique proved successful in locating salt plugs and associated oil traps, but DeGolyer was already experimenting with a refraction seismograph that responded to vibrations in the earth created by dynamite charges. Establishing the Geophysical Research Corporation as a part of his Amerada Corporation, DeGolyer employed J. C. Karcher of the University of Oklahoma Physics Department to lead this new operation. Refinements in the seismograph technique led to the reflection seismograph, which measured the reflection of sound waves from rock beds subjected to a dynamite charge in the earth above them. In February 1930 the reflection seismograph was responsible for the discovery of the Edwards, Okla., field, and it helped to open new oil fields in Illinois later in the decade.

A new dimension was added to oil prospecting with the use of airplanes for aerial mapping and then for carrying aloft magnetometers, used to measure the different magnetic attractions of rocks as a guide to the location of oil-bearing structures.

Despite such technological advances, the hazards of oil prospecting remain. From 1913 to 1975 the Internal Revenue Code authorized a percentage depletion allowance that aided oil companies to offset the costs of drilling dry holes. Termination of this tax concession was a victory for critics of oil company profits, but the risks and costs of finding oil remain. Using nontechnical prospecting methods, the odds of discovery are only about 1 in 24; for geological exploration they improve to roughly 1 in 10; and geophysical prospecting further improves the odds to 1 in 6. Nevertheless, it takes a seismic crew, on the average, more than two years to find a new, commercially successful source of petroleum.

Whereas the Drake well was only 69.5 feet deep, drilling in the 1970's was measured in miles. In some instances new, deeper drilling of abandoned dry holes produced important oil strikes, but some sites proved dry even after drilling a mile or more down. Much prospecting in the 1960's and 1970's was in offshore waters and such remote locations as Alaska and the North Sea, for the era of discovery of great, flowing wells in the United States seemed to be ended. The costs of prospecting and producing American wells under normal conditions does not compare favorably with similar ventures in such overseas areas as the Persian Gulf and North Africa. Nevertheless, the element of luck in oil prospecting combined with ever-advancing technology may unexpectedly produce a great oil strike that will erase the excessive and vulnerable dependence of the United States on other petroleum-rich countries for the nation's major source of energy.

[J. Stanley Clark, *The Oil Century;* James I. Crump, *Our Oil Hunters;* Everette DeGolyer, *The Development of the Art of Prospecting;* Ruth S. Knowles, *The Greatest Gamblers;* Harold F. Williamson and others, *The American Petroleum Industry.*]

ARTHUR M. JOHNSON

PEYOTE CULT, a religious movement that spread among the reservation Indians of the Plains in the late 19th century, after faith in the Ghost Dance had subsided. Peyote is a small spineless cactus that grows in the northern half of Mexico and a short distance north of the border in Texas. Sometimes inducing hallucinational visions when ingested, it was used in ceremonies by Indians in pre-Columbian Mexico, and it is still used by some Mexican tribes, such as the Tarahumare and Huichol. Its first appearance in the United States occurred about 1870, when it was brought from northern Mexico by the Mescalero Apache, who used it in connection with their own religious rites. Peyote became popular among the tribes of the southern Plains in the 1870's, including the Kiowa and Comanche, and subsequently its use diffused to many of the western tribes. In the southern Plains a full-fledged cult centering on the use of peyote developed. The eating of peyote was combined with hymn-singing and testimonials, with a fusion of Christian elements and native beliefs. The cult spread rapidly, despite the opposition of authorities; most peyotists are now members of the Native American Church, first chartered in Oklahoma in 1918.

[David Aberle, *The Peyote Religion Among the Navaho;* Weston LaBarre, *The Peyote Cult;* James S. Slotkin, *The Peyote Religion.*]

KENNETH M. STEWART

"PHANTOM SHIP," a vessel that mysteriously disappeared on a transatlantic voyage in 1646. On a June evening in 1648 an apparition of the ship allegedly appeared over New Haven harbor. As early as 1644 Theophilus Eaton and other merchants of New Haven Colony entrusted the construction of a 100-ton, oceangoing vessel to several feoffees at New Haven. Though "ill built" and "very walt sided," in due course the vessel was completed. Laden with a cargo of wheat, peas, hides, beaver, and plate; seventy passengers, including several leading merchants of New Haven; and manuscript writings of John Davenport and Thomas Hooker, the vessel sailed for England in January 1646. The vessel itself neither reached England nor returned to New Haven. Its loss was a severe blow to the commercial aspirations of the colony.

[Cotton Mather, *Magnalia Christi Americana;* John Winthrop, *Journal.*]

ISABEL M. CALDER

PHARMACEUTICAL INDUSTRY. Production of substances for the prevention or treatment of disease or other human ailments began in the American colonies as an unspecialized craft but by the mid-20th century was largely the province of a few specialized corporate enterprises that depended on a flow of creative product developments from well-financed research laboratories. In the colonial period medicinal materials, such as botanical extracts and mineral sub-

stances, were often compounded and distributed by physicians of limited training and even by the keepers of general stores. Late in the 18th century and early in the 19th, stimulated by the medicinal demands of the Revolution and influenced by changes in medical science (such as Edward Jenner's development of a smallpox vaccine), by the general acceptance of the system of chemistry developed by Antoine Laurent Lavoisier, and by the gradual professionalization of medicine, pharmaceutical production and distribution began to emerge as a specialized area of commerce. The first specialized drug houses appeared in Philadelphia, serving local retail customers as well as a wholesale trade among country doctors. During the first third of the 19th century, leaders of this trade supported the first steps toward the professionalization of pharmacy: the founding in Philadelphia (1821) of a professional organization, the College of Apothecaries (renamed College of Pharmacy in 1822); the beginning of collegiate education in pharmacy; and the founding of the *United States Pharmacopoeia,* an official compendium of medicinal materials.

During the second half of the 19th century the character of production of pharmaceutical preparations changed substantially. The large military demand during the Civil War encouraged large-scale, specialized, and even mechanized production, gradually diminishing the importance of compounding in local pharmacies. The rapid growth and dispersion of the population in the last decades of the century stimulated further entry of manufacturers into the field, many of whom were trained pharmacists or physicians who left their professions to produce pharmaceuticals and chemicals for the growing number of local pharmacies. In the late 19th and early 20th centuries many new substances were added to the pharmacopoeia, reflecting the influence of scientific work such as that of Rudolph Virchow in cellular pathology, of Robert Koch and Louis Pasteur in bacteriology, of Joseph Lister in sterilization and antisepsis, and of European chemists in elucidating the structure of organic compounds. Leadership in both scientific and commercial development came from Germany, Switzerland, and France. The introduction of aspirin in 1899 indicated the medical and commercial significance of chemical research so characteristic of German industry. Gradually chemists isolated the specific therapeutic agents in many of the traditional botanical materials, and tablets or capsules containing specific agents gradually replaced the old elixirs. In the early 20th century a few American companies, such as G. D. Searle and Parke, Davis and Company, introduced research facilities, but they enjoyed only limited success against the facilities of the larger and more established German and Swiss companies.

The two world wars did much to change the character and role of the American industry. The large military market and American and Allied civilian markets, cut off from the German suppliers, became the domain of American companies, which invested increasing sums in research and development. Moreover, American patents held by German firms—which patents were the key to German influence in American markets—then became available to American companies. The general character of the pharmacopoeia was changed by new therapeutic approaches that emerged during the first third of the century—including the development of chemicals, such as sulfa drugs, that specifically attack disease-causing agents without harming the human host; the identification of essential dietary substances, such as vitamins; and the identification of hormones, the regulative products of the glands of internal secretion, such as insulin. One of the most important new developments, antibiotics, was the product of British research from the late 1920's to the early 1940's, but leading American companies, such as Eli Lilly; Abbott; Upjohn; and Parke, Davis and Company, with the support of the government, introduced commercial production of the first antibiotic, penicillin, during World War II. After the war the leading companies invested heavily in antibiotic research and as a consequence introduced during the late 1940's and the 1950's a number of important new antibiotics, which helped to place the American industry in a position of international leadership in innovation and sales.

About two dozen corporations came to dominate the industry through their very high investment in scientific research and development, which provided a continual flow of new products, through patent and licensing policies, through substantial investment in sales and promotion of the new products, and through vertical integration and multinational operations. Their profit success brought these leading firms under congressional scrutiny during the late 1950's and the 1960's, which led to allegations that they enjoyed excessive profits in an oligopolistic market structure maintained through certain promotional and licensing practices. Nevertheless, this relatively small industry has—with occasional research and development support from foundations and government—promoted high standards of pharmaceutical quality and reliability and introduced many new pharmaceutical materials that played a vital role in the 20th century in the improvement of health and the extension of life in the United States and abroad.

[Williams Haynes, *American Chemical Industry;* Glenn Sonnedecker, *History of Pharmacy.*]

REESE V. JENKINS

PHARMACY. The need for men "skilful in all kinds of drugs" was frequently noted by explorers and promoters from the time of Richard Hakluyt and his support in 1584 of a voyage to Virginia to James Oglethorpe's founding of the colony of Georgia in 1732, but few came to British North America as practitioners of pharmacy. There are records of an apothecary shop in Boston as early as 1646 but of very few others in all British (and Dutch) North America in the 17th century.

By the end of the 18th century—and far into the 19th—there were four types of practitioners of pharmacy. There was first the physician, who not only dispensed but also compounded his own medicines. There was also the physician who kept a shop, known as a "Doctor's Shop," that was essentially a drugstore. In many communities in the mid-19th century, more shops were owned by physicians than by pharmacists. Second, there was the apothecary, the professional pharmacist, who, like his English model, not only compounded and dispensed drugs but also diagnosed and prescribed as well. Third, there was the druggist, later also to be called a pharmacist. The term "druggist" was originally applied to wholesalers—but wholesaler or not, the druggist compounded prescriptions in shops whose major concern was in pharmaceutical and related items. Fourth, there was the tradesman, of whom a variety took on a supply of drugs. Moreover, the general store often kept large stocks of medicines, and eventually many evolved into drugstores.

In the 19th century the American drugstore carried a full line of simples (crude drugs); had a prescription counter or section where medicinals and chemicals were compounded and dispensed; had a counter devoted to patent and proprietary medicines and perhaps a separate one devoted to nostrums; and handled a variety of other items, such as confections, perfumes, paints and glass, groceries, spices, and liquor. In midcentury the pharmacist—he was beginning to favor the designation over "pharmaceutist," although the terms "apothecary," "chemist," "druggist," and *Apotheker* continued in use—did a great deal of his own manufacturing. He spread his plasters and he prepared tinctures, ointments, syrups, confections, conserves, medicated waters, and perfumes. He made pills and powders of all kinds, and he manufactured his own soda water, fruit syrup, ink, and sealing wax. He was also adept at mixing paints.

New scientific and technological developments in the 19th century were eventually to erode this artisanal role of the pharmacist. By the late 1930's even the compounding of medicines from chemicals supplied by industrial manufacturers gave way to the dispensing of medications completely prepared by industry. By the 1960's only about 4 percent of all prescriptions required some combination or manipulation of ingredients. Similarly, the large-scale manufacture of proprietary medicines, and the concomitant flamboyant and often ruthless advertising and sale of them, not only undermined the artisanal and professional role of the pharmacist but also placed him in competition with price-cutters, grocers, chain stores, and, finally, supermarkets.

Pharmaceutical education began in the United States with the founding of the Philadelphia College of Pharmacy in 1821. The term "college" was intended at first only to suggest a society rather than a school, but the college was offering lectures almost from the start. Among its contributions to the field was the founding of the *American Journal of Pharmacy* in 1825, the first American serial publication devoted to the scientific and technical aspects of pharmacy.

Local societies of pharmacy, also calling themselves colleges, were formed in Boston, New York, Baltimore, Cincinnati, Chicago, and Saint Louis, and all of them sooner or later engaged in pharmaceutical instruction. By 1870 thirteen colleges of pharmacy had been established, and in 1900 about fifty were in operation. The program of instruction in any of these, usually private, proprietary institutions, was indeed meager, consisting merely of a series of lectures in the evening in rented rooms.

In 1868 the University of Michigan embarked on a full program of scientific training in pharmacy, offering laboratory and practical work as well as lectures, in chemistry, botany, materia medica, and toxicology. Eventually a full-time, day program of two years was developed. The University of Wisconsin followed suit in 1883, and nine years later pioneered in offering a four-year program leading to a bachelor's degree. Eventually the four-year program took hold around the country: the American Association of Colleges of Pharmacy, founded in 1900, adopted a two-

year curriculum as a minimum in 1907; a three-year curriculum in 1925, leading to the degree of Ph.G. (Graduate in Pharmacy) or Ph.C. (Pharmaceutical Chemist); a four-year baccalaureate curriculum in 1932; and a five-year curriculum in 1960.

The curriculum in colleges of pharmacy reflected the growing stature of pharmacy and the increasing demands for scientific training to keep pace with the rapid and revolutionary advances in medicine and therapeutics. The four-year and five-year programs represented a conscious effort to add a liberal arts base to the curriculum but resulted primarily in more extensive and intensive attention to pharmaceutical and related sciences. The modern pharmacist is trained in pharmaceutical chemistry, pharmacognosy, pharmacology, and pharmaceutics, as well as in practical pharmacy and pharmacy administration (in addition to basic training in chemistry, physics, and biology). The capstone of the curriculum has become pharmacology, and new programs in hospital and clinical pharmacy have been developed that are concerned with the pharmacist's direct and consultative responsibilities to patient and physician.

In the process of educational improvement the proprietary school has all but disappeared, and the college of pharmacy has taken a place as a university unit. This has meant not only the upgrading of academic standards but also the development of graduate programs. The University of Wisconsin was the first to award the Ph.D. in a pharmaceutical specialty, in 1902.

It was out of the early local colleges that the national organization of pharmacy developed. A meeting of representatives of five of the colleges created the American Pharmaceutical Association in 1852. This association has served as the scientific and professional organization of pharmacy. For the most part, the economic aspects of pharmacy have been left to the National Association of Retail Druggists, the forerunner of which dates from 1883, and to the state associations, which came into existence after a concerted effort by the American Pharmaceutical Association, begun in 1868. By 1875, eleven states had organized associations, and by 1890 forty-one of the forty-four states and one territory had such associations.

The first laws providing for the examination and licensing of pharmacists in an American jurisdiction were passed in Louisiana, where the Franco-Spanish tradition of pharmacy had prevailed: in the Territory of Orleans in 1808 and the state in 1816. The few other such attempts before the Civil War, in three southern states and a few localities elsewhere, were largely ineffectual, because of the influence of Jacksonian Democracy, which opposed such legislation generally. (The same tradition also precluded the limitation of the number of pharmacies in the United States, with the result that in the 1960's, the ratio of one pharmacy to 3,300 population was the highest ratio in any developed country.)

It was only after 1870 that state laws for the examining and licensing of pharmacists began to appear on the statute books under the pressure of the new state associations. By 1880, ten states or territories had such laws; by 1890, thirty-four; and by 1900, forty-seven. These laws all established state boards of pharmacy, composed of pharmacists, usually having some connection with the state association but technically a governmental agency. The boards examined candidates and, in accordance with statutory requirements, usually demanded four years of experience in pharmacy, with credit for college attendance, until about 1920, and the completion of a college program thereafter, as a prerequisite to examination. In the 1930's the requirement of a baccalaureate in pharmacy and a one-year internship became general; later the degree requirement was raised in accord with the five-year program.

Federal legislation pertaining to pharmacy has related to the prevention of the importation of adulterated drugs (going back to 1848); the regulation of the sale of narcotics (first under the Harrison Narcotics Act of 1914); and the concern for purity and proper branding, safety, and efficacy of drugs, under the Pure Food and Drug Act of 1906 and the revisions of it in 1938 and 1962, respectively.

In the mid-1970's it appeared that the profession was tending to become less oriented to the commodity-transfer function of the community pharmacy and more directed to its health-service function, and to the assumption, especially beyond the confines of a shop, of consultative responsibilities arising out of training in pharmacology and clinical pharmacy.

[G. Sonnedecker, *Kremer's and Urdang's History of Pharmacy*.]

DAVID L. COWAN

PHELPS-GORHAM PURCHASE, a land acquisition made in April 1788 from the legislature of Massachusetts by Oliver Phelps and Nathaniel Gorham. The tract of land consisted of all western New York beyond a line beginning eighty-two miles west of the intersection of the Delaware River with the boundary of New York and Pennsylvania and running north through Seneca Lake; a strip of land one mile wide running parallel to the Niagara River was excluded. The rival claims of New York and Massachusetts to the acquired territory were settled in 1786 by the Treaty of Hartford, which gave legal title (in essence, the right of first purchase from the Indians) to Massachusetts and the right of sovereignty to New York. The price agreed to by Phelps and Gorham for this tract was £300,000 Massachusetts currency, to be paid in the depreciated consolidated securities of the state. Difficulties soon arose, however, in securing title from the Indians. Despite the fact that Phelps secured the cooperation of Robert R. Livingston, who had been attempting to secure a 999-year lease for the same territory, and of the Niagara Genesee Company, a Canadian branch company also interested in the lands, he was able to persuade the Indians to part with only one-third of the land. The rise in value of the consolidated securities of Massachusetts following the prospect of federal assumption of state debts caused further difficulties. Unable to make the payments as agreed, despite a grant of an extension of time, Phelps and Gorham were forced in March 1790 to surrender to Massachusetts the two-thirds of their purchase not yet freed from the Indian rights. This reduced their holdings to two townships, for the previous year they had sold the rest of the remaining third to Robert Morris (*see* Pulteney Purchase). Even with their returns from this sale, and the privilege of paying the balance of their debt in specie, they found it difficult to meet their obligations, and the matter dragged on for years before it was settled.

[A. C. Flick, ed., *History of the State of New York*, vol. V; R. L. Higgins, *Expansion in New York*.]

A. C. FLICK

PHI BETA KAPPA SOCIETY, founded on Dec. 5, 1776, at William and Mary College, Williamsburg, Va., was the first undergraduate secret society among the colleges of the United States and differed little from other early college societies. The name was taken from the initial letters of its motto, Φιλοσοφία Βίου Κυβερνήτης ("Philosophy the guide of life").

It became an honor society with members, both men and women, elected on the basis of their class standing. The badge of the society is a golden key. The society had 184 chapters and about 215,000 members in 1970.

[William Thomson Hastings, *The Insignia of Phi Beta Kappa*.]

WILL D. HOWE

PHILADELPHIA. The tourist's Philadelphia of the Liberty Bell and Independence Hall, in southeastern Pennsylvania, 90 miles from New York City and 136 miles from Washington, D.C., constitutes the barest of introductions to the fourth largest city in the United States, with a population in 1970 of 1,950,098. The tourist's view includes little even of the city's history, neglecting especially the rich surviving physical evidence that Philadelphia was one of the first and greatest of the 19th-century industrial cities of America. Nevertheless, the tourist at Independence Hall can capture much of the essence of Philadelphia: it is an old and conservative city sustaining its importance largely on momentum gained in the past, and its future is the uncertain one of old northeastern American cities built almost too substantially, in that their very solidity hampers their adjustment to an age for which they were not designed.

It is something of a paradox that Philadelphia, the symbol of old American cities, was the last to be founded of the major colonial cities, partly because navigating the Delaware was a difficult venture. The Swedes planted the first permanent white settlements within the present city boundaries in the 1640's, but the history of Philadelphia begins essentially with William Penn's Pennsylvania charter of 1681; the selection by his surveyors of the site for his principal town and Thomas Holme's application of the famous checkerboard plan to the site; and Penn's arrival in 1682. Once begun, Philadelphia grew rapidly, both because Penn's tolerant government and active propagandizing attracted multinational immigration and because the new city tapped the most fertile nearby hinterland of any of the colonial towns. By the eve of the Revolution, some 28,400 people lived in Philadelphia and the adjacent districts, and the city was the largest in British America. James Logan and Benjamin Franklin and their circles had given the place a considerable cultural eminence as well, represented, for example, by the founding of the American Philosophical Society there in 1743. Given these factors and a central location, Philadelphia was an obvious site for intercolonial meetings, and despite much conservatism in the city, the first Continental Congress in 1774 and the second Continental Congress from 1775 through most of the war made Philadelphia a hub of the Revolution. Although Congress departed in 1783, the Constitutional Convention met at the State House in 1787, and the city was the capital of the United States from 1790 to 1800.

The federal period became Philadelphia's golden age. While President George Washington rode through the streets in an elegant coach and congressmen filled Congress Hall and the taverns, commercial, social, and cultural primacy among American cities as well as political leadership rested with Philadelphia. Indeed, jealousy lest the city become an American London or Paris overshadowing all other cities in the nation was a factor in keeping the presence of the capital merely temporary. The establishment of the first Bank of the United States there in 1791, following upon Robert Morris' Bank of North America, gave the city a financial preeminence it was to hold almost until the expiration of the charter of the second Bank of the United States in 1836. Yet Philadelphia's primacy could not endure. New York had always possessed a better harbor. Once upstate New York began to fill up with settlers, giving New York City a hinterland comparable to Philadelphia's, New York could forge ahead in population and commerce, as it did in the early years of the 19th century. The completion of the Erie Canal in 1825 assured New York's ascendancy; although Pennsylvania responded by building an elaborate combination of canals and railroads west from Philadelphia, the Appalachian Mountains prohibited Philadelphia from matching the advantages of New York's level route to the interior of the continent. By the time the Pennsylvania Railroad established a through line to Pittsburgh in 1854, the commercial superiority of New York was too great to be overcome.

Despite this eclipse, Philadelphia retained a vitality that it poured into growth in a new direction, as the most diversified American industrial city in the new age of factories and large-scale production. The variety of mineral and agricultural resources in the surrounding area permitted Philadelphia to be consistently the principal manufacturer of both textiles and products derived from the nearby iron mines and furnaces, notably locomotives. In industrial production, Philadelphia was not eclipsed; it contended for first place among the country's cities, a rank achieved for a time, as late as the end of the Civil War. In the era of most rapid industrialization, from the 1830's through the 1860's, the sprawling, bustling modern city emerged; its workers were rapidly transformed from home craftsmen into commuters to factories; and omnibuses and then horsecar lines appeared to carry them to and fro. The population surged from 111,210 in 1810 to 188,797 in 1830 and to 565,529 in 1860—these figures being for the whole of Philadelphia County, whose twenty-nine political divisions were consolidated into the city of Philadelphia in 1854. At that time probably only London, Paris, and

New York in the whole Western world surpassed in population the industrial metropolis on the Delaware.

Industrial Philadelphia celebrated its own achievements as well as the anniversary of American independence in the Centennial Exposition of 1876, a display principally of new industrial technology. But the exposition was a climax as well as a celebration; thereafter the course of Philadelphia history appears to run slowly downhill. By the time of the Centennial, the generation of business leaders who had guided Philadelphia during its great surge of industrialization was giving way to a second generation that chose to husband its inherited wealth in cautious investments. The political leaders of the city, separated from the business leaders in the course of industrialization, gave the kind of direction that made Lincoln Steffens' description of the city as "corrupt and contented" a byword. The Progressive movement came to Philadelphia only partially and late. After World War II the reform mayors Joseph S. Clark, Jr., and Richardson Dilworth led a Philadelphia renaissance; the 18th-century residential area called Society Hill was revitalized, and much of the old downtown area was reconstructed as a modern residential alternative to the suburbs. By the 1960's, however, the renaissance had lost its momentum, and the obsolescence of a city whose industrial, business, and social facilities were built largely in and for the 19th century remained a problem to aggravate all the other urban problems that Philadelphia shared with every major American city.

The port of Philadelphia (including the Delaware from Wilmington to Trenton) remained in the mid-1970's second to New York among American seaports in ship arrivals, and the largest freshwater port in the world. It was the largest petroleum port, and Philadelphia was the largest petroleum refining center, on the East Coast. Major freight yards and rail junctions of the Penn Central and Reading systems maintained the city as a railroad center. Philadelphia industry was never primarily heavy, basic industry; it remained a diversified manufacturing city of relatively small but numerous factories, including makers of metal products, textiles, food products, and chemicals. As an educational center, Philadelphia had fifteen colleges and universities and six medical schools; there were more than fifty colleges and universities in the metropolitan area. The Pennsylvania Academy of Fine Arts, founded in 1805 and the oldest art school and art museum in America, by the 20th century was one of several major art galleries, the most notable of the others being the Philadelphia Museum of Art, which opened in 1928. The Philadelphia

Orchestra, founded in 1900, remained one of the leading symphony orchestras of the world, a rank it attained under the conductorship of Leopold Stokowski from 1912 to 1936.

[E. Digby Baltzell, *Philadelphia Gentlemen: The Making of a National Upper Class;* Ellis Paxson Oberholtzer, *Philadelphia: A History of the City and Its People;* J. Thomas Scharf and Thompson Westcott, *History of Philadelphia, 1609–1884;* Sam Bass Warner, Jr., *The Private City: Philadelphia in Three Periods of Its Growth.*]

RUSSELL F. WEIGLEY

PHILADELPHIA, CAPTURE OF THE. On Oct. 31, 1803, during the Barbary Wars, the frigate *Philadelphia,* commanded by Capt. William Bainbridge and temporarily unsupported by other American warships blockading Tripoli, sailed too near the shore while pursuing an enemy craft and struck a hidden reef. Heroic efforts to release the frigate proved unavailing, and in the end the ship and its crew of 315 men were captured. This incident prolonged and made more difficult American negotiations with and operations against Tripoli—although the ill effects were subsequently somewhat minimized by Stephen Decatur's daring exploit in destroying the captured frigate after the Tripolitans had refloated it. With some eighty men, in the ketch *Intrepid,* Decatur, during the night of Feb. 16, 1804, boarded the *Philadelphia,* cleared it of the enemy, set it afire, and escaped from the harbor.

[H. Adams, *History of the U.S. During the Administrations of Jefferson and Madison;* G. W. Allen, *Our Navy and the Barbary Corsairs;* R. W. Irwin, *Diplomatic Relations of the U.S. With the Barbary Powers.*]

RAY W. IRWIN

PHILADELPHIA CORDWAINERS' CASE. In the fall of 1805 the journeymen cordwainers of Philadelphia went on strike to enforce their demands for the wage scale prevailing at New York and Baltimore and for a discontinuance of the rebate of wages for export work. Eight union leaders were then arrested on a charge of criminal conspiracy and tried in the mayor's court of Philadelphia. The court accepted the arguments of Jared Ingersoll for the prosecution and relied upon British authorities, since refuted, to establish the doctrine that "a conspiracy of workmen to raise their wages" was criminal at common law. Despite the efforts of defense counsel Caesar A. Rodney, the defendants were found guilty, but, as the court was chiefly concerned with establishing the principle, they were each fined $8.00. The strike was broken, and an important precedent was set for the criminal prosecution of labor union activities, which had multiplied with the rise of wholesale manufacturers. This was the first of six criminal conspiracy cases brought against union shoemakers in this period; four of the cases were decided against the journeymen.

[W. Nelles, "The First American Labor Case," *Yale Law Journal,* vol. 41 (1931).]

RICHARD B. MORRIS

PHILADELPHIA GAS RING, perpetrators of a notorious political scandal in the history of American municipal government. The Republican organization in Philadelphia, under the leadership of "Boss" James McManes, gained control of the city's gas department in the late 1860's, employed some 2,000 political henchmen therein, charged high rates and gave no service, and pocketed the proceeds. The trustees of the gas department, who became known as the "Gas Ring," ultimately controlled state as well as city elections. The organization was defeated in the 1880's by the Committee of One Hundred, a group of independent citizens who successfully prosecuted members of the "ring" and roused the electorate to vote for a reform candidate.

[James Bryce, *American Commonwealth.*]

FRANCES L. REINHOLD

PHILADELPHIA RIOTS. On May 6–8 and July 5–8, 1844, riots in Philadelphia climaxed the first phase of American nativistic agitation. Both periods of rioting followed minor clashes between Irish Catholics and native political organizations. Disorder quickly spread, as Protestants, their antipathies heightened by antipapal propagandists and by a recent Catholic attempt to end Bible-reading in the public schools, began systematic attacks on foreigners. During the actual rioting, Philadelphia resembled a war-torn city: military companies fought in the streets, cannon were mounted in the public squares, Catholic churches were burned, and hundreds of immigrants' homes were sacked by pillaging mobs. A score of persons were killed and nearly 100 wounded before militia ended the mob rule. Public reaction against this violence contributed to the downfall of the American Republican party and sent the whole nativistic movement into temporary eclipse.

[Ray A. Billington, *The Protestant Crusade.*]

RAY ALLEN BILLINGTON

PHILANTHROPIST, an early antislavery weekly newspaper established by Charles Osborn at Mt.

Pleasant, Ohio, in 1817. Benjamin Lundy contributed to it. Osborn sold it in 1818 to Elisha Bates, who continued it, with little success, for three more years as a broadly moral and religious reform advocate. The same title was used for an antislavery newspaper begun at New Richmond, Ohio, near Cincinnati, in 1836; James G. Birney was its editor. A mob destroyed the press, but the paper was printed for a short time in Warren County and delivered to Cincinnati by canal. Gamaliel Bailey, associated with Birney, became sole editor in 1837 and continued the paper for several years at Cincinnati.

[O. C. Hooper, *History of Ohio Journalism, 1793–1833.*]

EUGENE H. ROSEBOOM

PHILANTHROPY AND BENEVOLENCE. Native Americans aided the less fortunate and enriched their communities long before Europeans came to North America. But the newcomers' sense of superiority inclined them to believe that only they could be charitable. Spanish friars and English missionaries, such as John Eliot in 17th-century Massachusetts, labored to uplift native Americans with spiritual and material benefits. Eleazar Wheelock's famous Indian school, which became Dartmouth College, embraced intellectual goals as well. But colonists more often fought than blessed those with whom they struggled for land. This pattern of concern and animosity persisted throughout American history.

The Elizabethan Poor Law (1601), forcing localities to care for the needy, reflected unfavorably on English charity. Puritan leaders, notably John Winthrop and Cotton Mather, urged colonials to recognize God's plan, not man's law, by "doing good." Quakers imbibed this imperative from William Penn. Humanitarianism and revolutionary millenarianism, products of the 18th-century Enlightenment, likewise became parts of the American ethos. Inspired by such motives, colonists pursued philanthropic reputations. John Harvard inaugurated an important mode of giving when he endowed the first Anglo-American college in 1636. Benjamin Franklin helped found not only a school but also a hospital and a library, fulfilling the virtue of public service. John Woolman and Anthony Benezet, Quakers, remembered the poor and enslaved, about whom colonists often showed scant concern. Colonial treatment of dependent groups, while not unusual for the age, left much to be desired.

Stephen Girard, whose benefactions included a college for orphans in Philadelphia, stands out among wealthy philanthropists of the new nation. Benjamin

Rush, who established the first free medical clinic in the United States, exemplifies the role of reformers in benevolence. The optimism of the young republic provoked a veritable explosion of reform in Andrew Jackson's day. The organization of the New York Association for Improving the Condition of the Poor in 1841 by Robert M. Hartley and the founding of the Children's Aid Society in New York in 1853 by Charles Loring Brace stemmed from concern about the growing incidence of poverty in the industrializing society. Causes abounded—particularly Dorothea Dix's efforts to improve care of the mentally ill, Samuel Gridley Howe's actions in behalf of the sensorially handicapped, and the abolitionism of William Lloyd Garrison and Frederick Douglass.

The Civil War directed Americans' sympathies to the troops through such private organizations as the U.S. Sanitary Commission, a precursor of the American Red Cross. Northern blacks and whites also manifested concern for the newly freed slaves, from which emerged a joint private-public agency, the Freedmen's Bureau. For the first time on a major scale the federal government helped administer a welfare program for needy Americans. The contributions of blacks, particularly Douglass and Sojourner Truth, to various reforms of the time only hint at the history of black philanthropy in America, extending from colonial days well into the 20th century.

The Gilded Age produced philanthropists of the persuasion of Andrew Carnegie, and these "stewards of wealth" and their successors endowed American society with benefits in the areas of education, art, music, medicine, and science. The Social Gospel and Progressive movements of the turn of the century enlisted average citizens in charitable projects. Clara Barton's American Red Cross (1882) and the Charity Organization Movement reflected the growing desire to bring order to the rapidly expanding charity field. Founders of settlement houses—notably Jane Addams, who founded Hull House in Chicago in 1889, and Lillian Wald, who founded the Henry Street Settlement in New York City in 1893—urged that "dogooders" become more sophisticated, pointing toward social work as a profession. Moreover, the prominence of Barton, Addams, and Wald arose partly from the fact that philanthropy offered a unique career opportunity for American women.

The 20th century saw continued proliferation of charitable agencies and causes. The effort to rationalize giving produced cooperative campaigns, notably the Community Chest and the United Jewish Appeal.

Corporations became more philanthropic, and benevolent foundations, such as those of the Rockefeller and Ford families, became a major element in philanthropy. The 20th century also witnessed expanding governmental "charity" in the form of social security; public assistance; and aid to education, the arts, and the sciences. After the 1950's particularly, an affluent America discovered the persistent poverty of blacks, Indians, chicanos, and mountain people.

Coeval with domestic philanthropy has been U.S. philanthropy abroad. To foreign gifts, such as the aid given after the great San Francisco earthquake of 1906 and James Smithson's endowment of the Smithsonian Institution, Americans have responded to disasters and sought cultural challenges outside the nation's borders. Since the early 19th century, American missionaries have been major dispensers of education, medicine, and vocational knowledge and tools. Ad hoc groups have tackled specific crises, such as the Irish potato famine of the 1840's. Permanent organizations, particularly in the 20th century, have aided victims of famine, war, and other scourges. Important, but by no means exclusive in this regard, have been the (Quaker) American Friends Service Committee, the Church World Service, the Catholic Relief Services, the (Jewish) Joint Distribution Committee, and CARE (Cooperative for American Remittances Everywhere). Foundations also have been much in evidence, among them the Ford Foundation, the Rockefeller Foundation, and the Near East Foundation.

Congress was first asked to vote relief for foreigners when refugees from the Santo Domingo revolution crowded into the United States in the 1790's. Republicans defeated the measure, upholding strict construction of the Constitution. But in 1812 Congress approved funds for victims of the Venezuelan earthquake, and since then the government has repeatedly made appropriations for disaster victims abroad. Private support for the Greek war for independence in the 1820's, for Cubans in the 1890's, and for embattled Chinese and Spaniards in the 1930's has shown that "charity" can often become embroiled in world politics. The U.S. government has used aid itself to augment policy, as for example when it set up the American Relief Administration under Herbert Hoover to feed starving Europeans after World War I and the Marshall Plan after World War II. Sensitive to the implications of philanthropy abroad, the government has tried at times to control private aid, through the Neutrality Acts of the 1930's and the War Relief Control Board during World War II, and to involve private groups in governmental programs, through, for example, the U.S. Escapee Program of 1954 and the Peace Corps (established in 1961). The United States also endeavored to nationalize foreign aid—for example, the Point Four technical aid program—and to channel international relief through the United Nations.

Both foreign and domestic philanthropy have had their critics. Ralph Waldo Emerson and Nathaniel Hawthorne considered philanthropists naive in their seemingly monomaniacal efforts to make over the world. Radicals have attacked philanthropy as an unacceptable surrogate for the proper distribution of wealth. Do-gooders often appear sanctimonious to those compelled to accept their largesse, and critics have often detected more politics and self-interest than true benevolence in giving. Tax exemptions (since 1917) and other devices to encourage benevolence came under congressional scrutiny in 1948, 1952, and 1969, especially with regard to foundations, whose motives have been questioned and programs condemned for being either too radical or too conservative. Yet individual generosity in 1972, both to victims of major floods in the United States and to refugees of the Nicaraguan earthquake, and concern for Vietnamese war orphans suggest that many Americans continue to adhere to the ethic of personal charity.

[Robert Bremner, *American Philanthropy;* Merle Curti, *American Philanthropy Abroad.*]

CHARLES WETZEL

PHILIPPI, SKIRMISH AT (June 3, 1861), probably the first field action of the Civil War. A Confederate force of about 1,000 under Col. G. A. Porterfield, which had been burning railroad bridges in West Virginia, was surprised and routed at Philippi on a stormy night by Col. B. F. Kelley with a federal command of 3,000. The casualties were few.

[R. U. Johnson and C. C. Buel, eds., *Battles and Leaders of the Civil War,* vol. I.]

ALVIN F. HARLOW

PHILIPPINE INSURRECTION, the name most often applied to the **Filipino-American War** (1899–1902). Spain ceded the Philippine Islands to the United States following the Spanish-American War, by the Treaty of Paris, ratified in 1899. Except for the American force in Manila under Gen. Wesley M. Merritt and his successor, Gen. Elwell S. Otis, the islands were held by Filipino revolutionaries, whose desire for independence clashed with America's imperialistic intentions. Fighting began on Feb. 4, 1899. Otis pursued a cautious policy while awaiting reinforcements. Then, in October, he dispersed the Filipino army in an offensive north of Manila. Emilio Aguinaldo, the Filipino leader, fled into the mountains, and guerrilla warfare ensued.

American leaders hoped to pacify the islands by winning the support of the Filipino populace away from the revolutionaries. The army's work included legal and fiscal reform, organization of municipal governments and public-health programs, and creation of a public school system; but despite the efforts of a civilian commission headed by William Howard Taft and the pacification program of the military government under Otis and his successor, Gen. Arthur MacArthur, guerrillas continued harassing Americans and pro-American Filipinos. As the frustrations of the guerrilla war mounted, some Americans resorted to brutal retaliatory measures that matched the equally barbarous actions of some guerrillas.

President William McKinley's reelection victory over the antiimperialist William Jennings Bryan in November 1900 dealt a severe blow to insurgent morale, and MacArthur embarked upon a more forceful pacification program in December, having the largest number of American troops available at any time during the conflict (almost 70,000) and an ever-increasing number of Filipino scouts. Several thousand guerrillas and their supporters surrendered or were captured between November 1900 and mid-1901. Gen. Frederick S. Funston captured Aguinaldo in March 1901, and the Americans continued making progress in pacification throughout the year. In July Taft and his commission took control of the colonial government from the military; Gen. Adna R. Chaffee replaced MacArthur as military commander in the Philippines. The following year, after the surrender of Gen. Miguel Malvar on Luzon and Gen. Vicente Lucban on Samar, the U.S. secretary of war proclaimed the end of the Philippine Insurrection, but the newly formed Philippine Constabulary fought against recalcitrant guerrillas, bandits, and sporadic uprisings throughout the period of American rule.

The Philippine campaign left a bitter legacy. In the United States, vocal opponents of the war charged the army with brutality, prompting a Senate investigation and the court-martial of several officers, including Gen. Jacob H. Smith. Muslim Filipinos in Mindanao and the Sulu Archipelago did not participate in the revolution, and the American pacification against them is not usually considered part of the Filipino-American War.

[Teodoro A. Agoncillo, *Malolos: The Crisis of the Republic;* John M. Gates, *Schoolbooks and Krags: The United States Army in the Philippines, 1898–1902;* William T. Sexton, *Soldiers in the Sun;* Leon Wolff, *Little Brown Brother: How the U.S. Conquered the Philippines.*]
JOHN M. GATES

PHILIPPINE ISLANDS, an archipelago in the Pacific Ocean lying about 500 miles off the coast of Southeast Asia, has experienced the benefits and disadvantages of being the most westernized nation in the Far East. During the 20th century it successively served as the colony, subject ally, and diplomatic partner of the United States.

Covering an area of 115,600 square miles, the Philippine archipelago is the approximate size of the British Isles. Although composed of over 7,000 islands and reefs, its population is confined to eleven islands, the largest of which are Luzon and Mindanao. Predominantly Malay in stock, the population is Christian in its religious allegiance, as a result of the discovery and conquest of the islands by Spain in the 16th century. Ferdinand Magellan landed there in 1521, and the first permanent Spanish settlement was established by Miguel López Legazpe on Cebu in 1565. The Roman Catholic church accompanied and facilitated the rapid conquest of the islands by Spain, and the outstanding achievement of the long period of Spanish rule was the conversion of 90 percent of the Filipino population to the Catholic faith. Only in the southern island of Mindanao did the Spanish missionaries meet resistance. The inhabitants there were Muslim and, because of their religion, would be permanently and incorrectly labeled Moros by the Spaniards.

With the exception of a brief and partial occupation by the British in the 1760's, the Philippines remained a Spanish possession until 1898. In the 19th century there was a perceptible increase in the trade of the islands, but the success of Spanish administration was vitiated by absolutism, commercial restriction, and ecclesiasticism. The Spanish friars became a source of discontent as a result of their political control of the barrios and their monopolization of large areas of arable land. A small native professional class, influenced by European doctrines of nationalism and liberalism, began to seek more autonomy, and a brief revolt in

the 1870's was succeeded two decades later by the opening chapter of the Philippine Revolution. That revolution found its martyr in José Rizal, its organizer in Andres Bonifacio, and its most successful military figure in Emilio Aguinaldo. Although heartened by several early victories, Aguinaldo's guerrilla band was faced with a shortage of arms by August 1897 and the prospect of continued Spanish reinforcements. Extracting a large monetary payment and a vague promise of political and religious reforms from the Spanish governor-general, Aguinaldo and the other revolutionary leaders made peace by the Pact of Biacnabato and went into exile at Hong Kong.

The promised reforms were forgotten by the Spanish rulers, and in February 1898 guerrilla warfare recommenced in Luzon. The declaration of war against Spain by the United States in April appeared to offer the Filipino revolutionaries the opportunity for military success and independence. Shortly after Commodore George Dewey's naval victory at Manila Bay on May 1, 1898, Aguinaldo returned to the Philippines and with Dewey's encouragement raised a large and motley army that shortly drove the Spanish into the walled city of Manila. Dewey avoided a formal alliance with the insurgents, and Aguinaldo's initial confidence that the United States sought only to offer protection to an independent Philippines was undermined by the arrival of American troops, the arranged capitulation of Manila to the American forces alone, and President William McKinley's decision in October to instruct his commissioners to the Paris peace conference to demand of Spain the cession of the entire archipelago. Aguinaldo had earlier proclaimed the inauguration of the Philippine Republic and established its capital at Malolos. The likelihood of open conflict between the American and Philippine forces was accentuated in December 1898, when McKinley issued an executive order claiming American sovereignty throughout the islands and the troops under Gen. Elwell S. Otis sought to extend their lines beyond the city of Manila. On Feb. 4, 1899, two days before the U.S. Senate confirmed the Treaty of Paris, shots were exchanged at Santa Mesa, and the Filipino-American War began. In the official American view it was an "insurrection" inspired by a single tribe led by a power-hungry bandit chieftain, but Aguinaldo enjoyed mass support throughout the archipelago. The conflict required the expenditure by the United States of $400 million and cost 7,000 American casualties. The Philippines were declared pacified and the "insurrection" extinguished by proclamation of President Theodore Roosevelt on July 4, 1902.

A complex mixture of economic, strategic, and humanitarian considerations had persuaded the United States to claim and subjugate the Philippines. A belief that possession of the archipelago would assure American manufactures improved access to the supposedly limitless markets of China was perhaps the primary motive, but economic considerations were supplemented by those of naval strength, partisan advantage, missionary zeal, and international "duty."

It was under the auspices of the Republican party that the United States made a substantial effort to reconstruct the society and culture of the Filipino people in the years 1900–13. In this period American officials in the islands enjoyed relatively unrestricted power, and they achieved a measure of success in their determination to Americanize the political, educational, and judicial structures. The process began with the staged transfer of legislative and executive authority from the military to a civilian commission headed by William Howard Taft. Under the direction of Secretary of War Elihu Root and the Philippine Government Act of July 2, 1902, the Taft Commission proclaimed the establishment of American-style democratic government as the goal of American policy in the Philippines. Because of the "backward" condition of the people a long period of probationary tutelage would be necessary, but by carefully controlled stages the Filipinos should be allowed participation in all levels of government. In 1907 an elective assembly was instituted, representing the "Christian tribes" of the islands and selected by a restricted suffrage. This assembly served as the lower house of the Philippine national legislature, and the commission became the upper house. The head of the commission, given the title of governor-general, served as chief executive; acts of the legislature could be vetoed by both the governor and the U.S. Congress.

By 1912 the Filipino economy had experienced appreciable, if unbalanced, growth and was increasingly dependent on the American market. Although efforts to institute land reform and to modernize agricultural practices had failed, a system of public education had been successfully instituted at the primary level; the political unity of the islands had been promoted by improvements in communication and transportation; and a civil service system had been inaugurated and the judiciary reshaped in the American pattern.

While American rule was applauded by the wealth-

ier and more conservative Filipinos, political tensions arose as the Nacionalista party, pledged to "the complete independence" of the islands, gradually assumed a dominant position in the assembly. Its immediate goal was to lessen the power of the governor-general and commission and obtain legislative initiative for the assembly. When Woodrow Wilson took office as president in 1913, he appointed as governor-general Francis Burton Harrison. Harrison was openly sympathetic to the desire of Filipino leaders to shorten the period of tutelage. He purposefully accelerated the Filipinization of the civil service and acquiesced in the informal transfer of much of the authority of his office to Filipino department heads. By the Jones Act of 1916 an elective senate replaced the commission as the upper house of the legislature, and suffrage requirements were liberalized. The increasing role of the Filipinos in the operations of the government did not, however, mark any particular gain in social equality; drawn from a single class, the Filipino politicians exhibited little concern for the agrarian masses. In 1920 Harrison declared that the prerequisite of "stable" government had been achieved and recommended that independence be granted. Although neither Congress nor Harrison's Republican successors were prepared to accept his judgment, the process of effective Americanization of the islands was at an end.

Gen. Leonard Wood, appointed by President Warren G. Harding to succeed Harrison in 1921, sought to reclaim the supervisory powers of his office and to reassert the authority of the United States in the determination of Philippine social development. The inevitable result was a deadlock between the governor-general and the Philippine assembly. The instruments available to Wood were insufficient for effective domination. The Nacionalista party leaders, having shared executive authority in the Harrison years, sought to use the assembly's limited power of the purse to frustrate Wood and his "cavalry cabinet." A compromise of sorts was reached between Wood's successor, Henry L. Stimson, and the Filipino leaders Manuel Quezon and Sergio Osmeña, but by 1930 it was increasingly clear that Filipino demands for self-government would be satisfied only by national independence.

The decision to grant independence to the Philippines was the result of the initiative as well as the legislation of the U.S. Congress. That decision was in line with the long-term evolution of American Philippine policy, but its immediate causes were economic self-interest and isolationist fear. American agricultural producers urged independence under the erroneous belief that Philippine agricultural exports were depressing domestic prices in the home market; American labor leaders urged independence as a means of excluding Filipino immigration as well as the competition of cheap Filipino goods; American isolationists urged independence as a means of reducing the risk of United States involvement in a future Pacific war. The Philippines, once seen as a source of economic profit and strategic strength, had come to be viewed as an economic competitor and a diplomatic albatross. The Tydings-McDuffie Act of March 1934 provided for the complete independence of the islands following a transitional ten-year "commonwealth period." During that period the United States was to maintain its sovereignty over the islands, and certain Filipino exports were to suffer increasing tariff and quota restrictions. The Philippines, possessed of a colonial economy dependent on the American market, were promised independence and economic dislocation.

In accord with the provisions of the independence act, the Filipinos formulated and ratified a new constitution in 1935, and in November of that year the Philippine Commonwealth was formally established with Manuel Quezon as its president. Frank Murphy served as American high commissioner. American policy during the commonwealth period was rather anomalous. It called upon the Philippines to achieve economic and military viability but did little to further the efforts of the commonwealth government in either regard. The commonwealth period, scheduled to end in 1946, was interrupted by the Japanese invasion on Dec. 8, 1941.

Despite the gallant stand of Gen. Jonathan Wainwright at Corregidor, the combined American and Filipino forces were able to do no more than delay the skillfully orchestrated invasion, and by May 1942 the entire archipelago was in the hands of the Japanese, who set up a puppet Philippine republic under José P. Laurel and engaged in a propaganda campaign to persuade the Filipinos that they had been saved from their colonial masters. Some Filipinos collaborated with the Japanese by choice and more by necessity, but others joined the resistance movement, and a large majority remained faithful to the Philippine exile government under Osmeña in Washington and assisted the American force under Gen. Douglas MacArthur when it launched an amphibious invasion at Lingayen Gulf in January 1945. The destruction in Manila, where the Japanese fought a last-ditch battle, was but a symbol of the general devastation suffered by the Philippines during the years of occupation and war. When Osmeña returned from Washington to reestablish the commonwealth government, the economy was in a shambles.

The administration of President Harry S. Truman reaffirmed the intention of the United States to assist in the economic rehabilitation of the islands and to acknowledge full independence, which was indeed effected when the Republic of the Philippines came into being July 4, 1946. But congressional legislation respecting future trade relations furnished a source of grievance for the Filipinos. On Apr. 30, 1946, the U.S. Congress concurrently passed the Philippine Rehabilitation Act and the Philippine Trade Act. The former authorized $620 million for the repair of war damages and additional funds for public health and technological training programs if the Philippine legislature accepted the terms of the trade act. According to those terms, trade between the islands and the United States would be free until 1954, but fixed quotas were established on American products exported to the Philippines. After 1954, Philippine goods would be subject to an annual 5 percent tariff increase until the full rate of 100 percent was reached in 1974. In addition, the Filipinos were required to alter their constitution in order that citizens of the United States would be assured equal rights with citizens of the Philippines in the development of natural resources and the operation of public utilities. Protection of American capital was demanded as the price of rehabilitation aid and limited access to the American market. The Philippine legislature reluctantly agreed.

With the onset of the cold war, the Truman administration exhibited an increased concern for the military defense and economic viability of the Philippines and an increased willingness to furnish financial support on both counts. In March 1947 the United States negotiated with Manuel Roxas, the first president of the Philippine Republic, a military assistance agreement that gave the American army and navy a ninety-nine-year lease on twenty-three bases in the Philippines. It also stipulated that the United States would provide arms and technical advice to an expanded Philippine army; for Washington, as well as Manila, was concerned about a potential revolt by members of the Hukbalahap movement. Initially a branch of the resistance against the Japanese, the Huks subsequently directed their animosity against monopolistic landlords and the central government, and by 1950 they had declared open war on the government and were extending their guerrilla operations well beyond their home base in central Luzon. Upon the recommendation of a mission headed by Daniel W. Bell, the Truman administration accelerated its military and economic aid program, but it was Ramon Magsaysay who provided effective leadership against the Huks. Combining military counterinsurgency with social and economic reforms, Magsaysay, first as defense minister and then as president, gradually erased the rebellion and the threat of internal subversion. Concurrently, he sought to bring the agrarian masses into the political process and to implement an effective program of land reform.

During the 1950's, American foreign policy emphasized the strategic importance of the Philippines in a manner unequaled since the days of Commodore Dewey. The Mutual Defense Treaty of 1951 was followed by the inclusion of the Philippines in the Southeast Asia Treaty Organization in 1954 and a succession of military aid missions. American aid was primarily directed toward military assistance programs rather than economic diversification, and the reform programs instituted by Magsaysay lost much of their impetus after his death in a plane crash in 1957. The 1960's saw relatively little progress in such problem areas as tenancy and land monopoly, agricultural inefficiency, retrogressive tax policies, and the dependence of the export sector on the American market.

The Philippines remained in diplomatic alignment with the United States, but there was a rising body of opinion among Filipino politicians urging a more independent stand, one that sought to balance its special relationship to America with a closer association with its "natural partners" in Asia. Efforts to form a diplomatic or economic alliance with Malaysia and Indonesia proved ineffectual, but they reflected a determination no longer to serve as a subject ally of the United States. That determination was accentuated after 1972 by domestic political developments in the Philippines. Facing a secessionist rebellion in Mindanao and rising political opposition from liberal groups in Manila, President Ferdinand Marcos disbanded the Philippine assembly and began to rule by martial law. By 1975 he had proclaimed constitutional democracy unsuitable for the Philippines and established a personal dictatorship. American diplomats no longer boasted that the United States had created in the Philippines "a showcase for American democracy in Asia."

[Teodoro Agoncillo, *Malolos: Crisis of the Republic;* Oscar M. Alfonso, *A Short History of the Filipino People;* Onofro D. Corpuz, *The Philippines;* Garel A. Grunder and William E. Livezey, *The Philippines and the United States;* Joseph R. Hayden, *The Philippines: A Study in National Development;* Peter W. Stanley, *A Nation in the Making: The Philippines and the United States, 1899–1921.*]

RICHARD E. WELCH, JR.

PHILIPPINE SEA, BATTLE OF THE (June 19–20, 1944). During the offensive against Japan in the central Pacific beginning in November 1943, the Fifth Fleet of the U.S. Pacific Fleet assaulted strategically important Saipan in the Mariana Islands in June. This action forced Japan to commit its main fleet in battle for the first time in two years (*see* Midway, Battle of). Japan's aircraft carrier squadrons had been severely depleted by land-based Allied planes in the south Pacific and by the carrier planes of Task Force 58 since 1942, and thus most of the 450 undertrained pilots of Japanese carrier and island-based planes that tried to defend Saipan in the Battle of the Philippine Sea were easily shot down, as if in an "old-time turkey shoot," according to one American navy pilot.

Shadowed by American submarines, the Japanese Mobile Fleet, under Vice Adm. Jisaburo Ozawa, sortied for battle from Tawi Tawi in the Sulu Archipelago on June 13, two days before American marines assaulted Saipan. The main Japanese force of nine carriers and escorting battleships, cruisers, and destroyers rendezvoused east of the Philippine Islands with another battleship force, whose separate movements to that time had also been observed by the submarines and reported to Adm. Raymond A. Spruance, commander of the Fifth Fleet, off Saipan. Spruance mistook this information to mean that the Japanese fleet was approaching in two groups (as at Midway), when in fact Ozawa had concentrated all his ships for long-range shuttle flights to Guam and Tinian, his planes to attack the American vessels en route. Spruance thus removed his transports to safety 200 miles eastward, formed a gun force of prewar battleships off the west coast of Saipan, and held the fifteen fast carriers of Task Force 58 just west of there to meet the Japanese attack. On June 19, Ozawa's incoming planes, detected by the carriers' radar, were intercepted by Task Force 58 Grumman F6F Hellcat fighters and almost annihilated. The "Marianas Turkey Shoot," as this segment of the battle was called, lasted most of the day, during which some 300 Japanese planes were shot down and only 30 American planes lost.

Preoccupied with the aerial combat, Vice Adm. Marc A. Mitscher, commander of Task Force 58, could not cruise westward in search of the distant Japanese ships on June 19. Nevertheless, two Japanese heavy carriers sank from damage inflicted during the day by torpedoes from the American submarines *Albacore* and *Cavalla,* and that night Spruance released Mitscher and his carriers from protecting the beachhead. Ozawa tried to escape westward, but late on June 20 searching American carrier planes sighted his fleet over 300 miles from Task Force 58, far out in the Philippine Sea. A late afternoon carrier air strike sank one more Japanese carrier just after sunset, and many American planes had to ditch at sea when they ran out of fuel on the long return flight, but most pilots and aircrewmen floated in the life rafts until rescued by their ships or seaplanes. To some 475 Japanese aviators lost during the two-day battle, the American fleet lost 130 planes but no ships and only 76 pilots and aircrewmen. Stripped of its remaining trained pilots and three carriers in the battle, the Japanese fleet surrendered control of the Marianas and the central Pacific to the U.S. Navy; from these islands, B-29 very-long-range strategic bombers began to bomb Japan in November 1944, and with command of the sea, the Pacific Fleet was able to begin the blockade of the Asian littoral.

[S. E. Morison, *History of United States Naval Operations in World War II,* vol. VIII; C. G. Reynolds, *The Fast Carriers: The Forging of an Air Navy.*]

CLARK G. REYNOLDS

PHILIPSE'S PATENT, an enormous tract in Putnam County, N.Y., purchased by Adolphe Philipse from Lambert Dorlandt and Jan Sybrant, who had obtained a license to buy it from the Indians. In 1697, Philipse secured a patent from Gov. Benjamin Fletcher for this tract and some additional land, which was known as Philipse's Highland patent. Both the Highland patent and the manor of Philipsborough in Westchester County were inherited by Frederick Philipse, who on his death divided the Highland patent among his four younger children.

[William Pelletreau, *History of Putnam County.*]

A. C. FLICK

PHILOSOPHY. The word "philosophy" both begs and defies definition. William James once described this search for definition as comparable to a "blind man in a dark room looking for a black cat that is not there." One important clue to the more technical doctrines of leading American thinkers is their different conceptions of the proper content or role of philosophy. At least until the 19th century most avowed phi-

losophers assumed a special philosophic subject matter and defended philosophic understanding as a distinctive, and usually a lofty and comprehensive, form of knowledge. But, in a tradition going back at least as far as David Hume (1711–76), an increasing number of philosophers have denied any cognitive subject matter to philosophy. It is not, they believe, an empirical science or superscience nor is it directly competitive with such purely formal disciplines as mathematics. Logic and semantics remain the prime tools for philosophic analysis, but philosophers properly and competently deal only with meaning, not fact—with the proper formulation of questions, not the validity of answers. At least until 1950 this narrow conception of subject matter encouraged a steady erosion of metaphysics—of cosmology, ontology, teleology, and certain issues in epistemology—as the central concern of philosophers and supported a critical conception of philosophy either in restricted logical and analytical contexts closely related to the sciences or in the broad social and moral context so ably defended by John Dewey (1859–1952) and so closely tied to such normative subjects as aesthetics, ethics, and politics.

Because of the educational attainments and native brilliance of a few of its ministers and magistrates and the vital intellectual ferment sustained by its churches and colleges, New England first nurtured significant philosophical labors in English America. The Puritans articulated and implemented distinctive conceptions of popular sovereignty and natural law matured by 16th-century Calvinists and thus made an early contribution to American political theory. Reformed or Calvinist doctrines, although rarely expounded in a rigorous philosophical form by 17th-century Puritans, still entailed a substantially well-defined, neo-Augustinian ontology. A personal deity was the ground and source of all things. His timeless will encompassed, and gave cosmic meaning to, all human choice. Men had freedom and were fully responsible morally, but only as participants in a universe continuously dependent for its existence and lawful development upon God. Thus, man's very ability to love God was itself a gift, and Christian conversion was only the most dramatic illustration of God's ultimate control over man's destiny. Such doctrines found philosophical support in the greatest Calvinist apologist, Jonathan Edwards, who dominated American philosophy from about 1730 until his death in 1758 as the first significant American philosopher and perhaps the greatest of American philosophical theologians. Edwards defined God as "all being," correlated his attributes with Newtonian space, carefully delineated the horrible moral implications of doctrines of free will, developed highly aesthetic conceptions of virtue and piety, and explored in subtle detail the psychological dimensions of religious experience. At a technical level, his idealism was close to that earlier developed by George Berkeley (himself a two-year resident of Rhode Island) and to that of an American contemporary, Samuel Johnson.

Except to Edwards and his disciples, 18th-century America seemed peculiarly uncongenial to philosophical inquiry. Men such as John Adams, Benjamin Franklin, and Thomas Jefferson were fascinated with the physical sciences (natural philosophy) and with traditional issues in political theory, but they distrusted metaphysical speculation, remained blind to the most subtle concerns of theology, and unself-consciously revealed rather than rigorously articulated a body of aesthetic and ethical assumptions. But their concern with the sources and economic bases of political authority and with the institutional foundations of public virtue and good citizenship continued into the 19th century. College presidents (usually drawn from the ministry) traditionally taught required courses in moral philosophy or introduced new courses in political economy. Before the Civil War a stream of American ministers and scholars studied in Scottish universities and brought back to America a form of common-sense realism, a philosophic tradition that lasted out the century in many Presbyterian institutions. Secular American philosophers and political economists drew direct inspiration from English utilitarianism.

In New England a diverse group of ministers, scholars, and writers found new philosophical inspiration in German idealism and also began the soon typical trek of young scholars to German universities. Some so-called transcendentalists—Frederic Henry Hedge, Theodore Parker, and Octavius Brooks Frothingham—became rather careful students of Immanuel Kant, Johann Fichte, and Georg Hegel. The influential Ralph Waldo Emerson embraced a more lofty career than philosophy; he wanted to be poet-priest to a new American culture and composed brilliant sermons in the form of poems and essays. As a preacher he selected insights from many philosophic traditions but embraced none. Emerson suffered endless family afflictions, eventually probed the depths of despair, and always knew the horrible abyss of skepticism and cynicism that challenged any pious consent to, or celebration of, reality. Yet, out of long travail, he was able to affirm reality, and in his doctrine of self-reliance he offered an updated, aesthetic version of redemption. Although not a philosopher, Emerson was a sophisticated student of philosophy and thus has an almost Socratic position in American philosophy.

Various schools of idealism flourished in the late 19th century. In Saint Louis a circle of lay philosophers spread the glories of Hegel and also launched the *Journal of Speculative Philosophy* (1867–93), the first exclusively philosophical journal in the English language. Lay and academic philosophers cultivated myriad varieties of idealism—ethical, personal, dynamic, objective. The future of American philosophy was most apparent at Cornell University, where the Sage School led the way toward an academic and secular profession. But Josiah Royce, a precocious Californian who ended up in the great philosophy department at Harvard University, became the very symbol of idealism at its best. Royce joined the pragmatists in emphasizing the nonontological, instrumental nature of scientific knowledge but used this skepticism, or the very fact of error and doubt, to vindicate a comprehensive mind and an overarching truth, which contains or is man's own best self.

Charles Darwin's *Origin of Species* (1859) seemed to plunge man fully into nature and thus invited new conceptions of man, nature, and scientific explanation. The fullest response to these issues came from the American pragmatists. But in the immediate aftermath of the publication of the *Origin of Species* and by request of Darwin, Chauncey Wright, a versatile but eccentric mathematician and scientist, first showed how the peculiarities of symbolic language provided a naturalistic explanation of man's dominant position in nature. Wright's interest in language, but not his aversion to speculative metaphysics, continued in the even more eccentric Charles S. Peirce, who in his lonely musings made strikingly original contributions to semantics, symbolic logic, and the philosophy of science. Peirce, undisciplined in personal habits and plagued by marital problems, first matured a pragmatic conception of meaning and an operational conception of scientific method. But, for him, the very success of scientific inquiry depended upon a supporting, real world, which in his more soaring metaphysical excursions he defined as mind-like and always developing toward greater lawfulness. In less original and circumspect ways American followers of Herbert Spencer, notably John Fiske, extrapolated from Darwin a vast, cosmic law of evolution, which had profound implications for society.

William James defies classification. As a Harvard psychologist and philosopher, he responded to, or influenced, almost every philosophical movement of the 20th century. In his *Principles of Psychology* (1890) he broached a new, radical empiricism. In direct perception before classification by any concepts, James found an unbroken stream of consciousness containing a multicolored world full of relationships. Traditional epistemological problems evaporated when one no longer began with atomistic sensations that somehow had to be glued together to constitute a world, but with a holistic world that man subsequently cut up into analytical parts according to his purposes. This notion suggested that all reductionist and conceptual ontologies (materialism, idealism) are only retrospective characterizations of an experiential continuum, a position further developed by Dewey in his most significant book, *Experience and Nature* (1925). Yet James was never satisfied with any one formulation and at the end of his life seemed to affirm a kind of pluralistic idealism. The derivative status of concepts reinforced James's antipathy to scientism and led him to embrace the methodological insights of Peirce: the truth or validity of a proposition does not involve any correspondence with a preexistent world, but only its ability to guide man to certain expected experiences. Yet James would not follow Dewey in adhering to the rigorous implications of such a nonontological conception of science. He was always concerned with other than cognitive meanings—personal, religious, inspirational. Thus, he often confused the experiential consequences implied by a proposition and necessary to validate it with the personal satisfactions that come to one simply as a result of believing it true. When in this voluntaristic mood, James seemed to justify a wide variety of consoling beliefs that submitted to no conclusive evidence, and he often hopelessly confused the meaning of a new philosophic method that he called "pragmatic."

Dewey was the most systematic, comprehensive, and influential American philosopher. Educated at the University of Vermont and the Johns Hopkins University, he was early captivated by Hegelian idealism; he slowly responded to the naturalistic implications of Darwin's theories and to the challenging psychological theories of James. By 1900 he had espoused a broad, nonmaterialistic form of naturalism, which converted the objective mind of Hegel into the socially developed functions of language and culture. Dewey expanded the methodological insights of Peirce and James and often called his philosophy "in-

strumentalism." As much as James he probed into phenomenology—the attributes of pure experience—and into ontology, where he sought the most generic traits of an existential world he usually referred to as "nature." Experience, the departing point for inquiry and the source of verity for propositions, was even more significantly the source of quality and value for man. Dewey did his most profound work in axiology, in ethics and aesthetics. Finally, he felt a moral obligation to relate his philosophy to social problems, and thus his famous work in educational theory and in political reform.

Dewey, who died in 1952, was, with George Santayana and Alfred North Whitehead, the last of the giants. The age of towering individuals and great systems already seemed at an end. In the 1930's Nazi persecutions drove to America several members of the Vienna circle of logical positivists and some prominent German neo-Marxists, notably Herbert Marcuse. The positivists gained a large following just after World War II and helped stimulate an interest in the philosophy of science. Their iconoclastic attack on speculative philosophy, and the tremendous influence of English analytic philosophy, helped sway many philosophy departments toward specialized, highly technical, largely analytical concerns. Also in the postwar years, European existentialism, already well rooted in theology, had only limited impact on academic philosophers but created great interest among students and in literary circles. In Roman Catholic colleges sophisticated forms of Thomism that had long flourished there received new vigor from such European neo-Thomists as Jacques Maritain. In the 1960's the overweening interest in analytical approaches seemed on the decline, as more philosophers expressed an interest in phenomenology, in traditional metaphysics, and in normative theory. But any such judgment has to be largely impressionistic: American philosophy is much too diverse for easy characterization. But American philosophy was flourishing in the 1970's as never before in both rigor and technical proficiency, although it perhaps lacked an earlier breadth of interest and impact on the larger society.

[Paul K. Conkin, *Puritans and Pragmatists: Eight Eminent American Thinkers;* Max H. Fisch, ed., *Classic American Philosophers;* Andrew J. Reck, *Recent American Philosophy: Studies of Ten Representative Thinkers;* Herbert W. Schneider, *A History of American Philosophy;* Morton G. White, *Science and Sentiment in America: Philosophical Thought From Jonathan Edwards to John Dewey.*]

PAUL K. CONKIN

PHOENIX, the first important entirely American-built steamship, and the second such ship successfully engaged in the transportation of passengers and freight. It was designed by John Stevens of Hoboken, N.J., in 1806 and was launched Apr. 9, 1808. The ship was intended for service between New Brunswick, N.J., and New York, but the monopoly held by Robert Fulton and Robert R. Livingston prevented the vessel from entering waters subject to jurisdiction of New York State (*see* Fulton's Folly). Stevens sent it by sea to the Delaware River to run between Philadelphia and Trenton. Leaving New York, on June 8, 1809, the *Phoenix* reached Philadelphia on June 17, the first steamship to venture upon the open sea.

[J. H. Morrison, *History of American Steam Navigation.*]
STANLEY R. PILLSBURY

PHOENIXIANA; or Sketches and Burlesques, a literary work by George Horatio Derby (1823–61), an officer in the U.S. Topographical Engineers who wrote under the pseudonym John Phoenix. The volume, published in 1856, consisted of some thirty short humorous sketches and burlesques of current happenings; all of the vignettes had appeared in California newspapers and magazines between 1850 and 1855. The book was immediately successful and remained popular for a generation; twenty-nine editions or reprintings have been noted. In addition to being notable as an early example of American humor, *Phoenixiana* offers to the general historian a commentary, at once humorous and intelligent, upon the political and social conditions of mid-19th century America, particularly California.

[G. R. Stewart, *John Phoenix, Esq.*]
GEORGE R. STEWART

PHONOGRAPH. The concept of a device to record and reproduce sound goes back as far as Cyrano de Bergerac's *Comic History of the States and Empires of the Moon,* written in 1656. The prehistory of an actual instrument to record sound is at least as early as the Phonautograph of Léon Scott in Paris in 1857. This was used for recording and analyzing the pattern of sound waves as registered on the smoked surface of a metal cylinder. Because of the fragility of the film of lampblack it was not possible to play back the sound, nor is there any indication that such a course was even conceived. The machine did contain the essential elements later used in the phonograph, but it recorded laterally rather than vertically to the record surface, as Thomas A. Edison's machine did. Scott recorded on both cylinders and disks, and it may be that one of his instruments sparked the concept of Charles Cros, who in April 1877, twenty years later, lodged a sealed description of a proposed phonograph, including the name, with the French Academy of Sciences. This was published in October 1877. Meanwhile, on July 30, 1877, Edison filed a provisional specification with the British patent office and on Dec. 24, 1877, applied for a U.S. patent. His tinfoil phonograph was announced to the public in *Scientific American* on Nov. 17, 1877. As demonstrated at that time it was an impractical machine, little more than an interesting toy using fragile tinfoil records of little durability. He put it aside to devote his energies to developing the incandescent lamp, which promised greater returns.

In 1880, when Alexander Graham Bell received the $20,000 Volta Prize from the French Academy of Sciences for his work with the telephone, he founded the Volta Laboratory in Washington, D.C. Acoustical research, including work on both the telephone and the phonograph, was conducted at this laboratory. The most far-reaching result was a patent issued in 1886 to Chichester A. Bell and Charles Sumner Tainter, which included cutting the sound track into wax as opposed to indenting tinfoil, as described in Edison's patent. Although the issue was warmly contested, a distinction between the two methods was upheld by the courts, and Edison was obliged to operate under a license from the Bell and Tainter patent, although he had used the method before its issuance.

Early phonograph records gave little volume and were not durable. They had to be duplicated either mechanically by pantograph or acoustically. Neither method was satisfactory. These limitations were overcome by Emile Berliner in a series of patents between 1887 and 1895. The patents covered a wax-coated zinc disk on which the sound waves were cut laterally through the wax to the zinc. The exposed metal was then etched according to the pattern recorded in the wax. This process made a very durable loud-volume record described as sounding "like a partially educated parrot with a sore throat and a cold in the head." After several playings the harshest of the tones were softened, and the background or surface noise abated somewhat. A matrix or impression made from this original was successfully used to mold duplicates in hard rubber. The material was changed late in 1897 to a shellac composition, but it still depended on an etched zinc original.

In 1901 a patent was issued to Joseph W. Jones for cutting the original records in wax that was subsequently electroplated to allow duplication. The patent came as a surprise to Eldridge R. Johnson, who, in addition to manufacturing Berliner graphophones, had been making records by the same process, independently devised. After intense legal maneuvering Johnson was able to continue using the technique and in 1901 formed, with these records, the famous Victor Talking Machine Company. Edison met the challenge of greater volume and fidelity by perfecting his "gold molding" process, which had been initiated in 1892. Unfortunately, some of his earlier patents had revealed enough about the process to enable competitors to introduce successful records molded in Celluloid, a superior substance Edison was not able to use for many years because of patents held by others.

Although Edison's business expanded at a rapid rate for years, it never was able to overcome the lead taken by disk records and machines, particularly in the urban market. All aspects of the record business felt increasing competition from radio, starting in the 1920's. At the same time electricity began to be applied with very good effect to problems of the phonograph business that had never been satisfactorily resolved by purely acoustical and mechanical means. Electrical recording had been conceived and experimented with as early as 1882 by Berliner, but the telephone transmitter was too limited in tonal range for the successful conversion of music to electrical impulses.

A wire recorder foreshadowing tape recordings was invented in 1898 by the Danish electrical engineer Valdemar Poulsen, but it was largely unsuccessful for want of a suitable means of adequate amplification. The advent of the vacuum tube made suitable amplification easy, and mechanical recording became obsolete. The actual work was accomplished by Joseph P. Maxfield, H. C. Harrison, and associates at the Western Electric Company, the manufacturing branch of Bell Telephone, during 1924, making possible the manufacture of records that could reproduce a much greater range of cycles per second at a much higher volume. Coupled with the exponential horn advocated by Clinton R. Hanna and Joseph Slepian, these new records led to the creation of the Orthophonic Victrola, the last significant nonelectric phonograph to be produced. It was available with a record changer, not in itself a new development, but significant as the immediate forerunner of the coin-operated jukeboxes of the 1930's, produced by such makers as the Capehart, Seeburg, and Wurlitzer companies.

By that time all reproduction from records was electronic, following the trend set by recording techniques of a few years earlier. The new players were called radio-phonographs, and their history is closely allied to radio and high-fidelity technology. Record development made substantial advance in this era. During World War II, because of a shortage of shellac, a plastic, Vinylite, was substituted. This flexible material made the records unbreakable and greatly reduced surface noise. It was softer than the old shellac composition, and so it became desirable to reduce needle pressure. The weight of the needle was reduced, and a permanent sapphire needle was introduced, whose shape remained constant over a long time and closely conformed to the profile of the record groove, giving better support. This development made possible more closely spaced grooves and a longer playing time for each record. In 1948 the Columbia Record Company introduced microgroove records that made $33\frac{1}{3}$ revolutions per minute, the first to be made specifically for use only with a permanent stylus, the long-extinct Edison records excepted.

Electronics, low needle pressure and minimal record wear, very low surface noise, and long playing led to the development of stereophonic recording and playback, not a new concept but never before successfully implemented. A Parisian, Clement Adler, received a German patent for the telephone transmission of such sound in 1881, and various experiments were made in stereophonic radio broadcasting in the 1920's and 1930's. A. D. Blumlein of the Columbia Company in England patented, in 1930, a system of cutting the two separate recordings needed for stereo in one groove; one is recorded laterally and the other by the hill-and-dale technique. By early 1958 nine record companies were producing long-playing stereophonic records, and the necessary cartridges and switching gear were available at modest prices. This was the year stereo made its great leap into the consumer field. The greatest subsequent advance by the mid-1970's was the development of quadraphonic sound. This is achieved by either of two competing approaches. First to be marketed, in 1970, was the "Matrix" system invented by Peter Scheiber in 1969. The other is the "discrete" system originally developed by Victor of Japan between 1968 and 1971 and first introduced into the United States in 1972. Records in either system may be satisfactorily reproduced with all monaural and stereophonic equipment.

Because of complex electronic requirements, reproduction in quadraphonic sound depends on compatible specialized equipment.

[William F. Boyce, *Hi-Fi Stereo Handbook;* Roland Gelatt, *The Fabulous Phonograph, From Tin Foil to High Fidelity;* Théodose Achille Louis Du Moncel, *The Telephone, the Microphone and the Phonograph;* Harry F. Olson, *Modern Sound Reproduction;* Oliver Read and Walter Welch, *From Tin Foil to Stereo, Evolution of the Phonograph.*]

EDWIN A. BATTISON

PHOSPHATE INDUSTRY. *See* **Fertilizers.**

PHOTOGRAPHIC INDUSTRY. In 1839 the Frenchman Louis J. M. Daguerre introduced in Paris the first commercial photographic process, the daguerreotype. This novel process produced unique positive images on silvered plates that were exposed in cameras. Because of the perishability of the photosensitive materials and the complexity of the process, the practice of daguerreotypy, which soon became popular in the United States, was restricted to technically oriented persons who produced their own photosensitive materials at the site of the picture-taking. The daguerreotypists obtained the requisite optical apparatus from small optical instrumentmakers and chemical supplies from domestic and foreign chemical manufacturers. Within a decade the number of professional daguerreotypists increased substantially, and specialized photographic supply houses arose in the larger cities.

During the mid-1850's a variety of wet collodion processes replaced the daguerreotype. Fluid collodion served as carrier for the photosensitive halogen salts. At the site of exposure the photographer flowed the salted collodion onto glass for direct positive images in the ambryotype process, onto japanned iron plates for direct positive images in the tintype process, and onto glass for a negative from which a positive image was printed onto photosensitive paper in the popular negative-positive process. Owing to the perishability of the photosensitive negative and positive materials, their production remained with the professional photographers. The change in technology did influence many of the small producers of supplies for the photographer: for example, the Scovill Manufacturing Company of Waterbury, Conn., which had become the principal American producer of unsensitized daguerreotype plates, shifted its product line. While small producers of such new photographic supplies as tintype plates and unsensitized print paper did emerge

in the 1860's and 1870's, the most powerful firms in the industry were the Anthony and the Scovill companies, which dominated the jobbing function in photographic supplies and also engaged in the production of photographic papers, chemicals, cameras, and albums.

In the early 1880's dry gelatin supplanted wet collodion as the carrier of photosensitive salts on negative glass plates. Because the gelatin carrier preserved the photosensitivity of the halogen salts for many months, the technological change permitted centralized factory production of photosensitive materials for the first time. The traditional marketing and production companies in the industry did not take the lead in producing plates and papers; new firms assumed production leadership—Cramer, Seed, and Hammer in Saint Louis; American Aristotype in Jamestown, N.Y.; Eastman in Rochester, N.Y.; Stanley in Boston; and Nepera Chemical in Yonkers, N.Y. Many of them developed marketing departments independent of the jobbing firms of Scovill and Anthony. Although gelatin plates simplified the practice of photography and increased the number of amateur photographers, the technical complexities still deterred most people from practicing photography.

In 1884 George Eastman, despairing of the intense price competition in the dry-plate market, sought with William H. Walker, a Rochester cameramaker, to develop an alternative to dry plates. Improving substantially on a commercially unsuccessful system sold by Leon Warnerke in the 1870's in Britain, they introduced in 1885 a roll-film system. It consisted of a roll holder that slid into the back of the camera instead of the glass plates, and it employed roll film as the negative replacement for the glass plate. Although the well-designed and mass-produced Walker-Eastman roll holder met with enthusiasm initially, the lack of transparency of the paper film first employed by Eastman and the technical complexity of the later stripping film discouraged professional and amateur photographers from adopting the system. Recognizing the failure of this carefully patented system, Eastman reconceived his market and the roll-film system. In 1888 he addressed the enormously large and previously untapped mass amateur market by isolating the technical complexities from picture taking and by providing factory service to perform the technical functions. He added to the company's established production of photosensitive materials by designing a simple-to-operate, highly portable roll-film camera, the Kodak, and by providing factory service that included the unloading and reloading of the camera with film and the developing and printing of the pictures. With a highly successful advertising campaign featuring the slogan "You press the button—we do the rest," Eastman inaugurated photography for novices and revolutionized the industry. During the next decade numerous improvements were introduced, including a Celluloid base for film and daylight-loading film cartridges. The Eastman Kodak Company's tight patent control on the film system and its policy of continuous innovation helped it establish and maintain an almost exclusive position in the market.

As Eastman Kodak grew in size, it sought to broaden and strengthen its nonamateur product line by acquiring, during the decade from 1898 to 1908, a number of photographic-paper, plate-camera, and dry-plate companies in the United States and in western Europe. Despite the existence of a number of large competitors—including Ansco (a merger of the two old firms of Anthony and Scovill), Defender, Cramer, and Hammer in the United States; Ilford in Britain; and AGFA in Germany—Eastman Kodak held a substantial market share in photographic materials and apparatus both at home and abroad by 1910. George Eastman helped the company maintain this position through his continued emphasis on product quality, innovations, and patents. In recognition of the increasing importance of chemistry and physics to the industry, Eastman established in 1912 the Eastman Kodak Research Laboratory and appointed as its director the British photochemist C. E. Kenneth Mees. Within a decade of its founding the laboratory began to have a direct influence on the output of the Eastman Kodak production lines.

The introduction of the roll-film system stimulated the development of cinematographic apparatus. Early in the 20th century, concurrent with the rapid growth of amateur photography, an American cinematographic industry began to emerge, with innovators in cine projection equipment assuming the initial leadership. At the end of the first decade of the century a number of firms producing apparatus and commercial films combined their patents and other assets to form the Motion Picture Patents Company. It sought, through the control of basic apparatus patents and of the distribution of unexposed film, to limit competition in the motion picture industry, but adverse court decisions in an antitrust suit and a series of product and marketing innovations brought about the demise of the organization within a decade. Large new corporations that integrated production, distribution, and exhibition functions—and employed such innovations as multireel films and motion picture stars—emerged

by 1920 as the new leaders of the cine industry. These included Paramount, Fox, and Loew. The introduction of sound films in the late 1920's altered this structure somewhat as the innovators, Warner and RKO, joined the small group of leaders.

Meanwhile, the rapidly growing demand for raw cine film greatly stimulated film production at Eastman Kodak. After 1909 the production of cine film substantially exceeded the production for still photography. Although the company carefully avoided entry into the professional cine field, the territory of its largest customers, it did introduce home movie equipment with nonflammable film in the early 1920's. From the late 1920's onward the company developed and introduced a series of color processes for motion pictures. During the middle 1940's the motion picture industry enjoyed its greatest success, but soon the introduction of television inaugurated a quarter-century of decline. In response the industry introduced spectaculars; three-dimensional and widescreen productions; new exhibition methods, such as drive-in and shopping-center theaters to replace the giant downtown movie palaces of an earlier era; and, later, low-budget, sensational movies featuring sexuality and violence.

In still photography between World War I and World War II the German industry began to compete with the American. Whereas only minor improvements had been made in cameras for amateurs and in the reflex camera introduced to professional photographers at the turn of the century, German cameramakers, influenced by cinematography, introduced in the early 1920's small 35-mm cameras that appealed to journalists and serious amateur photographers. Also, in the late 1920's Ansco, which had faltered since its founding because of limited capital and technical resources, sold its assets to the I. G. Farben-Industrie and became the American outlet for the research-oriented German photographic industry. With the advent of World War II the U.S. government assumed ownership and operation of the firm, and the government relinquished ownership only in 1965, when the firm became a public corporation, General Aniline and Film (GAF).

In the post–World War II period four developments were of particular importance to the American industry. First, Eastman Kodak, as a result of its research and development, successfully introduced and promoted color-print photography. Second, Japan, manufacturer of high-quality miniature cameras for the serious amateur photographer, developed a dominant influence in that specialized sector of the American and international market. Third, in 1948 the Polaroid Corporation introduced to the market a new system of photography that produced finished prints direct from the camera. Edwin H. Land, designer of the Polaroid camera and principal researcher and shareholder in the firm, developed a well-protected system of patents that created an unassailable market position for his company. Fourth, Eastman Kodak, in response to the Polaroid challenge, introduced a series of Instamatic camera systems that further simplified negative-positive picture-taking. Three of these four developments reflect the importance of the research-and-development strategies and of the mass amateur-market emphasis of the American industry in its maintenance of international dominance in the 1970's despite the competitive efforts of German and Japanese firms.

[Reese V. Jenkins, *Images and Enterprise: Technology and the American Photographic Industry, 1839–1925;* Robert Taft, *Photography and the American Scene.*]

REESE V. JENKINS

PHOTOGRAPHY, MILITARY. Since its invention in 1839 photography has come to have an increasing number of military uses. Both still and motion-picture photography document combat, provide military intelligence and topographic data, aid military training, and help in mapping terrain. The first recorded use of photography for military subjects was a series of daguerreotypes of the Mexican War of 1846–48. The daguerreotypes, taken during battlefield lulls, were used as models for illustrations in popular journals. During the Crimean War (1854–56) the Englishman Roger Fenton was the first person to photograph battlefield scenes under fire. Because of bulky equipment and slow photographic materials, he could photograph only landscapes and portraits.

Most Civil War photographs, such as those of Mathew Brady and his assistants, were taken for a primarily civilian audience, although Union forces attempted on at least one occasion, in 1862, to take aerial photographs from a balloon. Because of technical limitations, it was principally the battlefield dead and ruins that were depicted; few pictures were taken of actual battles. Photography in the Spanish-American War of 1898 was also directed primarily at informing the general public.

World War I witnessed military recognition of the utility and technological improvements of photography. In 1915 the British at Neuve-Chapelle, France, used aerial photographs to prepare trench maps of enemy lines. By the end of the war each of the rival powers was taking thousands of aerial photographs

daily for intelligence purposes, and the art of photo interpretation became an important intelligence skill. Although restricted by the limitations of aircraft, aerial photography advanced during the war because of new high-speed shutters, improved lenses, and light-sensitive materials. Photography also took on new roles; it was used for training and indoctrination films and homefront information and propaganda.

Between the world wars military specialists —notably Gen. George W. Goddard—facilitated the further technical advancement of military photography. The development of lenses with longer focal lengths, high-speed processing equipment, sequence cameras, and infrared and color films made photography more flexible and useful for the military. Motion pictures also came to be used, principally for training and, for public consumption, for documentary purposes. An example of the peacetime, defensive use of military photography is to be found in the sophisticated photography during high-altitude reconnaissance flights over Cuba in 1962 where the presence of Soviet missiles was detected. Photography from satellites circling the earth is one of the latest technological advances to be put to military use.

[G. W. Goddard, *Overview: A Life-Long Adventure in Aerial Photography;* B. Newhall, *The History of Photography 1839–Present.*]

RICHARD A. HUNT

PHRENOLOGY. A theory of physiological psychology that posits that (1) the brain is the organ of mind, (2) the brain is a congeries of discrete organs that control different psychological functions, (3) the power of an organ depends on its size, (4) the shape of the skull corresponds to the organs beneath it, and (5) therefore it is possible to discern an individual's character by examining the size and shape of his skull.

The study was founded by two German physicians, Franz J. Gall and Johann K. Spurzheim, who practiced and lectured in the 1790's and the first two decades of the 19th century. The first American phrenologist, Charles Caldwell of Transylvania University, Lexington, Ky., began to lecture on the subject in 1821, but phrenology did not attract widespread attention until the lecture tours of Spurzheim in 1832 and the Scots phrenologist George Combe between 1838 and 1840. Both were warmly received in the leading intellectual and academic circles of the day.

Because of the claim that phrenology is an infallible guide to human nature and its improvement, it attracted some of the leading intellectuals and reformers of the 1830's and 1840's, including Henry Ward Beecher, Sarah M. Grimké, Samuel Gridley Howe, Horace Greeley, Horace Mann, and, later, Walt Whitman. Phrenologists were especially active in the campaigns for reform in educational, penal, and mental-illness institutions.

Phrenology reached its height as a respectable scientific movement in the 1840's, before experimental data on physiological psychology undermined its scientific credibility; but it flourished as a popular science and system of divination throughout the 19th century, owing largely to the efforts of two brothers, Orson S. and Lorenzo N. Fowler, and their brother-in-law, Samuel R. Wells. The center of the movement in America from 1836 until 1916 was the firm of Fowlers and Wells, with headquarters in New York City. The firm did head readings and character analysis, sold books, pamphlets, and plaster casts, published the *American Phrenological Journal and Miscellany* (1838–1911), trained phrenological lecturers, and even acted as a patent agency. Because of phrenology's emphasis on self-knowledge and improvement, its proponents often have been allied with movements for sex education, temperance, vegetarianism, hydropathy, and woman's rights.

[John B. Davies, *Phrenology: Fad and Science;* Madeleine B. Stern, *Heads and Headliners: The Phrenological Fowlers.*]

T. M. PARSSINEN

PHYSICS. From the colonial period through the early 19th century physics, which was then a branch of natural philosophy, was practiced by only a few Americans, virtually none of whom earned his living primarily in research. Some, like John Winthrop at Harvard, were college professors, who were expected and encouraged only to teach. Others were gentlemanly amateurs with private laboratories. The physics of that day ranged from astronomy and navigation to pneumatics, hydrostatics, mechanics, and optics. In virtually all these subjects Americans followed the intellectual lead of Europeans, especially the British. Along with the practitioners of other sciences, they were also inspired by Francis Bacon, who had urged scholars to study the facts of nature and had taught that knowledge led to power. Thus, American physicists emphasized the accumulation of experimental facts rather than mathematical theorizing, and they made no distinction between abstract and practical research, or what a later generation would call pure and applied science. The archetypical American

physicist was Benjamin Franklin, the retired printer, man of affairs, and deist, who was celebrated for his practical lightning rod as well as for his qualitatively speculative and experimental contributions to electrical science.

From the Jacksonian era through the Civil War, American physics became more specialized, with its subject matter narrowing to geophysics, meteorology, and such topics of physics proper as the older mechanics and the newer heat, light, electricity, and magnetism. The leading American physicist of the period was Joseph Henry, who discovered electromagnetic induction while teaching at the Albany Academy in Albany, N.Y. Later, he became a professor at Princeton and then the first secretary of the Smithsonian Institution. Imbibing the nationalism of the day, Henry worked to advance the study of physics and, indeed, of all science in America. With Henry's support, Alexander Dallas Bache, Franklin's great-grandson and the director of the U.S. Coast Survey, enlarged the scope of the agency to include studies in the geodesy and geophysics of the entire continent. In the 1850's the survey was the largest single employer of physicists in the country. Henry also channeled part of the Smithsonian's income into fundamental research, including research in meteorology. During Henry's lifetime, American physics became more professional; the gentlemanly amateur was gradually superseded by the college-trained physicist who was employed on a college faculty or by the government.

In the quarter-century after the Civil War, many physicists set themselves increasingly apart from utilitarian concerns and embraced the new ethic of "pure" science. At the same time, the reform of higher education gave physics a considerable boost by permitting students to major in the sciences, making laboratory work a standard part of the curriculum, creating programs of graduate studies, and establishing the advancement of knowledge, at least nominally, as an important function of the university and its professors. Between 1865 and 1890 the number of physicists in the United States doubled, to about 150. The profession included Albert A. Michelson, the first American to win the Nobel Prize in physics (1907), who measured the speed of light with unprecedented accuracy and invented the Michelson interferometer during his famed ether drift experiment in 1881. During the late 1870's and the 1880's, Henry A. Rowland won an international reputation for his invention of the Rowland spectral grating and for his painstakingly accurate determinations of the value of the ohm and of the mechanical equivalent of heat. Generally, American physics remained predominantly experimental, with the notable exception of the brilliant theorist Josiah Willard Gibbs of Yale, an authority in thermodynamics and statistical mechanics.

In 1893 Edward L. Nichols of Cornell University inaugurated the *Physical Review,* the first journal devoted to the discipline in the United States. Six years later Arthur Gordon Webster of Clark University helped found the American Physical Society, which in 1913 assumed publication of the *Review.* After the turn of the century, a sharp rise in electrical engineering enrollments created an increased demand for college teachers of physics. Employment opportunities for physicists rose elsewhere also. Some of the major corporations, notably General Electric and American Telephone and Telegraph, opened industrial research laboratories; and the federal government established the National Bureau of Standards, whose charter permitted it to enter a wide area of physical research. Before World War I, the graduation of physics Ph.D.'s climbed steadily, reaching 23 in 1914, when membership in the American Physical Society was close to 700.

Americans had not been responsible for any of the key discoveries of the 1890's—X rays, radioactivity, and the electron—that introduced the age of atomic studies. Like many of their colleagues in Europe, the older American members of the profession were disturbed by the development in the early 20th century of the quantum theory of radiation and the theory of relativity. But the younger scientists turned to the new atomic research fields, although not immediately to the new theories, with growing interest and enthusiasm. At the University of Chicago, Robert A. Millikan demonstrated that all electrons are identically charged particles (1909) and then more accurately measured the electronic charge (1913). Richard Tolman of the University of Illinois and Gilbert N. Lewis of the Massachusetts Institute of Technology delivered the first American paper on the theory of relativity (1908). By the beginning of World War I, modernist physicists like Millikan were moving into the front rank of the profession, which was focusing increasingly, at its meetings and in its publications, on the physics of the quantized atom.

During the war, physicists worked for the military in various ways, most notably in the development of systems and devices for the detection of submarines and for the location of artillery. Their success in this area helped bolster the argument that physics, like chemistry, could produce practical and, hence, economically valuable results. Partly in recognition of that fact, industrial research laboratories hired more physicists in the 1920's. Moreover, the funding for physical research rose considerably in both state and private universities. During the 1920's, about 650 Americans received doctorates in physics; and a number of them received postdoctoral fellowships from the International Education Board of the Rockefeller Foundation and from the National Research Council. After studying with the leading physicists in the United States and Europe, where the revolution in quantum mechanics was proceeding apace, many of these young scientists were well prepared for the pursuit of theoretical research.

By the end of the 1920's, the United States had more than 2,300 physicists, including a small but significant influx of Europeans, including Paul Epstein, Fritz Zwicky, Samuel Goudsmit, and George Uhlenbeck, who had joined American university faculties. During that decade, Nobel Prizes in physics were awarded to Millikan (1923), director (1921) of the Norman Bridge Laboratory of Physics and chief executive at the California Institute of Technology, and to Arthur H. Compton (1927) of the University of Chicago for his quantum interpretation of the collision of X rays and electrons. At the Bell Telephone Laboratories, Clinton J. Davisson performed the research in electron diffraction for which he became a Nobel laureate. By the early 1930's the American physics profession compared favorably in experimental achievement with its counterparts in Europe; and in theoretical studies its potential, although not yet its accomplishment, had also reached the first rank.

During the 1930's the interest of physicists shifted from the atom to the nucleus and to what were later called elementary particles. In 1932, while conducting research for which they would later win Nobel Prizes, Carl Anderson of the California Institute of Technology identified the positron in cosmic rays, and at the University of California at Berkeley, Ernest O. Lawrence successfully accelerated protons to one million volts of energy with his new cyclotron. Despite the depression, which at first reduced the funds available for physics research, U.S. physicists managed to construct cyclotrons, arguing that the exploration of the nucleus might yield the secret of atomic energy or that the radioactive products of cyclotron bombardment might be medically useful, especially in the treatment of cancer. All the while, more Americans earned Ph.D.'s in physics, and the profession was further enriched by such refugees from Nazi Europe as Albert Einstein, Hans Bethe, Felix Bloch,

Enrico Fermi, Emilio Segrè, and Edward Teller. By the end of the 1930's, the American physics profession, with more than 3,500 members, led the world in both theoretical and experimental research.

During World War II, physicists, mobilized primarily under the Office of Scientific Research and Development, contributed decisively to the development of microwave radar, the proximity fuze, and solid-fuel rockets. They also worked on the atomic bomb in various laboratories of the Manhattan Project, notably Los Alamos, N.Mex., which was directed by J. Robert Oppenheimer. Equally important, physicists began advising the military how best to use the new weapons tactically and, in some cases, strategically. After World War II, American physicists became prominent figures in the government's strategic advisory councils, and they played a central role in the debates over nuclear and thermonuclear weapons programs in the 1950's and 1960's. Recognized as indispensable to the national defense and welfare, physics and physicists received massive governmental support in the postwar decades, notably from the National Science Foundation, the Atomic Energy Commission, and the Office of Naval Research. Thus, the profession expanded rapidly, totaling more than 32,000 by 1972. About half of all American physicists were employed in industry, most of the rest in universities and colleges, and the remainder in federal laboratories. Many academic physicists did their research in groups organized around large, highly energetic particle accelerators.

With these accelerators, American physicists were among the world's leaders in uncovering experimental data about elementary particles, one of the central fields of postwar physics. Their achievements also included the work of Murray Gell-Mann in particle theory, Julian Schwinger and Richard P. Feynman in quantum electrodynamics, and Tsung Dao Lee and Chen Ning Yang in the nonconservation of parity. American physicists contributed significantly to such other important fields as plasma and low-temperature physics as well as astrophysics and relativity. In applied physics, William Shockley and John Bardeen invented the transistor and Charles H. Townes played a major role in the development of the laser. Between 1944 and 1974 American physicists won or shared in seventeen Nobel Prizes for both experimental and theoretical work.

[Herbert Childs, *An American Genius: The Life of Ernest Orlando Lawrence;* Stanley Coben, "The Scientific Establishment and the Transmission of Quantum Mechanics to the United States, 1919–1932," *American Historical Review,* vol. 76 (1971); Daniel J. Kevles, "On the Flaws of American Physics: A Social and Institutional Analysis," in George H. Daniels, ed., *Nineteenth-Century American Science,* and "Robert A. Millikan," *Dictionary of Scientific Biography;* Physics Survey Committee, National Research Council, *Physics in Perspective;* Nathan Reingold, "Joseph Henry," *Dictionary of Scientific Biography.*]

DANIEL J. KEVLES

PHYSICS, HIGH-ENERGY, the newest and most expensive branch of physics, is the study of elementary particles, the smallest bits of matter known to exist. Dozens of these particles had been discovered and studied by the mid-1970's. High-energy physics developed from nuclear physics, which had developed from atomic physics. These two branches of physics remain active, but are studied more for practical application than for scientific reasons. High-energy physics is the frontier of knowledge in physics and has no currently conceivable practical application for its research.

Elementary particles are produced naturally by the sun and other sources and reach the earth as "cosmic rays," which are detected and recorded in natural settings rather than in laboratories. These particles are available at much higher energy levels than can be produced in the laboratory, but they are difficult to detect because the "stream" of particles cannot be guided to desirable targets. Also, interaction of such particles with other physical matter in the atmosphere produces additional particles, thus complicating their detection and measurement. Particles must collide with the nucleus of the target matter in order to be observed, and it is theorized that one particle, the neutrino, may pass directly through 25,000 miles of earth without hitting the nucleus of another atom. Since most of an atom is empty space, the neutrino can pass between the electrons and nuclei of atoms.

In high-energy-physics laboratories, particle accelerators produce particles in large numbers under conditions that allow controlled observation. In general, the more powerful accelerators produce more particles per pulse of the machine, and more pulses of the machine per minute. Since World War II the United States has led in the field of high-energy physics because it has constructed more and bigger accelerators than any other country.

Early progress in atomic and nuclear physics was made primarily in England, at the universities of Manchester and Cambridge. Ernest Rutherford, a native of New Zealand who studied in England, proved in 1918 that an atom could be split into an electron and a nucleus. His students and colleagues in England developed methods in the 1920's for detecting elementary particles and by 1932 had built equipment that produced elementary particles in the laboratory. At this time, research in the United States was not developing in any great measure in any field, and physics was no exception.

A few years before World War II, American scientists began to build particle accelerators. Funds for these machines, expensive both to build and to operate, were obtained largely from private foundations for capital expenditures and from university budgets for operation. The University of California at Berkeley, under the direction of Ernest O. Lawrence, planned and built several machines, each more sophisticated and larger than its predecessor.

During World War II, British and American scientists informed their governments of the implications of nuclear physics for the war effort; and because Great Britain was not completely safe from the threat of invasion, some British scientists came to the United States and developed their ideas with American colleagues.

High-energy physics demands large-scale organization and support. The viability of this kind of organization for scientific research was evident during the Manhattan Project, which supported various laboratories, including the large one it operated at Los Alamos, N.Mex. After the war, the U.S. government continued to support nuclear physics research that focused more on higher energy levels and on elementary particles than on the problems of nuclear structure.

Financial support for such research increased greatly after 1945. At first, universities had their own accelerators, which were funded mostly by the Atomic Energy Commission, later joined by the National Science Foundation. These accelerators provided energies in the range of 100–700 million electron volts. When larger accelerators and supporting equipment were required, the expense did not seem justified or desirable for the exclusive use of one university. Thus, universities formed consortia and operated laboratories jointly for their own and other organizations' scientists. These jointly owned accelerators produced energies ranging up to 30 billion electron volts. The 30 billion electron-volt accelerator of the Brookhaven National Laboratory (Upton, N.Y.) has a diameter of 843 feet and has 240 magnets weighing a total of 4,400 tons. It delivers 25 pulses per minute with 2×10^{11} protons per pulse, and each proton travels 180,000 miles in the accelerator before being ejected into a target area.

The largest accelerator in the world by 1975 was at the Fermi National Accelerator Laboratory in Batavia, Ill. It has a design capability of 400 billion electron volts, with possible conversion to 1,000 billion electron volts. It cost about $250 million to build and at least $35 million annually to operate, even at less than full capacity. Since the construction of this accelerator, funds have shifted to fewer and larger accelerators. Besides the Fermi Laboratory, the Atomic Energy Commission operates three other national laboratories, but by the mid-1970's the operations time of their accelerators had been reduced to half. Although most of the advances in high-energy physics have been in experimental research and while most American winners of Nobel Prizes for high-energy physics research have been experimentalists, American theorists have also won Nobel Prizes, including Murray Gell-Mann and Richard P. Feynman. Despite excellent theoretical scientists, by the mid-1970's there had been little advance in accepted theory because the nature and behavior of elementary particles were yet to be understood.

[M. S. Livingston and J. P. Blewett, *Particle Accelerators;* C. N. Yang, *Elementary Particles.*]

JERRY GASTON

PHYSICS, NUCLEAR. The age-old goal of physicists has been to understand the nature of matter and energy. Nowhere in the 20th century have the boundaries of such knowledge been further extended than in the field of nuclear physics. From an obscure corner of submicroscopic particle research, nuclear physics has become the most prominent and fruitful area of physical investigation because of its fundamental insights and its applications.

In the first decade of the 20th century J. J. Thomson's discovery of the electron at Cambridge University's Cavendish Laboratory changed the concept of the atom as a solid, homogeneous entity—a "billiard ball"—to one of a sphere of positive electrification studded throughout with negative electrons. This "plum pudding" atomic model, with a different number of electrons for each element, could not account for the large-angle scattering seen when alpha particles from naturally decaying radioactive sources were allowed to strike target materials. Thomson argued that the alpha particles suffered a series of small deflections in their encounters with the target atoms, resulting in some cases in a sizable deviation from their initial path. But in the Manchester laboratory of Thomson's former pupil Ernest Rutherford,

297

Hans Geiger and Ernest Marsden, between 1909 and 1911, produced scattering data that showed too many alpha particles were bent through angles too large for such an explanation to be valid.

Instead of a series of small deflections, Rutherford suggested early in 1911 that large-angle scattering could occur in a single encounter between an alpha particle and a target atom if the mass of the atom were concentrated in a tiny volume. While the atomic diameter was of the order of 10^{-8} centimeters, this atomic core (or nucleus), containing virtually the atom's entire mass, measured only about 10^{-12} centimeters. The atom, therefore, consisted largely of empty space, with electrons circulating about the central nucleus. When an alpha-particle projectile closely approached a target nucleus, it encountered concentrated electrostatic repulsion sufficient to deflect it more than just a few degrees from its path.

The Danish physicist Niels Bohr absorbed these concepts while visiting Rutherford's laboratory and in 1913 gave mathematical formulation to the rules by which the orbital electrons behaved. The order and arrangement of these electrons were seen to be responsible for the chemical properties exhibited by different elements. Pursuit of this field led to modern atomic physics, including its quantum mechanical explanation, and bore fruit earlier than did studies in nuclear physics. Radioactivity was recognized as a nuclear phenomenon; and the emission of alpha particles, known by then to be nuclei of helium atoms; beta particles, long recognized as electrons; and gamma rays, an electromagnetic radiation, reopened the question of whether atoms were constructed from fundamental building blocks. The work in 1913 of Henry G.-J. Moseley, another former student of Rutherford's, showed that an element's position in the periodic table (its atomic number), and not its atomic weight, determined its characteristics. Moreover, he established that the number of positive charges on the nucleus (equal to its atomic number) was balanced by an equal number of orbital electrons. Since atomic weights (A) were (except for hydrogen) higher than atomic numbers (Z), the atom's nuclear mass was considered to be composed of A positively charged particles, called protons, and A-Z electrons to neutralize enough protons for a net nuclear charge of Z.

In 1919, Rutherford announced another major discovery. Radioactivity had long been understood as a process of transmutation from one type of atom into another, occurring spontaneously. Neither temperature, nor pressure, nor chemical combination could alter the rate of decay of a given radioelement or change the identity of its daughter product. Now, however, Rutherford showed that he could deliberately cause transmutations. His were not among the elements at the high end of the periodic table, where natural radioactivity is commonly found, but were among the lighter elements. By allowing energetic alpha particles from decaying radium C' to fall upon nitrogen molecules, he observed the production of hydrogen nuclei, or protons, and an oxygen isotope. The reaction may be written as

$$\frac{4}{2}\text{He} + \frac{14}{7}\text{N} \rightarrow \frac{1}{1}\text{H} + \frac{17}{8}\text{O},$$

where the superscript represents the atomic weight and the subscript the atomic number, or charge.

During the first half of the 1920's, Rutherford, now at Cambridge, where he had succeeded Thomson, was able to effect transmutations in many of the lighter elements. (In this work he was assisted primarily by James Chadwick.) But elements heavier than potassium would not yield to the alpha particles from their strongest radioactive source. The greater nuclear charge on the heavier elements repelled the alpha particles, preventing an approach close enough for transmutation. This finding suggested that projectile particles of energies or velocities higher than those found in naturally decaying radioelements were required to overcome the potential barriers of target nuclei. Consequently, various means of accelerating particles were devised.

In 1920, William D. Harkins, a physical chemist at the University of Chicago, conceived that the existence of a neutron would simplify certain problems in the construction of nuclei. In the same year, Rutherford (on the basis of incorrectly interpreted experimental evidence) also postulated the existence of such a neutral particle, the mass of which was comparable to that of the proton. Throughout the 1920's he, and especially Chadwick, searched unsuccessfully for this particle. In 1931, Walther Bothe and H. Becker, in Germany, detected a penetrating radiation when beryllium was bombarded by alpha particles, which they concluded consisted of energetic gamma rays. In France, Irène Curie and her husband, Frédéric Joliot, placed paraffin in the path of this radiation and detected protons ejected from that hydrogenous compound. They, too, believed that gamma rays were being produced and that these somehow transferred sufficient energy to the hydrogen atoms to break their chemical bonds. Chadwick learned of this work early in 1932 and immediately recognized that beryllium was yielding not gamma rays but the long-elusive neutron and that this particle was encountering protons of similar mass, transferring much of its kinetic energy and momentum to them at the time of collision. Since the neutron is uncharged, it is not repelled by atomic nuclei. Consequently, it can enter easily into reactions when it finds itself near a nucleus; otherwise it travels great distances through matter, suffering no electrostatic attractions or repulsions.

Werner Heisenberg, in Leipzig, renowned for his articulation of quantum mechanics and its application to atomic physics, in 1932 applied his mathematical techniques to nuclear physics, successfully explaining that atomic nuclei are composed not of protons and electrons but of protons and neutrons. For a given element, Z protons furnish the positive charge, while A-Z neutrons create a mass equal to the atomic weight A. Radioactive beta decay, formerly a strong argument for the existence of electrons in the nucleus, was now interpreted differently: the beta particles were formed only at the instant of decay, as a neutron changed into a proton. The reverse reaction could occur also, with the emission of a positive electron, or positron, as a proton changed into a neutron. This reaction was predicted by the Cambridge University theoretician P. A. M. Dirac and was experimentally detected in 1932 by Carl D. Anderson of the California Institute of Technology in cloud-chamber track photographs of cosmic-ray interactions. Two years later the Joliot-Curies noted the same result in certain radioactive decay patterns. The "fundamental" particles now consisted of the proton and neutron, nucleons with atomic masses of about 1, and of the electron and positron, with masses of about 1/1,840 of a nucleon.

The existence of yet another particle, the neutrino, was first suggested in 1931 by Wolfgang Pauli of Zurich in an address before the American Physical Society. When a nucleus is transmuted and beta particles emitted, there are specific changes in energy. Yet, unlike the case of alpha decay, beta particles exhibited a continuous energy distribution, with only the maximum energy seen as that of the reaction. The difference between the energy of a given beta particle and the maximum was thought to be carried off by a neutrino, the properties of which—zero mass and no charge—accounted for the difficulty of detecting it. In 1934, Enrico Fermi presented a quantitative theory of beta decay incorporating Pauli's hypothesis. Gamma radiation, following either alpha or beta decay, was interpreted as being emitted from the daughter nucleus as it went from an excited level to its ground state.

The neutron, the greatest of these keys to an understanding of the nucleus, helped to clarify other physical problems besides nuclear charge and weight. In 1913, Kasimir Fajans in Karlsruhe and Frederick Soddy in Glasgow had fit the numerous radioelements into the periodic table, showing that in several cases more than one radioelement must be placed in the same box. Mesothorium I, thorium X, and actinium X, for example, all were chemically identical to radium; that is, they were isotopes. This finding meant they each had 88 protons but had, respectively, 140, 136, and 135 neutrons. Also, in the pre–World War I period Thomson showed that nonradioactive elements exist in isotopic forms—neon, for example, having atomic weights of 20 and 22. His colleague F. W. Aston perfected the mass spectrograph, with which, during the 1920's, he accurately measured the masses of numerous atomic species. It was revealed that these masses were generally near, but not exactly, whole numbers, the difference being termed by Harkins and E. D. Wilson, as early as 1915, the "packing effect" and modified by Aston in 1927 as the "packing fraction." Nor, as was seen after 1932, were atomic masses the sums of Z proton masses and A-Z neutron masses, the difference being termed the "mass defect." The concept of nuclear building blocks (protons and neutrons) was retained; however, it was seen that a certain amount of mass was converted into a nuclear binding energy to overcome the mutual repulsion of the protons. This binding energy is of the order of a million times greater than the energies binding atoms in compounds or in stable crystals, which indicates why nuclear reactions involve so much more energy than chemical reactions.

The existence of deuterium, a hydrogen isotope of mass 2, present in ordinary (mass 1) hydrogen to the extent of about 1 part in 4,500, was suggested in 1931 by Raymond T. Birge and Donald H. Menzel at the University of California at Berkeley and shortly thereafter was confirmed by Harold C. Urey and George M. Murphy at Columbia University, in collaboration with Ferdinand G. Brickwedde of the National Bureau of Standards. The heavy-hydrogen atom's nucleus, called the deuteron, proved to be exceptionally useful: it entered into some nuclear reactions more readily than did the proton.

Shortly after their discovery in 1932, neutrons were used as projectiles to effect nuclear transmutations by Norman Feather in England and Harkins, David Gans, and Henry W. Newson at Chicago. Two years later the Joliot-Curies reported the discovery of yet another process of transmutation: artificial radioactivity. A target not normally radioactive was bombarded with alpha particles but continued to exhibit nuclear changes even after the projectile beam was stopped. Such bombardment has permitted the production of about 1,100 nuclear species beyond the 320 or so found occurring in nature.

During the mid-1930's, Fermi and his colleagues in Rome were most successful in causing transmutations with neutrons, particularly after they discovered the greater likelihood of the reactions occurring when the neutrons' velocities were reduced by prior collisions. When uranium, the heaviest known element, was bombarded with neutrons, several beta-particle-emitting substances were produced, which Fermi reasoned must be artificial elements beyond uranium in the periodic table. The reaction may be expressed as

$$\,_0^1 n + \,_{92}^{238}U \rightarrow \,_{92}^{239}U \rightarrow \,_{93}^{239}X + \,_{-1}^{0}e,$$

with a possible subsequent decay of

$$\,_{93}^{239}X \rightarrow \,_{94}^{239}Y + \,_{-1}^{0}e.$$

But radiochemical analyses of the trace amounts of new substances placed them in unexpected groupings in the periodic table, and, even worse, Otto Hahn and Fritz Strassmann, in Berlin, toward the end of 1938, were unable to separate them chemically from elements found in the middle part of the periodic table. It seemed that the so-called transuranium elements had chemical properties identical to barium, lanthanum, and cerium. Hahn's longtime colleague Lise Meitner, then a refugee in Sweden, and her nephew Otto R. Frisch, at that time in Bohr's Copenhagen laboratory, early in 1939 saw that the neutrons were not adhering to the uranium nuclei, followed by beta decay, but were causing the uranium nuclei to split (fission) into two roughly equal particles. They recognized that these fission fragments suffered beta decay in their movement toward conditions of greater internal stability.

With the accurate atomic-mass values then available, it was apparent that in fission a considerable amount of mass is converted into energy; that is, the mass of the neutron plus uranium is greater than that of the fragments. The potential for utilizing such energy was widely recognized in 1939, assuming that additional neutrons were released in the fission process and that at least one of the neutrons would rupture another uranium nucleus in a chain reaction. The United States, Great Britain, Canada, France, Russia, Germany, and Japan all made efforts in this direction during World War II. A controlled chain reaction was first produced in Fermi's "pile," or "reactor," in 1942 at the University of Chicago, and an uncontrolled or explosive chain reaction was first tested under the direction of J. Robert Oppenheimer in 1945 in New Mexico. Among the scientific feats of the atomic-bomb project was the production at Berkeley in 1940–41 of the first man-made transuranium elements, neptunium and plutonium, by teams under Edwin M. McMillan and Glenn Seaborg, respectively.

Like the fission of heavy elements, the joining together (fusion) of light elements is also a process in which mass is converted into energy. This reaction, experimentally studied as early as 1934 by Rutherford and his colleagues and theoretically treated in 1938 by George Gamow and Edward Teller, both then at George Washington University, has not been controlled successfully for appreciable periods of time; but its uncontrolled form is represented in the hydrogen bomb, first tested in 1952.

The growth of "big science," measured by its cost and influence, is manifest not only in weaponry and power-producing reactors but also in huge particle-accelerating machines. Alpha particles from naturally decaying radioelements carry a kinetic energy of between about 4 and 10 million electron volts (MeV). But, as only one projectile in several hundred thousand is likely to come close enough to a target nucleus to affect it, reactions occur relatively infrequently, even with concentrated radioactive sources. Cosmic radiation, which possesses far greater energy, has an even lower probability of interacting with a target nucleus. Means were sought for furnishing a copious supply of charged particles that could be accelerated to energies sufficient to overcome the nuclear electrostatic repulsion. This feat would both shorten the time of experiments and increase the number of reactions. Since electrical technology had little or no previous application in the range of hundreds of thousands or millions of volts, these were pioneering efforts in engineering as well as in physics.

In the late 1920's, Charles C. Lauritsen and H. R. Crane at the California Institute of Technology succeeded with a cascade transformer in putting 700,000 volts across an X-ray tube. Merle A. Tuve, at the Carnegie Institution of Washington, in 1930 produced protons in a vacuum tube with energies of more than a million volts. The next year, at Princeton, Robert J. Van de Graaff built the first of his electrostatic generators, with a maximum potential of about 1.5 million volts. In 1932, Ernest O. Lawrence and his associates at Berkeley constructed a magnetic resonance device, called a cyclotron because a magnetic field bent the charged particles in a circular path. The novelty of this machine lay in its ability to impart high energies to particles in a series of steps, during each revolution, thereby avoiding the need for great voltages across the terminals, as in other accelerators. The cyclotron soon exceeded the energies of other machines and became the most commonly used "atom smasher."

Although Americans excelled in the mechanical ability that could produce such a variety of machines, they were only beginning to develop theoretical and experimental research to use them. They also lacked the driving force of Rutherford. Since 1929, John D. Cockcroft and E. T. S. Walton had been building and rebuilding, testing and calibrating their voltage multiplier in the Cavendish Laboratory. Rutherford finally insisted that they perform a real experiment on it. The Russian George Gamow, and independently Edward U. Condon at Princeton with R. W. Gurney of England, had applied quantum mechanics to consideration of the nucleus. Gamow concluded that particles need not surmount the potential energy barrier of about 25 MeV, for an element of high atomic number, to penetrate or escape from the nucleus, but these particles could "tunnel" through the barrier at far lower energies. The lower the energy, the less likely it was that tunneling would occur, yet an abundant supply of projectiles might produce enough reactions to be recorded. With protons accelerated to only about one-fourth the height of the potential barrier, Cockcroft and Walton, in 1932, found lithium disintegrated into two alpha particles in the reaction

$$\mathrm{_1^1H + {_3^7}Li \rightarrow {_2^4}He + {_2^4}He.}$$

Not only was this the first completely artificial transmutation (Rutherford's transmutation in 1919 had used alpha-particle projectiles from naturally decaying radioelements), but in 1933 Kenneth T. Bainbridge's measurements at Harvard of the products' range, and therefore energy, combined with a precise value of the mass lost in the reaction, verified for the first time Albert Einstein's famous $E = mc^2$ equation.

The United States continued to pioneer in machine construction, often with medical and biological financial support: Donald W. Kerst of the University of Illinois built a circular electron accelerator, called a betatron, in 1940, and Luis W. Alvarez of Berkeley designed a linear proton accelerator in 1946. D. W. Fry in England perfected a linear electron accelerator

(1946), as did W. W. Hansen at Stanford. Since particles traveling at velocities near that of light experience a relativistic mass increase, the synchrotron principle, which uses a varying magnetic field or radio frequency to control the particle orbits, was developed in 1945 by Vladimir I. Veksler in Russia and by McMillan at Berkeley. By the 1970's, large accelerators could attain hundreds of millions, or even several billion, electron volts and were used to produce numerous elementary particles. Below this realm of high-energy or particle physics, recognized as a separate field since the early 1950's, nuclear physics research continued to be pursued in the more modest MeV range.

Besides the methods of inducing nuclear reactions and the measurements of the masses and energies involved, questions arose about what actually occurs during a transformation. Traditional instruments—electroscopes, electrometers, scintillating screens, electrical counters—and even the more modern electronic devices were of limited value. Visual evidence was most desirable. At Chicago in 1923, Harkins attempted unsuccessfully to photograph cloud-chamber tracks of Rutherford's 1919 transmutation of nitrogen. In 1921, Rutherford's pupil P. M. S. Blackett examined 400,000 tracks and found that 8 exhibited a Y-shaped fork, indicating that the alpha-particle projectile was absorbed by the nitrogen target into a compound nucleus, which immediately became an isotope of oxygen by the emission of a proton. The three branches of the Y consisted of the incident alpha and the two products, the initially neutral and slow-moving nitrogen having no track. Had the now-discredited alternative explanation of the process been true, namely, that the alpha particle merely bounced off the nitrogen nucleus, which then decayed according to the reaction

$$\mathrm{_2^4He + {_7^{14}}N \rightarrow {_2^4}He + {_1^1}H + {_6^{13}}C,}$$

a track of four branches would have been seen.

Experimental work by Harkins and Gans in 1935 and theoretical contributions by Bohr the next year clearly established the compound nucleus as the intermediate stage in most medium-energy nuclear reactions. Alvarez designed a velocity selector for monoenergetic neutrons that allowed greater precision in reaction calculations, while Gregory Breit at the University of Wisconsin and the Hungarian refugee Eugene P. Wigner at Princeton in 1936 published a formula that explained the theory of preferential absorption of neutrons (their cross sections): If the neutrons have an energy such that a compound nucleus can be formed at or near one of its permitted energy levels, there is a high probability that these neutrons will be captured.

It was recognized that the forces holding nucleons together are stronger than electrostatic, gravitational, and weak interaction (beta particle–neutrino) forces and that they operate over shorter ranges, namely, the nuclear dimension of 10^{-13} centimeters. In 1936, Bohr made an analogy between nuclear forces and those within a drop of liquid. Both are short range, acting strongly on those nucleons/molecules in their immediate neighborhood but having no influence on those further away in the nucleus/drop. The total energy and volume of a nucleus/drop are directly proportional to the number of constituent nucleons/molecules, and any excess energy of a constituent is rapidly shared among the others. This liquid-drop model of the nucleus, which meshed well with Bohr's understanding of the compound nucleus stage during reactions, treated the energy states of the nucleus as a whole. Its great success, discovered by Bohr in collaboration with John A. Wheeler of Princeton (1939), in explaining fission as a deformation of the spherical drop into a dumbbell shape that breaks apart at the narrow connection, assured its wide acceptance for a number of years.

The strongest opposition to this liquid-drop interpretation came from proponents of the nuclear-shell model, who felt that nucleons retain much of their individuality, that, for example, they move within their own well-defined orbits. In 1932, James H. Bartlett of the University of Illinois, by analogy to the grouping of orbital electrons, suggested that protons and neutrons in nuclei also form into shells. This idea was developed in France and Germany, where it was shown in 1937 that data on magnetic moments of nuclei conform with a shell-model interpretation.

To explain the very fine splitting (hyperfine structure) of lines in the optical spectra of some elements—spectra produced largely by the extranuclear electrons—several European physicists in the 1920's had suggested that atomic nuclei possess mechanical and magnetic moments relating to their rotation and configuration. From the 1930's on, a number of techniques were developed for measuring such nuclear moments—including the radio-frequency resonance method of Columbia University's I. I. Rabi—and from the resulting data certain regularities appeared. For example, nuclei with an odd number of particles have half units of spin and nuclei with an even number of particles have integer units of spin, while nuclei with an even number of protons and an even number of neutrons have zero spin. Evidence such as this suggested some sort of organization of the nucleons.

With the shell model overshadowed by the success of the liquid-drop model, and with much basic research interrupted by World War II, it was not until 1949 that Maria Goeppert Mayer at the University of Chicago and O. Haxel, J. H. D. Jensen, and H. E. Suess in Germany showed the success of the shell model in explaining the so-called magic numbers of nucleons: 2, 8, 20, 50, 82, and 126. Elements having these numbers of nucleons, known to be unusually stable, were assumed to have closed shells in the nucleus. Lead-208, for example, is "doubly magic," having 82 protons and 126 neutrons. More recent interpretations, incorporating features of both liquid-drop and shell models, are called the "collective" and "unified" models.

Aside from the question of the structure of the nucleus, after it was recognized that similarly charged particles were confined in a tiny volume, the problem existed of explaining the nature of the short-range forces that overcame their electrical repulsion. In 1935, Hideki Yukawa in Japan reasoned that just as electrical force is transmitted between charged bodies in an electromagnetic field by a particle called a photon, there might be an analogous nuclear-field particle. Accordingly, the meson, as it was called (with a predicted mass about 200 times that of the electron), was soon found in cosmic rays by Carl D. Anderson and Seth H. Neddermeyer. The existence of this particle was confirmed by 1938. But in 1947, Fermi, Teller, and Victor F. Weisskopf in the United States concluded that this mu meson, or muon, did not interact with matter in the necessary way to serve as a field particle; and S. Sakata and T. Inoue in Japan, and independently Hans A. Bethe at Cornell and Robert E. Marshak at the University of Rochester, suggested that yet another meson existed. Within the same year, Cecil F. Powell and G. P. S. Occhialini in Bristol, England, found the pi meson, or pion—a particle slightly heavier than the muon into which it decays and one that meets field-particle requirements—in cosmic-ray tracks. Neutrons and protons were thought to interact through the continual transfer of positive, negative, and neutral pions between them.

Although nuclear physics is sometimes said to have been born during the early 1930's—a period of many remarkable discoveries—it can more appropriately be dated from 1911 or 1919. What is true of the 1930's is that by this time nuclear physics was clearly defined as a major field. The percentage of nuclear-physics papers published in *Physical Review* rose dramatically; other measures of the field's prominence included research funds directed to it, the number of doctoral degrees awarded, and the number of fellowships tendered by such patrons as the Rockefeller Foundation. Although they were by no means the only scientists fashioning the subject in the United States, Ernest O. Lawrence at Berkeley and Oppenheimer at the California Institute of Technology and Berkeley were dominating figures in building American schools of experimental and theoretical research, respectively. This domestic activity was immeasurably enriched in the 1930's by the stream of refugee physicists from totalitarian Europe—men such as Bethe, Fermi, Leo Szilard, Wigner, Teller, Weisskopf, James Franck, Gamow, Emilio Segrè, and, of course, Einstein. Prominent Europeans had earlier taught at the summer schools for theoretical physics held at several American universities; now many came permanently. American domination of nuclear physics in the postwar decades resulted, therefore, from a combination of the wartime concentration of research in the United States and the simultaneous disruptions in Europe and from a combination of rising domestic abilities and exceptional foreign talent, financed by a government that had seen (at least for a while) that basic research was applicable to national needs.

[Samuel Glasstone, *Sourcebook on Atomic Energy;* M. Stanley Livingston, ed., *The Development of High-Energy Accelerators;* Charles Weiner, ed., *Exploring the History of Nuclear Physics;* Victor F. Weisskopf, *Physics in the Twentieth Century.*]

LAWRENCE BADASH

PHYSICS, SOLID-STATE. The term "solid state," although popularized by advertisers' tags on transistorized devices, refers properly to a field of basic research that has had broad practical application; namely, the branch of physics that deals with properties of condensed matter—solids and liquids. The multitude of properties studied (structure, cohesion, response to force, torque, heat, light, electric or magnetic fields) and the variety of materials that can be explored give this field enormous scope. It embraces many independent subfields, including the study of crystals, semiconductors, metallic surfaces, and the phenomenon of superconductivity.

"Modern" solid-state physics is based on the concepts and techniques of 20th-century atomic theory and quantum mechanics; solids and liquids are viewed as aggregates of atoms and molecules. Earlier concepts failed to explain the characteristic features of specific solids and liquids. Three events in the first quarter of the 20th century opened new dimensions for the study of solid-state physics: the application to solid-state phenomena (1907) of Albert Einstein's concept that light is quantized in tiny bundles called photons, the discovery that crystals diffract X rays (1912), and the development of a new quantum mechanics and quantum statistics (1925–26).

When a solid is heated, its temperature varies according to its specific heat, that is, the amount of heat added to a unit mass divided by its temperature change. Experiments show that for most simple solids, this ratio goes to zero in a characteristic way as the temperature approaches absolute zero. But this phenomenon could not be explained satisfactorily before 1907. In that year Einstein applied radical new ideas concerning the quantized nature of radiation to a model of a solid in which atoms were assumed to vibrate independently at the same frequency. At that time there were no definitive observations to confirm such a model. The qualitative success of Einstein's theory of specific heats, especially as refined a few years later by the Dutch physicist Peter Debye and then by the German physicist Max Born, in collaboration with the Hungarian physicist Theodore von Kármán, confirmed the quantum theory and its application to solid-state phenomena.

In 1912 scientists discovered an experimental method of "seeing" the internal arrangement of atoms in solids. Max von Laue, Walter Fredericks, and Paul Knipping, working in Munich, showed that X rays produce diffraction patterns when passed through crystals. These patterns were interpreted as the result of the scattering of the X rays by atoms arranged in a lattice. Many other crystal diffraction studies followed, including an extensive series by the British father-and-son team of Sir Lawrence and William Henry Bragg. Between 1925 and 1927 two American researchers, Clinton Davisson and Lester Germer, performed experiments at the Bell Telephone Laboratories in New York City in which beams of electrons were diffracted by crystals, confirming the French physicist Louis de Broglie's then controversial theory that under certain conditions particles behave like waves. By 1927 X-ray diffraction studies had revealed almost as much information about the arrangement of atoms in many simple crystals as was known a half-century later.

Nevertheless, there was still no adequate overview

for the physics of solids. Even the most promising theories—such as the free-electron theory of the German physicist Paul Drude and the Dutch physicist Hendrik Lorentz—contained problems that could not be resolved until quantum mechanics and quantum statistics were applied to the study of solids. Quantum mechanics was invented between 1925 and 1926 by the German physicist Werner Heisenberg and the Austrian physicist Erwin Schrödinger, based on more than a decade of intensive work by the Danish physicist Niels Bohr. A quantum statistics that could be applied to the particles in condensed matter was invented in 1926 by the Italian physicist Enrico Fermi and the British physicist Paul Dirac.

Between 1928 and 1933, a remarkably productive period in solid-state physics, new conceptual and mathematical tools were applied to the study of solids and liquids. Many leading European and American physicists were involved in this work, including Heisenberg, Wolfgang Pauli, Rudolf Peierls, Lothar Nordheim, Arnold Sommerfeld, Felix Bloch, Lev Landau, Yakov Frenkel, Léon Brillouin, Sir Alan Wilson, Eugene Wigner, John Van Vleck, and John Slater. A major breakthrough occurred in 1933 when Wigner and his student Frederick Seitz at Princeton developed the first successful quantum mechanics approach to the electronic structure of crystals. By 1934 some of the most dramatic properties of solids, such as magnetism and the electrical and thermal conductivities of metals, had received qualitative (if not quantitative) explanation. A concept of energy bands separated by gaps, which governed the distribution of electron energies in solids, helped explain why metals conduct electricity while insulators do not and why the electrical conductivity of a class of materials called semiconductors varies with temperature.

But the models of the new theory remained idealizations, at best applicable only to pure and perfect materials. Physicists could not verify their results with sufficient accuracy to extend them because in the 1930's the available materials contained far too many impurities and imperfections. By 1934 many theorists were turning their attention to other fields, including nuclear physics and quantum electrodynamics, which offered new intellectual challenges and greater opportunities for individual contributions at the forefront of physics.

While visible advances in solid-state physics were tapering off, a broader basis was being laid for future progress. A new generation of physics students was being trained, and for them graduate study included quantum mechanics, quantum statistics, and the new solid-state physics. In addition, a considerable number of established scientists and engineers were avidly studying quantum mechanics and the quantum theory of solids, particularly in the United States. At the same time conscious efforts were being made to upgrade and further develop American research and educational facilities in all fields of physics. These efforts were strengthened by the talents of more than 100 European physicists who had immigrated to the United States between 1933 and 1941 as a result of the political upheavals in Europe.

When World War II ended, scientists who wished to work in solid-state physics had available many new and useful techniques and much information that had been produced by wartime efforts. For example, during the war neutrons (neutral particles in the nucleus responsible for uranium fission) had been intensely studied; in the postwar period neutrons were found to be effective probes of solids, especially in explorations of magnetic properties of materials. Also during the war digital computing methods had been developed; and in the postwar period they were used by physicists to achieve a far greater degree of accuracy in solving problems of quantum mechanics. The intense study and development of microwave radar for wartime use resulted in a variety of new resonance techniques used for studying solids in the postwar period, such as microwave spectroscopy, in which microwave radiation is tuned to coincide with certain natural vibrational or rotational frequencies of atoms and molecules in applied magnetic fields. Methods were also developed during the war for producing perfect crystals (with accurately controlled impurity content) in large enough quantities for use in experimental studies. The methods of producing pure crystals of the semiconductors silicon and germanium, which had been used as microwave detectors and frequency converters, became so highly developed that an enormous number of careful studies in the postwar period employed silicon and germanium as prototypes for the study of solid-state phenomena in general. The Collins liquefier, developed just after the war at the Massachusetts Institute of Technology, made it possible for laboratories anywhere to obtain bulk liquid helium and study materials under the simplified conditions that prevail at very low temperatures.

Thus, by the late 1940's a seemingly mature field of solid-state physics was clearly growing in scope and also in terms of the number of physicists attracted to the field. By 1947 solid-state physics had become a large enough field to justify establishing a separate division for it within the American Physical Society.

In the postwar period solid-state physics also became even more closely tied to practical applications, which then stimulated new interest in the field and increased its funding. The invention and development of the transistor offers a striking example of the interplay of theory, technique, and application in solid-state physics during the late 1940's. These events began in January 1945 with the official authorization of a research group at the Bell Telephone Laboratories in New Jersey to work on the "Fundamental Investigation of Conductors, Semiconductors, Dielectrics, Insulators, Piezoelectric and Magnetic Materials"—in short, solids. The American physicist William Shockley, one of the two leaders of this group, was of the generation of physicists that had formally studied quantum mechanics and the quantum theory of solids before World War II. He believed that fundamental understanding of solids could lead to the invention of a semiconductor amplifier and directed the group's attention to silicon and germanium. By the end of 1947 two members of the group, the American physicists John Bardeen and Walter Brattain, had for the first time observed transistor amplification. Bardeen had also been trained in quantum mechanics in graduate school, and Brattain had been among those who had studied the quantum theory of solids informally during the 1930's. The transistor, which rectifies and amplifies electrical signals more rapidly and reliably than the more cumbersome, fragile, and costly vacuum tube, revolutionized communications, electronics, control apparatus, and data processing. It also increased the funding of solid-state physics, which in turn expanded the scale of basic research in the entire field.

Throughout the 1950's and 1960's theory, technique, and applications of solid-state physics all advanced rapidly. The long list of achievements made during those years toward more quantitative understanding of the properties of specific materials includes a theory for the detailed atomic structure and mechanism of atomic movements inside crystals, the specific role of impurities and imperfections on optical properties, the relationship of impurities and dislocations to crystal growth, computation of the energy associated with solid surfaces and interfaces, quantitative determination of such properties of materials as thermal and electrical resistivity and magnetoresistance, and a more complete theory for the mechanism of phase transformations.

The major breakthrough of the 1950's was the successful explanation of superconductivity in 1957 by

Bardeen and two other American physicists, Leon Cooper and J. Robert Schrieffer. In earlier theories the properties of macroscopic objects had been deduced by averaging the individual properties of large numbers of independent atomic systems—but two phenomena had resisted all explanation: superconductivity and superfluidity. The Bardeen-Cooper-Schrieffer (BCS) theory for superconductivity led the way to explanations of a whole series of so-called cooperative phenomena (which also include superfluidity, phase transitions, and tunneling) in which particles and sound-wave quanta move in unison while at the same time displaying strongly modified properties, including loss of electrical resistance at low temperatures in the case of superconductivity and loss of resistance to flow at low temperatures in the case of superfluidity.

Two of the most useful experimental techniques developed in the 1950's and 1960's were the Mössbauer effect (1957) and the Josephson effect (1962). The German physicist Rudolf Mössbauer found that atoms embedded in solids emit or absorb high-frequency electromagnetic waves (called gamma rays) without any measurable recoil. By establishing a resonance for—that is, by tuning—these recoilless radiations, a new method for the precise determination of frequencies was developed. The technique can be used to measure magnetic fields that could not previously be observed. Later, the young British physicist Brian Josephson proposed that a supercurrent can "tunnel" through a thin barrier separating two superconductors; this effect has since become the basis for many tunneling devices that can be used to replace transistors as rectifiers and amplifiers. They can be used for studying the internal structure of solids.

The list of the applications found for solid-state physics continued to grow rapidly. By the mid-1970's, in addition to countless varieties of electronic diodes and transistors, there were, for example, solid-state lasers (highly directional, monochromatic light sources) employed in such diverse applications as weaponry, welding, and eye surgery; magnetic bubble memories used in computers to store information in thin crystals; and superconductors for electromagnetics, which may play an important future role in the production and distribution of power.

By 1975 such rapid proliferation had already created entire industries; and the new, corporate enterprises had in turn stimulated business interest in solid-state physics. In terms of manpower solid-state physics was the largest single subfield of physics in the United States. More generally the field had had an enormous impact on day-to-day living in the 20th century: its applications were conspicuous in communications, travel, health care, warfare, power generation, education, accounting, finance, politics, law, and entertainment.

[J. Bardeen, "Solid State Physics: Accomplishments and Future Prospects," in S. Brown, ed., *Physics 50 Years Later;* D. A. Bromley, "Physics of Condensed Matter," in Physics Survey Committee, National Academy of Sciences, *Physics in Perspective,* vol. II; C. Kittel, *Introduction to Solid State Physics;* J. C. Slater, "The Current State of Solid-State and Molecular Theory," *International Journal of Quantum Chemistry,* vol. 1 (1967); C. S. Smith, "The Prehistory of Solid-State Physics," *Physics Today* (1965).]
LILLIAN HARTMANN HODDESON

PHYSIOLOGY developed along two major pathways in the United States. One was as a part of the growth of medical sciences in colleges and universities; the other has been closely associated with reformist and faddist movements of the 19th and 20th centuries. Physiology and its myriad subbranches have found great favor in health, hygiene, and temperance activities, bringing to large audiences popularized and frequently inaccurate versions of the "correct" functioning of animal and human bodily processes. Within this popular fund of knowledge reasonably validated information dealing with everything from diet to dyspepsia was interwoven with hearsay, fancy, and special group interpretations, leading to a wide diversity of opinion with respect to the truths of physiological matters.

Nevertheless, present-day biological curricula in primary and secondary schools have many of their roots in this popular physiology, simply because so many individuals in all walks of American life came under its influence over an extended period of time. During the 1830's and 1840's, for example, Sylvester Graham, an ordained minister whose name is memorialized in the graham cracker, preached the virtues of clean water, fresh air, unadulterated foods, and whole wheat flour. Dr. William A. Alcott, uncle of Louisa May Alcott, contributed to this crusade well into the 1860's. John Harvey Kellogg, of Kellogg's cereals, an ardent proponent of vegetarianism, tied his activities to the Seventh-Day Adventist movement, building his famous Battle Creek Sanitarium in Michigan in the late 19th century to care for those people whose physiology had gone amiss. These few, representing a larger body preaching and teaching with equal fervor (not always with altruistic motives), have kept America's attention focused on blood circulation, muscle tone, energy, proper excretory functioning, and sex.

By contrast, physiology as a branch of medicine had a poor following from the colonial era to well after the Civil War. As an experimental science it simply had no existence in the United States before the 1870's. The research activities that were conducted were almost exclusively individual enterprises, not institutional. John Young's digestion experiments at the University of Pennsylvania Medical College in 1803; William Beaumont's classical study of the digestive process, published in 1833; Silas Weir Mitchell's study of snake venoms (1860); and William J. G. Morton's introduction of ether anesthesia in 1846 are representative of the art prior to about 1870.

As an academic subject physiology was poorly taught. Medical colleges, even the prestigious ones in Philadelphia, New York, and Boston, included it as a short-term program, limited in scope. European textbooks dominated even those programs, and the courses were almost uniformly didactic in nature with little or no demonstration of physiological principles. Oliver Wendell Holmes at Harvard (1847–71) and John Call Dalton of the College of Physicians and Surgeons in New York (1855–83) were outstanding exceptions to this general rule.

The new era in American physiology was preceded by an increase in both the use of textbooks written in America and the number of individual investigators in physiology. Robley Dunglison, English-born physician to Thomas Jefferson, was a superb textbook author. His *Human Physiology* (1832) went through many editions and nearly 100,000 copies, and his *New Dictionary of Medical Science and Literature* (1833) became the standard of American medicine. Dalton and Austin Flint, Jr., both contributed textbooks on human physiology and carried out numerous experiments: Dalton, on bile and liver functions; Flint, on capillary circulation and the physiology of exercise.

The transition of physiology from a superficially treated subject to an experimental science and a field of study of major importance occurred in the 1870's, when scientists trained in the methodologies and philosophies of German and British institutions were engaged by a few American universities and colleges. H. Newell Martin was brought to Johns Hopkins University in 1876 to organize and teach a laboratory-oriented department of biology. Under Martin's direction physiology flourished as a branch of biology and attracted to the field such future eminences as

William Henry Howell and Henry Sewall. Howell, who succeeded Martin at Johns Hopkins, became the first professor of physiology in the medical school. He conducted extensive research on the circulatory system and was the author of the monumental *Textbook of Physiology* (1905). Sewall ultimately settled at the University of Colorado as professor of medicine with strong interests in clinical physiology.

At Harvard, Henry Pickering Bowditch, who had been trained in Germany, established and equipped the first physiological laboratory in the United States for student use in 1871 and ultimately incorporated physiology into the medical program. Two of his students, Harvey Cushing and Walter B. Cannon, became preeminent in their fields of study, the former in neurophysiology and neurosurgery, the latter in macroscopic physiology and the role of epinephrine (adrenaline) in stress situations. Cannon succeeded Bowditch in the chair of physiology at Harvard in 1906.

The pattern for the future development of physiology in the United States had been set. Disciples of Harvard and Johns Hopkins carried the idea of experimental physiology to other colleges and universities, training a second generation of young converts to the "new ways." Medical schools responded to the changes by converting textbook explications into student-laboratory activities, and after the publication of the 1910 Flexner Report on Medical Education, medical colleges that had not already done so reorganized their curricula. By the mid-1920's virtually all candidates for the M.D. degree were being subjected to an intensive program in physiology, one that united theory and hypothesis with experimental demonstration.

After that initial surge and its subsequent development, a coincidental increase in emphasis on medicine as a clinical subject tended to reduce or counter the importance of extensive physiological training. Literature in the medical sciences from the late 1920's onward was replete with arguments on the relative importance of physiology in the training of doctors.

Regardless of the medical aspect per se, contemporary physiology is a powerful discipline in its own right, no longer under the aegis of the medical profession. Nearly 50 percent of the membership of the American Physiological Society (APS), founded 1887, for example, held the Ph.D. degree in 1973; and although approximately half the APS members were employed in medical schools, the remainder taught or conducted research in graduate and undergraduate college programs. A large number of

teachers in the primary and secondary schools were at least part-time instructors of some aspects of physiology: growth, nutrition, exercise, hygiene. Such aspects most often included an extensive program in demonstration and experimental activities.

Another indication of the growth of physiology is seen in the large number of new disciplines or subbranches of study that are wholly or partially derived from macroscopic physiology: biochemistry, endocrinology, embryology, cardiology, and cellular physiology are but a few. Contemporary knowledge of vitamins, hormones, and enzymes; intermediate metabolism and bioenergetics; immunological processes; muscle chemistry; and the concept of regulatory feedback mechanisms in human control functions have emerged from many of these fields of study.

Also, physiology has benefited greatly from private institutions and federal agencies. The Carnegie and Rockefeller institutes have contributed much to research in nutrition, respiration, cardiology, and disease. The role played by the National Institutes of Health and the National Science Foundation in supporting physiological research is well documented.

This complex of multisupporting agencies and diversified areas of research coupled to a large number of publication outlets, along with developing technological changes in the methodologies of research, manifested itself in the form of teamwork in physiological investigations. Such individualist researchers as Beaumont became anachronisms. No clearer evidence can be adduced to illustrate this quantum jump in physiological studies than the simple statistic of the numbers engaged in such activities (compare the twenty-eight original members of the APS to the nearly 4,612 members in 1975). The popular media—magazines, newspapers, radio, and television—continued to disseminate information and misinformation on good health, hygiene, and muscle tone.

[Helen M. Barton, "A Study of the Development of Textbooks in Physiology and Hygiene in the United States and Canada," Ph.D. dissertation, Univ. of Pittsburgh (1942); Gerald Carson, *Cornflake Crusade;* Karl E. Rothschuh, *History of Physiological Thought,* translated by G. Risse.]

STANLEY L. BECKER

PIAVE RIVER, OPERATIONS ON (October–November 1918). During World War I, in October 1918, the American 332d Infantry Regiment, detached from the 83d Division, made frequent marches, principally for their effect upon Italian morale, behind the Piave River battlefront in Italy. On Oct. 27–28 the regiment assisted Italian forces in establishing bridgeheads on the Piave River, and on Oct. 30, as part of the Italian 31st Division, it joined in the operation that drove the Austrian forces from the Piave to the Tagliamento River.

ROBERT S. THOMAS

PICKAWILLANEE, an Indian village near the site of present-day Piqua, Ohio, was the western outpost of English traders before the French and Indian War (1754–63). It was founded in 1747 by the Miami, who left their village at the site of Fort Wayne, Ind., desiring British rather than French trade. By 1750 English traders had built storehouses at Pickawillanee and several were in residence there. Early in 1751 Christopher Gist, a surveyor and agent of the Ohio Company of Virginia, reported that the village consisted of about 400 families and was "daily encreasing."

In 1751 Pierre-Jacques de Taffanel, Marquis de La Jonquière, French governor of Canada, sent a party of Indians under French commanders to Pickawillanee to eject the English traders. Although the Ottawa forbade the passage of the expedition through their territory, a small force reached Pickawillanee, killed some of the Miami, and increased the Miami's hostility toward the French. Jonquière's successor, Charles Le Moyne, Baron de Longueuil, feared a general revolt of the Indians, and on June 21, 1752, an expedition of Indians commanded by Charles de Langlade attacked Pickawillanee, destroyed the traders' storehouses, captured several of the English traders (two were sent to France), and killed fourteen Miami.

After the Treaty of Logstown (1752), the English influence among the Miami waned, and the Indians returned to their old village in Indiana, leaving Pickawillanee deserted.

[C. A. Hanna, *Wilderness Trail;* L. P. Kellogg, *French Régime in Wisconsin and the Northwest.*]

SOLON J. BUCK

PICKENS, FORT. Upon the secession of Florida (Jan. 10, 1861) and the Confederate seizure of forts on the mainland at Pensacola, Lt. Adam J. Slemmer, with forty loyal Union troopers, escaped across Pensacola Bay to Santa Rosa Island and took possession of the long-unoccupied Fort Pickens. Short of food and ammunition, Slemmer's handful of men found themselves, in April 1861, in precisely the same situation as Maj. Robert Anderson's men at Fort Sumter.

A relief expedition, secretly organized by Secretary of State William Henry Seward (*see Powhatan Incident*) and energetically led by Capt. Montgomery C. Meigs and Lt. David D. Porter, reinforced Fort Pickens and saved it from capture. The fort remained an important federal stronghold throughout the war.

[R. S. West, Jr., *The Second Admiral.*]
RICHARD S. WEST, JR.

PICKETING, said the U.S. Supreme Court in 1941, is "the workingman's means of communication." The nonviolent competitive tactics of workers in labor disputes with employers have traditionally been limited to the strike, the secondary boycott, and the picket line. To get the person picketed to accede to the aims of the picketers, the tactics of picketing have been to impede deliveries and services; to cause employees to refuse to cross the line to work; to muster consumer sympathy to withhold patronage; and to be a "rallyround" symbol for the picketers and other workers. Their objective may be either to get recognition as the bargainers for employees or to gain economic demands.

Picketing has promoted interests other than those of workers, notably in protests against racial discrimination. But its history is very strongly linked to public policy regulatory of labor-management disputes. Very few states have comprehensive statutes governing labor disputes. At common law, state courts have been divided over the legality of picketing. Most have held it to be an unjustified infliction of economic harm. Some, as in California, in *Messner* v. *Journeymen Barbers* (1960), have refused to take sides in these competitive situations. They have reasoned that risks of loss among competitors should not be abated by courts, absent statutory regulation, since hardship does not make less legitimate the objectives of a union seeking organization, or of a nonunion shop resisting it, or of nonunion workers who may either join or resist. A number of courts, without statutory standards, enjoin picketing to forestall economic hardship, even though a decree merely shifts the loss from one competitor (the employer) to another (the union). Federal law is mostly statutory; it regulates picketing in terms of purposes and effects under the National Labor Relations Act of 1935, as amended in 1947 and 1959, and usually preempts state law.

In 1940 the Supreme Court added a constitutional dimension to the existing common law and to statutory law. In *Thornhill* v. *Alabama* it declared that picketing is a right of communication under the First and Fourteenth amendments, although regulation is available to curb numbers, threats, obstruction, fraud, misrepresentation, or violence. Still, the Court has had trouble in reconciling the conduct of patrolling with what, rather artificially, it has termed "pure speech"—oral communication, in contrast to overall communicative conduct—and in balancing regulatory policies against the communication values inherent in picketing. *Teamsters* v. *Vogt* (1957) seemed to strip constitutional insulation from picketers, leaving them open to sweeping injunctions, excepting only outright prohibition. But *Food Employees* v. *Logan Valley Plaza* (1968) cautioned that controls, improper for "pure speech" but proper for picketing because of the intermingling of protected speech and unprotected conduct, must still be applied to avoid impairment of the speech elements.

[D. Bok and J. Dunlop, *Labor and the American Community;* J. R. Commons et al., *History of Labour in the United States;* A. Cox, *Law and the National Policy;* C. O. Gregory, *Labor and the Law.*]

EDGAR A. JONES, JR.

PICKETT'S CHARGE (July 3, 1863), more properly the Pickett-Pettigrew charge, was the culminating event of the Battle of Gettysburg. Having failed on July 1 and 2 to rout the Union forces, Confederate Gen. Robert E. Lee decided to assault their center. For this purpose he designated George Edward Pickett's division; Henry Heth's division, temporarily commanded by J. J. Pettigrew; and two brigades of William Pender's division. After a preliminary bombardment by 125 guns, these troops—forty-seven regiments, 15,000 men—were ordered to advance an average of 1,300 yards eastward from Seminary Ridge to a "little clump of trees" on the front of the Second Corps along Cemetery Ridge. The assault was begun at about 2 P.M. and carried out with the utmost gallantry. It carried the column of attack to the Union position but failed for lack of support when the Union forces closed in from three sides. The Confederates, who were compelled to retreat under heavy fire, lost about 6,000 men. Three of Pickett's brigade commanders and most of his field officers were killed.

[D. S. Freeman, *R. E. Lee*, vol. III.]

DOUGLAS SOUTHALL FREEMAN

PIECES OF EIGHT, Spanish silver coins of eight reals (eight bits), first authorized by a law of 1497. Also known as pesos and Spanish dollars, they were minted in enormous quantities and soon became recognized and accepted throughout the commercial world as a reliable medium of exchange. Subsidiary coins—for example, four reals (half dollar, four bits) and two reals (quarter dollar, two bits)—were also minted. In 1728, Spain began coinage of the milled dollar to replace the piece of eight, the new coins being more difficult to clip or shave than the old ones.

The Spanish piece of eight or milled dollar had become familiar as the metallic basis of the monetary system in the British colonies in America, and consequently, Congress, in 1786, adopted the Spanish milled dollar as the basis of the U.S. coinage system; the first American dollars contained approximately the same amount of silver as their contemporary Spanish counterparts.

[D. R. Dewey, *Financial History of the United States;* J. P. Young, *Central American Currency and Finance.*]

WALTER PRICHARD

PIECEWORK, one of the oldest methods of paying for labor. It was known among ancient peoples, the payment often being in the form of food and the amount given depending upon the amount of work accomplished. In England it was in general use before the Industrial Revolution.

Piecework was common in American industry almost from the first, the amount of work assigned being called a stint or a "stent." It was the only form of incentive wage plan until the rise of industrial management brought the premium differential and task-and-bonus plans into widespread use. The principle upon which all these incentive plans is based is payment for results.

A variation of piecework that was in use in American industry during the last half of the 19th century was known as contract work. Andrew Carnegie, writing of his native Scottish village in the 1840's, described how the system functioned in the weaving industry: weavers owned their looms, got warps from large manufacturers, and were paid piece rates for weaving the cloth. In America this method was applied to many kinds of production, including that of machinery and tools; the one taking the contract to produce a certain quantity of goods for a specified price was called the "contractor." During the depression of the 1930's the contract work method was revived in some branches of the textile industry, notably silk-weaving, and continued throughout the century.

L. P. ALFORD

PIEDMONT REGION, geographically, the area of the eastern United States lying at the foot of the easternmost ranges of the Appalachian mountain system; historically, all the territory between these ranges and the fall line on the rivers. Below the falls many of the rivers are tidal estuaries, and the region is known as Tidewater. Up-country and backcountry are other terms sometimes used to designate the Piedmont region. The division of the Atlantic coastal plain into two regions has been profoundly important in American history. The Tidewater region, settled first, became the locale of conservative planters, merchants, and politicians. The Piedmont region was settled later, primarily by less wealthy and less cultured individuals. There they became small farmers rather than great planters or merchants. Socially and economically democratic, Piedmonters were generally at odds with the Tidewater population. Early sectionalism in America was based mainly on this differentiation. The gradual elimination of political discrimination and improved transportation have decreased but not eradicated the sectional significance of the Piedmont region.

[Charles Henry Ambler, *Sectionalism in Virginia.*]
ALFRED P. JAMES

PIEGAN. *See* **Blackfoot.**

PIEGAN WAR (1869–70). By a treaty in 1855 Gen. Isaac I. Stevens, governor of Washington Territory, fixed the hunting grounds of the Blackfoot confederacy—the northern Blackfoot, Blood, and Piegan—north of the Missouri River in Montana. Invasion of this territory by miners and ranchers in 1869 caused the Piegan to make retaliatory raids in which settlers near Fort Benton were killed. Col. E. M. Baker marched against the Piegan on Jan. 6, 1870, striking Chief Red Horn's camp on the Marias River on Jan. 23. Suffering from smallpox, the Indians were unprepared for the attack. Baker's detachment killed 173, including Red Horn and many women and children, with a loss of only one soldier. The attack drew censure from Congress and the press, and no further incidents occurred involving the Piegan.

[J. P. Dunn, *Massacres of the Mountains.*]
PAUL I. WELLMAN

PIERRE, FORT, developed from a small trading post established by Joseph LaFramboise, at the mouth of the Bad River on the west bank of the Missouri in October 1817. The Columbia Fur Company took the business over in 1822 and named the post Fort Tecumseh. In 1828 John Jacob Astor's interests bought the plant, and in 1832 built a new post, named Fort Pierre Chouteau. The "Chouteau" appellation did not become popular and was dropped. In 1855 the federal government bought the plant but dismantled it a year later. The village of Fort Pierre now occupies the area. For several decades the Fort Pierre trading post was the only settlement indicated on maps of the Dakota country.

In 1743, on the hilltop on which Fort Pierre was later constructed, the La Vérendrye brothers made claim to the Northwest for France and planted an inscribed plate in testimony to the taking. This plate was recovered in 1913.

DOANE ROBINSON

PIERRE'S HOLE, BATTLE OF (July 18, 1832). A noted trappers' rendezvous, Pierre's Hole was located in the Teton Mountains in eastern Idaho. The battle that took place there between the Gros Ventres and American fur traders was the most renowned struggle of the trapping era and witnessed the exploits of such prominent trappers and pathfinders as William L. Sublette, Nathaniel J. Wyeth, and Antoine Godin. Apparently the battle started when one of the trappers killed the Gros Ventres chief in revenge for the murder of his father by the Blackfoot, allies of the Gros Ventres. The Indians forted up in a swampy thicket of willows, and after an all-day fight the trappers were unable to dislodge them. A false rumor spread through the trappers' ranks that more Blackfoot were attacking their main camp, and so the bloody siege was abandoned.

[H. M. Chittenden, *History of the Fur Trade of the Far West.*]
CARL L. CANNON

PIETISM, the name given to the movement in German Protestantism that arose at the end of the 17th century and continued into the 18th century to combat the growing formalism in the Lutheran church. The father of the movement was Philip Jacob Spener, a Lutheran minister in Frankfort on the Main, Germany, who began the formation of *collegia pietatis,* or societies of piety, for the promotion of Bible study and prayer. He stressed Christianity as a life rather than as a creed; lay people were urged to take a larger part in the work of the church. In 1694 the University of

Halle was established through Spener's influence and became the principal pietistic center. In the American colonies the influence of pietism was exerted chiefly through the German Lutherans and the Moravians. Henry M. Mühlenberg was sent to America in 1742 largely through the efforts of the Halle pietists, and his leadership among the colonial Lutherans in the formative period served to emphasize that phase of Lutheranism. Count Nikolaus Ludwig von Zinzendorf, a pietist who spent six years at Halle, came to America in 1741 and set up several Moravian congregations. The American Moravians were the most pietistic of all the colonial religious bodies. Pietism was from the beginning strongly missionary in emphasis and for that reason had large significance in colonial America particularly.

[C. H. Maxson, *The Great Awakening in the Middle Colonies;* A. W. Nagler, *Pietism and Methodism.*]

WILLIAM W. SWEET

"PIG WAR." *See* **San Juan, Seizure of.**

PIKES PEAK, a famous mountain, altitude 14,110 feet, located in the Front Range of the Rocky Mountains in El Paso County, Colorado, was discovered in November 1806 by Lt. Zebulon M. Pike. Pike failed to ascend the peak because of heavy snow. It was first ascended by Edwin James, J. Verplank, and Z. Wilson of Maj. Stephen H. Long's expedition on July 14, 1820; Long named the peak after James, but popular usage by trappers and others of the name "Pikes Peak'" led to an official name change. Pikes Peak is the center for the region of Garden of the Gods, Manitou Hot Springs, the Ute Pass Highway, and the Cripple Creek gold mines. It is of historical significance as a landmark of early traders and trappers and as the name of the region now known as Colorado. The discovery of gold in 1858 brought large numbers to the region. Although many returned home in disappointment, further discoveries in 1859 attracted thousands more who crossed the Plains with the slogan "Pikes Peak or Bust" and who gradually opened up the various mining camps near Pikes Peak or settled in the valleys of the state.

[Enos A. Mills, *Rocky Mountain Wonderland;* John O'Byrne, *Pikes Peak or Bust.*]

MALCOLM G. WYER

PIKES PEAK GOLD RUSH. Gold was discovered at Ralston Creek, near present-day Denver, in 1850 by Cherokee goldseekers bound for California. Reports of this find, augmented by rumors of other discoveries, led in 1858 to the organization of parties to prospect the region. The expedition led by William G. Russell, comprising miners experienced in the goldfields of Georgia and California, was the most important but parties also came from Missouri and Kansas. Most of these prospectors, discouraged after a few days of unsuccessful search, returned to their homes. The remnant of the Russell party discovered some placer gold in Cherry Creek and other tributaries of the South Platte in July 1858. Word of these finds brought new hopefuls to the region in the fall. Exaggerated stories of the reputed goldfields circulated in the nation's press during the winter of 1858–59. Inasmuch as Pikes Peak was the best-known landmark, although seventy-five miles from the site of the discoveries, the region was called the Pikes Peak Gold Country, or Cherry Creek Diggings. The meager amount of dust found in 1858 hardly warranted so much excitement. But the country, suffering from the recent panic of 1857, grasped avidly at any hope of rehabilitation. Merchants and newspapers in the Missouri River towns, with an eye to spring outfitting, spread stories, which the Atlantic coast papers generally ridiculed and denied. Sixteen guidebooks (some by interested outfitting towns) were issued during the winter to instruct amateur prairie travelers and win them to particular routes, and this directed publicity built a great flood of goldseekers that traveled across the Plains in the spring. The principal routes were up the Platte, the Arkansas, and the Smoky Hill rivers, converging at the mouth of Cherry Creek. With wagons, on horseback, and afoot the goldseekers rushed mountainward. The Leavenworth and Pikes Peak Express, the first stage line to Denver, was established in 1859 as a result of these expeditions. Many early arrivals, finding the creek sands were not yellow with gold, and unenriched by a few days' futile search, turned back, crying "Pikes Peak Humbug." Fortunately, rich gold veins were found in the mountains, the first by John H. Gregory, near present-day Central City, May 6, 1859. It is estimated that 100,000 persons set out for the gold region, that half of them reached the mountains, and that only half of these remained, to found Colorado.

[L. R. Hafen, *Colorado, The Story of a Western Commonwealth.*]

LEROY R. HAFEN

PIKE'S SOUTHWESTERN EXPEDITION (1806–07), conducted by Lt. Zebulon M. Pike and a small band of U.S. soldiers, was organized to explore the Arkansas and Red rivers, to gather information about the abutting Spanish territory, and to conciliate the Indian tribes in the newly acquired territory of the United States (*see* Louisiana Purchase) extending southwestward toward Santa Fe and the Spanish border. Leaving Fort Bellefontaine (near Saint Louis) on July 15, 1806, the party traveled to the Pawnee towns in Kansas and then by way of the Arkansas River into Colorado. From here it crossed, in midwinter, the Sangre de Cristo Range to the Conejos, a tributary of the Rio Grande in New Mexico, and built a fort nearby. Learning of Pike's expedition in their territory, Spanish officials sent a detachment of soldiers to bring the men to Santa Fe. From there the Spanish authorities conducted Pike to Chihuahua and then by a circuitous route to the American border at Natchitoches, La., on July 1, 1807.

Pike's narrative, *An Account of Expeditions to the Sources of the Mississippi and Through the Western Parts of Louisiana,* published in 1810, afforded his countrymen their first description of the great Southwest, including military information valuable to the federal government. His men, few in number and poorly equipped, had braved possible Indian attack, the perils of starvation, the exposure of the Colorado Rockies in midwinter, and the prospect of perpetual confinement in a Spanish prison. Pike's journal was a valuable addition to the literature of New World exploration.

[Elliott Coues, ed., *The Expeditions of Zebulon M. Pike;* S. H. Hart and A. B. Hulbert, eds., *Zebulon Pike's Arkansaw Journal;* M. M. Quaife, ed., *The Southwestern Expedition of Zebulon M. Pike.*]

M. M. QUAIFE

PIKE'S UPPER MISSISSIPPI EXPEDITION

(1805–06). The acquisition of Louisiana in 1803 initiated a notable period of western exploration in which Lt. Zebulon M. Pike played a leading role. On Aug. 9, 1805, he left Saint Louis with twenty soldiers on a 70-foot keelboat to explore the Mississippi River to its source, conciliate the Indians in the area, assert the authority of the United States over British traders, and procure sites for military posts. Near Little Falls, Minn., Pike built a log fort and traveled for weeks in midwinter by sled and toboggan, ascending to what he thought were the upper reaches of the Mississippi and falsely named Leech Lake as the source of the river. He also met with British traders, urging them to obey the laws of the United States, held councils with the Indians, and made geographical observations. He

returned to Saint Louis on Apr. 30, 1806, with a record of achievement that won him the appointment to lead an expedition to the far Southwest. Although he had accomplished all that had been expected of him, the federal government neglected to follow up his achievement, whose chief practical result was its addition to existing geographical knowledge.

[Elliott Coues, ed., *The Expeditions of Zebulon M. Pike;* W. W. Folwell, *History of Minnesota,* vol. I.]

M. M. QUAIFE

PILGRIMS consisted of thirty-five members of an English Separatist church living in Leiden, the Netherlands, who, with sixty-six English sectarians and servants, sailed from Plymouth, England, on Sept. 16, 1620, on the *Mayflower* and founded Plymouth Colony in New England in December. Although outnumbered by the English contingent, the Leiden group were the prime movers and the backbone of the migration, and the Pilgrims are generally associated with the Leiden congregation of which they were a part. The congregation, one of many Puritan sects that opposed the Elizabethan Established Church settlement, originated at Scrooby, Nottinghamshire, England, an obscure village on a manor of the archbishop of York. Led by William Brewster, the archbishop's bailiff who had become a Puritan while at Cambridge, the sect formed as a Separating Congregationalist church between 1590 and 1607. By 1607 the congregation embraced 100 or more rural folk, including Elder Brewster; William Bradford, son of a prosperous Austerfield farmer; and John Robinson, nonconformist Cambridge graduate who became their minister in 1607.

A minority of Scrooby village, the congregation was persecuted by conforming neighbors and "investigated" by the Ecclesiastical Commission of York in November 1607. Thus, believing firmly in ecclesiastical independence and to avoid contamination in England, they determined to ensure religious and ecclesiastical purity by emigrating to Holland, where other English sectaries found liberty to worship and lucrative employment. After embarrassing difficulties with English officials, about 100 escaped to Amsterdam by August 1608, but Amsterdam heterodoxy troubled them. In May 1609, with Dutch permission, they settled at Leiden, where the local cloth industry largely employed their labors and the university stimulated their leaders. At Leiden the congregation approximately tripled in numbers (1609–18), and its polity and creed crystallized under the able leadership of Robinson and Brewster.

But as years passed they grew troubled and discontented. Their work was hard, their incomes small, and their economic outlook unfavorable. Their children were losing touch with their English background, and they lacked that ecclesiastical and civil autonomy deemed necessary for their purity and proper growth. Thus, they decided in the winter of 1616–17 to move to America, to the northern part of the Virginia Company's grant, under English protection, where they hoped to establish a profitable fishing and trading post. Deacon John Carver and Robert Cushman negotiated with the Virginia Company in the summer of 1617, hoping for official guarantees against English ecclesiastical interference. The Virginia Company encouraged them and gave them a charter (June 9, 1619). But they needed capital. When in February 1620 Thomas Weston, London Puritan merchant, proposed that they employ a charter that his associates held from the Virginia Company (dated Feb. 20, 1620, in the name of John Peirce and associates) and form a joint-stock company for seven years to repay financing of the trip, the Leiden people accepted. Specific terms were drawn up.

A bare majority, however, voted to remain in Leiden. The minority, taking Brewster as their "teacher," prepared to depart. A sixty-ton vessel, the *Speedwell*, was outfitted, and all was in readiness to sail when difficulties with the London financiers paralyzed the enterprise until June 10, when Cushman persuaded Weston to continue cooperation. The London associates hired the *Mayflower*, which by mid-July was provisioned and ready to sail. Aboard were some eighty men, women, and children, most of them engaged by Weston as laborers or servants, and probably not of the Separatist persuasion. On July 22 the Leiden people left Delftshaven in the *Speedwell* and joined the *Mayflower* at Southampton. There they quarreled over business terms with Weston, who finally left them "to stand on their own legs" and, with no settlement, they sailed on Aug. 15. But the *Speedwell* proved unseaworthy and, after repairs at Dartmouth and Plymouth, the decision was made to sail on the *Mayflower* alone. On Sept. 16, with some eighty-seven passengers, fourteen servants and workmen, and a crew of forty-eight, the *Mayflower* sailed from Plymouth. Only two of those aboard—Brewster and Bradford—came from the original Scrooby congregation.

After an uneventful voyage Cape Cod was sighted on November 19, north of the limit of their patent. There, deliberately abandoning their patent—which had given them legal departure from England—they determined to settle without legal rights on Massachusetts Bay. To quiet murmurs of the London men and maintain order, forty-one adult males drew up and signed the famous Mayflower Compact on Nov. 21, 1620, in which they pledged to form a body politic and submit to majority rule. The same day they landed in what is now Provincetown harbor. After considerable searching they discovered a harbor (Plymouth Harbor) on Dec. 21, landed the *Mayflower* there (Dec. 26), and spent the remainder of the winter building the town, combating illness (which reduced their number by forty-four by April). In March 1621, they chose a governor and other officers, but not until November 1621, when Weston arrived in the *Fortune,* did they come temporarily to terms with the London financiers and receive from the Council for New England a charter (dated June 11, 1621) that gave legal birth to Plymouth Plantation.

[William Bradford, *History of Plymouth Plantation;* John Demos, *A Little Commonwealth: Family Life in Plymouth Colony;* George D. Langdon, *Pilgrim Colony: A History of New Plymouth, 1620–1691*.]

RAYMOND P. STEARNS

PILLORY, a device for publicly punishing petty offenders, consisting of a frame with holes in which the head and hands of the standing prisoner were locked. It was not as common in the American colonies as was the more merciful stocks, in which the prisoner sat, fastened by the hands and feet. But one or the other was probably to be seen in every town in which a court sat.

CLIFFORD K. SHIPTON

PILLOW, FORT, "MASSACRE" (Apr. 12, 1864). Fifteen hundred Confederate cavalry under Gen. Nathan B. Forrest invested Fort Pillow, Tenn., on the land side, on the morning of Apr. 12, 1864. Before ordering the final assault that afternoon, Forrest warned the Union garrison of 557 men (295 white and 262 black) that unless they surrendered, he could "not be responsible for [their] fate." When the Union force refused to submit, the Confederates attacked and in a fierce fight drove the defenders out of the fort and, despite support of the Union gunboat *New Era,* into the Mississippi River. Forrest took prisoner 168 white and 58 black troops.

Surviving Union witnesses testified before federal authorities that on Forrest's orders, Confederates had refused quarter to surrendering soldiers, particularly blacks, and had massacred several hundred of them.

The general's biographers have rejected these accusations, but students of the period have concluded that although the charges may have been exaggerated, a number of the men garrisoned at the fort were indiscriminately killed after they had ceased to resist.

[Albert Castel, "The Fort Pillow Massacre: A Fresh Examination of the Evidence," *Civil War History*, vol. 4 (1958); Dudley T. Cornish, *The Sable Arm: Negro Troops in the Union Army, 1861–1865*.]

JOHN D. MILLIGAN

PILOT KNOB, BATTLE OF (Sept. 27, 1864). When Confederate Gen. Sterling Price and his men— between 12,000 and 15,000 strong—entered Missouri, the only federal force between them and Saint Louis was Brig. Gen. Thomas Ewing's command, about 1,000 men, holding Fort Davidson at Pilot Knob. Deciding to capture this stronghold before proceeding against Saint Louis, Price assaulted with two of his three divisions and suffered a bloody repulse, losing possibly 1,500 men. Finding his position untenable, that night Ewing retreated toward Leasburg. Price wasted three days in futile pursuit, permitting Saint Louis to be so strongly reinforced that he dared not attack it.

[Cyrus A. Peterson and Joseph M. Hanson, *Pilot Knob, The Thermopylae of the West*.]

JOSEPH MILLS HANSON

PIMA. Among American Indians of the Southwest, the Pima, along with their neighbors and linguistic relatives, the Papago, differ somewhat sharply in culture from both the Pueblo and the Navaho-Apache. Although characteristically southwestern in their development of an intensive agriculture, their farming methods suggest backgrounds in the prehistoric Hohokam culture of southern Arizona; the great period of the Hohokam, about A.D. 1100–1300, rivals that of the Pueblo of the same period. Both cultures were influenced by the rich civilization of Mexico, but in different ways, and there seems to have been little contact between them. The Pima-Papago may thus represent the terminal point of a cultural tradition that reached its climax in pre-Columbian times.

The Pima were located in the Salt and Gila river valleys in southern Arizona. The Papago, south of the Pima, inhabited the higher levels away from the rivers. The two tribes spoke closely related languages belonging to the Piman branch of Uto-Aztecan. Both tribes were contacted by the Jesuit missionary Eusebio Francisco Kino in his expeditions, which began in 1681. At that time, it is estimated, there were about 6,000 Papago and 4,000 Pima.

The sociocultural differences between the Pima and the Papago were minimal except in general ecological adaptations. The Pima, retaining the riverine focus, dug irrigation canals with wooden tools, a pattern that appeared early in the Hohokam culture, and became intensive cultivators. The Papago, driven away by the Apache from the rivers to the higher lands, came to depend less on agriculture and more on gathered plants, particularly the mesquite bean. Both groups built round, flat-topped single-family houses in small village communities. Both tribes had a strong sense of identity, the Pima especially having evolved a system of village chiefs and councils. A tribal chief was elected by the villages. Papago villages tended to remain autonomous. Because social changes resulted early from contacts with Europeans, some aspects of Pima-Papago political, social, and religious organization are not wholly clear. Both tribes had harvest festivals in four-year cycles, involving masked figures, a custom shared with other southwestern peoples. The Pima had a summer rain festival, involving the preparation of a wine made from the juice of the giant saguaro cactus. A ceremonial drunkenness was permitted at this time, a custom suggestive of the licensed drinking of pulque in Aztec Mexico: this is the sole appearance of an aboriginal alcoholic drink north of Mexico.

[E. F. Castetter and W. H. Bell, *Pima and Papago Indian Agriculture*; Ruth M. Underhill, *Papago Indian Religion*, and *Social Organization of the Papago Indians*.]

ROBERT F. SPENCER

PIMA REVOLT (1751) was an uprising by the Upper Pima in the area known to the Spaniards as Pimería Alta, which comprised much of what is now northern Sonora in Mexico and southern Arizona. Nine missions had been established by the Jesuit Father Eusebio Francisco Kino and were in operation in 1751. The revolt centered around the ambitions of one man, Luis Oacpicagigua, who aspired to be chief of all the Pima. He accused the Jesuits of oppression and planned a revolt to oust the Spaniards from the area, but he had little support among the Pima generally. The revolt began in Saric, in northern Sonora, where Oacpicagigua killed eighteen Spaniards whom he had invited to his house and then attacked the mission of Tubutama. Missionaries were slain at Caborca and Sonoita, and after 100 Spaniards in all had been killed, Oacpicagigua surrendered and was jailed.

[Russell C. Ewing, "The Pima Revolt of 1751," in Adele Ogden and Engel Sluiter, eds., *Greater America: Essays in Honor of Herbert Eugene Bolton;* Edward H. Spicer, *Cycles of Conquest.*]

KENNETH M. STEWART

PIMITOUI, FORT, was erected in the winter of 1691–92 on the right bank of the Illinois River near the site of the present city of Peoria, Ill., by Henry de Tonti and François Dauphin de La Forest. Because it was intended to replace Fort Saint Louis it was originally called by that name, but it soon came to be known by the Indian word for the widening of the river near which it was located, now called Peoria Lake. Fort Pimitoui—four log houses surrounded by 1,800 pickets—was the nucleus of the first permanent French settlement in the Illinois Country.

[C. W. Alvord, *The Illinois Country, 1673–1818.*]

PAUL M. ANGLE

PINCKNEY PLAN, a detailed plan of government, containing more than thirty provisions later incorporated in the Constitution, introduced by Charles Pinckney at an early session of the Convention of 1787. The plan has furnished an interesting subject for historical criticism, since the original was not preserved, and the alleged "Pinckney plan," printed many years later as part of the convention record, was obviously of later origin. Its general scope and contents, however, have been deduced from the convention debates.

[Max Farrand, *The Records of the Federal Convention;* J. F. Jameson, "Studies in the History of the Federal Convention of 1787," *American Historical Review,* vol. 9.]

W. A. ROBINSON

PINCKNEY'S TREATY (1795), or the **Treaty of San Lorenzo,** was the climax of twelve years of dispute with Spain over the western and southern boundaries of the United States and the navigation of the Mississippi River. Spain feared that territorial acquisitions along that river would lead to contraband traffic in the colonies of Louisiana and Florida and that commercial navigation of the river would lead to economic and political penetration dangerous to Spanish sovereignty in New Spain itself. The United States contended that its treaty of peace with Great Britain after the Revolution had made the Mississippi River and thirty-one degrees north latitude its recognized boundaries, and that riparian territorial sovereignty

rights upstream gave a "natural right" to free navigation in and out from the ocean, even though the lower reaches of the river were in undisputed Spanish possession.

The United States and Spain attempted, 1785–86, to reconcile their differences, but the effort failed (*see* Jay-Gardoqui Negotiations); and despite the new vigor of President George Washington's administration, the United States was unable to make headway until Spain became involved in the wars of the French Revolution. Then Europe's distress became America's advantage. By the Treaty of Basle (July 1795) Spain made a separate peace with France. Fearing English vengeance and perhaps Anglo-American alliance to guarantee the free navigation of the Mississippi, Spain suddenly gave in and met the American demands in a treaty signed by U.S. Minister to Great Britain Thomas Pinckney at San Lorenzo, Oct. 27, 1795. Among the major provisions, the treaty accepted the boundary claims of the United States (*see* Southern Boundary, Survey of the) at the thirty-first parallel, established commercial relations with Spain, stipulated that Spain would not incite the Indians on its frontier to attack Americans, and provided for the free navigation of the Mississippi by American citizens and Spanish subjects, with a three-year right of deposit at New Orleans, later at some other convenient place in Spanish territory. The treaty also provided for the adjudication by a mixed claims commission of spoliation claims arising over arbitrary captures by Spain of American neutral vessels.

[S. F. Bemis, *Pinckney's Treaty.*]

SAMUEL FLAGG BEMIS

PINE BARREN SPECULATIONS were perpetrated principally in Montgomery, Washington, and Franklin counties in Georgia, during the years 1793 and 1794, and rivaled the state's famous Yazoo sales fraud for notoriety. Through bribery or unbelievable carelessness, county officials issued warrants to a small group of speculators calling for more than 17 million acres of land, ten times the area actually in those counties. Philadelphia became the center for the sale of these worthless warrants to unsuspecting buyers and other speculators. The bankruptcy and ruin of Robert Morris, signer of the Declaration of Independence and chief financier of the American Revolution, were in part caused by this speculation.

[S. G. McLendon, *History of the Public Domain of Georgia;* E. M. Coulter, *A Short History of Georgia.*]

E. MERTON COULTER

PINE BLUFF, BATTLES AT. The first battle at Pine Bluff, Ark., took place on Oct. 25, 1863, during the Union conquest of Arkansas. Confederate Gen. Sterling Price's small force, battling two Union regiments, suffered heavy losses. The second battle at Pine Bluff took place on Feb. 22, 1865; Union cavalry successfully routed a portion of Gen. Edmund Kirby Smith's command.

[Robert L. Kerby, *Kirby Smith's Confederacy: The Trans-Mississippi South, 1863–65.*]

ALVIN F. HARLOW

PINE RIDGE INDIAN WAR. *See* **Messiah War.**

PINE TREE FLAG, a colonial flag of Massachusetts used as early as 1700. The pine tree of Massachusetts was the emblem of New England in general and seems to have been one of the earliest symbols of the union of the thirteen colonies. An evergreen was incorporated into the flags of the American forces from 1775 to 1777 in various ways, often with the motto "An Appeal to Heaven," and the pine tree and this motto were sometimes combined with the rattlesnake flag of the southern colonies with its motto, "Don't tread on me."

In September 1775 two American floating batteries attacked Boston under a pine tree flag. The six armed vessels commissioned by George Washington in 1775 also flew a pine tree flag. In April 1776 the Massachusetts council resolved that for its navy "the colors be a white flag, with a green pine tree, and the inscription, 'An Appeal to Heaven.' " An American flag of 1775 with a blue (sometimes red) field had a white canton bearing a red Saint George's cross; in the upper corner of the canton next to the staff was a pine tree.

[G. H. Preble, *Origin and History of the American Flag.*]

STANLEY R. PILLSBURY

PINE TREE SHILLING. To secure relief to a certain extent from a great need of currency, Massachusetts established a mint in June 1652. In the following year a crude silver coin was issued about the size of a modern half dollar but weighing only one-third as much. On the obverse was MASATHVSETS IN., between two beaded circles; within the inner circle was a pine tree from which the coin gets its name. On the reverse was NEWENGLAND. AN. DOM., between two beaded circles, and 1652, XII, within the inner one. The Roman numerals indicated the number of pence in a shilling. The mint was closed in 1684.

THOMAS L. HARRIS

PINKSTER was the Dutch Pentecost, celebrated in colonial New York and to some extent in Pennsylvania and Maryland, with picnicking, picking "pinkster" flowers (wild azaleas), and neighborly visiting. Gaily decorated booths were erected, as on Pinkster Hill (Capitol Hill), Albany, for the sale of gingerbread, cider, and applejack. The festival was later taken over by the city's black citizens, who elected a black governor, or "King Charley," dressed in colorful regalia, and paid him mock respect amid hilarious drinking, singing, and dancing. In *Satanstoe* (1845), James Fenimore Cooper described an 18th-century celebration in Long Island, where whites continued to participate. Forbidden in Albany in 1811, the Pinkster celebration soon disappeared.

[Alice Morse Earle, *Colonial Days in Old New York.*]

HAROLD E. DAVIS

PIONEERS. The terms "frontiersmen," "early settlers," and "pioneers" are applied indiscriminately in American history to those who, in any given area, began the transformation of the wilderness and the prairie into a land of homes, farms, and towns. In common usage, explorers, fur traders, soldiers, and goldseekers are not classed as pioneers unless they later settled down more or less permanently. They were the vanguard, the scouts of the westward movement. The pioneers constituted the shock troops of the main army.

Numerous differences with respect to region, period, and origin make it impossible to present a uniform description of the American pioneers. The English colonists were the first pioneers, but there were striking differences in character, purpose, and modes of life among the first inhabitants of such colonies as Massachusetts Bay, Pennsylvania, Virginia, and Georgia. The Germans and Scotch-Irish who pioneered the way into the interior of Pennsylvania and into the backcountry of Virginia and the Carolinas differed from their fellow settlers of English origin. By the time settlers began to pour over the mountains into the Mississippi Valley some of these differences were modified by the leveling effect of frontier experiences, but there were still noticeable variations in the types of pioneers and pioneer life. The first settlers in the various and distinct geographical regions of the Far West differed in some respects from each other and from the pioneers of the Middle West.

Some general similarities in character, motives, qualities, and life on the frontier may, however, be pointed out. It is safe to say that the pioneers as a class were people who had been in some degree and for some reason dissatisfied, maladjusted, or unsuccessful in the communities, whether in the United States or in Europe, from which they migrated. At the same time they were hardy, venturesome, optimistic, and willing to undertake the dangers and labors of taming the wilderness. The completely satisfied and the timid were not attracted to the outer fringe of civilization.

In one form or another, the desire to improve their economic status was undoubtedly the most universal and constant motive that impelled the pioneers westward. Cheap and fertile land was the most potent lure, and thus the term "pioneers" is confined largely to those who went west to take up land and make farms for themselves, although many were attracted by the opportunities for trade, mechanical occupations, and professional practice in newly established towns. Not all the pioneers were any more successful in their new homes than they had been in the places from which they came. A lengthy record of frontier failures, shiftlessness, and degeneration could be compiled from the writings of travelers and observers. Furthermore, numerous pioneers, finding their expectations too rosy-hued, sold out after a few years and went back to their native lands or towns.

Everywhere the lives of the pioneers were conditioned by the wilderness environment. Their homes were built of whatever materials the region afforded. The log cabin, with its earthen or puncheon floor, leaky roof, fireplace, and crude furniture, was the typical pioneer dwelling wherever trees were available. On the prairies, and especially in Kansas, Nebraska, and the Dakotas, the sod house took the place of the log cabin, whereas in some sections of the Southwest the adobe hut was the prevailing type of shelter. There is ample evidence that these crude and cheerless homes were often a severe trial to the wives and mothers. Their long days were filled with arduous and multitudinous tasks to be performed without what would now be regarded as the barest necessities. Both men and women suffered the psychological hardships of pioneer life—loneliness, fear of Indians, homesickness for relatives and old friends, and worry in times of sickness.

Unremitting toil was likewise the lot of the pioneer men whose visions were fixed on productive farms yielding a competence for themselves and their families. The task of clearing land covered with trees was one requiring strength and perseverance, and many years would pass before a quarter-section farm could be completely freed of trees and stumps. A small clearing was first made for vegetables, and thereafter

for several years the pioneer farmer devoted himself alternately to planting and caring for crops among trees deadened by girdling and to cutting down trees, rolling them into piles, burning or splitting them into fence rails, and afterward digging, chopping, and burning out the tenacious stumps. On the prairies the work of preparing land for cultivation was less difficult, but the breaking of the tough sod was by no means an easy task.

Food was usually plentiful. Pork was the meat most widely eaten in pioneer days, supplemented by wild game as frequently as possible. Wild fruits were available in some sections. Vegetables were raised in considerable variety, and corn in the form of cornmeal or hominy was a customary feature of the diet. Clothing as a rule was homemade of linsey-woolsey, a combination of linen and wool; and not infrequently the father made the shoes for the family.

With allowance for some exceptions, the pioneers as a whole were not a healthy people. The first settlements were often in the forests or on lowlands along streams. Poorly constructed dwellings and the exposure of pioneer life resulted in weakened constitutions. Because of these and other factors, epidemics frequently took a terrible toll in frontier communities. The rate of infant mortality was extremely high, and early graves claimed a shockingly great proportion of the mothers.

Pioneer life, however, was not all hardship, labor, and suffering. The pioneers were known generally to be a gregarious people, who seized every possible occasion to get together with their neighbors—at cabin raisings, logrollings, corn huskings, quilting parties, weddings, and camp meetings. They were generous and hospitable to strangers and travelers. All told, they were people well fitted to lay the foundations of civilization in the wilderness.

[Ray Allen Billington, *Westward Expansion: A History of the American Frontier;* Bernard De Voto, *Year of Decision, 1846;* David Lavendar, *Westward Vision: The Story of the Oregon Trail;* C. F. McGlashan, *History of the Donner Party, A Tragedy of the Sierras;* George R. Steward, *The California Trail: An Epic With Navy Heroes.*]

DAN E. CLARK

PIONEER STAGE LINE began operating in 1851 from Sacramento to Placerville, Calif., a distance of forty-four miles. In 1857 J. B. Crandall bought an interest in the line, drove an experimental coach over a rough trail through the Sierra Nevada to the Carson Valley, and began operating coaches regularly thereon. In 1860 control passed to Louis McLane (Wells, Fargo and Company's western manager), and from 1861 the Pioneer Stage Line was a link in their Overland Mail route, becoming one of the most famous stage lines of North America. A well-graded, 100-mile macadamized road was built from Carson City, Nev., to Placerville, which was watered daily in summer so that coaches ran at high speed. In 1865 formal announcement was made of the line's passing under Wells Fargo control, though it may have been owned by them long before.

[William Banning and George Hugh Banning, *Six Horses;* Alvin F. Harlow, *Old Waybills.*]

ALVIN F. HARLOW

PIOUS FUND CONTROVERSY. The Pious Fund of the Californias was established in the 17th century to maintain and support the Jesuit missions in Upper and Lower California. The Mexican government took over the administration of the fund in the 19th century. When the United States acquired Upper California in 1848 Mexico ceased payment of annuities. In 1875 a complaint was filed by the California bishops with the Permanent Court of Arbitration at The Hague. The appointed arbitrator, Sir Edward Thornton, decided that Mexico would have to pay $904,070.79, which was done. Two years later another claim was filed with the court and the missions were awarded $1,420,682.67 in annuities.

[John T. Doyle, *History of the Pious Fund of California.*]

ALVIN F. HARLOW

PIPE, INDIAN. Smoking varied in form among native American tribes: Indians of tropical South America and the Caribbean, the areas of original tobacco domestication, developed the cigar, while in Mexico and the Pueblo Southwest, corn-husk cigarettes prevailed. Not all tobacco-using native American tribes smoked, since the narcotic was also eaten, drunk, and snuffed. Pipe smoking was localized in a few areas, and there was considerable variation both in the form of pipes and in the materials from which they were made. Pipes of stone, wood, clay, and bone were used among various tribes of the differing culture areas of the present United States. Tubular pipes, not unlike a modern cigar holder, had a scattered distribution. The more conventional elbow pipe, with stem and bowl, appeared mostly in the Plains and Woodlands; this was the form introduced into Europe in the 16th century.

Folklore, not all of it accurate, surrounds the American Indian's use of the pipe. The common idea of the peace pipe, for example, is somewhat overdrawn, at least in respect to the sharing of a pipe to symbolize cessation of hostilities. Pipe-smoking rituals, it is true, were stressed by the Plains and Woodlands peoples, but it must be noted that tobacco and the items associated with it were sacred almost everywhere they appeared. A Plains Indian bundle, the wrapped tribal or group fetish, frequently contained a carved pipe bowl of catlinite, along with the reed or wooden stem, the calumet; the latter, carved, incised, and otherwise decorated, was often the more important element. In the Woodlands, the eastern Plains, and some of the Gulf area, the calumet, like wampum, might be carried by ambassadors between federated tribes and might symbolize states of war and peace, but it might also be employed in an appeal to spiritual beings. The passing of the pipe, solemnly ritualized as it was, became a social adjunct to its intertribal symbolic use.

[Harold E. Driver, *Indians of North America.*]

ROBERT F. SPENCER

PIPELINES, EARLY. In order to eliminate the risk, expense, and uncertainty of transporting oil by boat or wagon, Herman Jones proposed in November 1861, at a meeting at Tarr farm on Oil Creek, Pa., the laying of a 4-inch wooden pipe to Oil City. Although the idea met with favor, the state legislature refused to charter the company because of teamster opposition. In 1862 Barrows and Company of Tarr farm began operating the first successful pipeline, conveying oil from the Burning well to their refinery, about 1,000 feet away. Other early experiments with pipelines met with only partial success because of poor quality pipes, leaky lead joints, and faulty pumps, but they demonstrated the feasibility of the pipeline.

In the fall of 1865 Samuel Van Syckle began trenching and laying a 2-inch wrought-iron pipe from Pithole, Pa., to Miller farm on the Oil Creek Railroad, about five and a quarter miles distant. Just prior to completion of the project, disgruntled teamsters, who saw their occupation threatened, maliciously cut the line in several places. Nevertheless, on Oct. 9, Van Syckle finished his line and made the first test, in which eighty-one barrels of oil were forced through the pipe in one hour, the equivalent of 300 teams working ten hours. Van Syckle, who had been subject to ridicule until he demonstrated the line's usefulness, had the pleasure of seeing his persecutors silenced. Two weeks later another pipeline was completed from Pithole to Henry's Bend on the Allegheny River. The Van Syckle line proved so successful that a second pipe was laid to Miller farm and began delivering oil on Dec. 8, 1865. Four days later the Pennsylvania Tubing and Transportation Company completed a gravity line from Pithole to Oleopolis, Pa., that had a capacity of 7,000 barrels every twenty-four hours. Aroused over the prospect of the oil trade being diverted to other points, some of the Titusville businessmen organized the Titusville Pipe Company, laid a pipe to Pithole, about nine miles away, and began pumping oil in March 1866, at the rate of 3,000 barrels per day. During the same month, Henry Harley and Company laid two pipelines from Bennehoff Run to Shaffer farm on the Oil Creek Railroad, a distance of two miles.

While the pipelines reduced the cost of shipping oil to the uniform rate of $1.00 per barrel, they proved to be monopolies of the worst sort, keeping their prices just below the teamsters' in order to eliminate teaming, yet high enough so that producers derived little benefit. Even before the first pipeline to Miller farm had been completed, teamsters began leaving the oil fields, and when the Harley lines were completed, more than 400 teams left at one time. Those teamsters who remained made threats against the pipelines and even set fire to the Harley storage tanks at Shaffer, causing a loss of about $10,000. Rather than continue the violence, teamsters reduced the price of teaming, but their ruin was inevitable.

Van Syckle's partners suffered financial failure not long after the completion of their line. Although Van Syckle assumed payment of the debt and agreed that the First National Bank of Titusville should operate the line until the debt had been liquidated, he never managed to regain control. W. H. Abbott and Henry Harley bought Van Syckle's line and combined it with Harley's in 1867 to form the first great pipeline company, the Allegheny Transportation Company.

During the next few years short pipelines multiplied, crossing and paralleling one another in every direction. Competition was keen, and ruinous rate wars ensued. These were among the major factors that soon brought about the consolidation of the lines.

[Paul H. Giddens, *The Birth of the Oil Industry*.]

PAUL H. GIDDENS

PIPE STAVES, barrel staves, and hogshead staves were important articles of commerce and of domestic use in early America. All were rived from straight-grained logs of varying lengths, shaved smooth with a drawknife or plane, and given shape with a slight bulge of width in the middle, so that when hooped together from each end the resulting barrel, hogshead, or cask would be a double conoid. A pipe was a large cask, holding usually half a tun, that is, two hogsheads, or 126 wine gallons. Inasmuch as a large cask when filled was very heavy, pipe staves had to be thicker and stronger than barrel staves. Pipe staves were sent in large quantities to the wine-producing countries of Europe and the West Indies. The standard length of a pipe stave was 4½ feet; the width only a few inches; and they were usually made of white or red oak. Prices varied, depending on the quality, stage of manufacture (whether rough as rived or shaved and shaped), the commodity or currency given in exchange, and the time and place of the transaction. Staves packed close in shipping were preferred in outgoing cargoes to finished empty casks, which required much room.

[William B. Weedon, *Economic and Social History of New England*.]

JOHN W. WAYLAND

PIQUA, BATTLE OF (Aug. 8, 1780). In retaliation for a raid in early June 1780 by British Capt. Henry Bird and a force made up mainly of Indians, George Rogers Clark led nearly 1,000 frontiersmen up the Little Miami River against the Shawnee towns of Old Chillicothe (near Xenia) and Piqua (near Springfield), both in Ohio. Old Chillicothe was abandoned and burned, and the Indians fled to Piqua, some twelve miles distant. Clark divided his forces in an attempt to surround Piqua, but Col. Benjamin Logan, in command of one of the columns, became entangled in a grassy swamp and accomplished little. Many of the Shawnee fled at Clark's approach, leaving only a few Indians to sustain the American attack. The battle was hardly more than a long drawn-out skirmish, with only seventeen men lost on each side. After Clark used a small field cannon to dislodge the Indians from the fort in which they had taken refuge, they scattered into the forest, and Clark's men were able to burn the town, fields, and stores.

[E. O. Randall and D. J. Ryan, *History of Ohio*, vol. II.]

EUGENE H. ROSEBOOM

PIQUA, COUNCIL OF. *See* **Pickawillanee.**

PIRACY. From the early 17th century to the early 19th century the Atlantic and Gulf coasts were the sites of operations for numerous pirates who preyed on American shipping and caused great losses in ships and lives.

From New England's earliest settlement, its shipping suffered from pirates on its coast. In 1653 Massachusetts made piracy punishable by death; and its governors sometimes sent out armed ships to attack offshore pirates. On the other hand, colonial governors after 1650 granted "privateering" commissions to sea desperadoes and winked at their piracies—a popular procedure then. The Navigation Acts, passed by Great Britain from 1650 to 1696 halted all foreign ships from trading in the American colonies and led to colonial smuggling and eventually to piracy. Colonial merchants and settlers bought pirates' stolen goods and thus obtained necessary commodities at a cheap price. New York, Newport, R.I., and Philadelphia were rivals in this scandalous trade, with Boston, Virginia, and the Carolinas also buying stolen goods.

Richard Coote, Earl of Bellomont, was appointed governor of New York and New England in 1697 with orders to "suppress the prevailing piracy that was causing so much distress along the coast" and in that same year reported general colonial connivance with pirates, especially in New York, Rhode Island, and Philadelphia. One New York merchant secured $500,000 in seven years through the promotion of piracy.

The highest number of piracies was committed during the period 1705–25, and 1721–24 saw a reign of terror on the New England coast. English men-of-war ended this peril, but after the American Revolution piratical attacks on U.S. ships by French "privateers" brought on an undeclared war between France and the United States and led to the creation of the U.S. Navy. Piratical operations of English men-of-war on U.S. coasts and the high seas—including the impressment of American seamen—led to the War of 1812. The period 1805–25 witnessed a resurgence of piracy, which led to the maintenance and increase of the U.S. Navy, then busy at suppressing piracy and convoying ships. Over 3,000 instances of piracy were recorded between 1814 and 1824—half of them on U.S. shipping.

Beginning in 1805 the navy was engaged in warring on pirates on the Louisiana and Gulf coasts, which had long been haunted by pirates. The Barataria pirates were driven out in 1814, as well as the Aury-Laffite pirates from Galveston, Texas, in 1817. In 1816–24 the United States faced a perplexing problem in handling the piratical "privateers" of the new Latin-American republics. Congress finally was so

angered by these freebooters' depredations that in 1819 an act was passed prescribing the death penalty for piracy.

The Spaniards of Cuba and Puerto Rico sent out many pirates who captured American ships, murdered their crews, and nearly brought on a war between the United States and these two colonies of Spain. Congress denounced "this truly alarming piracy" in 1822, and in 1823–24 dispatched a strong naval squadron to suppress these pirates. By 1827 piracy had ended on all U.S. coasts.

[George Francis Dow and John H. Edmonds, *The Pirates of the New England Coast;* Gardner W. Allen, *Our Navy and the West Indian Pirates;* George Wycherley, *Buccaneers of the Pacific.*]

GEORGE WYCHERLEY

PISTOLE, a gold coin current in Spain, Italy, and America in the 18th century. Its value varied, but it was commonly worth fifteen English shillings. Its French equivalent was the louis d'or. During the first half of the 18th century Virginians spoke of values in terms of pistoles almost as readily as pounds.

CARL L. CANNON

"PIT," the popular name given to the trading floor of any commodity exchange, but most often applied to that of the Board of Trade of the City of Chicago, the largest commodity exchange in the United States. World opinion on the price of grains, gold and silver, plywood, and other commodities is registered at the "Pit." By providing opportunities for future buying (the making of contracts for future delivery) and hedging (the protection of the buyer against price changes), the "Pit" tends to promote a liquid market.

On Mar. 18, 1848, a call to organize a market for grain buyers and sellers was issued by a group of the leading commission merchants of Chicago. As a result, on Monday, Apr. 3, 1848, the Board of Trade was organized with a membership of eighty-two. The objectives were "to maintain a Commercial Exchange; to promote uniformity in the customs and usages of merchants; to inculcate principles of justice and equity in trade; to facilitate the speedy adjustment of business disputes; to acquire and disseminate valuable commercial and economic information; and, generally to secure to its members the benefits of cooperation in the furtherance of their legitimate pursuits."

In 1850 the Board of Trade was organized under a general statute for the incorporation of boards of trade and chambers of commerce, approved by the Illinois legislature on Feb. 8, 1849. On Feb. 18, 1859, the Board of Trade of the City of Chicago was incorporated by a special legislative act. The Board of Trade is governed by a board of directors; an appointed professional serves as president.

[Cedric B. Cowing, *Populists, Plungers, and Progressives: A Social History of Stock and Commodity Speculation.*]

BENJAMIN F. SHAMBAUGH

PITHOLE. In 1864 the United States Petroleum Company leased a portion of the Thomas Holmden farm on Pithole Creek, about six miles east of Oil Creek and equidistant from Titusville and Oil City, Pa. The company drilled a well that in January 1865 began flowing at the rate of about 250 barrels of oil a day, a figure that ultimately grew to 1,200 barrels a day. The United States well, as it was known, precipitated a wild stampede to the Holmden farm. Leases sold for fabulous sums; other wells were drilled; and a city called Pithole sprang into existence and became a whirlpool of excitement and speculation. In September 1865, the population reached 15,000, and the daily production exceeded 6,000 barrels. Then, within six months, after the failure of its wells, Pithole became a deserted city.

[Paul H. Giddens, *The Birth of the Oil Industry.*]
PAUL H. GIDDENS

PITT, FORT. The building of a temporary structure, commonly known as Fort Pitt, was begun in late 1858, after the British forces of Gen. John Forbes routed the French at the confluence of the Monongahela and Allegheny rivers on the present site of Pittsburgh. Named in honor of the British statesman William Pitt the Elder, the fort was completed in January 1759 and stood on the banks of the Monongahela, approximately 200 yards above the site of Fort Duquesne. On Sept. 3, 1759, Gen. John Stanwix personally directed the beginning of the work on a permanent fortification, correctly known as Fort Pitt and sufficiently formidable to assure British supremacy in the region. Although this fort was occupied in 1760, it was not completed until the summer of 1761, and the redoubt was added in 1764 by Col. Henry Bouquet. Fort Pitt was a five-sided structure surrounded by a ditch. A brick revetment supported the ramparts on the two sides facing the land. The three sides facing the rivers were supported by pickets. The British maintained a garrison at Fort Pitt to aid in

preserving order among the settlers and Indians until late 1772, when the troops were withdrawn. Only caretakers occupied the fort until January 1774, when John Connolly of Virginia took possession and renamed it Fort Dunmore (*see* Dunmore's War). Capt. John Neville, with a company sent out by the Virginia Provincial Convention, held control from September 1775 to June 1777, relinquishing his command to Gen. Edward Hand of the Continental forces. Except for one short interval, the fort was a base of operations for western campaigns during the Revolution (*see* Brodhead's Allegheny Campaign). Gen. William Irvine repaired the fort in 1782 but thereafter it was permitted to deteriorate.

R. J. FERGUSON

PITTMAN ACT, enacted Apr. 23, 1918, provided for the breaking up of not more than 350 million silver dollars and the export of said silver to India and the Orient to benefit the balance of payments of the United States and its allies in World War I. Provision was also made for the issuance of Federal Reserve bank notes to take the place of the silver dollars and certificates withdrawn from circulation and for their subsequent retirement and replacement with silver dollars and certificates through the purchase of silver from domestic producers, at not less than $1 per ounce.

[Milton Friedman and Anna Jacobson, *A Monetary History of the United States, 1867–1960.*]
FREDERICK A. BRADFORD

PITTSBURGH, a city in southwestern Pennsylvania, is situated where the Allegheny and Monongahela rivers form the Ohio. Pittsburgh early earned the sobriquet "Gateway to the West." In 1758, after British Gen. John Forbes and his force came upon the abandoned Fort Duquesne, Forbes renamed the site Pittsbourgh in honor of William Pitt the Elder. From 1759 to 1761 a permanent fort, also named after Pitt, was constructed. Laid out in 1764 by John Campbell, the small trading post that had recently survived attack by Ottawa forces, led by Pontiac, became successively a county seat in 1788, borough in 1794, and city in 1816. The same strategic situation that had made it the logical place for a fort controlling the upper Mississippi Valley also made it the entrepôt for the waves of migration to the West. With the opening of the Mississippi, Pittsburgh began its development as a commercial city. Its manufactures found their way to New Orleans and ultimately to Baltimore and

Philadelphia, first on flatboats, then by keelboat and river steamboat. The impetus given to nascent industry by the demands of westward migration was renewed by the War of 1812. At the same time western and southern areas that had been drawing on the city now began sending raw materials by steamboat to Pittsburgh. The demand for manufactured products, combined with the relative abundance of certain necessary raw materials, soon made the iron and glass industries of Pittsburgh of national importance. During the Civil War, Pittsburgh iron foundries and mills played an important role in supplying Union armies with cannon and armor plate. The transition from iron to steel was neither long nor difficult, and the city, under the guidance of certain prominent families—the Carnegies, Fricks, and Mellons—became the largest steel-producing area in the United States. During World War II Pittsburgh mills produced a third of the steel used in the war effort. After World War II the city began an extensive renovation of the Golden Triangle (the city's business district), razing old warehouses, factories, and other run-down buildings and replacing them with new office and civic structures, hotels, and parks. Smoke control legislation, first enacted in 1947, extensively reduced the air pollution that had once blighted the city. In 1970 the city's population was 520,117.

[Leland D. Baldwin, *Pittsburgh: The Story of a City;* Sarah H. Killikelly, *The History of Pittsburgh, Its Rise and Progress.*]

FRANK B. SESSA

PITTSBURGH, INDIAN TREATY AT (1775), was the result of a conference of the Indian tribes in that region with commissioners from the Virginia Assembly and Richard Butler, Indian agent for the Indian Department of the Continental Congress. The Delaware, Shawnee, Mingo, Seneca, Wyandot, and Ottawa tribes were restless and uneasy because of Dunmore's War of the previous year. Furthermore, the Shawnee Indians had taken captives and stolen black slaves from Virginians, which the commissioners sought to recover. The commissioners were also anxious to placate the Indians and procure their neutrality in the approaching struggle between Great Britain and the colonies.

Chief White Eyes of the Delaware was the spokesman for the Indians; George Morgan, the Indian trader, gave counsel to all; and Butler acted for the Indian Department. The treaty was a success. The Indians, after receiving promises that the Ohio River boundary would be respected, were satisfied and

agreed not to fight in the forthcoming struggle. The Shawnee agreed to return the captives and the stolen slaves, and the Seneca and Delaware engaged to assist them in that duty. The commissioners of Virginia sent letters to white settlers in the region requesting them not to cross the Ohio and to avoid irritating the Indians.

[Max Savelle, *George Morgan, Colony Builder.*]

R. J. FERGUSON

PITTSBURGH GAZETTE (variously the *Pittsburgh Gazette and Manufacturing and Mercantile Advertiser,* the *Pittsburgh Daily Gazette and Advertiser,* the *Pittsburgh Commercial Gazette,* the *Gazette Times,* and the *Pittsburgh Post-Gazette*) is generally considered to have been the first newspaper established west of the Allegheny Mountains. The founders, John Scull and Joseph Hall, Philadelphia printers, conveyed their press over the mountains in a Conestoga wagon and printed the first number of the paper on July 29, 1786.

[J. C. Andrews, *Pittsburgh's Post-Gazette.*]

J. CUTLER ANDREWS

PITTSBURGH RESOLUTIONS. On hearing of the battles at Lexington and Concord in April 1775, a meeting of the Virginia patriots in the vicinity of Pittsburgh was called for May 16. Both a committee of safety for the district of West Augusta, chaired by George Groghan, and a standing committee vested with emergency powers were established. In the resolutions passed at the meeting the patriots expressed their approval of the conduct of the minutemen of Massachusetts as well as their friendship for the Indians. An assessment was made on taxables in order to raise money to buy munitions for the militia, and the raising of independent military companies was encouraged.

[Neville B. Craig, *History of Pittsburgh.*]

LELAND D. BALDWIN

PITTSBURG LANDING. *See* **Shiloh, Battle of.**

PLACER MINING is a process in which gold or other mineral deposits are found loosely mixed with the sand at the bottom of a stream bed or similar alluvial deposit. It differs from lode mining where the minerals are always found in place. It was placer gold that started the gold rushes to California in 1849,

Pikes Peak in 1858, and the Klondike in Canada in 1896. The pure gold is washed from the sand or debris by means of a gold pan. Because of its weight, gold, if present, will gravitate to the bottom of the pan. Here the "colors" (tiny specks) or nuggets of gold are picked out with a tweezer or amalgamated with mercury. Improvements in placer mining, such as the rocker, sluicebox, long tom, hydraulic nozzle, boom dam, or dredge, are all designed to wash more gravel with a given amount of time and labor. The richest placer deposits have been in California and Alaska.

[C. F. Jackson and J. B. Knaebel, *Small Scale Placer-Mining Methods;* E. B. Wilson, *Hydraulic and Placer Mining.*]

PERCY S. FRITZ

PLAIN, FORT, was built in colonial times near the Mohawk River to protect the farmers near Canajoharie, N.Y., from the Iroquois. It sheltered the settlers from the Onondaga in 1777, and on numerous occasions during the American Revolution provided a rallying point for troop movements up the Schoharie Valley, as well as a refuge for the wounded. The importance of the fort ceased after 1781.

[W. M. Reid, *Old Fort Johnson.*]

CARL L. CANNON

PLAINS, GREAT. *See* **Great Plains.**

PLAINS OF ABRAHAM. *See* **Abraham, Plains of.**

PLANK ROADS, introduced into the United States from Canada about 1837, were first constructed in the state of New York and were widely adopted in South Carolina, Illinois, Ohio, and Michigan. Thousands of miles were built at a mileage cost of from $1,000 to $2,400. Roadways were first well drained, with ditches on either side. Then planks, 3 or 4 inches thick and 8 feet long, were laid at right angles to stringers, which were placed lengthwise on the road. Planks were prepared by portable sawmills that were set up in neighboring forests. For a time plank roads successfully competed with railroads, but were eventually replaced by paved roads.

[B. H. Meyer, *History of Transportation in the United States Before 1860.*]

CHARLES B. SWANEY

PLANNED ECONOMY. In contrast to the theory of individualism, under which each person carries on economic activities much as he pleases, is the theory of a planned economy, under which the government regulates and controls important elements of the economy in order to achieve certain economic goals. Advocates of the planned economy theory are in disagreement as to whether the planning, for the purpose of directing the economic system toward what they regard as socially desirable ends, should be done by the legislative or executive authority, or through the cooperative action of business. So far as the United States is concerned, such advocates are generally agreed that the planning should be national. The theory of a planned economy implies fact-finding to learn what needs must be met; limitation of production to meet those needs; and planning for future needs and for the development of new activities. Proposals for a planned economy were frequent after the beginning of the Great Depression in 1929. The theory was embodied to some extent in the New Deal program.

[George Soule, *Planning U.S.A.;* E. S. Woytinsky, *Profile of the United States Economy: A Survey of the Growth and Change.*]

ERIK MCKINLEY ERIKSSON

PLANNING, CITY. *See* **City Planning.**

PLAN OF 1776, a model set of articles for treaties to be negotiated with foreign powers by the newly independent United States. It was drawn up by a committee composed of John Adams, Benjamin Franklin, John Dickinson, and Robert Morris and was adopted Sept. 17, 1776. The plan remains significant because of its definition of neutral rights, that is to say, the freedom of the seas. The committee selected from 18th-century European treaties such definitions of neutral rights as appealed to small-navied powers: the doctrine of free ships, free goods; freedom of neutrals to trade in noncontraband between port and port of a belligerent (this a repudiation of the British Rule of the War of 1756); and restricted the category of contraband to a carefully defined list of arms, munitions, and implements of war, not including foodstuffs or naval stores. Blockade was not defined. These principles were written into the Franco-American Treaty of Amity and Commerce of 1778; into all other such treaties negotiated with European powers in the 18th century, excepting Great Britain; and into most of the first treaties of amity and commerce negotiated with

Latin-American republics. They also appeared in the Armed Neutrality of 1780 and of 1800; and the Declaration of Paris of 1856 confirmed as international law the principle of free ships, free goods, and also a definition of blockade.

[Samuel Flagg Bemis, *Diplomatic History of the United States;* Carlton Savage, *Policy of the United States Toward Maritime Commerce in War.*]

SAMUEL FLAGG BEMIS

PLAN OF UNION, an agreement made in 1801 between the Congregational Association of Connecticut and the general assembly of the Presbyterian church to combine their work on the frontier wherever the two bodies came together. The plan provided for the settlement of either a Presbyterian or Congregational minister over mixed congregations and for the settlement of a Presbyterian minister over a Congregational church, and vice versa. Its purpose was to "promote mutual forebearance and the spirit of accommodation" between adherents of both churches in frontier communities. As a whole it worked in the interest of Presbyterianism, owing to the more effective church polity of the latter and the willingness of Congregationalists to be absorbed in the West. It was repudiated by the old school Presbyterians in 1837 when the Presbyterians were divided into old and new school bodies and in 1852 by the Congregationalists.

[W. S. Kennedy, *The Plan of Union: Or a History of the Presbyterian and Congregational Churches of the Western Reserve;* W. W. Sweet, *Religion on the American Frontier,* vol. II.]

WILLIAM W. SWEET

PLANTATIONS, a term applied in New England to the system of planting new settlements, usually within a colony under the direction of its legislature. It did not originate in New England for it was already current in Virginia when the Pilgrims applied it to their colony—Plymouth Plantation. Still earlier, it was used in connection with the efforts of Sir Humphrey Gilbert and Sir Walter Raleigh to establish plantations or colonies in Ireland and the New World. It came to have a special significance in New England. Since the charter gave to the Massachusetts Bay Company the right to distribute its lands, the governing body, known as the general court, was able to select suitable leaders for a new planting and bestow upon them the authority to direct the whole enterprise. These leaders received the land for the new settlement in trust, they arranged the business details of the planting, they dis-

tributed the land, and they organized local government according to instructions given them. Sometimes actual settlement preceded the general court's authority, but usually the general court was lenient to squatter origin of settlements, provided it approved of the leaders. This system of authorized and controlled plantations in group units enabled the general court not only to distribute the colony's growing population and to govern it according to Puritan ideals and standards, but it also provided a frontier system of defense through the planning of buffer settlements. Other New England colonies copied it so that in time it came to be associated particularly with expansion in Puritan New England.

[C. M. Andrews, *The Colonial Period of American History,* vol. I.]

VIOLA F. BARNES

PLANTATION SYSTEM OF THE SOUTH was developed to meet the world demand for certain staple crops. While in 17th-century England the word "plantation" meant a colony, the relationship between the London Company and its plantation—Virginia (1607–24)—meant far more than that. The company transported the settlers, who were to be laborers, provided the taskmasters, fed and clothed the workers, and received the proceeds of their labor. Ten years' experience revealed numerous defects in operating a whole colony as one estate. Consequently, the company's possession was divided into smaller industrial units and private ownership granted; and when Virginia passed to the English crown (1624), it became a commonwealth of independent farms and private plantations. While tobacco was already known and used in England, the discovery in 1616 of a new method of curing it increased the demand and spurred large-scale production. The demand for labor thus created was filled by African slaves brought to the New World by Dutch traders, resulting in the adaptation of slaves to the system. This was the distinguishing feature of the plantation industry, because the racial factor and slave status of the laborers produced a fairly rigid regimentation. By the end of the 17th century the Virginia system was a model for the other southern colonies.

As finally evolved, the system employed large laboring forces (1,000 acres and 100 slaves was considered a highly productive unit), a division of labor, and a routine under the direction of a central authority to produce tobacco, rice, sugar, and cotton in large quantities for domestic and foreign markets. While tobacco and rice were important in the evolution of the system, cotton was the greatest force in making it dominant in southern economic life. The introduction of sea island cotton into Georgia (1786) and the invention of the cotton gin by Eli Whitney (1793) made possible the profitable growing of short staple cotton, and enabled the South to supply the English textile industry with the commercial quantities of raw cotton so urgently demanded. In 1800 the South exported 35,000 bales, in 1820 more than 320,000, and in 1860, 5 million bales. The plantation industry was in reality the "big business" of the antebellum South.

The plantations were self-sustained communities, with slave quarters, storehouses, smokehouses, barns, tools, livestock, gardens, orchards, and fields. The slaves were usually worked in gangs, although the task system was not uncommon; skilled slaves were employed in their special capacity; and care was taken to keep as large a number of slaves as possible busy throughout the year. The larger the plantation the more highly organized it was apt to be. In the absence of the owner, the establishment was directed by his agent, usually the overseer.

Climate and soil largely determined the location of the plantation system. The upper South (Maryland, Virginia, Kentucky, North Carolina) produced tobacco; the South Carolina and Georgia tidewater produced sea island cotton and rice; the rich bottoms of Louisiana, sugar cane; and throughout the Piedmont region short staple cotton held sway. Because slave labor was used, the "black belts" were identical with the plantation zones. After its development in Virginia, the plantation regime spread southwest with the national territorial expansion, until in 1860 most of the climatic zone available for staple production was affected.

The entire social and economic life of the South was geared to the plantation industry, although in 1850 two-thirds of all the white people of that section had no connection with slavery, and 1,000 families received over $50 million per year in contrast with about $60 million for the remaining 666,000 families. This concentration of wealth produced an economic power that dominated every field, similar to that of the northern industrial magnates of 1880.

While seemingly affluent, the plantation system was financially and commercially dependent on the eastern cities, especially New York. Such dependency reduced southern cities to mere markets and sent fluid capital as payment for insurance, freights, tariffs, and warehouse fees to New York and Philadelphia. Cotton was usually marketed through New York, and plantation supplies were purchased there or from northern agencies in the South. Soil exhaustion and erosion increased with the expansion of agriculture, the causes being the nature of the southern terrain, improper methods of cultivation, the lack of commercial fertilizer (before 1850), together with the continuous cultivation of the staples on the same land. A more efficient organization and operation of the system was imperative by 1860.

The plantation system with slave labor was destroyed by the Civil War and the decade of Reconstruction that followed. Some plantations operated thereafter on a crop-sharing basis under a centralized authority, as for example "Dunleith," in the Yazoo-Mississippi delta. Others operated on a wage-labor basis, but the vast majority broke up into small farms, operated by the individual owner, tenant, or sharecropper.

[John W. Blassingame, *The Slave Community;* Eugene D. Genovese, *The World the Slaveholders Made: Two Essays in Interpretation;* Robert M. Myers, ed., *The Children of Pride.*]

RALPH B. FLANDERS

PLANTS, NATIVE, STUDY OF. The study of American plants has attracted many naturalists, beginning with some of the early explorers. At first they had primarily utilitarian interests. Some edible plants were discovered, but the agriculture of North American Indians was neither ancient enough nor intensive enough for the development of important food crops (the Indians had brought their corn and tobacco from Middle America). Nor was North America to be an important source of new medicinal plants. But the quest for horticultural plants was considerably more successful. Because of lesser economic and aesthetic attractions, the ferns, mosses, and other nonflowering plants have become more slowly known than the flowering plants.

If one passes over the occasional descriptions of plants by explorers, such as those of John White, and over the few descriptions of American plants in European herbals, the first book on North American plants was that by the Parisian physician Jacques-Philippe Cornut. He devoted over half of his *Canadensium Plantarum* (1635) to descriptions of forty-four American plants, most of which were well illustrated. He did not collect the plants himself but relied on specimens growing in Parisian gardens. The earliest notable resident naturalist was an Oxford-educated minister and immigrant Virginia planter, John Banister, who came to America in 1678. He sent back to England specimens and descriptions of approximately 340 American plants, and he planned a treatise on the natural history of eastern Virginia, but it was not completed before his accidental death in 1692. Several decades later, another immigrant planter, John Clayton, compiled a *Flora Virginica*, which was edited, enlarged, and published by a Dutch patron, Johann Friedrich Gronovius. One of America's few immigrant physicians, Alexander Garden, who settled in Charleston, S.C., about 1754 and lived there for three decades, supplied his British countrymen and the Swedish naturalist Carl Linnaeus with both biological specimens and observations.

John Bartram was America's first prominent native-born plant explorer. On his farm near Philadelphia he grew many of the plants that he found on numerous trips. He also sent numerous specimens to British collectors. He published an account of his trip to Lake Ontario in 1751, which brought him fame both at home and abroad. His son, William Bartram, followed in his footsteps and in 1791 published a more widely acclaimed account of his own observations on a four-year (1773–77) trip through North and South Carolina, Georgia, and Florida.

The first collector of North American plants who distinguished himself by writing and illustrating an account of his discoveries was Mark Catesby, whose trip to America was paid for by British patrons. His *Natural History of Carolina, Florida, and the Bahama Islands* appeared in two volumes, in 1731 and 1743. Linnaeus described about 170 American plants in his *Hortus Cliffortianus* (1737), based on specimens growing in the garden of his Dutch patron, George Clifford. One of Linnaeus' students, Pehr Kalm, was sent to America by the Swedish Royal Academy of Science in 1748 "to enlarge the number and varieties of useful plants and trees in Sweden," and he explored from Philadelphia to the Great Lakes for more than two years. He reported many useful observations in his *Resa til Norra America* (1753–61). André Michaux came to America for a similar purpose on behalf of France in 1785, and before returning in 1796, he had explored from Florida and the Bahamas almost to Hudson Bay. He published his *Histoire des chênes de l'Amérique* in 1801, and his *Flora boreali-americana* appeared posthumously in 1803.

With the rise of higher education in America, university faculties became sources for the advancement and dissemination of knowledge about American plants. Benjamin Smith Barton, a professor of natural history, botany, and materia medica at the University of Pennsylvania, wrote the first botanical textbook published in America (1803). Both his nephew, William P. C. Barton, and one of his former students from Boston, Jacob Bigelow, began publishing their well-illustrated treatises on American medical botany in 1817.

By the beginning of the 19th century, plant explorers were already moving beyond the Atlantic states. Native Americans were often in the vanguard—the Meriwether Lewis and William Clark expedition of 1804–06, for example, returned with 177 species of plants after having lost others en route—but during the first half of the century Europeans continued to participate in the explorations. The explorers who started out from the Atlantic states were often allied with a college professor, notably B. S. Barton, John Torrey, and Asa Gray, or some other established naturalist who assisted in finding financial support and in publishing reports of the discoveries. Those explorers who started out from Europe with European support generally took their plants and observations back to Europe, where the results were published.

François André Michaux accompanied his father, André Michaux, on his American explorations, and in 1801 he returned to America to continue the work. He explored west to the Mississippi and published an account of his travels in 1804 and a study on growing North American trees in France in 1805; most important was his *Histoire des arbres forestiers de l'Amérique septentrionale* (1810–13). The English collector Thomas Nuttall was one of the most widely traveled of the early explorers in the West. In 1811 he traveled from Philadelphia to the Great Lakes and down the Mississippi River to New Orleans. He later traveled through the south Atlantic states and up the Arkansas River, and from 1834 to 1836 he traveled up the North Platte River, across the Rockies, and down the Columbia River to the Pacific. He then sailed to Honolulu and back to the southern coast of California before sailing to Boston via Cape Horn. He published his *Genera of North American Plants, and a Catalogue of the Species, to the Year 1817,* at Philadelphia in 1818. The plants of the California coast were first collected in 1791 by Thaddaeus Haenke, who was a member of the Malaspina expedition from Spain. In 1792–93 a Spanish royal botanical expedition to New Spain also collected plants of southern California. Martín Sessé was director of the expedition and his chief botanical assistant was José Mariano Mocino. Although they took their collections and observations to Spain in 1803, they were unsuccessful in having them published. Most of the written manuscripts were lost, but on the basis of their drawings and herbarium specimens other botanists later published accounts of their findings. The British were soon to follow. In 1792–94 the Scottish botanist Archibald Menzies, while accompanying George Vancouver on his voyage around the world, collected plants in California and Washington. David Douglas was the most successful explorer of the West for horticultural species. The Royal Horticultural Society sent him out from London on his first voyage to the United States in 1823, and he continued collecting for it until his accidental death in Hawaii in 1834. His contemporary, the British collector Thomas Drummond, who traveled in both Canada and Texas, also died at the task, at Havana, Cuba, in 1835.

Asa Gray was appointed professor of natural history at Harvard in 1842, and he soon became the dominant figure in American botany—as a collector and, more important, a classifier and organizer of botanical knowledge. He published the first of many editions of his *Manual of the Botany of the Northern United States* in 1848. Collectors in the West began sending him their plants to name, classify, and describe, and for years he performed valuable service as a clearinghouse, preventing the confusion of duplicate names for the same plant or of several plants with the same name. His domination gradually became oppressive, and it was an act of rebellion in 1881 when Edward Lee Greene began publishing his own names and descriptions without prior approval from Gray.

Many of the early American collectors in the West were attached to government exploring expeditions and, later, to government surveys. In contrast with the East, therefore, regional floras for the West were often published by the federal government. Greene and Edward Palmer were notable plant collectors who often traveled alone in the American West during the last three decades of the 19th century.

The modern study of American plants depends heavily on collections in herbaria. The herbaria made in America during the 18th century commonly went to Europe, and in the 19th century those that stayed in the country often were inadequately preserved. Thus, many of the important herbarium collections in America are less than a century old. The oldest permanent American herbaria, with dates of founding, are at the Academy of Natural Sciences, Philadelphia (1812); the University of Michigan (1838); the California Academy of Sciences (1853); the University of Missouri (1856); the Missouri Botanical Garden (1857); the Gray Herbarium at Harvard University (1864); and the U.S. National Herbarium (1868). The last of these is now the largest in the country.

[*Annals of the Missouri Botanical Garden*, vol. 61, no. 1 (1974); Sidney F. Blake and Alice C. Atwood, *Geographical Guide to the Floras of the World*, vol. I; Joseph Ewan, ed., *A Short History of Botany in the United States;* Harry B. Humphrey, *Makers of North American Botany;* Jean F. Leroy, ed., *Les botanistes français en Amérique du Nord avant 1850;* Susan D. McKelvey, *Botanical Exploration of the Trans-Mississippi West, 1790–1850.*]

FRANK N. EGERTON

PLASTICS. Natural plastics include horn, hoof, shell, shellac, and certain tars; animal horn, hoof, and tortoiseshell are albumenoids called keratin. Horn is plasticized by boiling water and then may be split, flattened, and delaminated along the annual growth rings. These thin laminates are molded, self-bonded, colored, carved, and machined. Animal-hoof glues are basic adhesives.

From horn, the horners, or hornsmiths, who came to America from England early in the 18th century fabricated combs, buttons, spoons, and other products; their lanthorn windows were converted to glass after 1740.

Combmaking from horn and shell was a business concentrated in Leominster, Mass., and Leominster plastics pioneers adapted to Celluloid, Bakelite, and acetate as the industry matured. Molding, extrusion, and calendering of plastics were pioneered by the rubber industry. The basic Edwin Chaffee rubber calender of 1833 is still used for coating fabrics and paper with vinyl, polyethylene, and other plastics. Molders of plastics followed the mold and pressing procedures of the rubber workers as they started to mold gutta-percha and shellac.

Gutta-percha, a rubberlike product of several trees of Malaysia, was introduced in Europe in 1832, and gutta-percha became the generic name for molded plastics, even though they were molded of shellac, rubber, or the pitch-bonded fillers. Shellac preparations, especially shellac-bonded wood flour, became important for molding and laminating and continued in that use until replaced by synthetics after World War II; shellac was the principal material used in phonograph records before the appearance of vinyl.

Nitrocellulose, a product of the action of nitric acid on cotton, was discovered in Germany in 1845. Its flammability ultimately brought it into use as a military propellant, under the name "guncotton." Solutions of nitrocellulose left, on evaporation, a plastic film that was called collodion, used in photography as early as 1851. At the same time, the compounding of nitrocellulose with other materials, especially camphor, was found to yield a bulkier plastic material. Introduced in England, molded nitrocellulose products were popular but less than satisfactory until technically improved by John W. Hyatt of Albany, N.Y., who introduced injection molding, solvent extrusion (forcing molten plastics through an opening), blow molding (similar to glass blowing), and other fabrication techniques. Hyatt's Celluloid, as he called it, introduced in 1869, made possible George Eastman's roll-film camera; Thomas A. Edison's motion picture; new forms of dentures, spectacle frames, collars, and side curtains; and a host of novelties. It also gave rise to a worldwide business and spawned many companies in the United States. The Celluloid Manufacturing Company (later Celanese), established in 1871, gave birth to the Hercules Plastics Corporation and the Atlas Powder, Nixon Nitration, and Foster Grant companies.

The combustibility of Celluloid placed a severe limit on its use, and a continuous attempt to produce similar, but nonflammable, plastics by reacting cotton with acids other than nitric acid yielded a cellulose acetate resin about 1890. One of its first uses was in the coating of airplane wings, but in 1908 it was replacing Celluloid in photographic film.

Bakelite, made from phenol and formaldehyde, is often considered the first truly synthetic plastics material, as its ingredients are not found in nature in a pure form. It takes its name from Leo H. Baekeland, a Belgian immigrant to the United States, who devoted the years 1902–10 to an attempt to reduce to a usable form the sticky product of certain organic reactions. The resin he succeeded in hardening by heat appeared just in time to serve as an insulating material in the embryonic electrical and automotive industries. Bakelite triggered the explosive growth of industrial plastics materials and remains one of the most important of them.

Other new plastics materials appeared with increasing frequency, including new urea resins resembling Bakelite. The process of thermosetting appeared in 1928, acrylics and polyethylene in 1931, vinyl resins in 1933, melamine in 1937, styrene about 1937, Teflon and epoxy in 1938, nylon in 1939, silicones in 1943, polypropylene in 1954, plastic foams (for example, urethane) about 1955, polycarbonate in 1959, and polysulfone in 1965.

Many of these materials had been discovered in the mid-19th century, when chemists—almost exclusively Europeans—were studying the properties of newly isolated organic compounds. Many of them exhibited polymerization, the property of agglomerating into large molecules having plastic properties for which nobody at the time felt any need. The early manufacturers naturally suggested uses, but their principal problem was in giving the plastics materials a usable form, and this was largely a mechanical problem. Hyatt had pioneered in the use of heat and pressure, extrusion, and blow molding. But these innovations were merely the beginning of plastics-forming technology, and subsequent improvements owed almost as much to European as to American enterprise. In the United States the Tennessee Eastman Company in particular developed cellulose acetate; E. I. Du Pont de Nemours, Celanese; and the research firm of Arthur D. Little concerned itself with the improvement of industrial thermoplastic resins. James T. Bailey, a glass technologist, in 1938 developed an automatic machine combining hot extrusion with blow molding for the manufacture of bottles. In 1947 he developed the "layflat tubing process" for film manufacture. In 1937 Ellis Foster introduced low-pressure molded plastics with glass filament reinforcement. W. H. Willert's reciprocating screw plasticizer-plunger of 1952 facilitated both injection and blow molding.

By the mid-1970's plastics were proven to be one of the answers to many of the pollution and waste disposal problems. Biodegradable materials had become available, and all plastics could be burned to convert their total energy values into heat. Flame retardant additives eliminated the combustion hazards that were present in the early plastics.

[J. Harry DuBois, *Plastics History, USA;* Williams Haynes, *Cellulose, The Chemical That Grows;* Carl B. Kaufman, *Grand Duke, Wizard and Bohemian—A Biographical Profile of Leo Hendrik Baekeland;* M. Kaufman, *The First Century of Plastics;* John K. Mumford, *The Story of Bakelite.*]

J. HARRY DUBOIS

PLATFORM, PARTY, a statement of governmental principle and policy made by a political party to enlist voter support for its candidates. Some historians have argued that the Virginia and Kentucky Resolutions of 1798–99 constituted the first party platform, but while there were numerous party manifestos and declarations of principle in the ensuing thirty years, the platform in its modern sense did not appear until the 1830's. Since 1840 it has been a regular feature of political campaigns. While state platforms have occasionally thrown considerable light on local con-

328

troversies or on sectional divergencies in the national parties, their importance has declined with the rise of the direct primary and the discrediting of the state conventions.

The platform is the responsibility of a committee of the national convention and inherits the disadvantages and defects of its creators. While considerable preliminary work has occasionally been given to their preparation, many platforms have shown hasty and careless drafting, a tendency to becloud or evade important issues, and a fondness for turgid rhetoric. On the other hand, controversies over particular issues, such as the "gold plank" in the Republican platform of 1896, have been of great historical importance.

Platforms have shown the characteristic American tendency to standardize. Past achievements of the party have been a regular feature of party platforms, as is denunciation of the opposing party, a feature that played an important part in the post–Civil War successes of the Republicans. Political parties have not hesitated to embarrass the State Department by declarations on domestic issues in foreign countries in the hope of placating or winning the support of groups of foreign-born voters. Opposing platforms have frequently much in common, and careful analysis is often required to find the real clash of issues. The major parties have invariably contained diverse and sometimes quarrelsome elements, and platform drafters have naturally had to keep this fact constantly in mind, with the result that they have too often turned out a mass of evasions, political platitudes, and inaccurate generalities. The American electorate has long since ceased to attach great importance to the platform, but rather has come to observe the interpretations and personal declarations of presidential and congressional candidates with increasing interest.

Minor party platforms have a great advantage—a fact that is evident in comparing, for example, the Free Soil and Whig platforms in 1848. The discordant elements in the Whig party forced evasion of the major question of the day, the expansion of slavery. The student of both social and political history cannot disregard party platforms, since they frequently constitute important sources of evidence of popular thought and eventual legislative action. This is especially true of the minor party platforms, such as the Greenback, Populist, and Prohibition parties, writing planks that later became bases of important national policies. The Progressive platform of 1912 exercised a decided influence on the domestic policies of both major parties, and various Socialist party platforms

influenced President Franklin D. Roosevelt's New Deal legislation in the 1930's—especially in the areas of Social Security, public power, and labor-management relations—and President Lyndon B. Johnson's civil rights legislation in the 1960's.

[Hugh A. Bone, *Party Committees and National Politics;* J. P. Gordy, *History of Political Parties in the United States;* C. E. Merriam and H. F. Gosnell, *The American Party System;* Kirk H. Porter and Donald B. Johnson, eds., *National Party Platforms, 1840–1968.*]

W. A. ROBINSON

PLATT AMENDMENT was the basis for Cuban-American relations from 1901 to 1934. Following the Spanish-American War the problem of the future relations between the United States and Cuba became a matter of earnest consideration in both countries. For the purpose of finding a solution, Gen. Leonard Wood, head of the U.S. military government in Cuba, convened the Cuban constituent assembly on Nov. 5, 1900, and instructed it to render an opinion on what the future relations "ought to be." Two unsatisfactory proposals were later submitted, whereupon the United States drew up its own plan. Although much of it was drafted by Secretary of War Elihu Root, it became known as the Platt Amendment after Sen. Orville H. Platt of Connecticut, chairman of the Senate committee on Cuban relations. To insure its passage it was attached as a rider to the army appropriations bill for the fiscal year ending June 13, 1902. It contained eight articles, the substance of which were: (I) Cuba was to make no treaty that would impair its independence, nor was it to alienate Cuban territory to a foreign power; (II) Cuba was not to assume or contract any public debt beyond its ability to meet out of "ordinary revenues"; (III) Cuba was to permit the United States "to intervene for the preservation of Cuban independence, the maintenance of a government adequate for the protection of life, property and individual liberty, and for discharging the obligations with respect to Cuba imposed by the Treaty of Paris on the United States now to be assumed and undertaken by the government of Cuba"; (IV) all acts of the United States during the occupation were to be validated; (V) Cuba was to continue the sanitation program started by the United States and, if necessary, extend it; (VI) title to the Isle of Pines was to be decided later; (VII) coaling and naval stations chosen by the United States were to be sold or leased; (VIII) the articles were to be embodied in a permanent treaty with the United States.

When the articles were submitted to the Cuban convention with the demand that they be incorporated into the Cuban constitution, a storm of indignation arose. The convention at first refused to agree and sent a delegation to Washington to protest. Particularly objectionable was Article III, which was viewed as depriving Cuba of its sovereign rights. In spite of assurances given by Root that the United States interpreted its right to intervene as applying only when Cuban independence was threatened by internal anarchy or foreign attack, the convention continued to balk. Not until the United States threatened to remain in the island did the convention, on June 13, 1901, agree to accept it. On May 22, 1903, the articles were written into a formal treaty. The arrangement, never popular in Cuba, aroused increasing bitterness as time went on, especially when later administrations at Washington showed a tendency to ignore the Root interpretation. While armed intervention was seldom resorted to, except in 1906–09 and again in 1917, there were numerous occasions when the United States exerted pressure of some sort. This so-called "intermeddling and interference" strengthened the demand for the repeal of the Platt Amendment, to which the United States acceded on May 29, 1934.

[David F. Healy, *The United States in Cuba, 1898–1902: Generals, Politicians, and the Search for Policy*.]

L. J. MEYER

PLATTE BRIDGE FIGHT (July 26, 1865). A large body of Sioux, Cheyenne, and Arapaho warriors converged in the hills north of the North Platte River in Colorado, to attack and destroy Platte Bridge, an important link on the trail to the West. Troops from the adjacent fort under Lt. Caspar Collins left the post to bring in a wagon train en route from Fort Laramie. Collins and four men were killed, and in a later fight to keep the telegraph lines intact another soldier was killed. The wagon train was wiped out, and twenty men accompanying it were slaughtered. The Indians also suffered heavily.

[A. W. Spring, *Caspar Collins*.]

CARL L. CANNON

PLATTE PURCHASE, a tract of almost 2 million acres that extended Missouri's northwest boundary to the Missouri River. It was purchased from the Indians by the federal government in 1836 for $7,500 cash together with specified quantities of merchandise, and annexed to Missouri on Mar. 28, 1837. The region was subsequently divided into six counties: Platte and Buchanan (Dec. 31, 1838), Andrew (Jan. 29, 1841), Holt (Feb. 15, 1841), and Atchison and Nodaway

(Feb. 14, 1845). It comprises about 4 percent of Missouri's total area.

[H. I. McKee, "The Platte Purchase," *Missouri Historical Review,* vol. 32.]

HOWARD I. MCKEE

PLATTE RIVER TRAIL through Nebraska and Wyoming owed its importance to South Pass near the southern end of the Wind River Range in southwest Wyoming, then the gateway of the Rockies. The Platte River heads at the pass, and the most direct route from the pass across 780 miles of plains to the Missouri River is down the Platte, which provides water for men and horses. Robert Stuart and six companions, carrying dispatches for the Pacific Fur Company from Astoria in Oregon Territory to Saint Louis, traversed the route in 1812–13. Maj. Stephen H. Long's expedition followed it part way to the Rockies in 1819. A brigade of William Henry Ashley's Rocky Mountain Fur Company definitely established the trail in 1825 while carrying supplies from the Missouri to trappers in the Rockies. From then on the route was traveled every year by trappers, missionaries, and homeseekers. Branches of the trail, with eastern termini on the Missouri at Westport, Fort Leavenworth, Atchison, and Saint Joseph, all converged on the Platte near Grand Island in what is now Nebraska. When a thousand Oregon homeseekers traversed the Platte Trail in 1843, they regarded it as merely a part of the Oregon Trail. It was also known as the California Trail, Mormon Trail, and Overland Route. The completion of the Union Pacific Railroad in 1869 ended its importance.

[H. M. Chittenden, *The American Fur Trade of the Far West;* Henry Inman, *The Great Salt Lake Trail.*]

BLISS ISELY

PLATTSBURGH, BATTLE OF (Sept. 11, 1814), an engagement on the western shore of Lake Champlain in New York. Sir George Prevost, governor general of Canada, invaded New York with 14,000 veterans, recently arrived from the Duke of Wellington's victorious army in Spain. He was opposed by Gen. Alexander Macomb's 1,500 American regulars and 2,500 militia, who were strongly entrenched south of the Saranac River in the village of Plattsburgh. Macomb's army was supported by a naval squadron of four small ships and ten gunboats under Comdr. Thomas Macdonough. The British invaders were assisted by another flotilla of about the same size commanded by Capt. George Downie.

Prevost planned a joint attack by land and by sea. He goaded Downie, whose fleet was not fully fitted, into attacking Macdonough, who lay at anchor in a well-chosen position in Plattsburgh Bay near Cumberland Head. Downie lost his ships and his life in a bloody battle lasting more than two hours. Macdonough's victory was chiefly the result of swinging about his flagship, the *Saratoga*, so as to make use of its uninjured broadside. Meanwhile, Prevost failed to fight his way across the Saranac and support Downie. Deprived of naval support, the British army was forced to retreat. Its defeat made peace more certain and cut short British designs of obtaining sole control of the Great Lakes by the Treaty of Ghent.

[A. T. Mahan, *Sea Power in Its Relations to the War of 1812.*]

EDWARD P. ALEXANDER

PLAY PARTY, a form of social diversion formerly very common in the hill region of the South. Young people would assemble to play games that were really a form of folk dancing to the accompaniment of singing. "Miller Boy," "Down to Rowser's," and "Little Brass Wagon" were common examples.

[B. A. Botkin, *The American Play Party Song;* Vance Randolph, "The Ozark Play-Party," *The Journal of American Folk Lore,* vol. 42.]

EDWARD EVERETT DALE

PLEASANT HILL, BATTLE OF (Apr. 9, 1864). On the night of Apr. 8, following his unsuccessful fight at Sabine Crossroads, La., Union Gen. Nathaniel P. Banks withdrew into strong positions at Pleasant Hill approximately twenty miles away to be ready to unite with the Union fleet in the Red River. Late in the afternoon of Apr. 9, Confederate Gen. Richard Taylor, with 12,000 troops, attacked Banks's 28,000 troops. At first successful, the Confederate exposed right flank was turned and the attack repulsed. The troops were thrown into disorder, part of the line being broken and scattered. The Confederate army retreated in confusion toward Shreveport. Banks did not pursue, but instead withdrew to the Red River.

[R. U. Johnson and C. C. Buel, eds., *Battles and Leaders of the Civil War,* vol. IV.]

THOMAS ROBSON HAY

PLEDGE OF ALLEGIANCE. As part of the celebration to mark the 400th anniversary of the discovery of America, President Benjamin Harrison in 1892 called for patriotic exercises in school. The pledge of allegiance, taken from a children's magazine, the *Youth's Companion,* was first recited by public-school children as they saluted the flag during the National School Celebration held that year. In 1942 Congress made the pledge part of its code for the use of the flag.

Authorship of the pledge was claimed by Francis Bellamy, an associate editor of the *Youth's Companion,* in 1923. The original wording was expanded by the National Flag Conference of the American Legion in 1923 and 1924, and the words "under God" were added by Congress in 1954. The text of the pledge is as follows: "I pledge allegiance to the flag of the United States of America and to the Republic for which it stands, one Nation under God, indivisible, with liberty and justice for all."

NORMA FRANKEL

PLESSY V. FERGUSON, 163 U.S. 537 (1896), upheld the validity of an 1890 Louisiana statute that required railroads operating in that state to provide "equal but separate accommodations for the white and colored races." For nearly sixty years after the *Plessy* decision the separate-but-equal doctrine enabled states to legislate segregation of races in almost all areas of public activity. In *Gong* v. *Rice,* 275 U.S. 78 (1927), the Court decided that a child of Chinese ancestry who is a citizen is not denied equal protection by being assigned to a public school provided for black children, when equal facilities are offered to both races.

Beginning in 1938, cases in the field of higher education foreshadowed the demise of the separate-but-equal doctrine, but it was not until the landmark ruling in *Brown* v. *Board of Education of Topeka* (1954) that the Supreme Court categorically held that "separate educational facilities are inherently unequal" and consequently a violation of the equal protection clause of the Fourteenth Amendment. After *Brown,* the Court quickly extended its desegregation principle to all varieties of public facilities, such as parks and golf courses. Although not explicitly overruled by the Court, the separate-but-equal formula, first enunciated in *Plessy,* has been tacitly buried as a legal doctrine.

[Alexander M. Bickel, "The Original Understanding and the Segregation Decision," *Harvard Law Review,* vol. 69 (1955); Harold W. Chase and Craig R. Ducat, eds., *Corwin's Constitution and What It Means Today;* J. Skelly Wright, "Professor Bickel, the Scholarly Tradition, and the Supreme Court," *Harvard Law Review,* vol. 84 (1971).]

HAROLD W. CHASE
ERIC L. CHASE

PLOESTI OIL FIELDS, AIR RAIDS ON (1941–44). Refineries located near Ploesti, Romania, provided one-third of the entire oil supply of the Axis in World War II. The concentration of such assets led planners to call Ploesti the most important target of the war and to believe its destruction possible. Two minor air attacks by the Russians in 1941 were ineffective. The United States lacked the airpower for decisive attacks in 1942, although Liberators en route to China were held in Egypt to bomb Ploesti. Thirteen were dispatched in June 1942, but the distance, small force, high altitude, and adverse weather made the attack ineffective. The Germans, anticipating further strikes, increased their defenses.

By mid-1943 the force was available for a one-time attack. Three U.S. Liberator groups based in England joined Maj. Gen. Lewis H. Brereton's two Ninth Air Force groups in Libya. For increased bombing accuracy Brereton planned a low-level attack; this unusual type of attack required special flying training on a simulated Ploesti constructed in the desert. At dawn on Aug. 1, 177 aircraft were airborne on a 2,300-mile mission. Simultaneous treetop strikes were planned against eight refineries. Success and safety depended largely on surprise, which was lost for several reasons. The attack was by group, with fierce battles ensuing in the developing inferno of the target area. Fifty-four aircraft were lost and fifty-five damaged by defending guns, fighters, balloons, and exploding bombs. Refinery production was reduced by about one-half.

No repeat attacks were made until Maj. Gen. Nathan F. Twining's Fifteenth Air Force struck from Italy in April 1944, opening a successful high-altitude campaign that continued until Aug. 19. Meeting the defenses of many heavy flak guns, German fighters, and a smoke screen, the attacks were costly, making Ploesti a dread target to the crews. Campaign bomber sorties numbered 5,287, with a 3.6 percent loss. The British contributed 900 night sorties. Combined with other force attacks on German refineries, the campaign deprived the Germans of much of the fuel essential for war.

[James Dugan and Carroll Stewart, *Ploesti*.]

LEON W. JOHNSON

PLOUGH PATENT. *See* **Lygonia.**

PLOW. *See* **Agricultural Machinery.**

PLOWDEN'S NEW ALBION was the first English colonizing grant of the present New Jersey area, the second in the United States to offer religious liberty. Two years after petitions to Charles I, the New Albion charter was issued June 21, 1634, to nine persons, including Sir Edmund Plowden (1592–1659), soon its sole owner. At their request it claimed title under the Irish crown. It was issued by Thomas Wentworth, first Earl of Strafford, lord deputy of Ireland, upon authority from Charles I, and enrolled in Dublin, where Plowden was stationed when the grant was made. The charter's religious provisions copied those of Maryland: Plowden, of a Shropshire Catholic family, apparently planned New Albion as another Catholic haven.

Plowden, who took upon himself the title Earl Palatine of New Albion, tried four times to settle his province. Financial troubles with his wife Mabel, daughter and sole heiress of Peter Marriner, delayed his start several years. On Aug. 30, 1639, Plowden wrote to Cecilius Calvert, second Lord Baltimore, that he would settle in New Albion next spring. Again domestic troubles intervened. In 1641 Plowden's colonizing prospectus—*A Direction for Adventurers to New Albion*—appeared. Also at this time, Charles I and Parliament requested Sir William Berkeley, governor of Virginia, to help Plowden settle his province on the Delaware, the Swedes having now been established there four years (*see* New Sweden Colony). In August 1642, just as civil war was beginning in England, Plowden sailed with his colonists to Virginia, where they spent the winter. The articles of his indentured settlers specified service in New Albion. Their predominant religion is not yet known.

Early in May 1643, a party of Plowden's people, while sailing with him outside Chesapeake Bay, apparently en route to settle his province, successfully mutinied against him, as recorded by the Swedish governor, Johan Björnsson Printz. Legal records thereafter indicate Plowden resided continuously in Virginia, reportedly hopeful of more settlers in spite of the English civil war. In the spring of 1648 he sailed to England, reporting at New Amsterdam and to Gov. John Winthrop in Boston his intention to return to America and "dispossess the Swedes."

In December 1648 *A Description of the Province of New Albion* was published in England with a long foreword signed "Beauchamp Plantagenet." This prospectus fancifully described New Albion; it detailed with considerable accuracy the New Albion charter, Virginia, and Plowden's life; and it reprinted the 1641 *Direction*. Plowden's third colonizing attempt, a large project, now developed. But last-minute lawsuits blocked it in April 1649. In 1650 "Plantagenet's" *Description* was reprinted, slightly revised, and on June 11, 1650, Oliver Cromwell's council of state issued a pass to New Albion for "seven score persons." This last venture collapsed, doubtless from political pressure, for it had been planned, after Cromwell's triumphs, as a Royalist asylum.

Numerous land suits kept Plowden in England until his death in 1659. He was buried July 20 at Saint Clement Danes, London. He had made his second son his heir, and additional confusion arose when the New Albion charter document was lost. Consequently, no Plowden contested Charles II's grant of these lands to James Stuart, Duke of York, in 1664. In 1772 chance disclosed the enrollment of Plowden's charter in Dublin. Francis Plowden, Sir Edmund's great-great-grandson, immediately but vainly petitioned George III for restoration of the province. In 1784 he sent to America an agent, Charles Varlo, whose recovery efforts also failed.

[Clifford Lewis III, "Some Recently Discovered Extracts From the Lost Minutes of the Virginia Council and General Court, 1642–1645, Together With Notes on Sir Edmund Plowden," *William and Mary Quarterly* (1940).]

CLIFFORD LEWIS III

PLUMB PLAN of public ownership of railroads to replace the Railway Administration after World War I was proposed by Glenn E. Plumb, counsel for the organized railway employees, and considered in Congress in 1919 as the Sims Bill. It was proposed that railroad properties be purchased at a government-appraised value subject to judicial review and be operated by a quasi-public corporation representing the government, operators, and classified employees; and that improvements be financed by federal and local funds, and profits be used to retire the public bonds, reduce rates, and increase railway wages. (*See also* Transportation Act of 1920.)

[K. Austin Kerr, *American Railroad Politics, 1914–1920.*]

MARTIN P. CLAUSSEN

PLUMMER GANG. Henry Plummer, elected sheriff of Bannack District (now Montana) May 24, 1863, organized a band of fifty outlaws, called the "Innocents," against whom 102 robberies and murders were charged. A vigilance committee, with which Wilbur Fisk Sanders (later senator) was associated,

was formed in December 1863 and within six weeks hanged most of the band. Among thirty-three executions was that of the notorious Joseph A. Slade.

[Hoffman Birney, *Vigilantes.*]

DON RUSSELL

PLYMOUTH, VIRGINIA COMPANY OF (1606–20), one of the two companies incorporated in the first Virginia charter of 1606. In 1605 a group of men representing the City of London and the outports of Bristol, Plymouth, and Exeter petitioned for a charter that would accord them the privilege of planting colonies in America. Although the petitioners were men bound by the ties of relationship, friendship, or common interest, the rivalry between London and the outports was such that the leaders wished to proceed with the project under separate companies. The charter of 1606 therefore created two companies, the Virginia Company of London, with permission to plant a colony in southern Virginia between thirty-four and forty-one degrees north latitude, to be called the First Colony of Virginia, and the Virginia Company of Plymouth, whose plantation, to be called the Second Colony of Virginia, was to be located to the north between thirty-eight and forty-five degrees north latitude, the overlapping area to be considered a neutral zone in which the colonies could not come within one hundred miles of each other.

The Plymouth Company, like the London Company, was to be under the jurisdiction of the royal council for Virginia, but had its own resident council of thirteen as government for its projected plantation. The enterprise was commercial in character, but to what extent the company could control the trade of its colony was not made clear in the charter. The leaders in the Plymouth Company were Sir John Popham and Sir Ferdinando Gorges, who became the mainstay of the enterprise after the death of Popham in 1607.

The Plymouth Company sent out its first expedition in the summer of 1606 to seek a place for a plantation. Unfortunately the vessel was captured by the Spanish near Puerto Rico, where it was driven by adverse winds, and the men carried off as prisoners to Spain from where a few of them made their way back to Plymouth with difficulty. A second vessel dispatched in the autumn of 1606 reached the coast of Maine in safety, and returned with such glowing accounts that the company sent out two ships in May 1607, the *Gift of God* and the *Mary and John,* carrying settlers. A plantation was begun near the mouth of the Sagadahoc (now Kennebec) River and Fort Saint George was built, but from the outset it did not prosper. Gorges ascribed its failure to an insufficiency of food supplies and "childish factions." The men were apparently not of the right type, lacking the self-discipline and the will to work necessary to all pioneer ventures. The winter cold, the burning of the storehouse and many dwellings, and the consequent shortage of supplies weakened the interest of the planters, while the death of some of the men whom Gorges had left in charge of the settlement, including the governor, George Popham, a nephew of Sir John, discouraged the company in England from pushing the enterprise further (*see* Popham Colony). Some of its members continued their interest in the fisheries and sent out several expeditions to fish and trade with the Indians. Profits from these activities were sufficient to convince men like Gorges of the potentialities of the region, and thus to pave the way for the reorganization of the project in 1620 under a new company, the Council for New England.

[C. M. Andrews, *The Colonial Period in America*, vol. I.]

VIOLA F. BARNES

PLYMOUTH PLANTATION. *See* **New Plymouth Colony.**

PLYMOUTH ROCK. There is no contemporary record that the Pilgrims landed on Plymouth Rock when they disembarked on Dec. 26, 1620, and it is not known who first set foot on the rock. Historian James Thacher states, on the authority of "the late venerable Deacon [Ephraim] Spooner," that when the latter was a boy, about the year 1741, he saw "Elder [Thomas] Faunce," then ninety-five years old, identify the present Plymouth Rock as that on which, according to his father (John Faunce, who came in the *Ann* in 1623), the Pilgrims landed. This tradition is accepted by Justin Winsor and later historians. Ann Taylor wrote in 1773 that her grandmother, Mary Chilton, was the first to step on the rock and a similar tradition persists regarding John Alden, but Winsor states that they both landed at a later date. The rock has been moved back from its original location in order to protect and display it.

[James Thacher, *History of the Town of Plymouth;* Justin Winsor, *Narrative and Critical History of America*.]

R. W. G. VAIL

PLYMOUTH TRADING POST. In 1632 Edward Winslow of the Plymouth Colony visited the Con-

necticut Valley to discover the possibilities of trade. After vain efforts to enlist the cooperation of the Massachusetts Bay Colony in the enterprise, Winslow, then governor of Plymouth, sent Lt. William Holmes to occupy the site he had selected for a trading post. Holmes sailed past the threatening Dutch who had established their House of Hope three months earlier at a site within the present limits of Hartford, Conn., and, with ready-made materials that he had brought, set up a trading post at the junction of the Farmington River with the Connecticut on Sept. 26, 1633. The trading post soon became the nucleus of the village of Matianuck, renamed Windsor in 1637. Traders and settlers from the Bay Colony began to enter the valley the next year and in 1635 located near the post, which was then in the charge of Jonathan Brewster. The Plymouth people soon found themselves crowded out and on May 15, 1637, sold their claims to all except the trading post and a small parcel of land to the Massachusetts settlers of Windsor (*see* River Towns of Connecticut).

[F. S. M. Crofut, *Guide to the History and Historic Sites of Connecticut*.]

GEORGE MATTHEW DUTCHER

"POCKET," a name given to the southwestern portion of Indiana, embracing ten counties within the area bounded by the Ohio, Wabash, White, and Blue rivers, because of its pendulous geographical relation to the rest of the state. Occasionally the southwesternmost congressional district is so designated. A letter written by Robert Dale Owen to William H. English, Mar. 1, 1851, indicates a common usage of the term at that time.

[T. J. De La Hunt, "The Pocket in Indiana History," *Indiana Magazine of History*, vol. 16.]

HARVEY L. CARTER

POCKET VETO, an indirect veto by which a U.S. president negates legislation without affording Congress an opportunity for repassage by an overriding vote. The Constitution (Article I, Section 7) provides that measures presented by Congress to the president within ten days of adjournment (not counting Sundays) and not returned by him before adjournment fail to become law. They are said to have been pocket vetoed. First employed by President James Madison, the pocket veto has been used by every president since Benjamin Harrison. Between 1789 and September 1972, 955 of the 2,260 vetoes recorded—or 42 percent—were pocket vetoes. During that period nine presidents, the last of whom was Dwight D. Eisenhower, pocketed more measures than they returned to Congress disapproved. Controversy over the practice has focused on the definition of "adjournment": presidential usage has included brief recesses, whereas congressional critics have argued that the term intends only lengthy or *sine die* adjournments.

[Joseph E. Kallenbach, *The American Chief Executive: The Presidency and the Governorship.*]

NORMAN C. THOMAS

POINTE COUPEE, on the west bank of the Mississippi River just below the mouth of Red River, was an early French settlement in Louisiana. It quickly became one of the more important French posts and remained such until the end of the French regime in 1762. Many Acadians settled there during the Spanish regime, and its population remained predominantly French.

[Henry E. Chambers, *History of Louisiana;* Charles Gayarré, *History of Louisiana.*]

WALTER PRICHARD

POINT FOUR of President Harry S. Truman's 1949 inaugural address urged international cooperation to teach self-help to poverty-stricken peoples through provision of technological knowledge and skills and through capital investment, whereby living standards might be raised and democracy strengthened. A 1950 appropriation of $35 million introduced U.S. outlays that reached $400 million by 1954. The United States supplied most of the aid from "free world" sources during the decade. Being vastly inclusive, espousing economic and social development throughout the free countries of Asia, Africa, and Latin America, Point Four necessarily confronted age-old institutions, customs, and vested interests. Its technicians encountered obstacles difficult to understand, capitalize, alter, or eradicate. Moreover, few areas possessed many facilities essential to that rapid industrialization recipient governments urgently sought. Yet progress appeared in agriculture, conservation, waterpower, technical skills, and installations. Although the administration of President Dwight D. Eisenhower tended to avoid use of the term, the validity of the Point Four principle continually widened its application. Offers of technical facilities and capital loans and grants to underdeveloped, uncommitted countries became a weapon sharpened by universal use in the cold war.

[Jonathan B. Bingham, *Shirt-Sleeve Diplomacy: Point Four in Action;* James W. Wiggins and Helmut Schoek, *Foreign Aid Reexamined.*]

JEANNETTE P. NICHOLS

POINT PLEASANT, BATTLE OF (Oct. 10, 1774), was one of the most notable conflicts between Indians and frontiersmen in the annals of the West (*see* Dunmore's War). Col. Andrew Lewis with about 1,100 men from the frontier of southwest Virginia marched 160 miles from Camp Union, on the levels of the Greenbrier River, to join Virginia Gov. John Murray, Earl of Dunmore, on the Ohio River, arriving at the mouth of the Kanawha River on Oct. 6, where they made camp in the point of the two rivers called Point Pleasant.

While resting and recruiting the men and awaiting the arrival of Col. William Christian with 250 of the rear guard, Lewis' army was attacked early in the morning of Oct. 10 by a large force of Shawnee, led by Chief Cornstalk, which had crossed the Ohio in the night. Lewis sent out two divisions under his brother, Col. Charles Lewis, and Col. William Fleming; both officers were soon wounded, the former fatally. The Indians fought desperately, hoping to drive the whites into the rivers. The fighting was in frontier fashion, with individual combats and sheltering behind trees and logs.

About one o'clock the Indians grew discouraged but continued desultory fighting until sunset, when they withdrew across the Ohio. The losses on both sides were heavy, the Virginians having more than 80 killed and 140 wounded. The losses of the Indians were about 200 killed.

[R. G. Thwaites and L. P. Kellogg, *Dunmore's War.*]

LOUISE PHELPS KELLOGG

POKAGON VILLAGE of the Saint Joseph River Potawatomi was situated in what is now Bertrand Township, Berrien County, in the southwest corner of Michigan. Not far from the site of the old Saint Joseph Mission, this village became the center of the revived Roman Catholic missions of the region when Father Stephen T. Badin was appointed resident missionary in 1830.

[C. B. Beuchner, "The Pokagons," *Indiana Historical Society Publication,* vol. 10; W. M. McNamara, *The Catholic Church on the Northern Indiana Frontier.*]

THOMAS T. MCAVOY

POKER, a popular American card game, probably developed from the French card game *poque,* which was played in French America during the late 18th century and early 19th century. The first known reference to poker in America appears in 1829 in the writings of the touring British actor Joseph L. Cowell. Especially popular as a gambling game first in the former Louisiana territory, and then throughout the South and nation in the decades prior to the Civil War, poker reached its glory in the boom years after the war. The exciting situations that poker offers, the taut crises, the readiness with which the game may be learned, and its adaptability to any number of players brought together by chance—all suited the flush times in Alabama, the boom times in California, and the roaring times all over the nation when railroads, factories, ranching, and other occupations were taking over an empire and making millionaires out of poor boys almost overnight. Jim Smiley's hearty eagerness to "take a chance on anything," in Mark Twain's *Jumping Frog of Calaveras County,* expresses the poker spirit of America. Poker players like Bret Harte's Mr. Oakhurst (in "The Outcasts of Poker Flat") and Cherokee Hall (in A. H. Lewis' *Wolfville* books) express the professional poker gambler, a type as familiar on Mississippi River steamboats as in Roaring Camp.

[G. H. Devol, *Forty Years a Gambler;* Allen Dowling, *The Great American Pastime;* John Philip Quinn, *Fools of Fortune.*]

J. FRANK DOBIE

POLAR EXPEDITION OF THE *JEANNETTE* (1879–81). After several years of planning, Lt. Comdr. George Washington De Long, with the financial support of James G. Bennett, publisher of the *New York Herald,* sailed in the Arctic steamer *Jeannette* from San Francisco on July 8, 1879, to the Bering Strait in an attempt to reach the North Pole. De Long sailed through the strait but soon became caught in the ice, drifting northward for twenty-one months and then foundering (June 12, 1881) in latitude 77°15′, longitude 155° east. De Long made his way with three boats to the New Siberian Islands, then tried to reach the Lena River in eastern Siberia. The boats became separated: one was lost; another reached the Lena; the third under De Long reached land, but he and his men all perished from starvation.

[Emma De Long, *The Voyage of the Jeannette;* A. A. Hoehling, *The Jeannette Expedition: An Ill-Fated Journey to the Arctic;* George W. Melville, *In the Lena Delta.*]

N. M. CROUSE

POLAR EXPLORATION. Exploration of the polar regions from North America began with the expedi-

tion of the 60-ton vessel *Argo* from Philadelphia in 1753 to explore, survey, and map the coast of Labrador to the entrance into Hudson Bay. John Churchman's petition to Congress in 1789 to subsidize his proposed expedition to Baffin Land (now Baffin Island) for scientific observations was rejected. Sealers and whalers—especially from New England—approached the arctic waters in Smith Sound and, in Antarctica, reached the Antarctic Peninsula. James Eights, a geologist on the Palmer-Pendleton sealing and exploring expedition to antarctic waters in 1829–31, postulated an antarctic continent. The U.S. exploring expedition of 1838–42 under Charles Wilkes explored, surveyed, and mapped the edge of the antarctic continent in the area near the Antarctic Peninsula and for 1,500 miles along the coast of East Antarctica, now called Wilkes Land.

Systematic exploration of the polar regions by the United States began in the 1840's. Inspired in part by a humanitarian interest in searching for Sir John Franklin's expedition, lost in the Canadian Archipelago, it was also in response to the clamor of sealers and whalers for arctic maps and geographical information and in response to the burning scientific interest of Matthew Fontaine Maury in the Arctic, especially its so-called open polar sea. As head of the U.S. Navy's Depot of Charts and Instruments, Maury was directly responsible for sending the first (Edwin Jesse De Haven, 1850–51) and second (Elisha Kent Kane, 1853–55) Grinnell expeditions into the North American Arctic, in which Kane reached 80°40′, and for encouraging the Isaac I. Hayes expedition (1860–61), in which Hayes reached 81°35′. These expeditions opened the route to the North Pole through Smith Sound. The navy also dispatched an exploring expedition, under John Rodgers and Cadwalader Ringgold (1853–56), to the North Pacific Ocean and into the Arctic Ocean to Wrangel Island to explore, survey, and map. In the late 1850's Maury sought in vain to get the active cooperation of the major nations in an assault on the South Pole combined with an exploration of Antarctica.

The Civil War delayed further official efforts in polar exploration until the ill-fated U.S.S. *Polaris* expedition under Charles Hall (1871–73) to the northeast coast of Greenland, during which Hall died and crew members suffered a very severe winter. In a disastrous expedition, the U.S.S. *Jeannette* under George De Long (1879–81) penetrated the Arctic Ocean through the Bering Strait, was beset in the ice, and for more than two years drifted west across the top of Siberia to a point near the mouth of the Lena

Delta, where it was crushed. The purchase of Alaska in 1867 initiated a broad program of exploration, surveying, and mapping by various government agencies—notably the Geological Survey, Coast and Geodetic Survey, navy, army, and revenue service—that has continued to the present. During the International Polar Year (1882–83) the Army Signal Office established stations at Point Barrow, Alaska, under P. Henry Ray and in Lady Franklin Bay (Fort Conger), Ellesmere Island, under A. W. Greely, from which extensive explorations and surveys were made of Ellesmere Island and the north coast of Greenland.

From 1885 to 1920 the dominant effort in polar exploration was to attain the North Pole. Although these explorations were private, they did have varying amounts of federal aid and active support. Most important were the seven successive explorations of Ellesmere Island, northern Greenland, and the adjoining Arctic Ocean by Robert E. Peary (1886–1909) that resulted in his reaching the North Pole on Apr. 6, 1909. Others include Frederick A. Cook's explorations of Ellesmere and Axel Heiberg islands (1907–09); and the Baldwin-Ziegler (1901–02) and the Fiala-Ziegler (1903–05) expeditions to Franz Josef Land in ill-fated attempts to reach the pole. The Jesup North Pacific expedition (1897–1902) and the Harriman Alaska expedition (1899) were privately subsidized scientific explorations, as were the National Geographic Society glaciological surveys of Alaska (1912–19). The Crocker land expedition, led by Donald B. MacMillan (1913–17), explored extensively in northwestern Greenland and Ellesmere Island. U.S. polar exploration had become almost exclusively arctic-oriented, although shortly after his return from the north in 1909 Peary strongly advocated sending expeditions to Antarctica, and at about the same time, Robert C. Murphy began his long life of scientific research in Antarctica with his ornithological and other observations in South Georgia (1912–13).

The introduction of the airplane into polar exploration changed the character and extent of U.S. activity by private as well as by government agencies between 1919 and 1941. Four U.S. Army Air Service aircraft flew from New York City to Nome, Alaska (1920). This was followed by a succession of momentous flights that went far in opening to view extensive areas of both the Arctic and the Antarctic. The arctic flights included the Roald Amundsen–Lincoln Ellsworth flight in 1925 from Spitsbergen north across the Polar Sea to eighty-eight degrees north latitude; the Donald B. MacMillan U.S. Navy (Richard E. Byrd) expedition (1925) to northwest Greenland, with flights by Byrd especially into Ellesmere Island; Byrd's flight from Spitsbergen to the North Pole and return in 1926; the George Hubert Wilkins–Carl Ben Eielson flight from Point Barrow, Alaska, across the Arctic Ocean to Spitsbergen in 1928; Wilkins' extensive flights and surveys of the Arctic Ocean north of Canada toward the pole in 1937–38; and Charles A. Lindbergh's survey flight of Greenland in 1931 for an arctic air route.

Significant terrestrial scientific explorations during the interwar years include those of Louise A. Boyd in the Norwegian and Greenland seas and along the east coast of Greenland (1928–41); the first exploration by a submarine, the *Nautilus,* below the ice of the Arctic Ocean northwest of Spitsbergen, by Wilkins (1931); a succession of scientific expeditions to western Greenland made by the University of Michigan under William H. Hobbs (1926–31); and the glaciological and topographic surveys in Alaska of the American Geographical Society (1926–41), led by William Fields and Walter A. Wood, and of the National Geographic Society (1919–41).

Following quickly upon initial successes flying in the Arctic, the United States directed its interests to Antarctica. Prior to World War II notable flights to Antarctica included flights by Wilkins in 1928–30 along most of the Antarctic Peninsula; four flights by Ellsworth (1933–39), including his long flight of 1935 from the northern tip of the Antarctic Peninsula to the Ross Ice Shelf beyond Marie Byrd Land; and Byrd's flight from Little America to the South Pole in November 1929. Byrd planned and commanded the first (1928–30) and second (1933–35) Byrd Antarctic expeditions, based at Little America I and II, and the U.S. Antarctic Service (1939–41) expedition, based at Little America III in West Antarctica and Stonington Island in the Antarctic Peninsula. From these bases Byrd and his staff carried out far-reaching air- and land-survey explorations into largely unknown regions, greatly modifying the map of West Antarctica and setting the pace for large-scale post–World War II activities.

During World War II the United States used its records of previous expeditions in the Arctic in a vast program of establishing transarctic air routes; locating air bases and meteorological and other scientific stations; and developing logistic support forces, especially in Alaska, northern Canada, Greenland, and Iceland. The U.S. Weather Bureau, Coast Guard, navy, army, and army air corps played leading roles in this further exploration.

Following World War II, through about 1956, the United States carried out an accelerated program of polar exploration and scientific investigation, primarily to test and improve on the experiences of the war years. In Antarctica the government launched an all-out program of exploration by the U.S. Navy Antarctic Developments Project (Operation Highjump, 1946–47), which involved ships, airplanes, oversnow vehicles, and personnel—the largest expedition ever sent to Antarctica. This program included the first use of helicopters and icebreakers in the area. Much of the continent was surveyed and mapped. The last private expedition to Antarctica was conducted by Finn Ronne as the Ronne Antarctic research expedition (1947–48). It explored, surveyed, and mapped in the Antarctic Peninsula, south into the Weddell Sea, and west around Alexander I Island. These expeditions were followed by the U.S. Navy Second Antarctic Developments Project (Operation Windmill, 1947–48), which explored, surveyed, and mapped the Ross Sea, the coast of West Antarctica, and Wilkes Land. During the austral summer of 1954–55, the icebreaker U.S.S. *Atka* circumnavigated the continent surveying the icefront and inspecting sites for bases for scientific stations to be used during the forthcoming International Geophysical Year (1957–58).

In the Arctic the decade after 1945 saw routine scientific (meteorological and geophysical) flights between Fairbanks and the North Pole, extensive surveys of the Arctic Ocean leading to the location and mapping of ice islands and their occupation by scientific stations; a continuous succession of army, navy, and air force logistic and scientific operations, often with Danish or Canadian collaboration; the establishment of the U.S. Navy Arctic Research Laboratory at Point Barrow, Alaska; successive penetrations of the Canadian Archipelago by navy task forces in experiments in logistics and tests; exploration for the building of the Distant Early Warning line; and surveys by navy task forces of the coast of northwest Greenland and of Ellesmere Island for bases, which culminated in the building of the giant Thule air base in Greenland.

The scientific aspect of U.S. polar exploration has been greatly accelerated since the beginning of the International Geophysical Year (1957–58), especially in Antarctica, where a remarkably high degree of international cooperation and participation has resulted from the Antarctic Treaty (June 21, 1961), signed by twelve governments. The logistics for a large program of permanent and temporary bases in Antarctica, as carried out by the U.S. Naval Support Force, and a scientific program directed by the Office of Polar Programs in the National Science Foundation have both been discussed in *Antarctic Journal of the United States* and its predecessor publications since 1959.

In the Arctic the program of exploration since World War II has been wide-ranging, including oceanographic and hydrographic surveys by U.S. Navy and Coast Guard ships of Chukchi, Beaufort, Greenland, and Norwegian seas and the continental shelf of the lands fronting onto the Arctic Ocean; the full transect of the Arctic Basin by nuclear inertial guidance submarines; an extensive program of long-range observational geophysical and aerial mapping; and the permanent establishment of a variety of scientific and logistic bases at strategic sites throughout the North American sector, some of which are on drifting ice islands. These activities have been discussed in *Arctic: Journal of the Arctic Institute of North America, Montreal* (since 1946) and in the *Polar Record,* published by Scott Polar Research Institute, Cambridge, England (since 1931).

[Kenneth J. Bertrand, *Americans in Antarctica, 1775–1948;* Herman R. Friis and Shelby G. Bale, Jr., *United States Polar Exploration;* L. P. Kirwan, *A History of Polar Exploration;* Paul A. Siple, *90° South: The Story of the American South Pole Conquest.*]

HERMAN R. FRIIS

POLICE. The ultimate basis of legal order is the likelihood that laws will be enforced, by physical coercion if need be. Police are the normal repository of these enforcement powers, holding a monopoly on the legitimate means of force in a society. They are responsible for maintaining the public order; promoting the public health, safety, and morals; and preventing and detecting violations of laws within a political jurisdiction.

Although continental European countries have traditionally maintained some form of national, professional police forces since the 17th century, the decentralized, local nature of American police agencies reflects their Anglo-Saxon origins. Before the 19th century England and its colonies relied on constables or sheriffs to maintain order, and their offices were outgrowths of still earlier localized systems of maintaining order, such as mutual pledges, tithing, and the watch and ward, or nightwatch.

The problems of lawlessness and disorder associated with industrialization and urbanization highlighted the inadequacies of these prior systems. The

London Metropolitan Police force, established in 1829, is generally regarded as the first modern city police department. Although Boston employed night-watchmen as early as 1636 and added a daywatch in 1838, the first consolidated city police force in America was created in New York in 1844. Early departments were characterized by political influence, corruption, and inefficiency. In the absence of urban problems, rural areas continued to be served by sheriffs.

Texas established a state police force, the Texas Rangers, in 1835, but most state police forces were not created until the 20th century, partly in response to problems posed by the automobile. While there is no federal police force as such, many police activities are performed by the Federal Bureau of Investigation, established in 1908, and a variety of specialized agencies, most of which are within the Department of Justice, the Treasury Department, and the Department of Defense.

[David J. Bordua and Albert J. Reiss, in Paul F. Lazarsfeld, ed., *The Uses of Sociology.*]

BARRY C. FELD

POLICE POWER, a power encompassed in the general power to govern, often phrased in terms of the power to legislate for the "public health, safety, welfare, and morals." In American constitutional theory the police power is usually conceived as a power of the state (as distinct from the powers of the national government) and thus often called the state police power.

Theoretically the powers of the federal government of the United States are enumerated in Article I, Section 8, of the Constitution, but the Tenth Amendment provides that "the powers not delegated to the United States by the Constitution, nor prohibited by it to the States, are reserved to the States respectively, or to the people." The Tenth Amendment is the constitutional basis for the state police power as a reserved power.

The broad conception of the police power and its ambiguous constitutional basis do not mean that it is without limit. Efforts by states to exercise police power (especially in relation to the regulation of property rights) have been challenged throughout American history, and Article I, Section 10, of the Constitution is an explicit list of limits on state power. While no longer of great significance, state efforts to regulate property rights were challenged in the early 19th century as a violation of the contract clause of Article

I, Section 10, which prohibits states from any legislation "impairing the Obligation of Contracts" (*Trustees of Dartmouth College* v. *Woodward,* 1819; *Charles River Bridge Company* v. *Warren Bridge Company,* 1837).

Efforts to invoke the Bill of Rights as a restraint on the power of the states were rejected in *Barron* v. *Baltimore* (1833), in which the Supreme Court ruled that only the national government was restrained by the Bill of Rights. Due process clauses in state constitutions were sometimes utilized to curb state police power, especially in relation to state attempts at economic and property regulation, for example, in *Wynhamer* v. *People* (1856).

Judicial protection of economic and property rights against regulatory attempts by the states reached its zenith in the early 20th century, under the due process clause of the Fourteenth Amendment, in *Lochner* v. *New York* (1905). The due process clause as a significant bar to state regulation of property (the "substantive due process" doctrine) has since been largely abandoned and reversed by the courts. The due process clause of the Fourteenth Amendment later became a significant restraining factor in other areas in which the state police power is exercised, especially criminal procedure—for example, in *Miranda* v. *Arizona* (1966).

State attempts to regulate may also be invalidated if they significantly encroach on an acknowledged power of the national government—especially the commerce clause of Article I, Section 8—even though they may be otherwise valid under the police power, on the ground that the supremacy clause of Article VI, Section 2, makes all laws of the United States supreme over state laws: for example, *Southern Pacific* v. *Arizona* (1945), in which an Arizona safety regulation limiting the maximum length of trains was invalidated because it burdened interstate commerce. State regulatory statutes may also be invalidated if they duplicate or clash with valid national regulation, on the basis of preemption, as in *Pennsylvania* v. *Nelson* (1956).

The national government has also exercised police powers, usually through exercising one of its enumerated powers for regulatory purposes: for example, the section of the Civil Rights Act of 1964 relating to public accommodations was upheld on commerce clause grounds, in *Heart of Atlanta Motel* v. *United States* (1964). Similarly, the Revenue Act of 1951, designed to control illegal professional gambling through imposition of a federal "bookie tax," was upheld in *United States* v. *Kahriger* (1953), under the provision in Article I, Section 8, that Congress has the power to lay and collect taxes.

[Harold W. Chase and Craig R. Ducat, eds., *Corwin's Constitution and What It Means Today*.]

STEFAN J. KAPSCH

POLICE STRIKE, BOSTON. *See* **Boston Police Strike.**

POLIOMYELITIS, also called infantile paralysis, is a disease caused by any of three types of viruses commonly found in the human intestine. Paralysis or death can result if these viruses enter the cells of the central nervous system (brain and spinal cord). In the first half of the 20th century paralytic poliomyelitis occurred in epidemic proportions in several industrialized nations, including the United States, Sweden, and Great Britain. These outbreaks occurred in the wake of the control (by vaccination and sanitation) of infectious diseases such as diphtheria and typhoid fever earlier in the century.

With the acceptance of the germ theory of disease, sanitary practices such as the sterilization of infants' food and clothing were adopted. Thus protected from exposure to microorganisms, infants could not readily develop new immunities to various diseases, including poliomyelitis; neither could they replace the temporary immunities acquired before birth once these immunities had disappeared. Until vaccines were available, such individuals were susceptible to attacks of paralytic poliomyelitis if and when the virus gained access to the bloodstream from the intestine and became established in nerve cells.

The first large polio epidemic in the United States occurred in 1916. The disease achieved national prominence in 1920 when Franklin D. Roosevelt suffered a severe attack. Later, Roosevelt helped to raise funds for poliomyelitis research. Beginning in 1934, a series of "President's Birthday Balls" was organized, the purpose of which was to raise the money for a therapeutic resort in Warm Springs, Ga., a favorite retreat of Roosevelt's. Fund-raising efforts were expanded in 1937 with the formation of the National Foundation for Infantile Paralysis. Basil O'Connor, one of Roosevelt's law partners, was named director of the foundation. Using the slogan "The March of Dimes," the foundation was successful in fund-raising campaigns, and large grants were made to scientists and institutions.

Such campaigns were accompanied by massive promotion and publicity. (In the 1940's and 1950's poliomyelitis was the disease most feared by American parents.) Summers were generally regarded as the "polio season," and the closing of swimming pools and other recreational facilities was commonplace. Although there were severe epidemics, the number of children crippled or killed by poliomyelitis was only a fraction of those who died from other diseases, including typhoid fever and tuberculosis. In 1952 more than 21,000 cases of poliomyelitis were reported.

In the 1940's virologists at the Johns Hopkins University discovered that polio is caused by more than one type of virus. Since a virus is characterized by its own particular immune reaction, scientists realized that a vaccine would have to be developed for each type of polio virus. It was suspected that there were three such viruses, but this conjecture had to be confirmed by determining the types of all known strains of poliomyelitis virus. The typing project, funded by the foundation, started in 1948. One of the virologists engaged in the project was Jonas Salk, then at the University of Pittsburgh.

In 1948 John F. Enders, in collaboration with Frederick Robbins and Thomas Weller at Children's Hospital in Boston, determined that poliomyelitis virus would grow in cell and tissue cultures of almost any kind of cell. Until that time it was believed that the virus would grow only in nerve cells. This belief deterred the development of poliomyelitis vaccines since vaccines made from viruses grown on nerve cells could cause a fatal reaction if injected. This consideration delayed the development of vaccines for almost twenty years.

In 1951–52 gamma globulin field trials were conducted. Gamma globulin, a blood protein in which antibodies are formed, was injected into several thousand children. This procedure afforded a temporary (about six weeks) immunity to poliomyelitis, but the procedure was expensive and was used only during epidemic situations. In order to prevent the development of a black market for gamma globulin, the foundation bought the entire supply.

Enders' work made polio vaccines a possibility. There were two opposing schools of thought relative to the vaccine. One school believed that vaccines made from killed viruses would be best; the other school thought that vaccines made from live but attenuated viruses would be better.

Salk, who received massive support from the foundation, began work on killed-virus vaccines in 1950. A field trial of Salk's vaccines was conducted in 1954. The vaccine for each of the three types was injected separately. About 400,000 children were involved. Some received actual vaccine. Others received a placebo and acted as a control group. The field trial was evaluated by Thomas Francis of the University of Michigan. The results of the trial were made public on Apr. 12, 1955: the vaccines were judged to be safe and about 70 percent effective. The vaccines were licensed two hours after the results were announced.

Following the announcement of the field-trial results, Salk became a national hero and received a presidential citation. Congressmen proposed that Salk receive a lifetime pension and that a Jonas Salk dime be struck.

Beginning in late April 1955, some 150 cases of paralytic poliomyelitis occurred among the vaccinated children, resulting in eleven deaths. The problem was traced to live virus in a batch of vaccine prepared by the Cutter Pharmaceutical Company. Because of this so-called Cutter incident, the Salk vaccine program was temporarily discontinued.

Research into live-virus vaccines was carried out by Herald R. Cox and Hilary Koprowski at the Lederle Division of the American Cyanamid Company and by Albert Sabin, who was funded by the National Foundation. In 1956 Cox and Koprowski carried out field tests of vaccines for two types of virus in Belfast, Northern Ireland. These tests were judged unsuccessful since live, virulent virus was excreted by the recipients. (The vaccines were swallowed rather than injected.) Field tests of Sabin's orally administered live-virus vaccine were carried out in the Soviet Union starting in 1957. Vaccines for all three types of virus were tested. These trials were judged completely successful, and the Sabin oral vaccines were licensed in 1960. But in 1962 there were several cases of paralytic poliomyelitis among those vaccinated.

By the 1970's the Sabin vaccine was used almost exclusively. Since 1965 paralytic poliomyelitis has become a rare disease, but this status can be maintained only by continued vaccination programs, as is evidenced by occasional cases in areas where vaccination programs have lagged.

[Saul Benison, *Tom Rivers: Reflections on a Life in Medicine and Science;* Richard Carter, *Breakthrough: The Saga of Jonas Salk;* Paul de Kruif, *Activities of the National Foundation for Infantile Paralysis in the Field of Virus Research;* Aaron E. Klein, *Trial by Fury: The Polio Vaccine Controversy;* J. R. Paul, *A History of Poliomyelitis.*]

AARON E. KLEIN

POLITICAL ASSESSMENTS of public officeholders and employees have long been used in the United States as a means of gaining funds for party operations. Generally, the assessment is made against the annual salary paid to the officeholder or employee and ranges from 1 to 5 percent.

Filing fees, which are exacted by parties of persons running in partisan primaries, can be a form of assessment; but the rationale in the case of filing fees is that they tend to prevent cluttering of the ballot by those having little chance of winning. Fees range from a few dollars to several hundred dollars, reaching more than $1,000 for some statewide offices. Several state courts have declared filing fees illegal.

Direct political assessment has been outlawed by the Political Activities acts of 1939 and 1940, known as the Hatch acts. These acts forbid "macing," or compelling, federal or state employees to contribute to a party, although "voluntary" contributions are often made nonetheless. Federal civil service rules have long forbidden the soliciting or receiving of any "assessment, subscription or contribution" on the part of officers or employees of the federal government. Several states have similar laws preventing the collection of contributions to a party from state and local public employees at local levels.

Holders of public office and public workers are often asked to contribute to party funds by buying costly reservations to party fund-raising dinners and other benefits. Technically, such contributions are on a voluntary basis, but subtle pressure can be applied through party-oriented supervisors to make many public workers, especially at the state level, feel obligated to contribute. Little of this type of assessment is obtained at federal levels of employment. Elective federal and state officials are prone to make contributions to party coffers, considering such contributions as evidence of their support of the party that helped to elect them.

Political assessment tends to prevail at state and local levels in the United States because no feasible plan for providing local parties with public funds has been devised. As greater public support of parties through income tax contributions occurs, the need for political assessments among the local parties should diminish.

[V. O. Key, Jr., *Politics, Parties and Pressure Groups.*]

PAUL DOLAN

POLITICAL CAMPAIGNS. *See* **Campaigns, Political; Campaigns, Presidential.**

POLITICAL EXILES TO THE UNITED STATES. The United States has been a haven for the politically oppressed of the world since 1562, when the first expedition of Huguenots reached Florida. The great Puritan immigration to Massachusetts beginning in 1630 and the equally great Cavalier immigration to Virginia in 1649 established in the New World two exile colonies of opposite political faiths—the former republican, the latter monarchical. Each in turn exiled its own dissenters, so that secondary exile communities developed in Connecticut, Rhode Island, New Hampshire, North Carolina, and part of Maryland. Pennsylvania welcomed the English Quakers and the Palatine exiles in the latter part of the 17th century. At about the same time, South Carolina and New York became places of refuge for French Huguenots.

Pennsylvania admitted the Swiss Mennonites in 1710, the Dunkards in 1719, and the Schwenkfelders in 1733—all politically persecuted in their home countries for their religious beliefs. Georgia became the home of the Salzburger exiles after 1734. Later, Congress granted a tract of land in central Ohio to Canadian refugees who had assisted the United States in the Revolution and could not return to their homes (see Refugee Tract). Following Pierre Dominique Toussaint L'Ouverture's black uprising in 1790, South Carolina became the major haven for French refugees from Haiti. After the French Revolution, many of the persecuted nobility came to the United States (see Castorland Company; Champ d'Asile).

In the 19th century the United States received the Burschenshaften refugees from Germany—those members of German student societies who were driven out for their political liberalism in the period 1817–20. Moreover, after the unsuccessful Polish uprising against Russia in 1830, Congress granted thirty-six sections of public land in Illinois and Michigan to Polish noblemen exiled for their part in the rebellion. The Socialist revolutions that swept over Europe in 1848 resulted in new exiles who also sought U.S. protection. Of these, the German "forty-eighters" were the most numerous. Lajos Kossuth and his Hungarian exiles were warmly welcomed in the United States (see New Buda). Russian pogroms against the Jews started in earnest in the 1880's, and periodically thereafter many Russian Jews sought refuge in the United States.

The wars and political upheavals of the 20th century have created vast refugee problems, and the United States has participated in the international programs dealing with these problems. Initially, U.S. efforts to aid refugees were comparatively limited. Many refugees from the regime of Adolf Hitler sought sanctuary in the United States, but because of the quota restrictions in the immigration laws compar-

atively few of them were received in this country. A firm and constantly increasing national commitment to help refugees developed after World War II. The United States participated in the International Refugee Organization, which was established to help resettle the large numbers of refugees produced by World War II. In 1948 Congress passed the Displaced Persons Act, under which 400,000 refugees were admitted to this country. The Refugee Relief Act of 1953 authorized the admission of 200,000 additional refugees from Communist countries. After the Hungarian revolt of 1956, approximately 38,000 people were admitted from Hungary. The 1960 Fair Share Act permitted the immigration of a limited number of refugee-escapees under the mandate of the UN high commissioner for refugees.

The foregoing were special laws and directives to deal with temporary situations. In 1965 a permanent statute was enacted to authorize the admission of 10,200 refugees annually. Moreover, the law has open-ended authority to deal with emergency situations by admitting refugees under parole, which eventually can be converted into permanent resident status. This parole authority has been utilized to admit over 400,000 refugees from Fidel Castro's Cuba. It has also been used to admit some Chinese refugees from Hong Kong and to deal with other special situations. Another provision in the immigration law authorizes the attorney general to withhold deportation in any case in which he finds that the deportee would be subject to persecution in the country to which he is destined.

The United States has continued to participate in international programs for the rehabilitation and resettlement of refugees, including the Intergovernmental Committee for European Migration (ICEM) and the United States Escapee Program (USEP). In 1968 the United States ratified the UN Protocol concerning the status of refugees. This act substantially incorporated a UN convention on the same subject and was designed to assure fair and humane treatment of refugees. In ratifying the protocol, the United Staes noted that its laws and policies had always assured such treatment. Moreover, a 1972 policy directive of the secretary of state, issued pursuant to directions from the president, reemphasized the commitment of the United States to the assurance of political asylum in this country and the need to give careful consideration to any such claim for political asylum. In 1975 the United States gave sanctuary to over 100,000 refugees from Vietnam who had fled that country when resistance to the Communist forces collapsed.

[Charles Gordon and Harry Rosenfield, *Immigration Law and Procedure.*]

CHARLES GORDON

POLITICAL PARTIES. As only one kind of political organization, the political party shares with other political organizations (for example, the interest group) the ability to increase the political effectiveness of individuals by bringing them into an aggregate. The importance and distinctiveness of parties as political organizations spring from their domination of electoral politics. Only the parties' labels identify the candidates on the ballots, and they provide the major cues to voters in elections.

That relationship of the parties to mass electoral politics is apparent in their evolution to their modern form. Originally legislative caucuses and elite nominating organizations, the American parties assumed their modern form with the expansion of the male suffrage in the first half of the 19th century, when they became for the first time political organizations with broad support in the electorate and with a network of constituency-based local parties. Thus, they became instruments for organizing and representing the expanding electorates. By the latter half of the century, in fact, they had in some cities become instruments by which the new masses of voters wrested control of cities from old patrician and economic elites.

The origin and development of the American political parties stand entirely apart from the U.S. Constitution. Nowhere are they mentioned in it or even anticipated. Throughout American history they have been instruments of the democratization of the Constitution as well as a result of that process. The parties and their system of loyalty transformed the electoral college and the entire process of electing an American president into something approaching a majoritarian decision.

American parties are also marked by a distinctive, three-part character that sets them apart from other political organizations. They are composed of an identifiable set of committees and activists (the party organization), a group of public officeholders and would-be officeholders (the party in government), and a large contingent of loyalists who consider themselves to be members of the party (the party in the electorate). Ordinary usage recognizes any of the three sectors as the party, or its spokesmen, and as in parties elsewhere, American party organizations and parties in government have contested for supremacy in the party and for control of its symbols and decisions. It is peculiar to the American party system that party organizations have rarely subjected the party's officeholders to even the mildest forms of direction or sanctions.

While the development of American parties was similar to that of parties in other Western democracies and for most of the same reasons, the American party system has always had special characteristics. In form it has long been marked by considerable decentralization, by nonbureaucratic, skeletal organizations, and by the persistence of only two competitive parties. That is to say, the American parties have always been loose confederations of state and local party organizations. Never have they developed the strong national executives or committees that parties elsewhere have. Never have they developed the membership organizations increasingly common in the 20th century in other parties. Largely without formal membership or a career bureaucracy, they have been manned at most levels—except perhaps within the classic urban machine—by only a few party functionaries investing only limited time and energy in the business of the party (*see* Political Parties, Organization of). And along with the British parties and very few others the major American parties have remained two in number. From the initial dualism of the Federalists and the Jeffersonians (Democratic-Republicans) the parties realigned in the 1820's into the Whigs, successors to the Federalist traditions, and the Democrats, led by Andrew Jackson; from 1860 on the Democrats and Republicans dominated the American party system (*see* Two-Party System).

Related to these formal, organizational characteristics have been the parties' chief functional trait: the pragmatic, almost issueless majoritarianism through which they piece together electoral majorities through strategies of compromise and accommodation. They have been much less involved in the business of doctrine or ideology than similar parties elsewhere. Platforms have revealed only modest differences between the two parties. Periodically one finds within the parties movements and candidates that have been intensely programmatic, but their records, even when they have succeeded in capturing the party's presidential nominations, have not been notable. One need only mention the three ill-fated Democratic candidacies of William Jennings Bryan (1896, 1900, and 1908), the Republican nomination of Barry M. Goldwater in 1964, and the Democrats' choice of George S. McGovern in 1972.

The American parties have found their major role as nominators and electors of candidates for public office. They waxed in the 19th century in their ability to confer the party label on candidates, first in party caucuses and then in the more widely consultative conventions that Jacksonian Democracy favored. Especially during the prevailing one-partyism of so much of American politics at the turn of the century, the excesses of party power in those nominations led to the advent of the direct primary in the years between 1900 and World War I. By the 1960's the party control of nominations was limited in some measure by primary laws in every state. In several states, to be sure, the primary law left some nominations to party conventions, and in others in which it did not, the parties devised ways (especially in preprimary endorsements) of affecting the primary-election outcomes. The quadrennial national conventions at which the parties choose their presidential candidates remain the most important vestige of the parties' unchallenged control of nominations.

Control of nominations has shifted from the party organization to the party in government; the same is true of the control of election campaigns. The vigorous political organization of the late 19th and early 20th century controlled, even monopolized, the major election resources. Its army of workers publicized the candidates, gathered information on the electorate, dominated the strategy, and "turned out" the voters on election day. Increasingly, especially after World War II, candidates raised their own campaign funds and recruited their own workers. And they have been able to find sources of campaign expertise other than the party organization—the opinion pollers, the political public relations firms, the mass media. Just as the primary ended the party organization's monopoly of nominations, the rise of the new campaign expertise threatens its control of the election campaign.

Nonetheless most American officeholders reach office on the ticket of one of the major American parties; American presidents and governors are party leaders, and in the mid-1970's all American legislatures (with the exception of the nonpartisan legislature in Nebraska) were organized along party lines. The parties do not find it easy to govern by enacting party-sponsored programs into public policy, and the legislative parties generally do not achieve high levels of cohesion in roll-call voting, leaving the passage of most major legislation to coalitions drawn from both parties. In fact, the percentage of "party votes"—roll calls in which a majority of one party opposes a majority of the other—has declined steadily in the U.S. Congress since the early years of the 20th century.

Only the American chief executives have overcome fragmented, decentralized party power in the United States to weld party support for their programs. So great is their role as party leaders that their program and performance become identified with their party, and elections are fought on the executive record. In that sense, the power of the political party has been joined to the new power of the American executive, particularly the president, especially in the 20th century. As coalitions led by the executive, American parties find their governing role conditioned above all by the American separation of powers. That role contrasts sharply with the role of the cohesive parties that support cabinets in the parliaments of most other Western democracies.

[Hugh A. Bone, *American Politics and the Party System;* V. O. Key, Jr., *Politics, Parties and Pressure Groups;* Everett C. Ladd, *American Political Parties;* Frank J. Sorauf, *Party Politics in America.*]

FRANK J. SORAUF

POLITICAL PARTIES, ORGANIZATION OF.
The organization of both the Democratic and Republican parties takes the form of a pyramid of party committees, beginning at the bottom with local ward, city, and county committees, extending through statewide committees, and building to a single national committee at the top. The personnel of these committees are chosen in a profusion of ways in the different states, some by voters at direct primaries, some by party caucuses and conventions, and some by the party committees below them in the pyramid. In addition, in both parties the national party convention is considered the highest authority of the national party; it defines the powers and the composition of the national committee.

Despite the formal hierarchical nature of the organizations, authority within them has always been decentralized. In some states the effective locus of power is the state committees, buttressed often by the prestige and power of the governor. In others power is further decentralized into autonomous city and county organizations, especially when they can control patronage appointments and election to public office. The national committees of the two parties, both of which date to the years before the Civil War, have never achieved any supremacy in the party organization. The president has customarily subordinated the national committee of his party to his own goals and leadership; in the opposition party the congressional leadership most frequently provides the voice for the national party. Furthermore, the national committees are weakened by being composed of delegates whose major political experience and loyalties are in and to state and local party organizations. Also, the original tradition of granting all state parties equal representation in the national committee emphasized their confederational nature; both parties in the 1960's and 1970's moved away from that tradition by adding extra members for states of greater party strength.

The basic forms of American party organization are to an unusual degree set by law—in this case the laws of the fifty states. Most of the state legislation on party organization was passed in the 19th century or reflects the legal patterns established then. Thus, the states hardened into law the organizational forms of the time: a party organization based on the local neighborhood and its electoral subdivisions (wards and precincts). For the state, the creation of party organization by legislative fiat was a part of its creating and administering the election machinery of the state; thus, the same organizational forms were generally mandated for all parts of the state, regardless of the party's differing organizational needs. Much of the state legislation setting up party organization also reflects the periodic attempts at reform of the parties. The great majority of states regulate party finance, and many also detail the processes and procedures party committees must employ.

Inside this formal structure mandated by the states *de facto* organization within the parties has varied greatly. At one organizational pole has been the big city "machine," an organization depending on armies of precinct and ward workers, on patronage for the dedicated, and on a loyal and compliant local electorate. It flourished especially in the urban centers of the Northeast from the 1880's to the 1950's, and it was typified by the Democratic Tammany Hall organization of New York City, the Boston machine of James M. Curley, and, into the 1970's, the Chicago and Cook County organization of Richard J. Daley. At the other extreme, especially in rural and small-town America, great numbers of local committees mandated by state statutes have long been largely unmanned and inactive. Most party organizations fall somewhere between these extremes, being typically led at the local level by a few stalwarts and officeholders and active only sporadically around election times.

To the basic structure of committees the American parties have periodically added various auxiliary party organizations. Both the Democrats and the Re-

publicans have long had women's and youth groups within them; they have generally been less effective and powerful than similar auxiliaries elsewhere. In both houses of Congress the members of each party have organized campaign committees to support the party's candidates for Congress; the four congressional committees have long histories—those in the House date to the late 1860's and those in the Senate to the years right after the adoption of the Seventeenth Amendment in 1913—and constitute a protection of the party's legislators from any dependence on the party's national committee. Less influential have been the periodic attempts of the governors of each party to organize themselves for action in party affairs. At the local levels the most influential development has been the addition, from the 1950's onward, of membership groups or clubs to the regular party committees. Usually organized by middle-class, well-educated partisans, they were developed as vehicles of greater programmatic emphasis in the activities of the parties and of greater internal democracy in their processes. In a word, they fought bossism and what they viewed as its consequences. The Democratic clubs in New York City and the Democratic clubs and the Republican League in California were typical examples in the 1950's and 1960's.

Along with changes in party organizations have come changes in the personnel that run them. Increasingly the parties attract younger, better educated, more affluent men and women, both in the regular party organization and in the auxiliary organizations. That change in turn reflects changes in the incentives to activity that the party can offer. In the late 19th century and into the 20th century the state and local party organizations controlled a wide variety of jobs and other preferments, such as the letting of government contracts, with which to reward party workers. A combination of reforms—chief among them the advent of civil service and other merit systems of public employment—robbed the parties of such patronage. After World War II the parties began increasingly to attract workers who were motivated by their commitment to ideas, issues, and programs. The new party activists were not only more committed to program than the general electorate was but also probably further away from the ideological center—Democratic workers were more liberal and Republican workers more conservative. At the same time the new activists were less tolerant of autocratic bossism than their earlier counterparts had been. Both the actual operation of the party organizations and the goals the organizations pursue in American politics are to some extent a reflection of the people they recruit to work for them and of their goals and aspirations in politics.

[Cornelius P. Cotter and Bernard C. Hennessy, *Politics Without Power*; Samuel J. Eldersveld, *Political Parties: A Behavioral Analysis*; M. Ostrogorski, *Democracy and the Organization of Political Parties*; James Q. Wilson, *The Amateur Democrat*.]

FRANK J. SORAUF

POLITICAL SCANDALS may be defined as shocking or amazing disclosures that involve disgraceful conduct by public figures or deeply offend public sensibilities. Scandals come in many forms—bribery of public officials, sale of justice and police protection, misappropriation of public property, illegal pressures on voters, corrupt collection and expenditure of money in elections, award of government contracts and franchises for political or financial favors, personal moral misconduct. Such scandals have shocked, angered, dismayed, or frustrated American citizens throughout the history of the country.

Improper handling of government secrets has sometimes erupted into scandal. Edmund Randolph, secretary of state under George Washington, was driven from office for allegedly improper relations with the French. Alger Hiss, in the 1950's, was accused of passing secrets to Communists but went to prison for perjury. In the 1970's the release to the press of the highly classified Pentagon Papers by Daniel Ellsberg shocked the nation because of both the manner and the substance of the disclosures.

Two sources of temptation to official corruption are the government's possession of extensive properties (land and forests, oil, gas, and other mineral deposits; buildings; stockpiles of many commodities) and the discretionary power of many units of government to award such lucrative favors as zoning changes; franchises; tax rulings; property assessments; operating permits based on health and safety inspections; bank charters; railroad, air, and bus routes; and broadcasting channels. To obtain such government property or to obtain preferential treatment, individuals and business firms often resort to sordid methods, and when they are exposed, political scandal results.

In 1872 a railroad scandal involving congressmen and other prominent politicians accepting stock in the Crédit Mobilier of America shook the nation. During the administration of Ulysses S. Grant (1869–77), the Whiskey Ring scandal, an extensive tax-evasion scheme; the Belknap scandal, the apparent bribery of the president's personal secretary; and the Black Fri-

day scandal, a conspiracy to corner the gold market, created widespread excitement. The Teapot Dome oil scandal of 1924 resulted in a prison sentence for Secretary of the Interior Albert B. Fall and the resignation of Secretary of the Navy Edwin Denby.

The history of American cities, particularly the larger ones, is studded with scandals. So many aspects of city living—building a house, operating a bar, planning a subdivision, getting a traffic ticket—involve such discretionary power on the part of local government that bribery, undue political pressure, and undercover deals are a constant possibility.

The award of government contracts for bribes or political favors has been exposed countless times, as has been the improper granting of governmental franchises that often mean quick wealth for the recipient. An example was the improper awarding of television licenses by the Federal Communications Commission in the 1950's.

The sale of justice is uncovered from time to time. The only federal officials ever removed by the U.S. Senate after impeachment have been federal judges. Police scandals involving bribery and the intimidation of policemen by criminal gangs are too numerous to recount.

Winning an election—even at the local level—often has great financial importance to the winner, and so corruption in elections is an ever-present threat. It was more widespread in the 18th and 19th centuries than in the 20th, but the election process continued to be flawed. Theft of votes, vote buying, double voting, shakedown of business and public employees for campaign contributions, and intimidation of opposition voters by gangs of bullies are traditional techniques.

Political scandals often involve personal, not official, acts. Alexander Hamilton's sweeping confession in 1791 of a sordid affair with a Maria Reynolds and the charges that President Andrew Jackson had married Rachel Robards before her divorce became final were major scandals. The refusal of other cabinet wives to accept the wife of Secretary of War John H. Eaton as a social peer resulted in the resignation of Jackson's entire cabinet, with the exception of the postmaster general, in 1831.

Dueling—and the resultant deaths—provided frequent 19th-century scandals. An alleged conflict of interest drove Sherman Adams, Dwight D. Eisenhower's chief of staff, from office. Disclosures that presidents Grover Cleveland and Warren G. Harding had fathered illegitimate children provided grist for the scandal mill.

The greatest American political scandal came in the 1970's. President Richard M. Nixon was forced to resign after his complicity in covering up the facts after a break-in of Democratic party offices in the Watergate Hotel in Washington, D.C., was revealed.

The permanent results of scandals are impossible to predict. Sometimes they are "one-day wonders," quickly fading into history. Some centers of scandal, such as Interior Secretary Fall, New York's William Marcy ("Boss") Tweed, Alger Hiss, and various figures in the Watergate scandal, served prison terms. Others—Nixon, Randolph, Aaron Burr, Spiro Agnew—suffered political disgrace as the result of scandal. Some—Huey Long of Louisiana, Ben Butler and James Michael Curley of Massachusetts, and Boies Penrose of Pennsylvania—seemed to turn controversy into a political asset.

More important are the legislative changes that sometimes take place. The growth of the civil service; regulation of Wall Street, banks, and public utilities; the secret ballot; campaign control laws; humanitarian reforms; and civil rights progress—many of these advances resulted wholly or in part from public reaction to political scandals.

Wherever government (and politics) operates, with its enormous power to reward and punish, men will try to obtain unwarranted favors by illegal means. When these efforts are exposed—by the media, by governmental investigations, by personal lawsuits, or by widespread gossip—scandal results.

[Burl Noggle, *Teapot Dome;* Lincoln Steffens, *Autobiography;* Robert Woodward and Carl Bernstein, *All the President's Men.*]

D. B. HARDEMAN

POLITICAL SCIENCE. In 1968 the eminent political scientist David Easton wrote: "Political Science in mid-twentieth century is a discipline in search of its identity. Through the efforts to solve this identity crisis it has begun to show evidence of emerging as an autonomous and independent discipline with a systematic structure of its own." But the search for identity has been characteristic of political science from its inception on the American scene. Initially the discipline was confronted with the task of demarcating its intellectual boundaries and severing its organizational ties from other academic fields, particularly history. Subsequently, confusion arose over goals, methods, and appropriate subject matter as political scientists tried to resolve the often conflicting objectives of its four main scholarly traditions: (1) legalism, or constitutionalism; (2) activism and reform; (3)

philosophy, or the history of political ideas; and (4) science. By the late 20th century the discipline had evolved through four periods as identified by Albert Somit and Joseph Tanenhaus in the major work on the history of the subject, *The Development of American Political Science: From Burgess to Behavioralism* (1967). The four periods are 1880–1903, 1903–21, 1921–45, and since 1945. In reviewing the organizational and intellectual history of American political science, it is helpful to use the time periods employed by Somit and Tanenhaus (much of what follows is drawn from their work).

1880–1903. Before 1880 the teaching of political science was almost nonexistent. Francis Lieber, generally considered the first American political scientist, held a chair of history and political economy at South Carolina College (being the second incumbent) from 1835–56. In 1858 he became professor of political science at Columbia College. Johns Hopkins University inaugurated the study of history and politics in 1876; but not until 1880, when John W. Burgess established the School of Political Science at Columbia University, did political science achieve an independent status with an explicit set of goals for learning, teaching, and research. Burgess, like Lieber, had been trained in Germany and sought to implement the rigor of his graduate training and the advances of German *Staatswissenschaft* ("political science") in the United States. Under his leadership the Columbia school became the formative institution of the discipline, emphasizing graduate education that was interdisciplinary, comparative in method, and oriented toward the development of political theories.

The discipline grew rapidly in the formative years 1880–1903. Theodore Woolsey, Woodrow Wilson, Burgess, Frank J. Goodnow, and A. Lawrence Lowell brought fame and direction to the field with their pioneering works. Columbia began publication of the *Political Science Quarterly* in 1886; Johns Hopkins published the *Johns Hopkins Studies in Historical and Political Science* (1882). New departments were formed; and the first American Ph.D.'s were awarded.

As with any new discipline, a lively debate ensued about the intellectual boundaries of political science, particularly as those boundaries related to history. There were those who envisioned the distinction in the words of Edward A. Freeman: "History is past politics and politics present history." Others eschewed the connection with history, arguing that law, economics, and sociology were more relevant to the discipline. How to study the discipline was also debated. Even at that early date advocates of a scientific approach contested the arguments of scholars who contended that the subject matter did not lend itself to the methods of the natural sciences.

Other notable developments during this period were the willingness of political scientists to diverge from a strict research orientation and to take an active part in public affairs, to deal with current political issues in their scholarship, and to take on the function of educating college students for citizenship and public affairs. Political scientists have remained committed to these tasks.

1903–21. With the establishment of the American Political Science Association in 1903, political science formally asserted its independence as a discipline. More important, the formation of an association provided a vehicle through which to pursue recognized common interests effectively. Annual conventions fostered a lively exchange of ideas and continued organizational development. In 1906 the association began publication of the *American Political Science Review,* which was soon to become the leading professional journal in the discipline, containing notes about personnel in the profession as well as scholarly articles.

Growth continued at a rapid pace throughout the period. The association's membership rose from 200 to 1,500. In a canvass of university programs prior to 1914, it was determined that 38 institutions had separate political science departments and that an additional 225 had departments that combined political science with other disciplines, most frequently with history or history and economics. It is estimated that the annual output of Ph.D.'s rose from between six and ten to between eighteen and twenty. The increase in domestically trained Ph.D.'s Americanized the profession, whereas previously the majority of new professionals had earned their degrees at German and French institutions. Concomitantly, undergraduate instruction came to focus more on American government and less on comparative and European government and politics. Original research and reviews in the journals emphasized American materials.

The second period is significant for the organizational progress made by the discipline; intellectually, the period is less interesting. As Somit and Tanenhaus described it, "With few exceptions . . . the political science of this period tended to be legalistic, descriptive, journalistic, conceptually barren, and largely devoid of what today would be called empirical data." The exceptions, however, were notable.

Henry Jones Ford, Jesse Macy, and Arthur F. Bentley continued to advocate the scientific approach; their arguments were to have substantial impact on the later development of the profession, for in the third era, 1921–45, the advocacy of science was to become the major intellectual development.

1921–45. The intellectual somnolence of the second era was abruptly interrupted in 1921 with the publication of Charles E. Merriam's "The Present State of the Study of Politics" in the *American Political Science Review.* Impressed with statistics and the rigor of psychology, Merriam called for a "new science of politics" characterized by the formulation of testable hypotheses (provable by means of precise evidence) to complement the dominant historical-comparative and legalistic approaches. The discipline, it was argued, should become more "policy-oriented." Merriam was joined in his effort by William B. Munro and G. E. G. Catlin—the three being considered the era's leading proponents of the "new science" movement. Merriam's work led to the formation of the American Political Science Association's Committee on Political Research; three national conferences on the science of politics; and, in all probability, the Social Science Research Council.

Opponents of "scientism" quickly emerged to challenge the advocates, most notably William Yandell Elliott, Edward S. Corwin, and Charles A. Beard. They questioned the existence of rigorous deterministic laws and the possibility of scientific objectivity by the proponents. They were concerned with the propriety of the participation of "scientists" in citizenship education and public affairs, endeavors that made objectivity difficult. The "scientists" responded by urging, in principle, that research become more important than education for citizenship and public affairs. But the Great Depression and World War II were countervailing forces to such events, and when the president of the association, William Anderson, listed in 1943 the preservation of democracy and "direct service to government" as the foremost obligations of political science, he was undoubtedly representing the prevailing view of political scientists.

The discipline continued to grow. The American Political Science Association doubled its membership. The number of Ph.D.'s awarded annually increased from thirty-five in 1925 to eighty in 1940; the number of universities granting degrees expanded. On the basis of efforts made in 1925 and 1934 to rate the quality of the various departments,

California, Chicago, Columbia, Harvard, Illinois, Michigan, Princeton, and Wisconsin ranked as the leaders.

Since 1945. The development of political science after 1945 was dramatic. The association more than trebled in size as a membership of 4,000 in 1946 grew to 14,000 in 1966. Over 500 independent political science departments were in existence. By the mid-1970's more than 300 Ph.D.'s were awarded annually by over seventy-five departments offering doctoral programs. There were at least twelve major professional journals. Four rankings of departmental quality were undertaken during the period. The 1969 ranking showed the following schools to be the twenty-two best with regard to graduate faculty: Yale; Harvard; California, Berkeley; Chicago; Michigan; Massachusetts Institute of Technology; Stanford; Wisconsin; Princeton; North Carolina; Columbia; California, Los Angeles; Minnesota; Cornell; Indiana; Northwestern; Rochester; Iowa, Iowa City; Oregon; Illinois; Johns Hopkins; and Washington, Saint Louis. All the departments that had rated highly in the previous era continued their excellence in the 1969 ratings.

The struggle over behavioralism (the quest for a more scientific study of politics) was of titanic proportions in the last period. The resolution of that conflict was still not clear in the 1970's. Even so, the quality and quantity of intellectual advances made by all the various subfields of modern political science (international relations; American government; comparative government; theory; public administration; public law) were significant. It is impossible to enumerate all these advances or the dimensions of the struggle over behavioralism that stimulated much of the intellectual progress, but political science in this period renewed an interest in the work of foreign political scientists, and an effort was made to make the discipline less provincial. Also, political science retained its emphasis on education for citizenship and participation in public affairs.

[David Easton, "Political Science," *International Encyclopedia of the Social Sciences;* Albert Somit and Joseph Tanenhaus, *The Development of American Political Science: From Burgess to Behavioralism;* Frank J. Sorauf, *Perspectives on Political Science.*]

HAROLD W. CHASE
ROBERT B. KVAVIK

POLITICAL SUBDIVISIONS are those legally defined governmental units that are utilized by a larger unit of government in order to perform its assigned tasks and that, strictly speaking, must be created by the larger unit of government. Most observers would therefore not consider the fifty states to be political subdivisions of the United States. Although the federal government often utilizes the states for administrative purposes, thirteen states preceded the national government historically, and constitutional theory holds that the states formed the national government.

Local subdivisions are more clearly creatures of the states and directly assist the states in the performance of their constitutional functions. Some of these subdivisions, such as counties (parishes in Louisiana and boroughs in Alaska), are divisions of the state created primarily for administrative purposes. Others are municipal corporations that perform general governmental functions as agents of the state and as units of local self-government. Still others, towns and townships, are administrative subdivisions of the county (although they may have existed prior to the county) that perform services in rural areas. Finally, a class of subdivisions known as special districts performs limited special governmental functions as authorized by state law. The 1972 census of governments found 3,044 counties, 18,517 municipalities, 16,991 townships, and 39,666 special districts in the United States.

The roles played by the various types of political subdivisions vary from state to state. Because of the different backgrounds of the American people in various regions of the country and because of differing political experiences, a unit that is of central importance to one state may be nonexistent in another. For example, the county is the most important subdivision in southern states, but counties were never organized in Rhode Island except as judicial districts and those in Connecticut were abolished as political subdivisions in 1960. Most functions performed by counties elsewhere in the United States are performed by towns in New England.

In those states having counties as significant subdivisions the number of counties grew with expanding state functions and increasing population density until the states had enough seats of administrative authority to render them accessible to the people. These units have proven to be remarkably persistent even though transportation and communications technology have made it possible for many states to reduce the number of counties without impairing governmental effectiveness.

349

Industrialization and urbanization in late 19th- and 20th-century America encouraged the incorporation of ever-increasing numbers of municipalities. Because these units could be created with relative ease by local citizens under the provisions of state law, they were frequently created as agencies of convenience for the local population rather than for the state. As the increasing density of urban settlement and a permissive view of incorporations made the urban environment confusing and progressively less manageable in the eyes of many reformers, some states took steps to restrict the incorporation of new cities, and the rate of numerical expansion of these subdivisions subsided greatly. Only 517 new municipalities were formed in the United States between 1962 and 1972, compared to 1,193 between 1952 and 1962.

Public lands in the West were surveyed and laid out in townships of thirty-six square miles by the federal government. As these lands became states, many midwestern states utilized modified townships as subunits of county government. These units have persisted in spite of frequent challenges by those who consider them obsolete.

Of the 39,666 special districts identified in 1972, 15,781 were school districts. Although the locally controlled school is a strong part of the American political tradition, high educational costs and encouragement by state governments have forced large-scale consolidations of these districts since 1955. Between 1962 and 1972 the number of school districts was reduced by 18,897. Other special districts are increasing rapidly in number. Because traditional subdivision boundaries do not coincide with the areas that need a particular service, a new unit is formed. Such special districts also have the advantage of providing a fresh tax base upon which to exercise those limited powers of taxation permitted to subdivisions by the states. Between 1962 and 1972, 5,562 were formed, making a total of 23,885 special districts, excluding school districts.

[Charles R. Adrian, *State and Local Governments;* George S. Blair, *American Local Government.*]

JOHN H. BAKER

POLITICAL THEORIES. The term "theory" is not used here in the rigorous sense intended by 20th-century social science but in the more commonplace way—to designate an organized body of interrelated speculation and reflection on a relatively broad subject. In this sense "political theory" is more exacting than "political thought," and yet it does not necessarily imply something as thoroughgoing as "political philosophy." Philosophy is radical—that is, it goes all the way to the roots of a subject—and thus it would perhaps be correct to say that there is no distinctively American political philosophy. Political thought in America, rather than going to the roots of things, rests on the root principles of modern Western European political philosophy. A discussion of American political thought implies consideration of those roots as well as the main themes and the main tenets of American political theory.

The roots of American political institutions are in the institutions of England and the political theory of America. The roots of American political theory are in the modern philosophical doctrine of natural rights and its concomitant, the social contract theory. Aristotle considered the view that contract might be taken as the basis of a political community but rejected it, reasoning as follows: The very meaning of community is the possession of things in common; if, as is implied by the social contract theory, all that men have together are agreed-upon rules whereby each can pursue his own good, they can hardly be said to have anything of substance in common. But modern political philosophy lowers the goal of politics from what Aristotle calls the noble, or the fair, life, to what Thomas Hobbes identifies as self-preservation. And that change in goal narrows the scope of politics. Many things come to be regarded as private that formerly had been thought to be of public concern. Thus, the doctrine of natural right, which had formerly served to raise the question what was by nature right—what one's duties were—was transformed into the doctrine of natural rights, which raised the question what individual claims human beings had independent of, and over against, the political community.

But this narrowing also meant that the size of the political community could be vastly increased—to which circumstance Alexander Hamilton referred when he asserted in *The Federalist* (Number 9) that the new science of politics enabled men to have a perfected republic and that the perfected republic would, in fact, be a very, very large republic. These, then, are the philosophical roots of American political theory: the elevation of the social contract to the rank of being the basis of political life; the reduction of the goal of politics from the fair or noble life to mere life; and the transformation of natural-right doctrine to natural-rights doctrine.

The main themes and tenets of American political

theory have remained constant. The themes are republicanism, constitutionalism, and federalism; the tenets are liberty and equality. The most influential American political theories, until well into the 20th century, were developed and forwarded by men who were active in political life. The principles of liberty and equality pronounced in the Declaration of Independence are the foundation of all later American views. The Declaration of Independence says men are equal, not in talents or capacities, but in that they have, by nature, a perfect equality of unalienable rights and that "among these are Life, Liberty and the Pursuit of Happiness." Thus, for example, although his neighbors or those in authority over him may take his liberty away from a human being, they can never take away his right to that liberty, for that right is his, not by a grant from government, but by nature. The enjoyment of these rights is, of course, in danger not only from aggression by rulers but also, and in fact first, from the violence of neighbors, wherefore the Declaration of Independence goes on to say that "to secure these Rights, Governments are instituted among Men." Implied is the view that the absence of government, or its weakness or ineptitude, is just as great a threat to the enjoyment of natural rights as is tyranny; also implied is an acceptance of the social contract theory.

Whether or not the Declaration of Independence then goes on to indicate what sort of government ought to be instituted as the surest way to secure these rights is a matter open to dispute, but the Constitution, which is meant to secure them, institutes a government that is described in *The Federalist* (Number 73) as "wholly and purely republican"; that is, it is a republic without any alloy of unrepublican features. By distinguishing between aristocracies and republics, *The Federalist* (Numbers 20, 39, and 43) indicates that there can be no such thing, properly speaking, as an "aristocratic republic." This point is emphasized by the assertion that the ultimate proof that the Constitution establishes an "unmixed republic" (Number 14) is its universal prohibition of titles of nobility (Numbers 39, 84, and 85); that is, no classes can be established. Inescapably, there will be classes in the sense that several individuals may be identified who, taken together, constitute a class—the rich or the poor, the wise or the foolish—but what is important is that no classes will be established.

The Constitution is conceived as setting up a republic that is relatively free of the vices of republics, of the injustices and inhumanities that a majority, blinded by passion or interest, can inflict on a defenseless minority. The Constitution aims at avoiding or moderating these vices without recourse to the traditional method of moderating politics, which was the "mixed regime"—mixed, that is, of elements of democracy and oligarchy. The American scheme attempts to achieve moderation in a regime "wholly and purely republican," in an unmixed republic in which all the members stand perfectly equal to each other in the crucial political respect, and in which political choice is the result of majority rule. Moderation is sought in such a regime, first, by ensuring that all political choices will be made by representative assemblies; second, by establishing a large enough nation to make it unlikely that any merely factious element can be a majority; and, third, by establishing a scheme of intricate devices that reinforce the effects of representation and largeness. One of the devices is bicameralism.

While the "great compromise" at the Constitutional Convention in 1787, which established popular representation in one house and representation by states in the other, served the ends of the American version of federalism, the purpose of bicameralism in the American scheme is neither federalism nor, as is sometimes said, a class distinction like that to be found between the two houses of the English Parliament. The purpose is to provide by means fully consistent with republican principles a moderating influence on the legislature—an influence that will by no means substitute minority for majority choice but will encourage the majority to reason out its choices rather than rush to them with impetuosity, from passion and prejudice. Thus, bicameralism in America is an element of the separation of powers, a manifold device meant to curb the potential excesses in the republic by republican means.

To speak of equality is to be reminded of the Constitution's compromise with its own principles by allowing slavery to continue. Stephen A. Douglas attempted to reconcile slavery and republican government through the doctrine of popular sovereignty. If a majority wanted slavery, he argued, it was permitted. But Abraham Lincoln argued that the very principle that was the only justification of majority rule—perfect political equality of the members—showed the injustice of slavery. Thus, the modern republic has a self-limiting principle that must be made effective if the republic is not to destroy itself. That is why what came in the 1960's to be called participatory democracy is inconsistent with the self-limiting, or limited, or liberal, or constitutional democracy of the Constitution. Participatory democracy suggests the unmediated participation of the whole citizen body in every political decision without the encumbrance of constitutional limitations.

The second great theme of American political theory is constitutionalism. Every country has a constitution in that it is somehow constituted, in the sense that there is some arrangement of the offices, honors, parts, and goals of the community. But there is another sense to the word "constitution," designating a specific codification of the arrangement, committed to writing. The English constitution is of the first kind; the American, of the second. Given this distinction, the United States cannot be properly said to have a "living constitution," as does Great Britain, for the living character of the English constitution rests on the omnipotence of Parliament. Thus, to the extent that a constitution is living, it is no longer limiting. So, while every country has a constitution, not every country has constitutional government. One of the distinctive features of American constitutional government is judicial review—judgment by the Supreme Court about the constitutional validity of statutes enacted by the Congress—first put into practice in 1803 in *Marbury* v. *Madison*. Each time the Court concludes that an act of Congress is unconstitutional and therefore cannot be enforced, it does so either in the name of some individual liberty guaranteed in the Constitution against government action or in the name of federalism.

The third great theme of American political theory is federalism. And in *The Federalist* (Number 9) Hamilton calls attention to the true principles of federalism: equal representation of the members in the federal councils; concern by the federal council with only intermember and external affairs, as opposed to internal political matters; and action by the federal council only on the member states and never on the individual persons of which the states are composed. In other words, according to Hamilton, there cannot properly be anything which could be called "federal government"; there can be a federation of governments, but where "federal" begins, "government" ends. But Hamilton then proceeds to demean the principles he has listed as unessential. His purpose was to soften the distinction between a "confederation" and a "consolidation" of the states, on which the adversaries of the proposed constitution relied. So successful was Hamilton in this matter that even though the new Constitution established a regime that was a mixture of federal and national principles (leaning heavily to the national side), it became the very standard of the new definition of federalism, which, in a nutshell,

is the division of powers between the central government and the member states. Thus, the statement at the beginning of Article I of the Constitution that "all legislative Powers herein granted" are given to the U.S. Congress, implies that a quantum of power not therein granted rests elsewhere or is held in abeyance. The Constitution nowhere explicitly grants any powers to the states, but the Tenth Amendment offers the reassurance that the states have whatever power is not given to Congress, not denied to the states by explicit prohibition, and not reserved to the people.

During the slavery controversy before the Civil War, John C. Calhoun developed the doctrine of the "concurrent majority" as a restraint on the national power in deference to sectional minorities. The burden of that doctrine would have been to restore some of the effects of the old federalism despite the nationalist, consolidationist effect of the Constitution. The Civil War effectively closed the question, and the Thirteenth, Fourteenth, and Fifteenth amendments to the Constitution resolved the contradiction that had allowed slavery, by declaring that everyone who is in the country is decidedly of the country—that is, that every member of the country is perfectly equal in the decisive political respect.

In the 20th century political republicanism, with its doctrine of individual rights to life, liberty, and property, came under heavy attack from various strains of Marxism that argued for what might be called economic democracy on the ground that political rights do not necessarily bring in their train economic benefits and that, in fact, the maldistribution of material benefits makes a mockery of political rights. In both England and America the response to this charge has been the development of the doctrines of the "welfare state"—the redress of the imbalance of material possessions without departure from the principles of private rights, including property rights.

[Morton J. Frisch and Richard G. Stevens, *American Political Thought: The Philosophic Dimension of American Statesmanship,* and *The Political Thought of American Statesmen.*]

RICHARD G. STEVENS

POLITICAL WRITINGS. All political writings are tracts, treatises, or some combination of the two. A tract aims at the achievement of some immediate political objective; a treatise aims at the understanding of some general political principle. Of course, even the baldest tract cannot help but appeal to principle, and even the most abstract treatise is motivated by some views of the political good. The most relevant, the most influential, and the most highly regarded of American political theories have been the work of American statesmen, but any account of American political writings would have to list other indigenous works and the works of distinguished visitors to America.

The first consequential political writing that strictly "belongs" to America is the Mayflower Compact, agreed to by the forty-one freemen aboard the *Mayflower* before debarking at Cape Cod, Mass., on Nov. 11, 1620. But the towering documents of America are the Declaration of Independence, written for the consideration and adoption of the Continental Congress by Thomas Jefferson in 1776, and the Constitution, prepared for submission to the Congress and ultimately for ratification by conventions of the American people, by the leading lights among the fifty-five delegates to the convention in Philadelphia in 1787. While the Constitution was pending before the people, a controversy over it ran in pamphlets and newspaper articles. Prominent among the writings in opposition to the Constitution were those by George Clinton, under the pseudonym "Cato," and those by Richard Henry Lee, called the "Letters of a Federal Farmer." But the most durable arguments were eighty-five articles written in favor of the Constitution by Alexander Hamilton, James Madison, and John Jay for New York newspapers under the pseudonym "Publius." Shortly before the series was completed in the newspapers, the group of eighty-five was published together as a book under the title *The Federalist* (1788). This is the preeminent work in American political thought. Other important works of the founding period were Thomas Paine's *Common Sense* (1776) and *The Rights of Man* (1792), and a long work by John Adams entitled *A Defence of the Constitutions of Government of the United States of America* (1787–88).

Once the Constitution was adopted, its interpretation became necessary. Important in that respect are Hamilton's financial reports to Congress (1790 and 1791) and Madison's Virginia Resolutions (1798–99) and Jefferson's Kentucky Resolutions (1798). But the chief issue to give rise to political writing was the problem of the Constitution's compromise with slavery, resolved finally by the Civil War, and the concomitant problems of the relation between the states and the United States. John C. Calhoun's *Disquisition on Government,* completed in 1848, and the magnificent debates between Abraham Lincoln and Stephen A. Douglas in the 1858 campaign for the U.S. Senate in Illinois are leading works. The two speeches of Lincoln that are cut into the stone walls of the Lincoln Memorial in Washington, D.C., must be mentioned: his Gettysburg Address (1863) and his second inaugural address (1865).

America was, so to speak, thrust into world affairs in the 20th century. Woodrow Wilson's "Peace Without Victory" speech (1917) and his "Fourteen Points" speech (1918) are evidences of the response to that fact, as is Franklin D. Roosevelt's "Four Freedoms" speech (1941). The internal companion of the crisis in world affairs was the crisis of the Great Depression. Crises in America have, for good reason, a way of expressing themselves in constitutional terms, and so some of Roosevelt's response to the depression can be seen in his "Fireside Chat" on reorganization of the judiciary (Mar. 9, 1937) and his address on Constitution Day (Sept. 17, 1937). Because so much in America turns on the Constitution, the opinions of U.S. Supreme Court justices in constitutional decisions are among the most important of American political writings: for example, John Marshall's opinion in *Marbury* v. *Madison* (1803; judicial review), *McCulloch* v. *Maryland* (1819; congressional power), and *Gibbons* v. *Ogden* (1824; commerce); Roger B. Taney's and Benjamin R. Curtis' opinions in *Dred Scott* v. *Sandford* (1857; slavery and citizenship); Oliver Wendell Holmes's in *Schenck* v. *United States* (1919; freedom of speech); Felix Frankfurter's and Hugo Black's in *Adamson* v. *California* (1947; rights of the accused); and Earl Warren's in *Brown* v. *Board of Education of Topeka* (1954; equality).

The most distinguished writings by visitors to America are Alexis de Tocqueville's *Democracy in America* (1835, 1840) and James, Viscount Bryce's, *The American Commonwealth* (1888). Academic writers played a more prominent role during the 20th century. Admirers of the British parliamentary system have had perhaps the longest influence. The beginning was Wilson's *Congressional Government* (1885), and the high point was reached in the publication of a document by the American Political Science Association in 1950 entitled *Toward a More Responsible Two-Party System: A Report.* Historical determinism and economic determinism, which came to full flower in Europe in the middle of the 19th century, never took hold as firmly in the United States as they did in Europe, but a version of those doctrines presented in Charles Beard's *An Economic Interpretation of the Constitution of the United States* (1913) was perhaps the most influential political book in academic circles and, in due course, in public opinion, in the 20th century. Positivism, an intellectual kin of historical determinism, has been more successful in America. One branch that flourished in the 1930's and 1940's was the "group theory of politics." A leading exponent is V. O. Key, Jr., in *Politics, Parties and Pressure Groups* (1942). The branch dominant in the 1950's and 1960's was behavioralism, the root principle of which is that there is a radical and unbridgeable gap between "facts" and "values." Perhaps no exponent of behavioralism in America stands above the others as does their intellectual forebear in Germany, Max Weber, but the preeminent American critic of behavioralism, as of historicism and in fact of all modern political philosophy laid on the grounds of Niccolò Machiavelli and Thomas Hobbes, is Leo Strauss, whose *Natural Right and History* appeared in 1953.

[Morton J. Frisch and Richard G. Stevens, *American Political Thought: The Philosophic Dimension of American Statesmanship,* and *The Political Thought of American Statesmen;* Herbert J. Storing, *Essays on the Scientific Study of Politics.*]

RICHARD G. STEVENS

POLK DOCTRINE. President James K. Polk's first annual message, Dec. 2, 1845, reaffirmed the Monroe Doctrine and at the same time extended the scope and narrowed the boundaries of the Monroe-Adams dictum by announcing American determination "that no future European colony or dominion shall, with our consent, be planted or established on any part of the North American continent," and American intention to resist "any European interference . . ." there. He thus added to the original idea of noncolonization of unoccupied territory that of "dominion," which has been defined as including acquisition "by voluntary transfer or by conquest of territory already occupied"; and emphasized opposition to "any interference." He also restricted the geographical radius of his prohibition to North America. This doctrine, applied in 1848 to discourage Yucatán from voluntarily ceding itself to some European power, was looked upon by Latin-American nations as a limitation upon their sovereignty.

[S. F. Bemis, ed., *The American Secretaries of State and Their Diplomacy,* vol. V.]

L. ETHAN ELLIS

POLLOCK'S AID TO THE REVOLUTION. With the opening of hostilities between the American colonies and Great Britain, the supply of gunpowder and arms heretofore purchased by the colonists in England and the West Indies was cut off. An agent sent by the governor of Virginia to New Orleans (1776) procured 10,000 pounds of powder through the mediation of Oliver Pollock with Luis de Unzaga y Amezaga, the Spanish governor. This was shipped to the upper Ohio River posts and to Philadelphia.

George Rogers Clark, after the capture of Kaskaskia (July 4, 1778), turned to Pollock for assistance as he had been directed to do by Virginia Gov. Patrick Henry. Arms, powder, blankets, sugar, coffee, and other supplies forwarded by Pollock enabled Clark to gain and hold possession of the Illinois Country. Serving also as commercial agent for the Continental Congress, Pollock continued to forward similar cargoes of goods procured from Spanish creditors for the use of the American army in the East.

By July 1779 Pollock's credit was exhausted and he was forced to mortgage his landholdings and dispose of his slaves. Neither the United States nor Virginia was able to meet his calls for financial assistance. By the close of the war, he had advanced for the American cause his entire property amounting to $100,000 and an additional $200,000 that he had borrowed. This amount surpasses the contribution of any other person to the direct cause of the Revolution.

[James Alton James, *Oliver Pollock, Life and Times of an Unknown Patriot.*]

JAMES A. JAMES

POLLOCK V. FARMERS LOAN AND TRUST COMPANY, 157 U.S. 429 (1895), a case in which the Supreme Court ruled that the income tax provision of the Gorman-Wilson tariff (1894) was unconstitutional on the ground that it was a direct tax and hence subject to the requirement of apportionment among the states according to population. In a prior hearing, only the tax on real estate income had been declared unconstitutional and the Court had divided evenly, four to four, regarding other forms of income. On a rehearing, the Court decided five to four against the income tax on personal property, owing to the fact that one justice, evidently David J. Brewer, now reversed himself to oppose the income tax, and another, Howell E. Jackson, who had not participated in the earlier hearing, voted with the minority. This decision inspired a popular attack on "judicial usurpation," resulting in the Democratic income tax plank of 1896 and leading ultimately to the passage of the Sixteenth Amendment (1913).

[Charles Warren, *The Supreme Court in United States History.*]

HARVEY WISH

POLL TAX. A tax levied on each person within a particular class (for example, adult male) rather than on his property or income is called a poll, head, or capitation tax. Poll taxes were employed in all the American colonies at one period or another. It was Virginia's only direct tax for years, and before the Revolution Maryland had practically no other direct tax. Poll taxes continued to be levied by most states through the 19th century and well into the 20th. In 1923 thirty-eight states permitted or required the collection of poll taxes. The amount of the tax varied from one to five dollars, and the proceeds were often allocated to specific public facilities, such as state schools or roads.

For many years states (five states as late as 1962) used the poll tax as a means of discouraging blacks from registering to vote by making the payment of the tax a prerequisite to the exercise of the right to vote. And the Supreme Court periodically upheld the states' right to do so, as in *Breedlove* v. *Suttles,* 302 U.S. 277 (1937).

In 1964 the Twenty-fourth Amendment to the Constitution was ratified, nullifying all state laws requiring payment of a poll tax as a condition "to vote in any [federal] primary or other [federal] election." Because the amendment made no mention of purely state elections, a few states continued the levy as a prerequisite for voting in state elections until 1966, when the Supreme Court, in *Harper* v. *Virginia Board of Elections,* 383 U.S. 663, ruled that a state violates the Fourteenth Amendment "whenever it makes the affluence of the voter or payment of any fee an electoral standard."

[Thomas I. Emerson and David Haber, *Political and Civil Rights in the United States.*]

HAROLD W. CHASE
ERIC L. CHASE

POLLY ADMIRALTY CASE. By the Rule of the War of 1756 Great Britain had contended that colonial trade of an enemy, which in time of peace had not been open to outside powers, could not in time of war be open to neutral carriage. During the wars of the French Revolution the British government accordingly confiscated neutral vessels carrying goods between France or its allies and their colonies. Partly as a means of diverting enemy colonial commerce through British ports, and partly as a means of ingratiating the neutral United States, then on the verge of hostilities with France, British orders in council of Jan. 25, 1798, allowed neutral vessels to carry the produce of any island or settlement of France, Holland, or Spain direct to a British port or to a port of their own country. This permitted the development of an American entrepôt traffic of West India goods to European ports after Americanization in the United States. In the case of the *Polly,* tried by British admiralty courts in 1802 (during the interim of peace), it was decided that this circuitous voyage (via the United States and Americanization of French colonial goods) to French enemy ports, was not a violation of the Rule of the War of 1756. (*See also Essex.*)

[A. T. Mahan, *Sea Power in Its Relations to the War of 1812.*]

SAMUEL FLAGG BEMIS

POLYGAMY. Polygamous living has been a custom practiced by certain sects and minorities, the most important of these in the United States being the Mormons and the Oneida Perfectionists. In the antebellum South, slaves were encouraged or permitted to mate according to the wishes of their owners, sometimes polygamously.

What is essentially polygamous living is practiced by many persons secretly, or with the knowledge of limited circles of acquaintances who approve or tolerate the situation. It is distinguished from prostitution in that it involves continuity of relationship, with affection and responsibility toward the extra mate. Such relationships, indicated by the terms "concubine," "mistress," and "lover," among others, have been described as occurring in many places in the American colonies and throughout American history. Toleration has varied from time to time and from place to place. Adultery is a crime in many states but is seldom prosecuted criminally. More often it forms the ground for a civil suit for divorce by the innocent party. Occasionally a person, concealing the facts or ignorant of the law, goes through the form of a marriage ceremony with his second or illicit partner; this constitutes bigamy, which is a crime, and furthermore the marriage thus attempted is legally null and void. Many divorces, if contested in the courts of the home state, would be found invalid, and hence the remarriage of the parties would be bigamous. In such case a civil suit for property is much more likely, in practice, than a criminal prosecution for bigamy. Some writers have said that the high U.S. divorce rate results in a form of "serial polygamy," as distinguished from "simultaneous polygamy."

[A. W. Calhoun, *A Social History of the American Family;* E. R. Groves, *The American Family.*]

JOSEPH K. FOLSOM

10

POMEROY CIRCULAR, a pronouncement of Salmon P. Chase for the presidency, was issued in January 1864 by a national executive committee of Radical Republicans over the signature of its chairman, Sen. Samuel C. Pomeroy. Distributed secretly at first, it was publicized through the *National Intelligencer,* Feb. 22. Unconditional Union men, believing President Abraham Lincoln's reelection undesirable and impossible, found that Chase, then secretary of the Treasury in Lincoln's cabinet, combined those qualities necessary for a more vigorous prosecution of the war. In explaining the circular to the Senate in March, Pomeroy asserted that the committee, without consulting Chase, had drafted him as their candidate. Meanwhile, the Chase boom had collapsed with the declaration of Ohio Unionists for Lincoln.

[John G. Nicolay and John Hay, *Abraham Lincoln: A History,* vol. VIII.]

WENDELL H. STEPHENSON

PONCE DE LEÓN'S DISCOVERY of Florida in 1513 added the mainland of North America to the Spanish dominions. In 1512 Juan Ponce de León secured a royal grant, with the title of *adelantado,* to conquer the island of Bimini to the north of Cuba where the fountain of youth presumably was located. Sailing from Puerto Rico on Mar. 3, 1513, he sighted the mainland on Mar. 27, and on Apr. 2 landed just north of the present site of Saint Augustine. The region was named Florida in honor of the Easter season. Reembarking, Ponce de León explored the eastern shore of Florida, doubled the cape, and passed along the Florida Keys, which he called the Martyrs. He continued along the western coast, probably reaching Pensacola Bay, and returned to Puerto Rico on Sept. 21. Besides taking possession of Florida, he discovered the Bahama Channel. Returning to Spain in 1514, he received a grant to colonize the islands of Florida and Bimini, but it was not until 1521 that he undertook the second expedition from Puerto Rico to Florida. Reaching the peninsula probably at Charlotte Harbor on the western coast, he and his party were attacked by hostile Indians, and in a battle the *adelantado* was severely wounded. The effort at colonization was abandoned, and the expedition returned to Havana, Cuba, where Ponce de León died.

[Frederick A. Ober, *Juan Ponce de León.*]

ROSCOE R. HILL

PONTCHARTRAIN, LAKE, in southeastern Louisiana, five miles north of New Orleans, was named by Pierre Lemoyne, Sieur d'Iberville, in 1699 in honor of Louis de Phélypeaux, Comte de Pontchartrain, French minister of marine. The lake is about 40 miles long and covers about 600 square miles. It was connected to New Orleans by canal in 1795, by railroad in 1831, and by ship canal in 1921. The Bonnet Carre spillway, completed in 1935 to protect New Orleans from Mississippi River floods, connects both lake and river thirty-five miles above the city. The lake is crossed by two causeways twenty-three miles in length, the first built in the mid-1950's and the second in the late 1960's (opened 1969), which form the longest bridge in the world. Lake Pontchartrain formed a link in the British inside passage to the Mississippi, 1763–83, and in the later overland route to the north and east.

[W. Adolphe Roberts, *Lake Pontchartrain.*]

WALTER PRICHARD

PONTCHARTRAIN DU DÉTROIT, FORT, was established by Antoine de la Mothe Cadillac on July 24, 1701. The original fort was a rectangular stockade one arpent (192.24 feet) square without the bastions; within were erected the church, the barracks, the storehouse, and other essential structures. Around it the Detroit River settlement grew up and eventually the city of Detroit. Frequently enlarged, and with various changes of name (Fort Lernoult, Fort Shelby, Detroit), the fortification continued to guard the settlement for 125 years.

[C. M. Burton, *City of Detroit, Michigan, 1701–1922,* and "Fort Pontchartrain du Detroit," *Michigan Pioneer Collections,* vol. 29.]

M. M. QUAIFE

PONTIAC'S WAR (1763–64), an uprising of Indians in 1763 after the end of the French and Indian War, in opposition to British expansion in the Great Lakes area. The leader and instigator of the struggle was an Ottawa chief named Pontiac, who devised a plan for a general uprising of the Indians and for a systematic destruction of the British forts and settlements. Pontiac seems to have been under the influence of the Delaware Prophet, who had earlier preached a return to the old Indian ways. Pontiac had long been hostile to the English and had fought against them at Gen. Edward Braddock's defeat in 1755.

Most of the Indians of the Great Lakes area had been on better terms with the French than with the English, and they were outraged when the British commander, Gen. Jeffrey Amherst, issued new and strict regulations that banned the credit and gifts that the Indians had been accustomed to receiving from the French.

Pontiac, following the teachings of the Delaware Prophet, attempted to forge unity among the Indians of the area and to induce them to join the Ottawa in a war against the English; he was convinced that the friendly French were preparing to reconquer their lost territories. Meanwhile, English settlers were moving into the area. Pontiac succeeded in convincing the Delaware, Shawnee, Chippewa, Miami, Potawatomi, Seneca, Kickapoo, and others that they should join him in his war on the British. In the spring of 1763 Pontiac convened a council of the Indian allies at the mouth of the Ecorse River, a few miles from Detroit, where he incited the hundreds of attending warriors to drive out the British.

The aroused warriors, at the end of May 1763, attacked every British fort in the area, taking eight out of ten of them and killing the garrisons. The main fortifications, Fort Pitt and Detroit, were, however, successfully defended, although under siege by the Indians. Because of the central location and military importance of Detroit, Pontiac himself directed the attack on it. He had planned a surprise attack; but the post commander, Maj. Henry Gladwin, was warned in advance, and the gates were closed. Pontiac laid siege to the fort, a tactic that was without precedent in Indian military history. During the summer the fort was relieved by reinforcements and military supplies from Niagara, but Pontiac continued to besiege it until November. Realizing that he could expect no assistance from the French and suffering defection of his Indian allies, Pontiac retreated to the Maumee River. Col. John Bradstreet entered Detroit with troops on Aug. 26, 1764, and prevented a renewal of the siege; but a formal peace was not concluded until July 24, 1766. Pontiac was unsuccessful in arousing the tribes along the Mississippi River to another effort, and in 1769 he was killed by an Illinois Indian.

[Francis Parkman, *History of the Conspiracy of Pontiac;* Howard H. Peckham, *Pontiac and the Indian Uprising.*]

KENNETH M. STEWART

PONTOTOC, TREATY OF (Oct. 20, 1832), negotiated by Gen. John Coffee, U.S. commissioner, with the Chickasaw at their council house in what is now Pontotoc County, northeast Mississippi. The treaty provided for the cession of Chickasaw lands (6,283,804 acres) in northeastern Mississippi and the removal of the tribe west of the Mississippi, thereby extinguishing the last Indian titles to lands in the state

(*see* Indian Removal). The United States promised the Indians the proceeds from the sales of the lands.

[H. R. Cushman, *History of the Choctaw, Chickasaw and Natchez Indians;* Mary Elizabeth Young, *Redskins, Ruffleshirts and Rednecks: Indian Allotments in Alabama and Mississippi 1830–1860.*]

MACK SWEARINGEN

PONY EXPRESS. During the late 1850's the question of the best route for the overland mail to California was a topic of great interest in the Far West. In September 1857 a contract was granted to John Butterfield and his Overland Mail Company, which began operation one year later over a circuitous southern route. The shortest time made on this route was twenty-two days. Many Californians, including Sen. William M. Gwin, believed that a central route was entirely feasible and would expedite the carrying of mail to the coast. It was Gwin who, early in 1860, induced William H. Russell, of the freighting firm of Russell, Majors and Waddell, to demonstrate the practicability of a central route in a dramatic manner by establishing a pony express. Of course, the hope of securing a lucrative mail contract was the motivating factor with the company (*see* Central Overland California and Pikes Peak Express).

The project was pushed vigorously. Starting at Saint Joseph, Mo., the route in general followed the well-known Oregon-California trail by way of Fort Kearny and Scottsbluff (Nebraska), Fort Laramie, South Pass, and Fort Bridger (Wyoming), and Salt Lake City. From there the trail went around the southern end of the Great Salt Lake, by way of Fort Churchill, Carson City (both in Nevada), and Placerville (California) to Sacramento. Stations were built at intervals of about fifteen miles, wherever stage stations did not already exist. Fleet, wiry, Indian ponies were purchased; and young, courageous, lightweight riders were hired. On Apr. 3, 1860, the service was inaugurated. It was like a giant relay, in which about seventy-five ponies participated in each direction. At each station the riders were given two minutes in which to transfer the saddlebags to fresh ponies and be on their way again. After riding a certain distance, one rider would hand the mail over to another, and so on, until the destination was reached. Day and night, summer and winter, over dusty plains and dangerous mountain trails, and frequently in the midst of hostile Indians, the ponies and their riders galloped at their best speed over the sections of the route allotted to them.

During the eighteen months of the operation of the pony express only one trip was missed. The service was weekly at first and later semiweekly. The best time ever made was in November 1860, when news of President Abraham Lincoln's election was carried in six days from Fort Kearny to Fort Churchill, then the termini of the telegraph lines that were being built from the Missouri River and California. When the two telegraph lines were joined on Oct. 24, 1861, all need for the pony express was eliminated.

The pony express was disastrous to the fortunes of Russell, Majors and Waddell. The cost of operation was greatly in excess of the revenue. In fact the company was virtually ruined by the experiment and was disappointed in its hope of gaining a valuable mail contract, which went to another firm. Furthermore, the enterprise was not even necessary as a demonstration of the feasibility of a central route. The outbreak of the Civil War made the selection of such a route inevitable.

[William Banning and George H. Banning, *Six Horses;* Glenn D. Bradley, *The Story of the Pony Express;* Le Roy Hafen, *The Overland Mail, 1849–1869.*]

DAN E. CLARK

POOLS, RAILROAD. Agreements between railroads to divide competitive business are called pools. Equalization was made either by dividing traffic or by dividing income. Since traffic pools limited the right of the shipper to route his own business, money pools were more common. The cattle eveners' pool, formed in 1875 to equalize traffic in livestock between Chicago and New York, was an example of the traffic type. The Chicago-Omaha pool, dividing business among three railroads, dated from 1870. Pooling agreements were common in the period from 1870 to 1887, but they were outlawed by Section 5 of the Interstate Commerce Act of 1887. They were succeeded by rate agreements, at least one of which, the Buffalo Grain Pool, was practically a pooling agreement. Even the rate agreements were held to be a violation of the Sherman Antitrust Act of 1890 in *United States* v. *Trans-Missouri Freight Association* (1897). In the Transportation Act of 1920 pooling agreements were legalized when approved by the Interstate Commerce Commission. But the railroads have not seen fit to make much use of this privilege. They had found other methods that seemed more suitable for their needs.

[D. P. Locklin, *Economics of Transportation.*]

HARVEY WALKER

POOR, CARE OF. *See* Poverty and Pauperism.

POOR RICHARD'S ALMANAC (1732–96), published in Philadelphia by Benjamin Franklin, contained, in addition to the usual almanac information on the weather, tides, eclipses, and medicinal remedies, maxims, saws, and pithy sayings written by Franklin. Each edition of *Poor Richard's Almanac* saw an increase in sales until 10,000 copies were printed annually, approximately one for every hundred people in the colonies. It eventually became the second most popular book in the American colonies, the Bible being first. It is probable that Franklin ceased to write for the almanac after 1748, when he began to devote most of his time and energy to public affairs, although he continued as its editor and publisher. In 1757, after editing the 1758 edition, he disposed of the almanac, which continued to appear until 1796. In 1758 Franklin collected the best of his writings from *Poor Richard's Almanac* in *Father Abraham's Speech,* more commonly known as *The Way to Wealth.* (*See also* Almanacs.)

[Benjamin Franklin, *Papers;* Carl Van Doren, *Benjamin Franklin.*]

E. H. O'NEILL

POOR WHITES, a term applied, frequently in scorn, to the lowest social class of white people in the South. Before the Civil War most early writers and travelers were interested only in the aristocracy and slaves and tended to dismiss almost all others as "poor whites." In the 1930's scholars began to draw a clearer distinction between what they thought were the comparatively few genuine poor whites in the antebellum period and the much greater numbers of artisans, yeoman farmers, and self-respecting mountaineers.

Whatever their numbers, the poor whites were a degraded class. Slaveless and usually located in isolated areas of poor soil such as the sandhills at the fall line or the "pine barrens" from the Carolinas to Mississippi, they became the victims of a vicious circle. A combination of malnutrition and disease deprived them of the energy necessary to rise out of the poverty that produced the very conditions that held them down. They thus became almost willing objects of contempt, as they lived in squalor, subsisted largely on a miserable fare of coarse cornmeal, sweet potatoes, beans or peas, and a little meat and gave birth to a numerous progeny afflicted like themselves with pellagra, malaria, tuberculosis, hookworm, and other chronic diseases.

An early theory that these agricultural slum dwellers were the descendants of English criminals, debtors, and the lowest class of indentured servants brought over in the colonial period is no longer given credence; nevertheless, their ignorance and lack of ambition made them despised even by the slaves. Disdaining manual labor, the men supported themselves primarily by hunting and fishing, while their gaunt, listless wives made halfhearted attempts to supplement their diet from small, poorly tended gardens.

After the Civil War the term took on a more elastic meaning as the rapid spread of sharecropping and farm tenancy engulfed even many of the formerly independent yeomanry in poverty. During the almost continuous agricultural depression that ran from the 1870's through the 1930's great numbers of southerners found themselves vulnerable to derision as "poor whites." The virtual eradication of hookworm, malaria, and pellagra in the 20th century, however, plus the spread of compulsory education, and finally the post–World War II agricultural revival eventually eliminated many of the problems plaguing these people and their numbers have declined.

[A. N. J. Den Hollander, "The Tradition of 'Poor Whites,' " in W. T. Couch, ed., *Culture in the South;* C. Vann Woodward, *Origins of the New South, 1877– 1913.*]

ROBERT W. TWYMAN

POPE-McGILL FARM ACT, also known as the Agricultural Adjustment Act of 1938, was approved on Feb. 16, 1938. Title I added amendments to the Soil Conservation and Domestic Allotment Act of 1936, which was continued in operation. Title II authorized the secretary of agriculture to complain to the Interstate Commerce Commission concerning freight rates on farm products and to set up four regional laboratories to find new uses for agricultural products. The Federal Surplus Commodities Corporation continued until June 30, 1942, when the Agricultural Marketing Service assumed many of its functions. Title III authorized the secretary of agriculture, under prescribed conditions, to proclaim national marketing quotas for tobacco, corn, wheat, cotton, and rice. Title IV had to do with "Cotton Pool Participation Trust Certificates," while Title V created the Federal Crop Insurance Corporation with a capital of $100 million within the Department of Agriculture to insure wheat crops against unavoidable losses.

ERIK MCKINLEY ERIKSSON

"POP-GUN" BILLS, tariff measures passed by the Democratic House of Representatives after the elec-

tions of 1890. Although blocked in the Senate, the "pop-gun" bills were effective in focusing attention on the defects in the McKinley Tariff of 1890 and creating issues for the campaign of 1892. The term arose when the Republicans contemptuously referred to the measures as "pop guns."

[Edward Stanwood, *American Tariff Controversies in the Nineteenth Century.*]

L. J. MEYER

POPHAM COLONY. Although English and European fishermen had long been taking cod along the New England coast, the first attempt by England to colonize the region was the ill-starred Popham Plantation on the Kennebec (formerly Sagadahoc) River in southeastern Maine in 1607–08. On May 31, 1607, the Plymouth Company of Virginia, proprietors of northern Virginia, spurred on by hopes of profitable farming of the rich resources of fish, lumber, furs, minerals, and medicinal herbs reported by the navigators Bartholomew Gosnold (1602), Martin Pring (1603), and George Waymouth (1605), sent out about 120 colonists on two ships, the *Mary and John* and the *Gift of God.* George Popham, nephew of Sir John Popham, chief justice of England and sponsor of the venture, was president and Raleigh Gilbert was admiral.

These men, having reached an island near the mainland, sailed south along the coast to Seguin Island and then landed at the mouth of the Kennebec River, on the western bank, in the middle of August 1607. They built a fort, which they named Saint George, a storehouse, fifty dwellings, and a church. The first Protestant church service was conducted here by the colony's Anglican clergyman, Richard Seymour. The settlers began the construction of a ship, a pinnace of 30 tons, *Virginia of Sagadahoc,* the first ship built by Englishmen in North America. They explored the river up to Merrymeeting Bay, the Androscoggin River to the Pejepscot River, Casco Bay on the coast to the west, and eastward to Pemaquid Point. They made friends with the Indians and traded with them. But things went wrong with the colony from the first. The reason for failure may lie in the fact that, in John Aubrey's words, the colony was stocked "out of all the gaols of England." Quarrels arose, and all but forty-five men had to be shipped home when the second ship left in December. On top of that disaster there came a savage Maine winter. Popham died on Feb. 5, 1608. Although ships brought supplies in the summer of 1608, they also brought news of the deaths in England of Sir John Popham and Gilbert's brother, Sir John Gilbert, who left him an inheritance of property. So, in September the settlers pulled up stakes and went home. A story, never verified by documentation, persisted for years that some colonists remained and joined the semipermanent fishing settlements to the east.

[Robert P. Tristram Coffin, *Kennebec;* William Strachey, *Historie of Travaile Into Virginia Brittanica, ca. 1616;* H. O. Thayer, *Sagadahoc Colony.*]

ROBERT P. TRISTRAM COFFIN

POPULAR SOVEREIGNTY, in a general sense, means the right of the people to rule. "Squatter sovereignty" literally means the right of people living anywhere without a government to form a body politic and practice self-government. When the theory that the people of a federal territory had the right to determine the slavery question for themselves was first enunciated, it was dubbed "squatter sovereignty" by its opponents. The term has persisted and is often used as the equivalent of popular sovereignty.

When Lewis Cass, senator from Michigan and later secretary of state, in a letter to A. O. P. Nicholson dated Dec. 24, 1847, declared that he was "in favor of leaving the people of any territory which may hereafter be acquired, the right to regulate [slavery] themselves, under the great general principles of the Constitution," he made the first clear statement of the principle of popular sovereignty. Acts organizing the territories of Utah and New Mexico were passed in 1850 (*see* Compromise of 1850). In neither territory was slavery prohibited or protected. It was simply provided that each of the territories should be admitted with or without slavery as its constitution might specify.

Sen. Stephen A. Douglas of Illinois made the Kansas-Nebraska Act a popular sovereignty measure that repealed the antislavery provision of the Missouri Compromise of 1820. That popular sovereignty would produce a bitter struggle for Kansas was as difficult to foresee as was the Civil War. The conflict that followed the passage of the Kansas-Nebraska Act was really decided by the forces controlling the westward movement of the 1850's. So superior were the drawing qualities of northern and southern frontier areas in competition with Kansas that only a small proportion of the migrating colonists reached that territory before 1860. The conditions prevailing between 1854 and 1860 were such that those interested in making Kansas a slaveholding state had no chance of success (*see* Border War). Even the modest contingent from the North, largely from Ohio, Indiana, and Illinois, greatly outnumbered the contribution from the entire South to Kansas. The southerners who settled in the territory were mainly nonslaveholders from the upper South, and many of them voted with the free-state element, when, on Aug. 2, 1858, it was finally determined by a large majority that Kansas would not become a slaveholding state (*see* Lecompton Constitution). Douglas' debates with Abraham Lincoln (Aug. 21–Oct. 15, 1858) came after the people of Kansas had made this decision, and there was no remaining federal territory where the conditions were so favorable to slavery.

Douglas opposed the admission of Kansas under the Lecompton Constitution on the ground that popular sovereignty had not been fairly applied when that constitution was first submitted to the people. Through the aid of Republicans, he won the Lecompton fight, which preceded the debates with Lincoln. The Dred Scott decision had come a year before the Lecompton contest. The opinion of Chief Justice Roger B. Taney troubled the leaders of the new Republican party, because it ran directly counter to the Wilmot Proviso principle. Lincoln believed that Taney had also played havoc with popular sovereignty, although Douglas declared that he had accepted the Court's decision. Before the beginning of the debates, the logic of the situation caused Douglas to discuss the effects of the decision on his principle of nonintervention. His Freeport Doctrine, in response to Lincoln's famous second question as to how the doctrine of popular sovereignty could be reconciled with the Dred Scott decision, was not new to either of the senatorial candidates. The assertion of Douglas that slavery could not exist in any territory where the territorial legislature refused to provide the necessary police regulations squared with the facts, and the people of a territory really could decide for themselves regardless of how the Supreme Court might in the future decide the abstract question of the right of a territorial legislature to prohibit slavery. When Sen. Albert G. Brown of Mississippi complained on the floor of the Senate on Feb. 23, 1859, that "Non-action goes a great way to exclude slave property from a territory, further perhaps than to exclude any other property," he was virtually repeating what Douglas had asserted at Freeport. On the basis of his belief that territorial legislatures would exclude slavery by nonaction, Brown voiced the demand that Congress provide the necessary legislation. It was then that Douglas added the second and final corollary to the doctrine of popular sovereignty, when he proclaimed that he would "never vote for a slave code in the territories by Congress."

[Eugene H. Berwanger, *The Frontier Against Slavery: Western Anti-Negro Prejudice and the Slavery Extension Controversy;* Eric Foner, *Free Soil, Free Labor, Free Men;* James A. Rawley, *Race and Politics: Bleeding Kansas and the Coming of the Civil War.*]

WILLIAM O. LYNCH

POPULATION, GROWTH AND MOVEMENTS OF.

The world's population has increased almost eightfold since the middle of the 17th century. Because the area now comprising the United States was virtually empty in 1650, it is not surprising that the population of the United States grew even more rapidly, but it is somewhat startling to realize that during the 320-year period to 1970 its exogenous population increased almost 4,000-fold. This works out to an average annual rate of growth of 2.6 percent, a figure well above the rate of increase in the 1970's of the world's less-developed regions, whose rapid growth is often spoken of as "explosive." To be sure, an increase of more than 2 percent in the poverty-stricken regions of dense settlement in the 1970's has a significance entirely different from the significance of much higher rates in the colonial and early federal eras. Writing in 1751, Benjamin Franklin pointed out that the experience of the fully settled European countries could not be taken as a guide to the growth in prospect for the colonies. A vast and empty land with abundant resources would, he thought, inevitably lead to high wages, early marriage, numerous offspring, and very rapid population growth. "Thus there are suppos'd to be now upwards of One Million English Souls in North-America. . . . This Million doubling, suppose but once in 25 Years, will, in another Century, be more than the People of England, and the greatest Number of Englishmen will be on this Side of the Water" ("Observations Concerning the Increase of Mankind, Peopling of Countries, etc."). And so it proved. The population of the United States grew at an average of almost 3 percent per year, causing it to double about every twenty-three years. Franklin's guess was one of the more accurate predictions ever made about population growth a century ahead. From 52,000 people in 1650, the population of the United States had grown to over 204 million by 1970.

Of course, the population was not all of English, or even British, descent, but after the early years' start, most of the growth came from the excess of births over deaths, which at the beginning of the 19th century is estimated to have been nearly 3 percent per year.

In the decade 1840–50 net immigration passed the 1 million mark, mounting to its maximum of 6.3 million from 1900 to 1910. During the Great Depression decade there was a net outward movement, but after that the total rose to almost 4 million in the 1960's. Despite this substantial immigration, the rate of population growth declined, with few breaks, from the beginning of the 19th century until the Great Depression. The gains through immigration were more than cancelled by the falling rates of natural increase, which dropped systematically from about 1830 to 1930, giving the United States one of the world's early and most sustained declines in natural increase.

Table 1 makes the reason clear. It is estimated that in the 1820's there were about 55 births a year per 1,000 population. These early figures should not be closely interpreted. There was no birth registration area before 1916, and the area did not come to include all of the United States until 1932. Births had to be estimated from the number of surviving children counted at the decennial censuses. Nevertheless, the figures are about right. The U.S. birth rate in the early 1800's was clearly higher than that of almost every country of Asia and Latin America in the 1970's. By 1935–39 the rate had fallen below 19. Then came wartime and postwar rebound, culminating in the "population explosion" of the 1950's, with a rate of nearly 25 per 1,000. It was followed by a sharp decline in the 1960's and 1970's, reaching 15 per 1,000 population in 1974. The birth rates for the nonwhite population, predominantly blacks, have been systematically higher than those for the whites, but since 1955 the decline has been even faster for the nonwhite than for the white population.

The rapid rate of growth in the early years was apparently also fostered by a favorable death rate for the time. Nothing very precise can be said about it because, without registration, deaths are more difficult to estimate than births. The death registration area was not started until 1900 and did not include the entire country until 1932. Nevertheless, there has been great improvement, the death rate for the total population dropping from 16.2 per 1,000 during 1900–05 to 9.4 in 1973, but the rate for the white population has changed little since 1950. The rate for the nonwhite population was substantially higher than that for the white until 1969, but then fell below it. This should not be interpreted to mean that the nonwhite population is healthier than the white: the death rate gives

Table 1. Estimated U.S. Birth Rates by Color
(per 1,000 population)

Period	Total [1]	White [2]	Nonwhite [2]
1820	55.0		
1830	53.3		
1840	51.8		
1850	47.9		
1860	44.3		
1870	44.8		
1880	39.8		
1890	35.7		
1900	32.2		
1910	30.3		
1920	27.8		
1930	21.2		
1935–39	18.8	18.0	25.9
1940–44	21.2	20.4	27.5
1945–49	24.1	23.4	30.3
1950–54	24.9	23.8	34.0
1955–59	24.9	23.6	34.7
1960–64	22.4	21.4	30.6
1965	19.4	18.3	27.6
1966	18.4	17.4	26.1
1967	17.8	16.8	25.0
1968 [3]	17.5	16.6	24.2
1969 [3]	17.8	16.9	24.4
1970 [3]	18.4	17.4	25.1
1971 [3]	17.2	16.2	24.7
1972 [3]	15.6	14.6	22.9
1973 [3]	14.9	13.9	21.9

[1] Source for totals 1820–1930: Irene and Conrad Taeuber, *People of the United States in the 20th Century*. Source for totals 1935–39 to 1960–64 and for White and Nonwhite figures: Robert D. Grove and Alice M. Hetzel, *Vital Statistics Rates in the United States, 1940–60*.

[2] Prior to 1933 the birth registration area did not cover the entire country, and even where births were registered, the registration was particularly incomplete for blacks. Births prior to 1916 are estimated from census counts of young children, but the amount of under-enumeration was particularly large for blacks.

[3] Monthly Vital Statistics Report, Summary Report, Final Natality Statistics (1973), vol. 23, no. 11. Supplement (Jan. 30, 1975).

the number of deaths per 1,000 population; it is determined by the risks of death across the span of life *and* by the age composition of the population; the non-whites, having higher birth rates, are more heavily loaded with young people for whom the risks of death are relatively low. The death rate tells little about the risks of death, but it does tell the rate at which the fund of life is depleted, and this rate in the mid-1970's was much the same for whites and non-whites.

The risks of death are better reflected by life expectancies. A life table treats the age-specific mortality of its base period as if it were that of a generation moving from birth to extinction. Such a generation, for example, having the male mortality of whites during 1900–02, would have lived an average of 48.2 years. Those of that generation who survived to the age of twenty would have lived on the average to the age of 62.2 years, and those who reached the age of 60 would have lived to an average age of 74.4 years. Nonwhites have been in an unsatisfactory position. In 1900 both the male and female nonwhites averaged 16 fewer years of life than the whites. Their position improved more rapidly than that of the whites, but even so by 1969 their expectation of life at birth was still 7 years less than that of the whites.

Nevertheless, the gains in life expectancy between 1900 and 1973 were remarkable: among males, 42 percent for whites and 90 percent for nonwhites; among females, 48 percent for whites and 100 percent for nonwhites. The greater longevity of females over males continues. In 1973, the life expectancy of females at age 60 exceeded that of males at age 60 by 30 percent for the whites and 24 percent for the nonwhites. Something of the dramatic way in which the reduction of mortality after 1900 changed the character of American life may be appreciated by the fact that among whites a newborn girl exposed to 1973's risks of death would have a better chance of reaching the age of 63 than her counterpart would have had of reaching the age of 5 on the tables of 1900–01. Nonwhite girls had a better chance of reaching age 65 than their counterparts had of reaching age 5 in 1900–01.

The varying rates of accretion by birth and migration, and depletion by death, have left their marks on the age composition of the population, as may be seen from Table 2. The higher birth rate of the nonwhite population is reflected in its higher burden of youth dependency, and the long-run decline of the birth rate is reflected in the reduction of that load as shown by the shrinking proportion of the population under fifteen years of age. The falling proportion of the population in the young working ages, 15 to 44, is also clearly evident, as is the rising proportion of people in the older working years. The falling proportion of females in the childbearing years is both consequence and cause of falling birth rates, and the higher proportions in the nonwhite than in the white population

Table 2. Percentage Age Distribution of the Population by Color and Sex for Coterminous United States
(selected dates) [1]

Date and Color	Male				Female			
	Under 15	15–44	45–64	65+	Under 15	15–44	45–64	65+
White								
1890	34.3	47.8	13.5	4.0	35.0	47.6	13.3	4.0
1910	30.9	49.2	15.4	4.3	32.1	48.7	14.4	4.6
1930	29.0	47.1	18.2	5.6	29.0	47.9	17.3	5.7
1950	27.0	44.3	20.9	8.0	25.6	44.7	20.7	8.9
1970 [2]	28.9	41.5	20.8	8.8	26.3	40.4	21.5	11.7
Nonwhite								
1890	41.8	43.7	11.0	2.8	41.8	45.2	9.8	2.8
1910	36.3	47.7	12.6	3.1	37.3	49.1	10.4	2.9
1930	32.6	48.6	15.5	3.2	32.8	51.4	12.7	3.0
1950	32.6	44.9	16.9	5.7	31.1	47.5	15.8	5.7
1970 [2]	36.6	41.1	15.9	6.3	33.4	42.7	16.6	7.3

[1] Unreported ages omitted.

[2] Includes Alaska and Hawaii.

Sources: U.S. Census, 1960; U.S. Census, 1970, General Population Characteristics, U.S. Summary.

account in part for the higher birth rates of the non-whites. Most pronounced of all is the rise of the old-age population. Between 1890 and 1970 the proportion of the population aged 65 and over more than doubled for males and increased more than 2.5 times for females.

These changes are reflected in the changing average age. The median age for white males rose from 23 years in 1890 to 30 in 1950 and fell, as a consequence of the postwar "baby boom," to 28 years in 1970. For the nonwhite males, it rose from 19 years in 1890 to 26 years in 1950 and fell to 22 years in 1970. The corresponding figures for white females were 22 to 31 years, falling to 30; and for nonwhite females, 18 to 26 years, falling to 24. The sharp decline of the birth rate after 1970 started the averages moving up again, continuing the shift of the population from a rather young to a mature one.

Internal migration, plus differences in the balance of births and deaths, have also changed the regional distribution of the population, as shown in Table 3. Only the West gained in its proportion of the national total after 1950; and since its rate of natural increase, along with that of the Northeast, was the lowest in the nation, the gains came from continuing in-migration. Each of these regions had a sharply reduced rate of growth in the last decade, and the decline was sharpest in the West, where the rate of growth was highest.

Table 3. Percentage Distribution and Average Annual Rate of Growth by Regions
(1950–70)

Region	Percent			% Average Annual Growth	
	1950	1960	1970	1950–60	1960–70
United States	100.0	100.0	99.9	1.7	1.3
Northeast	26.1	24.9	24.1	1.2	0.9
North Central	29.4	28.8	27.8	1.5	0.9
South	31.2	30.7	30.9	1.5	1.3
West	13.3	15.6	17.1	3.3	2.2

Sources: U.S. Census, 1960; U.S. Census, 1970, General Population Characteristics, U.S. Summary.

The most dramatic change in the nation's pattern of settlement is in the shift from the country to the city. As may be seen in Table 4, at the first U.S. census about 95 percent of the population lived in rural areas. By 1970 this proportion was down to 27 percent and, because of the ease of transportation, many of those who lived in the country worked in the city. The largest single factor underlying this change is the dramatic increase in the productivity of agriculture per man. In the early days of the Republic it probably

Table 4. Percentage Urbanization of U.S. Population

Year	Urban	Rural
1790	5.1	94.9
1840	10.8	89.2
1890	35.1	64.9
1910	45.7	54.3
1930	56.2	43.8
1950	59.6	40.4
1950 [1]	64.0	36.0
1970 [1]	73.5	26.5

[1] New Definition: The new definition of urban differs from the old mainly by including densely settled areas contiguous to, but outside, the limits of incorporated communities.

Sources: Irene and Conrad Taeuber, *People of the United States in the 20th Century;* U.S. Census, 1970, General Population Characteristics, U.S. Summary.

took about 75 percent of the labor force to produce the nation's food and fiber. In the 1970's less than 5 percent of the total was engaged in agriculture, although large populations were also engaged in supplying the transportation, machinery, fertilizer, and fuel on which agricultural production depended.

The drift to major metropolitan areas is shown by Table 5 in terms of the population in and outside Standard Metropolitan Statistical Areas (SMSAs). The SMSAs include all counties having a city of 50,000 or more population and the counties of urbanized char-

Table 5. Percentage Distribution of Population and Rates of Growth In and Outside Standard Metropolitan Statistical Areas (1950–70)

Type of Area	1950	1960	1970	Average Annual Increase 1950–60	1960–70
Total Population	100.0	100.0	100.0	1.7	1.3
SMSAs	59.2	63.3	68.6	2.4	2.1
Central Cities	34.7	32.4	31.4	1.0	1.0
Outside Central Cities	24.6	30.9	37.2	4.0	3.2
Outside SMSAs	40.8	36.7	31.4	0.7	−0.3

Sources: *Statistical Abstract of the United States* (1970); U.S. Census, 1970, General Population Characteristics, U.S. Summary.

acter contiguous to them. By 1970 these areas contained almost 69 percent of the population. It is to be noted, however, that a larger proportion of this metropolitan population lived outside the central cities than lived inside. Between 1950 and 1970 the suburbs grew more than three times as rapidly as the central cities.

Between 1960 and 1970, the population living outside the metropolitan areas declined. In each of the two intercensal periods 1950–60 and 1960–70, almost 50 percent of the nation's counties lost population; and about 33 percent of the counties had lost population steadily since the 1940's. The population went to the metropolitan areas, and more particularly to the coastal areas. If the U.S. coastline is considered to include that of the Great Lakes, then more than 50 percent of the nation's people lived within fifty miles of the coast by 1970. The United States has changed from a nation of country folk into a nation of people who complain about the cities but like to live near them, especially when they are near the water.

[American Council of Learned Societies, Committee on Linguistic and National Stocks in the Population of the United States, *Report in American Historical Association, Annual Report, 1931,* vol. 1; Ansley J. Coale and Melvin Zelnik, *New Estimates of Fertility and Population in the United States: A Study of Annual White Births From 1855 to 1960;* Evarts B. Greene and Virginia D. Harrington, *American Population Before the Federal Census of 1790;* E. P. Hutchinson, *Immigrants and Their Children, 1850–1950;* Irene Taeuber and Conrad Taeuber, *The People of the United States in the 20th Century;* Warren S. Thompson and P. K. Whelpton, *Population Trends in the United States;* U.S. Bureau of the Census, *A Century of Population Growth from the First Census of the United States to the Twelfth, 1790 to 1900.*]

FRANK W. NOTESTEIN

POPULISM emerged in the politically turbulent decade of the 1890's. It grew out of an agrarian movement of protest against some of the consequences of industrialization, reached its greatest intensity in the depression crisis following the panic of 1893, and lost its driving force just when success seemed imminent, during the presidential election of 1896.

For several reasons American agriculture had always moved in the direction of extensive, rather than intensive, farming. An abundance of land, a chronic shortage of labor, and improvements in agricultural technology had all led to an emphasis on productivity per man-hour rather than productivity per acre. Post–Civil War expansion of the railroad network and development of agricultural machinery had opened up vast areas of new land in the trans-Mississippi West. Between 1870 and 1900 the amount of farmland under cultivation doubled. Increased agricultural production in the United States—combined with increased production of agricultural regions in Canada, Australia, the Ukraine, and South America—contributed to a secular, or long-term, decline in agricultural prices throughout the world. In the United States the wholesale index of farm products went from 112 in 1870 to 71 in 1890. The total value of those products was on the rise, however, and not all farmers experienced a reduction of income as a result of price declines. Those who commanded sufficient capital to conduct their operations without incurring overburdening debts were usually able to succeed. Indeed, per capita farm income actually increased in the three decades after 1870.

Many farmers nevertheless experienced difficulties, and the incidence of rural distress in the late 1880's and the 1890's was particularly great in two of the nation's major agricultural areas: the old cotton-growing region of the South and the recently settled Plains region of the West. In the South heavy reliance on a single crop made farmers peculiarly subject to the deleterious effects of falling world prices. In the West the subhumid climate of the Plains made farming more costly and more risky than in eastern areas, where drought was less common. But in the early 1880's precipitation had been unusually great, and the promise of future prosperity had stimulated a land boom that, in turn, encouraged farmers to borrow more heavily than was justifiable. When the boom collapsed in the winter of 1887–88, the per capita private debt in Kansas was four times that in the nation as a whole. The maintenance of a crop-lien system in the South after the Civil War and the high rate of mortgage foreclosures in the Plains area during the late 1880's and the 1890's are indications of a relatively large number of marginal farms in both areas. And it was in the South and the trans-Mississippi West that agrarian causes won the most enthusiastic support; there the late 19th-century movement to organize farmers made the most significant gains.

The wave of agrarian protest that culminated in the Populist movement began with formation of local farmers' alliances in Texas and Arkansas during the 1870's. In the following decade those early organizations merged to form the National Farmers' Alliance and Industrial Union, popularly known as the Southern Alliance to distinguish it from the smaller Northwestern Alliance, founded in Chicago in 1880. Emphasizing economic activities, both organizations recruited members during the 1880's and by the end

of the decade could claim a combined membership of more than a million. The two alliances failed to unite as a political party, but they did hold concurrent conventions at Saint Louis in December 1889. There they agreed on the desirability of several measures, including an inflationary currency, government ownership of railroads, and legislation against alien landholding.

Sustained by the thought of a common purpose, leaders of dissident agrarians mustered their forces for the congressional and state elections of 1890. With the help of interested groups they formed independent parties in Kansas, Nebraska, the Dakotas, Minnesota, Colorado, Michigan, and Indiana. In the South members of the alliance concentrated on gaining influence within the Democratic party. The results were encouraging enough to arouse extensive support for a new national party, for aside from winning control of several state offices, the agrarians sent nine representatives and two senators to Congress. After a series of preliminary meetings the People's party came into being at a convention in Omaha, Nebr., in July 1892. Delegates nominated Iowa's James B. Weaver and enthusiastically adopted a platform calling for remedial legislation in the three areas of land, transportation, and finance. Specific planks included demands for free coinage of silver, an increase in the circulating medium, a graduated income tax, postal savings banks, government ownership of railroad and telegraph lines, and reclamation of alien landholdings. While Populists did not accomplish all they had hoped to achieve in the election, Weaver did carry four states and win twenty-two electoral votes.

The returns of 1892 proved gratifying enough to preserve optimism within the People's party, and after the onset of a severe depression in 1893, party organizers sought to take advantage of widespread economic discontent. In some areas they broadened their program to win the support of organized labor, Socialists, and advocates of the single tax; Populists of Wisconsin and Illinois, for example, even went so far as to endorse collective ownership of the means of production and distribution. But of all proposals with which the Populist party was identified, the free silver plank of the 1892 platform seemed to have the greatest appeal to voters. During the hard times of the 1890's, monetary reform could be presented not only as a stimulant to agricultural prices but also as a cure for the depression. Yet the attractions of silver divided Populist leadership. A middle-of-the-road faction, seeing bimetallism as an incidental issue, argued for a broader program, or at the least for adherence to the entire Omaha platform; fusionists, on the other hand, attracted by the possibility of victory, were persuaded that the People's party should join forces with others in the free silver camp. Confident that they could dominate affiliations with other groups, the fusionists looked forward to the election of 1896 as an opportunity to win the day for their entire platform by capturing the nation's free-silver sentiment.

The fusionist strategy prevailed, but Populists of each persuasion were disappointed in the way events unfolded. Assuming that both Republicans and Democrats would stand behind the gold standard and identify themselves with commercial and industrial interests, People's party leaders scheduled their national convention to follow the major party conventions. In so doing they hoped to pick up the support of disaffected silverites in both major parties. Contrary to expectations, however, bimetallists dominated the Chicago convention of the Democratic party; nominated the silverite William Jennings Bryan; and adopted a free-silver plank. When Populists convened in the wake of Bryan's dramatic triumph at Chicago, they found themselves facing distasteful alternatives: they could nominate their own candidate and defeat monetary reform, or they could endorse Bryan and destroy the People's party by merging with the Democrats. After a long and painful struggle, delegates accepted the second alternative.

As an organized political force, the Populist movement thus met defeat even before the candidates of 1896 entered the climactic stage of the campaign; and William McKinley's convincing triumph over Bryan removed whatever consolation the Populists might have salvaged from the election. With the return of prosperity after 1897, the United States moved into a new era in which agricultural interests developed new techniques, new organizations, and new strategies. Farm organizations gained considerable political influence as pressure groups in the 20th century, but the hope of building a national party on agrarian principles had disappeared.

[Robert F. Durden, *The Climax of Populism;* John D. Hicks, *The Populist Revolt;* Stanley L. Jones, *The Presidential Election of 1896;* Norman Pollack, *The Populist Response to Industrial America;* C. Vann Woodward, *Origins of the New South.*]

PAUL W. GLAD

PORCUPINE'S GAZETTE, issued from Mar. 4, 1797, to Oct. 26, 1799, was a daily and triweekly newspaper published at Philadelphia by William Cobbett ("Peter Porcupine"), a vituperative British jour-

nalist who advocated alliance with England and war against France and freely attacked many prominent citizens. Loss of a libel suit for $5,000, instituted by Dr. Benjamin Rush during the yellow fever epidemic, caused his failure, and he retreated to England in 1800.

[John W. Osborne, *William Cobbett: His Thought and His Times.*]

JULIAN P. BOYD

"PORK BARREL," a familiar term in American politics, generally applied to local projects and improvements for which appropriations are obtained by legislators for the benefit of their constituents. The phrase probably originated in the pre–Civil War practice on southern plantations of distributing salt pork to the slaves from large barrels. On such occasions there was generally a rush on the barrel as each slave tried to obtain as much as possible. Thus, the term is generally used, especially by journalists and reformers, in a derogatory sense, condemning such projects as a waste of public funds and a raid on the treasury. Elected officials generally see such projects differently, as tangible means of demonstrating to their constituents their diligence and concern for the state or district, as well as their personal power in the legislature. The classic example of a pork barrel is the periodic rivers and harbors bill, providing appropriations for dams, piers, bridges, and so on, and designating the location of such projects. Such bills fall within the jurisdiction of the Public Works committees of Congress.

As the activities of the federal government have expanded, so have the types of federal largesse available for distribution. Defense Department contracts and installations, which accounted for a large share of federal expenditures during and after World War II, provide one source. Other examples include the location of federal agencies and bureaus, research laboratories, space projects, and highways. Indeed, the pork barrel has been enlarged to include grants of government funds for special programs relating to education, health, pollution, and other areas involving the general welfare of the nation.

Except in the rivers and harbors bill, Congress generally does not exercise direct control over the specific location of projects or the allocation of grants, and so pork barrel distributions are usually effected through the influence of members of Congress on key executive decisionmakers. In making such decisions, the president or other members of the executive branch may use such projects as ways of winning legislative support for their policies. Within Congress, members of key committees, such as the Public Works committees or the Appropriations committees, may attempt to use proposed projects of this type in bargaining with their fellow legislators for support on other kinds of bills.

[Arthur Maass, *Muddy Waters;* James Murphy, "Partisanship and the House Public Works Committee," American Political Science Association paper (1968).]

DALE VINYARD

PORTAGES AND WATER ROUTES. Foremost among the factors that governed the exploration and settlement of the country were the mountain and the river systems, the former an obstacle, the latter an aid to travel. The English, who settled on the Atlantic coastal plain, were barred from the interior by the great wall of the Allegheny Mountains, and over a century was required to scale it and begin the descent of its western slope. The French, securing a foothold about the same time at the mouth of the Saint Lawrence River, found themselves on a waterway that offered ready access to the interior. By the Richelieu River–Lake Champlain route they might pass southward to the Hudson River, while numerous tributaries of the Ottawa and the Saint Lawrence rivers pointed the way to Hudson Bay. The humbling of the Iroquois (1666–67) opened the direct route to Lake Ontario, from which, save for the interruption at Niagara, more than a thousand miles of lake navigation invited the traveler (*see* Great Lakes).

Over the entire eastern half of primitive America stretched a forest, penetrated only by winding rivers or narrow trails. Wherever rivers ran, boats could be propelled, and the Indian canoe supplied a craft admirably adapted to the exigencies of wilderness travel, being light in weight and constructed of materials available almost everywhere. But travel by water was subject to interruption, either by rapids, shallows, or falls in a river, or at points where the transit from one river system to another must be made. At such places, boat and cargo had to be carried around the obstruction or across the intervening land. The term "portage" signifies both the act of transporting a boat and its cargo overland and the place where such a land carriage is necessary. At places where the volume of travel was considerable, either Indians or some white trader frequently maintained horses or oxen and carts for hauling boats across the portage.

The Ottawa River route to the upper Great Lakes was opened by the French explorer Samuel de Champlain, 1615–16. From Lake Erie the Ohio River might be reached by numerous routes: the Lake Chautauqua Portage to the Allegheny (at Warren, Pa.); the Presque Isle–Allegheny Portage (at Erie); the Maumee-Miami and the Maumee-Wabash (at Fort Wayne, Ind.) portages. From Lake Huron access to Lake Superior by the Saint Marys River or to Lake Michigan by the Straits of Mackinac was open. From Lake Superior one might pass by numerous river and portage routes to Hudson Bay, to the Mississippi River system, or to the great river systems that drain the vast interior plain of Canada into the Arctic Ocean. From Lake Michigan many routes led to the Mississippi system, the best-known portages being the Fox-Wisconsin at Portage, Wis.; the Chicago-Illinois at Chicago (*see* Chicago Portage); and the Saint Joseph-Kankakee at South Bend, Ind. (*see* Saint Joseph, Fort); while from the Saint Joseph, access was open to the Wabash and the Ohio rivers.

With the Mississippi system once gained, the entire heart of the continent from the Arctic to the Gulf of Mexico and westward to the Rockies lay open to the traveler. The encirclement of the English by the French precipitated the French and Indian War, which ended in the conquest of New France and the division of its territory between England and Spain (Treaty of Paris, 1763), but the waterways retained their importance as highways of trade and travel to the end of the wilderness period. At places where a break in transportation occurred (Niagara, Erie, Fort Wayne, Chicago, for example), forts were frequently placed and the foundations of future cities laid. Places like Detroit and Mackinac Island in northern Michigan owed their importance to their strategic location at points where the travel of a vast area centered.

Compared with modern standards, wilderness travel at best was laborious and time-consuming. If some rivers were deep and placid, others were swift and beset with shoals and rapids. Portage conditions, too, varied widely from place to place, or even at the same place under different seasonal conditions. Pierre de Céloron de Blainville in 1749 spent five days of arduous toil in traversing the ten-mile portage from Lake Erie to Lake Chautauqua, and two weeks in reaching the Allegheny at Warren, Pa.; and a Detroit merchant traveling by the waterways across Michigan to Chicago in 1790 required forty-eight days to reach his destination. Meriwether Lewis and William Clark in 1805 spent almost a month in making a portage of eighteen miles at Great Falls, Mont. The fact that travelers clung to the waterways under circumstances of such difficulty affords striking evidence of the still greater obstacles encountered by land.

[Seymour Dunbar, *A History of Travel in America;* A. B. Hulbert, *Portage Paths, The Keys of the Continent.*]

M. M. QUAIFE

PORT AUTHORITIES, quasi-public, tax-free organizations, generally regarded as the fastest growing units of local government in the United States. The Port Authority of New York and New Jersey (*see following article*) is the oldest in the United States and was modeled after the Port of London (England) Authority. It has made precedents and fashioned most of the law for many similar organizations and regional authorities that have come into being throughout the country since World War II.

Many of the larger port cities of the United States, in addition to New York, have established port authorities with varying degrees of power and coverage, as in Boston, Baltimore, Savannah, Mobile, Toledo, San Francisco, Los Angeles, Pensacola, and Norfolk. In some cases the port authority is a state-controlled unit, as in Maine, North Carolina, New Hampshire, Virginia, South Carolina, Georgia, Alabama, and Puerto Rico, but the jurisdiction of these port authorities is usually restricted. Many of the larger port authorities or port commissions have as extensive and varied jurisdiction as the Port Authority of New York and New Jersey.

Port authorities as a rule cannot levy taxes, but derive income from tolls, largely from bridges and tunnels, and rentals from airports, heliports, and marine and bus terminals. They can also borrow money, secured by tax-free bonds. The port authority is relatively free from political interference. Its operating head is usually an executive director, who is controlled by a board of commissioners of which he may be a member.

THOMAS ROBSON HAY

PORT AUTHORITY OF NEW YORK AND NEW JERSEY, a self-supporting, interstate corporate organization of New York and New Jersey, created in 1921 to protect and promote the commerce of New York Harbor and to develop terminal and transportation facilities in the bi-state area.

The Port of New York Authority, as it was originally called (the name was changed in 1972), was created by the joint efforts of Gov. Alfred E. Smith of New York and Gov. Walter Edge of New Jersey with a view to solving the problems caused by the artificial New York–New Jersey boundary line down the middle of the Hudson River, which split the natural unity of the port. Because it was an interstate treaty, approval of Congress was required. By the compact of organization, the Port Authority is permitted "to purchase, construct, lease and/or operate any terminal or transportation facility" and "to make charges for the use thereof." Its sphere of jurisdiction extends over a twenty-five-mile radius from the Battery, the southern extremity of Manhattan. Jurisdiction may be extended beyond this limit if approved by both New York and New Jersey governors and legislatures. The scope of the Port Authority extends to road transport terminals; shipping facilities, such as marine docks and terminals; airports and heliports; and bridges and tunnels.

Among the facilities built, owned, and operated by the Port Authority are the Goethals Bridge between Staten Island and Elizabeth, N.J. (opened 1928), the George Washington Bridge (1925–31), the Bayonne Bridge (1928–31), Lincoln Tunnel (first tube completed 1937; second, 1945; third, 1957), Port Authority Bus Terminal (1949–50; addition, 1975–78), and the George Washington Bridge Bus Station (opened 1963). Facilities built and operated by the Port Authority but owned by the city of New York include the New York City Passenger Ship Terminal (completed 1974). The Port Authority also operates the following facilities: Port Authority Trans-Hudson (PATH) System, Journal Square Transportation Center, the Holland Tunnel, Outerbridge Crossing, four airports (John F. Kennedy, LaGuardia, Newark, and Teterboro), two heliports (Port Authority-Downtown and Port Authority-West 30th Street), seven marine terminals, two truck terminals (Newark and New York City), the World Trade Center, and eight trade development offices (London, Tokyo, Zurich, and five in the United States).

The Port Authority's income from operations in 1974 was $77.9 million; total assets on Dec. 31, 1974, were more than $3.9 billion.

PORTER CASE. Gen. Fitz-John Porter was considered one of the ablest and best of the Union generals and was one of Gen. George B. McClellan's most intimate friends. On Nov. 27, 1862, he was arraigned before a court-martial in Washington, D.C., and charged with disobeying the orders of Gen. John Pope during the second Battle of Bull Run (Aug. 29–30, 1862). On June 21, 1863, Porter was found guilty and "forever disqualified from holding any office of trust or profit under the government of the United States." This verdict was the cause of much controversy until twenty-three years later when a bill was passed by Congress and signed by President Grover Cleveland that restored Porter to the U.S. Army on Aug. 7, 1886, with the rank of colonel. It has been charged that Porter was used as a scapegoat by the Radical Republicans and other enemies of McClellan on which to vent their revenge.

[W. S. Myers, *General George Brinton McClelland;* J. F. Rhodes, *History of the United States,* vol. IV.]

WILLIAM STARR MYERS

PORT GIBSON, BATTLE AT (May 1, 1863). Union Gen. John A. McClernand's van of Gen. Ulysses S. Grant's flank movement on Vicksburg, Miss., struck Gen. J. S. Bowen's outnumbered Confederates on a divided road ten miles from Bruinsburg and four miles from Port Gibson. Dual attacks were checked in bitter fighting, until McClernand's last reserve hit the southern flank while Grant personally directed reinforcements from James B. McPherson's corps against the northern flank. Bowen's brigades got away to Grand Gulf, north of Port Gibson.

[F. V. Greene, *The Mississippi.*]

ELBRIDGE COLBY

PORT HUDSON, SIEGE OF (March-July 1863). Following the Battle of Baton Rouge, Aug. 5, 1862, Confederate Gen. John C. Breckinridge occupied the high bluff at Port Hudson, twenty-five miles to the north, which was strongly fortified during the next few months to protect Confederate supplies coming down the Red River. Union Adm. David G. Farragut attacked Port Hudson on Mar. 14, 1863, in an attempt to join Gen. Ulysses S. Grant before his attack on Vicksburg, Miss., but only two gunboats succeeded in passing the fortifications, the others being disabled or driven back. While Grant invested Vicksburg, Gen. Nathaniel P. Banks besieged Port Hudson for six weeks. The fall of Vicksburg rendered Port Hudson useless to the Confederates, and on July 9, 1863, Gen. Frank Gardner surrendered this last Confederate stronghold on the Mississippi.

[R. U. Johnson and C. C. Buel, eds., *Battles and Leaders of the Civil War,* vol. III.]

WALTER PRICHARD

PORT REPUBLIC, BATTLE OF (June 9, 1862). After his defeat of Union Gen. John C. Frémont at Cross Keys, near Harrisonburg, Va., Confederate Gen. Thomas J. ("Stonewall") Jackson hurried to Port Republic and destroyed the bridge across the Shenandoah River there, thus dividing Frémont's force. On the following day, after a hard fight, Jackson defeated the two Union brigades south of the river, numerically much inferior to his own force (*see* Jackson's Valley Campaign).

[R. U. Johnson and C. C. Buel, eds., *Battles and Leaders of the Civil War,* vol. II.]

ALVIN F. HARLOW

PORT ROYAL, at the site of present-day Annapolis Royal on the southern shore of the Annapolis Basin, Nova Scotia, was the most important outpost of the French in Acadia against colonial New England. The earliest settlement of the name was begun in 1605 by Pierre du Guast, Sieur de Monts, deserted in 1608, reoccupied in 1610, and destroyed by Capt. Samuel Argall from Virginia in 1613, but rebuilt by French settlers. The Huguenot Claude de la Tour brought some Scottish settlers to Acadia in 1630 in behalf of Sir William Alexander, to whom James I of England had granted the region in 1621 (reconfirmed by Charles I in 1625), calling it Nova Scotia. Charles de Menou d'Aulnay obtained control in 1636, moved the fort to the site of the present town in 1643, and began a long rivalry with La Tour's son Charles, who, as governor of the French fort Saint Louis at Saint John, controlled much of the trade. On d'Aulnay's death in 1650, La Tour had possession until the place was captured by a New England expedition under Maj. Robert Sedgwick in 1654. Returned to the French in 1670, Port Royal in 1684 became the seat of their government in Acadia. It was the center from which they attacked New England shipping and the scene of much illicit trade with New Englanders. Captured by Sir William Phips in 1690, it was restored to the French by the Treaty of Ryswick in 1697. Several times threatened with attack from Boston, which in turn lived in daily fear of attack by a French fleet using Port Royal as a base, the town was finally taken by a great expedition in 1710 under Col. Francis Nicholson and Col. Samuel Vetch (*see* Queen Anne's War). Acadia was ceded to England by the Treaty of Utrecht. In the face of the Acadian citizenry, England's hold was precarious after the French built Louisburg on Cape Breton Island in 1713. Twice attacked and several times threatened in King George's War, Annapolis Royal (as it was called by the English) lost its strategic importance and also its position as seat of the government with the building of Halifax by the English in 1749.

[W. M. MacVicar, *A Short History of Annapolis Royal.*]
ROBERT E. MOODY

PORT ROYAL, a town on Port Royal Island in southeastern South Carolina. The French diplomat, soldier, and Huguenot leader Jean (Jan) Ribault in May 1562 settled twenty-eight or thirty Frenchmen, almost all Huguenots, on Parris Island where they constructed a fort, named Charlesfort after Charles IX of France, about three miles from the modern town of Port Royal. They named the harbor containing the island Port Royal from its size. It lies twenty miles north of the mouth of the Savannah River. Spanish navigators from Mexico and the West Indies had already named the harbor Santa Elena.

Ribault returned to France for reinforcements, and the settlers, soon discouraged, mutinied, killing their commander and abandoning their frail fortification. They constructed a tiny vessel and set sail for France. After fearful sufferings, they were rescued by an English cruiser and eventually reached their destination. To prevent further trespass in the region, the Spanish built Saint Augustine to the south in 1565 and destroyed the French Fort Caroline, built in 1564 on the Saint Johns River. Spain then built Fort San Felipe on the site of Port Royal in 1566, introduced farmers and missionaries, and explored the interior as far as the North Carolina mountains and eastern Alabama. Indians expelled the Spaniards and burned their fort in 1576, but in 1577 Spain built Fort San Marcos near the same spot. Sir Francis Drake's burning of Saint Augustine in 1586 forced Spain's abandonment that year of Port Royal. The English who under the authority of the Lords Proprietors of Carolina settled South Carolina in 1670 landed at Port Royal, but in a few days moved to the site of Charleston to eliminate the danger of attack by the Spanish. In 1684 fifty-one Scotch Covenanters settled at Port Royal but were driven off by Spaniards from Saint Augustine in 1686.

The modern town of Port Royal, immediately above Parris Island, was the center of a major cotton-growing region in the first half of the 19th century. The town was captured Nov. 7, 1861, by a Union fleet, and after the Civil War, Port Royal became mainly a fishing village and resort. The 1970 population was 2,865.

[Jeanette T. Connor, *Jean Ribault;* Woodbury Lowery, *Spanish Settlements Within the Present Limits of the United States;* D. D. Wallace, *History of South Carolina.*]
D. D. WALLACE

PORTSMOUTH, TREATY OF (Sept. 5, 1905), brought to a close the Russo-Japanese War and gave formal sanction to Japan's supplanting of Russian interests and political influence in Korea and southern Manchuria. It represented Japan's first forward step in territorial expansion on the Asiatic mainland. From the opening of the peace negotiations Russia had agreed to cede the special rights the czarist government held in southern Manchuria (notably the Liaotung Peninsula lease and what was to be called the South Manchuria Railway), but the conference almost broke up over Japan's demand for the further cession of the island of Sakhalin, north of Japan in the Sea of Okhotsk, and payment of an indemnity. At this point President Theodore Roosevelt, whose earlier intercession had been instrumental in bringing about the conference and for its being held in Portsmouth, N.H., again intervened, and both directly and through the German kaiser, William II, he brought such pressure as he could on the Russian and Japanese governments in favor of peace. As a result, Russia agreed to cede the southern half of Sakhalin while refusing to pay any indemnity, and Japan accepted these terms. Roosevelt was widely hailed for his contribution to peace and won the Nobel Peace Prize in 1906, but bitter resentment was created in Japan through loss of the expected indemnity.

[Tyler Dennett, *Roosevelt and the Russo-Japanese War.*]
FOSTER RHEA DULLES

POSSESSIONS, INSULAR. *See* **Insular Possessions.**

POSTAL SERVICE, UNITED STATES. The development and growth of the postal system in America have been inextricably linked to the development and growth of the United States itself. The postal system has acted as a unifying force for the nation, and it has helped foster America's commerce.

Between 1607 and 1775, the American postal system depended on the British crown for its existence and direction. During the earliest days of the colonial period letters were transmitted haphazardly, as colonists entrusted their mail to travelers and merchants. Letters to and from England were carried by captains of private vessels. But this "neighborly" arrangement was largely unsatisfactory; letters often failed to arrive at their destinations.

The first proposals for establishment of a post office in America seem to have come from New England in 1638. It was suggested that the king of England grant a patent for sixty years to someone who would set up this institution. Meanwhile, several colonies acted on their own. The general court of Massachusetts in 1639 established Richard Fairbanks' house in Boston as "the place appointed for all letters" to and from overseas. In 1657 the Virginia House of Burgesses approved "tobacco posts," making each plantation owner responsible for passing official messages and letters on to the next plantation. And the first intercolonial post was established by Gov. Francis Lovelace of New York in 1673, when monthly trips to Boston were inaugurated.

Despite these independent actions the handling of the mail was still generally unsatisfactory, and it was not until Feb. 17, 1692, that the crown issued a grant to Thomas Neale to set up and maintain a post office in the colonies for the term of twenty-one years. Neale was granted a monopoly, and he was to receive all profits from the business. In return he was to pay a rent of six shillings a year to the royal treasury. Neale himself never came to America to oversee his franchise; he appointed Andrew Hamilton, governor of New Jersey, as his deputy.

In 1711 the British Parliament reorganized and consolidated the postal system in all its dominions, including the colonies, and in 1730 Alexander Spotswood, a former governor of Virginia, was named postmaster general. Spotswood's most notable appointment was that of Benjamin Franklin as deputy postmaster at Philadelphia in 1737. Franklin, like other newspaper publishers of the time, wanted the position. Postal laws in the 18th century contained no provisions for introduction of newspapers into the mails and no rates of postage had been established for them. Thus, postmasters could make their own rules and, if desired, prevent competitors from using the mails. To Franklin's credit, he did not do this, but instead admitted all publications to the mails, charging a reasonable rate of postage.

In 1753 the crown appointed Franklin and William Hunter of Virginia joint postmasters general for the colonies. (John Foxcroft succeeded Hunter, who died in 1761.) During his tenure as a colonial postal official Franklin effected many improvements: for example, he surveyed new postal routes and established overnight delivery between Philadelphia and New York. In 1755 he established a direct packet line from England to New York and, later, to Charleston, S.C., giving the southern colonies direct communication with England.

By 1765 the colonies extended from Canada to Florida, and the crown had separated the colonial post office into a northern division and a southern division. The sparse settling of the South precluded the postal system's success there. The North fared much better, but the postal monopoly in the North was not popular, and it was easily evaded by those wishing to send their mail through private means.

Meanwhile, the winds of revolution were being inexorably fanned in the colonies; the number of dissidents was growing, and Paul Revere was among them. A rider for the colonial postal system as early as 1773, he was performing his postal duties when he warned the inhabitants of Boston on the night of Apr. 18, 1775, that the British were coming. Later that same year, on May 29, the newly formed Continental Congress appointed a committee headed by Franklin to set up a postal system independent of the crown, and in July, Congress established such a system with Franklin as its first postmaster general. Just a few months later, on Christmas Day, British postal service in the colonies came to an end when the crown closed its post office in New York City.

Although the Articles of Confederation contained a clause establishing a federal post office in the new United States, it was not until Oct. 18, 1782, that the Congress, acting under power granted by the Articles of Confederation, passed "An Ordinance for Regulating the Post-Office of the United States of America." When the Constitution went into effect in 1789, establishment of "Post Offices and post Roads" was called for under Article I, Section 8. There were about seventy-five post offices in the thirteen states and 2,400 miles of post roads to serve a population of 3 million. Legislation in 1789 and 1794 put the post office in the hands of the executive branch and established it as a permanent part of the federal government.

President George Washington, along with many government officials, recognized the importance of the postal system to the new nation, seeing it as a principal means by which Americans were bound together in loyalty to the central government. The post office made the national government visible to every American; in fact, the mail was Congress' chief means of communicating with constituents.

Washington's first appointee as postmaster general, in 1789, was Samuel Osgood of Massachusetts. Before the close of Washington's second term in office, the number of post offices, the number of miles of post road, and the amount of postal revenues had increased more than five times.

The Post Office Act of 1792 had set postage rates ranging from six cents for a single-page letter going as far as thirty miles to twenty-five cents for one going over 450 miles and had outlined the rules and regulations under which the post office was to operate. The act had also established postal policy, three important facets of which were the following: (1) The post office must be self-supporting; (2) it must use any profit to extend services; and (3) Congress, not the postmaster general, must establish the nation's post roads. At one point Congress actually became involved in constructing post roads, but President James Monroe put a stop to the practice.

As the new nation expanded in territory and population, so did the postal system. In 1794 the first letter carriers appeared in the cities. They were not paid salaries; instead, they collected two cents for each letter they delivered, in addition to postage. Joseph Habersham, postmaster general from 1795 to 1801, instituted government-owned coach service between Philadelphia and New York in 1799. By 1813 steamboats had become an important means of transporting the mail. In that year all steamship lines were declared post routes; in 1838 the railroads were also declared post routes. An 1845 law created the contractor system—the hiring of private, or star route, contractors to carry the mail between post offices. (By July 1973 there were about 14,500 contracts for air, highway, and waterway star route service.)

Carrying the mail on horseback was still an important means of conveyance, and the most glamorous era of transporting the mail lasted for only eighteen months, in 1860–61, when Pony Express riders linked the Far West to the rest of the nation. The bravery of these riders, who had to carry the mail across hundreds of miles of hazardous terrain and were constantly threatened by hostile Indians, became legendary. Their heroism was invaluable in keeping California on the side of the Union during the Civil War. The completion of the Pacific Telegraph in October 1861 was the death knell for the swift couriers.

In the late 18th and early 19th centuries the post office was subordinate to the Treasury Department, but as the system grew in importance, its value as a public service was recognized. The next logical step was taken by President Andrew Jackson on Mar. 9, 1829, when he named William T. Barry postmaster general, the first postmaster general to become a member of a president's cabinet. The move was not made to honor the post office, however, but to control it, and as a result of Jackson's action, the entire character of the postal system was changed. It became the chief patronage-dispensing agency of the political party in power, which led to many abuses in the century that followed, culminating in the legal demise of the Post Office Department and the birth of the U.S. Postal Service in 1971. After Jackson's first appointment the

terms of postmasters general were usually shorter than they had been, and most of the incumbents were not strong enough or did not have enough time in office to make permanent improvements in postal practices.

From the Jackson years to the eve of the Civil War, the postal service showed a phenomenal growth. While the population of the nation increased 144 percent, from 12.9 million to 31.4 million, the volume of mail grew more spectacularly—more than 1,200 percent, from 13.8 million letters to 184.3 million. In the mid-1840's the government's monopoly to deliver mail was reasserted and strengthened. Legislation was passed aimed at the elaborate system of private expresses that had grown up in the wake of high postage rates.

Postage stamps made their appearance in the United States shortly after their use was adopted in England in 1840. The first stamps in the United States were used by private expresses and local deliveries. Congress enacted a law on Mar. 3, 1847, authorizing the use of adhesive postage stamps in America for the first time. Put on sale in New York City on July 1, the first stamps portrayed Benjamin Franklin on the five-cent denomination and George Washington on the ten-cent stamp. In those early days stamps were designed to be issued to the postmasters on account, for sale to the public, providing an accurate and automatic check on the postage revenues. Before stamps were issued officially, letters accepted by postmasters for dispatch were marked "paid" by means of pen and ink or hand stamps of various designs. Such letters usually contained the town postmark and date of mailing. Some postmasters provided special stamps for use on letters as evidence of the prepayment of postage. These stamps of local origin are known as "postmasters' provisionals."

The new adhesive postage stamps were printed by private manufacturers until July 1, 1894, when the printing was transferred to the Bureau of Engraving and Printing. In 1869 the first stamps printed in two colors were issued, a novelty not repeated until 1901. The first commemorative series—featuring Christopher Columbus and the discovery of America—appeared in 1893, and the first airmail stamp (twenty-four cents) was issued in 1918. Beginning in 1957 the subjects of stamps were chosen by the Citizens Stamp Advisory Committee, which consisted of a cross section of people in the arts, history, philately, and business "whose judgment and taste can be relied upon to improve the quality of both subject choice and artistic presentation of stamps."

Development of the U.S. postal system continued in the mid-19th century with a momentary pause during the Civil War. Montgomery Blair, postmaster general under President Abraham Lincoln, wanted to keep the post offices open in the seceded states of the Confederacy as "the best means to communicate to the people of the South the judgement which I am confident the civilized world would pronounce against the rebellion, when its real purpose was distinctly seen." But he was unsuccessful. Not only were the offices closed, but the Confederacy established its own postal system, patterned after the U.S. Post Office. John H. Reagan of Texas, who was appointed postmaster general of the Confederacy, urged some people from the Post Office Department in Washington, D.C., to defect to the South and "to bring with them copies of the last annual report of the Postmaster-General and every form in the department together with the postal maps of the Southern States."

Reagan took a number of important actions to try to ensure the success of the postal system in the South. He had the Confederate congress authorize the continuation in office of the postmasters who had been in service under the government of the United States. He also raised the letter postage rate from three cents to five cents; later the rate was doubled to help the Confederate post office meet financial obligations. Unnecessary mail routes were discontinued and long routes were shortened to reduce the cost of service.

Operation of the Confederate postal system was seriously hampered almost from its inception on June 1, 1861. For one thing, it was difficult to send and receive foreign mail because of the blockading of southern ports by the Union fleet. Another problem was stamps. The first Confederate government postage stamp—the five-cent green stamp portraying President Jefferson Davis—was issued more than four months after the postal service went into business. It was difficult to find competent printing firms and even more difficult to procure adequate materials for printing. One result was a great variety and number of counterfeit stamps.

Later in the war another problem emerged. Service was disrupted by the invading Union forces. After the fall of Vicksburg, Miss., and Port Hudson, La., communication between Richmond, Va., the capital of the Confederacy, and the country west of the Mississippi River became "extremely uncertain." As a result a western branch of the postal service was established in Marshall, Tex., under James H. Starr. With the collapse of the Confederacy, the Confederate postal system passed out of existence. Reagan was taken prisoner of war but he was later freed and became a U.S. senator and chairman of the Committee on Postal Affairs. Not until 1878 did the South have as many post offices as it had had before the war in 1860.

During the war postal development in the North was slowed. On July 1, 1863, the day the Battle of Gettysburg began, free city delivery service was inaugurated when 449 letter carriers started to deliver mail in forty-nine cities. The postal monopoly had been confirmed three years earlier by a judicial decision, and in 1872 an ordinance established that Congress had the sole and exclusive right and power to establish and regulate post offices.

As the postal monopoly was consolidated, there were a number of developments, including agitation for a postal savings bank system. Although these demands began in 1871, postal savings banks were not authorized by law until June 25, 1910. The system went into operation on Jan. 1, 1911. Enactment of the law was ensured by the financial panic of 1907, which had generated demands for a guaranty of bank deposits. Other major purposes of the postal savings banks were to get money out of hiding and to attract the savings of immigrants who were accustomed to saving at post offices in their native countries. The interest return was set at 2 percent annually from the beginning, and the maximum amount that an individual could have insured in his account was $2,500. Use of the system reached a peak in 1947 when 4 million depositors had accounts totaling $3.4 billion. By June 30, 1965, the number of depositors had declined to 997,029, and the amount on deposit had tumbled to $344 million. The Post Office Department pressed Congress to phase out the postal savings system since dramatic changes had occurred in the economy of the country, resulting in the growth and strength, guaranteed by the Federal Deposit Insurance Corporation, of private banking facilities. Accordingly the postal savings banks were discontinued by Congress on Mar. 28, 1966.

As the country expanded in the closing decades of the 19th century, so did the post office. By the dawn of the 20th century, there were 76,688 individual post offices in the nation. But the expansion was marked by increasing postal deficits. There was a barrage of complaints about service and about how the Post Office Department itself was being run. In 1859 the House Committee on the Post Office considered a bill to turn the mails over to private hands but dismissed it as "inexpedient." Subsequently, proposals continued to be made to turn the post office over to private corporations, and the Hoover Commission in 1949 called for establishment of a government corporation to run the post office. Following a suggestion made by Postmaster General Lawrence F. O'Brien in 1967, President Lyndon B. Johnson appointed a commission, headed by Frederick R. Kappel, former board chairman of American Telephone and Telegraph Company, to make a study of what to do with the post office.

In June 1968, the committee issued its report, recommending that the Post Office Department be transformed into a public corporation, but no action was taken on this report. In January 1969, Winton M. Blount took office as postmaster general, backed by a pledge from President Richard M. Nixon to support real postal reform. Fifteen days later, on Feb. 5, 1969, Blount announced that patronage would be removed from the Post Office Department and that no more postmasters, rural carriers, or any other employees would be appointed with political recommendation—that all appointments would be made solely on the basis of merit. Despite enormous political pressure this policy prevailed, as Blount staffed the Post Office Department with executives from business and industry and began a massive introduction of business management techniques. In May 1969, just four months after he became a member of Nixon's cabinet, Blount proposed a basic and sweeping reorganization of the Post Office Department—and Nixon asked Congress to pass the Postal Service Act of 1969, calling for removal of the postmaster general from the cabinet and the creation of a self-supporting postal corporation wholly owned by the federal government.

But Congress did not act. There was a reluctance on the part of many congressmen to pass a law to relinquish the political patronage the Post Office Department had afforded them in the past. Their hand was forced in the spring of 1970, when a wildcat strike of letter carriers spread from New York City to other parts of the country, crippling postal service for more than a week. The dissent alarmed many congressmen, and the strike is believed to have accelerated the creation of the U.S. Postal Service. On Aug. 12, 1970, Nixon signed the Postal Reorganization Act, which took effect on July 1, 1971. The act created an independent government agency, removing the postmaster general from the president's cabinet and effectively eliminating politics and politicians from the management of postal affairs. The act also created a presidentially appointed nine-man board of governors to operate the postal establishment and to appoint the postmaster general and his deputy. The first postmaster general appointed by the board of governors was Blount, who also served as the first chairman of the board of governors. The act also authorized Congress to subsidize the Postal Service at a sliding rate for the first thirteen years of its existence; at the end of that period, it was expected, the Postal Service would be able to operate on a break-even basis. In addition the act allowed the service to borrow $10 billion through the sale of bonds to the public and established an independent presidentially appointed five-man Postal Rate Commission to set postage rates unless overruled by a unanimous vote of the board of governors (under the Post Office Department, rates had been set by Congress). Provisions for collective bargaining for postal workers were included in the act, but the right to strike was denied.

On Oct. 29, 1971, Blount resigned his post, and a few months later E. T. Klassen became the second postmaster general of the U.S. Postal Service.

[Gerald Cullinan, *The United States Postal Service;* August Dietz, *The Postal Service of the Confederate States of America;* Wayne E. Fuller, *The American Mail;* Roy L. Garis, *Principles of Money, Credit, and Banking;* Beverly S. King and Max G. Johl, *The United States Postage Stamps of the 20th Century;* Ross Allan McReynolds, *History of the United States Post Office, 1607–1931;* Everett Rich, *The History of the United States Post Office to the Year 1829;* Lindsay Rogers, *The Postal Power of Congress;* Daniel C. Roper, *The United States Post Office;* William Smith, *History of the Post Office in British North America;* State of California Department of Education Bulletin, *The United States Postal Service;* U.S. Post Office Department, *History of the Post Office Department.*]
WINTON M. BLOUNT

POSTAL TELEGRAPH COMPANY was organized June 21, 1881, with Elisha Gray's harmonic telegraph and a new patented wire as its chief assets. In 1883 John W. Mackay became interested and was elected president. The company was placed in receivership in 1884 and reorganized in 1886 as the Postal Telegraph Cable Company. Through Mackay's business genius it rapidly extended its lines and became the major rival to Western Union. In 1928 it became a part of the International Telephone and Telegraph Corporation, although retaining its own corporate identity.

[Alvin F. Harlow, *Old Wires and New Waves.*]
ALVIN F. HARLOW

POST ROADS. The earliest colonial mail carrying, between New York and Boston, and later, between

New York and Albany, in the late 17th century, traced routes that became great highways and are still known as the post roads. The names "Boston Post Road" and "Old (Albany) Post Road" on two meandering streets in New York City mark their lower courses. The Continental Congress began creating post roads during the revolutionary war. To designate a highway as a post road gave the government the monopoly of carrying mail over it; on other roads, anybody might carry it. At first the mail was conveyed on horseback; later it was carried in stagecoaches. But as late as 1825 Postmaster General John McLean reported that "The intelligence of more than half the Nation is conveyed on horseback." That a highway was a post road did not prevent its being impassable from mud at times, for little road improving was done in the early decades of U.S. history. Hugh Finlay, postal inspector, declared in 1773, for example, that the road between New London, Conn., and Providence, R.I., was "bad past all conception." In early days horseback travelers often sought the company of the post rider for guidance and protection; later, the mail coach was an important passenger carrier as well. The inns where the post rider stopped overnight or the mail coach paused for meals became noted and prosperous hostelries, and the post roads were the first to be improved. In 1787 connecting stretches of road reaching as far north as Portsmouth and Concord, N.H., as far south as Augusta, Ga., and as far west as Pittsburgh were declared post roads, as were others in the more settled area between; but many of the new routes were not expected to be self-supporting, and so were let out to contractors. Between 1790 and 1829 successive acts of Congress increased the post road mileage from 1,875 to 114,780. Steamboat captains carried many letters in the early days and collected the fees for them, until in 1823 all navigable waters were declared to be post roads, which checked the practice. Private letter-carrying companies after 1842 did much house-to-house mail business in the larger cities; but the postmaster general circumvented them in 1860 by declaring all the streets of New York, Boston, and Philadelphia to be post roads.

[Alvin F. Harlow, *Old Post Bags*.]
ALVIN F. HARLOW

POSTS, ARMY SUPPLY. Before the development of modern transportation the War Department found it difficult to provision army posts, many of which were located at great distances from settled communities. To offset high shipping costs, the government adver-

tised its contracts yearly in papers throughout the country, for in that way it hoped to reach some bidder close to a post who would probably submit a reasonable offer. Consequently, merchants everywhere had an opportunity to bid for the privilege of supplying pork, flour, whiskey, beans, vinegar, soap, and other needed items. Not all contracts went to merchants, but they obtained a large percentage because of their advantageous position. Thus, during the year merchants acquired considerable farm produce in barter for goods; they were familiar with the problem of transporting supplies; and they knew the best markets in which to purchase articles unobtainable locally. These factors, added to the advantages already held by merchants residing in the vicinity of posts, account for mercantile success in this line. For example, Hill and M'Gunnegle of Saint Louis held the contract for Jefferson Barracks during most of the decade of the 1830's; the Aulls of Lexington, Mo., supplied the nearby Fort Leavenworth at times; and J. M. D. Burrows of Davenport, Iowa, profited from a contract for Fort Snelling.

[Lewis E. Atherton, "James and Robert Aull—A Frontier Missouri Mercantile Firm," *Missouri Historical Review*, vol. 30; J. M. D. Burrows, *Fifty Years in Iowa*.]
LEWIS E. ATHERTON

POTASH (potassium carbonate) and soda (sodium carbonate) have been used from the dawn of history in bleaching textiles, making glass, and (from about A.D. 500) in making soap. Soda was principally obtained by leaching the ashes of sea plants, and potash from the ashes of land plants. In their uses they were more or less interchangeable, although not entirely so. Potash soap, for example, is soft, and soda soap, hard. The two were only vaguely differentiated before the mid-18th century. Soda was principally used around the Mediterranean and potash in the interior of Europe.

With the advent of gunpowder at the end of the Middle Ages potash found a new use, in the manufacture of saltpeter (in converting the calcium nitrate usually found in nature into potassium nitrate), and this was not a use for which soda could be substituted. Thus, the increasing demand for glass, soap, textiles, and gunpowder in 16th- and 17th-century Europe accelerated the decimation of the forests from which potash was obtained. Potash production was urged on the first settlers to Virginia, where the first factory, established in 1608, was a "glass house," and the first cargo to England included potash. England ob-

POTATOES

tained most of its potash from Russia, but a potash crisis about 1750 led Parliament to remit the duty and the Society of Arts of London to offer premiums for the production of potash in America. In the two decades after 1761 they distributed about £900 and fourteen gold medals for this purpose.

Potashmaking became a major industry in British North America. Thomas Jefferson listed potash as the sixth most important export in 1792 (after bread grains, tobacco, rice, wood, and salted fish). Great Britain was always the most important market, as the American potash industry followed the woodsman's ax across the country. After about 1820 New England was replaced by New York as the most important source; by 1840 the center was in Ohio. Potash production was always a by-product industry, following from the need to clear land for agriculture. In 1808 a complaint was made that the South Carolinians were so eager to get into cotton production that they simply burned up the forests, neglecting to collect either wood or ashes. William Brown's report in 1849 of "a four years residence" in America described a land-clearing party in Ohio. Ten acres of wood at a time were cut, and usable logs were removed if there was a sawmill nearby. The remainder was burned, a process that might take a week, and the ashes were collected—if there was a potash works nearby. The most urgent thing was to clear the land.

By 1850 potash had become popular as a fertilizer, while forests available for indiscriminate burning were becoming increasingly rare. But deep drilling for common salt at Stassfurt, Germany, revealed strata of potassium salts (mostly chlorides and sulfates), and production of this mineral potash began in 1861. The United States, having decimated its forests, joined most of the rest of the world in dependency on German potash. The dependency still existed when World War I cut off this source of supply. Frantic efforts produced some domestic potash, notably from the complex brines of some western saline lakes, especially Searles Lake, in the Mojave Desert of California. The wartime urgency was surmounted but left an awareness of the problem and directed attention to reports of potash salts having been brought up in drilling for oil. By following these clues, large deposits were found near Carlsbad, N.Mex. After 1931 a number of mines there supplied about 90 percent of the domestic requirement of potash, most of the remainder coming from Searles Lake. Ninety-five percent of this production was used in fertilizer.

["A Colonial Industry," *Bulletin of the Business History Society*, vol. 7 (1933); G. E. Mitchell, "The Potash Search in America," *Review of Reviews* (January 1912); J. W. Turrentine, *Potash*.]

ROBERT P. MULTHAUF

POTATOES. The so-called Irish potato, a native of the Andes, was introduced into England in the 16th century. A ship is known to have carried potatoes from England to Bermuda in 1613, and in 1621 the governor of Bermuda sent to Gov. Francis Wyatt of Virginia two large chests filled with plants and fruits then unknown to the latter colony, among them potatoes, which were planted and grown in the settlements along the James River. In 1622 a Virginia bark brought from Bermuda to Virginia about 20,000 pounds of potatoes. It seems that their cultivation did not spread widely during that century or, in fact, until a party of Scotch-Irish immigrants brought potatoes with them to Rockingham County, N.H., in 1719. Because of this introduction of the potato from Ireland and because the potato had become a major crop in Ireland by the end of the 17th century, "Irish" became a permanent part of its name. Some historians have asserted that this was the original introduction of potatoes to the American colonies; but Berthold Laufer of the Chicago Field Museum of Natural History quoted letters and documents to prove the century-earlier introduction into Virginia. Swedish botanist Peter Kalm found potatoes being grown at Albany in 1749. Thomas Jefferson wrote of cultivating potatoes, "both the long [sweet?] and the round [Irish?]." Decades later the Navaho Indians of the Southwest were found to be planting a small, wild variety common in some parts of Mexico. The Irish potato came to be a daily item on the American dinner table—especially in the North as an accompaniment for meats—and a major food crop in many states during the 19th century. Aroostook, the large, northernmost county of Maine, began extensive potato growing, and in 1935 that county's potatoes produced half of the agricultural income of Maine. Aroostook housewives are said to have been the first, or among the first, to make starch for their white garments by soaking potato pulp in water and then drying it. Starch sheds began to appear along the streams, and eventually Aroostook produced 90 percent of the nation's potato starch. The use of this starch declined greatly in the 20th century, and industrial alcohol appeared as a new means of saving the culls and the surplus.

Sweet potatoes (botanically, wholly unrelated to the Irish tuber) were being cultivated by the American

376

Indians before the arrival of Christopher Columbus, who, with the other members of his party, ate these potatoes and esteemed them highly. Because of the fact that they could be best grown in the South, and because they give an enormous yield (200 to 400 bushels per acre), they became a favorite vegetable in that section, while remaining unknown to the table in large areas of the North. To the southern poor, sweet potatoes were an inevitable accompaniment of opossum meat, although they were also served with fresh pork and other meats, and the sweet potato has often been the main item in the diet of some poor families, especially in winter. Their cultivation spread to California and gradually crept up the Atlantic coast as far as New Jersey.

By 1970 annual U.S. production of Irish potatoes had reached 319 million hundredweight; production of sweet potatoes in the same year totaled 13 million hundredweight.

[Berthold Laufer, *The American Plant Migration,* part 1; William Stuart, *The Potato.*]

ALVIN F. HARLOW

POT LIKKER AND CORN PONE. A well-known culinary combination peculiar to the South is corn pone (something between hoecake and corn bread) and pot likker (the juice of ham or fatback cooked with turnip, poke, or collard greens). In February 1931 Gov. Huey P. Long of Louisiana asserted that corn pone should be "dunked"; the *Atlanta Constitution,* which claimed authority on "all matters pertaining to pot likker, corn pone, dumplings, fried collards, sweet 'tater biscuits, 'simmon beer, and 'possum," contended it should be crumbled in the pot likker. Most people supported the "crumblers," but some politicians were careful to say that they liked it both ways.

HARVEY L. CARTER

POTOMAC, ARMY OF. The demoralization of the Union forces after the first Battle of Bull Run (July 21, 1861) left Washington, D.C., in an undefended state that might have proved disastrous had the Confederacy been able to take advantage of its opportunity. Immediately after congressional authorization for the acceptance of volunteers, the Division of the Potomac was created (July 25, 1861), and two days later Gen. George B. McClellan was placed in command. The immediate purpose was to guard the approaches to the Potomac River and thus to protect Washington. McClellan fell heir to "a collection of

undisciplined, ill officered, and uninstructed men," already demoralized by defeat. On Aug. 1 there were only about 37,000 infantry in the ranks, and the terms of many regiments were expiring. Four months later there were some 77,000 effectives available for active operations, aside from regiments on garrison and other duty. But the army was still growing.

McClellan's first job was to whip this heterogeneous mass of raw recruits into an effective fighting unit. The men were from all walks of life and every part of the country. Some were volunteers from foreign nations, and many could not speak English. McClellan was not allowed to expand the regulars or break them up to head volunteers, and many of the political generals at his disposal were useless. Also, he was hampered by the officious meddling and machinations of political leaders, while his own temperament was not such as to smooth out such difficulties. Nevertheless, in a very few months he evolved the best army the United States had had to that time, and so inspired it with a spirit of loyalty and feeling of destiny that all the interference from Washington during the remainder of the war could not permanently harm its morale.

Such an army was not allowed to exhibit its true worth until the war was half over. If McClellan overestimated the enemy in the Peninsular Campaign, it must be remembered that he was not allowed control of the intelligence service. Also, Washington officialdom far outdid him in that respect by withholding Gen. Irvin McDowell's 40,000 troops to guard against a possible attack on Washington by a third as many men under Confederate Gen. Thomas J. ("Stonewall") Jackson (*see* Jackson's Valley Campaign). When the Seven Days' Battles (June 26–July 2, 1862) resulted in the Union army reaching the James River, and in a better position to advance on Richmond than was to be achieved for two more years, McClellan was demoted beneath the incompetent Gen. John Pope, and the pick of the army was removed to join the latter at Aquia Creek. In caution McClellan was exceeded by Gen. George H. Thomas, in blunders by Gen. Ulysses S. Grant, in egotism and insubordination by Secretary of War Edwin M. Stanton. His tardiness in pursuit after Antietam (Sept. 17, 1862) was at least as excusable as that of Gen. George G. Meade after Gettysburg. But by July 1863 Washington officialdom had learned to give a general a chance while he was winning. In 1864 and 1865, with Meade still in command but Grant rather than Gen. Henry W. Halleck giving the superior orders, the Army of the Potomac was al-

lowed to complete the work that McClellan had outlined and begun in 1862.

[Bruce Catton, *The Army of the Potomac;* J. G. Randall,
The Civil War and Reconstruction.]

FRED A. SHANNON

POTOMAC COMPANY was organized in 1785 with
the idea that it would eventually achieve a waterway
connection between the Potomac and Ohio rivers.
George Washington was one of the incorporators and
was elected president. Work was begun that summer
on a short canal with locks around the Great Falls of
the Potomac, near the present site of Washington,
D.C.—the first corporate improvement of navigation
for public use in America. This canal was not completed until 1802. By 1808 there were four more short
canals between Washington and a point above
Harpers Ferry, the longest one 3,814 yards in length.
These were of great assistance to boatmen and rafts-
men in bringing their products down to tidewater; but
the project was not a paying one, and, when the
Chesapeake and Ohio Canal Company was organized, the Potomac Company willingly surrendered
its charter and rights to the new corporation in 1828.

[Alvin F. Harlow, *Old Towpaths.*]

ALVIN F. HARLOW

POTOMAC RIVER drains the western slopes of the
central Allegheny Mountains of West Virginia into
the Chesapeake Bay. Two main streams, the North
Branch and the South Branch, and several minor
streams unite to form the upper Potomac. A freshwater river for 287 miles, the Potomac below Washington, D.C., is a tidal estuary 125 miles in length
and from 2 to 8 miles wide.

Spaniards probably reached the Potomac estuary
before 1570. Capt. John Smith visited, described, and
mapped it in 1608. Capt. Samuel Argall, deputy governor of Virginia, and others sailed its waters in the
next decade. In the late 1620's Virginia traders
frequented its waters and shores. Probably agents of
George Calvert before 1632 explored the upper Potomac. After the founding of Maryland in 1634, the
Potomac was the early passageway of the colony. In
following decades its southern shores were gradually
settled by Virginians. But owing to the falls above
Washington, D.C., and at Harpers Ferry the upper
Potomac was long unimportant. In the second quarter
of the 18th century, Germans and Scotch-Irish crossed
it into the Shenandoah Valley, and about 1740

Thomas Cresap, militant Marylander, settled at Oldtown (also called Shawanese Oldtown) above the
junction of the South Branch and the Potomac, in
western Maryland. Slowly the Potomac Valley became a pathway to the Ohio Valley, utilized by the
Ohio Company of Virginia, by George Washington,
and by Gen. Edward Braddock. Over this route traveled the first settlers to the Monongahela country. Its
utilization was the basis of later enterprises, such as
the Potomac Company of 1785, the Cumberland
Road of 1807, the Baltimore and Ohio Railroad of
1827, and the Chesapeake and Ohio Canal Company
of 1828.

[Corra Bacon Foster, *Early Chapters in the Development
of the Potomac Route to the West;* Paul Wilstach, *Potomac
Landings.*]

ALFRED P. JAMES

POTSDAM CONFERENCE (July 17–Aug. 2,
1945), the last meeting during World War II of the
three allied chiefs of state—President Harry S. Truman, Prime Minister Winston Churchill, and Marshal
Joseph Stalin. Germany, but not Japan, had already
surrendered. Truman, Churchill (who was replaced
during the conference by the new prime minister,
Clement Attlee, after the British elections), and Stalin
fixed terms of German occupation and reparations
and replaced the European Advisory Commission (set
up at the Moscow Conference of Foreign Ministers in
October 1943) with the Council of Foreign Ministers
of the United States, Great Britain, France, and Russia, charged with preparing peace terms for Italy,
Romania, Bulgaria, Austria, Hungary, and Finland.
Since Russia had not yet declared war on Japan, the
Potsdam Declaration (July 26, 1945) was signed by
the United States and Great Britain only, although
with China's concurrence. The declaration called for
Japan to surrender but gave assurances that it would
be treated humanely. Although the discussions were
fairly cordial, the American delegation, disturbed by
indications of Russian noncooperation, left Potsdam
in a far less optimistic mood than President Franklin
D. Roosevelt's delegation had left Yalta.

CHARLES S. CAMPBELL

POTTAWATOMIE MASSACRE, the murder by
free-state men of five proslavery settlers near Dutch
Henry's Crossing at Pottawatomie Creek, Franklin
County, Kans., on the night of May 24–25, 1856 (*see*
Border War). The principal facts became known al-

most immediately. John Brown, four of his sons, and three others were accused of the murders; warrants were issued, but only one arrest was made (that of James Townsley). But the case never went to trial. Some proslavery newspapers gave fairly accurate statements of facts, but were confused in attributing motives. The free-state press misrepresented both. Brown's first biographer, James Redpath, endorsed by the Brown family, denied that Brown was present or even had prior knowledge of it. Not until the statement of Townsley was published in December 1879 did the Brown family and friends (with a few exceptions) admit the truth. From that date the Brown controversy centered on motives and justification rather than denial, but with little success in establishing either.

The primary issue in the spring of 1856 was enforcement of the so-called bogus laws. In various parts of the territory, threats were made against the courts and enforcement officers. The significant fact about the Pottawatomie victims is that, except for one of the victims, they were all members of the Franklin County grand jury or were associated otherwise with the session of court of Apr. 21–22. These facts place the massacre in the category of political assassination with a view to preventing enforcement of law by resort to a reign of terror.

[J. C. Furnas, *The Road to Harpers Ferry;* J. C. Malin, "The Hoogland Examination," *Kansas Historical Quarterly* (May 1938); O. G. Villard, *John Brown.*]

JAMES C. MALIN

POTTERY. In 1611 "4 potters of earth" were listed among tradesmen being sent to Virginia, and archaeologists have found evidence in Jamestown of pottery made locally by about 1630. In Massachusetts potters began work at Salem in 1635. For nearly two centuries thereafter American pottery in the European tradition remained at a folk level, as the work of growing clusters of potters became marked by regional characteristics. The prevailing output was lead-glazed, red earthenware, sometimes decorated with slip.

The arrival of German potters in the 18th century profoundly influenced the character of earthenware in the middle Atlantic colonies and in the interior regions of the South. Germanic pottery, often elaborately decorated with multicolored slips, was made in German and Swiss enclaves west of Philadelphia and in the Moravian community of Wachovia, N.C. Pennsylvania-German sgraffito-decorated presenta-

tion pieces, their designs scratched through a coating of slip to reveal the red body, have survived from the federal period. Excavations in Philadelphia have revealed the 18th-century fusion of German and English earthenware styles there.

The almost simultaneous beginning in the 1720's of the manufacture of blue-decorated, salt-glazed stoneware in Philadelphia and New York established a Rhenish-derived tradition that spread through the Northeast and Midwest after the Revolution. In Virginia the "Poor Potter of Yorktown" made English-style stoneware before 1740. Elsewhere in the South ash-glazed and salt-glazed stoneware was fashioned in rural potteries during the 19th and 20th centuries. Black potters played important roles there, including among their products grotesque, sculptural effigy jugs of apparent African ancestry.

Attempts to make "delftware" in New Jersey in 1688; porcelain in Savannah, Ga., in 1736; and Staffordshire-type "queensware" in Charleston, S.C., in 1771 met with little success. However, one of the Charleston queensware potters taught his art to the Wachovia Moravians, who then produced it successfully in an unusual cultural adoption. In Philadelphia, Bonnin and Morris briefly made English-type soft-paste porcelain in 1771–73, to be followed in 1827 by William Ellis Tucker's French-style porcelain.

An influx of British potters after 1825 led to factory production of molded stoneware, Rockingham, Parian, and porcelain ware. Centered first at Jersey City, N.J., they spread elsewhere, notably to East Liverpool, Ohio; Baltimore, Md.; and Bennington, Vt. The first successful hard-paste porcelain was manufactured at Greenpoint, N.Y., after 1862. An esthetic reaction against commercial Victorian wares precipitated "art potteries," stressing handcraft methods. Beginning in 1875 with the Chelsea (Mass.) Keramic Art Works, these included the Rookwood Pottery, Cincinnati; the Grueby Faience Company, Boston; and the Moravian Pottery, Doylestown, Pa. Out of this tradition developed the 20th-century studio potters, who, as artist-craftsmen, use clay for sculptural as well as useful forms. Factories in the 19th and 20th centuries, meanwhile, mass-produced common crockery, whiteware, semiporcelains, and bone china, as well as chemical stoneware, architectural terra cotta, and sewer pipe.

Traditional potters, following the frontier to Texas and California and lingering in cultural backwaters, continued to use kick wheels and wood-fired kilns in small shops differing little from 17th-century ones. It was probably 1971 before the last of those still capable of excellence in their products closed his North Carolina shop for the last time.

[E. A. Barber, *The Pottery and Porcelain of the United States;* Alexander Brown, ed., *The Genesis of the United States;* A. W. Clement, *Our Pioneer Potters;* J. L. Cotter, *Archaeological Excavations at Jamestown, Virginia;* L. W. Watkins, *Early New England Potters and Their Wares.*]

C. MALCOLM WATKINS

POULTRY CASE. *See Schechter Poultry Corporation v. United States.*

POVERTY AND PAUPERISM. "We were so poor," President Lyndon B. Johnson recalled of his childhood in Texas, "we didn't know there was such a thing as poverty." Like Johnson's family, countless Americans in every period of the nation's history have been poor in things owned and consumed. Many have also been poor in relation to more affluent neighbors. Until the 20th century neither circumstance occasioned much surprise or worry because hardship was such a common experience that it was taken for granted as a normal and generally wholesome condition of life. Want and inequality were so prevalent, were thought to be so natural, and were deemed to be so intimately related to personal behavior in terms of cause and cure that poverty hardly existed as a social issue. Only when the poor ceased to be self-supporting and sought public assistance did their situation become a problem requiring public attention. This special and limited aspect of poverty was traditionally designated pauperism—the condition of persons who in 20th-century terminology are said to be "on welfare." Whatever the choice of words, the relief of the dependent poor and the cost and consequences of their dependence have been subjects of continuing major concern since the earliest days of the settlement of America.

Colonial poor laws followed English precedents in assigning responsibility for financing and distributing poor relief to the local authorities. As a general rule, relief was reserved for persons who by birth or by a year or more of residence had established legal settlement in the town or county where assistance was sought. In accordance with the principle of local control, the kind and variety of relief varied from colony to colony and between different localities within each colony. Assistance was sometimes provided the poor in their own homes, but if able to work, both adult and child paupers were bound out to service to earn their keep. Except in the larger towns almshouses,

asylums, and similar institutions for the poor were rare.

The overthrow of English rule brought little change to the system except where disestablishment of the church transferred administration of relief from church to local government officers. New states adopted poor laws patterned after those of the seaboard states, those in the South and West giving responsibility for relief to the counties and those in New England to towns.

By about 1825 four methods of public assistance were in operation, often simultaneously within the same state: outdoor relief, that is, assistance to the needy in their own homes; auctioning individual paupers to the lowest bidder; contracting with a private individual to care for a group of paupers; or maintaining all the paupers in a town or county poorhouse. In the 19th century welfare reformers urged that institutional care in strictly supervised almshouses be substituted for other methods of public relief. If located on a farm, it was argued, the poorhouse might be partly self-supporting; moreover the rigor and discipline of institutional life would reform the inmates and deter impostors from seeking to live at public expense. In practice, almshouses proved to be not reformatories but custodial institutions for the aged, infant, infirm, and handicapped poor. Nevertheless, reformers continued to advocate cessation of outdoor relief on the assumption that private charity could and should relieve the deserving poor. During the middle and latter part of the 19th century numerous efforts were made to put private charity on a businesslike basis. The movement culminated in the 1870's and 1880's with the establishment in a number of cities of charity organization societies, forerunners of 20th-century family service agencies. The societies stressed thorough investigation of an applicant's need, counseling, and provision of services rather than financial assistance. The objective was to help the poor help themselves.

The acknowledged intent of 19th-century welfare reform was to stimulate self-support by making public assistance difficult to obtain and unpleasant to receive. This negative approach was accompanied by positive efforts to prevent pauperism by broadening economic and educational opportunities for the population as a whole. The Homestead Act of 1862; free, public, tax-supported schools; and state educational institutions for the deaf, blind, and mentally retarded were only a few of the measures advocated and adopted as preventives of pauperism.

Better provision for needy children was an essential

step toward breaking the cycle of dependency. Although numerous sectarian orphan homes were founded in the middle third of the 19th century, many unfortunate children continued to be sent to public poorhouses where they were reared with, and treated as, paupers. Nearly all reformers agreed on the unsuitability of conglomerate almshouses for child rearing and advocated removal of children from poorhouses to environments better suited to their development as responsible citizens. There was a difference of opinion about whether the children should be sent to special institutions to be brought up in the religious faith of their parents and subjected to close supervision or placed in private homes and allowed to grow up under the care and instruction of foster parents. Another course that was advocated was to provide a surviving parent—most often a widowed mother—with an allowance so that she could maintain her children in their own home under her care. This was the method endorsed by the first White House Conference on the Care of Dependent Children, held in 1909, which declared home life "the highest and finest product of civilization" and went on record as opposing the breakup of homes solely because of poverty.

The conference recommended that mothers' aid be financed by private charity rather than by public funds, but the mothers' pension laws adopted in forty-five states in the twenty years after 1911 authorized payments from money raised by taxation. Critics saw such programs as a retreat toward outdoor relief; advocates argued that mothers were the best guardians of their children's welfare and that it was sound policy to encourage them to devote their full time to the care of their homes and children. The laws were permissive rather than mandatory and were so administered that only mothers deemed "fit" and "proper" received aid. Nevertheless, by the 1920's almost as many dependent children were being cared for in their own homes as in institutions, and many more than in foster homes. This revolutionary change in methods of helping dependent children was to be continued and expanded under one of the provisions of the Social Security Act of 1935.

At about the turn of the century American reformers and publicists shifted their attention from pauperism to poverty. Poverty, declared such writers as Robert Hunter, was a bigger problem than pauperism. It included not only the dependent and destitute but also low-paid workers subject to unemployment, accidents, and other economic hazards not of their making and beyond their individual control.

Even before 1929 it became apparent to many that the want and insecurity of the poor were attributable less to personal failings of the sufferers than to inequality in the distribution of wealth and income and the haphazard operation of the economic machine.

The experience of the Great Depression embedded these convictions in the consciousness of a large segment of the American people. The depression shattered the myth that private charity could tide over the deserving poor in bad times. It also required state and federal governments to become much more involved in welfare activities than ever before. Between 1930 and 1933 states joined local governments in efforts to deal with unemployment relief. When President Franklin D. Roosevelt took office in March 1933, the federal government was already lending states and cities funds that provided 80 percent of all aid to the unemployed. After 1933 federal agencies made emergency grants to states and municipalities for cash and work relief. Beginning in 1935 the Works Progress Administration (WPA), the New Deal's major relief program, provided jobs for an average of 2 million persons a month for six years.

In contrast to WPA and other emergency programs the Social Security Act of 1935 sought to provide a long-term answer to problems of economic insecurity. As adopted, the act was modest in scope and coverage, but it was periodically amended to increase benefits and to bring more people under its protection. The 1935 law provided for a national system of old-age insurance financed by contributions from employers and employees; state-administered unemployment insurance financed by a federal payroll tax; grants-in-aid to states for federally approved, but state-administered, programs for maternal and child health; aid to the blind; aid to the aged not eligible for federal old-age insurance; and aid to dependent children. The public-assistance provisions of the act were included on the theory that even in times of prosperity the handicapped, the aged, and children without an adult breadwinner in the home would require public aid. The system of grants-in-aid avoided constitutional questions regarding the role of the national government in public assistance; it allowed federal participation in funding and establishment of standards while permitting states to maintain autonomy in operating public-assistance programs.

Numerous other New Deal reforms strengthened the position of organized workers and installed built-in stabilizers in the economy. Prosperity during and after World War II encouraged the belief that expanding productivity would solve the problems of poverty and dependency. In the late 1950's, however, pockets of poverty were discovered in such areas as Appalachia, and government reports called attention to a "low income population" seemingly immune to the benefits of economic growth.

In 1959 approximately 40 million Americans, constituting 22 percent of the population, lived in "poverty" as defined by the federal government. By 1970, according to federal agencies, the number of persons living in poverty had declined to about 26 million, or roughly 13 percent of the total population. The federal poverty index used to distinguish the poor from the nonpoor was the minimum income (periodically adjusted) deemed necessary for an individual or a family of specified size to obtain a subsistence level of food and other essential goods and services. In 1972 the poverty line was set at $2,032 for an individual and $4,113 for a "nonfarm" family of four. In 1969 one-third of poor families were headed by persons who worked full time or part time but failed to earn the poverty-line income. The population thus defined as living in poverty was composed mainly of children under sixteen years of age, persons sixty-five years of age or over, and women aged sixteen to sixty-four; 60 percent of the poverty population was white, 30 percent black, and 10 percent of Spanish-speaking, American Indian, or Asian stock.

President Johnson, in signing the Economic Opportunity Act of 1964, which launched his administration's war on poverty, announced that its purpose was "not to make the poor more secure in their poverty but to . . . help them lift themselves out of the ruts of poverty." The act, focusing most of its attention on disadvantaged youth, provided training to equip young people for work; it also incorporated programs to encourage involvement of the poor, organized and assisted by federally paid advocates, in efforts for community betterment.

Despite the officially recorded decline in poverty, welfare rolls and expenditures increased steeply in the 1960's. Between 1959 and 1969 the cost of federally assisted programs involving aid to the aged, the blind, and the disabled doubled and those involving aid to families with dependent children (AFDC) tripled. By 1972 the nation's welfare rolls exceeded 15 million persons, almost 11 million of whom were aided through the AFDC program. In 1969 President Richard M. Nixon proposed to eliminate AFDC in favor of a family assistance plan that would have assured a minimum income for all families but would also have required all recipients except persons unable to work and mothers of very young children to register for

work or training. Twice passed by the House of Representatives, the measure failed to receive approval in the Senate. Administration statements extolling "workfare" and denouncing "the welfare mess" and the emphasis in debates in and out of Congress placed on stringent work tests suggested that the nation's distrust of pauperism was still stronger than its determination to combat poverty.

[Edith Abbott, *Public Assistance;* Robert H. Bremner, *From the Depths: The Discovery of Poverty in the United States;* John K. Galbraith, *The Affluent Society;* Michael Harrington, *The Other America: Poverty in the United States;* Robert Hunter, *Poverty;* Robert J. Lampman, *The Low Income Population and Economic Growth;* Daniel P. Moynihan, *The Politics of a Guaranteed Income: The Nixon Administration and the Family Assistance Plan;* Ralph Pumphrey, "Social Welfare History," in *Encyclopedia of Social Work,* vol. II.]

ROBERT H. BREMNER

POVERTY POINT, a site, in Louisiana, peculiarly representative of an Archaic-stage prehistoric culture that once existed in the area. In addition to typical Archaic stone projectile points, grooved stone axes, adzes, celts, tubular pipes, and steatite and sandstone vessels, the site also contains some of the most impressive aboriginal earthworks and mounds in North America. A series of six low artificial ridges forming concentric octagons was constructed between 1300 and 200 B.C. on an ancient alluvial fan in a former channel of the Arkansas River. The largest of these earth ridges is more than 1,200 meters across. Gaps at the angles in the octagons allowed access to a central plaza. J. Ford and C. H. Webb have estimated that a minimum of 600 houses occupied the summits of the ridges at one time, and the large amount of refuse associated with these ridges further indicated to Ford and Webb that the Poverty Point octagon was a large planned town and an incipient urban development.

A 23-meter-high earth mound, apparently in the shape of a bird with outspread wings, was constructed immediately outside the settlement in a position 7 degrees south of due west. The purpose of this large mound, whose base is 200 meters across, remains a mystery, for by the mid-1970's it had not been excavated. Another mound, uncompleted but probably planned in a shape similar to that of the first, is located 2 kilometers north of the octagon about 7 degrees west of true north. The ground south and east of the site has been swept away by stream erosion, and so it must remain only speculation that there were effigy mounds in these areas too. Conical burial mounds and a small amount of fiber-tempered pottery indicate an advanced, transitional character for the site.

The compass orientation of the mounds and ridges and the presence of a variety of artifacts that have prototypes on the Gulf coast of Mexico suggest a complex, although unclear, relationship with the Middle American region. Figurines of clay representing nude females, pendants of hard stones representing birds' heads, small bead buttons, stone blades struck from prepared cores, and petaloid greenstone celts are among the artifacts indicating the culture had southern connections. Although millions of objects of fired clay that may have been used in hot-stone cookery litter the site and although one vegetable, squash, has been tentatively identified at a related site dating to about 1000 B.C., the subsistence pattern that supported this apparently planned town still remained a puzzle to archaeologists in the mid-1970's.

[James A. Ford and Clarence H. Webb, "Poverty Point," *Anthropological Papers of the American Museum of Natural History,* vol. 46; Jesse D. Jennings, *Prehistory of North America.*]

GUY GIBBON

POWDER. Little powder was manufactured in the thirteen colonies prior to the American Revolution. The principal supply of the colonists in 1775 was left over from the supplies of the French and Indian War. So limited were the facilities for its manufacture in the colonies that had it not been for the importation of 478,250 pounds of saltpeter and 1,454,210 pounds of black powder in the years from 1775 to 1777, the struggle for independence might have been lost. Less than 10 percent of the powder used by the revolutionary armies up to 1778 was produced in the colonies.

The production of powder on a large scale in the United States began with Éleuthère Irénée Du Pont, who, on the encouragement of Thomas Jefferson, bought equipment in France and set up a powder mill in 1801 near Wilmington, Del. Powder was successfully produced in 1804, and the company that Du Pont founded, E. I. Du Pont de Nemours and Company, continued to grow until it virtually controlled the production of explosives in the United States. It supplied the government with 150,000 pounds of black powder during the Barbary Wars, 750,000 pounds during the War of 1812, nearly 4 million pounds during the Civil War, and 2 million pounds of brown prismatic powder during the Spanish-American War.

In 1857 Lamont Du Pont patented the use of nitrate of soda in the manufacture of blasting powder for in-dustrial use. In 1872 the three largest powder producing agencies in the country, Laflin and Rand, Du Pont, and Hazard, combined to form the Gunpowder Trade Association, which dominated this field. The invention of dynamite by Alfred B. Nobel in 1866 and of smokeless powder by Paul Vieille in 1884 and, as Ballistite, by Nobel in 1887 complicated the manufacturing problem, but American firms soon adapted their plants for the manufacture of these products.

The U.S. circuit court in the district of Delaware in 1911 found the Du Pont corporation guilty of violating the provisions of the Sherman Antitrust Act and ordered a distribution of its assets among three companies. These three firms at one time produced 90 percent of the explosives manufactured in the United States.

World War I found the explosives industry in the United States undergoing a vast expansion. War orders from the Allied governments increased the daily output of smokeless powder in the United States from 50,000 pounds in 1914 to 1,250,000 pounds in 1917. In order to make the United States independent of outside imports of nitrate of soda, plants were built to produce nitrogen by the fixation process. The most famous of these plants was at Muscle Shoals, Ala. During World War I the most common explosive materials were black powder, trinitrotoluene (TNT), and amatol (a mixture of TNT and ammonium nitrate). During the period between World War I and World War II, and afterward, developments occurred that made ammonium nitrate one of the most important ingredients used in explosives in the United States. In the 1940's it became available in an inexpensive form for mixing with fuel oil. By the 1970's at least 70 percent of the high explosives used in the United States contained ammonium nitrate mixed either with fuel oil or in a water gel.

[William H. A. Carr, *The Du Ponts of Delaware;* William S. Dutton, *Du Pont, One Hundred and Forty Years;* A. P. Van Gelder and H. Schlatter, *History of the Explosives Industry in America;* T. Urbanski, *Chemistry and Technology of Explosives.*]

H. A. DEWEERD

POWDER RIVER CAMPAIGN. *See* **Sioux Wars.**

POWELL CASE. In 1967 Adam Clayton Powell, a veteran member of the U.S. House of Representatives, was denied membership in the House on the grounds of alleged misconduct before his reelection in 1966. Reelected in a special election in April 1967,

Powell chose not to seek membership, preferring to challenge the House's previous decision in U.S. courts. At issue was the question whether the House could deny membership on any grounds other than those stipulated in the Constitution, namely, age, citizenship, and residence. Both precedent and a long-standing claim that each chamber is the sole judge of a member-elect's qualifications placed Powell at a disadvantage. Nevertheless, in 1969 in *Powell* v. *McCormack* the Supreme Court ruled in his favor, declaring that the House had exceeded its constitutional authority. This was only a partial victory for Powell in that he was unable to win later judicial approval for recovery of back salary, seniority, and a $25,000 fine imposed upon him when he was seated in January 1969. But the Powell case also demonstrated the possibility of an arbitrary exercise of power by a chamber in judging the qualifications of members-elect and the need for an external check to guarantee the people's right to a representative of their own choice.

[P. A. Dionisopoulos, *Rebellion, Racism and Representation: The Adam Clayton Powell Case and Its Antecedents.*]

P. ALLAN DIONISOPOULOS

POWELL'S EXPLORATIONS. John Wesley Powell, professor of geology at the Illinois State Normal University, led two major expeditions down the Colorado River in the 19th century. Powell gained national prominence as a scientist because of these explorations and his findings. The first expedition, the more important one historically, was made in 1869. Powell organized a company of eleven men and in May, aboard four boats, entered the Colorado where the Union Pacific Railroad crosses the Green River, in western Wyoming. The expedition explored the length of the Green and Colorado rivers to the mouth of the Virgin River, in southeastern Nevada, passing through precipitous canyons and traversing treacherous rapids and waterfalls. The party did not emerge until Aug. 29, after a journey of 900 miles. So dangerous were the rapids that three of the men deserted before the end of the journey. Powell reported the expedition to Congress, which in 1870 appropriated funds for the exploration of adjacent rivers and territories. Powell undertook a second expedition (1871–72), which was the more scientifically productive of the two, and which included such eminent geologists as Grove Karl Gilbert and Clarence Dutton and the archaeologist William H. Holmes. The collaboration of these men did much to formulate the basic principles of structural geology. As a result of

the second expedition's success, Powell was named director of the Survey of the Rocky Mountain Region in 1877. Two years later all local surveys were merged in the U.S. Geological Survey, and Powell was made chief of this bureau in 1881; he served as chief until 1894. Among Powell's important publications resulting from his Colorado River explorations are *The Exploration of the Colorado River of the West* (1875) and *The Geology of the Eastern Portion of the Uinta Mountains* (1876).

[F. S. Dellenbaugh, *Canyon Voyage;* R. B. Stanton, *Colorado River Controversies;* Wallace Stegner, *Beyond the Hundredth Meridian: John Wesley Powell and the Second Opening of the West.*]

POWELL'S VALLEY, the most westerly of the long narrow valleys in southwestern Virginia and northeastern Tennessee. It leads directly to Cumberland Gap. In 1750 Thomas Walker explored the valley (*see* Loyal Land Company), and one of his party, Ambrose Powell, cut his name on a tree, hence the name. The first cabin in the valley was built in 1768 by Joseph Martin. There Daniel Boone's party was turned back, in 1773, from Kentucky after the Indians had killed his son and others. Through Powell's Valley passed the land route to Kentucky and the Wilderness Road. It was traversed by thousands of caravans.

[R. G. Thwaites and L. P. Kellogg, *Dunmore's War.*]
LOUISE PHELPS KELLOGG

POWER COMMISSION, FEDERAL. *See* **Federal Agencies.**

POWERS, SEPARATION OF. One of the fundamental America constitutional principles is the doctrine of separation of powers, under which governmental powers are vested in three different branches of government: the legislative, the executive, and the judicial.

While the idea of separation of powers may be traced back to Aristotle and Cicero, it was the Frenchman Charles de Secondat, Baron de Montesquieu, who first formulated it as a doctrine for safeguarding liberty. In his *Spirit of Laws* (*L'Esprit des Lois,* 1748), Montesquieu warned that there could be no liberty if the legislative, executive, and judicial powers, or any two of them, were exercised by one person or by one group of persons. A similar idea was expressed by Sir William Blackstone in his famous *Commentaries on the Laws of England* (1765–69).

The writings of these two were well known to leading Americans of the late colonial and early national periods. This is well demonstrated by the allusions to the principle of separation of powers in important constitutional documents of the period.

In the tenth resolve of the Declaration of Rights adopted by the First Continental Congress in 1774, the importance of the principle of separation of powers was clearly recognized. When the original state constitutions were drafted during the period of the Revolution, considerable attention was given to the application of the principle. The Virginia constitution emphatically declared that the powers of government should "be separate and distinct." The Massachusetts constitution of 1780 also had a definite statement requiring the separation of powers in the government of the commonwealth "to the end it may be a government of laws and not of men."

At the time of the framing of the U.S. Constitution in 1787, the doctrine of separation of powers was accepted without question by the national leaders. James Madison, George Washington, and Gouverneur Morris, to mention only a few of the prominent framers, subscribed to the principle. Yet it was not written directly into the Constitution. Rather, it was incorporated in the national document through the "distributing clauses," as the opening statements of the first three articles of the Constitution are called.

The framers of the fundamental law were well aware that it would be impossible to operate the three branches of the federal government as though they were in airtight compartments, with the functions of each so defined as to prevent any overlapping. This is demonstrated by the fact that they also gave application in the document to what is known as the principle of checks and balances. Through the operation of the two principles, the founding fathers believed each branch of the government could be kept within bounds. At least, they hoped to create a condition that would prevent any branch from exercising, in the words of James Madison, "directly or indirectly, an overruling influence over the others, in the administration of their respective powers."

A study of history since the Constitution was put into operation in 1789 reveals that this hope has not been fully realized. At no time has any one branch succeeded in securing or even attempted to secure for itself all the powers of government, although it is obvious that, at various times, one branch or another has been far more influential than either of the others. Thus, in the early years of the constitutional period, Congress was the dominant branch. Then, for a time,

the judiciary under the leadership of Chief Justice John Marshall, exerted what many believed to be an undue influence. But chiefly, the executive branch has tended to dominate the government. This has been notably true under such presidents as Abraham Lincoln, Theodore Roosevelt, Woodrow Wilson, Franklin D. Roosevelt, and Richard M. Nixon.

[S. P. Orth and R. E. Cushman, *American National Government;* Arthur T. Vanderbilt, *The Doctrine of the Separation of Powers and Its Present-Day Significance;* M. J. Vile, *Constitutionalism and the Separation of Powers.*]

ERIK MCKINLEY ERIKSSON

POWHATAN CONFEDERACY, a 17th-century chiefdom established by conquest among the Algonkin-speaking Indians of the Virginia coastal plain. Chief Powhatan (properly the name of his principal village) inherited dominion over some seven local groups ("tribes"). Thereafter he extended his sway north and south on the tidewater plain and across Chesapeake Bay to its eastern shore, until it embraced some thirty tributary groups, having an estimated population of 9,000. The center of Powhatan's domain lay on the James, Pamunkey, and Mattaponi rivers; yet within it the Chickahominy preserved their independence. Farmers who supplemented their agricultural produce through fishing, hunting, and gathering, these Virginia Algonkins dwelt in villages that were often fortified; the largest had over 200 inhabitants.

For the most part status among the leading families rested on a combination of wealth and ability. Powhatan exacted annual tribute from subordinate chiefs, and his own fields were worked by his immediate subjects. Opechancanough, one of two brothers who were to succeed him, had his seat at Pamunkey, a principal tributary. Beneath the chiefs in their various villages were officials serving both as advisers and as war leaders. Buttressing the ruling class was a priesthood serving in major villages at temples, each of which housed the image of a tribal deity together with the bones of past chiefs.

Powhatan and his chiefdom played a vital role in the early history of the Virginia colony. The early settlers were dependent for sustenance on the purchase or seizure of Indian foodstuffs, and during the "starving time" in 1609 some were lodged with the Indians. Powhatan was treated by the English as minor, barbaric royalty, and the marriage of his daughter Pocahontas to John Rolfe was instrumental in concluding peace between him and the English, freeing the latter to subdue the intervening Chickahominy. With the death of Powhatan in 1618, power passed by turns to Opechancanough, who remained obdurate and who in 1622 led his people into sudden and concerted war against the colonists. The colonists rallied from the blow and launched merciless reprisals until 1631. In 1644 the aged chieftain essayed a last, desperate campaign that ended in his defeat and death. Thereafter, the Virginia colony, in an early form of indirect rule, incorporated the chiefdom in subordinate status. In the last official act of the Tributary chiefs, as they were by then known, a delegation participated in the Treaty of Albany (1722) with the Iroquois.

[James Mooney, ''Powhatan,'' in F. W. Hodge, ed., *Handbook of American Indians North of Mexico;* Theodore Stern, ''Chickahominy: The Changing Culture of a Virginia Indian Community,'' *American Philosophical Society Proceedings,* vol. 96 (1952).]

THEODORE STERN

POWHATAN **INCIDENT.** During the early days of April 1861, just before the start of the Civil War, President Abraham Lincoln determined not to give up the two remaining federal forts in southern territory—Fort Sumter in the harbor at Charleston, S.C., and Fort Pickens in the harbor at Pensacola, Fla. Relief expeditions were ordered to the forts and sailed from New York on Apr. 8. Meanwhile, Secretary of State William H. Seward, in an attempt to maintain his supremacy in Lincoln's cabinet, secretly ordered the warship *Powhatan* to Fort Pickens instead of Fort Sumter, the more likely Confederate target, and secured Lincoln's signature to the necessary order. Controversy arose between Seward and Secretary of the Navy Gideon Welles over the Pickens relief expedition, and Lincoln ordered the *Powhatan* on Apr. 5 to join the expedition to Sumter. Seward telegraphed David Dixon Porter, commander of the *Powhatan,* over his own signature, but the ship was already on its way to Fort Pickens when the telegram was received. Porter declined to obey the order over Seward's name, stating that the presidential order took precedence. The Pickens expedition was successful, but without the *Powhatan*'s firepower, the relief of Sumter failed.

[A. Howard Meneely, *The War Department, 1861.*]

THOMAS ROBSON HAY

POWNALL, FORT, in Maine, was named after Gov. Thomas Pownall of Massachusetts Bay, who was largely responsible for its erection in 1759. This Brit-

ish fort, situated on the Penobscot River near what is now Fort Point, was one of the most defensible strongholds occupied by the British during the French and Indian War.

[W. D. Williamson, *The History of Maine.*]

ELIZABETH RING

POWWOW, a word drawn from an Algonkin stem referring to magical ritual, appears first in Massachusetts in 1624, used in this sense. By 1812 the meaning in English had changed, and the word was used to designate any gathering of American Indians, whether ceremonial or social. It is in this latter sense that the word continued to be used, often pejoratively, frequently referring to Indian dances and events for the benefit of outsiders.

[Deward E. Walker, Jr., *The Emergent Native Americans.*]

ROBERT F. SPENCER

PRAGMATISM, the name given to a worldwide philosophic movement that was most important in the United States in the late 19th and early 20th centuries. There were two centers in the United States. The one at the University of Chicago was led by John Dewey, who later taught at Columbia, and included James H. Tufts, George Herbert Mead, and Addison W. Moore. The other, with its nucleus at Harvard University, included Charles S. Peirce, William James, Josiah Royce, and Clarence Lewis.

Pragmatism arose as the most sophisticated attempt to reconcile science and religion in the wake of the widespread scholarly acceptance of Darwinian biology. The pragmatists argued that the truth of an idea lay primarily in its ability satisfactorily to orient individuals to the world of which they were a part, but also in its consistency with other ideas and its aesthetic appeal; ideas were plans of action and would be deemed true if action in accordance with them ''worked'' in the long run. Accordingly, the pragmatists accepted the findings and methods of the natural sciences and urged that these methods be applied in all areas of inquiry. But they also thought that religious ideas—for example, belief in the existence of God and in a benign universe—might be justified since, emotionally, they were a source of satisfaction and since such ideas also worked (that is, action in accordance with them met with success). These views were originally expressed in connection with the meaning of scientific concepts by Peirce (''How to Make Our Ideas Clear,'' in *Popular Science Monthly,*

1878). James's exposition was vigorously and forcefully popular, especially in his collected essays *Pragmatism* (1907). For James the chief virtue of the pragmatic account of truth was that it made philosophic speculation concrete and gave its adherents a creed to live by; Peirce dissociated himself from James's nontechnical theorizing. But even James limited the applications of pragmatist doctrine to the affairs of individuals, perhaps because of his early interest in physiology and psychology.

Dewey, steeped in the cultural thought of German idealism, used his version of pragmatism—he called it instrumentalism—to attack educational, social, and political problems, as in *The School and Society* (1899) and *Liberalism and Social Action* (1935). Throughout Dewey's long and prolific career he was involved in political controversy and led many liberal intellectual causes. Pragmatism in its crudest form became widely known as the rationale behind reformist politics: the political pragmatist was the liberal who restricted progressive goals to what was obtainable practically, to programs that could succeed. But for academic philosophers the epistemological implications of the work of earlier pragmatists became important, and in the writing of Clarence Lewis, *Mind and the World-Order* (1929), pragmatism was associated with a rigorous empiricism that had little significance for larger human issues.

[Charles Morris, *The Pragmatic Movement in American Philosophy;* Darnell Rucker, *The Chicago Pragmatists;* H. S. Thayer, *Meaning and Action: A Critical History of Pragmatism.*]

BRUCE KUKLICK

PRAIRIE of the United States is a geographical region whose eastern border is an irregular line running southeast through Minnesota, Wisconsin, and western Indiana and then extending southwest through Illinois, Missouri, Oklahoma, and Texas. Its western boundary merges into the Great Plains. The prairie is a vast area of grassland, as differentiated from the forested land to the east. When settlers first discovered this region, it was thought that the land was too infertile to produce trees and, therefore, that virtually all the valuable farming land was already occupied. One result of this belief was that frontiersmen, with an eye on the Canadian forests, clamored for war against Great Britain in 1812 (*see* War Hawks). So strongly did the idea persist that prairie soil was poor that the timberland was almost always settled first. For example, the rough, rocky portions of Missouri were settled before the rich prairies of the northeast-

ern area. The prairie land had the advantage of being much easier to bring under cultivation. In a few years a whole quarter-section could be bearing crops, whereas in forested areas a decade often found the settler with a comparatively small area cleared. One disadvantage of the prairie as a place for pioneering was the lack of timber for fuel and fencing.

[Ellen Semple, *American History and Its Geographic Conditions.*]

EVERETT DICK

PRAIRIE DOGS, burrowing rodents that formerly infested the Plains in immense numbers from Texas to Canada and the western slope of the Rocky Mountains. Since they lived underground in large colonies, threw up craters of earth at the surface of their burrows (excluding rain), and lived on grass, they destroyed vast areas of good grazing land. The cattlemen considered them pests for this reason and also because horses often broke their legs by stepping in their holes. Prairie dogs do not require any drinking water and do not, as commonly believed, associate on friendly terms with rattlesnakes and owls. Both of the latter are found in prairie dog colonies but live in abandoned burrows; they are natural enemies. One prairie dog colony in Trego County, Kans., extended one hundred miles with a breadth of a half to five miles. Farmers and ranchers have greatly reduced the number of prairie dogs mainly by poisoning, because of their destruction of crops and grass. Protected colonies can be found in South Dakota, Wyoming, Oklahoma, and Texas.

CARL L. CANNON

PRAIRIE DU CHIEN, a city in southwestern Wisconsin, was a French settlement commanding the western end of the Fox-Wisconsin Waterway from the Great Lakes to the Mississippi River. The site was first visited in 1673 by Louis Jolliet and Jacques Marquette. About 1685 Nicolas Perrot, a French officer, built at this site Fort Saint-Nicolas. It was not until the 18th century that the place acquired its present name from a Fox Indian chief named Alim (meaning "dog," who the French called Le Chien). The settlement of French traders and voyageurs began about the middle of the 18th century. Jean Marie Cardinal from the Illinois is known to have been there by 1754. After the cession in 1763 of all this region to the British by the Treaty of Paris, their traders mingled with the French, and during the expansion of the fur trade Prairie du Chien became an important mart. The explorer Jonathan Carver, who visited the village in 1766 and 1767, mentions the great concourse of traders who met each spring, and the rivalry between the British and Spanish traders from Saint Louis and New Orleans.

During the American Revolution a small fort was built by the British at Prairie du Chien, from which a raid was undertaken against the Spanish and Americans at Saint Louis and Cahokia, in southwestern Illinois. This fort was burned to prevent it from falling into the hands of the Americans and Spanish, who made a retaliatory raid.

In 1781 three French-Canadian settlers of Prairie du Chien purchased the site from the Indians, and the village began to grow. By the end of the century it contained about 100 houses and as many families, mostly of French-Canadian origin. Meanwhile, notwithstanding the cession of this region to the United States in 1783 by the Definitive Treaty of Peace, the British maintained a firm hold on the fur trade of the upper Mississippi, and few Americans entered the region. In 1803 some American commissions were granted the British fur traders, and in 1805 Lt. Zebulon M. Pike was sent up the Mississippi to assert the authority of the United States, but without much success.

On the outbreak of the War of 1812 all Americans were driven from the region, and the British enrolled the Indians in their forces. In 1814 Gen. William Clark came up the river from Saint Louis and built Fort Shelby at Prairie du Chien, raising the first American flag in what is now Wisconsin. The British sent an expedition from the Straits of Mackinac to dislodge the Americans. The Americans were defeated, and Fort Shelby became Fort McKay.

After the Treaty of Ghent (1814) Prairie du Chien was occupied permanently by the Americans. Fort Crawford was built in 1816 and American traders and settlers flocked thither. In 1817 the first priest came up the river, and about the same time the first school was begun. The chief traders for the American Fur Company were Joseph Rolette and Hercules Dousman. In 1818 the town became the seat of Crawford County.

Prairie du Chien became a steamboat port in the middle 19th century, the first steamboat going up the river in 1823, and in 1857 the railroad from Milwaukee entered the city. After the Civil War, the development of a variety of industries—the manufacture of fertilizer, cement, woolens, and building fixtures and butter production—led to the granting of a city charter in 1872. The city has remained small, its population in 1970 being only 5,540.

[L. P. Kellogg, *British Régime in Wisconsin and the Northwest*; P. L. Scanlan, *Prairie du Chien: French, British, American.*]

LOUISE PHELPS KELLOGG

PRAIRIE DU CHIEN, INDIAN TREATY AT, signed Aug. 19, 1825. The two great tribes of Chippewa and Sioux had been enemies for over a century and had drawn neighboring tribes into the feud. In 1824 a deputation to Washington, D.C., requested the federal government to set up boundaries between the tribal lands. The treaty of 1825 was called for that purpose. Gen. William Clark of Saint Louis and Gov. Lewis Cass of the Michigan Territory were the American commissioners. More than 1,000 tribal chiefs assembled. The Philadelphia artist, J. O. Lewis, was present, and painted many chiefs from life. A bower was built outside Fort Crawford at the village of Prairie du Chien, the garrison of which preserved order.

This treaty, unlike others made with the Indian, contained no cession of land. Boundaries were established, which the several tribes agreed to respect. The parties to the treaty were Sioux, Chippewa, Sauk and Fox, Potawatomi, Winnebago, and Iowa.

[C. J. Kappler, ed., *Indian Affairs, Laws and Treaties*; Peter L. Scanlan, *Prairie du Chien: French, British, American.*]

LOUISE PHELPS KELLOGG

PRAIRIE FIRES. In the autumn, after the luxuriant grass of the prairie had been frosted, a stroke of lightning, a match carelessly dropped, sparks from a locomotive, or the burning wads from the discharge of a shotgun were enough to start a blazing, leaping, consuming force that moved across the prairie with the speed of the wind, destroying crops, hay, barns, houses, and stock—and even taking the lives of people. The sky was pierced with spires of flame and a devouring inferno raced across the plain. Domestic and wild animals dashed madly ahead of the flame seeking safety. Sometimes entire settlements were devastated. The grand and startling spectacle was one of the greatest terrors to the settlers. So intense was the heat from a prairie fire in South Dakota in 1871 that the wall of the fire leaped across the Vermillion and James rivers as if attracted by a powerful magnet. The settlers in Wells County, N.Dak., in the 1880's observed that prairie fires starting far to the north would burn six weeks or more. Each day the smoke grew more dense until finally the sun would be obscured for days. At night the reflection of fire on the clouds could be seen drawing nearer and nearer. At times, towns were destroyed and communities were broken.

Very little could be accomplished fighting a head fire, but side fires could be put out. It was the unwritten although binding law that at the first word of warning every able-bodied man was to appear with fire-fighting equipment to help extinguish the blaze. A man who slept while neighbors fought fire was despised by the community. Buckets of water and wet sacks were often used to beat out the fire. Sometimes on the range a cow was killed, the body was split in half, and cowboys with ropes dragged each half of the carcass over the side fires, putting them out as fast as the men could ride.

Everyone venturing onto the prairie carried matches for personal safety. If caught by a prairie fire, the person burned a spot on which to stand. This technique of fighting fire by burning another area in the path of the fire is known as backfiring. Settlers protected their farms and ranges by plowing two sets of furrows around their property and burning off a wide strip between the two plowed areas. When the prairies were settled and the land broken, the dreaded prairie fires disappeared.

[Everett Dick, *The Sod House Frontier*.]
EVERETT DICK

PRAIRIE GROVE, BATTLE AT

PRAIRIE GROVE, BATTLE AT (Dec. 7, 1862), also known as the Battle of Fayetteville or Battle of Illinois Creek. After the Confederate defeat at Corinth, Miss., Confederate Gen. John Pemberton ordered Gen. Theophilus Holmes to send Thomas Hindman's Arkansas troops to Vicksburg, Miss. Resentful, Hindman planned to attack the Union forces under Gen. James Blunt before leaving the state. Learning that Gen. Francis Herron was coming up to reinforce Blunt at Prairie Grove, Ark., Hindman decided to destroy Herron first and then engage Blunt. Confederate Gen. John Marmaduke's cavalry was successful against Herron, but when Hindman advanced his infantry, instead of attacking he went into a defensive position. This tactic allowed Blunt to join Herron, and with superior numbers they forced Hindman to retreat in defeat to Van Buren, Ark.

[R. U. Johnson and C. C. Buel, eds., *Battles and Leaders of the Civil War*, vol. III.]
ROBERT S. THOMAS

PRAIRIE SCHOONER, a large wagon used for long-distance travel and freight transport in the 19th century. Originally, the wagon was made with the sides of the box sloping outward. Six or seven arching wooden bows supported a canvas cover. Seen in the distance, the vehicle so resembled a ship at sea as to suggest the name. The descendant of the old Conestoga wagon, in which Pittsburgh "stogies" were early transported to Philadelphia, the prairie schooner was also the ancestor of the modern truck and trailer. First brought into common use in the Santa Fe trade soon after 1821, it was later used by the Mormons, by California goldseekers, by emigrants to Oregon, by freighters operating on the Great Plains, and, in a modified form, by settlers seeking homesteads on the western prairies. Among the first prairie schooners used in the West were the "Murphy wagons," with iron axles, made in Saint Louis. Other types were made in Indianapolis, Chicago, and Kenosha, Wis. The prairie schooner was usually drawn by three to six yoke of oxen or by four to six mules. Its importance in the settlement and development of the West was enormous. It was not only the chief means for the transportation of goods, but it also provided a home for the pioneer family as it journeyed west in search of land.

[William Francis Hooker, *The Prairie Schooner*.]
EDWARD EVERETT DALE

PREEMPTION, the right of first purchase, a significant aspect of U.S. land law in the 19th century. Compact orderly settlement in groups or colonies and a continuous source of income for the federal Treasury were the principal motives for the early land policies of the U.S. government. Thus, settlement was restricted to surveyed areas, and the surveys were not made far in advance of demand (*see* Public Lands, Survey of). Inevitably, however, the lack of restraint and social control on the frontier led to the breakdown of these policies. Settlers pushed farther into the unsurveyed territory, even into Indian Country, and if forcibly removed, they would promptly return and reconstruct their homes when the troops had withdrawn. Since all lands when first brought on the market were put up at auction and sold to the highest bidder, the threat of the forthcoming government sale hung over the squatters like the sword of Damocles (*see* Public Land Sales). Their improvements might give value to their land, but they did not provide the necessary cash, always scarce on the frontier, to buy the land at the auction sale. There was always the danger that speculators might purchase their claims.

Furthermore, in the absence of land laws, squatters had difficulty in protecting their improvements against claim jumpers before the day of sale arrived.

The squatters early pressured Congress to grant them the right of preempting their claims in advance of the land sale, so the settlers would not be obliged to bid for their land against speculators. Congress, increasingly responsive to demands of the West, granted preemption rights to sixteen special groups before 1830, and between 1830 and 1840, it gave preemption rights on five occasions to all squatters then residing upon the surveyed lands. In 1841 a general law was passed, which gave the preemption right for up to 160 acres to any squatter who was then located on or in the future might settle on surveyed public lands. This act, although a victory for the West, by no means satisfied the settlers on the frontier. It applied to neither Indian reservations nor unsurveyed lands; it did not provide for free grants to actual settlers; and it retained the minimum price of $1.25 per acre.

Since squatters on surveyed lands before and on unsurveyed lands after 1841 were not sure of obtaining preemption rights, they organized claim associations to provide mutual protection. But such associations were powerless to aid, nor did the preemption law protect, the penniless settler who was threatened with the loss of his claim if he could not raise the money ($200 for 160 acres) necessary to buy the land before the government auction.

The 1841 preemption law remained in effect for fifty years, but in the late 19th century it was subject to serious abuses. In areas where the size of a squatter's claim to public land was limited, predatory interests found it possible to acquire large tracts by employing "floaters" to preempt land for them. False swearing, bribery of the land officers, laxity of supervision, and general western approval of such practices made evasion of the law easy. Finally, in 1891, when sentiment against the monopolization of the public lands by corrupt groups had become sufficiently aroused, the land system was given a thorough overhauling, and the preemption law was repealed. For thirty years it had outlived its usefulness. (*See also* Homestead Movement.)

[B. H. Hibbard, *History of the Public Land Policies;* R. M. Robbins, "Pre-emption—A Frontier Triumph," *Mississippi Valley Historical Review,* vol. 18.]

PAUL W. GATES

PREFERENTIAL VOTING, a method of voting under which the voter expresses a first choice, second choice, and sometimes third and further choices among the candidates nominated. It is frequently used as a substitute for primary elections, which it makes unnecessary. It is one feature of the Hare system of proportional representation and is also used in several different forms for majority elections of individual officials.

[C. G. Hoag and G. H. Hallett, Jr., *Proportional Representation.*]

GEORGE H. HALLETT, JR.

PREPAREDNESS, the name of a campaign to strengthen U.S. military forces after the outbreak of World War I in Europe. The movement was under way in 1914, before the war was more than a few months old, and it gathered momentum steadily as it became clear that the belligerents were interfering more and more with American interests and as the danger of American involvement in the struggle grew.

An early landmark in the preparedness movement was the publication of Theodore Roosevelt's *America and the World War* in January 1915. From that time forward Roosevelt was much in the public eye as an advocate of larger forces; his *Fear God and Take Your Own Part* (1916) was another literary contribution to the cause. Associated with him was Gen. Leonard Wood, and both men favored some form of universal military service. The most concrete result of Wood's efforts was the officers' training camp for business and professional men, conducted at Plattsburgh, N.Y., in the summers of 1915 and 1916. This enterprise, although small-scale compared with the mobilization effort later required, attracted much attention and had considerable effect on public opinion. During 1914 and 1915, moreover, two organizations came into being that thereafter played a great part in the preparedness campaign: the National Security League and the League to Enforce Peace. Both included in their membership many national figures, and although they approached the issue from different viewpoints, both were influential in advancing the cause of preparedness. Such books as F. L. Huidekoper's *The Military Unpreparedness of the United States* and Hudson Maxim's *Defenseless America* (both published in 1915) doubtless had some further effect.

Initially, the national administration was decidedly cool to the preparedness agitation, and President Woodrow Wilson was the target of much abuse from leaders of the movement, especially Roosevelt. As time passed the president apparently decided that preparedness was a logical corollary to his policy of attempting to compel the combatants to respect American rights. The turning point seems to have been the first German submarine campaign, which began in February 1915; from that time Wilson himself increasingly became an advocate of larger armaments. In December 1915 the administration presented to Congress a comprehensive national defense plan, which (after much discussion and numerous alterations) was enacted into law in the National Defense Act of June 3 and the naval appropriations act of Aug. 29, 1916. These statutes provided for an unprecedented increase in the country's armed forces. War with Germany came in April 1917, before the authorized army reorganization was more than begun; in addition, the new naval program proved to be misdirected, emphasizing construction of heavy ships rather than of the innumerable small craft needed for antisubmarine work. Thus, the material achievement of the preparedness agitation was small in comparison with the tremendous national effort of 1917–18, although it was not without value. Perhaps the campaign's most useful work had been in preparing the nation psychologically for the ordeal that lay ahead, and in particular for the imposition of compulsory service.

[John Garry Clifford, *The Plattsburg Training Camp Movement, 1913–1920;* Walter Millis, *Road to War.*]

C. P. STACEY

PRESBYTERIANISM. The name of the Presbyterian church is derived from its form of church government by a hierarchy of church courts composed of both teaching (clerical) and ruling (lay) elders, or presbyters. Doctrinally, Presbyterian churches are part of the Reformed tradition, founded by John Calvin of Geneva in the 16th century. Their most widely accepted standard is the Westminster Confession of Faith, which was drafted in 1646, during the English Civil War. The theology of the confession was influenced chiefly by the Puritan tradition. It stresses the role of the divine decrees, the use of the covenant system, the identification of the Lord's Day with the Christian sabbath, and the subjective operation of grace.

Although the Scotch-Irish have exerted considerable influence on the development of American Presbyterianism, the church has never been merely a reproduction of the Church of Scotland. Francis Mekamie, often called the founder of American Presbyterianism, organized the Presbytery of Philadelphia in 1706. By 1716 the church was large enough to form itself into a synod representing four presbyteries and thirty ministers. A large number of these clergymen were from New England, and conflict between the Scotch-Irish, led by John Thomson, and those clergymen was characteristic of early Presbyterian history. The original dispute concerned the terms of subscription to the Westminster standard, and implicitly the issue of the independence of the American church. It was settled by a compromise in 1729 that adopted a looser form of subscription than was current in Europe.

The Presbyterian church was both active in the Great Awakening and deeply divided over its significance. The center of Presbyterian Evangelical Calvinism was the Log College, established by William Tennent to train clergymen. Its graduates, partly under the influence of the Dutch Reformed pastor Theodore Frelinghuysen, were active revivalists and tended to form their own ecclesiastical party. Gilbert Tennent, the son of William, was the leader of the small revival that swept the middle colonies in the 1730's and was later a leading supporter of the evangelistic tours of George Whitefield. As the revival grew, so did tension between the two parties in the church. In 1741 Gilbert Tennent preached the so-called Nottingham sermon, "The Danger of an Unconverted Ministry," which heralded the coming division of the church into the Synod at New York, or New Side, formed by the Tennents and John Dickenson, and the Synod of Philadelphia, or Old Side, headed by Thomson. A reconciliation occurred only after the New Side made diplomatic advances to the Old Side pastors. But the controversy lay just beneath the surface, and the theological issues raised by evangelicalism were to contribute to the later Old School–New School schism.

In 1801 the Presbyterians joined the Congregationalists in the Plan of Union, which was intended to promote a joint endeavor in the winning of the West. The success of the plan, however, caused controversy, and as Congregationalism drifted toward a more liberal theology, it was abrogated. Most of the churches founded under the plan adhered to the New School theology.

Although the spread of Presbyterianism was initially hampered by its insistence on a learned ministry, its high standards enabled it to become the educator of the West. Presbyterians were the great college founders of the region, and, in the period before the Civil War, exercised the greatest cultural influence on that emerging society.

The question of slavery lay beneath many of the struggles in the Presbyterian church prior to the Civil War, and despite attempts by church leaders to resolve the issue, it refused to disappear. Although the abrogation of the Plan of Union in 1837 and the division of the church into New School and Old School groups were ostensibly over theological issues, it appears that the question of race was a hidden item on the agenda of the southern delegations. The New School Presbyterians were unable to maintain unity after 1857, when the small number of southern evangelicals withdrew from the parent body. The Old School remained united until hostilities actually began. After the Civil War, Old School and New School factions in both the North and South reunited, leaving the main division in Presbyterianism on regional lines, and as late as 1958 the Presbyterian Church in the United States (southern) refused merger with the northern body.

Since the Civil War the Presbyterian churches have been troubled by theological controversies that have threatened to destroy their precarious unity. The most serious of these was the fundamentalist-modernist controversy in the early part of the 20th century. The Old School theologians of Princeton Seminary formulated the defense of the traditional understanding of scripture against the higher criticism. In 1892 the general assembly of the northern church accepted the Princeton interpretation of the issue and suspended several seminary professors, most notably Charles A. Briggs of Union Seminary, from the ministry. In 1910 the general assembly passed a resolution declaring five fundamentals (inerrancy of the Bible, the virgin birth, substitutionary atonement, bodily resurrection, and the miracles of Christ) necessary articles of belief. Because of this decision, further discussion moved underground until the 1920's, when it reemerged over the teachings of Harry Emerson Fosdick, a Baptist serving the First Presbyterian Church of New York City. Given the choice of conforming or resigning, Fosdick resigned.

Since the early 1960's there have been signs that the Presbyterian church, at least in the North, has moved toward greater theological comprehensiveness. Following the merger of the Presbyterian Church in the United States of America and the United Presbyterian Church of North America in 1958, the new church began examining its confessional standards. The result of its deliberations was the adoption of the Book of Confessions, which added to the traditional Westminster standard such traditional symbols as the Apostles Scots Confession of 1560 and such modern statements of faith as the Barmen Declaration (1934) and the Confession of 1967. Although some lay groups protested the new position, it seemed to be firmly established in the mid-1970's.

The principal Presbyterian denominations and their 1974 membership figures are Associate Reformed Presbyterian Church, 28,711; Cumberland Presbyterian Church, 87,838; Orthodox Presbyterian Church, 14,871; Presbyterian Church in the United States (southern), 951,788; Reformed Presbyterian Church of North America, 5,560; Second Cumberland Presbyterian Church, 30,000; and United Presbyterian Church in the United States of America (northern), 2,908,958.

[Charles A. Anderson, *The Presbyterian Enterprise;* Gaius Jackson Slosser, *They Seek a Country: The American Presbyterians;* Ernest Trice Thomson, *Presbyterians in the South;* Leonard J. Trinterud, *The Forming of an American Tradition: A Re-examination of Colonial Presbyterianism.*]
GLENN T. MILLER

PRESERVATION MOVEMENT. The historic-preservation movement in the United States—the varied aspirations and actions of Americans to save their tangible historical and cultural heritage—began in 1850 when New York State became the first agency, public or private, to preserve officially a historic house as a museum: the Hasbrouck House, George Washington's headquarters at Newburgh, N.Y. Although there was great national enthusiasm to memorialize the first president, Congress rejected three proposals that the U.S. government acquire Mount Vernon, Washington's estate in Virginia. In 1858 a private group, the Mount Vernon Ladies' Association of the Union, rescued the estate.

The first federally purchased historic house was the Custis-Lee Mansion in Arlington, Va.; it was bought in 1883. The first federal park tract protected for historic value was Casa Grande, an excavated Indian pueblo in Arizona that was acquired by authorization of Congress in 1889.

The U.S. preservation movement can be followed through national legislation. The passage of the Antiquities Act in 1906 (Public Law 209) authorized the president to declare as national monuments historic landmarks, historic and prehistoric structures, and other objects of historic or scientific value located on lands owned or controlled by the government. The Historic Sites Act of 1935 (Public Law 74–292) declared it a national policy to preserve for public use historic sites, buildings, and objects of national significance for the people of the United States. The National Trust for Historic Preservation of 1949 authorized the establishment of a nonprofit, educational corporation to further the purpose of the Historic Sites Act; to facilitate public participation in preservation through service, education, and counsel; and to accept and administer properties significant in American history and culture for the public.

The National Historic Preservation Act of 1966 (Public Law 89–665) reaffirmed the national policy for preservation, acknowledged that governmental and nongovernmental preservation programs up to that time were inadequate to preserve the national heritage, and stated that although the major preservation burdens were borne and major efforts initiated by the private sector, the federal government should accelerate its activities and give maximum encouragement to the National Trust for Historic Preservation and to local and state governmental efforts. The preservation program of the National Park Service, a bureau of the Department of the Interior, was strengthened. Also, the National Register for Historic Places—which lists districts, sites, buildings, structures, and objects of local, regional, state, and national significance—was expanded. Heads of federal agencies were required to consider the effect on National Register properties of proposed federal projects. Conflicts between projects and properties were to be reported for comment to the Advisory Council on Historic Preservation, a unit established by the act. The act also authorized grants to the states for 50 percent of the cost of preparing statewide historic-preservation plans and historic-site surveys and gave assistance to preservation projects. Matching grants were authorized to the National Trust for its educational, technical, and properties programs.

Other national legislation that assists in the preservation of the American historical and cultural heritage includes the amended Surplus Property Act, 1944; the National Foundation on the Arts and the Humanities Act, 1965; the National Museum Act, 1966; the Demonstration Cities and Metropolitan Development Act, 1966; the Transportation Act, 1966; and the National Environmental Policy Act, 1969.

The 1966 National Historic Preservation Act and subsequent national preservation legislation were instigated by the rapid development of available land following World War II. Urbanization and increasing population brought highway construction, commercial and residential development, industry, and other developments that posed preservation problems.

Since 1850 historic preservation has developed from a pastime to a national movement. Preservationists work for private historical societies and action groups and for local, state, and federal public agencies. They are involved in the protection of one or many structures or a district with a total character greater than the sum of its individual elements. The National Trust sets national standards and provides direction for its members and the general public. In 1975 it had more than 75,000 individual members and affiliated organizations and a $5.8 million annual budget; it owned thirteen historic properties, which from June 1974 to June 1975 were visited by more than 230,000 people.

Government and such private groups as the National Trust are attempting to make preservation relevant to people of all income levels and to all racial and ethnic groups. Every American has a history and should have a tangible cultural heritage. Preservationists are concerned not only with the restoration and viewing of prime landmarks; they also advocate the rehabilitation of properties of lesser importance for rescue. The variety of properties in the urban and rural environment is vital to the quality of American life.

In the past, persons concerned about cultural values were not activists but appreciators; they were busy recording history and quietly enjoying it. Today preservationists are vigilantes participating in progress and are helping to make history by causing cultural values to be considered in all planning and development.

[David E. Finley, *History of the National Trust for Historic Preservation, 1947–1963;* Robert R. Garvey and Terry B. Morton, "The United States Government in Historic Preservation," *Momentum,* vol. 2 (1968); Charles B. Hosmer, Jr., *Presence of the Past—A History of the Preservation Movement in the United States Before Williamsburg;* U.S. Conference of Mayors and the Ford Foundation, Special Committee on Historic Preservation, *With Heritage So Rich.*]

TERRY B. MORTON

PRESIDENT, a forty-four-gun American frigate that saw extensive action in the War of 1812. Built in New York between 1794 and 1800, the ship first attracted public attention in 1811. Stationed off Chesapeake Bay, under the command of John Rodgers, it replied with a withering broadside to a suspicious shot fired in the darkness by the British sloop *Little Belt*. The *President*'s action, considered just retribution for British insults, delighted Americans. Rodgers subsequently fired the first shot of the War of 1812, in a chase of the *Belvidera;* he cruised extensively, but with no victories and few prizes.

After being blockaded in New York for a year, the *President,* then under Stephen Decatur, attempted to escape to sea on Jan. 14, 1815, but was overtaken, first by the British frigate *Endymion,* which it finally crippled, and then by the frigates *Tenedos* and *Pomone.* Surrounded by superior forces, Decatur, himself twice wounded, felt obliged to surrender, a decision later criticized by naval historian Alfred T. Mahan but approved by public opinion of Decatur's day. The *President* was taken to Bermuda and then to Spithead, England, but it never saw service under the British flag.

[A. T. Mahan, *Sea Power in Its Relations to the War of 1812.*]

WALTER B. NORRIS

PRESIDENT. The office of the president, created by the U.S. Constitution, is a depository of vast powers. First, there are the powers conferred by the Constitution. For example, the Constitution vests the executive power in the president and charges him to take care that the laws are faithfully executed. He is also commander in chief of the armed forces. Some of his constitutional powers, such as the veto, pertain to the legislative process.

Much of a president's authority is delegated to him by statute, to enable him to implement national policies. Covering a wide array of topics, from organization of the executive branch to tariffs and from labor-management relations to policy on national resources, such authority reflects the variety of functions and services of the late 20th-century American government. These powers, like the president's constitutional powers, are frequently granted in broad language and confer upon him considerable discretionary authority. The very complexity of modern government also means that many of these powers are not so much exercised by the president directly as by subordinates, in his name.

The third kind of power exercised by the president of the United States is extraconstitutional—what John Locke defined as the power to act "according to discretion for the public good without the prescription of law." A good example may be seen in some of the actions of President Abraham Lincoln during the Civil War: unauthorized expenditures of funds and independent raising of an army. In almost every instance of national emergency—a devastating depression, a major war—presidents have exceeded their constitutional and legal powers, and such actions have generally been legitimized through public approval. Such a tradition is at the core of the modern presidency: that the president as the sole representative of all the people possesses great power to preserve and protect the nation.

The presidency is an evolving, rather than a static, institution. While it is encrusted with custom and tradition, as an office it differs significantly from what was envisioned for it by its founders. It is a mixture of traditional and newly acquired functions. Like other institutions, the U.S. presidency has been conditioned by the forces and pressures that affect society generally and has thus been significantly altered over the years. Among the factors that have influenced its development are the following: (1) democratization of the means of nominating and electing the chief executive, lending substance to the claim that he is the only official elected by all the people; (2) ambiguity in the constitutional phrases defining presidential power and duties; (3) expansion in the role of the government, and the consequent creation of a vast bureaucracy under the president; (4) recurring periods of emergency and peril, during which the executive power seems to thrive and expand; and (5) the rise of the United States as a major world power and the preoccupation with foreign policy in the political arena, an area in which the president has long-standing advantages over the other branches of the government.

The office of president is also subject to the influence of personality. Each occupant of the office brings a personal dimension to it: his own political skills and abilities, his own vision and goals. Throughout history a number of broad presidential types have emerged. One is a literalist president, who functions in close obedience to the letter of the Constitution and the traditional separation of powers. Presidential powers are seen by such an incumbent mainly in a negative sense, restricting and confining; to him, Congress is in many ways the preeminent branch, needing little guidance or direction from the president. Such a chief executive plays the political role sparingly, preferring to remain above the battle. In the 19th century there were many such presidents—James Buchanan, Franklin Pierce, Ulysses S. Grant, James A. Garfield. Examples of 20th-century presidents of this type would include William H. Taft, Warren G. Harding, and Calvin Coolidge. At the other end of the continuum is a strong president. Such a president views his powers with a maximum liberality and, in the process of using them, frequently incites constitutional controversies; he establishes new precedents and breaks old ones. The

PRESIDENTS OF THE UNITED STATES

	DATE OF INAUGURATION	STATE OF RESIDENCE	PARTY
George Washington	1789	Virginia	Federalist
John Adams	1797	Massachusetts	Federalist
Thomas Jefferson	1801	Virginia	Democratic-Republican
James Madison	1809	Virginia	Democratic-Republican
James Monroe	1817	Virginia	Democratic-Republican
John Quincy Adams	1825	Massachusetts	Democratic-Republican
Andrew Jackson	1829	Tennessee	Democratic
Martin Van Buren	1837	New York	Democratic
William Henry Harrison	1841	Ohio	Whig
John Tyler [1]	1841	Virginia	Whig
James K. Polk	1845	Tennessee	Democratic
Zachary Taylor	1849	Louisiana	Whig
Millard Fillmore [1]	1850	New York	Whig
Franklin Pierce	1853	New Hampshire	Democratic
James Buchanan	1857	Pennsylvania	Democratic
Abraham Lincoln	1861	Illinois	Republican
Andrew Johnson [1]	1865	Tennessee	Union
Ulysses S. Grant	1869	Illinois	Republican
Rutherford B. Hayes	1877	Ohio	Republican
James A. Garfield	1881	Ohio	Republican
Chester A. Arthur [1]	1881	New York	Republican
Grover Cleveland	1885	New York	Democratic
Benjamin Harrison	1889	Ohio	Republican
Grover Cleveland	1893	New York	Democratic

PRESIDENTS OF THE UNITED STATES (*Continued*)

	DATE OF INAUGURATION	STATE OF RESIDENCE	PARTY
William McKinley	1897	Ohio	Republican
Theodore Roosevelt [1]	1901	New York	Republican
William Howard Taft	1909	Ohio	Republican
Woodrow Wilson	1913	New Jersey	Democratic
Warren G. Harding	1921	Ohio	Republican
Calvin Coolidge [1]	1923	Massachusetts	Republican
Herbert Hoover	1929	California	Republican
Franklin D. Roosevelt	1933	New York	Democratic
Harry S. Truman [1]	1945	Missouri	Democratic
Dwight D. Eisenhower	1953	New York	Republican
John F. Kennedy	1961	Massachusetts	Democratic
Lyndon B. Johnson [1]	1963	Texas	Democratic
Richard M. Nixon	1969	California	Republican
Gerald R. Ford [2]	1974	Michigan	Republican

[1] Vice-presidents who succeeded to the presidency upon the death of an incumbent president.

[2] Vice-president who succeeded to the presidency upon the resignation of a president.

emphasis of his activity is political, not legalistic. The president sees himself not merely as an administrative officer, but, in John F. Kennedy's phrase, as "the vital center of action in our whole scheme of government." This interpretation of function is represented by Andrew Jackson, Lincoln, Woodrow Wilson, Theodore Roosevelt, Franklin D. Roosevelt, and Kennedy. The third type of president takes a position about midway between the first two. He sometimes emphasizes the purely administrative aspects of the presidency and at other times the broader dimensions of the office. At one time he defers to Congress; subsequently he pushes and prods the legislators. The distinctive trait of such a president is that he views the essential presidential function defensively, using executive energy and weapons (such as the veto) to maintain an existing equilibrium. Examples include John Adams, John Quincy Adams, Martin Van Buren, and Grover Cleveland. Dwight D. Eisenhower might also belong in this category. Most modern commentators suggest that regardless of a particular incumbent's theory or view of the presidency, national demands and expectations push a president more and more to adopt the strong role.

The presidency has been a fairly flexible and adaptable institution. Originally selected by a few, the president is now popularly elected. Many 19th-century presidents regarded themselves primarily as administrators, but 20th-century presidents have performed a greater variety of roles, ranging from chief legislator to guardian of domestic peace and manager of prosperity. To help a president perform his expanded duties, an array of advisers, offices, and councils has been created, so that in some respects the presidency has been institutionalized. And it is likely that this development and adaptation will continue. The presidency will probably remain the focus of great demands and expectations. Its tasks and duties are so varied and complex and of such significance to the nation and the world that it has become one of the most powerful positions in the world. At the same time the circumstances of the age have subjected the president's leadership, domestic and foreign, to many limitations. His powers seem vast, but he is constrained in ways unknown to his predecessors, and when his powers are measured against the problems he confronts, they do not seem so great. And as a repository of high public hopes and expectations, presidential action or inaction must inevitably disillusion some people.

[Dorothy Buckton James, *The Contemporary Presidency;* Louis Koenig, *The Chief Executive;* Dale Vinyard, *The Presidency;* Aaron Wildavsky, *The Presidency.*]

DALE VINYARD

PRESIDENT, WAR POWERS OF. *See* War Powers of the President.

PRESIDENTIAL DISABILITY. Article II, Section 1, of the Constitution provides that if the president is unable to discharge the powers and duties of his office, they shall devolve on the vice-president. A number of presidents have been disabled for periods of time (James A. Garfield, Woodrow Wilson, Dwight D. Eisenhower). Until the Twenty-fifth Amendment was adopted in 1967, there were no prescribed procedures for establishing such inability or for determining when it had ceased—and without such procedures a vice-president might be reluctant to take action for fear he would be viewed as a usurper and provoke a constitutional crisis. But some presidents reached informal understandings with their vice-presidents on this issue (Eisenhower–Richard M. Nixon, John F. Kennedy–Lyndon B. Johnson, Johnson–Hubert H. Humphrey).

In 1967 the Twenty-fifth Amendment was adopted to deal, at least in part, with this problem. Disability extends not only to physical illness but also to mental illness or to a president who is missing or captured by an enemy. The determination of such disability can be made either by the president himself or by the vice-president acting with a majority of the cabinet or some "other body as Congress may by law provide."

In such cases the vice-president is to serve as acting president. The end of such disability can be determined by the president or, in the event the vice-president and cabinet do not agree with the president, by Congress. While certainly not a perfect solution, the amendment tends to clear up some ambiguities and to provide some rules and procedures for handling a potentially serious problem.

DALE VINYARD

PRESIDENTIAL ELECTIONS. *See* Campaigns, Presidential; Election of the President; Electoral College.

PRESIDENTIAL EXEMPTION FROM SUBPOENA. Following the passage of the Alien and Sedition Acts in 1798, Thomas Cooper, scientist and political philosopher, criticized acts of President John Adams and was tried for violation of the sedition act in 1800. Cooper asked the court to issue a subpoena for Adams so that he could prove the truth of the allegedly seditious statements. Justice Samuel Chase forbade summoning the president and declared the attempt to subpoena him an improper and indecent act.

The question of subpoenaing the president arose again during the trial of Aaron Burr in 1807. Chief Justice John Marshall declared that the president was subject to subpoena because no distinction was made as to persons subject to such compulsory processes of the Court. (English law did make an exception in the case of the king.) Marshall stated that if there was any ground on which a president could claim exemption, it must be that national business demanded his whole time. But this was no reason why the subpoena should not be issued, even though it might be a reason why the subpoena should not be obeyed. Marshall issued the subpoena, but President Thomas Jefferson flatly refused to appear. There was no way of forcing his appearance, and a precedent was established to the effect that the president could not be subpoenaed into court against his will.

In 1974 the Supreme Court faced the issue of whether or not President Richard M. Nixon could be compelled by a subpoena *duces tecum* to produce for use in a criminal case the tape-recorded conversations that ultimately played such an important role in his downfall (*see* Nixon, Resignation of; Watergate). The Court, in *United States* v. *Nixon,* 418 U.S. 683 (1974), decided that the president could, under this particular set of facts, be subpoenaed: "We conclude that when the ground for asserting privilege as to subpoenaed materials sought for use in a criminal trial is based only on the generalized interest in confidentiality, it cannot prevail over the fundamental demands of due process of law in the fair administration of criminal justice. The generalized assertion of privilege must yield to the demonstrated, specific need for evidence in a pending criminal trial.'' The Court went on to carefully explain how the federal district court trying the Watergate defendants should proceed: ''If a president concludes that compliance with a subpoena would be injurious to the public interest he may properly, as was done here, invoke a claim of privilege on the return of the subpoena. Upon receiving a claim of privilege from the Chief Executive, it became the further duty of the District Court to treat the subpoenaed material as presumptively privileged. . . .'' Citing *United States* v. *Burr,* the Court further stated that it was then the duty of the special prosecutor in the Watergate trial to show that the presidential material was ''essential to the justice of the [pending criminal] case'' and reaffirmed Marshall's 1807 comment that ''[I]n no case of this kind would a court be required to proceed against the President as against an ordinary individual.''

CHARLES MARION THOMAS
HAROLD W. CHASE

PRESIDENTIAL MESSAGES. The president of the United States has a number of opportunities to present messages to Congress. For example, Article II, Section 3, of the Constitution charges the president to give Congress information on the state of the Union, and tradition has dictated that he do so annually. This event is an important element in focusing congressional and public attention on a president's proposed programs and policies. It is frequently supplemented by special, detailed messages on individual areas of policy (education, civil rights, welfare reform). Other opportunities are provided by the Budget and Accounting Act of 1921, which imposes on the president the duty of presenting an annual executive budget to Congress, and by the Full Employment Act of 1946, which requires an annual economic report, largely prepared by the president's Council of Economic Advisers.

Such messages are reflective of the role the president plays in the legislative process. Some commentators have labeled the president the ''chief legislator.'' Members of Congress anticipate that such messages will be followed by administration bills,

backed up by bargaining and persuasion. Presidents in the 20th century have thus converted the message-giving authority into a legislative-planning and bill-originating function.

At times such messages, even if given before Congress, may be primarily designed to mobilize and mold public opinion in support of the president's policies and to induce the public to prod reluctant legislators. Presidential efforts easily command prime television time and front-page coverage by the press.

DALE VINYARD

PRESIDENTIAL SUCCESSION. Article II, Section 1, of the U.S. Constitution provides for the succession of the vice-president to the presidency of the United States in case of the death or resignation of the president or his removal from office. Eight presidents had died in office by 1975: William Henry Harrison, Zachary Taylor, Abraham Lincoln, James A. Garfield, William McKinley, Warren G. Harding, Franklin D. Roosevelt, and John F. Kennedy. One president, Richard M. Nixon, had resigned.

Before ratification of the Twenty-fifth Amendment in 1967, there was no clearly defined constitutional line of succession if the vice-president should succeed to the presidency and then die, but Congress, in 1947, had provided by law for such an eventuality by establishing a line of succession. The speaker of the House of Representatives was placed next in line after the vice-president; next came the president pro tempore of the Senate; and then the members of the cabinet, beginning with the secretary of state. An earlier act (1886) had placed the members of the cabinet in line after the vice-president.

The Twenty-fifth Amendment provides a means of filling the vice-presidential post in case of a vacancy, which had occurred sixteen times by 1975: seven vice-presidents had died in office, one had resigned, and eight had succeeded to the presidency. The amendment empowers the president to nominate a vice-president, subject to confirmation by Congress (majority vote in both chambers). If so confirmed, the new vice-president would then be eligible for succession to the presidency. This amendment was first used in 1973 upon the resignation of Spiro Agnew, when President Nixon nominated Rep. Gerald R. Ford for the position. Subsequently, when Nixon resigned and Ford became president, Ford nominated Gov. Nelson Rockefeller for the post.

The Twentieth Amendment, ratified in 1933, deals with another possible problem: if the president-elect dies or fails to qualify for office by the date of the inauguration, the vice-president-elect shall act as president. Furthermore, if neither the president-elect nor the vice-president-elect qualifies, Congress is empowered to declare who shall act as president.

[Harold W. Chase and Craig R. Ducat, eds., *Corwin's The Constitution and What It Means Today*.]

DALE VINYARD

PRESIDENTIAL TITLE. The title for the new chief executive of the United States was the subject of some controversy at the Constitutional Convention of 1787, as was the question of titular etiquette in general. The Committee of Detail recommended that "The Executive Power of the United States shall be vested in a single Person. His Stile shall be, 'The President of the United States of America'; and his Title shall be, 'His Excellency.' " The Committee on Style reported more simply, "The executive power shall be vested in a President of the United States of America," and this was the formulation adopted.

The contest over titles was continued into the First Congress. Shortly after he was installed as vice-president, John Adams lectured the Senate on the necessity and propriety of titles, and some three weeks of the opening deliberations were consumed in debating this matter. A Senate committee, after deciding that the ambassadorial "his excellency" was too paltry for the ruler of a young republic, urged that the chief executive be addressed as "His Highness, the President of the United States of America and Protector of their Liberties," and it is stated that this was the title George Washington preferred. The more republican House of Representatives remained obdurate, and the Senate, while feeling that "it would be proper to annex a respectable title to the office," was "desirous of preserving harmony with the House of Representatives" and agreed that "the present address be 'To the President of the United States,' without addition of title."

The practice of restricting the use of titles to the simple constitutional or statutory designation of the office has never been deviated from since. "Excellency" has sometimes been applied by private persons, but the formal style is to address the president or any officer in his official capacity solely by the title of his office.

[Max Farrand, ed., *The Records of the Federal Convention of 1787*; L. H. Irvine, *Dictionary of Titles*; Randolph Keim, *Society in Washington*.]

ERIC CYRIL BELLQUIST

PRESIDIO, a Spanish institution established primarily to hold the frontiers of Spain's territory in America against foreign aggressors and to protect the missions. Presidios were forts or posts where soldiers lived with their familes, cultivating the surrounding land. The number of soldiers varied; along the northern frontier there were seldom more than fifty residing at a presidio. The presidios were not entirely self-supporting because they received subsidies from the viceroy of Mexico. They were located in California, Arizona, New Mexico, Texas, the West Indies, and Spanish Florida, which at the time included Georgia and the Carolinas.

[L. E. Fisher, *Viceregal Administration in the Spanish American Colonies*.]

LILLIAN ESTELLE FISHER

PRESQUE ISLE, FORT, was constructed on the shore of Lake Erie at the site of present-day Erie, Pa., under the direction of an engineer attached to the French command of Capt. Pierre Paul Marin. Work was begun in the late spring of 1753 and was completed in June or July of that year. Made of chestnut logs 15 feet high, the fort was "about 120 feet square, [with] a log house in each square [corner], a gate to the southward and another to the N.ward." From 1753 to 1759 it served as a base of operations for the further projection of the Pennsylvania line of French forts—LeBoeuf, Machault, and Duquesne—and for the transportation of troops and supplies from Montreal to Duquesne. After the French abandoned Fort Presque Isle on Aug. 13, 1759, the British utilized it as a frontier outpost in dealing with hostile Indians of the region. During the general Indian uprising of 1763 (*see* Pontiac's War), the Indians captured the fort on June 22 and burned it. A subsequent fortification, designated as Presque Isle, was erected on a nearby site in the summer of 1795 to protect the commissioners who were laying out the town of Erie, but nothing was done to restore the original French fort.

R. J. FERGUSON

PRESS, FREEDOM OF THE. *See* **Freedom of the Press.**

PRESS GANG. The British government never devised an orderly procedure for impressment, or conscription, for naval service. In practice, captains of short-handed men-of-war sent armed details to scour English waterfronts or board merchantmen to exercise direct and immediate conscription. Lieutenants commanding these "press gangs" were ruthlessly undiscriminating. Their use in colonial ports was a minor cause of the American Revolution. Applied to American merchantmen by the British after independence, impressment was a major cause of the War of 1812.

[J. F. Zimmerman, *Impressment of American Seamen.*]
JIM DAN HILL

PRESSING TO DEATH. According to former English judicial practice, if a person accused of a felony contumaciously refused to plead either guilty or not guilty and so blocked a trial, weights might be placed on the person's chest until a plea was entered. The accused sometimes endured the *peine forte et dure* because if they were found guilty after pleading not guilty, their estates might be confiscated. The practice was apparently very rare in the American colonies, the only recorded instance of it being the case of Giles Corey, who was accused of witchcraft in Salem in 1692 and suffocated under the weights rather than endanger the inheritance of his children.

[G. L. Burr, .ed., *Narratives of the Witchcraft Cases, 1648–1706.*]
CLIFFORD K. SHIPTON

PRESSURE GROUPS are organized interests that seek to persuade governmental officials to adopt policies favorable to the group's goals. Typically a group's membership is restricted to particular categories with assumed common interests, such as the restriction of the American Medical Association to doctors and of the American Bankers Association to commercial bankers. Most political goals of pressure groups are relatively narrow—for example, the American Petroleum Institute's pressure for oil depletion deductions on taxes. Groups do, however, pursue policies that mix collective benefits for large segments of society with selective benefits for the pressure group. At least part of defense spending benefits the population at large while also selectively benefiting through purchases, jobs, and prestige its organized proponents (including the Aerospace Industries Association, the Machinists Union, and the Defense Department). Since their activities have negative implications in a democracy, pressure groups frequently try to minimize their visibility by using soft-sell tactics, by claiming to protect the public interest, and by

obscuring interest continuity through reliance on *ad hoc* groups for different issues.

The term "pressure group" is usually restricted to organized interests working within existing institutions to influence governmental policy by such activities as lobbying officials, electioneering for sympathetic candidates, demonstrating, and persuading and mobilizing public support for their goals. Pressure groups are normally distinguished from (1) the major political parties, which are primarily concerned with putting their people in office; (2) mass-based social movements, such as those of the Progressives and the Populists, which seek to reform the institutional system; and (3) revolutionary movements. The distinction between party and pressure group is not absolute, since many single-issue third-party movements in the United States, such as the Prohibition party, have functioned in a manner similar to that of pressure groups.

Normally, pressure activities are a by-product of the central concerns for which the group was formed. While governmental bureaucracies and business corporations apply lobbying pressure on Congress, the groups were not formed explicitly for that purpose. The same is true of national associations, most of which were formed for primarily economic purposes. About half of the national associations are business groups, and most of the remainder are professional, farm, and employee associations. The largest and best-known associations are multiinterest peak associations, such as the National Association of Manufacturers (NAM), the Chamber of Commerce, the American Farm Bureau Federation, and the American Federation of Labor–Congress of Industrial Organizations (AFL-CIO). Groups formed primarily for political purposes, including the Americans for Democratic Action, the Liberty Lobby, and the League of Women Voters, are much fewer in number than associations based on an economic interest and are usually smaller in membership and less well financed than politically active, specialized economic associations, such as the Teamsters union, the National Association of Milk Producers, and the National Association of Home Builders.

The pressure system as a whole has a clear bias in favor of business and upper-class interests. This disposition is a reflection of the disproportionate number of business groups among politically active groups and the overrepresentation of upper-income individuals with multiple memberships in politically active groups. The class bias is even more pronounced when one takes into account the political role of such non-partisan upper-class institutions as the Ford, Rockefeller, and Carnegie foundations; the Brookings Institution; the Council on Foreign Relations; and the Committee on Economic Development in shaping issues and influencing policy decisions.

These institutions and their antecedents—for example, the National Civic Federation and the American Association for Labor Legislation—have been influential in obtaining adoption of moderate reforms, including Progressive and New Deal legislation. Representing the progressive elements of the business community, they played a key role in surmounting the political pressure of the conservative wing of the business community led by the NAM and undercutting the radical proposals of the Socialist party and the Industrial Workers of the World in the early 1900's and of the Townsend Plan and Huey Long's share-the-wealth movement in the 1930's. The foundations and institutes continue to play low-key roles in the pressure system, but since World War II their focus has been on foreign policy.

[William Domhoff, *The Higher Circles;* E. S. Malecki and H. R. Mahood, *Group Politics;* E. E. Schattschneider, *The Semisovereign People;* David Truman, *The Governmental Process.*]

EDWARD S. MALECKI

PRIBILOF ISLANDS, in the Bering Sea, were first visited in 1786 by the Russian explorer Gerasim Pribylov. The islands were ceded to the United States by Russia at the time of the purchase of Alaska in 1867. As the summer breeding grounds of the largest known herd of seals they became the subject of a controversy between the United States, Great Britain, and other nations whose subjects were slaughtering the seals for their fur. In 1869 the U.S. Congress passed a law restricting the sealing. An American cutter seized Canadian vessels engaged in pelagic sealing in 1886. The British government vigorously protested, and an arbitration tribunal, agreed to in 1892, decided (in 1893) against the United States. The dispute was finally settled in 1911 by the North Pacific Sealing Convention between Great Britain, Russia, Japan, and the United States. The United States was given the right to regulate the killing of the seals, and the herd has increased from a low of 127,000 in 1911 to more than 2.5 million in the 1960's. Japan withdrew from the convention in 1941.

[J. H. Latané, *A History of American Foreign Policy.*]

CHARLES MARION THOMAS

PRICE-FIXING, a government action dating back to the time of Hammurabi, varies from restraints in inflation and discrimination to supports in time of deflation. Enforcement of restraints is difficult. Fixing prices by private agreement, ancient and common in business practice, is typically secret, unenforceable, and against public policy.

Northern colonial communities routinely regulated prices of necessaries. New York ordinances provoked strikes by coopers (1680) and bakers (1741). Massachusetts fixed beaver and corn as currency (1630) and set silver's value in previous contracts from 1727. Direct wage regulation was also common.

Unprofitable tobacco plagued colonial Virginia except in intervals such as 1682–1702. Its minimum prices of 1632–40, forbidden by royal ordinance in 1641, were followed by repeated stinting acts. Virginia also passed numerous rating acts equating tobacco currency to sterling.

Aside from Congress fixing the price of gold and silver, the federal government took little action between 1775 and 1917. The Continental Congress sidestepped the inflation problem. New England drafted schedules at price conventions in 1776–78, but Connecticut alone put them into effect. Enforcement proved impossible. Civil War prices remained largely free—northern foods were surprisingly cheap until 1864. Evidently the Confederacy's controls started too late to permit enforcement. By October 1864 compliance was so poor that legal ceilings, although extremely high, averaged only 37 percent of published market prices.

In World War I the War Industries Board imposed selective controls effectively and accumulated administrative experience. In 1942–45 the Office of Price Administration approached complete regulation of all prices and rents. Many orders began with a "freeze" (seller's prior maximum price) to be replaced later by "flat" pricing (uniform ceilings for comparable sellers). Upward adjustments were limited to hardship cases. Once begun, controls extended because goods flowed toward free markets. Black markets began flourishing near the end of the war, and practically all prices zoomed upward after the lid was lifted in 1946. Several states then assumed rent controls.

The Office of Price Stabilization imposed milder regulations during the Korean War. The persistence of creeping inflation during the late 1960's prompted the administration of Lyndon B. Johnson to establish guidelines on wage increases and pressure large concerns against raising prices. President Richard M. Nixon established the Cost of Living Council, the Price Commission, and the Pay Board, attacking the problem at strategic points, but avoiding enforcement of the World War II variety. Prices were still inching upward in 1975 despite much unemployment here and there.

After 1865, declining prices, cutthroat competition, and the emergence of giant concerns led eventually to the Granger laws and the Interstate Commerce and Sherman Antitrust acts. The utility policy set maximum rates to protect users, whereas the railroad policy also enforced minimum rates to protect small shippers. Later legislation follows these general objectives.

The Great Depression saw federal and state efforts to restore prices to former levels ("reflation"). Gold was boosted from $20.67 to $35 per troy ounce. The National Industrial Recovery Act let industries enact codes including minimum prices and wages (declared unconstitutional in 1935). The Agricultural Adjustment Act (also declared unconstitutional, in 1936) and later legislation provided higher prices and production controls. Still in effect in 1975, the parity-price program aimed to assure growers of leading crops prices in line with the prices they were paying. Minimum retail milk prices came in federal marketing areas and many states, and were also still in effect in 1975. Chain-store price cutting was attacked in the 1930's by fair-trade laws in forty-five states, allowing manufacturers to set minimum retail prices. The general inflation after 1945 saw several such laws repealed or invalidated in court, reflecting a notable shift of public policy away from favoring price supports.

Common and statute law treats price agreements as conspiracies in restraint of trade, but enforcement since 1711 has commonly taken the price situation into account. Beginning in 1817 saltmakers in western Virginia entered a long series of price and production agreements without court interference. Salt prices were low and other prices were declining. In *United States* v. *Trenton Potteries Company* (1927), however, the Supreme Court decided in favor of the government, rejecting contentions that the agreed-upon prices were not unreasonable. The most notable Supreme Court action came in 1961 (*United States* v. *General Electric et al.*), resulting in heavy fines, imprisonment of seven executives, and huge refunds. Nevertheless, agreements promise so much security to sellers that they may be expected to persist at various levels of trade.

The quotation of steel and cement prices from basing points was held illegal, as an aid to collusion by the Court in 1948 (*Federal Trade Commission* v. *Cement Institute et al.*), after buyers reported identical bids from various sellers. Retail prices of gasoline and new automobiles were still quoted in this way in the mid-1970's.

[Thomas S. Berry, *Western Prices Before 1861;* Lewis C. Gray and Esther K. Thompson, *History of Agriculture in the Southern United States to 1860;* Harvey C. Mansfield, *Short History of the OPA;* Dudley F. Pegrum, *Public Regulation of Business;* W. B. Weeden, *Economic and Social History of New England;* Chester W. Wright, *Economic History of the United States.*]

THOMAS SENIOR BERRY

PRICE IN MISSOURI (1861–64). Sterling Price, a former congressman and governor of Missouri and a general in the Mexican War, was elected on Feb. 18, 1861, as a Unionist, to the Missouri convention. The convention, of which Price became president, was to determine Missouri's attitude toward secession. The majority of its ninety-nine members favored a compromise between the North and the South that would preserve the Union.

Gov. Claiborne F. Jackson attempted to keep Missouri neutral during the Civil War. He refused to send the volunteers called for by President Abraham Lincoln and organized the state militia in an effort to keep Union troops out of the state. Union Capt. Nathaniel Lyon's capture of Camp Jackson, in Saint Louis, on May 10, 1861, drove Price into the secessionists' camp, and many Missourians, who had previously been in doubt, followed him.

Price, put in command of the Missouri State Guard by Jackson, organized his army in southwest Missouri and met Lyon at Wilson's Creek, near Springfield, on Aug. 10, 1861. Lyon was killed, and Price went north and captured Lexington on Sept. 20. The advance of Union Gen. John C. Frémont into southeast Missouri made Price's position dangerous, so he retreated to Springfield. When Union Gen. Samuel Curtis pushed after him, he retreated into Arkansas and joined forces with Confederate Gen. Earl Van Dorn. They fought Curtis at Pea Ridge, Ark., Mar. 6–8, 1862, and were forced to retreat.

Price and 5,000 of his men officially joined the Confederacy on Mar. 6, 1862, and after Pea Ridge, Price was transferred east of the Mississippi (*see* Iuka, Battle of). Subsequently, he returned to Arkansas and was engaged in the Red River campaign of 1864 and at Jenkins Ferry. Later that year he made his famous raid into Missouri. Entering from the southeast with 12,000 men on Sept. 19, he went north to Pilot Knob and then toward Jefferson City, but he could not capture the capital. He then swung west toward Independence and destroyed the railroads, bridges, and telegraph lines behind him. He was caught between Curtis' and Gen. Alfred Pleasanton's armies at Westport, in what is now Kansas City, and his army was nearly destroyed. After being pursued and forced to fight a series of costly rearguard actions, Price managed to escape into Arkansas with 6,000 men. The raid was a failure from every standpoint. Price did not return to Missouri until after the war.

[E. M. Violette, *History of Missouri.*]

W. FRANCIS ENGLISH

PRICE MAINTENANCE. Agreements on price maintenance can be of two types. In horizontal price maintenance producers or merchants handling a particular good agree among themselves to set a standard price. In vertical price maintenance a producer agrees with his retailers not to allow prices to fall below a minimum level. Both forms of price-fixing have been viewed unfavorably through much of American history, and each was forbidden by the Sherman Antitrust Act of 1890.

Although no one has ever seriously advocated legalization of horizontal price maintenance, small retailers began to solicit government support for vertical price maintenance in the early 20th century. Large, vertically integrated merchandising companies, such as Sears, Roebuck and Company and high-volume discount houses were undermining the traditional market structure. Because of their size these firms could operate on a smaller profit margin, underselling lower-volume merchants. Also, by bypassing the wholesaler they were able to obtain price concessions from manufacturers. Perhaps the event that precipitated political action was a 1911 Supreme Court ruling that effectively ended any possibility of price maintenance in interstate commerce. Despite heavy federal lobbying by the Fair Trade League, price maintenance laws were passed before 1936 only at the state level and applied only to goods that were manufactured and sold within the state.

In the Robinson-Patman Act of 1936 small merchants were successful in obtaining federal sanctions against price discrimination. Although this act reduced the competitive advantage of chain stores, it did not keep them from cutting prices in retail sales. With Congress reluctant to enter the field of retail price control, advocates of fair-trade legislation shifted their tactics toward removing federal restrictions and leaving the matter to the states. In 1937 the Miller-Tydings Enabling Amendment modified the Sherman act, removing restrictions on vertical price agreements. All but three of the states quickly enacted fair-trade laws that allowed manufacturers to set minimum retail prices.

Although price maintenance laws are widespread, they apparently have had little impact on the economics of retail merchandising. In the 1950's the federal courts exempted mail-order houses located in non-fair-trade states from these laws. Furthermore, manufacturers, the only ones in a position to police the operation of price agreements adequately, have been slow to press for their enforcement. As the W. A. Schaefer Pen Company found in its campaign of the 1950's, the cost of detecting price cutting and the legal fees involved in prosecution usually exceed any benefits. Except for particular items—such as liquor—in which the government takes a special interest, the laws were being widely circumvented in the 1970's. Even fair-trade advocates have been forced to concede that retail price maintenance has proven to be a rather futile effort.

[S. C. Hollander, "United States of America," in B. S. Yamey, ed., *Resale Price Maintenance.*]

ALAN D. ANDERSON

PRICES are ratios of exchange, usually for money, in sales of commodities, services, securities, land, and anything else of value. Essentially quantitative, they lie at the heart of economic affairs and govern the distribution of income among nations and individuals. They figure in such issues as the Navigation Acts, paper currency, the tariff, tight or easy money, bank charters, internal improvements, antitrust legislation, public utilities, and price control. Price variations guide an economy's development and measure its pulse. They follow secular trends, major tides (long swings), minor cycles, and seasonality. Price trends reflect the relative rates of growth in commodity output and the money supply. Upward trends favor debtors (including governments) at the expense of creditors, and conversely. Those with fixed incomes suffer when prices rise and benefit when they fall. American prices show four secular trends: downward in 1607–1720, upward in 1721–1814, downward in 1814–96, and upward after 1896.

The decline shown in fragmentary quotations before 1720 ran counter to the European price level, which rose until around 1680. Tobacco, the Chesapeake staple, depreciated sharply soon after settlement; yet production kept expanding. Planters sought thereafter to keep it above a penny a pound. Since prosperity intervened only occasionally (as after 1685), some growers turned to wheat and other crops. Indian corn, New England's original staple, gradually went down in price from about 10 or 11 shillings a bushel to a low in the period 1700–09 of 2 to 3 shillings. Other grains, wool, fish, and meats behaved similarly—wheat fell from 14 shillings to 4 shillings. Pennsylvania's cereals were equally cheap toward the end of the 17th century. These declines, basically caused by expansion of population and production, were probably moderated by successive devaluations of colonial shillings. However, prices remained low until colonial currencies later appeared in respectably large volume.

Distinct local price patterns developed during the 18th century. The New England price trough occurred in 1721, after some revival in 1710–20. Wheat was down to 3 shillings and corn to 1 shilling, and produce was accepted for taxes as in the 17th century. With expanding currency, particularly in the 1740's, Boston wheat appreciated over 600 percent to a peak in 1749, and silver rose from 12 to 60 shillings an ounce. This unique inflation collapsed in 1750 when Massachusetts Bay reverted to hard money, redeeming many notes with silver from England. Another boom occurred in 1756–63, but quotations receded well before 1775.

The middle colonies' grains settled to a fraction of a penny a pound about 1721, as did flour (9 shillings a hundredweight). Production evidently continued ahead of the market (mostly Lisbon and the West Indies). Paper money began to appear on a conservative basis (Benjamin Franklin printed New Jersey's). Prices stopped falling, but made no great advance until 1748–49. Virtually all colonies began expanding note issues in 1755. Philadelphia and New York price quotations (in domestic currency) held upward trends until the Revolution, measuring overall about 25 percent over 1750 and 60 percent over 1720. At the 1772 crest annual flour and wheat averages surpassed 20 and 7 shillings, respectively, for the first time in the century. Prices rose in Virginia during the French and Indian War but subsided when the currency was redeemed about 1765.

Charleston's price level must have risen before 1720, judging by the note issues after 1703. Later issues promoted chronic second-degree inflation, which apparently never advanced beyond control.

Sterling exchange, at 300 percent premium in 1722, rose to 600 percent by 1731. Thereafter South Carolina's price level was about 300 percent above Philadelphia's (North Carolina prices were probably much higher still). Rice prices were extremely unstable. South Carolina produce tended to rise after 1746—an index reached a peak of 137 in 1772, compared with 79 in 1732, 45 in 1746, 100 in 1750, and 102 in 1775.

The Revolution brought third-degree inflation, influencing American opinion for generations. Evidently Philadelphia, which has the best data, suffered the most. Its wholesale index stood at 90 in April 1775 (base 1771–73) and dropped to 85 by year's end (grains were subsiding). Then it took off, reaching 183; 193; 1,077; 7,989; and 14,800 in successive Decembers and spurting to 19,888 early in 1781. A currency reform brought the index down to 142. Superfine flour, under 22 shillings per hundredweight when hostilities began, sold at £187 six years later and then returned to 24 shillings. The local money was highly confusing during the war and included coin and several discounted issues after May 1781.

Wartime prices rose at various rates in the same or different markets. British occupation brought hard money into some localities. Philadelphia imported goods rose rapidly in 1777–78, domestic goods, in 1779–80. Charleston, already inflated, hardly felt the impact of the bills of credit issued by the Continental Congress (continentals) until 1777. The heaviest boom there (1780) was far under Philadelphia's. New England wartime quotations, divided between paper and hard money, also ranged well below Philadelphia's. The maximum hard-money quotations on Boston wheat (1782) measured some 50 percent above prewar. A New York index peaked at 318 during 1779–80, also implying a currency far more valuable than continentals.

In 1784–1861 commodities were so favored in speculation that newspapers carried prices-current with commendable regularity. Monthly index numbers, and quotations on many commodities, are available for Boston, New York, Philadelphia, Charleston, New Orleans, Cincinnati, and San Francisco for part or all of the period. The Hoover-Taylor annual index combines local series to show average price behavior. Comprehensive farm prices have been assembled for Vermont after 1790 and Virginia after 1800.

A notable deflation occurred in the 1780's. Reaction against soft currencies, continued growth of production, and abeyance of capital imports brought an acute money shortage. Although Charleston enjoyed a rice boom in 1786, prices elsewhere settled near the prewar level until 1788–89. Commerce and finance approached a standstill.

The establishment of the federal government and several eastern banks, including the first Bank of the United States, and outbreak of war in Europe turned markets sharply upward. They continued to improve until 1814, following short cycles with such troughs as the ones in 1802–03 and 1808. The 1814 peak was a high point in price history. A postwar boom then took place in commodities and western lands, culminating in panics, depression, and a deflation centering in 1821. Notes of new banks in the interior flowed into circulation, many of which were discounted at time of crisis. A wide discrepancy developed in regional moneys in 1820–22 because some interior banknotes continued to pass in that section.

The nation next experienced two tides, 1821–43 and 1843–62, marked by inflation over twelve to fifteen years and deflation thereafter. Immigration, exports of cotton and foodstuffs, international movements of capital and specie, public land sales, and construction were all factors. Twin peaks occurred in 1836–39 and 1855–57, followed by deep troughs in 1842–43 and 1860–62. The first tide featured credit and notes of state banks and the second Bank of the United States. The second saw California prices rise to two lofty peaks in 1849–52 when gold output temporarily outran commodity imports. Although leading banks in most states fostered more conservative currencies, the inflation and deflation of the 1850's were almost as great as before.

Over the years 1800–61 a noteworthy increase of farm prices accompanied the decline of freight rates to seaboard markets. The steady improvement of farmers' purchasing power was enhanced further by general declines in the prices of goods brought into the interior. This caused a remarkable appreciation in real estate in the interior. Moreover, price levels in leading markets approached each other because of improvements in regional currencies, transportation, and communication (particularly the telegraph).

The Civil War dispersed regional prices into three groups reflecting currencies and economic conditions. The North and Far West experienced second-degree inflations, and the Confederacy a third-degree inflation. New York's index ascended from 92 to 225 in 1864, and Cincinnati's from 92 to 235; Philadelphia's index, including cotton and textile prices at fixed weights, went from 105 to 309. Most commodities, such as metals and fibers and their derivatives, followed a conventional inflation pattern. However,

heavy production and the disruption of normal trade caused foods and farm products to remain unusually cheap in 1861–62, until military demands and the circulation of U.S. notes began taking effect. They dropped again in the 1863 season, when Philadelphia flour sank to $4.87 a barrel and Cincinnati's farm-products index fell to 115.

San Francisco saw a smaller price increase, primarily because gold coin remained standard (par) and U.S. notes (legal tenders) passed at a discount. The general index climbed from 108 to 183. Much of this increase came in 1864–65, and the western peak lagged eight or nine months behind the eastern peak.

The Confederacy's regional index reflected the heavy dependence on paper currency to finance the war. On a prewar base it ascended to 172; 686; 2,464; 4,285 in 1861–64 (Decembers) and to 9,211 in April 1865. The ascent slowed down at about 4,100 during 1864 because of a revaluation. Legal ceilings went without enforcement. Import prices quickly outran export prices, and different markets inflated to various degrees. In late 1864 goods were nearly twice as high in besieged Richmond as elsewhere. A wage index lagged far behind, attaining only 987 at war's end.

From 1865 to 1896 U.S. and world prices receded remarkably, reaching a record low. Regional price levels again moved toward uniformity, particularly after 1875. The New York wholesale index dropped from 225 to 66. The contraction periods of four-year cycles occasionally outlasted the expansions. Evidently production outran money supply, and the velocity of circulation was declining. A definitely upward trend characterized 1896–1914, commonly attributed to important gold discoveries in Alaska and South Africa. The world was approaching the crisis at the end of a major tide when World War I broke out.

The United States suffered much less inflation than Europe during World War I. America was a belligerent for only nineteen months, saw extremely heavy production, employed a more conservative fiscal policy, and used controls and priorities with some success. The wholesale level remained around 100 until 1916 but then rapidly advanced to 164 by April 1917 (base year, 1913). It was held to 195 at the armistice; but a postwar boom carried the index to 240 early in 1920. After a sharp deflation in 1921 it leveled off for most of the 1920's at 40 percent above 1913. Some felt price stability had finally been attained. Agricultural prices were much below others, whereas securities underwent a boom culminating in the crash in the New York stock market in October 1929.

The Great Depression developed in stages, spreading over much of the world. The Bureau of Labor Statistics (BLS) wholesale index subsided 10–20 percent each year until 1933, touching bottom at 85 (on the base 1913). Agricultural products and raw materials dropped most because heavy output faced severe competition in world markets. Manufacturers' prices resisted reduction. Some, such as the prices of Ford automobiles, increased to reflect quality improvements, but prices were eventually cut in most lines, such as radios and electric appliances, regardless of improvements in quality. Federal and state governments tried various approaches to "reflate" prices, some involving radical departures from past policy. By 1937 the BLS index had regained the 1930 level (124), but it suffered a relapse in 1938–39.

U.S. prices rebounded in the national defense epoch (1940–41), reaching 142 as the nation entered World War II. Under a crash program including price controls, rationing, priorities, and savings bonds, the BLS wholesale index was held to 152 during hostilities. Vigorous inflation broke out when controls were removed. If converted to the 1913 base, this index passed 230 by 1948, 253 by 1951, and 330 in 1972. This compares with maximums of 164, 196, 221, and 152 in the other major wars after 1812. Inflation even proceeded during some intervals of marked underemployment and threatened to become chronic. A universal phenomenon, it was much worse in several other nations. Authorities point to various causes: wars, liberal credit policies of governments and central banks, unbalanced budgets, business price policies, intransigent labor unions, and desertion of the gold standard.

The 1973 U.S. price level was low compared with past levels in the United States and with 1973 levels abroad when measured by Adam Smith's labor standard, because wage rates in the United States had been increasing rather more than commodity prices in previous decades. It took fewer U.S. labor hours to earn a steak or an automobile than labor hours anywhere else. Nevertheless, the inflation that began in 1933 and was continuing in the mid-1970's meant great hardship to pensioners and others with relatively fixed incomes, and deprived long-range creditors of an untold amount of purchasing power.

[T. S. Berry, *Western Prices Before 1861;* A. Bezanson et al., *Prices and Inflation During the American Revolution, Prices in Colonial Pennsylvania,* and *Wholesale Prices in Philadelphia 1784–1861;* A. H. Cole, *Wholesale Commodity Prices in the U.S. 1700–1861;* Congressional Joint Committee Hearings, *Employment, Growth and Price Levels: Part 2, Historical and Comparative Rates of Produc-*

tion, Productivity, and Prices (1959); E. M. Lerner, "Money, Prices and Wages in the Confederacy, 1861–65," *Journal of Political Economy,* vol. 63 (1955); G. F. Warren and F. A. Pearson, *Prices.*]

THOMAS SENIOR BERRY

PRIGG V. *COMMONWEALTH OF PENNSYLVANIA,* 16 Peters 539 (1842). In 1832 a slave fled from Maryland to Pennsylvania. Five years later Edward Prigg, an agent, seized her and, upon a magistrate's refusal to take cognizance of the case, returned her to the owner. Prigg was then indicted for kidnapping in the York County court under a Pennsylvania statute of 1826 prohibiting forcible seizure of fugitive slaves. Judgment for the commonwealth was affirmed by the Supreme Court of Pennsylvania in 1840. The state of Maryland then petitioned the U.S. Supreme Court for a writ of error. The opinion of the Court, written by Justice Joseph Story, declared the Pennsylvania statute unconstitutional because the federal Fugitive Slave Act of 1793 superseded all state legislation on the subject. Story's opinion also drew the conclusion, sharply contested by the dissenting justices, that no state could be required to enforce the federal statute. In consequence, a number of northern states passed so-called personal liberty laws, prohibiting state officials from cooperating with persons seeking to capture and return fugitive slaves.

[Albert B. Hart, *Slavery and Abolition;* Charles Warren, *The Supreme Court in United States History.*]

J. PAUL SELSAM

PRIMARY, DIRECT. The most widely used system in the 20th century for nominating candidates of a political party for elective office is the direct primary. Potential candidates of a given party for an office must obtain a designated minimum number of signatures of party members to allow their names to be printed on the ballots. Those candidates are then voted on by all the members of the given party in the election district on a prescribed date, ranging from early April to late September, according to state election laws and procedures. The winners of the direct primary for each office for each political party are allowed to represent their respective parties in the general election that takes place several months after the direct primary.

Before the early 1900's nominations for public office were made by the congressional and legislative caucuses' declaring nominees (from the birth of the United States through 1830) or by delegate conventions (from the 1830's until the early 1900's). Robert M. La Follette's Progressive movement in Wisconsin gave impetus to the principle of nominating candidates by direct voting of party members.

Democrats in Crawford County, Pa., first used the system on Sept. 9, 1842; the Republicans started to use the "Crawford County system" in 1860. Slowly but steadily, this system for nominating candidates became the standard method. It was accepted voluntarily at first and later enacted into state election laws.

Two types of direct primaries exist: closed and open. A closed primary, used by almost all states, is a direct primary in which evidence of party membership is required, either by enrollment before the election or by a statement of allegiance at the polls when the voter asks for the ballot of a given party. An open primary is a direct primary in which no party membership test is given, no record of the voter's choice of party ballot made, and no challenge made as to party affiliation.

[Charles E. Merriam and Louise Overacker, *Primary Elections;* National Municipal League, *A Model Direct Primary Election System.*]

RONALD F. STINNETT

PRIMARY, RUNOFF, a second direct primary, held shortly after the first primary, between the two candidates having the largest vote if neither has a majority. Found almost exclusively in the southern states, where nomination used to mean election in the Democratic party, the runoff primary became necessary because the vote became so divided among a large number of candidates that the candidate with the plurality of votes represented only a small percentage of the electorate. To assure that the candidate would represent the majority of a party, the runoff primary was devised and became law in a limited number of states. As the South and other parts of the country become more two-party oriented, which seems to be the trend, it is likely that fewer candidates will enter contests and the need for runoff primaries will diminish.

[William Goodman, *The Two-Party System in the United States.*]

RONALD F. STINNETT

PRIMARY, WHITE, one of several means used by white southern politicians in the first half of the 20th century to control black political power (*see* Suffrage, Afro-American). By preventing blacks from voting in Democratic primaries, southern whites effectively disfranchised them, since primaries are more important than general elections in one-party states. At first southern whites set up primary-election machinery so as to exclude most blacks, but without direct reference to race. In 1923 the Texas legislature enacted a law specifically declaring blacks ineligible to participate in the state's primary elections. In *Nixon* v. *Herndon* (1927) the U.S. Supreme Court ruled this statute a violation of the Fifteenth Amendment. The Texas legislature then passed a resolution authorizing the state Democratic executive committee to prescribe the specific qualifications of the party's members. When the Supreme Court invalidated the executive committee's action barring blacks from the party, the state party convention assumed authority to establish membership rules for the organization, voting that only white Texans were eligible to belong to the party and thus vote in primary elections. In *Grovey* v. *Townsend* (1935) the Court held this decision legal, since no state action was involved. But in *Smith* v. *Allwright* (1944) the Court ruled that since the primary was an integral part of the election process, the Texas Democratic party's decision to exclude blacks was unconstitutional. Supplemental decisions were handed down, and by midcentury the white primary was legally abolished not only in Texas but also in all other states.

[Louise Overacker, "The Negro's Struggle for Participation in Primary Elections," *Journal of Negro History,* vol. 30 (1945).]

MONROE BILLINGTON

PRIMOGENITURE. In general, primogeniture implies seniority by birth; legally, it connotes the right of the eldest son to inherit the estate of a parent to the exclusion of all other heirs. Its wide use in medieval England followed the introduction of continental feudalism by the Normans, who stressed the wishes of a lord to keep his holdings intact so as to ensure the rents, fees, and military services arising from these tenures. Otherwise, a vassal might distribute his tenure among his sons in a way that would defeat the economic basis of the feudal structure. By the 14th century practically all free tenures were subject to primogeniture, although by a statute of 1540 land held in fee simple, as well as many feudal tenures, could be willed. Feudal tenures were abolished in 1662, after which all freehold land could be willed. By this time feudalism, except for the manorial system, was in decline. And although feudalism influenced institutional development in America, it was chiefly in its manorial aspects that primogeniture affected the New World.

Primogeniture existed in all of the original thirteen colonies. In New England, except for Rhode Island, stout opposition gradually reduced this form of inheritance, so that by the Revolution it had practically disappeared. In Massachusetts, however, the parent had to will a double share to the eldest son. This rule was also in effect in Pennsylvania. In New York and the southern colonies, where economic and social forces favored large estates, primogeniture generally prevailed, much to the dissatisfaction of those who viewed the institution as an alien and undesirable practice. The movement for free and equitable inheritance was fostered by those sponsoring the American Revolution. Stimulated by the democratic philosophy of Thomas Jefferson, the Virginia assembly attacked primogeniture and finally, in 1785, abolished it. Georgia and North Carolina had done the same in 1777 and 1784, respectively. The other states followed this lead, although it was not until 1798 that Rhode Island abolished primogeniture. Since that date primogeniture has not been in effect anywhere in the United States, although in some states entailed estates descend to the eldest son.

[R. B. Morris, "Primogeniture and Entailed Estates in America," *Columbia Law Review,* vol. 27 (1927).]

W. FREEMAN GALPIN

PRINCE GEORGE, FORT, was built in November 1753 by Gov. James Glen of South Carolina. It was placed on the eastern side of the Keowee River, opposite the Cherokee town of Keowee. The fort was 200 feet square with earthen walls and timber ravelins. Intended to guard the frontier and protect Indian traders, it withstood successfully the Cherokee attacks of 1759–61.

[D. D. Wallace, *History of South Carolina.*]

R. L. MERIWETHER

PRINCETON, BATTLE OF (Jan. 3, 1777). Leaving three regiments at Princeton, N.J., British Gen. Charles Cornwallis arrived at the Delaware River near sunset on Jan. 2, 1777, to avenge George Washington's defeat of the Hessians at Trenton. Cornwallis found Washington's army of 5,000 men occupying a precarious position along Assunpink Creek. Convinced that the Continental troops had no means of escape and ignoring Sir William Erskine's counsel to attack immediately, Cornwallis decided to "bag him" in the morning. Advised by Gen. Arthur St. Clair,

Washington executed a brilliant military maneuver. At midnight, leaving his campfires burning, he quietly withdrew the main body of his army along an unpicketed road and gained the British rear. Approaching Princeton at about daybreak, the Americans encountered a force under Col. Charles Mawhood just leaving the village to join Cornwallis. Gen. Hugh Mercer's brigade engaged Mawhood's troops at close range but was driven back after bayonet fighting. Rallied by Washington and joined by new arrivals, the patriots, with deadly rifle fire, drove the enemy from the field and village; British losses were estimated at between 400 and 600 killed, wounded, or captured. Cornwallis, outgeneraled, withdrew his entire army in feverish haste to New Brunswick, to save a £70,000 war chest. Washington, his army wearied, took up a strong position at Morristown, having freed most of New Jersey and infused new life and hope into a cause that appeared all but lost.

[Alfred H. Bill, *Campaign of Princeton, 1776–1777.*]

C. A. TITUS

PRINCETON, **EXPLOSION ON THE** (Feb. 28, 1844). The *Princeton,* the first warship driven by a screw propeller, carried a 12-inch gun, the "Peacemaker," devised by R. F. Stockton, the ship's commander; it was the largest gun yet forged for the American navy. While a party of about 200 government officials, including President John Tyler, and their companions were cruising down the Potomac aboard the *Princeton,* the gun was fired to entertain the company. It burst and killed several persons, including Secretary of State Abel P. Upshur and Secretary of the Navy Thomas W. Gilmer.

[F. M. Bennett, *The Steam Navy of the United States.*]

WALTER B. NORRIS

PRINCETON UNIVERSITY. Founded in 1746 as the College of New Jersey, Princeton was the fourth college established in the American British colonies. It was inspired by the Great Awakening, and its founders were leaders in the New Light faction of the Presbyterian Church. The first president was the Rev. Jonathan Dickinson; the first classes were held at his home in Elizabeth, N.J. On his death the institution was transferred to Newark, and the Rev. Aaron Burr (the father of Thomas Jefferson's vice-president) became the second president. In 1756 the college was moved to the town of Princeton, and Nassau Hall was erected.

408

Princeton men contributed significantly to the forming of the nation: president John Witherspoon and two graduates, Richard Stockton and Benjamin Rush, signed the Declaration of Independence; nine alumni, including James Madison, William Paterson, and Oliver Ellsworth, sat in the Constitutional Convention of 1787.

Among the faculty in the 19th century was the famous physicist Joseph Henry, who became the first secretary of the Smithsonian Institution. Under the presidency of James McCosh the faculty was strengthened; graduate studies were introduced; and the School of Science, the predecessor of the School of Engineering and Applied Science, was established.

Woodrow Wilson, who took office as president of the university in 1902, six years after the college was named Princeton University, recruited many younger faculty members to staff the preceptorial method of instruction, insisting, however, that undergraduate and graduate programs be part of an integrated whole. Wilson's influence on the future course of the university was profound.

Further growth in facilities and curriculum took place under presidents John G. Hibben (1912–32) and Harold W. Dodds (1933–57); during Dodds's administration the Woodrow Wilson School of Public and International Affairs was established, the Firestone Library erected, and the James Forrestal Campus acquired. The presidency of Robert F. Goheen (1957–72) witnessed the expansion of the Woodrow Wilson School to embrace professional training for public service, the creation of new social facilities for undergraduates, the admission of women students, the enhancement of the curriculum, and many new buildings. In 1972 William G. Bowen became the seventeenth president of Princeton. As of September 1975 the university had 819 faculty members and 5,798 students (4,343 undergraduate and 1,455 graduate).

[C. G. Osgood and others, *The Modern Princeton;* T. J. Wertenbaker, *Princeton, 1746–1896.*]

JEREMIAH S. FINCH

PRINCIPIO COMPANY. A bloom forge, built in Maryland in 1715 at the head of Chesapeake Bay, was the origin of the Principio Iron Works. In 1718 the first quantity of bar iron exported from the colonies to England was made at this forge. In 1722 the members of the Principio Company included Joseph Farmer, Stephen Onion, William Chetwynd, Joshua Gee, William Russell, John England, and John Ruston—English capitalists, ironmasters, and mer-

chants. They built the Principio furnace, which went into operation in 1724. The next year the company made an agreement with Augustine Washington, father of George Washington, by which the former became a member of the company. Mines were opened on Washington's lands, and the Accokeek furnace, in Virginia, was built. On the death of Augustine Washington, Lawrence Washington fell heir to his father's iron interests. Not long after the death of Lawrence in 1752, the company abandoned the Accokeek furnace. By this time the company owned the Principio furnace and forge, North East forge, Kingsbury furnace, and Lancashire furnace, all in Maryland. Although changes in the partnership occurred from time to time through death and the sale of interests, the company remained intact until the Revolution. In 1780, when Maryland confiscated British property within the state, the existence of the company came to an end. The Washington interests as well as those of Thomas Russell were not affected, since these partners were loyal to the American cause.

[James M. Swank, *History of the Manufacture of Iron in All Ages;* Henry Whitely, "The Principio Company," *Pennsylvania Magazine of History and Biography,* vol. 11.]

ARTHUR C. BINING

PRINTERS, TRAMP, a class of itinerants that came into being early in the 19th century as a result of an excess of cheap apprentices; most were farm boys indentured in the shops of rural weeklies who quickly fled to larger towns already overcrowded with printers. Many such youths, forced to seek work from town to town, found the wandering journeyman's seemingly comfortless life a pleasantly irresponsible mode of existence. As the country expanded, itinerancy grew and acquired tradition, legend, and customs that made the "roadster's" path easier. After seeing a large part of the country, especially the untamed, opening West, in his younger days, the habitual wanderer then settled into a summer round in a chosen territory.

The tramp printer's chief mode of transportation was the railroad boxcar. Inveterates considered it disgraceful to pay a fare, and many refused work so long as money for food and drink could be panhandled from craft brothers holding steady situations. Nearly all tramps were devotees of the nickel bars and their free-lunch counters. On their travels they became seedy, and as age overtook them, stooped, bleary-eyed, and inclined to periodic drunkenness.

Tolerant conditions reached an apogee in the late 1880's. Subsequently, as the small, inefficient print-shops of the handset days gave way to composing machines and mass production, the tramps were restricted to the more remote, laggard shops. The last of the tramp printers disappeared only with the onset of depression in the 1930's.

GENE GEER

PRINTER'S DEVIL. When printing was first introduced in the 15th century in some European cities, it was associated with black magic because of the marvelous uniformity of printed works as compared with handwritten manuscripts. This air of mystery surrounding their trade was cherished by printers, who consequently dubbed their young helpers, blackened with ink, evil spirits, or "devils." In addition, some European apprentices were considered menials with no hope of advancement, and so received a disreputable name.

In America the chore boy or youngest apprentice was called the printer's devil, but the term had lost some of its evil import. The youth could follow the example of Benjamin Franklin and become a master, publisher, or writer. He learned to set type and to assist at the handpress, and so obtained a kind of education. His school was the printing office, which boasted of such graduates as Horace Greeley and Thurlow Weed. With the mechanization of printing, apprenticeship declined and the printer's devil became obsolete.

[W. W. Pasko, *American Dictionary of Printing and Bookmaking.*]

MILTON W. HAMILTON

PRINTING in the New World began in 1539 at Mexico City when Juan Pablos, an Italian living in Seville, was sent out to establish a branch of the flourishing house of Juan Cromberger. He was accompanied by his wife and two helpers. The archbishop of Mexico held out to them the promise of a busy traffic in religious works and particularly of primers in the Nahuatl Indian language to support the missionary activities. After the death of Cromberger in 1540 the junior partner took over the Mexican printing office and operated it for the next twenty years. The place of Pablos as prototypographer of the Americas has been challenged on scanty but respectable grounds, favoring Esteban Martín. There is documentary evidence that a printer of this name was in Mexico City and possibly at work there between 1535 and 1538. However, no known example of printing can be certainly credited to him and there is some

confusion about what he is supposed to have produced. A son-in-law of Juan Pablos, Pedro Ocharte, succeeded to the family business in 1563. From Mexico printing was introduced into South America at Lima, Peru, by Antonio Ricardo in 1584.

In the British settlements of North America the earliest press began work at Cambridge, Mass., in 1639. All the equipment, materials, and staff—consisting of Stephen Day, a locksmith by trade, and his son Matthew—arrived late in 1638. The proprietor, Josse Glover, the dissenting former rector of Sutton, Surrey, died on the voyage and his plans for the press were carried forward by his widow. A young clergyman and scholar, Henry Dunster, recently arrived from England, in 1640 was chosen first president of Harvard College; in June of 1641 he married Glover's widow and thus, incidentally, became master of the Cambridge press.

Evidently the first thing printed was "The Oath of a Free-man," a single sheet. The second item in the Cambridge press bibliography was an almanac. No example of either is known to survive. The third and earliest extant work to issue from the new press was the *Whole Booke of Psalmes* (1640). This considerable undertaking, popularly known as the Bay Psalm Book, was translated from the Hebrew by some not very clearly identified Cambridge divines. It was repeatedly revised and the first edition of 1,700 copies was followed by numerous reprintings, both American and British. The summit of achievement for the Cambridge press was attained in 1663: the *Holy Bible* containing the Old Testament and the New Testament, translated into Algonkin, the language of the Massachuset Indians, by the Reverend John Eliot. The printers were Samuel Green and Marmaduke Johnson. For the occasion they were provided from London with new type and a second press by the Corporation for Propagating the Gospel in New England.

The mechanisms and operations of the Cambridge press are best understood by reference to Joseph Moxon's *Mechanick Exercises on the Whole Art of Printing (1682–84)*, edited by Herbert Davis and Harry Carter. Glover's printing machine, the first imported into what is now the United States, was a "common press" of the cumbrous timber and metal construction generally used in Europe from the 15th to the beginning of the 19th century. It was known also as the two-pull press, since the screw could transmit to the platen only enough pressure to print half the form at a time. The Moxon book and a long line of "printer's grammars" deriving from it, at least in part, set forth the developmental record of printing from the 17th century well up toward the 20th century. The principal topics of Moxon's discourse—and these generally hold for successor authorities—are the art of printing, containing the office of a master printer and details of the press; the art of letter cutting; the art of moldmaking, sinking the matrices, and casting and dressing printing letters; the compositor's trade; and the pressman's trade. The illustrations, both the engravings from Moxon and additions by the modern editors, are important, as are the copious notes and references. Successor volumes, British and American, show the progress of all departments.

The efficient Stanhope and Columbian iron presses were introduced soon after 1800. They were still actuated by a bar drawn by the pressman. However, ingenious systems of levers, counterweights, and toggle joints made lighter work for him even though he was printing a full form at a single pull. Various refinements, such as the composition rollers that replaced the old wool-stuffed leather balls for inking the form, made the job more agreeable. The advancing 19th century produced successful experiments hitching the bed-and-platen press to steam power. Before midcentury the great majority of well-done books and magazines in the United States were printed on the power-propelled bed-and-platen Adams press. Immediately following this was the development of the cylinder press, the letterpress printers' standby for the next hundred years.

Letter Cutting and Typefounding. Pablos' contract to establish a printing business at Mexico City in the name of Juan Cromberger stipulated that type which became unusable through wear or damage would be melted down and replaced with new casting from home. This was to prevent a possible competitor from taking advantage of a supply of second-hand type. Pablos was not inclined to be too fastidious about the condition of his fonts, and perhaps the death of his senior partner interfered with the supply of new type from Spain. In 1550, Pablos took the problem in hand by engaging from Seville for three years the services of Antonio Espinosa, a skillful letter cutter, typefounder, and printer, and an assistant. In this way the New World establishment was brought into line with the independent state of typography in its beginnings, when the self-contained printing house had its own foundry and staff competent to make type. As explained by Moxon, the letter cutter draws the required character on the polished end of a piece of softened steel, which he then works with engraving tools and files until no metal interferes with the taking of a clean impression. He hardens and tempers the

punch and strikes it in a copper bar to a depth of one-sixteenth of an inch or so. Thus, he has an unjustified matrix or strike with the character in reverse sunk into it. The strike now needs to be justified; the bulges caused by displacement of the copper are dressed away and every surface polished true and the face parallel and to proper depth. The character, in the form of a justified matrix, is ready for casting. It is taken in the hand mold, and molten, highly fusible type metal is ladled from a furnace pot into the orifice, where it congeals instantaneously against the face of the matrix. The halves of the mold are separated to eject the newly cast character. The jet—that is, the extraneous metal attached to it—is broken off, and the type is dressed and rubbed on a smoothing stone and laid in its case, ready for the compositor.

The letter-cutting artist and his foundryman in the Pablos printing house made a remarkable improvement in the quality of output generally as well as in the matter of well-designed, clean-cut new fonts. After his term was completed Espinosa set up a shop of his own in Mexico to compete with Pablos and between 1559 and 1575 turned out a number of superior books. By Moxon's time, a century later, the art of letter cutting and all that went into the making of punches, molds, and matrices were jealously guarded craft secrets. For 200 years the types of the New World printers were imported from Europe. A very few instances of coping with emergencies prove the rule—as when Francisco Xavier de Ocampo, an engraver at the Mexican mint, in 1770 made a font of type, or when Benjamin Franklin contrived to supply a missing sort. At the same time, Abel Buell of Killingworth, Conn., a young jeweler and lapidary, announced that he had already embarked on the business of typefounding and hoped for encouragement by printers and all American patriots. The announcement was printed in a dozen lines from his own types, the crudeness of which emphasized the distance he had to go. However, he did achieve improvement if not perfection. Better types were made at Germantown, Pa., by Jacob Bay and Justus Fox during the War for Independence. From this point the future of type manufacture was firmly taken over by John Baine and his grandson and his fellow Scotsmen Archibald Binny and James Ronaldson. Their Philadelphia typefoundry, under experienced hands and sober management, began operations in 1796 and flourished for more than a century.

The earliest American type specimen book was issued by Binny and Ronaldson's Philadelphia foundry in 1812. A specimen sheet of 1806 has been reported, but no copy of it has ever come to light. A pamphlet dated 1809 showing ornaments is the first thing known in the way of a specimen from the foundry. The specimen book of types is prefaced by the partners' pledge "never to relax their assiduity, while there remains anything useful or ornamental to be added to their Foundery which can be found in the first Founderies of Europe." It advertises awareness of the coming plague of fat faces, although at heart these transplanted Scots were one with their countryman Dr. Edmund Fry, who damned the fad for "fancy letters of anomalous forms, with names inappropriate and disgraceful in a profession allied with scholarship." In the firm's type-specimen book of 1816 Ronaldson confessed that they had in some cases been forced to imitate the Europeans, against their better judgment.

The pursuit of high fashion in types and decorative material called for the exercise of the best technical skills and ingenuity on the part of letter cutters and foundrymen. As David Bruce, Jr., noted in his "Art of Type Founding: Its History in the United States," published in 1858 (*The Printer*, vol. I, no. 1), the few competent punch cutters were fully employed by some of the foundries on experiments with novelties seeking to attract printers. The ingenious Bruce knew what he was talking about, for among other celebrated successes he designed and cut Hancock Script for the Boston Type Foundry. Meanwhile he was constantly engaged in trying to perfect new machines and methods for printing processes and printers.

Mechanical Typecasting, Punch Cutting, Typesetting. The 19th-century inventions, adaptations, and developments in the printing field were extremely fertile. Early on a seemingly simple device ejected cast characters without the hand mold being taken apart; this device practically doubled production. William Church, a Vermonter who worked in England, in 1822 patented a machine for casting and composing type on workable principles. Bruce, in 1838, patented the pivotal typecaster, wherein a pump forced the fluid metal into the mold and matrix and produced better types at a much cheaper rate; from about 1840 this machine came into general use among typefounders. At just this time the typefounders—particularly those specializing in high-fashion novelty faces and ornaments—began exploiting the possibilities of "growing" matrices from actual type models in an electrolytic bath. The New York house of James Connor first made electrotype matrices for types in 1845. The process circumvented the demanding craft of cutting punches in hard metal

and making strikes; by using any printing surface in existence as a pattern, it could multiply copies to infinity, and these copies as matrices fitted to the molds of casting machines spewed mountains of type in short order.

Despite the commercial advantage of the electrotype offerings, printers of books, periodicals, newspapers, and other serious works preferred the durability and sharpness of types from steel punches engraved and matrices struck in solid metal. Such publication work more often than not went to press in the form of stereotype plates. That process demanded sound type with deep enough counters and clean edges for decent results. The reputation of typefounding companies continued to depend on the professional standing of their type cutters. Linn Boyd Benton of Milwaukee in 1884 patented a pantograph punch-cutting machine that took the individual drawing and engraving of each letter out of the hands of the craftsmen. It committed their process to a mechanical contrivance that cut out a metal pattern of any character drawn and then reproduced it in any size desired. The tiny cutting tools are power driven at high speed and are so sharp and accurate that the model is repeated in the slightest detail; little or no hand finishing is required. Benton's machine, capable of producing limitless numbers of precise copies of a model character or figure, solved a problem that had long blocked the efforts of experimenters working to perfect a composing machine.

Ottmar Mergenthaler of Baltimore had found the major obstacle to completing his Linotype was the lack of punches in the great quantities required to produce the vast numbers of matrices needed for his machine, which was in fact a self-contained typefoundry. More than 6,000 Mergenthaler Linotypes were in service before the century closed. Another hot-metal composing machine, the Monotype, was under development by Tolbert Lanston and J. S. Bancroft at the same time. Unlike the Mergenthaler Linotype, which set a line at a time and then cast it, the Monotype encoded copy as punched tape and set accordingly in a separate casting machine as individual characters. Together they sounded the doom of the great typefoundries.

Before the middle of the 20th century, 500 years after the beginnings of typographic printing in the western world, other means of achieving similar purposes much more speedily and cheaply were developing. They were often based on seemingly unrelated experiments in the fields of lithography and offset printing, photography and color processes, and techniques of automation and electronics. Through such systems the forward-looking printer might perform prodigies of production—for example, photosetting millions of characters of computer-arranged copy in an hour.

[J. Abbott, *The Harper Establishment;* T. L. De Vinne, *The Practice of Typography;* L. A. Legros and J. C. Grant, *Typographical Printing Surfaces;* T. MacKellar, *The American Printer;* D. B. Updike, *Printing Types: Their History, Forms and Use.*]

RAY NASH

PRINTING PRESS, EARLY AMERICAN. For over 100 years printing in America was done on presses imported from Europe. In 1750 Christopher Sower of Germantown, Pa., contrived a press for himself, but American manufacture did not begin until 1769 when Isaac Doolittle, a clockmaker of New Haven, Conn., built a press for William Goddard of Philadelphia. Around 1800, Adam Ramage, a Scotsman, began to manufacture in Philadelphia the presses that bore his name. All of these presses were of primitive design, operated by a hand lever that applied pressure to the platen by a central screw, held in a framework of wood. Ramage subsequently improved the press, enlarged the screw, and used more metal parts. He adapted or copied European innovations and carried on a sizable manufacturing business. In 1816 George Clymer made his Columbian press, which substituted direct leverage for the screw; and Otis Tuft used a toggle joint in place of the screw. Other pressmakers were John I. Wells of Hartford and Samuel Rust and Peter Smith of New York. The latter brought out the Washington handpress but sold the patent in 1825 to R. Hoe and Company. The power press was then coming into use, but these handpresses were used in smaller offices for many years.

The first regular manufacture of type in America was begun in 1769 by Abel Buell of Killingworth, Conn.; Buell's foundry was aided by the Connecticut assembly. German type was cast in 1770 by Christopher Sower, Jr., in Germantown. The Philadelphia firm of Binny and Ronaldson, established in 1796, was the first extensive typefoundry in America.

[Thomas MacKellar, *The American Printer;* L. C. Wroth, *The Colonial Printer.*]

MILTON W. HAMILTON

PRINTMAKING. Crude, homemade woodcuts, metal cuts, and copper engravings, often the work of printers and silversmiths serving local needs for book illustrations or printed currency, begin the history of printmaking in Britain's North American colonies. About 1670 John Foster, Boston's first printer, cut on wood and printed a stark memorial portrait of the Rev. Richard Mather. It is the earliest known print produced in North America. A hundred years later, the silversmith Paul Revere, copying a print already made by his townsman Henry Pelham, engraved on copper a scene portraying the Boston Massacre. Foster's woodcut and Revere's copperplate have been reproduced many times and are probably the best-known examples of early American graphic art.

A few professional printmakers came to the colonies from London. Notable among them was the mezzotint engraver Peter Pelham. His fourteen mezzotint portraits, most of them of New England divines, engraved in Boston between 1728 and 1751, are the most important series of 18th-century American prints.

Philadelphia and later New York were to preempt Boston's early leadership in the graphic arts. The small views of Philadelphia engraved on copper by William Birch and Thomas Birch, published in Philadelphia in 1800, and the engravings by Alexander Lawson of Alexander Wilson's studies of birds, illustrating Wilson's *American Ornithology* (Philadelphia, 1808–14), were the most ambitious printmaking enterprises yet accomplished in the young American cities. Forty years later, Philadelphia had some of the finest American practitioners of lithography; it was there that John James Audubon in the 1840's issued his great lithographed series *Viviparous Quadrupeds of North America.*

In New York Alexander Anderson taught himself wood engraving in the 1790's. He himself produced 6,000 prints before his death in 1870; more important was his introduction of the skills that made wood engraving a 19th-century industry, for many years the medium of American book and magazine illustration. The New York firm of Currier and Ives, beginning in the 1840's and continuing through the century, made a place for itself in history by producing and selling, on a vast scale, lithographed, hand-colored scenes and portraits for an emerging mass audience.

J. A. McNeill Whistler's departure from America in pursuit of his artistic goals was expressed as early as 1858 by his "French Set" of etchings, foreshadowing the emergence of American painter-engravers in the traditions of Paris and London. A fellow American abroad was Mary Cassatt, whose aquatints in color of the 1890's are prized examples of Impressionist printmaking.

Before the Civil War Winslow Homer began his career as an apprentice in a lithographer's shop. Best known for his paintings, for 18 years (1857–75) he designed many prints. His wood engravings in *Harper's Weekly* and other magazines in the 1870's include country scenes that catch the essence of a vanished America.

Many 20th-century American artists have explored printmaking. John Sloan's etchings, John Marin's etchings, George W. Bellows' lithographs, the etchings and lithographs of Reginald Marsh, and the etchings of Edward Hopper are landmarks of American art before World War II.

In the decades after 1945, the earlier tradition of small black-and-white prints gave way to larger works and to a preference for color. The silk-screen prints of Ben Shahn, the woodcuts of Antonio Frasconi, Leonard Baskin, and Carol Summers, and the lithographs and etchings of Jasper Johns are among many American prints of outstanding quality made in these years.

[Karen F. Beall, *American Prints in the Library of Congress;* Wendy J. Shadwell, *American Printmaking: The First 150 Years;* David McNeely Stauffer and Mantle Fielding, *American Engravers on Copper and Steel.*]

SINCLAIR HITCHINGS

PRISON CAMPS, CONFEDERATE. *See* **Andersonville; Castle Thunder; Confederate Prisons.**

PRISON CAMPS, UNION. Most captured Confederate soldiers were released on parole in the first year of the Civil War, but captured officers and civilian prisoners were confined by federal authorities in forts and other structures adapted temporarily as prisons: Fort McHenry in Maryland; Fort Lafayette, Fort Columbus, and Castle William in New York harbor; Fort Warren in Boston harbor; a former government building (old Capitol) in Washington, D.C.; Lynch's "slave pen" (Myrtle Street Prison) and J. M. McDowell's Medical College (Gratiot Street Prison) in Saint Louis; the state penitentiary at Alton, Ill.; and Camp Chase, a training camp for volunteers in Columbus, Ohio.

The veteran Lt. Col. William Hoffman was appointed the commissary general of prisoners on Oct. 7, 1861. He constructed a central depot for 1,200 inmates on Johnson's Island in Lake Erie, hopefully to consolidate the prisoners, when the capture of 14,000 Confederates at Fort Donelson (the night of Feb. 15–16, 1862) rendered the depot inadequate. The already chaotic collection of prisons was expanded to include a series of training camps: Camp Morton (Indianapolis), Camp Butler (Springfield, Ill.), Camp Douglas (Chicago), and Camp Randall (Madison, Wis.). Compounding the confusion, efficient guards and medical personnel were unavailable because the prisons were a minor aspect of the war effort, and the guard detachments were changed frequently, so there was little continuity in administration.

Hoffman tried to regulate the system by promulgating regulations for establishing a post fund, issuing rations, and inspecting the camps. As the number of prisoners increased, these efforts succeeded only partially. After the establishment of an agreement to exchange prisoners in June 1862, the number of inmates declined from 19,423 to 1,286, enabling Hoffman to close most of the camps and to consolidate the captives at Johnson's Island, Alton, and Camp Chase. When difficulties concerning prisoner exchange arose in early 1863, the number of inmates increased, closed camps were reactivated, and conditions deteriorated. The scarcity of substantial clothing, unsatisfactory sanitation, flimsy and overcrowded quarters, inadequate medical attention, inclement weather, and the emaciated condition of many soldiers when captured contributed to widespread sickness. To consolidate and regulate facilities Hoffman established large permanent prisons at Fort Delaware, Del., Rock Island, Ill., Point Lookout, Md., and Elmira, N.Y.

Although from April 1864 through January 1865 rations were reduced in an attempt to force southern authorities to improve the conditions of Union soldiers in Confederate prisons, there was no discernible increase in sickness or mortality. Conditions continued to be inadequate at various prisons, but the problems were the same ones that had plagued the camps from the beginning. Housing remained inadequate, and 20,000 prisoners were confined in tents at Point Lookout. Fort Delaware had unwholesome drinking water, and Rock Island suffered a smallpox epidemic (in 1864, from February to April, 770 men died). An unsanitary stagnant pond inside Elmira produced the highest mortality rate at that prison (from February to March in 1865, 917 prisoners died).

Starting in February 1865, when the Union prisons held over 65,000 inmates, the federal government began to return large numbers of soldiers to the Confederacy. After the surrender at Appomattox the Union prisons were closed quickly, so that by early July only a few hundred prisoners remained.

[William B. Hesseltine, *Civil War Prisons;* R. N. Scott et al., eds., *The War of the Rebellion: A Compilation of the*

Official Records of the Union and Confederate Armies, series 2.]

LESLIE GENE HUNTER

PRISONERS, EXCHANGE OF. *See* **Exchange of Prisoners.**

PRISONS AND PRISON REFORM. The prison as a place where sentences for crimes are served is a relatively modern social institution. Rarely used before the 19th century, imprisonment was to become between 1820 and 1900 the focus of criminal policy, at first in the United States and ultimately in nearly all nations of the world. The concept of imprisonment emerged from the work of the philosophers of the Enlightenment—Voltaire; Charles de Secondat, Baron de Montesquieu; and Cesare Bonesana, Marchese di Beccaria—and was reinforced by the efforts of Sir Samuel Romilly, Jeremy Bentham, and Sir William Blackstone, who in the 18th century led the attacks on the abuses of capital punishment in England.

In America the Quakers became the foremost leaders of prison reform. In 1682 they recorded their opposition to capital punishment by enacting William Penn's "Great Law," the humane criminal code of the Pennsylvania colony. They were strongly influenced by the work of their English coreligionist John Howard, whose *State of the Prisons in England and Wales* (1777) was to have profound effects on reform in England. Largely as the result of the efforts of the Quakers a cell block in the Walnut Street jail in Philadelphia was opened in 1790 as the penitentiary for the commonwealth, the first such institution in the United States.

By 1823 two competing models of prisons, the Pennsylvania system and the Auburn system, had emerged in the United States. The penitentiary system established by the Quakers was designed to save the offender through reflection and penitence. The competing system was represented by a prison constructed at Auburn, N.Y. The objective of the Auburn system was to produce obedient citizens. Prisoners were to be housed under conditions of stern discipline and employed in a system of congregate labor. Economic self-sufficiency in the operation of institutions was an important objective of the program. While the debate surrounding the relative values of the two systems was to continue well into the 1870's, the Auburn system was to become predominant for several reasons: The product of prison labor was needed, and if well managed, the institution could be operated at little cost to the taxpayer; in addition, it was believed that the institution could best provide the firm discipline that was seen as essential to reform the offender.

In the years before the Civil War, highly regimented industrial prisons that produced substantial quantities of goods were established in many states. After the war both business and labor protested the competition of prisonmade goods. Prisons became increasingly overcrowded and costs of new construction were prohibitive. Moreover, it appeared to many observers that the function of the prison as a place of reform had been forgotten and that the primary preoccupation of the system was to keep the prisoner in custody and exploit his labor.

At that point a significant new era in prison reform began. Enoch C. Wines, who became corresponding secretary of the Prison Association of New York, was to become the focal point of new reform efforts. For eighteen years Wines used his post to advance many proposals for the improvement of prison conditions. He also attempted systematically to collect information about prison conditions throughout the world. The results of this effort were incorporated in his *State of Prisons and of Child-Saving Institutions in the Civilized World,* published posthumously in 1880. Among the associates of Wines were Theodore Dwight, the first head of Columbia Law School; Z. R. Brockway, who was to direct the first reformatory at Elmira, N.Y.; John H. Griscom, son of the founder of the first house of refuge for children; Franklin Benjamin Sanborn; James G. Blaine; and Rutherford B. Hayes.

Largely on Wines's initiative a call was issued for a national congress on prison reform, which was convened at Cincinnati, Ohio, in October 1870. Hayes, then governor of the state, chaired the convention, which included more than 100 representatives of twenty-four states, Canada, and South America. The delegates heard more than thirty papers prepared for the meeting by prison reform leaders in Europe and the United States and debated a lengthy declaration of principles that had been drafted in advance of the meeting. The declaration, adopted by the congress, emphasized the responsibility of society for the reformation of criminals and noted that education, religion, and industrial training are valuable aids in such an undertaking; that discipline should build the self-respect of each prisoner; that his cooperation can best be secured with an indeterminate sentence under which his discharge is regulated by a merit system; that the responsibility of the state extends into the field of crime prevention; and that prison systems should be centrally controlled to assure a stable, non-political administration, trained officers, and reliable statistics. The declaration was not to be revised substantially until 1960, nearly 100 years after its adoption.

The Cincinnati congress was the forerunner of the first International Penal and Penitentiary Congress, convened in London in 1872. Wines was appointed U.S. commissioner to that congress by President Ulysses S. Grant. He was elected president both of the Congress and of the International Prison Commission (IPC), which was formed after the meetings. The IPC was later to become the International Penal and Penitentiary Commission (IPPC). The latter was the international organization primarily concerned with prison reforms until 1950, when its functions were transferred to the United Nations under the provisions of U.N. General Assembly Resolution 415V, Dec. 1, 1950. The IPPC organized and called international meetings at five-year intervals. Throughout their history these meetings concerned themselves with "the penitentiary and penitentiary science." By the mid-1970's the United Nations had held five international congresses: Geneva (1955); London (1960); Stockholm (1965); Kyoto, Japan (1970); and Geneva (1975).

Despite the optimism of the reformers of the late 19th century, American prisons changed little until the 1930's. The reformatory, newly created in 1876, failed to realize the high expectations of its founders, and the prison remained an essentially custodial institution that became increasingly insulated and isolated from society.

Before World War I attention was focused briefly on prison problems by study commissions established in New York and New Jersey and headed by Thomas Mott Osborne and Dwight W. Morrow, respectively. These studies, unfortunately, had a very limited immediate influence on prison reform. The country's preoccupation with the war; a decline in prison population; and a continuing high level of industrial productivity in prisons were factors that contributed to a lack of serious concern about prison problems. But a series of riots and major institutional disturbances during the 1920's again brought prisons to public notice. Prison reform once more became a major object of study with the organization of new crime study commissions in Illinois, Missouri, and New York in the late 1920's and the appointment by President Herbert Hoover in 1929 of the first federally sponsored study group, the National Commission on Law Ob-

servance and Enforcement, which was headed by George W. Wickersham, a one-time attorney general of the United States.

For the most part, despite the introduction of rudimentary programs of education and the wider use of recreational activities in some penal institutions, prisons continued to rely heavily upon repressive discipline as the principal form of management and control of the population. The period 1920–30 was marked, nonetheless, by the growing interest of behavioral scientists in the potential use of the prison for modifying human behavior and attitudes.

It was during this period, also, that the movement in the direction of diversifying institutions began. The recognition that all prisoners did not require confinement in maximum security cages led to the development of institutions of lesser custody. Walls were replaced by fences in institutions of medium security, and by the early 1940's camps and other open institutions had begun to become part of a classified system of institutional facilities in some states. Following World War II prison systems continued to plan and construct new types of institutions designed to meet the differential needs of identifiable offender groups.

During the late 1950's and early 1960's changes in prison programs were influenced by a number of developments. The work of the Joint Commission on Mental Health and Illness, which began in 1955, focused attention on the need for alternatives to the mental hospital and identified a wide range of community-based programs that might be employed in their stead. The efforts to create a broad base of community mental health activities stimulated a corresponding interest in such alternatives for correctional institutions. The state of North Carolina began to use a program of work release for felony offenders as a transition from the prison to the free community in 1957. Congress authorized the use of work release, study release, emergency furloughs, and community treatment centers (halfway houses) for adult federal offenders in 1965. Similar statutes were enacted in more than half the states within the next ten years.

The President's Commission on Law Enforcement and the Administration of Justice, in its report, *The Challenge of Crime in a Free Society* (1967), recommended the "wholesale strengthening" of community treatment of offenders and a much greater commitment of resources to their rehabilitation. It called for the establishment of correctional programs built around small centers located in the communities they serve. The commission noted that much could be done to improve existing facilities, but that improvements would require large increases in professional personnel; it declared that new regimes should involve all staff members and inmates in collaborative efforts toward rehabilitation. The report emphasizes the importance of improving prison industries and strengthening counseling, education, and vocational training programs; special importance is attached to efforts to reintegrate the offender into society.

The findings of the commission led to the creation in June 1968 of the Law Enforcement Assistance Administration (LEAA) as part of the U.S. Department of Justice, with the purpose of helping state and local governments reduce crime through the upgrading of facilities, personnel, and programs in all areas of the criminal justice system. Provision was made for grants of funds to each state annually for the development of comprehensive law enforcement plans and, after review and approval, for grants to the states for the implementation of the plans.

In 1970 the staff of the Joint Commission on Correctional Manpower and Training observed that the previous four decades had seen two parallel lines of action. One was the continuing humanitarian effort to upgrade the standards of living of those confined in institutions; the other was the introduction into the administrative structure of "classification," meaning a differentiation of inmate populations into custodial and security groupings, which brought about the opening of prison doors to the psychologist, the social worker, and the teacher, as well as others. In the prison system of New Jersey and in the federal prison system, classification became the device through which the efforts of professional staff were integrated; professional workers shared in individualized program planning for offenders and became increasingly involved in the day-to-day operations of the institutions.

A significant development has been the intervention of the courts since about 1965 in matters relating to postconviction rights of offenders. Throughout the greater part of the history of prisons in the United States the courts maintained a hands-off posture with respect to complaints presented by prisoners regarding the conditions of imprisonment. In the 1970's many came to see the courts, especially the federal courts, as "the major impetus and instrument for altering the conditions of confinement" (*The Emerging Rights of the Confined*). The courts have addressed themselves to a wide range of issues: the prisoner's access to courts and counsel; his exercise of religion; his rights to correspondence and visits; his access to the media; and his grooming and attire. In addition,

the courts are concerned with disciplinary matters, administrative interrogations and investigations, the adequacy of physical facilities, medical treatment, administrative liability, and rehabilitation. The courts have intervened largely in the direction of limiting arbitrary decisionmaking on the part of administrators, but the result has been the adoption of well-defined codes of administrative due process. The introduction of new concepts of fairness in the administration of prisons may well be the most significant development that took place in the first 200 years of the history of these institutions.

Prison riots and disturbances during the 1960's and early 1970's were again to play an important role in focusing public attention on the needs for prison reform. Of these, the riot at the New York State Correctional Facility at Attica in September 1971 was to have perhaps the most profound impact. The agonizing efforts to end the disturbance without loss of human life resulted in prolonged negotiations between the rioters and prison authorities in which thirty citizens served as observers and tried to act as mediators and which extended over several days. Television brought the struggle into millions of American homes. The tragic outcome—the decision to bring the riot under control by force of arms, which resulted in the deaths of forty-three prison officers and inmates—stimulated a widespread public concern about imprisonment and the role of the prison in American society.

Among professional workers there continues to be strong pressure in the direction of improving the standards of care of prisoners and of the management of institutions. The National Advisory Commission on Criminal Justice Standards and Goals, appointed by President Richard Nixon in October 1971, was provided $1.75 million by the LEAA to formulate for the first time national criminal justice standards and goals for crime reduction and prevention at state and local levels. Although the commission's report on corrections concluded that "the failure of major institutions to reduce crime is incontestable," it nonetheless called for substantial strengthening of the programs of such institutions. Similarly, the American Bar Association Commission on Correctional Facilities and Services, organized in 1970 with the strong support of Chief Justice Warren A. Burger, has produced a large number of reports designed to help upgrade and improve institutional standards in many areas.

Still another significant step taken to promote higher standards of practices was the organization in 1974 of the National Commission on Accreditation

417

for Corrections. The commission, a twenty-member body elected by the membership of the American Correctional Association, is broadly representative of the several components of the criminal justice system—law enforcement, the courts, correctional institutions, probation and parole, and the public. Drawing upon standards developed by affiliate bodies of the association, the American Bar Association Commission on Correctional Facilities and Services, and other professional bodies, it has moved toward establishing a system of voluntary accreditation of correctional agencies and institutions, both juvenile and adult. The commission is being guided in its work by the experience of other national accrediting bodies in the fields of medicine, education, child welfare, and the like.

The failure of the prison during the last fifty years to demonstrate its ability to rehabilitate offenders has contributed to a growing demand that the use of imprisonment be restricted to the punishment of persons so dangerous as to require their isolation from the community. The National Advisory Commission has strongly urged that states not "build new institutions for adults unless an analysis of the total criminal justice and adult corrections system produces a clear finding that no alternative is possible." A number of voluntary citizens groups, among them organized groups of ex-offenders, have taken the same position and urge the more extensive use of community alternatives to imprisonment for the nondangerous offender.

The debate about the future of imprisonment has produced a number of philosophical positions. At one extreme there is a small group that argues for the total abolition of prisons. The burden of their argument is that the prison is an anachronism and only its complete destruction will compel society to give serious attention to creating necessary alternatives. At the other extreme are those who urge a more extensive use of imprisonment as a method of punishment and a means of deterring crime. They would eliminate as unnecessary all institutional services except those required to provide a basic level of care.

The position that appears to have the strongest support is that while prisons should be used primarily for the purposes of punishment and deterrence, there is a need not only to maintain but to expand existing institutional programs. These, it is agreed, should be made available on a "non-coercive, facilitative" basis and that a prisoner's release from the institution should in no way depend on the extent to which he has become involved in them. The debate, like that between the protagonists of the Pennsylvania and Auburn systems more than a century ago, will undoubtedly be prolonged.

[Vernon Fox, *Introduction to Corrections;* Joint Commission on Correctional Manpower and Training, *Perspectives on Correctional Manpower and Training;* Joint Commission on Mental Illness and Health, *Action for Mental Health;* Blake McKelvey, *Prisons in America;* President's Commission on Law Enforcement and the Administration of Justice, *Task Force Report: Corrections;* David J. Rothman, *The Discovery of the Asylum;* South Carolina Department of Corrections, *The Emerging Rights of the Confined.*]

HERMAN G. MOELLER

PRISON SHIPS were used by both the Americans and the British during the Revolution for confining naval prisoners. The former maintained such ships at Boston and at New London, Conn., and the latter at Halifax, Nova Scotia; at Antigua, British West Indies; and at Wallabout Bay, Brooklyn. Conditions on the prison ships varied greatly according to the character of the officers and subordinates in charge, but the vessels moored in Wallabout Bay, particularly the *Jersey,* became notorious for the harsh treatment accorded the captives. Provisions were scanty, of bad quality, and poorly cooked. Fever and dysentery prevailed; the guards were brutal; and at night the prisoners, able-bodied and sick alike, were herded below decks in intolerable heat and stench. Both George Washington and the Continental Congress protested against this treatment, and Vice Adm. John Byron of the Royal Navy labored hard to better conditions. At least thirteen different prison ships were moored in Wallabout Bay or in the East or North rivers from 1776 to 1783. It has been estimated that some 11,500 men died on these ships.

[Thomas Dring, *Recollections of the Jersey Prison-ship;* E. L. Armbruster, *The Wallabout Prison Ships, 1776–1783;* G. W. Allen, *A Naval History of the American Revolution.*]

LOUIS H. BOLANDER

PRIVATEERS AND PRIVATEERING. The operations of Sir John Hawkins, Sir Francis Drake, and other 16th-century Elizabethan freebooters are often considered the historical starting point of privateering in America. But the participation of privately armed American colonists in the wars of England did not begin until more than a century later, during King William's War (1689–97). During Queen Anne's War (1702–13), a considerable number of privateers were commissioned by the colonial governors. Relatively few took to the sea during the short war with Spain in 1718, but under royal warrants the American governors, in 1739, again issued letters of marque and reprisal against Spain. In King George's War (1744–48) privateering began to assume the proportions of a major maritime business, and it is said that during the French and Indian War (1754–63) 11,000 Americans were engaged in such operations.

Upon the commencement of hostilities with the mother country in 1775, most of the colonies, notably Massachusetts and Rhode Island, issued letters of marque and reprisal, and three months before the Declaration of Independence, the Continental Congress sanctioned privateering "against the enemies of the United Colonies." The 1,151 American privateers operating during the Revolution captured about 600 British vessels, of which 16 were men-of-war. During the last three years of the war, the privateers carried the brunt of the fighting at sea. By 1781 there were in commission only three public cruisers, but 449 privately armed cruisers carrying 6,735 guns were in service. Although the operations of the privateers had been not only financially profitable but also an invaluable aid to the navy, the U.S. government soon joined the movement in Europe to abolish privateering. It reversed its position in 1798 in the face of the arrogant depredations of armed vessels sailing under the authority of republican France (*see* Franco-American Misunderstanding). Congress first dealt with this threat in an act of June 25, 1798, allowing American merchantmen to arm themselves for defensive purposes. An act of July 9, 1798, authorized them to apply for special commissions to make offensive war on all armed French vessels. By the close of the year at least 428 merchantmen had been armed (probably three-fourths of these had received official commissions), and before the close of hostilities in 1801, upward of 1,000 vessels had been armed. Since the armed merchantmen were not allowed to prey on unarmed commerce, fighting was generally secondary to trading; nevertheless, there were some notable encounters and valuable captures. In the War of 1812, 515 letters of marque and reprisal were issued, under which 1,345 British vessels are known to have been taken. All the seaboard states from Maine to Louisiana sent privateers to sea against Great Britain in either the Revolution, the War of 1812, or both, but the numbers contributed by each state varied greatly. Massachusetts led with a total of at least 457 ships, and Maryland followed with 281; in contrast, New Jersey and North Carolina probably contributed not more than four ships each.

With the return of world peace in 1815, many American and European privateers were unwilling to return to peaceful pursuits; some found service in Latin-American revolutions, and others became pirates. For the next twenty-five years the U.S. Navy was much engaged in the suppression of piracy. The Republic of Texas resorted to privateering in the early stage (1835–37) of its protracted war with Mexico. The United States, with its naval superiority, did not find it expedient to issue letters of marque and reprisal during the Mexican War (1846–48). The United States declined to accede to the Declaration of Paris (1856), outlawing privateering among the principal world powers, but when the Confederate States of America issued letters of marque, President Abraham Lincoln endeavored to treat the Confederate privateers as pirates, until he was checked by retaliatory measures. The privateers sailing from Louisiana, North Carolina, and South Carolina in 1861 enjoyed as profitable cruises as had their predecessors of 1812; but Confederate privateering declined after the first year, and a volunteer naval system was instituted. The United States' attempt at privateering in 1863 proved abortive, as did Chile's attempt against Spain in 1865, and privateering ended throughout the world with the downfall of the Confederacy.

[C. W. Kendall, *Private Men-of-War;* W. S. Maclay, *A History of American Privateers;* W. M. Robinson, Jr., *The Sea Dogs of Texas,* and *The Confederate Privateers.*]

WILLIAM M. ROBINSON, JR.

PRIVILEGE IN COLONIAL GOVERNMENTS comprises that body of rights and exemptions claimed by colonial legislatures in imitation of the British House of Commons. Privilege was sometimes claimed by virtue of charters and sometimes by inherent natural right, but it usually existed in practice by demand of the assembly and with the consent of the governor. As with the rights of Parliament itself, the exact extent of privilege in colonial governments cannot be measured because it was constantly changing. The five privileges usually petitioned for by the speaker of the house in London—freedom from arrest, freedom from molestation, freedom of speech, access to the crown, and favorable construction on all official acts of the house—had become practically universal in the colonies outside New England in the 18th century. Privilege was further expanded by extension to three classes of persons in addition to members—servants of members, officers of the house, and people who had given evidence. Privilege gradually extended to also include the rights to settle disputed elections, control members, and punish outsiders who abused individual members or insulted the house itself.

These claims to privilege were of practical importance, for by them the colonial assemblies tried to regulate the extent of the governor's power over them, as Parliament had tried to limit the power of the king. Many claims, such as the right to adjourn and dissolve assemblies and to establish new districts of representation, house control of the election of the speaker, and a veto power, were denied to the colonies by Great Britain, even though Parliament had won such claims over the king. Down to the Revolution such denials were not accepted by the colonies as final. The struggle to obtain additional privileges caused many a conflict between governor and assembly, and these disputes were made more acute by the fact that Parliament, in the last analysis, held the whip hand because it controlled the purse strings. By its authority taxes were levied and appropriations for expenses were made. Many a governor had to choose between making concessions to the colonial assemblies and receiving no salary. It can, therefore, be seen why parliamentary privilege was considered the very essence of representative government; by the exercise of such privilege the balance of power in the colonial assemblies could be kept with the people, through their legislature, rather than with the governor, who represented the British crown.

Parliament as well as the king disapproved of the independent position colonial assemblies achieved by claims to privilege, because such autonomy was incompatible with the theory that Parliament was the supreme legislative body for the empire and that the assemblies were subordinate to it. As long as the assemblies were, in practice, in a position of equality with the House of Commons on money matters by taxing themselves, conflicts over privilege did not jeopardize the empire. When, in 1764, Great Britain denied the colonists' claims to be taxed only through their assemblies, it brought to a crisis the long-standing larger issue of the relationship of the colonial assemblies to Parliament.

VIOLA F. BARNES

PRIVILEGES AND IMMUNITIES OF CITIZENS

are dealt with in two clauses in the U.S. Constitution. The first, in Article IV, Section 2, guarantees that citizens of each state shall be entitled to all privileges and immunities of citizens in the several states. There had been a similar provision in the Articles of Confederation, but the meaning of this new section was far from clear. It provided no definition of privileges and immunities, no test of state citizenship, and no indication whether the citizen was entitled to these privileges in his own state or when he was temporarily in other states, or both.

The first authoritative definition was given by Justice Bushrod Washington on circuit in *Corfield* v. *Coryell* (1823); the privileges and immunities protected, he said, were those "which are, in their nature, fundamental; which belong, of right, to the citizens of all free governments." As illustrations, he suggested protection by the government and the right to acquire and possess property, to bring court actions, and to travel from one state to another.

Whatever these rights are, according to the Supreme Court ruling in the Slaughterhouse Cases (1873), the Constitution requires that, as the states grant or establish privileges and immunities to their own citizens, "the same, neither more nor less, shall be the measure of the rights of citizens of other States within [their] jurisdiction." However, states can treat out-of-state citizens differently from their own citizens when there are reasonable grounds for doing so. Thus, the right to vote is limited to citizens of the state. Out-of-state students can be charged higher tuition fees in state universities. Fees for hunting and fishing licenses can be higher for out-of-state residents, since they do not contribute by local taxes to the upkeep of the public domain, but the fees cannot be prohibitive. Practitioners of certain professions vital to the public interest, such as medicine and law, cannot practice outside the state in which they are licensed without new certification. Corporations cannot claim protection under the provision.

While the right to travel across interstate boundaries had been earlier upheld by the Supreme Court on the basis of Article IV, Section 2, in *Edwards* v. *California* (1941), a statute barring indigents from entering that state was ruled unconstitutional as a burden on interstate commerce; only two justices relied on the privileges and immunities clause. In *Shapiro* v. *Thompson* (1969), invalidating a state law imposing a one-year waiting period before new residents of a state would be eligible for public assistance, the Court decided that the right of interstate travel derived from the nature of the federal union, not from any particular constitutional provision.

The second privileges and immunities clause, in the Fourteenth Amendment, forbids states to make or enforce any law abridging the privileges and immunities of citizens of the United States. It was one of three standards written into the post–Civil War amendment for the purpose of, but not limited to, protecting the rights of the newly freed blacks. The other two provisions were the equal protection clause and the due process clause. Debates on the Fourteenth Amendment in Congress made it clear that the privileges and immunities clause was regarded as the most important of these three, and it was expected to be a major restraint on state denial of civil rights. However, in the Slaughterhouse Cases the Supreme Court interpreted the language narrowly to protect only those rights peculiar to national citizenship (such as access to the seat of government and the writ of habeas corpus) and made it inapplicable to the whole field of property rights and to trials in state courts. Attention then turned to the due process clause and the equal protection clause, with much greater success, and the wide interpretation given to those two provisions has made the privileges and immunities clause of the Fourteenth Amendment almost a dead letter.

[C. Herman Pritchett, *The American Constitution.*]

C. HERMAN PRITCHETT

PRIVY COUNCIL, a body of advisers to the English crown. At the time English colonization in America began in the 17th century, the council filled a place roughly corresponding to that now occupied by the cabinet. The council contained all of the ministers of state, who held leading positions in administration. Its purview extended to virtually the entire empire. Thus, as new colonies became established, they fell under the special care of the council. This body heard appeals from colonial courts, and colonial laws were referred to it for approval or veto (*see* Royal Disallowance). In addition, a succession of bodies formed for the oversight of the colonies, culminating with the Board of Trade and Plantations of 1696, were either committees of the Privy Council or boards acting under its control and reporting to it.

[C. M. Andrews, *The Colonial Period of American History,* vol. I.]

FRANK B. HURT

PRIZE CASES, CIVIL WAR. In 1863 the Supreme Court upheld President Abraham Lincoln's exercise, at the outbreak of the Civil War, of emergency powers not previously authorized by Congress. After the firing on Fort Sumter, Lincoln, by executive proclamations (in April and May 1861), virtually declared war, called for volunteers, enlarged the regular army, suspended the writ of habeas corpus, and blockaded

various southern ports. Not until July did Congress, meeting in special session, retroactively legalize these executive measures. Meanwhile, under the presidential blockade certain merchant vessels were captured as prizes by the Union navy for attempting to run the blockade. These seizures were challenged in court, and eventually the Supreme Court held, in a narrow five-to-four decision, that Lincoln's blockade by executive proclamation was constitutional and that civil war had "legally" existed between April and July 1861, even though Congress did not recognize a state of war until July 13. (*See also Amy Warwick* Admiralty Case.)

[J. G. Randall, *Constitutional Problems Under Lincoln.*]

MARTIN P. CLAUSSEN

PRIZE COURTS derive their name from their function, which is to pass on the validity and disposition of prizes, a term referring to the seizure of a ship and/or its cargo by the maritime forces of a belligerent, not its land forces. Jurisdictional pronouncements of prize courts have expanded the definition of lawful capture of property at sea to include the territorial waters and navigable rivers of occupied enemy territory and have accepted as legitimate the seizure of vessels in dry docks, ports, and rivers.

According to the U.S. Prize Act of 1941, the seizure of aircraft may also fall under the jurisdiction of prize courts. Whether the broad principles of judicial prize doctrine can be adopted to capture by aircraft remained a subject of legal argument in the mid-1970's. Under the U.S. Prize Act the term "vessels of the Navy" explicitly includes aircraft, provided they are manned by navy personnel. The evolution of prize law may extend application to all types of military aircraft.

Although belligerents are operating under the rules of international law when conducting seizures, the prize courts themselves are national instrumentalities. Their structures, rules of procedure, and disposition of the prizes emanate from national law. They may apply the principles of international law to determine the validity of seizures and the liability to condemnation, but in many cases the rules of international law are applied by virtue of their adoption by the national legal system or incorporation into it. They may also be modified by domestic enactments and regulations. It is not surprising, therefore, that worldwide prize-court decisions have lacked uniformity and have not always reflected a high degree of recognition of, and respect for, international law regarding capture and condemnation.

In the United States, jurisdiction in prize matters belongs to the federal district courts, with the right of appeal to the circuit court of appeals and ultimately the Supreme Court. The domestic courts are authorized to appoint special prize commissioners to act abroad.

The twelfth convention of the Hague Peace Conference of 1907 attempted to establish an international prize court to function as a court of appeal in prize cases heard before national courts, but how the court was to be constituted presented many difficulties. Although a consensus was reached on the court's composition, the convention was never ratified because some countries, especially Great Britain, feared that in the absence of a well-defined comprehensive international prize law the court would assume international legislative functions. Thus, an international prize court never came into existence.

The thirteenth Hague convention, the Hague Convention Concerning the Rights and Duties of Neutral Powers in Naval War, signed in 1907, formally affirms customary rules of international law. It also stipulates that a prize court cannot be set up by a belligerent on neutral territory—as was attempted by the French minister to the United States, Edmond C. Genêt, at the outbreak of the war between Great Britain and France in 1793, in connection with various French consulates in the United States. Articles 21 and 22 of this convention also stipulate that a prize may only be brought into a neutral port on the basis of unseaworthiness, stress of weather, or exhaustion of fuel or provisions and that the vessel must leave the neutral port as quickly as possible. When, during World War II, a German warship had captured a British passenger liner, the *Appam,* and brought it to Newport News, Va., the U.S. district court ruled that the above articles prohibited that neutral port from becoming a place of asylum.

[Andrew W. Knauth, "Prize Law Reconsidered," *Columbia Law Review,* vol. 46 (1946).]

WERNER FELD

PRIZEFIGHTING. The history of American prizefighting, so far as fan interest is concerned, is largely a history of the heavyweights, though many fighters in the lighter-weight divisions have captured the public's imagination. The sport was introduced in America when visiting British sailors in the first half of the 19th century showed the superiority of "stand-up boxing"—long practiced in England—over the less scientific fighting methods of American tars. In bouts held in the back rooms of waterfront saloons, the straight left and right cross held mastery. Fascination with boxing in England influenced the sons of southern plantation owners who studied in England to stage matches between husky slaves on their return to America. Wagers were sometimes enormous; entire plantations sometimes changed hands. One slave, Tom Molineaux, earned his freedom by winning a huge bet for his master. Molineaux then went to England and had two epic bouts with the English champion Tom Cribb.

It has been well established that most prizefighters in America have been immigrants or their immediate descendants or native blacks—willing to accept the grueling training required to try to make their fortunes. John L. Sullivan, son of Irish immigrants, did much to make the sport popular in the last part of the 19th century. His fight in New Orleans on Sept. 7, 1892, against James J. Corbett, also of Irish descent, caused intense interest all over America. In a startling upset, Corbett won by a knockout. Corbett lost the title in 1897 to "Ruby" Robert Fitzsimmons, the lightest man to hold the championship. Two years later Fitzsimmons was knocked out by the powerful James J. Jeffries.

For reasons not always salutary, the sport's golden age was the period from 1910 to 1930. After John A. (Jack) Johnson, a black from Galveston, Tex., wrested the world's heavyweight title from Tommy Burns in 1908, a wide search was made in America for a "white hope"—a Caucasian who could beat Johnson and regain for whites the prestige the title represented to many. In 1910, after Johnson soundly defeated Jeffries—far from his prime—riots erupted in many American cities. Showings of the fight films were banned lest more rioting ensue. In 1915, in Havana, Cuba, Johnson was knocked out by Jess Willard, who was in turn defeated by William Harrison (Jack) Dempsey in 1919. The most outstanding promoter of the era was George Lewis (Tex) Rickard, a former Yukon gold miner, who built up huge attendance by showmanship. Dempsey's two fights with James Joseph (Gene) Tunney (1926, 1927), promoted by Rickard, excited the nation as no sports events had up to that time. Tunney, a studious former marine, won both contests.

After Tunney retired in 1928, interest in the sport lagged until Joe Louis (Joseph Louis Barrow), a powerful puncher from Alabama, captured the heavyweight title from the "Cinderella Man," James J. Braddock, in June 1937. Louis' previous knockout by the German Max Schmeling in 1936 was an astounding upset. Their second bout, in 1938, having political overtones, was an emotional as well as an athletic event. A determined Louis knocked out the German in the first round in Madison Square Garden, New York City. "Jersey Joe" Walcott took the crown from Louis in 1951, and Rocky Marciano (Rocco Marchegiano) beat Walcott in 1952. Marciano retired in 1955 without having lost a fight. The most controversial fighter of the 1960's and early 1970's was the voluble Cassius Clay, later known as Muhammad Ali. Clay won the championship in 1964 from Sonny Liston, but was deprived of his title and his license to box for refusing to serve in the army. (Clay had unsuccessfully asked to be exempt from service because of his adherence to the Black Muslim faith.) His license, but not the title, was restored in 1970. Like Clay, Joe Frazier and George Foreman were Olympic champions before winning their professional titles in 1970 and 1973, respectively. Floyd Patterson, another Olympian, was the first heavyweight to have lost the championship (held 1956–59) and won it back (1960). The second was Clay, who defeated Foreman in October 1974.

Among American fighters of the lighter weights, the greatest include middleweight Jack ("Nonpareil") Dempsey (1884–91); welterweight Kid McCoy (1896); lightweight Joe Gans (1902–08); middleweight Stanley Ketchell (1907–10), a white hope who lost to Johnson; lightweight Battling Nelson (1908–10); lightweight Benny Leonard (1917–25); middleweight Harry Greb (1923–26); middleweight Mickey Walker (1926); Henry Armstrong, who held three championships at once (1938)—featherweight, welterweight, and lightweight; light heavyweight Billy Conn (1939–41); and light heavyweight Archie Moore (1952–60).

[John Durant, *The Heavyweight Champions;* Finis Farr, *Black Champion—The Life and Times of Jack Johnson;* Nat Fleischer, *Gene Tunney, The Enigma of the Ring;* Hugh Fullerton, *Two-Fisted Jeff;* Mel Heimer, *The Long Count;* Alexander Johnston, *Ten—and Out!;* Rex Lardner, *The Legendary Champions,* and *Ali.*]

REX LARDNER

PRIZE MONEY. The Continental Congress thriftily adopted the European practice of justifying low naval pay by splitting with captains and crews the proceeds from captured enemy vessels sold by prize courts. Privateers, which were privately owned, received all the proceeds from a sale, and they generally had an easy time recruiting crews. The main difference between an American naval vessel and a privateer in quest of the same merchantman prey showed in encounters with British warships: the naval commander was honor-bound to fight, whereas a privateer captain considered fighting to be poor business and would not fight unless cornered. In raiding British commerce during the Revolution, more than 1,000 privateers took about 600 prizes sold for the then great total of $18 million, far more than the meager bag brought in by the fifty-three men-of-war in the Continental navy. The privateer champion was the *Rattlesnake,* which netted $1 million from a single cruise in the Baltic.

Although Congress declined to authorize privateers for the curious Quasi-War with France (1798–1800), the merchantmen's armament for self-defense had to be legalized. A few enterprising captains succeeded in stoutly defending themselves to the extent of taking fourteen French armed cruisers. Meanwhile, forty-nine men-of-war of the new U.S. Navy made ninety-five captures on the basis of the 1798 prize law. The government's half went into a naval pension fund, while for a lone ship the captors' half was divided into twenty equal parts, three for the captain, two shared by the lieutenants and master, two among marine and warrant officers, three among midshipmen and chief petty officers, three among the petty officers, and seven among the seamen and marines. If the capturing ship was in a squadron, the naval half was divided among ships in firing range, and the commodore given one-twentieth. If the prize was an armed foe of equal or superior strength, captors received all proceeds. An enemy combatant sunk in battle merited a purse based upon its armament. Fortune in this undeclared naval war with France brought prize money ranging from $1,027 to John Barry and the 44-gun *United States* for the privateer *Tartuffe* to $27,000 to George Little and the 28-gun *Boston* for the *Esperance.* The capture of the French 36-gun frigate *Insurgente* by Thomas Truxtun and the 38-gun *Constellation* brought $84,500 when purchased by the U.S. Navy Department for commissioning.

The war against commerce-poor Tripoli (1801–05) found Congress ultimately considering $100,000 for the survivors or heirs of Stephen Decatur and his seventy volunteers who in the *Intrepid* audaciously retook and blew up the unfortunate U.S. frigate *Philadelphia.*

In the War of 1812, 492 American privateers took 1,344 prizes, most of them in 1814 during the last six months of the war. U.S. naval vessels, while nowhere near as successful as the privateers, made some spectacular captures. Typical combat awards were $50,000 voted to Isaac Hull and the crew of the 44-

gun *Constitution* for the 38-gun *Guerrière* and $25,000 to Jacob Jones and the 18-gun *Wasp* over the equal H.M.S. *Frolic*. For the battles of Lake Erie and Lake Champlain, Oliver Hazard Perry and Thomas Macdonough were each personally awarded $12,140, huge amounts when compared with their annual pay of $720; prize money for ordinary seamen was $209. These combat awards paled against the $350,000 for the rich merchantman *Volunteer* taken by Samuel Evans and the 38-gun *Chesapeake*.

Prize money was trifling in the Mexican War (1846–48). Nine small prizes were seized at Tabasco by Perry's twenty-one-unit squadron. The richest was worth $2,000.

Although the Confederacy had only a minor portion of the prewar U.S. merchant marine, blockading was lucrative for the Union navy. Foreigners gambled for huge profits to be made running the blockade, and about 1,400 runners lost the gamble. Proceeds ranged from $1.11 for a Confederate sloop (after deduction of $108.85 for court costs) to $510,914 for the steamer *Memphis*. Among the Union admirals serving at $5,000 per annum, prize money enriched Samuel P. Lee by $109,690, David Dixon Porter by $91,529, Samuel F. Du Pont by $57,093, and David G. Farragut by $56,509. Commander John Jay Almy received $54,509; Lt. Commander William Budd, $38,766; Lt. William B. Cushing, $15,529 plus $56,056 for his *Albemarle* exploit; and Ensign O. E. S. Roberts, $8,577 (each was the leading recipient in his rank).

In the growth of the navy, requiring assignment of able officers to shore duties, it became manifest that resultant denial of opportunities for prize money at sea was unjust. Thus, at the conclusion of the Spanish-American War (1898), Congress voted $2 million for navywide distribution, and in 1900 it abolished the prize law and enacted a reasonable pay scale.

R. W. Daly

PROCLAMATION MONEY was coin valued according to a proclamation of Queen Anne issued on June 18, 1704, and in effect until 1775. Under this proclamation, the various colonial valuations of Spanish pieces of eight, the most common coins in the American colonies, were superseded by a uniform fixed valuation of six shillings. This attempt to unify the silver currency of the colonies failed in practice.

[A. McF. Davis, "Currency and Banking in the Province of Massachusetts-Bay," *American Economic Association Publications*, vol. 1, series 3.]

Stanley R. Pillsbury

PROCLAMATION OF 1763, a document issued by the British government regulating the settlement of land in North America. It was prepared in part by William Petty Fitzmaurice, Lord Shelburne, president of the Board of Trade, but was completed after his resignation by his successor, Wills Hill, Lord Hillsborough, and was proclaimed by the crown on Oct. 2. By it, parts of the territory in America acquired through the Treaty of Paris earlier in the year were organized as the provinces of Quebec, East Florida, West Florida, and Grenada; the laws of England were extended to these provinces; and provision was made for the establishment of general assemblies in them. Settlement within the new provinces was encouraged by grants of land to British veterans of the French and Indian War.

The part of the proclamation most significant for American history was that aimed at conciliating the Indians. The governors of the provinces and colonies were forbidden to grant lands "for the present, and until our further Pleasure be known . . . beyond the Heads or Sources of any of the Rivers which fall into the Atlantic Ocean from the West and North West." An Indian reservation was thus established south of the lands of the Hudson's Bay Company, west of the province of Quebec and of the Appalachian Mountains, and north of the boundary line of the Floridas, the thirty-first parallel. Settlement upon the Indian lands was prohibited, and settlers already on such lands were commanded "forthwith to remove themselves." Furthermore, private purchases of land from the Indians were forbidden; those that had been made in the Indian reservation were voided; and future purchases were to be made officially, by the governor of the colony involved, for the crown alone. Indian traders were to be licensed and to give security to observe such regulations as might be promulgated.

Although the proclamation was issued hurriedly at the time of Pontiac's War, the sections relating to the Indian lands and Indian trade had been maturely considered. For more than a decade successive ministries had been dissatisfied with the management of Indian relations by the different colonies. The rivalry among the colonies for Indian trade, and in some cases for western lands, had led to abuses by the governors of their power over trade and land grants. Attempting to advance their own interests or those of their respective colonies, the governors ignored the interests of the Indians and aroused a justified resentment. The success of the French in conciliating the Indians was an argument in favor of a unified system of imperial control of Indian affairs and the restriction of settlement.

The appointment in 1756 of two superintendents of Indian affairs, for the northern and southern districts, had been the first step toward the British government's control of Indian relations. Thereafter, the letters of Sir William Johnson, superintendent of the northern Indians, informed the Board of Trade of Indian grievances and urged the fixing of a line west of which settlement should be prohibited. The danger from the Indians during the French and Indian War automatically fixed such a line at the Appalachian Mountains, and after the war proclamations by the military authorities continued this line. Settlers, however, disregarding the proclamations, swarmed over the mountains, and their encroachments were one of the causes of Pontiac's War. The proclamation of 1763 was an attempt to check the advance of pioneering until some agreement securing the Indians' consent to such settlement could be made. The proclamation fixed the settlement line temporarily at the watershed—a conspicuous landmark—but did not and was not intended to change the boundaries of the old colonies; nevertheless, it was resented in the colonies as an interference in their affairs. After Pontiac's War, negotiations with the Indians resulted in the treaties of Hard Labor, Fort Stanwix, and Lochaber, by which a new line, more acceptable to the colonists, was drawn. In 1774 the Quebec Act added the remainder of the Indian reservation north of the Ohio River to the province of Quebec, but this act aroused resentment in some of the thirteen colonies already close to rebellion, since it was seen as an attempt to deprive them of their claims to western lands.

[C. W. Alvord, *Mississippi Valley in British Politics*.]

SOLON J. BUCK

PROCLAMATIONS, official or general notices to the public. Such notices are issued by American political executives either in connection with the conduct of government or for ceremonial purposes. Proclamations related to governmental conduct include those always issued by the president or the governor when an emergency situation requires the establishment of martial law, as in the case of Abraham Lincoln's Proclamation of 1861. Governmental proclamations may also be issued when it is necessary to order troops into a troubled or afflicted area to protect life and property and maintain order, without martial law, as in some strike situations; or when a sudden turn of events requires executive action, as in the case of Lincoln's Emancipation Proclamation of 1863, President Andrew Johnson's Proclamation of Amnesty of 1865, President Woodrow Wilson's Armistice Proclamation of 1918, or President Franklin D. Roosevelt's Bank Holiday Proclamation of 1933.

Ceremonial proclamations may be issued in connection with the observance of legal holidays. For example, on Thanksgiving it has become customary for the president or the governor or both, as the responsible heads of state, to issue proclamations calling upon the people to cooperate in the appropriate observance of the day. Similar proclamations are issued to commemorate some significant event in national or local history or for publicity purposes, as when a week is designated to call the public's attention to an industrial or agricultural product.

W. BROOKE GRAVES

PRODUCTIVITY, CONCEPT OF. The term "productivity" is generally used broadly to denote the ratio of economic output to any or all associated inputs, in real terms. Only when output is related to all associated tangible inputs in total-productivity measures is the net saving of real costs, and thus the effect of technological innovations and other factors increasing productive efficiency, indicated. Partial-productivity ratios of output to one input-class, such as labor (usually measured as output per man-hour), reflect substitutions among factors, as well as changes in productive efficiency.

The earliest studies of output per man-hour in the United States were made in the late 19th century by the Bureau of Labor in the Department of the Interior. Under the direction of Commissioner Carroll D. Wright the labor-displacing effects of machinery were measured. The next broad studies were made by the National Research Project of the Works Progress Administration in the 1930's, again because of concern with possible "technological unemployment." Measurement of output per man-hour in major industries and sectors of the United States was made a regular part of federal government statistical programs in 1940 under the Bureau of Labor Statistics in the U.S. Department of Labor. The focus after World War II was on (1) the contribution of productivity to economic growth and (2) the use of the trend-rate of productivity advance as a guide to noninflationary wage increases under the voluntary stabilization programs of the 1960's and the wage-price controls that were in effect from late 1971 to 1974.

Estimates of productivity also were provided in a series of studies sponsored by the National Bureau of Economic Research beginning in the 1930's and expanded after World War II to include capital productivity and total productivity. The summary volume by

John W. Kendrick, *Productivity Trends in the United States* (1961), provided an impetus for various investigations of the sources of economic growth and explanations of the productivity "residual," with particular emphasis on the contribution of human capital formation.

JOHN W. KENDRICK

PROFITEERING. Popularized during World War I, the term "profiteering" refers to the making of unconscionable profits. The presumption is that profit is just and useful, but profiteering is grossly unreasonable and destructive to society.

Profiteering has appeared especially in times of economic stress and widespread shortages. During the American Revolution, speculators bought paper money at low prices and then made inordinate profits when the value of the money fluctuated. During the War of 1812 profiteers sold sugar at fifty cents a pound and salt at five dollars a bushel. Profiteers were also active during the Mexican War and during the Civil War, when the government paid excessive prices to contractors who furnished matériel to the army. When President Grover Cleveland turned to J. P. Morgan for aid in coping with the panic of 1893, Morgan provided the necessary assistance but made a profit of $7.5 million on the deal. World War I and World War II were characterized by heroism and sacrifice—accompanied by profiteering in munitions and other supplies and commodities. In 1973–75, when petrochemical and other shortages became acute, oil corporations reported per annum profits that ranged up to about 800 percent.

Instances of profiteering have been accompanied by efforts to control such activities. Derided as meretricious and impotent and assailed as so hyperactive and dysfunctional as to impair industry's capacity to serve American consumers and compete in world markets, antiprofiteering controls embrace governmental and nongovernmental agencies and actions. Included are publicity through mass communications media; pressures by consumer and other interest groups; antitrust and antimonopoly laws; legislative investigations; creation of bureaucratic agencies to check on unfair methods of competition; government regulation or ownership of industrial enterprises; judicial decisions that determine the legality of specific merger, pricing, or other corporate behavior; price ceilings; and governmental attempts to increase the supply or channel the distribution of scarce items. (*See also* Revolutionary War, Profiteering in.)

[*Profiteering*, 65th Congress, 2nd session, Senate Document No. 248; *The Industrial Reorganization Act*, Hearings Before the Subcommittee on Antitrust and Monopoly of the Committee on the Judiciary, 93rd Congress, 1st session.]

NORMAN JOHN POWELL

PROFIT SHARING. Annual bonuses, particularly to white-collar or administrative workers, have a long European history. Plans to distribute a percentage of profits to all workers appeared in the United States shortly after the Civil War. These plans were largely confined to medium-size family or paternalistic companies and never became widespread before their general abandonment during the Great Depression. The difficulties in such schemes were formidable: many employers feared the effect on prices and competitors from a public disclosure of large profits; it was hard for managers to see how a share in profits could affect the productivity of many types of labor; workers feared that the promise of a bonus based on profits was in fact an excuse for a low-wage, antiunion policy; and most working-class families preferred a reliable to a fluctuating income. As a consequence, when unions became strong in the manufacturing field after 1940, their leaders proposed fixed fringe benefits such as group insurance, pensions, or guaranteed annual wages, rather than profit sharing.

An allied movement, particularly popular in the prosperous 1920's, was the purchase of stock in the company by employees. Management offered easy payments and often a price lower than the current market figure. It was hoped, as in the case of profit sharing, that the plan would reduce labor turnover and give workers a stronger interest in company welfare. The decline in value of common stocks in the Great Depression to much less than the workers had paid for them, especially when installment payments were still due, ended the popularity of such schemes.

Annual bonuses in stock, cash, or both have been continued in many companies as an incentive to employees in managerial positions. Especially when managerial talent has been scarce, as in the booms of the middle 1950's or 1960's, options to buy large amounts of stock over a span of years at a set price have been used to attract executives.

[Thomas C. Cochran, *American Business in the Twentieth Century*; John R. Commons et al., *History of Labor in the United States, 1896–1932*, vol. III.]

THOMAS C. COCHRAN

PROGRESS AND POVERTY, the magnum opus of American economist Henry George (1839–97) and the bible of his Single Tax movement. The germinal 48-page essay upon which the book was based, "Our Land and Land Policy," published in 1871, advocated the destruction of land monopoly by shifting all taxes from labor and its products to land. *Progress and Poverty* was begun in September 1877 as "an inquiry into industrial depression and of increase of want with increase of wealth." Its publication in 1880 established a major American contribution to the literature of social reform and exerted an appreciable influence upon modern theories of taxation.

[Henry George, Jr., *Henry George.*]

HARVEY WISH

PROGRESSIVE MOVEMENT was a diffuse reform effort of the first two decades of the 20th century. It had supporters in both major political parties and pursued a number of goals, ranging from prohibition and woman suffrage to antitrust legislation, industrial regulation, tax reform, and workmen's compensation. Some historians, noting the variety of politicians and issues embraced by the term, have questioned the propriety of speaking of anything so coherent as a "movement." The term nevertheless usefully describes the attempt to depart from 19th-century laissez-faire policies and to make government both more democratic and more effective in redressing the imbalances of power that large-scale industrialism had produced. In 1912 some of the people committed to those goals formed an important third party, the Progressive, or Bull Moose, party.

The new party's origins can be traced to Theodore Roosevelt's presidency, 1901–09. Roosevelt's proposals for the regulation of transportation and industry, tax reform, labor laws, and social welfare legislation helped to shape a loose coalition of Republican senators and representatives, mostly from the Midwest, who were eager to make their party an instrument of reform. To continue the advances his administration had made, Roosevelt handpicked his successor for the Republican presidential nomination in 1908, William Howard Taft, who was thought to be friendly to the midwestern progressives while still acceptable to the conservative wing of the party.

Once in the White House, Taft proved so much more responsive to the Republican Old Guard than to the progressives that he produced a fateful rebellion within his party. The battle lines began to form during the special session of Congress that Taft called in 1909 to draft new tariff legislation. At the outset the progressives tried to enlist Taft's help in their fight to restrict the powers of the autocratic, reactionary speaker of the House, Joseph G. ("Uncle Joe") Cannon of Illinois. Taft, although sympathetic to the progressives' campaign against the speaker, refused to give them sufficient aid, and Cannon survived the fray with his powers only slightly reduced. Taft also disappointed the midwesterners on the tariff issue, where they expected his support for lower schedules. Again he had proved an undependable ally, and the new Payne-Aldrich tariff actually raised import rates. At the same time Taft wavered in his commitment to income tax legislation, another cherished progressive goal.

In the regular session of Congress Taft intensified progressive disaffection by proposing in his railroad bill a court of commerce to adjudicate disputed rulings of the Interstate Commerce Commission. Almost all the courts had proved unfriendly to regulatory measures, and progressives wanted to curb judicial power, not extend it. Taft further alienated progressives when he supported his secretary of the interior, Richard A. Ballinger, against Gifford Pinchot, the chief forester in the Department of Agriculture, who charged that Ballinger had betrayed Roosevelt's conservation policies.

The progressive ranks included senators Robert M. La Follette of Wisconsin, Jonathan P. Dolliver and Albert B. Cummins of Iowa, Albert J. Beveridge of Indiana, Moses E. Clapp of Minnesota, Joseph L. Bristow of Kansas, William E. Borah of Idaho, Jonathan Bourne of Oregon, and Rep. George W. Norris of Nebraska. By 1910 Taft had resolved to purge the insurgents, as they were known, in the election of that year. But the results boded ill for Taft. The Republican Old Guard suffered widespread casualties at the polls; the Democrats gained control of the House for the first time in eighteen years. The "Grand Old Party" was left more bitterly divided than ever.

In the wake of the election the insurgents formed the National Progressive Republican League in a meeting at La Follette's home on Jan. 21, 1911. Ostensibly created to advocate progressive principles, the league was widely regarded as a device for La Follette to wrest the Republican presidential nomination from Taft in 1912. That suspicion was confirmed when La Follette, on June 17, 1911, announced his candidacy for the nomination.

Theodore Roosevelt, in the meantime, had watched the developing schism in his party with increasing discomfort. Although he campaigned for both regulars and insurgents in the election of 1910, he showed his progressive sympathies in a famous speech expounding his "New Nationalist" philosophy at Osawatomie, Kans., on Aug. 31, 1910. Still, while rankled by Taft's policies, Roosevelt remained aloof from the National Progressive Republican League. Many of its members preferred him to La Follette as a presidential nominee, but Roosevelt remained convinced until well into 1911 that 1912 would be a Democratic year; better to stick with Taft and let the Old Guard bear responsibility for defeat, he reasoned, thus clearing the way for reorganization of the party along progressive lines before the 1916 election.

On Oct. 27, 1911, the Taft administration announced its intention to bring an antitrust suit against the United States Steel Company. The suit attacked U.S. Steel's 1907 acquisition of the Tennessee Coal and Iron Company, a merger that Roosevelt, then president, had personally approved in a meeting with J. P. Morgan. Incensed at Taft's repudiation of that decision, and at the implication that he had been a party to wrongdoing, Roosevelt announced late in February 1912 that his "hat was in the ring." Most of La Follette's backers, many of whom had been covertly promoting Roosevelt's candidacy, almost immediately declared their support for the former president. There followed a bitter series of battles for delegates to the Republican National Convention, scheduled to meet June 18, 1912, in Chicago. Taft, by organizing the largely black Republican delegations from the southern states and by controlling the national committee, clearly had the upper hand. Of the 254 contested seats at Chicago, 235 went to pro-Taft delegates, and only 19 to Roosevelt men. On a vote of 561 to 107 the convention nominated Taft, while 344 Roosevelt delegates simply refused to vote. Roosevelt, backed by many of the rank and file but by few party professionals, determined to abandon his lifelong Republicanism and form a new party. Assured of financial support by publisher Frank A. Munsey and by George W. Perkins, an associate of J. P. Morgan and a director of U.S. Steel and International Harvester, Roosevelt called for the first Progressive National Convention to meet in Chicago on Aug. 5, 1912.

That convention, made up of reformers of every stripe but dominated by urban, middle-class persons with little previous experience in national politics, adopted a remarkably advanced platform. Condemning what it called "the unholy alliance between corrupt business and corrupt politics," the platform called for the adoption of primary elections; the short ballot; initiative, referendum, and recall measures; the direct election of U.S. senators; and woman suffrage. It advocated federal legislation establishing minimum standards of industrial safety and health; minimum wages for women; the eight-hour day in many industries; medical, old-age, and unemployment insurance; stronger regulation of interstate business (Perkins, to the distress of many delegates, succeeded in eliminating an antitrust plank from the platform); a tariff commission; public ownership of natural resources; graduated income and inheritance taxes; improved educational services for immigrants; and government supervision of securities markets. It endorsed collective bargaining, the establishment of industrial research laboratories, government-business cooperation to extend foreign commerce, the creation of a department of labor, and the prohibition of child labor. It strongly opposed the power of the courts to nullify social and economic legislation.

Roosevelt and Gov. Hiram W. Johnson of California, vice-presidential nominee, running best in the big cities, finished second in the national balloting, with 4.1 million popular and 88 electoral votes. But at the state and local levels, the party did less well. It was able to field full slates in only fifteen states. Including incumbent Republicans who had joined the Progressives, the party in 1913 could count only one governor, two senators, sixteen representatives, and 250 local elected officials. Many Progressives blamed their relatively poor showing at the polls on the influence of Perkins, who, they claimed, had too close an association with Wall Street. Roosevelt, however, stood by Perkins and in 1913 thwarted an attempt to oust him from the chairmanship of the national executive committee.

When the elections of 1914 produced more disasters for the party (every important Progressive save Hiram Johnson was defeated) and when, after the outbreak of World War I, the questions of neutrality and preparedness threatened further to divide it, many Progressives began to consider fusion with the Republicans. The two parties held their presidential nominating conventions simultaneously in June 1916, in Chicago. There, after Roosevelt had declined the Progressive nomination, the national committee, on a divided vote, agreed to endorse the Republican candidate, Charles Evans Hughes. Most Progressives thereupon rejoined the party they had left in 1912, a few became Democrats, and a die-hard contingent persevered until April 1917, when in a final convention in Saint Louis it merged with the Prohibition party.

The Progressive bolt, by splitting Republican strength, had made possible Woodrow Wilson's victory in 1912. It had also removed liberal influence from the Republican party just when liberals were on the verge of controlling it. When they returned four years later, they were largely without power; their departure had helped to ensure conservative dominance of the Republican party for some years to come. Their action had, however, demonstrated the strength of liberal sentiment in the country and helped move the Democrats in a progressive direction. Wilson, especially in 1915–16, pursued several policies calculated to woo the Progressive voters of 1912 into the Democratic ranks. And the Progressive platform of 1912 constituted a charter for liberal reform for the next fifty years.

[Alfred D. Chandler, Jr., "The Origins of Progressive Leadership," in Elting E. Morison, ed., *The Letters of Theodore Roosevelt*, vol. VIII; Benjamin Parke DeWitt, *The Progressive Movement*; George E. Mowry, *Theodore Roosevelt and the Progressive Movement*; Robert H. Wiebe, *The Search for Order, 1877–1920.*]

DAVID M. KENNEDY

PROGRESSIVE PARTY (1947–52). Established in 1947 and expiring shortly after the 1952 national elections, the Progressive party claimed that it was the true heir to the philosophy of Franklin D. Roosevelt and condemned the administration of Harry S. Truman for its alleged failures at home and abroad. The party opposed the administration's loyalty-security program, called for bolder civil rights and welfare measures, charged that the large military budgets fostered bellicosity, blamed the administration in large measure for the cold war, and offered a policy of accommodation with the Soviet Union. In 1948 the party selected as its candidates Henry A. Wallace, formerly vice-president under Roosevelt, and Glen H. Taylor, senator from Idaho. Polls initially predicted that the party would receive about 7 percent of the popular vote, cut into Democratic strength, and cost Truman the election. But the Czechoslovakian coup and the Berlin blockade, both interpreted widely as proof of Communist aggression, and the charges of growing Communist influence in the party cut deeply into its potential support. The party won 1,157,172 votes, or 2.4 percent of the popular vote, with more than 60 percent of that from New York and California and most of it from New York City and Los Angeles. The crushing defeat, growing anticommunism in America, and renewed charges of Communist domination soon weakened the party. In 1950 it was injured when its executive board opposed American intervention in the Korean War, and Wallace, along with

many others, resigned. In 1952 the party ran Vincent W. Hallinan, an attorney, and Charlotta Bass, a black newspaper publisher, and received 140,023 votes, 56,647 of those from New York City.

BARTON J. BERNSTEIN

PROHIBITION. The ratification of the Eighteenth Amendment to the U.S. Constitution, completed Jan. 29, 1919, and the subsequent enactment by Congress of the Volstead Act marked the culmination of a long campaign in the United States against the manufacture and sale of alcoholic beverages. Although the origin of the movement is to be found in colonial protests against the excessive use of intoxicants, the temperance crusaders did not turn from moral suasion to legal coercion until the middle of the 19th century. Thereafter, three periods of legislative activity are apparent. First, between 1846 and 1855, following the lead of Maine, thirteen states passed prohibition laws. Within a decade, however, nine of these measures had been either repealed or declared unconstitutional. After Kansas, in 1880, had written prohibition into its constitution, there was a revival of the temperance movement, stimulated by the persistent efforts of the Prohibition party (1869), the Woman's Christian Temperance Union (1874), and, most powerful of all, the Anti-Saloon League (1893). Again results were impermanent, for by 1905 only Kansas, Maine, Nebraska, and North Dakota were prohibition states.

The failure of the brewers and distillers to set their houses in order and the judicious political tactics of the Anti-Saloon League prepared the way for the final drive to outlaw the saloon. A wide range of motivations influenced the voters as they went to the polls under local option laws in the various states. The ardent reformers relentlessly pressed their arguments that the liquor interests represented a demoralizing force in American politics, that the mechanization of industry placed a premium upon the sober employee, and that the taxpayer really paid the bills for a business that was filling the poorhouses and prisons with its victims. On the eve of the United States' entrance into World War I, there were prohibition laws in twenty-six states, of which thirteen could be described as "bone-dry." Wayne B. Wheeler, Ernest H. Cherrington, and other leaders of the Anti-Saloon League, who had already mobilized the forces of evangelical Protestantism, were quick to associate prohibition with winning the war. Congressional action reinforced their arguments.

By December 1917, both the Senate and the House of Representatives had approved a resolution, originally proposed by Sen. Morris Sheppard of Texas, to add an amendment to the Constitution prohibiting the "manufacture, sale or transportation" of intoxicating liquors for beverage purposes. Within thirteen months ratification by the legislatures of three-quarters of the states had been secured, and a year later the Eighteenth Amendment went into effect. Meanwhile, Congress had placed restrictions upon the manufacture of intoxicants, to conserve grain during the war, and had provided that from July 1, 1919, until the termination of the war (which actually ended in 1918) no distilled spirits, beer, or wine should be sold for beverage purposes.

The opponents of Prohibition soon directed their attack against the efforts of governmental agents to enforce the law. They approved the banishment of the saloon, but they insisted that it had been replaced by illegal "speakeasies" and nightclubs; that the illicit traffic in intoxicants was breeding "rum runners," racketeers, and gangsters; that corruption was rampant in federal and state enforcement units; and that disrespect for all law was becoming a characteristic of those who flouted the liquor laws with impunity. The supporters of the Eighteenth Amendment, on the other hand, admitted that enforcement was far from perfect but proclaimed Prohibition's benefits—reduced poverty, increased bank deposits, and expanding industry. For them it was a basic factor in the nation's prosperity from 1923 to 1929.

But popular disgust over the failure of enforcement grew so steadily, especially after the onset of the Great Depression, that the Democratic National Convention in 1932 demanded repeal of the Eighteenth Amendment. The Democratic landslide in the November elections persuaded Congress that the time for action had come. In the short session (Feb. 20, 1933) a resolution was approved providing for an amendment to accomplish repeal. Submitted to conventions in the several states, the Twenty-first Amendment was ratified in less than a year. Before ratification, Congress, on Mar. 22, 1933, had legalized the sale of beverages containing no more than 3.2 percent alcohol, wherever state law did not contravene.

Repeal of the Eighteenth Amendment ended the first experiment on the part of the American people in writing sumptuary legislation into the fundamental law of the land. The liquor problem was turned back to the states.

[J. C. Furnas, *The Life and Times of the Late Demon Rum;* Charles Merz, *Dry Decade;* Andrew Sinclair, *Prohibition: The Era of Excess;* James H. Timberlake, *Prohibition and the Progressive Movement.*]
JOHN A. KROUT

PROHIBITION PARTY, oldest of the third parties in the United States, was organized in 1869 after nearly three-quarters of a century of temperance agitation had failed to influence the platforms of the major parties. The campaign of 1872 marked its initial appearance in national politics. Nine states were represented at its first national convention in Columbus, Ohio, Feb. 22, 1872. James Black of Pennsylvania was nominated for president. Prior to 1872 Prohibition candidates for state offices had been nominated in some states. In its early years the party was strongest in Ohio and New York, holding the balance of power in the latter in the presidential election of 1884. Candidates have appeared in every presidential campaign since 1872 but have never won any electoral votes. The peak of the party's popular support was reached in 1892 when its candidate for president, John Bidwell, received 271,000 votes. In 1896 the money question temporarily split the party (*see* Presidential Campaigns: Campaign of 1896).

Through its educational activities and its strong appeal to the moral sentiment of the people, the party exerted an influence for a more effective governmental policy toward the liquor problem. While its primary object has been the prohibition of the manufacture and sale of intoxicating liquors, it has advocated other political, economic, and social reforms, many of which have subsequently been endorsed by the major parties.

[W. B. Hesseltine, *The Rise and Fall of Third Parties;* Howard P. Nash, *Third Parties in American Politics.*]
GLENN H. BENTON

PROMONTORY POINT, Utah, was the site of the dramatic completion, on May 10, 1869, of the first transcontinental railroad. A motley crowd gathered to witness the final ceremonies. Following prayers and brief but grandiloquent speeches, President Leland Stanford of the Central Pacific Railroad, using a silver sledgehammer, nervously drove the last golden spike into a polished California laurel tie. Western Union telegraph apparatus was connected with the spike, and these final strokes were instantly heralded in all cities of the United States. Two locomotives, *Jupiter* and *119,* hastened to move forward until their noses touched, and a cheering crowd confirmed a single-word telegram: "Done."

[Edwin L. Sabin, *Building the Pacific Railroad.*]
OSCAR OSBURN WINTHER

PROPAGANDA may be defined as any form of controlled communication for the purpose of influencing the opinions, emotions, attitudes, or behavior of an intended audience. It is the communication of messages that aim to propagate a point of view favorable to an advocate. The advocate may be a single individual acting alone or an official of an organization. The scope and depth of propaganda efforts vary widely in a direct relation to the resources in personnel and communications media assigned to the effort. Any person or group with a message, an audience to receive the message, and a communications carrier may become an advocate or sponsor of propaganda.

The purposes that guide propaganda efforts may be specific or broad and general. Specific purposes can be evaluated for effectiveness when an audience takes some action that can be observed; for example, when enemy soldiers surrender or abandon the fight in direct response to messages that urge them to do so. Communications to convince an electorate to support a political candidate are similarly direct and specific in purpose and comparably susceptible to evaluation through polls and election results. General purposes are usually related to situations and audiences wherein slight, subjective changes in audience perceptions will constitute the desired effect. This can sometimes be achieved by bringing a particular fact or event to the attention of the audience. General purposes normally contribute to or reinforce other types of actions designed to achieve the purposes of the sponsor, for example, as a contribution to other actions designed to influence a nation that is potentially hostile to swing toward neutrality or alliance.

Methods and techniques in propaganda encompass the entire range of words, sounds, symbols, and actions that depict ideas or bits of information. The propaganda is carried and delivered through equally diverse media. Loudspeakers and leaflets that contain writing, drawing, and photographs are widely used in battlefield propaganda. Organizations come into being specifically to direct propaganda to international and domestic audiences. These organizations normally develop media appropriate to their messages and audiences and also use existing news media, posters, paid advertising, public gatherings, official statements, and word-of-mouth communications between key individuals.

Although the distinctions are frequently unclear or indefinite, there are differences between propaganda and associated uses of communication to inform or instruct. An editorial or cartoon designed to influence an audience is propaganda. A news account or photograph that depicts portions of an event is not. If a sponsor or an advocate uses that news account or photograph to depict a point of view and/or to encourage certain perceptions by an audience, it becomes propaganda. The content of propaganda may be true or false, real or fabricated. The consistent distinction is in whether the communication is sponsored to influence or is prepared and disseminated to contribute to entertainment or general knowledge.

Nations and individuals have used persuasive communications from the beginnings of recorded history, but the use of the term "propaganda" is comparatively modern. Its usage probably dates from the mid-17th century, when it was used by the Roman Catholic church in the name of its missionary organization for the propagation of the faith. In earlier years, when word traveled slowly and audiences were necessarily small, the communications consisted mainly of exchanges between leaders and officials of the nations and institutions involved. Messages were conveyed by emissary, courier, letter, rumor, and face-to-face meeting. When propaganda was used as an instrument of national policy, government leaders developed procedures to convince audiences of their capabilities and intentions to undertake the actions promised in the propaganda messages. Information intended to confirm the capability to prosecute a war or to enforce political or economic sanctions was released to the audience nation, either directly or through third-nation parties. Demonstrations of economic or combat prowess were staged in a manner to attract the attention of the audiences and reinforce the credibility and strength of the propaganda messages.

Propaganda is practiced extensively and pervasively during war and in short-of-war hostilities. While the conduct of war to inflict casualties on an enemy is not properly within the realm of propaganda, virtually all the other actions of one nation to influence the leaders and people of another nation are so deeply woven into propaganda purposes as to merit inclusion of those actions within broad-scope propaganda. (Terrorism, murder, and political assassination, sometimes referred to as "propaganda of the deed," are not properly characterized as propaganda. While such acts may have influences that coincide with the purposes of propaganda, the very nature of the acts places them beyond the realm of propaganda.) Wartime propaganda is directed to enemy, neutral, friendly, and home (national) audiences. Purposes, messages, and media are tailored to existing perceptions of each audience and its receptiveness to the media that can be applied to reach it. Home, friendly, and allied audiences are usually urged to strengthen their resolve and intensify their efforts to gain victory. The messages to hostile audiences are designed to lessen the effectiveness of enemy actions. Themes normally include the carrot-and-stick approach, including promises of improvement in conditions through nonresistance or cooperation, and threats of harm if resistance continues. Communication to hostile audiences is sometimes called psychological warfare, and that term has been adopted by the U.S. military services to describe the propaganda and other psychological actions directed toward hostile foreign groups.

America has employed propaganda in each of the nation's wars. By the time of the Revolution newssheets and pamphlets had come into wide use; they were adapted to carry the speeches and writings of leaders who sought to build a willingness to go to war. Those leaders consistently proclaimed that British legislation threatened to take away the liberties that had already been established. The Declaration of Independence, used to unify the colonists and justify the Revolution, still stands as an example of highly effective propaganda. Beginning with the Battle of Bunker Hill, British soldiers were regularly urged to contrast the rigors and danger of their situation with the relative comfort and safety enjoyed by their officers. The increased communications capabilities effected by the time of the Civil War made it possible for each side in that conflict to conduct active propaganda, making appeals designed to strengthen its cause and weaken the opponent. The Emancipation Proclamation issued by President Abraham Lincoln in January 1863, irrespective of its force or merit, was a masterful propaganda stroke, for once the war became characterized as a crusade against slavery, it became very difficult for any European government to support the Confederacy.

During World War I Britain led the way in the practice of skillful propaganda. With an extensive news service and experience in international communications, Britain developed extensive propaganda networks that reached almost all civilian audiences in the western world. The U.S. effort in that war centered on the exploitation of basic vulnerabilities—such as shortage of food and medical care—of German soldiers. During subsequent wars the United States gradually expanded the search for vulnerability in the enemy that could provide a basis for propaganda to reduce enemy morale and degrade combat effectiveness. Modern military propagandists strive to classify enemy groupings according to

needs, hopes, and fears that can be exploited by messages that will contribute to thoughts and/or doubts on their part that favor attainment of U.S. national and military objectives. During World War II the United States established the Office of War Information, which exercised some control over the news and information disseminated at home and internationally. There was no comparable organization or policy during the Korean and Vietnam wars, although U.S. military forces engaged in extensive battlefield propaganda during both of those conflicts.

The experiences gained during World War II and in the subsequent occupation of Germany and Japan caused the United States to provide continuing policies and capabilities to conduct communications with foreign audiences. The Smith-Mundt (Information and Education Exchange) Act of 1948 directed the secretary of state to "provide for the preparation and dissemination abroad of information about the United States, its people and its policies, through press, publications, radio, motion pictures and other information media, and through information centers and instructors abroad." The International Information Administration (IIA) of the Department of State was assigned to conduct the information program. In 1953 the United States Information Agency (USIA) was established to replace the IIA. The purpose of the USIA is to help achieve U.S. foreign policy objectives by influencing public attitudes in other nations, and to advise other agencies on the implications of foreign opinion for present and contemplated U.S. policies, programs, and official statements. The USIA operates four media services: broadcasting (Voice of America), the Information Center Service, the Motion Picture and Television Service, and the Press and Publications Service. The services provide materials to overseas missions, known as the United States Information Service (USIS), whose posts abroad perform under the direction of the ambassador and conduct public information, public relations, and cultural activities intended to inform or influence foreign public opinion.

The dramatic increase in the volume and speed of communications during the 20th century tended to make propaganda a part of everyday domestic life in America as propaganda sponsors came to include virtually all fields of interest that depend on an audience or clientele for success in an enterprise. The many departments and levels of government have been especially active in dissemination of information. While those who manage the information flow may strive for objectivity and balance, a large part of the output contains points of emphasis designed to enhance views favorable to the sponsor, thus deserving to be called propaganda. The variety of associations and agencies that propagate a point of view tends to provide a contrast and balance in the release of information and makes it possible for any person to acquaint himself with all sides of an issue. Among the most active sponsors of propaganda are political parties, labor and trade unions, manufacturing and business associations, and professional societies or associations.

[Harwood L. Childs, *A Reference Guide to the Study of Public Opinion;* Philip Davidson, *Propaganda and the American Revolution, 1763–1783;* Harold D. Lasswell, *Propaganda Technique in the World War;* Harold D. Lasswell, Ralph D. Casey, and Bruce L. Smith, *Propaganda and Promotional Activities—An Annotated Biliography.*]

W. E. BARBER

PROPERTY. The most important division of property is that between real and personal. In general, real property consists of land and things permanently attached to land; such things, which either are immovable or ordinarily go with land when it is conveyed, include trees, buildings, and fences. Personal property consists of all other property that is capable of ownership.

Another classification, cutting across both of the above classes, divides property into corporeal and incorporeal. The former term refers to tangibles, such as land, livestock, implements, furniture, automobiles, and the like; the latter refers to intangibles, such as contract rights, franchises, claims against others because of personal injuries, notes, stocks, bonds, insurance policies, and rights of action of various kinds. Corporeal personal property is also known as chattels or goods.

In a popular sense, property usually consists of concrete things or substances, but in the eyes of the law, it more frequently consists of legal relations between a person called the owner and other people. The owner's legal rights constitute his property. Hence, when one owns property, he has a "bundle of legal rights," the most essential one being the power of more or less exclusive control. Such things as air, light, water in streams, birds, fish, and wild animals, not being capable of exclusive control, are not capable of ownership, until reduced to possession.

The feudal system of land tenures introduced in England by William the Conqueror was based on the theory that all land was owned by the king, who allotted it among his lords; they in turn parceled out its

use among the villeins, who tilled the land. The interests thus created were not absolute, but conditional upon military and other services being rendered to the lord and king. Through the years the rights of the lords to such services were gradually reduced by statutes, until a more or less absolute ownership (called free and common socage) was created in the villeins.

This was the type of land ownership in England when the American colonies were settled, and it was this system that was transplanted to America. Hence, the American law of real property is based on that of England after the feudal system had disappeared. Although all land titles in the United States originate with the state, the state, having no right to services, is not an overlord in the feudal sense. There are, however, important limitations on ownership of land. No type of ownership can be said to be absolute. Owners may not use land in such a way as to create public nuisances or injure their neighbors. Property may be taken for taxes and is subject to execution for the payment of debts. It is also liable to escheat (reversion to the state) if a deceased owner has no will or heirs, and it is subject to the power of eminent domain and to curtailment under the police power.

The subjection of both real and personal property to the police power is of growing importance. Public utilities, such as transportation, communication, and electric light and power companies, are said to be businesses "affected with a public interest." In contrast to strictly private businesses they must serve all who apply and are subject to close legislative regulation as to rates charged and quality of service rendered. Since a business is property, this regulation constitutes an encroachment upon ownership. But the line between such a business and one that is said to be private has grown less distinct with the years. With the passage of civil rights legislation in the 1960's, "public accommodations" (such as restaurants, bars, and hotels) were required to serve all prospective customers, regardless of race or ethnic background. In addition, many businesses formerly classed as private are now subject to such governmental supervision as the public interest seems to demand. For example, federal, state, and local laws regulate the operations of food processors and packers, require manufacturers to install antipollution equipment, prescribe safety standards in mines and plants, set minimum wages for workers, and prohibit construction of commercial buildings in specified zones. All such laws restrict the use of property and may even reduce its value. Although state and federal legislative power to curtail the use of private property is limited by the due process clauses of the Fifth and Fourteenth amendments to the U.S. Constitution, court decisions indicate that this protection is less absolute than formerly. Property interests once regarded as immune from interference have now been brought within the scope of legislative treatment.

Although title to land or an interest therein may be acquired by adverse possession, statutes in all U.S. states provide for the conveyance or transfer of land by deed, a document required to be signed by the grantor and delivered to the grantee.

In most states, interests in land that are inheritable under the law (see Freeholder) pass, upon the death of the owner, to the owner's heirs or, if there is a will, to the devisees named in it. Statutes in all U.S. states provide for the recording, in a public office, of deeds, mortgages, and other instruments affecting title to land, so that notice may be given to the world of the facts relative to the title. Instruments not so recorded, although valid as between the parties to them, do not affect others who have no notice of them. A document in which the various links in the chain of title are copied, so that the history of ownership may be examined, is known as an abstract of title.

Title to personal property may be transferred by mere delivery or by agreement. No formal document of transfer comparable to a deed is usually required. Upon the death of the owner of personal property, the title passes to the executor or administrator. The next of kin of the owner have no rights with respect to the property until the debts of the owner have been paid and the estate finally settled.

Statutes regarding property interests have been passed in all states. Many of them are simply a codification of certain common law rules. Others have materially changed the law. Examples of the latter are statutes broadening the scope of the term "heirs" by abolishing primogeniture, abolishing or modifying the fee tail estate, granting to married women the power to own and control both real and personal property, and providing for a system of recording deeds, mortgages, and other instruments affecting property titles and simplifying the form of such instruments.

In the United States, a noteworthy movement affecting the ownership and transfer of various types of personal property is that toward uniformity in the laws of the various states. Most states have now enacted identical statutes covering such subjects as negotiable instruments, bills of lading, warehouse receipts, and the sales of goods.

[John Rogers Commons, *Legal Foundations of Capitalism;* Pearl J. Davies, *Real Estate in American History.*]

GEORGE W. GOBLE

PROPERTY INSURANCE. *See* **Insurance.**

PROPERTY QUALIFICATIONS. The Twenty-fourth Amendment to the Constitution (Jan. 23, 1964) effectively outlawed property qualifications for voting in federal elections by abolishing all poll or other taxes as requirements for voting. This prohibition was extended to state elections by a 1967 Supreme Court decision (*Harper* v. *Virginia Board of Elections*), which held that state poll taxes were in violation of the Fourteenth Amendment's requirement of equal protection of the laws. A 1973 Supreme Court decision, however, permitted states to limit voting to property owners in "special" districts. In a six-to-three decision, the majority held that a state "could rationally conclude that landowners are primarily burdened and benefited by the establishment and operation of watershed districts, and may condition the vote accordingly."

The rationale behind property qualifications in the American states was that only property owners possessed "stock" in the state, which was regarded as a corporation. Almost all states had property requirements for voting at the time of the American Revolution. The Massachusetts requirement was typical, requiring that a voter had to own either real estate yielding an annual income of 40 shillings or other property worth £40.

In the early 19th century the newly admitted western states had few property requirements for voting, and the eastern states tended to reduce the requirements. For example, when Ohio became a state in 1803 the only property requirement for voting was that voters pay a county tax, or "work out" a tax on the public highway. By 1820 even Massachusetts gave the vote to those who paid a county or state tax. By the time of the Civil War virtually all property requirements for voting had been eliminated. After the Civil War many southern states enacted poll taxes in order to disfranchise blacks.

JOHN H. FENTON

PROPHET DANCE is the name given to a cult movement that arose among the Indian tribes of the Plateau area of the Pacific Northwest before the end of the 18th century. Although it may have had its roots in native beliefs about death and rebirth, the cult appears to have been indirectly influenced by alien intrusions before the whites ever entered the area. The later nativistic Ghost Dance may have had its source in the Prophet Dance, for both the Prophet Dance and the

Ghost Dance emphasized beliefs in the impending destruction of the world and its subsequent renewal, concomitant with the return of the dead Indians. The dance, usually circular, was considered to be an imitation of the dances of the dead, and it was believed that intensive concentration on the dance would hasten the day of reunion with the departed. Inspired leaders related prophecies that they had earlier received in visions. The cult spread to most of the Plateau tribes and also diffused to many of the Northwest Coast Indians. Between 1830 and 1845 some elements of Christian derivation were added to the Prophet Dance, including the cross and the prescription for the observance of the Sabbath.

[David F. Aberle, "The Prophet Dance and Reactions to White Contact," *Southwestern Journal of Anthropology,* vol. 15; Leslie Spier, *The Prophet Dance of the Northwest and Its Derivatives: The Source of the Ghost Dance;* Wayne Suttles, "The Plateau Prophet Dance Among the Coast Salish," *Southwestern Journal of Anthropology,* vol. 13; Deward E. Walker, Jr., "New Light on the Prophet Dance Controversy," *Ethnohistory,* vol. 16.]

KENNETH M. STEWART

PROPHET'S TOWN. In 1808, at a site on the west bank of the Wabash River just below the mouth of the Tippecanoe River (in present-day Tippecanoe County, Ind.), Tenskwatawa, an orator and reformer known as the Shawnee Prophet and brother of Tecumseh, established his headquarters. Groups of northwestern tribesmen, dissatisfied with white encroachments on their land, gathered at Prophet's Town to plan a concerted resistance. After the Battle of Tippecanoe in 1811, the Shawnee Prophet abandoned the town, and Gen. William Henry Harrison destroyed it.

[Benjamin Drake, *Life of Tecumseh and of His Brother, The Prophet;* Logan Esarey, *A History of Indiana From Its Exploration to 1850.*]

EUGENE H. ROSEBOOM

PROPORTIONAL REPRESENTATION, an electoral device, the intent of which is to make a representative body a faithful image of its electorate. Ideally, the system gives legislative voting strength proportionate to the electoral strength of every shade of societal opinion. Proportional representation dates at least to the French Revolution. Over 300 variations have been devised. Although it is the most common method of election in the Western democracies, the use of proportional representation in the United States has been rare. It has been tried by several cities, notably Cincinnati; Boulder, Colo.; and New York. In the late 1960's the system was adopted by the Democratic party for selecting delegates to the Democratic National Convention. Debate over the use of proportional representation has tended to focus on the consequences of the system—especially instability of governments—rather than on its inherent logic or principle. Proponents argue that proportional representation prevents excessive centralization of government, strengthens parties by making candidates more dependent on them, and increases voter interest and participation in elections. Opponents contend that the system vitiates democracy on the interparty and intraparty levels. Little empirical evidence has been collected to support either position.

Technically, proportional representation is achieved by devising a quota that determines the minimum number of votes required for election. The number of seats a party wins is the number of votes it receives divided by the quota. The simplest quota is the Hare quota, which is found by dividing the total number of votes cast by the number of seats to be filled. Important quotas are the Droop, d'Hondt, and Sainte-Laguë quotas. Some proportional representation systems require surplus or wasted votes (votes that do not count up to a quota) to be transferred from one party to another in accordance with a voter's rank-ordering of his preferences on the original ballot. Complex systems weigh the first, second, third, and so on, preferences of a voter in determining results. Elections are usually at large or employ multimember districts. The greater the number of seats to be filled, the greater proportionality of representation possible. Logically, the greater the number of seats available—assuming the size of the electorate to be constant—the lower the quota. The lower the quota, the more likely it is that small groups will be willing to contest an election, since the odds of their winning are greater—more so than in a majority vote system. Proportional representation elections using party lists allow the voter to influence which of the party's candidates will be selected to fill the seats allotted to the party.

[F. A. Hermens, *Democracy or Anarchy?;* C. G. Hoag and G. H. Hallett, Jr., *Proportional Representation.*]

ROBERT B. KVAVIK

PROPRIETARY AGENT, a business representative of the proprietor of an American colony. The Duke of York (later James II) in New York; the Carolina board; Cecilius Calvert, Lord Baltimore, in Maryland; and William Penn in Pennsylvania all found it necessary to employ agents to attend to colonial business both in London and in America. Sir John Werden served as the Duke of York's agent in England, and John Lewin went to the colony as special agent to report on financial conditions. Before 1700 Henry Darnall served Lord Baltimore as a private agent in Maryland, and this office was continued through the colonial era. Proprietors frequently acted as their own agents in London. Until his health failed, Penn transacted in London all important business relating to his province. F. J. Paris frequently acted during the 18th century as London agent for the Penn family and other private interests. For many years James Logan was the efficient agent of Penn and his sons in the Quaker colony, looking after the survey and sale of lands, the collection of proprietary revenue, and the management of estates.

[E. P. Lilly, *The Colonial Agents of New York and New Jersey;* Mabel P. Wolff, *The Colonial Agency of Pennsylvania.*]

WINFRED T. ROOT

PROPRIETARY PROVINCES. The proprietorship succeeded the trading company as a device employed to build England's colonial empire (*see* Colonial Policy, British). The proprietary provinces had a familiar precedent in English history, being patterned, in general, upon the ancient Palatinate of Durham, in which the feudal lord enjoyed sweeping powers that enabled him to guard the English border against Scottish forays. Originating in a royal grant bestowing broad territorial and political powers upon a single person or a small group (the lord proprietor or the lords proprietors), the proprietary province was virtually a feudal jurisdiction in which, with specified exemptions, the lord proprietor exercised sovereign powers. He could appoint all officials; create courts, hear appeals, and pardon offenders; make laws and issue decrees; raise and command a militia; and establish churches, ports, and towns. The charters of Maryland and Pennsylvania contained the important limitation requiring the proprietor to make laws by and with the consent of the freemen. These provinces were, thus, feudal only in name. The proprietors were forced to accede to the insistent demands of the people and to yield to them political privileges and powers (*see* Colonial Assemblies). The land of the proprietary province, however, constituted a great private domain. The proprietor granted it to settlers on his own terms. He could mortgage it for debt, as William Penn did. New provinces could come into existence by subgrants. Estates could be transferred into new hands by purchase.

By 1630 the trading company venture of the Virginia Company had proved a failure, and the Council for New England was moribund. Thus, when the next important royal grant was made, that of Maryland to Cecilius Calvert, Lord Baltimore, in 1632, it was of the feudal, or proprietary, type. Seven years later, when Sir Ferdinando Gorges received a royal charter for Maine, as compensation for his part in the Council for New England, the grant was also of the feudal or proprietary type, and as such it was sold by Gorges' heir, in 1677, to Massachusetts.

When, in 1664, an English fleet ended Dutch rule in New Netherland, the king granted the region, comprising what came to be known as New York, New Jersey, and Delaware, to the Duke of York as a proprietary. When, in 1685, the duke became King James II, New York, the part of the proprietary still remaining in his hands, became a royal colony.

The area of New Jersey had, in 1664, been subgranted by the Duke of York to John Berkeley (Lord Berkeley of Stratton) and Sir George Carteret, and in 1682 the duke had subgranted Delaware to William Penn. In 1674 Berkeley sold his share of New Jersey for £1,000, and West Jersey, as the region was known, soon came into the hands of a board of Quakers. In 1680 another group purchased East Jersey from the Carteret estate. The proprietary right to both of these areas, so far as the land is concerned, still exists in the councils of the proprietors of New Jersey.

By the charters of 1663 and 1665 a group of eight men, royal courtiers and colonial planters, received the broad area of Carolina, in which two colonies came into existence under one board. The proprietary continued until 1729, when the owners, wearying of the unprofitable colonial business, sold their proprietary rights to the king, with the exception of one parcel that came to be known as the Granville Grant.

Pennsylvania, founded under a charter issued to William Penn in 1681, was the last of the proprietary colonies. Thereafter the policy was definitely in the direction of the royal colony. At the outbreak of the Revolution there remained of the proprietary colonies only Pennsylvania and Delaware, in the hands of the Penn family, and Maryland, in the hands of the Calvert family.

The Revolution cut the political ties between Great Britain and the colonies and thereby placed ultimate political and territorial power in America in the people of the several states. Popular and independent state governments were promptly created, and the huge estates of the Penn and Calvert heirs were con-

PROSTITUTION

fiscated and disposed of in harmony with popular desires. The state governments were not generous in the process of confiscation. The largest estate, that of the Penn family, was valued at about £1 million, but the legislature paid the Penns £130,000. The Maryland government gave Lord Baltimore £10,000 for his confiscated land, a sum deemed so inadequate that the British government paid him an additional £90,000. The Granville estate also passed into the control of the state.

A feudal and proprietary land system thus ceased to be. The large private estates became public property, and the legislatures abolished quitrents, which had been paid to the proprietors. The land was sold in smaller portions, thus making for economic democracy, and the sale of confiscated lands helped to pay for the war.

[J. F. Jameson, *American Revolution Considered as a Social Movement;* C. P. Nettels, *Roots of American Civilization.*]

WINFRED T. ROOT

PROSPECTORS are persons who explore for minerals. For many 19th-century American prospectors the hope of one day striking it rich was a lifelong preoccupation. William Green Russell is typical. Twice (1849 and 1853) he went from the Georgia gold mines to California's rich deposits. In 1858 he led a party to the foothills north of Pikes Peak and found the placer deposit that, greatly exaggerated, precipitated the Pikes Peak gold rush. In 1859 he led another party from Georgia to rich deposits in Russell Gulch above Central City, Colo. After the Civil War he returned again to Colorado, and the last two summers before he died he spent placer mining in the San Luis Valley.

Most prospectors were not placer miners by trade as was Russell. George Jackson was a hunter and trapper who was first touched by the gold fever during the California rush. When he made his discovery at Idaho Springs, Colo., he was equipped with a hunting knife and tin cup instead of a pick and pan. Bob Womack, who precipitated the Cripple Creek gold rush in 1893, was a cowboy and ranch hand who had the gold fever. Even when riding the range he could not resist picking up unusual pieces of rock. George Washington Carmack, who discovered Bonanza Creek in the Klondike on Aug. 10, 1896, combined prospecting and trading with the Yukon Indians.

The 19th-century prospectors' explorations accelerated the settlement of the West. The influx of miners and then settlers after gold discoveries forced

the Cherokee from Georgia, the Sioux from the Black Hills of South Dakota, and the Arapaho, Cheyenne, and Ute from Colorado.

By the mid-20th century prospecting in the United States was being done, for the most part, by representatives of giant corporations, who relied heavily on geological research and sophisticated detection equipment. Increasingly, the minerals being sought were those related to energy production, notably petroleum and uranium.

[G. C. Quiett, *Pay Dirt.*]

PERCY S. FRITZ

PROSTITUTION was not regarded as a serious social problem in the United States until the last part of the 19th century. Previously Americans had followed the practice of English common law in ignoring prostitution, regarding it as a crime only when it became an offense to public decency. In most areas of America during the colonial and early national periods prostitution was a more or less irregular occupation for a few women. Only where there was a great excess of men over women, as in the French colonies on the Gulf of Mexico, was it in any way institutionalized. By the middle of the 19th century the growth of the industrial cities and the opening of the western frontier had led to an increase in prostitution, which by general agreement was concentrated in segregated or red-light districts. The growth of these districts and the mounting concern over venereal disease resulted in two differing approaches to prostitution. One group, led by the New York physician W. W. Sanger, wanted to require compulsory medical inspection of prostitutes and to confine all prostitution to the red-light districts. During the Civil War some army commanders adopted such plans, but the only city to do so was Saint Louis between 1870 and 1874. Agitation against the Saint Louis plan came not only on moral grounds but also on public health grounds as an increasing number of physicians began to have doubts about the ability to detect venereal disease through the required inspection.

The second group wanted to abolish prostitution altogether. It was greatly influenced by the efforts of Josephine Elizabeth Butler in England, but the group was also tied into efforts by women to gain greater emancipation. Many of the activists of the pre–Civil War antislavery movement also joined in the cause, and an increasing number of cities and states acted to curtail prostitution in the last two decades of the 19th century. The abolitionist movement gained immea-

437

surably when a number of venereal specialists, especially Prince A. Morrow of New York, decided that the consequences of syphilis and gonorrhea were so horrible that traditional attitudes and institutions had to be changed. The result was the formation of the American Social Hygiene Association, which gave "scientific" backing to the abolition movement. The reluctance of law enforcement officials to move against the tolerated houses was overcome by the Iowa Injunction and Abatement Law of 1909, which was widely copied by other states. Under this law any taxpayer might institute an action in equity against property used for prostitution. The U.S. government also entered the field with laws against procuring and transporting women across state borders for immoral purposes (federal Mann Act or White Slave Traffic Act of 1910). The army's decision in World War I to inspect the soldiers rather than prostitutes also proved a boost in the campaign against tolerated houses. By the 1920's legally tolerated districts had mostly disappeared. For a brief period prostitution became a source of income for organized crime, but the difficulties of establishing a monopoly on what was essentially a free-lance occupation made prostitution only a minor aspect of the underworld's activities.

After the end of World War II, when effective cures for venereal disease had been developed, legal attitudes toward prostitution began to be questioned again. The American Law Institute and the American Civil Liberties Union have urged that sexual activities between consenting adults not be subject to criminal penalties. Instead they would return to the earlier common-law regulation of prostitution. In the mid-1970's several states were considering action in this area. Only in Nevada was prostitution legally tolerated on a county-by-county basis. Most authorities feel that even if legalized, prostitution would continue to decline because of the changing moral standards in the United States. As women began to gain equality—economically, politically, and sexually—the double standard that accepted prostitution as a necessary evil was increasingly challenged. Perhaps the decisive factor for change was the development of effective contraceptives.

[Vern L. Bullough, *History of Prostitution;* John C. Burnham, "Medical Inspection of Prostitutes in America in the Nineteenth Century," *Bulletin of the History of Medicine,* vol. 45 (1971); David Pivar, *The New Abolitionism: The Quest for Social Purity, 1876–1900;* Robert E. Riegel, "Changing American Attitudes Toward Prostitution," *Journal of the History of Ideas,* vol. 29 (1968); W. W. Sanger, *History of Prostitution;* Charles Winick and Paul M. Kinsie, *The Lively Commerce;* H. B. Woolston, *Prostitution in the United States.*]

VERN L. BULLOUGH

PROTECTION. *See* **Tariff.**

PROTECTIVE WAR CLAIMS ASSOCIATION, one of the first of many similar organizations, began operations in 1863 in New York and Philadelphia under the sponsorship of the U.S. Sanitary Commission. It was formed to assist in settling claims of soldiers, sailors, and their relatives and to prevent imposture, fraud, and false claims. Prominent men, including Gen. Winfield Scott, Henry W. Bellows, Hamilton Fish, John Jacob Astor, and Peter Cooper, were active in its management.

THOMAS ROBSON HAY

PROTRACTED MEETING, a religious convocation especially common during the 19th century in the rural districts of the South and West. It probably originated much earlier, however, and existed at times in nearly every part of the United States. Although often similar in nature to a revival meeting, a protracted meeting was nevertheless somewhat different, since its purpose was not only to create a rebirth of religious fervor and swell the ranks of church members but also to provide the religious people of a community with spiritual sustenance and social contacts. The protracted meeting was usually held in the late summer, during the period of leisure existing between the cultivation and the harvesting of crops. It was generally conducted by some well-known minister assisted by local pastors. Services were held each evening, commonly in the open under a large arbor, and often lasted several hours. After hymns had been sung and prayers offered, the leader delivered the sermon and then called for sinners to come forward to the "mourner's bench" to be prayed for. During these prayers "personal workers" would plead with the sinners to confess their transgressions and accept salvation. The protracted meeting sometimes resembled the camp meeting, if attended by many people from a distance. It usually lasted two or three weeks, closing only when attendance and interest began to lag.

[Everett Dick, *The Sod House Frontier;* Guion Griffis Johnson, "The Camp Meeting in Ante Bellum North Carolina," *The North Carolina Historical Review,* vol. 10.]

EDWARD EVERETT DALE

PROVIDENCE, DIVINE. *See* **Divine Providences.**

PROVIDENCE ISLAND COMPANY, which functioned from 1630 to 1641, was incorporated for the purpose of colonizing the islands of Providence, Henrietta, and Association in the Caribbean. Those locations were chosen because they offered opportunities for illicit trade and buccaneering in the nearby Spanish colonies. The company's promoters were wealthy and aristocratic English Puritans, many of whom were also connected with Puritan colonization projects on the North American continent. Although profit was the promoters' objective, they were also interested in founding a colony for Puritans. The company, like its predecessors, the Virginia and Bermuda companies, financed its plantation by means of a joint stock held by adventurers and planters, the capital and profits to remain undistributed for seven years. From the outset the undertaking failed to prosper. Soil and climate were unfavorable, and the location of the colony in the heart of Spanish territory was a constant source of danger. After 1635 the company expanded its program by attempting to colonize on the mainland of Central America. Since its leaders in England were by then no longer in sympathy with the Puritans in Massachusetts, they tried to divert to Providence Island English Puritans planning to go to New England; they even attempted to transplant to the islands New England Puritans who found the atmosphere in that region uncongenial. A group headed by John Humphry left Massachusetts in 1641 to settle in Providence, but shortly before its arrival the colony was conquered by a Spanish expedition.

[A. P. Newton, *The Colonizing Activities of the English Puritans.*]

VIOLA F. BARNES

PROVIDENCE PLANTATIONS is the original name for the first colonial settlement in Rhode Island, made by Roger Williams in June 1636. The name was chosen to commemorate "God's providence to [Williams] in his distress," after he fled from Massachusetts to escape religious persecution. Williams bought a large tract of land from the Indians, and in 1638 he joined with twelve other settlers in forming a land company. A covenant was drawn up in 1637 providing for majority rule "only in civill things," thus permitting religious liberty. The first home lots were laid out along the present North Main Street of Providence. Under the parliamentary charter of 1644, Providence was joined with Newport and Portsmouth as the Incorporation of Providence Plantations in the Narragansett Bay in New England. A communal gristmill was established by John Smith in 1646. Thirty years later, during King Philip's War, the growing town of 1,000 people suffered severely from Indian

attack. Although not as important a center of colonial commerce as Newport, Providence did handle some shipping, and wharves and warehouses began to be constructed in 1680. The city's first newspaper, the *Providence Gazette,* was established in 1762 by William Goddard, and in 1770, Rhode Island College (now Brown University) moved there from Warren. The term "Providence Plantations" still remains as part of the official title of the state of Rhode Island.

[W. A. Greene, *The Providence Plantation for Two Hundred and Fifty Years.*]

JARVIS M. MORSE

PROVINCETOWN PLAYERS, the most distinguished American little theater group, first produced plays in 1915 in Provincetown, Mass. The group's discovery of Eugene O'Neill and its production during two summers of numerous successful dramas prompted it to establish the Playwrights' Theater in New York City's Greenwich Village. Although the Provincetown Players was essentially a cooperative, the dominant and adventurous George Cram Cook was its leader. Its great days ended in 1922, when the success of *The Emperor Jones* took O'Neill's plays to Broadway and when Cook and Susan Glaspell sailed for Greece, but two later groups carried on until 1929.

[Helen Deutsch and Stella Hanau, *The Provincetown;* Susan Glaspell, *The Road to the Temple.*]

DOROTHY DONDORE

PROVINCIAL CONGRESSES were the extralegal, or revolutionary, assemblies that sprang up in most of the colonies in the early stages of the American Revolution; they became the agencies whereby the transition was effected from dependent colony to independent state. In some instances the term "convention" was used instead of "congress." Distinct connotations seemed not yet to have crystallized, although there was some donning and doffing of one title or the other, as if in an effort to make a distinction. "Congress," long used in the colonies to designate occasional or irregular assemblages of delegates or agents for purposes of a conference, was the more familiar term. It was also more adaptable to the new purposes of the revolutionary provincial assemblies. New Hampshire, Massachusetts, and North Carolina inclined to the title "provincial congress"; Virginia uniformly called its extraordinary assemblies "conventions"; New York used both titles at different times. In any case, the last of the revolutionary assemblies that undertook the task of formulating a system of government employed the name "conven-

PRUDHOMME BLUFFS

tion," and that name has become the accepted designation of a constitution-forming body.

The provincial congresses or conventions had various though similar origins. For the most part they were generated by or through the local committees that flourished in the towns and counties of every colony (*see* Committees of Correspondence; Committees of Safety). In some instances the colonial assembly was the promoting agency. In Massachusetts, for instance, the assembly merely transformed itself into a provincial congress. Virginia pursued a similar course. In other cases the assembly, shorn of participation by governor and council, became virtually a provincial congress without change of name. Rhode Island and Connecticut, for instance, effected their changeovers to independent statehood under their old charters.

The earliest revolutionary assemblies (they were recorded under a variety of titles, including "general meeting," or "meeting of the principal gentlemen") were called together primarily for the purpose of choosing delegates to the proposed Continental Congress, which convened in September 1774. The next group of assemblies met to select delegates to the Second Continental Congress, which opened in May 1775, to take action on the proposed "Association" (the plan to terminate trade with Great Britain until colonial grievances were redressed) and to consider the unsettled state of affairs. The Second Continental Congress, in its turn, further promoted the provincial congresses by tentatively advising certain of them (New Hampshire, South Carolina, and Virginia, on Nov. 3, Nov. 4, and Dec. 4, 1775, respectively) to set up their own governments; on May 10, 1776, the Continental Congress urged all provincial congresses to do so.

To a greater or lesser degree that very process had meanwhile been going on. First called as advisory rather than as lawmaking bodies, the provincial congresses had already severed virtually every tie to British authority, and, presumably acting as representatives of the sovereign people, they had gradually taken over the functions of government, either directly or through committees of safety of their own creation. It remained only for each colony to definitely set up its own system of government; and after the adoption of the Declaration of Independence, every colony, now an independent state, began that process.

[J. F. Jameson, "Early Political Uses of the Word Convention," *American Antiquarian Society's Proceedings*, vol. 12; A. C. McLaughlin, *A Constitutional History of the United States;* A. M. Schlesinger, *The Colonial Merchants and the American Revolution.*]

EDMUND C. BURNETT

PRUDHOMME BLUFFS (Écores Prudhomme), also known as the Third Chickasaw Bluffs, is located on the Mississippi River about 150 miles below the mouth of the Ohio. Being a strategic point, it was the site of a fort erected by the French explorer Robert Cavelier, Sieur de La Salle, in 1682, and of a new Spanish fort occupied shortly before 1795; the position was not fortified continuously during the intervening period.

[John W. Monette, *History of the Discovery and Settlement of the Valley of the Mississippi.*]

WALTER PRICHARD

PRUSSIA, TREATIES WITH. In 1785 the United States made a treaty with Prussia that embodied the principles of the Plan of 1776 plus additional principles of the so-called Plan of 1784. The latter provided for preemption rather than confiscation of defined contraband and, in case of war between the two treaty parties, for considerate treatment of enemy aliens and their property within each enemy's domains. The treaty was renewed with some alterations in 1799 and 1828 and continued until World War I.

[Alexander De Conde, *Entangling Alliance: Politics and Diplomacy Under George Washington;* Patrick O. T. White and A. S. Eisenstadt, eds., *Conducting the Diplomacy of the New Nation, 1793–1815.*]

SAMUEL FLAGG BEMIS

PSYCHOLOGICAL WARFARE. Joshua's trumpets at the Battle of Jericho suggest that psychological warfare, or psywar, is probably as old as warfare itself. But official agencies to organize this effort were not designated until the Allied and Axis powers did so during World War I. The U.S. Committee on Public Information (Creel Committee) marked the United States's foray into formal propaganda activities; and in quite a different application, the propaganda section of the American Expeditionary Forces staff headquarters represented the first official U.S. experiment in the military use of psywar.

Psywar is not a substitute for military operations but a complement; it is divided into two broad categories. Strategic psywar usually targets the enemy in its entirety—troops, civilians, and enemy-occupied areas. Tactical psywar usually supports localized combat operations by fostering uncertainty, creating dissension, and sometimes causing the enemy to surrender.

American World War I psywar techniques were primitive by later standards. Following the English and French lead, the United States used the leaflet as the primary vehicle for the delivery of moral and surrender-type messages. These were delivered to the target audiences by hedgehoppers, balloons, and, to a lesser degree, by modified mortar shells. Their ploy was to alienate the German troops from their "militarist" and "antidemocratic" regimes. Later the Nazis were to suggest that the German army had not been defeated but had been victimized by Allied propaganda.

Psywar activities were dropped in the interwar period and were not resumed until World War II. Hastily improvised propaganda agencies were set up; these jealously fought over spheres of interest and mission assignments. It was only when the Office of War Information (OWI) and the Office of Strategic Services (OSS) were formed and their respective functions later redefined (Executive Order 9312 on Mar. 9, 1943) that this infighting ceased.

On the theater level, psywar operations differed widely from one command to another because Executive Order 9312 required commander approval for all plans and projects. Under General Dwight D. Eisenhower, Allied psywar activities were managed by an Anglo-American military staff in cooperation with such propaganda agencies as the OWI and the OSS. In the Pacific commands and subcommands there were varying degrees of official acceptance for psywar, except for Adm. William F. Halsey's command, which would have nothing to do with psychological warfare and would not allow OWI and OSS civilians to have clearances for this area. As the war progressed, this nonconventional weapon of war slowly won grudging official approval and a place on the staffs of Pacific commands. Leaflets were by far the most prevalent means of delivery, but loudspeaker and radio broadcasts were also employed.

[W. E. Daugherty and M. Janowitz, *A Psychological Warfare Casebook*; P. M. A. Linebarger, *Psychological Warfare*.]

DON E. MCLEOD

PSYCHOLOGY. Until the 19th century, psychology appeared in America only as a part of philosophical teaching and thinking. American theories of mind and basic assumptions about man's behavior were taken completely from contemporary European thinkers. Jonathan Edwards, the early 18th-century religious philosopher, was notable for his originality in the use of the ideas of John Locke to explain not only theological but psychological aspects of perceiving and willing.

In the first part of the 19th century teachers of required moral philosophy courses in colleges spent much time on psychological problems. Most teachers followed the Scottish school of commonsense philosophers, who held that in addition to sensations, inherent moral sense informed a person's mind. Influenced by Immanuel Kant and his students, faculty psychology later added the idea that a human mind has the faculties of intellection, feeling, and willing. Each teacher made his own version and synthesis of faculty and commonsense psychologies. The best known were those of Thomas C. Upham of Bowdoin College and Laurens P. Hickok of Union College. All these moral philosophers connected the human mind to the idea of an immaterial soul and immortality.

As the 19th century progressed, philosophical writers and teachers incorporated other European ideas. Particularly influential were the works of association psychologists, such as John Stuart Mill and Herbert Spencer, and the neurophysiologists, who were providing a nervous system correlate for the association of ideas. In the mid-19th century, phrenology provided an important model for a scientific psychology. By the later part of the century, philosophers increasingly were called upon to discuss the physiological basis of thinking. In 1887 religious philosopher George Trumbull Ladd of Yale published the first American textbook of psychology that incorporated the experimental work that was making Germany the fountainhead of what was coming to be called "the new psychology."

A number of Americans studied the new psychology in Germany. Typically the new psychologist presented a trained subject with a sensory stimulus and then recorded what the subject reported was going on in his own mind. By 1874 William James, who had specialized in the teaching of psychology at Harvard, had a few instruments for classroom purposes; but the first formal experimental laboratory in the United States was established by G. Stanley Hall at Johns Hopkins in 1883. Six years later Hall founded another laboratory at Clark University. In the meantime James McKeen Cattell, who had just returned from Europe, began another laboratory at the University of Pennsylvania. By the 1890's many other laboratories were opening; and because the development of psychology coincided with the expansion of the American university, graduate school, and scientific laboratory, the discipline was able to establish itself rapidly; by early in the 20th century it had largely separated itself from philosophy departments. Self-consciously trying to make the discipline constitute a science, the pioneers sought successfully to establish other institutional badges of identity. In 1887 Hall set up the *American Journal of Psychology,* and in 1894 Cattell and J. Mark Baldwin issued the *Psychological Review.* The American Psychological Association was founded in 1892, and by 1899 it had 127 members.

Initially American psychology followed to an astonishing extent a charming two-volume textbook published in 1890 by James and acclaimed all over the world. James eclectically surveyed the literature of his day, including neurophysiological, experimental, and philosophical works. He also discussed the general biological setting and such areas as emotion, instinct, and hypnotism that were not strictly experimental. He introduced the concept of the stream of consciousness and emphasized an adaptive, action-oriented view of man.

By the time of World War I, American psychologists—even those educated in Europe—were emphasizing viewpoints that differentiated their own discipline from their counterparts overseas. One emphasis was individual differences (as opposed to psychological uniformities), pioneered especially by Cattell, who used tests to measure such differentiations. Another was functionalism, the emphasis on the growing, adaptive organism (in contrast to adult, mechanical mental structures). In 1898 Edward L. Thorndike pioneered experimentation in animal psychology in the area of learning and so began both the use of animal experiments and an interest in mental adaptability (soon known as learning theory). In 1913 John B. Watson of Johns Hopkins introduced behaviorism, an emphasis on performance rather than conscious thought, and experiment under scientifically controlled conditions; thus, he made animal studies the model for human psychology. Wits remarked that while with the new psychology the discipline had lost its soul, now it had lost its mind and had even lost consciousness. Americans were extremely anxious to apply psychology to human problems and made many attempts to carry laboratory experiments over to the areas of advertising, education, law, and industrial production—and, to some extent, implicitly, social problems.

The great opportunity to apply psychology came with World War I, when the armed services utilized psychologists in a number of capacities but most notably to apply newly introduced intelligence tests to all army recruits. Mental tests of all sorts created a large market for psychological services thereafter, and the profession grew very rapidly. By 1930 there were 1,100 members of the American Psychological Association. Clearly also, by the interwar years American psychologists dominated the discipline in almost every field throughout the world. Animal psychology was theirs by 1910 and more traditional fields by 1929, partly because of research funding and rapid university growth and acceptance of the discipline.

Animal psychology, particularly the inference that animal reactions reveal patterns of human behavior, was an American hallmark of psychology; and the special field that dominated the best efforts was learning theory. (One critic suggested that the *Journal of Experimental Psychology* be renamed the *Journal of Rat Learning.*) But American efforts also proliferated in the applied and clinical fields, especially with mental tests and the influx of psychoanalysts into the United States in the 1930's. A special new interest of the pre–World War II era was personality theory, which combined clinical with genetic and learning viewpoints.

During World War II, psychologists again made themselves useful, and by 1945 there were over 4,000 members of the American Psychological Association. An ambitious group centered at Yale determined to bring psychologists into American life as much as possible, largely by expanding the work of clinical and applied psychologists. The group obtained training subsidies from the National Institute of Mental Health, and in the 1950's and 1960's expanded the profession dramatically. In 1970 there were over 30,000 members of the American Psychological Association. In the years between 1940 and 1962 the number of university-affiliated members declined from 75 percent (over 50 percent in departments of psychology) to 47 percent (only 29 percent in departments of psychology). This vast increase in numbers of clinicians caused the establishment of an intricate certification apparatus, although in most states medical opposition was effective in preventing formal licensing. During the 1960's the number of unqualified "psychologists" in private practice declined substantially as the national demand for mental health services was increasingly furnished by trained personnel. Psychologists were particularly conspicuous in the lavishly funded community mental health programs initiated in that decade.

With tremendous infusions of manpower and research funding, psychologists after World War II greatly refined and sophisticated their research. Neobehaviorism and learning theory were supplemented as central fields by a renewed interest in cognitive processes, while genetic, abnormal, and social psychology all flourished. Perhaps the most notable development was an increasing emphasis on individual competence and persistent life-style that brought together leading theories of both psychoanalytic psychology and experimental learning theory. In practice, however, tension continued between academic experimentalists and applied clinicians, who had differing ideas of what psychology is and should be.

[Edward G. Boring, *A History of Experimental Psychology;* Hamilton Cravens and John C. Burnham, "Psychology and Evolutionary Naturalism in American Thought, 1890–1940," *American Quarterly,* vol. 23 (1971); Jay Wharton Fay, *American Psychology Before William James;* Henryk Misiak and Virginia Staudt Sexton, *History of Psychology, An Overview;* Gardner Murphy, *Historical Introduction to Modern Psychology;* Robert I. Watson, "The Historical Background for National Trends in Psychology: United States," *Journal of the History of the Behavioral Sciences,* vol. 1 (1965).]

JOHN C. BURNHAM

"PUBLIC BE DAMNED." On Sunday afternoon, Oct. 8, 1882, as a New York Central Railroad train bearing W. H. Vanderbilt, president of the railroad, was approaching Chicago, two newspaper reporters boarded the train and interviewed Vanderbilt on various phases of the railroad industry. In the course of the interview, Vanderbilt was asked whether he planned to match the "express passenger" service just inaugurated by the Pennsylvania Railroad. Vanderbilt remarked that such service was unprofitable, and to a question about "the public benefit," he is reported to have replied, "The public be damned," adding that the public's only interest in the railroads was to get as much as possible out of them for the least cost. Vanderbilt did not know how the interview had been reported until it was printed in the *New York Times* and other newspapers, whereupon he wired the *Times* denying that he had used the "language reported." He stated that "both my words and ideas are misreported and misrepresented." The reporters alleged that Vanderbilt's language had been reported accurately and stood willing to "make affidavits as to the correctness of their reports." Publication of the interview caused widespread critical comment.

THOMAS ROBSON HAY

PUBLIC CREDIT ACT, a federal statute enacted after Alexander Hamilton's "First Report on the Public Credit" of Jan. 14, 1790. The act provided for the payment of the government's obligations at par with interest (except that Continental currency was to be redeemed at 100 to 1 in specie); the assumption of state debts for services or supplies during the Revolution; and the authorization of loans to meet these obligations. The act was approved Aug. 4, 1790. The act helped get the support of security holders for the new government.

[D. R. Dewey, *Financial History of the United States.*]
JAMES D. MAGEE

PUBLIC DEBT. *See* **Debt, Public.**

PUBLIC DOMAIN. The public domain is distinguished from national domain and acquired land. National domain arises from political jurisdiction; acquired land is either bought or received as gifts for national parks, monuments, forests, wildlife refuges, post-office sites, and other such purposes. The first portion of the public domain or public land was created by cessions of their western land claims by seven of the original thirteen states: Massachusetts, Connecticut, New York, Virginia, North Carolina, South Carolina, and Georgia. These seven states retained the ungranted land within their present boundaries as did the other original states and Maine, Vermont, West Virginia, Kentucky, Tennessee, and Texas. Between 1802 and 1867 huge additions to the national domain and the public domain were made through the Louisiana Purchase in 1803, the Florida Purchase in 1819, the annexation of Texas in 1845 and the Texas cession of 1850, the division of the Oregon country in 1846, the huge purchase from Mexico in 1848, the Gadsden Purchase of 1853, the purchase of Alaska in 1867, and the annexation of Hawaii in 1898.

From the outset there were two views concerning the policy that should govern the disposal of the public lands. The first, sponsored by Alexander Hamilton, was that the government's need of money to retire its revolutionary war debt and to meet its expenses required it to pledge the public domain for the payment of that debt and to extract from it the greatest possible income. The other view, held by Thomas Jefferson, was that farmer-owners with a stake in the land made the most responsible citizens and that the public lands should be easily accessible to them at little cost. Hamilton's view prevailed for a time and, indeed, was reluctantly accepted by Jefferson, who yielded to necessity. The basic established price varied from $1.00 to $2.00 per acre until 1820, when credit was abolished and the minimum price became $1.25 per acre. This may not have been a high price to the investors Hamilton hoped would purchase large tracts of land, but to frontiersmen lacking capital or credit it was more than they could raise. Their solution was to squat on public land, improve it, and try to raise a crop or two to make their payments before their trespass was discovered. Squatters wanted protection against speculators who might try to buy their somewhat improved tracts. Squatters protected themselves through claim associations, which provided mutual assistance to all members. But the squatters also wanted the legal recognition of their right of preemption—that is, a prior right to purchase their claim before auction at the minimum price, without having to bid against speculators. They won a number of special preemption acts and in 1841 sustained a major victory with the adoption of the Distribution-Preemption Act, which permitted persons to settle anywhere on surveyed land in advance of its official opening; to improve the land; and, when the auction was announced, to purchase up to 160 acres at the minimum price of $1.25 an acre. Squatterism—first banned, although not successfully; then tolerated; and finally sanctioned—had thus prevailed, and a major breach in the revenue policy was made.

In 1854 the Graduation Act provided a further breach by reducing the price of land that had been on the market for ten or more years in proportion to the length of time it had been subject to sale, the lowest price being 12.5 cents. In 1862 the West gained its major triumph in the Homestead Act, which made public lands free to settlers who would live on and improve tracts of up to 160 acres for five years. Unfortunately, a substantial portion of the best arable lands had already been alienated through sale to speculators, grants to states, and direct grants to corporations to aid in the construction of canals and railroads. Grants to states and railroads alone amounted to well over 300 million acres. All this land was to be sold for the market price and was beyond the reach of many pioneer settlers.

Individual speculators and land companies invested heavily in land during boom periods, 1816–19, 1833–37, and 1853–57. Holdings of from 10,000 to 50,000 acres were not uncommon; a score or more ranged up to 100,000 acres; and partnerships held as much as 500,000 acres. By anticipating settlers, investors, as well as land grant railroads and states, raised the cost of farmmaking; dispersed population

widely on the frontier; delayed the introduction of roads, churches, and transportation facilities; contributed to the early appearance of tenancy; aggravated relations with the Indians; and in some regions were responsible for the development of rural slums. On the other hand, they provided credit to hard-pressed pioneers; aided in bringing settlers to the West through their advertising and promotional works; and introduced improved farming techniques that by example contributed to better agricultural practices. At the time public attention centered on the damaging effects of intrusions by speculators and led to demands for the limitation in the sale of public land and the halt to further grants to railroads. After the adoption of the Homestead Act, little newly surveyed land was opened to unlimited purchase, although unsold land that had been offered previously continued to be subject to unrestricted entry.

Farmers in the High Plains west of the ninety-ninth meridian, where the annual rainfall was less than 20 inches and where a portion of the land had to be left fallow each year, needed more than 160 or even 320 acres for the extensive cultivation that was necessary. Congress met this difficulty by increasing the quantity that farmmakers could acquire by enacting the Timber Culture Act of 1873, the Desert Land Act of 1877, and the Timber and Stone Act of 1878. Combined with the Preemption and Homestead acts, these measures permitted individuals to acquire up to 1,120 acres in the semiarid High Plains and in the intermountain and desert regions. Like all poorly drafted land legislation, the acts became subject to gross abuse by grasping persons anxious to engross as much land as possible through the use of dummy entrymen and roving, uprooted people willing to serve their ends.

Growing criticism of the abuse of the settlement laws and the laxity of the land administration led in 1889–91 to the adoption of a series of measures to restrict total acquisition of public lands under all laws to 320 acres, to halt all purchases of potential agricultural lands other than those specifically intended for farmmaking, and to eliminate or insert additional safeguards in acts most subject to abuse.

Notwithstanding the extensive abuse of the land system and its incongruous features that somewhat minimized the effectiveness of the measures designed to aid homesteaders in becoming farm owners, the public land states enjoyed a remarkable growth rate. In the 1850's, the first decade for which there are statistics, 401,000 new farms were created in the public land states. Thereafter the number grew even more

PUBLIC DOMAIN

rapidly. By 1890 additional farms numbering 2 million had been established in the public land states. Never before had so many farmers subjected such a large area to cultivation as occurred in those years.

The censuses of 1880 and 1890, giving alarming figures of mortgage debt outstanding on farms and the high proportion of farms that were tenant-operated, combined with the growing feeling that soils, minerals, and forests were being wastefully used, turned people's thoughts to further reform in land management and to conservation. Instead of a policy of transferring all public lands to individuals, railroads, and states as rapidly as possible, it was determined to retain a portion of the land in public ownership. To this end, an amendment to the General Revision Act of 1891 authorized the president to withdraw from public entry forest lands on which organized management policies could be introduced. Under President Theodore Roosevelt's leadership gross withdrawals were pushed to nearly 160 million acres.

Next in the planned use of the natural resources by government was the Reclamation Act (Newlands Act) of 1902, which provided that the income from the sale of public lands be used for construction of high dams on western rivers to store water for the irrigation of dry lands and thus to provide for a new farmers' frontier. With supplementary appropriations for construction of dams, the government gave an enormous boon to the development of the eleven far western states; but the provisions of the act that were designed to make small farmers the major beneficiaries (the antispeculator and excess-lands provisions) have been frustrated, and instead large individual and corporate owners have derived the greatest returns.

In 1916 the National Park Service was created to administer areas of superlative natural beauty that were being set aside from the public lands as permanent reserves—Yosemite, Yellowstone, Hot Springs, Glacier, Sequoia, Mount Rainier, Grand Canyon, and Crater Lake. These and other places of outstanding aesthetic, geologic, and historical interest were thus prevented from despoilment by curiosity seekers and commercial interests.

Rapid and unscientific exploitation of mineral lands by destructive and wasteful practices induced Roosevelt to order the withdrawal of 66 million acres suspected of being underlain with valuable coal deposits and a smaller acreage of suspected oil-bearing land. Lands having coal, potash, phosphate, and nitrate deposits were also withdrawn from entry, although the surface rights might be left alienable. In 1920 the Mineral Leasing Act provided some control over the exploitation of these withdrawn lands for the first time and, as a sweetener to the West, allocated 37.5 percent of the proceeds from leasing to the states in which the lands were located and 57.5 percent to reclamation projects, thereby assuring a principal and growing source of funds for such projects. The remaining 5 percent went to the states in which lands were allocated for schools.

Summary of Accessions of the United States

	National Domain (acres)	Public Domain (acres)
Area conceded by Great Britain in 1783 and by the Convention of 1818 (Lake of the Woods boundary)	525,452,800	
Cessions of seven states to the United States		233,415,680
Louisiana Purchase (1803)	523,446,400	523,446,400 *
Florida Purchase (1819)	43,342,720	43,342,720 *
Red River Basin (Webster-Ashburton Treaty, 1842)	29,066,880	29,066,880
Annexation of Texas (1845)	247,050,480	
Oregon Compromise (1846)	180,644,480	180,644,480
Treaty With Mexico (1848)	334,479,360	334,479,360 *
Purchase From Texas (1850)		78,842,880
Gadsden Purchase (1853)	18,961,920	18,961,920 *
Alaska Purchase (1867)	365,481,600	365,481,600
Hawaiian Annexation (1898)	3,110,820	

* Between 40 million and 50 million acres included in the public domain were in private claims of land granted by Great Britain, France, Spain, and Mexico, which when proved valid were patented and were not subject to disposal by the United States.

445

Roosevelt was also persuaded by his conservation-minded advisers, notably Gifford Pinchot, to withdraw 3.45 million acres of public lands as possible sources for power sites. Under the Water Power Act of 1920 a system of licensing the power sites was authorized, but it was not until the 1930's and 1940's that the great hydroelectric power development of the federal government was undertaken.

The last important withdrawal of public lands from entry was made in 1934. The harmful effects of overgrazing on the ranges of the West had become so evident that even the livestock industry was persuaded to accept federal control. It was provided that in the future the remaining grazing lands in public ownership were to be leased under close supervision. To administer these lands a Division of Grazing was set up in the U.S. Department of the Interior. Congress preferred to create a new administrative agency rather than to permit the Forest Service, which had gained much valuable experience in administering the range lands within the national forests, because this latter agency had shown independence as well as excellent judgment in protecting its lands. The Division of Grazing started off well, but it also ran into bitter opposition for its failure to play politics, was virtually starved by Congress by inadequate appropriations, and was later consolidated with the General Land Office in the Bureau of Land Management.

A century and a half of unparalleled prodigality in managing the public domain had made possible the alienation of most of the best agricultural, forest, and mineral lands of the United States, but there still remained a noble fragment in federal ownership under organized management. By the 1970's there were 186 million acres in the national forests, 26 million acres of which were acquired land bought for watershed protection and other conservation objectives. They included stands of Douglas fir, sugar pine, ponderosa pine, and Sitka spruce in California, Oregon, Washington, and the Rocky Mountain states, where steeply sloped land must be carefully protected from fire and overgrazing to prevent silting of reservoirs and irrigation districts. In the mid-1970's the Bureau of Land Management (BLM) administered 140 million acres in grazing districts and remaining desert lands and some 300 million acres of unsurveyed land in Alaska, subject to selection by the state of 103.35 million acres and by the native tribes of 40 million acres, as provided in legislation of 1972. Included in the BLM lands are some of the richest stands of Douglas fir, the result of the forfeiture of the Oregon and California railroad land grant.

Best known of the public lands are the 19 million acres in the national parks, part of which came from the public domain and part through gift (Mount Desert Island) or exchange of public land outside the parks for privately owned inholdings. Of the original 1.23 million acres in the fifty states, the public domain comprised some 350 million acres in 1975. Public policy in the mid-1970's was directed to acquiring additional tracts of seashore, mountain, and lakeside to meet the recreational needs of an expanding population with more time for outdoor enjoyment.

[Paul W. Gates, *History of Public Land Law Development; One Third of the Nation's Land: A Report to the President and to the Congress by the Public Land Law Review Commission.*]

PAUL W. GATES

PUBLIC HEALTH. English settlers who came to the American colonies during the early and middle decades of the 17th century brought with them a long-standing dread of the bubonic plague, but they never had to fight that scourge in the New World. They did take community action to try to control certain other diseases, to prevent famine, and to take care of sanitary problems. The sporadic sanitary measures of small colonial towns—street cleaning, regulation of privies, and control of slaughterhouses and fish stalls, for example—were based as much on considerations of aesthetics as of health. Measures taken against infectious diseases were largely limited to fasting and prayer. Diseases that were regarded as clearly contagious, particularly smallpox, called forth vigorous public action. Port cities established quarantine stations to guard against infected ships; travelers along the roads were inspected at ferry landings or tollhouses; pesthouses were established to isolate infected persons; and sometimes houses and goods were fumigated. For the most part sanitary measures as well as measures to control infectious disease were *ad hoc* actions directed by temporary local committees. Even the yellow fever epidemics in the late 18th century did not lead to permanent boards of health. But by 1800 some communities were keeping vital statistics regularly as well as hiring occasional health officials, chiefly sanitary inspectors and port quarantine officers, who were usually part-time political appointees.

The great population increase and national growth of the 19th century brought a corresponding expansion of public health activities and organizations. These developments generally reflected the pressures of rapid urbanization, the evolution of medical ideas, and the workings of the era's dynamic spirit of moral and social uplift. But more immediate stimulus came from recurring epidemics of cholera after 1830 and from the example of French and British sanitary reforms. Before midcentury, cities had to take over and expand water and sewer systems; to provide for garbage removal; and to inspect slum housing, factories, and schools. At the same time, faced with ever-larger numbers of sick poor, they were compelled to build public dispensaries and hospitals, to inaugurate public vaccination programs, and to foster health education. Many of these and other activities were undertaken on the basis of statistical arguments, which became increasingly convincing after the launching of effective state vital statistics registration systems in the 1840's and 1850's. Such data, along with the facts uncovered in city and state sanitary surveys, pointed up the need for permanent health bodies. Such organizations were begun in the state of Louisiana and the city of Providence, R.I., as early as 1855; in New York City in 1866; and in Massachusetts in 1869.

Public health workers were groping toward professionalism before the Civil War, partly through a series of national quarantine and sanitary conventions held between 1857 and 1860. These meetings, however, like the work of the wartime U.S. Sanitary Commission, were motivated almost as much by moral as by public health considerations. Only after the war, with the founding of the American Public Health Association in 1872, was a real basis established for scientific sanitary and health work. During the 1870's, as earlier, public hygienists paid most of their attention to cleansing the environment. Within fifteen or twenty years, upon the arrival of the bacteriological era, health officers began to be guided by new knowledge about microorganisms that caused particular diseases. Increasingly boards of health became impatient with their general sanitary activities and in the decades after 1885 focused instead on the laboratory diagnosis of disease, on the control of specific infected individuals, and on the development of immunizing agents.

Before the last quarter of the 19th century the federal government played a relatively small role in public health. From 1819 onward, army medical officers were making epidemiological observations at posts all over the country; but after the Civil War such personnel were increasingly involved with vital statistics, bacteriological research, tropical medicine, and other areas of public health work. The first federal civilian agency with broad public health responsibilities was the National Board of Health. This body was created in 1879 with high hopes, but it faded after 1883 because of political squabbling. The Marine Hospital Service, which went back to 1798 but became effectively organized only in 1870, acquired federal quarantine functions in the early 1890's. Then, in a series of reorganizations, expansions, and changes of name over the next twenty years, it gradually evolved into the U.S. Public Health Service. By 1910 the service's scientific activities included the regulation of serums and toxins, the conduct of field epidemiological investigations, and the carrying out of laboratory research. Several other federal agencies also launched significant health-related activities: the Agriculture Department's Bureau of Animal Industry beginning in the 1880's, its Bureau of Chemistry about the same time, and the Children's Bureau from its establishment in 1912.

Continuing expansion of public health work in the 20th century was supplemented by private health agencies that sprang up to help educate the public, foster research, and promote legislation. Life insurance companies also began vigorous health education and welfare programs, while philanthropy created a number of important public health organizations. Particularly significant were the Rockefeller Sanitary Commission's hookworm eradication campaign in the South (1909–14), the creation of the Rockefeller Foundation in 1915 to support international health programs, and the training of public health personnel.

Meanwhile, public health emerged as a sophisticated medical and scientific discipline. Departments and schools of public health were established after 1910, beginning with those at the Massachusetts Institute of Technology, Harvard, and Johns Hopkins. Specialties developed in such subfields as sanitary engineering, bacteriology, public health nursing, vital statistics, and epidemiology. Health officers began to try to evaluate their activities quantitatively.

In the early 20th century many health officials thought their new knowledge and methods would soon eradicate the infectious diseases and turn the United States into a sanitary utopia. While such diseases as typhoid fever, diphtheria, and scarlet fever did decline greatly, other events, such as the influenza pandemic of 1918–19, pointed up the great difficulties that remained. Not the least of these has been the changing in type of diseases themselves. In more recent years other types of problems have become evident. Prominent among these has been the failure of society to cope with man's renewed and accelerated pollution of his environment. Again, just as changes in moral standards and sexual attitudes brought on venereal disease control measures during World War I, so the impact of rapid population increase after World War II has been bringing society around to the point of accepting birth control as public policy. Finally, as concepts of the role of government have gradually changed over the years, so the early 20th-century rejection of health insurance has been slowly undergoing modification, to the point where a comprehensive system of state medicine does not seem to be far off.

[John B. Blake, *Public Health in the Town of Boston, 1630–1822;* James H. Cassedy, *Charles V. Chapin and the Public Health Movement;* John Duffy, *A History of Public Health in New York City;* Mazyck P. Ravenel, *A Half Century of Public Health;* Charles E. Rosenberg, *The Cholera Years;* Barbara G. Rosenkrantz, *Public Health and the State;* Wilson G. Smillie, *Public Health: Its Promise for the Future;* Ralph C. Williams, *The United States Public Health Service, 1798–1950.*]

JAMES H. CASSEDY

PUBLICITY ACTS. In order to restrict the evils of stock inflation and overcapitalization and the sale of bogus securities, Congress passed the Publicity Acts of 1903 and 1909, often referred to as the federal Blue Sky laws. These acts, the initial ones in the regulation and control of securities, have been reinforced by similar measures in the states and by the Federal Securities Act (1933) and the Securities Exchange Act (1934). The act of 1903 created the Bureau of Corporations with power "to investigate into the organization, conduct, and management of the business of any corporation, joint stock company, or corporate combination engaged in commerce among the several states and with foreign nations"; common carriers were exempted. The act of 1909 made illegal and subject to punishment the making of a contract for the sale or purchase of securities on credit or margin without the actual sale or purchase being made; the making of a contract for the sale or purchase of securities on credit or margin when they reach a certain market price, without an actual bona fide sale or purchase taking place; and the making of a contract providing for payment of the difference between contract and market price, the securities not having been actually delivered or received.

[Rinehard J. Swenson, *The National Government and Business;* James T. Young, *The New American Government and Its Work.*]

W. BROOKE GRAVES

PUBLICITY AND CORRUPT-PRACTICES LAWS. Publicity laws are an integral part of corrupt-practices legislation; the latter is a more general term referring to the regulation of money in the political process. Historically, electoral practices such as bribery, treating, intimidation, coercion, and personation were prohibited under the common law and then regulated by statute beginning in the 19th century.

Legislative enactments at the federal and state levels have taken five basic forms: (1) To meet the problems of rising costs and the disparities in funds available to various candidates, laws set ceilings on expenditures. (2) To spare candidates from obligations to special interests, laws have prohibited contributions from certain sources and sometimes have limited the size of individual contributions. Corporations, national banks, and labor unions are prohibited from contributing at the federal level and in some states, but corporate and labor executives may contribute funds of their own. Through political-action affiliates, labor unions and corporations may collect voluntary contributions from members, employees, and stockholders and their families for election campaigns; they also expend funds for educational or non-partisan political activities. (3) To provide the public, both during and after campaigns, with knowledge of monetary influences on elected officials and to help curb excesses and abuses by increasing risks for those engaging in sharp practices, statutes have required certain candidates and committees to make specified disclosures of information about contributions and expenditures. (4) To prevent "spoils system" practices under which government workers are forced to support political campaigns, legislation like the Hatch Act (1939) was enacted to protect civil service employees (generally excepting those in top policymaking positions) from pressured solicitation. (5) To prevent partisan domination of the airwaves, federal law obliges broadcasters to yield rival candidates equal amounts of free time on the air. Not very successful attempts have been made to restrict use of the mails by incumbents.

Federal provisions controlling political finance are principally contained in the Federal Election Campaign Act (FECA) of 1971, which was revised extensively in the FECA amendments of 1974. Federal law requires comprehensive disclosure of candidate and committee receipts and expenditures. Federal law limits amounts contributed by individuals and groups and by candidates to their own campaigns, and it limits amounts that can be spent by, or on behalf of, candidates for federal office. This law is a notable improvement over corresponding provisions of the predecessor Federal Corrupt Practices Act, which was in effect from 1910—although substantially recodified in 1925—until 1972. Historically, federal and state publicity and corrupt-practices laws generally lacked precision, leading to interpretations permitting evasion and avoidance. Often enforcement was lax because administrative and enforcement authorities achieved office through political means and were subject to political pressures. The 1971–74 federal act is more tightly drawn than most, and many state laws have been tightened in the same time frame. Federal law requires candidates for nomination or election to federal office and political committees raising or spending in excess of $1,000 on their behalf to file periodic reports, before and after election, disclosing all receipts and expenditures, itemizing full information to identify each person contributing in excess of $100 and each lender or endorser of a loan, and all transfers of funds between committees. The Federal Election Commission receives the reports and administers the law. The commission is a bipartisan agency. The law provides that the president, the speaker of the House, and the president pro tempore of the Senate appoint to the commission two members, one from each of the parties, all subject to confirmation by Congress. The secretary of the Senate and the clerk of the House are ex officio, nonvoting members of the commission; and their offices serve as custodian of reports for candidates for House and Senate. Commissioners serve six-year, staggered terms, with a rotating one-year chairmanship. The commission receives campaign fund reports and makes them available for public inspection; makes rules and regulations (subject to veto within 30 legislative days); maintains a cumulative index of reports filed and not filed; makes special and regular reports to Congress and the president; and serves as an election information clearinghouse. The commission has power to render advisory opinions; conduct audits and investigations; subpoena witnesses and information; and go to court to seek civil injunctions. Criminal cases are referred by the commission to the attorney general for prosecution. Penalties vary in several sections of the law.

Major restrictions in the 1974 amendments limit contributions to $1,000 per individual for each primary, runoff, or general election, with an aggregate contribution limit of $25,000 to all federal candidates annually; to $5,000 per organization, political committee, and national and state party organizations for each election, but no aggregate limit on the amount organizations can contribute in an election or on the amount organizations can contribute to party organizations supporting federal candidates; to $50,000 for president, $35,000 for U.S. senators, and $25,000 for representatives by candidates and their immediate families. In addition, individuals are limited to $1,000 for independent expenditures on behalf of a candidate; and cash contributions in excess of $100 are prohibited, as are contributions by foreigners.

Other provisions establish the following expenditure limits: In the presidential prenomination period, $10 million total per candidate may be spent for all state primaries and other expenses. In a state presidential primary, a candidate is limited to spending no more than twice the amount a Senate candidate in that state is allowed to spend, as noted below. In a presidential general election, a $20 million per candidate limit applies. For presidential nominating conventions, a $2 million ceiling is provided for each major political party, and lesser amounts for minor parties, to make the arrangements and operate the convention; this amount does not include candidate or delegate expenses.

For each candidate in U.S. Senate primaries, the limit is $100,000 or 8 cents per eligible voter, whichever is greater. For each candidate in U.S. Senate general elections, the ceiling is $150,000 or 12 cents per eligible voter, whichever is greater. In House primary or general election campaigns, $70,000 in each is the maximum permitted spending per candidate. The Senate spending limits apply to House candidates who represent a whole state in an at-large district.

The national party is allowed to spend $10,000 per candidate in House general elections; $20,000 or 2 cents per eligible voter, whichever is greater, for each candidate in Senate general elections; and 2 cents per voter in presidential general elections. These expenditures are in addition to each candidate's individual spending limit.

Fund-raising costs of up to 20 per cent of the candidate spending limit are allowed as an overage above the limit. For example, the spending limit for House candidates is effectively raised from $70,000 to $84,000, and for candidates in presidential primaries from $10 million to $12 million if the excess can be documented as spent for fund-raising purposes.

The expenditure limits are adjusted according to rises in the Cost of Living Index. Exemptions from the spending limits are expenditures of up to $500 for food and beverages, invitations, and unreimbursed travel expenses by individual volunteers; and spending on "slate cards" or sample ballots paid for by a state or local committee of a political party.

The FECA amendments of 1974 have other provisions, including amendments to existing prohibitions on corporate, labor-union, and government-contractor contributions. For a period of forty-five days before a primary and sixty days preceding a general election, broadcasters' charges for air time cannot exceed the lowest unit rate charged other advertisers for the same class and amount of time. At other times and for newspaper advertising, charges must be at the same rates as for comparable time or space by other users.

Some degree of disclosure of political finances, with inconsistency and variation, is required by forty-nine states, in most cases requiring both candidates and committees to file reports, detailing sources of funds and types of expenditures, both before and after the primary and general elections. In some states, municipal contests are excluded. Half of the states have bipartisan commissions similar in composition and powers to the Federal Election Commission.

Various states have differing forms of limitations on amounts candidates can spend and on amounts individuals can contribute and have prohibitions on contributions from certain sources. The federal regulatory scheme also includes provisions in the Revenue Act of 1971 as amended by the FECA amendments of 1974. (*See also* Campaign Resources.)

[Herbert E. Alexander, *Money in Politics.*]
HERBERT E. ALEXANDER

PUBLIC LAND COMMISSIONS were established by the U.S. government on four occasions to review federal land policies and to make recommendations for their improvement or redirection. The first of these was authorized by Congress in 1879, when widespread abuse of the settlement laws existed; corruption was prevalent in the local land offices and in the awarding of lucrative surveying contracts; the General Land Office was understaffed and far behind in its work; and a mass of conflicting land laws and administrative orders required revision. Five distinguished men long associated with public land administration were appointed to the commission, the best known of whom was John W. Powell, explorer of the Grand Canyon and author of the *Report on the Lands of the Arid Region.* The testimony they took during a three-month tour of the West revealed scandalous management of the surveys, illegal sale of relinquishments, and exploitative activities by land attorneys and agents, and it indicated that serious damage was being done to rich valley lands in California by hydraulic mining. Recommendations for change included abolition of the unnecessary re-

ceivers' office in each land district, better salaries for the staff of the General Land Office, classification of the public lands, sale of the grazing lands, and exchange of lands between the railroads and the government to block areas for more effective management. Congress was not moved to action, although some of the reforms were adopted in 1889–91, by which time the best of the arable land had gone into private ownership. Thomas Donaldson, a member of the commission, left its most lasting contribution, *The Public Domain,* a 1,300-page history and analysis of land policies that has since become a basic source of information about land policies. It bore down heavily on the misuse of the settlement laws.

In 1903 President Theodore Roosevelt appointed the second commission with Gifford Pinchot, then head of the Bureau of Forestry in the Department of Agriculture, as its most important member. After hearings in Washington, D.C., and in the West, the commission recommended the repeal of the Timber and Stone Act of 1878, as had the first commission. It also urged the appraisal of timber and other lands before they were sold; the establishment of grazing districts to be administered by the Department of Agriculture, with fees to be charged for use of the public ranges for grazing; the repeal of the lieu land feature of the Forest Management Act of 1897; and additional safeguards in the Homestead Act of 1862 and Desert Land Act of 1877. Congress was not receptive, although the lieu land provision was repealed and the forest reserves were transferred from the Department of the Interior to the Agriculture Department's Bureau of Forestry under Pinchot.

Western livestock, lumber, and mining interests did not like the dynamic leadership of Pinchot, one of the founders of the modern conservation movement, and they brought about his dismissal by President William Howard Taft in 1910. These interests were pressing for the cession of the public lands to the states in which they were located, thereby reviving an issue that had agitated the public land states for a century. They also opposed executive withdrawals of public lands that kept them from entry by private individuals and companies. They wanted no more government controls on public lands. Until 1929 their influence was responsible for relaxation of controls in the Department of the Interior, while the public lands were being overgrazed and their carrying capacity was seriously declining. Conservationist forces were not moribund but rather were regrouping their forces to protect the national forests from passing into private hands and to provide management of the public domain rangelands previously uncontrolled. President

Herbert Hoover may have sensed this ground swell and shrewdly decided to anticipate it with a proposal to convey the remaining public lands not subject to controlled use by a government agency to the western states, which, he said, had "passed from swadling cloths and are today more competent to manage" them than the federal government. In response to his request, Congress authorized the appointment of the third commission, known as the Committee on the Conservation and Administration of the Public Domain. A carefully picked committee, dominated by westerners, recommended that the public lands, minus mineral rights, be turned over to the states in the hope that they would establish grazing control but that if they did not, the United States should undertake to do so in the recalcitrant states. The committee also recommended a procedure to eliminate those portions of the national forests it was not deemed desirable to retain. Conservationists throughout the country, not agreeing with the president that the record of the states was better than that of the National Forest Service in administering both forest and rangelands under its jurisdiction, sprang to arms in opposition to the recommendations. Most western states were also distressed at the recommendations, for they felt that without the mineral rights there was little to be gained from the cession of the lands. No action was taken.

The fourth and best-financed of the public land commissions came into existence in 1964, when many issues affecting the public lands were in need of serious attention and measures relating to them were already under consideration in Congress. Rather than deal with these questions in a piecemeal fashion, Congress decided to create the Public Land Law Review Commission, which, through use of the best expert aid in the universities and government agencies, would attempt an overall examination of the many overlapping and conflicting programs and make recommendations to the Congress for new legislation. Again, failing to recognize that the public lands belong to the nation and that people of all states are deeply concerned about their management, whether they are national forests, parks, grazing districts, or wildlife refuges, the commission was strongly slanted toward the western viewpoint. Its final report, *One Third of the Nation's Land,* contained homilies about planning for future needs and multiple use but placed emphasis on giving commercial interests more leeway in utilizing and acquiring ownership of the public lands, although requiring that they pay more for those privileges. The report showed westerners' dislike of the use of executive authority to effect land withdrawals, opposition to higher fees for grazing privi-

leges, and preferences for state, as against federal, administrative authority. It also reflected the general public's concern for retaining public lands in government ownership and for multiple use of the lands, but it favored "dominant use," which was generally interpreted to mean timber cutting and mining above other uses. Conservationists long accustomed to regarding the National Forest Service as the best administrative agency dealing with land matters were troubled by the proposal to consolidate it with the Bureau of Land Management. Environmentalists feared that the commission's failure to recommend the repeal of the Mining Act of 1872, which had been responsible for some of the most serious errors of the past in land administration, showed a marked insensitivity to public attitudes.

[Paul W. Gates with a chapter by Robert W. Swenson, *History of Public Land Law Development.*]

PAUL W. GATES

PUBLIC LANDS. *See* **Public Domain.**

PUBLIC LANDS, FENCING OF. The range cattle industry on the Great Plains was based on the use of the public domain for grazing purposes. There was no serious objection to this practice as long as the range remained open and the country was not wanted by settlers. After the invention of barbed wire during the 1870's, however, complaints began to pour into the General Land Office that illegal enclosures of public land were being made. By this means land companies were able to control large ranges, including streams and other watering places, and keep other cattlemen out. Settlers were also demanding access to the land, and fence-cutters' wars were frequent occurrences.

A series of investigations revealed a startling situation. In 1884 the commissioner of the General Land Office reported thirty-two cases of illegal fencing. One enclosure contained 600,000 acres, another forty townships; one cattleman had 250 miles of fence. Investigations during the succeeding years showed a rapid increase in illegal fencing, until 531 enclosures were reported in 1888, involving more than 7 million acres of the public domain. Congressional legislation and a presidential proclamation in 1885 ordered the removal of the fences, but it was not until 1889 that any real progress was made in eliminating the illegal practice of fencing public land.

[Commissioner of the General Land Office, *Annual Reports* (1884–90); Louis Pelzer, *The Cattlemen's Frontier.*]

DAN E. CLARK

PUBLIC LANDS, SURVEY OF. The first settlers in America measured out their lands for individual or public holdings on the basis of "metes and bounds," the shape of a tract being determined by natural features, such as the shoreline of a lake or a river, the ridges of hills and mountains, or even by the desirability of certain land as compared with other adjoining land. The lack of system permitted the first settlers to pick and choose to an almost unlimited degree. There had been in Europe some attempt at regular surveys, but they did not predominate and were not introduced at all promptly in America.

The colonies did begin a system of surveys for outlining towns. Massachusetts attempted to lay them out in six-mile square tracts. Connecticut likewise attempted a five-mile square town, and the square town, or township, was, in a small way, attempted in South Carolina. Several land schemes provided for the township system of subdivision soon after the middle of the 18th century.

The difficulties connected with the indiscriminate surveys of most colonies, especially in the South (including Kentucky and Tennessee), had impressed a large number of people interested in a feasible system of measurements and designations with the desirability of a rectangular survey. In the debate on this subject many genuine objections were brought forth, for example, that rectangular surveys would cut across streams, valleys, and ridges in undesirable and awkward ways: shutting one division off from a suitable building site and another from a watercourse, giving all of one kind of land to one tract and all of another kind to another tract.

The present rectangular survey was adopted as a feature of the Land Ordinance of 1785. It provides for the survey of all public land into townships six miles square (see Seven Ranges, Survey of). The townships are numbered running north and south from certain east-west baselines (see Geographer's Line). Certain meridians are designated as primary meridians, and a north-south row of townships parallel to these meridians is called a range. Such rows are numbered running east and west from the primary meridians. A township is divided into thirty-six sections, each a mile square. The sections are numbered beginning from the northeastern corner and moving west, then east along the second row, then west again along the third row, and so forth, bringing number thirty-six to the southeastern corner. This survey system applies, with a few local exceptions, to all states of the Union except the thirteen original states and Vermont, Maine, Kentucky, Tennessee, West Virginia, Hawaii, and Texas, the last-named state having a similar system of its own.

Under the 1785 survey system it is possible to designate a certain forty-acre tract of land with a few words and numbers. The designation is absolutely definite and could not apply to any other land whatever. For instance, a tract of land numbered Sec. 10; T. 94 N.; R. 40 west of the Fifth Principal Meridian could be found nowhere else than in northwestern Iowa. The Fifth Principal Meridian runs north from the mouth of the Arkansas River in Arkansas. The baseline governing this part of the country runs west from the mouth of the Saint Francis River in the same state. Thus, the particular section 10 designated will be found in the ninety-fourth township to the north of this baseline, and in the fortieth one to the west of the line designated as the Fifth Principal Meridian.

The rectangular survey system, with all its inaccuracies, is a system of great convenience. Even though it is not literally an American invention, its widespread use in the United States led to its acceptance in a large portion of the New World.

[Thomas Donaldson, *The Public Domain, 1884;* B. H. Hibbard, *A History of the Public Land Policies;* Payson J. Treat, *The National Land System, 1785–1820.*]

BENJAMIN HORACE HIBBARD

PUBLIC LAND SALES. It was the practice of the United States after the Indian title to land had been surrendered and the land surveyed and divided into townships of 36 square miles and sections of 640 acres and half, quarter, and eventually quarter-quarter sections (40 acres), to offer the sections at public auction. The minimum price was $2.00 an acre until 1820 and $1.25 an acre thereafter. Credit was allowed before 1820, but later the successful bidder had to pay the full cash price on the day of sale. Public auction sales in Illinois, Wisconsin, Michigan, Mississippi, and Alabama drew great crowds in 1816–19, 1835–37, and 1854–57 to much excitement. The sales reached their peak in 1836, when 25 million acres were sold and the receipts constituted nearly one-half of the total revenue of the government. Some of the buying was by petty speculators attempting to enclose more land than they had capital to develop, but more was bought by eastern capitalist speculators and land companies organized to buy undeveloped land on the frontier and sites for prospective cities. The American Land Company, which had a capitalization of $1 million, was the best known of these large speculative organizations. Anxiety about their claims led squatters to organize claim associations to prevent competitive bidding and provide a form of registration of boundaries before the county organization and title registration had been established. In a few instances prices were bid to absurd levels, as in potential cotton districts of Mississippi and Alabama, but it was usual to forfeit the contracts without making any payment; then at the next sale the lands could go for the minimum price. Worker demands for "lands for the landless" led the government to slow down the public offering of land at auction in the late 1850's and after 1862 leave most public land open only to entry by settlers under the preemption and homestead laws. In a series of acts during 1888–91, Congress halted the unlimited sales of land that had been brought into the market before 1870.

[Everett Dick, *The Lure of the Land;* Paul W. Gates, *History of Public Land Law Development.*]

PAUL W. GATES

PUBLIC LAND STATES are the thirty "sovereign" commonwealths created by the United States out of territory (1) ceded by the older states (Ohio, Indiana, Illinois, Michigan, Wisconsin, Alabama, and Mississippi); (2) acquired by purchase (Florida, Alaska, and all the states west of the Mississippi River except Texas, Oregon, Washington, and Idaho); or (3) acquired from England by the Oregon Treaty of 1846 (Washington, Oregon, and Idaho). Within these thirty public land states there were 35 million acres in land claims given by predecessor governments and reservations established by Virginia and Connecticut that never became part of the public lands of the United States. But the rest were public lands owned by the national government, and so the residents of those states looked to Congress for aid in building roads, canals, and railroads; endowing public schools, universities, and agricultural colleges; draining wetland; and irrigating dry land. This entrepreneurial role of the U.S. government helped counteract states' rights parochialism.

[Benjamin H. Hibbard, *History of Public Land Policies.*]

PAUL W. GATES

PUBLIC OPINION, a term that has been in common usage in the United States since the latter part of the 18th century. No definition has won general acceptance, although many have been suggested. Analysis of many of these led Harwood L. Childs, Princeton University professor of politics, to conclude in 1962 that public opinion is "used to refer to any collec-

tion of individual opinions." Opinion pollsters and scholars of the 20th century customarily define the specific collections of persons to whom they refer as various "publics" rather than "the public." In general usage the term often implies the opinion of the public at large, a considerable majority of all the people, or of the voting public.

The vagaries of definition have hardly detracted from interest in public opinion. Over the years a great deal of attention has been given to the subject by politicians, journalists, historians, and social scientists, for however defined, public opinion is widely recognized as being vitally related to many democratic processes—not only governmental, but social and economic as well. Such has not always been the case. In its earliest usage the "public" in "public opinion" was equated with "the people" or, more specifically, the landholders or propertyowners in whom the franchise was vested.

The general thesis that the political history of the United States has been largely a long struggle between vested rights and the public interest, with the former being gradually eroded as popular suffrage and individual rights have expanded, provides a loose frame of reference for changes in the broad usage of the term "public opinion."

Public opinion is commonly associated with concepts integral to democracy and consequently receives very close attention. Majority rule, consent of the governed, and representative government can hardly be discussed without reference to public opinion; nor can referenda, for example, or propaganda.

Consideration of public opinion is morally and ethically essential in the context of government in the United States and in most other countries of the free world; it is a practical necessity for any form of government. Consequently, systematic efforts to measure and evaluate the opinions of masses of people and special groups of people are more or less universal. By no means limited to governmental agencies, such efforts are undertaken by private and institutional agencies interested in public opinion from various perspectives.

Public opinion research burgeoned after 1935. Both American and world associations for public opinion research came into being. The Gallup Poll, originated by George H. Gallup in the 1930's, became the prototype of public opinion polling around the world, as many other widely known polling organizations were developed, mostly in the decade 1935–45: the Harris Poll, the Opinion Research Corporation, and the National Opinion Research Center;

many regional, state, and even local companies; and nonprofit research groups, such as the Bureau of Applied Social Research at Columbia University, the Survey Research Center at the University of California, Berkeley, and the Survey Research Center at the University of Michigan. Many of these and other organizations belong to the National Council on Public Polls (founded 1969), which distributes information to journalists, broadcasters, and public officials concerning appropriate standards for conducting public opinion polls and reporting on their results.

A number of these polling organizations specialize in predicting voting behavior in national, state, and local elections based on surveys of samples of the voting population. Their published and private reports on the popularity of political figures and on trends in public opinion and attitude on a variety of topics are also well known. Other organizations study more esoteric and philosophical problems of public opinion, the opinions of special publics, methodology of survey research, propaganda and mass communications, and opinion formation and leadership. Commercially oriented organizations tend toward market research activities, such as studying the psychological motivations behind buying behavior and corporate-image analyses. Some limit their practice to, or specialize in, advising political officeholders and candidates about their images or popularity and the implications of alternative actions or positions they might take— all based, at least in part, on public opinion research.

Substantial efforts are made to relate opinions or attitudes to actions and to determine the reasons for the development of opinions and attitudes and the relationship of education, mass communications, propaganda, cultural, and societal factors to both public opinion and behavior. Elections, the adoption of legislation, and the formation and implementation of public policies frequently provoke complex analyses of their relationship to public opinion. In 1961 V. O. Key, Jr., epitomized the views of many social scientists when he said that "the sharp definition of the role of public opinion as it affects different kinds of policies under different types of situations presents an analytical problem of extraordinary difficulty."

Since the early years of the Republic there has been a tendency for some observers to attempt to correlate an increasingly well-informed populace and electorate with the expansion of democratic processes in the sense of making governmental policies and practices more responsive to public opinion. Faith in this potential has persisted despite parallel increase in the awareness of the extent to which the United States functions as a pluralistic society with a constant need to balance complex interests. Political theorists and realists alike have tended to believe that such factors as the spread of public education and the development of mass media of communication inevitably engender increased governmental responsiveness to public opinion, in terms of both broad policies and specific issues concerning which the voting public can conceivably become well informed.

During the first half of the 20th century, techniques for manipulating and controlling public opinion and actions based on these advances began to be recognized as an increasing threat to such hopes. This was especially true as these techniques were successfully exercised in the form of propagandist activities by national governments and powerful social and economic institutions, sometimes working in concert. Phrases such as "the engineering of consent" to describe opinion formation processes began to suggest the effectiveness of forces antithetical to the leadership of informed public opinion.

To some observers the development of enlightened public opinion has seemed unlikely. They have viewed the role of public opinion in a democracy as an inherent defect in the form of government and likely to bring about its downfall as the technological revolution and international tensions combine to require governmental action of a degree of sophistication that the great mass of the people cannot and will not support. Others believe that the masses of people and their institutions are being corrupted by the propagandist activities of elected officials and leaders who constitute a sort of democratic ruling class. For example, in the 1960's the French historian Jacques Ellul concluded that tools of propaganda and not public opinion guide men's destinies and that the very prospects for democratic freedom are bleak unless the peoples of all the world soon awaken to this danger and take appropriate action to protect themselves. Simultaneously, in the United States, Key declared that "the critical element for the health of a democratic order consists in the beliefs, standards and competence of those who constitute the influentials, the opinion leaders . . . if a democracy tends toward indecision, decay and disaster, the responsibility rests here, not in the mass of the people."

[Harwood L. Childs, *Public Opinion: Nature, Formation and Role;* Jacques Ellul, *Propaganda: The Formation of Men's Attitudes;* V. O. Key, Jr., *Public Opinion and American Democracy;* Walter Lippmann, *Public Opinion.*]

PAUL M. DOUGLAS

PUBLIC OWNERSHIP. Since the federal government was acting within fairly strict constitutional

limits in the first half of the 19th century, the states were active in promoting economic development. The sale of public lands provided revenue for internal improvements. Pennsylvania, Massachusetts, New York, and Virginia were active in promoting a system of mixed enterprise. Most of this ownership was in social overhead or utilities, especially in canal and road building.

On the federal level, the only important public ownership was in the first and second Bank of the United States, chartered in 1791 and 1816 for twenty-year periods. The government subscribed to one-fifth of the capital of both banks and appointed their directors. Although these banks did provide some central banking functions, they were essentially private, profit-making institutions. For this reason, their policies were highly controversial and their charters were not extended.

Under the U.S. Constitution the states possess residual powers; they may undertake any economic activities not reserved for the federal government. But they have not been active in the field of business ownership. Some states have established banks, flour mills, and housing programs and have offered loans to farmers. Others have only miscellaneous holdings, such as a power company in Nebraska, a railroad in California, the New Jersey Turnpike, the basic magnesium plant in Nevada.

Most government ownership has been on the federal level. The Congress was authorized under the Constitution to establish a post office and a mint, to build post roads, and to provide for the common defense. Federal ownership was limited to those areas throughout the 19th century. In 1904 the federal government reentered the field of corporate enterprise when it purchased the Panama Railroad Company, which was part of the Canal Zone. This company was reincorporated in 1948 as the Panama Canal Company. In addition to the railroad, it also operates a steamship line from New York, docks and piers, an oil company, stores, hotels, restaurants, power facilities, and other services. Under the Shipping Act of 1916 the U.S. Shipping Board was authorized to form one or more corporations to purchase, construct, equip, maintain, and operate merchant vessels. At the beginning of World War I the Shipping Board formed the Emergency Fleet Corporation. The Merchant Marine Act (Jones Act) of 1920 changed the name to the Merchant Fleet Corporation, and the corporation was given the responsibility of establishing new routes and of operating ships that were not sold to private interests. During World War I, the Mississippi Barge Lines was operated as a part of the federal

inland waterways service, and this company was incorporated in 1924 as the Inland Waterways Corporation. Its assets included a switching railroad in Alabama and terminal facilities in three cities. In 1953 the corporation was terminated by an act of Congress, at the recommendation of President Dwight D. Eisenhower.

In addition to transportation, public ownership has been most notable in the light and power industry. In 1925 less than 4 percent of all electric power for public use was produced in publicly owned and operated plants; in 1960 the figure was closer to 20 percent. The beginnings of public power on a large scale date to World War I, but it was the Tennessee Valley Act of 1933 that created a broad program for flood control, navigational aids, power production, and reforestation. The Tennessee Valley Authority (TVA) brought electricity to the region, fostered rapid industrialization, and supplied energy for the atomic energy plants at Oak Ridge and at Paducah, Ky. Once the TVA was shown to be feasible, other hydroelectric projects became realities. The largest of these are the Bonneville in Oregon, Grand Coulee in Washington, McNary in Oregon, Shasta in California, Hungry Horse in Montana, and Garrison in North Dakota.

There was also a great expansion in the lending operations of the national government. In 1916 the twelve federal farm banks were set up, and these continued to operate in the mid-1970's as an important source of long-term mortgage funds for farmers. But the largest loan agency, the Reconstruction Finance Corporation (RFC), was a product of the Great Depression. It began operations in July 1932 to rescue foundering businesses by granting temporary loans. Gradually the powers of the RFC were broadened. In 1933 it was permitted to subscribe to preferred stock in sound banks; and in 1939 it was allowed to assist in the financing of wartime agencies to make loans to new industries that could not obtain funds from commercial banks. Like the Inland Waterways Corporation, the RFC was ordered to be liquidated in 1953. In the twenty-one years of its operation it earned over $1 billion; when it was disposed of, it held assets of $1.7 billion, including ownership of synthetic rubber plants and metal reserves. It had made loans to 5,835 going banks, 2,780 closed banks, 1,183 building and loan associations, 98 railroads, and 12,102 industrial concerns. It has also invested in the preferred stock of 6,882 banks and 10 insurance companies.

While the total of federal assets continued to grow, the bulk of the assets was not in areas that competed directly with private business in the mid-1970's. Federal facilities accounted for more than 20 percent of all public construction in the United States, but they were mostly in water resources, power generation, space facilities, research complexes, defense establishments, office buildings, and museums. The government often obtains ownership by default; thus, in the years 1959 to 1972 it obtained ownership of the Jersey Central, Boston and Maine, Lehigh Valley, and Erie Lackawanna railroads.

A phenomenon of public ownership since World War II is the "off-budget" agency—the privately owned, but government-chartered, enterprise. These include the federal land banks, the federal National Mortgage Association, and the Communications Satellite Corporation. Other off-budget agencies are wholly owned and controlled by the federal government, such as the U.S. Postal Service and the U.S. Railway Service.

In the 1970's the area of greatest controversy over public versus private ownership remained the field of power generation. The argument centered on whether there should be more regulation or more ownership. Historically, government regulation forestalled the movement for government ownership. But regulation had not been totally satisfactory, and the cry arose once again for more government ownership of utilities and mass transportation systems. Despite the growing dissatisfaction with regulation, there was still very little public ownership in the United States in 1975.

[Sidney D. Goldberg, *The Government Corporation;* Carter Goodrich, *Government Promotion of American Canals and Railroads, 1800–1890;* Ford P. Hall, *Government and Business;* James Goodwin Hodgson, *Government Ownership of Utilities;* Jula E. Johnsen, *Federal and State Control of Water Power;* John McDiarmid, *Government Corporations and Federal Funds;* U.S. General Accounting Office, *Reference Manual of Government Corporations.*]

A. C. BOLINO

PUBLIC REVENUE. *See* **Revenue, Public.**

PUBLIC UTILITIES, a group of industries that share, to a greater or lesser degree, a number of common economic and legal characteristics. Alternative names for the public utility group ("regulated industries" and "public service industries") identify two of these characteristics. Standing between the privately owned competitive firms, on the one hand, and government departments or bureaus, on the other, public utilities are for the most part profit-oriented,

privately owned firms, the regulation of which, it is felt, cannot safely be left to the operation of competitive market forces. At the same time—at least in the United States—it is believed that their continued operation under private ownership is preferable to government ownership. Since public ownership is shunned and competition is considered to be an inadequate regulator, government regulation replaces control through market processes.

The "public service industries" label further identifies these firms in terms of their relationship to the publics they serve: in the language of court decisions, these are firms "affected with a public interest." According to Chief Justice Morrison R. Waite (*Munn* v. *Illinois,* 1877), property "does become clothed with a public interest when used in a manner to make it of public consequence, and affect the community at large. When, therefore, one devotes his property to a use in which the public has an interest, he, in effect, grants to the public an interest in that use, and must submit to be controlled by the public for the common good."

Since all firms are in some measure affected with a public interest, and it is the rare firm that completely escapes some form of government regulation, the public utility classification is, and always has been, somewhat arbitrary. Among the industries that have at one time or another been classified as public utilities, with constituent firms subject to formal regulation, are (1) industries providing transportation (common carriers—railroads, bus lines, trucking companies, pipelines); (2) industries providing services incidental to transportation (stockyards, warehouses, elevators, docks, terminals); (3) industries providing services facilitating communication (telegraph, telephone, radio and television broadcasting); (4) industries furnishing facilities that provide power, light, heat, and refrigeration; and (5) industries furnishing facilities that provide water and sanitation. The list tends to grow during certain periods and shrink at others, depending on changing economic circumstances and legal interpretations.

Although developments since about the 1870's have given public utilities great public prominence, the public utility concept itself is of ancient origin. Various writers trace the origin of the concept at least as far back as the Middle Ages, citing the influence of the "just price" doctrines of the church fathers and Scholastics, regulation of the guilds, and the medieval concepts of status and "common callings." With the close of the Middle Ages and the joining together of local economies into national economies, new influences came into play, especially the granting of domestic monopolies and the creation of the great regulated and joint-stock trading companies. The latter were regarded in one sense as extensions of the state—private companies charged with carrying out important public functions. This attitude, along with the common-law suspicion of uncontrolled monopolies and the associated right of regulation of the common callings, carried over into the American colonies and later into the practices of state and federal governments. The early corporations in America were chartered by special legislative acts. Along with each grant of special privilege went the understanding that the corporation so chartered was to serve the public interest.

Just how to guarantee that the utility company would serve the public adequately proved to be a matter of considerable difficulty. It was complicated in the beginning by the fact that, with capital and entrepreneurial talent both scarce, controls discouraged entry into the public utility field. In fact, the history of the 19th century is marked by the need to provide government support for such undertakings. Under these circumstances, consumers of the public utility service were forced to seek protection from the courts under the common law when confronted with discriminatory or inadequate services or excessive rates. Judicial regulation, though, was both costly and time-consuming. State governments were forced by public pressure to provide alternative arrangements for control.

One such alternative presented itself as an aspect of the legislative granting of charters: what the state gave the state could take away in the event of unsatisfactory performance. Even before the Dartmouth College decision (*Trustees of Dartmouth College* v. *Woodward,* 1819) this approach had been vigorously and often successfully protested by the owners of property used in the provision of public utility services, on the very grounds validated by the Dartmouth College case: a corporation charter was not a revocable gift, but instead a contract for services, revocable only by mutual agreement. The Dartmouth College decision did not end the use of regulation by charter. State legislators simply built additional restrictions and controls into the charter itself and supplemented them by the passage of control statutes and the establishment of investigatory commissions. But in the face of rapidly changing economic circumstances, this proved to be an awkward, hit-or-miss procedure. An alternative arrangement, the "mixed corporation," whereby state governments provided

part of the capital and secured some degree of control, also proved not to be viable.

As the 19th century wore on, the practice of regulating by charter fell into disfavor. With the expansion of industry and commerce the mere process of legislative chartering became more and more cumbersome, as well as more venal. In addition, the generalized principles of competition and economic freedom, as developed in the writings of Adam Smith and the other classical economists, ultimately became accepted as truth, making suspect the belief that government supervision and control were necessary to ensure adequate economic performance: competition between the firms in each industry would take care of that problem. General or free incorporation spread rapidly from the 1830's onward, and all levels of government—federal, state, and municipal—relied increasingly on the forces of competition to protect the public interest. The distinction between public utilities and other industries narrowed.

That the distinction was a vital one became manifest in the period after the Civil War. Users of railroad services often found themselves confronted with what they regarded as exorbitant, discriminatory demands by sole providers of what had by then become a vitally necessary service. Competition did work to the benefit of the consumer in an overall fashion; passenger and ton-mile freight rates fell rapidly during the last third of the century. But customers served by only one railroad complained that their rates were artificially high because the railroad had to recoup losses suffered where competition was intense, such as between urban centers. The result was a rising demand in several midwestern states for legislation to control freight rates and discriminatory practices. Before this Granger movement had run its course, it had led to the passage of state laws, in the Midwest and elsewhere, setting limits on railroad rates and limiting the ability of railroads to discriminate between customers. Opposition to the practice of legislative control was intense, but it received a sharp setback in 1877 when the U.S. Supreme Court (*Munn* v. *Illinois*) laid down the dictum that when property was devoted to a public calling, it was subject to public control. Further expansion of state control was abruptly curbed in 1886 when the Supreme Court, in *Wabash, Saint Louis and Pacific Railroad Company* v. *Illinois,* reversed a previous position and ruled that no state could exercise any control over commerce beyond its limits. The two cases combined said clearly that regulation itself, at least for any business classified as a public utility, could no longer be questioned but that regulation of firms operating across state lines would have to be a federal function.

There is evidence that the public utility leadership was less hostile to the idea of federal regulation than its public pronouncements suggested. In industries marked by heavy overhead costs there are real dangers of cutthroat competition and bankruptcy, especially in periods of slack demand. Since the general state of the economy in the 1880's was not good and the efforts of railroads to cope with the situation by pooling arrangements had been struck down, railroad leaders could well have felt that "sympathetic" federal control would at least be tolerable. Besides, there was the ever-present danger that the alternative to unrestrained private operation would be outright government ownership.

The rudiments of federal control of the railroads came into being the year after the *Wabash* case, in the form of the Interstate Commerce Act, which laid down general principles of regulation and established the Interstate Commerce Commission (ICC) to administer the act. Federal regulation was established in principle, but effective regulation in practice proved to be far more difficult to institute.

One of the difficulties was that the ICC was not given the right to set rates and fix tariffs, but only to initiate action in the courts if it was believed rates were too high. Given the economic environment of the times, it perhaps is not surprising that of sixteen rate cases appealed to the Supreme Court for enforcement between 1887 and 1905, fifteen were decided in favor of the carriers and only one in favor of the commission. With the passage of additional federal legislation after the turn of the century, the commission had effective power to control freight rates. And even then the legal guidelines laid down by the Supreme Court for ratemaking ("fair return on a fair value," *Smyth* v. *Ames,* 1898) were both restrictive and ambiguous.

Another difficulty was that railroads alone were singled out in this early period for regulation by the federal government. It was awkward to regulate the railroads but ignore activities, such as express and sleeping-car services, that were inseparable from railroading. The loophole was closed by amendments to the Interstate Commerce Act during the first decade of the 20th century. And the federal legislature also extended the jurisdiction of the commission to areas lying well outside transportation—to telephone, telegraph, and cable companies. As other public utilities developed, they were placed under the jurisdiction of specialized federal commissions, such as the Federal Power Commission and Civil Aeronautics Board.

While the federal government was working out procedures for regulating public utilities engaged in interstate commerce, a parallel movement was under way on the part of state and municipal governments. Municipal governments had the task of assuring adequate local utilities (street railways, gas, electricity, water, and telephone) at reasonable rates. The extension of the franchise provided an opportunity for control. Franchise periods of different length were tried, with indifferent success, and in the period of competition franchises were often granted to competing companies. Gradually it was learned that franchises for a definite period of tenure worked best and that a single supplier, carefully regulated, was preferable to competitive services. But by that time (about the turn of the century), the growth in the size of utility companies and their combination into large statewide networks, coupled with the difficulty of controlling local corruption, forced a shift from municipal to state regulation.

State governments began to take the need for greater controls seriously. They moved in the direction of establishing strong commissions that could provide continuous supervision of the intrastate public utilities and permit the setting of general standards of control. In general the public utility commissions fixed rates that would justify reasonably adequate service and facilities, by administrative order on the basis of the common law.

By the end of the 1920's the role of public utilities in the American economy appeared to be firmly established. A long series of court tests had led to a determination of which industries were to be considered public utilities and which were not—and therefore which industries were to be subjected to government regulation and which were to be left to control by the marketplace. Another series had served to clarify, in some measure, guidelines under which commissions could operate in setting utility rates. And in the regulatory commissions, federal and state governments seemed to have found the optimum control device. The secure role of the public utilities was reflected in the vigorous movement of public utility securities in the booming stock market.

Later this hard-won consensus largely evaporated. The extension by the Supreme Court of the right of government control of industries lying outside the public utility field (*Nebbia* v. *New York,* 1934), as well as the comprehensive regulation of virtually all industries during the New Deal period, during World War II, and in the price control era of the early 1970's, served to blur the distinction between ordinary competitive firms and public utility companies.

Any distinction based on the concept of "natural monopoly" has proved to be illusory as alternative ways of providing basic public services have appeared, especially in transport and communications. Having earlier determined that public utilities were, or should be, monopolies, the regulatory commissions recognized only belatedly, and with reluctance, the need to take competitive forces into account in their control activities. The public, meanwhile, adopted a somewhat jaundiced view of public utilities. Their stock market losses when the public utility holding-company empires collapsed in the 1930's began the process of disillusionment. Deterioration of service and environmental pollution also contributed. But perhaps of greatest importance was the conviction that the regulatory process was not working. Regulation of the railroads proved disastrous. The ICC rarely exercised its authority to coordinate railroad operations, rationalize technology, or raise the railroads from their path of decline. As overseer of a self-governing cartel, its concern was not to promote efficiency in the railroads but to slow it down elsewhere. To that end, it placed formidable barriers on entry into the trucking business. There as elsewhere the public became convinced that the regulated industries had captured the regulatory commissions, with the result of excessive payment for inadequate services.

By the mid-1970's some tentative moves had been made in the direction of recognizing that one public utility industry cannot be singled out for control without taking into account repercussions on other regulated industries. More sophisticated economic analysis was being used in ratemaking, looking more to the future and less to the past. "Externalities" in the provision of public utility services were being recognized and taken into account. But how to provide effective overall coordination and control in the public utility sector in a rapidly changing American economy remained a question.

[Martin T. Farris and Roy J. Sampson, *Public Utilities: Regulation, Management, and Ownership;* Paul J. Garfield and Wallace F. Lovejoy, *Public Utility Economics;* Martin G. Glaeser, *Public Utilities in American Capitalism;* Charles F. Phillips, Jr., *The Economics of Regulation;* Clair Wilcox, *Public Policies Toward Business.*]

MAX E. FLETCHER

PUBLIC WORKS ADMINISTRATION. *See* **New Deal.**

PUEBLO. Several significant points may be made about the Pueblo Indians of Arizona and New Mex-

ico. Their remarkably resistant and vital culture, unlike that of many other native American tribes, has lasted almost intact despite more than four centuries of European inroads. In general, the Pueblo (the word is Spanish, meaning "town," "village"), actively preserving their ancient way of life, share an essentially uniform culture and society. But their languages differ. Four major linguistic families are represented, along with a number of related but mutually unintelligible languages. The modern Pueblo continue a series of traditions that have their roots deep in prehistory; they are one of the few native American peoples whose historic development can be traced as a continuum from as early as A.D. 300.

Spanish knowledge of the Pueblo dates from 1539, when the Franciscan missionary Marcos de Niza reported on the fabled Seven Cities of Cíbola. The 1540–42 expedition of Francisco Vásquez de Coronado apparently visited all the then extant pueblos, including Zuni, site of the golden-city legend. Spanish contacts with the Rio Grande Pueblo and occasional visits to the western Hopi and Zuni continued until missionary and military pressures instigated the Pueblo Revolt of 1680–96. Although some new towns were built and others abandoned, the Pueblo were centered in Arizona and New Mexico by 1700. In some aspects of life the Pueblo yielded to Spanish influence, but they tended also to retain their aboriginal theocratic organization. Spanish political patterns were imposed mainly on the Rio Grande Pueblo; they established an elected secular officialdom, but side by side with it the sacred priesthoods continued to stand—the rainmaking and fertility cults that inject so solemn a religious note into Pueblo life. Nominally Christian, the Pueblo have effected a syncretism of aboriginal modes and Roman Catholic elements. Saints became identified with the native spirit realm, and the Spanish-built churches, however important, were eclipsed by the presence of the kiva, the semisubterranean ritual chamber where the agricultural fetishes continue to be kept.

The Pueblo offer a classic example of the point that uniformity of culture need not be accompanied by uniformity of language, the Pueblo evidently being a composite of peoples from different areas who were drawn into a desert farming pattern. The Uto-Aztecan speech phylum, with its branches of Aztec-Tanoan and Shoshonean, appears, Hopi being affiliated with the Shoshonean branch. The Tanoan speakers, who are found in the east, fall into three subgroupings linguistically: Tewa, found in the towns of Nambe, Tesuque, San Ildefonso, San Juan, Santa Clara, Pojoaque (extinct), and Hano, the latter reflecting a late migration to the Hopi country; Tiwa, in Isleta, Sandia, Taos, and Picuris; and Towa, in Jemez and the extinct Peco. The three Tanoan branches—Tewa, Tiwa, and Towa—are mutually unintelligible. Zuni, in western New Mexico, formerly consisting of seven towns, speaks a language seemingly unrelated to any other in native America. The central Pueblo speak Keresan, also an unrelated group. The seven Keresan towns are Acoma and Laguna in the west and Zia, Sant'Ana, San Felipe, Santo Domingo, and Cochiti on the Rio Grande and the tributary Jemez.

Archaeologists trace the beginnings of the Pueblo to the so-called Basket Maker horizon, a desert focus of incipient desert agriculture two millennia old. The great period of the Pueblo, covering a 300-year span from A.D. 1000 to 1300, was marked by population concentration in such sites as Mesa Verde, Chaco Canyon, and other prehistoric monuments. These were marked by the characteristic Pueblo architecture, with multistoried buildings of coursed stone and adobe. The great sites were abandoned because of drought.

Some differences in societal structure appear between the western and eastern Pueblo despite similarities in material culture, farming patterns, and religious orientations. Hopi and Zuni in the west strongly stress matrilineal kinship, having elaborate clan organizations based on affiliation through the female line. In the east there is paternal development with dual divisions of village society, the so-called moiety organizations. All the Pueblo are remarkable for their unity, their stress on peaceful internal cooperation, and the intricacies of their ritual and societal structures.

[Fred Eggan, *Social Organization of the Western Pueblos;* Robin Fox, *The Keresan Bridge;* Elsie Clews Parsons, *Pueblo Indian Religion,* and *Social Organization of the Tewa of New Mexico;* Kenneth M. Stewart, "Zuni," in Robert F. Spencer et al., *The Native Americans.*]

ROBERT F. SPENCER

PUEBLO INCIDENT. On Jan. 23, 1968, twenty miles from Wonsan, North Korea, four North Korean patrol craft ordered the U.S.S. *Pueblo* to heave to. When it failed to do so, the vessels brought it under fire. Engaged in the collection of electronic intelligence, the *Pueblo* did not resist, and it was seized along with eighty-three crewmen. According to U.S. sources, the ship was seventeen miles offshore, in international waters. North Korea charged that it was an "armed spy boat" in the territorial waters of North Korea. The U.S. government gained release of the

crew (one man had died from wounds suffered during the capture) eleven months later by signing an apology, which it simultaneously repudiated. The ship remained in North Korea.

When the ship's company returned to the United States, the Navy Department convened a court of inquiry on the surrender of the ship in the face of navy regulation 0730, which directs that no commanding officer shall permit his ship to be searched as long as he has the power to resist. The court, after lengthy hearings, recommended general courts-martial for the commanding officer, Comdr. Lloyd Bucher, and for Lt. Stephen R. Harris, the electronics-intelligence officer. Three other officers, including Rear Adm. Frank L. Johnson, Bucher's operational superior, also came under fire. After pondering the matter, Secretary of the Navy John H. Chafee concluded that courts-martial would not help matters. On May 6, 1969, he announced that no disciplinary action would be taken. A panel of the House Armed Services Committee charged that serious deficiencies existed in the military command structures of the navy and the Department of Defense. Secretary of Defense Melvin Laird ordered a review of the civilian-military chain of command.

[Trevor Armbrister, *A Matter of Accountability;* Ed Brandt, *The Last Voyage of the U.S.S. Pueblo;* U.S. Congress, House Document, *Inquiry Into the U.S.S. Pueblo and EC-121 Plane Incidents* (1969).]

PAUL B. RYAN

PUEBLO REVOLT (1680–96), in New Mexico, was engineered by Popé, a Tewa Indian of San Juan Pueblo, one of forty-seven Pueblo religious leaders who in 1675 had been flogged by the Spaniards for practicing Pueblo religious rites. The Spanish, who then numbered only about 2,500 in all of New Mexico, had been making strenuous efforts to extirpate pagan beliefs and ceremonies, and potential rebellion had been brewing among the Indians. The Spanish colony itself had approached the brink of demoralization and disorganization because of persistent conflict between the ecclesiastical and civil authorities. Popé preached a return to the old Indian ways, plus the elimination of the missions and the driving out of the Spaniards. He held secret meetings in an effort to unify the Pueblo, who had been too disunited for effective action. A day for simultaneous uprising was agreed upon, but word leaked out in advance. Nevertheless, all the Pueblo north of Isleta, N.Mex., participated. In a concerted uprising the Indians destroyed all the missions and killed about 400

Spaniards. The rest of the Spaniards fled south to El Paso. Attempts at reconquest by the Spaniards were unsuccessful prior to 1692, by which time the brief unity of the Pueblo had been shattered by internal dissension. In 1692 the Spanish expedition under Diego de Vargas was resisted by some Pueblo but not by others. Santa Fe was taken, and by 1696 Spanish control over the Pueblo of the Rio Grande area had been firmly reestablished.

[J. M. Espinosa, *First Expedition of Vargas Into New Mexico, 1692;* Franklin Folsom, *Red Power on the Rio Grande;* C. W. Hackett and C. C. Shelby, *Revolt of the Pueblo Indians of New Mexico and Otermin's Attempted Reconquest, 1680–1682;* Robert Silverberg, *The Pueblo Revolt.*]

KENNETH M. STEWART

PUERTO RICO. The island of Puerto Rico is the smallest and most easterly of the Greater Antilles, which form the broken northern boundary of the Caribbean Sea. Before coming under the jurisdiction of the United States by the Treaty of Paris of 1899, Puerto Rico was a colony of Spain for more than four hundred years. Discovered by Christopher Columbus on his second voyage in 1493, the island was colonized in 1508 by Juan Ponce de León. The scarce gold deposits and the sparse Indian population were both soon exhausted by the Spaniards, who retained the island principally as a key outpost in the first line of defense of their wealthier colonies in Mexico and Central and South America. Although attacked by the Dutch in 1625 and the British in 1798, Puerto Rico did not fall to a foreign power until 1898, during the Spanish-American War.

After the war the United States retained Puerto Rico as its first colony in the tropics. Substantial private investments were made in the establishment of large agricultural corporations dedicated to the cultivation and refining of sugarcane. Public funds were directed primarily toward the areas of health and education, which had been widely ignored by the Spanish colonial administration.

The islanders, although largely of Spanish stock, with African and some Indian admixtures, accepted the change of sovereignty with favor, expecting it would bring them a more democratic form of government. Although they were granted American citizenship in 1917, it was not until 1947 that they were given the right to elect their own governor. The first elected Puerto Rican governor was Luis Muñoz Marín. With the permission of the U.S. government and the approval of the people of Puerto Rico, he created a new form of government with extensive, but not unlimited, local autonomy. This government, known as the Commonwealth of Puerto Rico, was established through a constitutional convention held in 1952, and under it local autonomy is restricted only by the U.S. Constitution and laws of Congress that specifically mention Puerto Rico. Puerto Rico elects a nonvoting resident commissioner to Congress. Legal cases can be appealed from the insular supreme court through the federal court system to the U.S. Supreme Court.

The existing relationship with the United States was approved by more than 60 percent of those voting in a plebiscite in 1967. A sizable minority, 38.9 percent of those voting, expressed support for eventual statehood for Puerto Rico. A small group in favor of independence, estimated at roughly 10 percent of the population, boycotted the plebiscite.

Although Puerto Rico lies within the customs barrier of the United States, federal tax laws, including income and excise taxes, do not apply to the island. Federal taxes collected on imports and exports and excise taxes on Puerto Rican products are returned to the insular government. During World War II, funds thus returned to the local government grew to substantial amounts, and the government utilized this unexpected income to initiate a highly successful industrial development program, known as Operation Bootstrap.

For the first fifty years under American control Puerto Rico was primarily a producer of agricultural products, such as sugar, pineapples, coffee, and tobacco. So successful, however, was Operation Bootstrap in bringing industrial enterprises to the island that by 1957 the contribution of the industrial sector of the economy surpassed that of the agricultural sector to the gross insular product. After that time agricultural production continued to decline, and correspondingly, industries continued to grow and multiply—where sugarcane used to grow, for example, extensive petrochemical plants were built—although industries found it necessary to import almost all the raw material they required. In the 1970's tourism was making an important contribution to the island economy, and Puerto Rico had an important potential source of income in the form of untapped minerals, such as copper, nickel, and some iron.

The people of Puerto Rico, as a result of the industrialization of their economy, came to enjoy one of the highest standards of living in the Caribbean, although poverty remained in some of the slums of the large cities and in some of the remote valleys in the mountainous interior of the island. The population of the predominantly Roman Catholic island grew rapidly. With a population density of about 900 persons per square mile in 1975, Puerto Rico has been the source of a migration of about a million people to the United States.

[Kal Wagenheim, *Puerto Rico: A Profile;* Henry Wells, *The Modernization of Puerto Rico.*]

THOMAS MATHEWS

PUGET SOUND, an arm of the Pacific Ocean located in northwestern Washington. Long before Puget Sound was actually discovered and explored, 18th-century maps pictured an inland sea in that region because geographers had given credence to fictitious accounts of voyages to such a sea. The British expedition under Capt. George Vancouver was the first to explore Puget Sound (1792), although other vessels had previously seen and entered the Juan de Fuca Strait, which leads to the sound from the Pacific. Among those who had seen the strait before Vancouver were the English sea captains Charles Barkley and John Meares and the American Capt. Robert Gray.

Vancouver's men circumnavigated the sound in the ship's boats during the early summer of 1792. Many of the chief geographical features were given the names still used. The sound itself was named for one of Vancouver's officers, Lt. Peter Puget.

Lt. Charles Wilkes of the U.S. Navy surveyed the sound in 1841 and strongly urged the U.S. government to acquire it; he described it as the best harbor north of San Francisco. Pioneer settlement began in 1841. Important ports have developed along the shores of Puget Sound, and the establishment in 1891 of the Puget Sound Naval Shipyard at Bremerton created an immense industry in ship repair and construction.

[Edmund S. Meany, *History of the State of Washington.*]

ROBERT MOULTON GATKE

PUJO COMMITTEE. In February 1912 the House of Representatives passed a resolution directing its Committee on Banking and Currency to ascertain whether there existed in the United States a concentration of financial and banking power in the hands of a few individuals, "a money trust." A subcommittee, headed by Rep. Arsène Pujo of Louisiana, with Samuel Untermeyer of New York as counsel, conducted hearings, at which J. P. Morgan, George F. Baker, and other financiers testified. After examining a great

mass of evidence, the committee issued a majority report declaring that existing banking and credit practices resulted in a "vast and growing concentration of control of money and credit in the hands of a comparatively few men." This disclosure led eventually to the passage of the Federal Reserve Act (1913) and the Clayton Antitrust Act (1914).

[L. D. Brandeis, *Other People's Money.*]

THOMAS S. BARCLAY

PULASKI, FORT, named for Casimir Pulaski, Polish military commander in the American Revolution, is located on Cockspur Island in Savannah harbor, commanding both channels of the Savannah River. Construction began in 1829 and was completed in 1847. Georgia state troops seized Fort Pulaski in January 1861, but on Apr. 11, 1862, after a fifteen-minute bombardment by Union forces under the command of Capt. Q. A. Gillmore, it was recaptured and held by Union forces for the remainder of the Civil War. The fort was designated Fort Pulaski National Monument in 1924.

[R. U. Johnson and C. C. Buel, eds., *Battles and Leaders of the Civil War,* vol. II.]

ROBERT S. THOMAS

PULLMAN COMPANY. *See* **Pullmans; Pullman Strike; Railroads, Sketches.**

PULLMANS, the railroad sleeping cars that, when introduced in the mid-19th century, popularized long-distance rail travel. In 1836–37 the Cumberland Valley Railroad of Pennsylvania installed sleeping car service between Harrisburg and Chambersburg by adapting the ordinary day coach to sleeping requirements. Each car contained four compartments of three bunks each, built on one side of the car, and there was one rear section for washing facilities. Passengers could read only by candlelight and were warmed by box stoves. The seats and floors of most cars were filthy, and compartments were usually crowded. Travel under such circumstances could be justified only as a painful duty. A New York cabinetmaker, George M. Pullman, arrived in Chicago during 1855 to apply his inventive ability to altering these conditions. At Bloomington, Ill., in 1858, Pullman remodeled two Chicago and Alton coaches into sleeping cars, each of which contained ten sleeping sections, two washrooms, and a linen locker. Although this venture proved unprofitable, Pullman decided in 1864 to create a more elaborate car, which was equipped at a cost of $20,178.14, a huge amount for car construction in that day. The "Pioneer," as it was called, was enlarged in height and width and contained a folding upper berth, sliding seats, artistically decorated furnishings, special car springs, and better lighting, heating, and ventilation. In 1867 the Pullman Palace Car Company was incorporated, with a capitalization of $1 million. In the same year, the new luxurious sleeping-car model, the "President," included a kitchen, the predecessor of the dining car. In 1870 a Pullman car completed its first transcontinental journey. The Pullman Company introduced to the United States the brilliant Pintsch gaslight as an illuminant in 1883 and was a pioneer in the introduction of electric lighting. Other improvements followed, and competitors were outdistanced. Pullman service, by introducing comfort to transportation, revolutionized travel both in the United States and abroad.

[Joseph Husband, *The Story of the Pullman Car*.]
HARVEY WISH

PULLMAN STRIKE. As a result of the panic of 1893, various railroad companies suffered heavy losses, which led them to curtail their operations and to reduce the wages of their employees. The Pullman Palace Car Company, which manufactured railroad sleeping cars, lowered the wages of its employees an average of 25 percent. This company, organized in 1867, carried on its chief operations at Pullman, a town which it owned just south of Chicago. When wages were reduced, no reduction was made in the rentals and fees charged employees in the company town. About 4,000 disgruntled employees joined Eugene V. Debs's American Railway Union in the spring of 1894. On May 11, 1894, about 2,500 Pullman employees quit work and forced the closing of the shops. Thereafter attempts were made to arbitrate the differences between the company and its employees, but the former took the view that there was nothing to arbitrate. Nor would the company consent to bargain with the union, although Pullman officials expressed readiness to deal with employees individually.

The local strike soon developed into a general railroad strike, when members of the American Railway Union refused to handle Pullman cars. First, twenty-four Chicago-based railroads, whose affairs were handled by the General Managers' Association, were tied up. This led to a general railroad tie-up throughout the western United States by June 28. In

another two days the strike had spread to practically all parts of the country. One result was serious delay in the transportation of mail. At this juncture federal judges William A. Woods and Peter S. Grosscup issued a "blanket injunction," prohibiting all interference with trains. The injunction was defied, and violence was resorted to by the strikers. Thereupon, President Grover Cleveland ordered federal troops into Chicago on July 4. Following their arrival, there was much mob violence and destruction of railroad property. Rioting occurred in cities as far west as Oakland, Calif., and on July 5, federal troops were put on strike duty in California. By July 13 some trains were running under military guard, and a few days later the strike was broken. By July 20 all federal troops were out of Chicago. During the strike Debs was arrested and his subsequent conviction for violation of a federal injunction led to a lengthy campaign to curb the use of blanket injunctions in labor disputes. This campaign ultimately resulted in the passage of the Norris–La Guardia Anti-Injunction Act of 1932.

[W. H. Carwardine, *The Pullman Strike;* Almont Lindsey, *The Pullman Strike*.]
ERIK MCKINLEY ERIKSSON

PULP. *See* **Paper and Pulp Industry.**

PULTENEY PURCHASE (1791), the residue of the Phelps-Gorham Purchase (from Massachusetts), comprised over 1 million acres in Steuben, Ontario, and Yates counties and parts of Monroe, Wayne, Allegany, Livingston, and Genesee counties, all in western New York. These "Genesee lands" were purchased for £75,000 from William Franklin, Robert Morris' London agent, by a group calling itself the Pulteney Associates. Charles Williamson, the group's first American agent, laid out Bath, N.Y., in 1793. The last transaction of the Pulteney Associates was recorded in December 1926.

[A. M. Sakolski, *The Great American Land Bubble*.]
THOMAS ROBSON HAY

PUMP-PRIMING, government spending during a recessionary period, in an attempt to stimulate private spending and the expansion of business and industry. The phrase derives from the operation of an old-fashioned pump, in which a small leather suction valve must be moistened, or primed, with water so that it will function properly.

Economic pump-priming was begun in 1932 under President Herbert Hoover, when the Reconstruction Finance Corporation was created to make loans to banks, railroads, and other industries. President Franklin D. Roosevelt, who began his administration in March 1933 with an economy program, became convinced by the fall of 1933 that pump-priming was necessary to achieve economic recovery. Thereafter, through the Reconstruction Finance Corporation, the work-relief agencies, the Public Works Administration, and other organizations, billions of dollars were used for priming the pump. These expenditures averaged $250 million a month in 1934 and 1935 and about $330 million a month in 1936, but only about $50 million a month at the end of 1937. The recession of 1937 caused the Roosevelt administration to again resort to extensive pump-priming in 1938.

In the post–World War II period, pump-priming has become an unquestioned function of government economic policy. Some government programs, such as unemployment insurance, automatically act as pump-primers, since government expenditures must increase as people lose jobs during a recession. Since the 1960's, putting more disposable income into the economy by cutting taxes (rather than or as well as by raising government expenditures) has come to be a widely accepted economic policy. The policy is exemplified by the income tax rebate and tax-rate reduction legislation of 1975.

ERIK McKINLEY ERIKSSON

PUNISHMENT, CRUEL AND UNUSUAL. The Eighth Amendment to the Constitution of the United States declares: "Excessive bail shall not be required, nor excessive fines imposed, nor cruel and unusual punishments inflicted." The amendment is almost identical to the tenth guarantee in the English Bill of Rights of 1689; however, the words "ought not to be required" appear in the English document, instead of the more positive words "shall not be required." Considered a fundamental guarantee of liberty, prohibition of "cruel and unusual punishments" was included in a number of the original state constitutions of the revolutionary period, notably those of Virginia, Maryland, North Carolina, and Massachusetts. Naturally, when a national Bill of Rights was adopted in 1791, the guarantee was included to prevent excesses by the government such as had been common in 17th-century England.

In the 1960's the issue of whether capital punishment was "cruel and unusual" became prominent.

Civil libertarians contended that, in view of changing societal attitudes, killing criminals was per se objectionable and that the death sentence was being so rarely meted out in applicable cases that its imposition had become arbitrary and discriminatory. In 1972 the U.S. Supreme Court, in *Furman* v. *Georgia,* did strike down all capital punishment statutes, but only on the grounds that the death sentence was being administered arbitrarily. In the wake of the decision several states enacted laws that, in essence, mandated capital punishment for certain crimes, removing any discretion judges or juries had in handing down the sentence.

[E. M. Eriksson and D. N. Rowe, *American Constitutional History;* C. Ellis Stevens, *Sources of the Constitution of the United States.*]

ERIK McKINLEY ERIKSSON

PUNISHMENTS, COLONIAL. Although punishments in colonial America were generally harsh, the New England colonies and the Quaker colonies of Pennsylvania and West Jersey had, in general, a more humane set of criminal penalties than prevailed in New York and the South. In New York larceny was punished by multiple restitution and by whipping. In the South the death penalty was at times enforced, in accord with English law, for theft of more than twelve pence from a person, but in the majority of instances multiple restitution was exacted, as, for example, under a Maryland act of 1715.

In Massachusetts barbarous or inhumane tortures were forbidden almost from the beginning. However, the Puritan code leaned in the direction of exemplary and humiliating punishments, such as the ducking stool for the scold, the stocks for the vagrant, the letter "A" sewn on the garment for the adulterer, and the branding iron for the burglar; drunkards were required to sit astride a wooden horse with an empty pitcher in one hand. Hanging was the normal method of capital punishment, and it was by this method, not by burning, that persons convicted of witchcraft in New England were executed.

In West Jersey only treason and murder were capital offenses, and in Pennsylvania murder alone was punishable by death. Imprisonment at hard labor was prescribed in most cases for noncapital crimes, but by 1700 the Quakers had abandoned their early humane theories with regard to punishment.

In New York and the South two tendencies stand out conspicuously—the extreme severity of the penalties prescribed and the almost exclusive employment of fines or some form of corporal punishment.

Whipping, branding, mutilations, confinement in the stock or pillory, and ducking were among the most prevalent forms of corporal punishment. At times whippings were carried to excess. (The New Englanders observed the Mosaic law setting thirty-nine stripes as the maximum penalty.) In addition to hanging, burning and quartering were also employed in New York and the South as means of capital punishment. Many of the blacks convicted in the "Negro Plot" of 1741 were burned at the stake. Others were sent to a penal colony, a method also used in New England for dealing with captive Indians in wartime. Treason was punished by dismembering the body of the executed person and disposing of the parts in various communities. For the murder of an overseer, a Maryland black in 1745 was sentenced to have his right hand cut off, to be hanged, and then to be quartered. Except in New England, for treason and other felonies, all the offender's goods and chattels were forfeited to the king, and a treason conviction also brought with it a loss of inheritance rights and the right to transmit property to one's heirs.

Both in New England and in the South mutilation was not uncommon. In the South, for contempt of court, an ear might be cut off or a tongue pierced with a hot iron. In Virginia an ear might be nailed to the pillory and then cut off to punish a slave for running away. For slander, in Virginia, the tongue might be bored through with an awl, and the convicted party might be forced to pass through a guard of forty men, being "butted" by each, and then be kicked down or "footed" out of the fort or trailed behind a boat. For criticizing the authorities in Virginia, one might be pilloried with a placard, lose both ears, serve the colony a year, be unable to become a freeman, have one's ears nailed to the pillory, or be laid "neck and heels" in irons and fined. Castration might be ordered by the court for any slave convicted of attempting to rape a white woman.

[Julius Goebel, Jr., and T. Raymond Naughton, *Law Enforcement in Colonial New York;* Edwin Powers, *Crime and Punishment in Early Massachusetts, 1620–1692.*]

RICHARD B. MORRIS

PURCHASING POWER. *See* **Money.**

PURE FOOD AND DRUG MOVEMENT. The American colonies, inheriting British practice, enacted local laws to fight gross adulteration of bread, butter, and beer and to strive for honest and proper weighing, packing, and storing of various foods.

Maritime colonies enacted fish inspection statutes. Drug laws were virtually nonexistent, although fraud provisions of the common law provided some protection against quacks. States continued such colonial legislation, and toward the middle of the 19th century, as exposure of adulteration began to mount, states and municipalities expanded laws striving to protect milk, meat, and other susceptible foods. During the Granger period, farmer lobbies successfully sought state statutes attacking adulteration of fertilizer, feedstuffs, and butter. Chemists on state payrolls began to expose a more sophisticated adulteration, by which almost every processed food could be cheapened through the mediation of organic chemistry; chemicals were employed to intensify flavor, modify color, soften texture, even convert apple scraps and hayseeds into "strawberry jam." Consumers, living increasingly under urban conditions and buying packaged products on a national market, suffered some loss of ability to judge the quality of the food they ate. By 1900 most states had enacted general food laws, but few of them were effective.

The first federal law in the field, passed in 1848, forbade the importation of adulterated and spurious drugs; it was poorly enforced. During the quarter of a century after 1880, more than a hundred food and drug bills were introduced into Congress, which enacted special laws concerning tea, oleomargarine, filled cheese, mixed flour, renovated butter, meat exports, and opium imports. A general law, with broad provisions covering all foods and drugs, was passed in 1888 for the District of Columbia. The first such general bill for the nation was introduced in 1879; versions of it passed either the Senate, in 1892, or the House, in 1902 and 1904, but not both houses during the same congressional session.

State food and drug officials, especially chemists, worked to secure a national law. So too did the more responsible food processors and pharmaceutical manufacturers, whose wares faced ruinous competition from adulterated goods and who found the effort to abide by divergent state laws oppressive. Most food producers favored national regulation. Their cause was effectively supported by Harvey W. Wiley, formerly Indiana state chemist, who became chief of the Division (after 1901, Bureau) of Chemistry in the Department of Agriculture in 1883. He made pure food the division's principal project, conducting a sixteen-year analysis of food adulteration and testing food preservatives on a group of volunteer civil servants. Wiley's "poison squad" experiments, widely reported, helped dramatize the pure-food issue, as had the "embalmed beef" fright during the Spanish-American War. At the turn of the century a revitalized American Medical Association became a powerful lobbying force in behalf of a law. So too did the General Federation of Women's Clubs. Wiley skillfully organized these pressure groups and worked with sympathetic members of Congress. Muckraking journalism aroused public opinion, especially Samuel Hopkins Adams' exposure in *Collier's* of patent-medicine evils in 1905.

Obstacles to the law included doubts about constitutionality, especially among southern congressmen, and the complexity of economic interests to be regulated. Major efforts at conciliation both outside and inside Congress failed, as alum and cream-of-tartar baking powder interests, propreservative and antipreservative catsupmakers, and straight whiskey distillers and rectifiers contested for advantage. What crusading and compromise had failed to achieve, public alarm accomplished. Descriptions of unhygienic conditions in the meat-packing industry contained in Upton Sinclair's novel *The Jungle* (1906) hit the public's stomach. Amidst the furor, the food and drug bill passed, as did a meat-inspection bill. President Theodore Roosevelt signed them both.

The Pure Food and Drugs Act of 1906 forbade interstate and foreign commerce in adulterated and misbranded food and drugs. Offending products could be seized and condemned; offending persons could be fined and jailed. Drugs had either to abide by standards of purity and quality listed in the *United States Pharmacopoeia* or the *National Formulary* or to meet individual standards chosen by their manufacturers and stated on labels. Food standards were not provided, but the law prohibited the adulteration of food by the removal of valuable constituents, the substitution of ingredients so as to reduce quality, the addition of deleterious ingredients, the concealment of damage, and the use of spoiled animal or vegetable products. Making false or misleading label statements regarding a food or drug constituted misbranding. The presence and quantity of a short list of narcotic drugs had to be stated on the labels of proprietary medicines.

The law's elastic definitions and imprecise administrative directions brought trouble. Wiley, whose Bureau of Chemistry received authority to propose regulatory actions, believed in rigorous enforcement, especially against chemical preservatives, saccharin in canned foods, and rectified whiskey. His efforts angered some farmers and processors who made their political weight felt. Secretary of Agriculture James

Wilson and Roosevelt created machinery to checkmate Wiley's initiative. In 1912 Wiley resigned.

Walter Campbell, Wiley's chief inspector, developed under Wiley's successors the project system of enforcement, by which the bureau concentrated on major abuses, giving threats to health priority over injuries to purse. The most extensive and obvious transgressions prevailing before passage of the law were drastically reduced: polluted, decomposed, and filthy foods; foods contaminated with lead and arsenic through careless manufacturing procedures; gross adulteration of botanical drugs; and, after the 1912 Sherley Amendment to plug a loophole found by the Supreme Court, proprietary medicines misbranded with "false and fraudulent" claims as cures for cancer, consumption, or epilepsy. Increasingly violations became more clever and difficult to detect, demanding the development of new scientific methods, such as the R. J. Howard mold count for tomato products and sophisticated bioassay techniques for determining drug potency. Enforcement turned more toward inspection of factory conditions.

The courts in general gave the law a liberal interpretation, although treating convicted violators leniently, with light fines and almost no imprisonments. These mild sentences, meager appropriations from Congress, and appeals from trade groups led the bureau toward efforts at preventive enforcement by educating industry to improve processing procedures. Often the bureau sought help from industry to determine feasible standards for enforcement within existing technology, as when contact committees from the two pharmaceutical trade associations gave counsel regarding hypodermic tablets, which was then written into enforcement regulations.

Debate over relations between regulators and regulated began early and never ceased. In the political climate of the 1920's a propinquity aiming at voluntary enforcement seemed natural, although to critics, like Wiley, the bureaucrats seemed to have sold out to businessmen to the neglect of consumers. The onset of depression intensified condemnation of the regulators, as in *100,000,000 Guinea Pigs* (1933) by Arthur Kallet and F. J. Schlink.

Campbell, by now commissioner, and his aides had long recognized weaknesses in the 1906 law and the inadequacy of amendments defining apples (1912) and butter (1923), requiring the labeling of net weight (1913), and drawing a line between standard and substandard canned foods (1930). In 1933, under the aegis of Rexford G. Tugwell, assistant secretary in the Department of Agriculture, a strong consumer-oriented measure went to the Congress from the Food and Drug Administration (FDA)—the new name adopted in 1927.

The affected industries, having had no share in drafting the bill, found great fault with it. A five-year period of attritional compromise began, managed by Sen. Royal S. Copeland, a homeopathic physician. The abandonment of a provision setting up quality-grade labeling and the elimination of advertising control provisions won support for the bill from food processing and publishing industries. The FDA and the Federal Trade Commission (FTC) engaged in a bitter battle for control over food and drug advertising, which was won by the FTC, which secured an increase in its authority in the Wheeler-Lea Act of 1938. Other concessions gained support of the food and drug revision bill from the pharmaceutical industry. Apple growers, fearing stringent control of pesticide residues, and makers of proprietary medicines furnished the most persistent opposition. New, tough, divergent state laws again helped bring industry to desire a national measure.

President Franklin D. Roosevelt gave only lukewarm support. Muckrakers viewed compromise as emasculation. Organized medicine seemed largely indifferent. The press and popular magazines showed little of their turn-of-the-century interest and afforded the issue scant coverage. A coalition of women's organizations provided the FDA its major lobbying weight. The general public hardly knew a new campaign was under way until, in 1937, catastrophe struck. A small firm issued a liquid dosage form of one of the new wave of wonder drugs, sulfanilamide, without testing the solvent, diethylene glycol, for safety, and more than 100 deaths resulted. Thus, again public alarm helped to get a lagging bill through Congress.

Despite the compromises, the Food, Drug, and Cosmetic Act of 1938 greatly strengthened consumer protection. It increased penalties and added a new legal weapon, the injunction. Foods injurious to health could be more stringently controlled, and labeling, especially for special dietary foods, was made more informative. The FDA was empowered to establish food standards that had the effect of law. Cosmetics and therapeutic devices came under regulation for the first time. The government was no longer required to prove fraudulent intent concerning false therapeutic claims in the labeling of proprietary medicines. False labeling was extended to now include not only erroneous positive statements but also the failure to include adequate warnings. Under a section directly resulting from the "Elixir Sulfanilamide" tragedy, new drugs could not be marketed until their manufacturers had convinced the FDA of their safety.

This "new drug" provision furnished a precedent for one of the major regulatory developments occurring after 1938, the trend toward preventive law. Whereas the FDA had formerly expended its energy mainly in tracking down violators after their violations had occurred and bringing them to court, it had become too hazardous to wait, for the chemotherapeutic revolution had brought scores of new drugs, potent for good, but, in their side-effects, powerful for ill. A chemogastric revolution, involving new pesticides in the growing of foods and new additives in their processing, also raised questions of safety, which a select subcommittee of the House of Representatives investigated during 1950–52. Congress enacted laws requiring proof of safety prior to marketing for pesticides (1954), food additives (1958), and color additives (1960). Laws forbade the marketing of insulin and antibiotics until the FDA had tested and certified each batch. An important new step, premarketing proof of drug efficacy, was added in 1962 to the 1938 requirement of proof of safety. Individual legal actions declined, and the dealing with problems in broad across-the-board fashion rose in importance. Forced recalling of goods from the marketplace by their manufacturers became a major regulatory weapon. And these developments involved increasingly close consultation between regulators and regulated about extremely complex matters.

Besides acquiring new duties within its traditional areas of control, the FDA constantly acquired new tasks by act of Congress. Modest controls over household containers of caustic poisons (1927) were expanded (1960) and extended to flammable fabrics (1953, 1967), products emitting radiation (1969), and toys (1969). In 1972 the FDA was given responsibility for regulating biological products, such as vaccines, which the Public Health Service had controlled since 1902.

The FDA had great difficulty in keeping up with the massiveness and complexity of its many regulatory mandates. Drug testing during World War II had been regarded by the agency as a patriotic contribution: no additional appropriations were requested or added during the war. In a fiscal rut, the FDA had fewer personnel in 1955 than in 1941. Key congressmen, displeased by rulings adverse to constituents, were responsible for budget cuts. Public opinion offered no counterweight, for the public scarcely knew the agency existed, and the press paid the FDA scant

467

attention. A citizens' advisory committee pointed in 1955 to the need for expanding the FDA's resources, and its plea was echoed by a second such committee in 1962. Congress responded by steadily increasing appropriations, a more than forty-fold increase between 1955 and 1975, when the FDA received nearly $200 million.

Both citizens' committees also found fault with the FDA's organization and procedures, particularly shortcomings of scientific competence. Congress, while giving the FDA more money and new tasks, also markedly increased the degree and continuity of oversight. Especially significant were hearings on the drug industry before Sen. Estes Kefauver's Subcommittee on Antitrust and Monopoly during 1959–62. Not only did the committee reveal that one high FDA official had received an extremely large honorarium for editing drug journals in the field he was charged with regulating, but it also discovered loopholes in the law regarding the manufacture and promotion of prescription drugs. A remedial bill received congressional approval under the impact of a scare over thalidomide, a soporific drug that had been taken by pregnant women in Europe and resulted in many malformed babies. Only a few American cases occurred, because the FDA barred marketing of the drug. The law tightened controls governing premarketing drug research involving human subjects and placed the advertising of prescription drugs under the FDA's jurisdiction. After 1962 the FDA undertook a long-term broad-scale resurvey, first of prescription drugs and then of nonprescription drugs, with respect to safety and efficacy.

The combination of the Kefauver committee and the thalidomide scare brought a glare of publicity on the FDA. Thereafter neither the news media nor congressional committees neglected the agency. A new wave of critics came with the ecological crisis. Environment-minded consumers, most notably Ralph Nader and his associates, condemned the FDA's policies as industry-oriented, as not severe enough in their definitions of hazards to health. Crises over cyclamate sweeteners, mercury in fish, and hexachlorophene in soaps and cosmetics, among others, continued to disturb the public and the Congress. Such dissatisfaction led to a broad consumer-product safety law, passed in 1972, which took from the FDA and gave to the new Consumer Product Safety Commission regulatory authority over consumer products not traditionally within the FDA's purview, leaving to FDA control foods, drugs, medical devices, and cosmetics. Responding to the climate of opinion, the FDA greatly increased consumer input into its decisionmaking.

Meat inspection under the Department of Agriculture was expanded to cover other than red meats. Dangerous drugs, such as barbiturates, amphetamines, and LSD, which might be abused, became subject to special regulation by the FDA under a 1965 law. In 1968 the FDA's Bureau of Drug Abuse Control was fused with the Bureau of Narcotics to form the Bureau of Narcotics and Dangerous Drugs in the Department of Justice. In 1973 the name of this bureau was changed to the Drug Enforcement Administration.

Buttressing federal efforts, states and cities continued regulating in the food and drug field, with laws of varying severity and enforcement of varying rigor. Some private organizations, such as the American Medical Association, the American Dental Association, the American Pharmaceutical Association, and the National Better Business Bureau, developed programs that influenced both the practice of their members and marketing standards for food and drugs. Initial steps were taken toward international controls over food and drug abuses—for example, to develop standardized definitions for foods.

[Oscar E. Anderson, Jr., *The Health of a Nation;* Oscar E. Anderson, Jr., James Harvey Young, and Wallace F. Janssen, "The Government and the Consumer: Evolution of Food and Drug Laws," *Journal of Public Law,* vol. 13 (1964); Food and Drug Administration, *Annual Reports;* Charles O. Jackson, *Food and Drug Legislation in the New Deal;* Wallace F. Janssen, "America's First Food and Drug Laws," *FDA Consumer,* vol. 9 (1975); James Harvey Young, *The Medical Messiahs,* and *American Self-Dosage Medicines.*]

JAMES HARVEY YOUNG

PURITANS AND PURITANISM. The terms "Puritans" and "Puritanism" originated in England in the 1560's, when they were used to describe the people who wished to reform the Church of England beyond the limits established by Queen Elizabeth I and who strove to "purify" it of what they considered the remnants of Roman Catholicism. Puritanism was first formulated as an ecclesiastical protest and was at the beginning devoted to attacking clerical vestments, the use of medieval ceremonial, and the structure of the official hierarchy; Puritans wished to substitute a church government modeled upon the example of the apostles in the New Testament. However, this preoccupation with polity and ritual must be interpreted as an expression rather than the substance of Puritanism. Puritans were men of intense piety, who took literally and seriously the doctrines of original sin and salvation by faith; they believed that true Christians should obey the will of God as expressed in divine revelation, and they condemned the Church of England because they found its order impious and anti-Christian. After 1603 their opposition to the church became allied with the parliamentary opposition to the royal prerogative; in the 1640's Puritans and Parliamentarians united in open warfare against Charles I.

Puritanism was thus a movement of religious protest, inspired by a driving zeal and an exalted religious devotion, which its enemies called fanaticism, but which to Puritans was an issue of life or death. At the same time, Puritanism was connected with the social revolution of the 17th century and the struggle of a rising capitalist middle class against the absolutist state. It was a religious and social radicalism that in England proved incapable of maintaining unity within its own ranks and, during the 1650's, split into myriad sects and opinions. The process of division began in the 16th century when "Separatists" broke off from the main body of Puritans. A small congregation of these extremists fled to America and established the Plymouth colony in 1620, although the major contribution of Puritanism to American life was made through the settlement established by the Massachusetts Bay Company at Boston in 1630. This band of Puritans was inspired to migrate by a conviction that the cause had become hopeless in England after the dissolution of the Parliament of 1629. Within the next decade some 20,000 persons came to Massachusetts and Connecticut and there built a society and a church in strict accordance with Puritan ideals. Ruled by vigorous leaders, these colonies were able to check centrifugal tendencies, to perpetuate and to institutionalize Puritanism in America long after the English movement had sunk into confusion and a multiplicity of sects. Yet in so far as Puritanism was but the English variant of Calvinism and was theologically at one with all Reformed churches, New England Puritanism must be viewed as merely one of the forms in which the Calvinist version of Protestantism was carried to America; its influence, therefore, must be considered along with that of Scotch-Irish, Dutch, or French Protestantism.

In the United States the word Puritanism has become practically synonymous with New England, simply because New England (except for Rhode Island) achieved a social organization and an intellectual articulation that trenchantly crystallized the Puritan spirit. Puritanism can be said to have affected American life wherever Calvinism has affected it, but most markedly at those points where persons of New England origin have been influential.

[William Haller, *The Rise of Puritanism;* M. M. Knappen, *Tudor Puritanism;* Perry Miller and T. H. Johnson, *The Puritans;* R. H. Tawney, *Religion and the Rise of Capitalism.*]

PERRY MILLER

PURPLE HEART, ORDER OF THE. *See* **Decorations, Military.**

PUT-IN BAY NAVAL BATTLE. *See* **Erie, Lake, Battle of.**

QUAKER HILL, BATTLE AT. *See* **Rhode Island, Sullivan in.**

QUAKERS, members of the **Society of Friends,** first came to America shortly after Quakerism emerged from the ferment of the Puritan Revolution in England. The society was founded by George Fox, who began preaching in 1647, as a democratic, apostolic Christian sect, and since it had no place for priest or minister, bishop or presbyter, it seemed to threaten church and government alike. Fox's doctrine that God's Inner Light illuminates the heart of every man and woman converted many who, despite fierce persecution, roamed the dales and towns of England as ministers of the new gospel. Ann Austin and Mary Fisher carried the message to Barbados in 1655 and thence to Boston in 1656. There the Puritan authorities imprisoned them, burned their Quaker books, and finally shipped them back to Barbados. Zealous Quaker missionaries, continuing to invade the Massachusetts Bay Colony, suffered fines, flogging, and banishment. Three men and one woman who defied the ban were hanged on Boston Common between 1659 and 1661. In Rhode Island, on the other hand, leading families embraced the new faith and established the "yearly meeting" for worship and church business at Newport in 1661. Quakers appeared in Maryland in 1656 and in Virginia in 1657. When Fox himself visited the colonies in 1672 he found Friends scattered all along the mainland coast from North Carolina to New England.

Continuing persecution at home prompted an increasing emigration of British Quakers to the New World. Settlements in West Jersey preceded the

"Holy Experiment" that William Penn, convert to Quakerism, undertook in 1681 in Pennsylvania. Thousands of British Quakers and a few Rhineland pietists found refuge in Penn's colony. Uniting with their brethren in New Jersey and Delaware, the Pennsylvania Friends organized a yearly meeting in 1681, which became the most influential in America. Other yearly meetings, independent of the Philadelphia meeting but in close touch with it, took form in Maryland (1672), New York (1695), and North Carolina (1698). Each followed the pattern of church organization that had developed in England; subordinate quarterly meetings were established, with monthly meetings the basic congregational units of the society. Friends met for worship to wait upon the Lord, maintaining a silence broken only by occasional sermons and prayers by men and women who felt the Spirit move them. They renounced ritual and the outward sacraments and eschewed music and art. The very simplicity of their worship and the austerity of their meetinghouses made for a certain dignity and beauty, and the uprightness of their lives lent grace to the plainness of Quaker speech and apparel.

As persecution almost ceased after the British Toleration Act of 1689, except for occasional fines for refusal to do military service or pay tithes to an established church, quietism rather than active proselytism became the rule. Friends perfected their organization as a "peculiar people" and punished by disownment breaches of the discipline, such as marrying out of the society. Although in colonies such as Pennsylvania they had played a prominent role in government, they withdrew from politics after the mid-18th century, primarily because of the conflict between their pacifism and the military necessities of the French and Indian War and the American Revolution. After the Revolution the westward movement drew many of them, particularly from Virginia and North Carolina, over the mountains to the slave-free soil of the Northwest Territory. Gradually they spread to the Pacific Coast, establishing yearly meetings in Ohio (1813), Indiana (1821), Iowa (1863), Kansas (1872), Illinois (1875), Oregon (1893), California (1895), and Nebraska (1908). Another stream of emigration led through western New York and into Ontario, Canada.

The evangelical movement that splintered 19th-century American Protestantism also brought schism to the Society of Friends. The Great Separation of 1827–28, beginning in Philadelphia, produced Orthodox and Hicksite groups, the former evangelical and the latter more Unitarian in tendency. The Hicksites

avoided further separations and united in the biennial General Conference in 1902. But among the Orthodox, evangelicalism produced schism after schism, beginning with a small Wilburite, or Conservative, separation in New England in 1845. The Philadelphia yearly meeting forestalled further division by ceasing to correspond with other Orthodox bodies in 1857 and by refusing to join the Orthodox Five Years Meeting, which began to take form in 1887. The isolation and evangelicalism of the western frontier so affected Friends in the West that their "churches," paid pastors, and missionary activities made them hardly distinguishable from their non-Quaker evangelical neighbors.

Theological differences diminished in the 20th century among Friends in the eastern United States and Canada, who largely followed the older Quaker practice of unprogrammed, nonpastoral worship. A series of reunions of the Orthodox and Hicksite yearly meetings took place, beginning in Philadelphia, New York, and Canada in 1955. On the other hand, the fundamentalist-modernist controversy gave fresh life to evangelical fervor in some western Orthodox meetings. Oregon withdrew from the Five Years Meeting in 1926—after 1965 called Friends United Meeting—as did Kansas in 1937; and in 1966 they both joined Ohio and Rocky Mountain yearly meetings in forming the Evangelical Friends Alliance.

The Quaker doctrine of the Inner Light encouraged humanitarian social activities even as it had fostered religious mysticism and quietism. Whereas Quakers had attacked the slave trade and slavery in the 18th and 19th centuries and made notable contributions in the fields of Indian relations, prison reform, education, woman's rights, temperance, and the care of the insane, their modern descendants sought to apply Quaker principles to the problems of war and social maladjustment. The American Friends Service Committee, organized in 1917 to enable Friends to substitute noncombatant relief work for military service, united all Quaker groups in promoting their peace testimony. The committee's pioneering in crisis situations in the United States and abroad brought them and their English counterpart, the Friends Service Council, the Nobel Peace Prize in 1947.

Friends opposed the Vietnam War from the beginning and highlighted their peaceful campaign against the war by attempting to bring relief to suffering civilians on both sides. As in World War II some went to prison rather than have anything to do with the Selective Service System, while others accepted alternative service under civilian auspices. Most avoided the more militant peace demonstrations of the 1960's, but some of the younger members came to believe that only through a radical approach to militarism, racism, poverty, and other sources of social unrest could they measure up to the standards of early Quakerism.

No longer a peculiar people in matters of dress and language, no longer rigid in enforcing a strict discipline against mingling with the world's people, no longer disowning people for marrying out of meeting or even for accepting military service if conscience so dictated, 20th-century Quakers showed great diversity among themselves and many similarities to other Christians around them. Nevertheless, their peace testimony in particular and their emphasis on the Inner Light set them apart as a unique group, and for all their diversity they joined together in 1937 in a Friends World Committee for Consultation, which drew Quakers together from throughout the world. In 1973 the Society of Friends included approximately 118,000 members in the United States and Canada. While rural membership seemed to be declining somewhat, new growth in metropolitan areas and university centers indicated an increasing interest in Quaker principles and their application to religious worship and the problems of modern life. (*See also* Friends, Society of.)

[Errol T. Elliott, *Quakers on the American Frontier*; Daisy Newman, *A Procession of Friends: Quakers in America*; Elbert Russell, *The History of Quakerism*.]
THOMAS E. DRAKE

QUANTRILL'S RAID (Aug. 21, 1863). William Clarke Quantrill, at the head of a band of 448 Missouri guerrillas, raided Lawrence, Kans., in the early dawn. The town was taken completely by surprise and was undefended; the local militia company was unable to assemble, and the few federal soldiers were stationed across the Missouri River. The raiders first stormed the Eldridge Hotel. After it had been surrendered and set on fire, the raiders scattered over the town, killing, burning, and plundering indiscriminately. All the business buildings—about 185—and more than half of the dwellings were totally or partially destroyed. The known dead numbered more than 150. Withdrawing at the approach of federal troops, the guerrillas, although pursued, were able to reach Missouri with few losses.

Unlike other border raids of the Civil War, this was not a mere harrying foray, but a general massacre. It was no doubt prompted by the old bitterness against Lawrence for its part in the Kansas conflict, the contest for control of the region between proslavery and abolitionist forces (*see* Border War). But the excuse given was reprisal for Sen. Jim Lane's raid on Osceola, Mo., earlier in the year. Quantrill, who had lived in Lawrence under the name of Charlie Hart and had been driven out as an undesirable, was probably motivated by a personal grudge.

[W. E. Connelley, *Quantrill and the Border Wars;* Richard Cordley, *History of Lawrence, Kansas.*]
SAMUEL A. JOHNSON

QUARTERING. *See* **Billeting.**

QUARTERING ACT. The first quartering act in the colonies was passed in March 1765 for a two-year term; it required the colonies to provide barracks for British troops. A second act, 1766, provided for quartering troops in inns and uninhabited buildings. The Quartering Act of June 2, 1774, known as one of the Coercion Acts, was passed by Parliament to permit effective action by the British troops sent to Boston after the Tea Party in 1773. In 1768 the Boston Whigs, taking advantage of the absence of barracks in Boston, had attempted to quarter the British troops in Castle William (a fort on an island in Boston harbor) rather than in the town itself where they were urgently needed. To forestall a like effort, the Quartering Act of 1774 provided that when there were no barracks where troops were required, the authorities must provide quarters for them on the spot; if they failed to do so, the governor might compel the use of occupied buildings. The Boston patriots, however, refused to allow workmen to repair the distilleries and empty buildings that Gen. Thomas Gage had procured for quarters and thus forced the British troops to remain camped on the Boston Common until November 1774. (*See also* Billeting.)

[Edward Channing, *History of the United States*, vol. III.]
JOHN C. MILLER

QUASI-JUDICIAL AGENCIES are administrative bodies that, although different in character and function from courts, adjudicate while engaging in public administration. The Interstate Commerce Commission (created in 1887) is the most striking example of the thousands of agencies active at all governmental levels, where variously constituted, large and small administrative units engage in rulemaking, adjudication, investigation, prosecution, supervision, and advisement.

QUASI-JUDICIAL AGENCIES

In quasi-judicial agencies the adjudicatory function looms large, in relation to diverse kinds of matters, notably complaints, applications, and benefits. The process goes back to 1789 when two federal adjudicatory agencies were established, one dealing with import duties and the other with military pensions. Thus began a trend involving the exercise of judicial power by a constantly increasing number of agencies, two-thirds of which had been created even before the New Deal. Franklin D. Roosevelt's presidency (1933–45) marked a growing awareness of the agencies' revolutionary role within the American legal setup and the beginning of persistent attempts to curb such agencies. The most significant of these was the conservatively motivated Walter-Logan bill, the veto of which blocked this attempt to impose judicial review on agency adjudicatory powers. Compromise was achieved in the 1946 Administrative Procedure Act prescribing uniform procedures for agency hearings, greater publicity for administrative regulations, broader judicial review, and separation of prosecutorial and decisional functions through an increase in the independence of hearing examiners. In the mid-1970's the act remained the fundamental statute governing the adjudicative and regulatory phases of administration. Amendments, of course, have had to be added to meet emerging problems—witness the 1966 Freedom of Information Act (itself amended a dozen ways in 1974). Also, the National Environmental Policy Act signed into law in 1970 has had widespread and unprecedented repercussions on the whole administrative process.

Constitutionally, there has been considerable controversy regarding the legitimacy of a so-called "headless fourth branch" within a governmental structure intended to be tripartite. Judicial decision has lessened headlessness by recognizing executive power of removal over purely administrative agencies (*Myers* v. *United States,* 1926), but with respect to independent regulatory commissions, removal is limited (*Rathbun* v. *United States,* 1935).

A melding of powers, rather than their separation, has long been in process, excesses being controllable by checks and balances. Thus, under due process of law, notice and hearing are generally required in administrative adjudications. Moreover, opportunity for judicial review exists if due process is violated. Resort to an ombudsman, a mediator between the bureaucracy and those affected by it, offers a possible solution to the increasing incidence of discretionary justice. But by the mid-1970's no fully satisfactory solution had been found for the control of administrative operations, often involving the exercise of informal and unreviewed (if not unreviewable) discretion. As Supreme Court Justice Robert H. Jackson observed, "The mere retreat to the qualifying 'quasi' . . . is a smooth cover which we draw over our confusion" (*Federal Trade Commission* v. *Ruberoid,* 1952).

[Robert E. Cushman, *Independent Regulatory Commissions;* Kenneth Culp Davis, *Administrative Law and Government;* James M. Landis, *The Administrative Process;* Peter Woll, *American Bureaucracy.*]

ROYAL CLARENCE GILKEY